Psychology

Psychology

Third Edition

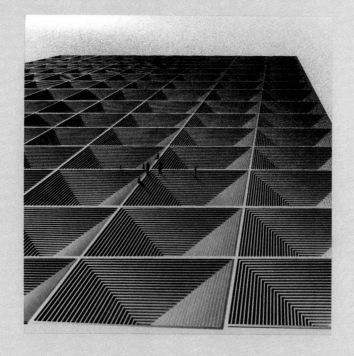

Carole Wade
College of Marin

Carol Tavris

HarperCollinsCollegePublishers

Acquisitions Editor: Margaret W. Holden
Project Editor: Robert Ginsberg
Design Supervisor: Dorothy Bungert
Text Design: Circa 86, Inc.
Cover Design and Part Openers: Bass/Yager & Associates
Photo Researcher: Sandy Schneider
Production Manager: Willie Lane
Compositor: York Graphic Services, Inc.
Printer and Binder: Von Hoffmann Press, Inc.
Cover Printer: The Lehigh Press, Inc.

Psychology, Third Edition

Library of Congress Cataloging-in-Publication Data

Wade, Carole.
    Psychology/Carole Wade, Carol Tavris.—3rd ed.
        p.   cm.
    Includes bibliographical references and index.
    ISBN 0-06-500217-2 (student ed.)   ISBN 0-06-501251-8 (instructor's ed.)
    1. Psychology.   I. Tavris, Carol.   II. Title.
    BF121.W27 1993
    150—dc20   92-17531
                                                              CIP

93 94 95 96   10 9 8 7 6 5 4 3 2

Contents at a Glance

v

Contents

PART 1

An Invitation to Psychology

P A R T

2

*Biological Bases of
Behavior*

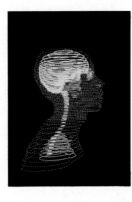

PART

3

*Learning,
Thinking,
and Feeling*

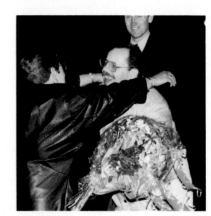

PART

4

Development of the Individual

P A R T

5

*Health and
Disorder*

P A R T

6

*Principles of Social
Life*

To the Instructor

"May you live in interesting times," goes an old Chinese curse. Well, these are certainly interesting times for psychologists. The field seems to be exploding in all directions at once. The long-simmering controversy between research and clinical practice has heated up, sometimes to the boiling point. "New age" cults, beliefs, and philosophies, with a quasi-scientific veneer, continue to pose a serious challenge to scientific psychology; it is getting harder and harder for the public to distinguish reputable psychological work from what R. D. Rosen (1977) once called "psychobabble." And, perhaps most passionately, arguments over multiculturalism—over whether and how to incorporate into the basic curriculum the experiences of diverse racial, ethnic, and cultural groups—have erupted on many campuses.

These developments present some difficult but exciting challenges for psychology teachers and textbook authors. In this book, we embrace those challenges by confronting the question of how our discipline can best fulfill its mission of understanding human behavior and contributing to human welfare. Psychology, we feel, is not only a body of knowledge; it is a way of approaching and analyzing the world. Indeed, it's a way of asking questions about everything from the smallest curiosities to the largest matters of life and death. Our goal, therefore, is not only to convey the basic content of psychology, but also to get students to reflect on and use what they learn—to show them what it is like to *think* like a psychologist.

■ CRITICAL AND CREATIVE THINKING

From our first edition, our approach has been based on critical thinking, an important movement in educational reform. We believe that in order to become critical thinkers, students must reject the common view that knowledge is something to be ingested, digested, and regurgitated. By the time they finish this book, students should understand that to "do" psychology, one must be imbued, paradoxically, with both intellectual caution and an open mind. They should appreciate that knowledge is advanced when people resist leaping to conclusions on the basis of personal experience alone (so tempting in psychological matters!), when they apply rigorous standards of evidence, and when they listen to competing views.

People often equate critical thinking with debunking. In our approach, however, critical thinking is not simply *negative* thinking. Sometimes, of course, critical thought does require skepticism and doubt. But it also involves the ability to generate ideas, see implications, be creative with explanations, and ask imaginative questions. It means breaking out of preconceived categories. It means being open-minded (although not so open-minded, as the philosopher Jacob Needleman observes in Chapter 1, "that your brains fall out"). We emphasize all of these *positive* aspects in our approach.

In this new edition, we have strengthened our commitment to the teaching of critical thinking, not only by doing more of it in the text, but also by adding *critical thinking questions* to many of our self-tests (called Quick Quizzes), so that students will have plenty of opportunities, as they read, to practice specific critical thinking skills. These items, which are identified by a "flash" symbol such as the one in the margin, vary in difficulty and are appropriate for students of varying abilities. They invite the student to reflect on the implications of findings and consider how psychological principles might illuminate real-life issues.

For example: What kinds of questions should a critical thinker ask about a new biological treatment for depression? How might a hypothetical study of testosterone and hostility be improved? What are the behavioral assumptions underlying experimental "learnfare" programs that now exist in some states? How might findings on motivation, circumstance, and culture help us think critically about the reasons for an employee's chronic tardiness? Note that although we offer some possible ways of responding to such questions, most of them do not have a single correct answer, and students may have valid, well-reasoned answers that differ from our own. These items require more than debunking; they require real thought.

Other aspects of our approach to critical and creative thinking include:

• *An extended discussion, in the first chapter, of what critical and creative thinking is (and isn't).* This discussion includes eight specific guidelines to critical thinking and an explanation of why critical thought is particularly relevant to the study of psychology (see pages 27–32). A pictorial essay (on pages 36–37) further illustrates the guidelines discussed.

• *Marginal* **"signposts"** *consisting of provocative questions that alert students to some (though by no means all) of the critical discussions in the text.* These signposts, accompanied by the flash symbol for easy identification, are *not*, in themselves, illustrations of critical thinking. Rather, they serve as pointers to critical analyses in the text of a chapter and invite the reader into the discussion.

• *A special feature in each chapter titled* **Think About It,** *which raises psychological, social, or philosophical issues that have no easy answers.* These essays pose provocative questions for the student to ponder. (Some instructors require students to choose one or more of these for term papers.) Topics new to this edition include whether television is killing off reading, how far "fetal protection" policies should go, and whether people from different cultural groups can learn to live together in mutual acceptance of their differences or are doomed to conflict because of them.

• *Coverage of methods—how the evidence was gathered and evaluated—in discussions of findings throughout the text.* When we report a finding, we also ask: How should this research be evaluated? Was the study designed well? What is the finding's larger significance? For example, some studies find a statistically significant male-female difference on certain traits, but often these differences are small and of no consequence in the real world (see Chapter 2).

Ultimately, we believe, students will not develop an enduring disposition to think critically if their textbook does not make critical analysis an integral part of its narrative. *Critical thinking cannot be tacked on.* We therefore weave critical analysis into the text itself, throughout this book. We apply it to concepts that many students approach uncritically, such as astrology, "premenstrual syndrome," and the "instinctive" nature of love and desire. We also apply it to some assumptions that *psychologists* have accepted unquestioningly, including stages in adult development, the decisive importance of childhood to later life, the hierarchical nature of motives, and the automatic nature of drug effects. By probing beneath assumptions and presenting the most recent evidence available, we hope to convey the excitement and open-ended nature of psychological research and inquiry.

■ ON INTEGRATING GENDER AND CULTURE INTO MAINSTREAM PSYCHOLOGY

When we wrote the first edition of this book some years ago, we felt the time had finally come for psychologists to acknowledge that universal principles of behavior cannot be deduced from a narrow sample of humanity. College students were growing more diverse; they included older adults (who are often amused at "findings" based on 19-year-olds) and people of many ethnicities (who are often baffled by "findings" based solely on Anglo-Americans). A substantial body of knowledge had accumulated on gender roles and male-female differences (and less often, similarities). Studies were showing that culture is not merely a superficial gloss on human behavior, but a profound influence that affects virtually all aspects of life.

At the time, the idea of "mainstreaming" issues of age, gender, ethnicity, and culture in college textbooks was still considered radical. Today, some instructors still fear that the introduction of these topics will compromise the scientific nature of the field and that they represent a rejection of the entire Western curriculum. For many instructors, however, the issue is no longer whether to include these topics, but how best to do it. Our own belief has always been that male and Western biases in psychology undermine the *scientific* generality of its findings, and that we should not throw out existing knowledge but rather expand its frontiers. Further, we believe the relevant studies and the larger perspectives on these issues should be raised *where they occur in the main body of the text*. Relegating this information to separate chapters or boxed features, we feel, conveys the idea that white people or Westerners or young people or men are the norm and that the groups discussed separately are the exception, peripheral to the main business of psychology.

On the matter of gender, for example: Are there sex differences in the brain? This controversial issue belongs in the text of the brain chapter. Do women and men differ in the meanings and motives they attach to love and sex? That topic belongs in the motivation chapter. Do men and women express emotion differently? That question should be addressed in the emotion chapter. On the matter of culture: Not all cultures regard the "self" or the "individual" as Westerners do or place the same priority on competition. This fact has consequences for personality theory, and thus belongs in the discussion of personality. Cultures differ in the display rules of emotion; what, if anything, does that tell us about the universality of emotional experience? People are supposed to have a biologically built-in need for "closure," especially for unfinished tasks; then how come the Hopi could leave their houses half-built and go on to other tasks? Cultures differ in how infants are treated from the very moment of birth; what effect does this have on the milestones of infant development? We hope to show how the answers to these and other questions illuminate our understanding of human development and behavior.

Users of previous editions will find much new material that is relevant to an increasingly multicultural society. For example, in the chapter on intelligence, we go beyond traditional deficit models by including research on how school systems can capitalize on the linguistic traditions and *strengths* of minority children. In the section on adolescence, we discuss the conflict between ethnic identity formation and acculturation during the teenage years. And in our discussion of mental disorders, we include an extended analysis and critique of how the *Diagnostic and Statistical Manual of Mental Disorders* has misdiagnosed "mental illness" for women, homosexuals, and African Americans.

Integrating such issues into a textbook requires some choices about how to label groups: black or African American, Hispanic or Latino, Eskimo or Inuit, Indian or Native American, white or Anglo-American? Group labels are still in flux, as people struggle with their ethnic identities and their place in the larger culture. In this textbook we have based our choices on the context in which the terms appear, realizing that our specific decisions may not please everyone. For example, Hispanic seemed appropriate to us when discussing population groups, but Latino seemed better for identifying certain cultural tastes and customs. Also, we have replaced Eskimo with Inuit, the term preferred by this group. But we use "black" more often than African American because it is still the term most commonly used by both blacks and others in society. Rather than focus on which terms are most "correct," we encourage teachers to raise the question of labels in their own classrooms. What do students prefer to call themselves and other groups? Their answers will reveal a great deal about their ethnic identities and sense of place in society.

We wish to emphasize that although we have expanded our integration of research on culture and gender, we have not written an anthropology text or a women's studies book. We have written a psychology text: one that, we hope, will expand a student's vision and understanding of the many and varied influences on the human being; one that, we hope, teaches that a scientific psychology must be the study of all human beings.

■ APPLICATIONS: TAKING PSYCHOLOGY WITH YOU

Few disciplines have as many real-world implications as does psychology. Psychological principles and findings can be applied to individuals, groups, institutions, and society as a whole. We cover such applications not only in the main body of the text but also in a feature at the end of each chapter called **Taking Psychology with You.** Drawing on research reported in the chapter, this feature tackles topics of practical concern, such as coping with the stresses of life, helping a friend who is suicidal, managing anger, rearing children, improving memory (and appreciating forgetfulness!), and resisting friendly and not-so-friendly tactics of persuasion. Some of the discussions are about "taking critical thinking with you," as in Chapter 2 (how to avoid the pitfalls of "intuitive statistics") and Chapter 12 (how not to misinterpret the normal occurrence of astonishing coincidences).

The final "Taking Psychology with You" feature is an **Epilogue,** which represents a unique effort to show readers that the vast number of seemingly disparate studies and points of view they have just read about *are* related. The epilogue contains two real-life problems that most students can be expected to encounter, if they haven't already: the end of a love relationship and difficulties at work. We show how various topics discussed in previous chapters can be applied to understanding and coping with these situations. Readers learn that solving a real problem requires more than finding the "right" study from the "right" school of psychology. Many instructors have told us that they find this epilogue a useful way to help students integrate some of the diverse approaches of contemporary psychology. Asking students to come up with research findings that might apply to other "problems in living" makes for a good term-paper assignment as well.

■ INVOLVING THE STUDENT

One of the sturdiest findings about learning is that it requires the active encoding of material. In this textbook, three features in particular encourage students' active involvement and provide pedagogical support:

• *A separate handbook called* **Learning to Think Critically: The Case of Close Relationships.** This handbook, which has been updated and is free to all students whose instructors order it, illustrates how critical and creative thinking skills and psychological research can be applied to beliefs about love, intimacy, attraction, and commitment. Some instructors assign this booklet to teach critical thinking skills, either at the beginning of the course or along with Chapter 8, on thought and problem solving. Others assign it in tandem with Chapter 18, on social psychology, focusing on the research content of the handbook.

• *Quick Quizzes—periodic self-tests that encourage students to check their own progress, and to go back and review if necessary.* These quizzes do more than just test for memorization of definitions; they tell students whether they comprehend the issues. Mindful of the common tendency to skip quizzes or to peek at the answers, we have used various formats and have included entertaining examples in order to motivate students to test themselves. As we mentioned, in this edition many of the quizzes also include critical thinking items. We believe that the incorporation of these items makes this pedagogical feature, more than ever, a useful one for students of all abilities.

• *A **running glossary** defines boldfaced technical terms on the pages where they occur (or on the facing page) for handy reference and study.* Students are enthusiastic about this feature. All entries can also be found in a cumulative glossary at the back of the book.

Other special features include chapter outlines, lists of key terms, and chapter summaries in numbered paragraph form.

■ WHAT ELSE IS NEW?

In addition to the sharpened focus on critical and creative thinking, and additional material on human diversity, this edition includes revised content and updated research throughout. We have purposely avoided making purely "cosmetic" changes, especially in the stories and examples that students enjoy. We did, however, add a great deal of recent, cutting-edge research, and we reorganized some sections to make them clearer and easier to study and teach. Here are some highlights:

Chapter 2 (research methods) contains an updated section on the animal research issue, and concludes with a new, introductory-level discussion of the "postmodern" movement and its implications for traditional approaches to psychological inquiry.

Chapter 3 (the nervous system, the brain, and hormones) contains new research challenging the assumption that central nervous system neurons can't regenerate after injury; a reorganized discussion of neurotransmitters, with new findings on the role of serotonin imbalances in Alzheimer's disease and childhood autism; and new case reports of brain-damaged patients that demonstrate extreme specificity of functioning in the brain.

Chapter 4 (biological rhythms and states of consciousness) contains an expanded critical analysis of "PMS" and a discussion of the possible role of male hormones in mood and behavior; a new section on dreams as opportunities for problem solving; a fuller discussion of the activation-synthesis theory of dreaming; and new studies that account for reports of "past-lives regression" under hypnosis.

Chapter 5 (sensation and perception) has been extensively reorganized to make the material easier to follow; contains new research on olfaction; and includes an updated discussion of nonconscious perceptual processes, with fascinating new research that has investigated claims of subliminal perception and subliminal persuasion.

Chapter 6 (learning) contains an updated discussion of the role of classical conditioning in drug tolerance; new research on the effects of punishment in the real world; and a new "Think About It" box that examines the possible relationship between media violence and real-world violence.

Chapter 7 (memory) contains new material on the study of implicit memory; a new discussion of cross-cultural research on semantic categorization in recall; new research on the brain systems involved in memory; and more material on autobiographical memory, including a critical discussion of cases of sudden recall of repressed memories and new research on the fragility of "flashbulb" memories.

Chapter 8 (thought and language) contains a reorganized section on inductive versus deductive reasoning, with new, more precise definitions; a new "Think About It" box on how television and reading affect the ability to think clearly and critically; new sections on the confirmation bias and the hindsight bias as sources of irrationality; and an updated discussion of animals' ability to acquire language, with a critical discussion of anthropomorphism *and* anthropocentrism.

Chapter 9 (emotion) includes an extensively reorganized introduction that moves away from the old question, "Which comes first, body or cognition?" (a question that promoted a misleading mind/body dualism), and instead emphasizes the major concerns of emotion research today. The chapter reviews new findings and research directions that resolve the age-old organic/mental debate; contains more material on the physiology of emotion and on cultural influences in emotion; and has an expanded and clarified concluding section that more thoroughly "puts the elements together" in discussing gender and emotion (i.e., physiology, attributions, feeling, expression, emotion work, display rules, etc.).

Chapter 10 (motivation) contains new studies on the genetics of body shape and weight gain; a new, separate section on sexual motives and theories of sexuality, with an expanded discussion of sexual coercion and new material contrasting sociobiology with script/learning theories; a discussion of the "glass ceiling" and how it affects work motivation for minorities and women; and more on the cultural influences on motivation and behavior.

Chapters 11 and 12 (human diversity) have been reordered: Mental testing and individual differences in ability are now covered first, in Chapter 11; personality testing and individual differences in personality are now covered in Chapter 12 along with theories of personality. *This is a major change* that we believe will improve students' ability to understand the material.

Chapter 11 (abilities) includes a new, timely discussion of performance-based assessment; an expanded discussion of specific environmental influences on individual differences in ability; new cross-cultural and cross-ethnic research that can help explain group differences in performance on intelligence tests; and new discussions of practical and emotional intelligence.

Chapter 12 (personality) has been reorganized. Trait studies now precede theories of personality, because traits are the elements of personality that the theories attempt to explain. In addition, the chapter contains a new section on *biological* theories of personality, incorporating material on heredity from the former Chapter 12; a new box on culture, personality, and the self; and new coverage of contemporary psychodynamic theories, such as object-relations theory.

Chapter 13 (child development) contains much more research, including meta-analytic studies, on the effects of child-rearing techniques, day care in infancy and early childhood, and divorce; a new "Think About It" on the "fetal protection" movement; and more material on the development of guilt and shame as "moral emotions."

Chapter 14 (adolescence and adulthood) contains an expanded discussion of the psychology of adolescence, including gender differences in personality and self-esteem, "possible selves," and ethnic identity versus acculturation as developmental issues for adolescents; more material on the diversity of American families (including families headed by single parents and gay parents) and of life milestones; and a new section on the effects of divorce on couples.

Chapter 16 (abnormal psychology) contains an expanded and more detailed discussion of the difficulties of diagnosing and defining certain mental disorders, including a critique of the DSM; an expanded discussion of the controversies surrounding multiple personality disorder; and late-breaking work on the schizophrenias.

Chapter 17 (psychotherapy) includes new work on the role of narratives—the accounts that people generate to explain the main events of their lives—in psychotherapy; and new research on drug therapies, including information on their uses and limitations and on racial and gender differences in responses to drugs.

Chapter 18 (social psychology) contains more material on heroes and dissenters—the positive side of social influence; and an expanded discussion of the nature of prejudice and the meanings and forms of racism.

A detailed explanation of deletions, additions, and changes in this edition is available to all adopters of the previous edition, so that they will not have to guess why we made particular changes. We hope this support will make the transition from one edition to the next as painless for instructors as possible. You can obtain this description from your HarperCollins representative or by writing to: Marketing Manager, Psychology, HarperCollins College Publishers, 10 E. 53rd Street, New York, NY 10022.

■ SUPPLEMENTS PACKAGE

Psychology, Third Edition, is supported by a complete teaching and learning package. To help instructors integrate the individual components of the package into their courses, HarperCollins has provided an "Integrator"—a chapter-by-chapter indexing and cross-referencing guide to many of the instructional resources accompanying the text. The Integrator is conveniently located in the instructor's free edition of the text.

Print Supplements and Transparencies

INSTRUCTOR'S RESOURCE KIT. Written by Eva Conrad, of San Bernardino Valley College, and Mark Rafter, of Chaffey Community College, in consultation with the textbook authors, this manual contains a wealth of teaching aids for each chapter: learning objectives, chapter outlines, lecture supplements, classroom demonstrations, critical thinking exercises; mini-experiments, self-test exercises and suggestions for additional readings; and an extensive guide to audiovisual materials. This instructor's kit is housed in a three-ring binder for easy reproduction of student handouts. The roomy binder also makes a great storage unit for collecting your own favorite lecture supplements and teaching materials.

TEST BANK. A comprehensive assortment of multiple-choice and essay test items per chapter is featured in this class-tested supplement written by Grace Galliano of Kennesaw State College. Reviewed by content and testing experts, it offers questions that test conceptual knowledge and are referenced by learning objectives, cognitive type, and difficulty level. Each chapter includes several scenario questions that tell stories and then ask students to respond to questions by synthesizing concepts from the text.

STUDY GUIDE. Written by Judith Sugar, Jeanette Cleveland, and Kevin Murphy of Colorado State University, this highly acclaimed manual has been extensively updated to reflect the new coverage in the third edition. It includes learning objectives, chapter outlines, thinking questions illustrating concepts in the text, and three sets of practice tests with answers.

PRACTICE TESTS. Shrink-wrapped with student copies of the text, this supplement provides a sample multiple-choice test written by the test bank author for each chapter.

TRANSPARENCIES. A new Introductory Psychology Transparency Package contains 100 full-color acetates, some from the text. The package features many transparencies specifically designed for large lecture halls.

Software Supplements

TESTMASTER COMPUTERIZED TESTING SYSTEM. This flexible, easy-to-master computer test bank includes all the test items in the test bank. The TestMaster software allows you to edit existing questions and add your own items. Tests can be printed in several different formats and can include figures such as graphs and tables. Available for IBM and Macintosh computers.

SUPERSHELL COMPUTERIZED TUTORIAL. Created by Eva Conrad and Mark Rafter, this interactive program helps students learn the major facts and concepts through drill and practice exercises and diagnostic feedback. SuperShell provides immediate correct answers and the text page numbers on which the material is discussed. Missed questions appear with greater frequency; a running score of the student's performance is maintained on the screen throughout the session. It is available for IBM computers.

LECTURESHELL. The chapter outlines of the entire text are available for the IBM computer for use in creating your own lecture outlines.

JOURNEY II. You can take students through a concept-building tour of the psychology experiment, the nervous system, learning, development, and psychological assessment with this program developed by Intentional Educations. Each module is self-contained and comes complete with step-by-step pedagogy. This program is available for IBM and Macintosh computers.

Media Supplements

NEW! PSYCHOLOGY ENCYCLOPEDIA III LASERDISC. This supplement is on the cutting edge of audiovisual capabilities for the introductory psychology classroom. Drawing from extensive focus group research, HarperCollins has created a multimedia laserdisc that combines a broad-based classical approach to introductory concepts of psychology, using seven minutes of newly developed computer animation, classic and contemporary archival motion footage, colorful graphics, and over 200 still images, including critical thinking and test-question frames. Extensively reviewed to ensure accuracy, original animation demonstrates the biological and physiological concepts of psychology (accompanied by voice-over narration). Motion footage compilations include archival footage of classic experiments as well as up-to-date demonstrations of difficult psychological concepts.

In addition, the laserdisc is accompanied by an Instructor's Guide that includes a detailed table of contents and bar code directory for easy access to individual frames. Also included are numerous suggestions for integrating the disc into classroom lectures and activities. Through this unique addition, professors will be able to use multimedia visuals to bring the introductory psychology curriculum to life during lecture presentations.

■ ACKNOWLEDGMENTS

Like any other cooperative effort, writing a textbook requires a support team. The following reviewers and consultants made many valuable suggestions during the development of the first, second, and third editions of *Psychology*, and we are indebted to them for their contributions.

Benton E. Allen
Mt. San Antonio College

Susan M. Andersen
University of California, Santa Barbara

Lynn R. Anderson
Wayne State University

Emir Andrews
Memorial University of Newfoundland

Patricia Barker
Schenectady County Community College

Ronald K. Barrett
Loyola Marymount University

Allan Basbaum
University of California, San Francisco

Carol Batt
Sacred Heart University

Bill E. Beckwith
University of North Dakota

David F. Berger
SUNY at Cortland

Michael Bergmire
Jefferson College

Philip J. Bersh
Temple University

Richard Bowen
Loyola University of Chicago

Laura L. Bowman
Kent State University

John R. Braun
University of Bridgeport

Sharon S. Brehm
SUNY at Binghamton

Sylvester Briggs
Kent State University

Gwen Briscoe
College of Mt. St. Joseph

Barbara Brown
DeKalb College

Robert C. Brown, Jr.
Georgia State University

Peter R. Burzynski
Vincennes University

Jean Caplan
Concordia University

Bernardo J. Carducci
Indiana University Southeast

Paul Chance
Laurel, DE

Samuel Clement
Marianopolis College

Eva Conrad
San Bernardino Valley College

Richard L. Cook
University of Colorado

Robert Cormack
New Mexico Institute of Mining and Technology

Wendi Cross
Ohio University

Robert M. Davis
Purdue University School of Science, IUPUI

Michael William Decker
University of California, Irvine

Geri Anne Dino
Frostburg State University

Ronald Finke
SUNY at Stony Brook

John H. Flowers
University of Nebraska-Lincoln

William F. Ford
Bucks County Community College

Donald G. Forgays
University of Vermont

Sheila Francis
Creighton University

Grace Galliano
Kennesaw State College

Mary Gauvain
Oregon State University

Ron Gerrard
SUNY at Oswego

Margaret Gittis
Youngstown State University

Carlos Goldberg
Indiana University-Purdue University at Indianapolis

Carol Grams
Orange Coast College

Patricia Greenfield
University of California, Los Angeles

Richard A. Griggs
University of Florida

Sami Gulgoz
Auburn University

Len Hamilton
Rutgers University

George Hampton
University of Houston

Neil Helgeson
The University of Texas at San Antonio

John E. Hesson
Metropolitan State College

Robert Higgins
Oakland Community College

John P. Hostetler
Albion College

John Hunsley
University of Ottawa

James Johnson
University of North Carolina at Wilmington

Timothy P. Johnston
University of North Carolina at Greensboro

Chadwick Karr
Portland State University

Yoshito Kawahara
San Diego Mesa College

Geoffrey Keppel
University of California, Berkeley

Harold O. Kiess
Framingham State College

Gary King
Rose State College

Jack Kirschenbaum
Fullerton College

Donald Kline
University of Calgary

Stephen M. Kosslyn
Harvard University

George S. Larimer
West Liberty State College

S. David Leonard
University of Georgia

Herbert Leff
University of Vermont

Robert Levy
Indiana State University

Lewis Lieberman
Columbus College

R. Martin Lobdell
Pierce College

Nina Lott
National University

Bonnie Lustigman
Montclair State College

Debra Moehle McCallum
University of Alabama at Birmingham

D. F. McCoy
University of Kentucky

C. Sue McCullough
Texas Woman's University

Elizabeth McDonel
University of Alabama

Susanne Wicks McKenzie
Dawson College

Mark B. McKinley
Lorain County Community College

Ronald K. McLaughlin
Juniata College

Frances K. McSweeney
Washington State University

Marc Marschark
University of North Carolina at Greensboro

Monique Martin
Champlain Regional College

Mary Jo Meadow
Mankato State University

Dorothy Mercer
Eastern Kentucky University

Laura J. Metallo
Five Towns College

Maribel Montgomery
Linn-Benton Community College

Douglas G. Mook
University of Virginia

T. Mark Morey
SUNY College at Oswego

James S. Nairne
University of Texas at Arlington

Douglas Navarick
California State University, Fullerton

Robert A. Neimeyer
Memphis State University

Nora Newcombe
Temple University

Linda Noble
Kennesaw State College

Keith Oatley
Ontario Institute for Studies in Education

Peter Oliver
University of Hartford

Patricia Owen-Smith
Oxford College

David Page
Nazareth College

M. Carr Payne, Jr.
Georgia Institute of Technology

Dan G. Perkins
Richland College

Gregory Pezzetti
Rancho Santiago Community College

Wayne Poniewaz
University of Arkansas, Monticello

Paula M. Popovich
Ohio University

Robert Prochnow
St. Cloud State University

Janet Proctor
Purdue University

Reginald L. Razzi
Upsala College

Gary Ross-Reynolds
Nicholls State University

Joe Rubinstein
Purdue University

Nancy Sauerman
Kirkwood Community College

H. R. Schiffman
Rutgers University

David A. Schroeder
University of Arkansas

Marvin Schwartz
University of Cincinnati

Shelley Schwartz
Vanier College

Joyce Segreto
Youngstown State University

Kimron Shapiro
University of Calgary

Phillip Shaver
University of California, Davis

Susan A. Shodahl
San Bernardino Valley College

Dale Simmons
Oregon State University

Art Skibbe
Appalachian State University

William P. Smotherman
SUNY at Binghamton

Samuel Snyder
North Carolina State University

Tina Stern
DeKalb College

A. Stirling
John Abbott College

Milton E. Strauss
Johns Hopkins University

Judith Sugar
Colorado State University

Shelley E. Taylor
University of California, Los Angeles

Barbara Turpin
Southwest Missouri State University

Ronald J. Venhorst
Kean College of New Jersey

Wayne A. Viney
Colorado State University

Benjamin Wallace
Cleveland State University

Phyllis Walrad
Macomb Community College

Charles R. Walsmith
Bellevue Community College

Phillip Wann
Missouri Western State College

Thomas J. Weatherly
DeKalb College-Central Campus

Mary Wellman
Rhode Island University

Gary L. Wells
University of Alberta

Warner Wilson
Wright State University

Loren Wingblade
Jackson Community College

Our editorial and production team at HarperCollins has been, as always, superb, and we are enormously grateful to these talented people for their hard work and commitment to quality. In particular, we thank psychology editor Anne Harvey, for her unwavering confidence in us and in this book; marketing manager Barbara Cinquegrani, for expertly organizing and implementing the marketing plan; and project editor Robert Ginsberg, whose humor, calm manner, and excellent organizational skills helped us to meet our deadlines without ever feeling (too) pressured. Under Dorothy Bungert's direction, the book has acquired a clean new design that weaves the many elements together with clarity and elegance. As critical thinkers, we don't believe in mind reading, of course, yet photo researcher Sandy Schneider often did seem to be reading our minds about how to visually illustrate abstract concepts or raise thought-provoking questions.

We cannot begin to thank Saul Bass for once again giving us a unique and stunning cover design, and for adding immeasurably to the visual impact of this new edition with a series of striking part-opening illustrations. Saul's work conveys the mystery, the challenge, the risk, and the rewards in thinking critically and creatively, and represents art and psychology at their best. Our appreciation also goes to Art Goodman, Nancy Von Lauderbach and the rest of the fine staff at Saul Bass/Herb Yager and Associates.

Most of all, we thank Howard Williams and Ronan O'Casey, who from the beginning of this endeavor have bolstered us with their love, humor, and good cheer, not to mention an endless supply of freshly brewed coffee.

We have enjoyed writing this book, and we hope you will enjoy reading and using it. Your questions, comments, and reactions on the first two editions helped us make many improvements. Please let us hear from you.

CAROLE WADE
CAROL TAVRIS

To the Student

If you are reading this introduction, you are starting your introductory psychology course on the right foot. It is always a good idea to get a general picture of what you are about to read before charging forward, just as it is best to find out what Wyoming looks like before moving there from Maine.

Our goal in writing this book is to guide you to *think critically* and imaginatively about what you read, and to *apply* what you learn to your own life and the real world. We ourselves have never gotten over our initial excitement about psychology, and we have done everything we can think of to make the field as absorbing for you as it is for us. However, what you bring to this book is as important as what we have written. This text will remain only a collection of pages with ink on them unless you choose to interact with its content. The more actively you are involved in your own learning, the more successful the book and your course will be, and the more enjoyable, too.

In our years of teaching, we have found that certain study strategies can vastly improve learning, and so we offer the following suggestions. Do not read the text in the same way as you might a novel, taking in large chunks at a sitting. To get the most from your studying, we recommend that you read only a part of each chapter at a time. And instead of simply reading silently, try to *restate* what you have read in your own words at the end of each major section. Some people find it helpful to write down main points on a piece of paper or on index cards. Others prefer to recite main points aloud to someone else or to themselves (which may require some privacy!). Do not count on getting by with just one reading of a chapter. Most people need to go through the material at least twice, and then review the main points several times before an exam.

Individuals often develop their own unique strategies for studying, and we don't want to discourage you from doing so. Whatever approach you use, though, it should involve an active response to the material. Here are some hints for enhancing your learning:

• A good first step is to read the chapter title and outline to get an idea of what's in store. Browse through the chapter, looking at the pictures and reading the headings.

• Every chapter contains several *Quick Quizzes* that permit you to test your understanding and retention of what you have just read and your ability to *apply* the material to examples. Do not let the word "quiz" give you a sinking feeling. These quizzes are for your practical use and, we hope, for your enjoyment. When you can't answer a question, do not go on to the next section; pause right then and there, review what you've read, and then try again.

• Some of the Quick Quizzes contain a special critical-thinking item, denoted by a "flash" symbol such as the one in the margin. The answers we give for these items are only suggestions; you may come up with different (and possibly better) ones. Quizzes containing critical-thinking items are not really so "quick," because they ask you to reflect on what you have read and to apply certain guidelines to critical thinking that are introduced in Chapter 1. But if you take the time to respond thoughtfully to these questions, we think you will learn more and become a more sophisticated user of psychology.

• Every important new term in this textbook is printed in **boldface** and is defined in the margin of the page on which it appears or on the facing page. The marginal glossary permits you to find all key terms and concepts easily, and will help you when you study for an exam. A full glossary also appears at the end of the book.

• "Critical thinking signposts," found in the margins and accompanied by the "flash" symbol, indicate where critical thinking analyses or issues appear in the text.

• When you have finished a chapter, read the *summary*. Some students tell us they find it useful to write down their own summary first, then compare it with the book's.

• Use the *key terms* list at the end of each chapter as a checklist. Try to define and discuss each term in the list to see how well you understand and remember it. If you need to review a term, a page number is given to tell you where it is first mentioned in the chapter.

There are some other features of this book that you should know about. In each chapter, a *Think About It* box poses a provocative question that has no easy answer. We hope you will have as much fun pondering these questions as we did writing about them. Another box, called *A Closer Look at . . .* , examines various research specialties within psychology in depth. At the end of each chapter, a feature called *Taking Psychology with You* draws on research to suggest ways you can apply what you have learned to everyday problems and concerns, such as living with stress, coping with life's transitions, and getting a better night's sleep, and to more serious ones, such as coping with life's "crises" or helping a suicidal friend.

You will notice that discussions of studies and theories are followed by one or more *citations* in parentheses. A citation tells the reader where the original research report or theoretical work was published. It consists of the author's name and the date of publication—for example: (Smith, 1984). The full reference, with the name of the article or book and other information, can be found in a *bibliography* at the end of the book. Students often find citations useful, especially for locating material for term projects and reports.

At the back of the book you will also find an *author index* and a *subject index*. The author index lists the name of every author cited in the book and the pages where the person's work is discussed. If you want to review a study by someone named Snodgrass, but you can't recall where it was covered, look under "Snodgrass" in the author index. The subject index provides a listing of all the major topics mentioned in the book. If you want to review material on, say, depression, you can look up "depression" in the subject index.

Most psychology books stop abruptly with the last chapter, leaving the reader with the impression that early lessons have little to do with later ones. At the end of this book, you will find an *Epilogue* that shows you how you can integrate and use the findings and theories you have read about to understand events, make wise decisions, and cope with life's inevitable challenges and changes. We consider the Epilogue to be important because it suggests how you can carry psychology out of your classroom and into the "real world."

We also recommend the Study Guide that is available at your bookstore to help you study and expand upon the material in this book. The Study Guide contains review material, exercises, and practice tests that show you how to apply the concepts in the book.

We have done our utmost to convey our own enthusiasm about psychology, but in the end, it is your efforts as much as ours that will determine whether you find psychology to be exciting or boring, and whether the field will matter in your own life. We welcome your ideas and reactions so that we will know what works for you and what doesn't. In the meantime, welcome to psychology!

CAROLE WADE
CAROL TAVRIS

About the Authors

Carole Wade earned her Ph.D. in cognitive psychology at Stanford University. She began her academic career at the University of New Mexico (where she initiated a new course on gender roles); was professor of psychology for ten years at San Diego Mesa College; and currently teaches undergraduate courses in psychology at the College of Marin. She is coauthor (with Sarah Cirese) of *Human Sexuality* and coauthor (with Carol Tavris) of *The Longest War: Sex Differences in Perspective*. A former associate editor of *Psychology Today*—where she met Dr. Tavris—Dr. Wade has a long-standing interest in making psychology accessible to students and the general public through public lectures, workshops, general interest articles, and the electronic media. For many years she has focused her efforts on the teaching and promotion of critical thinking skills; she is a member of the Standing Committee on Critical Thinking and Psychology of the National Council for Excellence in Critical Thinking Instruction. She is a past chair of the American Psychological Association's Public Information Committee and a past member of the APA's Committee on Undergraduate Education, and was a member of the Steering Committee for the APA's National Conference on Enhancing the Quality of Undergraduate Education. Dr. Wade is a Fellow of Divisions 1 and 2 and a member of Divisions 8, 9, and 35 of the American Psychological Association, and is a charter member of the American Psychological Society.

Carol Tavris earned her Ph.D. in the interdisciplinary social psychology program at the University of Michigan, and ever since has sought to bring interdisciplinary research from the many fields of psychology to the public. She is author of *The Mismeasure of Woman*, which won the 1992 Distinguished Media Contribution Award from the American Association from Applied and Preventive Psychology and the Heritage Publications Award from Division 35 of the APA. Dr. Tavris is also the author of *Anger: The Misunderstood Emotion;* and coauthor (with Carole Wade) of *The Longest War: Sex Differences in Perspective*. She has written on psychological topics for a wide variety of magazines, journals, and edited books, and also contributes essays to the *Los Angeles Times*. Highly regarded as a national and international lecturer, she has given keynote addresses and workshops on, among other topics, critical thinking, anger, gender, and psychology and the media. She has taught at the Human Relations Center of the New School for Social Research in New York and in the psychology department at UCLA. Dr. Tavris is a Fellow of Divisions 1, 9, and 35 of the American Psychological Association and a member of Division 8; a charter member and Fellow of the American Psychological Society; a member of the International Society for Research on Emotion; a member of the Authors Guild and of PEN Center USA; and a Fellow of the Committee for the Scientific Investigation of Claims of the Paranormal.

AN INVITATION TO PSYCHOLOGY

1

What Is Psychology?

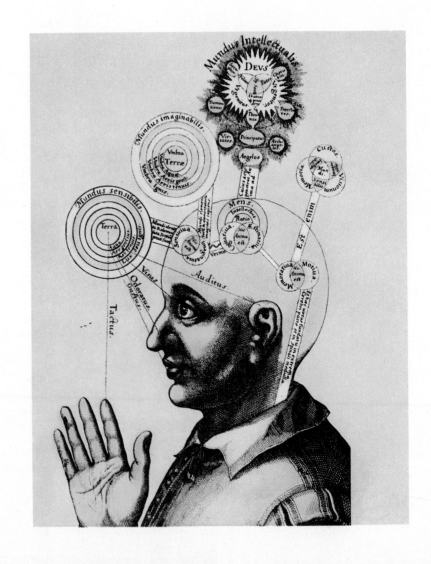

*The purpose of psychology
is to give us a completely different idea
of the things we know best.*

PAUL VALÉRY

In 1945, a 15-year-old Jewish girl named Anne Frank died of typhus at Bergen-Belsen, a notorious Nazi death camp. She had spent the previous two years with her parents, her sister, and four others in a cramped apartment in Amsterdam, hiding from German troops occupying Holland. Unable to go outside, the group depended entirely on Christian friends for food and other necessities. Anne, who was a gifted writer and astute observer, recorded in her diary the fears, frustrations, and inevitable clashes of people forced to live 24 hours a day in close proximity. Yet she never despaired or lost her sense of wonder at life's joys. With humor and grace, she described the pleasure of family celebrations, the thrill of first love, the excitement of growing up. Shortly before the Gestapo discovered the hideout, Anne wrote, "It's really a wonder that I haven't dropped all my ideals, because they seem so absurd and impossible to carry out. Yet I keep them, because in spite of everything I still believe that people are really good at heart. I simply can't build up my hopes on a foundation consisting of confusion, misery, and death."

Anne Frank (1929–1945)

Many years later, and thousands of miles away, Charles "Tex" Watson grew up, apparently uneventfully, in a small American town. A handsome boy, Charles attended church, earned high grades, and competed successfully in football, basketball, and track. During his junior year in high school his fellow students named him the outstanding member of his class. Then, a few years after leaving home for college, Watson fell in with the Charles Manson cult. Manson was a charismatic figure who convinced his followers that he was divinely chosen to lead them and demanded their blind obedience. In 1969, on Manson's orders, the cult savagely slaughtered seven innocent people in Los Angeles. Tex Watson, the young man who had earlier seemed so full of promise, cold-bloodedly carved his initials on the chest of one of the victims.

Why did Anne Frank, living in the constant shadow of death, retain her love of humanity? Why did Tex Watson, who apparently had everything to live for, turn to brutal acts of violence? How can we explain why some people are overwhelmed by petty problems, while others, faced with real difficulties, remain mentally healthy? What principles can help us understand why some human beings are confident players in the game of life, while others angrily reject its basic rules?

If you have ever asked yourself such questions, welcome to the world of psychology. You are about to explore a discipline that studies the many complexities and contradictions of human behavior. Psychologists take as their subject the entire spectrum of brave and cowardly, wise and silly, intelligent and foolish, beautiful and brutish things that human beings do. Their aim: to examine and explain how human beings—and animals, too—learn, remember, solve problems, perceive, feel, and get along with others.

Many people, when they hear the word *psychology*, think immediately of mental disorders and abnormal behavior. But psychologists do not confine their attention to extremes of behavior. They are just as likely to focus on commonplace experiences—experiences as universal and ordinary as rearing children,

3

remembering a shopping list, daydreaming, and even gossiping. Most of us, after all, are neither saints nor sinners but a curious combination of both positive and negative qualities. Psychology, in short, is not only about martyrs and murderers; it is also about *you*.

■ A MATTER OF DEFINITION

Psychology has always had a way of outgrowing its definitions. At the start of this century, most psychologists considered psychology to be the study of mental life, the mind, or consciousness. Within a few years, however, such definitions came under attack as vague and unscientific. As we shall see, between the 1920s and the 1950s many psychologists preferred to define their discipline as the study of behavior, because what people do—unlike what they think or feel—can be directly observed and measured. But this definition also came under attack. To those who still wanted to study thinking, dreaming, and all the other fascinating things that go on between people's ears, confining psychology to behavior made no more sense than confining literature to short stories or history to descriptions of military battles.

Today, most psychologists are willing to make room for both behavior and mind in their work. In this book we, too, take a broad approach. We define **psychology** as *the scientific study of behavior and mental processes and how they are affected by an organism's physical state, mental state, and external environment.*

We realize that this brief definition of psychology is a little like defining a car as "a vehicle for transporting people from one place to another." Such a definition is accurate as far as it goes, but it doesn't tell you what a car looks like, how a car differs from a train or a bus, how a Ford differs from a Ferrari, or how a carburetor works. Similarly, to get a good, clear picture of what psychology is, you need to have more information—about its methods, its findings, its ways of interpreting data. Your course and the rest of this textbook will give you this information.

Psychology's Main Goals

We can begin with psychology's main goals. These goals are straightforward: to (1) *describe*, (2) *understand*, (3) *predict*, and (4) *control* or *modify* behavior and mental processes.

In a sense, every human being is an amateur psychologist, because everyone wants to describe, understand, predict, and control behavior and mental processes, both their own and those of other people. Suppose your best friend has just nagged you for the three hundredth time about your tendency to subsist solely on pizza, potato chips, and soda pop. You might describe the behavior ("Frieda is always badgering me about the way I eat"); attempt to understand its cause ("She's a health nut"); make a prediction about the future ("If I don't do something, I'm going to be nagged for the rest of my life"); and try to bring about a change ("I'll eat wheat germ and drink carrot juice once a week, and then maybe she'll leave me alone").

But if psychologists' goals are the same as everyone else's, what makes psychology a special discipline? The answer is that most people form opinions about human behavior and experience in a casual way. Most psychologists, in contrast, follow rigorous and systematic procedures, to be described in the next chapter. They resist reaching for conclusions until they have evidence that can be checked and verified by others. They test their ideas. For example, do lie detectors work? A nonpsychologist might base an opinion on conjecture, media accounts, or the claims of professional lie detector interpreters. Psychologists, however, have studied the question by comparing the results of lie detector tests taken by people already known by the researcher to be guilty or

■ **psychology**
The scientific study of behavior and mental processes and how they are affected by an organism's physical state, mental state, and external environment. The term is often represented by Ψ, the Greek letter psi *(usually pronounced "sy").*

innocent of a crime. Lie detectors, it turns out, are highly inaccurate: As we will see when we get to Chapter 9, many innocent people fail lie detector tests, and many guilty people pass with flying colors.

There has sometimes been heated, even bitter, debate among both psychologists and nonpsychologists about psychology's fourth goal, the control or modification of behavior and mental processes. When psychologists talk about changing behavior, they are thinking about improving education and child rearing, increasing work productivity, reducing crime, teaching social skills, helping people get rid of unwanted habits, and making other useful contributions to society. However, some people worry that governments or ambitious individuals will use the control techniques of psychology to set themselves up as Big Brother and manipulate the unsuspecting.

Defenders of behavioral control point out that psychologists did not invent the idea. In fact, all of us control others, and in turn are controlled by others, each and every day. The last time you tried to attract someone's romantic interest, get a child to do something he or she didn't want to, or win an argument, *you* were attempting to exert behavioral control. Even people who consider themselves easygoing, live-and-let-live types inevitably control others, whether intentionally or not—by their actions, their responses, their facial expressions, and even their silences.

The findings of any science can be used in ways that help or hurt people, depending on the political decisions made by society. Psychologists who include control as a goal believe that psychological findings and principles, if used wisely, can contribute to human welfare and happiness. We all exert control anyway, they say. We might as well know what we are doing.

QUICK QUIZ

Pause now to be sure you understand psychology's goals. Below are four statements that a psychologist might make. Name the main goal met by each statement: description, understanding, prediction, or control.

1. Children begin to combine words at about age 2.
2. You can overcome your fear of snakes by gradually exposing yourself to pictures of snakes and eventually to real snakes.
3. The more meaningful a paragraph is, the better it will be remembered.
4. One reason men are slightly better on the average than women in mathematical problem solving is that men have taken more math courses.

ANSWERS:

1. description 2. control 3. prediction 4. understanding

(*Note:* This self-test does not ask you to parrot back a memorized list of psychology's goals but rather to recognize an example of each. If you can do this, you have not merely memorized; you have understood. If you had any difficulty, we strongly recommend rereading the preceding section before going on.)

Psychology and Common Sense

Psychology is a popular topic, and much of its vocabulary has crept into everyday speech. If someone says that Annette "unconsciously" hates her father or that Frank was "conditioned" by his unhappy childhood to be moody, the speaker is using the language of psychology.

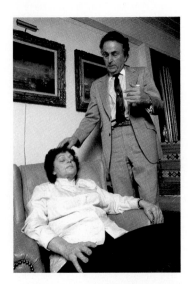

Do hypnotized people remember past events with special clarity, or do they make things up that never happened and only appear to "remember" them? Whichever answer we gave you, you might say, "I knew that all along." (You'll find out the actual answer in Chapter 4.)

Because many psychological terms are in common usage, people sometimes conclude that psychology is nothing but common sense. The wisdom of the ages, they say, already tells us why people act as they do, so who needs psychologists or their data? And indeed, psychological research sometimes does confirm what many people already believe to be true. Often, however, the obviousness of a finding is only an illusion. Armed with the wisdom of hindsight, people maintain that they "knew it all along," when in fact they did not (Locke & Latham, 1991).

Consider this demonstration: An instructor tells an introductory psychology class that "according to research, couples whose careers require them to live apart are more likely to divorce than other couples." Most students, upon hearing this finding, will claim they are not surprised. After all, as everyone knows, "out of sight, out of mind." But then, in another class, the instructor changes the report, this time saying that couples whose careers require them to live apart are *less* likely to divorce than other couples. This "finding" is exactly the reverse of the first one, yet, again, most students will claim they could have predicted it. After all, as everyone knows, "absence makes the heart grow fonder." Both results, once they are "known," seem intuitively obvious, whether true or not (Myers, 1980; Wood, 1984).

Familiar sayings can be used to support opposing results because "common sense" is full of contradictions. And common sense also greatly oversimplifies matters. A psychologist would want to go beyond "common sense" to determine the *conditions* under which absence might or might not make the heart grow fonder. One important factor, for example, is the degree of emotional attachment felt by a couple before their separation; absence often intensifies a bright flame but extinguishes a weak one (S. Brehm, 1985).

Despite the illusion of obviousness, psychological research also yields frequent surprises. For example, according to popular belief, "the child is father to the man" (or mother to the woman, as the case may be); that is, early experiences determine how a person "turns out," for better or for worse. But actually, although childhood certainly influences adulthood, a human being is never a finished product. As we will see in Chapters 13 and 14, many abilities, behaviors, and attributes can change throughout life in response to new situations. Even children traumatized by abuse, neglect, or war can become happy, secure adults if their circumstances improve (Thomas & Chess, 1984).

This, of course, is good news. Sometimes, however, psychological research tells us things we may not *want* to know. For example, studies show that most people are willing to inflict physical harm on another person if they are told to do so by an authority figure. Those inflicting the harm are likely to suffer terrible emotional distress because of their actions, but they obey anyway (Milgram, 1963, 1974). This is a disturbing finding, with important political and moral implications. To take another example: Despite all the warnings against judging a book by its cover, most people do exactly that. Research shows that good-looking individuals are more likely than others to attract dates and get jobs. Attractive people even receive shorter jail sentences (Berscheid, 1985). This is sobering information for a society that considers itself to be democratic and egalitarian.

Psychology, then, may or may not confirm what you already believe about human nature. We want to emphasize, though, that findings do not *have* to be surprising to be scientifically important. Psychologists may enjoy announcing results that startle people, but they also seek to extend and deepen understanding of generally accepted facts. After all, long before the laws of gravity were discovered, people knew that an apple would fall to the ground if it dropped from a tree. But it took Isaac Newton to discover the principles that explain why the apple falls and why it travels at a particular speed. Psychologists, too, seek to deepen our understanding of an already familiar world.

People sometimes think that psychology is "only common sense." But common sense does not tell us why people dress up in funny outfits, do self-destructive things like starving themselves to death, or jump off a bridge suspended only by a bungee cord.

Psychology's Relatives

Psychology belongs to a family of disciplines known as the social (or sometimes the behavioral) sciences. All of these sciences encourage us to analyze human problems objectively and to search for reliable patterns in behavior. All teach us to appreciate both the similarities and the differences among individuals and groups. But there are some important differences in emphasis.

Sociology is the study of groups and institutions within society, such as the family, religious institutions, the workplace, and social cliques. A sociologist might study, for example, how family roles change when women enter the paid work force, or how and why urban gangs come into being. In general, sociologists pay less attention than psychologists do to personality traits and individual differences. However, one specialty, *social psychology*, falls on the border between psychology and sociology; it focuses on how social groups and situations affect an individual's behavior, and vice versa.

Anthropology is concerned with the physical and cultural origins and development of the human species. Anthropologists typically focus on a large social unit—a tribe, a community, or even an entire society. They explore human diversity by comparing the customs and beliefs of different cultures, and often they participate in the group they are observing. In contrast, most psychologists study behavior only in their own society, and they take specific behaviors or mental processes as the topic for analysis, rather than the society itself. Again, however, there is overlap between the fields. Some anthropologists study psychological issues, and in the growing field of *cross-cultural psychology*, researchers are investigating differences and similarities among cultures and are learning which psychological principles apply only to certain societies and which are widespread.

Two other disciplines are often counted as social sciences. *Economics* is the study of how people produce, distribute, and consume goods and services. *Political science* is the study of political behavior and the establishment and conduct of government. Each of these two sciences bites off just a piece of the behavioral pie; in contrast, psychology, sociology, and anthropology all search for general principles of human nature.

Of all the social sciences, psychology relies most heavily on laboratory experiments and observations. At the same time it is the most personal of the social sciences, focusing more than the others on the individual and his or her well-being. Psychology also makes more use of biological information than the other disciplines do (except for physical anthropology, which is concerned with the physical evolution of the human species). In fact, some psychologists classify psychology with the biological and life sciences rather than the social sciences. But whereas the discipline of biology is concerned with the structure and functioning of *all* living things, from trees to turtles, psychologists are interested in biological findings mainly for the light these findings may shed on behavior or mental activities. A psychologist might study the communication of nerve cells in the brain, for example, in order to better understand the processes of learning and memory.

Psychology also has links with several other fields, including linguistics, computer science, neuroscience, and management science. Most of the findings in this book come from research done by psychologists, but we will occasionally refer to results from related disciplines as well. When scholars and scientists cultivate only their own gardens, they may miss ways to improve their intellectual harvest. Now and then it's a good idea to glance over to see what is happening in someone else's yard.

■ PSYCHOLOGY'S PAST: FROM THE ARMCHAIR TO THE LABORATORY

Men and women have always speculated about what makes people tick. And most of the great thinkers of history, from Aristotle to Zoroaster, have raised questions that today would be called psychological. Philosophers, physicians, historians, and political theorists have all wanted to know how people take in information through their senses, use information to solve problems, become motivated to act in particular ways, and undergo emotional or mood changes. But unlike modern psychologists, scholars of the past did not rely heavily on **empirical** evidence—evidence gathered by careful observation, experimentation, and measurement. Their observations were often simply anecdotes or descriptions of individual cases.

This does not mean that the forerunners of modern psychology were always wrong. Often they were right. Hippocrates, the ancient Greek known as the father of modern medicine, observed patients with head injuries and inferred that the brain must be the ultimate source of "our pleasures, joys, laughter, and jests as well as our sorrows, pains, griefs, and tears." And so it is.

But without empirical methods, the forerunners of psychology also committed some terrible blunders. Even Aristotle, one of the first great philosophers to advocate the use of empirical methods, did not always use them correctly himself. He thought that the brain could not possibly be responsible for sensation since the brain itself feels no pain, and he concluded that the brain was simply a radiator for cooling the blood. Aristotle was absolutely right about the brain being insensitive, but he was wrong about the brain being a radiator, and about many other things. (For instance, he believed that small people have poor memories!)

A good example of how prescientific psychology could lead down a blind alley comes from the seventeenth century. At that time, when physics and physiology were still young sciences, scholars were puzzled about how living things could move about. The great French mathematician and philosopher René Descartes [Day-CART] suggested that animals operated much like machines. Descartes concocted a complicated theory of motion that compared muscles and tendons to engines and springs (Jaynes, 1973b). But he could not quite bring

■ **empirical**
Relying on or derived from observation, experimentation, or measurement.

himself to call his own species a mere mechanical contraption. Human beings, he decided, possessed a mind, or immortal soul, which for him was the same thing. According to Descartes, this mind/soul squeezed the pineal [pie-NEE-ul] gland, a small blob of tissue in the center of the brain, this way and that. The pineal gland, the bridge between the soul and the body, in turn caused "animal spirits" (brain fluids) to flow down nerves, which Descartes believed were hollow tubes leading to muscles. When brain fluid entered a muscle it made it billow out like a balloon, resulting in the movement of a limb. Most of these ideas, which seem so outlandish today, were based on pure speculation.

It would be wrong, however, to ridicule the outmoded ideas of the past—as the psychologists of the future may do someday when they look back at *us*. Even without scientific methods, the great thinkers of history often had insights and made observations that led to later advances. Descartes, for example, argued that stimulating a sense organ caused a signal of some sort to travel to the brain, which then *reflected* the signal back to the muscles. Thus was born the concept of a *reflex*. Although Descartes' description of reflexes was not anatomically correct, his work led to the idea that the actions of living things are determined by *stimuli*, or physical changes in the environment, an idea that greatly influenced psychology some three centuries later. More generally, by rejecting the then-common belief that human behavior is governed by unknowable forces, by openly doubting conventional wisdom, and by searching for physical explanations of behavior, Descartes helped promote scientific thinking.

Still, until the nineteenth century, psychology was pretty much a hit-or-miss sort of business. It was not recognized as a separate field of study, and there were few formal rules on how it was to be conducted.

This sketch by René Descartes shows his concept of reflex action. Energy from the fire (A) travels to a cavity in the brain (F) and is reflected back to a muscle that moves the foot (B). Descartes failed to distinguish between pathways that carry signals to and from the brain, and he thought movement occurred when "animal spirits" flowed down hollow nerves. However, his basic notion, that behavior occurs in response to physical events in the environment, had a strong influence on later stimulus-response psychology.

The Birth of Modern Psychology

People love to date the beginning of things. They celebrate not only their own birthdays but also those of their marriages, their countries, their clubs, their schools. Psychologists are no different. They have decided, by common agreement, that psychology as a formal science was born in the year 1879, with the establishment of the first official psychological laboratory in Leipzig, Germany.

The "father" of psychology, it is generally agreed, was a German researcher named Wilhelm Wundt [VILL-helm Voont] (1832–1920). Wundt was trained in medicine and philosophy. Over some 60-odd years he turned out volume after volume on psychology, physiology, natural history, ethics, and logic. What

Wilhelm Wundt (1832–1920), third from left, with co-workers.

most people remember about Wundt, however, is that he was the first person to announce (in 1873) that he intended to make psychology a science.

Actually, psychology had many fathers (and several mothers too, although their accomplishments were often unacknowledged or were even credited to others [Scarborough & Furumoto, 1987]). Various philosophers, such as John Locke in England, had paved the way by arguing that all knowledge must be based on sensory experience and not on speculation or pure reasoning. By the time Wundt set up his laboratory, a number of individuals in both Europe and North America were already doing some psychological research and teaching some psychological topics. The Leipzig laboratory, however, was the first to be formally established and to have its results published in a scholarly journal. Although it started out as just a few rooms in an old building, it soon became the "place to go" for anyone who wanted to become a psychologist. Many of America's first psychologists got their training there.

Researchers in Wundt's laboratory did not study the entire gamut of topics that today's psychologists do. Most concentrated on sensation, perception, reaction times, imagery, and attention, and avoided learning, personality, and abnormal behavior. Wundt himself doubted that higher mental processes, such as abstract thinking, could be studied experimentally. He thought such topics were better understood by studying culture and natural history.

One of Wundt's favorite research methods was called trained introspection. **Introspection** involved the careful observation and analysis by specially trained people of their own mental experiences, under controlled conditions. Looking inward wasn't as easy as it sounds. Wundt's introspectors had to make 10,000 practice observations before they were allowed to participate in an actual study. Once trained, they might take as long as 20 minutes to report their inner experiences during a 1.5-second experiment (Lieberman, 1979). Wundt hoped trained introspection would yield reliable, verifiable results. Ironically, however, although Wundt made his mark on history by declaring psychology to be an objective science, introspection was soon abandoned by other psychologists because it wasn't objective enough.

Two Early Psychologies

Wundt's ideas were popularized in America in somewhat modified form by one of his students, E. B. Titchener (1867–1927). Titchener's brand of psychology became known as **structuralism.** Structuralists hoped to analyze sensations, images, and feelings into their most basic elements, much as a chemist might analyze water into hydrogen and oxygen atoms. For example, a person might listen to a metronome clicking and report exactly what he or she heard. Most people said they perceived a pattern (such as, CLICK click click CLICK click click), even though the clicks of a metronome are actually all the same. Or a person might be asked to break down all the different components of taste when biting into an orange (sweet, tart, wet, etc.).

But structuralism soon went the way of the dinosaur. After you have discovered the building blocks of a particular sensation or image and how they link up, then what? Years after structuralism's demise, Wolfgang Köhler (1959) recalled how he and his colleagues had responded to it as students: "What had disturbed us was . . . the implication that human life, apparently so colorful and so intensely dynamic, is actually a frightful bore."

The structuralists' reliance on introspection also got them into hot water. To see why, imagine that you are a structuralist who wants to know what goes on in people's heads when they hear the word *triangle*. You round up some trained introspectors, say *triangle*, and ask them about their mental experience. Most of your respondents report a visual image of a form with three sides and three corners. Elbert, however, reports a flashing red form with equal angles,

■ **introspection**
A form of self-observation in which individuals examine and report the contents of their own consciousness.
■ **structuralism**
An early approach to psychology that stressed analysis of immediate experience into basic elements.

and Endora insists she saw a revolving colorless form with one angle larger than the other two. Which attributes of *triangle* would you conclude were basic? This is exactly what happened in structuralist studies; people disagreed. Some even claimed they could think about a triangle without forming any visual image at all (Boring, 1953).

Another early school of psychology was called **functionalism.** One of its leaders was William James (1842–1910), an American philosopher, physician, and psychologist who argued that searching for building blocks of experience was a waste of time, because the brain and the mind are constantly changing. Permanent and fixed ideas—of triangles or anything else—do not appear periodically before the "footlights of consciousness." Attempting to grasp the nature of the mind through introspection, wrote James (1890/1950), is "like seizing a spinning top to catch its motion, or trying to turn up the gas quickly enough to see how the darkness looks."

Where the structuralists simply asked *what* happens when an organism does something, the functionalists asked *how* and *why.* That is, they focused on the *function*, or purpose, of behavior. This emphasis on function was inspired in part by the evolutionary theories of British naturalist Charles Darwin (1809–1882). Darwin had argued that a biologist's job is not merely to describe, say, the brilliant plumage of a peacock or the drab markings of a lizard but also to figure out how these attributes enhance survival. (Do they help the animal attract a mate? Hide from its enemies?) Similarly, the functionalists wanted to know how various behaviors help a person (or animal) adapt to the environment. They looked for underlying causes and practical consequences of specific behaviors and mental strategies. Unlike the structuralists, they felt free to pick and choose among many methods and to broaden the field of psychology to include the study of children, animals, religious experiences, and what James called the "stream of consciousness."

As a distinct school of psychology, functionalism had a rather short life. It seems to have lacked the sort of precise theory or program of research that inspires passion or wins recruits. Also, it endorsed the study of consciousness just as that concept was about to fall out of favor. However, the functionalists' emphasis on the causes and consequences of behavior was to set the course of modern psychology.

William James (1842–1910)

■ **functionalism**
An early approach to psychology that stressed the function or purpose of behavior and consciousness.

QUICK QUIZ

Check your memory of the preceding section by choosing the correct response from the pair in parentheses.

1. Psychology has been a science for about (2000/100) years.
2. The forerunners of modern psychology depended heavily on (casual observation/empirical methods).
3. Credit for founding modern psychology is generally given to (William James/Wilhelm Wundt).
4. Early psychologists who emphasized how behavior helps an organism adapt to its environment were known as (structuralists/functionalists).
5. Introspection was rejected as a research method because it was too (subjective/time consuming).

ANSWERS:

1. 100 2. casual observation 3. Wilhelm Wundt 4. functionalists 5. subjective

The astonishing diversity of human behavior is vividly captured in Pieter Brueghel's depiction of Dutch proverbs, rhymes, and folk sayings. Psychologists approach the study of this diversity from five major perspectives.

■ PSYCHOLOGY'S PRESENT: BEHAVIOR, MIND, BODY, AND CULTURE

During the first half of the twentieth century, several psychological movements contended for a place in the sun, some briefly, others more successfully. Today, five major perspectives predominate in psychology; they are the *behavioral, psychodynamic, cognitive, physiological,* and *sociocultural* perspectives.

Now, we know that at this early point in your study of psychology, attempting to remember a bunch of abstract theories can be like trying to hold water in a sieve. So we are going to try to make these five major approaches more memorable for you by discussing how they might apply to a concrete issue, the issue of violence. Human violence takes a multitude of different forms: spouse and child abuse, street crime, political terrorism, mass murder, war. Armchair speculation has done little to curb violence or prevent the suffering it causes, but we believe that psychological theories and research can help people understand why violence occurs and can even point to some possible solutions. As we describe the major perspectives in psychology, see if you can predict how each one might go about explaining why human beings are so often willing to inflict physical harm on one another.

The Behavioral Perspective

In 1913, a psychologist named John B. Watson (1878–1958) published a paper that rocked the still-young science of psychology. In "Psychology as the Behaviorist Views It," Watson argued that if psychology were ever to be as objective as physics, chemistry, and biology, it would have to give up its preoccupation with the mind and consciousness. Psychologists, he said, should throw out introspection as a method of research and reject terms like *mental state, mind,* or *emotion* in explanations of behavior. They should stick to what they can observe and measure directly: acts and events actually taking place in the environment. In short, they should give up mentalism for **behaviorism.** A structuralist might study pain by asking people what a pinprick felt like. A behaviorist would simply observe what happened if you stuck someone's finger with a pin—tears, withdrawal of the hand, or whatever.

Watson wrote approvingly of studies by the Russian physiologist Ivan Pavlov (1849–1936). Pavlov had shown that many kinds of automatic or involuntary behavior, such as salivating at the sight of food, were simply learned responses to specific changes, or stimuli, in the environment. Like Pavlov, Watson believed that certain basic laws of learning could explain the behavior of both human beings and animals. Later, another psychologist, B. F. Skinner (1904–1990), extended the behavioral approach, with important modifications, to voluntary acts, such as turning on a light switch, riding a bike, or getting dressed. Skinner showed that the consequences of an act powerfully affect the probability of its occurring again (see Chapter 6).

When it was first presented, behaviorism excited not only psychologists but also sociologists and political scientists. Here, at last, was a way for the social sciences to be hardheaded and earn the respect of a skeptical world. In many ways, stimulus-response or "S-R" psychology, as it was informally called, narrowed the scope of psychology. But in other ways it broadened it, for (like functionalism) it fostered the study of groups that could not be studied at all through introspection, including animals, infants, and mentally disturbed persons. Behaviorism soon became the predominant American school of experimental psychology and remained so until the early 1960s.

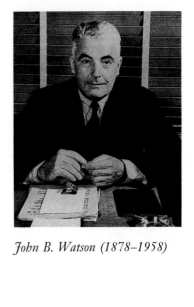

John B. Watson (1878–1958)

■ **behaviorism**
An approach to psychology that emphasizes the study of objectively observable behavior and the role of the environment as a determinant of human and animal behavior.

For behavioral psychologists, human behavior, even such an ordinary event as an intimate conversation between friends, is explainable largely in terms of its environmental consequences. One such consequence is the rewarding attention we get from others.

Critics of behaviorism sometimes accuse behaviorists of denying that ideas and thoughts exist—of believing "that human beings do not think or ponder or worry, but instead only *think* that they do" (C. Sherif, 1979). But this is a misconception. In everyday conversation, behaviorists are as likely as anyone else to say that they think or feel this or that. They realize that they themselves are conscious! It's true that Watson wanted to eliminate thoughts, emotions, and visual images as topics of psychological study, but as we will see in Chapter 6, Skinner held that private events could be studied, so long as they were treated as types of behavior. Verbal reports, said Skinner, could provide imperfect clues to these events. Where Skinner and other behaviorists parted company with nonbehaviorists was in their insistence that mental events could not *explain* behavior. For behaviorists, thoughts and feelings were simply behaviors to be explained. The prediction and control of behavior depended on specifying the environmental conditions that maintained the behavior, not in describing people's thoughts or feelings. That is why behaviorists viewed discussions of "the mind" with suspicion.

Today, many psychologists feel comfortable about combining elements of classic behaviorism with approaches that do incorporate the study of thinking and consciousness. Instead of focusing on discrete stimuli, they look at general ways in which the environment affects behavior. One outgrowth of behaviorism, *social learning theory*, continues to acknowledge the importance of environmental consequences, but also emphasizes how observation and imitation affect learning and how expectations, perceptions, and interpretations influence human social behavior.

What can behavioral approaches tell us about violence and aggression? Behaviorists, as you might guess, do not probe the inner lives or motives of violent people. Instead, behaviorally oriented research identifies the sorts of situations that promote violence and the kinds of payoffs it earns for its perpetrators. For example, studies have found that aggressiveness in children increases when a teacher unwittingly rewards aggression with attention (Serbin et al., 1973). Conversely, violent behavior can be reduced or eliminated by withdrawing the rewards that maintain it and by rewarding cooperative, friendly behavior instead (Fixsen et al., 1978). Laboratory studies also suggest that some children learn to be aggressive by imitating the aggressive behavior of others, including behavior depicted on television and in movies (Bandura, 1973; Eron, 1980). It follows that a society that wishes to reduce violence should not present aggressive bullies or lawless vigilantes as role models to be admired, and that parents should not model violence in the home by using it against their children or each other.

Because of its practical applications, the behavioral approach has touched many lives. Behavioral techniques have helped people eliminate unreasonable fears, quit smoking, lose weight, toilet train infants, and acquire better study habits. In addition, behavioral research has given psychology some of its most reliable findings. Behaviorism's insistence on precision and objectivity has done much to advance psychology as a field.

The Psychodynamic Perspective

In 1900, a few years before John Watson published his behaviorist manifesto, an obscure Viennese physician published a book called *The Interpretation of Dreams*. The book was not exactly what you would call an overnight sensation. In fact, during the next eight years the publisher managed to sell only 600 copies. Who could possibly have known that the author's ideas would eventually alter psychology, medicine, philosophy, literature, and art?

That author was Sigmund Freud (1856–1939), whose name today is as much a household word as Einstein's. A neurologist by training, Freud originally

Sigmund Freud (1856–1939), with his daughter Anna, who also became an influential psychoanalyst.

hoped for a career as a medical researcher, but research did not pay well and family responsibilities forced him to go into private practice as a physician. In his practice, Freud was a good listener. As he listened to his patients' reports of depression, nervousness, and obsessive habits, he became convinced that many of their symptoms had mental, not bodily, causes. Their distress was due, he concluded, to conflicts, memories, and emotional traumas that often went back to early childhood. Freud's ideas eventually evolved into a broad theory of personality, and both his theory and his methods of treating people with emotional problems became known as **psychoanalysis.**

Freud argued that our most important impulses and motives are sexual and aggressive in nature. Because these primitive urges are threatening, we push them out of consciousness, deep into our *unconscious* minds. We are not aware of them as we go blithely about our daily business. Yet they do make themselves known, in hundreds of small ways. Freud (1905a) wrote, "No mortal can keep a secret. If the lips are silent, he chatters with his fingertips; betrayal oozes out of him at every pore." Unconscious thoughts find expression in dreams, slips of the tongue, apparent accidents, and even jokes. Virtually all behavior is meaningful, no matter how trivial it may seem. But whereas a behaviorist is concerned with observable acts, a psychoanalyst tries to dig below the surface of a person's behavior to uncover the roots of personality. Whereas a behaviorist emphasizes the external environment, the psychoanalyst emphasizes processes that go on within the individual. In effect, the psychoanalyst is an archeologist of the mind.

Unlike the behaviorists, Freud viewed aggression not as a learned behavior but as a basic human instinct, lodged in the unconscious part of the mind. The duty of society, he said, is to get people to channel their aggressive energy into productive, socially useful activities. Aggressive energy that is not channeled into productive activity will inevitably be released in violent actions, such as murder and war. It follows that if society wishes to minimize aggression, it must establish clear rules about its expression and reinforce those rules, and it must provide people with ways to rechannel their aggressive impulses. A Freudian might say that the corner butcher, a world-famous surgeon, and an Olympic athlete are all channeling their aggressive energy in healthy directions.

Psychoanalysis continues today as a school of therapy and an approach to explaining human nature. Its major role has been as an influence on modern **psychodynamic** theories of personality, which emphasize unconscious dynamics within the individual—such as inner forces, conflicts, or instinctual energy (see Chapter 12).

Critics, however, have faulted psychodynamic theories, including psychoanalysis, for being based on a limited number of patients in therapy, and they have found many psychodynamic assumptions, such as the claim that aggression is instinctive, difficult to verify scientifically. Critics also note that psychodynamic approaches blame an individual's distress almost entirely on the person's own complexes and hang-ups, ignoring possible political and social explanations. Nonetheless, most psychologists believe that this approach has increased our understanding of the ways in which people unconsciously protect themselves from anxiety and emotional conflict. By making us aware that we are not always the best judges of our own motives and behavior, psychodynamic theories have contributed to psychology and human understanding.

The Cognitive Perspective

For decades, behaviorism and psychoanalysis ruled in psychology, with the former governing most research and the latter guiding most psychotherapy. Then, in the 1950s, changes began to occur. The rather gloomy outlook of the psychoanalysts gave way to a more balanced view of human nature, and the mind again became a respectable topic of scientific study.

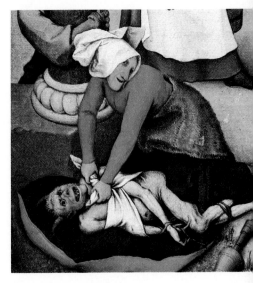

For psychoanalysts, behavior is explained primarily by unconscious needs and motives. Everyone, in this view, struggles to control instinctive "demons" of aggression and sexuality that threaten to disrupt civilization.

■ **psychoanalysis**
An approach to psychology that emphasizes unconscious motives and conflicts. It encompasses both a theory of personality and a method of psychotherapy.

■ **psychodynamic**
A term referring to psychological theories that explain behavior in terms of unconscious energy dynamics within the individual—such as inner forces, conflicts, or the movement of instinctual energy.

The reaction to both psychoanalytic pessimism and behavioristic "mindlessness" emerged initially in the form of a "third force" in psychology, called **humanistic psychology** (or sometimes simply *humanism*). One of the founders of this approach, Abraham Maslow (1908–1970), noted that Freud had based his ideas largely on contacts with unhappy people who were plagued by hostility, fear, and depression. Although Freud reportedly once said that the meaning of life was to be found in work and love, rarely did he discuss joy, compassion, and the nobler aspects of human nature. Behaviorists, too, ignored human hopes and aspirations, though for different reasons. But, wrote Maslow (1971), "When you select out for careful study very fine and healthy people, strong people, creative people, saintly people, sagacious people . . . then you get a very different view of mankind. You are asking how tall can people grow, what can a human being become?"

Humanists differed from other psychologists in emphasizing free will. Human behavior, they said, is not completely determined by either the immediate environment or past experiences; we are able to make choices and control our destinies. Nor did humanists give high priority to discovering general laws of behavior. Their mission was to help people express themselves creatively, understand themselves, and achieve their full human potential. Because of these goals, critics accused humanism of being vague and unscientific, of being more a philosophy of life than a psychology. And indeed, humanism never did translate into a broad program of empirical research; its impact was primarily on personality theory (Chapter 12) and psychotherapy (Chapter 17). However, humanists did succeed in directing psychology's attention to the study of human thoughts, values, and purposes.

During the 1950s and 1960s, this new emphasis on the workings of the human mind gathered momentum from another source as well. The development of the computer encouraged scientists to study problem solving, informational "feedback," and other mental processes. The result was the rise of **cognitive psychology.** (The word *cognitive* comes from the Latin for "to know.") Cognitive psychologists argued that in order to understand how people use language, acquire moral codes, experience emotions, or behave in social groups, psychologists must know what is going on in people's heads. They must study how people attend, perceive, think, remember, solve problems, and form beliefs. However, cognitive researchers did not wish to return to the structuralists' heavy dependence on introspection. Instead, they developed new ways to infer mental processes from observable behavior. For example, by examining the kinds of errors people make when they try to recall words from a list, cognitive psychologists can draw conclusions about whether words are stored in memory in terms of sound or meaning (see Chapter 7).

Cognitive psychology does not yet have a unifying theory, and unlike the other "brands" of psychology discussed so far, it has lacked an acknowledged spokesperson. Yet hardly a topic in psychology has remained unaffected by what is sometimes called the "cognitive revolution." Cognitive researchers have studied how people explain their own behavior, understand a sentence, solve intellectual problems, reason, form opinions, and remember events. They have busily rushed into areas of study where behaviorists once feared to tread, such as sleeping, dreaming, hypnosis, and drug-induced states of consciousness.

How would a cognitive psychologist analyze the problem of violence? Cognitive research has shown that our actions are influenced by how we perceive events and how we interpret the intentions of others. People who are quick to become violent often assume, even in the absence of much evidence, that others are insulting them. If someone does something they dislike, they attribute the action to meanness and malice. They see provocation everywhere. They accept negative stereotypes about those who are different from themselves, and divide the world up into "us" versus "them." In contrast, nonviolent people are

■ **humanistic psychology**
An approach to psychology that emphasizes personal growth and the achievement of human potential more than the scientific understanding, prediction, and control of behavior.

■ **cognitive psychology**
An approach to psychology that emphasizes mental processes in perception, memory, language, problem solving, and other areas of behavior.

Cognitive psychologists emphasize people's perceptions, thought processes, and explanations of events. When a problem arises, a person's behavior will depend in part on whether he or she interprets it as a challenge or "cries over spilt milk."

able to take another person's perspective. If someone does something they dislike, they are apt to say, "He had a bad day" instead of "He's a rotten person." They avoid blowing disputes out of proportion. They can generate alternative ways of solving disagreements. Thus, in the cognitive view, the solution to violence (and to other human problems as well) is to change destructive and distorted thinking patterns.

Like every other approach to psychology, the cognitive perspective has its critics. They point out that although perceptions and interpretations are important, we must not overlook the impact of external events—job conditions, family situations, difficult losses—on our behavior. Critics also complain that often there is no way to choose between competing cognitive explanations. However, the cognitive approach is one of the strongest forces today in psychology, and its findings have made psychology a far more complete science.

The Physiological Perspective

Many people, when they first start studying psychology, are surprised to find that psychologists are interested not only in actions and thoughts, but also in genes, hormones, and nerve cells. However, the physiological approach to psychology has been an important one from the very beginning. Wilhelm Wundt's best-known work was called *Principles of Physiological Psychology*, and for good reason: He and most other early researchers expected their science to rest on a firm foundation of anatomy and biology. During the 1920s and 1930s, interest in both mental and brain processes flourished within *Gestalt psychology*, a movement that had begun in Germany in 1912. In German, *gestalt* means "pattern" or "configuration." The Gestalt psychologists studied how people interpret sensory information as patterns in order to acquire knowledge (see Chapter 5).

The basic idea behind **physiological psychology** is that all actions, feelings, and thoughts are associated with bodily events. Electrical impulses shoot along the intricate pathways of the nervous system. Hormones course through the bloodstream, signaling internal organs to slow down or speed up. Various chemical substances flow across the tiny gaps that separate one microscopic brain cell from another. Physiological psychologists want to know how these bodily events interact with events in the external environment to produce perceptions, memories, and behavior.

In the past few decades, new techniques have made it possible to explore areas of an organism's "inner space" where no one has ventured before (see Chap-

■ **physiological psychology**
An approach to psychology that emphasizes bodily events and changes associated with actions, feelings, and thoughts.

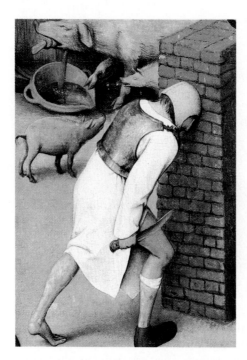

Some people literally bang their heads against a wall. Physiological psychologists look for the causes of such abnormal behavior, and of normal actions as well, in brain circuits and bodily processes.

ter 3). One result has been a better understanding of how mind and body interact in illness and in health. Researchers are learning that although bodily processes can affect one's moods and emotions, the converse is also true: Emotions, attitudes, and perceptions can influence the functioning of the immune system and thus a person's susceptibility to certain diseases (Chapter 15). Physiological research has also renewed interest in the age-old debate over the relative contributions made by "nature" (genetic dispositions) and "nurture" (upbringing and environment) in the development of abilities and personality traits (Chapters 11 and 12).

Many physiological psychologists hope that their discoveries, along with those of biochemists and other scientists, will help solve some of the mysteries of mental problems. Some of that research might help us understand certain types of violence. Experiments with animals show that stimulation of particular brain areas tends to produce behavior associated with rage, whereas stimulation of other areas produces calm, placid behavior. Some cases of sudden, unprovoked violence by human beings may be traceable to brain tumors, injuries, and diseases or to more subtle neurological disorders (Lewis, 1981; Moyer, 1983).

As we will see, findings in physiological psychology can tempt people to reduce complex psychological issues to the actions of hormones, nerve cells, genes, and enzymes, and to ignore important psychological and social factors. People often think that the explanation for some puzzle of human behavior must be *either* physiological or psychological, and they fail to appreciate how complex the interactions between body and mind really are. But the physiological approach has a useful message for us all: We cannot know ourselves if we do not know our bodies. That is why physiological discoveries are found in many sections of this book.

The Sociocultural Perspective

Most psychologists (with the exception of strict behaviorists) study forces within the individual—biological, cognitive, or motivational—that affect a person's behavior. During the 1930s and 1940s, some psychologists began to question this **intrapsychic** (within the person) focus. They wanted to know how dictators like Adolf Hitler could persuade people to commit the kinds of atrocities that

■ **intrapsychic**
Within the mind or self.

led to the deaths of Anne Frank and millions of others. They wondered why apparently nice people often hold hateful racial or ethnic stereotypes and whether such attitudes could be changed. They asked how cultural values and political systems affect everyday experience. We call the view that emerged from these questions the **sociocultural perspective.**

Researchers working from this perspective have shown that most of us (including psychologists) tend to overlook how social contexts shape nearly everything we do—how we perceive the world, express joy, manage our households, rear our children. We tend to overestimate the contribution of personality traits to our own behavior and the behavior of others and underestimate the influence of the particular historical, cultural, and social situation in which we happen to find ourselves. We are like fish who, having always lived in water, are unaware of its existence. We assign blame and give credit, without noticing that context, rather than personality, has determined an outcome.

Psychologists who emphasize the "socio" side of the sociocultural perspective examine how a person's behavior is affected by a particular situation or by social roles. For example, they might study how gender roles influence the expression of emotion (Chapter 9), how access to job opportunities affects people's goals and ambitions (Chapter 10), or how groups affect attitudes (Chapter 18). Psychologists who emphasize the "cultural" side of the perspective study how differences among cultures affect behavior (Cole, 1990; Triandis, 1990). They might look at how a society's emphasis on individualism or loyalty to the group affects people's motives and goals (Chapter 10), how cultural expectations about children's family responsibilities affect moral development (Chapter 13), or how cultural attitudes toward personal control affect the experience of stress (Chapter 15).

In the sociocultural view, the reasons for violence and cruelty do not reside in instincts, brain circuits, or personal dispositions, but in social and cultural rules about when to aggress and against whom, and in economic and political arrangements. When groups or societies are small and close-knit, and when individuals must cooperate to survive, people tend to fear and avoid aggression. The Inuit (Eskimos), for example, often regard the mildest protest, the slightest raised tone, the merest hint of a frown, as a serious threat. The Inuit consider anger to be dangerous and intolerable, appropriate only for babies, the insane, the sick—and *kaplunas*, white people (J. Briggs, 1970). In contrast, societies that value competition or power often foster aggression, both within the society and against outsiders. (Consider our own culture's fondness for guns,

■ **sociocultural perspective**
An approach to psychology that emphasizes social and cultural influences on behavior.

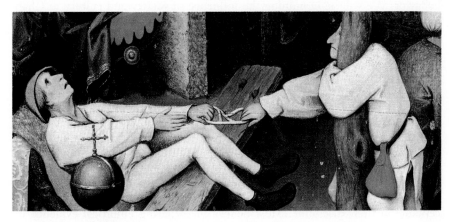

For psychologists who take a sociocultural perspective, human behavior depends on many outside influences, ranging from the immediate situation to the larger culture. They might ask why relationships in some societies are a tug-of-war, whereas those in other societies are more cooperative.

Sense and Nonsense About Human Experience

You have probably heard that human beings are different from other animals because we have language, use tools, or can think. But to communications psychologist George Gerbner (1988), we are unique because we tell stories—and live by the stories we tell. All of us have a need to explain ourselves and the workings of the world around us. We are constantly constructing stories that will make sense of confusing, surprising, or unfair events. Which stories are right? Marriages have broken up and wars have been waged over that question.

Psychology and other sciences offer certain kinds of stories about human behavior; they are called "theories." But psychology has plenty of nonscientific competitors. Are you having romantic problems? An astrologer may advise you to choose an Aries instead of an Aquarius as your next love. Are you unable to make decisions? A

"channeler" will put you in touch with a 5,000-year-old equivalent of Dear Abby. Are you fighting the battle of the bulge? An expert in "past lives regression" will explain that the problem is not in your unhappy childhood but in your unhappy previous life; perhaps in the fourteenth century you were a starving serf.

Nonscientific approaches to human experience share psychology's basicgoals of describing, explaining, predicting, and modifying behavior. Moreover, by analyzing personality and dispensing advice, many of their practitioners operate in effect as unlicensed psychological counselors. You hear about their famous clients all the time—movie stars, rock singers, Wall Street brokers, even politicians. During former President Ronald Reagan's term of office, Nancy Reagan sought the advice and consent of an astrologer before permitting White House staffers to set her husband's schedule.

When deciding which stories about human behavior to believe, it helps to distinguish two questions that are often confused: *Does it work?* and *Is it true?* Many stories "work" for people; that is, they help people feel better, provide entertainment, reassure people that they are normal, or simplify a complicated world. But for a story, theory, or system to be *true,* or valid, it must consistently explain or predict behavior or events with better than chance accuracy.

boxing matches, and violent movies.) To reduce violence, then, there must be social change, not merely personal change.

The sociocultural perspective can lead to glib generalizations about ethnic groups, nations, and cultures. But because we human beings are social animals, this perspective can also expand our ability to understand and predict human behavior. We will be examining the influence of society and culture in Chapter 18 and in our discussions of perception, emotion, child development, and many other topics.

A Note on Psychology's Multiple Personalities

The differences among the various schools of psychology are very real; they have produced passionate arguments, and sometimes stony silences, among their defenders. But not all psychologists feel they must swear allegiance to one approach or another. Many, if not most, are *eclectic*, using what they believe to be the best features of diverse theories and schools of thought. Further, most psychologists agree on certain broad guidelines about what is and what is not acceptable in their discipline. Most believe in gathering empirical evidence instead of arriving at conclusions through reasoning alone. Nearly all reject supernatural explanations of events—evil spirits, psychic forces, miracles, and so forth. This insistence on rigorous standards of proof sets psychology

Throughout history, people have turned to religion for answers to ultimate questions of life and death, spirituality, and meaning. Religious explanations are for the most part impossible to test for accuracy; they are a matter of faith. But other nonscientific systems of belief are testable in principle, although their followers often ignore the basic rules of evidence. One such rule is that you have to make predictions in advance of, not after, the fact. For example, you don't get to observe an earthquake and then argue that the planets predicted it.

When you look closely, you find that nonscientific or pseudoscientific predictions are rarely correct *in advance*. For example, in a review of many studies, Geoffrey Dean (1986/87, 1987) found that predictions made by highly trained astrologers have only chance-level accuracy. Their occasional on-target predictions are the result of shrewd guesses ("Mideast tensions will continue"), vagueness ("A tragedy will hit the country this spring"), or inside information ("Movie star A will marry director B"). And astrologers are no better at describing individuals' personalities based on their birth charts; they actually do *worse* than they would simply by guessing. Dean concludes that astrology is "psychological chewing gum, satisfying but ultimately without real substance."

Even when people know about a system's inadequacies, they may ignore them, out of a need to believe. The task of the skeptical person is to separate belief from evidence, and to consider all of the available information, including any counterevidence. James Randi, a magician who devotes his time to debunking pseudoscientific claims, once sent a birth chart to a noted astrologer for analysis. The astrologer, thinking the chart was Randi's own, sent back a glowing description of a virtuous, steadfast fellow. In fact, the chart was based on the birthdate, birth hour, and birthplace of a convicted rapist.

In this book, you will learn that psychology tells more than one "story." A psychoanalyst's explanation of your personality will not be the same as a cognitive psychologist's, and neither "story" will be the same as a behaviorist's. In later chapters, we will be offering you ways to think critically about various psychological approaches as well as about those of psychology's nonscientific competitors.

In the meantime, ask yourself what else you need to know to evaluate a theory besides the fact that it is coherent and appealing, and you want it to be true. What is the harm in accepting an explanation of human behavior that has no evidence to support it? Why does it matter whether we attribute our fates to the alignment of heavenly bodies, past lives, spirit guides, "psychic energy," or our own decisions and actions? Think about it.

apart from other, nonscientific explanations of human experience (see "Think About It").

Some psychologists hope that in time they will be able to resolve their differences and settle on a limited set of fundamental principles that apply to all forms of behavior (Kimble, 1990). Some even hope for a single, unifying *paradigm*—a guiding model or theory—that will define what psychologists should study and how they should study it. They hope that such a paradigm will do for psychology what the laws of motion did for physics and evolutionary theory did for biology. Given the complexity of their subject matter, however, a unifying paradigm may be as elusive as the Holy Grail. Even as psychologists yearn for unity, individual researchers are heading off in different directions. While some seek the answers to psychological problems in biology, others are tracing psychological problems to social pathology—to poverty, unemployment, racism, sexism, ageism, and urban crowding. While some want to bring psychology back to its philosophical roots, others are investing their energy in computer simulations and space-age technology. Grand theories have been replaced by more specific ones that address particular kinds of questions. Human behavior does not seem to lend itself to simple, all-encompassing theories. It is like a giant mosaic made up of many fragments, so complicated that no single approach can take in the whole picture. Put all the approaches together, though, and the result is a rich, multicolored, absorbing psychological portrait.

QUICK QUIZ

A. Like violence, anxiety is a common problem. To find out if you fully understand the five major perspectives in psychology, try to match each possible explanation of anxiety on the left with a perspective on the right.

1. Anxious people often think about the future in distorted ways.
2. Anxiety is due to forbidden, unconscious desires.
3. Anxiety symptoms often bring hidden rewards, such as being excused from exams.
4. Excessive anxiety can be caused by a chemical imbalance.
5. A national emphasis on competition and success promotes worry and anxiety about failure.

a. behavioral
b. psychodynamic
c. sociocultural
d. physiological
e. cognitive

B. Different assumptions about human behavior can lead to different conclusions. What assumption distinguishes cognitive psychology from behaviorism? What assumption distinguishes psychoanalysis from the sociocultural perspective?

ANSWERS:

A. 1. e 2. b 3. a 4. d 5. c **B.** Cognitive psychologists assume that thoughts and feelings can explain behavior; behaviorists assume that thoughts and feelings are behaviors to be explained. Psychoanalysts assume behavior is driven largely by internal (intrapsychic) factors, such as unconscious urges and personality traits; the sociocultural perspective assumes that behavior is determined largely by social and cultural contexts.

■ WHAT PSYCHOLOGISTS DO

Now you know the main viewpoints that guide psychologists in their work. But what do psychologists actually do with their time between breakfast and dinner?

When most people hear the word *psychologist* they probably imagine a therapist listening intently while a client, perhaps stretched out comfortably on a couch, pours forth his or her troubles. Many psychologists do in fact fit this image (though chairs are more common than couches these days). However, many others do not.

In North America, about two-thirds of all people working in psychology have doctorates and most of the rest have master's degrees. The professional activities of psychologists generally fall into three categories: 1) research, 2) education, and 3) health or mental health services, which is often referred to as psychological practice. These activities are carried out in a variety of different work settings, as you can see in Figure 1.1.

Within the field of psychology, tensions have been increasing between the different "kinds" of psychologists. Those engaged in scientific research often worry that some practitioners are giving the field a bad name by using counseling and therapy techniques that have not been scientifically tested and validated. A few years ago, such concerns contributed to the formation of the American Psychological Society, an organization devoted to the needs and interests of psychology as a science. On the other hand, practitioners often feel that psy-

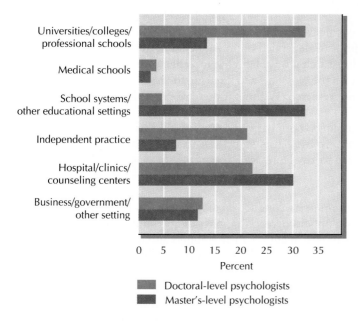

FIGURE 1.1

Where psychologists work
This graph shows the primary employment settings of doctoral- and master's-level psychologists. (The percentages do not total 100 because of rounding and because a few persons surveyed failed to specify a setting.) As the text notes, many psychologists work in more than one setting. (Based on Stapp, Tucker, & VandenBos, 1985.)

chological scientists live in an "ivory tower" and show too little concern for helping people solve problems in the real world. As for those psychologists whose professional commitment is mainly to teaching, they sometimes feel that their concerns are ignored by both researchers and practitioners!

Many psychologists, however, wear more than one professional hat, moving flexibly between teaching, research, and practice. An academic at a university might spend half the day doing laboratory research and the other half teaching psychology courses. A "scientist-practitioner" might see patients in a mental health clinic three days a week and do research in a hospital on the causes of depression the other two. And despite the stresses and strains within psychology, many psychologists feel that keeping science and practice within a single discipline is important if psychological research is to remain relevant and psychological practice is to be based on a reliable understanding of human behavior.

Psychological Research

Psychological researchers work for universities and colleges, the government, the military, schools, and business. Some, seeking knowledge for its own sake, work in **basic psychology,** or "pure" research. Others, concerned with the practical uses of knowledge, work in **applied psychology.** A psychologist doing basic research might ask: "How do children, adolescents, and adults differ in their approach to moral issues such as honesty?" An applied psychologist might ask, instead: "How can knowledge about moral development be used to prevent juvenile delinquency?" A psychologist in basic science might ask: "Can a nonhuman primate, such as a chimpanzee or a gorilla, learn to use sign language?" An applied psychologist might ask: "Can techniques used to teach language to a chimpanzee be used to help mentally impaired or disturbed children who do not speak?"

Over the past century, applied psychologists have made important contributions in areas such as health, education, marketing, management, consumer behavior, industrial design, personnel selection, and urban planning. For many years, however, the "pure" approach had far more prestige among psychologists than the applied approach (C. W. Sherif, 1979). This began to change during World War II, when the U.S. government encouraged psychological scientists to apply their findings to the training, education, and health care problems facing the country. Many well-known psychologists answered the call. Today, most

■ **basic psychology**
The study of psychological issues in order to seek knowledge for its own sake rather than for its practical application.
■ **applied psychology**
The study of psychological issues that have direct practical significance and the application of psychological findings.

psychologists recognize that basic and applied psychology are both necessary. Although basic psychology can sometimes lead to useful discoveries by accident, such accidents cannot be depended on to happen. On the other hand, insisting that psychological research always be relevant is like trying to grow flowers by concentrating only on the blossoms and ignoring the roots (E. L. Walker, 1970). Basic research is root research. Without it there would be little scientific knowledge to apply.

Psychologists' findings, both basic and applied, fill this book, so you can get a good idea of *what* psychologists study and teach by scanning the Table of Contents on pages vi to xiv. Here are a few of the major nonclinical specialties in psychology:

• *Experimental psychologists* conduct laboratory studies of learning, motivation, emotion, sensation and perception, physiology, human performance, and cognition. We will discuss many of their findings in Chapters 3 through 10. (Don't be misled by the term *experimental*, though; other researchers also run experiments.)

• *Educational psychologists* study psychological principles that explain learning and search for ways to improve learning in educational systems. Their interests range from the application of findings on memory and thinking (see Chapters 7 and 8) to the use of rewards to encourage achievement (see Chapters 6 and 10).

• *Developmental psychologists* study how people change and grow over time, physically, mentally, and socially. In the past their focus was mainly on childhood, but many now study adolescence, young adulthood, the middle years, or old age. We will take a close look at their findings in Chapters 13 and 14.

• *Industrial/organizational psychologists* study behavior in the workplace. They are concerned with group decision making, employee morale, work motivation, productivity, job stress, personnel selection, marketing strategies, equipment design, and many other issues. We will discuss their findings at several points in this book, but especially in Chapter 10.

• *Psychometric psychologists* design and evaluate tests of mental abilities, aptitudes, interests, and personality. Nearly all of us have had first-hand experience with one or more of these tests—in school, at work, or in the military. We will discuss test construction and the controversies that surround testing in Chapter 11.

• *Social psychologists* study how groups, institutions, and the social context influence individuals and vice versa. Among their interests are conformity, obedience, competition, cooperation, leadership styles, and prejudice. We will take up these topics in Chapter 18.

The Practice of Psychology

Over the past two decades, the proportion of practicing psychologists has steadily increased; today, well over two-thirds of new psychology doctorates are going to practitioners (Kohout & Wicherski, 1991). Psychological practitioners work in general hospitals, mental hospitals, clinics, schools, counseling centers, and private practice. Their object is to understand and improve physical and mental health. Some are *counseling psychologists,* who generally help people deal with problems of everyday life, such as test anxiety, family and marital problems, or low job motivation. Others are *school psychologists,* who work with parents, teachers, and students to enhance students' performance and emotional development. The majority, however, are *clinical psychologists,* who diagnose, treat, and study mental or emotional problems and disabilities. Clinicians are trained to do psychotherapy with highly disturbed people as well as those who are simply troubled or unhappy or who want to learn to handle their problems

better. (As we will see in Chapter 17, there are many different kinds of psychotherapy.)

In almost all states, a license to practice clinical psychology requires a doctorate. Most clinical psychologists have a Ph.D., some have an Ed.D. (doctorate in education), and a smaller but growing number have a relatively new degree called a Psy.D. (doctorate in psychology, pronounced "sy-dee"). Whichever degree they earn, clinical psychologists typically do four or five years of graduate work in psychology, plus at least a year's internship under the direction of a practicing psychologist. Clinical programs leading to a Ph.D. or Ed.D. are designed to prepare a person both as a scientist and clinical practitioner; they require completion of a dissertation, a major scholarly work (usually involving research) that contributes to knowledge in the field. Programs leading to a Psy.D. focus on professional practice and do not usually require a dissertation. However, they do require the student to complete a research study, theoretical paper, literature review, or some other scholarly project.

People often confuse the terms *clinical psychologist*, *psychotherapist*, *psychoanalyst*, and *psychiatrist*, but these terms do not mean the same thing. Anyone who does psychotherapy is a psychotherapist; and in most states almost anyone can say that he or she is a "therapist" of one sort or another, so checking credentials is important. A psychoanalyst is a person who practices one form of therapy, psychoanalysis. To call yourself a psychoanalyst, you must get specialized training at a recognized psychoanalytic institute, and must usually undergo extensive psychoanalysis yourself. **Psychiatry** is the medical specialty concerned with mental disorders, maladjustment, and abnormal behavior. Psychiatrists are medical doctors (M.D.s) who have had three or four years of general medical training, a yearlong internship in general medicine, and a three-year residency in psychiatry. During the residency period a psychiatrist learns to diagnose and treat psychiatric patients under the supervision of a more experienced physician. Some psychiatrists go on to do research on mental problems rather than work with patients.

Although there are many similarities in what psychiatrists and clinical psychologists do, there are also important differences. Psychiatrists are more likely than psychologists to treat severe mental disorders. They tend to be more medically oriented because they have been trained to diagnose physical problems that can cause mental ones. In addition, psychiatrists can write prescriptions and clinical psychologists cannot (or at least not yet; many psychologists are currently pressing for prescription-writing privileges). Psychiatrists, however, sometimes are not thoroughly trained in the theories and methods of modern psychology. These differences can affect approaches to treatment (see Chapter 17). For example, if a patient is depressed, a psychiatrist will often prescribe an

Psychologists may be researchers and/or practitioners. In the photograph on the left, Patricia Goldman-Rakic (center) and her colleagues use newly developed technology to study the brain mechanisms underlying mental processes. In the photograph on the right, a clinical psychologist helps a client cope with an emotional problem.

■ **psychiatry**
The medical specialty concerned with mental disorders, maladjustment, and abnormal behavior.

antidepressant drug. A psychologist is more likely to look for the psychological and social origins of depression.

Psychologists and psychiatrists are not the only professionals who do mental health work; so do marriage, family, and child counselors, school counselors, and social workers. These professionals ordinarily treat general problems in adjustment and not serious mental disturbance. Licensing requirements vary somewhat from state to state but usually include a master's degree in psychology or social work and one or two years of supervised experience.

Psychology in the Community

In the past few decades psychology has probably expanded faster than any other field, in terms of scholars, publications, and specialties. The American Psychological Association, psychology's largest professional organization, now has 47 divisions. Some of these divisions represent the major fields described in this chapter, such as developmental psychology and physiological psychology; others represent special research or clinical interests, such as the psychology of women, sports psychology, environmental psychology, and the psychological study of gay and lesbian issues. Look around your community and you are apt to find psychologists. Besides teaching, doing research, and treating patients, they advise commissions on how pollution and noise affect mental health. They educate judges and juries about the reliability of eyewitness testimony. They assist the police in emergencies involving hostages or disturbed persons. They conduct public opinion surveys. They run suicide prevention "hot lines." They advise zoos on the care and training of animals. They help coaches improve the athletic performance of their teams. And on and on.

No wonder people are a little fuzzy about what a psychologist is. Cognitive psychologist George Miller has related what happens when he tells people his profession:

> Some people say: "So you're a psychologist. I think my wife's calling," and off they go. Then there's the opposite reaction: "So you're a psychologist. Well I'm something of a psychologist myself," and they describe how they trained their dog to bring in the newspaper. Other people ask about their children's test scores, and still others want me to interpret their dreams. All I can say is: "I'm not that kind of psychologist!" (in J. Miller, 1983, pp. 15–16)

Psychologists work in many settings, from classrooms to courtrooms. This woman is a prison psychologist.

QUICK QUIZ

Let's try a game of "What's My Line?" Which kinds of psychologist are most likely to have the following job descriptions?

1. Studies emotional development during childhood.
2. Does laboratory studies of visual perception in animals.
3. Treats eating disorders of patients in a mental health clinic.
4. Consults with industry on marketing strategies.

ANSWERS:

1. developmental 2. experimental 3. clinical 4. industrial/organizational

■ THINKING CRITICALLY AND CREATIVELY ABOUT PSYCHOLOGY

These days, most people know that you have to exercise the body to keep it in shape. But they assume that thinking doesn't take any effort at all, and certainly no practice. You just do it, like breathing. But thinking does need practice. All around us we can see examples of flabby thinking, lazy thinking, emotional thinking, and nonthinking. Sometimes people justify their mental laziness by proudly telling you they are "open-minded." "It's good to be open-minded," replies philosopher Jacob Needleman, "but not so open that your brains fall out."

We believe that one of the greatest benefits of studying psychology is that you learn not only how the brain works in general but how to use yours in particular—by thinking critically. **Critical thinking** is the ability and willingness to assess claims and make objective judgments on the basis of well-supported reasons. It is the ability to look for flaws in arguments and resist claims that have no supporting evidence. *Critical thinking, however, is not merely negative thinking.* It also fosters the ability to be *creative and constructive*—to generate possible explanations for findings, think of implications, and apply new knowledge to a broad range of social and personal problems. You can't really separate critical thinking from creative thinking, for it is only when you question *what is* that you can begin to imagine *what can be*.

Here is an example of what we mean. Many people, when faced with a setback to their expectations, narrow their horizons instead of expanding them. We know a fellow named Victor whose entire dream in life was to be a veterinarian. Victor's love of animals was legendary: At 3, he wouldn't let you kill a bug in his presence. But Victor wasn't admitted to any of the veterinary schools he applied to, and his reaction was panic and despair: "My whole life is ruined!" At first, Victor was not thinking critically; he had divided his possibilities into only two alternatives: become a veterinarian, or nothing. But by examining this assumption and by thinking creatively about all the possible occupations that would make use of his love of animals, Victor realized his choices were endless: pet-shop owner, Hollywood "pet therapist," animal trainer, designer of humane zoos, organizer for an endangered-species group, ecologist, wildlife photographer. . . .

Does critical thinking sound hard? It's not, really, once you get into the proper spirit and pick up a few skills. Researchers find that people don't usually use such skills until their mid-20s or until they have had many years of higher education—if then (Kitchener & King, 1989; Schmidt, 1985; Welfel & Davison, 1986). That does not mean, however, that people *can't* think critically.

■ **critical thinking**
The ability and willingness to assess claims and make objective judgments on the basis of well-supported reasons.

Even young children often do so, though they may not get much credit for it. We know one fourth-grader, who, when told that ancient Greece was the "cradle of democracy," replied, "But what about women and slaves, who couldn't vote and had no rights? Was Greece a democracy for them?" That's critical thinking. And it is also creative thinking, for once you question the basic assumption that Greece was a democracy for everyone, you can begin to imagine other interpretations of ancient Greek civilization.

However, we do agree with the growing number of educators, philosophers, and psychologists who believe that the American educational system shortchanges students by not encouraging them to think critically and creatively. Too often, say these critics, both teachers and students view the mind as a bin for storing "the right answers" or a sponge for "soaking up knowledge." The mind is neither a bin nor a sponge. Remembering, thinking, and understanding are all active processes. They require judgment, choice, and the weighing of evidence. Unfortunately, children who challenge prevailing opinion at home or in school are often called "rebellious" rather than "involved." As a result, say the critics, many high school and college graduates cannot formulate a rational argument or see through misleading advertisements and propaganda that play on emotions. They do not know how to go about deciding whether to have children, make an investment, or support a political proposal. They do not know how to come up with imaginative solutions to their problems. In short, they cannot use their heads.

Critical thinking involves a set of skills that you can apply to any subject you study or problem you encounter. But it is particularly relevant to psychology, for three reasons. First, the field itself includes the study of thinking, problem solving, creativity, curiosity, and other components of this process, and so by its very nature fosters critical and creative thinking. In one study, graduate students in psychology substantially improved in their ability to reason about the events of everyday life, whereas graduate students in chemistry showed no improvement (Lehman, Lempert, & Nisbett, 1988). Second, the field of psychology generates many competing findings on topics of immediate personal and social relevance, and people need to be able to evaluate these findings and their implications. Third, the public's appetite for psychological information has created a huge market for what R. D. Rosen (1977) called "psychobabble": pseudoscience and quackery covered by a veneer of psychological language. Critical thinking can help you separate psychology from psychobabble.

In part, learning to think critically means following the rules of logic. But there are also more general guidelines involved (Ennis, 1985; Paul, 1984; Ruggiero, 1988). Here are eight of the essential ones, which we emphasize throughout this book.

ASK QUESTIONS; BE WILLING TO WONDER. What is the one kind of question that most exasperates parents of young children? "Why is the sky blue, Mommy?" "Why doesn't the plane fall?" "Why don't pigs have wings?" Unfortunately, as children grow up, they tend to stop asking "why" questions. (Why do you think this is?)

"The trigger mechanism for creative thinking is the disposition to be curious, to wonder, to inquire," writes Vincent Ruggiero (1988). "Asking 'What's wrong here?' and/or 'Why is this the way it is, and how did it come to be that way?' leads to the identification of problems and challenges." Some occupations actually teach their trainees to think this way. Industrial engineers are taught to walk through a company and question everything, even procedures that have been used for years. But other occupations prefer to give trainees "received wisdom" and discourage criticism.

We hope that you will not approach psychology as "received wisdom," but will ask many questions about the theories and findings we present in this book.

It's fine to be an optimist, but critical thinkers also try to separate truth from fiction.

Be on the lookout, too, for questions about human behavior that are *not* answered in the chapters that follow. If you do that, you will not only be learning psychology, you will also be learning to think like a psychologist.

DEFINE THE PROBLEM. Once you've raised a question, the next step is to identify the issues in clear and concrete terms. "What makes people happy?" is a fine question for midnight reveries, but it will not lead to answers unless you have specified what you mean by "happy." One psychologist defined a "happy marriage" as one that had lasted ten years and produced two children (Toman, 1976). Would you agree with that definition?

The inadequate formulation of a question can produce misleading or incomplete answers. For example, asking "Can animals learn language?" assumes that "language" is an all-or-none ability, and allows for only two possible answers, yes or no. But putting the question another way—"Which aspects of language might certain animals be able to acquire?"—takes into account the fact that language requires many different abilities. It also acknowledges that there are differences among species, and opens up a range of possible answers, as we will see in Chapter 8.

EXAMINE THE EVIDENCE. Have you ever heard someone in the heat of argument exclaim, "I just know it's true, no matter what you say" or "That's my opinion; nothing's going to change it" or "If you don't understand my position, I can't explain it"? Have you ever made such statements yourself? Accepting a conclusion without evidence, or expecting others to do so, is a sure sign of uncritical thinking (or of no thinking at all). It implies that all opinions are equal, and they are not. A critical thinker asks, *What evidence supports or refutes this argument and its opposition? How reliable is the evidence?* If it is not possible to check the reliability of the evidence, the critical thinker considers whether its source has been reliable in the past.

Some well-known popular beliefs have been widely accepted on the basis of poor evidence or even no evidence at all. For example, many people believe that it is psychologically and physically healthy to "ventilate" their anger at the first person, pet, or piece of furniture that gets in their way. Actually, years of research in many different fields suggest that sometimes expressing anger is beneficial, but more often it is not. Often it makes the angry person angrier, makes the target of the anger angry back, lowers everybody's self-esteem, and fosters hostility and aggression (see Chapter 9). Yet the belief that expressing anger is always healthy persists, despite the lack of evidence to support it. Can you think of some reasons why this might be so?

ANALYZE ASSUMPTIONS AND BIASES. Critical thinkers evaluate the assumptions and biases that lie behind arguments—beliefs that are taken for granted and biases about how the world works. They ask how these assumptions and biases influence claims and conclusions in the books they read, the political speeches they hear, the news programs they watch, and the ads that bombard them every day. Here is an example: The manufacturer of a popular pain reliever advertises that hospitals prefer its product over all others. The natural assumption—the one the advertiser wants you to make—is that this product is better than all others. Actually, hospitals prefer the product because they get a bigger discount on it than on its competitors.

Critical thinkers also are aware of their own assumptions and are willing to question them. For example, many people are biased in favor of their parents' ways of doing things. When faced with difficult problems, they will reach for familiar solutions, saying, "If my dad voted Republican (or Democratic), then I should," or "I was brought up to believe that the best way to discipline children is to beat them." But critical thinking requires us to examine our biases when the evidence contradicts them. All of us, of course, carry around a headful of assumptions about how the world works: Do people have free will or are they constrained by biology and upbringing? Are government programs the solution to poverty or would private programs do better? If we don't make our assumptions explicit, our ability to interpret evidence objectively can be seriously impaired.

AVOID EMOTIONAL REASONING: "IF I FEEL THIS WAY, IT MUST BE TRUE." Emotion has a place in critical thinking. Without it, logic and reason can lead to misguided or destructive decisions and actions. Indeed, some of the most cold-blooded murderers in history have been bright, even brilliant, thinkers. But when "gut feelings" replace clear thinking, the results are equally dangerous. "Persecutions and wars and lynchings," observes Edward de Bono (1985), "are all a result of gut feeling."

Because our feelings seem so right, it is hard to understand that people with opposing viewpoints feel just as strongly. But they usually do, which means that feelings alone are not a reliable guide to the truth. As you begin this book, you may hold strong, passionate beliefs about child rearing, drugs, astrology, ideal body weight, the origins of intelligence, the nature of "mental illness," men and women, whites and blacks, Americans and Japanese, heterosexuals and homosexuals. Try to set these feelings aside so they won't interfere with your consideration of evidence bearing on such topics. Keep in mind the words of English poet and essayist Alexander Pope: "What reason weaves, by passion is undone."

DON'T OVERSIMPLIFY. A critical thinker looks beyond the obvious, resists easy generalizations, and rejects either/or thinking. For example, when life serves up a miserable situation, should you deny your problems ("Everything's fine; let's go to the movies") or face them head-on? Either answer oversimplifies. As we will see in Chapter 15, sometimes denial can keep people from solving their problems, but at other times it helps them get through painful situations that can't be changed.

Often in an argument you will hear someone generalize from one tiny bit of evidence to the whole world. An example is arguing by anecdote: One crime committed by a paroled ex-convict means the whole parole program is bad; one friend of yours who hates his or her school means that everybody who goes there hates it. Anecdotal generalizations are the source of stereotyping as well: One dishonest welfare mother means they are all dishonest; one encounter with an unconventional Californian means that they are all "flaky." A critical thinker wants more evidence than one or two stories before drawing generalizations. The same applies to thinking about one's own life. For example, many people generalize from one negative event to a whole pattern of defeat, creating no end of misery: "I did poorly on this test, and now I'll never get through college or have a job or kids or anything."

Is this a UFO? Some people, reasoning emotionally, believe passionately in the existence of "flying saucers" from outer space. They jump from "I want them to exist" to "They do exist." (To find out more about this particular "UFO," see page 32.)

CONSIDER OTHER INTERPRETATIONS. A critical thinker creatively formulates hypotheses that offer reasonable explanations of characteristics, behavior, and events. The ultimate goal is to find an explanation that accounts for the most evidence with the fewest assumptions. But critical thinkers are careful not to shut out alternative explanations too soon. They generate as many interpretations of the evidence as possible before settling on the most likely one.

Consider, for example, a study of Swedish couples in which those who lived together before marriage were 80 percent more likely to separate or divorce than those who had lived apart (Bennett, Blanc, & Bloom, 1988). How would you interpret these results? *Time* magazine promptly concluded that "premarital cohabitation may be hazardous to your marriage," and Dear Abby advised a reader that if she wanted her forthcoming marriage to last she shouldn't cohabit beforehand. But there is another plausible conclusion: that people who cohabit before marriage are less committed to the institution of marriage and therefore more inclined to leave an unhappy marriage. This was the interpretation the researchers themselves favored.

TOLERATE UNCERTAINTY. Ultimately, learning to think critically teaches us one of the hardest lessons of life: how to live with uncertainty. As we have seen, it is important to examine the evidence before drawing conclusions. Sometimes, however, there is little or no evidence on which to base any conclusions. Sometimes the evidence merely allows us to draw tentative conclusions. And sometimes, exasperatingly, the evidence seems good enough to permit strong and sturdy conclusions . . . until new evidence throws our beliefs into disarray. Critical thinkers are willing to accept this state of uncertainty. They are not afraid to say, "I don't know" or "I'm not sure." This admission is not an evasion but a spur to further creative inquiry.

The desire for certainty often makes people uncomfortable when they go to experts for "the" answer and the experts cannot give it to them. Patients may demand of their doctors, "What do you mean you don't know what's wrong with me? Find out and fix it!" Students may demand of their professors, "What do you mean it's a controversial issue? Just tell me the answer!" Critical thinkers, however, know that the more important the question, the less likely it is to have a single simple answer.

The need to accept a certain amount of uncertainty does not mean that we must live without beliefs and convictions. "The fact that today's knowledge may be overturned or at least revised tomorrow," says Ruggiero (1988), "could lead us to the kind of skepticism that refuses to embrace any idea. That would be foolish because, in the practical sense, it is impossible to build a life on that view. Besides, it is not the embracing of an idea that causes problems—it is the refusal to relax that embrace when good sense dictates doing so. It is enough to form convictions with care and carry them lightly, being willing to reconsider them whenever new evidence calls them into question."

Like the man who was delighted to learn he had been speaking prose all his life, many people are pleased to find that they already know some of these basic guidelines of critical and creative thinking. They do it, we might say, without thinking about it. Still, all of us could benefit from shaping up our mental muscles. In the remaining chapters, you will have many opportunities to apply critical thinking to psychological theories and to everyday life. From time to time, questions in the margin, accompanied by a little flash symbol like the one next to this paragraph, will draw your attention to discussions in which critical and creative thinking is particularly important. (Feel free to find others!) The photographs on pages 36 and 37 give a preview of some of the issues to be discussed. The flash symbol will also appear from time to time in Quick Quizzes to signal a question that gives you practice in critical thinking skills.

These odd objects may look like spaceships, but they are really lenticular (lens-shaped) clouds over Santos, Brazil. When people reason emotionally about UFOs, or anything else, they may overlook relevant evidence and ignore alternative interpretations.

Keep in mind, though, that critical thinking is as much an attitude as it is a set of skills. We are all less open-minded than we think. We take comfort from believing that only *other* people are biased or need to think more clearly. Critical thinking requires a willingness to submit even your most cherished beliefs to honest analysis. That is why intelligent people are not always critical thinkers. Clever debaters can learn to poke holes in the arguments of others, while twisting facts or conveniently ignoring arguments that might contradict their own position. But true critical thinking, according to philosopher Richard W. Paul (1984), is "fair-mindedness brought into the heart of everyday life."

Critical thinking is not for people who want psychology to give them final answers and simple solutions. Psychological facts do not simply pile up like a collection of postage stamps or trading cards. As new facts are added to our store of knowledge, others are discarded. Existing facts are continually being reorganized, reinterpreted, and assigned new meanings.

Some philosophers of science actually argue that, in a sense, all scientific theories *must* eventually fail. As knowledge grows, so does ignorance, for the more we know, the more questions we think to ask (Kuhn, 1981). As findings accumulate, existing theories become strained. Eventually they cannot explain all the evidence, no matter how they are stretched. It is like trying to fit a queen-sized sheet on a king-sized bed. When you tuck the sheet in at the head of the bed, it is too short at the bottom; when you tuck it in at the bottom, it is too short at the top. Eventually you have to get a new sheet or a new bed. Similarly, the scientist eventually is forced to show that new findings are wrong or get a new theory.

Does all this mean that there is no such thing as intellectual progress? Not at all. After each failure, a new and better theory arises from the ashes of the previous one, explaining more facts, solving more puzzles. This can be frustrating for those who want psychology and other sciences to hand them some absolute truths. But it is exciting for those who love the pursuit of understanding as much as the collection of facts. As neuroscientist John C. Eccles (1981) recalled, his training taught him to "rejoice in the refutation of a cherished hypothesis, because that, too, is a scientific achievement and because much has been learned by the refutation."

If you are ready to share in the excitement of studying psychology—if you, like Eccles, love a mystery—then you are ready to read on.

TAKING PSYCHOLOGY WITH YOU

What Psychology Can Do For You— And What It Can't

If you intend to become a psychologist or mental health professional, you have an obvious reason for taking a course in psychology. But psychology can contribute to your life in many ways, whether you plan to work in the field or not. Here are a few things psychology can do for you:

• *Make you a more informed person.* One purpose of education is to acquaint people with their cultural heritage and with humankind's achievements in literature, the humanities, and science. In contemporary society, being a well-informed person requires knowing something about psychology. One psychologist has written, "What geology was to the early nineteenth century, biology to the late nineteenth century, and physics to the first half of the twentieth century, so psychology is . . . [to] . . . the latter half of the twentieth century, its central major science" (Jaynes, 1973a). Geologists, biologists, and physicists might not agree, but certainly psychology plays a large role in our culture.

• *Satisfy your curiosity about human nature.* When the Greek philosopher Socrates admonished his fellow human beings to "know thyself," he was only telling them to do what they wanted to do anyway. The topic that seems to fascinate human beings most is human beings. Psychology, along with the other social sciences, literature, history, and philosophy, can contribute to a better understanding of yourself and others.

• *Help you increase control over your life.* Throughout this book we will be suggesting ways in which you can apply the findings of psychology to your own life. Psychology cannot solve all your problems, but it does offer techniques that may help you handle your emotions, improve your memory, and eliminate unwanted habits. It can also foster an attitude of objectivity that is useful for analyzing your behavior and your relationships with others.

• *Help you on the job.* Some people reading this book will probably go on to become psychologists. Others will find a bachelor's degree in the field useful for getting a job in a helping profession, for example, as a welfare caseworker or job rehabilitation counselor. People with a bachelor's degree in psychology also teach the subject in high schools. Still other readers, whether they earn a psychology degree or not, will go on to jobs (or already have jobs) in which psychological insights are useful. Anyone who works as a nurse, doctor, social worker, member of the clergy, police officer, or teacher can put psychology to work on the job. People who have lots of contact with others—waiters, flight attendants, bank tellers, receptionists—can make psychology work for them. Finally, psychology can be useful to those whose jobs require them to predict people's attitudes and behavior—for example, salespeople, labor negotiators, politicians, advertising copywriters, merchandise buyers, personnel managers, product designers, market researchers, magicians. . . .

• *Give you insights into political and social issues.* Examine the front page of any newspaper: Most of the stories you find there are likely to raise questions studied by psychologists. Crime, drug abuse, discrimination, and war are not only social issues but psychological ones. Psychologists argue among themselves about whether they should use the results of their research to advocate specific public policies on such issues. Most agree, though, that reliable information, scientifically arrived at, can help society achieve its political and social aims whether or not scientists help determine those aims. Psychological knowledge alone cannot solve the complex political, social, and ethical problems that fill the news, but it can help you make informed judgments about them. Knowing, for example, that involuntary crowding often leads to stress and abnormal behavior may affect your views on conditions in schools and prisons. Knowing that being sexually harassed lowers a person's self-esteem and sense of control may influence your views on antiharassment legislation.

As you can see, we are optimistic about psychology's role in the world. But we want to caution you that sometimes people expect things from psychology that it cannot deliver; for example:

• *It can't tell you the meaning of life.* Some people follow individual psychologists the way others follow religious leaders and gurus, hoping for enlightenment (Albee, 1977). There is no such thing, however, as instant wisdom. A personal philosophy about the purpose of life requires not only the acquisition of knowledge but also reflection and a willingness to learn from life's experiences.

• *It won't relieve you of personal responsibility for your actions.* It is one thing to understand the origins of offensive or antisocial behavior and another thing to *excuse* it. Knowing that your short temper is a result, in part, of your unhappy childhood doesn't give you a green light to yell at your neighbors. Nor does scientific neutrality mean that *society* must be legally or morally neutral. A better understanding of the psychological origins of child beating may help us reduce child abuse and treat offenders, but we can still hold child beaters accountable for their behavior.

• *It doesn't provide simple answers to complex psychological questions.* You have already found out in this chapter that psychologists, like other scientists, often disagree among themselves. By the time you finish this book, you will have discovered that there is controversy even about such basic issues as the causes of mental disturbance and the existence of stable personality traits. Many psychological questions have no simple answers on which everyone can agree. To say that psychology has limitations, however, is not to underestimate the contributions it can make to our lives.

Over two decades ago, in a presidential address to the American Psychological Association, George Miller (1969) called on his colleagues to "give psychology away." It was time, he said, for them to emerge from their laboratories and make an impact on the world around them. They should not assume the role of experts jealously guarding their professional secrets. "Psychological facts," he said, "should be passed out freely to all who need and can use them."

Ever since, critics have complained that psychologists don't know enough to "give it away." Some say that too much of psychology is common sense, and others make the opposite claim—that human behavior is infinitely mysterious, so psychologists might as well pack up their laboratories and go home. We don't agree. Behavioral scientists know the questions they raise are difficult—harder than those tackled by such "hard" sciences as physics and chemistry (J. Diamond, 1987). You can't put an attitude, emotion, or thought in a test tube or measure it with calipers. But that doesn't mean human behavior is beyond understanding. Even love is yielding its secrets.

At the end of each chapter, starting with the next one, you will have the opportunity to decide whether psychology does, in fact, have something to give away. The "Taking Psychology with You" section will suggest ways to apply psychological findings to your own life—in your relationships, on the job, or at school. We hope this information helps you understand, predict, and control events in your own personal world.

SUMMARY

1. Psychology is the study of behavior and mental processes and how they are affected by an organism's external and internal environment. Its goals are to describe, understand, predict, and control behavior and mental processes, using rigorous and systematic procedures. There has been some controversy over the goal of control.

2. Psychological findings sometimes confirm, but often contradict, "common sense." When psychological results do seem obvious, it is often because people overestimate the ability they might have had to predict the outcome of a study in advance. In any case, a result does not have to be surprising to be scientifically important.

3. Psychology has links with other social sciences, particularly with sociology and anthropology, and also with biology, but there are important differences in emphasis.

4. Until the late 1800s, psychology was not a science. A lack of empirical evidence often led to serious errors in the description and explanation of behavior. But psychology's forerunners also made valid observations and had useful insights. Descartes is a good example.

5. The official founder of scientific psychology was Wilhelm Wundt, whose work led to an approach called *structuralism*. Structuralism emphasized the analysis of immediate experience into basic elements. It was soon abandoned, because of its reliance on introspection. Another early approach, *functionalism*, emphasized the purpose of behavior. It, too, did not last long as a distinct school of psychology, but it greatly affected the course of psychological science.

6. Five points of view predominate today in psychology. The *behavioral perspective* emphasizes the study of observable behavior and rejects mentalistic explanations. The *psychodynamic perspective*, which originated with Freud's theory of psychoanalysis, emphasizes unconscious motives, conflicts, and desires. The *cognitive perspective* emphasizes mental processes in perception, problem solving, belief formation, and other human activities. The *physiological perspective* emphasizes bodily events associated with actions, thoughts, and feelings. The *sociocultural perspective* emphasizes how social and cultural rules, values, and expectations affect individual beliefs and behavior. Each of these approaches has made an important contribution to psychology, and each also has its critics. Many, if not most, psychologists draw on more than one "school" of psychology.

7. Psychologists teach, do research, and provide mental health services. Applied psychologists are concerned with the practical uses of psychological knowledge. Basic psychologists are concerned with knowledge for its own sake. Psychological specialties include, among others, experimental, educational, developmental, industrial/organizational, psychometric, social, counseling, school, and clinical psychology.

8. One of the greatest benefits of studying psychology is the development of *critical thinking* skills and attitudes. The critical thinker asks questions, defines problems clearly and accurately, examines the evidence, analyzes assumptions and biases, avoids emotional reasoning, avoids oversimplification, considers alternative interpretations, and tolerates uncertainty. Critical thinking is not for those who want psychology to give final answers and simple solutions, but it can open up many exciting paths in the pursuit of understanding.

KEY TERMS

Use this list to check your understanding of terms in this chapter. If you have trouble defining a word, you can find it on the page listed.

psychology 4
sociology 7
anthropology 7
cross-cultural psychology 7
empirical 8
Wilhelm Wundt 9
introspection 10
structuralism 10
functionalism 11
William James 11
Charles Darwin 11
John B. Watson 13
behaviorism 13
Ivan Pavlov 13
B. F. Skinner 13
Sigmund Freud 14
psychoanalysis 15
psychodynamic 15
humanistic psychology 16
Abraham Maslow 16

cognitive psychology 16
physiological psychology 17
intrapsychic 18
sociocultural perspective 19
paradigm 21
basic psychology 23
applied psychology 23
experimental psychologist 24
educational psychologist 24
developmental psychologist 24
industrial/organizational
  psychologist 24
psychometric psychologist 24
social psychologist 24
counseling psychologist 24
school psychologist 24
clinical psychologist 25
psychiatry 25
critical thinking 27

Thinking Critically and Creatively About Psychology

In the pages ahead, we will apply the eight guidelines to critical and creative thinking discussed in Chapter 1 to a variety of psychological topics.

1. Ask questions; be willing to wonder. *The sight of this Chinese man standing alone against awesome military might inspired millions of people around the world. What gives some people the courage to risk their lives for their beliefs? Why, in contrast, do so many people "go along with the crowd" and mindlessly obey authority? Social psychologists have probed these questions in depth, as we will see in Chapter 18. (© Stuart Franklin/Magnum)*

2. Define the problem. *People talk about "intelligence" all the time, but what is it exactly? Does the musical genius of a world-class violinist like Anne-Sophie Mutter count as a kind of intelligence? Is intelligence confined to what IQ tests measure, or does it also include other kinds of wisdom, knowledge, and "smarts"? We will be taking up these issues in Chapter 11. (© Crickmay/Daily Telegraph/International Stock Photo)*

3. Examine the evidence. *Amazed onlookers watch as illusionists Siegfried & Roy demonstrate "levitation" on a Las Vegas street corner. Illusionists take advantage of the fact that people are willing to trust the evidence of their own eyes, even when such evidence is misleading, as discussed in Chapter 5. (© Chris Callis)*

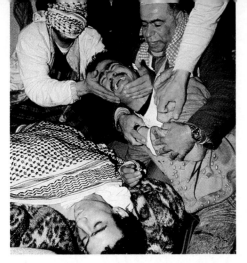

4. Analyze assumptions and biases. *Cultural and personal biases lead many people to believe that men are "naturally" less expressive emotionally than women. But which men, which cultures, and which emotions? This Palestinian man, grieving over his dead son, does not fit Western stereotypes. As we will see in Chapter 9, cultural display rules have a powerful influence on when, how, and to whom we express our feelings. (© Tannenbaum/Sygma)*

5. Avoid emotional reasoning. *Chances are that this photograph inspires an emotional reaction in you. Passionate feelings about controversial issues like abortion can keep us from considering other viewpoints. The resolution of differences requires that we move beyond emotional reasoning ("I feel this way strongly, so I must be right") and think dialectically, weighing point and counterpoint, as discussed in Chapter 8. (© Dennis Brack 1989/Black Star)*

6. Don't oversimplify. *Is the left side of the brain entirely analytic, rational, and sensible? Is the right side always intuitive, emotional, and spontaneous? As we will see in Chapter 3, the two hemispheres of the brain do have some specialized "talents," but it's easy to exaggerate the differences. (Courtesy of Natural Nectar Corporation)*

7. Consider other interpretations. *These young Jamaican children, members of the Rastafarian church, are smoking ganja (marijuana), which their religion regards as a "wisdom weed." Will they react in the same way as a North American who buys the drug on the streets and smokes it alone or at a party? Many people attribute the effects of psychoactive drugs solely to properties of the drug itself. An alternative explanation, however, supported by much evidence, emphasizes the importance of setting, motives, and cultural expectations, as we will see in Chapters 4 and 16.*

8. Tolerate uncertainty. *Some questions have no easy answers, and may even be unanswerable in principle. For example: What are the origins of sexual orientation? Many theories have been offered, but no single explanation can account for the many variations of homosexuality or of heterosexuality, as we will see in Chapter 10. (© Jim Anderson 1983/Woodfin Camp & Assoc.)*

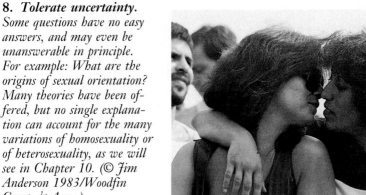

2

How Psychologists Know What They Know

The negative cautions of science
are never popular.

MARGARET MEAD

In recent years, no question has aroused more passionate debate, both pro and con, than the question of whether children make up stories about sexual abuse. Some people argue that no child would ever lie about being abused. Others say that children can't tell real life from fantasy, and that they tend to say whatever adults expect. The two sides hold different assumptions about what children know, what they remember, and what they can be induced to say. People on both sides often reach their conclusions on the basis of little more than emotion and "gut feeling."

How might a psychologist approach this question? To begin, a psychologist would want to assess the credibility of children in a more systematic manner. And that is just what Gail Goodman and her associates have done, in a program of studies stretching over ten years (Goodman & Helgeson, 1988).

In these studies, the researchers set out to learn, among other things, whether children would voluntarily reveal that their genitals had been touched and whether children could be persuaded to say something had happened when it had not. In one study, the children, ages 5 and 7, had all undergone routine physical checkups. Half had been examined genitally and anally for rashes, infections, tears, and other signs of trauma. The others had been examined for scoliosis (curvature of the spine). The researchers began by asking the children to act out what happened during the exam, using dolls and doctor toys. Then they interrogated the children, using intentionally misleading questions, such as "How many times did the doctor kiss you?" Goodman and her associates found that children whose genitals had been touched usually did not reveal that fact spontaneously during the doll play. On the other hand, children whose genitals had not been touched almost never said they had, even when prompted to do so by leading questions. This finding, confirmed by other studies, is an important one, because *without* leading questions, young children who have been abused often will not volunteer information they feel is embarrassing or shameful.

Of course, the findings of psychological research are only one consideration in evaluating any particular case involving charges of sexual abuse. Sexual abuse is one of the worst things that can happen to a child, but a false accusation of sexual abuse is also one of the worst things that can happen to an adult—which is why we need a justice system that attempts to separate fact from fiction in specific instances. Nor do the results mean that children are *never* suggestible. Like adults, they can sometimes be influenced to report an event in a certain way, depending on the frequency of the suggestions and the insistence of the person making them. Sometimes 3-year-olds give misleading responses because they don't understand the terms used by an adult; one little girl in Goodman's studies thought "private parts" meant her elbows! And occasionally, Goodman found, a child will spontaneously give a false response about being touched or undressed. But in her studies, children's reports were usually quite accurate.

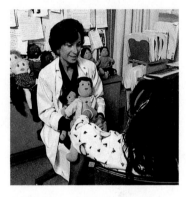

Psychologists have developed methods of studying children's recall and the extent of their suggestibility.

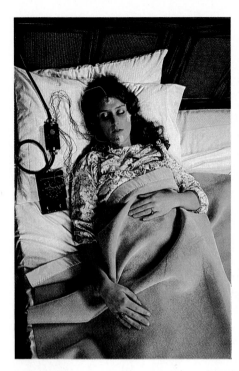

Innovative research methods have enabled psychologists to study many questions that once seemed unanswerable. Here, a volunteer in a sleep experiment slumbers while researchers measure her brain and muscle activity. If awakened during periods of rapid eye movement, she is likely to report that she has been dreaming.

You can see, then, why research methods, the focus of this chapter, are so important to psychologists. *These methods are the tools of the psychologist's trade.* They allow researchers to separate the kernel of truth from the chaff of unfounded belief. They offer a way to sort out conflicting views and can sometimes help clarify emotional issues, like the one about children's credibility. They also replace overly simplistic questions ("Do children lie?") with more sophisticated and valuable ones ("How should questions be worded to help children be as accurate and truthful as possible?"). As we will see at several points in this book, an innovative or clever research method can even reveal answers to questions that previously seemed impossible to study.

■ SCIENCE VERSUS PSEUDOSCIENCE

Perhaps you are saying to yourself, "Okay, okay . . . psychologists have to know about research methods. But what can knowing about these methods do for me (besides help me pass this course)? Why can't we just get right to the findings?" In this section, we will give you two answers. Then we will look at the assumptions and procedures that you need to understand if you are to distinguish good science from bad.

Why Study Methodology?

One reason to study methodology is that it can help you identify fallacies in your own or other people's thinking. For instance, we all have a tendency to look for evidence that supports our ideas and ignore evidence that doesn't, and sometimes this bias can have profound personal consequences. Consider, again, the painful issue of sexual abuse. Adults who were physically or sexually abused early in life are often afraid to have children of their own because they think

TABLE 2.1

Examining the Evidence

Is an abused child likely to become an abusive parent? People often base their answer solely on confirming cases, represented by the upper left-hand cell of this table. Psychological researchers consider all four types of evidence in the table.

Abused as a child?

		Yes	**No**
Abusive as a parent?	**Yes**	Abused children who become abusive parents	Nonabused children who become abusive parents
	No	Abused children who do not become abusive parents	Nonabused children who do not become abusive parents

their experience has ruined them as parents. Social workers, judges, and other professionals sometimes make the same assumption: One judge denied a woman custody of her children solely because the woman had been abused as a child, even though she had never harmed her children. However, the notion that "abuse inevitably breeds abuse" is usually based solely on confirming cases— cases of abused children who became abusive adults. What about children who suffer abuse but do not grow up to mistreat their children? A person knowledgeable about scientific methodology would consider both groups, as well as people who were not abused as children and then grew up to be—or not to be—abusive parents (see Table 2.1). As we will see in Chapter 13, when you take all the existing data into account, you find that although being abused is definitely a risk factor for becoming an abusive parent (and for other destructive behaviors as well), most abused children do *not* grow up to mistreat their own offspring (Kaufman & Zigler, 1987; Widom, 1989).

Many other mental stumbling blocks interfere with the ability to describe, understand, and predict behavior accurately. You will find some further examples in "Taking Psychology with You" at the end of this chapter.

A second reason for studying methodology is to become a more critical consumer of psychological findings. Psychology can be useful to you in many ways, but you should not accept every reported finding uncritically. You are constantly being bombarded with conflicting claims about matters that can affect your life—claims about how you should break bad habits, manage your emotions, dress for success, settle disputes, overcome shyness, or reduce stress. Not all studies on such matters are created equal, and some advice from self-styled "experts" is based on no evidence at all. As psychologists, we hope that when you hear and read about psychological issues, you will consider how the information was obtained and how the conclusions were reached, using guidelines in this chapter.

A psychologist has published a paper in which she states that all the abusive parents in a sample from a large midwestern city were mistreated as children. Does this mean that any child who is abused will grow up to become an abusive parent?

What Makes Research Scientific?

When we refer to psychologists as scientists, we do not mean that they work with complicated gadgets and machines or wear white lab coats (although some psychologists do). The scientific enterprise has more to do with attitudes and procedures than with apparatus. Philosophers and scientists have written many fat books on the features that distinguish science from other ways of knowing. We can't go into all these features, but here are a few key characteristics of the ideal scientist:

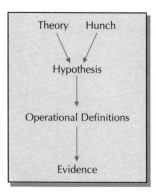

1. *Precision.* Scientists start out with a **hypothesis,** a statement that attempts to describe or explain behavior. Initially, the hypothesis may be stated in very general terms, as in "Anxiety increases sociability." But before any research can be undertaken, the hypothesis must be put into more specific terms; for example, "People who are anxious about a threatening situation tend to seek out others who face the same threat."

Some hypotheses are suggested by previous findings or casual observation. Others are derived from a general **theory,** an organized system of assumptions and principles that purports to explain certain phenomena and how they are related. A scientific theory is not just a bunch of hunches or opinions (as in "It's only a theory"). Theories that come to be accepted by a large part of the scientific community are consistent with many different observations and inconsistent with only a few (Stanovich, 1992).

A hypothesis leads to explicit predictions about what will happen in a particular situation. In a prediction, vague terms like *anxiety* or *threatening situation* are given **operational definitions** that specify how they are to be observed and measured. For example, *anxiety* might be defined as a score on an anxiety questionnaire and *threatening situation* as the threat of an electric shock. The prediction might be, "If you raise people's anxiety scores by telling them they are going to receive electric shocks, and then give them the choice of waiting alone or with others in the same situation, they will be more likely to choose to wait with others than they would if they were not anxious." The prediction is then tested, using careful and systematic procedures.

In contrast, pseudoscientists—people who pretend to be scientific but aren't—often hide behind vague and empty statements and make predictions that are nearly meaningless. If your astrological forecast tells you that "today will be a good time to take care of unfinished tasks," what have you learned? Isn't every day a good one for crossing things off your "to do" list?

2. *Skepticism.* Scientists do not accept ideas on faith or authority; their motto is "Show me!" Some of the greatest scientific advances have been made by those who dared to doubt what everyone else assumed to be true: that the sun revolves around the earth, that illness can be cured by applying leeches to the skin, that madness is a sign of demonic possession. In the everyday world of the researcher, skepticism means accepting conclusions, both new and old, with caution. Caution, however, must be balanced by an openness to new ideas and evidence. Otherwise, the scientist may wind up as shortsighted as the famous physicist Lord Kelvin, who at the end of the nineteenth century reputedly declared with great confidence that radio had no future, X-rays were a hoax, and "heavier-than-air flying machines" were impossible.

3. *Reliance on empirical evidence.* Unlike plays and poems, scientific theories and hypotheses are not judged by how artistically pleasing or entertaining they are. An idea may initially generate excitement simply because it is plausible, imaginative, or appealing. But no matter how true or right it may seem, eventually it must be backed by evidence if it is to be taken seriously. As Nobel-Prize-winning scientist Peter Medawar (1979) wrote, "the intensity of the conviction that a hypothesis is true has no bearing on whether it is true or not." Moreover, the evidence for a scientific idea must be *empirical,* that is, based on careful and systematic observation. A collection of personal accounts or anecdotes, or an appeal to authority, will not do.

Consider the plausible notion that *infantile autism,* a profound mental disorder that first appears in early childhood, is caused when a child is rejected by an emotionally cold mother (Bettelheim, 1967). Some clinicians once accepted this idea, even though it was based solely on therapists' personal observations of a limited number of cases. But when researchers carefully observed parents of autistic children and gave them standard personality tests, they found them to be no different on average from parents of normal children (DeMyer, 1975;

■ **hypothesis**

A statement that attempts to predict or account for a set of phenomena. Scientific hypotheses specify relationships among events or variables and are supported or disconfirmed by empirical investigation.

■ **theory**

An organized system of assumptions and principles that purports to explain a specified set of phenomena and their interrelationships.

■ **operational definition**

A precise definition of a term in a hypothesis that specifies the operations for observing and measuring it.

Koegel et al., 1983). Unfortunately, thousands of mothers had already suffered needless guilt and remorse because they had been told they were responsible for their children's disorder. Today there is general agreement that autism stems from a neurological problem, and not from any psychological problems of the parents.

4. *Willingness to make "risky predictions."* A scientist must state an idea in such a way that it can be *refuted*, or disproved by counterevidence. This principle, known as the **principle of falsifiability,** doesn't mean the idea *will* be disproved, only that it *could* be if certain kinds of facts were to be discovered. Another way of saying this is that a scientist must predict not only what will happen, but also what will *not* happen. A willingness to make such "risky predictions" forces scientists to take negative evidence seriously. Any researcher who refuses to go out on a limb and risk disconfirmation is not a true scientist.

This last characteristic is a little tricky, so let's take an example. Most psychologists view *parapsychology*, the study of extrasensory perception (ESP) and other "psychic" phenomena, as a pseudoscience. One objection, among many, is that parapsychologists often ignore the principle of falsifiability (Radner & Radner, 1982). If someone who claims to have ESP does better than chance at guessing a series of symbols on hidden cards, parapsychologists exclaim, "Aha, ESP at work!" But if the person performs only at chance levels, they may say that the person had a bad day or that the "vibes" were bad. And if the person does worse than chance, they may say that ESP was working, but in the opposite direction! It really doesn't matter how the ESP "demonstration" turns out, because the parapsychologist has all the bases covered in advance.

Many critics of psychoanalysis find it guilty of the same thing. If a person recalls some conflict in childhood that psychoanalysts think is universal, the psychoanalysts say, "Aha, evidence for our theory!" If a person can't recall such a conflict, the psychoanalysts say it must have been repressed (forced into the unconscious mind so that it can't be remembered). Thus there is no evidence that can count against the theory. *Any theory that purports to explain everything that could conceivably happen is unscientific.*

5. *Openness.* Scientists must be willing to tell others where they got their ideas, how they tested them, and what the results were. They must do this clearly and in detail so that other scientists can repeat, or *replicate*, their studies and verify the findings.

Replication is an important part of the scientific process, because sometimes a finding turns out to have been only a fluke. Some years ago a team of researchers trained flatworms to cringe in response to a flashing light. Then they killed the worms, ground them into a mash, and fed the mash to a second set of worms. This cannibalistic diet, the researchers reported, sped up acquisition of the cringe response in the second group of worms (McConnell, 1962). As you can imagine, this report generated tremendous excitement. If worms could learn faster by ingesting the "memory molecules" of their fellow worms, could memory pills be far behind? Students joked about grinding up professors; professors joked about doing brain transplants in students. But alas, the results proved difficult to replicate, and talk of memory pills eventually faded away.

Do psychologists and other scientists always live up to the lofty standards expected of them? Of course not. Being human, they may put too much trust in their personal experiences. They may deceive themselves. They may permit ambition to interfere with openness. They may fail to put their theories fully to the test: It is always easier to be skeptical about someone else's ideas than about your own pet theory. Even Albert Einstein sometimes resisted data that might have disconfirmed his own ideas.

Commitment to one's theories is not in itself a bad thing. Passion is the fuel of progress. It motivates researchers to think boldly, defend unpopular ideas,

Can this "dowser" find water by pointing a stick at the ground? Believers in parapsychology often ignore the negative evidence.

■ **principle of falsifiability**
The principle that a scientific theory must make predictions that are specific enough to expose the theory to the possibility of disconfirmation; that is, the theory must predict not only what will happen, but what will not happen.

and do the exhaustive testing that is often required. But passion can also cloud perceptions and in a few sad cases has even led to fraud. That is why science must be a *communal affair*. Scientists are expected to share their evidence and procedures with others. They are expected to submit their results to "peer review" before going public. They must persuade skeptical colleagues that their position is well supported. The scientific community—in our case, the psychological community—acts as a jury, scrutinizing and sifting the evidence, approving some viewpoints and relegating others to the scientific scrap heap. This public process gives science a built-in system of checks and balances. Individuals are not necessarily objective or even rational, but science forces them to justify their claims.

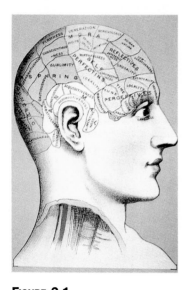

FIGURE 2.1

A wrong-headed theory
Nineteenth-century phrenologists thought that different parts of the brain accounted for specific traits of character and personality, and that these traits could be "read" from bumps on the skull. Like many pseudoscientific theories before and since, phrenology was wildly popular—and nonsense.

QUICK QUIZ

Test your understanding of science by identifying which of its rules was violated in each of the following cases.

1. For years, author and editor Norman Cousins told how he had cured himself of a rare and life-threatening disease through a combination of humor and vitamins. His book, *Anatomy of an Illness*, became a huge best-seller.
2. Alfred Russel Wallace (1823–1913) hit upon the theory of evolution at about the same time that Charles Darwin did. Later he became fascinated by attempts to communicate with the dead. To prove that communication with spirits was possible, he had professional mediums conduct seances. He trusted these mediums and was persuaded by their demonstrations.
3. Joseph Gall (1758–1828) was an Austrian physician who thought character was revealed by the bumps on a person's skull. He reported that he had examined many thieves who had large bumps above the ears. Gall also found people with "stealing bumps" who were not thieves. In such cases, he explained, a bump for "religiosity" or some other admirable trait held the person's thieving impulses in check (see Figure 2.1).

ANSWERS:

1. Cousins offered only a personal account and ignored disconfirming evidence. 2. Wallace was gullible rather than skeptical. 3. Gall failed to obey the principle of falsifiability; his theory was impossible to refute by counterevidence because he could explain anything away by referring to one or another "bump."

■ FERRETING OUT THE FACTS: DESCRIPTIVE STUDIES

Psychologists use several different methods in their research, depending on the kinds of questions they want to answer. These methods are not mutually exclusive. Just as a police detective may use a magnifying glass *and* a fingerprint duster *and* interviews of suspects to figure out "who done it," psychological "sleuths" may draw on different techniques at different stages of an ongoing investigation.

Many psychological methods are **descriptive** in nature. That is, they allow a researcher to describe and predict behavior but they often do not allow the researcher to choose one explanation over other, competing ones. Some descriptive methods are used primarily by clinicians to describe the behavior of

■ **descriptive methods**
Methods that yield descriptions of behavior but not necessarily causal explanations.

individuals. Others are used primarily by researchers to compare groups of people and arrive at generalizations about human behavior. Certain methods can be used in either way. In this section we will discuss the most common descriptive methods. As you read, you might want to list each method's advantages and disadvantages on a piece of paper. When you finish this and the next two sections, check your list against the one in Table 2.3 on p. 59.

Case Studies

A **case study** (or *case history*) is a detailed description of a particular individual. It may be based on careful observation or formal psychological testing. It may include information about the person's childhood, dreams, fantasies, experiences, relationships, and hopes—anything that will increase insight into the person's behavior. Case studies are most commonly used by clinicians, but they are occasionally used by academic researchers as well. They are especially valuable in the investigation of a new topic. Many early language researchers started out by keeping detailed diaries on the language development of their own children. A case study can be a rich source of hypotheses for future research.

Case studies illustrate psychological principles in a way that abstract generalizations and cold statistics never can, which is why we have peppered this book with them. They also produce a more detailed picture of an individual than other methods do. Often, however, case studies depend on people's memories of the past, and such memories may be both selective and inaccurate. Moreover, because case studies focus on individuals, they have drawbacks that limit their usefulness for psychologists who want to generalize about human behavior. The person who is the subject of a case study may be unlike most other people, or even those of the same economic class or age group. Also, it is often hard to know how to choose one interpretation of a case over another.

Still, case studies can be enlightening when practical or ethical considerations prevent information from being gathered in other ways. Let's take an example. Many psychologists believe that a "critical period" for language learning occurs between infancy and late childhood. They argue that a child who fails to learn a language during that period will be unable to catch up completely later on, no matter how much special tutoring the person gets. How can psychologists test this hypothesis? Obviously, they cannot put children in solitary confinement until adolescence and then suddenly expose them to language. However, they can study the tragic cases of children who were abandoned or isolated by their parents and were therefore prevented from acquiring language until they were rescued, sometimes after many years of solitude. These "experiments of nature" often leave many questions unanswered: How long was the child alone? At what age was the child isolated or abandoned? Was the child born mentally retarded? Did the child have a chance to learn any language before the ordeal began? But they can also provide valuable information.

In 1970, social workers discovered a 13-year-old girl whose parents had locked her up in one small room since age $1\frac{1}{2}$. During the day they usually strapped her in a child's potty seat. At night they confined her to a straitjacket-like sleeping bag. The mother, a battered wife who lived in terror of her husband, barely cared for the child. The father barked and growled at the little girl like a dog and physically abused her. There was no television or radio in the home, and no one spoke a word to the child. If she made the slightest sound, her father beat her with a large piece of wood.

Genie, as researchers later called her, hardly seemed human when she was finally set free from her terrifying prison. She did not know how to chew or stand erect and she was not toilet trained. She slobbered uncontrollably, masturbated in public, and spit on anything that was handy, including herself and other people. When she was first observed by psychologists, her only sounds

■ **case study**
A detailed description of a particular individual under study or treatment.

This picture was drawn by Genie, the adolescent girl described in the text, who endured years of isolation and mistreatment. It shows one of Genie's favorite pastimes: listening to researcher Susan Curtiss play classical music on the piano. Genie's drawings were used along with other case material to study her mental and social development.

were high-pitched whimpers. She understood only a few words, probably learned shortly after her release.

Yet Genie was alert and curious. Placed in a hospital rehabilitation center and then a foster home, she made rapid progress. She developed physically, learned some basic rules of social conduct, and established relationships with others. Gradually she began to use words and understand short sentences. Eventually she was able to use language to convey her needs, describe her moods, and even lie. However, her grammar and pronunciation of words remained abnormal even after several years. Susan Curtiss (1977) studied Genie's language development as part of her doctoral work and concluded that Genie's case supported the "critical period" hypothesis.

Ironically, then, the unusual and even bizarre circumstances of one person's life can shed light on a general question about human nature. Most case studies, however, are *sources* rather than *tests* of hypotheses. You should be cautious about "pop psych" books that present only testimonials and vivid case histories as "evidence."

Observational Studies

In **observational studies,** the researcher carefully and systematically observes and records behavior without interfering in any way with the behavior. Unlike case studies, observational studies usually involve many different **subjects.** Often an observational study is the first step in a program of research; you need a good description of behavior before you can explain it.

The primary purpose of *naturalistic observation* is to describe behavior as it occurs in the natural environment. Ethologists like Jane Goodall and the late Dian Fossey have used this method to study apes and other animals in the wild. Psychologists use naturalistic observation wherever people happen to be—at home, on playgrounds, and in schoolrooms and offices.

In one study using naturalistic observation, a social psychologist and his students ventured into a common human habitat—bars. They wanted to know whether people who drink in bars consume more alcohol when they are in groups than when they are alone. They visited all 32 pubs in a midsized city, ordered beers, and proceeded to record on napkins and pieces of newspaper how much the other patrons imbibed. They found that drinkers in groups consumed more than individuals who were by themselves. Those in groups didn't drink any faster; they just lingered in the bar longer (Sommer, 1977).

■ **observational study**
A study in which the researcher carefully and systematically observes and records behavior without interfering in any way with the behavior. Involves naturalistic or laboratory observations.
■ **subjects**
Animals or human beings used in research.

Psychologists often venture into "the field" to do observational studies. The man asking for a handout is actually a psychologist studying how people react to panhandlers. A tape recorder hidden under his shirt records their responses.

Note that the student researchers in this study did not rely on their impressions or memories of how much people drank. In observational studies, it is important to *count*, *rate*, or *measure* behavior. This procedure helps to minimize the tendency of most observers to notice only what they expect or want to see. Careful record keeping ensures accuracy and allows different observers to cross-check their observations. Cross-checking is necessary to make sure the observations are reliable, or consistent, from person to person.

Note, too, that the researchers took pains to avoid being obvious about what they were doing. If they had marched in with video cameras and announced that they were psychology students, people might not have behaved naturally. In other studies, researchers have concealed themselves entirely. When such precautions are taken, naturalistic observation gives us a glimpse of subjects as they really are, in their normal social contexts. However, it does *not* tell us what caused their behavior. For example, the barroom results do not necessarily mean that being in a group makes people drink a lot. People may join a group because they are already interested in drinking and find it more comfortable to hang around the bar if they are with others.

Sometimes it is preferable or necessary to make observations in the laboratory rather than in the "real world." In *laboratory observation*, the method is still descriptive, but the psychologist has more control. He or she can use sophisticated equipment, determine how many people will be observed at once, maintain a clear line of vision while observing, and so forth. Suppose, for example, that you want to know how infants of different ages respond when left in the company of a stranger. You could observe children at a nursery school, but most would probably already be toddlers and would know the nursery school personnel. You could visit private homes, but that might be slow and inconvenient. The solution would be to have parents and their infants come to your laboratory, observe them together for a while through a one-way window, then have a stranger enter the room and, a few minutes later, have the parent leave. You could record signs of distress, interactions with the stranger, and other behavior. You would find that very young infants carry on cheerfully with whatever they are doing when the parent leaves. However, by the age of about 8 months they often burst into tears or show other signs of what child psychologists call "separation anxiety" (Ainsworth, 1979).

A shortcoming of laboratory observation, however, is that the presence of researchers and special equipment may cause subjects to behave differently than they would in their normal surroundings. Also, laboratory observations, like

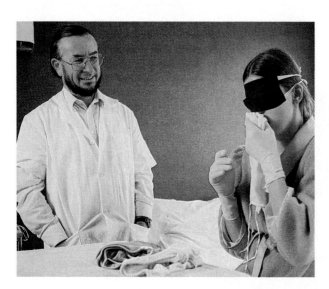

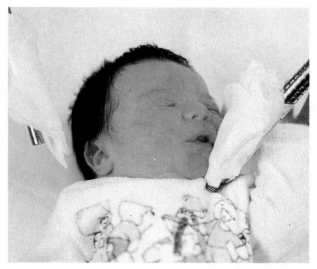

Can mothers and infants recognize one another's odors? It might be hard to tell in the natural environment, with its many distractions and scents—for example, the background fragrance of dinner cooking. But in the laboratory, researchers have better control over the factors they are investigating. Using laboratory methods, French ethologist Hubert Montagner (1985) has shown that infants as young as three days are calmer when they get a whiff of gauze worn by their mothers than when they smell gauze worn by other women. Moreover, by then mothers can distinguish their own baby's shirt from the shirts of other newborns on the basis of smell alone.

naturalistic observations, are more useful for describing behavior than for explaining it. When we observe infants protesting whenever a parent leaves the room, we cannot be sure *why* they are protesting. Is it because they have become attached to their parents and dependent on having them nearby, or have they simply learned from experience that crying brings attention and affection? It is hard to answer such questions on the basis of observational studies alone.

Surveys

A quick way to get information about people is to ask them for it. Questionnaires and interviews that ask people directly about their experiences, attitudes, or opinions are called **surveys.** Most people are familiar with surveys in the form of national opinion polls, such as the Gallup poll. Surveys have been done on many topics, from consumer preferences to sexual preferences—and sometimes they not only reflect people's attitudes and behavior but also influence them (see "Think About It").

Surveys produce bushels of data, but they are not easy to do well. The biggest hurdle is getting a **sample,** or group of subjects, that is **representative** of the larger **population** that the researcher wishes to describe. Suppose you want to know what college sophomores think about affirmative action. You can't question every college sophomore in the country, because that is not practical; instead, you must choose a sample. Special selection procedures can be used to ensure that this sample will be representative, that is, that it will contain the same proportion of women, men, blacks, whites, poor people, rich people, Catholics, Jews, and so on, as the general population of college sophomores. A sample's size is less critical than its representativeness; a small but representative sample may yield extremely accurate results.

In contrast, surveys and polls that fail to use proper sampling methods may yield questionable results. A newspaper that asks its readers to vote yes or no by telephone on a controversial question is hardly conducting a scientific poll. Only those who feel quite strongly about an issue (*and* read the newspaper) are

■ **surveys**
Questionnaires and interviews that ask people directly about their experiences, attitudes, or opinions.

■ **sample**
A group of subjects selected from a population for study in order to estimate characteristics of the population.

■ **representative sample**
A sample that matches the population in question on important characteristics, such as age and sex.

■ **population**
The entire set of individuals from which a sample is drawn.

likely to call in, and those who feel strongly may be likely to take a particular side. A psychologist or statistician would say that the poll suffers from a **volunteer bias:** Those who volunteer probably differ from those who stay silent.

Many magazines—*Redbook, Cosmopolitan, Playboy, The Ladies' Home Journal*— have done highly publicized surveys on the sexual habits of their readers, but these surveys, too, are vulnerable to the volunteer bias. Readers motivated to respond to these surveys may be more (or possibly less) sexually active, on the average, than those who do not respond. In addition, people who read magazines regularly tend to be younger, more educated, and more affluent than the American population as a whole, and these characteristics may affect the results. When you read a survey, always ask what sorts of people participated. A biased, nonrepresentative sample does not necessarily mean that a survey is worthless or uninteresting, but it does mean that the results may not hold for other groups.

A final problem with surveys is that people sometimes lie. This is especially likely when the survey is about a touchy topic ("What? Me do that? Never!"). The likelihood of lying is reduced when respondents are guaranteed anonymity. Also, there are some ways to check for lying—for example, by asking a question several times in different ways. But not all surveys use these techniques, and even when people do not intentionally lie, they may misremember. Still, if surveys are conducted and interpreted carefully they can be very informative.

✳ Your favorite magazine has just published a sensational survey of its female readers called "The Sex Life of the American Wife." The survey reports that "Eighty-seven percent of all wives like to make love in rubber boots." Is this claim justified? What would be a more accurate title for the survey?

■ **volunteer bias**
A shortcoming of findings derived from a sample of volunteers instead of a representative sample.

THINK ABOUT IT

Surveys, Public Opinion, and You

• According to a nationwide survey, 87 percent of all high school students have had sexual intercourse.

• According to a nationwide survey, 37 percent of all high school students have had sexual intercourse.

Do you find yourself wanting to believe one of these results rather than the other because it matches your own sexual history? Would one figure make you feel normal and the other make you feel odd? Might either finding influence you to change your own behavior? If so, you are not alone. Opinion polls and surveys not only reflect, but can also *affect,* people's feelings and behavior.

Many people form their views by studying a sample of one—themselves. Or perhaps they expand the sample a bit to include their sister, their best friend, and the neighborhood grocer. They assume that their own beliefs and actions, or those of people they know, are typical of "most people." Gary Marks and Norman Miller (1987) call this tendency the *false consensus effect.* By overestimating the degree of agreement between themselves and others, say Marks and Miller, people maintain their self-esteem and reduce the

discomfort of feeling different or "weird." But the false consensus effect can also keep people from recognizing other points of view and can make them discount information that challenges their own ways.

In addition to thinking that everyone is like them, people tend to think that they ought to be like everyone else. As a consequence, when they find themselves in the minority, they may become apathetic, feeling that "there's no point trying to do anything." Or they may do things they consider wrong, or alter their beliefs, because "everybody" (according to the surveys) is doing something or feels a certain way, and they don't want to be different. Sociologist Elisabeth Noelle-Neumann (1984) argues that this tendency to unconsciously tailor opinions and values to fit prevailing trends makes "public opinion" a potent form of social control. She describes a German election in which two parties were neck and neck, until polls gave one party a slight edge. "And then, right at the end, people jumped on the bandwagon," she writes. "As if caught in a current, 3–4 percent of the votes were swept in the direction of the general expectation of who was going to win."

How can people resist the false consensus effect? What can be done to limit the influence of political polls during elections? How will you be influenced by studies in this book showing that your own opinions or habits are not shared by "everybody"? Think about it.

Tests

Psychological tests are procedures used to measure personality traits, emotional states, aptitudes, interests, abilities, and values. Like surveys, they may require people to answer a series of written or oral questions, but they tend to elicit information less directly than surveys do. Answers are often totaled to yield a single numerical score, or a set of scores, that reveals something about the person. Psychological tests are used in educational and job settings and in clinical work to evaluate individuals, promote self-understanding, or evaluate treatments and programs, and in scientific research to draw generalizations about groups. Some tests measure beliefs, feelings, or behaviors of which an individual is aware. Others are designed to tap unconscious feelings or motives. Psychological tests are an improvement over simple self-evaluation because many people have a distorted view of their own abilities and traits.

Test construction, administration, and interpretation require specialized training. It is extremely difficult to construct a test that is **valid** (measures what it sets out to measure) and **reliable** (yields the same results from one time and place to the next). A test that purports to measure creativity is not valid if it actually measures verbal sophistication. A vocational interest test is not reliable if it tells Tom he would make a wonderful engineer but a poor journalist, and then gives different results when Tom takes the test again a week later. The "psychological tests" frequently found in magazines and newspapers often are neither valid nor reliable. They are simply lists of questions that someone thought sounded good.

■ **psychological tests**
Procedures used to measure personality traits, emotional states, aptitudes, interests, abilities, and values.

■ **valid test**
A test that measures what it was designed to measure.

■ **reliable test**
A test that yields consistent results from one time and place to another.

QUICK QUIZ

A. Which descriptive method would be most appropriate for studying each of the following topics? (We did not make up these topics.)

1. Ways in which the games of boys differ from those of girls
2. Changes in attitudes toward nuclear disarmament after a television movie about nuclear holocaust
3. The math skills of U.S. versus Japanese children
4. Physiological changes that occur when people watch violent movies
5. The development of a male infant who was reared as a female after his penis was accidentally burned off during a supposedly routine circumcision involving electrocauterization

a. case study
b. naturalistic observation
c. laboratory observation
d. survey
e. test

B. Over a period of 55 years, an 80-year-old British woman sniffed large amounts of cocaine, which she obtained legally under British regulations for the treatment of addicts. Yet the woman appeared to show no negative effects, other than drug dependence (Brown & Middlefell, 1989). What does this case tell us about the dangers or safety of cocaine?

ANSWERS:

ANSWERS:

A. 1. b 2. d 3. e 4. c 5. a B. Not much. "Snorting" cocaine may be relatively harmless for some people, such as this woman, but extremely harmful for others. Also, the cocaine she received may have been less potent than cocaine purchased on the street. Critical thinking requires that we resist generalizing from a single case.

■ LOOKING FOR RELATIONSHIPS: CORRELATIONAL STUDIES

In descriptive research, psychologists often want to know whether two or more phenomena are related, and if so, how strongly. To obtain this information, they do **correlational studies.** If a researcher simply surveys college students to find out how many hours a week they spend watching television, the study is not a correlational one. However, if the researcher looks for a relationship between hours in front of the television set and grade point average, then it is.

The word **correlation** is often used as a synonym for "relationship." Technically, however, a correlation is a numerical measure of the *strength* of the relationship between two or more things. The "things" may be events, scores, or anything else that can be recorded and tallied. In psychological studies, such things are called **variables** because they can vary in quantifiable ways. Height, weight, age, income, IQ scores, number of items recalled on a memory test, number of smiles in a given time period—anything that can be measured, rated, or scored can serve as a variable.

Correlations always occur between *sets* of observations. Sometimes the sets come from one individual. Suppose you measured both a person's temperature and the person's alertness several times during the day. To check for a relationship between temperature and alertness, you would need several measurements, or values, for each variable. Of course, your results would hold only for that individual. In psychological research, sets of correlated observations usually come from many individuals or are used to compare groups of people. For example, in research on the origins of intelligence, psychologists look for a relationship between the IQ scores of parents and children. To do this, they must gather scores from a *set* of parents and from the children of these parents. You cannot compute a correlation if you only know the IQs of one particular parent-child pair. To say that a relationship exists, you need more than one pair of values to compare.

A **positive correlation** means that high values of one variable are associated with high values of the other, and that low values of one variable are associated with low values of the other. Height and weight are positively correlated, for example; so are IQ scores and school grades. Rarely is a correlation perfect, however. Some tall people weigh less than some short ones; some people with average IQs are superstars in the classroom and some with high IQs get poor grades. Figure 2.2(a) shows a positive but not perfect relationship between educational level and annual income.

A **negative correlation** means that high values of one variable are associated with *low* values of the other (see Figure 2.2[b]). In the automobile business, the older the car, the lower the price, except for antiques and models favored by collectors. As for human beings, in general the older adults are, the fewer miles they can run and the fewer hairs they have on their heads. See if you can think of some other variables that are negatively correlated. Remember, though, a negative correlation indicates that a certain kind of relationship exists. If there is *no* relationship between two variables, we say they are *uncorrelated.* Shoe size and IQ scores are uncorrelated.

The statistic used to express a correlation is called the **coefficient of correlation.** This number conveys both the size of the correlation and its direction. A perfect positive correlation has a coefficient of +1.00. Suppose you weighed ten people and listed them in order, from lightest to heaviest. Then suppose you measured their heights and listed them in order, from shortest to tallest. If the names on the two lists were in exactly the same order, the correlation between weight and height would be +1.00. (Table 2.2 gives some examples of small, moderate, and large positive correlations.) A perfect negative correlation has a coefficient of −1.00. If you hear that the correlation between two variables is +.80, it means that they are very strongly related. If you hear that the correlation is −.80, the relationship is just as strong, but it is negative.

■ **correlational study**
A descriptive study that looks for a consistent relationship between two phenomena.

■ **correlation**
A measure of how strongly two or more variables are related to each other.

■ **variables**
Characteristics of behavior or experience that can be measured or described by a numeric scale. Variables are manipulated and assessed in scientific studies.

■ **positive correlation**
An association between increases in one variable and increases in another.

■ **negative correlation**
An association between increases in one variable and decreases in another.

■ **coefficient of correlation**
A measure of correlation that ranges in value from −1.00 to +1.00.

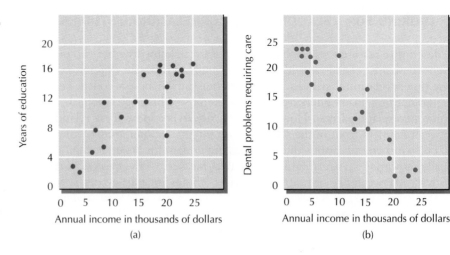

FIGURE 2.2

Correlations
Graph (a) shows a positive (but not perfect) correlation between education and income in a group of men. Each dot represents a man. You can find each man's educational level by drawing a horizontal line from his dot to the vertical axis. You can find his income by drawing a vertical line from his dot to the horizontal axis. Graph (b) shows a negative correlation between average income and the incidence of dental disease for groups of 100 families. Each dot represents one group. In general, the higher the income, the fewer the dental problems. (From Wright, 1976.)

When there is no association between two variables, the coefficient is zero or close to zero.

Correlations allow researchers, using statistical techniques, to make general predictions about a variable if they know how it is related to another one. But because correlations are rarely perfect, predictions about a particular *individual* may be inaccurate. If you know that a person is well educated, you might predict, in the absence of any other information, that the person is fairly well off, because education and income are positively correlated. You would not be able to say exactly how much the person earned, but you would probably guess that the person's income was relatively high. You could be wrong, though. Some people with doctorates earn low salaries, and some people with only a grade school education make fortunes.

Correlational studies in the social sciences are common and are often reported in the news. But beware—they can be misleading. The important thing to remember is that *a correlation does not show causation*. It is easy to assume that if A predicts B, A must be causing B—that is, making B happen—but that is not necessarily so (see Figure 2.3). The number of storks nesting in certain Eu-

TABLE 2.2

Some positive correlations

Small (about .10)

Viewing television violence—Aggressive behavior
Stress—Physical illness
IQ score—Grade in a particular course

Moderate (about .30)

Psychotherapy—Adjustment
Self-esteem—Grades in school
Similar values—Interpersonal attraction

Large (about .50)

IQ score—Grade point average
Wife's satisfaction—Husband's satisfaction
Belief in God—Church attendance

(Adapted from Kenny, 1987.)

ropean villages is reportedly correlated (positively) with the number of human births in those villages. In other words, knowing when the storks nest allows one to predict when more births than usual will occur. But clearly that doesn't mean that storks bring babies or that babies attract storks. Human births seem to be somewhat more frequent at certain times of the year (you might want to speculate on the reasons), and the peaks just happen to coincide with the storks' nesting periods.

The coincidental nature of the correlation between nesting storks and human births may seem obvious, but in other cases, unwarranted conclusions about causation are more tempting. For example, there is a significant correlation between circulation rates of adult magazines like *Penthouse* and *Playboy* and rates of reported rape (Scott & Schwalm, 1988). States such as Alaska and Nevada, with high rape rates, tend to have high sales of such magazines. States such as Maine and West Virginia, with low rape rates, tend to have low sales. Does this mean that reading adult magazines makes men more likely to commit rape? Perhaps so, but it is also possible that in places with high rape rates, men who are already prone to rape are especially likely to buy erotic magazines. Or other factors, such as attitudes toward women, may affect both magazine sales and rape statistics.

The moral of the story: When two variables are associated, one variable may or may not be causing the other.

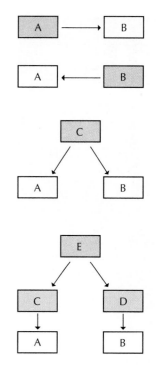

FIGURE 2.3

Correlation and causation
If two variables, A and B, are correlated, one is not necessarily causing the other. There are many possible patterns of causation, including the four shown here. (The arrows indicate the direction of causation, and C, D, and E represent other variables.)

QUICK QUIZ

1. Are you clear about correlations? Find out by identifying each of the following findings as indicative of either a positive correlation or a negative correlation.
   a. The higher a child's score on an intelligence test, the less physical force her mother is likely to use in disciplining her.
   b. The higher a male monkey's level of the hormone testosterone, the more aggressive he is likely to be.
   c. After a certain age, the older people are, the less frequently they tend to have sexual intercourse.
   d. The hotter the weather, the more crimes against persons (such as muggings) tend to occur.

✳ 2. Now see if you can generate two or three alternative explanations for each of the above findings.

ANSWERS:

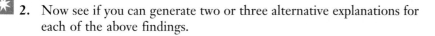

1. **a.** Negative correlation **b.** Positive correlation **c.** Negative correlation **d.** Positive correlation 2. **a.** Physical force may impair a child's intellectual growth; brighter children may elicit less physical discipline from their parents; brighter mothers may have brighter children and may also tend to use less physical force. **b.** The hormone might cause aggressiveness or acting aggressively might stimulate hormone production. **c.** Older people may have less interest in sex than younger people; older people may have less energy for sex; older people may think they are supposed to have less interest in sex and behave accordingly; older people may have trouble finding sexual partners. **d.** Hot temperatures may make people edgy and cause them to commit crimes; potential victims may be more plentiful in warm weather because more people stroll outside and go out at night; criminals may find it more comfortable to be out committing their crimes in warm weather than in cold. (Note: Our explanations for these correlations are not the only ones possible.)

Everyone knows that alcohol and the operation of heavy machinery don't mix—but what about the effects of nicotine on such work? What sort of experiment might answer that question?

■ **experiment**
A controlled test of a hypothesis in which the researcher manipulates one variable to discover its effect on another.
■ **independent variable**
A variable that an experimenter manipulates.
■ **dependent variable**
A variable that an experimenter predicts will be affected by manipulations of the independent variable.

■ HUNTING FOR CAUSES: THE EXPERIMENT

Researchers often propose explanations of behavior on the basis of descriptive studies, but for actually tracking down the causes of behavior they rely heavily on the experimental method. An **experiment** allows the researcher to *control* the situation being studied. Instead of being a passive recorder of what is going on, the researcher actively does something that he or she thinks will affect the subjects' behavior, then observes what happens as a result.

Experimental Variables

Suppose you are a psychologist and you come across reports that cigarette smoking improves performance on simple reaction time tasks. You do not question these findings, but you have a hunch that the nicotine in cigarettes may have the opposite effect on more complex or demanding kinds of behavior, such as driving. You know that on the average, smokers have more vehicular accidents than nonsmokers, even when differences in alcohol consumption, age, and other factors are taken into account (DiFranza et al., 1986). But this relationship doesn't prove that smoking *causes* accidents. Smokers may simply be greater risk takers than nonsmokers, whether the risk is lung cancer or trying to beat a red light. Or perhaps the distraction of falling cigarette ashes or of fumbling for matches explains the relationship, rather than smoking itself. So you decide to do an experiment. In a laboratory, you ask smokers to "drive" on a Monte Carlo–type road, using a computerized driving simulator equipped with a stick shift and a gas pedal. The object, you tell them, is to maximize distance by driving as fast as possible while avoiding rear-end collisions. At your request, some of the subjects smoke a cigarette immediately before climbing into the driver's seat. Others do not. You are interested in comparing how many collisions the two groups have. (The basic design of this experiment is illustrated in Figure 2.4. You may want to refer to the figure from time to time as you read the next few pages.)

The aspect of an experimental situation manipulated or varied by the researcher is known as the **independent variable.** The reaction of the subjects—the behavior that the researcher tries to predict—is called the **dependent variable.** Every experiment has at least one independent and one dependent variable. In our example, the independent variable is nicotine use: one cigarette versus none. The dependent variable is the number of rear-end collisions.

Ideally, everything about the experimental situation *except* the independent variable is held constant, that is, kept the same for all subjects. You would not have some people use a stick shift and others an automatic, unless shift type were an independent variable. Similarly, you would not have some people go through the experiment alone and others perform in front of an audience. Holding everything but the independent variable constant ensures that whatever happens is due to the researcher's manipulation and nothing else. It allows you to rule out other interpretations.

Understandably, students often have trouble keeping independent and dependent variables straight. You might think of it this way: The dependent variable—the outcome of the study—*depends* on the independent variable. When psychologist Smith sets up an experiment, she thinks, "If I do (such and such), the subjects in my study will do (such and such)." The first "such and such" represents the independent variable; the second represents the dependent variable. Most variables may be either independent or dependent, depending on what the experimenter is manipulating and trying to predict. If you want to know whether eating chocolate makes people nervous, then the amount of chocolate eaten is the independent variable. If you want to know whether feeling nervous makes people eat chocolate, then the amount of chocolate eaten is the dependent variable.

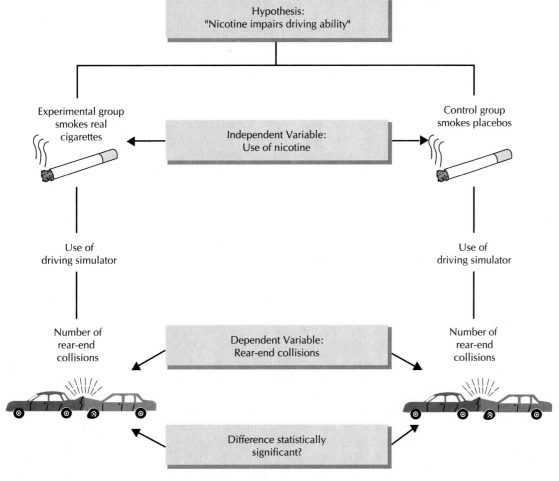

FIGURE 2.4

Do smoking and driving mix?
The text suggests an experiment to test the hypothesis that the nicotine in cigarettes impairs driving skills. The independent variable is use or nonuse of nicotine. The dependent variable is the number of rear-end collisions while operating a driving simulator.

QUICK QUIZ

Name the independent and dependent variables in studies designed to answer the following questions:

1. Whether sleeping after learning a poem improves memory for the poem
2. Whether the presence of other people affects a person's willingness to help someone in distress
3. Whether people get agitated from listening to rock-and-roll

ANSWERS:

1. Opportunity to sleep after learning is the independent variable; memory for the poem is the dependent variable. 2. The presence of other people is the independent variable; willingness to help others is the dependent variable. 3. Exposure to rock-and-roll is the independent variable; agitation is the dependent variable.

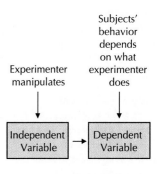

✳ *You've developed a new form of therapy that you believe cures anxiety: Sixty-three percent of the people who go through your program improve. Why shouldn't you rush out to open an Anxiety Clinic?*

■ **control condition**
In an experiment, a comparison condition in which subjects are not exposed to the same "treatment" or manipulation of the independent variable as in the experimental condition.

■ **random assignment**
A procedure for assigning people to experimental and control groups in which each individual has the same probability as any other of being assigned to a given group.

■ **placebo**
An inactive substance or fake treatment used as a control in an experiment or given by a medical practitioner to a patient.

■ **single-blind study**
An experiment in which subjects do not know whether they are in an experimental or control group.

Experimental and Control Conditions

Experiments usually require both an experimental condition and a comparison, or **control condition.** In the control condition, subjects are treated exactly like those in the experimental condition, except that they are not exposed to the same "treatment" or manipulation of the independent variable. Without a control condition, you can't be sure the behavior you are interested in would not have occurred anyway, even without your manipulation. In some studies, the same subjects can be used in both the control and experimental conditions; they are said to "serve as their own controls." In other studies, subjects are assigned to either an *experimental group* or a *control group*.

In the nicotine experiment, the people who smoke before driving make up the experimental group, and those who refrain from smoking make up the control group. We want these two groups to be roughly the same in terms of average driving skill. It wouldn't do to start out with a bunch of reckless road-runners in the experimental group and a bunch of tired tortoises in the control group. We probably also want the two groups to be similar in average intelligence, education, smoking history, and other characteristics, so that none of these variables will affect our results. To accomplish this, we can use **random assignment** to place people in the groups. We might randomly give each person a number, then put all those with even numbers in the experimental group and all those with odd numbers in the control group. At the beginning of the study, each subject will have the same probability as any other subject of being assigned to a given group. If we have enough subjects in our study, individual differences among them are likely to be roughly balanced in the two groups. However, for some characteristics, such as sex, we may decide not to depend on random assignment. Instead, we may deliberately assign an equal number of people from each category (e.g., male and female) to each group.

Sometimes researchers use several different experimental or control groups. For example, in our nicotine study, we might want to examine the effects of different levels of nicotine by having people smoke one, two, or three cigarettes before "driving," and comparing each of these experimental groups to each other and to a control group of nonsmokers as well. For now, however, let's focus just on experimental subjects who smoked one cigarette.

We now have two groups. We also have a problem. In order to smoke, the experimental subjects must light up and inhale. These acts might set off certain expectations—of feeling relaxed, getting nervous, feeling confident, or whatever. These expectations, in turn, might affect driving performance. It would be better to have the control group do everything the experimental group does *except* use nicotine. Therefore, let's change the experimental design a bit. Instead of having the control subjects simply refrain from smoking, we will give them a **placebo,** or fake treatment. Placebos, which are used frequently in drug research, often take the form of pills or injections containing no active ingredients. Assume that it's possible in the nicotine study to use phony cigarettes that taste and smell like the real thing but contain no active ingredients. Our control subjects will not know their cigarettes are fake and will have no way of distinguishing them from real ones. Now if they have substantially fewer collisions than the experimental group, we will feel safe in concluding that nicotine increases the probability of an auto accident. (Placebos, by the way, sometimes produce effects that are as strong or nearly as strong as those of a real treatment. Thus phony injections are often surprisingly effective in eliminating pain. Such placebo effects are a puzzle awaiting scientific solution.)

Experimenter Effects

Because expectations can influence the results of a study, subjects should not know whether they are in an experimental or control group. When this is so (as it usually is), the experiment is said to be a **single-blind study.** But subjects are not the only ones who bring expectations to the laboratory; so do researchers. Their expectations (and hopes for a reportable result) may cause them to inadvertently influence the participants' responses through facial expressions, posture, tone of voice, or some other cue.

Several years ago, Robert Rosenthal demonstrated how powerful such **experimenter effects** can be. He had students teach rats to run a maze. Half the students were told their rats had been bred to be "maze bright," half that their rats had been bred to be "maze dull." In reality, there were no genetic differences between the two groups of rats. During the course of the experiment, the supposedly brainy rats actually did learn the maze more quickly! If an experimenter's expectations can affect a rodent's behavior, reasoned Rosenthal, surely they can affect a human being's. He went on to demonstrate this in many other studies (R. Rosenthal, 1966).

Unfortunately, the cues an experimenter may give subjects can be as subtle as the smile on the Mona Lisa. In fact, the cue may *be* a smile. In one of his studies, Rosenthal found that male researchers were far more likely to smile at female subjects than at males. Since one smile tends to invite another, such behavior on the part of the experimenter could easily ruin a study on friendliness or cooperation. "It may be a heartening finding to know that chivalry is not dead," noted Rosenthal, "but as far as methodology is concerned it is a disconcerting finding."

A smile is nice, but not if it produces an experimenter effect.

One solution to the problem of experimenter effects is to do a **double-blind study.** In such a study, the person running the experiment (the one having actual contact with the subjects) does not know which subjects are in which groups until the data have been gathered. Double-blind procedures are common in drug research. Different doses of a drug are coded in some way, and the person administering the drug is kept in the dark about the code's meaning until after the experiment. To run the nicotine study in a double-blind fashion, we would keep the person dispensing the cigarettes from knowing which ones were real and which were placebos. In psychological research, double-blind studies are often more difficult to design than those that are merely single-blind. The goal, however, is always to control everything possible in an experiment.

Because experiments allow conclusions about cause and effect, they have long been the "method of choice" in psychology. However, like all methods, the laboratory experiment has its limitations. As we noted earlier, the laboratory creates a very special kind of setting, one that may call forth certain kinds of behavior rarely seen elsewhere. Moreover, the laboratory encourages a certain kind of relationship between researchers and their subjects, one in which the researcher determines what the questions are and which behaviors will be recorded. In their desire to cooperate, subjects may act in ways that they ordinarily would not. Thus the psychologist confronts a dilemma: The more control he or she exercises over the situation, the more unlike real life it may be. For this reason, many psychologists are calling for more field research, or careful study of behavior in natural contexts.

■ **experimenter effects**
Unintended changes in subjects' behavior due to cues inadvertently given by the experimenter.
■ **double-blind study**
An experiment in which neither the subjects nor the researchers know which subjects are in the control group(s) and which in the experimental group(s) until after the results are tallied.

QUICK QUIZ

1. What's wrong with these two studies?
    a. A kidney specialist and a psychiatrist treated mentally disordered patients by filtering their blood through a dialysis machine (normally used with kidney patients). They reported several cases of dramatic improvement, which they attributed to the removal of an unknown toxin (Wagemaker & Cade, 1978).
    b. A sex researcher surveyed women on their feelings about men and love. She sent out 100,000 lengthy questionnaires to various women's groups and got back 4,500 replies (a 4.5 percent return).

On the basis of these replies, she reported that 84 percent of women are dissatisfied with their relationships, 98 percent want more communication, and 70 percent of those married five years or more have had extramarital affairs (Hite, 1987).

2. Suppose you hear that a researcher reported a dramatic improvement in the functioning of Alzheimer's patients who took an experimental drug. As a critical thinker, what questions would you want to ask about this study? Try to come up with as many questions as you can.

ANSWERS:

1. **a.** The dialysis study had no control group and was not double-blind. Patients' expectations that the fancy "blood-cleansing" equipment would wash their madness out of them might have influenced the results, and so might the researchers' expectations. In later studies, using double-blind procedures, control subjects had their blood circulated through the machine but the blood was not actually filtered. Little improvement occurred in either the experimental or the control condition, and the real treatment was no better than the fake treatment (Carpenter et al., 1983). **b.** Because of the way the sample was recruited and the low return rate, the findings may be flawed by a volunteer bias. Although the study produced thought-provoking information on the feelings of many women, figures and percentages from the study are not necessarily valid for the general population. **2.** Some possible questions: How many people were studied? Was there a control group? If so, did the control subjects receive placebos? How were patients assigned to the experimental and control groups? Were double-blind procedures used? How was "improved functioning" measured? How long did the effects last? Did the effects make any difference in the everyday lives of the patients or their families? Were there any negative effects? Has the experiment been replicated by other researchers?

■ EVALUATING THE FINDINGS: WHY PSYCHOLOGISTS USE STATISTICS

If you are a psychologist who has just done an observational study, a survey, or an experiment, your work has only just begun. Once you have some results in hand, you must do three things with them: (1) describe them, (2) assess how meaningful they are, and (3) figure out how to explain them.

Descriptive Statistics: Finding Out What's So

Let's say that 30 people in the nicotine experiment smoked real cigarettes and 30 smoked placebos. We have recorded the number of collisions each person had on the driving simulator. Now we have 60 numbers. What can we do with them?

The first thing we must do is summarize the data. The world does not want to hear how many collisions each person had. It wants to know what happened in the "nicotine group" as a whole, compared to what happened in the control group. To provide this information, we need numbers that sum up our data. Such numbers are known as **descriptive statistics,** and are often depicted in graphs and charts.

A good way to summarize the data is to compute group averages. The most commonly used type of average is the **arithmetic mean.** (For two other types, see the Appendix.) It is calculated by adding up all the individual scores and dividing the result by the number of scores. We can compute a mean for the nicotine group by adding up the 30 collision scores and dividing by 30. Then we

■ **descriptive statistics**
Statistics that organize and summarize research data.

■ **arithmetic mean**
An average that is calculated by adding up a set of quantities and dividing the sum by the total number of quantities in the set.

TABLE 2.3

Research Methods in Psychology: Their Advantages and Disadvantages

Method	Advantages	Disadvantages
Case history	Good source of hypotheses. Provides in-depth information on individuals. "Experiments of nature" shed light on situations/ problems that are unethical or impractical to study in other ways.	Individual may not be representative or typical. Difficult to know which subjective interpretation is best.
Naturalistic observation	Allows description of behavior as it occurs in the natural environment. Often useful in first stages of research program.	Allows researcher little or no control of the situation. Observations may be biased. Does not allow firm conclusions on cause and effect.
Laboratory observation	Allows more control than naturalistic observation. Allows use of sophisticated equipment.	Allows researcher only limited control of the situation. Observations may be biased. Does not allow firm conclusions on cause and effect. Behavior in the laboratory may differ from behavior in the natural environment.
Survey	Provides large amount of information on large numbers of people.	If sample is nonrepresentative or biased, it may be impossible to generalize from the results. Responses may be inaccurate or untrue.
Test	Yields information on personality traits, emotional states, aptitudes, abilities.	Difficult to construct tests that are valid and reliable.
Correlational study	Shows whether two or more variables are related. Allows general predictions.	Does not permit identification of cause and effect.
Experiment	Allows researcher to control the situation. Permits researcher to identify cause and effect.	Situation is artificial and results may not generalize well to the real world. Sometimes difficult to avoid experimenter effects.

can do the same for the control group. Now our 60 numbers have been boiled down to 2. For the sake of our example, let's assume that the nicotine group had an average of 10 collisions, while the control group's average was only 7.

It is easy to be misled by the term *average*. It does *not* necessarily mean "typical." It could be that no one in our nicotine group actually had 10 collisions. Remember, the mean merely summarizes a mass of data. Perhaps half the people in the nicotine group were motoring maniacs and had 15 collisions, while the others were more cautious and had only 5. Perhaps almost all the subjects had 9, 10, or 11 collisions. Perhaps accidents were evenly distributed between zero and 15. The mean does not tell you about the variation in subjects' responses; there are other statistics for that. One, the **range,** gives the difference between the lowest and highest scores in a distribution of scores. If the lowest number of collisions in the nicotine group was 5 and the highest was 15, the range would be 10. Another, the **variance,** is more informative. Basically, the variance is a number that tells you how clustered or spread out the individual scores are around the mean (see Figure 2.5). Knowing about variance can help you understand certain passionate debates in psychology. The concept of variance has been important, for example, in arguments over the meaning of group differences in IQ (see Chapter 11). But when research is reported in the mass media, the public usually hears only about the mean.

There are other kinds of descriptive statistics as well, including the coefficient of correlation, which we covered earlier. Descriptive statistics are discussed in greater detail in the Appendix.

■ **range**
A measure of the spread of scores, calculated by subtracting the lowest score from the highest score.
■ **variance**
A measure of the dispersion of scores around the mean.

Averages can be misleading, if you don't know how much events deviated from the statistical mean and how they were distributed.

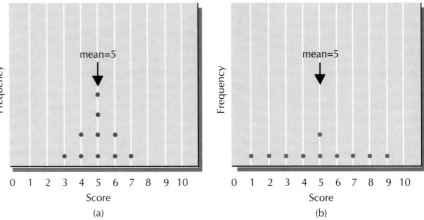

FIGURE 2.5

Same mean, different variances
In both distributions of scores the mean is 5, but in (a) the scores are clustered around the mean, whereas in (b) they are widely dispersed. (From Wright, 1976.)

Inferential Statistics: Asking "So What?"

At this point in our nicotine study, we have one group with an average of 10 collisions and another with an average of 7. Should we break out the champagne? Try to get on TV? Call our mothers?

Better hold off. Descriptive statistics do not tell us whether the outcome is anything to write home about. Perhaps if one group had an average of 15 and the other an average of 1 we could get excited. But rarely does a psychological study produce what one of our colleagues calls an "interocular" effect—one that hits you between the eyes. In most cases there is some possibility that the difference between the two groups was due simply to chance. Perhaps the people in the nicotine group just happened to be a little more accident-prone during the study, and their behavior had nothing to do with smoking. It would be surprising if the two groups had *exactly* the same number of collisions.

To find out how significant the data are, the psychologist uses **inferential statistics.** They permit a researcher to draw *inferences* (conclusions based on evidence) about the findings. There are many inferential statistics to choose from, depending on the kind of study and what the researcher wants to know. Like descriptive statistics, inferential statistics involve the application of mathematical formulas to the data (see the Appendix).

Inferential statistics do not merely describe or summarize the data. *They tell the researcher how likely it is that the result of the study occurred by chance.* More precisely, they reveal the probability of obtaining an effect as large as (or larger than) the one observed, if manipulating the independent variable actually has no reliable effect on the behavior in question. It is impossible to rule out chance entirely. However, if the likelihood of the result occurring by chance is extremely low, we say the result is **statistically significant.** This means that the probability that the difference is "real" is overwhelming—not certain, mind you, but overwhelming. By convention, psychologists consider a result significant if it would be expected by chance 5 or fewer times in 100 repetitions of the study. (Another way of saying this is that the result is significant at the .05, or "point oh five," level.)

■ **inferential statistics**
Statistical tests that allow researchers to assess how likely it is that their results occurred merely by chance.
■ **statistically significant**
Term used to refer to a result that is extremely unlikely to have occurred by chance.

Inferential statistics are necessary because a result that seems unlikely may not be so unlikely after all. For example, how probable do you think it is that in a room of 25 people, at least 2 will have the same birthday? Most people think it is very unlikely, but in fact the odds are better than even. Even if there are only 10 people in the room, the chances are 1 in 9. Among U.S. presidents, two had the same birthday (Warren Harding and James Polk) and three died on the fourth of July (John Adams, the second president; Thomas Jefferson, the third; and James Monroe, the fifth). Surprising? No. Such "coincidences" are not statistically striking at all.

With inferential statistics, we can find out if an experimental result would be truly a rare event if only chance were operating. In our nicotine study (as summarized in Figure 2.4), they would tell us how likely it is that the difference between the nicotine group and the placebo group occurred by chance. If the difference could be expected to occur by chance in 6 out of 100 studies, we would have to say that the results failed to support the hypothesis. That is, we would be forced to conclude that the difference we obtained might well have occurred merely by chance. You can see that psychologists refuse to be impressed by just any old result.

Statistically significant results allow psychologists to make predictions about human behavior. It is important to understand, however, that these predictions are generalizations about behavior and are usually stated as probabilities ("On average, we can expect 60 percent of all students to . . ."). They do not usually tell us with certainty what a particular *individual* will do in a situation. Probabilistic results are typical of all the sciences. Medical research, for example, can tell us that the odds are high that someone who smokes will get lung cancer, but because many different variables interact to produce any particular case of cancer, research can't tell us for sure whether Aunt Bessie, a two-pack-a-day smoker, will come down with the disease.

By the way, a nicotine study similar to our hypothetical example, but with somewhat different and more complicated procedures, has actually been done (Spilich, June, & Renner, 1992). Smokers who lit up before driving got a little farther on the simulated road, but they also had significantly more rear-end collisions on average (10.7) than temporarily abstaining smokers (5.2) or nonsmokers (3.1). After hearing of this research, the head of Federal Express banned smoking on the job among all of the company's 12,000 drivers (George J. Spilich, personal communication).

QUICK QUIZ

Check your understanding of the descriptive/inferential distinction by placing a check in the appropriate column for each phrase:

	Descriptive statistics	Inferential statistics
1. Summarize the data	_____	_____
2. Give likelihood of data occurring by chance	_____	_____
3. Include the mean	_____	_____
4. Give measure of statistical significance	_____	_____
5. Tell you whether to call your mother	_____	_____

ANSWERS:

1. descriptive 2. inferential 3. descriptive 4. inferential 5. inferential

From the Laboratory to the Real World: Interpreting the Findings

The last step in any study is to figure out what the findings mean. Trying to understand behavior from uninterpreted findings is like trying to become fluent in Swahili by reading a Swahili-English dictionary. Just as you need the grammar of Swahili to tell you how the words fit together, the psychologist needs hypotheses and theories to explain how the facts that emerge from research fit together.

Sometimes it is hard to choose between competing explanations. Does nicotine disrupt driving by impairing coordination? By increasing a driver's vulnerability to distraction? By interfering with the processing of information? By clouding judgment or distorting the perception of danger? In general, the best explanation is the one that accounts for the greatest number of findings and makes the most accurate predictions about new findings.

Often the explanation for a finding will need to take into account many different factors because in psychology most effects have more than one cause. We saw earlier, for example, that being abused as a child does not inevitably turn a person into an abusive parent. Various influences, including life stresses, exposure to violence on television, and the nature of the abuse, interact in complicated ways to determine the kind of parent a person eventually becomes (Widom, 1989). Fortunately, with special statistical procedures, psychologists can often analyze how much each factor contributes to a result and how various factors interact.

In interpreting any particular study, we must be careful not to go too far beyond the facts or generalize inappropriately. We saw earlier that in surveys the sample must be representative of the population that the researcher is interested in. The same holds for other types of studies, including experiments. Historically, many studies in psychology have been done only with young, white, middle-class, male college students as subjects (Sherif, 1979). Findings from such studies may not apply to people of color, older people, low-income people, females, or nonstudents. Even when findings do generalize to many groups, there may be several explanations that fit the facts equally well, which means that more research will be needed to determine the best explanation. Rarely does one study prove anything. That is why you should be suspicious of headlines that announce a "Major Scientific Breakthrough!!!" Scientific progress usually occurs gradually, not in one fell swoop.

Sometimes the best interpretation of a finding does not emerge until a hypothesis has been tested in different ways. Although the methods we have de-

Laboratory and field studies are both important in psychological research. An industrial/organizational psychologist might be interested in doing a field study to investigate the management style of the man who is pointing. Instead of staying in an office, this man "manages by wandering around," moving from one production group to another during the day. How might this technique affect employee morale and productivity?

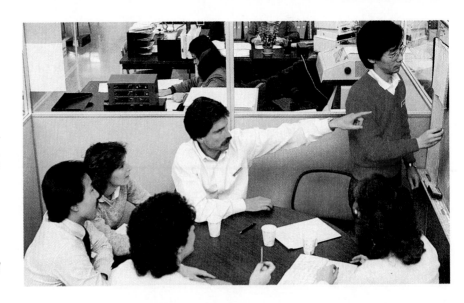

scribed tend to be appropriate for different questions (see Table 2.4), there is growing agreement that different methods can also complement each other. That is, one method can be used to confirm, disconfirm, or extend the results obtained with another. If the findings of studies using various methods converge, there is greater reason to be confident about them. On the other hand, if they conflict, researchers will know they must modify their hypotheses or do more research.

As an example, consider research on aging. When psychologists compare the mental test scores of young and old people, they usually find that younger people outscore older ones. This type of research, in which groups are compared at a given time, is called **cross-sectional.** Other researchers, however, have used **longitudinal studies** to investigate mental abilities across the life span. In a longitudinal study, people are followed over a period of time and reassessed at periodic intervals. In contrast to cross-sectional studies, longitudinal studies find that as people age they often continue to perform as well as they ever did on many types of mental tests. A general decline in ability does not usually occur until the seventh or eighth decade of life (Baltes, Dittman-Kohli, & Dixon, 1984). Why do results from the two types of studies conflict? Apparently, cross-sectional studies measure generational differences; younger generations tend to outperform older ones, perhaps because they are better educated or more familiar with the types of items used on the tests. Without longitudinal studies, we might falsely conclude that mental ability inevitably declines with age.

Sometimes psychologists agree on the reliability and meaning of a finding, but not on its ultimate significance for theory or practice. Statistical significance

■ **cross-sectional study**
A study in which groups of subjects of different ages are compared at a given time.
■ **longitudinal study**
A study in which subjects are followed and periodically reassessed over a period of time.

TABLE 2.4

Psychological Research Methods Contrasted

Psychologists may use different methods to answer different questions about a topic. To illustrate, this table shows some ways in which the methods described in this chapter can be used to study different questions about aggression. The methods listed are not necessarily mutually exclusive. That is, sometimes two or more methods can be used to investigate the same question. As discussed in the text, findings based on one method may extend, support, or disconfirm findings based on another.

Method	Purpose	Example
Case study	To understand the development of aggressive behavior in a particular individual; to formulate research hypotheses about the origins of aggressiveness.	Developmental history of a serial killer.
Naturalistic observation	To describe the nature of aggressive acts in early childhood.	Observation, tally, and description of hitting, kicking, etc. during free-play periods in a preschool.
Laboratory observation	To find out if aggressiveness in pairs of same-sex and opposite-sex children differs in frequency or intensity.	Observation through a one-way window of same-sex and opposite-sex pairs of preschoolers. Pairs must negotiate who gets to play with an attractive toy that has been promised to each child.
Survey	To find out how common domestic violence is in the United States.	Questionnaire asking anonymous respondents (in a sample representative of the U.S. population) about the occurrence of slapping, hitting, etc. in their homes.
Tests	To compare the personality traits of aggressive and nonaggressive persons.	Administration of personality tests to violent and nonviolent prisoners.
Correlational study	To examine the relationship between aggressiveness and television viewing.	Administration to college students of a paper-and-pencil test of aggressiveness and a questionnaire on number of hours spent watching TV weekly; computation of correlation coefficient.
Experiment	To find out whether high air temperatures elicit aggressive behavior.	Arrangement for individuals to "shock" a "learner" (actually a confederate of the experimenter) while seated in a room heated to either 72°F or 85°F.

A study reports that women are "significantly" better than men at tongue twisters. On closer examination, you find that women are "better" by an average of three seconds. Does this finding make any difference in real life?

alone does not provide the answer, because *statistical significance does not always imply real-world importance.* A result may be statistically significant at the "point oh-five level," but at the same time be small and of little consequence in everyday life. Psychologists are now using an important new technique called *meta-analysis* to find out when this is so. Meta-analysis statistically combines the results of many studies, instead of assessing each study's results separately. It tells the researcher how much of the variation in scores across all the studies examined can be explained by a particular variable. Meta-analysis has turned up some interesting surprises. For example, "well-established" sex differences in verbal ability, spatial-visual ability, aggressiveness, and suggestibility, although usually reliable, turn out to be quite small (see Chapter 3). In most cases, gender accounts for only 1 to 5 percent of the variance in scores, and verbal differences have declined over the years almost to the vanishing point (Eagly & Carli, 1981; Feingold, 1988; Hyde, 1981, 1984b; Hyde, Fennema, & Lamon, 1990; Hyde & Linn, 1988). In plain English, this means that a person's gender is a poor clue to the person's performance in these four areas (see Figure 2.6).

■ KEEPING THE ENTERPRISE ETHICAL

Scientists sometimes have an image problem. Their insistence that nothing be taken for granted and their tendency to turn answers into questions is sometimes seen as threatening. Fear of science has found expression in "mad scientist" books, such as Mary Shelley's *Frankenstein*, and science-gone-amok films, such as *Blade Runner, Terminator*, and (in a lighter vein) *Honey, I Shrunk the Kids.* Psychologists, who generally view themselves as nice people, tend to dismiss such fears as irrational. But it is true that the control exercised by scientists in their laboratories can be abused. The world learned that lesson at the Nuremberg trials in 1945, when 20 Nazi doctors were convicted of conducting sadistic experiments on concentration camp inmates, all in the name of science.

The American Psychological Association (APA) recognizes the need for ethical guidelines and has a formal code that all members must follow, both in clinical practice and in psychological research. The APA code calls on psychological scientists to respect the dignity and welfare of their subjects. It states that human subjects must voluntarily consent to participate in a study and must know enough about it to make an intelligent decision, a doctrine known as *informed*

FIGURE 2.6

Is this a meaningful difference? *Group differences that are statistically significant are not always useful for predicting behavior. For example, seventh-grade boys do better on the average than seventh-grade girls on the mathematics section of the Scholastic Aptitude Test. But as this graph shows, the difference, although reliable, is tiny, and male and female scores greatly overlap. Thus, it is impossible to predict with any confidence whether a particular boy will outperform a particular girl. (From Sapolsky, 1987, based on data from Benbow & Stanley, 1983.)*

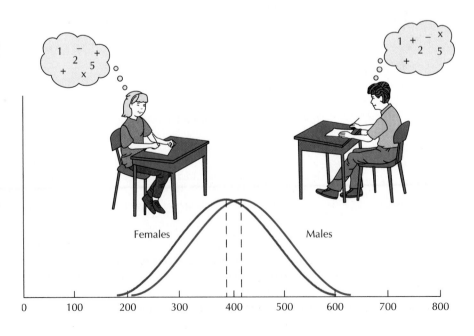

consent. Once a study begins, a subject must be free to withdraw from it at any time. Federal regulations also govern scientific research, and in most colleges and universities, an ethics committee must approve all proposed studies. Most issues that arise are not very controversial, but two issues have provoked continuing debate: the use of animals and the practice of deception.

Should Animals Be Used in Research?

Animals are used in about 7 or 8 percent of psychological studies. Ninety-five percent of the animals are rodents (American Psychological Association, 1984). Psychologists are especially partial to the Norwegian white rat, which is bred specifically for research purposes and is relatively cheap and healthy. But they also occasionally use pigeons, cats, monkeys, apes, and other species. Most studies—for example, observations of hamsters' mating habits—involve no harm or discomfort to the animals. Others, however, have involved physical or psychological harm, such as experiments in which infant monkeys are reared apart from their mothers and as a consequence develop abnormal patterns of behavior. Some studies require the animal's death, as, for example, when rats brought up in deprived or enriched environments are sacrificed so that their brains can be examined for specific effects.

Some psychologists who study animals are interested in comparing different species or hope to learn more about a particular species. Their work generally falls into the area of basic science, but often there are practical benefits. Understanding the behavior of a gull may help animal workers when an oil spill or an unusual weather condition threatens gulls' survival. Understanding how pandas conduct their courtship rituals can help zoos breed pandas in captivity and save them from extinction. Using behavioral principles, farmers have been able to reduce crop destruction by birds and deer without resorting to their traditional method—shooting the animals.

Other psychologists who use animals are primarily interested in principles that apply to both animals and people. Many animals have biological systems or behavioral patterns similar to those of human beings. Using animals often gives the researcher more control over variables than would otherwise be possible. In some cases, practical or ethical considerations prevent the use of human beings as subjects. And studying animals can clarify important theoretical issues. For example, we might not want to attribute the greater life expectancy of women solely to "life style" factors and health practices if we find that a male-female difference exists in other mammals as well.

Animal studies have led to many improvements in human health and well-being. Findings from these studies have helped psychologists and other researchers develop methods for treating enuresis (bed-wetting) and fecal incontinence (loss of bowel control); teach retarded children to communicate; devise behavioral therapies for treating emotional problems and substance abuse; combat life-threatening malnutrition caused by chronic vomiting in infants; rehabilitate patients with neurological disorders and sensory impairment; teach people to control stress-related symptoms such as high blood pressure and headaches; treat suicidal depression; develop better ways to reduce chronic pain; train animal companions for the disabled; and understand the mechanisms underlying memory loss and senility—to name only a few benefits (Greenough, 1991; N. Miller, 1985). Many such breakthroughs have been the unforeseen result of basic laboratory studies using animals (Feeney, 1987).

Not all animal studies have led to benefits for human beings, however, and in recent years, animal research has provoked an emotional controversy. Much of the criticism has centered on the medical and commercial use of animals, but psychologists have also come under fire. A few years ago, a Maryland psychologist studying the nervous system was convicted of cruelty to animals after he cut the nerve fibers controlling limb sensation in 17 monkeys. The purpose of

Animals are often used to study the biological bases of emotion and motivation. Here, electrical stimulation of certain brain areas, delivered by remote control, has produced rage in two previously peaceful monkeys.

his research was to find ways to restore the use of crippled limbs in stroke victims. The charges alleged abusive treatment of the animals. The psychologist's conviction was eventually reversed on appeal, but by then the government had withdrawn its funding of the project.

Unfortunately, debates over animal research have often degenerated into angry name-calling, or worse. One animal rights group calls psychological research with animals "an American holocaust." Groups of animal rights activists have vandalized laboratories and threatened and harassed researchers and their families. On the other side, some scientists have overlooked philosophical differences in the animal rights movement and have branded all animal rights and animal welfare activists as terrorists. On both sides, people have staked out extreme positions. In a recent survey, fully 85 percent of committed animal rights activists (versus only 17 percent of a comparison group) endorsed the statement, "If it were up to me, I would eliminate all research using animals" (Plous, 1991). For their part, some psychologists have refused to acknowledge that confinement in laboratories can be psychologically and physically harmful for certain kinds of animals.

One positive result of the debate, however, is that many researchers are now looking for ways to balance the need for animal research with an increased concern for animal welfare. The APA ethical code has always contained provisions covering the humane treatment of animals, and in 1985, more comprehensive guidelines were issued by a special APA committee. Recent years have also seen stricter federal animal welfare regulations governing the housing and care of research animals. By federal law, every experiment involving vertebrates must now be reviewed by a committee comprised of representatives from the research institution and the community.

Most psychological organizations, however, oppose proposals to ban or greatly reduce animal research. In psychological research using animals, alternative methods suggested by animal welfare groups, such as computer simulations, are not always feasible. Brain research would virtually halt if animals could not be used. The APA and other organizations feel that protective legislation for animals is desirable but must not jeopardize productive research that increases scientific understanding and improves human welfare.

Should Psychologists Lie to Their Subjects?

Another emotional issue has to do with human subjects. Unlike a laboratory rat, human beings may be able to figure out what a study is all about. In many cases, this knowledge can affect their behavior and wreck the research. If you realize that a study is about altruism, the willingness to help others, you may try to outdo Mother Teresa as a Good Samaritan. If you guess that the study is about verbal ability, you may become as talkative as a sportscaster at the Super Bowl.

The obvious way around this problem is to disguise the purpose of the study or, to put it more bluntly, lie. Deception is common in psychological research, especially in social psychology. Its practice has borne bountiful fruit, as we will see again and again in later chapters. But sometimes it has also caused anxiety or embarrassment for the subjects.

One study that sparked a bonfire of criticism was reported by Stanley Milgram in 1963. Milgram wanted to know how many people would obey an authority figure when ordered to violate their own ethical standards. But that is not what the subjects were told. Instead, they were led to believe that the study concerned the effect of punishment on memory. Each subject was assigned the role of "teacher" in a learning situation, with another person (who was actually in league with the experimenter) acting as the "learner." Whenever the learner made an error, the teacher was supposed to administer punishment by pulling a series of levers on a "shock generator machine." The levers had labels ranging from "Slight Shock" to "Danger: Severe Shock," with two levers at the very end simply marked "XXX." Actually, the machine was fake and the "shock" was never delivered, but the subjects didn't know that.

Milgram's experiment is one of the best-known studies in psychology, and we will discuss it further in Chapter 18. Right now, we will simply tell you that a whopping 65 percent of the subjects went all the way, eventually pulling the last lever (XXX). But their obedience cost them great emotional pain. Many, said Milgram, were observed to "sweat, tremble, stutter, bite their lips, groan, and dig their fingernails into their flesh," and these "were characteristic rather than exceptional responses to the experiment."

After the study was over, subjects were interviewed and were told about its true purpose. Procedures were taken "to assure that the subject would leave the laboratory in a state of well-being." The subject met the supposed victim, and "an effort was made to reduce any tensions that arose as a result of the experiment." Not everyone was convinced, however, that such procedures were effective. A rising tide of concern about the morality of deception and its possibly harmful effects on subjects eventually led to a tightening of controls. Today, although deception is still widely used, it is done more cautiously. According to the APA's ethical guidelines, before using deception a researcher must determine whether it is justified by the study's potential scientific, educational, or applied value and must explore possible alternatives that do not require deception. The investigator must protect subjects from physical and mental discomfort or harm, and if any risk exists, must tell them. Many studies conducted a decade or two ago probably could not be done in the 1990s. Milgram's study, which won the American Association for the Advancement of Science award for social-psychological research in 1964, is one of them.

Psychologists who defend deception say that in practice the risks to subjects are minor. The few follow-up surveys that have been done generally support this claim. Most people, looking back on their participation in deceptive research, say they think the stress was justified by the knowledge gained. Even those in Milgram's study felt that way. Eighty-four percent of them said later they were glad they had participated, and only 1.3 percent expressed regret; the rest were neutral (Milgram, 1974). Defenders of deception also point out that many kinds of information cannot be obtained without it (Baron, 1981).

Critics of deception, however, feel that procedures with the potential for causing emotional harm are still too widespread. They cite reports of subjects who were disillusioned or felt ashamed after they learned some unpleasant truths about themselves in a psychological study. They claim that "debriefing"—telling the subject about the study's true purpose after it is all over—does not always help. These critics, including some psychologists, argue that deception deprives subjects of free choice and treats them as mere pawns in the research game. They also worry that the use of deception may undermine psychology's credibility with the public and contribute to lowered standards of integrity (Baumrind, 1985; R. Goldstein, 1981).

▪ SCIENCE UNDER SCRUTINY

The continuing debates over animal research and deception show that research methods in psychology can arouse as much controversy as research findings do. Controversy exists not only about ethics but also about what particular methods can and cannot reveal. Methods are the very heart of science, so it is not surprising that psychologists spend considerable time discussing and debating their procedures for collecting, evaluating, and presenting data.

In recent years, such debates have gone far beyond such matters as when to use questionnaires versus interviews, or how to best analyze the data. Heated exchanges are now raging in all the sciences and humanities about the very meaning of knowledge itself. For the past three centuries, the answer seemed clear enough. Knowledge was the discovery of some reality existing "out there," and the way to find it was to be objective, value-free, and detached (in other words, as unlike a normal human being as possible). The purpose of a theory was to map or reflect this reality. A clear line was assumed to exist between the knower, on one side, and the phenomenon under study, on the other—and the knower wasn't supposed to cross the line.

Today, many scholars are questioning these fundamental assumptions. They argue that detached objectivity, which has long been considered the cornerstone of Western science, is only a myth. In this view, which is sometimes referred to as *postmodernism*, the observer's values, categories, and perceptions inevitably affect how events are studied, how they are explained, and even how they take place. Knowledge isn't so much discovered as it is *created* (Gergen, 1985; Guba, 1990; Hare-Mustin & Maracek, 1990; Rosaldo, 1989; Watzlawick, 1984). Our understanding of things does not merely mirror what's "out there"; it organizes and orders it. Linguist George Lakoff (1987) gives an example from one of the natural sciences. In 1735, the Swedish botanist Carl Linnaeus introduced a way of classifying plants that has been used as the objective standard ever since. Linnaeus's system relied largely on the shape of the fruit. Why didn't Linnaeus use the shape of the leaves, or the color of the fruit, or some other attribute that might make "common sense"? According to his son, the reason was convenience rather than the dictates of some reality "out there": fruit shape was "clearly marked, readily appreciated, [and] easily described in words."

Postmodern views of science have been influenced by two of the psychological perspectives we discussed in Chapter 1. Cognitive psychologists have shown that people's emotions and behavior depend on how they interpret the world, rather than on some "real" state of affairs. And sociocultural psychologists have shown that social and cultural roles profoundly influence how people view the world and the conclusions they draw about reality. Scientists, being people, are no exception. Because they do their work at a particular time and in a particular culture, they bring with them shared assumptions and world views that influence what counts as a fact and what parts of reality get noticed.

For example, when Western sex roles went unquestioned, and when the vast majority of Western scientists were men, primatologists making field observations tended to focus on large, intimidating male animals, who spent their time displaying dominance, pursuing sex partners, and bossing the apparently prim and passive females around. The primatologists were not purposely ignoring the females; male behavior was simply of more interest to them, and, because it seemed to conform to their own notions of gender, more conspicuous—so that is what they noticed. But when women began to enter the field, they noticed some other things (Hrdy, 1981; Lancaster, 1975; Small, 1984). For example, they saw that in several monkey species, a mother's rank largely determines her offspring's rank, so female dominance is important in the life of the troop. Among vervet monkeys, females achieve strength through unity, banding together and ganging up on males who try to take too much food or frighten an infant. And in many species, as we will see in Chapter 10, the males are not promiscuous playboys nor are the females coy maidens. In some species, both sexes are monogamous; in others, females will mate with as many males as they can fit into their social calendar.

Some people react to postmodern views with alarm, thinking that these criticisms mean "anything goes" and therefore spell the end of science. After all, in science, as we have emphasized throughout this chapter, anything does *not* go. However, new ways of looking at knowledge also have the potential for expanding and enriching our understanding of behavior. The observations by female primatologists didn't mean that previous observations were wrong, only that they were incomplete and gave a misleading impression. When old assumptions were questioned, a new and fuller picture became possible.

Postmodern debates now reverberating through the halls of science are especially challenging for psychologists. Their goal has always been to understand the behavior and mental processes of human beings. Now they are being challenged to expand their horizons by analyzing their own behavior as psychologists and by examining how their values, gender, place in society, and cultural categories affect their conclusions. Still, some things will remain the same: an insistence on rigor and standards of evidence, a reliance on verifiable results, and an emphasis on critical thinking. That is why we hope that as you read the following chapters, you will resist the temptation to skip descriptions of how studies were done. If the assumptions and methods of a study are faulty, so are the results and the conclusions based on them. Ultimately, what we know about human behavior is inseparable from how we know it.

TAKING PSYCHOLOGY WITH YOU

"Intuitive Statistics": Avoiding the Pitfalls

Everyone uses intuition and hunches to generate hypotheses about human behavior. Scientists are required to confirm their hypotheses through careful research and rigorous statistical analysis. In daily life, though, people usually test their ideas through casual observation and the use of "intuitive statistics," notions about probabilities that may or may not be correct. These unscientific methods often work well but can sometimes lead to errors. You can take Chapter 2 with you by watching out for common statistical mistakes in your own thinking.

For example, you have learned how misleading it can be to "accentuate the positive and eliminate the negative" by ignoring nonoccurrences of a phenomenon (see p. 41). Sherlock Holmes, the legendary detective, was aware of the value of nonoccurrences. In one adventure he invited a police inspector to consider "the curious incident of the dog in the nighttime." The inspector protested that the dog did nothing in the nighttime. Holmes replied that *that* was the curious incident: The dog's silence proved that the intruder in the mystery was someone well known to the dog (Ross, 1977). Like Sherlock Holmes, we all need to be aware of what nonoccurrences can tell us.

Other "intuitive statistics" can also trap us in false conclusions. For example, how would you answer the following questions?

1. If black has come up three times in a row on the roulette wheel, would you be inclined to bet next on red or on black?
2. Where are you more worried about safety, in a car or plane?

3. If your psychology instructor has a friend who is a professor and that person is rather shy, is slight of stature, and likes to write poetry, is the friend's field more likely to be Chinese studies or psychology?

When presented with the first question, many people say that it is red's "turn" to win. Yet black and red are equally likely to win on the fourth play, just as they were on the first three (assuming that the wheel is fair). How could the probabilities change from one play to the other? A roulette wheel has no memory! The same is true for tossing coins. If you get three heads, the chance of a head on the fourth toss is still .50. The probability of a head or tail does not change from toss to toss, and it is perfectly normal to get a run of either heads or tails, though over the long run (if the coin is fair), there will be a balance of heads and tails. But many people fail to realize this. They succumb to the Gambler's Fallacy, the belief that a "run" of one event alters the chances of that event occurring again. The Gambler's Fallacy is common outside the casino as well. Many people think that parents with three girls are "due" for a boy, but the odds are the same as they always were (50 percent for most people; more or less than 50 percent when the man happens to produce a larger-than-average supply of male-producing or female-producing sperm).

What about the second question? You may already know that airplanes are far safer than cars, even controlling for number of passenger miles traveled. Yet most of us still feel safer in cars, because we overestimate the probability of an event when examples are readily available (Tversky & Kahneman, 1973). We can all recall specific airplane disasters; they make headlines because so many people die at once. A single vivid plane crash lingers longer in memory than the many auto accidents regularly reported in the local newspaper. Thus airplane fatalities *seem* more likely. (On the other hand, we don't want to simplify: driving may not be riskier for everyone. Your age, driving habits, and seat belt use, and the type of car you drive, all affect your risk of dying in a traffic accident.)

Finally, on the third question, many people predict that the instructor's friend is in Chinese stud-ies (Ross, 1977). But this is unlikely, since there are very few professors of Chinese studies in the United States and there are thousands of professors of psychology. Also, a psychology instructor is likely to have more friends in psychology than in Chinese studies. People go astray on this question because they are influenced by their stereotypes about people and ignore statistical probabilities.

We have led you through this little exercise to show you how intuitions can be clouded by biases and fallacies despite people's best efforts to be rational. The scientific approach is the psychologist's way of avoiding such pitfalls.

SUMMARY

1. Research methods are the tools of the research psychologist's trade. A knowledge of methodology can also benefit nonpsychologists, by alerting them to errors in thinking and making them astute consumers of psychological findings.

2. The ideal scientist is skeptical of claims that rest solely on faith or authority; relies on empirical evidence; states hypotheses and predictions precisely; is open about his or her work; and is willing to comply with the principle of falsifiability and make "risky predictions." The public nature of science gives it a built-in system of checks and balances.

3. *Descriptive methods* are more useful for describing and predicting behavior than for explaining its causes. Some descriptive methods are used by both clinicians and researchers.

4. *Case studies* are detailed descriptions of particular individuals. Unusual cases sometimes shed light on general questions about behavior that would be difficult to study in other ways. But case studies are typically sources rather than tests of hypotheses because the person under study may not be representative of people in general.

5. In *observational studies*, the researcher carefully and systematically observes and records behavior in an objective fashion, without interfering in any way with the behavior. *Naturalistic observation* is used to obtain descriptions of how subjects behave in their natural environment. *Laboratory observation* allows more controlled observation and the use of special equipment. Behavior in the laboratory may differ in certain ways from behavior in natural contexts.

6. *Surveys* are questionnaires or interviews that ask people directly about their experiences, attitudes, and opinions. Precautions must be taken to obtain a *sample* that is *representative* of the *population* in question.

7. *Psychological tests* measure personality traits, emotional states, aptitudes, interests, abilities, and values. A good test must be valid (measure what it sets out to measure) and reliable (yield consistent results).

8. In descriptive research, studies that look for a relationship between two or more phenomena are known as *correlational*. A *correlation* is a measure of the strength of the relationship between variables. Correlations may be positive or negative. A correlation does *not* necessarily show causation.

9. *Experiments* allow the researcher to control the situation, manipulate an *independent variable*, and assess the effects of the manipulation on a *dependent*

variable. Random assignment is usually used to place people in experimental and control groups. In some studies, control subjects receive *placebos*. Precautions, such as *single-blind* and *double-blind* procedures, must be taken to prevent the expectations of the subjects or the experimenter from affecting the results. Like laboratory observations, experiments create a special kind of social situation that may call forth behavior not typical in other environments. However, experiments have been the method of choice for drawing conclusions about cause and effect.

10. Psychologists use *descriptive statistics*, such as the *mean, range,* and *variance*, to summarize their data. They use *inferential statistics* to find out how likely it is that the results of a study occurred merely by chance. The results are *statistically significant* if this likelihood is very low.

11. In interpreting findings, it can be hard to choose between competing explanations. Often explanations will need to take into account many different factors. Care must be taken to avoid going beyond the facts, overgeneralizing, or exaggerating the real-world significance of the findings. It is often useful to use one method to confirm, disconfirm, or extend results obtained by another. For example, the results of *cross-sectional* and *longitudinal* studies can be compared.

12. The fact that psychological research methods can affect subjects in unintended ways raises certain ethical problems. Two particularly controversial issues are the use of animals in research and the use of deception in studies of human subjects.

13. Many fundamental assumptions about scientific research are currently under scrutiny. *Postmodernism* rejects the notion that knowledge is the discovery of objective truth. Postmodern critics argue that cultural values, assumptions, and categories affect what counts as a fact and how findings are interpreted. Although some scholars view postmodern views with alarm, these new views may expand and enrich our understanding of human behavior.

KEY TERMS

PART TWO

BIOLOGICAL BASES OF BEHAVIOR

3

Neurons, Hormones, and the Brain

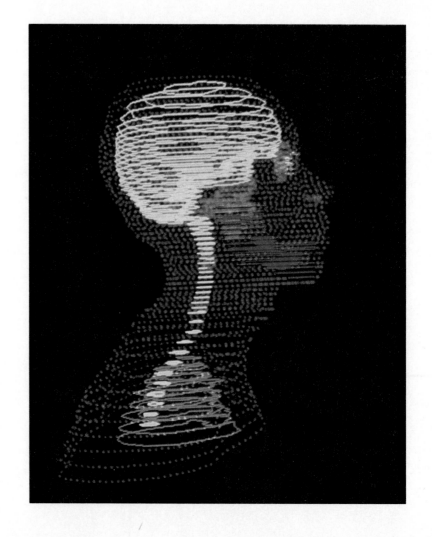

It's amazing to think that the body feeds the brain sugar and amino acids, and what comes out is poetry and pirouettes.

NEUROLOGIST ROBERT COLLINS

D r. P., a cultured and charming musician of great repute, had a problem. Though his vision was sharp, he no longer recognized people or objects. He would pat the heads of water hydrants and parking meters, thinking them to be children, or chat with pieces of furniture and wonder why they wouldn't reply. He could spot a pin on the floor but did not know his own face in the mirror. Neurologist Oliver Sacks (1985), who examined Dr. P., recalls that while Dr. P. was looking around for his hat, "He reached out his hand and took hold of his wife's head, tried to lift it off, to put it on. He had apparently mistaken his wife for a hat!"

Dr. P.'s problem was damage in the part of the brain that controls visualization, due perhaps to a tumor or disease. This damage prevented Dr. P. from recognizing things, remembering the past visually, or even dreaming in visual images. As Sacks notes, the man who mistook his wife for a hat was stranded in "a world of lifeless abstractions."

Cases of brain damage like Dr. P.'s show us clearly that the brain is the bedrock of behavior. **Neuropsychologists,** along with other **neuroscientists** from a variety of disciplines, explore that bedrock, searching for the basis of behavior in the structure, biochemistry, and circuitry of the brain and the rest of the nervous system. Among their many interests are the biological foundations of consciousness (Chapter 4), perception (Chapter 5), memory (Chapter 7), emotion (Chapter 9), intelligence (Chapter 11), stress (Chapter 15), and mental disorders (Chapter 16). We will discuss their findings at many places in this book. In this chapter, we describe the structure of the brain and the rest of the nervous system as background for our later discussions.

At this moment your own brain, assisted by other parts of your nervous system, is taking in these words. Whether you are excited or bored, your brain is registering a reaction. As you continue reading, your brain will (we hope) store away much of the information in this chapter for future use. Later on, your brain may enable you to smell a flower, climb the stairs, greet a friend, solve a personal problem, or laugh at a joke. But the brain's most startling accomplishment is its knowledge that it is doing all these things. This self-awareness makes brain research different from the study of anything else in the universe. The scientist uses the cells, chemicals, and circuitry of his or her own brain to understand the cells, chemicals, and circuitry of the brain.

No wonder William Shakespeare once called the brain "the soul's frail dwelling house." Actually, though, the brain is more like one room in a house filled with many rooms and passageways. The "house" is the nervous system as a whole. Before we can understand the windows, walls, and furniture of that house, we need to examine the overall floor plan.

■ **neuropsychology**
The field of psychology concerned with the neural and biochemical bases of behavior and mental processes.
■ **neuroscience**
An interdisciplinary field of study concerned with the structure, function, development, and biochemistry of the nervous system.

■ THE NERVOUS SYSTEM: A BASIC BLUEPRINT

The purpose of a nervous system is to gather and process information, produce responses to stimuli, and coordinate the workings of different cells. Even the lowly jellyfish and the humble worm have the beginnings of such a system. In very simple organisms, which do little more than move, eat, and eliminate wastes, the "system" may be no more than one or two nerve cells. In human beings, who do such complex things as dance, cook, and take psychology courses, the nervous system contains billions of cells. This intricate network has two main parts: the **central nervous system (CNS)** and the **peripheral nervous system (PNS)** (see Figure 3.1).

The Central Nervous System

The central nervous system receives, processes, interprets, and stores incoming sensory information—information about tastes, sounds, smells, color, pressure on the skin, the state of internal organs, and so forth. It also sends out orders destined for muscles, glands, and body organs. The central nervous system has two components: the brain and the spinal cord. We will consider the brain in some detail a little later.

The **spinal cord** is actually an extension of the brain. It runs from the base of the brain down the center of the back, protected by a column of bones, and acts as a sort of bridge between the brain and the parts of the body below the neck. But the spinal cord is not merely a bridge. It also produces some behaviors on its own, without any help from the brain. These behaviors, called spinal **reflexes,** are automatic, requiring no conscious effort. For example, if you accidentally touch a hot iron, you will immediately pull your hand away, even before the brain has had a chance to register what has happened. Nerve impulses

■ **central nervous system**
The portion of the nervous system consisting of the brain and spinal cord.

■ **peripheral nervous system**
All portions of the nervous system outside the brain and spinal cord. Includes sensory and motor nerves.

■ **spinal cord**
A collection of neurons and supportive tissue running from the base of the brain down the center of the back, protected by a column of bones (the spinal column).

■ **reflex**
An automatic response to a stimulus.

FIGURE 3.1 _____

The central and peripheral nervous systems
The central nervous system, shown here in gold, consists of the brain and spinal cord. The peripheral nervous system, shown in purple, consists of 43 pairs of nerves that transmit information to and from the central nervous system. Twelve pairs of cranial nerves in the head enter the brain directly. Thirty-one pairs of spinal nerves enter the spinal cord at the spaces between the vertebrae (bones) of the spine.

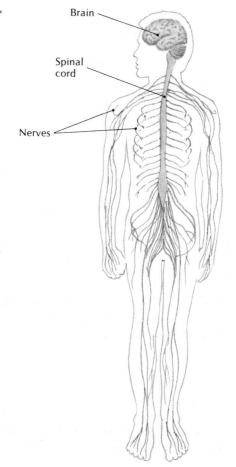

Brain

Spinal cord

Nerves

bring a message to the spinal cord (hot!), and the spinal cord immediately sends out a command via other nerve impulses, telling muscles in your arm to contract and pull your hand away from the iron. (Reflexes above the neck, such as sneezing and blinking, involve the lower part of the brain rather than the spinal cord.)

The neural circuitry underlying a reflex is called a *reflex arc*. In the case of some reflexes, such as the jerking of a knee when it is tapped, the reflex arc is extremely simple. In other cases, it is quite complex. For example, if you step on a piece of glass, you will reflexively withdraw your foot and at the same time shift your weight in subtle ways to maintain your balance. Such adjustments require the coordination of many neural messages entering and exiting from the spinal cord.

The neural circuits underlying many spinal reflexes are linked to other neural pathways that run up and down the spinal cord, to and from the brain. Because of these connections, reflexes, although not requiring conscious awareness, can sometimes be influenced by thoughts and emotions. An example is erection in men, a spinal reflex that can be inhibited by anxiety or distracting thoughts, and initiated by erotic thoughts. Further, some reflexes can be brought under conscious control. If you concentrate, you may be able to keep your knee from jerking when it is tapped. Similarly, most men can learn to voluntarily delay ejaculation, also a spinal reflex.

The Peripheral Nervous System

The peripheral (meaning "outlying") nervous system handles the central nervous system's input and output. It contains all portions of the nervous system outside the brain and spinal cord, right down to nerves in the tips of the fingers and toes. Science fiction writers love to write stories about disembodied but functioning brains. In reality, a brain that could not get information about the world by means of a body equipped with a peripheral nervous system would have nothing to think about. It would be as worthless as a radio without a receiver. In the peripheral nervous system, **sensory nerves** carry messages from special receptors in the skin, muscles, and other internal and external sense organs to the spinal cord, which sends them along to the brain. These nerves put us in touch with both the outside world and the activities of our own bodies. Motion-producing **motor nerves** carry orders from the central nervous system to muscles, glands, and internal organs. They enable us to move our bodies, and they cause glands to contract and secrete various substances, including chemical messengers called *hormones*.

The peripheral nervous system is further divided into two parts: the somatic (bodily) nervous system and the autonomic (self-governing) nervous system. The **somatic nervous system,** sometimes called the *skeletal nervous system,* controls the skeletal muscles of the body and permits voluntary action. When you turn off a light or write your name, your somatic system is active. The **autonomic nervous system** regulates blood vessels, glands, and internal (visceral) organs like the bladder, stomach, and heart. When you happen upon the secret object of your desire and your heart starts to pound, your hands get sweaty, and your cheeks feel hot, you can blame your autonomic nervous system.

The autonomic nervous system works more or less automatically, without a person's conscious control. We say "more or less" because some people may be able to heighten or suppress certain autonomic responses intentionally. In India, some yogis reportedly can slow their heartbeat and metabolism (energy consumption) so dramatically that they can survive in a sealed booth long after most of us would have suffocated to death. In the 1960s and 1970s, Neal Miller (1978) and his colleagues showed that ordinary people, too, can control internal, or visceral, responses, using a technique called **biofeedback.** Biofeedback involves the use of monitoring devices to track the bodily process in question

■ **sensory nerves**
Nerves in the peripheral nervous system that carry sensory messages toward the central nervous system.

■ **motor nerves**
Nerves in the peripheral nervous system that carry messages from the central nervous system to muscles, glands, and internal organs.

■ **somatic nervous system**
The subdivision of the peripheral nervous system that controls skeletal muscles. Also called skeletal nervous system.

■ **autonomic nervous system**
The subdivision of the peripheral nervous system that regulates the internal organs and glands.

■ **biofeedback**
A technique for controlling bodily functions by attending to an instrument that monitors the function and signals changes in it.

Some patients with spinal cord injuries lose consciousness when they sit upright because their blood pressure plunges. Here, Neal Miller, a pioneer in biofeedback research, trains a patient to control her blood pressure at will so that she can lead a fuller life.

and signal a person whenever he or she makes the desired response. Typically a light goes on or a tone sounds each time the response occurs. Instructions may include specific methods for producing the response, or the person may simply be told to try to increase the frequency of the signal.

There is little question that biofeedback can help people control *voluntary* responses. For example, it has helped teenagers with scoliosis (curvature of the spine) alter their posture and overcome the disorder (Dworkin & Dworkin, 1988). Some people can also learn to control autonomic responses, such as blood pressure, blood flow, heart rate, and skin temperature, and some clinicians are using biofeedback training to treat high blood pressure, asthma, and migraine headaches (although there is great controversy about success rates). It is not clear, however, whether the control that occurs over autonomic responses is direct or indirect. When people learn to raise or lower their heart rate, for example, are they doing so directly, or are they producing the response indirectly by using skeletal muscles in the chest to speed up or slow down their breathing, which in turn affects their heart rate? In early experiments on this issue, Miller and his colleagues taught rats to alter their heart rates by rewarding the animals whenever their rates changed in the desired direction (N. Miller, 1969). To prevent the rats from using chest or other skeletal muscles, the researchers paralyzed them with the drug curare. But research since then has failed to replicate these results (Dworkin & Miller, 1986). Today, we still do not have an explanation for the autonomic effects of biofeedback.

One other nervous system division is important for you to know about. The autonomic nervous system is itself divided into two parts: the **sympathetic nervous system** and the **parasympathetic nervous system.** These two parts work together—but in opposing ways—to adjust the body to changing circumstances (see Figure 3.2). To simplify a bit, the sympathetic system acts like the accel-

Sympathetic division

Dilates pupils
Weakly stimulates salivation
Stimulates sweat glands
Accelerates heartbeat
Dilates bronchial tubes in lungs
Inhibits digestion
Increases epinephrine,
  norepinephrine secretion
  by adrenal glands
Relaxes bladder wall
Decreases urine volume
Stimulates glucose release by liver
Stimulates ejaculation in males

Parasympathetic division

Constricts pupils
Stimulates tear glands
Strongly stimulates salivation
Slows heartbeat
Constricts bronchial tubes in lungs
Activates digestion
Inhibits glucose release by liver

Contracts bladder wall
Stimulates genital erection (both
  sexes) and vaginal lubrication
  (females)

FIGURE 3.2

The autonomic nervous system
The two divisions of the autonomic nervous system have different functions. In general, the sympathetic division prepares the body for an expenditure of energy, and the parasympathetic division restores and conserves energy. Sympathetic nerve fibers exit from areas of the spinal cord shown in yellow in this illustration. Parasympathetic nerve fibers exit from the base of the brain and from areas of the spinal cord shown in purple.

erator of a car, mobilizing the body for action and an output of energy. It makes you blush, sweat, and breathe more deeply, and it pushes up your heart rate and blood pressure. The parasympathetic system is more like a brake. It doesn't stop the body, but it does tend to slow things down or keep them running smoothly. It conserves energy and helps the body store it. If you have to jump out of the way of a speeding motorcyclist, sympathetic nerves increase your heart rate. Afterward, parasympathetic nerves slow it down again and keep its rhythm regular. Both systems are involved in emotion and stress.

QUICK QUIZ

Speaking of stress, you may be feeling a bit overwhelmed by the many terms introduced in the last few paragraphs. Pause now to test your memory by mentally filling in the missing parts of the nervous system "house."

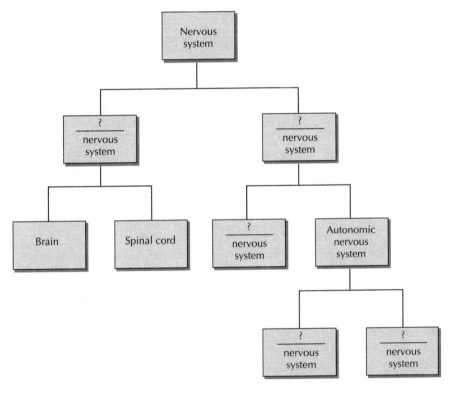

ANSWERS:

Check your answers against Figure 3.3 on the next page. If you had any difficulty, or if you could label the parts but could not remember what they do, review the preceding section. Then try again.

COMMUNICATION IN THE NERVOUS SYSTEM: THE NUTS AND BOLTS

The blueprint of the nervous system just described provides only a general idea of its structure. When we examine the system more closely, we discover that it is made up in part of **neurons,** or nerve cells. These neurons are held in place by **glial cells** (from the Greek for "glue"). Glial cells, which outnumber neurons by a factor of 5 to 10, also provide the neurons with nutrients, insulate them, and remove cellular "debris" when they die. Some neuroscientists think

■ **sympathetic nervous system**
The subdivision of the autonomic nervous system that mobilizes bodily resources and increases the output of energy during emotion and stress.

■ **parasympathetic nervous system**
The subdivision of the autonomic nervous system that operates during relaxed states and conserves energy.

■ **neuron**
A cell that conducts electrochemical signals; the basic unit of the nervous system. Also called a nerve cell.

■ **glial cells**
Cells that hold neurons in place, insulate neurons, and provide them with nutrients.

FIGURE 3.3

How the nervous system is organized

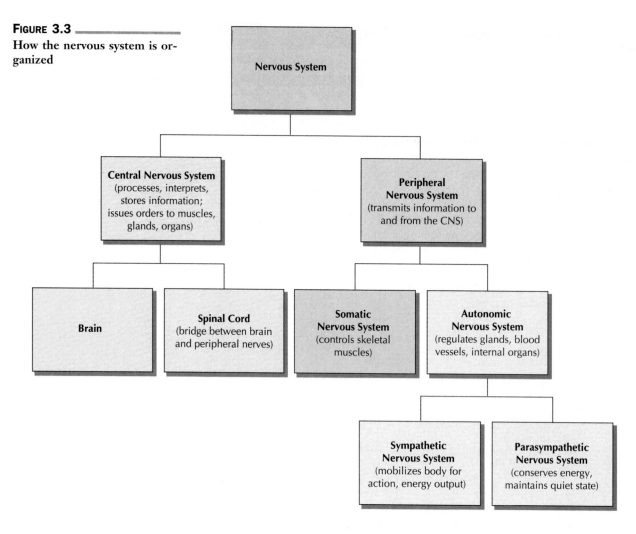

glial cells may also carry signals between various parts of the nervous system (Cornell-Bell et al., 1990), although it is not yet clear what kind of information they might transmit.

What is clear is that the neurons are communication specialists. They transmit information to, from, or inside of the central nervous system, and are often called the building blocks of the nervous system. They do not look much like blocks, however. They are more like snowflakes, exquisitely delicate, differing from each other greatly in size and shape (see Figure 3.4).

In the giraffe, a neuron that runs from the spinal cord down the animal's hind leg may be nine feet long! In the human brain, neurons are microscopic.

FIGURE 3.4

Different kinds of neurons
Neurons vary in size and shape, depending on location and function. Over 200 types of neurons have been identified in mammals.

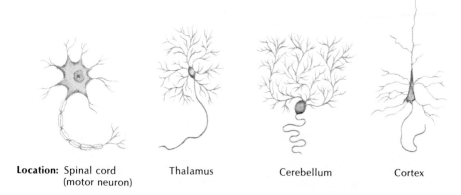

Location: Spinal cord   Thalamus   Cerebellum   Cortex
          (motor neuron)

No one is sure how many neurons the brain contains, but a typical estimate is 100 billion, about the same number as there are stars in our galaxy, and some estimates go as high as a *trillion*. Perhaps even more impressive is the fact that all these neurons are busy most of the time.

The Structure of the Neuron

As you can see in Figure 3.5, a neuron has three main parts: a *cell body*, *dendrites*, and an *axon*. The **cell body** is shaped roughly like a sphere or a pyramid. It contains the biochemical machinery for keeping the neuron alive. It also determines whether the neuron should "fire," that is, transmit a message to other neurons. The **dendrites** of a neuron look like the branches of a tree; indeed, the word *dendrite* means "little tree" in Greek. Dendrites act like antennas, receiving messages from other nerve cells and transmitting them toward the cell body. The **axon** (from the Greek for "axle") is like the tree's trunk, though more slender. It transmits messages away from the cell body to other neurons or to muscle or gland cells. Axons commonly divide at the end into branches, called *axon terminals*. In adult human beings, axons vary from only a tenth of a millimeter to a few feet in length. Dendrites and axons give each neuron a double role: As one researcher puts it, a neuron is first a catcher, then a batter (Gazzaniga, 1988).

In the peripheral nervous system, the fibers of individual cells (axons and sometimes dendrites) collect together in bundles called **nerves,** rather like the lines in a telephone cable. (In the central nervous system, similar bundles of neuron fibers are called *tracts*.) The human body has 43 pairs of peripheral nerves, one nerve from each pair on the left side of the body and the other on the right. Most of these nerves enter or leave the spinal cord, but the 12 pairs that are in the head, the *cranial nerves*, go directly to and from the brain. In Chapter 5, we will have more to say about three cranial nerves involved in sensory processing: the olfactory nerve, involved in smell; the auditory nerve, involved in hearing; and the optic nerve, involved in vision.

Most axons are insulated by a layer of fatty material called the **myelin sheath,** which is derived from glial cells. One purpose of this covering is to prevent sig-

■ **cell body**
The part of the neuron that keeps it alive and determines whether it will fire.

■ **dendrites**
Branches on a neuron that receive information from other neurons and transmit it toward the cell body.

■ **axon**
Extending fiber of a neuron that conducts impulses away from the cell body and transmits them to other neurons.

■ **nerve**
A bundle of nerve fibers (axons and sometimes dendrites) in the peripheral nervous system.

■ **myelin sheath**
A fatty insulating sheath surrounding many axons.

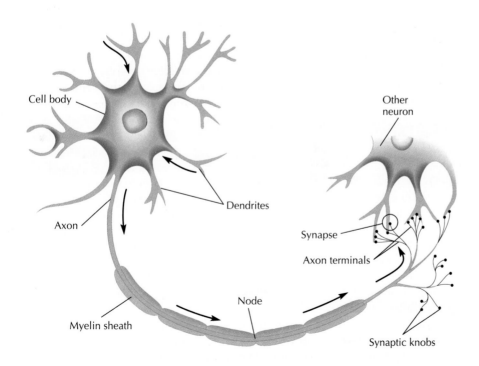

Cell body

Axon

Myelin sheath

Node

Dendrites

Synapse

Axon terminals

Synaptic knobs

Other neuron

FIGURE 3.5
The structure of a neuron
Incoming neural impulses are received by the dendrites of a neuron and transmitted to the cell body. Outgoing signals pass along the axon to terminal branches. The arrows show the direction in which impulses travel.

nals from adjacent cells from interfering with each other. Another is to speed up the conduction of neural impulses. The myelin sheath is divided into segments that make the axon look a little like a string of link sausages. Beneath the myelin sheath, conduction of a neural impulse is impossible because conduction involves the passage of certain ions (charged particles) across the cell's membrane and the myelin inhibits this movement. Instead, when a neural impulse travels down the axon, it "hops" from one break in the "string" to another. This action allows the impulse to travel faster than it could if it had to move along the entire axon. Nerve impulses travel more slowly in babies than in children and adults because babies' myelin sheaths have not fully developed.

Until a few years ago, neuroscientists thought that neurons in the human central nervous system could neither regenerate to any significant degree, nor reproduce; if these cells were injured or damaged, that was it. But new animal studies have challenged these assumptions. In one study, researchers got severed axons in the spinal cords of rats to regrow by blocking the effects of certain nerve-growth inhibiting substances found in the myelin sheath (Schnell & Schwab, 1990). In another, researchers induced severed optic nerves in hamsters to regenerate by laying down a "trail" of transplanted nervous tissue from the animals' legs (Keirstead, Rasminsky, & Aguayo, 1989). And Canadian neuroscientists have discovered that certain undifferentiated cells from the brains of mice, when immersed in a growth-promoting protein in the laboratory, will produce new neurons, which then continue to divide and multiply (Reynolds & Weiss, 1992). One of the researchers, Samuel Weiss, says this result was hard to believe at first: "It challenged everything I had read; everything I had learned when I was a student" (quoted in Barinaga, 1992).

Each year brings new findings on neurons, findings that would once have seemed the stuff of science fiction. Many of these results, if replicated, will not only alter our understanding of the nervous system, but may also lead to unprecedented new treatments for neurological damage. As we saw in Chapter 2, the willingness to question conventional wisdom is a characteristic of the ideal scientist. Critical thinking about commonly accepted assumptions ("Neurons in the central nervous system can't regenerate, period"), when combined with a search for empirical evidence, makes possible new discoveries and a more complete understanding.

How Neurons Communicate

We have called neurons communications specialists. But neurons do not form an unbroken chain, with each neuron directly touching one other, end to end. If they did, the number of connections would be inadequate for the vast amount of information the nervous system must handle. Instead, individual neurons are separated by minuscule spaces called *synaptic gaps*, where the axon terminal of one neuron almost meets a dendrite or the cell body of another. The entire site—the axon terminal, the gap, and the membrane of the receiving dendrite or cell body—is called a **synapse**. Because a neuron's axon may have hundreds or even thousands of terminals, a single neuron may have synaptic connections with a great many other cells. As a result, the number of communication links in the nervous system runs into the trillions or perhaps even the quadrillions.

Although we seem to be born with nearly all the neurons we will ever have, many synapses have not yet formed at birth. Research with animals shows that axons and dendrites continue to grow as a result of both physical maturation and experience with the world. Tiny projections on dendrites called *spines* increase both in size and in number. Throughout life, new learning results in new synaptic connections in the brain, with complex environments producing the greatest changes (Greenough & Anderson, 1991; Greenough & Black, 1992). Conversely, some unused synaptic connections may be lost as cells or their

■ **synapse**
The site where transmission of a nerve impulse from one nerve cell to another occurs; includes the synaptic knob, synaptic gap, and receptor sites of the receiving cell.

branches die (Camel, Withers, & Greenough, 1986). Clearly, the brain is not fixed and "hardwired," but is continually changing in response to challenges and changes in the environment.

Neurons speak to one another—or in some cases to muscles or glands—in an electrical and chemical language. A neural impulse—a wave of electrical voltage—travels down a transmitting nerve cell's axon somewhat as fire travels along the fuse of a firecracker. (The physics of this process involve the sudden inflow of positively charged sodium ions followed by the outflow of positively charged potassium ions.) When an impulse reaches an axon terminal's buttonlike tip (*synaptic knob*), it must get its message across the synaptic gap to another cell. At this point, *synaptic vesicles*, tiny chambers in the synaptic knob, open and release a few thousand molecules of a chemical substance called a **neurotransmitter** (or *transmitter* for short). Like sailors carrying a message from one island to another, these molecules then diffuse across the gap (see Figure 3.6).

Once across the gap, the transmitter molecules bind briefly with special molecules called *receptor sites* on the receiving neuron, fitting these sites much as a key fits into a lock. This produces certain changes in the membrane, or enclosing cover, of the receiving cell. The result is a brief change in electrical potential caused largely by the momentary inflow of positively charged sodium ions across the membrane. The ultimate effect of this change is either *excitatory* (a voltage shift in a positive direction) or *inhibitory* (a voltage shift in a negative direction), depending on which receptor sites have been activated. If the effect is excitatory, the probability increases that the receiving neuron will fire; if it is inhibitory, the opposite is true. Inhibition in the nervous system is extremely important. Without it, we could not sleep or coordinate our movements. Excitation of the nervous system would be overwhelming, producing convulsions.

What any given neuron actually does at any given moment depends on the net effect of all the neurons that are "talking" to it. Only when the cell's voltage reaches a certain threshold will it fire. Thousands of messages, both excitatory and inhibitory, may be coming into the cell. Essentially the neuron must average them. But how it does this, and how it "decides" whether or not to fire, is still a puzzle.

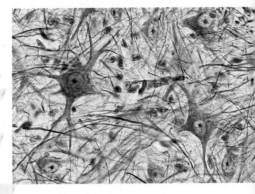

This photograph, taken through a microscope, reveals the delicate fibers of a human motor neuron.

■ **neurotransmitter**
A chemical substance that is released by a transmitting neuron at the synapse and that alters the activity of a receiving neuron.

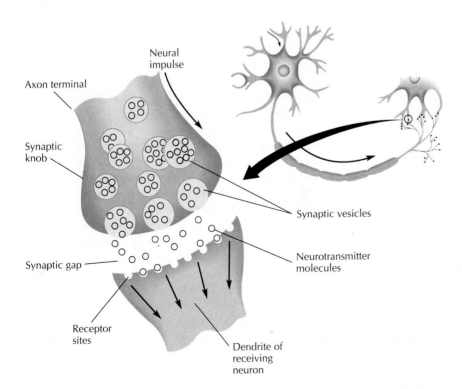

FIGURE 3.6
Neurotransmitter crossing a synapse
Neurotransmitter molecules are released into the synaptic gap between two neurons from vesicles (chambers) in the transmitting neuron's axon terminal. After crossing the gap, the molecules bind to receptor sites on the receiving neuron. As a result, the electrical state of the receiving neuron changes and it becomes either more or less likely to fire an impulse, depending on the type of transmitter substance. A neuron may have synaptic connections with hundreds or even thousands of other neurons.

Labels in figure:
- Neural impulse
- Axon terminal
- Synaptic knob
- Synaptic gap
- Receptor sites
- Synaptic vesicles
- Neurotransmitter molecules
- Dendrite of receiving neuron

The message that reaches a final destination depends on how frequently particular neurons are firing, how many are firing, what types are firing, and where they are located. It does *not* depend on how strongly individual neurons are firing, however, because a neuron always fires in an *all or none* fashion. That is, the neuron's axon either does fire or doesn't fire, but if it does, it gives the impulse everything it's got.

Chemical Messengers in the Nervous System

It takes a lot of nerve to make up the nervous system "house," but that house would remain dark and lifeless without chemical couriers such as the neurotransmitters. We now look more closely at neurotransmitters, and at another class of chemical messengers, the hormones.

NEUROTRANSMITTERS: VERSATILE COURIERS. As we have seen, neurotransmitters make it possible for one neuron to excite or inhibit another. Dozens of different substances are known or suspected to be transmitters, and the number keeps growing. Each particular neurotransmitter binds only to certain specific types of receptor sites. This means that if some of those "sailors" we mentioned (the transmitter molecules) get a little off course and reach the wrong "islands" (receiving neurons), their messages will fall on "deaf ears" (no binding will occur). The existence of different neurotransmitters and receptor sites ensures that messages go only where they are supposed to go.

Neurotransmitters exist not only in the brain, but also in the spinal cord, the peripheral nerves, and certain glands. These substances play critical roles in mood, memory, and physical and psychological well-being. Various harmful effects can occur when particular neurotransmitters are in either too great or too short a supply. For example:

• The degeneration of brain cells that produce and use the neurotransmitter *dopamine* appears to cause the symptoms of Parkinson's disease, a condition characterized by tremors, muscular spasms, and muscular rigidity. Injections of dopamine do not help because dopamine molecules cannot cross the "blood-brain barrier" (a system of densely packed capillary and glial cells) to enter brain tissue. However, symptoms can be lessened by the administration of levodopa (L-dopa), which is a precursor, or building block, of dopamine.

• Imbalances in the neurotransmitters dopamine, *norepinephrine*, and *serotonin* may underlie schizophrenic disorders, which are characterized by such symptoms as delusions, hallucinations, incoherent word associations, and inappropriate emotional reactions. These neurotransmitters may also be involved in some cases of bipolar disorder, characterized by alternating episodes of depression and mania.

• Deficiencies in a number of neurotransmitters have been implicated in Alzheimer's disease, a devastating condition, most common in the elderly, that causes memory loss, personality changes, and eventual disintegration of all physical and mental abilities. For example, in Alzheimer's patients, many of the brain cells responsible for producing *acetylcholine* have been destroyed, and this deficit may help account for memory loss. Also, in the early stages of the disease, serotonin receptors normally present in certain layers of brain cells nearly disappear (Cross, 1990). This deficit could be related to the increased aggressiveness and moodiness often observed in Alzheimer's patients.

• Elevated levels of serotonin seem to be involved in childhood autism (du Verglas, Banks, & Guyer, 1988). Autism is a severe disorder characterized by self-stimulation (for instance, rocking and twirling) and a lack of social responsiveness. Autistic children usually do not speak, establish eye contact, or respond to other people. Often they seem insensitive to pain, and some seriously hurt themselves by banging their heads against walls, biting their fingers, or poking themselves with sharp objects. A serotonin abnormality, along with a number of other biochemical and brain abnormalities, may help explain this puzzling condition.

We want to warn you, however, that establishing a cause-and-effect relationship between neurotransmitter abnormalities and behavioral abnormalities is extremely difficult, and many conclusions remain tentative. As one writer notes, "nothing is black-and-white when it comes to the gray matter of the brain" (R. Cowen, 1989). The study of neurotransmitters is complicated by the fact that each one plays multiple roles (see Table 3.1). The effect of a given substance depends on the location of the neurons it serves and whether it excites or inhibits those neurons. Also, the functions of different substances often overlap. And it is always possible that something about a disorder leads to the neurotransmitter problem, instead of the other way around. Although drugs that boost or decrease levels of particular neurotransmitters are sometimes effective in treating various disorders, that does not necessarily mean abnormal neurotransmitter levels are *causing* the disorders. After all, aspirin can relieve a headache, but headaches are not caused by a lack of aspirin!

One particularly intriguing group of chemical messengers in the brain is known collectively as *endogenous opioid peptides*, or more popularly as **endorphins.** Endorphins have effects similar to those of natural opiates; that is, they reduce pain and promote pleasure. Some endorphins function as neurotransmitters, but most act primarily as **neuromodulators,** which increase or decrease the action of specific neurotransmitters.

Endorphins were identified some two decades ago. Candace Pert and Solomon Snyder (1973) were doing research on morphine, a pain-relieving and mood-elevating opiate that derives from heroin, which is made from poppies. They found that morphine works by binding to certain receptor sites in the brain. This seemed odd: As Snyder later recalled, "We doubted that animals had evolved opiate receptors just to deal with certain properties of the poppy plant" (quoted in Radetsky, 1991). Pert and Solomon reasoned that if opiate re-

■ **endorphins [en-DOR-fins]**
Neuromodulators that are similar in structure and action to opiates; involved in pain reduction, pleasure, and memory. Known technically as endogenous opioid peptides.

■ **neuromodulators**
Chemical messengers in the nervous system that increase or decrease the action of specific neurotransmitters.

TABLE 3.1	

Magic Molecules

These are some of the better understood neurotransmitters and some of their known or suspected effects.

Acetylcholine (uh-seet-ul-COE-leen)	Involved in muscle action, cognitive functioning, memory, emotion.
Norepinephrine (nor-ep-uh-NEF-rin)	Increases heart rate and slows intestinal activity during stress. Involved in learning, memory, wakefulness, emotion. Abnormal levels associated with mania and depression.
Serotonin (sair-uh-TOE-nin)	Linked to sleep, appetite, heightened sensory states, pain suppression, emotion. Deficit associated with severe depression.
Dopamine (DOE-puh-meen)	Involved in voluntary movement, learning, memory, emotion. Deficit associated with Parkinson's disease. Abnormally high level linked by some researchers to schizophrenia.
GABA (gamma amino butyric acid)	The major inhibitory neurotransmitter in the brain. Abnormal GABA activity implicated in sleep and eating disorders and in various convulsive disorders. Some studies suggest an inability to use GABA underlies Huntington's disease.
Endorphins (en-DOR-fins)	Neuromodulators involved in pain suppression, appetite, blood pressure, mood, perception of pleasure, learning, memory.

ceptors existed, the body must produce its own internal, or endogenous, morphinelike substances, which they called endorphins. Soon they, as well as other researchers, confirmed this hypothesis.

Endorphin levels seem to shoot up when an animal or person is either afraid or under stress. This is no accident; by making pain controllable in such situations, endorphins give a species an evolutionary advantage (Levinthal, 1988). When an organism is threatened, it needs to do something fast—fight, flee, or cope. Pain, however, can interfere with action: If a mouse pauses to lick a wounded paw it may become a cat's dinner; if a soldier is overcome by his injury, he may never manage to get off the battlefield. Of course, as we all know, the body's built-in system of counteracting pain is only partly successful, especially when painful stimulation is prolonged. Researchers are now searching for ways to stimulate endorphin production or administer endorphins directly in order to alleviate pain. Some techniques may already exist. For example, there is some evidence that acupuncture eases pain in part by causing endorphin levels to rise (Watkins & Mayer, 1982). (For more on the role of endorphins in pleasure, see "A Closer Look at Neuropsychology.")

Many researchers believe that unlocking the mysteries of neurotransmitters and neuromodulators will set off a revolution in our understanding of both mind and body, and may even help us improve their functioning. For example, during the past few years, surgeons in several countries have experimentally grafted dopamine-producing brain or adrenal gland tissue from miscarried fetuses into the brains of people suffering from Parkinson's disease. Although it is uncertain whether these grafts actually survive, there have been some reports of a re-

A CLOSER LOOK AT NEUROPSYCHOLOGY

The Biology of Pleasure

Like other psychologists, neuropsychologists want to explain the miseries of human life—stress, mental confusion, pain, disease. But they also hope to explain the joys of life—the satisfaction of eating a bowl of chocolate ice cream, the comfort in the arms of a lover, the euphoria of a good laugh. They search for the sources of pleasure in the cells and circuits, enzymes, and electric signals of the nervous system.

Some early clues to the neural basis of pleasure were uncovered by James Olds and Peter Milner, who reported the existence of specific "pleasure centers" in the area of the brain known as the limbic system (see page 93 of the text). They found that a rat could be trained to press a lever on the side of its cage to get its limbic system buzzed with electricity delivered through tiny electrodes (Olds, 1975; Olds & Milner, 1954). Some rats would press the bar thousands of

times an hour, for 15 or 20 hours at a time, until they collapsed from exhaustion. When they revived, they went right back to the bar. The little hedonists couldn't be lured away by water, food, or even the provocative gestures of an attractive rat of the other sex. (You may be either relieved or disappointed to know that human beings do not act like rats in this regard. Patients who have volunteered to have their pleasure areas stimulated as a treatment for depression say the experience is generally "pleasant" [Sem-Jacobsen, 1959]. But the earth doesn't move, and electrical "self-stimulation" cannot cure depression or provide an electrical "high.")

Today, researchers believe that brain stimulation such as that used in the Olds and Milner studies activates various neural pathways, rather than discrete "centers," and that changes in neurotransmitter or neuromodulator levels must be involved. Several lines of research have focused on the possible role played by endorphins, the nervous system's opiatelike chemicals. The limbic system contains some of the highest concentrations of endorphins and endorphin receptors in the brain, and endorphins may not only relieve pain but also promote pleasure.

In one unusual study, neuroscientist Avram Goldstein (1980) asked students to name personal experiences that gave them an emotional

duction in such symptoms as muscular tremors and rigidity (Freed et al., 1990; Lindvall et al., 1990). In other research, when rats suffering alcohol-induced memory problems have received grafts of fetal rat brain tissue rich in acetylcholine, their memories have improved (Arendt et al., 1988.) However, at present, brain tissue transplants in human beings are considered highly risky, and the long-term results are not known.

Are neurotransmitters the key to new treatments for medical and psychological disorders? Or are the interactions among the different substances so complex that tinkering with them will be unfeasible, or even dangerous? While scientists try to answer such questions, many of us are already doing things that affect our own neurotransmitters, usually without knowing it. Various drugs used recreationally or for medical purposes either block or enhance the effects of particular neurotransmitters (see Chapter 4). Even ordinary foods can influence the availability of neurotransmitters in the brain, as we discuss in "Taking Psychology with You" at the end of this chapter.

HORMONES: LONG-DISTANCE MESSENGERS. **Hormones** are chemical substances that are produced in one part of the body but affect another. They originate primarily in **endocrine glands,** which release them directly into the bloodstream (see Figure 3.7). The bloodstream then carries them to organs and cells that may be far from their point of origin. Some endocrine glands are activated by nervous system impulses. Conversely, hormones affect the way the nervous system functions. The parts of the nervous and endocrine systems that interact are often referred to as the *neuroendocrine system.*

■ **hormones**
Chemical substances that are secreted by organs called glands *and affect the functioning of other organs.*

■ **endocrine glands**
Internal organs that produce hormones and release them into the bloodstream.

thrill. Nearly all mentioned listening to a musical passage, and many reported feeling a "tingling" sensation during such experiences. Using a double-blind procedure (see Chapter 2), Goldstein then had some of the "tinglers" listen to their favorite music before and after receiving either a placebo or an injection of naloxone, a chemical that blocks the effects of endorphins. Whether their tastes ran to rock or Rachmaninoff, in some people naloxone reduced the frequency and intensity of tingles. The implication: Endorphins may mediate musical enjoyment.

Other research, using animals, has demonstrated a link between endorphins and the pleasures of social contact. In one series of studies, Jaak Panksepp and his colleagues (1980) gave low doses of morphine or endorphins to young puppies, guinea pigs, and chicks. After the injections, the animals showed much less distress than usual when separated from their mothers. (In all other respects they behaved normally, and they did not appear sedated.) The injections seemed to provide a biochemical replacement for the mother, or more specifically, for the endorphin surge presumed to occur during contact with her. Conversely, when young guinea pigs and chicks received a chemical that *blocks* the effects of opiates, crying increased. These findings suggest that an endorphin-stimulated euphoria may

be a child's initial motive for seeking affection and social comfort. In effect, a child attached to his or her parent is a child addicted to love.

If a biochemical need for endorphins prompts an infant to seek closeness with others, could excess endorphins *interfere* with normal attachment? Several researchers think so. They argue that such an excess might explain certain symptoms of childhood autism, including extreme withdrawal from others. So far, findings on autistic children's endorphin levels are inconclusive. However, small-scale studies find that when these children are given an opioid blocker, sometimes their behavioral symptoms decrease and they become more sociable (Campbell et al., 1989; Herman, 1991; LeBoyer, Bouvard, & Dugas, 1988).

Future research is likely to tell us more about the neurochemistry of love, attachment, and other pleasures, as well as the consequences when that neurochemistry goes awry. But keep in mind that research findings and conclusions in this area are still preliminary. Also, in normal life, the effects of endorphins are subtle, and happiness is more than a matter of chemistry. Even if we could monitor every cell and circuit of the brain, we still would want to understand the circumstances, thoughts, and social rules that determine whether we are gripped by hatred, consumed by grief, lifted by love, or transported by joy.

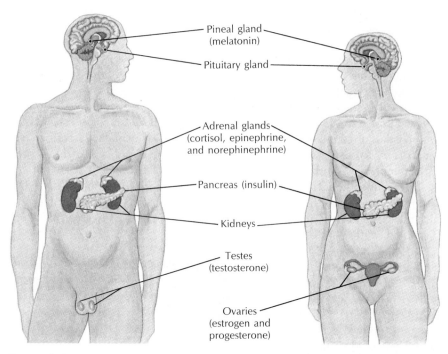

Pineal gland (melatonin)

Pituitary gland

Adrenal glands (cortisol, epinephrine, and norephinephrine)

Pancreas (insulin)

Kidneys

Testes (testosterone)

Ovaries (estrogen and progesterone)

Figure 3.7

Some endocrine glands
This figure shows parts of the endocrine system that are of particular interest to psychologists. The hormones named in the diagram have various known or suspected effects on behavior or emotion.

Hormones have dozens of jobs, from promoting bodily growth to aiding digestion to regulating metabolism. Certain hormones are of particular interest to psychologists:

1. *Insulin,* which is produced by the *pancreas,* plays a role in the body's use of glucose (a sugar) and affects appetite (see Chapter 10).

2. *Melatonin,* which is secreted by the *pineal body,* a small gland deep within the brain, appears to regulate certain biological rhythms (see Chapter 4).

3. Various hormones produced by the *adrenal glands,* organs that are perched right above the kidneys, are involved in emotion and responses to stress. Each adrenal gland is composed of an outer layer, or *cortex,* and an inner core, or *medulla.* The outer part produces *cortisol,* which increases blood-sugar levels and enhances energy. The inner part produces *epinephrine* (adrenaline) and *norepinephrine* (noradrenaline). When these hormones are released in your body, they activate the sympathetic nervous system, which in turn prepares you for action.

4. Sex hormones are secreted by tissue located within the gonads—testes in men, ovaries in women. There are three main types of sex hormones. All three occur in both sexes, but in differing amounts. *Androgens* (the most important of which is *testosterone*) are masculinizing hormones produced mainly in the testes but also in the ovaries and adrenal cortex. Androgens produce the physical changes males experience at puberty, cause pubic and underarm hair to develop in females, and appear to influence sexual arousal in both sexes (see Chapter 10). *Estrogens* are feminizing hormones produced primarily in the ovaries but also in the testes and adrenal cortex. They produce the physical changes females experience at puberty and influence the course of the menstrual cycle. *Progesterone* is a hormone that contributes to the growth and maintenance of the uterine lining in preparation for the implantation of a fertilized egg. It is produced mainly in the ovaries, but small amounts are also produced in the

■ **sex hormones**
Hormones that regulate the development and functioning of reproductive and sex organs and stimulate the development of male and female sexual characteristics.

testes and adrenal cortex. In the next chapter, we will examine the possibility that fluctuating sex hormones affect mood and behavior.

Note that although we have discussed neurotransmitters and hormones as separate substances, they are not always chemically distinct. The two classifications are like clubs that admit some of the same members. A particular chemical, such as norepinephrine, may belong to more than one classification depending on where it is located and what function it is performing. Nature has been efficient, giving various substances more than one task to perform.

QUICK QUIZ

A. Each definition below is followed by a pair of words. Which word best fits the definition?

1. Basic building blocks of the nervous system (*nerves/neurons*)
2. Cell parts that receive nerve impulses (*axons/dendrites*)
3. Site where communication between neurons takes place (*synapse/myelin sheath*)
4. Opiatelike substance in the brain (*dopamine/endorphin*)
5. Chemicals that make it possible for neurons to communicate (*neurotransmitters/hormones*)
6. Hormone closely associated with emotional excitement (*epinephrine/estrogen*)

B. Imagine that you are depressed, and you hear about a treatment for depression that affects the levels of several neurotransmitters thought to be involved in the disorder. Based on what you now know about neurotransmitters, what questions would you want to ask before deciding whether to try the treatment?

ANSWERS:

A. 1. neurons 2. dendrites 3. synapse 4. endorphin 5. neurotransmitters 6. epinephrine. B. You might want to ask, among other things, about side effects (each neurotransmitter has several different functions, all of which might be affected by the treatment); about evidence that the treatment works; and about whether there is any reason to believe that your own neurotransmitter levels are abnormal or whether there are other possible explanations for your depression.

■ EAVESDROPPING ON THE BRAIN

A disembodied brain is not very exciting to look at. Stored in a formaldehyde-filled container, it is merely a putty-colored, wrinkled glob of tissue that looks a little like a walnut whose growth has gotten out of hand. It takes an act of imagination to envision this modest-looking organ writing *Hamlet*, discovering radium, painting *The Last Supper*, or inventing French cuisine. Obviously, you can't judge a book, or a brain, by its cover.

In a living person, of course, the brain is encased in a thick protective vault of bone. How, then, can scientists study it? One approach is to study patients who have had a part of the brain damaged or removed because of disease or injury. Another, called the lesion method, involves damaging or removing sections of brain in animals, then observing the effects.

The brain can also be probed by using devices called **electrodes.** Some electrodes are coin-shaped and are simply pasted or taped on the scalp. They de-

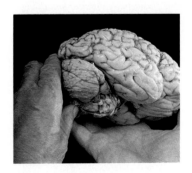

The human brain: Its modest appearance gives no hint of its powers.

tect the electrical activity of millions of neurons in particular regions of the brain and are widely used in research and medical diagnosis. The electrodes are connected by wires to a machine that translates the electrical energy from the brain into wavy lines on a moving piece of paper or visual patterns on a screen. That is why we refer to electrical patterns in the brain as "brain waves." Different wave patterns are associated with sleep, relaxation, and mental concentration, as we will see in Chapter 4.

A brain wave recording is called an **electroencephalogram (EEG).** A standard EEG is useful, but not very precise, because it reflects the firing of many cells at once. "Listening" to the brain with an EEG machine is like standing outside a sports stadium: You know when something is happening, but you can't be sure what it is or who is doing it. But fortunately, computer technology can be combined with EEG technology to get a clearer picture of brain activity patterns associated with specific events and mental processes. To analyze such patterns, or **evoked potentials,** researchers use a computer to extract all the background "noise" being produced by the brain, leaving only the pattern of electrical response to the event.

For even more specific information, researchers use needle electrodes. These are very thin wires or hollow glass tubes that can be inserted into the brain, either directly in an exposed brain or through tiny holes in the skull. Only the skull and membranes covering the brain need to be anesthetized; the brain itself, which processes all bodily sensation and feeling, paradoxically feels nothing when touched. Therefore a human patient or an animal can be awake and not feel pain during the procedure. Needle electrodes can be used both to record electrical activity from the brain and to stimulate the brain with a weak electrical current. Stimulating a given area often results in a particular sensation or movement. *Microelectrodes* are so fine that they can be inserted into single cells.

During the past few years, even more amazing doors to the brain have opened. One method, the **PET scan (positron-emission tomography),** goes beyond anatomy to record biochemical changes in the brain as they are happening (see Figure 3.8). It takes advantage of the fact that nerve cells convert glucose, a sugar, into energy. A researcher can inject a patient with a glucoselike substance that contains a harmless radioactive element. This substance accumulates in brain areas that are particularly active and are consuming glucose rapidly. The substance emits radiation, which is a telltale sign of activity, like cookie crumbs on a child's face. The radiation is detected by a scanning device, and the result is a computer-processed picture of biochemical activity on a display screen, with different colors indicating different activity levels. Although PET scans were designed to diagnose physical abnormalities, they can be used to find out which parts of the brain are active during particular activities and emotions. These pictures can tell us what happens in the brain when a person hears a song, feels depressed, or shifts attention from one task to another. Already they have yielded some evidence that certain brain areas in people with emotional disorders are abnormally quiet or active.

■ **electrodes**
Devices used to apply electric current to tissue or detect neural activity.

■ **electroencephalogram (EEG)**
A recording of neural activity detected by electrodes.

■ **evoked potentials**
Patterns of brain activity produced in response to specific events.

■ **PET scan (positron-emission tomography)**
A method for analyzing biochemical activity in the brain, using injections of a glucoselike substance containing a radioactive element.

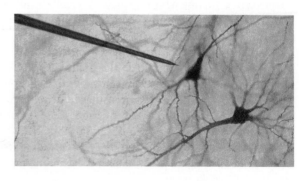

A microelectrode is used to record the electrical impulses generated by a single cell in the brain of a monkey.

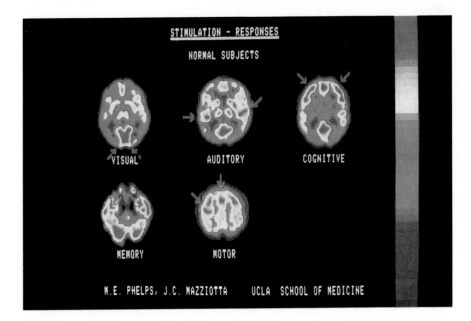

FIGURE 3.8

Metabolic activity in the brain during various tasks

In these PET scans, red indicates areas of highest activity, and violet areas of lowest activity. The arrows point to regions that are most active when a person looks at a complicated visual scene (top left), listens to a sound (top center), performs a mental task (top right), recalls information from stories heard previously (bottom left), or moves the right hand (bottom center).

Another technique, **magnetic resonance imaging (MRI),** allows the exploration of "inner space" without injecting chemicals, and produces some of the most accurate images yet of living body and brain tissue. Powerful magnetic fields and various radio frequencies are used to produce vibrations in the nuclei of atoms making up body organs. These vibrations are picked up as signals by special receivers. A computer then analyzes the signals, taking into account their strength and duration, and converts them into a high-contrast picture. Like the PET scan, MRI is used both for diagnosing disease and studying normal brains, but unlike the PET technique, MRI does not map activity over time.

Still newer techniques, though not yet widely used for psychological research, have appeared on the horizon. SPECT scans (single-photon emission computed tomography) are similar to PET scans but use new kinds of radioactive tracers and are cheaper than PET scans (Holman & Tumeh, 1990). An experimental new device called MANSCAN (mental activity network scanner) uses electrodes to record electrical signals from 124 points on the scalp, takes a new reading every four milliseconds, and uses a computer to map ongoing, changing neuronal activity within a three-dimensional magnetic resonance image of the brain. The result is something like a movie of brain cell activity. In one study, MANSCAN computers identified neurological signs of mental fatigue in fighter pilots before their performance actually deteriorated (Gevins et al., 1990).

In sum, the brain can no longer hide from researchers behind the fortress of the skull. It is now possible to get a clear visual image of our most enigmatic organ, in living color, without so much as lifting a scalpel.

■ **magnetic resonance imaging (MRI)**

A method for studying body and brain tissue, using magnetic fields and special radio receivers.

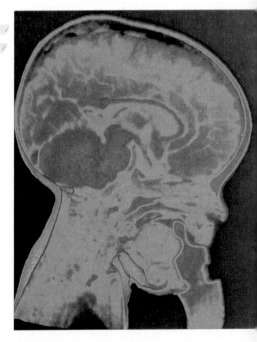

This magnetic resonance image shows a child's brain—and the bottle given to him to quiet him during the seven minutes it took to obtain the image.

■ A TOUR THROUGH THE BRAIN

Neurosurgeon Joseph Bogen (1978) once suggested that a 30-story replica of the brain be built so that people could learn about brain anatomy the way they learn about a neighborhood—by strolling through it. No one has followed up on that suggestion, so we must make do with an imaginary tour. Pretend, then, that you have shrunk to microscopic size and that you are wending your way through the "soul's frail dwelling house." That house is commonly thought of as having three main sections: the *hindbrain*, *midbrain*, and *forebrain*. The more reflexive or automatic a behavior is, the more likely it is to be controlled by

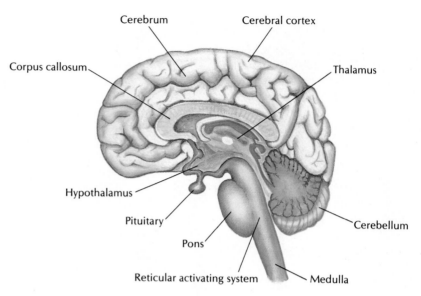

FIGURE 3.9 ━━━━━━━━━━━━━━━━━━━━━━━━━

The human brain
This drawing, a cross section, shows the brain as though it were split in half. The view is of the inside surface of the right half. The pons, medulla, cerebellum, and lower part of the reticular activating system make up what has traditionally been called the hindbrain. The reticular activating system extends into an area called the midbrain. The other structures labeled in the figure belong to the forebrain.

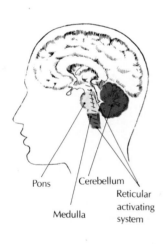

■ **brain stem**
The part of the brain at the top of the spinal cord; responsible for automatic functions such as heartbeat and respiration.
■ **reticular activating system**
A dense network of neurons found in the core of the brain stem; arouses the cortex and screens incoming information.
■ **cerebellum**
A brain structure that regulates movement and balance.

areas in the hindbrain and midbrain. The more complex a behavior, the likelier it is to involve the forebrain. Major structures of the brain are shown in Figure 3.9.

The Hindbrain: Vital Functions

Our guided tour begins at the base of the skull, with the **brain stem,** which began to evolve some 500 million years ago in segmented worms. The brain stem looks like a stalk rising out of the spinal cord. Pathways to and from upper areas of the brain pass through its two main structures, the *medulla* and the *pons.* The pons is involved in (among other things) sleeping, waking, and dreaming. The medulla is responsible for prewired functions that do not have to be consciously willed, such as breathing and heart rate. Hanging has long been used as a method of execution because when it breaks the neck, nervous pathways from the medulla are severed, stopping respiration (Bailey, 1975).

Another important structure, extending from the core of the brain stem into the midbrain and forebrain, is the **reticular activating system (RAS).** This dense network of neurons, which has connections with many higher areas of the brain, screens incoming information. Irrelevant information is filtered out. Important information is passed on to higher centers. The RAS also arouses the higher centers when something happens that demands their attention. Without the RAS, we could not be alert, nor perhaps even conscious.

Standing on the brain stem and looking toward the back part of the brain, we see a structure about the size of a small fist, bulging out from the pons. It is the **cerebellum,** or "lesser brain," which contributes to a sense of balance and coordinates the muscles so that movement is smooth and precise. If your cerebellum were damaged, you would probably become clumsy and uncoordinated. You might have trouble using a pencil, threading a needle, or riding a bicycle.

The Midbrain: Important Way Stations

The midbrain contains neural tracts that run to and from the upper and lower portions of the brain. Various areas of the midbrain perform special functions. For example, one area receives information from the visual system and is involved in eye movements. Some researchers consider the midbrain to be part of the brain stem. In this book, we will not be concerned with details about the structure of the midbrain.

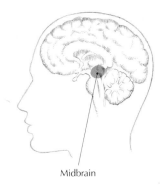

Midbrain

The Forebrain: Emotions, Memory, and Thought

Standing atop the midbrain, we see that the largest part of the brain, the forebrain, is still above us. The complexity of the human brain's circuitry far exceeds that of any computer in existence, and much of its most complicated wiring is packed into the uppermost part of the brain, the **cerebrum,** where the higher forms of thinking take place. Compared to many other creatures we may be ungainly, feeble, and thin-skinned, but our well-developed cerebrum enables us to overcome these limitations and creatively control our environment, for better or for worse.

The cauliflower-like cerebrum is divided into two separate halves, or **cerebral hemispheres,** connected by a large band of fibers called the **corpus callosum.** In general, the right hemisphere is in charge of the left side of the body, and vice versa. As we will see later, the two sides also have somewhat different talents.

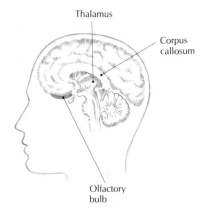

Thalamus

Corpus callosum

Olfactory bulb

Several structures in the forebrain are invisible from the outside. One is the **thalamus,** the busy traffic officer of the brain. As sensory messages come into the brain, the thalamus directs them to various higher centers. For example, the sight of a sunset sends signals that the thalamus directs to a vision center. The only sense that completely bypasses the thalamus is the sense of smell, which has its own private switching station, the *olfactory bulb*. The olfactory bulb lies near areas that control emotion. Perhaps that is why particular odors—the smell of fresh laundry, gardenias, a steak sizzling on the grill—often rekindle memories of important experiences in one's life.

Beneath the thalamus sits a tiny, bean-shaped structure called the **hypothalamus** (*hypo* means "under"). The small size of the hypothalamus is no indicator of its importance. It is involved in powerful drives associated with the survival of both the individual and the species—hunger, thirst, emotion, sex, and reproduction. It regulates body temperature by triggering sweating or shivering. It controls the complex operations of the autonomic nervous system.

Hanging down from the hypothalamus, connected to it by a short stalk, is a cherry-sized structure that is *not* made up of neurons. It is the **pituitary gland,** an endocrine gland. The pituitary is often called the body's "master gland" because it controls many other endocrine glands. The master, however, is really only a supervisor. The true boss is the hypothalamus. The hypothalamus sends chemicals to the pituitary that tell it when to "talk" to the various endocrine glands. The pituitary, in turn, sends hormonal orders to the glands.

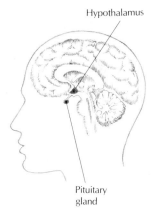

Hypothalamus

Pituitary gland

The hypothalamus has many connections to a set of loosely interconnected structures that form a sort of border on the underside of the brain's "cauliflower." Together these structures make up the **limbic system** of the brain (see Figure 3.10). (*Limbic* comes from the Latin word for "border." Some brain specialists include the hypothalamus and parts of the thalamus in the limbic system.) The limbic system is heavily involved in emotions, such as rage and fear, that we share with other animals.

An important part of the limbic system is the **hippocampus,** which has a shape that must have reminded someone of a sea horse, for that is what its name means. This structure is larger in human beings than in any other species. One of its duties seems to be to compare sensory messages with what the brain has

FIGURE 3.10

The limbic system
Structures of the limbic system play an important role in memory and emotion.

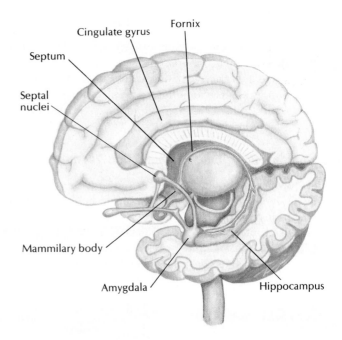

Cingulate gyrus
Fornix
Septum
Septal nuclei
Mammilary body
Amygdala
Hippocampus

■ **cerebrum [suh-REE-brum]**
The largest brain structure, comprising the upper part of the forebrain; it is in charge of most sensory, motor, and cognitive processes in human beings. From the Latin for "brain."

■ **cerebral hemispheres**
The two halves of the cerebrum.

■ **corpus callosum**
The bundle of nerve fibers connecting the two cerebral hemispheres.

■ **thalamus**
The brain structure that relays sensory messages to the cerebral cortex.

■ **hypothalamus**
A brain structure involved in emotions and drives vital to survival, such as fear, hunger, thirst, and reproduction; regulates the autonomic nervous system.

■ **pituitary gland**
A small endocrine gland at the base of the brain that releases many hormones and regulates other endocrine glands.

■ **limbic system**
A group of brain areas involved in emotional reactions and motivated behavior.

■ **hippocampus**
A brain structure thought to be involved in the storage of new information in memory.

■ **amygdala**
A brain structure involved in the arousal and regulation of emotion; may also play a role in the association of memories formed in different senses.

learned to expect about the world. When expectations are met, the hippocampus tells the reticular activating system, the brain's arousal center, to "cool it." It wouldn't do to be highly aroused in response to *everything*. What if neural alarm bells went off every time a car went by, a bird chirped, or you felt your saliva trickling down the back of your throat?

The hippocampus has also been called the "gateway to memory" because (along with certain other brain areas) it seems to enable us to store new information for future use. We know about this role of the hippocampus in part from research on brain-damaged patients with severe memory problems. One man, known to researchers as H. M., was studied for many years by Brenda Milner, and is still being studied today (Corkin, 1984; Milner, 1970; Ogden & Corkin, 1991). In 1953, when H. M. was 27, surgeons removed most of his hippocampus, along with part of another limbic structure, the **amygdala** (which is involved in emotion). The operation was a last ditch effort to relieve H. M.'s severe and life-threatening epilepsy. People who have epilepsy, a neurological disorder that has many causes and that takes many forms, often experience seizures. Usually the seizures are brief, mild, and controllable by drugs, but in H. M.'s case, they were unrelenting and uncontrollable.

The operation did, in fact, achieve its goal: Afterward, the young man's seizures were milder and could be managed with medication. His memory, however, had been affected dramatically. Although H. M. continued to recall most events before the operation, especially those that had occurred several years before, he could no longer remember new experiences for much longer than 15 minutes. They vanished like water down the drain. Milner and H. M.'s doctors had to reintroduce themselves every time they saw him. He would read the same issue of a magazine over and over again without realizing it. He could not recall the day of the week, the year, or even his last meal. Today, years later, he will occasionally recall an unusually emotional event, such as the assassination of someone named Kennedy. He has managed to learn some new manual, perceptual, and problem-solving skills, which may draw on a different part of the brain than do facts and events. However, he forgets the training sessions. For the most part, he does not store new information about events; history stopped for H. M. on the day of his operation. H. M. says that living his life is like constantly waking from a dream. We will meet H. M. again, in Chapter 7.

The Cerebral Cortex: The Brain's Thinking Cap

Working our way right up through the top of the brain, we find that the forebrain is covered by several thin layers of densely packed cells known collectively as the **cerebral cortex.** (Although the cerebral cortex is part of the forebrain, because of its importance we are discussing it separately.) Cell bodies in the cortex, as in many other parts of the brain, are crowded together and produce a grayish tissue; hence the term *gray matter*. In other parts of the brain and nervous system, long, myelin-covered axons prevail, producing *white matter*. The cortex contains almost three-fourths of all the cells in the human brain (Schneider & Tarshis, 1986). In only 1 square *inch* of the cortex there are around 10,000 miles of synaptically connected nerve cells. In the entire cortex there are enough connections to stretch from the earth to the moon and back again, and then back to the moon (Davis, 1984).

Standing atop the cortex, we note that it has many deep crevasses and wrinkles. The folds and fissures in the brain's surface enable it to contain its billions of neurons without requiring us to have the heads of giants—heads that would be too big to permit birth. In other mammals the cortex is less crumpled, and in the rat it is quite smooth.

From our vantage point on the brain's surface we can see that deep grooves or fissures divide the cerebral cortex into four distinct regions, or lobes (see Figure 3.11):

• The *occipital lobes* (from the Latin for "in back of the head") are at the lower back part of the brain. Among other things, they contain the *visual cortex*, where visual signals are processed. Damage to the visual cortex can cause impaired visual recognition or blindness.

• The *parietal lobes* (from the Latin for "pertaining to walls") are at the top of the brain. They contain the *somatosensory cortex*, which receives information about pressure, pain, touch, and temperature from all over the body. The sensory information tells you what the movable parts of your body are doing at every moment. Different parts of the somatosensory cortex are associated with different body parts. The areas associated with the hands and the face are disproportionately large because these parts are particularly sensitive.

• The *temporal lobes* (from the Latin for "pertaining to the temples") are at the sides of the brain, just above the ears, behind the temples. They are involved in memory, perception, emotion, and language comprehension, and they contain the *auditory cortex*, which processes sounds.

• The *frontal lobes*, as their name indicates, are located toward the front of the brain, just under the skull in the area of the forehead. They contain the *motor cortex*, which issues orders to the 600 muscles of the body that produce voluntary movement. They also seem to be responsible for the ability to make plans, think creatively, and take initiative.

The descriptions we have given are simplified ones; in reality, there is considerable overlap in what the various lobes do. Still, when a surgeon probes these four pairs of lobes with an electrode, different things tend to happen. If current is applied to the somatosensory cortex, in the parietal lobes, the patient may feel tingling in the skin or a sense of being gently touched. If the visual cortex, in the occipital lobes, is stimulated, the person may report a flash of light or swirls of color.

But in most areas of the cortex, nothing happens after electrical stimulation. These "silent" areas, which are sometimes called the *association cortex*, appear to be responsible for higher mental processes. The silent areas of the cortex are just beginning to reveal their secrets. Psychologists are particularly interested in new information about the forwardmost part of the frontal lobes, the *prefrontal cortex*. This area barely exists in mice and rats and takes up only 3.5 per-

"Well, time for our weekly brain-stem storming session."

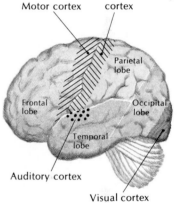

FIGURE 3.11

Lobes of the cerebrum
In this drawing, crosshatched areas show regions specialized for movement and bodily sensation, and dotted areas show regions specialized for vision and hearing.

■ **cerebral cortex**
A collection of several thin layers of cells covering the cerebrum; it is largely responsible for higher functions. Cortex is Latin for "bark" or "rind."

cent of the cerebral cortex in cats, about 7 percent in dogs, and 17 percent in chimpanzees. In human beings, it accounts for fully 29 percent of the cortex (M. Pines, 1983).

Scientists have long known that the frontal lobes must have something to do with personality. The first clue appeared in 1848, when an accident drove an inch-thick iron rod clear through the head of a young railroad worker named Phineas Gage. The rod (which is still on display at Harvard University) entered beneath the left eye and exited through the top of the head, destroying much of the front of the brain. Miraculously, Gage survived this trauma. What's more, he retained the ability to speak, think, and remember. But his friends complained that he was "no longer Gage." In a sort of Jekyll and Hyde transformation, Gage changed from a mild-mannered, friendly, efficient worker into a foul-mouthed, ill-tempered, undependable lout who could not hold a steady job or stick to a plan.

Other sorts of damage to the frontal lobes, including tumors and war injuries, suggest that they are involved in planning, goal setting, and intention, or what is commonly called "will." They govern the ability to do a series of tasks in the proper order and to stop doing them at the proper time. The pioneering Soviet psychologist A. R. Luria (1980) studied many cases in which damage to the frontal lobes disrupted these abilities. One man observed by Luria kept trying to light a match after it was already lit. Another planed a piece of wood in the hospital carpentry shop until it was gone, and then went on to plane the workbench.

Scientists are now starting to map the circuitry of the frontal lobes. Their subjects are brain-injured patients and monkeys. Their tools are the sophisticated techniques discussed earlier—microelectrodes, injections of radioactive substances, and brain scans. These researchers hope to link specific areas of the frontal lobes with specific mental abilities.

QUICK QUIZ

Match each of the descriptions on the left with one of the terms on the right.

1. Filters out irrelevant information	a. reticular activating system
2. Known as the "gateway to memory"	b. cerebrum
3. Controls the autonomic nervous system; involved in drives associated with survival	c. hippocampus
4. Consists of two hemispheres	d. cerebral cortex
5. Wrinkled outer covering of the brain	e. frontal lobes
6. Site of the motor cortex; associated with planning, thinking creatively, taking initiative	f. hypothalamus

ANSWERS:

1. a 2. c 3. f 4. b 5. d 6. e

Phineas Gage's skull and a cast of his head, on display at the Harvard Medical School, show the extent of the injury that so dramatically altered his behavior and personality. You can see where the tamping iron penetrated the skull.

■ THE TWO HEMISPHERES OF THE BRAIN

We have seen that the cerebrum is divided into two hemispheres that control opposite sides of the body. Although similar in structure, the hemispheres have somewhat separate talents, or areas of specialization. This raises an interesting question: Should the hemispheres be considered equal partners in human functioning, or is one like a senior partner and the other only a junior partner?

Two Minds in One Skull: Split Brains

In a normal brain, the two hemispheres communicate with one another across the corpus callosum, the bundle of fibers that connects them. Whatever happens in one side of the brain is instantly flashed to the other.

What would happen, though, if the communication lines were cut? An early clue occurred in a case study published in 1908. A mentally disturbed woman repeatedly tried to choke herself with her left hand. She would try with her right hand to pull the left hand away from her throat, but she claimed that the left hand was beyond her control. She also did other destructive things, like throwing pillows around and tearing her sheets, but only with her left hand. A neurologist suspected that the woman's corpus callosum had been damaged so that the two sides of the brain could no longer communicate. When the woman died, an autopsy showed that he was right (Geschwind, in J. Miller, 1983).

This case suggests that the two sides of the brain can experience different emotions. What would happen if they were completely out of touch? Would they think different thoughts and store different memories? In 1953, Ronald E. Myers and Roger W. Sperry took the first step toward answering this question by severing the corpus callosum in cats. They also cut parts of the nerves leading from the eyes to the brain. Normally, each eye transmits messages to both sides of the brain. After this procedure, a cat's left eye sent information only to the left hemisphere and its right eye only to the right hemisphere.

At first the cats did not seem to be affected much by this drastic operation. But Myers and Sperry showed that something profound had happened. They trained the cats to perform various tasks with one eye blindfolded. For example, a cat might have to push a panel with a square on it to get food but ignore a panel with a circle. After the task was learned, the researchers switched the blindfold to the cat's other eye and tested the animal again. Now the cats behaved as if they had never learned the trick. Apparently, one side of the brain didn't know what the other side was doing. It was as if the animals had two minds in one body. Later studies confirmed this result with other species, including monkeys (Sperry, 1964).

In all the animal studies, ordinary behavior, such as eating and walking, remained normal. Encouraged by this finding, a team of surgeons led by Joseph Bogen decided in the early 1960s to try cutting the corpus callosum in patients with debilitating, uncontrollable epilepsy. In some forms of epilepsy, disorganized electrical activity spreads from an injured area to other parts of the brain.

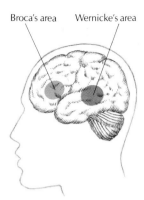

Broca's area   Wernicke's area

The surgeons reasoned that in such cases cutting the connection between the two halves of the brain might stop the spread of electrical activity from one side to the other. As in H. M.'s case, the operation was a last resort.

The results generally proved quite successful. Seizures were reduced and sometimes disappeared completely. As an added bonus, these patients gave psychologists a chance to find out what each half of the brain can do when it is quite literally cut off from the other. It was already known that the two hemispheres are not mirror images of one another. In most people, language is largely handled by the left hemisphere: speech production in an area of the left frontal lobe known as *Broca's area*, meaning and language comprehension in an area of the left temporal lobe known as *Wernicke's area*. Therefore, a person who suffers brain damage because of a stroke (a blockage in or rupture of a blood vessel in the brain) is much more likely to have language problems if the damage is in the left side than if it is in the right. How would splitting the brain affect language and other abilities?

In their daily lives, "split-brain" patients did not seem much affected by the fact that the two sides of their brains were incommunicado. Their personalities and general intelligence remained intact; they could walk, talk, and in general lead normal lives. Apparently connections in the undivided brain stem kept body movements normal. But in a series of ingenious studies, Sperry and his colleagues (and later other researchers as well) showed that perception and memory had been profoundly affected, just as they were in earlier animal research. In 1981, Sperry received a Nobel Prize for this work.

To understand this research, you must know a little more about how nerves connect the eyes to the brain. (The human patients, unlike Myers and Sperry's cats, did not have these nerves cut.) If you look straight ahead, everything in the left side of the scene before you—the "visual field"—goes to the right half of your brain, and vice versa. This is true for *both* eyes (see Figure 3.12).

The basic procedure was to present information only to one or the other side of the subjects' brains. In one early study (Levy, Trevarthen, & Sperry, 1972),

FIGURE 3.12 _____

Visual pathways
Each hemisphere of the brain receives information about the opposite side of the visual field. For example, if you stare directly at the corner of a room, everything to the left of the juncture is represented in your right cerebral hemisphere and everything to the right is represented in your left cerebral hemisphere. This is so because half the axons in each optic nerve cross over (at the optic chiasma) to the opposite side of the brain. Normally, each hemisphere immediately shares its information with the other one. However, in split-brain patients, severing of the corpus callosum prevents such communication from occurring.

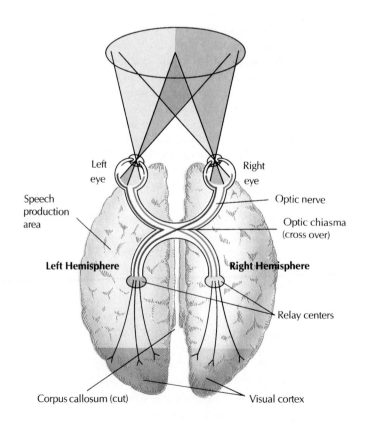

Left eye
Right eye
Speech production area
Optic nerve
Optic chiasma (cross over)
Left Hemisphere
Right Hemisphere
Relay centers
Corpus callosum (cut)
Visual cortex

the researchers took photographs of different faces, cut them in two, and pasted different halves together (see Figure 3.13). The reconstructed photographs were then presented on slides. The person was told to stare at a dot on the middle of the screen, so that half the image fell to the left of this point and half to the right. Each image was flashed so quickly that there was no time for the person to move his or her eyes. When the subjects were asked to say what they had seen, they named the person in the right part of the image. But when they were asked to *point* with their left hands to the face they had seen, they chose the person in the left side of the image. Further, they claimed they had noticed nothing unusual about the original photograph! Each side of the brain saw a different half-image and automatically filled in the missing part. Neither side knew what the other side had seen.

Why did the patients name one side of the picture but point to the other? Speech centers are in the left hemisphere. When the person responded with speech, it was the left side of the brain talking. When the person pointed with the left hand, which is controlled by the right side of the brain, the right brain was giving *its* version of what the person had seen.

In another study, the researchers presented slides of ordinary objects, and then suddenly flashed a slide of a nude woman. Both sides of the brain were amused, but because only the left side has speech, the two sides responded a bit differently. When the picture was flashed to her left hemisphere, one woman laughed and identified the picture as a nude. When it was flashed to her right hemisphere, she said nothing but began to chuckle. Asked what she was laughing at, she said, "I don't know . . . nothing . . . oh—that funny machine." The right hemisphere could not describe what it had seen, but it reacted emotionally, just the same (Gazzaniga, 1967).

FIGURE 3.13

Divided brain, divided view
Split-brain patients were shown composite photographs, then asked to pick out the face they had seen from a series of intact photographs. These patients said they had seen the face on the right side of the composite, yet they pointed with their left hands to the face that had been on the left. Because the two hemispheres of the brain could not communicate, the verbal left hemisphere was aware of only the right half of the picture and the relatively mute right hemisphere was aware of only the left half.

A Question of Dominance

Some popular self-improvement programs promise to sharpen up your logical "left brain" and liberate your artistic "right brain." Why do so many people get carried away with the right brain/left brain dichotomy? Does the evidence support their enthusiasm—and their programs?

Since the initial split-brain studies, many others have been carried out. (Several dozen people have undergone the split-brain operation during the past three decades.) Research on left-right differences has also been done with people whose brains are intact. Electrodes and measurements of blood flow have been used to gauge activity in the left and right sides of the brain while people perform different tasks. The results confirm that nearly all right-handed people and a majority of left-handers process language mainly in the left hemisphere. The left side also seems superior to the right in various kinds of logical, symbolic, and sequential tasks, such as solving math problems and understanding technical material. Because of these cognitive abilities, many researchers refer to the left hemisphere as *dominant*. They believe that the left side usually exerts control over the "minor" right hemisphere. One well-known split-brain researcher, Michael Gazzaniga (1983), has argued that without help from the left side, the right side's mental skills would probably be "vastly inferior to the cognitive skills of a chimpanzee." He also believes that the left hemisphere is constantly trying to explain actions and emotions generated by brain parts whose workings are nonverbal and outside of awareness.

You can see in split-brain patients how the left brain concocts such explanations. In one classic example, a picture of a chicken claw was flashed to a patient's left hemisphere, a picture of a snow scene to his right. The task was to point to a related image for each picture from an array, with a chicken the correct choice for the claw and a shovel for the snow scene. The patient chose the shovel with his left hand and the chicken with his right. When asked to explain why, he responded (with his left hemisphere) that the chicken claw went with the chicken, and the shovel was for cleaning out the chicken shed. The left brain had seen the left hand's response but did not know about the snow scene, so it interpreted the response by using the information it did have (Gazzaniga, 1988). In people with intact brains, says Gazzaniga, the left brain's interpretations account for the sense of a unified, coherent identity. (For more on the brain and self-awareness, see "Think About It.")

Other researchers, including Sperry (1982), have rushed to the right hemisphere's defense. The right side, they point out, is no dummy. It is superior in problems requiring visual-spatial ability, the ability you use to read a map or follow a dress pattern, and it excels in facial recognition. (The unfortunate Dr. P., at the beginning of this chapter, had damage in the right hemisphere.) It is involved in creating and appreciating art and music. It recognizes nonverbal

"It's finally happening, Helen. The hemispheres of my brain are drifting apart."

(Drawing by Lorenz; © 1980 The New Yorker Magazine, Inc.)

THINK ABOUT IT

Where Is Your "Self"?

When you say, "I am feeling unhappy," who is the "I" doing the feeling? When you say, "I've decided to have a hot dog instead of a hamburger," who is the "I" doing the choosing? When you say, "My mind is playing tricks on me," who is the "me" watching your mind play those tricks, and who is being tricked? Brainteasers like these have been baffling philosophers for thousands of years. How can the self observe itself? Isn't that a little like a finger pointing at its own tip?

The ancient Egyptians reportedly believed that the "self" controlling actions and thoughts was a little man, a *homunculus,* residing in the head. Descartes, as we saw in Chapter 1, thought the soul made contact with the body in the brain's pineal gland. Western religions resolved the problem by teaching that there is an immortal self or soul that exists entirely apart from the mortal brain. But most modern brain scientists (with a few notable exceptions) consider mind to be a matter of matter. Although they may have personal religious convictions about a soul, most assume that "mind" or "self-awareness" can be explained in physical terms as a product of the cerebral cortex; there is no "ghost in the machine." What is not clear, however, is why damage to the cortex, or even removal of an entire hemisphere, usually leaves a person's sense of self intact.

Some scientists suggest that the sense of self is merely a reflection, a kind of byproduct, of some sort of overall control mechanism in the brain. But neurologist Richard Restak (1983) notes that many of our actions and choices seem to occur without direction by a conscious self: "There is not a center in the brain involved in the exercise of will any more than there is a center in the brain of the swan responsible for the beauty and complexity of its flight. Rather, the brains of all creatures are probably organized along the lines of multiple centers and various levels." Similarly, brain researcher Michael Gazzaniga (1985) suggests that the brain is organized as a loose confederation of independent "modules," or mental systems, all working in parallel. The sense of a unified self or consciousness is an illusion; it occurs because the one verbal module, an "interpreter" (usually in the left hemisphere), is constantly constructing a theory to explain the actions, moods, and thoughts of the others.

Curiously, such views come close to those of Eastern spiritual traditions. Buddhism, for example, teaches that the "self" is not a unified "thing" but a collection of thoughts, perceptions, concepts, and feelings that change from moment to moment. The unity and permanence of the self are considered a mirage. Such notions are contrary to what most of us in the West, including psychologists, have always assumed about our "selves."

What do you think about the existence and location of your "self"? And who, by the way, is doing the thinking?

---

sounds, such as a dog's barking. The right brain also seems to have some language ability. Typically it can read a word briefly flashed to it and can understand an experimenter's instructions. In a few split-brain patients, language ability has been quite well developed. Research with other brain-damaged people finds that the right brain actually outperforms the left at understanding familiar idioms and metaphors (such as "turning over a new leaf") (Van Lancker & Kempler, 1987).

Some brain researchers have also credited the right hemisphere with having a unique cognitive style, one that is holistic (sees things as wholes) and intuitive, in contrast to the left hemisphere's more rational and analytic mode. Neuropsychologist Jerre Levy (1983) concludes that the right hemisphere is active, responsive, and highly intelligent. "Could the eons of human evolution have left half of the brain witless?" she asks. "Could a bird whose existence is dependent on flying have evolved only a single wing?"

However, many researchers are concerned about popular interpretations of such conclusions. Books and programs that promise to "beef up your brain,"

It's easy to exaggerate differences between the left and right brain hemispheres.

they observe, tend to oversimplify and exaggerate hemispheric differences. Most studies find these differences to be relative, not absolute—a matter of degree. Moreover, the "talents" of the two hemispheres do not always divide up as one might expect, and the "intuitive, holistic" right hemisphere is not always a hero. For example, as we will see in Chapter 9, certain regions of the left hemisphere seem to be specialized for the processing of positive emotions, such as happiness, whereas certain regions of the right hemisphere are specialized for negative emotions, such as fear, anger, and depression. Finally, in most real-life activities, the two hemispheres seem to cooperate naturally as partners, with each making a valuable contribution to our effectiveness (Kinsbourne, 1982; J. Levy, 1985). As Sperry (1982) himself has noted, "The left-right dichotomy . . . is an idea with which it is very easy to run wild."

QUICK QUIZ

A. Keeping in mind that both sides of the brain are involved in most activities, see if you can identify which side is *most* closely associated with each of the following:

1. Enjoying a musical recording
2. Wiggling the left big toe
3. Giving a speech in class
4. Balancing a checkbook
5. Recognizing a long-lost friend

B. Over the past two decades, thousands of people have taken courses and bought tapes that promise to turn them into right-brained types. What characteristics of human thought might explain the eagerness of some people to glorify "right-brainedness" and disparage "left-brainedness" (or vice versa)?

ANSWERS:

A. 1, 2, and 5 are most closely associated with the right side; 3 and 4 with the left. B. One possible answer: Human beings like to make sense of the world, and one easy way to do that is to divide humanity into opposing categories, such as right-brained versus left-brained types. This sort of dualistic, either-or thinking can lead to the conclusion that "fixing up" one of the categories (e.g., left-brained types) will make individuals happier and the world a better place. (If only it were that simple!)

■ TWO STUBBORN ISSUES IN BRAIN RESEARCH

If you have mastered the definitions and descriptions in this chapter, you are prepared to read popular accounts of advances in neuropsychology intelligently. You will soon find that many mysteries remain about how the brain works in memory, thought, and emotion. We end this chapter with two of them.

How Specialized Are Separate Brain Parts?

One of the most persistent questions in brain research has been this: Where are specific memories, habits, perceptions, and abilities stored? Most theories assume that different brain parts perform different jobs and store different sorts of information. This concept, known as **localization of function,** goes back at least to Joseph Gall (1758–1828), an Austrian anatomist who thought personality and character traits were reflected in the development of different areas of the brain (see Figure 2.1 on page 44). Objective research eventually showed that Gall's theory of *phrenology* was completely wrong-headed (so to speak) but that his basic notion of specialization had merit. Particular functions, such as visual processing, language production, and the generation of mental images, were traced to specific brain areas; the motor cortex and the various centers of sensation were located; and split-brain studies showed that the two cerebral hemispheres have somewhat different talents.

In addition, clinical research has shown that brain damage can have extremely specific effects, depending on exactly where the damage is. In one recent study, two female stroke patients both had problems with verbs! One woman could read or speak verbs but had trouble writing them; the other could only do the reverse. The first woman had no trouble writing down the word *crack* after hearing the sentence "There's a crack in the mirror" (in which *crack* is a noun), but she could not write the word after hearing "Don't crack the nuts in here" (in which *crack* is a verb). The other woman could write *crack* as both a noun and a verb, but couldn't speak it as a verb (Caramazza & Hillis, 1991). In another study (Cubelli, 1991), two brain-damaged patients were unable to correctly write down the vowels in words, but had no trouble writing the consonants! Researchers have also studied patients who can recognize manufactured items, such as photographs, tools, or books, but not natural objects, or who can recognize most natural objects but cannot distinguish among animals, or fruits, or vegetables (Damasio, 1990).

Because of such findings, localization remains the guiding principle of modern brain theories. However, there is another, minority view. It holds that perceived, learned, or remembered information is *distributed* across large areas of the brain, perhaps even the entire cortex. One of the first to make this argument was Karl Lashley, who many years ago set out to find where specific memories were stored in the rat's brain. His search turned out to be as frustrating as looking for a grain of sugar in a pile of sand. Lashley trained rats to run a complicated maze in order to find food, then destroyed a part of each rat's cortex. Destroying any section of the cortex led to some loss of the behavior, but the size of the area damaged was more important than where the damage was located, and even when Lashley removed over 90 percent of a rat's visual cortex, the animal could still find its way through the maze. After a quarter of a century, Lashley (1950) finally gave up searching for specific memory traces. He jokingly remarked that perhaps "learning just is not possible." More seriously, he concluded that every part of the cortex must somehow influence every other part.

How might the brain function as an integrated whole? According to theorist E. Roy John (1976; John et al., 1986), when we learn that Columbus discovered America or remember that 6 times 8 equals 48, it is not because certain

Is a piece of information stored in one specific spot or distributed throughout the brain? Researchers have generally assumed that only one answer can be true. Could both be true?

■ **localization of function**
Specialization of particular brain areas for particular functions.

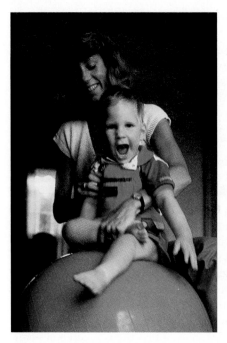 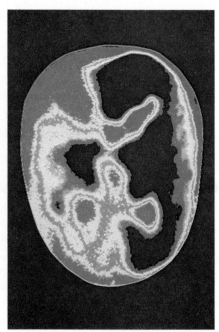

The child on the left, Ryan, suffered from continual, life-threatening seizures that could not be controlled by medication. When he was 15 months old, a PET scan (right) showed that much of his left hemisphere was diseased and not functioning properly, and surgeons removed the affected areas. The seizures diminished and Ryan's development improved dramatically. Cases like these demonstrate the remarkable plasticity of the human brain.

cells fire or because a particular connection among cells is formed. What matters is the *average pattern* of cell activity throughout the brain. This pattern, John believes, has a particular rhythm. The billions of cells in the brain are like the members of a gigantic orchestra. Each instrument is making noise in a more or less random way, as when an orchestra is tuning up. When a particular thought or memory occurs, most of the instruments in one section start to play a tune that has a definite rhythm. However, some instruments in other sections do so as well.

Another holistic approach compares brain processes to holography (Pribram, 1971, 1982). Holography is a system of photography in which a three-dimensional image is reproduced by means of light-wave patterns that are recorded on a photographic plate or film (the hologram). Information about any point in the image is distributed throughout the hologram. Thus any given area of the hologram contains the information necessary for producing the entire image. Similarly, some forms of knowledge may be dispersed throughout the brain, just as Karl Lashley thought.

Holistic theories have the virtue of being able to explain the remarkable flexibility of the brain (psychologists call it *plasticity*). Sometimes people who cannot recall simple words after a stroke regain normal speech within a matter of months. Similarly, people who cannot move an arm after a head injury may regain use of it after therapy. A few individuals have even survived and functioned well in their lives after a drastic surgical procedure, the removal of an entire cerebral hemisphere. Perhaps patients who have recovered from brain damage have learned to use entirely new strategies to accomplish the mental and physical tasks in question. Another possibility, however, is that the brain is, indeed, like a giant orchestra, and the players know one another's music. If one violinist can't make it to the performance, another violinist or perhaps a cellist may be able to fill in.

Well, then, is information in the brain localized or distributed? The best way out of this dilemma may be to recognize that both answers can be true. Neuropsychologist Larry Squire (1986, 1987) observes that any particular perception, habit, or memory includes many bits and pieces of information, often gathered from more than one sense: sounds, images, locations, facts. Specific collections of neurons in the brain may handle specific pieces of information, and many such collections, distributed across wide areas of the brain, may participate in representing an entire event. This view reconciles apparently opposite positions: The parts of the event are localized but the whole is distributed. However, we still are a long way from knowing how the many aspects of a memory or ability finally link together to form a whole. Nor do we understand yet why some people recover from damage to the brain while others, with similar damage, are permanently disabled.

Are There "His" and "Hers" Brains?

A second stubborn controversy concerns the existence of sex differences in the brain. Efforts to distinguish male from female brains have a long and not always glorious history in psychology. During the nineteenth century, "findings" on male–female brain differences often flip-flopped in a most suspicious manner (Shields, 1975). At first, scientists doing dissection studies reported that women's frontal lobes were smaller than men's, and that their parietal lobes were larger. This presumably explained women's intellectual shortcomings. Then, around the turn of the century, people began (mistakenly) to attribute intellect to the parietal lobes rather than the frontal lobes. Suddenly there were reports that women had *smaller* parietal lobes and larger frontal lobes. You probably won't be surprised to learn that these researchers often knew the sex of the brains they were dissecting.

Since the 1960s, newer theories about male–female brain differences have come and gone just as quickly. A few years ago there was speculation that women were more "right-brained" and men were more "left-brained." It soon became clear, however, that the abilities popularly (and often incorrectly) associated with the two sexes did not fall neatly into one or the other side of the brain. The left side was more verbal (presumably "female"), but it was also more mathematical (presumably "male"). The right side was more intuitive ("female"), but it was also more spatially talented ("male").

Perhaps no topic in brain research is as subject to muddy thinking and unwarranted conclusions as sex differences in the brain. Does the evidence warrant significant conclusions about real-life behavior?

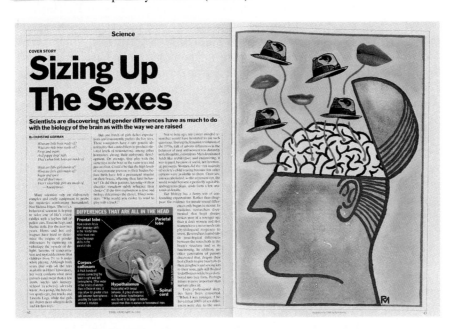

Popular magazines have been quick to run stories on purported differences in the brains of males and females. Often these articles (such as this one from Time*) conclude, from interesting but still tentative findings, that gender differences in behavior must be biologically based. Is this conclusion justified? What kind of evidence is necessary to establish a link between an observed brain difference and an observed behavioral difference? And why do studies of gender differences make the covers of national magazines when studies that find gender similarities do not?*

To evaluate the issue of sex differences in the brain, we need to ask two separate questions: Do physical differences actually exist in male and female brains? And if differences do exist, what do they have to do with behavior?

Let's consider the first question. A number of anatomical sex differences have been observed in studies of animal brains, especially in areas related to reproduction. In rats, for example, hormone differences before birth result in nerve cell clusters in the hypothalamus that differ in size in males and females. There are also sex differences in the levels of various neurotransmitters in rats' brains (McEwen, 1983). And in male rats, the right half of the cerebral cortex is thicker than the left in most areas, while in females the opposite tends to be true, though most of the left-right differences are not statistically significant (Diamond et al., 1983).

Human sex differences, however, have been more elusive. Of course, we would expect to find male–female brain differences that are related to the regulation of sex hormones and other aspects of reproduction. However, most recent work has focused on how brain differences might produce differences in the way that men and women think—and here, the picture is much murkier. A few years ago, for example, two anthropologists autopsied 14 human brains and reported that one section of the corpus callosum was larger in females than in males (de Lacoste-Utamsing & Holloway, 1982). (The corpus callosum, you will recall, connects the two cerebral hemispheres.) Many writers concluded that in women, the two hemispheres must communicate more efficiently. Men's brains, they decided, are more **lateralized;** that is, men rely more heavily on one or the other side of the brain when performing particular tasks, whereas women are more likely to use both sides. More recent studies, however, using magnetic resonance imaging to study *living* brains, get conflicting results. Some researchers find sex differences (Allen et al., 1987), but others don't (Bleier, 1988; Bleier, Houston, & Byne, 1986).

Some researchers have tried to study male–female brain differences indirectly, by observing what happens to men and women after a stroke (Inglis & Lawson, 1981; McGlone, 1978). One finding is that left-hemisphere damage is more likely to cause language problems in men than in women. Some people think this means, again, that men's brains are more lateralized, and that women are more likely to use both hemispheres to process language. But others draw a different conclusion: that a smaller left-hemisphere area controls language in women, so damage is more likely to miss this area in women and leave language abilities intact (Kimura & Harshman, 1984).

In sum, sex differences in the human brain, which have made headlines in recent years, are controversial. Also, when differences are reported, they tend to be smaller than in animals. This brings us to the second question: If reliable physiological differences do exist, what do they mean? Speculations are as plentiful as ants at a picnic, but the fact is that no one really knows the answer to this question. To have an answer, we would need to know how brain organization and chemistry affect human abilities and traits in general, and we don't.

Those who believe that brain differences can explain psychological differences often take the psychological differences for granted, relying on popular stereotypes or obsolete findings rather than recent evidence. As a result, they fail to realize that some of the differences they wish to explain no longer exist! For example, several brain researchers have suggested that brain differences might account for male–female differences in verbal ability. But as we saw in Chapter 2, verbal differences (which used to favor women) seem to have nearly disappeared (Feingold, 1988; Hyde & Linn, 1988). Other differences, most notably mathematical and spatial-visual ones, have been exaggerated. Men do outperform women in math, but typically in only selected (e.g., gifted) samples, not in the general population (Hyde, Fennema, & Lamon, 1990). And men excel on the average in only one type of spatial ability, the ability to rotate ob-

■ **lateralization**
Specialization of the two cerebral hemispheres for particular psychological operations.

jects mentally; on other measures, the sexes perform equally (Linn & Petersen, 1985).

It can be tempting to reach for biological explanations for complex behaviors. But when thinking about sex differences in the brain, or about any of the findings discussed in this chapter, two important points need to be kept firmly in mind.

First, brain organization—the proportion of brain cells found in any particular part of the brain—varies considerably from person to person. Therefore, any sweeping generalizations about the brain, whether they are about the left and right hemispheres, localization of function, or sex differences, are bound to be oversimplifications. As Roger Sperry (1982) notes, "The more we learn . . . the stronger the conclusion becomes that the individuality inherent in our brain networks makes that of fingerprints or facial features gross and simple by comparison."

Second, different experiences and environments may affect the way brains are organized to do various jobs. A cross-cultural example may make this point clear. The brains of the Japanese may not be lateralized in the same way as the brains of Westerners (including Americans of Japanese descent). There is some evidence that the Japanese process nonverbal human and animal sounds and Japanese instrumental music in the left hemisphere rather than the right, where we would expect them to be processed on the basis of split-brain studies. One possible explanation (a speculation, far from proven) is that because the Japanese language is rich in vowel sounds, and therefore has a musical quality, the left hemisphere learns to process nonverbal sounds (Sibatani, 1980; Tsunoda, 1985). Similarly, different experiences could conceivably result in some differences yet to be identified in men's and women's brains.

As we have seen in this chapter, the more we know about our physical selves, the better we understand our psychological selves. Yet biological research does not always answer behavioral questions. Physiological findings are most illuminating when they are integrated with what we know about personal perception and cultural experience. Analyzing a human being in terms of physiology alone is like analyzing the Taj Mahal solely in terms of the materials used to build it.

TAKING PSYCHOLOGY WITH YOU

Food For Thought: Diet and Neurotransmitters

"Vitamin improves sex!"

"Mineral boosts brainpower!"

"Chocolate chases the blues!"

Claims like these have long given nutritional theories of behavior a bad reputation. In the late 1960s, when Nobel laureate Linus Pauling proposed that some mental illnesses might result from an unusual need for massive doses of particular vitamins, few serious researchers listened. Mainstream medical authorities classed Pauling's "orthomolecular psychiatry" with such infamous cure-alls as snake oil and leeches.

Today most mental health professionals remain skeptical of unorthodox nutritional treatments for mental illness. But they may have to eat at least some of their words, as respect grows for the role that various nutrients might play in mood and performance. The underlying premise of these treatments, that diet affects the brain and therefore behavior, is getting a second look. Well-publicized claims that sugar or common food additives lead to undesirable behavior in otherwise normal people remain controversial. However, in some cases of disturbance, diet may make a difference. In one recent double-blind study, researchers asked depressed patients to abstain from refined sugar and caffeine. Over a three-month period, these patients showed significantly more improvement in their symptoms than did control patients who refrained from red meat and artificial sweeteners (Christensen & Burrows, 1990).

Some of the most exciting work on diet and behavior has looked at the role played by nutrients in the synthesis of neurotransmitters, the brain's chemical messengers. Certain nutrients serve as precursors, or building blocks, for particular neurotransmitters. Tryptophan, an amino acid found in protein-rich foods (dairy products, meat, fish, and poultry), is a precursor of the neurotransmitter serotonin. Tyrosine, another amino acid found in proteins, is a precursor of norepinephrine, epinephrine, and dopamine. Choline, a component of the lecithin found in egg yolks, soy products, and liver, is a precursor of acetylcholine.

In the case of tryptophan, the path between the dinner plate and the brain is an indirect one. Tryptophan leads to the production of serotonin, which appears to reduce alertness, promote relaxation, and hasten sleep. Since tryptophan is found in protein, you might think that a high-protein meal would make you drowsy, and carbohydrates (sweets, bread, pasta, potatoes) would leave you relatively alert. Actually, the opposite is true. High-protein foods contain several amino acids, not just tryptophan, and they all compete for a ride on carrier molecules headed for brain cells. Because tryptophan occurs in foods in small quantities, it doesn't stand much of a chance *if* all you eat is protein. It is in the position of a tiny child trying to push aside a crowd of adults for a seat on the subway. Carbohydrates, however, stimulate the production of insulin, and insulin causes all the other amino acids to be drawn out of the bloodstream while having little effect on tryptophan. So carbohydrates increase the odds of tryptophan making it to the brain (Wurtman, 1982).

Paradoxically, then, a high-carbohydrate, no-protein meal should make you relatively calm or lethargic and a high-protein one should promote alertness. Studies with human beings support this conclusion (Spring, Chiodo, & Bowen, 1987; Wurtman & Lieberman, 1982–83). It follows that if you have a 10:00 A.M. class, you might do better to include some meat or eggs in your breakfast than to eat only a sweet roll or sugared cereal. On the other hand, if you want a slumber-promoting snack at bedtime, a drink high in carbohydrates, like fruit juice, might be helpful.

Keep in mind, though, that research in this area is just beginning. Studies with human beings have shown links between diet and behavior, but they have not conclusively pinned down the neurochemistry. Individuals differ in how they respond to different nutrients. Also, the effects are subtle (many other factors also influence mood and behavior), and some of them depend on the age of the subjects and the time of day a meal is eaten. Alan Gelenberg, a psychiatrist who has studied tyrosine, has noted that health food publications tend to exaggerate his findings. "Then some health food stores stock something they call tyrosine—who knows what's in it—and people are writing from all over wanting to know how much they should take" (quoted in Weisburd, 1984). The dangers of dietary fadism became clear in the late 1980s, when several thousand users of tryptophan became severely ill with a rare blood and connective-tissue disorder, and some people died. One study suggested that some people may have had trouble metabolizing the substance (Clauw et al., 1990).

Clearly, nutrients can and do affect the brain and behavior. But these nutrients interact in complex ways. If you don't eat protein, you won't get enough tryptophan, but if you go without carbohydrates, the tryptophan found in protein will be useless. The moral of the story is that if you're looking for brain food, you are most likely to find it in a well-balanced diet.

SUMMARY

1. The nervous system is the bedrock of behavior. For purposes of description, it is divided into the *central nervous system* (CNS) and *peripheral nervous system* (PNS). The CNS, which includes the brain and spinal cord, processes, interprets, and stores information and issues orders destined for muscles, glands, and organs. The PNS transmits information to and from the CNS by way of sensory and motor nerves.

2. The peripheral nervous system is made up of the *somatic nervous system*, which controls voluntary actions, and the *autonomic nervous system*, which regulates blood vessels, internal organs, and various glands. The autonomic system usually functions without conscious control. Some people can learn to control their autonomic responses to some degree, using *biofeedback* techniques, but it is not clear whether this control is direct or indirect.

3. The autonomic nervous system is divided into the *sympathetic nervous system*, which mobilizes the body for action, and the *parasympathetic nervous system*, which conserves energy.

4. *Neurons*, supported by glial cells, are the basic units of the nervous system. Each neuron consists of a *cell body*, *dendrites*, and an *axon*. In the peripheral nervous system, axons (and sometimes dendrites) collect in bundles called *nerves*. It has always been thought that neurons in the human central nervous system could not be induced to regenerate or multiply, but recent research has challenged these assumptions.

5. The site where communication occurs between two neurons is called a *synapse*. When a wave of electrical voltage reaches the end of a transmitting axon, *neurotransmitter* molecules are released into the *synaptic gap*. When these molecules bind to receptor sites on the receiving neuron, the receiving neuron becomes either more or less likely to fire. The message that reaches a final destination depends on how frequently particular neurons are firing, how many are firing, what types are firing, and where they are located.

6. Neurotransmitters play a critical role in mood, memory, and psychological well-being. Abnormal levels of particular neurotransmitters have been implicated in Parkinson's disease, Alzheimer's disease, childhood autism, and other disorders. However, it is difficult to establish a cause-and-effect relationship between a particular neurotransmitter problem and a particular behavioral disorder.

7. *Endorphins*, which are neuromodulators that affect the action of neurotransmitters, resemble opiates in both structure and function. Like opiates, they reduce pain and promote pleasure. As we saw in "A Closer Look at Neuropsychology," endorphins may be linked to the pleasures of social contact.

8. *Hormone* levels affect, and are affected by, the nervous system. Insulin, melatonin, adrenal hormones, and sex hormones have been of special interest to psychologists. Some substances seem to act as both neurotransmitters and hormones.

9. Researchers study the brain by observing brain-damaged patients, operating on the brains of animals, and using such techniques as electroencephalograms (EEGs), PET scans, and magnetic resonance imaging (MRI).

10. In the *hindbrain*, the *brain stem* controls automatic functions such as heartbeat and breathing. The *reticular activating system* screens incoming information and is responsible for alertness. The *cerebellum* contributes to balance and muscle coordination.

11. In the *forebrain*, the *thalamus* directs sensory messages to appropriate centers. The *hypothalamus* is involved in emotion and in drives associated with survival and controls the autonomic nervous system through messages sent to the *pituitary gland*. The *limbic system* is involved in emotions that we share with other animals and contains pathways involved in pleasure. One limbic structure, the *hippocampus*, plays a critical role in storage of long-term memories.

12. The *cerebrum*, the upper part of the forebrain, consists of two hemispheres. Because the *cerebral cortex*, or outer covering of the cerebrum, is convoluted, it can contain billions of neurons without requiring the brain to be too big for the skull. The occipital, parietal, temporal, and frontal lobes of the cortex have specialized (but partially overlapping) functions. The *association cortex* appears to be responsible for higher mental processes.

13. Split-brain studies of patients who have had the *corpus callosum* cut show that the two cerebral hemispheres have somewhat different "talents." In most people, language is processed mainly in the left hemisphere, which generally appears to be specialized for logical, sequential tasks. The right hemisphere appears to be specialized for visual-spatial tasks, facial recognition, and appreciation of art and music. However, in most mental activities, the two hemispheres cooperate as partners, with each making a valuable contribution.

14. Most brain theories emphasize that different brain parts perform different jobs and store different sorts of information, a concept known as *localization of function*. Some researchers, however, argue that perceived, learned, or remembered information is *distributed* across large areas of the brain and that the brain functions as an integrated whole. Both views may have merit: Specific locations in the brain may handle specific pieces of information, and many such collections, distributed across wide areas of the brain, may participate in representing an entire event, perception, or skill.

15. Sex differences have been observed in anatomical studies of animal brains. Sex differences in human brains, however, have been more elusive, and there is controversy about their existence and their meaning. It is unclear how reported brain differences are related to sex differences in human behavior. Several proposals fail to take into account that various sex differences in ability have been decreasing or even disappearing.

16. Individual brains vary considerably in their organization, and different experiences and environments may affect brain development. These points should be kept in mind when interpreting brain findings. Such findings are most illuminating when they are integrated with psychological and cultural ones.

KEY TERMS

neuropsychology 75
neuroscience 75
central nervous system 76
peripheral nervous system 76
spinal cord 76
reflex 76
sensory nerves 77
motor nerves 77
somatic nervous system 77
autonomic nervous system 77
biofeedback 77
sympathetic nervous system 78
parasympathetic nervous system 78
neuron 79
glial cells 79
cell body 81
dendrites 81
axon 81
axon terminals 81
nerve 81
myelin sheath 81
synaptic gap 82
synapse 82
synaptic knob 83
synaptic vesicles 83
neurotransmitter 83
excitatory and inhibitory effects 83
endorphins 85
neuromodulators 85
hormones 87
endocrine glands 87
neuroendocrine system 87

sex hormones 88
insulin 88
melatonin 88
adrenal glands 88
adrenal cortex and medulla 88
cortisol 88
epinephrine 88
norepinephrine 88
sex hormones 88
electrodes 89
electroencephalogram (EEG) 90
evoked potentials 90
PET scan 90
magnetic resonance imaging (MRI) 91
hindbrain 91
midbrain 91
forebrain 91
brain stem 92
medulla 92
pons 92
reticular activating system (RAS) 92
cerebellum 92
cerebrum 93
cerebral hemispheres 93
corpus callosum 93
thalamus 93
hypothalamus 93
pituitary gland 93
limbic system 93
hippocampus 93

4

Body Rhythms and Mental States

Like a bird's life, [consciousness] seems to be made of an alternation of flights and perchings.

WILLIAM JAMES

In Lewis Carroll's immortal story *Alice in Wonderland*, the ordinary assumptions of everyday life keep dissolving in a sea of logical contradictions. First Alice shrinks to within only a few inches of the ground, then she shoots up taller than the treetops. The crazy antics of the inhabitants of Wonderland make her smile one moment and shed a pool of tears the next. "Dear dear!" muses the harried heroine. "How queer everything is today! And yesterday things went on just as usual. I wonder if I've been changed in the night? Let me think: *was* I the same when I got up this morning? I almost think I can remember feeling a little different. But if I'm not the same, the *next* question is, 'Who in the world am I?' Ah, *that's* the great puzzle!"

In a way, we all live in a sort of Wonderland. For a third of our lives we reside in a realm where the ordinary rules of logic and experience are suspended: the dream world of sleep. Throughout the day, mood, alertness, efficiency, and **consciousness** itself (the awareness of oneself and the environment) are in perpetual flux, sometimes shifting as dramatically as Alice's height.

The techniques and concepts described in the previous chapter are being used to learn more about these fascinating fluctuations. Starting from the assumption that mental and physical states are as intertwined as sunshine and shadow, psychologists, along with other scientists, are exploring links between subjective experience and predictable changes in brain activity, hormone levels, and the action of neurotransmitters. They have come to view changing **states of consciousness** as part of an ebb and flow of experience over time, associated with predictable bodily events. For example, dreaming, traditionally classified as a state of consciousness, is also part of a 90-minute cycle of brain activity. Alternating periods of dreaming and nondreaming during the night occur in a regular pattern, or **biological rhythm.**

Examining subjective experience in terms of ongoing rhythms is a little like watching a motion picture of consciousness. Studying subjective experience in terms of distinct states is more like looking at separate snapshots of consciousness. In this chapter, we will first run the motion picture, to see how functioning and consciousness vary predictably over time. Then we will zoom in on one specific "snapshot," of the world of dreams, and examine it in some detail. Finally, we will turn to some ways in which people try to "retouch the film" by deliberately altering consciousness.

■ BIOLOGICAL RHYTHMS: THE TIDES OF EXPERIENCE

Wouldn't you like to know beforehand when you were about to have a bad day or be in top form? People who sell "biorhythm charts" claim you can. They cite an old theory that 28-day mood cycles, 33-day intellectual cycles, and 23-day physical cycles begin at birth and continue like clockwork throughout life. Half of each cycle is said to be positive and half negative, and the point at which a

■ **consciousness**
The awareness of the environment and of one's own existence, sensations, and thoughts.
■ **states of consciousness**
Distinctive and discrete patterns in the functioning of consciousness, characterized by particular modes of perception, thought, memory, or feeling.
■ **biological rhythm**
A periodic, more or less regular fluctuation in a biological system; may or may not have psychological implications.

cycle changes from positive to negative is said to be "critical"—ripe for errors, accidents, and illness. Proponents of this theory will tell you that Clark Gable, Harry Truman, and other famous people had heart attacks or died on "critical" days. They may also cite "scientific studies" showing that accidents declined after bus drivers or pilots were warned to be particularly careful on critical days.

Purveyors of biorhythm charts would have us believe that various famous people died when they did because their "biorhythms" were in a trough. What facts does this explanation leave out?

Can you spot the weaknesses in this "evidence"? One problem is that the anecdotal accounts ignore *negative* data, all the cases of people who have remained perfectly healthy on critical days or died on noncritical ones. As for the "studies," they failed to include safety warnings to workers who were *not* entering a "critical" period. Without control groups, biorhythm studies merely show that warning people to be careful makes them more careful. Even on the face of it, the biorhythm theory is implausible. Why should such rhythms start at birth, rather than at conception or during fetal development? Besides, we know that the human body is not rigidly regular; illness, fatigue, stress, excitement, exercise, and drugs can all affect how we function.

When people have taken the trouble to test the biorhythm theory scientifically, by examining occupational accidents or the performance of sports stars, they have consistently failed to find any support whatsoever for it (Englund & Naitoh, 1980; Louis, 1978; Wheeler, 1990). Yet biorhythm charts continue to be marketed. Apparently, one human characteristic that does not fluctuate much is gullibility! On the other hand, it *is* true that human beings, unlike robots and computers, do not operate in an unvarying way 24 hours a day, 7 days a week, 52 weeks a year. We've got rhythm. In fact, we experience dozens of periodic, more or less regular ups and downs in physiological functioning. Biological "clocks" in our brains govern the waxing and waning of hormone levels, urine volume, body temperature, blood pressure, and even the responsiveness of brain cells to stimulation. Such physiological fluctuations are what scientists mean by biological rhythms.

Biological rhythms are typically synchronized with external events, such as changes in clock time and daylight. But many rhythms will continue to occur (though perhaps with a somewhat different average length) even in the absence of all external time cues; they are *endogenous*, or generated from within. These rhythms fall into three categories:

1. *Circadian rhythms occur approximately every 24 hours.* The best-known circadian rhythm is the sleep-wake cycle, but there are hundreds of others that affect physiology and performance. For example, body temperature fluctuates about 1 degree Fahrenheit each day, peaking, on average, in the late afternoon and hitting a low point, or trough, in the wee hours of the morning.

■ **circadian [sur-CAY-dee-un] rhythm**
A biological rhythm with a period (from peak to peak or trough to trough) of about 24 hours. From the Latin circa, "about," and dias, "a day."

■ **infradian [in-FRAY-dee-un] rhythm**
A biological rhythm that occurs less frequently than once a day. From the Latin for "below a day."

■ **ultradian [ul-TRAY-dee-un] rhythm**
A biological rhythm that occurs more frequently than once a day. From the Latin for "beyond a day."

2. *Infradian rhythms occur less frequently than once a day.* In the animal world, infradian rhythms are common: birds migrate south in the fall, bears hibernate in the winter, and marine animals become active or inactive depending on bimonthly changes in the tides. In human beings, the female menstrual cycle, which occurs every 28 days on the average and is characterized by changing hormone levels, is an example of an infradian rhythm.

3. *Ultradian rhythms occur more frequently than once a day.* An extraordinary array of physiological changes and behaviors follow a roughly 90-minute schedule when social customs do not intervene. They include stomach contractions, certain hormone levels, appetite for food, oral behavior (smoking, pencil chewing, snacking), susceptibility to visual illusions, performance on verbal and spatial tasks, and alertness (Friedman & Fisher, 1967; Klein & Armitage, 1979; Kripke, 1974; Lavie, 1976). Even daydreaming follows an ultradian rhythm: At the peak of each cycle, thoughts and images are likely to be emotional or even bizarre; at the trough, thoughts are more realistic and concern the here-and-now, personal problems, or future plans (Kripke & Sonnenschein, 1978). However, the most frequently studied ultradian rhythm, as we will see, occurs during sleep.

With better understanding of these internal tempos, we may be able to design our days to take the best advantage of our bodies' natural cycles. Let's look more closely at the forms these cycles may take.

Circadian Rhythms

Circadian rhythms exist in plants, animals, insects, and human beings. They reflect the adaptation of organisms to the many changes associated with the rotation of the earth on its axis, such as changes in light, air pressure, temperature, and wind.

During ordinary living, time cues abound and our bodies adapt to a strict 24-hour schedule. To explore endogenous rhythms, therefore, scientists must isolate volunteers from sunlight, clocks, environmental sounds, and all other cues to time. Artificial light is kept constant, varied by the researcher, or turned on and off by the volunteers when they retire or awaken. Some hardy souls have spent weeks or even months alone in caves and salt mines, linked to the outside world by only a one-way phone line and a cable transmitting physiological measurements to the surface. More often, volunteers live in specially designed bunkers equipped with stereo systems, comfortable furniture, and temperature controls.

In a typical study, a person sleeps, eats, and works whenever he or she wishes, free of the tyranny of the timepiece. Living on a self-imposed schedule in this way is called *free-running*. In the absence of time cues, some people live a "day" that is far shorter or longer than 24 hours, but most people soon settle into a "day" that averages about 25 hours in length. During each successive cycle the person tends to go to sleep a little later and get up a little later (see Figure 4.1). Temperature, blood pressure, and hormone cycles usually follow suit (Aschoff & Wever, 1981; Moore-Ede, Sulzman, & Fuller, 1984).

Researchers originally thought that one biological "clock" or pacemaker in the brain might directly control the dozens of different human circadian rhythms. It now seems that several self-sustaining but interrelated clocks are ticking away in different parts of the brain. These clocks seem to be linked to each other and also to a "super clock," or overall coordinator, located in a tiny

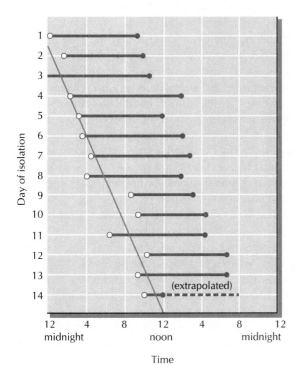

FIGURE 4.1

The days grow longer
This is a chart of sleep periods for a volunteer living in isolation from all time cues. Open circles show when the person went to bed; solid circles show when the person rose. Like most volunteers living in isolation, this individual tended to retire and awaken later and later as the study wore on—in this case, an average of 49 minutes later each day. The pattern is represented by the diagonal red line. (From Webb & Agnew, 1974.)

A morning glory is only "glorious" in the morning. Animals and human beings also have daily physical and behavioral rhythms.

area of the hypothalamus. Normally the various rhythms they govern are synchronized, just as wristwatches can be synchronized. Their peaks may occur at different times, but they occur in phase with one another; if you know when one rhythm peaks, you can predict when another will. This synchrony seems to be choreographed by rising and falling levels of various hormones and neurotransmitters (Moore-Ede & Sulzman, 1981).

One hormone, **melatonin,** which is secreted by the pineal gland deep within the brain, is responsive to changes in light and dark and may keep the "super clock" in phase with the light-dark cycle (Reppert et al., 1988). (Animal studies suggest that information about light and dark reaches the pineal gland via a neural pathway that leads from the eyes through the hypothalamus and on to the pineal gland.) Melatonin treatments were used successfully to synchronize the disturbed sleep-wake cycle of a blind man whose sleep problems apparently stemmed from his inability to sense light and dark (Arendt, Aldhous, & Wright, 1988).

When a person's normal routine changes, circadian rhythms may be thrown out of phase with one another. Such *internal desynchronization* often occurs when people take airplane flights across several time zones. Sleep and wake patterns usually adjust quickly, but temperature and hormone cycles can take several days to return to normal. The resulting "jet lag" affects mental and physical performance. A mini-version of jet lag seems to occur in some people when they have to "spring forward" into daylight savings time, losing an hour from the 24-hour day. They may sleep less well than usual and feel a little out of sorts during the week following the time change. In contrast, "falling back" into standard time, which produces a 25-hour day and time for some extra sleep, does not seem to be a strain (Monk & Aplin, 1980).

Internal desynchronization also occurs when workers must adjust to a new shift. Efficiency drops, the person feels tired and irritable, accidents become more likely, and sleep disturbances and digestive disorders may occur. For people like police officers, emergency room personnel, airline pilots, truck drivers, and nuclear power plant operators, the consequences can be very serious. In 1991, a National Commission on Sleep Disorders noted that lack of alertness in night-shift equipment operators may have contributed to the *Exxon Valdez* oil spill and the accidents at the Three Mile Island and Chernobyl nuclear power plants.

■ **melatonin**
A hormone secreted by the pineal gland; it is involved in the regulation of circadian rhythms.

Travel is often exhausting, and jet lag can make it worse. Because most people, when freed from the clock, have a natural day that is somewhat longer than 24 hours, jet lag tends to be more noticeable and long-lasting after eastbound travel (which shortens the day) than after westbound (which lengthens it).

Night work itself is not always a problem: With a schedule that always stays the same (even on weekends), people may adapt. However, many swing and night-shift assignments are made on a rotating basis, so circadian rhythms never have a chance to resynchronize. Moreover, shift workers often fail to sleep enough during the day. Ideally, a rotating work schedule should follow circadian principles by switching workers as infrequently as possible and by always moving them forward to a later schedule rather than backward to an earlier one. (For example, if you've been working from midnight to 8:00 A.M., your next shift should be 8:00 A.M. to 4:00 P.M.) Recent research also suggests that night workers would be more alert on the job if they could work under very bright lights and then, during the day, sleep in a completely darkened room (Czeisler et al., 1990).

We want to emphasize that circadian rhythms are not perfectly regular and they are easily modified by daily experiences. Hormones rise and fall in a characteristic pattern, but stress can alter the pattern. Exposure to moderate levels of light at critical times can temporarily shut down body temperature and hormone rhythms completely (Jewett, Kronauer, & Czeisler, 1991). Moreover, circadian rhythms differ from individual to individual: Some people are feeling their oats by 10 in the morning; others aren't ready for action until 4 in the afternoon. Research with animals suggests that such differences may be at least partly genetic (Ralph & Menaker, 1988). You may be able to learn about your own personal pulses through careful self-observation.

The Menstrual Cycle and Other Long-term Rhythms

According to Ecclesiastes, "To every thing there is a season, and a time for every purpose under heaven." Modern science agrees: Long-term (infradian) cycles have been observed in everything from the threshold for tooth pain to mortality and conception rates.

In some cases of severe depression, symptoms occur every winter, when periods of daylight are short, and clear up every spring, as daylight increases. This pattern, called "seasonal affective disorder" (SAD), seems to disappear in some people when they spend time each day sitting in front of extremely bright fluorescent lights (N. Rosenthal et al., 1985). Some researchers think the winter doldrums are related to fluctuations in melatonin. Melatonin usually peaks during the night and falls with the approach of day; in many winter depressives, the cycle seems to begin and end later than in other people (Lewy et al., 1987). But it is hard to prove that human long-term cycles are endogenous. The winter blues could also be caused by the mental association of short days with cold weather, inactivity, or even the holidays, which some people find depressing. Similarly, some people report *summer* depression (Wehr, Sack, & Rosenthal, 1987), but this does not necessarily mean depression follows an internally generated biological rhythm. Perhaps summer depressives are simply people who can't take the heat.

One infradian rhythm that clearly *is* endogenous is the menstrual cycle. Several hormones in human females ebb and flow over a period of roughly 28 days, the length of the lunar month. During the first half of the cycle, an increase in estrogen causes the lining of the uterus to thicken in preparation for a possible pregnancy. At midcycle, ovulation occurs and the ovaries release a mature egg, or ovum. After ovulation, the ovarian sac that contained the egg begins to produce progesterone, which helps prepare the uterine lining to receive the egg. Then, if conception does not occur, estrogen and progesterone levels fall, the uterine lining sloughs off as the menstrual flow, and the cycle is ready to begin again.

For psychologists, the interesting question is whether or not emotional or intellectual changes are correlated with the physical ones. Folklore and tradition say that menstruating women are emotionally unstable. Doctors and counselors, who are sometimes influenced more by folklore and tradition than they care to admit, have often agreed.

Recently, a cluster of symptoms associated with the days preceding menstruation—including fatigue, backache, headache, tension, depression, and mood swings—has come to be thought of as an "illness" and has been given a label, "premenstrual syndrome (PMS)." Some popular books refer to "millions" of sufferers or assert that "most" women have "PMS," although there are no statistics to back up such claims. Proposed explanations of the syndrome include progesterone deficiency, estrogen/progesterone imbalance, water retention, high sodium, and a fall in the level of endorphins, the brain's natural opiates. Yet despite more than a decade of biomedical research, there is no consistent support for *any* of these theories. In one recent study, researchers gave "PMS" patients a drug that blocks the hormonal changes characteristic of the premenstrual period; the women still reported symptoms, indicating that hormone changes could not be the cause (Schmidt et al., 1991). Nor is there convincing evidence that any particular "treatment"—including progesterone, the most commonly prescribed remedy—works better than a placebo, despite many anecdotes and testimonials (Freeman et al., 1990; Parlee, 1989).

Discussions of "PMS" often fail to distinguish between physical and emotional symptoms, and this distinction is critical in evaluating the phenomenon. Women vary tremendously in the physical symptoms they have. Some women have none, some have many, and for some, symptoms change in severity over the years. Physical symptoms, which typically include cramps and water retention, usually have a physical basis; there is no controversy there. But there is reason to question claims that *emotional* symptoms are reliably and universally tied to the menstrual cycle. Although many women report having "PMS" and are grateful that researchers are finally paying attention to women's reproductive issues, remember that self-reports can be a poor guide to reality, no matter how valid they feel to the person doing the reporting (see Chapter 2). A woman might easily attribute a blue mood to her impending period, although at other times of the month she would blame a grouchy professor, a disappointing date, or a stressful day. She may notice that she feels depressed or irritable when these moods happen to occur premenstrually, but overlook times when such moods are *absent* premenstrually, and wrongly conclude that she "typically" gets moody before her periods.

Many women believe they are more irritable premenstrually. Then why do their own daily reports fail to bear them out? And why do men report as many mood changes as women do over the span of a month?

Most important, a woman's perceptions of her own emotional ups and downs can be influenced by expectations and menstrual myths. To get around this problem, psychologists have polled women (and sometimes men) about their psychological and physical well-being *without revealing the true purpose of the study* (for example, Alagna & Hamilton, 1986; Burke, Burnett, & Levenstein, 1978; Englander-Golden, Whitmore, & Dienstbier, 1978; Parlee, 1982; Slade, 1984; Vila & Beech, 1980). Using a double-blind procedure, some researchers have had people report symptoms for a single day and have then gone back to see what phase of the cycle the women were in. Others have had people keep daily records over an extended period of time. Here's what they find:

• Overall, women and men *do not differ* in the emotional symptoms they report or the number of mood swings they experience in the course of a month. However, when both sexes fill out a checklist titled "Menstrual Distress Questionnaire," men magically lose their irritability, depression, fatigue, and backaches.

• A few women do become irritable or depressed before menstruation—and others become more energetic and happy. For most women, however, the relationship between cycle stage and symptoms is *weak or nonexistent*. They may *recall* their moods as having been more unpleasant before or during menstruation, but, as you can see in Figure 4.2, their own daily reports fail to bear them out (McFarlane, Martin, & Williams, 1988).

• There is *no* reliable relationship between cycle stage and work efficiency, problem solving, motor performance, or any other behavior that matters in real life (Golub, 1988).

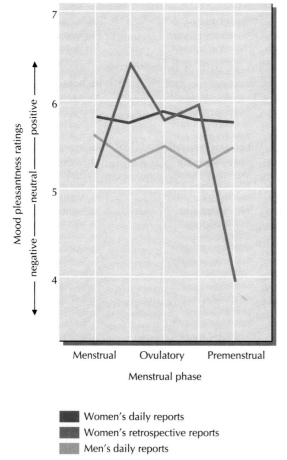

FIGURE 4.2

Mood changes in women and men: Are they cyclical?
In a study that challenged popular stereotypes about "PMS," college students of both sexes recorded their moods daily for 70 days without knowing the purpose of the study. This graph shows three of the study's findings. First, at no time of the month were the women grumpier or feeling less pleasant than the men. Second, when women were asked to recall their moods, they said their moods had been lower premenstrually. Third, the women's daily reports showed that actually their moods did not *change significantly over the menstrual cycle: their moods were just as stable as those of the men (McFarlane, Martin, & Williams, 1988).*

Results like these, reported many times over the past 15 years, are unknown to most people and are often ignored by doctors, therapists, and (especially) the media (Tavris, 1992).

Of course, men also have their emotional ups and downs. Is there a hormone–mood link in men? Testosterone, an important androgen (masculinizing hormone), fluctuates daily in all men, reaching a peak in the morning. It also seems to follow a longer, infradian cycle in some men, the length of the cycle varying from one individual to another (Doering et al., 1974). So far, the evidence on the relationship of testosterone levels to mood is sparse, conflicting, and hard to interpret. In one study, which measured daily mood and hormone changes in young men for a month, high testosterone levels predicted high hostility for some men, but low hostility for others (Doering et al., 1975). In another study, testosterone rose in men who were feeling elated after winning a $100 prize in a tennis match (Mazur & Lamb, 1980), but in a third study, teenagers with characteristically high testosterone levels had a tendency to feel sad, not elated (Susman et al., 1987).

Recently, in a study of 4,462 men, James Dabbs and Robin Morris (1990) found that unusually high testosterone levels were associated with delinquency, drug use, having many sex partners, abusiveness, and violence—and were not associated with any positive behaviors. These results do not mean that men are victims of their hormones or that high testosterone levels constitute a "syndrome." (The causes of antisocial behavior are far more complicated than that, and besides, the findings were only correlational.) But it is interesting to ask why analogous claims are so often made about women. Perhaps one reason is that the visible monthly reminder of women's hormonal changes makes it easier to blame negative moods or behavior on their biology.

In actuality, the evidence shows that few people of *either* sex are likely to undergo dramatic personality shifts because of their hormones. To be sure, hormonal abnormalities may produce psychological symptoms, just as a brain tumor might. One's circumstances also affect physical or emotional symptoms: In one study, full-time homemakers with young children reported the most severe "PMS" (Sanders et al., 1983). Chronic pain or discomfort may affect mood in both women and men. But for most people, the relationships between body rhythms and mental states are subtle and varied. An increased state of arousal or sensitivity may contribute to nervousness and restlessness—or to creative energy and vitality.

Symptoms are certainly not "all in your head"; physical changes and mood changes are real. The body provides the clay for our symptoms; it's real clay—but it's only clay. Learning and culture mold that clay, by teaching us which symptoms are important or worrisome and which are not. The impact of any bodily change, whether it is circadian, ultradian, or infradian, depends on how we interpret it and how we choose to respond to it.

QUICK QUIZ

Has your concentration peaked, or is it in an ultradian trough? Take this quiz to find out.

1. In the absence of time cues, most people would live a day that is about _____ hours long.
2. Jet lag occurs because of internal _____.
3. Which type of biological rhythm describes the menstrual cycle? (a) circadian, (b) infradian, (c) ultradian.

4. You are a psychologist studying testosterone in men. You tell your subjects that testosterone peaks in the morning and that you believe this hormone causes hostility. You then ask them to fill out a "Hypertestosterone Syndrome (HTS) Survey" in the morning and again at night. Based on menstrual cycle findings, what result might you get? How could you improve your study?

ANSWERS:

1. 25 2. desynchronization 3. b 4. Because of the expectations the men now have about testosterone, they may be biased to report more hostility in the morning. It would be better to keep them in the dark about your hypothesis; give them a questionnaire with a neutral title (such as "Health and Mood Checklist"), and measure their actual hormone levels early and late in the day (since individuals vary in the timing of their peaks). Also, you might add a control group of women, to see whether their hostility levels vary in the same way as men's.

The Rhythms of Sleep

Perhaps the most perplexing of all our biological rhythms is the one governing sleeping and wakefulness. Human beings and most animals curl up and go to sleep once every 24 hours. The reason remains something of a mystery. After all, sleeping puts an organism at risk: Muscles that are usually ready to respond to danger relax, and senses grow dull. As the late British psychologist Christopher Evans (1984) noted, "The behavior patterns involved in sleep are glaringly, almost insanely, at odds with common sense." Then why is sleep such a profound necessity?

WHY WE SLEEP.   One likely function of sleep is to provide a "time-out" period, so that the body can restore depleted reserves of energy, eliminate waste products from muscles, repair cells, or recover physical abilities lost during the day. The idea that sleep is for physical rest and recuperation accords with the undeniable fact that at the end of the day we feel tired and crave sleep. Though most people can function fairly normally after a day or two of sleeplessness, sleep deprivation that lasts for four days or longer is extremely uncomfortable. In animals, forced sleeplessness leads to damaged internal organs and eventually death (Rechtschaffen et al., 1983). The same thing may be true for people. There is a case on record of a man who abruptly began to lose sleep at age 52. After sinking deeper and deeper into an exhausted stupor, he developed a lung infection and died. An autopsy showed he had lost almost all of the large neurons in two areas of the thalamus that have been linked to sleep and hormonal circadian rhythms (Lugaresi et al., 1986).

Oddly enough, however, when people go many days without any sleep, they do not then require an equal period of time to "catch up"; one night's rest usually eliminates all symptoms of fatigue (Dement, 1978). And in ordinary life, the amount of time we sleep does not necessarily correspond to how active we have been during the day; even after a relaxing day on the beach, we usually go to sleep at night as usual. For these reasons, simple rest or energy restoration cannot be the sole purpose of sleep.

Many researchers believe that sleep must have as much to do with brain function as with bodily restoration. Only animals with brains or at least an integrated bundle of central nervous system tissue show unmistakable signs of sleep (Evans, 1984). As we have noted, after losing a single night's sleep most people still function pretty well. However, mental flexibility, originality, and other aspects of creative thinking may suffer (Horne, 1988). In a recent study, young men who fell asleep within minutes when given the chance (indicating that they needed more sleep than they were getting) performed more poorly than other

During the Great Depression of the 1930s, marathon dancers competed for prize money by trying to dance longer than other contestants—and inadvertently demonstrated some of the effects of sleep deprivation.

Whatever your age, sometimes the urge to sleep is irresistible. However, the physical and psychological functions of sleep are still not fully understood.

subjects on tasks that required vigilance or divided attention (Roehrs et al., 1990). Laboratory studies and observations of people participating in "wake-athons" have shown that after several days of sleep loss, people become irritable and begin to have hallucinations and delusions (Dement, 1978; Luce & Segal, 1966).

The brain, then, needs periodic sleep. Researchers are now trying to find out how sleep may contribute to the regulation of brain metabolism, the maintenance of normal nerve cell activity, and the replenishment of neurotransmitters. What's clear, however, is that during sleep, the brain is not simply resting. Indeed, most of the brain remains quite active, as we are about to see.

THE REALMS OF SLEEP.   Until the 1950s, the nature of sleep seemed beyond the reach of science. Then a breakthrough occurred: In 1953, a student in a laboratory where infants were being studied noticed that the babies' eyes often darted around beneath their lids as they slept. It was the sort of unplanned observation that can set off a chain reaction in science. By using the electroencephalograph, a machine that uses small, circular electrodes placed on the scalp to measure the brain's electrical activity (see Chapter 3), researchers were able to correlate the eye movements of sleepers with changes in their "brain wave" patterns. Adult volunteers were soon spending their nights sleeping in laboratories while scientists observed them and measured changes in their brain activity, muscle tension, breathing, and other physiological responses.

Today it is clear that sleep is not an unbroken state of rest, as was once thought. In adults, periods of **rapid eye movement (REM)** alternate with periods of fewer eye movements, or *non-REM* (NREM), in an ultradian cycle that recurs, on the average, every 90 minutes or so. The REM periods last from a few minutes to as long as an hour, averaging about 20 minutes in length. Whenever they begin, the pattern of electrical activity from the sleeper's brain changes to resemble that of alert wakefulness. Non-REM periods are themselves divided into shorter, distinct stages, each one associated with a particular brain wave pattern (see Figure 4.3).

When you first climb into bed, close your eyes, and relax, your brain emits bursts of **alpha waves** in a regular, high-amplitude, low-frequency rhythm of 8–12 cycles per second. Alpha is associated with relaxing or not concentrating on anything in particular. Gradually these waves slow down even further and you drift into the Land of Nod, passing through four stages, each deeper than the previous one.

■ **rapid eye movement (REM) sleep**

Sleep periods characterized by eye movement, loss of muscle tone, and dreaming.

■ **alpha waves**

Relatively large, slow brain waves characteristic of relaxed wakefulness.

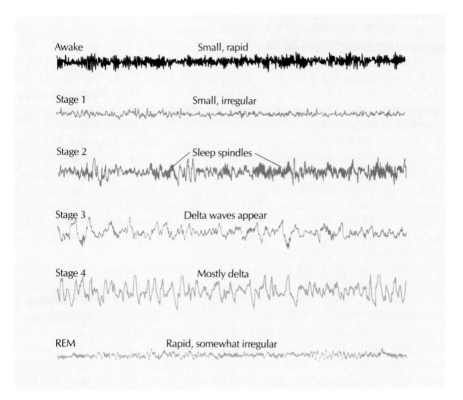

FIGURE 4.3

Brain wave patterns during sleep
Most types of brain waves are present throughout sleep, but different ones predominate at different stages.

1. *Stage 1.* Your brain waves become small and irregular, indicating activity with low voltage and mixed frequencies. You feel yourself drifting on the edge of consciousness, in a state of light sleep. If awakened, you may recall fantasies or a few visual images.

2. *Stage 2.* Your brain emits occasional short bursts of rapid, high-peaking waves called *sleep spindles.* Light sounds or minor noises probably won't disturb you.

3. *Stage 3.* In addition to the waves characteristic of stage 2, your brain occasionally emits very slow waves of about 1 to 3 cycles per second, with very high peaks. These **delta waves** are a sure sign that you will be hard to arouse. Your breathing and pulse have slowed down, your temperature has dropped, and your muscles are relaxed.

4. *Stage 4.* Delta waves have now largely taken over, and you are in deep sleep. It will take vigorous shaking or a loud noise to awaken you, and you won't be very happy about it. Oddly enough, though, if you talk or walk in your sleep, this is when you are likely to do so.

This sequence takes about 30 to 45 minutes. Then it reverses, and you move back up the ladder from stage 4 to 3 to 2 to 1. At that point, about 70–90 minutes after the onset of sleep, something peculiar happens. Stage 1 does not turn into drowsy wakefulness, as one might expect. Instead, your brain begins to emit long bursts of very rapid, somewhat irregular waves, similar to those produced during stage 1. Your heart rate increases, your blood pressure rises, and your breathing becomes faster and more irregular. There may be small, convulsive twitches in the face and fingers. In men, the penis becomes somewhat erect as vascular tissue relaxes and blood fills the genital area faster than it exits. In women, the clitoris enlarges, the vaginal walls become engorged, and vaginal lubrication increases. At the same time, most of your skeletal muscles go as limp as a rag doll, preventing your aroused brain from producing physical movement. Though you are supposedly in a "light" stage of sleep, you are hard to awaken. You have entered the realm of REM.

■ **delta waves**
Slow, regular brain waves characteristic of stage 3 and stage 4 sleep.

Because cats sleep so much—up to 80 percent of the time!—it's easy to catch them in the various stages of slumber. A cat in NREM sleep (top) remains upright, but during REM sleep (bottom) its muscles go limp and it flops onto its side.

Because the brain is extremely active while the body is almost devoid of muscle tone, REM sleep has also been called "paradoxical sleep." It is during these periods that you are most likely to dream (Aserinsky & Kleitman, 1955; Dement, 1955). Even people who claim they never dream at all will report dreams if awakened in a sleep laboratory during REM sleep. In fact, they are just as likely to do so as other people (Goodenough et al., 1959). Dreaming is also sometimes reported during non-REM sleep, but less often, and the images are less vivid and more realistic than those reported during REM sleep.

The study of REM has opened a window on the world of dreams. We now know, for example, that dreams do not take place in an instant, as people used to think, but in "real time." When volunteers are awakened 5 minutes after REM starts, they report shorter dreams than when they are awakened after 15 minutes (Dement & Kleitman, 1957). If you dream that you are singing all the verses to "A Hundred Bottles of Beer on the Wall," your dream will probably last as long as it would take you to sing the song. Most dreams take several minutes, and some may last half an hour.

REM and non-REM sleep continue to alternate throughout the night, with the REM periods tending to get longer and closer together as the hours pass (see Figure 4.4). An early REM period may last only a few minutes, whereas a later one may go on for 20 or 30 minutes and sometimes as long as an hour. (That is why people are likely to be dreaming when the alarm goes off in the morning.) In the later part of sleep, stages 3 and 4 become very short or disappear. But the cycles are far from regular. An individual may bounce directly from stage 4 back to stage 2, or go from REM to stage 2 and then back to REM. Also, the time between REM and non-REM is highly variable, differing from person to person and also within a particular individual. In fact, scientists must use sophisticated statistical methods to "see" the regularity in the REM and non-REM cycles.

The purpose of REM sleep is still a matter of debate, but clearly it does have a purpose. If you wake people every time they lapse into REM sleep, nothing dramatic will happen. When finally allowed to sleep normally, however, they will spend a much longer time than usual in the REM phase. Electrical brain activity associated with REM may burst through into quiet sleep and even into wakefulness. The subjects seem to be making up for something they were deprived of. Many people think that in adults, at least, this "something" has to do with dreaming.

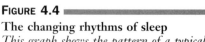

FIGURE 4.4

The changing rhythms of sleep
This graph shows the pattern of a typical night's sleep for a young adult. Time spent in REM sleep is represented by the colored bars. REM periods tend to lengthen as the night goes on. In contrast, stages 3 and 4, which dominate non-REM sleep early in the night, may disappear as morning approaches. (From Kelly, 1981a.)

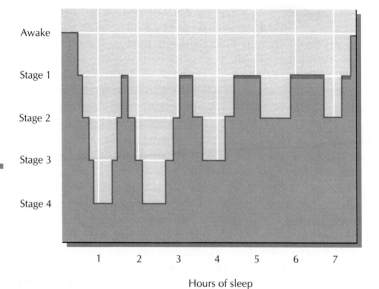

Match each term with the appropriate phrase.

1. REM periods   **a.** delta waves and talking in one's sleep
2. alpha   **b.** irregular brain waves and light sleep
3. stage 4 sleep   **c.** relaxed but awake
4. stage 1 sleep   **d.** active brain but inactive muscles

ANSWERS:

1. d 2. c 3. a 4. b

■ EXPLORING THE DREAM WORLD

Every culture has its theories about dreams. In some, dreams are thought to occur when the spirit leaves the body to wander the world or speak to the gods. In the Bible, dreams provided revelations: It was while dreaming, for example, that Joseph learned there was to be a famine in Egypt. A Chinese Taoist of the third century B.C. pondered the possible reality of the dream world. He told of dreaming that he was a butterfly merrily flitting about. "Suddenly I woke up and I was indeed Chuang Tzu. Did Chuang Tzu dream he was a butterfly, or did the butterfly dream he was Chuang Tzu?"

In dreaming, the focus of attention is inward, though sometimes an external event such as the ringing of an alarm clock can influence the dream. While a dream is in progress, it may be vivid or vague, terrifying or peaceful, colorful or bland. It may also seem to make perfect sense—until you wake up. Then it is often recalled as illogical and bizarre. The flow of a dream is usually not as smooth as the flow of waking consciousness; events occur without transitions. REM dreams, which as we noted are usually more vivid than non-REM dreams, are often reported as adventures or stories. Non-REM dreams tend to be described as vague, fragmentary, unemotional, and commonplace.

Ordinarily, during dreaming you have no background awareness of where you are or of your own body. Some people, however, report dreams in which they know they are dreaming and they feel as though they are conscious. These **lucid dreams,** which occur at times of high cortical arousal, seem to involve a split in consciousness known as **dissociation.** During the dream, consciousness seems to divide into a dreaming part and an observing part. Some people have learned, with training, to produce lucid dreams at will and control the action in them, much as a scriptwriter decides what will happen in a movie (Garfield, 1974; LaBerge, 1986, 1990). In the sleep laboratory, they may even be able to signal that they are having a lucid dream by moving their eyes in a prearranged way!

Studies of lucid dreamers have stirred up an issue that has been bothering sleep researchers for years: Do the eye movements of REM sleep correspond to events in a dream? Some researchers think that eye movements are no more related to dream content than are inner ear muscle contractions, which also occur during REM sleep (Kelly, 1981b). Every mammal studied except the spiny anteater goes through REM sleep, as do human fetuses, but we might not want to credit mice, opossums, or human fetuses with what we ordinarily call dreams. Further, although children's eyes move during REM sleep, the imagery in children's dreams tends to be static until age 6 or so, and their cognitive limitations keep them from creating true narratives in dreams until age 7 or 8 (Foulkes, 1990; Foulkes et al., 1990). On the other hand, in adult dreamers eye move-

■ **lucid dream**
A dream in which the dreamer is aware of dreaming.
■ **dissociation**
Separation of consciousness into distinct parts.

ments resemble those of waking life, when the eyes and head move in synchrony as the person moves about and changes the direction of his or her gaze—even though during dreaming the head and body stay still (J. H. Herman, 1992). Moreover, studies of skilled lucid dreamers find that their eye movements correspond to preplanned actions in their dreams (Schatzman, Worsley, & Fenwick, 1988). These findings suggest that in adults, at least, the eyes may indeed track dream images, actions, and events.

Why do these dream images arise at all? Why doesn't the brain just *rest*, switching off all thoughts and images and launching us into a coma? Why, instead, do we spend our nights flying through the air, battling monsters, or flirting with an old flame in the fantasy world of our dreams?

Dreams as Unconscious Wishes

The Iroquois Indians of North America believed that dreams express hidden wishes and desires, and many cultures around the world have developed rituals for the purpose of analyzing the underlying meanings of dreams (Krippner & Hillman, 1990). In psychology, one of the first theorists to take dreams seriously was Sigmund Freud, the founder of psychoanalysis, who also emphasized hidden messages from the mind. After analyzing many of his patients' dreams and some of his own, Freud concluded that our nighttime fantasies provide a "royal road to the unconscious." In dreams, said Freud, we are able to gratify forbidden or unrealistic wishes and desires, often sexual, that have been forced into the unconscious part of the mind. If we did not dream, energy invested in these wishes and desires would build up to intolerable levels, threatening our very sanity.

In Freud's psychoanalytic theory of dreaming, no matter how absurd a dream may seem, it has meaning and logic. But if a dream's message arouses anxiety, the rational part of the mind must disguise and distort it. Otherwise the dream would wake the dreamer up, intruding into consciousness. In dreams, therefore, one person may be represented by another—for example, a father by a brother—or even by several different characters. Similarly, thoughts and objects are translated into symbolic images. A penis may be disguised as a snake, umbrella, dagger, or other elongated object; a vagina, as a tunnel, entrance way, or cave; and the human body, as a house.

To understand a dream, Freud said, we must distinguish its *manifest* content, the aspects of it that we consciously experience during sleep and may remember upon wakening, from its *latent* or hidden content, the unconscious wishes and thoughts being expressed symbolically. Freud warned against the simple-minded translation of symbols, however. Each dream had to be analyzed in the context of the dreamer's waking life as well as the person's associations to the dream's contents. Not everything in a dream is symbolic. Sometimes, Freud cautioned, "a cigar is only a cigar."

Most psychologists today accept Freud's notion that dreams are more than incoherent ramblings of the mind, but many quarrel with his interpretations, which they find farfetched. Critics of psychoanalysis point out that there are no clear rules for interpreting the latent content of dreams and there is no objective way to know whether a particular interpretation is correct.

Dreams as Problem Solving

Many psychologists believe that most dreams reflect not deep-seated or infantile wishes but the ongoing emotional preoccupations of waking life—concern over relationships, work, sex, or health (Webb & Cartwright, 1978). In this view, the symbols and metaphors in dreams convey the dream's true meaning, rather than disguising it. One psychologist, Gayle Delaney, tells of a woman who

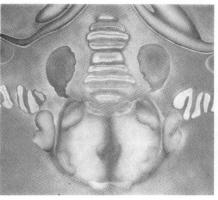
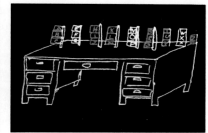

These drawings, from dream journals kept by two sleep research subjects, show that dream images can be either abstract or literal. The two fanciful paintings on the left represent the dreams of a person who worked all day long with brain tissue—which they rather resemble. The desk on the right was sketched in 1939 by a scientist to illustrate his dream about a mechanical device for instantly retrieving quotations—a sort of early desktop computer.

dreamed she was swimming underwater. Her eight-year-old son was on her back, his head above the water. Her husband was supposed to take a picture of them, but for some reason he wasn't doing it, and she was starting to feel as if she was going to drown. To Delaney, the message was obvious: The woman was "drowning" under the responsibilities of child care and her husband wasn't "getting the picture" (in Dolnick, 1990). Another psychologist, Alan Siegel (1991), tells of a father-to-be who dreamed of swimming downhill, with instructions from his wife's labor coach, and emerging in the locker room wrapped in a towel. When asked for his interpretation, the man said the dream meant he should swim more at the gym! To Siegel, however, the dream was about dealing with impending childbirth and parenthood.

According to Rosalind Cartwright, dreams give us an uninterrupted opportunity to deal with particularly emotional issues, even if we forget the dreams later. When we are relatively free of problems, we may simply use dreams to exercise our creativity, but during a crisis, our dream machinery goes into high gear, and emotional concerns activate certain images in memory. Cartwright (1989, 1991) finds that in depressed people going through a divorce, the first dream of the night often comes sooner than it does for others, lasts longer, and is more emotional and storylike—and that this pattern relates to recovery. The content of these people's dreams suggests that they are working on issues of loss and new responsibilities. Cartwright (1990) suggests that getting through a divorce (and by implication, other crises) takes "time, good friends, good genes, good luck, and a good dream system."

Dreams as Information Processing

A different approach views dreams as opportunities for mental housekeeping. Christopher Evans (1984) argued that the brain must periodically shut out sensory input so that it can process and assimilate new data and update what has already been stored. It divides new information into "wanted" and "unwanted" categories, makes new associations, and revises old "programs" (to use a computer analogy) in light of the day's experiences. The data it works on include not only recent events, but also ideas, obsessions, worries, wishes, and thoughts about the past. What we recall as dreams are really only brief snippets from an ongoing process of sorting, scanning, and sifting that occurs during REM sleep and possibly throughout the night. Because they give us only a glimpse of the night's mental activity, they naturally seem odd and nonsensical when recalled.

A somewhat similar idea has been proposed by Francis Crick, co-discoverer of the structure of DNA, and his colleague, Graeme Mitchison. Crick and Mitchison (1983) argue that during REM periods, the brain jettisons mental garbage—information it doesn't need, undesirable ways of behaving, accidental connections in the brain. In short, we dream in order to forget. Crick and

Mitchison speculate that random firing from the brain stem sets off the undesirable connections that have overloaded the cortex, including fantasies, obsessions, and hallucinations, thereby defusing them. The subjective result of this firing is a dream. In this view, there is no reason to search through the garbage for tidbits of meaning. Trying to remember dreams defeats their purpose and could lead to mental disorders—an idea guaranteed to anger psychoanalysts!

Information-processing approaches to dreaming might explain why REM sleep occurs in fetuses, babies, and animals as well as in adult human beings. They, too, need to "sort things out." Newborns, in fact, spend about 50 percent of their sleeping hours in REM sleep, versus only 20 percent for adults. Since everything that is happening to them is new, perhaps they have more writing and revising of "programs" to do. As we noted, however, children's cognitive immaturity prevents them from creating the kinds of narratives and images that adult human beings experience during dreaming.

Dreams as Interpreted Brain Activity

Some recent theories of dreaming draw heavily on physiological research. One, the **activation-synthesis theory,** was first proposed by Allan Hobson and Robert McCarley (1977) and later elaborated by Hobson (1988, 1990). According to this theory, dreams are not, in Shakespeare's words, "children of an idle brain." Rather, they are the result of neurons firing spontaneously in the lower part of the brain, specifically in the pons. These neurons control eye movement, gaze, balance, and posture, and send messages to areas of the cortex responsible during wakefulness for visual processing and voluntary action. Such sleeptime signals have no psychological meaning in themselves, but the cortex tries to make sense of them by *synthesizing*, or combining, them with existing knowledge and memories to produce some sort of coherent interpretation—just as it would if the signals had come from sense organs during ordinary wakefulness. When neurons fire in the part of the brain that handles balance, the cortex may generate a dream about falling. When signals occur that would ordinarily produce running, the cortex may manufacture a dream about being chased. Since the signals themselves lack coherence, the interpretation—the dream—is also likely to be incoherent and confusing. And since cortical neurons that control storage of new memories are turned off during sleep (because certain neurotransmitter levels are low), we typically forget our dreams upon waking.

Hobson (1988) suggests an explanation for why REM sleep and dreaming do not occur continuously through the night. Giant cells found in the reticular activating system of the pons, sensitive to the neurotransmitter acetylcholine, appear to initiate REM sleep. They then proceed to fire in unrestrained bursts, like a machine gun. Eventually, however, the gun's magazine is emptied, and other neurons, which inhibit REM sleep, take over. "If synapses are like cartridges," writes Hobson, "it may be that is why REM sleep ends; no more synaptic ammunition." Only when the neurons "reload" can firing, and REM sleep, resume. In support of this idea, Hobson notes that when sleeping volunteers are injected with drugs that stimulate acetylcholine, REM sleep and dreaming increase. When they are injected with a drug that negates the effects of acetylcholine, REM sleep and dreaming decrease (Gillin et al., 1985).

Wishes, according to Hobson, do not cause dreams; brainstem mechanisms do. But that doesn't mean dreams are meaningless. According to Hobson (1988), the brain "is so inexorably bent upon the quest for meaning that it attributes and even creates meaning when there is little or none to be found in the data it is asked to process." By studying these attributed meanings, you can learn about your unique perceptions, conflicts, and concerns—not by trying to dig

■ **activation-synthesis theory**
The theory that dreaming results from the cortical synthesis and interpretation of neural signals triggered by activity in the lower part of the brain.

below the surface of the dream, as Freud would, but by examining the surface itself. Or you can relax and enjoy the nightly entertainment that dreams provide.

The activation-synthesis model is a well developed approach to dreaming that takes both physiology and cognition into account. However, like all dream theories, it has its critics. Some argue that the cortex, far from "merely submit[ting] docilely to incoming volleys" from the pons, takes an active role in controlling REM sleep and dreaming (J. H. Herman, 1992). In a review of current knowledge about dreams and sleep, John Antrobus (1991) concludes that contrary to most theories, including Hobson's, dreaming is really just a modification of what goes on when we are awake. During REM sleep, as in wakefulness, the parts of the cortex involved in perceptual and cognitive processing are highly activated. The difference is that when we are asleep we are cut off from sensory input and feedback from our own movements, and so the only input to the various processing "modules" of the brain is their own output. It is this restricted input, argues Antrobus, that accounts for the bizarre imagery in dreams, rather than the difficulty of synthesizing and interpreting spontaneous and meaningless signals originating in the pons. Antrobus cites research in his laboratory indicating that mental activity during wakefulness would be much like that during dreaming—with the same hallucinatory quality—if the person could be totally cut off from all external stimulation.

Well then, how are we to evaluate the various theories of dreaming? Each explanation seems to fit certain kinds of evidence: the "aha" reactions of patients undergoing psychotherapy (psychoanalytic explanations); the dream experiences of people going through a crisis (problem-solving explanations); the existence of REM sleep in animals and infants (information-processing explanations); and physiological evidence (the activation-synthesis theory). At present, however, no one theory seems to explain all dreams, and all the theories are proving difficult to test. Perhaps it will turn out that different kinds of dreams have different purposes and origins. Much remains to be learned about the purpose of dreaming and even of sleep itself.

QUICK QUIZ

A dreamer imagines himself as an infant crawling through a dark tunnel looking for something he has lost. Which theory of dreams would be most receptive to each of the following explanations?

1. The dreamer has recently misplaced a valuable watch and is worried about possible memory problems.
2. While the dreamer was sleeping, neurons in his pons that would ordinarily stimulate leg muscle movement were active.
3. The dreamer has repressed an early sexual attraction to his mother; the tunnel symbolizes her vagina.
4. The dreamer has broken up with his lover and is working through the emotional loss.

ANSWERS:

1. The information-processing approach (the dreamer is processing information about a recent experience) 2. The activation-synthesis theory 3. Freudian psychoanalytic theory 4. The problem-solving approach.

■ ALTERED STATES OF CONSCIOUSNESS

Dreaming is an ordinary state of consciousness that everyone experiences. Are there other, equally fascinating states we can enter if we unlock the right doors? William James (1902/1936), who was fascinated by alterations in consciousness, thought so. After inhaling nitrous oxide ("laughing gas") he wrote, "Our normal waking consciousness, rational consciousness as we call it, is but one special type of consciousness, whilst all about it, parted from it by the filmiest of screens, there lie potential forms of consciousness entirely different."

James believed that psychologists should study these other forms of consciousness, but for half a century few took his words seriously. Consciousness was out of favor as a topic of scientific concern. Then, during the 1960s, attitudes changed. During that decade of political and social upheaval, millions of people began to explore techniques for deliberately producing alternate or **altered states of consciousness.** Some began to practice *meditation*, the focusing of consciousness in order to eliminate distracting thoughts and quiet the mind (see Chapter 15). Others began to experiment with drugs. In psychology, researchers became interested in whether hypnosis could change consciousness. Some writers argued that altering consciousness would enhance creativity and deepen insight (see "Think About It"). For psychologists and others, the "filmy screen" described by James finally began to lift.

■ **altered (alternate) state of consciousness**
A deliberately produced state of consciousness that differs from ordinary wakefulness or sleep.

■ **psychoactive drug**
A drug capable of influencing perception, mood, cognition, or behavior.

Consciousness-altering Drugs

Perhaps the fastest, and also the riskiest, way to alter consciousness is to use a **psychoactive drug** to alter the body's biochemistry. A drug is psychoactive if it can influence perception, mood, thinking, memory, or behavior. Nearly every human society has discovered at least one such substance, natural or artificial,

All cultures seem to find ways to alter ordinary consciousness. The Maulavis of Turkey (left), the famous "whirling dervishes," spin in an energetic but controlled manner in order to achieve religious rapture and unite their souls with Allah. In many cultures, people learn to meditate (right) as a way to quiet the mind, experience immediate reality, and achieve spiritual enlightenment.

Does Consciousness Need Altering?

• In Jerusalem, hundreds of male Hasidic Jews celebrate the completion of the annual reading of the holy Torah by dancing in the streets. Although it is warm and the men are dressed in long black coats, they go on for hours, never tiring. For them, dancing is not a diversion; it is a path to religious ecstasy.

• In South Dakota, several Sioux Indians sit naked in the darkness of the sweat lodge, a circular hut covered with hides and blankets. A medicine man offers prayers and leads chants. Then he throws water on a pit of red-hot rocks, and a crushing wave of heat envelops the participants. They must concentrate all their thoughts on coping with it. Their reward will be euphoria, the transcendence of pain, and according to Sioux belief, possible connection with the Great Spirit of the Universe.

• Deep in the Amazon jungle, a young man is training to be a *shaman*. For weeks he has starved himself. Now he enters a trance, aided by a whiff of hallucinogenic snuff made from the bark of the *Virola* tree. As a full shaman he will be expected to enter trances regularly and to communicate with animals, spirits, and supernatural forces.

These three rituals, seemingly quite different, are all aimed at release from the confines of ordinary consciousness. Cultures around the world have devised such practices, often as part of their religions. In India, a *sadhu* (Hindu holy man) uses yoga to achieve a state of sublime detachment that makes him insensitive to pain as he calmly lies on a bed of sharp cactus spines. The Maulavis of Turkey, the "whirling dervishes," use spinning dances to accomplish much the same thing. As Muslims, they dance mainly to unite their souls with Allah, but their trances also enable them to show their faith by fearlessly piercing their cheeks or touching burning coals. Hinduism, Sufiism, and Buddhism, and some forms of Judaism and Christianity, all use meditation as a way of achieving emotional detachment, a direct experience of the moment, and transcendence of the self—a state of spiritual enlightenment known in Eastern cultures as *satori, nirvana, kensho,* or *samadhi.*

Because attempts to alter consciousness appear to be universal, some writers believe they reflect a basic human need. Psychopharmacologist Ronald Siegel (1989) calls the motive to alter mood or consciousness a "fourth drive" (after sex, thirst, and hunger). In *The Natural Mind* (1972/1986), physician Andrew Weil argues that this need enables us to shift to a more intuitive, creative mode. Children, he says, are trying to alter consciousness when they purposely hyperventilate or when, like the dervishes, they whirl around and around. Adults in our culture, having learned that such behavior is silly or inappropriate, resort to alcohol and other recreational drugs instead. However, as both Siegel and Weil note, the fact that all or most societies have ways of altering consciousness does not mean that every method of doing so is beneficial, safe, or desirable. Drugs that might be fairly benign in their natural state (e.g., coca in the coca leaf) may turn toxic when purified and taken in large doses (e.g., in the form of "crack" cocaine). Further, cultures and individuals may have different motives for trying to disrupt everyday ways of perceiving and thinking.

Is there actually a basic need to go beyond the ordinary states of wakefulness and sleep? Are people looking for a natural high when they schuss down the ski slope, push themselves to their physical limits in the Boston Marathon, or (much more commonly) make love? In our culture, when is the search for an altered state a sign of creativity and growth, and when is it a sign of boredom, escapism, or emotional distress? What do you think?

and has used it in rituals or recreationally. Many animals, too, like to get chemically high. Baboons ingest tobacco, elephants love the alcohol in fermented fruit, and reindeer and rabbits seek out intoxicating mushrooms (R. Siegel, 1989).

In our society, where the "drugs of choice" are caffeine, nicotine, and alcohol, the use of drugs, especially illicit ones, is an emotionally charged issue. Drug dependence, whether psychological or physical, can lead to social prob-

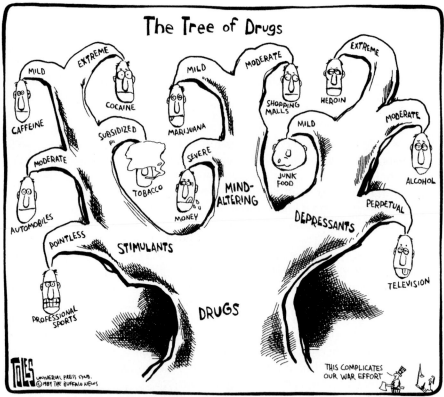

This cartoon, which pokes fun at the things people do to alter consciousness and make themselves feel better, reminds us that many "stimulants" and "depressants" are neither chemical nor illegal.

lems and personal tragedy. Many drugs, if used frequently or excessively, can do grave damage to body organs, interfere with the ability to work or study, and turn careful drivers into dangerous ones. (Dependence and addiction are discussed further in Chapter 16.) However, because drugs are so controversial, people tend to lump them all together, overlooking the fact that two substances labeled "drugs" may be totally unalike chemically and may have vastly different effects on the nervous system. Extremely potent drugs may be confused with others that have only subtle effects or are safe in moderate amounts.

People may also fail to recognize that light use can have different consequences than heavy use. Recent research finds that using a drug (especially marijuana or hashish) only once a month or less seems to have little impact on the social or personal adjustment of most teenagers, and tends to be just one aspect of youthful experimentation (Newcomb & Bentler, 1988; Shedler & Block, 1990). However, heavy use of hard drugs interferes with nearly every aspect of a teenager's life, from relationships to schoolwork. One longitudinal study that followed teenagers into young adulthood found that excessive drug use was itself an attempt to deal with existing emotional problems. But adolescents who coped by habitually using several different drugs were more likely to prolong their problems (Scheier, Newcomb, & Bentler, 1990).

We should keep in mind that legal drugs may be as harmful as some illegal ones, if not more so. Tobacco use contributes to about 400,000 deaths in the United States every year—about 20 times the number of deaths from all other forms of drug use *combined* (U.S. Department of Health and Human Services, 1989). Indeed, nicotine dependence is one of the most common preventable causes of death. However, because tobacco-related deaths usually occur years after the onset of smoking, people tend to think of cigarettes as less harmful than many other drugs.

PHYSICAL EFFECTS. Many psychoactive drugs are legally prescribed in the treatment of physical and mental disorders. There are also dozens of illegal drugs in the United States. Psychoactive drugs work primarily by acting on brain neurotransmitters, the substances that enable messages to pass from one nerve cell to another (see Chapter 3). Some cause more or fewer neurotransmitter molecules to be released at a synapse. Others prevent the reabsorption ("reuptake") of a neurotransmitter after its release. Still others block the effects of a neurotransmitter on a receiving nerve cell. Figure 4.5 shows how cocaine increases the amount of norepinephrine and dopamine in the brain by blocking the reabsorption of these substances. Animal studies suggest that repeated use of certain drugs, including "designer drugs" (potent synthetic chemicals that are easy to concoct and modify), causes permanent brain damage. For example, the drug "Ecstasy" (MDMA) may permanently damage cells that produce serotonin (Ricaurte et al., 1988).

The use of some psychoactive drugs, such as heroin and tranquilizers, leads to **tolerance:** As time goes by, more and more of the drug is needed to get the same effect. When habitual heavy users stop taking a drug (whether it causes tolerance or not), they may suffer severe **withdrawal symptoms**, such as nausea, abdominal cramps, muscle spasms, depression, and sleep problems, depending on the drug. Tolerance and withdrawal are often assumed to be purely physiological, but in Chapter 6 we will see that learning also plays a role.

Most drugs can be classified as *stimulants, depressants, opiates,* or *psychedelics,* depending on their effects on the central nervous system and their impact on behavior and mood (see Table 4.1). The following descriptions do not include the many "designer" drugs in use, or antipsychotic drugs, which are used to treat certain mental disorders and are covered separately in Chapter 17.

1. Stimulants, such as cocaine, amphetamines ("uppers"), and nicotine, speed up activity in the central nervous system. In moderate amounts, they tend to produce feelings of excitement, confidence, and well-being or even euphoria. In large amounts, they make a person anxious, jittery, and hyperalert, and interfere with sleep. In very large doses, they may cause convulsions, heart failure, and death.

Amphetamines are synthetic drugs usually taken in pill form. Cocaine ("coke") is a natural drug, derived from the leaves of the coca plant. (It has nothing to do with chocolate, which comes from the cacao bean.) Rural workers in Bolivia and Peru chew coca leaf every day, without apparent ill effects. In this country, the drug is usually inhaled ("snorted") or injected, or smoked in the highly refined form known as "crack." These methods give the drug a more immediate, powerful, and dangerous effect. Amphetamines and cocaine make users feel peppy but do not actually increase energy reserves. Fatigue, irritability, and depression may occur when the effects of the drugs wear off.

■ **tolerance**
Increased resistance to a drug's effects with continued use; as tolerance develops, larger doses are required to produce effects once brought on by smaller ones.
■ **withdrawal symptoms**
Physical and psychological symptoms that occur when someone addicted to a drug stops taking it.
■ **stimulants**
Drugs that speed up activity in the central nervous system.

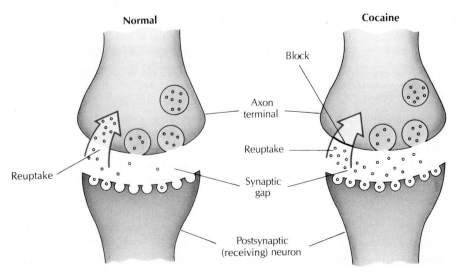

FIGURE 4.5

Cocaine's effect on the brain
Cocaine blocks the ability of brain cells to reabsorb the neurotransmitters dopamine and norepinephrine, so levels of these substances in the brain rise. The result is overstimulation of certain brain circuits and a brief euphoric "high." Then, when the drug wears off, a depletion of dopamine may cause the user to "crash" and become sleepy and depressed.

2. Depressants, such as alcohol, tranquilizers, and barbiturates, slow down activity in the central nervous system. Also known as *sedatives* or *hypnotics,* they usually make you feel calm or drowsy, and may reduce anxiety, guilt, tension, and inhibitions. In large amounts, they may produce insensitivity to pain and other sensations. In very large doses, they may, like stimulants, cause convulsions and death.

People are often surprised to learn that alcohol is a central nervous system depressant. In small amounts, alcohol may affect behavior much as a stimulant would because it first suppresses nerve cell activity in parts of the brain that normally inhibit behavior. Behavior that might ordinarily be checked, such as loud laughter and clowning around, is disinhibited. Like barbiturates and opiates, alcohol can be used as an anesthetic, and if you drink enough, you will eventually pass out. Extremely large amounts of alcohol can kill, by inhibiting the nerve cells in the brain centers that control breathing and heartbeat. Every so often the newspapers report how someone died after consuming large amounts of alcohol during a night of partying.

Drinking, unlike illicit drug use, is a socially accepted custom in our culture. An estimated 70 to 100 million Americans imbibe socially. In a recent survey, 57 percent of high school seniors and 75 percent of college students said they had used alcohol during the past month; 32 percent of the high school seniors and 41 percent of the college students said they had consumed five or more drinks at one sitting during the past two weeks (Johnston, O'Malley, & Bachman, 1991).

Because of alcohol's effect on judgment, drinkers often are unable to gauge their own competence. Even moderate amounts of alcohol can affect perception, response time, coordination, and balance, despite the drinker's own impression of unchanged or even improved performance (Poley, Lea, & Vibe, 1979). Liquor also affects memory, possibly by interfering with the work of the neurotransmitter serotonin. Information stored before a drinking session remains intact during the session but is retrieved more slowly (Stempel, Beckwith, & Petros, 1986). The ability to store new memories for later use also suffers, even after two or three drinks (Parker, Birnbaum, & Noble, 1976). Consuming small amounts does not seem to affect *sober* mental performance, but even occasional heavy drinking impairs later abstract thought. In other words, a Saturday night binge is more dangerous than a daily drink.

3. Opiates include opium, derived from the opium poppy; morphine, a derivative of opium; heroin, a derivative of morphine; and certain synthetic drugs, such as methadone. All these drugs relieve pain, mimicking the action of endorphins, and most have a powerful effect on the emotions. When injected, they may produce a sudden feeling of euphoria, called a "rush." There may be a decrease in anxiety and a decrease in motivation, although the effects vary. When habitual users stop taking an opiate, they may suffer serious withdrawal symptoms.

4. Psychedelic drugs include substances that alter consciousness by producing hallucinations, changing thought processes, or disrupting the normal perception of time and space. Some, such as lysergic acid diethylamide (LSD), are made in the laboratory. Others, such as mescaline (from the peyote cactus) and psilocybin (from various species of mushrooms), are natural. Unlike the hallucinations characteristic of some mental disturbances, which are typically sounds and voices, the hallucinations produced by psychedelics are usually visual. Emotional reactions to psychedelics vary from person to person, and from one time to another for a particular individual. A "trip" may be mildly pleasant or unpleasant, a mystical revelation, or a nightmare.

Two commonly used drugs fall outside the usual classifications: anabolic steroids and marijuana. *Anabolic steroids* are synthetic derivatives of testosterone, taken in pill form or by injection, that have a variety of legitimate medical uses.

■ **depressants**
Drugs that slow down activity in the central nervous system.
■ **opiates**
Drugs, derived from the opium poppy, that relieve pain and commonly produce euphoria.
■ **psychedelic drugs**
Consciousness-altering drugs that produce hallucinations, change thought processes, or disrupt the normal perception of time and space.

TABLE 4.1

Some Psychoactive Drugs and Their Effects

	Type of Drug	Common Effects	Results of Abuse/Addiction
Amphetamines	Stimulant	Wakefulness, alertness, raised metabolism, elevated mood	Nervousness, headaches, loss of appetite, high blood pressure, delusions, psychosis, heart damage, convulsions, death
Cocaine	Stimulant	Euphoria, excitation, boost of energy, suppressed appetite	Excitability, sleeplessness, sweating, paranoia, anxiety, panic, depression, heart damage, heart failure, injury to nose if sniffed
Tobacco (nicotine)	Stimulant	Varies, from alertness to calmness, depending on mental set, setting and prior arousal; decreases appetite for carbohydrates	Nicotine: heart disease, high blood pressure, impaired circulation Tar: lung cancer, emphysema, mouth and throat cancer, many other health risks
Caffeine	Stimulant	Wakefulness, alertness, shortened reaction time	Restlessness, insomnia, muscle tension, heartbeat irregularities, high blood pressure
Alcohol (1–2 drinks)	Depressant	Depends on setting, mental set; tends to act like a stimulant because it reduces inhibitions, anxiety	
Alcohol (several/ many drinks)	Depressant	Slowed reaction time, tension, depression, reduced ability to store new memories or retrieve old ones, poor coordination	Blackouts, cirrhosis, organic damage, mental and neurological impairment, psychosis, possibly death
Tranquilizers (e.g., Valium); Barbiturates (e.g., pheno-barbital)	Depressant	Reduced anxiety and tension, sedation	Increased dosage needed for effects; impaired motor and sensory functions, impaired permanent storage of new information, withdrawal symptoms; possibly convulsions, coma, death (especially when taken with other drugs)
Opium, heroin, morphine	Opiate	Euphoria, relief of pain	Loss of appetite, nausea, constipation, withdrawal symptoms, convulsions, coma, possibly death
LSD, psilocybin, mescaline	Psychedelic	Exhilaration, visions and hallucinations, insightful experiences	Psychosis, paranoia, panic reactions
Marijuana	Mild psychedelic (classification controversial)	Relaxation, euphoria, increased appetite, reduced ability to store new memories, other effects depending on mental set and setting	Throat and lung irritation, lung damage (if smoked), impaired immunity; long-term effects not well established

They are thought to increase muscle mass and strength when combined with weight-bearing exercise, and for this reason have been used illegally for years by athletes, especially weight lifters. As reports of use by high school and even junior high school athletes have surfaced, concern about these drugs has grown. Numerous negative physical effects have been reported, including heart and liver disease and decreased testicular size (Pope & Katz, 1988). Whether anabolic steroids are psychoactive, however, is still an open question. There have been reports of both positive psychological effects (increased sex drive, increased confidence, reduced fatigue during training) and negative ones (increased aggression, irritability, hostility, anxiety, and even psychosis). However, many of these reports have been anecdotal. There have been few studies on the effects of anabolic steroids, and many of them have used questionable sampling strategies or relied on unverified self-reports (Bahrke, Yesalis, & Wright, 1990). Because of these and other methodological problems, no firm conclusions can be drawn yet about either the physical or psychological effects of these drugs.

Marijuana ("pot," "grass") is probably the most widely used illicit drug in the United States. It is smoked or, less commonly, eaten in foods like brownies or cookies. Some researchers classify marijuana as a mild psychedelic. Others feel that both in its chemical makeup and in its psychological effects, marijuana falls outside the major classifications. We know that the major active ingredient in marijuana is tetrahydrocannabinol (THC), derived from the hemp plant, *Cannabis sativa*. Little is known yet about how THC acts on the nervous system. In some respects, it appears to be a mild stimulant, increasing heart rate and making tastes, sounds, and colors seem more intense. But users report both mild euphoria and relaxation, or even sleepiness. Time often seems to go by slowly.

In moderate doses, marijuana can interfere with the transfer of information to long-term memory, a characteristic it shares with alcohol. In large doses it can cause hallucinations and a sense of unreality. Some studies also find that the drug impairs coordination, concentration, visual perception, and reaction times, though it is not clear how long these effects last. It also depresses the immune system. That is what we know. Surprisingly, considering that marijuana use is so widespread, there is still plenty that we don't know. There have been few long-term studies of the drug, and few facts about it are well established (see Gallagher, 1988).

Existing work on marijuana raises as many questions as it answers. For example, in the 1970s, an interdisciplinary research team studied a group of working-class Costa Rican men who had smoked an average of almost 10 marijuana cigarettes daily for 17 years. They found no significant physical or psychological differences between these men and a matched group of nonusers. Recently, another team restudied some of the same men. On tests that were used earlier, there was no evidence of deterioration in the marijuana users, although the men had now been smoking for 30 years on the average. On three *new* tests, of sustained attention, organizing skills, and short-term memory, the users did do worse than the control subjects, but the differences were subtle (Page, Fletcher, & True, 1988).

Are you more impressed by these men's normal performance on the old tests or by their somewhat inferior performance on the new tests? Those who are worried about marijuana's effects emphasize the latter. In the United States, they point out, even slight impairment of performance might be troublesome

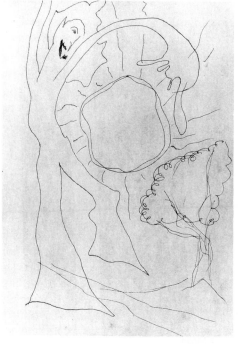

An LSD "trip" may be a ticket to agony or ecstasy. Both of these drawings were done while under the influence of the drug.

because many of us hold jobs requiring mental exertion and alertness. Others, however, note that very few Americans smoke 10 joints a day for 30 years. Also, the marijuana used in Costa Rica is far more potent than most varieties available in the United States. Moreover, the slight deficits that were observed in Costa Rica could have been due to the temporary effects of recent smoking and not to any permanent effects of long-term use. The subjects were asked to abstain from smoking for two days before being tested, but it can take days or even weeks for the body to rid itself of THC.

Heavy, prolonged use of marijuana does pose physical dangers (see Table 4.1). Even mild use can cause lung damage when the drug is smoked (Bloom et al., 1987; Wu et al., 1988). However, we cannot yet draw any firm conclusions about psychological consequences, and again, we must be careful not to confuse light or mild use with heavy use. Marijuana is clearly milder in its effects than alcohol, and many researchers doubt that occasional use poses psychological problems for most people. In 1990, an advisory panel of scientists for the state of California recommended legalizing the cultivation of marijuana for personal use, after concluding that the drug causes less individual and social damage than alcohol and cigarettes. The state attorney general's office, however, declined to print their recommendations.

BEYOND PHYSIOLOGY: THE PSYCHOLOGY OF DRUG EFFECTS. People often talk about the effects of a drug as if such effects were automatic, the inevitable result of the drug's chemistry ("I couldn't help being an obnoxious slob; the booze made me do it"). But as we noted in Chapter 3, trying to understand behavior solely in terms of physiology almost always leads to oversimplification. If we want to understand drugs, we must know more than their chemical properties. Drug responses depend on a person's physical condition, experience with the drug, mental set, and environmental setting.

One person takes a drink and flies into a rage. Another has a drink and "mellows out." What qualities of the user rather than the drug might account for this difference?

• *Physical condition* includes body weight, individual tolerance for the drug, and initial state of arousal. A drug may have a different effect after a tiring day than after a rousing quarrel. It may also affect a person differently at one time of the day than another because of the body's circadian rhythms.

• *Experience with the drug* refers to the number of times it has been used and the levels of past usage. Trying a drug—a cigarette, an alcoholic drink, a stimulant—for the first time is often a neutral or unpleasant experience. But reactions may change once a person has become familiar with the drug's effects.

• *Mental set* refers to expectations about the drug's effects, the reasons for taking the drug, and the presence or absence of a desire to justify some behavior by being "under the influence." For example, some people drink to become more sociable, friendly, or seductive; others drink solely to have an excuse for violence. Because so many crimes of violence are committed when the participants have been drinking, and because so many marital quarrels accompany drinking, alcohol is often assumed to "release" anger and aggression. However, the ultimate source of aggression is not in the alcohol but in the mind of the drinker. About half of all men arrested for assaulting their wives claim to have been drinking at the time. Yet research finds that most of these men do *not* have enough alcohol in their bloodstream to qualify as legally intoxicated, and most have *not* been drinking immediately prior to being violent (Gelles & Straus, 1988). Further, the link between alcohol and aggression disappears when people believe they will be held responsible for their actions while drunk (Critchlow, 1983).

People's expectations of how a drug will affect them play a part in how they respond to it. Several studies have identified a "think-drink" effect by comparing people who are *actually* drinking liquor (vodka and tonic) with those who *think* they are drinking liquor but are actually getting only tonic and lime juice.

The motives for using a drug, expectations about its effects, and the setting in which it is used all contribute to a person's reactions to the drug.

(Vodka has a subtle taste, and most people cannot tell the real and phony drinks apart.) Men behave more belligerently when they think they are drinking vodka than when they think they are drinking plain tonic water, regardless of the actual content of the drinks. Both sexes report feeling sexually aroused when they think they are drinking vodka, whether they actually get vodka or not (Abrams & Wilson, 1983; Marlatt & Rohsenow, 1980).

Even alcoholics are influenced by mental set. Alcoholics who have a couple of tonics, thinking they are drinking vodka, develop a "craving" for more liquor. A researcher reported the case of an alcoholic who sometimes could drink a dozen whiskeys without a sign of inebriation. At other times he staggered around and became antagonistic after two drinks. His reactions depended on his mood before drinking, which in turn depended on how he was getting along with the people who mattered to him (Rioch, 1975). Expectations and prior mood probably play a role in all psychological drug reactions, including those to coffee and cigarettes.

• *Environmental setting* greatly affects an individual's response to a drug. Setting is the reason that a person can have one glass of wine at home alone and feel sleepy, but have three glasses of wine at a wedding party and feel full of pep. It is the reason that a person might feel happy and "high" drinking with good friends but fearful and nervous drinking with strangers. In one study of reactions to alcohol, researchers found that most of the drinkers became depressed, angry, confused, and unfriendly. Then it dawned on them that *anyone* might become depressed, angry, confused, and unfriendly if asked to drink bourbon at 9:00 A.M. in a bleak hospital room—the setting for the experiment (Warren & Raynes, 1972).

Now, none of this means that alcohol and other drugs are merely placebos. Drugs do have physiological effects, many of them quite powerful. However, people must learn from their culture how to interpret these effects and how to behave when they occur. Most Americans start their day with a cup of coffee because it increases alertness. (Textbook authors could not survive without it.) But when coffee was first introduced in Europe, there were protests against it. Women said it made their husbands impotent and inconsiderate—and maybe it did. Conversely, in the nineteenth century, Americans looked on marijuana as a mild sedative with no "mind-altering" properties. They didn't expect it to give them a high, and it didn't; it merely put them to sleep (Weil, 1972/1986). Today's marijuana is more potent, but motives for using it have also changed. Young users are often expressing their rejection of conventional adult roles and social institutions (D. Kandel, 1984), and that may affect their reactions.

Public attitudes can affect overall patterns of drug use, as well as reactions to specific drugs. Gallup polls indicate that attitudes of North Americans toward both illicit and legal drugs have become more negative in recent years,

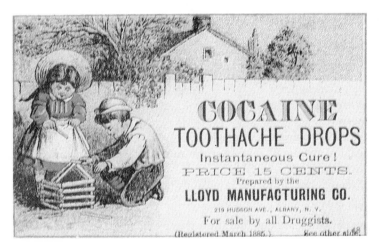

Before its sale was banned in the 1920s, cocaine was widely touted as a cure for everything from toothaches to timidity. The drug found its way into teas, tonics, throat lozenges, and even soft drinks (including, briefly, Coca-Cola, which derived its name from the coca plant). Ingesting it had a less powerful effect than sniffing, injecting, or smoking it, as is done today. However, as cocaine use became associated in the popular mind with criminality and as concerns about abuse grew, public opinion turned against it.

and alcohol, cigarette and illicit drug use are all declining. High school and college students increasingly see drugs as dangerous and socially unacceptable. Although teenagers and young adults in the United States are still more likely to use illicit drugs than their counterparts in other industrialized countries, reported usage has fallen (see Table 4.2). In 1990, a third of all high school seniors said they had taken at least one illicit drug during the past year, down from a peak of 54 percent in 1979 (Johnston, O'Malley, & Bachman, 1991). The decrease in usage has occurred among young people of all social classes, racial groups, and geographic areas, and even among those who do poorly in school and are frequently truant. (The figures do not include teenagers who drop out of school, however.)

Unfortunately, many people in our society still learn drug reactions that include substance abuse and social abusiveness. The findings in this chapter raise important questions to consider as you think about this problem: Given the universality of drug use, is total prohibition of all drugs the answer? Which drugs, if any, should be prohibited? Can we create mental sets and environmental settings that promote the harmless use of some drugs?

TABLE 4.2

Drug Use Among High School Seniors

These figures, from an annual national survey of nearly 16,000 seniors, show the percentages who used various drugs within the previous year, or, in the case of alcohol and cigarettes, the previous month. Although alcohol and cigarette use have declined since the surveys began in 1975, alcohol consumption fell only slightly during the past few years and cigarette smoking, which declined in the general population, remained stable among young people throughout the 1980s. Use of most other drugs, however, has fallen steadily.

Drug	Usage in 1990	Usage in peak year
At least one illicit drug	32.5	54.2 (1979)
Marijuana	27.0	50.8 (1979)
Cocaine (all types)	5.3	13.1 (1985)
Crack cocaine	1.9	3.9 (1987)
Tranquilizers	3.5	10.8 (1977)
Stimulants	9.1	20.3 (1982)
LSD	5.4	7.2 (1975)
PCP	1.2	7.0 (1979)
Alcohol	57.1*	72.1 (1978)
Cigarettes	29.4*	38.8 (1976)

*Percentage using within past 30 days.

Source: Based on Johnston, O'Malley, & Bachman, 1991.

QUICK QUIZ

A. See if you can name the following:

1. An illegal stimulant
2. Two drugs that interfere with the formation of new long-term memories
3. Three types of depressant drugs
4. A legal "recreational" drug that acts as a depressant on the central nervous system
5. Four factors that influence a person's psychological reactions to a drug

B. A bodybuilder who has been illegally taking anabolic steroids says the drugs make him feel more aggressive. What are some other possible interpretations?

ANSWERS:

think he is more aggressive and his behavior may contradict his self-perceptions. (or other drugs he is taking) may be making him more aggressive; or he may only building gym may encourage aggressiveness; other influences in the person's life effect); bodybuilding itself may increase aggressiveness; the culture of the body-builder's increased aggressiveness may be due to his expectations (a placebo experience with the drug, mental set, and the environmental setting. **B.** The body-tranquilizers, and alcohol **5.** the person's physical condition, prior ex-**A. 1.** cocaine; also some amphetamines **2.** marijuana and alcohol **3.** barbiturates,

Hypnosis

Hypnosis is usually defined as a heightened state of suggestibility or responsiveness. It is *not* sleep; brain waves during hypnosis are similar to those of ordinary wakefulness. The person almost always remains fully aware of what is going on and remembers the experience later, unless explicitly instructed to forget it. Even then, the memory can be restored by a prearranged signal. To induce hypnosis, the hypnotist typically suggests that the person being hypnotized feels relaxed, is getting sleepy, and feels the eyelids getting heavier and heavier. In a singsong or monotonous voice, the hypnotist assures the subject that he or she is sinking "deeper and deeper," without actually falling asleep. Sometimes the hypnotist has the person concentrate on a certain color or small object. Some people can be hypnotized while they are doing something active, such as riding a bicycle (Bányai & Hilgard, 1976).

People who have been hypnotized report that the focus of attention turns outward, toward the hypnotist's voice. The experience is sometimes likened to total absorption in a good book, a play, or a favorite piece of music. People who can easily become absorbed in such activities, who can suspend ordinary reality and become involved in the world of imagination, make good subjects (J.R. Hilgard, 1979). Not surprisingly, children are in general more easily hypnotized than adults, who often have learned to be wary of fantasy and are unwilling to suspend ordinary perceptions of reality. However, most people are at least somewhat susceptible to hypnotic suggestions.

There is no evidence that people can be hypnotized against their wills or forced under hypnosis to do things they would not otherwise consider. An individual must *choose* to turn initiative over to the hypnotist and cooperate with the hypnotist's suggestions (Lynn, Rhue, & Weekes, 1990). However, like drugs, hypnosis can be used to justify letting go of inhibitions. ("I know this looks silly, but after all, I'm hypnotized.") Hypnotized people may also do unusual things

■ **hypnosis**
A condition in which attention is focused and a person is extremely responsive to suggestion.

if they accept a suggestion that they are in an appropriate situation for doing so. They may take off their clothes if they are convinced they are in the shower or attack someone they are led to believe has killed one of their friends.

Because hypnotic suggestions may affect perception, memory, or motivation, hypnosis has found many applications in both medicine and psychology. It has been used effectively to treat headaches; anesthetize people undergoing dental work, surgery, or childbirth; eliminate unwanted habits such as smoking or nail biting; improve study skills; reduce nausea in cancer patients undergoing chemotherapy; and even pump up the confidence of athletes. Psychologists have done extensive research on pain reduction under hypnosis. In a typical experiment, a hypnotized volunteer places an arm in ice water for several seconds, then rates the pain. Normally, this is an excruciating experience. But when subjects are told that they will feel no pain, they report little or none, nor do they show any obvious signs of distress, such as groaning or grimacing. After the hypnotic session ends, they continue to deny that they felt pain (Hilgard & Hilgard, 1975).

Yet many psychologists believe there is less to hypnosis than meets the eye. They note that claims about the "powers" of hypnosis are often overblown or poorly supported. For example, studies on how hypnotic suggestions might bolster the immune system have lacked good controls, and when proper procedures are used, the effects tend to disappear (Stam, 1989). Further, there is good evidence that unhypnotized people, if encouraged to relax, concentrate, and do their best, can respond in the same way as hypnotized people to suggestions for pain reduction, increased self-esteem, and all the rest.

Then what is going on? Is hypnosis really an altered state of consciousness, subjectively and objectively different from ordinary wakefulness? Or is it something else—and if so, what?

HYPNOSIS AS AN ALTERED STATE.   The traditional view of hypnosis has been that it is a true altered state. Although hypnosis has not been consistently linked with predictable changes in brain waves, eye movements, skin resistance, or other physiological responses, Ernest Hilgard, who has studied hypnosis for many years, argues that such responses are not critical for concluding that hyp-

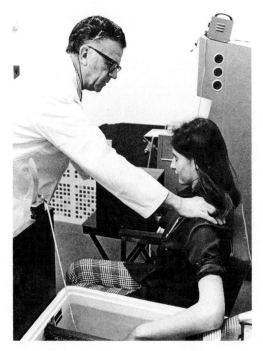

Ordinarily, a person whose arm is immersed in ice water feels intense pain. But Ernest Hilgard has found that if hypnotized people are told the pain will be minimal, they report little or no discomfort, and, like the young woman shown here in one of Hilgard's studies, they seem unperturbed.

nosis is different from ordinary waking consciousness. After all, he notes, scientists readily accepted the reality of dreams and the existence of sleep as a separate state before anyone knew about rapid eye movements or EEG patterns.

Hilgard's own belief is that hypnosis is an altered state that involves *dissociation*, the split in consciousness we mentioned when discussing lucid dreams (E.R. Hilgard, 1977). In dissociation, one part of the mind operates independently from another. In many hypnotized persons, says Hilgard, only one of the parts goes along with the hypnotic suggestion. The other part is like a *hidden observer*, watching but not participating. Unless given special instructions, the hypnotized person remains unaware of the observer.

Hilgard and his colleagues have attempted to question the "hidden observer" directly. For example, using the ice water procedure, they tell hypnotized subjects that although they will feel no pain, the nonsubmerged hand will be able to signal the level of any hidden pain by pressing a key. In this situation, many people say they feel little or no pain while at the same time their free hand is busily pressing one of the keys. After coming "out" of hypnosis these people continue to insist that they were pain-free—unless the hypnotist suggests that the "hidden observer" will be able to issue a separate report.

HYPNOSIS AS GOAL-DIRECTED FANTASY.   Other psychologists believe that hypnosis is really only "goal-directed fantasy," in which the person uses imagination in an attempt to comply with the hypnotist's suggestions. Theodore Barber notes that there is no truly objective way to verify that the hypnotized person is in a separate state (Barber, 1979; Barber & Wilson, 1977). In fact, says Barber, the notion of a hypnotic state is circular; that is, the explanation of it restates the problem. How do we know that a person is hypnotized? Because he or she obeys the hypnotist's suggestions. And why does the person obey those suggestions? Because the person is hypnotized!

Barber and more recently Nicholas Spanos (1986) point out that all the apparently astounding things that people do while "under" hypnosis can also be done in the waking state, *if* people are sufficiently motivated and *if* they believe they can succeed. For example, when a stage hypnotist has a hypnotized person stretch out rigid as a plank between two chairs, with the head on the back of one chair and ankles on the back of another, nothing special is actually occurring. Most unhypnotized people can do the same thing—they only think they can't. Barber and Spanos do not deny that hypnotic suggestion leads to feats of great strength, pain reduction, hallucinations, or even the disappearance of warts. However, they cite impressive evidence that suggestion alone, without the special procedures of hypnosis, can produce exactly the same results.

What about the frequent claim that under hypnosis, people can relive their fourth birthday party or a childhood trauma? Stage hypnotists, "past-lives channelers," and even some psychotherapists have reported dramatic "childlike" performances by people who have been "age-regressed" to earlier years or even earlier centuries. They use this apparent evidence of their own eyes to argue that people literally revert to an earlier mode of psychological functioning. But is it true?

Michael Nash (1987) has reviewed 60 years of scientific studies on this question. The research clearly shows that when people are "regressed" to infancy, their brain wave patterns and reflexes do not become infantile. Outgrown emotional disorders do not reappear. Nor do they reason as children do or show child-sized IQs. Their mental and moral performance, says Nash, remains "essentially adult in nature." What about enhanced recall of childhood events? Once again, the answer is negative. Hypnosis does *not* reliably improve memory for early experiences, even though hypnotized people often swear it does. In one of Nash's own studies, hypnotized individuals tried to recall what their

Under hypnosis, Jim will cheerfully describe the chocolate cake at his fourth birthday or remember a former life as a twelfth-century French peasant. As it turns out, lemon cake was served at that birthday, and Jim can't speak twelfth-century French. What are some possible explanations of these vivid "memories"?

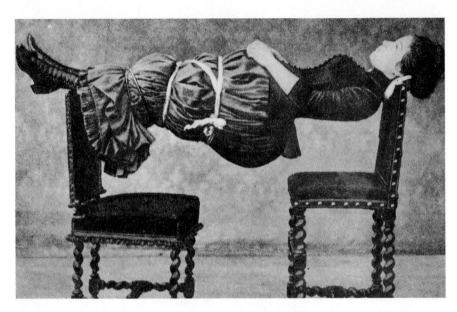

Amazing, right? Or maybe not. Although the chair trick is a staple of the stage hypnotist's repertoire, most unhypnotized people can do it, too. The only way to find out if hypnosis produces unique results is to do controlled research—with control groups.

favorite comforting object was at age 3 (teddy bears, blankets, and the like). Only 23 percent were accurate, compared to 70 percent of a nonhypnotized control group! (Mothers independently verified the accuracy of these memories.)

Of course, Nash says, people do undergo dramatic changes in behavior and subjective experience when they are hypnotically regressed. For example, they may use baby talk or report that they feel 4 again. But the reason is not that they *are* 4, simply that they are willing to play the role. They will do the same when they are hypnotically *progressed* ahead—say, to age 70 or 80—or regressed to "past lives." Their belief that they are 7 or 70 or 7,000 may be sincere and convincing, but it is all in their minds.

In a fascinating series of studies, Nicholas Spanos and his colleagues (1991) instructed hypnotized Canadian university students to regress past their own birth to a previous life. About a third of the students reported they could do so But when they were asked, while "reliving" a past life under hypnosis, to name the leader of their country, say whether the country was at peace or at war, or describe the money used in their community, the students could not do it. One student, who thought he was Julius Caesar, said the year was 50 A.D. and he was emperor of Rome—but Caesar died in 44 B.C. and was never crowned emperor (and besides, dating years as A.D. or B.C. did not begin until several centuries after 50 A.D.).

In these studies, all of the students who believed they were reliving a past life under hypnosis were actually weaving events, places, and persons from their present lives into their accounts. Spanos and his colleagues found that descriptions of past lives, and people's acceptance of their regression experiences as "real," were also influenced by the instructions of the hypnotist. The researchers conclude that the act of "remembering" another "self" involves the construction of a fantasy that accords not only with one's own beliefs but the beliefs of others—a fantasy that may be experienced as real. They suggest that a similar process occurs when people under hypnosis report a hidden observer, multiple personalities, spirit possession, or "memories" of UFO abductions.

Even under the best of circumstances, when the focus is an event from real life, people find it hard to distinguish an authentic memory from their inferences about what must have happened (see Chapter 7). Under hypnosis, the natural tendency to confuse fact and speculation is increased both by a desire to please the hypnotist and by the fact that hypnosis encourages fantasy and vivid imagery. Consider what happens when hypnosis is used to jog the mem-

Drawing by M. Stevens; © 1987 The New Yorker Magazine, Inc.

Why is it that people who report "past lives" never seem to recall an average, ordinary existence? Why do so many think they were emperors, courtesans, crusaders, or priestesses?

ories of crime victims and trial witnesses. In some cases, it leads to a happy ending. After the 1976 kidnapping of a busload of schoolchildren in Chowchilla, California, the bus driver was hypnotized and was able to recall all but one of the license plate numbers on the kidnappers' car. That clue provided a breakthrough in the case. But in other cases, hypnotized witnesses have been wrong. Research finds that although hypnosis does sometimes boost the amount of information recalled, it also increases errors, perhaps because hypnotized people are more willing than nonhypnotized people to guess, or because they mistake vividly imagined possibilities for actual memories (Dinges et al., 1992; Dywan & Bowers, 1983; Whitehouse et al., 1988). Because pseudomemories and errors are so common in hypnotically induced recall, both the American Psychological Association and the American Medical Association are on record as opposing the use of "hypnotically refreshed" testimony in court.

HYPNOSIS AS ROLE PLAYING.   But, you say, hypnosis *looks* like an altered state: There are the drooping eyelids, the fixed gaze, the slumped posture. However, hypnosis does not have to involve these bodily reactions. When it does, it is probably because most people know from films or nightclub acts how a hypnotized person is *supposed* to behave. Indeed, Theodore Sarbin and his colleagues believe that role playing is the very essence of hypnosis (Coe & Sarbin, 1977; Sarbin, 1991). In this view, the hypnotized person is playing the part of a hypnotized person, a part that has analogies in ordinary life, where we willingly submit to the suggestions of parents, teachers, doctors, therapists, and television commercials. The person is not merely faking or playacting. The role of hypnotized person, like many social roles, is so engrossing and involving that actions occur without conscious intent.

Sometimes objective tests can penetrate the role. Imagine that a person has been given a hypnotic suggestion to become deaf until she receives a tap on the shoulder. The suggestion seems to work; even the crash of cymbals behind her back fails to get her attention or startle her. But then the researcher has the subject participate in a procedure called *delayed auditory feedback*. As she reads a paragraph aloud, her words are recorded and played back to her through earphones with half a second delay. People with normal hearing respond to delayed auditory feedback with stuttering, slurring, and hesitation. They speak more loudly than usual and mispronounce words. (The same thing can happen when a bad long-distance telephone connection produces an echo of your own voice.) Studies have shown that hypnotized subjects, though apparently deaf to their own voices, will respond in exactly the same way as would a hearing person (Barber, 1979). Therefore, they must be able to hear.

But why don't they realize that they can hear? Recent research on a related phenomenon, "hypnotic blindness," suggests that hypnotized people use active strategies to experience what the hypnotist tells them to experience. They do not merely focus on the hypnotist's words; they try their best to meet the demands of the hypnotic setting. For example, when shown a page with a word on it, a person told to be "blind" may think of a white curtain coming down over the page and then manage to believe that he or she is not seeing the word (Bryant & McConkey, 1990).

Where does this leave us? The preponderance of evidence casts doubt on the idea that hypnosis is a profound alteration in consciousness. Yet, as with dream theories, the evidence sometimes allows for differing interpretations, and so the debate is likely to continue. Whatever hypnosis is, by studying it psychologists can learn much about human suggestibility, the power of imagination, and the way we perceive the present and remember the past.

QUICK QUIZ

A. True or false:

1. Most people are at least somewhat susceptible to hypnotic suggestions.
2. According to Hilgard, hypnosis is a state of dissociation involving a "hidden observer."
3. Hypnosis gives us special powers we do not ordinarily have.
4. Hypnosis reduces errors in memory.

B. Some people believe that hypnotic suggestions can bolster the immune system and even help cure cancer. However, findings on this issue (mostly in the form of case reports) are contradictory, and positive results have been hard to replicate (Stam, 1989). One researcher has dismissed this problem by saying that a negative result just means the hypnotist was untalented or lacked the "right" kind of personality. As a critical thinker, can you spot what's wrong with his reasoning? (Think back to the qualities of the ideal scientist discussed in Chapter 2.)

ANSWERS:

A. 1. T 2. T 3. F 4. F B. The researcher's argument violates the principle of falsifiability. If a result is positive, he counts it as evidence. But if a result is negative, he refuses to count it as counterevidence ("Maybe the hypnotist just wasn't good enough"). With this kind of reasoning, there is no way to tell whether the hypothesis is right or wrong.

As we have seen in this chapter, changes in consciousness, however they are initiated, allow us to explore how our expectations and explanations of behavior affect what we do and how we feel. States of consciousness are interesting in and of themselves. And under scientific scrutiny, hypnosis, drug-induced states, dreams, and biological rhythms—phenomena once thought beyond the pale of science—can also deepen our understanding of the intimate relationship between body and mind.

How to Get a Good Night's Sleep

You hop into bed, turn out the lights, close your eyes, and wait for slumber. An hour later, you're still waiting. Finally you drop off, but at 3:00 A.M., to your chagrin, you're awake again. By the time the rooster crows, you have put in a hard day's night.

Insomnia affects most people at one time or another, and many people most of the time. In search of relief, Americans spend hundreds of millions of dollars each year on sleeping aids. Their money is not well spent. Over-the-counter pills are almost worthless for inducing sleep, and prescription drugs can actually make matters worse. Barbiturates greatly suppress REM sleep, a result that eventually causes wakefulness, and also suppress stages 3 and 4, the deeper stages of sleep. Any effectiveness they do have usually disappears within a few days. Other medications, known as benzodiazepines, lead to tolerance more slowly, but they produce a breakdown product that stays in the body during the day and causes diminished alertness and hand-eye coordination problems (Kelly, 1981a). Says one well-known sleep researcher, "Let me put a person on sleeping pills for a month, and I'll guarantee broken sleep" (Webb, quoted in Goleman, 1982).

Studies of sleep suggest some better alternatives. Here are some basic principles:

• *Be sure you actually have a sleep problem.* Many people only *think* they don't sleep well. People complaining of insomnia often greatly overestimate how long it takes them to nod off and underestimate how much sleep they actually get (Bonnet, 1990). In one study, 55 people reporting for help at a sleep clinic were observed for several nights in the laboratory. Most took less than 30 minutes to fall asleep. Only 30 got less than six-and-a-half hours of sleep per night, and only 26 were awake more than 30 minutes total during the night (Carskadon, Mitler, & Dement, 1974).

The amount of time spent sleeping is not a good criterion of insomnia in any case. Some people need a lot of sleep; in fact, some research suggests that most of us would be more alert during the day if we could sleep longer at night (Roehrs et al., 1989). Yet some apparently healthy people seem to get by fine on as little as three or four hours. As people age, they typically sleep more lightly, and often break up sleep into nighttime snoozing and an afternoon nap. If you function well with less sleep than most people get, you probably shouldn't worry about it, since worrying itself can cause insomnia (Lichstein & Fanning, 1990).

• *Get a correct diagnosis of the sleep problem.* Once you know you have a problem, you need to identify the cause. Disruption of sleep can result from psychological disturbances, such as severe depression. It can also result from physical disorders. In *sleep apnea,* breathing periodically stops for a few moments, causing the person to choke and gasp. This can happen hundreds of times a night, often without the person knowing it, and may lead to high blood pressure or irregular heartbeat. There are several causes of sleep apnea, from blockage of air passages to failure of the brain to control respiration correctly. A person with apnea needs medical evaluation. In *narcolepsy,* another serious disorder, an individual is subject to irresistible and unpredictable daytime attacks of sleepiness lasting from 5 to 30 minutes. For reasons not yet clear, narcoleptics often lapse immediately into REM sleep, even during the briefest naps. Some researchers think that as many as a quarter of a million Americans may suffer from this condition, many without knowing it.

• *Avoid excessive use of alcohol or other drugs.* Many drugs interfere with normal slumber. Alcohol suppresses REM sleep and tranquilizers like Valium and Librium reduce stage 4 sleep. Coffee, tea, cola, and chocolate all contain caffeine, which is a stimulant.

• *Don't associate the bedroom with wakefulness.* When environmental cues are repeatedly associated with some behavior, they can come to trigger the behavior (Bootzin, Epstein, & Wood, 1991). If you don't want your bedroom to trigger wakefulness, avoid reading, studying, and watching TV there. Also avoid lying awake for hours waiting for sleep, since your frustration will cause arousal that can be associated with the bedroom. If you can't sleep, get up and do something else, preferably something dull, in a different room. When you feel drowsy, try sleeping again. If necessary, repeat the process until you fall asleep easily.

• *Take care of your health.* This may sound like a grandmother's advice, but good health habits are probably important for good sleep. Nutrition is one area to watch. As we saw in Chapter 3, the amino acid *tryptophan* promotes the onset of sleep, and there may be other dietary influences on alertness and relaxation. Exercise during the day also seems to enhance sleep, but it should be avoided right before bedtime, since in the short term it heightens alertness.

Finally, since much if not most insomnia is related to anxiety and stress, it makes sense to get to the source of your problems. You can't expect to sleep well with adrenaline pouring through your bloodstream and worries crowding your mind. In an evolutionary sense, sleeplessness is an adaptive response to danger and threat. As Woody Allen once said, "The lamb and the lion shall lie down together, but the lamb will not be very sleepy." When your anxieties decrease, so may your sleepless nights.

SUMMARY

1. *Consciousness* is the awareness of oneself and the environment. *States of consciousness* are distinct patterns of consciousness, and changes in these states are often associated with *biological rhythms*, periodic, more or less regular fluctuations in physiological functioning. *Circadian* fluctuations occur about once a day; *infradian* fluctuations occur less often; and *ultradian* fluctuations occur more frequently than once a day, often on a 90-minute cycle.

2. Circadian rhythms appear to be governed by biological "clocks" in the brain that seem to be linked to each other and to an overall coordinator in the hypothalamus. These rhythms are studied by allowing people to "free run." When volunteers live in isolation from all time cues they typically live a "day" of about 25 hours. In normal life, when a person's usual routine changes, circadian rhythms may be *desynchronized*, that is, thrown out of phase with one another.

3. Infradian rhythms of many types have been observed, including seasonal fluctuations in vulnerability to depression. However, it is hard to prove that they are endogenous—that is, that they originate within the body and are not due to social or cultural conventions or other external factors.

4. One infradian rhythm that is endogenous is the menstrual cycle, during which various hormones rise and fall predictably. Physical symptoms associated with the cycle usually have a biological cause. However, well-controlled (blind) studies on "PMS" do not support claims that emotional symptoms are reliably and universally tied to the menstrual cycle. Overall, women and men do not differ in emotional symptoms reported or number of mood swings experienced in the course of a month. Expectations and learning affect how we interpret bodily and emotional changes. Few people of either sex are likely to undergo dramatic monthly mood swings or personality changes because of hormones.

5. Sleep, which recurs on a circadian rhythm, seems necessary not only for bodily restoration but also normal brain function. During sleep, periods of *rapid eye movement*, or *REM*, alternate with non-REM sleep in an ultradian rhythm. For descriptive purposes, non-REM sleep is divided into four stages associated with certain brain wave patterns. During REM sleep, the brain is active and there are other signs of arousal, yet most of the skeletal muscles are limp; thus REM sleep has also been called "paradoxical sleep." Dreams are reported most often during REM sleep, and everyone dreams every night.

6. The *psychoanalytic explanation* of dreams is that they allow us to gratify forbidden or unrealistic wishes and desires that have been forced into the unconscious part of the mind. Thoughts and objects may be disguised as symbolic images that provide clues to the dream's meaning. Most psychologists today accept the notion that dreams are more than incoherent ramblings of the mind, but many quarrel with specific psychoanalytic interpretations.

7. The *problem-solving explanation* of dreams emphasizes the opportunity they provide for working through emotional issues, especially during times of crisis. Cartwright's findings on divorced people provide support for this explanation.

8. The *information-processing explanation* of dreams views them as opportunities for mental housekeeping. According to Christopher Evans, sleep gives the brain an opportunity to scan and sort through new data, and dreams are snippets from an ongoing process that is otherwise inaccessible to consciousness. A similar idea, advanced by Francis Crick and Graeme Mitchison, holds that during REM periods the brain jettisons mental "garbage." These theories could explain why REM sleep occurs in human infants and animals, who also need to "sort things out."

9. The *activation-synthesis theory* of dreaming, proposed by Allan Hobson, holds that dreams occur when the cortex tries to make sense of spontaneous neural firing initiated in the pons. The resulting interpretation is a dream. In this view, dreams do not disguise unconscious wishes, but they can reveal a person's perceptions, conflicts, and concerns. The activation-synthesis theory is well developed, but not everyone agrees that the physiological evidence supports it, and alternative explanations of the evidence have been proposed.

10. In all cultures, people have found ways to produce *altered* or *alternate* states of consciousness. For example, *psychoactive drugs* alter the body's biochemistry, primarily by acting on brain neurotransmitters. Most psychoactive drugs can be classified as *stimulants*, *depressants*, *opiates*, or *psychedelics*, depending on their central nervous system effects and their impact on behavior and mood, but some drugs, such as anabolic steroids and marijuana, fall outside these categories.

11. The effects of a psychoactive drug cannot be explained solely in terms of its chemical properties. Reactions to a drug are also influenced by the user's physical condition, prior experience with the drug, and mental set and by the environmental setting. Public attitudes affect drug reactions and patterns of drug use.

12. *Hypnosis* is usually defined as a heightened state of suggestibility or responsiveness. Some researchers consider it to be an altered state that involves *dissociation*, or a split in consciousness. Others regard it as goal-directed fantasy or as a form of role playing in which the role is so engrossing that the person interprets it as "real." These two interpretations can account for apparent age and past-life "regressions" and hypnotically induced "blindness" and "deafness." Like drug-induced states, dreams, and biological rhythms, hypnosis can help shed light on the intricate relationship between body and mind.

KEY TERMS

consciousness *113*	free-running *115*
states of consciousness *113*	melatonin *116*
biological rhythm *113*	internal desynchronization *116*
endogenous *114*	menstrual cycle *117*
circadian rhythm *114*	"premenstrual syndrome" *118*
infradian rhythm *114*	REM sleep *122*
ultradian rhythm *114*	non-REM sleep *122*

Sensation and Perception

Minds that have nothing to confer
Find little to perceive.

WILLIAM WORDSWORTH

When he was only 10 months old, S. B. went blind. An infection damaged his corneas, the transparent membranes on the front surfaces of the eyes, leaving him sightless. As he grew into adulthood, S. B. adjusted well to his disability; a cheerful and independent man, he married, supported himself, and led an active life. But through the years he continued to dream of regaining his sight.

At last, when S. B. was 52, a doctor successfully performed corneal transplant surgery. Almost as soon as the bandages were removed, S. B. was able to identify common objects and letters of the alphabet. Within days he could make his way down corridors without touching the walls, and could even tell time from a large wall clock. But there were also some strange gaps in his visual world. Although his eyes now functioned well, he seemed blind to objects or parts of objects that he had not previously touched. He could not read facial expressions well or recognize pictures of scenery. Gradually his visual abilities improved, yet his perception of the world months after surgery remained limited and distorted by his previous sensory experiences. When asked to draw a bus, he produced the sketch in the margin—leaving out the front end, which he had never felt with his hands. In many ways S. B. continued to lead the life of a blind man until his death three years after the operation (Gregory & Wallace, 1963).

S. B.'s story is an unusual one, but it contains some lessons for us all. Like S. B., we all depend on our senses for our everyday understanding of physical reality. Also like S. B., we have only a partial perception of that reality. Even with normal eyesight and hearing, we are blind to most of the electromagnetic energy waves around us and deaf to most of the pressure waves that fill the air. And because of expectations shaped by our previous experiences, even with normal sensory abilities we may look but not see, listen but not hear.

Yet despite these limitations, our sensory and perceptual capacities are astonishingly complex and sensitive. In this chapter, you will learn how your sense organs take in information from the environment and how your brain interprets and organizes that information to construct a reliable model of the world. The boundary between these two processes is not always easy to draw, because they occur so quickly and because some organization occurs even before incoming signals reach the brain. However, as a way of conceptualizing what is going on, psychologists have traditionally called the first process *sensation* and the second *perception*.

Sensation is the detection and encoding of changes in physical energy caused by environmental or internal events. The cells that detect such changes are called **sense receptors** and are located in the *sense organs*—the eyes, ears, tongue, nose, skin, and internal body tissues. The receptors for smell, pressure, pain, and temperature are structural extensions (dendrites) of sensory neurons. The receptors for vision, hearing, and taste are distinct cells separated from sensory neurons

■ **sensation**
The detection or direct experience of physical energy in the external or internal environment due to stimulation of receptors in the sense organs.

■ **sense receptors**
Specialized cells that convert physical energy in the environment into electrical energy that can be transmitted as nerve impulses to the brain.

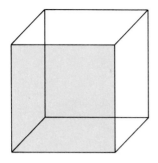

by synapses. The sensory processes made possible by these sense receptors produce an immediate awareness of sound, color, form, and other basic building blocks of consciousness. They tell us what is happening, both inside our bodies and in the world beyond our own skins.

Without sensation, we would have nothing to laugh, cry, or think about. Yet sensation is essentially the handmaiden of **perception,** the set of processes that organize and interpret the sensory impulses. Perception tells us where one object begins and another ends. It assembles the building blocks of sensory experience into meaningful patterns. The sense of vision produces a two-dimensional image on the back of the eye, but we *perceive* the world in three dimensions. The sense of hearing brings us the sound of a C, an E, and a G played simultaneously on the piano, but we *perceive* a C-major chord.

Look at the drawing of the cube in the margin. If you stare at the cube, it will flip-flop in front of your eyes. The surface on the outside and front will suddenly be on the inside and back, or vice versa. You *sense* only some black lines on a field of white. However, because your brain can interpret the sensory image in alternate ways, you *perceive* two different cubes. The ambiguity is not in the picture but in the eye (actually, the brain) of the beholder. Something similar happens when you repeat certain speech sounds. Say the word "say" over and over again. "Say" will soon become "ace," and then "ace" will shift back to "say." The sound signal does not change, only your perception of it.

Psychologists study sensation and perception because together these processes are the foundation of learning, thinking, and acting. Much of the research in this area is of the "pure," or basic, sort. But knowledge about sensation and perception is often put to practical use, for example, in the design of color television sets, hearing aids, and robots that "see," "hear," and "feel," and in the training of flight controllers, astronauts, and others who must make important decisions based on what they sense and perceive.

■ OUR SENSATIONAL SENSES

At some point you probably learned that there are five senses corresponding to five sense organs: vision (eyes), hearing (ears), taste (tongue), touch (skin), and smell (nose). The senses have been categorized in this way at least since Aristotle's time. Actually, however, there are more than five senses, though scientists disagree about the exact number. The skin, which is the organ of touch or pressure, also senses heat, cold, and pain, not to mention itching and tickling. The ear, which is the organ of hearing, also contains receptors that account for a sense of balance. The internal muscles contain receptors responsible for a sense of bodily movement.

All of our senses evolved to help us survive. Even pain, which causes so much human misery, is indispensable, for it alerts us to illness and injury. In rare cases, people have been born without a sense of pain. Although free of the hurts and aches that plague the rest of us, they lead difficult lives. Because they feel none of pain's warnings, they burn, bruise, and cut themselves more than other people do. One young woman developed inflamed joints because she failed to turn over in her sleep or shift her weight while standing, acts that people with normal pain sensation perform automatically. At the age of only 29 she died from massive infections, due in part to skin and bone injuries (Melzack, 1973).

Sensory experiences contribute immeasurably to the quality of life, even when they are not directly helping us survive. They entertain us, amuse us, inspire us. If we really pay attention to our senses, said poet William Wordsworth, we can "see into the life of things" and hear "the still, sad music of humanity."

■ **perception**
The process by which the brain organizes and interprets sensory information.

The Riddle of Separate Sensations

Sensation begins with the sense receptors. When these receptors detect an appropriate stimulus—light, mechanical pressure, or chemical molecules—they convert the energy of the stimulus into electrical impulses that travel along nerves to the brain. This conversion of one form of energy into another is known as **transduction.** Sense receptors are biological transducers. Radio receivers, which convert radio waves into sound waves, are mechanical transducers, as are Geiger counters, television sets, and electronic eyes.

Sense receptors are like military scouts who scan the terrain for signs of activity and relay a message when they detect something. These scouts cannot make many decisions on their own. They must transmit what they learn to field officers—sensory neurons in the peripheral nervous system. The field officers in turn must report to generals at a command center—the cells of the brain. The generals are responsible for analyzing the reports, combining information brought in by different scouts, and deciding what it all means.

The various "field officers" in the sensory system all use exactly the same form of communication, a neural impulse. It is as if they must all send their messages on a bongo and can only go "boom." How, then, are we able to experience so many different kinds of sensations? The answer is that the nervous system *encodes* the messages, using two basic kinds of code (Schneider & Tarshis, 1986). One kind, which is *anatomical*, was first described as far back as 150 A.D. by the Greek physician Galen, and was elaborated on in 1826 by the German physiologist Johannes Müller in his *doctrine of specific nerve energies.* According to this doctrine, different sensory modalities exist because signals received by the various sense organs stimulate different nerve pathways, which terminate in different areas of the brain. Signals from the eye cause impulses to travel along the optic nerve to the visual cortex. Signals from the ear cause impulses to travel along the auditory nerve to the auditory cortex. Light and sound waves produce different sensations because of these anatomical differences.

Although some of the physiological details proposed by Müller have since been shown to be wrong, his fundamental concept is generally correct. The doctrine of specific nerve energies implies that what we know about the world ultimately reduces to what we know about the state of our own nervous system. Therefore, if sound waves could stimulate nerves that end in the visual part of the brain, we would "see" sound. In fact, a similar sort of crossover does occur when you close an eye, press lightly on the side of the lid, and "see" a flash of light. The pressure apparently produces an impulse that travels up the optic nerve to the visual area of the brain.

Anatomical encoding, however, does not completely solve the riddle of separate sensations. It accounts well for our ability to distinguish visual from auditory signals, but linking the different skin senses to distinct nerve pathways has proven difficult. The doctrine of specific nerve energies also fails to explain variations of experience within a particular sense—the sight of pink versus red, the sound of a piccolo versus the sound of a tuba, or the feel of a pinprick versus the feel of a kiss. An additional kind of code is therefore necessary.

This second kind of code has been called *functional* (Schneider & Tarshis, 1986). Functional codes rely on the fact that particular receptors and neurons fire, or are inhibited from firing, only in the presence of certain sorts of stimuli. At any particular time, then, some cells in the nervous system are firing and some are not. Information about *which* cells are firing, *how many* cells are firing, and the *rate* at which cells are firing constitutes a functional code.

Functional encoding may occur all along a sensory route, starting in the sense organs and ending in the brain. There is still controversy, however, about how functional encoding eventually yields an overall perception of a stimulus. For example, most current theories of vision assume that as impulses travel from the

■ **transduction**
The conversion of one form of energy to another. Sensory receptors are biological transducers.

eye to the lower brain centers and on to higher ones, individual nerve cells abstract more and more information about the visual image. How do they do this? Recall from Chapter 3 that as various neurons converge at a synapse, their overall *pattern* of firing determines whether the neuron on the other side of the synapse is excited or inhibited. The firing (or inhibition) of that neuron, then, actually conveys information to the *next* neuron along the sensory route about what was happening in many other cells. Eventually a single "hypercomplex" cell in the cortex of the brain may receive information that was originally contained in the firing of thousands of different visual receptors. However, many researchers believe that the final perception of a visual stimulus ultimately depends not just on the firing of a single hypercomplex cell but on the simultaneous activation of many different cells in different parts of the brain (E. Kandel, 1981).

Measuring the Senses

Just how sensitive are our senses? The answer comes from the field of **psychophysics,** which is concerned with how the physical properties of stimuli are related to our psychological experience of them. Drawing on principles from both physics and psychology, psychophysicists have studied how the strength or intensity of a stimulus affects the strength of sensation in an observer.

ABSOLUTE THRESHOLDS. One way to find out how sensitive the senses are is to present people with a series of weak stimuli, or signals, and ask them to say which ones they can detect. The smallest amount of energy that a person can detect reliably is known as the **absolute threshold.** The word *absolute* is a bit misleading, however, because people detect borderline signals on some occasions and miss them on others. "Reliable" detection is said to occur when a person can detect a stimulus 50 percent of the time.

If you were having your absolute threshold for brightness measured, you might be asked to sit in a dark room and look at a wall or screen. You would then be shown flashes of light varying in brightness. Your task would be to say whether you noticed a flash. Sometimes you would miss seeing a flash, even though you had noticed one of equal brightness on other trials. At other times you would have a "false alarm," thinking that you saw a flash when there was none. Such errors seem to occur in part because of random firing of cells in the nervous system, which produces something like the background noise in a stereo system.

By studying absolute thresholds, psychologists have found that our senses are very sharp indeed. If you have normal sensory abilities you can see a candle flame on a clear, dark night from 30 miles away. You can hear a ticking watch in a perfectly quiet room from 20 feet away. You can taste a teaspoon of sugar diluted in two gallons of water, smell a drop of perfume diffused through a three-room apartment, and feel the wing of a bee falling on your cheek from a height of 1 centimeter (Galanter, 1962).

Yet, despite these impressive sensory skills, our senses are tuned in to only a narrow band of physical energies. For example, as mentioned earlier, we are sensitive visually to only a tiny fraction of all electromagnetic energy (see Figure 5.1). Other species can pick up various sorts of signals that we cannot. Dogs can detect high-frequency sound waves that are beyond our range, as you know if you have ever called your pooch with a "silent" doggie whistle. Bats and porpoises can hear sounds two octaves beyond our range. Bees can see ultraviolet rays, and snakes can see tiny changes in temperature. As we discuss in "Think

■ **psychophysics**
The area of psychology concerned with the relationship between physical properties of stimuli and sensory experience.

■ **absolute threshold**
The smallest quantity of physical energy that can be reliably detected by an observer.

The electromagnetic spectrum

Wavelength

| 3000 mi. | 1 mi. | 100 ft. | 1 ft. | .01 ft. | .0001 ft. | 10 nm. | 1 nm. | .001 nm. | .00001 nm. |

| Radio | TV | Microwaves | Infrared | U-V | X-rays | Gamma rays | Cosmic rays |

Infrared   Visible spectrum   Ultraviolet

| 1500 | 1000 | 700 | 600 | 500 | 400 | 300 |

Wavelength in nanometers

FIGURE 5.1 _____

The visible spectrum of electromagnetic energy
Our visual system detects only a small fraction of the electromagnetic energy around us.

About It" on page 156, sensory differences among species raise some intriguing questions about the true nature of "reality."

DIFFERENCE THRESHOLDS.   Psychologists also study sensory sensitivity by having people compare two stimuli and judge whether they are the same or different. A subject might be asked to compare the weight of two blocks, the brightness of two lights, or the saltiness of two liquids. The smallest difference in stimulation that a person can detect reliably (again, half of the time) is called the **difference threshold,** or *just noticeable difference (j.n.d.).* When you compare two stimuli, A and B, the difference threshold will depend on the intensity or size of A. The larger or more intense A is, the greater the change must be before you can detect a difference. If you are comparing the weights of two pebbles, you might be able to detect a difference of only a fraction of an ounce, but not if you are comparing two massive boulders.

According to **Weber's Law** (named for Ernst Weber, who proposed it in the early 1800s), when a person compares two stimuli, the size of the change necessary to produce a just noticeable difference is a *constant proportion* of the original stimulus. Consider those pebbles and boulders again. Assume, for the sake of argument, that one pebble weighs 5 ounces, and you can just detect the difference between the two pebbles when the second one weighs $\frac{1}{10}$ of an ounce more ($\frac{1}{50}$ of 5 ounces). Assume, too, that the first massive boulder weighs 100 pounds. How much must the second boulder weigh in order for you to tell the difference? The answer is 102 pounds—an addition of $\frac{1}{50}$ of 100 pounds, or 2 pounds. In both cases, the *proportion* of change necessary to produce the just

■ **difference threshold**
The smallest difference in stimulation that can be reliably detected by an observer when two stimuli are compared. Also called just noticeable difference (j.n.d.).
■ **Weber's Law**
Law of psychophysics stating that the change necessary to produce a just noticeable difference is a constant proportion of the original stimulus.

The sunflower on the left was photographed in normal light. The one on the right, photographed under ultraviolet light, is what a butterfly (which is equipped with ultraviolet receptors) might see. The bright spots are nectar sources—invisible to the naked eye of a human being.

THINK ABOUT IT

In Search of the Real World

Three baseball umpires were arguing about how to tell balls from strikes. The first said, "I calls 'em as I sees 'em." The second said, "I calls 'em as they is." The third, obviously feeling superior, said, "They ain't nothin' until I calls 'em!"

This old story raises an issue pondered by philosophers through the ages: Is reality "out there" in the environment or "in here" in a person's mind? Suppose a tree falls in the forest and there is no one around to hear the crash. Is there a noise? *Objectivists* say yes. They believe in the objective reality of a material world that exists completely apart from the perceiver. *Solipsists* (from the Latin words for "alone" and "self") say no. They argue that reality exists solely in the mind of the perceiver. For a solipsist, even the tree has no independent reality. Psychologists usually take the middle ground in this debate. They accept that there is a physical reality, that a falling tree disturbs air molecules and produces pressure waves. But they also note that hearing, like all sensations, is a subjective experience, and so *noise* cannot be said to occur unless someone experiences it.

Since sensation is a subjective experience, our ideas about reality must be affected by our sensory abilities and limitations. That is, things appear to us as they do not only because of *their* nature but because of *ours*. If the entire human race were totally deaf, we might still talk about pressure waves, but we would have no concept of sound. Similarly, if we were all completely color blind, we might still talk about the wavelengths of light, but we would have no concept of color.

The human way of sensing and perceiving the world is certainly not the only way. Because different species have different needs, their bodies are attuned to different aspects of physical reality. Bees are blind to red, but they can see ultraviolet light, which merely gives human beings a sunburn. Since different parts of flowers reflect ultraviolet light at different rates, flowers that appear to us to be a single color must look patterned to a bee. Neither our perception nor the bee's is more "correct."

Some animal sensory systems seem to have no equivalent at all in human beings. Snakes have an organ, in a pit on the head, that detects infrared rays. This organ permits them to sense heat given off by the bodies of their prey. The slightest change in temperature sends a message racing to the snake's brain. There the message is combined with information from the eyes, so that the snake actually sees an infrared pattern—and locates its prey with deadly accuracy even in the dark (Newman & Hartline, 1982). The sensory abilities of other animals, too, seem like something out of a science fiction story. For example, some fish apparently sense distortions of electrical fields through special receptors on the surface of their bodies (Kalmijn, 1982).

Our sensory windows on the world, then, are partly shuttered. But we can use reason, ingenuity, and technology to pry open those shutters. Ordinary perception tells us that the sun circles the earth, but the great astronomer Copernicus was able to figure out nearly five centuries ago that the opposite is true. Ordinary perception will never let us see ultraviolet and infrared rays directly (unless evolution or genetic engineering drastically changes the kind of organism we are), but we know they are there, and we can measure them.

If science can enable us to overturn the everyday evidence of our senses, who knows what surprises about "reality" are still in store for us? Think about it.

noticeable difference is the same. Weber's Law applies to stimuli in the midrange of many dimensions, from weight to smell. The value of the proportion depends on which dimension is being measured (see Table 5.1).

In everyday life, we may sometimes think we can detect a difference between stimuli when we can't. For example, many people say they prefer one of the two leading colas to the other, and ads often capitalize on that claim. As a class project, undergraduate students at Williams College put cola preference claims to the test. They presented tasters with three glasses of cola, two of one leading brand and one of the other (or vice versa), and asked them which drink they liked most and least. Each taster was given three trials. Most of the tasters were

Table 5.1

Weber's Law

When you are trying to detect a change in some stimulus, the larger it is, the larger the change must be for you to notice it. According to Weber's Law, the "just noticeable difference" is a constant proportion of the original stimulus. Below are the proportions for various sensory dimensions. Notice that a change in loudness can be detected when the change is equivalent to one-tenth of the original stimulus. In contrast, a change in the brightness of light can be detected when the change is equivalent to only one-sixtieth of the original stimulus. Weber's Law tends to break down when stimulation is very weak or very strong.

Dimension	Ratio
Brightness (white light)	$\frac{1}{60}$
Weight (lifted weights)	$\frac{1}{50}$
Pain (heat on skin)	$\frac{1}{30}$
Hearing (moderately loud tone, middle pitch)	$\frac{1}{10}$
Pressure (on skin)	$\frac{1}{7}$
Smell (raw rubber)	$\frac{1}{4}$
Taste (table salt)	$\frac{1}{3}$

inconsistent in their preferences, indicating that they had trouble telling the two brands apart (P. Solomon, 1979).

SIGNAL DETECTION THEORY. Despite their usefulness, the procedures we have described for measuring sensory thresholds have a serious limitation. Measurements for any given individual may be affected by the person's general tendency, when uncertain, to respond, "Yes, I noticed a signal (or a difference)" or "No, I didn't notice anything." Some people are habitual yea sayers, willing to gamble that the signal was really there. Others are habitual nay sayers, cautious and conservative. In addition, motives and expectations can influence how a person responds on any given occasion. If you are in the shower and you're expecting an important call, you may think you heard the telephone ring when it didn't. In laboratory studies, when observers want to impress the experimenter, they may lean toward a positive response.

Fortunately, these problems of *response bias* are not insurmountable. According to **signal detection theory,** an observer's response in a detection task can be divided into a *sensory process,* which depends on the intensity of the stimulus, and a *decision process,* which is influenced by the observer's response bias. There are methods for separating these two components. For example, the measurement of an absolute threshold includes some trials ("catch trials") in which no stimulus is presented and others in which a weak stimulus is presented. Yea sayers will have more "hits" than nay sayers when a weak stimulus is presented, but they will also have more "false alarms" when no stimulus is presented. As the number of catch trials increases, people in general will become more likely to say "nay." All this information can be fed into a complex mathematical formula that yields separate estimates of a person's response bias and sensory capacity. The individual's true sensitivity to a signal of any particular intensity can then be predicted.

The old method of measuring thresholds assumed that a person's threshold was determined entirely by the stimulus. Signal detection theory assumes that the "threshold" depends on a decision actively made by the observer. Signal detection methods have many real-world applications, from screening applicants for jobs requiring keen hearing to training air traffic controllers, whose decisions about the presence or absence of a blip on a radar screen may mean the difference between life and death.

■ **signal detection theory**
A psychophysical theory that divides the detection of a sensory signal into a sensory process and a decision process.

Sensory Adaptation

You're in a dark room, isolated from sight, sound, smell, and taste. Will you hallucinate and beg to be released, or will you find the experience restful and soothing? What might affect your reaction?

Variety, they say, is the spice of life. It is also the essence of sensation, for our senses are designed to respond to change and contrast in the environment (see Figure 5.2). When a stimulus is unchanging or repetitious, sensation fades or disappears. Receptors get "tired" and temporarily stop responding, or nerve cells higher up in the sensory system temporarily switch off. The resulting decline in sensory responsiveness is called **sensory adaptation.** You know that adaptation has occurred when you can no longer feel your watch on your wrist or smell a gas leak that you noticed when you first entered the kitchen.

We never completely adapt to extremely intense stimuli—a terrible toothache, the odor of ammonia, the heat of the desert sun. And we rarely adapt completely to visual stimuli, whether they are weak or intense. Eye movements, both voluntary and involuntary, cause the location of an object's image on the back of the eye to keep changing, so that visual receptors don't have a chance to "fatigue." But in the laboratory, researchers can stabilize the image of a simple pattern, such as a line, at a particular point on the back of a person's eye. They use an ingenious device consisting of a tiny projector mounted on a contact lens. Though the eyeball moves, the image of the object stays focused on the same receptors. After a few minutes, the image begins to fade and disappear.

What would happen if our senses adapted to *most* incoming stimuli? Would we sense nothing, or would the brain substitute its own images for the sensory experiences no longer available by way of the sense organs? In early studies of **sensory deprivation,** researchers studied this question by isolating male volunteers from all patterned sight and sound. Vision was restricted by a translucent visor; hearing by a U-shaped pillow and noise from an air conditioner and fan; and touch by cotton gloves and cardboard cuffs. The volunteers took brief breaks to eat and use the bathroom, but otherwise they simply lay in bed, doing nothing. The results were dramatic. Within a few hours, many of the men felt edgy. Some were so disoriented that they quit the study the first day. Those who stayed longer became confused, restless, and grouchy. Many reported hallucinations—at first simple images, then more bizarre visions, like a squadron

■ **sensory adaptation**
The reduction or disappearance of sensory responsiveness that occurs when stimulation is unchanging or repetitious.
■ **sensory deprivation**
Absence of normal levels of sensory stimulation.

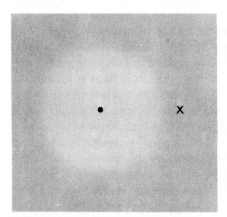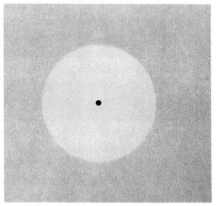

FIGURE 5.2

Now you see it, now you don't
Sensation depends on change and contrast in the environment. Hold your hand over one eye and stare steadily at the dot in the middle of the circle on the right. You should have no trouble maintaining an image of the circle. However, if you do the same with the circle on the left, the image will fade. The gradual change from light to dark does not provide enough contrast to keep the visual receptors in your eye firing at a steady rate. The circle only reappears if you close and reopen your eye or if you shift your gaze to the X.

The effects of sensory deprivation depend on the circumstances. Choosing to spend an hour in a solitary "flotation tank" is one thing; being imprisoned in a dark cell, alone, is another.

of marching squirrels, or a procession of marching eyeglasses. Few men were willing to remain in the study for more than a few days (Heron, 1957).

These findings made headlines, of course. But the notion that sensory deprivation is unpleasant or even dangerous turned out to be an oversimplification (Suedfeld, 1975). In many of the studies, the experimental procedures themselves probably aroused anxiety. Participants were told about "panic buttons," asked to sign "release from legal liability" forms, and given inadequate orientation sessions. Later research, using better methods, showed that hallucinations are less dramatic and less disorienting than at first thought. In fact, many people enjoy time-limited periods of deprivation, and some perceptual and intellectual abilities actually improve. Like any human experience, the response to sensory deprivation is affected by a person's expectations and interpretations of what is happening. Reduced sensation can be scary if you are locked in a room for an indefinite period, but relaxing if you have retreated to that room on your own for a little time out.

Still, it is clear that the human brain requires a certain amount of sensory stimulation during daily life to function normally. The absence of sensory input during sleep may help explain the sometimes bizarre imagery of dreams (see Chapter 4). And the need for sensory stimulation during waking life may help explain why people who live alone often keep the radio or television set running continuously and why prolonged solitary confinement is a form of torture.

Sensory Overload

If too little stimulation can be bad for you, so can too much. Excessive stimulation can lead to fatigue and mental confusion. If you have ever come home from a crowded department store or a noisy sports event nervous, exhausted, and with a splitting headache, you know firsthand about sensory overload.

When people find themselves in a state of overload, they often cope by blocking out unimportant sights and sounds and focusing only on those they find interesting or useful. Psychologists have dubbed this the "cocktail party phenomenon," because at a cocktail party a person typically focuses on just one conversation, ignoring other voices, the clink of ice cubes, music, and bursts of laughter. The competing sounds all enter the nervous system, enabling the person to pick up anything important—even the person's own name, spoken by someone several yards away. Unimportant sounds, though, are not fully processed by the brain.

The capacity for **selective attention** protects us in daily life from being overwhelmed by all the sensory signals impinging on our receptors. The brain is not forced to respond to everything the sense receptors send its way. The "generals" in the brain can choose which "field officers" get past the command center's gates. Those that don't seem to have anything important to say are turned back.

What would stock and commodity traders, who operate amid constant pandemonium, do without selective attention, the ability to focus on some messages while blocking out others?

■ **selective attention**
The focusing of attention on selected aspects of the environment and the blocking out of others.

QUICK QUIZ

1. Even on the clearest night, some stars cannot be seen by the naked eye because they are below the viewer's _____ threshold.
2. Mark is asked to judge whether two bars differ in length. When one bar is 10 millimeters long, the just noticeable difference is 1 millimeter (the second bar must be 11 millimeters before a difference is detected). Suppose the first bar is 20 millimeters long; what will the just noticeable difference be then?
3. If you jump into a cold lake, but moments later the water no longer seems so cold, sensory _____ has occurred.
4. If you are immobilized in a hospital bed, with no roommate and no TV or radio, and you feel edgy and disoriented, you may be suffering the effects of _____.
5. During a break from your job as a waiter you decide to read. For 20 minutes, you are so engrossed that you fail to notice the clattering of dishes or orders being called out to the cook. This is an example of _____.

 6. In real-life detection tasks, is it better to be a "nay-sayer" or a "yea-sayer"?

ANSWERS:

1. absolute 2. 2 millimeters (The j.n.d. is a constant proportion of the first stimulus, in this case 1/10.) 3. adaptation 4. sensory deprivation 5. selective attention 6. Neither; it depends on the consequences of a "miss" or "false alarm" and the probability of an event occurring. You might want to be a "yea-sayer" if you're just out the door, you think you hear the phone ringing, and you're expecting a call about a job interview. You might want to be a "nay-sayer" if you're just out the door, you think you hear the phone, and you're on your way to a job interview and don't want to be late.

■ VISION

Vision is the most frequently studied of all the senses, and with good reason. More information about the external world comes to us through our eyes than through any other sense organ. Because we are most active in the daytime, we are "wired" to take advantage of the sun's illumination. Animals that are active at night tend to rely more heavily on hearing.

What We See

The stimulus for vision is light; even cats, raccoons, and other creatures famous for their ability to get around in the dark need *some* light to see. Visible light may come from the sun or other stars or from light bulbs, and is reflected off objects. Light travels in the form of waves, and the way we see the world—our sensory experience—is affected by the characteristics of these waves:

1. Hue, the dimension of visual experience specified by the various color names, is related to the wavelength of light—that is, to the distance between the crests of a wave. Shorter waves tend to be seen as violet and blue, and longer ones as orange and red. (We say "tend to" because other factors also affect color perception, as we will see later.) The sun produces white light, a mixture of all the visible wavelengths. Sometimes drops of moisture in the air act like a prism: They separate the sun's white light into the colors of the visible spectrum, and we are treated to a rainbow.

■ **hue**

The dimension of visual experience specified by the various color names and related to the wavelength of light.

2. Brightness is the dimension of visual experience related to the amount, or intensity, of the light that an object emits or reflects. Intensity corresponds to the amplitude (maximum height) of the wave. Generally speaking, the more light an object reflects, the brighter it appears. However, brightness is also affected by wavelength: Yellows appear brighter than reds and blues when physical intensities are actually equal. (For this reason, some fire departments have switched from red engines to yellow ones.)

3. Saturation (colorfulness) is the dimension of visual experience related to the **complexity of light**—that is, to how wide or narrow the range of wavelengths is. When light contains only a single wavelength it is said to be "pure," and the resulting color is said to be completely saturated. At the other extreme is white light, which lacks any color and is completely unsaturated. In nature, pure light is extremely rare. Usually we sense a mixture of wavelengths, and we see colors that are duller and paler than completely saturated ones.

Note that hue, brightness, and saturation are all *psychological* dimensions of visual experience, whereas wavelength, intensity, and complexity are *physical* properties of the visual stimulus, light.

An Eye on the World

Light enters the visual system through the eye, a wonderfully complex and delicate structure that is often compared, rather loosely, to a camera. As you read this section, examine Figure 5.3. Notice that the front part of the eye is covered by the transparent *cornea*. The cornea protects the eye and bends incoming light rays toward a *lens* located behind it. A camera lens works by moving closer to or farther from the opening. However, the lens of the eye works by subtly changing its shape, becoming more or less curved to focus light from objects that are close by or far away. The amount of light that gets into the eye is controlled by muscles in the *iris*, the part of the eye that gives it color. The iris surrounds the round opening, or *pupil*, of the eye. When you enter a dim room, the pupil widens, or dilates, to let more light in. When you emerge into bright sunlight, the pupil gets smaller, allowing in less light. You can see these changes by watching your eyes in a mirror as you change the lighting.

The visual receptors are located in the back of the eye, or **retina.** In a developing embryo, the retina forms from tissue that projects out from the brain, not from tissue destined to form other parts of the eye; thus the retina is actu-

■ **brightness**
Lightness or luminance; the dimension of visual experience related to the amount of light emitted from or reflected by an object.

■ **saturation**
Vividness or purity of color; the dimension of visual experience related to the complexity of light waves.

■ **complexity (of light)**
Refers to the number of different wavelengths contained in light from a particular source.

■ **retina**
Neural tissue lining the back of the eyeball's interior that contains the receptors for vision.

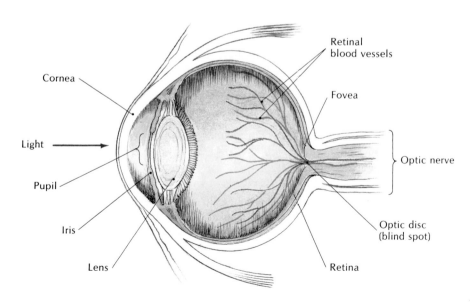

Figure 5.3
Major structures of the eye
Light passes through the pupil and lens and is focused on the retina at the back of the eye. The point of sharpest vision is at the fovea.

FIGURE 5.4

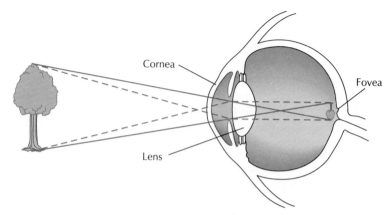

The retinal image
When we look at an object, the light pattern focused on the retina is upside down. René Descartes was probably the first person to demonstrate this fact. He took an ox's eye, cut a piece from the back of it, and replaced the piece with paper. When he held the eye up to the light, he saw an upside-down image of the room on the paper! Retinal images are also mirror-reversed; light from the right side of an object hits the left side of the retina, and vice versa.

ally an extension of the brain. As Figure 5.4 shows, when the lens of the eye focuses light on the retina, the result is an upside-down image (which can actually be seen with an instrument used by eye specialists). Light from the top of the visual field stimulates light-sensitive receptor cells in the bottom part of the retina, and vice versa. The brain interprets this upside-down pattern of stimulation as something that is right side up.

About 120 to 125 million receptors in the retina are long and narrow and are called **rods.** Another 7 or 8 million receptors are cone-shaped and are called, appropriately enough, **cones.** The center of the retina, or *fovea*, where vision is sharpest, contains only cones, clustered densely together. From the center to the periphery, the ratio of rods to cones increases, and at the outer edges, there are virtually no cones.

Rods are more sensitive to light than cones are. They enable us to see in dim light and at night. Since they occupy the outer edges of the retina, they also handle side vision. That is why you can sometimes see a star from the corner of your eye although it is invisible when you gaze straight at it. But rods cannot distinguish different wavelengths and therefore are not sensitive to color. That is why it is often hard to distinguish colors clearly in dim light. The cones, on the other hand, are differentially sensitive to specific wavelengths of light and allow us to see colors. However, the cones need plenty of light to respond. They don't help us much when we are trying to find a seat in a darkened movie theater.

We have all noticed that it takes some time for our eyes to adjust fully to the darkness. This process of **dark adaptation,** which involves chemical changes in the rods and cones, actually occurs in two phases. The cones adapt quickly, within 10 minutes or so, but never become very sensitive to the dim illumination. The rods adapt more slowly, taking 20 minutes or longer, but are ultimately much more sensitive. After the first phase of adaptation, you can see better but not well; after the second phase, your vision is as good as it will get.

Rods and cones are connected by synapses to *bipolar neurons*, which in turn communicate with neurons called **ganglion cells** (see Figure 5.5). Usually a single cone communicates (via a bipolar neuron) with a single ganglion cell; it has a "private line." Rods, in contrast, must communicate via a "party line." That is, whole groups of rods, covering a particular area of the retina, send their messages to a single ganglion cell. This is an example of the kind of sensory encoding we discussed earlier.

The axons of the ganglion cells converge to form the *optic nerve*, which carries information out through the back of the eye and on to the brain. Where the optic nerve leaves the eye, at the *optic disc*, there are no rods or cones. The absence of receptors produces a blind spot in the field of vision. Normally we are unaware of the blind spot because (1) the image projected on the spot is hitting a different, "nonblind" spot in the other eye; (2) our eyes move so fast that we can pick up the complete image; and (3) the brain tends to fill in the gap. You can find your blind spot by following the instructions in Figure 5.6.

 rods
Visual receptors that respond to dim light but are not involved in color vision.

■ **cones**
Visual receptors involved in color vision.

■ **dark adaptation**
A process by which visual receptors become maximally sensitive to dim light.

■ **ganglion cells**
Neurons in the retina of the eye that gather information from receptor cells (by way of intermediate bipolar cells); their axons make up the optic nerve.

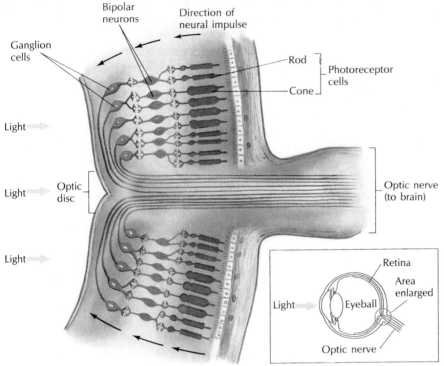

FIGURE 5.5

The structures of the retina
For clarity, all cells in this draw-ing are greatly exaggerated in size. Notice that in order to reach the receptors for vision (the rods and cones), light must pass through the ganglion and bipolar cells as well as the blood vessels that nourish them. Normally we do not see the shadow cast by this network of cells and blood vessels. It always falls on the same place on the retina, and such stabilized images are not sensed (see text). But when an eye doctor shines a moving light into your eye, the treelike shadow of the blood ves-sels falls on different regions of the retina and you may see it—a rather eerie experience.

Why the Visual System Is Not a Camera

Because the eye is often compared with a camera, it is easy to assume that the visual world is made up of a mosaic of dots, as in a photograph. But unlike a camera, the visual system is not a passive recorder of the external world. Instead of simply registering spots of light and dark, neurons in the system build up a picture of the world by detecting its meaningful features.

Simple features of the environment, such as spots of light and dark, are coded in the ganglion cells and in an area in the thalamus of the brain. In mammals, more complex features are coded in special **feature detector** cells in the visual cortex. This fact was first demonstrated by David Hubel and Torsten Wiesel (1962, 1968), who painstakingly recorded impulses from individual cells in the brains of cats and monkeys. (In 1981, they received a Nobel Prize for their work.) Hubel and Wiesel found that different neurons were sensitive to differ-ent patterns projected on a screen in front of the animal's eyes. Most cells re-sponded maximally to moving or stationary lines that were oriented in a par-ticular direction and located in a particular part of the visual field. One type of cell might fire most rapidly in response to a horizontal line in the lower right part of the visual field, another to a diagonal line at a certain angle in the up-per left part of the visual field. In the real world, such features make up the boundaries and edges of objects.

FIGURE 5.6

Find your blind spot
The optic disk, where the fibers of the optic nerve leave the eye, has no visual receptors and is therefore a blind spot. To find the blind spot in your left eye, close your right eye and look at the magician. Then slowly move the book toward and away from yourself. The rabbit should disap-pear when the book is between 9 and 12 inches from your eye.

The image that reaches the brain, then, is not a mosaic of light and dark dots but a combination of lines and angles that the brain somehow integrates into a pattern that makes sense. The process of integration is still not clear to scientists, but progress is being made. Many researchers now think the important visual features of the environment are variations in brightness over broad areas of space rather than edges at a particular point. When researchers present an observer with gratings (series of light and dark bars), some cortical cells respond to a series of many narrow stripes, and others respond to a series of fewer, wider stripes (DeValois & DeValois, 1980). Studies also suggest that it is not only the frequency of a cell's firing that contains information but also the pattern or rhythm with which it fires (Richmond et al., 1987). Clearly, the nervous system is extraordinarily "smart," searching for and analyzing separate scraps of sensory information and then putting all the bits and pieces together to construct an overall picture.

How We See Colors

For 200 years, psychologists and physiologists have been trying to figure out why we see the world in living color. One approach, the **trichromatic theory** (also known as the *Young-Helmholtz theory*), assumed that there were three mechanisms in the visual system, each especially sensitive to a certain range of wavelengths, and that these interacted in some way to produce all the different color sensations. Another approach, the **opponent-process theory,** assumed that the visual system treated various pairs of colors as opposing or antagonistic, which would explain why we can describe a color as bluish green but not as "reddish green." Modern research suggests that both views are valid, and that each explains a different level of processing.

The trichromatic theory applies to the first level of processing, which occurs in the retina. The retina contains three different types of cones. One type responds maximally to blue (or more precisely, to the band of wavelengths that gives rise to the experience of blue), another to green, and a third to red. The hundreds of colors we see result from the combined activity of these three types of cones.

Total color blindness is usually due to a genetic problem that causes cones of the retina to be absent or malfunctional. The visual world then consists of black, white, and shades of gray. Many animal species are totally color blind, but the condition is extremely rare in human beings. Most "color blind" people are actually *color deficient*. Usually the person is unable to distinguish red and green; the world is painted in shades of blue, yellow, and gray. In rarer instances, a person may be blind to blue and yellow and see only reds, greens, and grays. Color deficiency is found in about 8 percent of white men, 5 percent of Asian men, and 3 percent of black men and Native American men (Sekuler & Blake, 1985). Because of the way the condition is inherited, it is very rare in women. Fortunately for people who are color deficient, this condition does not interfere drastically with daily living. A person who is blind to red and green can respond correctly to traffic lights, for instance, because the lights differ in position and brightness as well as hue.

The opponent-process theory applies to the second stage of color processing, which occurs in bipolar and ganglion cells in the retina and in neurons in the thalamus of the brain. These cells, known as *opponent process cells*, either respond to short wavelengths but are inhibited from firing by long wavelengths, or vice versa (DeValois, 1960; DeValois & DeValois, 1975; Hurvich & Jameson, 1974). Certain opponent-process cells respond in opposite fashion to red and green; they fire in response to one and turn off in response to the other. Others respond in opposite fashion to blue and yellow. (A third system responds in opposite fashion to white and black and thus yields information about bright-

■ **feature detectors**
Cells in the visual cortex that are sensitive to specific features of the environment.

■ **trichromatic theory**
A theory of color perception that proposes three mechanisms in the visual system, each sensitive to a certain range of wavelengths; their interaction is assumed to produce all the different experiences of hue.

■ **opponent-process theory (of color)**
A theory of color perception that assumes that the visual system treats various pairs of colors as opposing or antagonistic.

ness.) The net result is a color *code* that is passed along to the higher visual centers. Opposing colors cannot be coded at the same time, which is why we never see a reddish green or a bluish yellow.

Opponent-process cells that are *inhibited* by a particular color seem to produce a burst of firing when the color is removed, just as they would if the opposing color were present. Similarly, cells that *fire* in response to a color stop firing when the color is removed, just as they would if the opposing color were present. These facts seem to explain why we are susceptible to *negative afterimages* when we stare at a particular hue—why we see, for instance, red after staring at green (Figure 5.7). A sort of neural rebound effect occurs: The cells that switch on or off to signal the presence of "red" send the opposite signal ("green") when the red is removed. If you stare intently at the green screen of a computer monitor for a long time, you may occasionally see the world through rose-colored glasses when you turn your gaze away—a demonstration of the opponent process in action.

Unfortunately, two-stage theories do not yet provide a complete explanation of color vision. The wavelengths reflected by an object do not by themselves account for whether we see the object as mauve or magenta, purple or puce. Edwin Land (1959), inventor of the Polaroid camera, showed that the perceived color of an object depends on the wavelengths reflected by *everything around it*. Thus you never see a good, strong red unless there are other objects around that reflect the green and blue part of the spectrum. Land worked out precise rules that predict exactly how an object will appear, given the wavelengths reflected by all the objects in a scene. So far, however, researchers have not been able to explain fully how the *brain* follows these rules.

Constructing the Visual World

We do not see a retinal image; that image is merely grist for the mill of the mind, which actively *interprets* the image and *constructs* the world from the often fragmentary data of the senses (see Figure 5.8). In the brain, where we ultimately see, hear, taste, smell, and feel, sensory signals are combined from moment to moment to produce a model of the world. This is the process of perception.

FORM PERCEPTION. To make sense of the world, we must know where one thing ends and another begins, and we must do this in all our sensory modalities. In vision we must separate the teacher from the podium, in hearing we must separate the piano solo from the orchestral accompaniment, and in taste we must

FIGURE 5.7 _____

Change of heart

To produce a negative afterimage, stare at the black dot in the middle of the heart for at least 20 seconds. Then shift your gaze to a white piece of paper or white wall. You should see an image of a red heart with a blue border.

FIGURE 5.8 _____

Perception is meaningful
Perceptual processes actively organize and interpret data from our senses. For example, chances are that you see more than a random collection of light and dark splotches in this picture. If not, try holding the picture a little farther away from you.

separate the marshmallow from the hot chocolate. This process of dividing up the world occurs so rapidly and effortlessly that we take it completely for granted—until we must make out objects in a heavy fog or words in the rapid-fire conversation of someone speaking a foreign language.

The Gestalt psychologists, whom we introduced in Chapter 1, were among the first to study how people organize the world visually into meaningful units and patterns. In German, *gestalt* means "pattern" or "configuration." The Gestalt psychologists' motto was "The whole is more than the sum of its parts." They observed that when we perceive something, certain properties emerge from the whole configuration that are not found in any particular component. When you watch a movie, for example, the motion you "see" is nowhere in the film, which consists of separate static frames projected at 24 frames per second.

Although the Gestalt psychologists had ideas about the physiology of visual perception that are no longer accepted, many of their observations remain useful. For instance, they noted that we always organize the visual field into *figure and ground*. The figure stands out from the rest of the environment, which provides a formless background (see Figure 5.9). Some things stand out as figure by virtue of their intensity or size; it is hard to ignore the blinding flash of a camera or a tidal wave approaching your piece of the beach. Unique objects also stand out, such as a banana in a bowl of oranges. Moving objects in an otherwise still environment, such as a shooting star, will usually be seen as figure. Indeed, it is hard to ignore a sudden change of any kind in the environment. Remember, our brains are geared to respond to change and contrast. However, selective attention, the ability to concentrate on some stimuli and filter out others, gives us some control over what we perceive as figure and ground.

FIGURE 5.9 _____

Figure and ground
Both the photograph (a) and the drawing (b) have two possible interpretations, which keep alternating depending on which part is seen as figure and which as ground. Do you see the silhouettes and the goblet in the photograph and the word in the drawing?

(a)

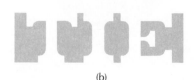

(b)

Here are some other Gestalt strategies that the visual system uses to group sensory building blocks into perceptual units:

1. *Proximity.* Things that are near each other tend to be grouped together. Thus you perceive the dots on the left as three groups of dots, not as 12 separate, unrelated ones. Similarly, you perceive the pattern on the right as vertical columns of dots, not as horizontal rows:

2. *Closure.* The brain tends to fill in gaps in order to perceive complete forms. This is fortunate, since we often need to decipher less than perfect images. The following figures are easily perceived as a triangle, a face, and the letter *e*, even though none of the figures is complete:

3. *Similarity.* Things that are alike in some way (for example, in color, shape, or size) tend to be perceived as belonging together. In the figure on the left, you see the circles as forming an *x*. In the one on the right, you see horizontal bars rather than vertical columns because the horizontally aligned stars share the same color:

4. *Continuity.* Lines and patterns tend to be perceived as continuing in time or space. You perceive the figure on the left as a single line partially covered by a circle rather than as two separate lines touching a circle. In the figure on the right, you see two lines, one curved and one straight, instead of two curved and two straight lines:

One psychologist has estimated that adults in our society must readily discriminate among 30,000 different familiar objects (Biederman, 1987). Gestalt and other perceptual principles help explain why we have trouble discriminating some of these visual forms. Objects manufactured by human beings may be designed with little thought for how the mind works, which is why it can be a major challenge to figure out how to use a new washing machine, camera, or VCR (Norman, 1988). Good design requires, among other things, that crucial distinctions be visually obvious. For instance, knobs and switches with different functions should differ in color, texture, or shape, and should stand out as "figure." But on some VCRs, it is hard to tell the rewind button from the fast-forward button.

Fortunately, with a little ingenuity, and a knowledge of perceptual principles, design flaws can often be overcome. Clever control-room operators in one nuclear power plant solved the problem of similar knobs on adjacent switches by placing distinctively shaped beer-keg handles over them, one labeled Heinekin's, the other Michelob (Norman, 1988). Can you think of some ways to overcome problems of poor design in your own environment?

DEPTH AND DISTANCE PERCEPTION.   Ordinarily we need to know not only what something is, but where it is. Touch gives us this information directly. Vision does not and so we must use various cues to *infer* an object's location by estimating its distance or depth.

To perform this remarkable feat, we rely in part on **binocular cues**—cues that require the use of two eyes. The eyes are about $2\frac{1}{2}$ inches apart on the face. As they converge on objects close by or far away, the angle of convergence changes, providing information about distance (see Figure 5.10). The two eyes also receive slightly different retinal images of the same object. You can easily prove this by holding a finger about 12 inches in front of your face and looking at it with only one eye at a time. Its position will appear to shift when you change eyes. Now hold up two fingers, one closer to your nose than the other. Notice that the amount of space between the two fingers appears to change when you switch eyes. The slight difference in lateral (sideways) separation between two objects as seen by the left eye and the right eye is called **retinal disparity.** Since retinal disparity increases as distance between two objects increases, the brain can use retinal disparity to infer depth and calculate distance. Retinal disparity is mimicked by 3-D movies and slide viewers (stereoscopes), which project two images, one as seen by the left eye and one as seen by the right, to create the illusion of depth.

Binocular cues only help us locate objects up to about 50 feet away. For objects farther away, we rely on **monocular cues,** cues that work with only one eye. One such cue is *interposition:* When an object is interposed between the viewer and a second object, partly blocking the view of the second object, the first object is perceived as being closer. Another monocular cue is *linear perspective:* When two lines known to be parallel appear to be coming together or converging, they imply the existence of depth. For example, if you are standing between railroad tracks, they appear to converge in the distance. A third monocular cue is *relative size:* The smaller the retinal image of an object, the farther away the object appears to be. These and other monocular cues are illustrated in Figure 5.11.

■ **binocular cues**
Visual cues to depth or distance requiring two eyes.

■ **retinal disparity**
The slight differences in lateral separation between two objects as seen by the left eye and the right eye.

■ **monocular cues**
Visual cues to depth or distance that can be used by one eye alone.

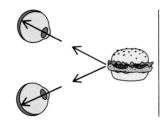

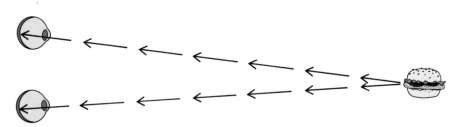

FIGURE 5.10

Convergence
Convergence, the coordinated turning of the eyes toward an object, provides an important binocular cue to depth and distance. If an object is in the center of your visual field, then the closer it is, the more your two eyes must turn inward to focus on it. The resulting muscular sensations are obvious when you "cross" your eyes by trying to look at your own nose.

(a)

(b)

(c)

(d)

(e)

(f)

FIGURE 5.11

Monocular cues to depth

Most cues to depth do not depend on having two eyes. Some monocular (one-eyed) cues are: (a) Interposition *(partial overlap). An object that partly blocks or obscures another one must be in front of the other one, and is therefore seen as closer. (b)* Motion parallax. *When an observer is moving, objects seem to move at different speeds and in different directions. The closer an object, the faster it seems to move. Close objects also appear to move backward, while distant ones seem to move forward. (c)* Light and shadow. *Light and shadow give objects the appearance of three dimensions. (d)* Relative size. *The smaller the image of an object on the retina, the farther away it appears. (e)* Relative clarity. *Because of particles in the air (from fog, smog, or dust), distant objects tend to look hazier, duller, or less detailed. (f)* Texture gradients. *In a uniform surface, distant parts of the surface appear denser; that is, the elements that make it up seem spaced more closely together. (g)* Linear perspective. *Parallel lines will appear to be converging in the distance; the greater the apparent convergence, the greater the perceived distance. This cue is often exaggerated by artists to convey an impression of depth.*

(g)

When size constancy fails.

VISUAL CONSTANCIES: WHEN SEEING IS BELIEVING. You might be able to see what things are and where they are, but your perceptual world would be a confusing place without another important perceptual skill. Lighting conditions, viewing angles, and the distances of stationary objects are all continually changing as we move about, yet we rarely confuse these changes with changes in the objects themselves. This ability to perceive objects as stable or unchanging even though the sensory patterns they produce are constantly shifting is called **perceptual constancy.** The best studied constancies are visual. They include the following:

1. *Shape constancy.* We continue to perceive objects as having a constant shape even though the shape of the retinal image changes when our point of view changes. If you hold a Frisbee directly in front of your face, its image on the retina will be round. When you set the Frisbee on a table, its image becomes elliptical, yet you continue to identify the Frisbee as round.

2. *Location constancy.* We perceive stationary objects as remaining in the same place even though the retinal image moves about as we move our eyes, heads, and bodies. As you drive along the highway, telephone poles and trees fly by—on your retina. But you know that objects like telephone poles and trees move by themselves only in cartoons, and you also know that your body is moving, so you perceive the poles and trees as staying put.

3. *Brightness constancy.* We continue to see objects as having a more or less constant brightness even though the amount of light they reflect changes as the overall level of illumination changes. Snow remains white even on a cloudy day. In fact, it is possible for a black object in strong sunlight to reflect more light than a white object in the shade. We are not fooled, though, because the brain registers the total illumination in the scene, and we automatically take this information into account in the perception of any particular object's brightness.

4. *Color constancy.* We see an object as maintaining its hue despite the fact that the wavelength of light reaching our eyes may change somewhat. For example, outdoor light is "bluer" than indoor light, and objects outdoors therefore reflect more "blue" light than those indoors. Conversely, indoor light from a lamp is rich in long wavelengths, and is therefore "yellower." Yet objects usually look the same color in both places. The explanation involves sensory adaptation, which we discussed earlier. Outdoors we quickly adapt to short wavelength (blue) light, and indoors we adapt to long wavelength light. As a result, our visual responses are similar in the two situations. Also, as we saw earlier, the brain takes into account all the wavelengths in the visual field when computing the color of a particular object. If a lemon is bathed in bluish light, so, usually, is everything else around it. The increase in blue light reflected by the lemon is "cancelled" in the visual cortex by the increase in blue light reflected by the lemon's surroundings, and so the lemon continues to look yellow.

5. *Size constancy.* We continue to see an object as having a constant size even when its retinal image becomes smaller or larger. A friend approaching on the street does not seem to be growing; a car pulling away from the curb does not seem to be shrinking. Size constancy depends in part on familiarity with objects. You *know* people and cars don't change size just like that. It also depends on the apparent distance of an object. When you move your hand toward your face, your brain registers the fact that the hand is getting closer, and you correctly perceive its unchanging size. There is, then, an intimate relationship between perceived size and perceived distance.

VISUAL ILLUSIONS: WHEN SEEING IS MISLEADING. Perceptual constancies allow us to make sense of the world, or at least of the thin slice of it that our senses are designed to detect. Occasionally, however, we can be fooled, and the result is a

■ **perceptual constancy**
The accurate perception of objects as stable or unchanged despite changes in the sensory patterns they produce.

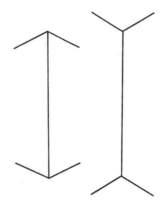

perceptual illusion. For psychologists, illusions are valuable because they are *systematic* errors that provide us with hints about the perceptual strategies of the mind.

Although illusions can occur in any sensory modality, visual illusions have been studied most frequently. Visual illusions sometimes occur when the strategies that normally lead to accurate perception are overextended to situations where they don't apply. Compare the two lines in the margin. If you are like most people, you perceive the line on the right as slightly longer than the one on the left. Yet if you measure the lines, you will find that they are exactly the same length. This is the Müller-Lyer illusion, named after the man who first described it, in 1889.

One explanation for the Müller-Lyer illusion is that the figures contain perspective cues that normally suggest depth (Gregory, 1963). The line on the left is like the near edge of a building; the one on the right is like the far corner of a room. The two lines produce the same-sized retinal image, but the one with the outward-facing branches suggests greater distance. We are fooled into perceiving it as longer because we automatically apply a rule about the relationship between size and distance that is normally very useful. The rule is that when two objects produce the same-sized retinal image, and one is farther away, the farther one is larger. The problem, in this case, is that there is no actual difference in the distance of the two lines, so the rule is inappropriate. A similar explanation has been proposed for other "geometrical" illusions.

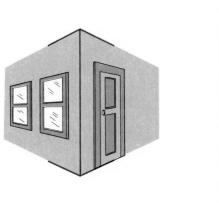

Just as there are size, shape, location, brightness, and color constancies, so there are size, shape, location, brightness, and color illusions. Some illusions are simply a matter of physics. Thus a chopstick in a half-filled glass of water looks bent because water and air refract light differently. Other illusions are due to misleading messages from the sense organs, as in sensory adaptation. Still others, like the Müller-Lyer illusion, seem to occur because the brain misinterprets sensory information. Figure 5.12 (on page 172) shows some simple but startling visual illusions.

Although illusions are distortions, in everyday life most are harmless, or even useful or entertaining. For example, electric signs often take advantage of the fact that when lights flash on and off in certain patterns, images occur successively across the retina, much as they do when actual objects move, and so we perceive the images in the sign as moving. The result of this apparent motion, or *phi phenomenon*, may be dancers kicking up their heels on a Las Vegas billboard, stock prices rolling along the Big Board at the New York Stock Exchange, or reindeer prancing merrily in someone's Christmas decorations.

■ **perceptual illusion**
An erroneous or misleading perception of reality.

FIGURE 5.12

Some visual illusions
Although perception is usually accurate, we can be fooled. In (a) the cats as drawn are all the same size; in (b) the two figures are the same size; in (c) the diagonal lines are all parallel; and in (d) the sides of the square are all straight. To see the illusion depicted in (e), hold your index fingers 5 to 10 inches in front of your eyes, as shown, then focus straight ahead. Do you see a floating "fingertip frankfurter"? Can you make this apparition shrink or expand? Why do you think this illusion occurs?

(a)

(b)

(c)   (d)   (e)

QUICK QUIZ

1. How can two Gestalt principles help explain why you can make out the Big Dipper on a starry night?
2. True or False: Binocular cues help us locate objects that are very far away.
3. Hold one hand about 12 inches from your face and the other one about 6 inches away. (a) Which hand will cast the smaller retinal image? (b) Why don't you perceive that hand as smaller?

ANSWERS:

1. *Proximity* of certain stars encourages you to see them as clustered together to form a pattern; *closure* allows you to "fill in the gaps" and see the contours of a "dipper." 2. false 3. a. The hand that is 12 inches away will cast a smaller retinal image. b. Your brain takes the differences in distance into account in estimating size; also, you know how large your hands are.

■ HEARING

Like vision, the sense of hearing, or *audition*, provides a vital link with the world around us. When damage to the auditory system causes hearing loss, the consequences go beyond the obvious loss of auditory information. Because we use hearing to monitor our own speech, when deafness is present at birth or occurs early in life speech development is hindered. When people lose their hearing, they sometimes come to feel socially isolated, because social relationships rely so heavily on hearing others.

What We Hear

The stimulus for sound is a wave of pressure created when an object vibrates (or, sometimes, when compressed air is released, as in a pipe organ). The vibration (or release of air) causes molecules in a transmitting substance to move together and apart. This movement produces variations in pressure that radiate in all directions. The transmitting substance is usually air, but sound waves can also travel through water and solids. That is why, in old westerns, Indians would sometimes put an ear to the ground to find out if anyone was approaching.

As with vision, certain psychological aspects of our auditory experience are related in a predictable way to physical characteristics of the stimulus, in this case, a sound wave:

1. Loudness is the dimension of auditory experience related to the intensity of a wave's pressure. Intensity corresponds to the amplitude, or maximum height, of the wave. The more energy pushing the wave, the higher it is at its peak. Loudness is also affected by pitch—how high or low a sound is. If low and high sounds produce waves with equal amplitudes, the low sound may seem quieter.

Sound intensity is measured in units called *decibels* (dB). A decibel is one-tenth of a bel, a unit named for Alexander Graham Bell, the inventor of the telephone. The average absolute threshold of hearing in human beings is zero decibels. Decibels are not equally distant, as inches on a ruler are. A sound of 60 decibels (such as that of a sewing machine) is not one-fifth louder than one at 50 decibels (such as that of a refrigerator), but ten times louder. Table 5.2 (on p. 174) shows the intensity in decibels of some common sounds.

2. Pitch is the dimension of auditory experience related to the frequency of the sound wave and, to some extent, its intensity. **Frequency** refers to how rapidly the air (or other medium) vibrates, that is, the number of times per second the wave cycles through a peak and a low point. One cycle per second is known as 1 *Hertz* (Hz). The human ear normally detects frequencies in the range of 16 Hz (the lowest note on a pipe organ) to 20,000 Hz (the scraping of a grasshopper's legs).

A remarkable new line of research, however, is finding that under special conditions people can detect *ultrasonic* frequencies previously thought to be beyond the range of human hearing. Martin Lenhardt and his colleagues (1991) have used a special laboratory device, placed directly against the skull, to deliver signals as high as 90,000 Hz through bone conduction. They find that even profoundly deaf people can clearly perceive words presented at 28,000 to 40,000 Hz in this manner. These results suggest that bone-conducted ultrasonic frequencies are processed by different auditory structures (yet to be identified) than audible frequencies are. If that is true, the findings may one day lead to a new type of hearing aid for the hearing-impaired.

3. Timbre is the distinguishing quality of a sound. It is the dimension of auditory experience related to the complexity of the sound wave—to how wide or narrow a range of frequencies the wave contains. A pure tone consists of only one frequency, but in nature pure tones are extremely rare. Usually what we hear is a complex wave consisting of several subwaves with different frequencies. A particular combination of frequencies results in a particular timbre. Timbre is what makes a note played on a flute, which produces relatively pure tones, sound different from the same note played on an oboe, which produces very complex sounds.

When many frequencies are present but are not in harmony, we hear noise. When all the frequencies of the sound spectrum occur, they produce a hissing sound called *white noise*. White noise is named by analogy to white light. Just as white light includes all wavelengths of the visible light spectrum, so white noise includes all frequencies of the sound spectrum.

■ **loudness**
The dimension of auditory experience related to the intensity of a pressure wave.

■ **pitch**
The dimension of auditory experience related to the frequency of a pressure wave; height or depth of a tone.

■ **frequency (of a sound wave)**
The number of times per second that a sound wave cycles through a peak and low point.

■ **timbre**
The distinguishing quality of a sound; the dimension of auditory experience related to the complexity of the pressure wave.

TABLE 5.2

Sound Intensity Levels in the Environment

The following decibel levels apply at typical working distances. Each ten-point increase on the decibel scale represents a tenfold increase in sound intensity over the previous level. Even some everyday noises can be hazardous to hearing if exposure goes on for too long a time.

Typical Level (Decibels)	Example	Dangerous Time Exposure
0	Lowest sound audible to human ear	
30	Quiet library, soft whisper	
40	Quiet office, living room, bedroom away from traffic	
50	Light traffic at a distance, refrigerator, gentle breeze	
60	Air conditioner at 20 feet, conversation, sewing machine	
70	Busy traffic, noisy restaurant (constant exposure)	Critical level begins
80	Subway, heavy city traffic, alarm clock at 2 feet, factory noise	More than 8 hours
90	Truck traffic, noisy home appliances, shop tools, lawnmower	Less than 8 hours
100	Chain saw, boiler shop, pneumatic drill	Less than 2 hours
120	Rock concert in front of speakers, sandblasting, thunderclap	Immediate danger
140	Gunshot blast, jet plane at 50 feet	Any length of exposure time is dangerous
180	Rocket launching pad	Hearing loss inevitable

Source: Reprinted with permission from the American Academy of Otolaryngology—Head and Neck Surgery, Washington, D.C.

An Ear on the World

As Figure 5.13 shows, the ear has an outer, a middle, and an inner section. The soft, funnel-shaped outer ear is well designed to collect sound waves, but hearing would still be quite good without it. The essential parts of the ear are hidden from view, inside the head.

A sound wave passes into the outer ear and through an inch-long canal to strike an oval-shaped membrane called the *eardrum*. The eardrum is so sensitive that it can respond to the movement of a *single molecule!* A sound wave causes it to vibrate with the same frequency and amplitude as the wave itself. This vibration is passed along to three tiny bones in the middle ear, the smallest bones in the human body. The bones move, one after the other, which has the effect of intensifying the force of the vibration. The third bone pushes on a membrane that opens into the inner ear.

The actual organ of hearing, the *organ of Corti*, is a chamber inside the **cochlea,** a snail-shaped structure within the inner ear. The organ of Corti plays the same role in hearing that the retina plays in vision. It contains the all-important receptor cells, which in this case look like bristles and are called hair cells, or *cilia.* Exposure to extremely loud noise for a brief period of time, or more moderate levels of noise for a sustained period, can damage these fragile cells. They flop over, like broken blades of grass, and if the damage reaches a certain point, hearing loss occurs. In our society, with its ubiquitous office machines, automobiles, power saws, leaf blowers, jackhammers, and stereos (often

■ **cochlea (kock-lee-uh)**
A snail-shaped, fluid-filled organ in the inner ear, containing the receptors for hearing.

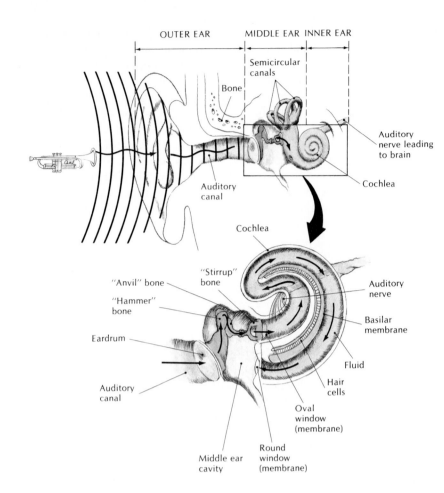

FIGURE 5.13

Major structures of the ear
Sound waves are collected by the outer ear and channeled down the auditory canal, causing the eardrum to vibrate. These vibrations are then passed along to the tiny bones of the middle ear. Movement of these bones intensifies the force of the vibrations and funnels them to a small membrane separating the middle and inner ear. The receptor cells for hearing (hair cells) are located in a small organ within the snail-shaped cochlea. The receptors initiate nerve impulses that travel along the auditory nerve to the brain.

played at full blast and listened to through headphones), such impairment is common. According to one estimate, three of every five entering college students already have impaired hearing, most of them because of damage to the cilia (Lipscomb, 1972). Our noisy environment also helps explain why so many older people cannot hear as well as they once did (especially the higher frequencies), although some receptor cells in the ear are also lost normally with age.

The hair cells of the cochlea are embedded in the rubbery *basilar membrane,* which stretches across the interior of the cochlea. When pressure reaches the cochlea, it causes wavelike motions in fluid within the cochlea's interior. These motions push on the basilar membrane, causing it to move in a wavelike motion. Just above the hair cells is yet another membrane. As the hair cells rise and fall, their tips brush against it and they bend. This causes the hair cells to initiate a signal that is passed along to the *auditory nerve,* which then carries the message to the brain. The particular pattern of hair cell movement is affected by the manner in which the basilar membrane moves. The pattern determines which neurons fire and how rapidly they fire, and the resulting code determines the sort of sound we hear.

Could anyone ever imagine such a complex and odd arrangement of bristles, fluids, and snail shells if it didn't already exist?

Constructing the Auditory World

Just as we do not see a retinal image, so we do not hear a chorus of brushlike tufts bending and swaying in the dark recesses of the cochlea. Just as we do not see a jumbled collection of lines and colors, so we do not hear a disconnected

The spiraled interior of a guinea pig's cochlea, shown here, is almost identical to that of a human cochlea.

cacophony of pitches and timbres. Instead, we use our perceptual powers to organize patterns of sound and construct a meaningful auditory world.

For example, in class, your psychology instructor hopes you will perceive his or her voice as *figure* and the hum of a passing airplane, cheers from the athletic field, or distant sounds of a construction crew as *ground*. Whether these hopes are realized will depend, of course, on where you choose to direct your attention (so stay awake!). Other Gestalt principles also seem to apply to hearing. The *proximity* of notes in a melody tells you which notes go together to form phrases; *continuity* helps you follow a melody on one violin when another violin is playing a different melody; *similarity* in timbre and pitch helps you pick out the soprano voices in a chorus and hear them as a unit; *closure* helps you understand a radio announcer's words even when static makes some of the individual sounds unintelligible.

Besides organizing sounds, we also need to know where they are coming from. We can estimate the *distance* of a sound's source by using loudness as a cue. For example, we know that a train sounds louder when it is 20 yards away than when it is a mile off. To locate the *direction* a sound is coming from, we depend in part on the fact that we have two ears. A sound arriving from the right reaches the right ear a fraction of a second sooner than it reaches the left. It may also provide a bit more energy to the right ear (depending on its frequency) because it has to get around the head to reach the left ear. It is hard to localize sounds that are coming from directly in back of you or from directly above your head because they reach both ears at the same time. When you turn or cock your head, you are actively trying to overcome this problem. Many animals don't have to do this; they can move their ears independently of the head.

People who are hearing-impaired in one ear have trouble telling where sounds are coming from. Even those with normal hearing find it difficult to locate objects through sound alone, as you know if you have ever played blindfold games like Marco Polo. Our eyes provide fuller information on distance than our ears do because they provide direct perception of a three-dimensional world.

QUICK QUIZ

1. Which psychological dimensions of hearing correspond to the intensity, frequency, and complexity of the sound wave?
2. Willie Nelson has a nasal voice and Ray Charles has a gravelly voice. Which psychological dimension of hearing describes the difference?
3. A loud or sustained noise can permanently damage the _____ of the ear.
4. During a lecture, a classmate draws your attention to a buzzing fluorescent light that you had not previously noticed. What will happen to your perception of figure and ground?

ANSWERS:

1. loudness, pitch, timbre 2. timbre 3. hair cells (cilia) 4. The buzzing sound will become figure and the lecturer's voice will become ground, at least momentarily.

■ OTHER SENSES

Psychologists have been particularly interested in vision and audition because of the importance of these senses to human survival. However, research on the other senses is growing dramatically, as awareness of how they contribute to our lives increases and new ways are found to study them.

Taste: Savory Sensations

Taste, or *gustation*, occurs because chemicals stimulate thousands of receptors in the mouth. These receptors are located primarily on the tongue, but there are also some in the throat and on the roof of the mouth. If you look at your tongue in a mirror you will notice many tiny bumps. Each bump contains many **taste buds** along its sides. The buds, which up close look a little like a segmented orange, are commonly referred to, mistakenly, as the receptors for taste. The actual receptor cells, however, are inside the buds, 15 to 50 to a bud (estimates vary). These cells send tiny fibers out through an opening in the bud; the receptor sites are on these fibers. The receptor cells are replaced by new cells every 10 days or so. However, over time, the total number of taste buds (and therefore receptors) declines, which is why older people can often enjoy strong tastes that children may detest.

There appear to be four basic tastes: *salty, sour, bitter,* and *sweet,* each produced by a different type of chemical. Most taste receptors are particularly sensitive to one of these four tastes. And because of the way the taste buds are distributed across the tongue, different parts of the tongue also tend to "specialize" in particular tastes, as you can see in Figure 5.14. When you bite into an egg or a piece of bread or an orange, its unique flavor is composed of some combination of the four basic taste types. The physiological details, however, are still not well understood. For example, it is not yet clear whether the four basic tastes are really points on a continuum, as colors are, or are distinct and associated with different types of nerve fibers.

Human beings are born with a sweet tooth. Only a few drops of sugar water will calm a crying newborn infant and raise an infant's pain threshold, perhaps because the sugar somehow activates endorphins, the body's natural opiates (Smith, Fillion, & Blass, 1990). Our species also seems to have a natural dislike for bitter substances, probably because many poisonous substances are bitter. But taste is also a matter of culture. For example, although raw oysters, raw smoked salmon, and raw herring are appetizing to many North Americans, other forms of raw seafood that are popular in Japan (sea urchin, octopus, yellowtail) have only recently gained a following and are still rejected by many.

Individual tastes also vary. The French have a saying, *Chacun à son goût* (each to his own taste). Why do some people within a culture gobble up a dish that makes others turn green? Experience undoubtedly plays a role. As we will see in Chapter 6, one can acquire a taste or a distaste for a particular food. Recent evidence indicates that individual differences in taste sensitivity are also related to the density of taste buds; human tongues may have as few as 500 and as many as 10,000 taste buds (Miller & Reedy, 1990). Genetic differences probably make people more or less sensitive to the chemicals in particular foods (Bartoshuk, 1980). Some people experience a bitter taste from saccharin, but others do not; some people notice that water tastes sweet immediately after they eat artichokes, but others taste no difference.

■ **taste buds**
Nests of taste receptor cells.

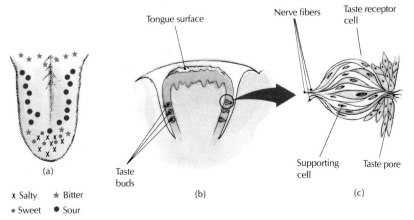

(a)

x Salty   ★ Bitter
● Sweet   ● Sour

Tongue surface

Nerve fibers

Taste receptor cell

Taste buds

Supporting cell

Taste pore

(b)

(c)

FIGURE 5.14

Taste receptors
(a) Various areas of the tongue are differentially sensitive to the four basic tastes, at least when the solution being tested is weak. (b) An enlarged view of the tongue's surface. (c) An enlarged view of a single taste bud.

The attractiveness of a particular food can be affected by its temperature and texture. As Goldilocks found out, a cold bowl of porridge isn't nearly as delicious as one that is properly heated. And any peanut butter fan will tell you that chunky and smooth peanut butters just don't taste the same. Even more important for taste is a food's odor. Subtle flavors, such as chocolate and vanilla, would have little taste if we could not smell them (see Figure 5.15). The dependence of taste on smell explains why you have trouble tasting your food when you have a stuffy nose. Most people who chronically have trouble tasting things probably have a problem with smell, not taste per se. The total loss of taste is extremely rare; taste expert Linda Bartoshuk (1990) says that in a decade of evaluating disorders of smell and taste, she met only two people who could not taste a thing.

Smell: The Sense of Scent

The great author and educator Helen Keller, who was blind and deaf from infancy, once called smell "the fallen angel of the senses." Yet our sense of smell, or *olfaction*, although seemingly crude when compared to a bloodhound's, is actually quite good—and more useful than most people realize. People can detect thousands of different odors. And they can smell some substances before they can be detected by odor-sensitive machines, which is why human beings are often hired to detect odors in chemical plants and laboratories and to detect the freshness of fish at fish markets.

The receptors for smell are specialized neurons embedded in a tiny patch of mucous membrane in the upper part of the nasal passage, just beneath the eyes (see Figure 5.16). These receptors—about 5 million of them in each nasal cavity—respond to chemical molecules in the air. Certain types of molecules seem to fit certain receptors the way a key fits a lock. Somehow their effects combine to yield the yeasty smell of freshly baked bread or the spicy fragrance of a eucalyptus tree. But the neural code for smell, like that for taste, is still poorly understood.

One complicating factor is that there are many words to describe smells (rotten, burned, musky, fruity, spicy, flowery, resinous, putrid . . .), but researchers do not agree on which smells are basic. Recent research suggests that there may

FIGURE 5.15

Taste test

The green bars show the percentages of people who could identify a substance dropped on their tongues when they were able to smell it. The blue bars show the percentages who could identify a substance when they were prevented from smelling it. (From Mozell et al., 1969.)

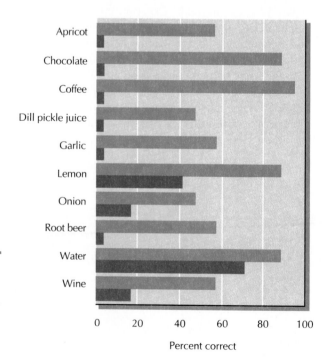

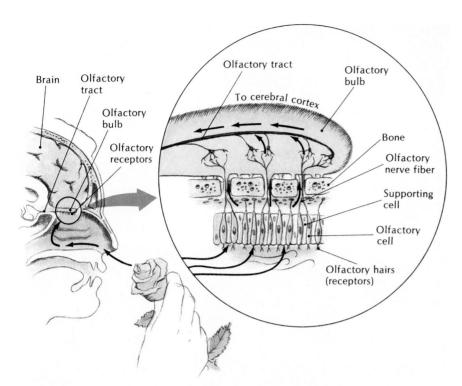

FIGURE 5.16

Receptors for smell
Airborne chemical molecules (vapors) enter the nose and circulate through the nasal cavity, where the smell receptors are located. Sniffing draws more vapors into the nose and speeds their circulation. Vapors can also reach the nasal cavity through the mouth by way of a passageway from the throat.

be as many as a thousand different receptor types, with each possibly responding to only a few kinds of odor molecules (Buck & Axel, 1991). This kind of system is quite unlike the one involved in vision, where only three basic receptor cell types are involved, or the one involved in taste, where there are four basic types.

Signals from the receptors travel to the olfactory bulb in the brain. However, the discovery of so many different receptor types means that a great deal of the processing necessary for odor discrimination may occur within the nose itself. Such a system may have originally evolved because most animals were heavily dependent on smell for finding food or detecting predators, and with their small brains, they needed a lot of specialized receptor cells to do the actual work of olfaction. Through evolution we apparently acquired the same basic plan.

Although smell is less vital for human survival than for the survival of other animals, it is still important. We sniff out danger by smelling smoke, food spoilage, or poison gases. Thus a deficit in the sense of smell is nothing to turn up your nose at. Such a loss can come about because of infection or disease. It can also occur because of cigarette or pipe smoking. In a recent study, people had to take a whiff of 40 common odors, such as pizza, motor oil, and banana. Smokers were nearly twice as likely as nonsmokers to show impaired ability. The results showed that a person who has smoked two packs a day for 10 years must abstain from cigarettes for 10 more years before odor detection will return to normal (Frye, Schwartz, & Doty, 1990).

Folklore tells us that smells not only aid survival but also contribute to the sexual "chemistry" that seems to exist between certain people. Researchers, however, have had trouble proving it. Interest has centered on *pheromones*, odorous chemical substances released by one member of a species that affect the physiology or behavior of other members. In many species, pheromones play a role in sexual behavior. A female cat in heat will attract, through scent, all the unneutered tomcats in the neighborhood. A female moth emits pheromones to entice male suitors who are miles away. There is some evidence that human beings, too, produce pheromones, a fact that has inspired one American perfume company to bring out a pheromone-based scent that it promises will "trigger

Smell has not only evolutionary but cultural significance. These pilgrims in Matsuyama, Japan, are purifying themselves with holy incense for good luck and health. Incense has always been an important commodity; the gifts of the Magi, after all, included frankincense and myrrh.

an intense magnetic reaction" in persons of the other sex. But before you head for the perfume counter, we should tell you that there is no evidence that eau de pheromone can influence, let alone *compel*, human sexual behavior, or increase sexual allure. Natural or learned reactions to smells may well play some role in sex, but in sexual matters, human beings are generally more affected by what the brain learns and the eyes see than what the nose knows (Wade & Cirese, 1991).

Human odor preferences, like taste preferences, vary. In some societies, people use rancid fat as a hair pomade, but anyone in our culture who did so would quickly have a social problem. Within a particular culture, context and experience are all-important. The very same chemicals that contribute to unpleasant body odors and bad breath also contribute to the pleasant bouquet and flavor of cheese (Labows, 1980).

Senses of the Skin

The skin's usefulness is more than just skin deep. Besides protecting our innards, our 2 square yards of skin help us identify objects and establish intimacy with others. By providing a boundary between ourselves and everything else, the skin also gives us a sense of ourselves as distinct from the environment.

The skin senses include *touch* (or pressure), *warmth*, *cold*, and *pain*. At one time it was thought that these four senses were associated with four distinct kinds of receptors, or "end organs," but this view is now in doubt. Although there are spots on the skin that are particularly sensitive to cold, warmth, pressure, and pain, no simple, straightforward correspondence between the four sensations and the various types of receptors has been found. Recent research has concentrated more on the neural codes involved in the skin senses than on the receptors themselves.

Pain, which is both a skin sense and an internal sense, has come under special scrutiny. Pain differs from other senses in an important way: When the stimulus producing it is removed, the sensation may continue—sometimes for years. Chronic pain disrupts lives, puts stress on the body, keeps people from their jobs, and causes depression and despair. (For some ways of coping with pain, see "Taking Psychology with You.")

According to the **gate-control theory** of pain, the experience of pain depends partly on whether pain impulses get past a "gate" in the spinal cord and thus reach the brain (Melzack & Wall, 1965). The gate is made up of neurons that can either transmit or block pain messages from the skin, muscles, and internal organs. Pain fibers (like other kinds of fibers in the nervous system) are always active. When injury to tissue occurs, certain fibers open the gate. Normally, though, the gate is closed, either by impulses coming into the spinal cord from larger fibers that respond to pressure or by signals coming down from the brain itself. According to the gate-control theory, chronic pain occurs when disease, infection, or injury damages the fibers that ordinarily close the gate, and pain messages are able to reach the brain unchecked.

The gate-control theory may help explain the strange phenomenon of *phantom pain*, in which a person continues to feel pain that seemingly comes from an amputated limb or from a breast or internal organ that has been surgically removed. Although sense receptors that were in the body part no longer exist, the pain can nonetheless be excruciating. An amputee may feel the same aching, burning, or sharp pain from gangrenous ulcers, calf cramps, throbbing toes, surgical wounds, or even ingrown toenails that he or she endured before the surgery (Katz & Melzack, 1990).

One explanation of phantom pain is that impulses normally responsible for closing the pain "gate" are reduced or eliminated by the amputation or operation. Without these inhibitory impulses, pain fibers near the spinal cord are able to get their messages through, and pain pathways are permanently activated. Another possible explanation is that pain-producing activity in the brain, once it begins, somehow continues on its own without any further impulses from the spinal cord. This would explain why amputees who undergo complete transection (horizontal cutting) of the spinal cord may still report phantom pain (Melzack, 1990).

During the past three decades, researchers have learned that the occurrence of pain involves the release of several chemicals at the site of tissue damage and in the spinal cord and brain, including an important neurotransmitter called *substance P*. These chemicals promote inflammation and cause pain nerves to fire. Conversely, the suppression of pain involves the release of various endorphins in the brain (see Chapter 3). One effect of the endorphins is to prevent pain fibers from releasing substance P (Jessel & Iversen, 1979; Ruda, 1982).

Thus pain is far more complex than scientists thought when the gate-control theory was first proposed. However, although certain aspects of the gate-control theory have turned out to be incomplete (or even wrong), in its general outlines the theory remains useful. It correctly predicts that mild pressure, as well as other types of stimulation, can interfere with severe or protracted pain by closing the spinal gate, either directly or by means of signals sent from the brain. When we vigorously rub a banged elbow, or apply ice packs, heat, or mustard plasters to injuries, we are acting on this principle. The idea of fighting fire with fire in order to close the pain gate has led to the development of a pain relief device that delivers small amounts of electric current into certain spinal cord nerves. This device can be installed under the skin, and patients can control the amount of stimulation themselves, with a resulting decrease in the pain they feel.

Much remains to be learned, not only about the four basic skin sensations, but also about itch, tickle, sensitivity to vibration, the sensation of wetness, and different types of pain. Researchers are trying to break the neural codes that explain why gently pricking pain spots with a needle produces itch; why lightly touching adjacent pressure spots in rapid succession produces tickle; and why

■ **gate-control theory**
The theory that the experience of pain depends in part on whether pain impulses get past a neurological "gate" in the spinal cord and thus reach the brain.

the simultaneous stimulation of warm and cold spots produces not a lukewarm sensation but the sensation of heat. Decoding the messages of the skin senses will eventually tell us how we are able to distinguish sandpaper from velvet and glue from grease.

The Environment Within

We usually think of our senses as pipelines to the "outside" world, but two senses keep us informed about the movements of our own bodies.

Kinesthesis tells us where our various body parts are located and lets us know when they move. It uses pain and pressure receptors located in the muscles, joints, and tendons (tissues that connect muscles to bones). Without kinesthesis you could not touch your finger to your nose with your eyes shut. In fact, you would have trouble with any voluntary movement. Think of how hard walking is when your leg has "fallen asleep" or how clumsy chewing is when a dentist has numbed your jaw with an anesthetic.

Equilibrium, or the sense of balance, gives us information about our bodies as a whole. Along with vision and touch, it lets us know whether we are standing upright or on our heads and tells us when we are falling or rotating. Equilibrium relies primarily on three **semicircular canals** in the inner ear (see Figure 5.13 on page 175). These thin tubes are filled with fluid that moves and presses on hairlike receptors whenever the head rotates. The receptors initiate messages that travel through a part of the auditory nerve that is not involved in hearing.

Normally, kinesthesis and equilibrium work together to give us a sense of our own physical reality, something we take utterly for granted but shouldn't. Oliver Sacks (1985) tells the heartbreaking story of a young British woman named Christina who suffered irreversible damage to her kinesthetic nerve fibers because of a mysterious inflammation. At first Christina was as floppy as a rag doll; she could not sit up, walk, or stand. Then, slowly, she learned to do these things, relying on visual cues and sheer willpower. But her movements remained unnatural; she had to grasp a fork with painful force or she would drop it. More important, despite her remaining sensitivity to light touch on the skin, she could no longer experience herself as physically embodied: "It's like something's been scooped right out of me, right at the centre. . . ."

■ **kinesthesis (KIN-es-THEE-sis)**
The sense of body position and movement of body parts. Also called kinesthesia.

■ **equilibrium**
The sense of balance.

■ **semicircular canals**
Sense organs in the inner ear that contribute to equilibrium by responding to rotation of the head.

*Martha Graham photograph courtesy Barbara Morgan.
Martha Graham, Letter to the World (Kick). 1940.*

On the left, Olympic gold medalist Greg Louganis executes a winning dive that requires precise positioning of each part of his body. "I have a good kinesthetic awareness," says Louganis, with some understatement. "I am aware of where I am in space." Above is famed dancer and choreographer Martha Graham, who turned kinesthesis and balance into artistry.

With equilibrium, we come, as it were, to the end of our senses. We have seen that the gathering of sensory data about the external and internal world is far from straightforward. A hundred sensory signals reach the brain each second. The brain, where we ultimately see, hear, taste, smell, and feel pleasure and pain, combines and integrates these signals to produce a model of reality from moment to moment. How does it know how to do this? Are our perceptual abilities inborn, or must we learn them? We turn next to this issue.

QUICK QUIZ

Can you make some sense out of the following sensory problems?

1. April always has trouble tasting foods, especially those with subtle flavors. What's the most likely explanation?
2. May has chronic shoulder pain. How might the gate-control theory explain it?
3. June, a rock musician, discovers she can't hear as well as she used to. What's a likely explanation?

ANSWERS:

1. An impaired sense of smell, possibly due to disease, illness, or cigarette smoking. 2. Nerve fibers that normally close the pain "gate" may have been damaged. Or it may be that pain-producing activity in the brain is, for some reason, continuing even without pain impulses from the spinal cord. 3. Hearing impairment has many causes, but in June's case we might suspect that prolonged exposure to loud music has damaged the hair cells of her cochlea.

■ PERCEPTUAL POWERS: ORIGINS AND INFLUENCES

The Gestalt psychologists argued that the basic strategies for organizing the world are *innate*, that is, wired into our brains from the beginning. Other psychologists have argued that babies have almost none of the perceptual powers that adults have and must acquire them through experience and learning. William James once described the infant's world as nothing but a "blooming, buzzing confusion." Modern research suggests that the truth lies somewhere between these two extremes.

Inborn Abilities and Perceptual Lessons

One way to study the origins of perceptual abilities is to see what happens when the normal perceptual experiences of early life are prevented from happening. Researchers have found that when newborn animals are reared in total darkness for a period of weeks or months, or fitted with translucent goggles that permit only diffuse light to get through, or exposed only to certain types of patterns, vision develops abnormally. In one study, for example, kittens were fitted with special collars that kept them from turning their heads or seeing their own bodies. For five hours a day they lived in a cylinder with walls that were covered entirely with either vertical or horizontal black and white stripes. The rest of the time they were housed in a completely dark room. When tested after several months, the kittens exposed only to vertical stripes seemed blind to all horizontal contours, and those exposed only to horizontal stripes seemed blind to all vertical ones (Blakemore & Cooper, 1970).

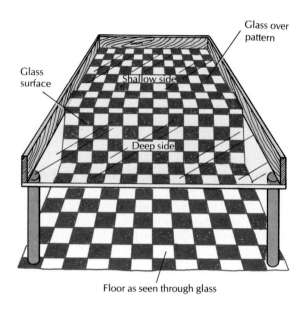

FIGURE 5.17

A cliff-hanger
Infants as young as 6 months usually hesitate to crawl past the apparent edge of a "visual cliff," which suggests that they are able to perceive depth.

How would you interpret these results? Your first inclination may be to say that early experience is necessary for the *initial* development of the skills in question—that cats are blind to both horizontal and vertical lines at birth. There is another possibility, however: Normal experience may merely ensure the survival of skills *already present* at birth. Physiological studies suggest that this second interpretation is the correct one, at least in the case of line perception. The brains of newborn kittens are equipped with the same "feature detector" cells that adult cats have. But when kittens are not allowed to see lines of a particular orientation, cells sensitive to those orientations deteriorate or change, and perception suffers. For example, when a kitten wears a special mask that permits it to see only vertical lines with one eye and horizontal lines with the other, cells in its visual cortex later respond only to vertical or horizontal orientations rather than the full range of orientations that is usual in cats (Hirsch & Spinelli, 1970).

Human infants, too, seem to be born with certain basic perceptual abilities. They are nearsighted at first, but their visual acuity develops rapidly. They can discriminate size and color very early, possibly even at birth, and can distinguish complex patterns after only a few weeks (see Chapter 13). Even depth perception occurs early and may be present from the beginning.

Testing an infant's perception of depth requires considerable ingenuity. One favorite procedure is to place infants on a device called a "visual cliff" (Gibson & Walk, 1960). The "cliff" is a pane of glass covering both a shallow surface and a deep one (see Figure 5.17). The infant is placed on a board in the middle, and the child's mother tries to lure the baby across either the shallow or deep side. Babies as young as 6 months of age will crawl to their mothers across the shallow side but will refuse to crawl out over the "cliff." Their hesitation shows that they have depth perception.

Infants younger than 6 months are unable to crawl, but they can still be tested on the visual cliff. At only 2 months of age, babies show a drop in heart rate when placed on the deep side of the cliff, but no change when they are placed on the shallow side. A slowed heart rate is usually a sign of increased attention. These infants may not be frightened the way an older infant would be, but apparently they can notice the difference in depth (Banks & Salapatek, 1984). Other studies suggest that within the first few months of life, infants use depth cues to achieve size constancy (T. G. R. Bower, 1981).

Another line of evidence also supports the notion that certain abilities are prewired: case histories of people who have gained sight after a lifetime of blindness (Senden, 1960). Like S. B., whose case we described at the start of this chapter, these individuals may have many visual limitations. On the other hand, even though they have never seen before, when their bandages are removed they can distinguish figure from ground, scan objects, and follow moving objects with their eyes. Thus these abilities, at least, seem to be inborn.

The world of the infant, then, is far from the blooming, buzzing confusion that William James took it to be. A young child's perceptual world may not be identical to an adult's, but if learning to perceive is compared to going to school, nature has allowed us to skip kindergarten and possibly even the first grade.

Psychological and Cultural Influences on Perception

The fact that some perceptual processes appear to be innate does not mean that all people perceive the world in the same way. A camera doesn't care what it "sees." A tape recorder doesn't ponder what it "hears." A robot arm on a factory assembly line holds no opinion about what it "touches." But because human beings care about what they see, hear, taste, smell, and feel, psychological factors can influence what they perceive and how they perceive it:

1. *Needs.* When we need something, have an interest in it, or want it, we are especially likely to perceive it. For example, studies show that hungry individuals are faster than others at seeing words related to hunger when the words are flashed briefly on a screen (Wispé & Drambarean, 1953).

Several decades ago, two researchers discovered that the desire of sports fans to see their team win can affect what they see during a game. Sports fans, of course, tend to regard their own team as the good guys and the opposing team as the dirty rats. In the study, Princeton and Dartmouth students were shown a movie of a football game between their two teams. The game, which Princeton won, was a rough one. Several players were injured, including Princeton's star quarterback. Princeton students viewing the film saw Dartmouth players commit an average of 9.8 rule infractions. They considered the game "rough and dirty." Dartmouth students, on the other hand, noticed only half as many infractions by their team. They considered the game rough but fair (Hastorf & Cantril, 1954).

2. *Beliefs.* What a person holds to be true about the world can affect the interpretation of ambiguous sensory signals. Suppose you spot a round object hovering high in the sky. If you believe that extraterrestrials occasionally visit the earth, you may "see" the object as a spaceship. But if you think such beliefs are hogwash, you are more likely to see a weather balloon. An image of a crucified Jesus on a garage door in Santa Fe Springs, California, caused great excitement among people who were ready to believe that divine messages may be found on everyday objects. The image was found to be caused by two streetlights that merged the shadows of a bush and a "For Sale" sign in the yard.

3. *Emotions.* Emotions can also influence our interpretation of sensory information. A small child, afraid of the dark, may see a ghost instead of a robe hanging on the door, or a monster instead of a beloved doll. Pain, in particular, seems affected by emotion (Melzack & Dennis, 1978). Soldiers who are seriously wounded often deny being in much pain, even though they are alert and are not in shock. Their relief at being alive may offset the anxiety and fear that

People often see what they want to see. This apartment building in a small French town drew huge crowds when some people thought they saw the face of Jesus on it. Actually, the pattern on the wall was the result of damage caused by water leaking from faulty plumbing in one of the apartments.

FIGURE 5.18

Overcoming perceptual expectations
Can you draw a chair this well? If not, perhaps your perceptual expectations about chairs are getting in the way. Renowned art educator Betty Edwards (1986) uses several techniques to help people see (and then draw) what is really "out there." One of her assignments is to draw the empty spaces *between the lines or shapes of an object, instead of the object itself. That technique produced this student's drawing. Why not try it yourself with some simple object, such as a chair, a cup, or your own hand with your index finger touching your thumb? You may find yourself perceiving the world around you in a fresh new way.*

contribute so much to pain (although other explanations are also possible). Conversely, depression can make pain worse than it would otherwise be (Fields, 1991).

4. *Expectations.* Previous experiences often lead us to perceive the world in a certain way (see Figure 5.18). The tendency to perceive what you expect is called a **perceptual set.** Perceptual sets can come in handy. For example, at a noisy party you may not catch every sound the person talking to you makes. But if she says, "How do you . . ." and then extends her hand, you may "hear" the word *do.* But perceptaul sets can also keep us from perceiving things. In Center Harbor, Maine, local legend has it that veteran newscaster Walter Cronkite was sailing into port one day when he heard a small crowd on shore shouting "Hello, Walter . . . Hello, Walter." Pleased, he waved and took a bow. Only when he ran aground did he realize what they had really been shouting: "Low water . . . low water." (By the way, there is a misspelled word right before this story. Did you notice it? If not, probably it was because you expected all the words in this book to be spelled correctly.)

In turn, our needs, beliefs, emotions, and expectations are all affected by the culture we live in. Culture can even affect certain perceptual processes that we usually regard as universal and automatic, such as those that produce pain. In one recent study of people who had just had their ears pierced, Asians reported more pain than did Caucasians, who in turn reported more pain than Afro-West Indians (Thomas & Rose, 1991). Cultural differences in the subjects' attitudes toward minor injury appeared to play a role in their responses.

Different cultures also give people practice with certain kinds of perceptual environments (see Figure 5.19). In a classic study done in the 1960s, researchers found that members of certain African tribes were much less likely to be fooled by the Müller-Lyer illusion and other geometric illusions than were Westerners. Westerners, the researchers observed, live in a "carpentered" world, full of rectangular structures built with the aid of saws, planes, straight edges, and carpenter's squares. Westerners are also used to interpreting two-dimensional photographs and perspective drawings as representations of a three-dimensional world. As a result, they learn to interpret acute and obtuse angles as right angles extended in space—just the sort of habit that would increase susceptibility to the Müller-Lyer illusion. The rural Africans in the study, living in a less carpentered environment and in round huts, seemed more likely to take the lines in the figures literally, as two-dimensional, which could explain why they were less susceptible to the illusion (Segall, Campbell, & Herskovits, 1966).

■ **perceptual set**
A habitual way of perceiving, based on expectations.

This research was followed by a flurry of replications in the 1970s, showing that it was culture, rather than race, that produced the differences between groups (Segall et al., 1990). Since then there has been almost no further work on the fascinating intersection of culture and visual illusions. However, as we will be seeing throughout this book, culture affects perception in many other ways: by shaping our stereotypes, directing our attention, and telling us what is important to notice and what is not.

■ PUZZLES OF PERCEPTION

We come, finally, to two puzzling questions about perception that have captured the public's imagination for years. The first is: Can we perceive, through our usual sensory channels, what is happening in the world, without conscious awareness? The second is: Can we perceive what is happening in the world without using our usual sensory channels at all?

Conscious and Nonconscious Perception

Many aspects of perception occur outside of awareness. As we have seen, before something can be recognized or identified, its basic features must be analyzed. In the case of vision, we must make out edges, colors, textures, and differences in the reflectance of light. We must separate figure from ground, calculate distance or depth, and adjust for changing patterns of stimulation on the retina. All this we do without any conscious intention or awareness.

Research on persons blinded by damage to the visual cortex provides striking evidence for the nonconscious nature of certain basic perceptual processes. When these people are presented with a brief flash of light, they deny seeing it. But when they are asked to *guess* where the light is by pointing to it or by directing their eyes toward it, they do much better than chance, although they continue to deny seeing anything (Bridgeman & Staggs, 1982). Some patients can even distinguish a vertical line from a horizontal one, or an *X* from an *O*, with better than chance accuracy. Such "blindsight" may occur because messages from the eyes reach parts of the brain other than the visual cortex, areas that handle elementary kinds of visual information without a person's conscious awareness.

What about more complicated perceptual tasks, like registering and deciphering speech? Research on selective attention and the "cocktail party phenomenon," discussed earlier, shows that even when we are oblivious to unattended speech sounds, we are processing and recognizing them at some level.

Other tantalizing evidence of nonconscious perception comes from research on people anesthetized and unconscious during surgery. Many surgeons report that after an operation some patients show signs of having heard remarks made by doctors and nurses while the patient was still "under." Several controlled studies support these observations (Bennett, 1988; Millar & Watkinson, 1983; Stolzy, Couture, & Edmonds, 1986).

In one study, for example, researchers suggested to anesthetized surgical patients that they later pull on an ear during a postoperative interview. On the average, these patients pulled on their ears six times more often than did patients in a control group, although they had no recollection of having heard the suggestion (Bennett, Davis, & Giannini, 1985). In another study, surgical patients were exposed to a taped list of word pairs (such as *ocean–water*) while they were anesthetized and apparently unconscious. After their operations, the patients had no conscious memory for the word pairs. But when they were given the first word from each pair and were asked to say any word that popped into mind, they were somewhat more likely than they would otherwise have been to respond with the associated words presented during surgery (Kihlstrom et al., 1990).

The sorts of nonconscious processes we have been discussing all involve stimuli that would be *above* the absolute threshold if a person were consciously attending to them. Is it also possible to perceive and respond to messages that are *below* the threshold—too quiet to be consciously heard (in the case of hearing) or too brief or dim to be consciously seen (in the case of vision), even when you are trying your best to hear or see them? Perhaps you have seen ads for products that will allow you to take advantage of such *subliminal perception*. Or perhaps you have heard that subliminal perception doesn't really exist. What are the facts?

First, there is considerable evidence that a simple visual stimulus can affect a person's responses to certain tasks even when the person has no awareness of seeing the stimulus. For example, in one study, people subliminally exposed to a face tended to prefer the face over one they did not "see" in this way (Bornstein, Leone, & Galley, 1987). In another study, words were briefly flashed on a screen and immediately "masked" by a pattern of *X*s and *O*s. Subjects said they could not read the words, or even tell whether a word had appeared at all. But when an "invisible" word (e.g., *bread*) was followed by a second, visible word that was either related in meaning (e.g., *butter*) or unrelated (e.g., *bubble*), the subjects were able to read the related word faster (Dagenbach, Carr, & Wilhelmsen, 1989).

For only $29.95, a "subliminal perception tape" promises to tune up your sluggish motivation. It's true that many perceptual processes occur outside of awareness, but does that mean that "subliminal" tapes can change your behavior or improve your life?

Findings like these are remarkable and potentially very important for theories of how the mind works. They have convinced many psychologists that people often know more than they know they know (Greenwald, 1992; T. Moore, 1991). In fact, nonconscious processing appears to occur not only in perception, but also in memory, thinking, and decision making, as we will see in Chapters 7 and 8. However, the *real-world* implications of subliminal perception are not as dramatic as you might think. Even in the laboratory, where researchers have considerable control, the phenomenon is often hard to demonstrate, and subtle changes in procedure can affect the results. The strongest evidence comes from studies using simple stimuli (faces or single words, such as *bread*), rather than complex stimuli such as sentences ("Eat whole-wheat bread, not white bread"). Moreover, while visual subliminal perception may occur under certain conditions, subliminal *persuasion*, the subject of many popular books and magazine articles, is quite another matter. Careful research has uncovered no basis whatsoever for believing that Madison Avenue can seduce us into buying soft drinks or voting for political candidates by flashing subliminal slogans on television or slipping subliminal images into magazine ads (T. Moore, 1988; Pratkanis & Aronson, 1992). Nor is there any evidence that so-called "subliminal" messages recorded backward on music albums can affect either behavior or attitudes (Vokey & Read, 1985).

What about subliminal tapes that promise, for only $29.95, to help you lose weight, stop smoking, reduce stress, or improve your sex life? Such tapes earn $50 million a year, and a majority of Americans assume they're effective. But spectrographic analysis shows that many of these tapes contain no intelligible subliminal signal (Merikle, 1988). And even when there is some sort of signal, research fails to support any of the manufacturers' claims (Moore, 1991). In one recent study using a double-blind procedure, over 200 college students and other adults listened every day to commercially available tapes that claimed to improve memory or boost self-esteem. Some people thought they were using memory tapes but were actually using self-esteem tapes, or vice versa. Others listened to correctly labeled tapes. These people had all volunteered and they wanted the tapes to work. At the end of a month, about half thought they had improved in the area corresponding to the label they had received, *whether the label was correct or not*. But in reality, there were *no* actual improvements beyond a general placebo effect (Greenwald et al., 1991).

If you want to improve yourself or your life, we encourage you to do so—but you'll probably have to do it the old-fashioned way, by working at it.

QUICK QUIZ

 In 1990, the parents of two young men who had killed themselves brought suit against the rock group Judas Priest. A subliminal message on one of the band's albums, said the parents, had provoked the suicides. What was wrong with this claim?

ANSWER:

First, there is no evidence that such messages can affect behavior. Second, millions of other people listened to the album without killing themselves. Third, many other factors could have led to the suicides, such as delinquency, drug and alcohol abuse, and family violence (Pratkanis & Aronson, 1992). The parents, understandably upset about their sons' deaths, engaged in emotional reasoning ("Who can I blame?") without considering these other, painful, explanations. (The parents, by the way, lost their suit.)

Extrasensory Perception: Reality or Illusion?

Eyes, ears, mouth, nose, skin—we rely on these organs for our experience of the external world. Some people, however, claim they can send and receive messages about the world without relying on the usual sensory channels, by using *extrasensory perception*, or *ESP*.

Reported ESP experiences fall into four general categories. (1) *Telepathy* is direct communication from one mind to another without the usual visual, auditory, and other sensory signals. If you try to guess what number someone is thinking of or what card a person is holding out of sight, you are attempting telepathy. (2) *Clairvoyance* is the perception of an event or fact without normal sensory input. If a man suddenly "knows" that his wife has just died, yet no one has informed him of the death, he might be called clairvoyant. (3) *Precognition* is the perception of an event that has not yet happened. Fortune-tellers make their livings by claiming to read the future in tea leaves or a person's palm. (4)

Out-of-body experiences involve the perception of one's own body from "outside," as an observer might see it. The person feels that he or she has left the physical body entirely. Such experiences are often reported by persons who have been near death, but some people say they can bring them on at will.

Some types of ESP are more plausible than others, given what we know about the physical world. Normal perception depends on the ability to detect changes in energy. Conceivably telepathy could involve something similar: the sending and receiving of changes in energy through channels that have not yet been identified. Other forms of ESP, however, challenge everything we suppose to be true about the way the world and the universe operate. Precognition, for instance, contradicts our usual assumptions about time and space. If it exists, then tomorrow is as real as today and future events can be known, even though they cannot have caused physical changes in the environment.

It might be fun to have ESP—especially before a tough exam or a blind date. However, it's one thing to wish ESP existed and another to conclude that it does. What kind of evidence would convince you that ESP is real, and what kind is only wishful thinking?

EVIDENCE—OR COINCIDENCE? Much of the "evidence" for extrasensory perception comes from anecdotal accounts. Unfortunately, people are not always reliable reporters. They often embellish and exaggerate, or recall only parts of an experience. They also tend to "forget" incidents that don't fit their beliefs, such as "premonitions" of events that fail to occur. Many ESP experiences could merely be unusual coincidences that are memorable because they are dramatic (see Chapter 2). What passes for telepathy, clairvoyance, or precognition could also be based on what a person knows or deduces through ordinary means. If Joanne's father has had two heart attacks, her "premonition" that her father will die shortly (followed, in fact, by her father's death) may not really be so impressive.

The scientific way to establish that a phenomenon exists is to produce it under controlled conditions. Extrasensory perception has been studied extensively by researchers in the field of **parapsychology.** In a typical study, a person might be asked to guess which of five symbols will appear on a card presented at random. A "sender" who can see the card before it is presented tries to transmit a mental image of the symbol to the person. A deck of 25 cards is usually used. Though most people do no better than chance at guessing the symbols, in some studies a few people have consistently done somewhat better than chance. But ESP studies have often been sloppily designed, with inadequate precautions against fraud and improper statistical analysis. When skeptical researchers try to repeat the studies, they usually get negative results. The better controlled the study, the less likely it is to produce support for ESP.

We are not saying that ESP abilities are impossible; some scientists continue to view the issue as unresolved. But most feel that the thousands of experiments done in the past 40 years have failed to make a convincing case for ESP. After an exhaustive review, the National Research Council has concluded that there is "no scientific justification . . . for the existence of parapsychological phenomena" (Druckman & Swets, 1988).

LESSONS FROM A MAGICIAN. Despite the lack of evidence for ESP, in national polls about half of all Americans say they believe in it. Perhaps you yourself have had an experience that seemed to involve ESP or have seen a convincing demonstration by someone else. Surely you can trust the evidence of your own eyes—or can you? We will answer with a true story that contains an important lesson, not only about ESP but about ordinary perception as well.

Several years ago, physician Andrew Weil (whose writings on altered states of consciousness we discussed in Chapter 4) set out to investigate the claims of an Israeli psychic named Uri Geller (Weil, 1974a, 1974b). Geller seemed able to bend keys without touching them, start broken watches, and guess the nature of simple drawings hidden in sealed envelopes. Although he had performed

■ **parapsychology**
The study of purported psychic phenomena, such as ESP and mental telepathy.

"Seeing is believing," goes the old saying, but is it? The engraving on the left shows "a living half woman." The one on the right reveals how the illusion is produced: A diagonal mirror reflects the floor or carpet pattern, so onlookers think they see an unbroken expanse of floor. The moral: Be skeptical when someone claims to possess "supranormal" powers, even if you "saw it with your own eyes."

as a stage magician in his native country, he denied using trickery. His powers, he said, came from energy from another universe.

Weil, who believed in telepathy, felt that ESP might be explained by principles of modern physics and was receptive to Geller's claims. When he met Geller at a private gathering, he was not disappointed. The psychic correctly identified a cross and a Star of David sealed inside separate envelopes. He made a stopped watch start running and a ring sag into an oval shape, apparently without touching them. He made keys change shape in front of Weil's very eyes. Weil came away a convert. What he had seen with his own eyes seemed impossible to deny . . . that is, until he met The Amazing Randi.

James Randi is a well-known magician who is dedicated to educating the public about psychic deception. To Weil's astonishment, Randi was able to duplicate much of what Geller had done. He, too, could bend keys and guess the contents of sealed envelopes. But Randi's feats were only tricks, and he was willing to show Weil exactly how they were done. Weil suddenly experienced "a sense of how strongly the mind can impose its own interpretations on perceptions; how it can see what it expects to see, but not see the unexpected."

Weil was dis-illusioned—literally. He was forced to admit that the evidence of one's own eyes is *not* always reliable. Even when he knew what to look for in a trick, he could not catch The Amazing Randi doing it. Weil learned that our sense impressions of reality are not the same as reality. Our eyes, our ears, and especially our brains can play tricks on us.

The great Greek philosopher Plato once said that "knowledge is nothing but perception," but in fact simple perception is *not* always the best path to knowledge. The truth about human behavior is most likely to emerge if we are aware of how our beliefs and assumptions shape and alter our perceptions. As we have seen throughout this chapter, we do not passively register the world "out there." We mentally construct it.

Living with Pain

Temporary pain is an unpleasant but necessary part of life, a warning of disease or injury. Chronic pain, which is ongoing or recurring, is another matter, a serious problem in itself. According to one estimate, 86 million Americans have some form of chronic pain (Bonica, 1980). Back injuries, arthritis, migraine headaches, serious illnesses such as cancer—all can cause unrelieved misery to pain sufferers and their families. The direct and indirect financial costs to victims and the health care system run into billions of dollars every year.

At one time, the only way to combat pain was with drugs or surgery, which were not always effective. Today, we know that the experience of pain is affected by attitudes, actions, emotions, and circumstances, and that treatment must take into account psychology as well as biology. Even social roles can influence a person's response to pain. For example, in pain experiments done in the laboratory, men tend to "tough it out" longer than women do. But a real-world study of people in constant pain for more than six months found that men suffered more severe psychological distress than women, possibly because the male role made it hard for them to admit their pain or accept a decrease in productivity (Snow et al., 1986).

Many pain treatment programs encourage patients to manage their pain themselves instead of relying entirely on health care professionals. Usually these programs combine several strategies:

• *Painkilling medication.* Doctors used to worry that patients would become addicted to painkillers or develop a tolerance to them. They would give a minimal dose, then wait until the effects wore off and the patient was once again in agony before giving more. This approach was ineffectual and ignored the fact that addiction depends in part on the motives for which a drug is taken and the circumstances under which it is used (see Chapters 4 and 16). The method now recommended by experts (although doctors and hospitals do not always follow the advice) is to give pain sufferers a continuous dose of painkiller in whatever amount is necessary to keep them pain-free, and to allow them to do this for themselves when they leave the hospital. This strategy leads to *reduced* dosages rather than increasing ones and usually does not lead to drug dependence or tolerance (Hill et al., 1990; Taub, 1984).

• *Spouse or family involvement.* When a person is in pain, friends and relatives understandably tend to sympathize and excuse the sufferer from regular responsibilities. The sufferer takes to bed, avoids physical activity, and focuses on the pain. As we will see in Chapter 6, attention from others is a powerful reinforcer of whatever behavior produces the attention. Also, focusing on pain tends to increase it, and inactivity can lead to shortened muscles, muscle spasms, and fatigue. So sympathy and attention can sometimes backfire and may actually prolong the agony (Flor, Kerns, & Turk, 1987). For this reason, many pain experts now encourage family members to resist rewarding or reinforcing the pain and instead reward activity, exercise, and "wellness." This approach, however, must be used carefully, preferably under the direction of a competent professional, since a patient's complaints about pain are an important diagnostic tool for the physician (Rodgers, 1988). Also, there have been many cases in which lack of compassion about a patient's pain has led to undermedication and needless suffering.

• *Behavioral self-management.* In behavioral therapy, patients learn to identify how, when, and where their pain occurs. This knowledge helps them determine whether the pain is being reinforced or maintained by external events. Just being in control of one's pain can have a powerful pain-reducing effect. Behavior therapy may also include muscle "reeducation"; for example, instead of tensing muscles in response to pain, which only makes the pain worse, patients can learn to relax them (Keefe & Gil, 1986).

• *Biofeedback, hypnosis,* and *progressive relaxation.* These techniques have all been successful with some patients. (We discussed biofeedback in Chapter 3, hypnosis in Chapter 4.) It is unclear, however, whether biofeedback and progressive relaxation are applicable to all types of chronic pain.

• *Cognitive-behavioral therapy.* Attention, expectancies, and beliefs can affect how a person experiences pain. Cognitive-behavioral strategies teach people to identify negative thoughts about pain; recognize connections between thoughts, feelings, and pain; substitute adaptive thoughts for negative ones; and use various coping strategies (such as distraction, relabeling of sensations, and imagery) to alleviate suffering (Turner & Chapman, 1982). All of these techniques increase feelings of control and reduce feelings of inadequacy.

For further information about help for pain, you can contact pain clinics or services in teaching hospitals and medical schools. There are many reputable clinics around the country, some specializing in specific disorders. But take care: There are also many untested therapies and quack practitioners who only prey on people's pain.

SUMMARY

1. *Sensation* is the detection or encoding of changes in physical energy caused by environmental or internal events. *Perception* is the process by which sensory impulses are organized and interpreted.

2. Separate sensations can be accounted for by anatomical codes (the *doctrine of specific nerve energies*) and functional codes in the nervous system. There is still controversy about how functional encoding yields an overall perception of a stimulus.

3. Psychologists in the area of *psychophysics* study sensory sensitivity by measuring *absolute and difference thresholds*. The *theory of signal detection* assumes that an observer's response in a detection task consists of both a sensory process and a decision process, and allows improved estimates of individual thresholds.

4. Our senses respond to change and contrast in the environment, and when stimulation is unchanging *sensory adaptation* occurs. However, too much stimulation can be overwhelming, which is why we exercise *selective attention*.

5. Vision is affected by the wavelength, frequency, and complexity of light. The visual receptors—*rods* and *cones*—are located in the *retina* of the eye. Rods are responsible for vision in dim light; cones are responsible for color vision. The visual world is not a mosaic of light and dark spots but a collection of lines and angles detected and integrated by special *feature detector cells* in the visual cortex of the brain.

6. The *trichromatic* and *opponent-process* theories of color vision apply to different stages of processing. In the first, three types of cones respond selectively to different wavelengths of light. In the second, cells in the visual system known as *opponent-process cells* respond in opposite fashion to short and long wavelengths.

7. Perception involves the active construction of a model of the world from moment to moment. The *Gestalt principles* (such as figure and ground, proximity, closure, similarity, and continuity) describe visual strategies used in form perception. Gestalt and other perceptual principles can be used to improve the design of everyday objects.

8. We localize objects in visual space by using both *binocular* and *monocular* cues. Shape, location, brightness, color, and size *constancies* allow us to perceive objects as stable despite changes in the sensory patterns they produce. Visual *illusions* occur when sensory cues are misleading or when we misinterpret cues; illusions provide useful hints about perceptual processing.

9. Hearing, or *audition*, is affected by the intensity, frequency, and complexity of pressure waves in the air or other transmitting substance. The receptors for hearing are hair cells (cilia) embedded in the *basilar membrane*, in the interior of the *cochlea*. The sounds we hear are determined by patterns of hair cell movement.

10. Gestalt principles seem to apply to auditory as well as visual perception. When we localize sounds we use subtle differences in how pressure waves reach the two ears.

11. Taste, or *gustation*, is a chemical sense. There are four basic tastes, associated with different receptors. Responses to a particular taste depend on culture, genetic differences among individuals, the texture and temperature of the food, and above all, the food's smell.

12. Smell, or *olfaction*, is also a chemical sense. No basic odors have been identified, and the code for smell remains to be worked out. Recent research suggests that there may be as many as a thousand different receptor types for smell, and that much of the processing for smell occurs within the nose itself. Cultural and individual differences affect people's responses to particular odors. *Pheromones* have not been shown to play a role in human sexual responses.

13. The skin senses include touch (pressure), warmth, cold, and pain. There does not seem to be a simple connection between these four senses and different types of receptors, as was once thought.

14. Pain is both a skin sense and an internal sense. According to the *gate-control theory*, the experience of pain depends on whether neural impulses get past a "gate" in the spinal cord and reach the brain. This theory, although not correct in all its details, has led to important advances in pain treatment. Pain also depends on the release of certain chemicals at the site of tissue damage, and pain suppression involves the release of endorphins in the brain.

15. *Kinesthesis* tells us where our various body parts are located, and *equilibrium* tells us the orientation of the body as a whole. Together these two senses provide us with a feeling of physical embodiment.

16. Studies of animals, human infants, and blind people who have recovered their sight suggest that many fundamental perceptual skills are inborn or acquired shortly after birth. However, without certain experiences early in life, cells in the nervous system deteriorate, change, or fail to form appropriate neural pathways, and perception is impaired.

17. Psychological influences on perception include needs, beliefs, emotions, and expectations. All of these influences are in turn affected by culture, which gives people practice with certain kinds of experiences. Because psychological factors affect the way we construct the perceptual world, the evidence of our senses is not always reliable.

18. Many basic perceptual processes occur outside of awareness and without conscious intention. Research on selective attention and on anesthetized surgical patients indicates that even complex nonconscious processing can occur. Moreover, in the laboratory, simple visual subliminal messages can influence behavior. However, there is no evidence that complex behaviors can be manipulated subliminally in everyday life.

19. *Extrasensory perception* refers to such paranormal abilities as telepathy, clairvoyance, precognition, and out-of-body experiences. Studies of ESP have been difficult to replicate, and most scientists feel that the case for ESP is flawed and unconvincing.

KEY TERMS

sensation   *151*

sense receptors   *151*

perception   *152*

transduction   *153*

anatomical codes   *153*

doctrine of specific nerve
  energies   *153*

functional codes   *153*

psychophysics   *154*

absolute threshold   *154*

difference threshold/j.n.d.   *155*

Weber's Law   *155*

signal detection theory   *157*

sensory adaptation   *158*

LEARNING, THINKING, AND FEELING

6

Learning

[R]eward and punishment . . . these are the spur and reins whereby all mankind are set on work, and guided.

JOHN LOCKE

I t's January 1, a brand new year. The sins and lapses of the old year are behind you; you're ready for a fresh start. Optimistically, you sit down to record your New Year's resolutions:

1. Lose 10 pounds; no more chocolate ice cream.
2. Raise grades; spend more time studying.
3. Be easier to get along with; control temper.
4. Get more exercise; take up jogging.
5. Control spending; pay off credit card.
6. Overcome shyness; stop blushing when called on to speak.
7. (You fill in the blank.)

How likely are you to achieve these goals? Some people do fulfill most of their resolutions. For others, the road to frustration is paved with good intentions. Within weeks, days, or even hours they find themselves backsliding ("Well, maybe just one *small* dish of ice cream"). They may end up feeling like the proverbial old dog, unable to learn new tricks.

In fact, however, all of us *can* learn new tricks. By studying the laws of learning, we can improve our ability to change behavior in desirable ways—as we will see in this chapter.

In everyday speech, learning is often taken to mean classroom activities, such as diagramming sentences or memorizing the facts of geography, or the acquisition of practical skills, such as carpentry or sewing. But to psychologists, **learning** is *any* relatively permanent change in behavior that occurs because of experience (excluding changes due to fatigue, injury, or disease). Experience is the great teacher, altering an organism's nervous system and, through the nervous system, its behavior. Learning provides the essential link between the past and the future, enabling an organism to adapt appropriately to changing circumstances in order to survive and thrive. It is a fundamental process in all animals, from the lowliest backyard bug to the loftiest human scholar.

Not all behavior, however, is learned. Some emerges simply as a result of maturation, the natural process of growth and development. And in many animals, a great deal of behavior is due to inborn, unlearned reflexes, simple automatic responses to specific stimuli. Human beings, too, are born with reflexes. If you touch a baby's face, the baby will turn toward your hand, and if you touch its lips, it will make sucking motions. These reactions help the infant find and use the nipple during nursing. Later, when they are no longer needed, these automatic responses disappear, but many others, such as the knee-jerk, eyeblink, and sneeze reflexes, remain.

In the study of animal behavior, complex chains of interrelated reflexes have traditionally been called **instincts,** or more technically, *fixed action patterns* (Tinbergen, 1951). These patterns of behavior, relatively uninfluenced by learning,

■ **learning**
A relatively permanent change in behavior (or behavioral potential) due to experience.

■ **instinct**
A complex pattern of behavior that occurs without learning in every member of a species in response to a specific stimulus. Also called fixed action pattern.

199

Not all behavior is learned; in many animals, responses to particular stimuli are instinctive—such as the glorious display of the male peacock when he is courting. People's courtship rituals can be quite dramatic too, but they have to be learned.

■ **imprinting**
The tendency of some animals, especially birds, to follow and form a permanent attachment to the first moving object they see or hear after birth.

■ **sensitive period**
A period in the development of an organism that is optimal for the acquisition of a particular behavior.

■ **behaviorism**
An approach to psychology that emphasizes the study of objectively observable behavior and the role of the environment as a determinant of behavior.

occur in every individual of a species. Some instincts are common to several different species. Others are "species-specific," representing an adaptation unique to a particular type of organism. A spider will spin a perfect web even if it has never seen one before. A male stickleback fish will instinctively attack any other male that approaches its territory during the mating season, its belligerence automatically triggered by the invader's distinctive red belly.

Fixed action patterns, however, are not always as "fixed" as was once thought. In birds, mammals, and even lower species such as fish, biology and the environment interact to produce behavior. For example, soon after birth, some animals will follow and become attached to the first thing they see or hear that happens to move, a behavior known as **imprinting.** Ordinarily, the "thing" on which the animal imprints is its mother, but experience can dictate otherwise. When ethologist Konrad Lorenz hatched young geese in an incubator, they imprinted on *him*, following him around and responding to his calls as if he were their mother (Lorenz, 1937). In the laboratory, ducklings have imprinted on decoys, rubber balls, and wooden blocks (Hess, 1959). Imprinting is most likely to take place during a brief **sensitive period** of development. (Researchers used to speak of a *critical period*, but because the readiness to imprint sometimes declines gradually, they changed their terminology.) Once it has occurred, imprinting is usually hard to reverse, even when the "mother" is an inanimate object that can offer neither food nor affection. These facts suggest that imprinting is a special type of learning that occurs because at a particular stage in development the animal's nervous system is geared to respond to a conspicuous moving object in a certain way.

Some human behaviors resemble fixed action patterns—for example, universal facial expressions such as smiling or raising the eyebrows in friendly greeting. However, scientists disagree about the place of instinct in more complex human behaviors. On one side, *sociobiologists* maintain that even complicated forms of human behavior can have an instinctive basis. They believe that over the course of evolution certain behavioral patterns have been selected because these patterns have aided individuals in propagating their own genes or those of their biological relatives. According to the sociobiologists, social customs that enhance the odds of such transmission survive in the form of kinship bonds, courtship rituals, altruism, taboos against female adultery, and many other aspects of social life (Wilson, 1975). Other scientists argue that all of these customs can be explained in terms of learning. They acknowledge that our biological heritage may make certain kinds of learning either difficult or easy, but they doubt that true instincts occur in human beings.

Because our species learns more frequently and impressively than any other, each of us acquires not only those characteristics typical of our species but also thousands of attributes that make us unique as individuals. We are liberals, conservatives, rock fans, Bach buffs, gourmet cooks, fast-food fanatics, optimists or pessimists because of our experiences in life and what we have learned from them.

In this chapter we will examine some basic types of learning that help account for our similarities and our diversity. Research on these topics has been heavily influenced by **behaviorism,** the view that psychologists should explain behavior in terms of observable events rather than hypothetical mental processes. Behavioral research has led to the discovery of many powerful principles of animal and human behavior. However, as we will see later in this chapter, not all psychologists believe that these principles are sufficient to explain learning. Cognitive psychologists, in particular, argue that omitting mental processes from explanations of human learning is like omitting passion from descriptions of sex: You may explain the form, but you miss the substance. To nonbehaviorists, learning is not so much a change in behavior as a change in *knowledge* that has the *potential* for affecting behavior.

■ CLASSICAL CONDITIONING: NEW REFLEXES FROM OLD

At the turn of the century, the great Russian physiologist Ivan Pavlov (1849–1936) was studying salivation in dogs, as part of a research program on digestion. His work on digestion would shortly win him the Nobel Prize in physiology and medicine. Pavlov's procedure was to make a surgical opening in a dog's cheek and insert a tube that conducted saliva away from the animal's salivary gland so it could be measured. To stimulate the reflexive flow of saliva, Pavlov placed meat powder or other food in the dog's mouth. This procedure was later refined by others (see Figure 6.1).

Pavlov was a truly dedicated scientific observer. (Many years later, when he was dying, he carefully dictated his sensations for posterity!) During his salivation studies, Pavlov noticed something that most people would have overlooked or dismissed as trivial. After a dog had been brought to the laboratory a number of times, it would start to salivate *before* the food was placed in its mouth. The sight or smell of the food, the dish in which the food was kept, even the sight of the person who delivered the food or the sound of the person's footsteps, were enough to start the dog's mouth watering. This new salivary response clearly was not inborn but was acquired through experience.

At first Pavlov treated the dog's excessive drooling as an annoying "psychic secretion," but after reviewing the literature on reflexes, he realized that he had stumbled onto an important phenomenon. He called that phenomenon a "conditional" reflex—conditional because it depended on environmental conditions. Later, an error in the translation of his writings resulted in "conditional" becoming "conditioned," the word most commonly used today.

Pavlov soon dropped what he had been doing and turned to the study of conditioned reflexes, to which he would devote the last three decades of his life. Why were his dogs salivating to aspects of the environment other than food?

Principles of Classical Conditioning

Pavlov decided that it was fruitless to speculate about his dogs' thoughts, wishes, or memories. Instead he analyzed the environment in which the conditioned reflex arose. The original salivary reflex, according to Pavlov, consisted of an

FIGURE 6.1

A modification of Pavlov's method
Pavlov's work inspired others to refine his techniques. In this apparatus, saliva collected from a dog's cheek flowed down a tube and was measured by the movement of a needle on a revolving drum.

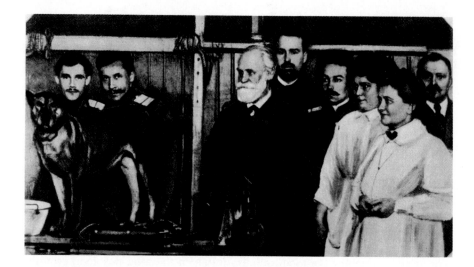

Ivan Pavlov is in the center, flanked by his students and a canine subject.

unconditioned stimulus (US), food, and an **unconditioned response (UR),** salivation. By an unconditioned stimulus, Pavlov meant a stimulus—any thing or event—that elicited a response automatically or reflexively. By an unconditioned response, he meant the response that was automatically produced:

US   UR

Learning occurs, Pavlov said, when some neutral stimulus is regularly paired with an unconditioned stimulus. The neutral stimulus then becomes a **conditioned stimulus (CS),** which elicits a learned or **conditioned response (CR)** that is similar to the original, unlearned one. In Pavlov's laboratory, the sight of the food dish, which had not previously elicited salivation, became a CS for salivation:

■ **unconditioned stimulus (US)**
The classical conditioning term for a stimulus that elicits a reflexive response in the absence of learning.

■ **unconditioned response (UR)**
The classical conditioning term for a reflexive response elicited by a stimulus in the absence of learning.

■ **conditioned stimulus (CS)**
The classical conditioning term for an initially neutral stimulus that comes to elicit a conditioned response after being associated with an unconditioned stimulus.

■ **conditioned response (CR)**
The classical conditioning term for a response that is elicited by a conditioned stimulus; occurs after the conditioned stimulus is associated with an unconditioned stimulus.

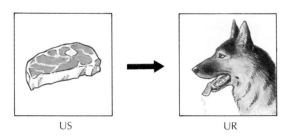

CONDITIONING

Neutral stimulus   US

AFTER CONDITIONING

CS   CR

In a series of experiments, Pavlov showed that virtually any stimulus can become a conditioned stimulus for salivation—the ticking of a metronome, the musical tone of a tuning fork, the vibrating sound of a buzzer, a triangle drawn on a large card, even a pinprick or electric shock. None of these stimuli "naturally" elicits salivation, but if paired with food, all of them will. The process by which a neutral stimulus becomes a conditioned stimulus has become known as **classical conditioning** (also sometimes called *Pavlovian* or *respondent conditioning*).

Because the terminology of classical conditioning can be hard to learn, let's pause for a Quick Quiz break before going on.

QUICK QUIZ

See if you can name the four components of classical conditioning in these two situations.

1. Five-year-old Samantha is watching a storm from her window. A huge bolt of lightning is followed by a tremendous thunderclap, and Samantha jumps at the noise. This happens several more times. There is a brief lull and then another lightning bolt. Samantha jumps in response to the bolt.
2. Gregory's mouth waters whenever he eats anything with lemon in it. One day, while reading an ad that shows a big glass of lemonade, Gregory notices his mouth watering.

ANSWERS:

1. US = the thunderclap; UR = jumping elicited by the noise; CS = the sight of the lightning; CR = jumping elicited by the lightning. 2. US = the taste of lemon; UR = salivation elicited by the taste of lemon; CS = the picture of a glass of lemonade; CR = salivation elicited by the picture.

Since Pavlov's day, researchers have established that nearly any automatic, involuntary response can become a conditioned response—for example, heartbeat, stomach secretions, blood pressure, reflexive movements, blinking, or muscular contractions. For optimal conditioning, the conditioned stimulus should precede the unconditioned stimulus, not follow it or occur simultaneously. This makes sense, for in classical conditioning, the conditioned stimulus becomes a kind of signal for the unconditioned stimulus. It enables the organism to *prepare* for an event that is about to happen. In Pavlov's experiments, for instance, a bell or buzzer was a signal that meat was coming, and the dog's salivation was preparation for digesting food. The optimal interval between the presentation of the CS and the presentation of the US depends on the kind of response being conditioned. In the laboratory, the optimal interval is often less than a second!

To a surprising extent, the principles that govern the learning of classically conditioned responses are common to all species, from worms to *homo sapiens.* Here are some of the most important ones.

EXTINCTION. Conditioned responses do not necessarily last forever. If, after conditioning, the conditioned stimulus is repeatedly presented without the unconditioned stimulus, the conditioned response eventually disappears and **extinction** is said to have occurred (see Figure 6.2). Suppose you train a dog to salivate to the sound of a bell, but then you ring the bell every five minutes and do *not* follow it with food. The dog will soon stop salivating to the bell; salivation has been extinguished. However, if you come back the next day and ring the bell,

■ **classical conditioning**
The process by which a previously neutral stimulus acquires the capacity to elicit a response through association with a stimulus that already elicits a similar response. Also called Pavlovian *and* respondent *conditioning.*

■ **extinction**
The weakening and eventual disappearance of a learned response. Occurs in classical conditioning when the conditioned stimulus is no longer paired with the unconditioned stimulus.

FIGURE 6.2

Acquisition and extinction of a salivary response
Graph (a) shows what happens when a neutral stimulus is consistently followed by an unconditioned stimulus for salivation. The neutral stimulus also comes to elicit salivation; that is, it becomes a conditioned stimulus. *Graph (b) shows what happens when the conditioned stimulus is repeatedly presented without the unconditioned stimulus. The conditioned salivary response weakens and eventually disappears; it is* extinguished.

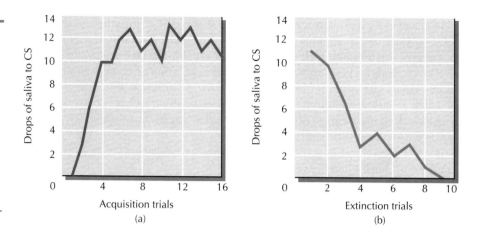

(a)

(b)

the dog may salivate again for a few trials. The reappearance of the response is called **spontaneous recovery.** Because of spontaneous recovery, eliminating a conditioned response usually requires more than one extinction session.

HIGHER-ORDER CONDITIONING. Sometimes a neutral stimulus can become a conditioned stimulus by being paired with an already established CS, a procedure known as **higher-order conditioning.** Say a dog has learned to salivate to the ringing of a bell. Now you present a flash of light before ringing the bell. With repeated pairings of the light and the bell, the dog may learn to salivate to the light (although the light will probably elicit less salivation than the bell does). The procedure looks like this:

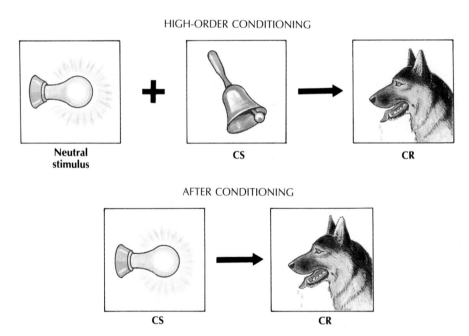

■ **spontaneous recovery**
The reappearance of a learned response after its apparent extinction.
■ **higher-order conditioning**
In classical conditioning, a procedure in which a neutral stimulus becomes a conditioned stimulus through association with an already established conditioned stimulus.

It may be that words acquire their emotional meanings through a process of higher-order conditioning. When they are paired with objects or other words that already elicit some emotional response, they, too, may come to elicit that response (Chance, 1988a; Staats & Staats, 1957). For example, a child may learn a positive response to the word *birthday* because of its association with gifts and attention. Conversely, the child may learn a negative response to certain national labels, such as *Swede, Turk,* or *Jew,* if those words are paired with already disagreeable words, such as *dumb* or *dirty.* Higher-order conditioning, in other words, may contribute to the formation of prejudices.

STIMULUS GENERALIZATION AND DISCRIMINATION. After a stimulus becomes a conditioned stimulus for some response, other, similar stimuli may produce the same reaction—a phenomenon known as **stimulus generalization.** For example, a dog conditioned to salivate to middle C on the piano may also salivate to D, which is one tone above C, even though D was not paired with food. Stimulus generalization is described nicely by an old English proverb: "He who hath been bitten by a snake fears a rope."

The mirror image of stimulus generalization is **stimulus discrimination,** in which *different* responses are made to stimuli that resemble the conditioned stimulus in some way. Suppose you condition your poodle to salivate to middle C on the piano. Now you play middle C on a guitar. If the dog does not salivate to the note on the guitar, we can say that the dog has discriminated between the two sounds. In this case, the discrimination has occurred naturally. But it is also possible to teach a discrimination explicitly by the selective presentation of the unconditioned stimulus. Again, suppose your dog has been conditioned to salivate to middle C on the piano and that because of generalization the dog also salivates to D. If you repeatedly play D without following it by food (but continue to follow C by food), eventually the dog will stop salivating to D and will respond only to C.

Classical Conditioning and the Real World

If a dog can learn to salivate to the ringing of a bell, so can you. In fact, you probably *have* learned to salivate to the sound of a lunch bell, not to mention the sight of the refrigerator, the word *steak*, the sight of a waiter in a restaurant, and a voice calling out "Dinner's ready!" But the role of classical conditioning goes far beyond the learning of simple observable reflexes. Here are some other ways that classical conditioning affects us in everyday life.

Whether we say "yum" or "yuck" to certain foods may depend on a past experience involving classical conditioning.

ACCOUNTING FOR TASTE. We probably learn to like and dislike many things, including particular foods, through a process of classical conditioning. Martin Seligman, who has studied learned behavior in the laboratory, tells how he himself was conditioned to hate béarnaise sauce. Seligman and his wife went out for dinner and ordered one of his favorite dishes, filet mignon with béarnaise sauce. Shortly afterward, Seligman happened to come down with the flu. Naturally, he felt nauseated and wretched. His misery had nothing to do with the béarnaise sauce, of course, yet the next time he tried it, he found he disliked the taste (Seligman & Hager, 1972). Similar conditioned food aversions sometimes occur in cancer patients when the food is followed by nausea-inducing chemotherapy (Bernstein, 1985).

Food and odor preferences have also been conditioned in the laboratory. One researcher trained slugs to associate the smell of carrots, which slugs normally like, with a bitter-tasting chemical, which they detest. Soon the slugs were avoiding the smell of carrots. The researcher then demonstrated higher-order conditioning by pairing the smell of carrots with the smell of potato. Sure enough, the slugs began to avoid the smell of potato as well (Sahley, Rudy, & Gelperin, 1981).

Sometimes we like a food, but our bodies refuse to tolerate it. This happens with allergies—you adore chocolate, but your skin breaks out in hives whenever you eat it. Certain allergic reactions may be classically conditioned. In a study with guinea pigs, researchers paired the smell of either fish or sulphur with injection of a substance that the animals were already allergic to. After only ten pairings, the animals became allergic to the odor alone. Their blood histamine levels rose, just as they would have after exposure to a true allergen (Russell et al., 1984). People, too, may learn to be allergic to certain substances that have been associated with substances to which they were already sensitive.

■ **stimulus generalization**
After conditioning, the tendency to respond to a stimulus that resembles one involved in the original conditioning. In classical conditioning, it occurs when a stimulus that resembles the conditioned stimulus elicits the conditioned response.

■ **stimulus discrimination**
The tendency to respond differently to two or more similar stimuli.

LEARNING TO LOVE.   Classical conditioning involves involuntary bodily responses, and many such responses are part and parcel of human emotions. It follows that this type of learning may explain how we acquire emotional responses to particular objects and events.

One of the first psychologists to recognize this implication of Pavlovian theory was John B. Watson. Watson, the founder of American behaviorism, believed that emotions were simply collections of gut-level muscular and glandular responses. A few such responses, said Watson, are inborn. For the sake of convenience he called them fear, rage, and love, but he was really referring to patterns of movement and changes in breathing, circulation, and digestion, not subjective feelings. In Watson's analysis, "love" included the smiling and burbling that babies are apt to do when they are stroked and cuddled. The stroking and cuddling are unconditioned stimuli; the smiling and burbling are unconditioned responses. According to Watson, an infant learns to "love" other things when they are paired with stroking and cuddling. The thing most likely to be paired with stroking and cuddling is, of course, a parent. Learning to love a parent, then, (or anyone else, for that matter) is really no different from learning to salivate to the sound of a bell—at least in Watson's view. (Most modern psychologists believe the process is much more complicated.)

A similar process may help explain unusual desires and preferences, such as *masochism*, the enjoyment of pain. We mentioned earlier that Pavlov could condition dogs to salivate to a pinprick or an electric shock. The animals showed none of the bodily upset usually associated with these painful stimuli. In fact, they seemed to enjoy being pricked or shocked. Similarly, masochism in human beings may result when painful stimuli are associated with an unconditioned stimulus for pleasure or satisfaction.

CONDITIONED FEARS AND PHOBIAS.   Negative emotions, as we already indicated in our discussion of higher-order conditioning, can also be classically conditioned. Interest has focused especially on fears and phobias (irrational fears of certain objects or situations). According to behaviorists, fears and phobias are conditioned responses to stimuli that were originally neutral. The original conditioning incident or incidents need not be remembered; the emotional response remains long after its origin has faded into the mists of memory.

To demonstrate how fears and phobias might be acquired, John B. Watson and Rosalie Rayner (1920) deliberately established a rat phobia in an 11-month-old boy named Albert. The ethics, procedures, and findings of their study have since been questioned (B. Harris, 1979). However, the study is a classic, and its main conclusion, that fears can be conditioned, is well accepted.

"Little Albert" was a rather placid tyke who rarely cried. When Watson and Rayner gave him a furry white rat to play with, he was initially delighted. (Contrary to widespread opinion, fear of rats, bugs, spiders, snakes, and other creepy-crawlies is not innate.) However, like most children, Albert *was* afraid of loud noises. Whenever a steel bar behind Albert's head was struck with a hammer, Albert would jump and fall sideways onto the mattress he was seated on. The noise was an unconditioned stimulus for the unconditioned response of fear.

Having established that Albert liked rats, Watson and Rayner set about teaching him to fear them. Once again they offered him a rat, but this time, as Albert reached for it, one of the researchers struck the steel bar. Startled, Albert fell onto the mattress. The researchers repeated this procedure several times. Albert began to whimper and tremble. Finally, the rat was offered alone, without the noise. Albert fell over, cried, and crawled away as fast as he could; the rat had become a conditioned stimulus for fear. Further tests showed that Albert's fear generalized to other hairy or furry objects, including white rabbits, cotton wool, a Santa Claus mask, and even John Watson's hair.

Unfortunately, Watson and Rayner did not have an opportunity to reverse the conditioning. (The circumstances are unclear.) Later, however, Watson and

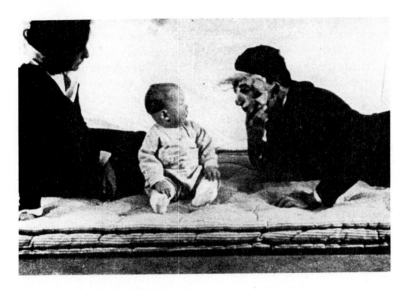

This photograph, made from a 1919 film, shows John Watson, in a mask, testing "Little Albert" for stimulus generalization. (Photo courtesy of Prof. Benjamin Harris)

Mary Cover Jones did accomplish a reversal in a 3-year-old named Peter (M. Jones, 1924). Peter was deathly afraid of rabbits. His fear was, as Watson put it, "home-grown" rather than psychologist-induced. Watson and Jones eliminated it with a method called **counterconditioning,** which involved pairing the rabbit with another stimulus—a snack of milk and crackers—that produced pleasant feelings incompatible with the conditioned response of fear. At first, the researchers kept the rabbit some distance from Peter, so his fear would remain at a low level. Otherwise, Peter might have learned to fear milk and crackers! But gradually, over several days, they brought the rabbit closer and closer. Eventually Peter was able to sit with the rabbit in his lap, playing with it with one hand while he ate with the other. A variation of this procedure, called *systematic desensitization*, was later devised for treating phobias in adults (see Chapter 17).

THE POWER OF DRUGS. Many researchers believe that classical conditioning has important implications for understanding certain aspects of drug addiction (Poulos & Cappell, 1991; Siegel & Sdao-Jarvie, 1986). In the most recent formulation of this view, a drug's effect is seen as the unconditioned stimulus for a *compensatory* bodily response, a response that opposes the drug's effect. When morphine, for example, causes numbness to pain, the body attempts to compensate by becoming increasingly sensitive to pain. Environmental cues, such as needles or a particular location, that are paired with the drug's effects may then become conditioned stimuli for this compensatory response.

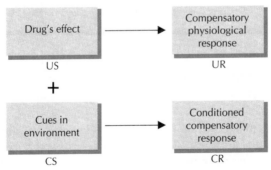

This analysis can explain why *tolerance* to drugs often develops (see Chapter 4). In the presence of environmental cues associated with drug taking, a compensatory response occurs, so more of the drug is needed to produce the usual effects. On the other hand, a drug dose that would ordinarily be safe, given an

■ **counterconditioning**
In classical conditioning, the process of pairing a conditioned stimulus with a stimulus that elicits a response that is incompatible with an unwanted conditioned response.

addict's tolerance level, may be lethal when the drug is used in novel circumstances, because the usual conditioned compensatory response doesn't occur. The result may be sudden and seemingly inexplicable death.

Experiments with both animals and human beings, using a wide variety of drugs, support this theory. In one study, male college students drank large amounts of beer at the same place on each of four consecutive days. On the fifth day, some of the students downed their beers at a new place. Students who remained at the original location scored higher on tests of intellectual and perceptual-motor skills, apparently because their bodies had learned to moderate the effects of alcohol in the presence of familiar cues (Lightfoot, 1980). In another study, researchers gave rats a strong dose of heroin. Some of the rats were already "experienced" with the drug. In inexperienced rats, the injection was almost always fatal, but in experienced ones the outcome depended on the setting: Two-thirds of the rats injected while in a strange environment died, versus only a third of those who remained in a familiar place (Siegel et al., 1982).

The importance of environmental cues may help explain why in-hospital drug treatment programs so often fail: When people return to the neighborhoods where they used to take drugs, conditioned stimuli elicit the usual compensatory responses. In the absence of the drug, such responses are now experienced as a return of unpleasant withdrawal symptoms, and a craving for the drug again develops (Siegel, 1983). The implication is that people who want to overcome drug dependence either must relocate to a new environment or must receive treatment that systematically exposes them to familiar features of their usual environment until their conditioned physiological responses to these cues become extinguished.

QUICK QUIZ

Supply the correct term to describe the outcome in each situation:

1. After a child learns to fear spiders, he also responds with fear to ants, beetles, and other crawling bugs.
2. A toddler is afraid of the bath, so her father puts just a little water in the tub and gives the child a lollipop to suck on while she is being washed. Soon the little girl loses her fear of the bath.
3. A factory worker notices that his mouth waters whenever a noontime bell signals the beginning of his lunch break. One day the bell goes haywire and rings every half hour. By the end of the day, the worker has stopped salivating to the bell.

ANSWERS:

1. stimulus generalization 2. counterconditioning 3. extinction

■ OPERANT CONDITIONING: THE CARROT AND THE STICK

At the end of the nineteenth century, in the first known scientific effort to study anger, G. Stanley Hall (1899) asked people to describe angry episodes they had experienced or observed. One informant told of a 3-year-old girl who broke out in furious, seemingly uncontrollable sobs when she was punished by being kept home from a ride. In the middle of her tantrum, the little girl suddenly stopped crying and calmly asked if her father (who she obviously hoped might rescue her) was in. Told no, she immediately resumed her sobs.

Children, of course, cry for many valid reasons—pain, discomfort, fear, illness, fatigue—and these cries deserve an adult's sympathy and attention. However, careful studies show that even infants only a few weeks old will also learn to cry when they are *not* in physical distress if adults respond to such cries (Gewirtz, 1991). The child described by Hall's informant had learned, from prior experience, that an outburst of sobbing would bring her attention and possibly the ride she wanted—that it stood a reasonable chance of working. Her behavior, which some might simply label "naughty," was perfectly understandable, because it followed one of the most basic laws of learning: *Behavior becomes more or less likely depending on its consequences.*

An emphasis on consequences is at the heart of **operant conditioning** (also called *instrumental conditioning*). In classical conditioning, the animal's or person's behavior does not have any environmental consequences. Thus in Pavlov's procedure, the dog receives food whether it salivates or not. But in operant conditioning, the organism's response (say, the little girl's sobbing) *operates* or produces effects on the environment. These effects, in turn, influence whether or not the response will occur again. Classical and operant conditioning also tend to involve different types of responses. In classical conditioning, the response is reflexive, an automatic reaction to something happening in the environment (for example, the sight of food or the sound of a bell). Generally speaking, responses in operant conditioning are not reflexive and are more complex—for example, riding a bicycle, writing a letter, climbing a mountain, or throwing a tantrum.

Classical and operant conditioning often occur in the same situation. For example, when Little Albert learned to fear the rat, his trembling was classically conditioned. But when he learned to avoid the rat by crawling away (a response that had the effect of reducing his fear), that was an example of operant conditioning. (In "A Closer Look at Consumer Psychology" on page 210, we discuss how both classical and operant conditioning contribute to that perennially popular pastime, consumer spending.)

Operant conditioning has been studied since the turn of the century. Edward Thorndike (1898) set the stage by observing cats as they tried to escape from a "puzzle box" to reach some food that was just outside. At first the cat would engage in blind trial and error, scratching, biting, or swatting at parts of the cage in an unorganized way. Then, after a few minutes, the animal would chance on the successful response (loosening a bolt, pulling a string, hitting a button) and get the reward. Placed in the box again, the cat now took a little less time to escape. And after several trials, the cat immediately made the correct response. According to Thorndike's *law of effect*, the correct response had been "stamped in" by its satisfying effects (getting the food). In contrast, annoying or unsatisfying effects "stamped out" behavior. Behavior, said Thorndike, is controlled by its consequences.

This general principle was elaborated and extended to complex forms of behavior by B. F. (Burrhus Frederic) Skinner (1904–1990), who has been called the greatest of all American psychologists. Calling his approach "radical behaviorism," Skinner was careful to avoid such terms as "satisfying," which might imply certain assumptions about how an animal feels or what it wants. For Skinner, the explanation of behavior was to be found by looking outside the individual rather than within—a position he continued to defend up until his death in 1990.

Despite Skinner's fame (or perhaps because of it), his position is often distorted by the general public, psychology students, and even some psychologists. For example, many people think Skinner denied the existence of human consciousness and rejected the study of thinking. It is true that Skinner's predecessor, behaviorist John Watson, thought psychologists should study only public (external) events, not private (internal) ones. But Skinner maintained that we *can* study private events, by observing our own sensory responses and the ver-

Reprinted with special permission of King Features Syndicate, Inc.

An instantaneous learning experience.

In operant conditioning, behavior is controlled by its consequences.

■ **operant conditioning**
The process by which a response becomes more or less likely to occur, depending on its consequences.

A CLOSER LOOK AT CONSUMER PSYCHOLOGY

Buy, Buy, Buy

You are strolling through the mall one day when an item in a store window happens to catch your eye. You want it. You *must* have it. Never mind that you can't really afford it; before you can say "MasterCard," you've bought it.

A *consumer psychologist* would want to know why you gave in to the impulse. Was there something about the window display that especially appealed to someone like you? Did some clever commercials for the product wear down your resistance? The field of consumer psychology addresses these questions and many others. As you might guess, researchers in this field are in demand by advertisers, manufacturers, and retailers who want advice on how to capture the attention of potential customers and get people to open their wallets.

Consumer psychologists have shown that many of Madison Avenue's techniques are based on principles of conditioning, whether advertising executives realize it or not. For example, Gerald Gorn (1982) showed that associating an item with pleasant stimuli induces people to like the item itself. Gorn had college students view slides of either a beige or blue pen. During the presentation, half the students heard a song from a recent musical film and half heard a selection of classical Indian music. (Gorn made the reasonable assumption that the show tune would be more appealing to most Americans.) Later the students were allowed to choose one of the pens.

Almost three-fourths of those who heard the popular music chose a pen that was the same color as the one they had seen in the slides. An equal number of those who heard the Indian music chose a pen that *differed* in color from the one they had seen. This is an instance of classical conditioning: The music was an unconditioned stimulus for internal responses associated with pleasure or displeasure, and the pens became conditioned stimuli for similar responses. You can see why television commercials often pair products with music, attractive people, or other appealing stimuli.

Advertising is not the only influence on spending. Credit cards, as some of us know all too well, have a power of their own. Handing over your card to a salesperson is immediately rewarded by the delivery of a desired item into your hands; the payment isn't due until much later. Thus, through a process of operant conditioning, credit card use becomes more likely. Even the mere presence of a credit card increases the likelihood and magnitude of spending. When a card is repeatedly paired with the responses involved in spending, it becomes a stimulus for "spending behavior." Through a process of classical conditioning, it may also come to elicit positive emotional responses (Feinberg, 1986).

If you are a seller, you will want to use this information to attract customers—say, by displaying signs of the credit cards you accept. But when you are on the other side of the counter, a knowledge of conditioning principles can help you control your own spending. To avoid impulse buying, you might purposely leave your credit cards at home. To reduce your susceptibility to a commercial, you might turn down the sound. And next time you find yourself about to reach for an item at the end of the supermarket aisle that wasn't on your list, think of Pavlov and Skinner.

bal reports of others and the conditions under which they occur. For Skinner, the private events we "see" when we examine our own "consciousness" are simply the early stages of behavior, before the behavior begins to act on the environment. These private events are as "real" or "physical" as public ones, Skinner said, although they are less accessible and harder to describe (Skinner, 1972, 1990).

Because Skinner thought the environment could and should be manipulated to alter behavior, some critics have portrayed him as cold blooded or even sinister. Poet Stephen Spender once called one of Skinner's books "fascism without tears." But Skinner, who in person was a quiet and mild-mannered man, felt that it would be unethical *not* to try to improve human behavior by applying behavioral principles. In recognition of his efforts, the American Humanist Association honored him with its Humanist of the Year Award.

B. F. Skinner, at work on a scale model of a Skinner box.

One of the best-known controversies regarding Skinner occurred when he invented the Air-Crib, an enclosure for his younger daughter, Deborah. This "baby box," as it came to be known, was set up to eliminate the usual discomforts suffered by babies, including heat, cold, wetness, and confinement by bedding. For example, it had temperature and humidity controls, so Deborah could go without any clothes. Many people were appalled, and for years, rumors circulated that Deborah had grown up to be psychotic. Actually, both of Skinner's daughters turned out to be perfectly normal. One became a successful artist, the other a professor of educational psychology. The latter raised her own two daughters in an Air-Crib.

While some other psychologists, notably the humanists, have argued for the existence of free will, Skinner steadfastly supported the view of *determinism*. Free will, he believed, is an illusion. Environmental consequences may not automatically "stamp in" operant behavior, but they do determine the probability that an action will occur. Skinner refused to credit mental events—plans, goals, thoughts, or motives—for his own or anyone else's accomplishments. Indeed, he regarded his own life as just a long case history of environmental influences. "So far as I know," he wrote in the third volume of his autobiography (1983), "my behavior at any given moment has been nothing more than the product of my genetic endowment, my personal history, and the current setting."

Reinforcers and Punishers: A Matter of Consequence

In Skinner's analysis, which has inspired an enormous body of research on operant conditioning, a response can lead to one of three types of consequences. The first type is neutral as far as future behavior is concerned: It neither increases nor decreases the probability that the behavior will recur. If a door handle squeaks each time you turn it, and the sound does not affect whether you turn the door handle again in the future, the squeak is a neutral consequence.

A second type of consequence involves **reinforcement**. In reinforcement, a reinforcing stimulus, or *reinforcer*, strengthens or increases the probability of the response that it follows. When you are training your dog to heel, and you offer it a doggie biscuit or a pat on the head when it does something right, you are using reinforcement (see Figure 6.3). Reinforcers are roughly equivalent to rewards. Strict behaviorists avoid the term *reward* because it is the organism, not the response, that is rewarded. The response is *strengthened*. Also, in com-

■ **reinforcement**
The process by which a stimulus or event strengthens or increases the probability of the response that it follows.

FIGURE 6.3

Reinforcement in action
The dog's response, heeling (a), is followed immediately by a reinforcer, in this case praise and a pat (b). As a result, the response is strengthened (c).

(a)   (b)   (c)

mon usage, a reward is something earned that results in happiness or satisfaction. But technically, any stimulus is a reinforcer if it strengthens the preceding behavior, whether or not the organism experiences pleasure or any other positive state. Conversely, no matter how pleasurable a stimulus is, it is not a reinforcer if it does not increase the likelihood of a response. Like many psychologists, however, we ourselves have no objection to the use of *reward* as an approximate synonym of *reinforcer*.

The third type of consequence involves **punishment.** Punishment occurs when the stimulus or event that follows a response *weakens it or makes it less likely to recur*. Any aversive (unpleasant) stimulus or event may be a *punisher*. When your dog runs into the street and is nearly killed by a passing car, running into the street is then less likely to occur when cars are present (see Figure 6.4). (Later we will see that deliberate punishment as a way of controlling behavior has many drawbacks.)

Reinforcement and punishment are not as simple as they may seem. In our example of reinforcement, something pleasant (a doggie biscuit or a pat on the dog's head) followed the dog's response (heeling). This type of procedure is known as **positive reinforcement.** However, reinforcement can also involve the *removal* of something *unpleasant*, in which case it is called **negative reinforcement.** For example, if you politely ask your roommate to turn off some music you can't stand, and your roommate immediately complies, the likelihood of your being polite when making similar requests will probably increase. Your politeness has been strengthened by the removal of the unpleasant music.

As Table 6.1 shows, the positive-negative distinction can also be applied to punishment: something unpleasant may occur (positive punishment) or something pleasant may be removed (negative punishment). The terms "positive" and "negative," however, are more often applied to reinforcement. These terms are often a great source of confusion to students. You will master them more quickly if you understand that "positive" and "negative" have nothing to do with "good" or "bad." They refer to *procedures*—giving something or taking some-

■ **punishment**
The process by which a stimulus or event weakens or reduces the probability of the response that it follows.
■ **positive reinforcement**
A reinforcement procedure in which a response is followed by the presentation of, or increase in intensity of, a reinforcing stimulus; as a result, the response becomes stronger or more likely to occur.
■ **negative reinforcement**
A reinforcement procedure in which a response is followed by the removal, delay, or decrease in intensity of an unpleasant stimulus; as a result, the response becomes stronger or more likely to occur.

FIGURE 6.4

Punishment in action
The dog's response, running into the street when cars are present (a), is followed immediately by a punisher, nearly being hit by a car (b). As a result, the response is weakened (c).

(a)   (b)   (c)

TABLE 6.1

Types of Reinforcement and Punishment

In operant conditioning, a response increases or decreases in likelihood depending on its consequences. The occurrence of a pleasant stimulus or the removal of an unpleasant one reinforces the response. The occurrence of an unpleasant stimulus or the removal of a pleasant one constitutes punishment, which weakens the response.

What event follows the response?

	Stimulus presented	Stimulus removed
Response increases	**Positive reinforcement** For example: Completion of homework assignments increases when followed by praise.	**Negative reinforcement** For example: Use of aspirin increases when followed by reduction of headache pain.
Response decreases	**Positive punishment** For example: Nail biting decreases when followed by the taste of a bitter substance painted on the nails.	**Negative punishment** For example: Parking in "no parking" zones decreases when followed by loss of money (a fine).

(left axis label: What happens to the response?)

thing away. Both positive and negative reinforcement make a response more likely. If someone praises Ludwig for doing his homework, that is positive reinforcement. If Ludwig's headache goes away after he takes an aspirin, that is negative reinforcement (of aspirin taking). Think of a positive reinforcer as something that is added or obtained, and a negative reinforcer as the avoidance of or escape from something. After Little Albert learned to fear the white rat, crawling away was negatively reinforced by escape from the now fearsome rodent. Negative reinforcement of "escape behavior" and "avoidance behavior" explains why so many fears are long-lasting. By avoiding a feared object or situation, you also avoid opportunities for extinguishing the fear.

Understandably, people often confuse negative reinforcement with positive punishment, since both involve an unpleasant stimulus. To keep the two straight, remember that punishment *decreases* the likelihood of a response. Reinforcement—either positive or negative—*increases* it. In real life, punishment and negative reinforcement often go hand in hand. If you use a choke collar on your dog to teach it to heel, a yank on the collar *punishes* the act of walking. But release of the collar *negatively reinforces* the act of standing still by your side.

QUICK QUIZ

Which kind of consequence is illustrated by each of the following? (You may want to refer to Table 6.1 if you have difficulty with these.)

1. A child is nagging her father for a cookie; he keeps refusing, but she keeps pleading. Finally, unable to stand the aversive stimulation any longer, he hands over the cookie. For him, the ending of the child's pleas is a _____. For the child, the cookie is a _____.
2. A woman wants her husband to take more responsibility for household chores. One night he clears the dishes. She touches him affectionately on the arm. The next night he again clears the dishes. Her touch was probably a _____.

3. A hungry toddler gleefully eats his oatmeal with his hands after being told not to. His mother promptly removes the cereal and takes the messy offender out of the high chair. The removal of the cereal is a _____.

✳ 4. During "happy hours" in bars and restaurants, typically held in the late afternoon, drinks are sold at a reduced price and appetizers are often free. What undesirable behavior may be rewarded by this practice?

ANSWERS:

1. negative reinforcer; positive reinforcer 2. positive reinforcer 3. punisher (or more precisely, a negative punisher) 4. One possible answer: The reduced prices, free appetizers, and convivial atmosphere all reinforce heavy alcohol consumption just before the commuter rush hour and thus may contribute to drunk driving (see Geller & Lehman, 1988).

Secondary Reinforcement

Food, water, light stroking of the skin, and a comfortable air temperature are naturally reinforcing because they satisfy biological needs. They are therefore known as **primary reinforcers.** Similarly, pain and extreme heat or cold are inherently punishing and are therefore known as **primary punishers.** Primary reinforcers and punishers are powerful controllers of behavior, but they also have their drawbacks. For one thing, the organism may have to be in a deprived state for a stimulus to act as a primary reinforcer; a glass of water isn't much of a reward to someone who just drank three full glasses. Also, there are ethical problems with using primary punishers or taking away primary reinforcers.

Fortunately, behavior can be controlled just as effectively by **secondary reinforcers** and **secondary punishers,** which are learned. Money, praise, a smile, a friendly greeting, applause, good grades, awards, and gold stars are common secondary reinforcers. Criticism, demerits, a frown, catcalls, scoldings, bad grades, and angry gestures are common secondary punishers. Most behaviorists believe that secondary reinforcers and punishers acquire their ability to influence behavior by being paired with primary reinforcers and punishers. If that reminds you of classical conditioning, reinforce yourself with a pat on the back! Indeed, secondary reinforcers and punishers are often called *conditioned* reinforcers and punishers.

Just because a reinforcer (or punisher) is secondary doesn't mean it is any less potent than a primary reinforcer (or punisher). Money, it has been said, makes the world go round. That may or may not be true, but it certainly has a great deal of power over most people's behavior. Not only can it be exchanged for primary reinforcers such as food and shelter, but it also brings with it other secondary reinforcers, such as praise and respect. However, like any conditioned stimulus, a secondary reinforcer will eventually lose its ability to affect behavior if it cannot be paired at least occasionally with one of the stimuli originally paired with it. In 1930, a child who found a penny would be thrilled at the goodies it could buy. Today, U.S. pennies are so worthless that billions of them go out of circulation each year because people throw them away or leave them on the ground when they drop.

Principles of Operant Conditioning

Thousands of studies have been done on operant conditioning, the majority using animals. A favorite experimental tool is the Skinner box, a cage equipped with a device (called a magazine) that delivers food into a dish when an animal makes a desired response (see Figure 6.5). Skinner originally created this apparatus by adapting a Sears, Roebuck ice chest.

■ **primary reinforcer**
A stimulus that is inherently reinforcing, typically satisfying a physiological need; an example is food.
■ **primary punisher**
A stimulus that is inherently punishing; an example is electric shock.
■ **secondary reinforcer**
A stimulus that has acquired reinforcing properties through association with other reinforcers.
■ **secondary punisher**
A stimulus that has acquired punishing properties through association with other punishers.

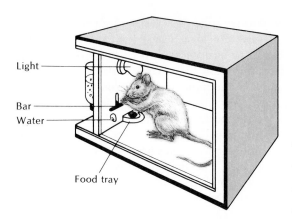

FIGURE 6.5
The Skinner box
Rats have been popular research subjects in studies using this device. When a rat presses a bar, a food pellet or drop of water is automatically released. Skinner's own favorite subjects, however, were pigeons, which are typically trained to peck at a disk or key.

Early in his career, Skinner (1938) used the Skinner box for a classic demonstration of operant conditioning. A rat that had previously learned to eat from the magazine was placed in the box. Since no food was present, the animal proceeded to engage in typical ratlike behavior, scurrying about the box and randomly touching parts of the floor and walls. Quite by accident it happened to press a lever mounted on one wall. Immediately a pellet of tasty rat food fell into the food dish. The rat continued its movements and again happened to press the bar. Plop! Another pellet. With additional repetitions of bar pressing followed by food, the animal's random movements began to disappear, replaced by more consistent bar pressing. Eventually Skinner had the rat pressing the bar as fast as it could shuttle back from the magazine.

By using the Skinner box and similar devices, psychologists have discovered many reliable principles of operant conditioning.

EXTINCTION.   In operant conditioning, as in classical, **extinction** is a procedure that causes a previously learned response to stop occurring. In operant conditioning, it takes place when the reinforcer that maintained the response is removed or is no longer available. At first there may be a spurt of responding, but then the responses gradually taper off and eventually cease. Suppose you put a coin in a vending machine and get nothing back. You may throw in another coin, or perhaps even two, but then you will probably stop trying. The next day you may put in yet another coin, an example of *spontaneous recovery*. Eventually, however, you will probably give up on that machine. Your response will have been extinguished.

IMMEDIATE VERSUS DELAYED CONSEQUENCES.   In general, the sooner a reinforcer or punisher follows a response, the greater its effect. This is especially true for animals and children, but human adults also respond more reliably when they don't have to wait too long for a paycheck, a smile, or a grade. When there is delay, other responses occur in the interval, and the connection between the desired or undesired response and the consequence may not be made. Suppose your naughty pooch has urinated on the rug, but you have been away and don't discover the soiled spot until later. Now you swat the poor dog for its misbehavior. This punishment won't work because the dog cannot possibly associate the swat with its misbehavior. Instead, a more recent behavior, such as approaching you as you enter the room, will be weakened. Holding the dog's nose next to the offending spot and then swatting your pet won't help either: You will merely be punishing the dog for putting its nose in that position! In operant conditioning, timing is all important.

STIMULUS GENERALIZATION AND STIMULUS DISCRIMINATION.   In operant conditioning, as in classical, **stimulus generalization** may occur. That is, responses may

■ **extinction**
The weakening and eventual disappearance of a learned response. In operant conditioning, it occurs when a response is no longer followed by a reinforcer.

■ **stimulus generalization**
In operant conditioning, the tendency for a response that has been reinforced (or punished) in the presence of one stimulus to occur (or be suppressed) in the presence of other, similar stimuli.

generalize to stimuli not present during the original learning situation. For example, a pigeon that has been trained to peck at a picture of a circle may also peck at a slightly oval figure. But if the bird does not peck at the oval when it is presented, then **stimulus discrimination** has occurred. If you wanted explicitly to train the bird to make this discrimination, you would present both the circle and the oval, giving reinforcers whenever the bird pecked at the circle but withholding reinforcers when it pecked at the oval.

A somewhat different kind of discrimination occurs when an animal or human being learns to respond to a stimulus only when some other stimulus, called a **discriminative stimulus,** is present. The discriminative stimulus signals whether a response, if made, will "pay off." In a Skinner box, for example, a light may serve as a discriminative stimulus for pecking at a circle. When the light is on, pecking brings a reward; when it is off, pecking is futile. The light is said to exert **stimulus control** over the pecking by setting the occasion for reinforcement to occur if the response is made. However, the response is not *compelled,* as salivation was compelled by the ringing of the bell in Pavlov's classical conditioning studies. It merely becomes more probable (or occurs at a greater rate) in the presence of the discriminative stimulus.

Human behavior is controlled by many discriminative stimuli, both verbal ("Store hours are 9 to 5") and nonverbal (traffic lights, doorbells, the ring of a telephone, the facial expressions of others). Learning to respond correctly when these stimuli are present is an essential part of operant learning. In a public place, if you have to go to the bathroom, you don't simply walk through any door that leads to a toilet. The words *Women* and *Men* are discriminative stimuli for entering. One word tells you the response will be rewarded by the opportunity to empty a full bladder, the other that it will be punished by the jeers or protests of others. Similarly, when you go fly fishing, a smooth surface on a lake may cause you to put away your gear, whereas ripples and splashes tell you your efforts are likely to be rewarded by dinner. In the language of behaviorism, the jumping of a trout is a discriminative stimulus for the fishing behavior of a human being.

In everyday life, failure to make appropriate discriminations can lead to accidents and errors. A behaviorist would say that when we go into the next room to do something and then can't remember why we're there, it is because the discriminative stimuli for the response are no longer present (Salzinger, 1990). But insufficient generalization also causes problems. For example, "personal growth" workshops provide participants with lots of reinforcement for emotional expressiveness and self-disclosure. Participants often feel that their way of interacting with others has been dramatically transformed. But when they return to normal life, where the environment is full of the same old reinforcers, punishers, and discriminative stimuli, they may find, to their chagrin, that their new responses have failed to generalize. A grumpy boss or cranky spouse may still be able to "push their buttons."

LEARNING ON SCHEDULE. Reinforcers can be delivered according to different schedules, or patterns over time. When a response is first acquired, learning is usually most rapid if the response is reinforced each time it occurs. This procedure of reinforcing every response is called **continuous reinforcement.** However, once a response has become reliable, it will be more resistant to extinction if it is rewarded on a **partial** or **intermittent schedule of reinforcement,** which involves reinforcing only some responses, not all. Skinner (1956) reported that he first happened on this property of partial reinforcement when he ran short of food pellets for his rats and was forced to deliver reinforcers less often. (Not all scientific discoveries are planned!) Years later, when the eminent psychologist Hans Eysenck asked Skinner how he could tolerate being misunderstood so often, Skinner replied that he only needed to be understood three or four times a year—presumably on an intermittent schedule of reinforcement.

✴ After a weekend of "getting in touch" with your feelings, you are full of patience and goodwill toward others. Then why do you lose your temper just as easily on Monday morning as you did on Friday afternoon?

■ **stimulus discrimination**
In operant conditioning, the tendency of a response to occur in the presence of one stimulus but not in the presence of other, similar stimuli that differ from it on some dimension.
■ **discriminative stimulus**
A stimulus that signals when a particular response is likely to be followed by a certain type of consequence.
■ **stimulus control**
Control over the occurrence of a response by a discriminative stimulus.

Many kinds of intermittent schedules have been studied. *Ratio schedules* deliver a reinforcer after a certain number of responses have occurred. *Interval schedules* deliver a reinforcer if a response is made after the passage of a certain amount of time since the last reinforcer. The number of responses that must occur or the amount of time that must pass before the payoff may be *fixed* (constant) or *variable*. Combining the ratio/interval patterns and fixed/variable patterns yields four basic types of intermittent schedules (see Figure 6.6). These variations in how the reinforcers are delivered have powerful effects on the rate, form, and timing of behavior—effects that most people are not aware of. Let's look more closely at these variations.

1. On a **fixed-ratio (FR) schedule,** *reinforcement occurs after a fixed number of responses.* An FR-2 schedule delivers a reinforcer after every other response, an FR-3 schedule delivers a reinforcer after every third response, and so forth. Fixed-ratio schedules produce very high rates of responding. In the laboratory, a rat may rapidly press a bar several hundred times to get a single reward. Outside the laboratory, fixed-ratio schedules are often used by employers to increase productivity. A salesperson who must sell a certain number of items before getting a commission or a factory worker who must produce a certain number of products before earning a given amount of pay (a system known as "piecework") are on fixed-ratio schedules. An interesting feature of high fixed-ratio schedules is that performance drops off just after reinforcement. If a writer must complete four chapters before getting a check, interest and motivation will sag right after the check is received.

2. On a **variable-ratio (VR) schedule,** *reinforcement occurs after some average number of responses, but the number varies from reinforcement to reinforcement.* A VR-5 schedule would deliver a reinforcer *on the average* after every fifth response but sometimes after one, two, six, or seven responses, or any other number, as long as the average was five. Variable-ratio schedules produce extremely high, steady rates of responding. The responses are more resistant to extinction than when a fixed-ratio schedule is used. The prime example of a variable-ratio schedule outside the laboratory is delivery of payoffs by a slot machine. A player at a "one-armed bandit" knows that the average number of responses necessary to win is set at a level that makes money for the house. Hope springs eternal, though. The gambler takes a chance on being in front of the machine during one of those lucky moments when fewer responses bring a payoff.

■ **continuous reinforcement**
A reinforcement schedule in which a particular response is always reinforced.

■ **intermittent (partial) schedule of reinforcement**
A reinforcement schedule in which a particular response is sometimes but not always reinforced.

■ **fixed-ratio (FR) schedule**
An intermittent schedule of reinforcement in which reinforcement occurs only after a fixed number of responses.

■ **variable-ratio (VR) schedule**
An intermittent schedule of reinforcement in which reinforcement occurs after a variable number of responses.

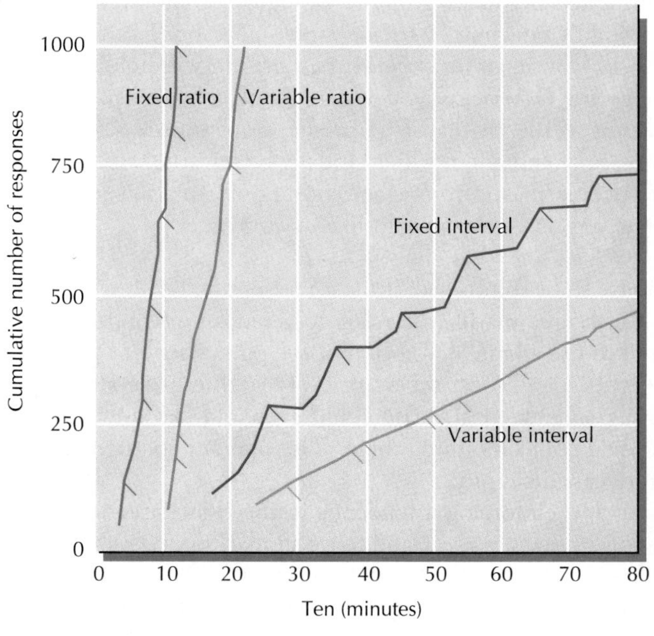

FIGURE 6.6

Reinforcement schedules and behavior
Different schedules of reinforcement produce different learning curves, *or patterns of responding over time. In research using the Skinner box, these curves can be recorded by a device called a cumulative recorder. Each time a response occurs, a pen moves up a notch on a moving strip of paper. The faster the rate of responding, the steeper the curve. In this figure, each crosshatch indicates the delivery of a reinforcer. Notice that when a fixed-interval schedule is used, responses drop off immediately after reinforcement, resulting in a "scalloped" curve. (Adapted from B. F. Skinner, "Teaching machines," November 1961, p. 96. Copyright © 1961 by Scientific American, Inc. All rights reserved.)*

"Boy, do we have this guy conditioned. Every time I press the bar down he drops a pellet in."

3. *On a* **fixed-interval (FI) schedule,** *reinforcement of a response occurs only if a fixed amount of time has passed since the previous reinforcer.* A rat on a FI-10-second schedule gets a food pellet the first time it presses the bar after the passage of a 10-second interval. Pressing the bar earlier does not hasten the reward. Animals on fixed-interval schedules seem to develop a sharp sense of time. After a reinforcer is delivered, they often stop responding altogether. Then as the end of the interval approaches, responding again picks up, reaching a maximum rate right before reinforcement. Outside the laboratory, fixed-interval schedules are not common, but certain behavior patterns do resemble those seen on such schedules. Suppose your sweetheart, who is away for a month, writes you a love letter every day. If the letter usually arrives at about noon, you probably won't check the mailbox at 8:00 A.M., but will start checking as noon approaches. Once the delivery is received, you will not check again until the next day (Houston, 1981).

4. *On a* **variable-interval (VI) schedule,** *reinforcement of a response occurs only if a variable amount of time has passed since the previous reinforcer.* A VI-10-second schedule means that the interval will average 10 seconds but will vary from reinforcement to reinforcement. Since the animal or person cannot predict when a reward will come, responding is relatively low but steady. When you go fishing, you do not know whether a fish will bite in 5 seconds or 30 minutes or not at all. Under these conditions (assuming you really want that fish), you may steadily check your line every few minutes (Houston, 1981).

A basic principle of operant conditioning is that if you want a response to persist after it has been learned, you should reinforce it intermittently, not continuously. If an animal has been receiving continuous reinforcement for some response and then reinforcement suddenly stops, the animal will soon stop responding. Because the change in reinforcement is large (from continuous to none at all), the animal will easily distinguish the change. But if reinforcement has been only intermittent, the change is not so dramatic, and the animal will keep responding for some period of time. Pigeons, rats, and people on intermittent schedules of reinforcement have responded in the laboratory thousands of times without reinforcement before throwing in the towel, especially on variable schedules. Animals will sometimes work so hard for an unpredictable, infrequent bit of food that the energy they expend is greater than that from the reward; theoretically, the animal could actually work itself to death (Hill, 1985).

It follows that if you want to get rid of a response, you should be careful *not* to reinforce it intermittently. If you are going to extinguish undesirable behavior by ignoring it—a child's tantrums, a friend's midnight phone calls, a parent's unasked-for advice—you must be *absolutely consistent* in withholding reinforcement (your attention). Otherwise, you will probably only make matters worse. The other person will learn that if he or she keeps up the screaming, calling, or advice giving long enough, it will eventually be rewarded. One of the most common errors people make, from a behavioral point of view, is to reward intermittently the responses they would like to eliminate.

SHAPING.   For a response to be reinforced, it must first occur. But suppose you want to train a rat to pick up a marble, or a dog to stand on its hind legs and turn around, or a child to use a knife and fork properly, or a friend to play terrific tennis. Such behaviors, and most others in everyday life, have almost no probability of appearing spontaneously. You could grow old and gray waiting for them to occur so you could reinforce them. The operant solution to this dilemma is a procedure called **shaping.**

In shaping, you start by reinforcing a tendency in the right direction, then gradually require responses that are more and more similar to the final, desired response. The responses that you reinforce on the way to the final one are called **successive approximations.** In the case of the rat and the marble, you might

■ **fixed-interval (FI) schedule**
An intermittent schedule of reinforcement in which a reinforcer is delivered for the first response made after a fixed period of time has elapsed since the last reinforcer.

■ **variable-interval (VI) schedule**
An intermittent schedule of reinforcement in which a reinforcer is delivered for a response made after a variable period of time has elapsed since the last reinforcer.

■ **shaping**
An operant conditioning procedure in which successive approximations of a desired response are reinforced. Used when the desired response has a low probability of occurring spontaneously.

■ **successive approximations**
In the operant conditioning procedure of shaping, behaviors that are ordered in terms of increasing similarity or closeness to the desired response.

deliver a food pellet if the rat merely turned toward the marble. Once this response was well established, you might then reward the rat for taking a step toward the marble. After that, you could reward it for approaching the marble, then touching the marble, then putting both paws on the marble, and finally holding it. With the achievement of each approximation, the next one would become more likely, making it available for reinforcement.

Using shaping and other techniques, Skinner was able to train pigeons to play Ping-Pong with their beaks and to "bowl" in a miniature alley complete with a wooden ball and tiny bowling pins. Rats have learned equally impressive behaviors (see Figure 6.7). Animal trainers routinely use shaping to teach dolphins to run flags up flagpoles, bears to ride bicycles, and dogs to act as the "eyes" of the blind.

Shaping can be equally effective with human beings. According to one story (probably apocryphal, though it could have happened), some university students once used the secondary reinforcement of eye contact to shape the behavior of a famous professor who was an expert on operant conditioning. They decided to get him to deliver his lecture from one particular corner of the room. Each time he moved in the appropriate direction, they looked at him. Otherwise, they averted their gaze. Eventually, the professor was backed into the corner, never suspecting that his behavior had been shaped.

SUPERSTITION.   So far, we have been talking about responses that directly bring about some consequence. But a consequence can be effective even when it is entirely coincidental. Skinner (1948) demonstrated this fact by putting eight pigeons in boxes and rigging the boxes so that food was delivered every 15 seconds, even if the bird didn't lift a feather. But pigeons, like rats, are often in motion, so when the food came, each animal was doing *something*. That something was then reinforced by the food. The behavior, of course, was reinforced entirely by chance, but it still became more likely to occur, and thus to be reinforced again. Within a short time six of the pigeons were practicing some sort of consistent ritual—turning in counterclockwise circles, bobbing the head up and down, swinging the head to and fro, or making brushing movements toward the floor. None of these activities had the least effect on the delivery of the reinforcer; the birds were simply "superstitious."

Coincidental reinforcement may account for many human superstitions. A baseball pitcher happens to scratch his left ear, then strikes out a star batter on

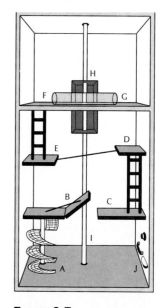

FIGURE 6.7

A rat's route
To demonstrate the effectiveness of shaping and other operant procedures, a researcher trained a rat to perform a long sequence of activities in an apparatus resembling this one. Starting at point A, the rat climbs a ramp to B, crosses a drawbridge to C, climbs a ladder to D, crosses a tightrope to E, climbs another ladder to F, crawls through a tunnel to G, runs to H and enters an elevator, descends in the elevator to I, and runs out of the elevator to J, where it presses a lever and finally receives food. (After Cheney, in Chance, 1988a.)

Animals can learn to do some surprising things, with a little help from their human friends and the application of operant conditioning techniques. Water skiing, anyone?

✳ *"Good luck" objects and rituals—a lucky hat, knocking wood—don't "work" most of the time. Why do people superstitiously continue to believe in them?*

Farmers sometimes put "hex" signs like this one on the sides of their barns to ward off evil spirits. Why do such superstitions persist?

the other team. Ever after, he scratches his left ear before pitching. A student always uses a "lucky" pen for taking tests because she used it on the first exam of the semester and got an A. Why, though, don't such superstitions extinguish? After all, the pitcher isn't always going to pitch a perfect game, nor is the student always going to be brilliant. One answer: Intermittent reinforcement may make the response particularly resistant to extinction. If coincidental reinforcement occurs occasionally, the superstitious behavior may continue indefinitely (Schwartz & Reilly, 1985). The fact that our little rituals only "work" some of the time ensures that we will keep using them.

There are other reasons, as well, why superstitions occur and persist. Many superstitions are part of one's culture, and are reinforced by the agreement, approval, or attention of others. We don't have to have an accident after walking beneath a ladder to believe that this behavior brings bad luck. Also, superstitions give people the illusion of control over the uncontrollable. It's not surprising that people often look for evidence to justify their superstitions, but ignore contrary evidence. As Paul Chance (1988b) points out, if a child finds a four-leaf clover and a few days later trips over a dollar, adults may point to the four-leaf clover's power. But if nothing particularly lucky happens to the child until puberty, no one points to the clover's failure. When people survive a plane crash, they often attribute their escape to prayer. "The chances are good that those who did not survive also prayed for all they were worth," notes Chance, "but they are now too dead to testify about the value of the procedure." As for good-luck charms and the like, as long as nothing awful happens when a person is carrying the charm, the person is likely to credit it with protective powers, but if something bad does occur, the person can always say that the charm has "lost" its powers. Chance says that he himself no longer has any superstitions. "A black cat means nothing to me now, nor does a broken mirror. There are no little plastic icons on the dashboard of my car, and I carry no rabbit's foot. I am free of all such nonsense, and I am happy to report no ill effects—knock wood."

QUICK QUIZ

Are you ready to apply the principles of operant conditioning? In each of the following situations, choose the best alternative and give your reason for choosing it:

1. You want your 2-year-old to ask for water with a word instead of a grunt. Should you give him water when he says "wa-wa" or wait until his pronunciation improves?
2. Your roommate keeps interrupting you while you are studying though you have asked her to stop. Should you ignore her completely or occasionally respond for the sake of good manners?
3. Your father, who rarely writes to you, has finally sent a letter. Should you reply quickly or wait a while so he will know how it feels to be ignored?

ANSWERS:

1. You should reinforce "wa-wa," an approximation of *water*, because complex behaviors need to be shaped. 2. You should ignore her completely because intermittent reinforcement could cause her interruptions to persist. 3. You should reply quickly if you want to encourage letter writing, because immediate reinforcement is more effective than delayed reinforcement.

Reprinted with special permission of King Features Syndicate, Inc.

Just Deserts? The Problem with Punishment

In a novel called *Walden Two* (1948/1976), Skinner imagined a utopia where re-inforcers were used so wisely that undesirable behavior was rare. His book gives a revealing glimpse of how a behaviorist might go about designing an entire community by using "behavioral engineering." But in the real world, boners, bloopers, and bad behavior abound. We learn bad habits as well as good ones, maladaptive behaviors as well as useful ones. Then we are faced with how to get rid of the bad habits and behaviors.

An obvious approach might seem to be punishment. Many adults think that if you spare the rod, you will spoil the child. The United States is one of the few Western countries that still permits corporal (physical) punishment of students by principals and teachers. (States vary in their policies.) In the United States, the physical punishment of children has religious roots, in the belief that you must beat children or their innate wickedness will land them in hell (Greven, 1991). According to one estimate, at least half of all American schoolchildren are at some time exposed to physical or psychological punishment (Hyman, 1988). Boys, minority children, and poor white children are the most likely to be hit. Our penal system is also based on the principle of punishment as a de-terrent. Yelling, scolding, fining, and firing are familiar features of life, and many people feel rewarded by a temporary feeling of control and power when they punish others. But does all this punishment work?

In the laboratory, unpleasant stimuli do make the behaviors they follow less likely to recur. Punishment is also sometimes effective in the real world. Some highly disturbed children have been known to chew their own fingers to the bone, stick objects in their eyes, or tear out their hair. You can't ignore such behavior because the children are seriously injuring themselves. You can't re-spond with concern and affection because you may unwittingly reward the be-havior. In this case, punishment works: Clinical studies find that immediately punishing the self-destructive behavior eliminates it (Lovaas, 1977; Lovaas, Schreibman, & Koegel, 1974). Mild punishers, such as a spray of water in the face, are just as effective as strong ones, such as electric shock; sometimes they are even more effective. A firm "No!" can also be established as a conditioned punisher.

The effects of punishment, however, are far less predictable than many peo-ple realize. Consider the problem of domestic violence. In a widely publicized real-life experimental intervention, men who were arrested for assaulting their wives or girlfriends were less likely to repeat the offense within six months than men who were merely talked to by the police or ordered to stay away from the victim for a few hours (Sherman & Berk, 1984). On the basis of these results, police departments across the United States adopted mandatory arrest policies in cases of domestic assault. Then more research came along showing that the conclusions were premature: Although arrests do temporarily prevent a repeat attack, they do not usually deter domestic violence *in the long run* (Dunford, Huizinga, & Elliott, 1990; Hirschel et al., 1990; Sherman, 1992). A moral dilemma exists, then, between the immediate need to protect the victim and the long-term need to eliminate the violence entirely.

Further, sociologist Lawrence Sherman and his colleagues (Sherman, 1992; Sherman et al., 1991) have noted that if arrest is the aspirin of criminal justice, the "pill" has different effects on different people at different doses. In their research, they found that brief arrests of two or three hours were generally most effective in initially reducing the chances of renewed domestic violence (when compared with a warning), although this effect disappeared within a few weeks. However, for unemployed men in the inner city, both brief and lengthy arrests actually *increased* the long-term chances of a repeat attack. The researchers speculate that in unemployed men living in ghetto areas, initial fear of being arrested again may wear off quickly, to be replaced by anger at the woman who "caused" the arrest or at women in general.

Because of such complexities, well-intentioned but simplistic efforts to "crack down" on wrong-doers often fail to produce the desired results. Laboratory and field studies show that punishment also has the following other disadvantages as a method of behavior control:

1. *People often administer punishment inappropriately or when they are so enraged that they are unable to think through what they are doing and how they are doing it.* They swing blindly or yell wildly, applying punishment so broadly that it covers all sorts of irrelevant behaviors. Indeed, even when people are not carried away by anger, they often misunderstand the proper application of punishment. One student told us his parents used to punish their children before leaving them alone for the evening because of all the naughty things they were going to do. Naturally, the children didn't bother being angels.

2. *The recipient of punishment often responds with anxiety, fear, or rage.* These emotional "side effects" may then generalize to the entire situation in which the punishment occurs—the place, the person delivering the punishment, and the circumstances—through a process of classical conditioning. Such reactions tend to create more problems than the punishment solves. For example, instead of becoming obedient or respectful, a teenager who has been severely punished might strike back or run away. As we saw in the case of domestic violence, emotional reactions to punishment may even produce an increase in the undesirable behavior that the punishment was intended to eliminate.

3. *The effects of punishment are sometimes temporary, depending heavily on the presence of the punishing person or circumstances.* We can probably all remember some transgressions of childhood that we never dared commit when our parents were around but which we promptly resumed as soon as they were gone. All we learned was not to get caught.

4. *Most misbehavior is hard to punish immediately.* Recall that punishment, like reward, works best if it quickly follows a response, especially with animals and children. Outside the laboratory, quick punishment is often hard to achieve.

5. *Punishment conveys little information.* If it immediately follows the misbehavior, it may tell the recipient what *not* to do. But it doesn't communicate what the person (or animal) *should* do. For example, spanking a toddler for messing in his pants will not teach him to use the potty chair.

6. *An action intended to punish may instead be reinforcing because it brings attention.* Indeed, angry attention may be just what the offender is after. If a mother yells at a child who is throwing a tantrum, the very act of yelling may give him what he wants—a reaction from her. In the schoolroom, teachers who scold children in front of other students, thus putting them in the limelight, often unwittingly reward the very misbehavior they are trying to eliminate.

Is this scene familiar? Harried parents often resort to physical punishment, without being aware of the many negative consequences for themselves and their children. Based on your reading of this chapter, what alternatives does this mother have?

Because of these drawbacks, most psychologists believe that punishment, especially severe punishment, is a poor way to eliminate unwanted behavior and in general should be regarded only as a last resort. When punishment is used, it should not involve physical abuse, it should be accompanied by information about what kind of behavior would have been more appropriate, and it should be followed, whenever possible, by the reinforcement of desirable behavior.

Fortunately, in most situations there is a good alternative to punishment: extinction of the responses you want to discourage. Of course, extinction is sometimes difficult to achieve. It is hard to ignore the child nagging for a cookie before dinner, the roommate interrupting your concentration, or the dog barking its lungs out. Also, the simplest form of extinction, simply ignoring the behavior, is not always appropriate. A teacher cannot ignore a child who is clobbering a playmate. The dog owner who ignores Fido's backyard barking may soon hear from the neighbors. A parent whose child is a TV addict can't ignore the behavior, because television is rewarding to the child. One solution: Combine extinction of undesirable acts with reinforcement of alternative ones. If a child is addicted to TV, the parent might ignore the child's pleas for "just one more program" and at the same time encourage behavior that is incompatible with television watching, such as playing outdoors.

Warnings and threats of punishment often don't work.

Putting Operant Principles to Work

The use of operant techniques (and also classical ones) in real-world settings is called **behavior modification.** Many behavior modification programs rely on a technique called the **token economy.** Tokens are secondary reinforcers that have no real value in themselves (for example, points or script money) but are exchangeable for primary reinforcers or other secondary reinforcers. They provide an easy way to reinforce behavior on a continuous schedule. Once a particular behavior is established, tokens can be phased out and replaced by more "natural" intermittent reinforcers, such as praise.

Behavior modifiers have carried learning principles out of the narrow world of the Skinner box and into the wider world of the classroom, athletic field, prison, mental hospital, nursing home, rehabilitation ward, day-care center, factory, and office. Behavior modification has its critics. They fear that its widespread use will crush creativity and turn people into sheep. To these critics, operant conditioning seems mechanistic, cold-blooded, and unethical, especially when it involves the use of punishment or the withholding of reinforcers. But behaviorists contend that society needs *more*, not less, behavior modification. They point out that unethical manipulation existed long before behavioral principles were known. Reinforcement, punishment, and extinction are always occurring, whether in a planned or unplanned way. The important question is whether society is willing to use behavioral procedures wisely to achieve humane goals.

Consider the enormous scope of behavioral successes in real life. Behaviorists have taught parents how to toilet train their children (Azrin & Foxx, 1974) and teachers how to be "behavioral change agents" (Besalel-Azrin, Azrin, & Armstrong, 1977). They have taught autistic children who have never before spoken to use a vocabulary of several hundred words (Lovaas, 1977). They have trained barely functioning disturbed and mentally retarded adults to communicate, dress themselves, mingle socially with others, and earn a living in the community (Lent, 1968; McLeod, 1985). They have taught brain-damaged patients to control socially inappropriate behavior, focus attention, and improve their language abilities (McGlynn, 1990). And they have helped ordinary folk eliminate unwanted habits, such as smoking and nail biting, or acquire wanted ones, such as practicing the piano or studying. They have even used operant procedures, once thought applicable only to voluntary behavior, to modify such "in-

■ **behavior modification**
The application of conditioning techniques to teach new responses or reduce or eliminate maladaptive or problematic behavior.

■ **token economy**
A behavior modification technique in which secondary reinforcers called to-kens, which can be collected and exchanged for primary or other secondary reinforcers, are used to shape behavior.

Behavioral principles have many practical applications. This capuchin monkey has been trained to assist her paralyzed owner by picking up objects, opening doors, helping with feeding, and performing a variety of other everyday tasks.

voluntary" responses as heart rate and blood pressure (although the mechanism by which this process occurs remains controversial, as we saw in Chapter 3).

All too often, say behaviorists, society either ignores the consequences of behavior or applies operant principles haphazardly. For example, in many states, nursing homes for the elderly receive more state aid for bedridden patients than for those who can get about. Thus there is no financial incentive for helping patients become independent. To take another example: Many health insurance plans will not pay for checkups when a person is well. Health care professionals believe that some serious, costly illnesses could be avoided if they were caught early during routine exams. Unfortunately, when insured patients are denied reimbursement for taking such preventive measures, they are not likely to do so. On the positive side, some schools and large companies are establishing "wellness" programs and giving prizes for improved health habits. Some insurance companies now reward nonsmokers by reducing the cost of their premiums.

■ COMPLICATING FACTORS IN THE MODIFICATION OF BEHAVIOR

We have made behavioral modification sound pretty easy. In the real world, though, it sometimes fails or even backfires. Human beings may feel manipulated and refuse to cooperate. Situations are often so complex and uncontrolled that well-planned programs can go awry, especially if those who must implement them have not been adequately trained. In one study, a token economy system that had worked well with juvenile offenders in a pilot project fell apart when it was tried in a different institution. The people in charge neglected to smile as they handed out the tokens, and apparently the young men took their stern expressions as an insult (related by Pryor, 1984). Operant techniques may also fail when the underlying cause of the behavior is not altered. For example, rewarding your partner's cheerfulness may not do much good if his or her gloominess is caused by a boring job. The real solution may be for the person to change jobs.

Effective behavior modification is not only a science but an art. (In "Taking Psychology with You" we offer some guidelines for mastering that art.) Let us look at two other complicating factors.

When Play Becomes Work:
Intrinsic Versus Extrinsic Reinforcers

One complication is that human beings (and probably animals, too) work not only for **extrinsic reinforcers,** such as money and gold stars, but also for **intrinsic reinforcers,** such as enjoyment of the task. As behavior modifiers carried operant conditioning into real-world settings, it became obvious that extrinsic reinforcement can turn into too much of a good thing. In fact, it can sometimes kill intrinsic motivation.

Consider what happened when psychologists had nursery school children draw with felt-tip pens (Lepper, Greene, & Nisbett, 1973). The children already liked this activity and readily took it up during free play. First the researchers recorded how long each child spontaneously played with the pens. They then told some children that if they would draw with felt-tip pens for a man who had come "to see what kinds of pictures boys and girls like to draw with magic-markers," there would be a prize, a "Good Player Award" complete with gold seal and red ribbon. After drawing for six minutes, each child got the promised award. Other children did not expect a reward and were not given one. A week later, the researchers again observed the children's free play. Those children who had expected and received a reward were playing with the pens less than those who had not received an award. Further, they were spending much less time with the pens than they had before the start of the experiment (see Figure 6.8). Similar results occurred when older children were or were not promised awards for working on academic subjects.

Why should extrinsic rewards undermine intrinsic motivation? The researchers in these studies suggested that when we are paid for an activity, we interpret it as work. It is as if we say to ourselves, "I'm doing this because I'm being paid for it. Since I'm being paid, it must be something I wouldn't do if I didn't have to." When the reward is withdrawn, we refuse to "work" any longer. Others have suggested that extrinsic rewards given by others are often seen as controlling, and therefore they reduce a person's sense of autonomy, self-determination, and choice ("I guess I should just do what I'm told to do") (Deci & Ryan, 1987). Still a third (more behavioral) explanation is that extrinsic re-

⚹ People often work hard for money and good grades. Unhappily, these rewards can also kill the intrinsic pleasure of the activity. Could that be why so many college students stop reading after they graduate?

■ **extrinsic reinforcers**
Reinforcers that are not inherently related to the activity being reinforced. Examples are money, prizes, and praise.
■ **intrinsic reinforcers**
Reinforcers that are inherently related to the activity being reinforced. Examples are enjoyment of the task and the satisfaction of accomplishment.

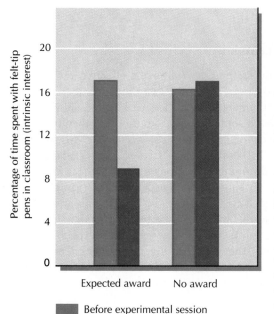

FIGURE 6.8 _____

Turning play into work
Preschool children were promised a prize for drawing with felt-tip pens, an activity they already liked. Time voluntarily spent with the pens temporarily increased. But after the prize was awarded, the children spent less time with the pens than they had before the study. In contrast, children who were not promised or given an award continued to show interest in the activity. Such results suggest that extrinsic rewards can sometimes reduce intrinsic motivation.

inforcement sometimes raises the rate of responding above some optimal, enjoyable level. Then the activity really does become work.

The temporary quality of extrinsically rewarded behavior is captured in a folktale about an old man whose peace and quiet were constantly disturbed by some rowdy children. The old man called the children over and said, "I like to hear you play. If you'll come every day and make noise, I'll pay you each a quarter." Naturally, the children agreed, and that day they got their quarters. The next day, the old man said, "I'm a little low on cash, so I can only pay you twenty cents." The children were disappointed, but they accepted. Each day the fee continued to fall, until it was only five cents. "Well!" snorted the children, "We're not going to make noise for only five cents. It's not worth the effort." Off they went, leaving the old man to enjoy his tranquillity.

There is a trade-off, then, between the short-term effectiveness of extrinsic rewards and the long-term effectiveness of intrinsic ones. Extrinsic rewards work: How many people would trudge off to work every morning if they never got paid? In the classroom, a teacher who offers incentives to an unmotivated student may be taking the only course of action open. But if a behavior is to last when the teacher isn't around, extrinsic reinforcers eventually must be phased out. As one mother wrote in a *Newsweek* essay, "The winners [of prizes for school work] will . . . suffer if they don't discover for themselves that they can gain the pleasure of health and strength from exercise, the joy of music from songs, the power of mathematics from counting and all of human wisdom from reading" (Skreslet, 1987). The fact that our school system relies heavily on grades and other extrinsic incentives may help explain why the average college graduate reads few books.

We do not want to leave the impression, however, that extrinsic reinforcers always decrease intrinsic motivation. Many businesses and industries now recognize that workers' productivity depends both on pay incentives *and* on having interesting, challenging, and varied kinds of work to do (see Chapter 10). Money and praise do not necessarily interfere with intrinsic motivation when extrinsic rewards are clearly tied to competence rather than mere performance and when the activity is already well learned (Deci, 1975). Also, people who are extremely interested in an activity or task to begin with are likely to keep doing it even when extrinsic reinforcers are withdrawn (Mawhinney, 1990).

Biological Constraints on Learning

Certain biological constraints on learning also limit the effectiveness of operant procedures. What an animal can learn depends on the physical characteristics of its body; a fish cannot be trained to climb a ladder. Further, animals seem to be biologically prepared to learn some responses more easily than others. In an article entitled "The Misbehavior of Organisms," Keller and Marian Breland (1961), two psychologists who became animal trainers, described some fascinating failures in operant conditioning. The Brelands found that animals often had trouble learning tasks that should have been easy. For example, a pig was supposed to drop large wooden coins in a box. Instead, the pig would drop the coin, push at it with its snout, throw it in the air, and push at it some more. This behavior actually delayed reinforcement, so it was hard to explain in terms of operant principles. Apparently the pig's rooting instinct (its tendency to use its snout to uncover edible roots) interfered with the desired learning. The Brelands called this tendency to revert to an instinctive behavior **instinctive drift.**

Both operant and classical procedures seem to work best when they capitalize on inborn tendencies. Consider the psychologist mentioned earlier who

Drawing by Lorenz; © 1986 The New Yorker Magazine, Inc.

"That is the correct answer, Billy, but I'm afraid you don't win anything for it."

■ **instinctive drift**

The tendency of an organism to revert to an instinctive behavior over time; can interfere with learning.

learned to hate béarnaise sauce. This incident differed from laboratory conditioning in many ways. Learning occurred after only one pairing of the sauce with illness and with a considerable delay between the conditioned and unconditioned stimuli. In addition, neither the psychologist's wife nor the plate from which he ate became conditioned stimuli for nausea, though they, too, were paired with illness. Controlled research suggests that certain animals (including, apparently, psychologists) are biologically prepared to associate sickness with taste rather than, say, with light and sound (Garcia & Koelling, 1966; Seligman & Hager, 1972). This tendency enhances the species' survival: Eating bad food is more likely to be followed by illness than are certain sights or sounds.

Biology also places constraints on the learning of other associations. For example, in human beings it is easier to establish a conditioned fear of spiders, snakes, or heights than of butterflies, flowers, or toasters, probably because during the evolution of our species the former objects presented a danger. As we will see in Chapter 13, many psychologists believe that human beings are also biologically "prepared" to learn a complex type of behavior that gives our species a distinct advantage: language.

Operating conditioning procedures work best when they capitalize on an animal's natural responses. For example, it's easy to train pigs to hunt for truffles, a fungus that grows underground, because pigs have a natural rooting instinct.

QUICK QUIZ

A. According to behavioral principles, what is happening here?

1. An adolescent whose parents have hit him for minor transgressions since he was small runs away from home.
2. A young woman whose parents paid her to clean her room while she was growing up is a slob when she moves to her own apartment.
3. Two parents scold their young daughter every time they catch her sucking her thumb. The thumb sucking continues anyway.

B. Several states are trying to reduce truancy and school failures by experimenting with various forms of punishment. For example, families on welfare may lose part of their payments if their children regularly skip school, students who earn poor grades may lose after-school activities or driving privileges, and students who quit high school may have to forfeit their driver's licenses. What assumptions underlie such programs?

ANSWERS:

A. 1. The physical punishment was painful, and through a process of classical conditioning, the situation in which it occurred also became unpleasant. Since escape from an unpleasant stimulus is negatively reinforcing, the boy ran away. **2.** Extrinsic reinforcers are no longer available, and room-cleaning behavior has been extinguished. Also, extrinsic rewards may have displaced the intrinsic satisfaction of having a tidy room. **3.** Punishment has failed, possibly because it rewards thumb sucking with attention or because thumb sucking still brings the child pleasure whenever the parents aren't around. **B.** We do not know yet the effectiveness of such programs, but in any case, they rest on the following assumptions (among others): (a) The threat of punishment will motivate students to do better instead of alienating or discouraging them; (b) the problem is in the students, not the schools or the community; (c) if a student isn't doing well, the student must not be working hard; (d) enforcement will be adequate and the punishers used will be effective; (e) extrinsic and intrinsic reinforcers can't do the job without punishment. (Based on your reading of this chapter, can you think of some reasons why some or all of these assumptions may be valid or invalid for certain students?)

■ CONNECTIONS OR COGNITIONS: WHY DOES LEARNING OCCUR?

Conditioning alters behavior. But why?

For half a century, most American learning theories held that learning could be completely explained by specifying the behavioral "ABCs"—*antecedents* (events preceding behavior), *behaviors*, and *consequences*. Early behaviorists, such as John Watson, assumed that what was learned was simply a stimulus-response connection. Skinner (1974) and later behaviorists rejected this simple approach, and discussed complex cues for responding, classes of behavior, and the way that rules, in the form of language, can control behavior. But almost all behaviorists agreed that nothing was to be gained by theorizing about how hypothetical mental operations might explain behavior.

In the 1960s, a new view, labeled "expectancy theory," emphasized that when an organism behaves in a certain way, it acts *as if* it has certain expectations (Bolles, 1972; Bolles et al., 1980). Pavlov's dogs acted *as if* they expected the ringing of the bell (the CS) to be followed by food (the US). Skinner's rats acted *as if* they expected bar pressing to be followed by food. Expectancy theorists did not speculate about what an animal (or person) might consciously experience during learning, but their views were a step in the direction of a more mentalistic view of learning.

Today, in classical conditioning research, many psychologists contend that what an organism actually learns is *information* conveyed by one stimulus about another. In studies supporting this view, Robert Rescorla showed that the mere pairing of an unconditioned stimulus and a neutral one is not enough to produce learning; the neutral stimulus must reliably *signal*, or *predict*, the unconditioned one (Rescorla, 1968, 1988; Rescorla & Wagner, 1972). Suppose we want to teach rats to fear a tone. Following the usual procedure, we would repeatedly sound the tone before an unconditioned stimulus for fear, such as electric shock. After 20 pairings, the rats would probably show signs of fear upon hearing the tone. But now suppose we do this experiment again—on 20 trials the tone precedes the shock—but this time we randomly intersperse another 20 trials in which the shock occurs *without* the tone. With this method, the tone is paired with the shock just as often as in the standard procedure, but it signals shock only half of the time. Thus the shock is equally likely whether the tone is present or not. Under these conditions, the tone does not provide any information about the shock, and hardly any conditioning occurs.

From this and similar findings, Rescorla (1988) concludes that "Pavlovian conditioning is not a stupid process by which the organism willy-nilly forms associations between any two stimuli that happen to co-occur. Rather, the organism is better seen as an information seeker using logical and perceptual relations among events, along with its own preconceptions, to form a sophisticated representation of its world." Not all learning theorists agree with this conclusion or with the findings on which it is based (Papini & Bitterman, 1990). The important point here, however, is that concepts such as "expectancy," "information seeking," "preconceptions" and "representations of the world" have opened the door to a more cognitive view of learning.

Behaviorists have often clashed with more cognitively oriented psychologists over three other kinds of learning: *latent learning, observational learning*, and *insight*.

Latent Learning: Delayed Performance

Behaviorism emphasizes behavior. Sometimes, however, learning takes place without any obvious behavioral change. In a classic experiment, psychologists placed three groups of rats in mazes and observed their behavior each day for

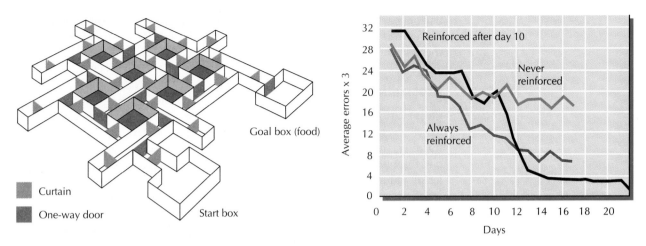

FIGURE 6.9

Latent learning

Rats were placed in a maze like the one on the left. Rats that always found a food reward in the goal box made fewer errors over time, as shown by the gray curve on the graph. In contrast, rats that never found food showed little improvement, as shown by the red curve. A third group of rats found no food for the first ten days and then were given food on the eleventh day. As the black curve shows, these animals showed rapid improvement from then on, quickly equaling the performance of the rats that received food from the start. This result suggests that learning involves cognitive changes that can occur even in the absence of reinforcement, although such changes may not be acted upon until a reward becomes available.

over two weeks. The rats in Group 1 always found food at the end of the maze. Group 2 never found food. Group 3 found no food for ten days but then received food on the eleventh. The Group 1 (reinforced) rats, as you might expect, quickly learned to head straight for the end of the maze without going down blind alleys, whereas Group 2 rats did not learn to go to the end. But the Group 3 rats were different. For ten days they appeared to follow no particular route. But on the eleventh day, when food was introduced, they quickly learned to run to the end of the maze. As Figure 6.9 shows, by the next day they were doing as well as Group 1 (Tolman & Honzik, 1930).

Group 3 had demonstrated **latent learning,** learning that is not immediately expressed in an overt response. A great deal of human learning also remains latent until circumstances allow or require it to be expressed in performance. We learn how the world is organized, which paths lead to which places, and which actions can produce which payoffs. This knowledge permits us to be creative and flexible in reaching our goals.

Behaviorists have usually dealt with latent learning by defining learning as a change in behavior or in the *potential* for behavior. Cognitive psychologists, however, argue that latent learning poses certain problems for behavioral theories. Not only does it occur in the absence of any obvious reinforcer, but it also raises questions about what, exactly, is learned during learning. The rats who were not given food until the eleventh day had no reason to run toward the end during their first ten days in the maze. Yet clearly they had learned *something*. One of the psychologists who designed the experiment felt that this "something" was a **cognitive map**—a mental representation of the spatial layout of the maze (Tolman, 1948). Other studies of latent learning also seem to involve knowledge, not behavior. When a reinforcer is eventually introduced, it does not actually produce new learning; it merely motivates the person or animal to use already existing knowledge stored in memory. What's more, the be-

■ **latent learning**
A form of learning that is not immediately expressed in an overt response. Occurs without obvious reinforcement.

■ **cognitive map**
A mental representation of the environment.

havior may take many forms. You can find your way to the supermarket in a car, even if in the past you have always walked there. The learned "responses," then, are not muscle movements—but what are they?

Observational Learning: The Copycat Syndrome

Observational learning, sometimes called *vicarious conditioning,* has also led many psychologists toward a more cognitive view of learning. In observational learning, the learner observes a *model* (another animal or person) making certain responses and experiencing the consequences. Sometimes the learner mimics or imitates the responses shortly after observing them. At other times the learning remains latent. A young child may observe a parent setting the table, threading a needle, or tightening a screw, but not act on this learning for several years. Then the child finds he knows how to do these things, even though he has never before done them. He did not learn by doing, but by watching.

None of us would last long without observational learning. We would have to learn about avoiding oncoming cars by walking into traffic and suffering the consequences, or about swimming by jumping into a deep pool, or about staying warm by going out in a snowstorm without clothes. Learning would be not only dangerous but also inefficient. Parents and teachers would be busy 24 hours a day shaping children's behavior. Bosses would have to stand over their employees' desks, rewarding every little link in the complex chains we call typing, report writing, and widget assembling.

Observational learning can also explain how children acquire certain attitudes and responses, both positive and negative. In a classic study, nursery school children viewed a short film of two men, Rocky and Johnny, playing with toys (Bandura, Ross, & Ross, 1963). (The children apparently didn't think this behavior was odd.) In the film, Johnny refuses to share his toys and Rocky responds by clobbering him. Rocky's actions are rewarded because he winds up with all the toys. Poor Johnny sits dejectedly in the corner, while Rocky marches off with a sack full of his loot and a hobby horse under his arm. After watching the film, each child was left alone for 20 minutes in a playroom full of toys, including some of the items shown in the film. Watching through a one-way mirror, the researchers found that the children were much more aggressive in

■ **observational learning**
A learning process in which an individual learns new responses by observing the behavior of another (a model) rather than through direct experience. Sometimes called vicarious conditioning.

Like father, like daughter. Parents can be powerful role models.

their play than a control group that had not viewed the film. Sometimes the children's behavior was almost a direct imitation of Rocky's. At the end of the session, one little girl even asked the experimenter for a sack!

Albert Bandura (1973) has noted: "Children have been apprehended for writing bad checks to obtain money for candy, for sniping at strangers with BB guns, for sending threatening letters to teachers and for injurious switchblade fights after witnessing similar performances on television." Children also learn attitudes and behaviors from real models. This may be one reason why parents who hit their children for hitting playmates and siblings tend to rear children who are hitters, and why yellers ("Be quiet!") tend to rear yellers. The children do as their parents do, not as they say. Keep in mind, however, that observational learning is complex and interacts with many other influences, as we discuss in "Think About It" on page 232.

Behaviorists recognize the importance of observational learning and believe that it can be explained in stimulus-response terms. But social learning theorists and other psychologists conclude that observational learning cannot be understood without taking into account the thought processes of the learner (Bandura, 1977). In observational learning, as in latent, the performance of a response is often delayed until long after learning has occurred, and the nature of the reinforcer during learning is not easily identified. Once the learner does perform the response, it is often carried out smoothly and without error, even though the learner has never done it before. Cognitivists believe that what the learner learns is not a response, but *knowledge* about responses and their consequences.

Insight Learning: The "Aha!" Phenomenon

Sometimes learning seems to occur in a flash. You suddenly "see" how to solve an equation, fix your carburetor, or finish a puzzle. This sort of learning, called **insight,** seems to involve a new way of perceiving logical and cause-and-effect relationships. You do not simply respond to stimuli; you solve a problem.

Not only humans but also chimpanzees seem capable of insight. In the 1920s, Wolfgang Köhler (1925) put chimpanzees in situations in which some tempting bananas were just out of reach, and then watched to see what they would do. The apes turned out to be very clever. If the bananas were outside the cage, the animal might pull them in with a stick. If the bananas were hung overhead, and there were boxes in the cage, the chimpanzee might pile up the boxes and climb on top of them to reach the fruit. Often the solution came after the animal had been sitting quietly for a while without actively trying to reach the bananas. It looked as though the animal was thinking about the problem and suddenly saw the answer.

Behaviorists argue that insight can be explained in terms of an organism's prior reinforcement history, without resorting to cognitive explanations (Windholz & Lamal, 1985). To a behaviorist, insight is just a label for a sudden change in behavior; it does not explain behavior. In this view, nothing is to be gained by resorting to mentalistic notions; insight simply involves the combination of previously learned patterns.

Behaviorists observe that even animals not credited with higher mental processes seem capable of what looks suspiciously like "insight," as long as they have had certain experiences. In one ingenious study, researchers trained four pigeons to push boxes in a particular direction and also to climb onto a box to peck a toy banana overhead in order to obtain grain. The birds were also taught not to fly or jump at the banana. Then they were left alone with the banana overhead and the box at the edge of the cage. The pigeons quickly solved their feeding problem by pushing the box beneath the banana and climbing onto it, just as Köhler's chimps had done (see Figure 6.10). Here is how the researchers described the behavior of one bird: "It paced and looked perplexed, stretched

When a chimpanzee suddenly finds a way to reach some bananas, we say it has "insight." But what if a pigeon does the same thing? Can a birdbrain have insight?

■ **insight**
A form of learning that occurs in problem solving and appears to involve the (often sudden) understanding of how elements of a situation are related or can be reorganized to achieve a solution.

Media Violence: Getting Away with Murder

• An inner city teacher decided to take some gang members to a hospital so they could see up close the results of violence on their streets. While they were there, they spotted a fellow gang member on a hospital gurney, bloodied and moaning in pain from a gunshot wound. The victim looked up and said, in a tone of astonishment, "I had no idea it hurt."

• In a Connecticut town, a group of teenage boys looking for excitement telephoned an order for Chinese food so that they could rob the delivery man. When he refused to hand over the cartons of food, one of the teenagers impulsively shot and fatally wounded him. Later the boys calmly ate the food.

Many people are worried about what seems to be an epidemic, among young people, of insensitivity and even obliviousness to the real pain caused by violence. Although the reasons for this trend are complex, many psychologists and social critics put the blame, in part, on television and movies. Social-learning theory predicts that children will imitate violent acts, or at least become more aggressive, if they are exposed to portrayals of violence in which the perpetrator is rewarded. A great deal of media violence certainly

fills the bill: During the course of growing up, children in the United States and many other countries view endless killings and maimings that leave out all negative consequences. Victims are merely "blown away." Death doesn't mean grief, mourning, or pain; it means disappearing from the screen.

Yet, surprisingly, research findings on the effects of media violence are less consistent than most people might think. In this chapter, we discussed a classic study showing that some children become more aggressive from watching aggression on television; other research has found the same thing (Comstock et al., 1978; Eron, 1980; Geen, 1978). But in the real world children view many kinds of programs and movies and there are many influences on aggression, ranging from prejudice to a history of family violence. Some psychologists, reviewing the available evidence, conclude that the impact of media violence on real violence has not been convincingly demonstrated (Freedman, 1988; Milavsky, 1988). Others, reviewing the same evidence, reach the opposite conclusion (Singer & Singer, 1988).

Which view is right? Certainly not everyone who watches *The Terminator,* or even four "Freddy" films in a row, runs out to commit mayhem. Yet movies and television programs are almost certainly powerful shapers of values, attitudes, and reactions to events, including violent events. Critics of media violence point out that most research on the issue was done during the 1970s. Since then, depictions have become far more graphic, especially in action and slasher films, which are

(a)

(b)

(c)

FIGURE 6.10

Smart bird

"Now, let's see . . . ." In Robert Epstein's laboratory, a pigeon looks at a cluster of toy bananas strung overhead (a), pushes a small box beneath the bananas (b), then climbs on the box to peck at them (c). The bird previously learned separate components of this sequence through a process of operant conditioning. Behaviorists view this accomplishment, which resembles that of chimpanzees, as evidence against the cognitive view of insight. Cognitive psychologists disagree. What do you think?

routinely shown on non-network TV stations and which feature, with monotonous regularity, people being sawed in half by chain saws, impaled, or blown to bits. To many young people, these films are a joke, fun, and the rush of epinephrine the movies produce is enjoyable. To many psychologists, however, graphic violence is no joke. They believe that with repeated exposure to mindless murder, viewers' responses of horror or disgust tend to extinguish, people become numb to the consequences of brutality, and increasingly gruesome depictions are needed to produce an emotional effect. Support comes from studies of slasher films, which often link erotic scenes with grisly violence. In the laboratory, viewers of such films tend to become calloused in their attitudes toward women and toward real-life rape victims (Linz, Donnerstein, & Penrod, 1988).

Of course, violence has always been a part of storytelling, in fairy tales, myths, novels, and plays. Modern media violence, however, whether bloodless or gory, is often notable not only for what it shows but for what it leaves out: the human face and personality of the victim, the sorrow of those they leave behind (even bad guys usually have friends and families), and perhaps most important, alternative ways of resolving conflicts. People can identify with victims and survivors when violence has meaning; they will cry even for Bambi, a cartoon deer. But it is hard to feel empathy when killing is just a matter of awesome special effects.

Even news reports of real violence are often sanitized. Since World War II, government censors have been concerned about journalists want

ing to portray the realities of war: rape, disease, and bodies torn apart in battle (Fussell, 1989). Since the Vietnam conflict, the first "TV war," battlefields and body bags have been off limits to cameras, presumably because seeing the real carnage of war might affect public support for it. During the 1991 Persian Gulf war, television viewers saw only sleek aircraft taking off and videos of "smart bombs" "surgically" destroying buildings. They did not get to witness the chaos and fear of battle; enemy fatalities were called "collateral damage." Whether or not you supported this particular war, you might ask yourself how such censorship—the images of war shown on the screen and those that were not shown—might have affected your reactions.

Because the causes of violence—and apathy about violence—are complicated, it is hard for researchers to establish with certainty that media violence and real violence are linked, or that media violence and emotional apathy are linked. Then what should parents and policy makers do? Should they do nothing? Should they support laws that limit the amount of violence in films and on TV, or would that be unwarranted censorship? Violent films make barrels of money for their producers, which of course reinforces the production of these films. Can viewers extinguish violent-film-making behavior by refusing to buy tickets to slasher and other violent action films or by turning the dial when such films are shown on TV—and would they be willing to do so? What effect have media depictions of violence had on your own ability to understand the reality of a violent death? Think about it.

toward the banana, glanced back and forth from box to banana and then energetically pushed the box toward it, looking up at it repeatedly as it did so, then stopped just short of it, climbed, and pecked" (Epstein et al., 1984). Yet few people would want to credit pigeons with complex thought.

To behaviorists, insight is the *result* of learning, not a way of learning. Other psychologists maintain that although insight may require using previously learned responses to solve problems, in human beings (and possibly chimpanzees) it requires *mentally* combining these responses in new ways. In truth, psychologists do not yet have much insight into how insight operates.

■ COGNITIVE THEORIES: PEERING INTO THE BLACK BOX

We close with a story, told many years ago by social-learning theorist Albert Bandura (1969). Once upon a time, there was a big-game hunter who came face to face with a hungry lion. As the hunter prepared to shoot the charging beast, the gun jammed. Terrified, the hunter closed his eyes and began to pray. Moments passed but nothing happened. Surprised and puzzled, the hunter slowly opened his eyes to find the lion also bowed in prayer. "Thank God," the hunter exclaimed, "you are responding to my prayers!" The lion replied, "Not at all. I'm saying grace."

A cognitive psychologist would say that because the poor hunter did not know the lion's goals, intentions, and motives, he lacked a complete understanding of its behavior. We may not want to speculate about the mental life of real lions, but people, argue the cognitivists, are also not "empty organisms." They are full of attitudes, beliefs, and expectations that affect the way they acquire and store information, make decisions, reason, and solve problems. Cognitive psychologists like to compare the mind to an engineer's hypothetical "black box," a device whose workings must be inferred because they can't be observed directly. By carefully examining the box's inputs and outputs, cognitive psychologists construct plausible models of what is happening inside the box. By carefully designing imaginative experiments, they objectively study such "mentalistic" phenomena as attention, silent rehearsal of information, imagery, and thinking.

Despite the differences between behavioral and cognitive approaches, in actual practice, they are often treated as different levels of analysis, rather than conflicting ones. Further, many therapists now combine behavioral principles with cognitive ones to treat people in psychotherapy (see Chapter 17). Nonetheless, as we will see in the next two chapters, cognitive psychologists have staked out for study many areas that behaviorists have traditionally regarded as foreign territory—areas in the vast country of the mind.

TAKING PSYCHOLOGY WITH YOU

Shape Up!

Operant conditioning can seem deceptively simple. Some popular books reinforce this impression. In the early 1980s, a tiny but expensive book called *The One Minute Manager* became an enormous best-seller simply by advising managers to use praise and constructive criticism. In practice, though, behavior modification can be full of unwanted surprises, even in the hands of experts. Here are a few things to keep in mind if you want to modify someone's behavior.

• *Accentuate the positive.* Most people notice bad behavior more than good and therefore miss opportunities to use reinforcers. Parents, for example, often scold a child for bed-wetting but fail to give praise for dry sheets in the morning; or they punish a child for poor grades but fail to reward studying.

• *Reinforce small improvements.* A common error is to withhold reinforcement until behavior is perfect. Has your child's grade in math improved from a D to a C? Has your favorite date, who is usually an awful cook, managed to serve up a half-decent omelet? Has your messy roommate left some dirty dishes in the sink but vacuumed the rug? It's probably time for a reinforcer.

On the other hand, you don't want to overdo praise or give it insincerely. Gushing about every tiny step in the right direction will cause your praise to lose its value, and soon nothing less than a standing ovation will do.

• *Find the right reinforcers.* You may have to experiment a bit to find which reinforcers a person (or animal) actually wants; one person's meat, as they say, is another's poison. In general, it is good to use a variety of reinforcers since using the same type over and over again can get boring. Reinforcers, by the way, do not have to be *things.* You can also use valued activities, such as going out to dinner, to reinforce other behavior.

• *Always examine what you are reinforcing.* It is easy to reinforce undesirable behavior merely by responding to it. Suppose someone is always yelling at you at the slightest provocation or with no provocation at all. You find the yelling enraging and humiliating, and you want it to stop. If you respond to it at all, whether by crying, apologizing, or yelling back, you are likely to reinforce it. An alternative might be to explain in a calm voice that you do not respond to complaints unless they are communicated without yelling—and then, if the yelling continues, leave. When the person does speak civilly, you can reward this behavior with your attention and good will.

Since you are with yourself more than anyone else, it may be easier to modify your own behavior than someone else's. You may wish to reduce your nibbling, eliminate a smoking habit, or become more outgoing in public. Let's assume for the sake of discussion that you aren't studying enough. How can you increase the time you spend with your books? Some hints:

• *Analyze the situation.* Are there circumstances that keep you from studying, such as a friend who is always pressuring you to go out or a rock band that practices next door? If so, you need to change the "discriminative stimuli" in your environment during study periods. Try to find a comfortable, cheerful, quiet, well-lit place. Not only will you concentrate better, but you may also have positive emotional responses to the environment that may generalize to the activity of studying.

• *Set up realistic goals.* If you usually study only 30 minutes a day, don't suddenly hit the books for 5 hours straight. All you will do is make studying so miserable that you will try to avoid it. Instead, reward yourself for small, steady improvements—perhaps 30 minutes the first day, 45 the next, and 60 the third.

• *Reinforce getting started.* The hardest part of studying can be getting started. (This is true of many other activities, too, as writers, joggers, and people who prepare their own income tax returns can tell you.) You might give yourself a small bit of candy or some other reward just for sitting down at your desk or, if you study at the library, setting out to get there.

• *Keep records.* Chart your progress in some way, perhaps by making a graph. This will keep you honest, and the progress you see on the graph will serve as a secondary reinforcer.

• *Don't punish yourself.* If you didn't study enough last week, don't brood about it or berate yourself with self-defeating thoughts, such as "I'll never be a good student" or "I'm a failure." Think about the coming week instead.

Above all, be patient. Shaping behavior is a creative skill that takes time to learn. Like Rome, new habits cannot be built in a day.

SUMMARY

1. Not all behavior is learned. A great deal of animal behavior is instinctive. Some animals also show *imprinting* during a *sensitive period* of development. Sociobiologists maintain that even complicated forms of human behavior can have an instinctive basis. Other social scientists acknowledge that our biological heritage may make certain kinds of learning difficult or easy but doubt that true instincts occur in human beings.

2. Under the influence of *behaviorism*, research on learning has led to the discovery of important principles governing two basic types of learning, classical conditioning and operant conditioning.

3. *Classical conditioning* was first studied by Russian physiologist Ivan Pavlov. He noted that when a neutral stimulus is paired with an *unconditioned stimulus (US)* that elicits some reflexive *unconditioned response (UR)*, the neutral stimulus comes to elicit a similar response. The neutral stimulus is then called a *conditioned stimulus (CS)*, and the response it elicits, a *conditioned response (CR)*. Subsequent studies demonstrated such phenomena as *extinction, stimulus generalization, stimulus discrimination*, and *higher-order conditioning*.

4. Classical conditioning may account for the acquisition of likes and dislikes, positive emotions, and fears and phobias. John Watson and his colleagues showed how fears may be learned, and then unlearned through a process of *counterconditioning*. Classical conditioning may also be involved in such aspects of drug addiction as tolerance and withdrawal.

5. The basic principle of *operant conditioning* is that behavior becomes more or less likely to occur depending on its consequences. Research in this area is closely associated with B. F. Skinner, who has been called the greatest of all American psychologists.

6. The consequences of behavior may be neutral, reinforcing, or punishing. *Reinforcement* strengthens or increases the probability of a response. *Punishment* weakens or decreases the probability of a response. Reinforcement (as well as punishment) may be either positive or negative. *Positive reinforcement* occurs when something rewarding is added to a situation. *Negative reinforcement* is the removal of an unpleasant stimulus. Reinforcement may also be characterized as primary or secondary. *Primary reinforcers* are naturally reinforcing and usually satisfy a biological need. *Secondary reinforcers* acquire their ability to strengthen responses through their association with other reinforcers.

7. Such phenomena as extinction, stimulus generalization, and stimulus discrimination occur in operant as well as classical conditioning. In general, immediate consequences have a greater effect on a response than do delayed consequences.

8. The pattern of responding in operant conditioning depends in part on the *schedule of reinforcement. Continuous reinforcement* leads to the most rapid learning, but *intermittent,* or *partial, reinforcement* makes a response resistant to extinction. Intermittent schedules deliver a reinforcer after a certain amount of time has passed since the last reinforcer (*interval* schedules) or after a certain number of responses are made (*ratio* schedules). Such schedules may be *fixed* or *variable.* If you want to get rid of a response, you should be careful not to reinforce it intermittently.

9. *Shaping* is used to train behaviors with a low probability of occurring spontaneously. Reinforcers are given for *successive approximations* to the desired response, until the desired response is achieved.

10. Accidental or coincidental reinforcement can effectively strengthen behavior and probably helps account for the learning of superstitions and their persistence, although other factors are also involved.

11. Punishment can sometimes be effective in eliminating undesirable behavior, but it has many drawbacks and may have unintended consequences. It is often administered haphazardly; it may produce rage and fear; its effects are often temporary; it is hard to administer immediately; it conveys little information about what kind of behavior is desired; and an action intended to punish may instead be reinforcing because it brings attention. Extinction of undesirable behavior, combined with reinforcement of desired behavior, is generally preferable to the use of punishment.

12. *Behavior modification,* the application of operant principles, has been used in many settings with success. However, problems also occur. For example, dependence on *extrinsic reinforcers* may undermine *intrinsic* motivation. Also, biological constraints may interfere with learning.

13. In the 1960s and 1970s, expectancy theory and new theories of classical conditioning opened the door to more cognitive interpretations of learning. Behaviorists and cognitive psychologists have often clashed over three other types of learning. *Latent learning* takes place in the absence of any obvious reinforcement and does not involve an immediate (observable) response. In *observational learning,* the learner imitates the behavior of a model; performance may be either immediate or delayed. *Insight* is learning that seems to occur suddenly and involves the solving of a problem. Behaviorists believe these forms of learning can be understood in terms of the conditioning history of the organism. Cognitive psychologists believe that what is learned is knowledge rather than behavior.

14. In the past few decades, cognitive theories of learning have become increasingly influential in psychology. Cognitive psychologists attempt to explain how such mental phenomena as attention, imagery, and thinking can affect learning. The behavioral and cognitive approaches are quite different. However, many psychologists treat them as different levels of analysis and use concepts and techniques from both.

KEY TERMS

7

Cognition I: Memory

Better by far that you should forget and smile
Than that you should remember and be sad.

CHRISTINA ROSSETTI

What is your earliest memory?

Swiss psychologist Jean Piaget (1951) once reported one of his own early memories—nearly being kidnapped at the age of 2. Piaget remembered sitting in his pram, watching his nurse as she bravely defended him from the kidnapper. He remembered the scratches she received on her face. He remembered a police officer with a short cloak and white baton who finally chased the kidnapper away. There was only one small problem: When Piaget was 15, his nurse wrote to his parents confessing that she had made up the entire story. Piaget noted, "I therefore must have heard, as a child, the account of this story . . . and projected it into the past in the form of a visual memory, which was a memory of a memory, but false."

A young woman we know tells of a more serene early memory. She was about 5 years old, on a car trip in Ireland with her parents. From the window she was looking out on velvety green hills. The sun was emerging after a downpour, and there was a spectacular rainbow. The image of her father is especially vivid in her mind's eye. "It's all so clear, so real," she says, "that sometimes I can close my eyes and go there." There is only one small problem: Our friend was completely blind until age 7, and her father died when she was 4.

Chances are that if you ask someone in your own family to compare notes on a shared early memory—or even one that's not so early—you will find discrepancies, meaning that at least one of you is wrong. All of us remember things that never happened and forget things that did take place. Even recent memories can evaporate like the morning dew. We watch the evening news, and half an hour later can't relate the lead story. We enjoy a meal, and quickly forget what we ate. We study our heads off for an exam, only to find to our dismay that the information isn't all there when we need it. Where on earth did it go?

Yet memory is also a marvel of the human mind. Who fought whom in World War II? When are presidential elections held? What is the tune of your national anthem? How do you use an automated teller machine? What's the most embarrassing thing that ever happened to you? You can probably answer most of these questions—and *hundreds of thousands* of others—without hesitation. Our brains are crammed with facts, descriptions, and skills, and a good thing, too. **Memory,** the capacity to retain and retrieve information, confers competence; without it we would be as helpless as infants, unable to negotiate even the most trivial of our daily tasks, from brushing our teeth to turning on the television set. It also confers a sense of personal identity; we are each the sum total of our personal recollections, which is why we feel so threatened when people tell us our memories are wrong. Individuals and cultures alike rely on a remembered history for a sense of coherence and meaning. Memory preserves the past and guides the future.

People usually refer to memory as if it were a single ability or faculty, as in, "I must be losing my memory" or "He has a memory like an elephant's." Actually, however, the term *memory* covers a complex collection of abilities, processes, and mental systems. In this chapter, we will see how these abilities, processes, and systems allow us to remember, and why, despite our best efforts, we so often forget.

■ **memory**
The capacity to retain and retrieve information; also refers to the mental structure or structures that account for this capacity, and to the material that is retained.

239

Rudolph the
Red-Nosed Reindeer
had eight reindeer
friends. Name as many
of them as you can.

FIGURE 7.1

Who were Rudolph's friends?
This is a test of recall. After you have done your best to remember all eight names, turn to page 242 for a recognition test on the same information.

■ **recognition**
The ability to identify previously encountered material.

■ **recall**
The ability to retrieve and reproduce from memory previously encountered material.

■ **explicit memory**
Conscious, intentional recollection of an event or item of information.

■ **implicit memory**
Unconscious retention in memory, as evidenced by the effect of a previous experience or previously encountered information on current thoughts or actions.

■ **TAKING MEMORY'S MEASURE**

To understand how memory works, you must know a little about how psychologists measure it. The ability to remember is not an all-or-nothing phenomenon; it depends on the type of performance required. Students who express a preference for multiple-choice, essay, or true-false exams already know this.

One common type of memory test measures **recognition,** the ability to identify information you previously observed, read, or heard about. The information is given to you, and all you have to do is say whether it is old or new, or perhaps correct or incorrect, or pick it out of a set of alternatives. Your job, in other words, is to match a current stimulus with what you have stored in memory. In the classroom, true-false and multiple-choice tests ask for recognition. In contrast, tests of **recall** measure the ability to retrieve from memory information that is not currently present. Essay and fill-in-the-blank exams and memory games such as Trivial Pursuit require recall.

As all students know, recognition tests can be quite difficult (some might say "tricky"), especially when false items closely resemble correct ones. Under most circumstances, however, recall is the greater challenge (see Figure 7.1). This difference was once demonstrated in a study of people's memories of their high school classmates (Bahrick, Bahrick, & Wittlinger, 1975). The subjects, aged 17 to 74, first wrote down the names of as many classmates as they could remember. Recall was poor; most recent graduates could write only a few dozen names, and those out of school for 40 years or more recalled an average of only 19. Even when prompted with yearbook pictures, the youngest subjects failed to name almost 30 percent of their classmates and the oldest ones failed to name over 80 percent. Recognition, however, was far better. The task was to look at ten cards, each containing five photographs, and say which picture on each card was that of a former classmate. Recent graduates were right 90 percent of the time. More important, so were people who had graduated 35 years earlier. Even those out of high school for *over 40 years* could identify three-fourths of their classmates, and the ability to recognize names was nearly as impressive.

The kind of memory measured by recognition and recall tests is often called **explicit memory,** because it involves conscious recollection of an event or item of information. However, information can also be retained even when there is no conscious remembering. Such unconscious or **implicit memory** may affect our current thoughts or actions, even though we are no longer consciously aware of the original information or event (Graf & Schacter, 1985; Schacter, 1987). To get at this subtle sort of knowledge, researchers use indirect methods.

One indirect memory test, the *relearning method* (or *savings method*), was devised by Hermann Ebbinghaus over a century ago. It requires you to relearn information or a task that you learned earlier. Even if you cannot recall or recognize the material, if you learn it more quickly the second time around you must be remembering something from the first experience, whether you realize it or not. Another commonly used method, *word-stem completion*, asks you to read or otherwise process a list of words, then later try to complete word stems (such as DEF) with the first word that comes to mind (such as *define* or *defend*). Even when recognition or recall for the original list is poor, people who were exposed to the list are more likely than control subjects to complete the word fragments with words from the list. The fact that the original words "prime" certain responses on the word completion task shows that people can retain more implicit knowledge about the past than they realize (Richardson-Klavehn & Bjork, 1988; Roediger, 1990).

Researchers have often shown great ingenuity in uncovering evidence of implicit memory. In Chapter 5 we described two studies that used surgical patients as subjects (Bennett, Davis, & Giannini, 1985; Kihlstrom et al., 1990). These patients were exposed to suggestions or lists of word pairs while they were "under" anesthesia. After surgery they could not consciously remember the suggestions or words. However, they were more likely than control subjects to follow the suggestions or repeat words from the lists on a test of "priming," showing that some implicit memory for the stimuli remained (and also that the material might have been nonconsciously perceived in the first place).

In another study, two patients with brain damage were unable to recognize familiar faces. When they were shown photographs of both familiar and unfamiliar people, they reported no conscious recognition of the pictures. But electrical conductance of the skin (a measure of autonomic nervous system arousal) changed while they were looking at the familiar faces, indicating that some sort of primitive, nonconscious recognition must, in fact, have been taking place (Tranel & Damasio, 1985).

■ THE INFORMATION-PROCESSING APPROACH TO MEMORY

Besides good methods, researchers need a general framework or approach for planning studies and interpreting the results.

In the past, philosophers compared memory to a tablet of hot wax that would preserve anything that chanced to make an imprint on it. Today many people think of memory as a mental tape recorder, automatically recording, in both audio and video, every moment of their lives. However, both of these metaphors are misleading. Not everything that happens to us or impinges on our senses is tucked away for later use. If it were, our minds would be cluttered with all sorts of mental "junk"—the temperature at noon Thursday, the price of hamburger two years ago, a phone number needed only once. Memory must be selective.

Most cognitive models of memory view the human mind not as a wax tablet or a tape recorder but as an information processor, analogous in some ways to a computer, only far more complex. These information-processing models borrow liberally from the language of computer programming: Instead of stimuli, there are "inputs"; instead of responses, there are "outputs"; and between the inputs and outputs, information is actively processed in a series of "subroutines." Though the mind of a machine differs in many ways from that of a human being (see Chapter 8), information-processing approaches have proven useful. They capture an essential fact: *that the brain does not passively record information but actively alters and organizes it.*

Encoding, Storage, and Retrieval

According to information-processing theories, remembering begins with **encoding,** the conversion of information to a form that the brain can process and store. Our memories are not an exact replica of experience. Sensory information is changed in form almost as soon as it is detected (see Chapter 5), and the form retained for the long run is much different from the original stimulus. For example, when you hear a lecture, you may hang on every word, but you do not store those words verbatim. Instead, you convert sentences to units of meaning, possibly in the form of *propositions* (Anderson & Bower, 1973). Propositions are similar to sentences, but they express unitary ideas and are made up of abstract concepts rather than words. Thus the sentence "The clever psychologist made an amazing discovery" contains three propositions that can be expressed by the words *the psychologist was clever, the psychologist made a discovery,* and *the discovery was amazing.* A man who emigrated from Germany at a young age and forgot all his German would still remember facts learned in the first grade because such information is stored as propositions, not as strings of German (or English) words.

Most psychologists believe that information can also be stored in the form of auditory or visual images—melodies, sounds, "pictures in the mind's eye."

■ **encoding** *(in memory)*
The conversion of information into a form that can be stored and retrieved.

Rudolph the Red-Nosed Reindeer had eight reindeer friends. From the following list, see if you can identify their correct names:

Blitzen
Cupid
Kumquat
Bouncer
Dander
Dasher
Donder
Blintzes
Dancer
Prancer
Flasher
Trixie
Masher
Comet
Pixie
Vixen

If you took the recall test in Figure 7.1 (page 240), now try this recognition item. Which test was easier?

■ **storage** *(in memory)*
The maintenance of material over time.
■ **retrieval**
The recovery of material stored in memory.

Visual images are often particularly memorable. In one study of visual memory, Roger Shepard (1967) had students view 612 colored pictures on slides. Then the pictures were paired with new ones, and the students had to select the ones they had previously seen. Immediately after the original presentation, recognition was 96.7 percent, and four months later it was still better than 50 percent. Subsequent research showed that even if the original set of slides contained 2,560 different photographs, recognition remained high (Haber, 1970).

Other forms of encoding may also be possible. For example, memories for specific motor skills, such as those involved in swimming or riding a bicycle, may be encoded and stored as sets of kinesthetic (muscular) instructions. Memories for motor skills are extremely long-lasting. If you learned to swim as a child, you will still know how to swim at age 30, even if you haven't been in a pool or lake for years.

With certain kinds of information, encoding takes place automatically; you don't have to make a deliberate effort. Think about your bedroom. When were you last there? What color are the walls? Where is the bed located? You can probably provide this information easily, even though you never made an effort to encode it. In general, people automatically encode their location in space and time and the frequency with which they experience various situations (Hasher & Zacks, 1984). But other kinds of information require *effortful* encoding. To retain such information, you might have to label it, associate it with other material, or rehearse it until it is familiar. A friend of ours tells us that in her ballet class, she knows exactly what to do when asked to perform a *pas de bourrée*, yet she often has trouble recalling the term itself. Because she rarely uses it, she probably has not bothered to encode it well.

Unfortunately, people sometimes count on automatic encoding when effortful encoding is needed. For example, students may assume they can encode the material in a textbook as effortlessly as they encode the color of their bedrooms, and then they wind up in trouble at test time.

Once encoding takes place, the next steps are **storage,** the maintenance of the material over time, and **retrieval,** the recovery of stored material, or what a computer programmer might call the "accessing" of information. When memory works well, encoding leads to storage and storage permits retrieval. Sometimes, however, information is temporarily encoded but is not retained for the long run. As we will see, even when information does get stored, a person may have trouble "finding" it in memory.

QUICK QUIZ

How well do you remember what you just learned?

1. Years ago, Gloria learned to play poker, but she played only a few times, and eventually she forgot all the rules. Then a friend offered to teach her to play again, and in only two sessions Gloria relearned everything she had forgotten. Gloria had retained some _____ memory for the rules of poker.

2. The three basic memory processes are _____, storage, and _____.

3. Do the preceding two questions ask for recall, recognition, or relearning? (And what about *this* question?)

ANSWERS:

1. implicit 2. encoding, retrieval 3. The first two questions both measure recall. The third question measures recognition: The options are given and you simply have to recognize the correct one.

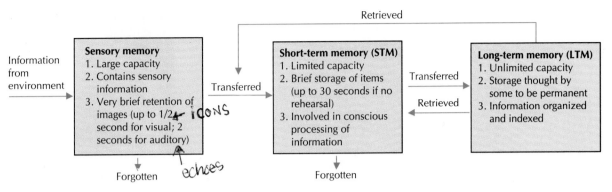

FIGURE 7.2

Three memory systems

Most memory models distinguish three separate but interacting memory systems, as shown in this diagram (although some models would draw the arrows a bit differently). When information does not transfer from sensory memory to short-term memory, or from short-term memory to long-term memory, it is assumed to be forgotten. Once in long-term memory, information can be retrieved for use in analyzing incoming sensory information or for temporary mental operations performed in short-term memory.

Three Systems of Memory

After information is encoded, what happens to it? Most people think of memory as a single "place" or system. But in many information-processing models, memory consists of three separate, interacting systems. The first is **sensory memory**, which retains incoming sensory information for at most a second or two, until it can be processed further. The second is **short-term memory (STM)**, which holds a limited amount of information for a brief period of time, perhaps up to 30 seconds or so, unless a conscious effort is made to keep it there longer. The third system is **long-term memory (LTM)**, which accounts for the more or less permanent storage of information.

According to one leading model of memory, first proposed by Richard Atkinson and Richard Shiffrin (1971), information can pass from sensory memory to short-term memory and in either direction between short-term and long-term memory (see Figure 7.2). To encode this model, which is sometimes informally called the "three box model," in your own memory, you might think of "memory" as a library building that contains an entry area, a work area, and the stacks. A new piece of information passes through the entry area to the work area, where a decision is made about whether it should remain in the permanent collection. If the answer is yes, the information is stored in the stacks. From there, it can be called up for temporary use in the work area. This analogy does not imply, however, that there are actually three separate places in the brain corresponding to the three memory storehouses. Talking about memory systems as places is merely a convenience. The three systems are actually clusters of mental processes that occur at different stages.

The "three-box" model has dominated research on memory for nearly three decades. However, it does not explain all the findings, and in recent years many other models have been proposed. Advocates of these models disagree on how information passes from one kind of memory system to another and how information gets encoded and stored in each system. Some question the very notion of distinct memory systems. They argue that there is just one system, with different mental processes called on for different tasks. Details about competing models of memory are beyond the scope of this book, and until the dust settles, we cannot say which one is best. In this chapter we have decided to retain the notion of separate systems—sensory, short-term, and long-term—because it offers a convenient way to organize the major findings on memory and it also fits certain biological facts about memory to be described later.

■ **sensory memory**
A memory system that momentarily preserves extremely accurate images of sensory information.

■ **short-term memory (STM)**
A limited capacity memory system involved in the retention of information for brief periods. It is used to store recently perceived information and information retrieved from long-term memory for temporary use.

■ **long-term memory (LTM)**
The memory system involved in the long-term retention of information; theoretically, it has an unlimited capacity.

If you swing a flashlight rapidly in a circle, you see an unbroken circle of light instead of a series of separate points, because the successive images remain briefly in sensory memory.

■ FLEETING IMPRESSIONS: SENSORY MEMORY

In standard information-processing models of memory, all incoming sensory information must make a brief stop in *sensory memory*, the entry area of memory. Sensory memory includes a number of separate memory subsystems, or **sensory registers**—as many as there are senses. Information in sensory memory is short-lived. Visual images, or *icons*, remain for a maximum of half a second in a visual register. Auditory images, or *echoes*, remain for a slightly longer time, by most estimates up to two seconds or so, in an auditory register.

Sensory memory acts as a sort of holding bin, retaining information just until we can select items for attention from the stream of stimuli bombarding our senses. In most models of memory, *pattern recognition*, the preliminary identification of a stimulus on the basis of information already contained in long-term memory, occurs during the transfer of information from sensory memory to short-term memory. Information that does not go on to short-term memory vanishes forever, like a message written in disappearing ink.

Images in sensory memory are fairly complete. How do we know that? In a clever experiment, George Sperling (1960) briefly presented people with visual arrays of letters similar to this one:

$$X \quad K \quad C \quad Q$$
$$N \quad D \quad X \quad G$$
$$T \quad F \quad R \quad J$$

In previous studies, subjects had been able to recall only four or five letters, no matter how many were initially shown. Yet many people insisted that they had actually seen more items. Some of the letters, they said, seemed to slip away before they could be reported. To overcome this problem, Sperling devised a method of "partial report." He had people report the first row of letters when they heard a high tone, the middle row when they heard a medium tone, and the third row when they heard a low tone:

$$X \quad K \quad C \quad Q \quad \leftarrow \quad \text{High tone}$$
$$N \quad D \quad X \quad G \quad \leftarrow \quad \text{Medium tone}$$
$$T \quad F \quad R \quad J \quad \leftarrow \quad \text{Low tone}$$

■ **sensory registers**
Subsystems of sensory memory. Most memory models assume a separate register for each sensory modality.

If the tone occurred right after presentation of the array, people could recall about three letters from a row. Since they did not know beforehand which row they would have to report, they therefore must have had most of the letters in sensory memory. However, if the tone occurred after a delay of even one second, people remembered very little of what they had seen. The letters had slipped away.

We have often wondered if the visual sensory register could be involved in a poorly understood (and still controversial) phenomenon called **eidetic imagery.** A person with eidetic imagery, usually a child, can reportedly look at a picture for several seconds, look away, and then "see" a literal image of the picture projected on the wall or on a blank sheet of paper. The image is experienced as "out there" rather than in "the mind's eye." Like images in sensory memory, eidetic images are accurate, but they last considerably longer, for at least half a minute and often for several minutes. While they remain, the person seems able to "read" information from them just as from a real picture. Eidetic images arise spontaneously. In fact, any attempt by the "eidetiker" to memorize a picture by naming or labeling the items in it seems to prevent formation of the image. Perhaps the eidetic image is actually an image from the visual sensory register that for some reason has stayed around longer than usual.

Eidetic imagery seems to occur in about 8 children out of 100 (Haber, 1974). It usually disappears by adolescence, perhaps because by then language is the dominant way of processing new information. Since eidetic images usually cannot be reinstated once they disappear, eidetikers cannot recall events or memorize material better than anyone else. In fact, in daily life eidetic images are a potential nuisance. Imagine what would happen if you had eidetic images that kept popping back into view or that lasted a long time. You might turn a page of music only to see a previous page's notes superimposed on the new ones! To avoid such confusion, eidetikers prevent images from forming by changing their gaze frequently, and forcefully blink in order to "erase" images.

In normal processing, too, sensory memory needs to clear quickly to prevent sensory "double exposures." It also acts as a filter, keeping out extraneous and unimportant information. Our brains store trillions of bits of information during our lifetimes. Processing everything detected by our senses, including irrelevancies, would lead to inefficiency and frustration.

If the sensory register did not clear quickly, multiple images might interfere with the accurate perception and encoding of information.

■ MEMORY'S WORK AREA: SHORT-TERM MEMORY

Like sensory memory, *short-term memory (STM)* retains information only temporarily—for up to about 30 seconds by most estimates, although some think the maximum interval may extend to a few minutes. In short-term memory, the material is no longer an exact sensory image but an encoding of one, such as a word or a number. In the "three-box" model, this material either transfers into long-term memory or decays and is lost forever. (There are, however, ways to keep material in short-term memory beyond the usual limits, as we will see.)

Certain cases of brain injury demonstrate the importance of transferring new information from short-term memory into long-term memory. You may recall the tragic case of H. M., which we described in Chapter 3 (page 94). Ever since much of H. M.'s hippocampus was surgically removed in 1953, he has suffered from **anterograde amnesia,** the inability to form long-term memories for new events and facts (Corkin, 1984; Milner, Corkin, & Teuber, 1968; Ogden & Corkin, 1991). H. M. does store information on a short-term basis; he can hold a conversation and appears normal when you first meet him. As we will see later, he also retains some implicit memory. However, for the most part H. M. cannot retain information about new facts and events for longer than a few minutes. Therefore he cannot learn new words, songs, stories, or faces. According to Suzanne Corkin, who has studied H. M. extensively, H. M. does have some "islands of remembering." For example, he sometimes recalls that both his parents are dead, and he knows that he has memory problems and that

■ **eidetic [eye-DET-ik] imagery**
An image of a visual stimulus that appears to exist in the external environment instead of in "the mind's eye" and that can be "read" for information.

■ **anterograde amnesia**
Loss of the ability to form long-term memories for new facts and events.

the operation done on him has never been done since. But these "islands" are the exceptions in a vast sea of forgetfulness. H. M. cannot recognize anyone he has met since 1953, including the people who have studied him for decades. Although he is now in his 60s, he does not know how old he is and usually guesses his age as much younger. He can read the same magazine over and over without realizing that he has read it before. He can learn some new motor and perceptual skills, but he cannot recall learning them. Today, this gentle, good-natured man can no longer recognize a photograph of his own face; he is stuck in a time warp from the past. Most psychologists attribute H. M.'s terrible memory deficits to a problem in transferring explicit memories from short-term storage into long-term storage—although it is also possible that his problem is in maintaining information in long-term storage once it gets there. (Put H. M. in your long-term memory, as we will be seeing him again in this chapter.)

Besides retaining new information for brief periods, short-term memory also holds information that has been retrieved from long-term memory for temporary use. For this reason, short-term memory is often called *working* memory. When you do an arithmetic problem, working memory contains the numbers and the instructions for doing the necessary operations ("add the right-hand column, carry the 2"), plus the intermediate results from each step. The ability to bring information from long-term memory into working memory is *not* disrupted in patients like H. M. They can do arithmetic, converse, relate events that occurred before their injury, and do anything else that requires retrieval of information from long-term into short-term memory.

Chunks of Experience

We all know what it is like to look up a telephone number, dial it, get a busy signal, and then find after a moment that we have forgotten it. The number has vanished from short-term memory. The same thing happens when you are introduced to someone and two minutes later find yourself groping unsuccessfully for her name. Is it any wonder that short-term memory has been called a "leaky bucket"?

According to most memory models, if the bucket did not leak it would quickly overflow, because at any given moment short-term memory can hold only a few items. Years ago, George Miller estimated its capacity to be "the magical number 7 plus or minus 2" (G. A. Miller, 1956). (Five-number zip codes and seven-number telephone numbers fall conveniently in this range.) More recently, others have questioned whether Miller's magical number is so magical after all. Estimates of STM's capacity have ranged from 2 items to 20, with most of the estimates at the lower end. Some theorists believe it is not STM per se that is limited, but the processing capacity available to the entire memory system at any one time. Everyone agrees, however, that the number of items that short-term memory can handle at any one time is quite small.

If this is so, then how do we remember the beginning of a spoken sentence until the speaker reaches the end? After all, most sentences are longer than just a few words. According to most models of memory, we overcome this problem by grouping small bits of information into larger units, or **chunks.** The real capacity of STM, then, is not a few bits of information but a few chunks. A chunk may be a word, a phrase, a sentence, or even a visual image, and it depends on previous experience. For most of us, the acronym *FBI* is one chunk, not three, and the date *1492* is one chunk, not four. In contrast, the number *9214* is four chunks and *IBF* is three—unless your address is 9214 or your initials are IBF. To take another, more visual example: If you are not familiar with football and look at a field full of players, you probably won't be able to remember their positions when you look away. But if you are a fan of the game, you may see a single chunk of information—say, a wishbone formation—and be able to retain it for some time.

■ **chunk**
A meaningful unit of information; may be comprised of smaller units.

ing over (rehearsing) the concept, you might encode the information that a re-inforcer follows a response, strengthens the response, and is similar to a reward. You might also note that the word *reinforcer* starts with the same letter as *reward*. And you might think up some examples of reinforcement and of how you have used it in your own life and could use it in the future. The more you elaborate the concept of reinforcement, the better you will remember it.

A related strategy for prolonging retention is **deep processing,** or the processing of meaning. If you simply process the physical or sensory features of a stimulus, such as how the word *reinforcement* is spelled and how it sounds, your processing will be *shallow* even if it is elaborate. If you recognize patterns and assign labels to objects or events ("Reinforcement is an operant procedure"), your processing will be somewhat deeper. If you fully analyze the meaning of what you are trying to remember (semantic encoding), your processing will be deeper yet. Deep processing is often more effective than shallow processing for remembering information, but not always. For example, if you are trying to memorize a poem, you will want to pay attention to (and elaborately encode) the sounds of the words and the patterns of rhythm in the poem, and not just the poem's meaning.

The Serial Position Curve

The occurrence of rehearsal in short-term memory has often been invoked to explain a phenomenon called the **serial position effect.** When a person is asked to recall a list of items (for example, words) immediately after the list is presented, the retention of any particular item depends on its position in the list (Glanzer & Cunitz, 1966). Recall is best for items at the beginning of the list (the **primacy effect**) and at the end of the list (the **recency effect**). When retention of all the items is plotted, the result is a U-shaped curve (see Figure 7.5). In daily life, a serial position effect occurs when you are introduced to a roomful of people and find you recall the names of the first few people and the last few the best.

According to the "three-box" model, the first few items on a list are remembered well because they were well rehearsed. Since short-term memory was relatively "empty" when they entered, there was little competition among these items for rehearsal time, and so they made it into long-term memory. The last few items are remembered well for a different reason: At the time of recall, they are still sitting in short-term memory and can simply be "dumped." (If there is a 30-second delay after presentation of the list and people are prevented from rehearsing, the recency effect usually disappears, presumably because the items in STM have decayed.) The items in the middle of a list, however, are not so well retained because by the time they get into short-term memory it is

■ **deep processing**
In the encoding of information, the processing of meaning rather than simply the physical or sensory features of a stimulus.
■ **serial position effect**
The tendency for recall of the first and last items on a list to surpass recall of items in the middle of the list.
■ **primacy effect**
The tendency for items at the beginning of a list to be well recalled.
■ **recency effect**
The tendency for items at the end of a list to be well recalled.

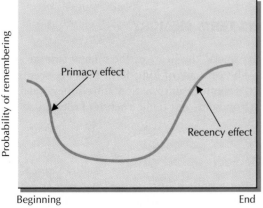

FIGURE 7.5

The serial position effect
When people try to recall a list of similar items immediately after learning it, they tend to remember the first and last items on the list best and the ones in the middle worst. This effect occurs with all sorts of materials.

already "crowded"; as a result, many of these items don't get much rehearsal, and they drop out of short-term memory before they can be stored in long-term memory.

This explanation seems to make sense—except for two things. First, under certain conditions, the last items on a list are well remembered even when the test is delayed past the time when short-term memory has presumably been "emptied" and filled with other information (Greene, 1986). In other words, the recency effect occurs even when, according to the "three-box" model, it shouldn't. Second, serial position curves occur in rats when they have to remember a series of places in a maze (Kesner et al., 1984), and obviously, rats don't verbally rehearse. Clearly, some process besides verbal rehearsal and short-term memory "dumping" must be going on to produce the primacy and recency effects, but researchers are not yet sure what it is.

QUICK QUIZ

Find out if the findings discussed so far have transferred from your short-term memory to your long-term memory.

1. Horace repeats his grocery list over and over to himself as he walks down the supermarket aisle. What strategy is he using to keep the items in short-term memory?
2. For most people, the abbreviation *U.S.A.* consists of _____ informational "chunk(s)."
3. _____ memory holds images for a fraction of a second.
4. If a child is trying to memorize the alphabet, which sequence should present the greatest difficulty: *abcdefg, klmnopq,* or *tuvwxyz?* Why?
5. Camille is furious with her history professor. "I read the chapter three times, but I still failed the quiz," she fumes. "The quiz must have been unfair." What's wrong with Camille's reasoning, and what are some other possible explanations for her poor performance?

ANSWERS:

1. maintenance rehearsal 2. one 3. sensory 4. *klmnopq,* because of the serial position effect 5. Camille is reasoning emotionally and is not examining the assumptions underlying her explanations. Perhaps Camille relied on automatic rather than effortful encoding, used maintenance instead of elaborative rehearsal, and used shallow instead of deep processing when she studied. She may also have tried to encode everything, instead of encoding selectively.

■ FINAL DESTINATION: LONG-TERM MEMORY

Just as the heart of a library is the stacks, the heart of the mental storage system is *long-term memory (LTM)*. The capacity of long-term memory seems to have no practical limits. The vast amount of information stored there enables us to learn, get around in the environment, and build a sense of identity and a personal history.

Organization in Long-term Memory

Because long-term memory contains so much information, we cannot search through it exhaustively, as we can through short-term memory. The information must be organized and "indexed," just as items in a library are. Research on organization in long-term memory has tended to focus on words and other verbal material.

One way to index words (or the concepts they represent) is by the semantic categories to which they belong. *Chair*, for example, belongs to the category *furniture*. In a well-known study, people had to memorize 60 words that came from four semantic categories: animals, vegetables, names, and professions. The words were presented in random order, but when people were allowed to recall them in any order they wished, they tended to recall them in clusters corresponding to the four categories (Bousfield, 1953). This finding has since been replicated many times.

Evidence on the storage of information by semantic category also comes from a case study of a stroke victim called M. D. (Hart, Berndt, & Caramazza, 1985). Two years after suffering several strokes, M. D. appeared to have made a complete recovery, with one very odd exception: He had trouble remembering the names of fruits and vegetables. M. D. could easily name a picture of an abacus or a sphinx but not a picture of an orange or a peach. He could sort pictures of animals, vehicles, and food products into their appropriate categories, but did poorly with pictures of fruits and vegetables. On the other hand, when M. D. was *given* the names of fruits and vegetables, he immediately pointed to the corresponding pictures. Apparently, he still had a store of information about fruits and vegetables, but his brain lesion prevented him from using their names to get to the information when he needed it, unless the names were provided by someone else. Although this evidence comes from only one patient, it supports the idea that information about a particular concept (such as *peach*) is linked in some way to information about the concept's semantic category (such as *fruit*).

Many models of long-term memory represent its contents as a vast *network* or grid of interrelated concepts (Anderson, 1983; Collins & Loftus, 1975). Such models assume that semantic networks are a fundamental human way of organizing information. The way we use this network, however, depends on experience and education. For example, cross-cultural studies of rural children in Liberia and Guatemala have shown that the more schooling children have, the more likely they are to use semantic categories in recalling lists of objects (Cole & Cole, 1989). This makes sense, because in school, children must memorize a lot of information in a short time, and semantic grouping can help. Unschooled children, having less need to memorize lists, do not cluster items and do not remember them as well. But this does not mean that unschooled children have poor memories. When the task is a meaningful one for them—say, recalling objects that were part of a story or a village scene—they remember the objects extremely well (Cole & Cole, 1989; Rogoff & Waddell, 1982).

We organize information in long-term memory not only by semantic groupings but also in terms of the way words sound or look. Have you ever tried to recall some word that was on the "tip of your tongue"? In daily life, nearly everyone experiences such **tip-of-the-tongue states,** especially when trying to recall the names of acquaintances or famous persons, the names of objects or places, or the titles of movies, television programs, or books (Burke et al., 1991). Researchers study this phenomenon by having people record tip-of-the-tongue experiences in daily diaries. They are also able to reproduce this frustrating experience in the laboratory by presenting people with definitions of uncommon words and asking them to supply the words. When a word is on the tip of the tongue, people often come up with words that are similar in meaning to the right word before they finally recall it. In addition, the incorrect guesses often have the correct number of syllables, the correct stress pattern, the correct first letter, or the correct prefix or suffix (A. Brown, 1991; Brown & McNeill, 1966). Thus verbal information in long-term memory seems to be "indexed" by sound and form, and is retrievable on that basis.

Although there are certain basic ways of organizing long-term memories, culture affects how we encode, store, and retrieve information. Navaho healers, who use stylized, symbolic sand paintings in their rituals, must be able to commit to memory dozens of intricate visual designs. No permanent, exact copies are made, and after each ceremony the painting is destroyed.

■ **tip-of-the-tongue state**
The subjective certainty that information is available in long-term memory even though one is having difficulty retrieving it.

What Is Stored in Long-term Memory?

Researchers are currently studying other ways in which we organize information in long-term memory, such as by its familiarity, personal relevance, or association with other information. The method used in any given instance probably depends on the nature of the memory. For example, information you have stored about the major cities of Europe is probably organized differently from information about your first date.

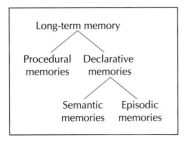

To understand the organization of long-term memory, then, we need to understand what kinds of information can be stored there (see Figure 7.6). Most theories distinguish skills or habits ("knowing how") from abstract or representational knowledge ("knowing that"). **Procedural memories** are memories of knowing how—for example, knowing how to comb your hair, use a pencil, or swim. **Declarative memories** are memories of "knowing that." Declarative memories, in turn, come in two varieties (Tulving, 1985). **Semantic memories** are internal representations of the world, independent of any particular context. They include facts, rules, and concepts. On the basis of your semantic memory of the concept *cat*, you can describe a cat as a small, furry mammal that typically spends its time eating, sleeping, and staring into space, even though a cat may not be present when you give this description and you probably won't know how or when you learned it. **Episodic memories,** on the other hand, are internal representations of personally experienced events. They allow you to "travel back" in time. When you remember how your furry feline once surprised you in the middle of the night by pouncing on your face as you slept, you are retrieving an episodic memory. As we will see later in the chapter, the distinction between procedural and declarative memories is supported by recent brain research.

FIGURE 7.6

Memories are made of this
According to a widely accepted way of classifying memories, long-term memory contains procedural memories *("knowing how") and* declarative memories *("knowing that"). Declarative memories, in turn, consist of* semantic memories *(general knowledge), and* episodic memories *(personal recollections). You might draw on procedural memories to ride a bike, semantic memories to identify a bird, and declarative memories to recall your graduation or wedding. Can you come up with some other examples for each type of memory?*

Reconstructing the Past

You have encoded some information, you have rehearsed it, and now it is stored away in long-term memory, properly organized and indexed. What happens next?

Despite our library analogy, recovering information from long-term memory is not like checking out a book from the library. It is more like checking out a few pages, then figuring out what the rest of the book must have said. As Frederic Bartlett found out back in 1932, when he asked people to read and later remember brief stories, retrieval is a *reconstructive* process. When we remember information, we typically add, delete, and change elements in ways that help us make sense of the material. Since Bartlett's time, dozens of memory studies have found this to be true for everything from stories to conversations. Often we cannot tell what we originally stored and what we have reconstructed. It all feels like one "memory."

A poignant story about H. M. illustrates the process of reconstruction at work (Ogden & Corkin, 1991). After eating a large chocolate Valentine's Day heart, H. M. stuck the shiny red wrapping in his shirt pocket. Two hours later, while searching for his handkerchief, he pulled out the paper and looked at it in puzzlement. When researcher Jenni Ogden asked why he had the paper in his pocket, he replied, "Well, it could have been wrapped around a big chocolate heart. It must be Valentine's Day!" Ogden could hardly contain her excitement about H. M.'s apparent recall of a recent episode. But a short time later, when she asked him to take out the paper again and say why he had it in his pocket, he replied, "Well, it might have been wrapped around a big chocolate rabbit. It must be Easter!"

Of course, H. M. *had* to reconstruct the past; his damaged brain could not recall it in any other way. But those of us with normal memory abilities also reconstruct, far more than we realize. Suppose someone asks you to describe a previous birthday. You may have some direct recollection of what took place, especially if it was emotionally significant. But you have also stored information gleaned from family stories, photographs, or home videos. You take all these bits and pieces and build one integrated account from them, and you may not be able to identify which information came from which source. (As we saw in Chapter 4, this sort of reconstruction also occurs when people are "age regressed" under hypnosis. The information they unwittingly add may or may not be an accurate reflection of what really happened.)

Not only do we reconstruct at the time of recall, but we alter information even as it is being stored. Most cognitive psychologists believe that whenever we are exposed to new information, we integrate it with what we already know or believe. That is, instead of simply filing separate items away, we incorporate the information into an existing web of knowledge, or **cognitive schema.** In everyday life, such schemas are useful because they help us make sense of separate pieces of information and thus remember them better. Many educators believe that one reason American students frequently find history difficult is that they are asked to memorize dates, facts, and events that seem to have no connection with one another. Having an overall concept of the story of American history, and of the major issues involved, makes it easier to remember any specific bit of information. Cognitive schemas can also lead to misremembering, however, if we distort or modify new information in order to make it "fit" our already existing beliefs. Sometimes, when information won't fit their schemas, people simply ignore it or forget it.

Although we can all produce some familiar facts without much reconstruction, literal recall is probably the exception, not the rule. In general, remembering is an *active* process that involves not only dredging up stored information but also putting two and two together to reconstruct the past. This process helps the mind work efficiently. We can store just the essentials of an experi-

■ **procedural memories**
Memories for the performance of particular actions and skills, or "knowing how."

■ **declarative memories**
Memories of facts, rules, concepts, and events, or "knowing that"; semantic and episodic memories.

■ **semantic memories**
Memories that reveal general knowledge, including facts, rules, concepts, and propositions.

■ **episodic memories**
Memories for personally experienced events and the contexts in which they occurred.

■ **cognitive schema**
An integrated network of knowledge, beliefs, and expectations concerning a particular topic.

The justice system depends on eyewitnesses to state "the facts and just the facts"—but are the facts always reconstructed accurately?

ence, then use our general knowledge to figure out the specifics when we need them. But sometimes the reconstructive nature of memory gets us into hot water.

The Eyewitness on Trial

Imagine that as you leave an office building, you see a man running in the direction of a blue Dodge. You glance away for a moment, and when you look back, you see that someone in the Dodge is pulling away from the curb. You are not paying any special attention to this chain of events. Why should you? But just then, a woman emerges from the building, points wildly at the receding car, and shouts, "Stop that man, he stole my purse!" Soon the police arrive and ask you to tell what you saw.

If we compare memory to a film, you have actually stored only some of the frames: a man running toward a car, the car pulling away. Asked now to recall, you are likely to fill in the frames that are missing, the ones that would presumably show the man climbing into the car. In other words, you *infer* (deduce) what must have happened. Now you have a complete "film" in your mental archives, but you may be unable to tell which parts were "shot" during the original event and which were added later. ("I saw a brown-haired man, about 5 feet 10 inches tall, with a mustache, and wearing a blue shirt, run over to the blue Dodge, get in, and drive away.") To make matters worse, the frames you stored at the time of the event were probably hazy or incomplete, so you have probably gone back and retouched them. What has happened is a little like the perceptual closure we discussed in Chapter 5, except that in this case the closure has occurred in memory.

Will any harm result from your reconstruction? That depends. Perhaps the man you saw really did drive off in the car. Then again, perhaps someone else was the purse snatcher, and the man you saw was someone else. Because memory is reconstructive, eyewitness testimony is not always reliable, even when the witness feels completely confident in the accuracy of his or her report.

Unfortunately, there is no easy solution to this problem. For example, it does little good to give a lie detector test to a witness who is unwittingly reconstructing an event. Not only is the reliability of lie detectors questionable (see Chapter 9), but also someone who reconstructs the past is not deliberately lying and should therefore pass the test. The consequences can be serious. Eyewitness testimony plays a vital role in our justice system; without it, many guilty people would go free. But convictions based on such testimony occasionally turn out to be tragic mistakes. Errors are especially likely to occur when the suspect's race differs from that of the witness (Brigham & Malpass, 1985; Luce, 1974). Perhaps negative racial attitudes or lack of familiarity prevent people

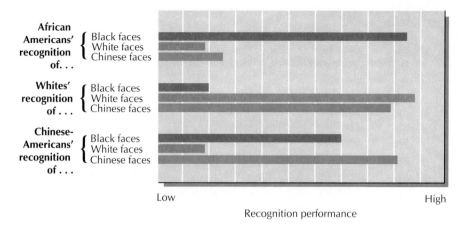

African Americans' recognition of. . .
{ Black faces
White faces
Chinese faces

Whites' recognition of . . .
{ Black faces
White faces
Chinese faces

Chinese-Americans' recognition of . . .
{ Black faces
White faces
Chinese faces

Low   Recognition performance   High

FIGURE 7.7

"They all look alike to me"
People are generally best at recognizing differences among faces in their own racial group. In one study, African Americans recognized different black faces much more easily than white or Chinese faces. White people could distinguish white and Chinese faces easily but not black ones. Chinese Americans could distinguish Chinese faces, but had some trouble with black faces and great difficulty with white ones (Luce, 1974).

from attending to the distinctive features of members of other races. Whatever the reason, every race seems to have this problem (see Figure 7.7).

To complicate matters, our reconstructions of past events are heavily influenced by the way questions about those events are put to us. In a study of leading questions, Elizabeth Loftus and John Palmer (1974) showed people short films depicting multicar traffic accidents. Afterward they asked some of the viewers, "About how fast were the cars going when they *hit* each other?" Other viewers were asked the same question, but with the verb changed to *smashed, collided, bumped,* or *contacted.* These words imply different speeds, with *smashed* implying the greatest speed and *contacted* the least. Sure enough, the estimates of how fast the cars were going varied, depending on which word was used. *Smashed* produced the highest average speed estimates (40.8 mph), followed by *collided* (39.3 mph), *bumped* (38.1 mph), *hit* (34.0 mph), and *contacted* (31.8 mph).

In a similar study (Loftus & Zanni, 1975), some people were asked, "Did you see a broken headlight?" and others were asked, "Did you see the broken headlight?" Two other pairs of questions also differed only in the use of *a* or *the.* Note that the question with *the* presupposes a broken headlight, and merely asks if the witness saw it. The question with *a* makes no such presupposition. The researchers found that people who received questions with *the* were far more likely to report having seen something that had not really appeared in the film than were those who received questions with *a.* If a tiny word like *the* can lead people to remember what they never saw, you can imagine how the leading questions of police detectives and courtroom lawyers might influence a witness's recall. What we remember, it seems, is not always what happened.

A witness viewing a police lineup relies on recognition memory, which is generally superior to recall. But lineups have a serious drawback. Sometimes witnesses compare the suspects and pick the one most like the criminal, even though all the suspects are actually innocent. Observing suspects one at a time, instead of in a group, reduces such false identifications without reducing correct identifications (Cutler & Penrod, 1988). The moral: The accuracy of memory depends on the methods used to invoke it.

QUICK QUIZ

See if you can reconstruct what you have just read in order to answer the following questions.

1. Suppose you must memorize a long list of words that includes the following: *desk, pig, gold, dog, chair, silver, table, rooster, bed, copper,* and *horse.* You can recall the words in any order you wish. How are you likely to group these words in recall? Why?

2. When you roller-skate, are you relying on procedural, semantic, or episodic memory? How about when you recall the months of the year, or when you remember falling off your roller skates on an icy January day?

3. Harvey tells Susan that he spilled cranberry juice on his rug, adding no other information. Later, when Susan retells the story, she says, "Harvey stained his rug." What does this tell you about retrieval from long-term memory?

4. In psychotherapy, hundreds of people, many of them diagnosed with a multiple personality disorder, have reported witnessing or taking part in bizarre satanic rituals involving animal and human torture and sacrifice. Yet law enforcement investigators have been unable to confirm any of these reports. Based on what you know about long-term memory, how might you explain such "memories"?

ANSWERS:

1. *Desk, chair, table,* and *bed* would probably form one cluster; *pig, dog, rooster,* and *horse* a second cluster; and *gold, silver,* and *copper* a third. Concepts tend to be organized in long-term memory in terms of the semantic categories they belong to, such as *furniture, animals,* and *metals.* 2. procedural; semantic; episodic 3. Retrieval from long-term memory is reconstructive. (Susan "remembers" the rug being stained, although Harvey didn't tell her it was.) 4. Memories of satanic ritual abuse, or at least many such memories, may be constructions that mix fantasy with fact. As psychiatrist George Ganaway (1991) notes, therapists who uncritically accept the widespread existence of satanic abuse cults may ask leading questions and make leading comments to their patients. Suggestible patients may then "remember" experiences that did not happen, "borrowing" ideas and descriptions from fictionalized accounts, or they may confuse ritual abuse with other forms of abuse that did happen. Networks of patients and therapists who subscribe to a belief in satanic ritual abuse may provide reinforcement and support for such false memories. (Do you see how similar mechanisms might explain "memories" of being abducted by aliens from outer space?)

■ MEMORY AND THE BRAIN

So far, we have been discussing memory solely in terms of information processing. Psychologists would also like to know what happens physiologically in the brain while all that processing is going on. More specifically, they would like the answers to three questions: (1) What changes occur in neurons and synapses (the small gaps between neurons) when we store information about an event or task? (2) Where in the brain do these changes occur? (3) How might hormones and other substances regulate or improve memory? In work on these issues, researchers draw on many of the concepts already covered in this chapter and in Chapter 3. (It might help you to encode the following information if you review Chapter 3.)

Changes in Neurons and Synapses

Nearly all scientists agree that memory involves chemical and structural changes at the level of neurons. But why do some memories last only a few seconds or minutes, whereas others persist for years or even a lifetime? Why, when a blow on the head or an electroconvulsive shock disrupts brain activity, do people often lose information stored during the past few minutes but not information stored weeks or years ago?

One answer is that *short-term memory and long-term memory involve different kinds of brain changes.* Short-term retention does not seem to involve permanent structural changes. Instead, temporary changes occur within neurons that alter their ability to release neurotransmitters, the chemicals that carry messages from one cell to another. Evidence comes from studies with the lowly sea snail, *Aplysia* (Kandel & Schwartz, 1982), and other organisms that have small numbers of easily identifiable neurons. These primitive animals can be taught simple conditioned responses. When retention is only for the short term, a neuron's readiness to release neurotransmitter molecules temporarily increases or decreases, depending on the kind of response being learned.

Long-term memory, on the other hand, seems to involve permanent structural changes in the brain. Thus, when rats learn new motor skills and retain them over time, their cerebellums show more dendritic growth and more synaptic connections than do those of rats who have merely exercised, or rats that have been inactive "couch potatoes" (Black et al., 1990).

To mimic what they think may happen during the formation of a long-term memory, researchers apply brief, high-frequency electrical stimulation to groups of neurons in the brains of animals. In various brain areas, especially the hippocampus, this stimulation leads to a long-lasting increase in the strength of synaptic responsiveness known as **long-term potentiation** (McNaughton & Morris, 1987; Teyler & DiScenna, 1987). In other words, certain synaptic pathways become more excitable. Long-term potentiation seems to occur because of a complicated sequence of chemical reactions in receiving neurons, including the synthesis of certain proteins (Lynch, 1986; Lynch & Baudry, 1984). One result is that the tiny spines (projections) that cover the dendrites of the receiving neuron change shape, becoming rounder. This change in turn causes decreased electrical resistance and an increase in the responsiveness of the receiving neuron to the transmitting neuron. It is a little like what would happen if you increased the diameter of a funnel's neck to permit more flow through the funnel.

Other, related, changes also occur in long-term potentiation (and presumably, the formation of long-term memories). For example, dendrites branch out, and certain types of synapses increase in number (Greenough, 1984). These changes all take time, which may explain why long-term memories remain vulnerable to disruption for a while after they are stored. It takes a period of **consolidation,** or stabilization, before a memory solidifies. This process appears to be a gradual rather than an all-or-nothing process. If an animal gets electroconvulsive shock within the first hour after learning a task, it will forget what it has learned, which indicates that little if any consolidation has occurred. If the shock is delivered several hours or a few days after learning, the memory will be unaffected, which implies that by then consolidation has taken place. But *repeated* sessions of shock will again disrupt the memory, showing that the process is not yet complete (Squire, 1987). Consolidation can continue in animals for weeks and in human beings for several years.

Keep in mind that the brain changes we have described are correlational. That is, they accompany the retention of learning, but no one can be absolutely certain that they actually reflect the storage of information. One way to find out might be to look at what happens in the brain after an animal's memory

■ **long-term potentiation**
A long-lasting increase in the strength of synaptic responsiveness, thought to be a biological mechanism of memory.

■ **consolidation**
The process by which a long-term memory becomes durable and stable.

for some task (say, running a maze) begins to dim (Squire, 1987). Do the physical changes disappear, too? Future research will tell.

Locating Memories

We have been describing changes in neurons, but which neurons are they? Most scientists believe that memory traces (the neural changes associated with specific memories) are confined to specific areas, or *localized*. However, some theorists argue that any given memory is *distributed* across large areas of the brain. These two views can be reconciled by recognizing that the typical "memory" is actually a complex cluster of information. When you recall meeting a man yesterday, you remember his greeting, his tone of voice, how he looked, and where he was. These different pieces of information may be processed separately and stored at different sites, with all these sites participating in the representation of the event as a whole. If this is so, then memories are both "localized" and "distributed" (Squire, 1986).

Recently, researchers have discovered that particular brain structures seem to be responsible for the formation of certain types of memories (see Figure 7.8). Generally speaking, the formation of procedural memories (skills and habits) involves different structures and pathways than does the formation of declarative memories (facts and episodes). Declarative memories, you will recall, are those you draw on when identifying a flower or recalling a vacation trip. The formation of declarative memories involves the hippocampus, the amygdala, and parts of the temporal lobe cortex. The hippocampus is especially important: Damage that is limited to this structure results in profound amnesia for facts and events (Press, Amaral, & Squire, 1989). Procedural memories—the kind you draw on to ride a bike, solve a jigsaw puzzle, or slam your foot on the brake—seem to involve various other brain areas. In work with rabbits, Richard Thompson (1983, 1986) has shown that one kind of procedural memory, a simple, classically conditioned response to an unpleasant stimulus, is associated with specific changes in the cerebellum, the roundish structure at the back of the brain. After Thompson conditioned rabbits to blink in response to a tone, he discovered predictable changes in electrical activity in particular parts of the cerebellum. If he removed or destroyed the affected brain tissue, the animals immediately forgot the response.

But be careful: In the case of declarative memories, at least, we are talking about brain circuits involved in the *formation* and perhaps the temporary stor-

FIGURE 7.8

Brain areas critical for memory
The regions shown are particularly important in the formation or storage of memories.

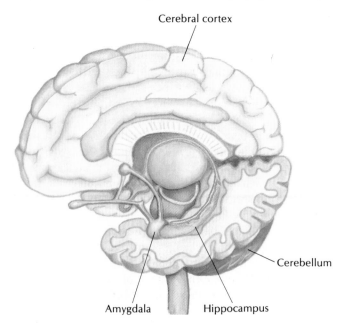

Cerebral cortex

Cerebellum

Amygdala

Hippocampus

age of memories, and *not* necessarily areas where the permanent changes required for long-term retention occur. Research with animals suggests that the ultimate destinations of declarative memories are not in the hippocampus or the amygdala, but rather in various parts of the cerebral cortex. More specifically, long-term storage may take place in the same cortical areas that were involved in the original perception of the information (Mishkin & Appenzeller, 1987).

The formation of declarative and procedural memories in different brain areas could explain a curious finding about H. M. Despite his inability to form new semantic and episodic memories, H. M. can, with sufficient practice, acquire new cognitive, perceptual, and motor *skills*, such as solving a puzzle, reading mirror-reversed words, or playing tennis—even though he does not remember the training sessions. Other patients with similar brain damage have shown the same pattern of memory loss, as have monkeys with lesions in the hippocampus and amygdala (Mishkin & Appenzeller, 1987). Apparently, the parts of the brain involved in procedural memory have remained intact.

Patients like H. M. not only retain procedural memories, but they also retain some implicit memory for verbal material. For example, if H. M. sees the word *define* on a list and later has to complete the stem "DEF" with the first word that comes to mind, he is likely to say *define* rather than some other word, just as people with normal memories do after seeing the list (Keane, Gabrieli, & Corkin, 1987). Some psychologists argue that such performance differences on explicit and implicit memory tasks occur because the tasks tend to involve different encoding or retrieval processes (Roediger, 1990). Others believe that there must be separate systems in the brain for different kinds of implicit and explicit tasks (Sherry & Schacter, 1987; Tulving & Schacter, 1990). As Figure 7.9 shows, this view was bolstered recently by PET scans from normal subjects, which revealed differences in the location of brain activity when the subjects performed explicit versus implicit memory tasks (Squire et al., 1992).

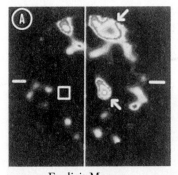
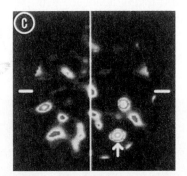

Explicit Memory   Implicit Memory

FIGURE 7.9

Brain activity in explicit and implicit memory

These PET scans show average changes in blood flow for several subjects as they performed different kinds of memory tasks (Squire et al., 1992). In scan "A," yellow and red represent increased blood flow, but the same colors represent decreased blood flow in scan "C." Scan A shows that when people recalled words from a list—a test of explicit memory—neural activity increased in the right part of the hippocampus (lower arrow) and the right prefrontal cortex (upper arrow). (The right hemisphere may have been more active than the left because the task emphasized the visual form of the words rather than their sound or meaning.) In contrast, scan C shows that when people read the list and later just said the first words that came to mind in response to word stems—a test of implicit memory—there was a far smaller increase in activity in the hippocampus. In addition, activity in the right part of the visual cortex decreased (see arrow), presumably because seeing the initial list reduced the visual processing necessary for the word stems. Taken together, these findings support the view that different areas of the brain are involved in explicit and implicit memory tasks.

Hormones and Memory

Have you ever smelled fresh cookies and recalled a tender scene from your childhood? Do you have a vivid memory of the first time you fell in love? In his classic novel *Remembrance of Things Past*, Marcel Proust evoked powerful emotional memories of tastes, sensations, and feelings. For the rest of us, too, emotional memories are often especially vivid and intense. The explanation may reside in our hormones.

Hormones appear to affect memory by regulating, or modulating, the storage of information. For example, various hormones released by the adrenal glands during stress, including epinephrine (adrenaline) and certain steroids, appear to enhance memory (McGaugh, 1990). They do so, however, only at low or moderate levels. If you administer epinephrine to animals right after learning, their memory improves, but if the dosages are too high, memory suffers. Assuming that these findings apply also to human beings, they imply that if you want to remember information well, you should aim for an arousal level somewhere between "hyper" and "laid back."

How can hormones affect the remembrance of things past? One idea is that epinephrine affects the release of norepinephrine in the amygdala, which in turn sends out messages to other brain areas involved in memory storage (McGaugh, 1990). Another possibility involves, of all things, sugar. Paul Gold (1987) notes that epinephrine causes the level of glucose (a sugar) to rise in the bloodstream. Although epinephrine does not seem to enter the brain from the bloodstream readily, glucose does. Once in the brain, glucose may enhance memory either directly or by altering the effects of various neurotransmitters. This "sweet memories" effect seems to occur both in aged rats and mice and in elderly human beings. In one fascinating study, healthy older people fasted overnight, drank a glass of lemonade sweetened with either glucose or saccharin, and then took two memory tests. The saccharine-laced drink had no effect on their performance, but drinking lemonade with glucose greatly boosted their ability to recall a taped passage 5 or 40 minutes after hearing it and their long-term ability to recall words from a list (Manning, Hall, & Gold, 1990).

Which of these students will remember best? Keep in mind that a moderate degree of emotional arousal enhances memory. One explanation may be biological: Retention seems to be best when hormones associated with arousal reach an optimal level.

The apparent ability of hormones to regulate memory fits well with the view of many scientists that moderate emotional arousal is an essential ingredient in learning and memory. Arousal may signal the brain that an event or piece of information is important enough to store. Or it may ensure that a person or animal will pay attention to what is happening so that encoding can take place. But the exact mechanisms remain unclear and controversial.

In this area, as in others in the biology of memory, we still have much to learn. Each new finding on the biology of memory nudges the neuroscientist's dream of describing behavior in physical terms a bit closer to reality, but biological findings can be as slippery as any others. Technical obstacles often make it difficult to get reliable results, and a finding with one animal or procedure may not apply to others. New discoveries about the brain's role in memory are being made at a tremendous rate, but many of these findings are provisional, and as yet there is no comprehensive biological model of memory. We do not yet know how the brain actually encodes information, how "distributed" circuits link up with one another, or how a student is able to locate and retrieve information at the drop of a multiple-choice item.

QUICK QUIZ

1. Speaking of multiple-choice items, is *long-term potentiation* associated with (a) increased responsiveness of a receiving neuron to a transmitting neuron, (b) a decrease in receptors on a receiving neuron, or (c) reaching your true potential?
2. The cerebellum has been associated with _____ memories, and the hippocampus and amygdala have been associated with _____ memories.
3. True or false: Hormone research suggests that if you want to remember well, you should be as relaxed as possible while learning.
✴ 4. After reading the findings on glucose and memory, should you immediately start gulping down lemonade? Why or why not?

ANSWERS:

1. a 2. procedural, declarative 3. false 4. You probably shouldn't pig out on sugar yet. Results from elderly people, using certain measures of memory on which older people tend to show deficits, will not necessarily generalize to younger people with normal memories (although they might). Also, in some people, frequent glucose consumption may have adverse health consequences.

■ FORGETTING OF THINGS PAST

Have you ever, in the middle of some experience, told yourself, "I'm never going to forget this; I'm going to remember every detail," only to find later that the experience has receded into the misty recesses of your mind? As we suggest in "Think About It" on page 262, not all forgetting is bad. Most of us, however, would like to remember better than we do.

As we have seen, sometimes "forgetfulness" simply means the material wasn't well encoded in the first place. You can't remember what you never really learned. But suppose you do encode the information as well as you can. You might still forget. Although we do not yet know what accounts neurologically or biochemically for forgetting, cognitive psychologists have proposed many theories about what happens mentally.

NEVER FORGETS

SOMETIMES FORGETS

ALWAYS FORGETS

The Benefits of Forgetting

Who has not wished, at some time or other, for a "photographic memory"? It's bad enough that we forget so much that we have worked diligently to learn in school. How can we formulate a realistic assessment of ourselves if our recollection of the past is both inaccurate and incomplete?

Yet a perfect memory is not the blessing that one might suppose. Soviet psychologist Alexander Luria (1968) once told of a journalist, S., who could remember giant grids of numbers and long lists of words after seeing them for only a few seconds. This man could reproduce these grids and lists both forward and backward, even after the passage of 15 years. He also remembered the circumstances under which he had originally learned the material.

S. used various memory "tricks" to accomplish his astonishing feats, many involving the formation of visual images. But you shouldn't envy him, for he had a serious problem: He could not forget. Images he had formed in order to remember kept creeping into consciousness, distracting him and interfering with his ability to concentrate. At times he even had trouble holding a simple conversation because the other person's words would set off a jumble of associations. In fact, Luria called him "rather dull-witted." Eventually, unable to work at his profession, S. took to supporting himself by traveling from place to place as a performer, demonstrating his abilities for audiences.

Perhaps you still think a perfect memory would be a terrific thing to have. Imagine, then, for a moment, what it would be like to remember *everything*. Each time you recalled the past, you would dredge up not only the diamonds of experience but the pebbles as well. Remembering might take hours instead of moments. The clutter in your mind might grow beyond your ability to organize it efficiently. With a perfect memory, you might also remember things better off forgotten. Would you really want to recall every angry argument, every embarrassing episode, every painful moment of your life? How would total recall affect your relationships with relatives and friends? Could it be that the success of a close relationship depends on a certain amount of forgiving forgetfulness? Could it be that self-confidence and optimism are only possible if we lock some grievances in a back drawer of memory, and stop ruminating on them?

Like remembering, a certain degree of forgetting contributes to our survival and our sanity. Where is the line between adaptive forgetting and disruptive forgetting? If you had the choice, what would you recollect with greater clarity, and what would you allow to fade? Think about it.

Decay

One "commonsense" view of forgetting, the **decay theory**, holds that memory traces simply fade with time if they are not "called up" now and then. Earlier we saw that decay occurs in sensory memory, and it seems to occur in short-term memory as well if we don't rehearse the material.

However, the mere passage of time does not seem to account so well for forgetting in long-term memory. We have all had the experience of forgetting something that happened only yesterday while remembering an event from many years ago. Indeed, some knowledge is still accessible decades after learning. In one study, people who had taken Spanish in high school or college were able to do well on Spanish tests up to 50 years later, although most had hardly used Spanish at all in the intervening years (Bahrick, 1984). Most forgetting occurred in the first few years after learning. This period was followed by a quarter century of stability and then, again, a decline (although scores were still impressive). The better that people had done in their original courses and the more courses they had taken, the better they did years later. Recent research finds that people can also remember their high school algebra for many decades, even if they haven't used it, *if* they had a chance to reuse and review their algebra in a college calculus course (Bahrick & Hall, 1991). Decay alone, then, does not seem to explain lapses in long-term memory.

■ **decay theory** (*of forgetting*)
The theory that information in memory eventually disappears if it is not reactivated; it appears to be more plausible for short-term than long-term memory.

New Memories for Old

A second "commonsense" view of forgetting holds that once material is learned, it remains forever in one's mental library, but for various reasons it may be difficult to retrieve. Evidence for this view has come in part from studies of electrical brain stimulation. Stimulating various parts of the brain before surgery sometimes evokes reports of vivid memories from the distant past, thought by the patient to be long forgotten (Penfield & Perot, 1963). In one case, for example, a woman told of rehearing a concert she had attended years before; she even hummed along with the music.

The notion that memory is permanent is certainly appealing, which may explain why for many years people unquestioningly accepted the brain stimulation evidence as persuasive. But then Elizabeth Loftus (1980) looked again and discovered that electrically stimulated "memories" have actually occurred in very few patients. Moreover, these "memories" seem more like reconstructions than accurately retrieved events. Loftus also pointed out what in retrospect should have been obvious: The recovery of *some* information stored long ago does not mean that *all* memories from the past remain available.

According to Loftus, there is no solid evidence that long-term memories do last forever. On the contrary, she argues, information in long-term memory can be completely wiped out by new, misleading information, or at least be made permanently inaccessible. Loftus cites a study in which she and her colleagues used a leading question to mislead people into thinking they had seen either a stop sign or a yield sign while viewing slides of a traffic accident. Other people were not misled and accurately identified the sign they had actually seen. Later, all the subjects were told the purpose of the study and were asked to guess whether or not they had been misled. Almost all of those who had been misled continued to insist that they had seen the sign whose existence had been "planted" in their minds by the leading question (Loftus, Miller, & Burns, 1978).

Other studies, too, suggest that new, incorrect information can "erase" or replace old, correct information, just as rerecording on an audio or videotape will obliterate the original material. We should note, however, that not everyone agrees with this conclusion. For example, some psychologists believe that misleading information does not actually "erase" the original information, but simply biases a person to accept the misinformation as correct (McCloskey & Zaragoza, 1985). In psychology, as in all other sciences, researchers often agree on the facts but must tolerate uncertainty over the best interpretation of those facts.

Interference

Another type of forgetting occurs because similar items of information interfere with each other in either storage or retrieval (see Figure 7.10). The information may be in memory, but you confuse it with other information. This type of forgetting, which occurs in both short- and long-term memory, is especially common when you have to recall isolated facts.

Suppose you are at a party and you meet someone named Julie. A half hour later you meet someone named Judy. You go on to talk to other people, and after an hour you again bump into Julie, but by mistake you call her Judy. The second name has interfered with the first. This type of interference, in which new information interferes with the ability to remember old information, is called **retroactive.** It is often illustrated by a story about an absent-minded professor of ichthyology (the study of fish) who complained that whenever he learned the name of a new student he forgot the name of a fish.

Since new information is always entering memory, we are all vulnerable to the effects of retroactive interference—or at least most of us are. Studies of

✳ When their brains are electrically stimulated, some people seem to "relive" long-forgotten experiences. Should we conclude that all our memories are permanently on file, waiting to be retrieved?

■ **retroactive interference**
Forgetting that occurs when recently learned material interferes with the ability to remember similar material stored previously.

FIGURE 7.10

Interference in memory
Retroactive interference occurs when new information interferes with memory for previously stored material. Proactive interference occurs when previously stored material interferes with memory for new information.

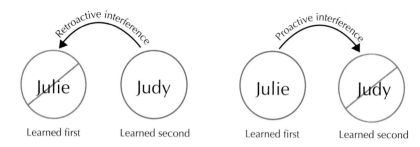

H. M. find that his memories of childhood and adolescence are unusually detailed and clear, and rarely change. H. M. can remember actors and singers famous in his childhood, the films they were in, and who their costars were. He knows the names of friends from the second grade. Presumably, these memories from early in life have not been subject to interference from memories since the operation—because there have been no new memories!

Interference also works in the opposite direction. Old information (such as the French we've learned in high school) may interfere with the ability to remember new information (such as the Italian we're trying to learn now). This type of interference is called **proactive.** Over a period of weeks, months, and years, proactive interference may cause more forgetting than retroactive, simply because we have stored up so much information that can potentially interfere with anything new. But fortunately, we can also use our old information to elaborately encode new information and thus improve our ability to remember.

Motivated Forgetting

Sigmund Freud believed that people unconsciously "forget" information that is too threatening to live with. Freud called this process of keeping dangerous memories out of consciousness *repression* (as we discuss further in our coverage of Freud's theories in Chapter 12). Today, however, many psychologists prefer a more general term, **motivated forgetting,** and note that there are many reasons why a person might be psychologically motivated to "hide" certain memories, including embarrassment, guilt, shock, and a desire to protect one's pride. Motivated forgetting may explain some cases of **retrograde amnesia,** in which people can remember historical incidents and form new memories, but forget friends, relatives, or events from the past that are too painful to remember (see Chapter 16).

Evidence for repression and motivated forgetting comes mostly from clinical reports of people in psychotherapy who appear to have remembered long-buried memories. In addition, in recent years, sensational news stories have appeared about people claiming to remember repressed traumas from early childhood. However, these people's stories, although compelling, are often difficult to verify. In one case, Eileen Franklin, a woman whose best childhood friend was beaten to death with a rock 20 years earlier, said she looked at her own daughter one day and suddenly had a vivid memory of watching her father doing the killing. He was subsequently convicted and sentenced to life in prison on the basis of her testimony, although every detail that Eileen Franklin reported was in the public record at the time of the crime and there was no other evidence against him.

Most psychologists think that the process of motivated forgetting does occur, and they certainly do not dispute the reality of traumatic experiences that all too many people have endured. (Eileen Franklin's father, for example, repeatedly terrorized his family.) Yet because of what psychologists have learned about memory, cases such as that of Eileen Franklin raise unsettling issues. How

People sometimes appear to recall a long-buried trauma from the past. Given what we know about motivated forgetting and the reconstructive nature of memory, how are we to judge these memories? Are they sufficient to convict someone of a crime?

■ **proactive interference**
Forgetting that occurs when previously stored material interferes with the ability to remember similar, more recently learned material.

■ **motivated forgetting**
Forgetting because of a desire to eliminate awareness of painful, embarrassing, or otherwise unpleasant experiences.

■ **retrograde amnesia**
Loss of the ability to remember events or experiences that occurred before some particular point in time.

are we to know when a "memory" is being accurately retrieved or reconstructed? Should the validity of "recovered" memories—either our own or those of other people—be accepted in a court of law? To what extent are memories of events from long ago contaminated by what a person has heard from others since the event occurred, or by other traumatic experiences?

Cue-dependent Forgetting

Often, when we need to remember, we rely on *retrieval cues*, items of information that can help us find the specific information we're looking for. When we lack such cues, we may feel as if we have lost the "call number," or perhaps some part of the call number, for an entry in the mind's library. The information doesn't get lost *from* long-term memory; it gets lost *in* long-term memory (Ashcraft, 1989). Such **cue-dependent forgetting** is perhaps the most common type of forgetting of all.

Retrieval cues may work by getting us into the general area of memory where an item is stored, or by making a "match" with information that is linked in memory with the item in question. Thus, if you are trying to remember the last name of a particular actor, knowing the person's first name or the name of a recent movie the actor starred in might help. A student of ours remembered where he left his psychology textbook by remembering the right cue—an image of the student union coffee shop where he had gone after class on the day he misplaced the book.

Cues that were present at the time you learned a new fact or had a personal experience are apt to be especially useful as retrieval aids. That may explain why remembering is often easier when you are in the same physical environment as you were when an event occurred: Cues in the present context match those from the past. Many people have suggested that the overlap between present and past cues may also lead to a *false* sense of having been in exactly the same situation before; this is the strange phenomenon of *déjà vu* (from the French for "already seen"). Ordinarily, however, contextual cues help us remember the past more accurately.

Even imagining features of a past situation can help us recall an experience that occurred in that situation. Many police departments now encourage witnesses to reconstruct the circumstances of a crime and to recall without interruption everything they can about what they saw, even details that seem unimportant. Such "cognitive interview" strategies, which were devised by psychologists, increase the number of retrieval cues available and produce better recall than standard "and-then-what-did-he-do" techniques (Geiselman, 1988).

Your mental or physical state may also act as a retrieval cue, evoking a **state-dependent memory.** For example, if you are drunk when something happens, you may remember it better when you are once again drunk than when you are sober. (This is not an endorsement of drunkenness! Your memory will be best if you are sober during both encoding and recall.) If your emotional arousal is especially high or low at the time of an event, you may remember that event best when you are once again in the same state of arousal. One research team has speculated that when victims of violent crimes have trouble recalling details of the experience, it may be in part because they are far less emotionally aroused than they were at the time of the crime (Clark, Milberg, & Erber, 1987).

Some researchers have proposed that retrieval of a memory is best when a person's *mood* is the same as it was when the memory was first encoded and stored, presumably because mood serves as a retrieval cue. Findings on this notion, however, have been frustratingly inconsistent (Bower & Mayer, 1989). Better support exists for a somewhat different idea, that what really counts is the match between your current mood and the *kind of material being remembered.*

■ **cue-dependent forgetting**
The inability to retrieve information stored in memory because of insufficient internally or externally generated cues.

■ **state-dependent memory**
The tendency to remember something when one is in the same physical or mental state as during the original learning or experience.

Charlie Chaplin's film City Lights *provides a classic illustration of state-dependent memory. After Charlie saves the life of a drunken millionaire, the two spend the rest of the evening in boisterous merry-making. The next day, however, after sobering up, the millionaire fails to recognize Charlie and gives him the cold shoulder. Then, once again, the millionaire gets drunk—and once again he greets Charlie as a pal.*

This effect seems to occur mainly when people are feeling happy: that is, you are likely to remember happy events or ideas better when you are feeling happy than when you are feeling sad (Mayer et al., 1990; McCormick & Mayer, 1991).

Until we understand the links between mood and memory more fully, you may find it enlightening to notice your own thoughts and memories when you are feeling elated or down in the dumps. When you are happy, do you remember only your victories and not your defeats? When you are blue, do you find yourself dwelling on all the rotten things that have happened to you, or do you cheer yourself up by remembering the great time you had last weekend?

QUICK QUIZ

1. A boy who saw his brother drown cannot recall the incident. What sort of forgetting has probably occurred?
2. Willard was a fan of Judy Garland in the 1950s and 1960s. Later, he became a fan of Garland's daughter, singer/actress Liza Minelli. Now Willard often mistakenly refers to Ms. Minelli as "Judy." Why doesn't he remember her name correctly?
3. When a woman at her twentieth high school reunion sees her old friends, she recalls incidents she had thought were long forgotten. Why?

ANSWERS:

1. motivated forgetting or repression 2. proactive interference 3. The sight of her friends provides retrieval cues for the incidents.

■ AUTOBIOGRAPHICAL MEMORIES: THE WAY WE WERE

What do our memories about our own lives tell us? Do they reveal actual events that occurred—or events that we wish had occurred? Do they tell us what we were like then—or what we are like now?

[An autobiography] is a story of oneself in the past, read in the light of one's present self.   —LLOYD MORGAN

Early in this chapter we noted that memory provides each of us with a sense of identity. This sense of ourselves evolves and changes as we build up a store of episodic memories about events we have experienced first-hand. For most of us, the memories we have of our own lives are by far the most fascinating. We offer them to others as entertainment ("Did I ever tell you about the time . . . ?"); we manipulate them—some people even *publish* them—in order to create a certain image; we probe them to learn more about who we are (Ross, 1989).

Childhood Amnesia: The Missing Years

One curious thing about autobiographical memories is that few of us recall any events from earlier than the third or fourth year of life. Of course, we all retain procedural memories from the toddler stage, when we first learned to use a fork, drink from a cup, and pull a wagon. We also retain semantic memories acquired early in life: the rules of counting, the names of people and things, knowledge about all manner of objects in the world. But as adults we cannot remember being fed in infancy by our parents, taking our first steps, or uttering our first halting sentences. We are victims of **childhood amnesia.**

People often find childhood amnesia difficult to accept. There is something disturbing about the fact that our early years are beyond recall—so disturbing that some people adamantly deny it, claiming to remember events from the second or even the first year of life. But most psychologists believe these "memories" are merely reconstructions based on photographs, family stories, and imagination. Like Piaget's kidnapping, the "remembered" event may not even have taken place.

Some researchers believe that childhood amnesia occurs because brain areas used to store events, notably the hippocampus, are not well developed in infancy (Nadel & Zola-Morgan, 1984; Schacter & Moscovitch, 1984). Also, as adults we use very different cognitive schemas from those we use in early childhood, schemas that are not useful for reconstructing early events from the memory fragments we stored at the time (Neisser, 1967). Only after we enter school do we learn to think as adults do, using language to organize our memories and storing not only events but also what we think about them. In addition, as preschoolers we may encode our experiences far less elaborately than we do as adults because our information-processing abilities are still limited. As a result, we may have few cues for retrieving our early memories later on in life (White & Pillemer, 1979).

Recent longitudinal research with children suggests still other explanations for the puzzling loss of early memories. It turns out that preschoolers can actually remember past events quite well. In fact, Robyn Fivush and Nina Hamond (1991) have found that four-year-olds can often remember experiences that occurred before age two-and-a-half. But, these researchers note, young children are still trying to figure out how the world works, and they tend to focus on the routine, familiar aspects of an experience (eating lunch, going to sleep, playing with toys) rather than the distinctive, novel aspects that would make the event more memorable in the long run. Also, young children have not yet mastered the social conventions for reporting events; they do not know what is important and interesting to others. Instead, they tend to rely on adults' questions to provide retrieval cues ("Where did we go for breakfast?" "Who did you go trick-or-treating with?"), and this dependency on adults may prevent them from building up a stable core of remembered material that will still be available when they are older.

Whatever the explanation for childhood amnesia, our first memories may provide some useful insights into our personalities. Some psychologists believe that these memories are not random but instead reflect our basic concerns, ambitions, and attitudes toward life (Kihlstrom & Harackiewicz, 1982). Think back to your own earliest memories. Do you think the kinds of events and experiences you recall reveal anything important about you?

She may be having a great birthday party, but this toddler will be unable to recall it when she grows up. Like the rest of us, she will fall victim to "childhood amnesia."

■ **childhood amnesia**
The inability to remember events and experiences that occurred early in life.

Memories of a Lifetime

A century ago, Hermann Ebbinghaus established a method for studying memory that was adopted by generations of psychologists. Ebbinghaus wanted to measure "pure" memory loss, independent of personal experience. Using himself as a subject, he memorized long lists of nonsense syllables, such as *bok, waf,* or *ged,* and tested his retention over a period of several days or weeks. He reported (1885/1913) that most forgetting occurred soon after the initial learning and then tapered off (see Figure 7.11).

A hundred years later, Marigold Linton, also using herself as a subject, decided to chart the curve of forgetting over years rather than days. Linton was interested in how people forget real-life personal events, not nonsense syllables. Every day for 12 years she recorded on a 4-×-6-inch card two or more things that had happened to her that day. Eventually she accumulated a catalogue of thousands of discrete events, both trivial ("I have dinner at the Canton Kitchen: delicious lobster dish") and significant ("I land at Orly Airport in Paris"). Once a month, she took a random sampling of all the cards accumulated to that point, noted whether she could remember the events on them, and tried to date the events. Reporting on the first 6 years' results, Linton (1978) told how she had expected a forgetting curve similar to that reported by Ebbinghaus. Instead, as Figure 7.12 shows, she found that long-term forgetting was slower and proceeded at a much more constant pace.

As you might expect, details tended to drop out of Linton's memories with the passage of time. A similar study, by Willem Wagenaar (1986), found the same thing. Wagenaar thought that he would surely remember certain critical details about the events he recorded. Yet within a year he forgot 20 percent of these details, and after five years he forgot 60 percent. However, when he gathered cues from witnesses about ten events that he appeared to have forgotten, he was able to recall something about all ten events, which suggests that some of his forgetting was cue-dependent.

From his own research and that of others, Michael Ross (1989) concludes that even when we appear to remember what we said, did, or believed months or years ago, many of our "memories" are actually based on our *present* traits and beliefs, and on our *implicit theories* about how changeable certain traits or beliefs are. (The theories are "implicit" because we may never have expressed them to anyone, even ourselves.) For example, Ross finds that most people have an implicit theory that feelings and attitudes are consistent over time. As a result, whether recalling their past opinions of a dating partner, their past drug

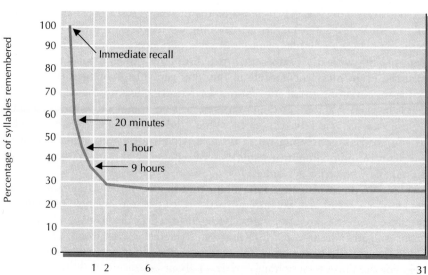

FIGURE 7.11

Ebbinghaus's forgetting curve
When Hermann Ebbinghaus tested his own retention of a list of nonsense syllables, he found that memory loss was rapid soon after initial learning and then tapered off.

Percentage of syllables remembered

Immediate recall

20 minutes

1 hour

9 hours

Elapsed time since learning (in days)

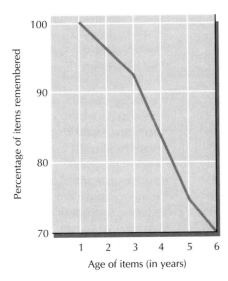

Percentage of items remembered

Age of items (in years)

FIGURE 7.12

A forgetting curve for personal events
When Marigold Linton tested her own memory for personal events over a period of several years, she obtained a forgetting curve quite different from that of Ebbinghaus (see Figure 7.11). Her memory loss was minimal at first, but then retention fell off at a gradual but steady rate.

use, or their past incomes, they tend to think they have not changed much—even when the evidence shows they have. In one study, 91 percent of people who had changed their political affiliation in a four-year period reported that they had *not* changed (Niemi, Katz, & Newman, 1980). Remarkably, if they were currently Republicans they forgot that they had only recently been Democrats, and vice versa!

Conversely, when their implicit theories predict change, people are likely to "forget" information showing that they haven't really changed much at all. An implicit theory predicting change, Ross observes, seems to explain why (as we saw in Chapter 4) many women "remember" mood changes associated with their menstrual cycles, even though their own daily diaries fail to confirm their memories. As we will see in Chapter 17, implicit theories of change raise a problem in evaluating psychotherapy and self-help programs. Most people have an implicit theory that these programs will change their lives. As a result, they "remember" themselves as having been worse off before the program than they really were.

Of course, even with the passage of time, some personal memories never lose their vividness. Events that mark important transitions (marriage, getting a first job) are more memorable than other events. And as we age, certain periods of our lives seem to stand out. Specifically, in old age, people seem to remember more from adolescence and early adulthood than from midlife, a phenomenon known as the "reminiscence bump" (Fromholt & Larsen, 1991; MacKavey et al., 1991). Perhaps the younger years are especially memorable because they were full of transitions. Or perhaps people are especially apt to weave events from their youth into a coherent "story" or narrative, and thus remember them better ("After I graduated from college I was in no hurry to marry, but then I met the love of my life, and before I knew it . . .") (Fitzgerald, 1988).

Events that were particularly surprising, shocking, or emotional also seem to hold a special place in memory. Such experiences may seem like moments frozen in time, with all the details seemingly intact. A number of years ago, Roger Brown and James Kulik (1977) labeled these memories **flashbulb memories** because that term captures the surprise, illumination, and seemingly photographic detail that characterize them. Brown and Kulik speculated that the capacity for flashbulb memories may have evolved because such memories had survival value. Remembering the details of a surprising or dangerous experience tended to help people avoid similar situations in the future. Since it was not possible for an individual to know which details would ultimately prove useful, flashbulb memories contained a large number of details. This interpretation fits well with the finding mentioned earlier, that certain hormones released during emotional arousal enhance memory.

■ **flashbulb memories**
Vivid, detailed recollections of the circumstances in which one learned of or perceived some significant or surprising event, or of the event itself.

Some shocking or emotional events seem like snapshots forever lit up in memory. But are these "flashbulb" memories really so illuminating, or do they have less "wattage" than we realize?

But despite their vividness, even flashbulb memories are not always complete or accurate. For example, many people swear they saw the assassination of President Kennedy on television, as it was taking place. Yet in reality, no television cameras were present during the assassination, and the only film of the event, made by a bystander, was not shown until later.

Similarly, many people say they know exactly where they were and what they were doing when they learned of the 1986 explosion of the space shuttle *Challenger*, as well as who told them the news and what their own reactions were—yet several studies done since the tragedy show that memories for the event are often dimmer than they appear. In one study, done a few days after the explosion, most people could provide many details about the experience, but nine months later, when they were questioned again, there was a shift to more general answers, and fully a quarter of the subjects gave some responses that were inconsistent with their original reports (McCloskey, Wible, & Cohen, 1988). In another study, college students, on the morning after the event, reported how they had heard the news. But three years later, when they again recalled how they learned about the incident, not one student was entirely accurate, and a third of them were *dead wrong*, although they *felt* they were remembering accurately (Neisser & Harsch, 1992). A third study found that after eight months, only those people who had been upset rather than calm at the news of the disaster *and* who had often recounted their experience in learning about it could relate many details of the incident with a high degree of confidence (Bohannon, 1988).

Because of such findings, psychologists disagree about how "special" flashbulb memories really are. Some shocking or surprising events do remain extremely memorable, especially when the person doing the remembering was personally involved in the event and did not simply hear about it from someone else. Research finds, for example, that if you were living in the San Francisco Bay Area in 1989, you probably remember quite accurately where you were and what you were doing when the Loma Prieta earthquake hit on October 17, and what action you took just afterward (Neisser, Winograd, & Weldon, 1991; Palmer, Schreiber, & Fox, 1991).

It is clear, however, that even with flashbulb memories and other vivid memories for public and personal events, facts tend to get mixed with a little fiction. Some of the details we "remember" so clearly probably are added after the event, as we try to tie our own life stories to the broader saga of history (Neisser, 1982). Having read this chapter, you should not be surprised at this. As we have seen, we are not merely actors in our personal life dramas. We also write the scripts.

Do you recall where you were and what you were doing when you learned about the tragic explosion of the space shuttle Challenger *on January 28, 1986? If so, you may have a "flashbulb memory" of that moment.*

How to . . . Uh . . . Remember

"YOU SIMPLY ASSOCIATE EACH NUMBER WITH A WORD, SUCH AS 'TABLE' AND 3,476,029."

Someday drugs may help people with memory deficiencies and increase normal memory performance. For the time being, however, those of us who hope to improve our memories must rely on mental strategies. Formal memory techniques are known as *mnemonics* [neh-MON-iks]. Some mnemonics take the form of easily memorized rhymes ("Thirty days hath September/April, June, and November . . ."). Others use formulas ("*Every good boy does fine*" for remembering which notes are on the lines of the treble clef in musical notation). Still others use visual images or verbal associations. These tricks work for a variety of reasons. Some force you to encode the material actively and thoroughly. Some make the information meaningful and thus easier to store and retrieve. Still others reduce the amount of information to be stored by "chunking" it. The phone number 466-3293, for example, is better remembered in terms of the corresponding letters, which form a meaningful chunk: GOOD-BYE (appropriate, perhaps, for a travel agency).

Books on how to improve your memory often suggest more elaborate mnemonics. A favorite is to remember a list of items by taking a mental stroll through your house, forming a visual image of each item at a particular location (the "method of Loci"). Later you repeat the tour, picking off each item as you go. Such aids can help those who must learn lists of relatively meaningless material for immediate recall, or remember long

speeches. They are also tricks of the trade for stage performers with apparently amazing memories. Recent research, however, suggests that for long-term retention, elaborate mnemonics are no more effective than rote rehearsal, and are sometimes even worse (Wang & Thomas, 1992; Wang, Thomas, & Ouellette, 1992). In one survey of memory researchers, most said they did not use such mnemonics themselves (Park, Smith, & Cavanaugh, 1990). After all, why bother to memorize a grocery list with the "mental stroll" method when you can simply write down what you plan to buy?

A better route to a good memory is to follow some general guidelines based on the principles in this chapter. They include the following:

• *Pay attention!* It seems obvious, but often we fail to remember because we never encoded the information in the first place. For example, which of these is the real Lincoln penny?

Most people have trouble recognizing the real penny because they have never attended carefully to the details of a penny's design (Nickerson & Adams, 1979). We are not advising you to do so, unless you happen to be a coin collector or a counterfeiting expert. Just keep in mind that when you do have something to remember, you will do better if you encode it well. (The real penny, by the way, is the left one in the bottom row.)

• *Encode information in more than one way.* The more elaborate the encoding of information, the more memorable it will be. Elaboration can take many forms. In addition to remembering a telephone number by the sound of the individual digits, you might note the spatial pattern they make as you punch them in on a pushbutton phone.

• *Add meaning.* The more meaningful material is, the more likely it is to link up with information already in long-term memory. Meaningfulness also reduces the number of chunks of information you have to learn. Thus, if your license plate happens to be 236MPL, you might think of 236 maples.

• *Make up a story.* Facts or words to be memorized are often more meaningful and therefore more memorable if they are woven into a coherent story or narrative (Bower & Clark, 1969). The narrative provides a kind of cognitive schema into which the separate items of information fit. If you need to remember the parts of the digestive system for a physiology course, for example, you might construct a narrative about what happens to a piece of food after it enters a person's mouth, then repeat the narrative out loud to yourself, a roommate, or a study partner.

• *Use visual imagery.* Memory for pictures is often better than memory for words (Paivio, 1969). You can make up your own mental "pictures" when you have to memorize verbal information. If you are in the import-export business and need to remember the main exports of several different countries, instead of trying to store, say, "Brazil: coffee," you might imagine a map of Brazil with a big coffee mug superimposed on it. Some people find that the odder the image, the better.

• *Take your time.* If you must remember large amounts of verbal material, leisurely learning, spread out over several sessions, will probably produce better results than harried cramming. (*Reviewing* material just before you are tested on it, however, can be helpful since it places the information at the top of your "cognitive deck.") In terms of hours spent, "distributed" (spaced) learning sessions are more efficient than "massed" ones. Thus you may find that you retain information better after three separate one-hour sessions than after one session of three hours.

• *Take time out.* If possible, minimize interference by using study breaks for rest or recreation. Sleep is the ultimate way to reduce interference. In a classic study, students who slept for eight hours after learning lists of nonsense syllables retained them better than students who went about their usual business (Jenkins & Dallenbach, 1924). Sleep is not always possible, of course, but periodic mental relaxation usually is.

• *Overlearn.* You can't remember something you never learned well in the first place. Overlearning—studying information even after you think you know it—is one of the best ways to ensure that you'll remember it.

• *Monitor your learning.* People who remember well tend to score well on tests of *metamemory*, the ability to monitor and be aware of one's own retention. By testing yourself frequently (use the Quick Quizzes!), rehearsing thoroughly, and reviewing periodically, you will have a better idea of how you are doing. Don't try to evaluate your own learning immediately after reading the material, though; because the information is still in short-term memory, you are likely to feel a false sense of confidence about your ability to recall it later. If you delay making a judgment for at least a few minutes, your evaluation will probably be more accurate (Nelson & Dunlosky, 1991).

Whatever strategies you use, you will find that active learning produces more retention than merely reading or listening passively. The mind does not gobble up information automatically; you must take some pains to make the material digestible. Even then, you should not expect to remember everything you read or hear. Nor should you want to. Piling up facts without distinguishing the important from the trivial is just confusing. It is what you do with what you know that counts. Books on memory written by reputable scientists may help you boost your recall, but books or courses that promise a "perfect," "photographic," or "instant" memory fly in the face of what psychology knows about the workings of the mind. Our advice: Forget them.

SUMMARY

1. *Memory* involves a complex collection of abilities, processes, and mental systems. It is not an all-or-nothing phenomenon, but depends on the type of performance required. In tests of *explicit memory* (conscious recollection), *recognition* is usually better than *recall*. In tests of *implicit memory*, past experiences may affect current thoughts or actions even when these experiences are not consciously remembered.

2. Most cognitive models of memory take an *information-processing approach*, describing memory as the *encoding, storage,* and *retrieval* of information. Sensory information is encoded almost as soon as it is detected and is stored in the form of propositions, images, or sets of instructions.

3. In many information-processing models, memory consists of three separate but interacting systems: sensory memory, short-term memory, and long-term memory. *Sensory memory* briefly retains information in the form of literal sensory images, such as *icons* and *echoes*, so that it can be further processed. We speculated that sensory memory may be involved in a poorly understood phenomenon called *eidetic imagery*. In normal processing, sensory memory acts as a filter, keeping out unimportant information.

4. *Short-term memory (STM)* retains recently received information temporarily, perhaps up to 30 seconds, although *rehearsal* can extend retention. Short-term memory also acts as a working memory for the processing of information retrieved from long-term memory for temporary use. The capacity of STM is extremely limited but this capacity can be extended if information is organized into larger units, by *chunking*.

5. According to most models of memory, information that is not transferred to long-term memory from short-term memory decays and is lost. *Elaborative rehearsal* is more likely to result in transfer to long-term memory than is *maintenance rehearsal*. And deep processing is usually a more effective retention strategy than shallow processing, although there are exceptions.

6. *Long-term memory (LTM)* handles the more or less permanent storage of information. Its contents appear to be organized and indexed largely in terms of meaning, but other features of information, such as the sounds of words, are also stored. The way people use their network of semantic associations in long-term memory depends on experience and education.

7. *Procedural memories* are memories for how to perform specific actions, or "knowing how." *Declarative memories* are memories of "knowing that" and include *semantic memories* (internal representations of the world, including facts, rules, and concepts) and *episodic memories* (internal representations of personally experienced events).

8. Remembering information stored in long-term memory is in part a reconstructive process, and reconstruction may distort what was originally learned or experienced. Distortions also occur because initial storage is influenced by cognitive *schemas* and because memory can be affected by racial biases and leading questions. These facts pose serious problems for the legal system, which must rely to some extent on eyewitness testimony.

9. Short-term memory seems to involve temporary changes within neurons that alter their ability to release neurotransmitters. In contrast, long-term memory involves permanent structural changes in neurons and synapses. *Long-term potentiation*, an increase in the strength of synaptic response, may be an important mechanism of long-term memory. Neural changes underlying memory take time to develop, which may explain why long-term memories require a period of *consolidation*.

10. Declarative memories appear to be formed in the hippocampus, the amygdala, and parts of the temporal lobe cortex; procedural memories appear to be stored in various other brain areas. These facts might explain why brain-damaged patients with *retrograde amnesia* (such as H. M.) can often acquire new cognitive, perceptual, and motor skills. Different brain systems may also be involved in explicit and implicit memory tasks.

11. Various hormones produced during emotional arousal appear to regulate or modulate the storage of information in memory. Recent research suggests that epinephrine causes the level of glucose to rise in the bloodstream, and that glucose enhances memory either directly or by altering the effects of various neurotransmitters.

12. Once information is encoded, forgetting can occur for various reasons. Information in sensory and short-term memory appears to *decay* if it does not receive further processing. Long-term memories are more permanent, but some argue that these memories can be "erased" by new, contradictory information. Forgetting in LTM also occurs because of interference among items, either *proactive* or *retroactive*. Some memory lapses appear to be due to repression, or *motivated forgetting*, although it is hard to confirm the validity of "buried" memories that are subsequently recalled.

13. Perhaps the most common kind of forgetting is *cue-dependent forgetting*, which occurs because *retrieval cues* are inadequate. Among the most effective retrieval cues are ones that were present at the time of the initial learning or experience. A person's mental or physical state may act as a retrieval cue, evoking a *state-dependent memory*. There is evidence that we find it easier to remember happy material when we are feeling happy than when we are sad.

14. Autobiographical memories provide each of us with a sense of personal identity. They are missing from the first two or three years of life, a phenomenon known as *childhood amnesia*. Autobiographical memories seem to be forgotten at a slower and steadier rate than the nonsense materials so often used in laboratory experiments. According to one theory, our memories of our past beliefs and actions are often based on our present traits and beliefs and our "implicit theories" of how flexible various traits and beliefs are.

15. *Flashbulb memories* have a special vividness and clarity, freezing a moment in time when we learned about or perceived a surprising or shocking event. However, even flashbulb memories may be embellished or distorted, for remembering is, above all, a reconstructive process.

KEY TERMS

memory *239*
recognition *240*
recall *240*
explicit and implicit memories *240*
relearning method *240*
priming *240*
encoding *241*
proposition *241*
storage *242*
retrieval *242*
sensory memory *243*
short-term memory (STM) *243*
long-term memory (LTM) *243*
sensory registers *244*
eidetic imagery *245*
anterograde amnesia *245*
working memory *246*
chunks *246*
rehearsal *247*
maintenance versus elaborative rehearsal *248*
deep versus shallow processing *249*

serial position effect *249*
primacy and recency effects *249*
tip-of-the-tongue state *251*
procedural memories *252*
declarative memories *252*
semantic memories *252*
episodic memories *252*
cognitive schema *253*
long-term potentiation *257*
consolidation *257*
decay theory *262*
retroactive interference *263*
proactive interference *264*
motivated forgetting/ repression *264*
retrograde amnesia *264*
cue-dependent forgetting *265*
state-dependent memory *265*
childhood amnesia *267*
implicit theory *268*
flashbulb memories *269*
mnemonics *271*

8

Cognition II: Thought and Language

What a piece of work is man! How noble in reason! How infinite in faculties! . . . in apprehension how like a god!

WILLIAM SHAKESPEARE

A great many people think they are thinking when they are merely rearranging their prejudices.

WILLIAM JAMES

He's thinking—but how well *is he thinking?*

Every day, in the course of ordinary living, we must all make plans, draw inferences, analyze relationships, and organize the flotsam and jetsam of our mental world. These powers of thought led our forebears to give our species the immodest name *homo sapiens*, Latin for wise or rational man. But just how "sapiens" are we, really? In the previous chapter we saw that memory both impresses and disappoints; so, too, do our powers of thought and reason. Consider:

• Early in life we all master the concept of time and learn how clocks arbitrarily divide it into hours, minutes, and seconds. Yet every spring, when daylight savings time begins, there are people who fret about tampering with "God's time." One letter writer in Colorado even complained to a local newspaper that the "extra hour" of sunlight was burning up her front lawn!

• A recent national survey of ethnic attitudes (T. Smith, 1991) asked people to rank the social standing of 58 groups, including one called the Wisians. Although three-fifths of the respondents said they knew too little about the Wisians to rank them, the others had no such reservations, assigning the group a relatively low average score of 4.12 on a 9-point scale. In reality, there were no "Wisians"; they had been made up by the researchers.

• A few years ago, the pilots of an Air Florida flight were going over a pretakeoff checklist. When the de-icer was mentioned, a crew member automatically responded "off," without giving it much thought. After all, it's always warm in Florida, isn't it? Unfortunately, on this occasion, the weather was icy. The plane crashed, killing 74 people.

Clearly, the human mind, which has managed to come up with poetry, penicillin, and pantyhose, has its limitations as well as its leaps of inspiration. We may be able to go to the moon, but we are also capable of illogic, mindlessness, and overconfidence in our own opinions. In this chapter, we will examine our abilities to think, reason, solve problems, and use language, and we will also explore some sources of our mental shortcomings.

276

■ THOUGHT: USING WHAT WE KNOW

Thinking is defined most simply as the mental manipulation of information. This capacity frees us from the confines of the immediate present: We can think about the camping trip we took three years ago, the party we are planning for Saturday night, the War of 1812. It also carries us beyond the boundaries of physical reality: We can think about unicorns and utopias, Martians and magic. Because we can think, we do not need to grope our way blindly through our problems but can solve them intelligently and creatively.

The Elements of Cognition

When we take action, we physically manipulate the environment. When we think, we *mentally* manipulate internal representations of objects, activities, and situations. However, we do not manipulate all the information potentially available to us, any more than we memorize everything we read, see, or hear. If we did, making the simplest decision or solving the most trivial problem would be a time-consuming, and perhaps impossible, task. Imagine trying to decide whether to go out for a hamburger if that meant thinking about every hamburger you ever ate, saw a commercial for, or watched someone devour. Thinking is possible because our internal representations simplify and summarize information that reaches us from the environment.

CONCEPTS.   One type of representation, or unit of thought, is the **concept.** The concept of a concept is a tricky one. Essentially, a concept is a mental category that groups objects, relations, activities, abstractions, or qualities having common properties. The instances of a concept are seen as roughly similar. For example, *golden retriever, cocker spaniel, Weimaraner,* and *German shepherd* are all instances of the concept *dog,* and *anger, joy, sadness, fear,* and *surprise* are instances of the concept *emotion.* Because concepts simplify the world, we do not have to learn a new name for each thing, relation, activity, abstract state, or quality we encounter, nor treat each instance as though it were unique. You may never have seen a *Basenji* or eaten *escargots,* but if you know that the first is an instance of *dog* and the second an instance of *food,* you will know how to respond.

We form concepts not only through direct contact with objects and situations, but also by contact with *symbols,* things that represent or stand for something else. Symbolic representations include words, mathematical formulas, maps, graphs, pictures, and even gestures. Symbols stand not only for objects but also for operations (for example, the symbols + and ÷), relationships (for example, = and <), and qualities (for example, the dot in musical notation that symbolizes an abrupt or staccato quality).

Certain concepts, called **basic concepts,** have a moderate number of instances and are naturally easier to acquire than those that have either few or many instances (Rosch [formerly Heider], 1973). What is the object pictured in the margin? You will probably call it an apple. The concept *apple* is more basic than *fruit,* which includes many more instances and is more abstract. It is also more basic than *McIntosh apple,* which is quite specific. Similarly, *book* is more basic than either *printed matter* or *novel.* Children seem to learn basic-level concepts earlier than others, and adults use them more often than others, because basic concepts convey an optimal amount of information in most situations.

All the qualities associated with a concept do not necessarily apply to every instance: Some apples are not red; some dogs do not bark; some birds do not fly or perch on trees. But all the instances of a concept do share a "family resemblance." Moreover, everyone within a culture can easily tell you which instances are most representative, or *prototypical,* of the concept (Rosch, 1973).

■ **thinking**
The mental manipulation of information stored in the form of concepts, images, or propositions.
■ **concept**
A category used to class together objects, relations, activities, abstractions, or qualities that share common properties.
■ **basic concepts**
Concepts that have a moderate number of instances and that are easier to acquire than those having few or many instances.

A bachelor, according to the dictionary, is an unmarried man—period. In real life, however, some instances of a concept are more representative, or prototypical, than others. It is easy to label Eddie Murphy a bachelor, but what about the Pope, or Robert Redford, who is divorced, or Woody Allen, when he was Mia Farrow's "significant other" for many years? And what about a gay man in a committed relationship: Is he a bachelor?

Which dog is doggier, a golden retriever or a chihuahua? Which fruit is more fruitlike, an apple or a pineapple? Which activity is more representative of sports, football or weight lifting? When we need to decide whether something belongs to a concept, we are likely to compare it to a prototype.

PROPOSITIONS AND IMAGES. Concepts are the building blocks of thought, but they would be of limited use if we simply stacked them up mentally. We must also represent how they are related to one another. As we saw in Chapter 7, one way we accomplish this seems to be by storing and using **propositions.** Propositions are units of meaning that are made up of concepts and that express a unitary idea. A proposition may express nearly any sort of knowledge *(Hortense raises Basenjis)* or belief *(Basenjis are beautiful).* Propositions, in turn, may be linked together in complicated, constantly shifting networks.

Most psychologists believe that **mental images** are also important in thinking (Kosslyn, 1983; Paivio, 1983). Most people report experiencing visual images, pictures in the mind's eye. Although no one can directly "see" another person's visual images, cognitive psychologists are able to study them indirectly. One method is to measure how long it takes people to rotate an image, scan from one point to another, or "read off" some detail. The results suggest that visual images are like images on a television screen: that is, we can manipulate them, they occur in a mental "space" of a fixed size, and small ones contain less detail than larger ones (Kosslyn, 1980; Shepard & Metzler, 1971).

Most people also report auditory images, for instance, when thinking about a song or a conversation, and many report images in other sensory modalities— touch, taste, smell, or pain. Some even report kinesthetic images, feelings in the muscles and joints. In the course of everyday life, many mental images have no obvious purpose. However, people do sometimes use their images to visualize the possible outcomes of a decision, understand or formulate verbal descriptions, boost motivation, or improve mood (Kosslyn et al., 1990). Imagining yourself performing a motor skill, such as diving or sprinting, may even improve your actual performance (Druckman & Swets, 1988).

Indeed, people in fields as diverse as sports and science have reported on the usefulness and effectiveness of mental imagery. East European athletes pioneered the use of visual imagery to rehearse a skill mentally before performing it, and many athletic coaches recommend the technique today. Albert Einstein said that he relied heavily on visual and kinesthetic imagery for formulating ideas. The happiest thought of his life, he once recalled, occurred in 1907, when he suddenly imagined a human observer falling freely from the roof of a house and realized the person would not experience a gravitational field in his immediate vicinity. This insight led to Einstein's formulation of the principle of general relativity, and physics was never again the same.

■ **proposition**
A unit of meaning that expresses a unitary idea and is made up of concepts.

■ **mental image**
A mental representation that mirrors or resembles the thing it represents. Mental images can occur in many and perhaps all sensory modalities.

QUICK QUIZ

1. Stuffing your mouth with cotton candy, licking a lollipop, and chewing a piece of beef jerky are all instances of the _____ *eating.*
2. Which concept is most basic: *furniture, chair,* or *high chair?*
3. In addition to concepts and images, _____ have been proposed as a basic form of mental representation.

ANSWERS:

1. concept 2. *chair* 3. propositions

How Conscious Is Thought?

Most of us, when we think about thinking, have in mind certain mental activities, such as solving problems or making decisions, that are carried out in a deliberate way with a conscious goal in mind. As we saw in previous chapters, however, not all mental processing is conscious. Many perceptual processes, from discerning the contours of objects to judging distance and depth, occur without our conscious intent. Implicit or unconscious memories may affect our actions even when we cannot consciously recall an event. Thinking, too, involves certain mental processes that lie outside of awareness.

Subconscious processes are mental activities that can be brought into consciousness when necessary. They allow us to handle more information and perform more complex tasks than if we depended entirely on conscious thought, because they can occur simultaneously, or in parallel, with other tasks (Kahneman & Treisman, 1984). Consider all the automatic routines that we perform "without thinking," though they might once have required careful, conscious attention: knitting, typing, driving a car, decoding the letters in a word in order to read it. Because of the capacity for automatic processing, with proper training people can even learn to perform simultaneously such complex tasks as reading and taking dictation (Hirst, Neisser, & Spelke, 1978).

Nonconscious processes are processes that remain outside of awareness but which nonetheless affect behavior. For example, most of us have had the odd experience of having a solution to a problem "pop into the mind" after we have given up trying to find one. Similarly, people will often say they rely on "intuition" rather than conscious reasoning to solve a problem. According to Kenneth Bowers and his colleagues (1990), the experience of intuition is actually an orderly process involving two stages. First, clues in the problem automatically activate certain memories or knowledge, and you begin to see a pattern or structure in the problem, although you can't yet say what it is. This nonconscious perception guides you toward a hunch or hypothesis. Then, in the second stage, your perception becomes conscious, and you become aware of a possible solution. This stage may feel like a sudden revelation ("Aha, I've got it!") but, actually, considerable mental work has already occurred, even though you were not aware of it.

Certain decisions to act also seem to be made without awareness. In a fascinating study, physiologist Benjamin Libet (1985) told volunteers to flex a wrist or finger whenever they felt like it. As soon as the urge to flex occurred, the person noted the position of a dot revolving on a clocklike screen. Electrodes monitored changes in brain activity occurring immediately before the volunteers' muscular movements, changes known as "readiness potentials." Libet found that readiness potentials occurred about half a second before muscle movement, but conscious awareness of an intention to move the muscle (as

Fortunately for this father, some well-learned tasks, such as typing, do not require much conscious thought; we perform them automatically, so we can do other things at the same time.

■ **subconscious processes**
Mental processes occurring outside of conscious awareness but accessible to consciousness when necessary.

■ **nonconscious processes**
Mental processes occurring outside of and not available to conscious awareness.

inferred from reports of dot position) occurred about three-tenths of a second *after* that. In other words, the brain seemed to be initiating action before the person was aware of it.

Libet drew an analogy between these results and what happens when a sprinter hears a starter's pistol go off. The sprinter will take off in less than a tenth of a second after the gun fires, yet that is too short a time to perceive the sound consciously. According to Libet, the runner must be responding unconsciously; then, after the sound enters awareness, the mind "corrects" the sequence, so the person thinks he or she heard the sound before actually moving. Libet's results are in agreement with current speculations about how the brain works (see Chapter 3).

In daily life, of course, much of our thinking is conscious—but we may not be thinking very *hard*. Like the pilots who left the de-icer off, we may act, speak, and make decisions out of habit, without stopping to analyze what we are doing or why we are doing it. Ellen Langer (1989) has called this mental inertia *mindlessness*. She notes that mindless processing keeps us from recognizing when a change in context requires a change in behavior. In one study by Langer and her associates (1978), a researcher approached people as they were about to use a photocopier and made one of three requests: "Excuse me, may I use the Xerox machine," "Excuse me, may I use the Xerox machine, because I have to make copies," or "Excuse me, may I use the Xerox machine, because I'm in a rush." Usually, people will let someone go before them *if* the person has a legitimate reason, as in the third request. In this study, however, people also complied when the reason sounded like an authentic explanation but was actually meaningless ("because I have to make copies"). They heard the form of the request, but not its content, and mindlessly stepped aside.

The mindless processing of information has certain benefits: If we stopped to think twice about everything we did, we would get nothing done ("Okay, now I'm reaching for my toothbrush; now I'm putting a quarter inch of toothpaste on it; now I'm brushing my upper right molars"). But it can also lead to errors and mishaps, ranging from the trivial (putting the butter in the dishwasher or locking yourself out of the car) to the serious (accepting racial stereotypes or driving carelessly).

Jerome Kagan (1989) argues that fully conscious awareness is really only needed when we must make a deliberate choice, when events happen that can't be handled automatically, and when unexpected moods and feelings arise. "Consciousness," he says, "can be likened to the staff of a fire department. Most of the time, it is quietly playing pinochle in the back room; it performs [only] when the alarm sounds." That may be so, but most of us would probably benefit if our mental "fire fighters" paid a little more attention to their jobs. Cognitive psychologists have devoted a great deal of study to mindful, conscious thinking, and to the barriers that sometimes keep us from reasoning clearly, making decisions rationally, and solving problems creatively.

Which cereal to buy? Without a certain degree of mindlessness, the decisions of everyday life would be overwhelming. But mindlessness also leads to miscalculations and poor choices. This consumer could be blindly loyal to the brand he has bought for years, or he could devote time and effort to making a thoughtful decision.

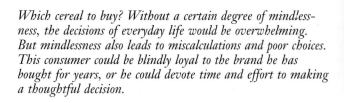

■ REASONING

Reasoning is purposeful mental activity that involves operating on information in order to reach conclusions. Unlike impulsive or "intuitive" responding, reasoning requires us to draw inferences from observations, facts, or assumptions. In reasoning, we use the concepts, propositions, and images stored in memory to review the past, make judgments, and solve problems.

Sources of Rationality

Philosophers and logicians distinguish various kinds of reasoning. Two of the most basic types are *deductive reasoning* and *inductive reasoning*, which both involve drawing conclusions from a series of observations or propositions *(premises)*.

In **deductive reasoning,** if the premises are true then the conclusion *must* be true. Often deductive reasoning takes the form of a *syllogism*, a simple argument consisting of two premises and a conclusion:

premise	All human beings are mortal.
premise	I am a human being.
conclusion	Therefore I am mortal.

We all think in syllogisms all the time, although many of our premises are implicit rather than clearly spelled out in our minds: "I never have to work on Saturday. Today is Saturday. Therefore, I don't have to work today." However, applying deductive reasoning to abstract problems that are divorced from everyday life does not seem to come so naturally; it depends on experience and schooling. In a study of the Kpelle Tribe in Africa (Scribner, 1977), researchers gave an unschooled farmer this problem: "All Kpelle men are rice farmers. Mr. Smith is not a rice farmer. Is he a Kpelle man?" The farmer insisted that the information provided did not allow a conclusion:

KPELLE MAN: I don't know the man in person. I have not laid eyes on the man himself.

RESEARCHER: Just think about the statement.

KPELLE MAN: If I know him in person, I can answer that question, but since I do not know him in person I cannot answer that question.

Because the Kpelle farmer was accustomed to drawing on personal knowledge alone to reach conclusions, he could not approach the task analytically. Yet in the exchange with the researcher, the man showed that he *could* reason deductively:

premise	If I do not know a person, I cannot draw any conclusions about that person.
premise	I do not know Mr. Smith.
conclusion	Therefore I cannot draw any conclusions about Mr. Smith.

In **inductive reasoning,** the premises provide support for the conclusion, but the conclusion *could* still be false. The conclusion does not follow *necessarily* from the premises, as it does in deductive reasoning. Often people think of inductive reasoning as the drawing of general conclusions from specific observations, as when you generalize from past experience: "I had three good meals at that restaurant; they sure have great food." But modern philosophers and logicians observe that an inductive argument can have general premises. Two logicians (Copi & Burgess-Jackson, 1992) give this example:

■ **reasoning**
The drawing of conclusions or inferences from observations, facts, or assumptions.

■ **deductive reasoning**
Reasoning in which the conclusion follows necessarily from certain premises.

■ **inductive reasoning**
Reasoning in which the premises provide support for a certain conclusion, but it is still possible for the conclusion to be false.

All cows are mammals and have lungs.
All whales are mammals and have lungs.
All humans are mammals and have lungs.
Therefore probably all mammals have lungs.

And inductive arguments can also have specific conclusions:

Most people with season tickets to the concert love music.
Jeannine has season tickets to the concert.
Therefore Jeannine probably loves music.

Science depends heavily on inductive reasoning. In their studies, researchers make many careful observations, then draw some conclusions that they think are probably true. But in inductive reasoning, no matter how much supporting evidence you gather, it is always possible that new information will show you are wrong. For example, you might discover that the three good meals you ate at that restaurant were not at all typical—that, in fact, all the other dishes on the menu are awful. Or you might learn that Jeannine bought season tickets to the concert only to impress a friend.

Logic alone is often inadequate for solving the messy problems of life for other reasons as well. First, even literate people often have trouble thinking logically. For example, they may say that the following syllogism is valid, when in fact it is not:

All birds have beaks.
That creature has a beak.
Therefore that creature is a bird.

"That creature" may well be a bird, but the conclusion does not follow from the premises. Other animals may also have beaks. Errors of this type occur because people reverse a premise. In this case, they convert "All birds have beaks" to "All beaked animals are birds." The reversed premise is plausible because few people are aware of any instances of *beaked creature* besides birds—but this premise is not the one that was given.

Second, different people often reach different conclusions even when they are thinking logically, because they disagree in their premises. Logic only tells us that *if* certain premises are true, a certain conclusion must follow (deductive reasoning) or is probably true (inductive reasoning). But logic does not tell us whether or not the premises *are* true. Controversial issues tend to be those in which premises cannot be proven true or false to everyone's satisfaction. For example, your position on abortion rights will probably depend on your premises about when meaningful human life begins, what rights an embryo has, the physical and psychological health of women, and a woman's right to control her own body.

Third, even when we feel fairly confident about our premises, there may be no clearly correct solution to a problem (Galotti, 1989). In formal reasoning problems—the kind you might find, say, on an intelligence test or a college entrance exam—the information you need for drawing a conclusion is specified clearly and there is a right answer. But in everyday *informal* reasoning problems, information may be incomplete; many approaches and viewpoints may compete, and you have to decide which one is most reasonable, based on what you know (see Table 8.1). Should the government raise taxes or lower them? What is the best way to improve public education? Is this a good time to buy a car? To think rationally about such issues, you need more than inductive and deductive logic. You also need some real-world knowledge, and the ability to think *dialectically*.

"If people would only be logical, they could get along." But logic is not enough when people start with different assumptions and values. How can people who are operating from different premises reach agreement?

TABLE 8.1

Two kinds of reasoning

In formal reasoning, we apply rules of logic to solve well-specified problems. In informal, or everyday, reasoning, we make plans, evaluate arguments, and choose options in order to solve problems that are less clearly defined. Below are some differences between the two modes of thinking.

Formal	Informal
All premises are supplied	Some premises are implicit, and some are not supplied at all.
There is typically one correct answer.	There are typically several possible answers that vary in quality.
There are often established methods of inference that apply to the problem.	There are rarely established procedures for solving the problem.
You usually know when the problem is solved.	It is often unclear whether the current "best" solution is good enough.
The problem is often of limited real-world interest.	The problem typically has personal relevance.
Problems are solved for their own sake.	Problems are often solved as a means of achieving other goals.

SOURCE: Adapted from Galotti, 1989.

Dialectical reasoning is the ability to evaluate opposing points of view. Philosopher Richard Paul (1984) describes it as a process of moving "up and back between contradictory lines of reasoning, using each to critically cross-examine the other." This is what juries are supposed to do to arrive at a verdict. A jury decision is not reached by applying some formula or set of procedures but (ideally) by open-minded consideration of arguments for and against, point and counterpoint. Dialectical reasoning is at the core of the critical thinking strategies we encourage in this book. When we ask you to examine evidence, question assumptions, or consider alternative interpretations, we are really asking you to reason dialectically.

Many people have trouble with dialectical reasoning because their self-esteem depends on being right and having their beliefs accepted by others. We all have our convictions, of course, but the inability to listen with an open mind

■ **dialectical reasoning**
A process in which opposing facts or ideas are weighed and compared, with a view toward determining the truth or resolving differences.

Deductive and inductive reasoning alone will not enable the members of this jury to reach a conclusion. They will also need to reason dialectically, weighing the evidence for and against guilt or innocence and the reasonableness of the arguments made by the attorneys.

to competing views is a major obstacle to critical thinking. Another obstacle is impatience. Some critics believe that the replacement of reading by television watching is partly to blame for the growing inability of young people to weigh opposing points of view. Television news often gives us "sound bites" instead of fully developed arguments, encouraging us to form quick, impulsive opinions instead of carefully considered ones (see Figure 8.1). The medium through which we get our information may affect our ability to evaluate the message, as we discuss further in "Think About It."

Sources of Irrationality

As we have noted, in many areas of life, we must make judgments and decisions under conditions of uncertainty. We can't know for sure whether the stock market will rise or fall, whether we will like an apartment we are considering renting, whether we'll have rain or sunshine during our vacation. Faced with incomplete information and the need to make a judgment or decision, we must

---

THINK ABOUT IT

Has Television Killed Off Reading—And If So, So What?

You find yourself with a free evening, and decide to spend a quiet, cozy evening at home. A novel someone gave you for your birthday beckons from the bookshelf. The TV listings tempt you with a new sitcom. Which do you pick, the book or the tube?

A growing number of academics, writers, and social commentators think you'll make the wrong choice. We bet you can guess what it is.

Reading, the critics say, appears to be going out of fashion. More books are being published than ever before, but many are sold as gifts and are not necessarily read or even skimmed. In an article called "The Death of Reading," writer Mitchell Stephens (1991) notes that more and more people are reading no books at all, and fewer and fewer people say they read yesterday's

newspaper. Poet and writer Katha Pollitt (1991) contends that college teachers get as worked up as they do about which literary works to teach— the traditional Western "classics" or works from many cultures by both sexes—in part because they assume students won't read anything else. "While we have been arguing so fiercely about which books make the best medicine," Pollitt says, "the patient has been slipping deeper and deeper into a coma." The curriculum debate, says Pollitt, misses the point that if students don't read *on their own,* they won't like reading and will forget the books on the required reading list the minute they finish them, no matter what the books are.

One reason people are reading less these days is that they are doing something else instead: watching TV, typically for 20 to 30 hours a week. The problem, say many critics, is not just television's content, which is often mindless, but the medium itself, which creates mindlessness. We watch TV primarily to amuse ourselves, but in fact, far from cheering us up, television has a negative impact on both mood and alertness. In a series of studies involving 1,200 subjects, Robert Kubey and Mihalyi Csikszentmihalyi (1990) found that although television relaxes people while they are watching, afterward they are likely to feel more tense, bored, irritable, and lonely than they did before, and less able to concentrate. In contrast, reading tends to leave people more relaxed, in a better mood, and with improved concentration.

Television may also discourage the development of imagination and creativity. Patricia Green-

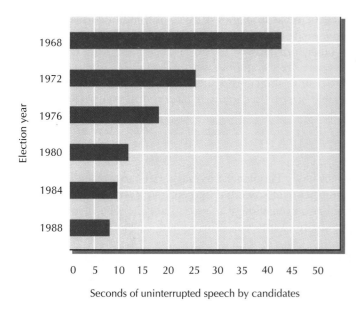

Election year

1968
1972
1976
1980
1984
1988

0 5 10 15 20 25 30 35 40 45 50

Seconds of uninterrupted speech by candidates

FIGURE 8.1

The shrinking sound bite
Since 1968, the average number of seconds of uninterrupted speech by political figures during network news coverage of U.S. presidential campaigns has declined steadily (Hallin, 1991). At this rate, candidates will soon have barely enough time to say, "Vote for me." Length is no guarantee of substance, of course; and brevity, as Shakespeare said, is the soul of wit. But critics worry that chopping political discourse into fleeting "sound bites" discourages people from critically analyzing the issues.

field and Jessica Beagles-Roos (1988) found that children *remember* more of a story when they see it on TV than when they hear it on radio (because visual images help memory), but their thinking becomes more *imaginative* when they hear the story on radio (because they have to imagine what the characters look like and what they are doing). The researchers fear that children who are raised on television "may have more information but be less imaginative, less verbally precise, and less mentally active" than earlier generations raised with only radio.

The medium that supplies our information about the world may also influence our ability to think critically. In his book *Amusing Ourselves to Death,* Neil Postman (1985) notes that because television lumps serious issues with silly ones, sells politicians the same way it sells cereal, and relies on a format of quick cuts and hot music, it discourages sustained, serious thought. Mitchell Stephens (1991) makes a similar point: "All television demands," he writes, "is our gaze." We can make dinner, play with the cat, or even daydream while watching it.

Television, say these critics, teaches us to judge not only products but also politicians by their ability to divert us. If an argument is too complex, if it takes more of our time than a "sound bite," we can just switch the channel. In contrast, reading gives us the opportunity to examine connections among statements and spot contradictions. It requires that we sit still and follow extended arguments. It frees us from the here and now, and encourages us to think in terms of abstract principles and not just personal experience.

Defenders of television feel the criticisms are unfair. There are many possible causes of reading's decline: the press of modern life, the popularity of outdoor sports and physical fitness, the time demands of juggling work and family responsibilities. Television not only entertains, but it also supplies information and intellectual enrichment (especially through public television programming). It gives families something to do together. It provides a diverse population with a common culture. *Mindful* television viewing, in which you analyze and discuss what you're seeing, can be mentally enriching (Langer & Piper, 1988). And who knows, perhaps television will eventually be put to better use, in ways that haven't yet been thought of; after all, it took a century and a half after the printing press was invented for someone to think of producing novels and newspapers (Stephens, 1991).

What do you think of these arguments? Are there books you can't wait to read, or has reading become a chore (and if so, why)? Would you read more books if you watched less television? Do you know as much about world events after watching the nightly news as you do after reading a newspaper? Is disapproval of television just a reactionary, backward-looking response to a successful new technology? If not, what can be done to see that people control the TV knob instead of allowing themselves to be controlled by it? Think about it.

"This CD player costs less than players selling for twice as much."

Mindlessness is a common source of irrationality.

■ **heuristic**
A rule of thumb that guides problem solving but does not guarantee an optimal solution. Heuristics are often used as shortcuts in solving complex problems.

■ **availability heuristic**
The strategy of estimating the probability of a certain type of event by how easy it is to think of or recall examples or instances; the more available such examples or instances in memory, the higher the estimate.

fall back on **heuristics,** habitual strategies or rules of thumb that may or may not produce a solution or the desired outcome. When you check the fuse box first during a power outage, or answer all the easy questions on a test before tackling the hard ones, you are using a heuristic.

Often heuristics are helpful and appropriate, but not always. Some heuristics are subject to predictable biases. Psychologists have shown that personal, economic, and political decisions cannot be explained without taking these biases into account (Simon, 1973; Tversky & Kahneman, 1986). Here are some of their findings.

EXAGGERATING THE IMPROBABLE. People tend to exaggerate the probability of very rare events. Therefore they will sometimes accept risk even though a gain is improbable, and avoid risk even though a loss is unlikely. The first tendency helps explain the popularity of lotteries. The second explains why people buy earthquake insurance.

As we saw in Chapter 2, people are especially likely to exaggerate the likelihood of rare but catastrophic events. One reason is the **availability heuristic,** the tendency to judge the probability of a certain type of event by how easy it is to think of examples or instances. The availability heuristic can explain why, in one study, people overestimated the frequency of deaths from tornadoes and underestimated the frequency of deaths from asthma, which occur 20 times as often but do not make headlines. It also explains why these same people estimated deaths from accidents and disease to be equally frequent, even though 16 times as many people die each year from disease as from accidents (Lichtenstein et al., 1978).

In everyday life, people will sometimes work themselves up into a froth about unlikely events, such as dying in an airplane crash, yet irrationally ignore real dangers to human life that are harder to visualize, such as a growth in cancer rates due to depletion of the ozone layer in the earth's atmosphere. Similarly, parents are often more frightened about real but unlikely threats to their children, such as being kidnapped by a stranger or having an adverse reaction to an immunization (both extremely unlikely), than they are about problems more common in children, such as depression, delinquency, or poor school performance (Stickler et al., 1991).

LOSS AVERSION. In general, people making a decision try to avoid risks or losses. For example, suppose you had to choose between two health programs to combat a disease expected to kill 600 people. Which would you prefer, a program that would definitely save 200 people, or one with a one-third probability of saving all 600 people and a two-thirds probability of saving none? When subjects (including physicians) were asked this question, most said they preferred the first program. In other words, they rejected the riskier, though potentially more rewarding, solution in favor of a sure gain. The same study, however, found that people *will* take a risk if they see it as a way to *avoid loss.* Subjects were asked to choose between a program in which 400 people would definitely die and a program in which there was a one-third probability of nobody dying and a two-thirds probability that all 600 would die. If you think about it for a while, you will see that the alternatives are exactly the same as in the first problem, but are merely worded differently. Yet this time, most people chose the second solution. They rejected risk when they thought of the outcome in terms of lives saved, but they accepted risk when they thought of the outcome in terms of lives lost (Tversky & Kahneman, 1981).

Few of us will have to face a decision involving hundreds of lives, but we may have to choose between different medical treatments for ourselves or a relative. Our decision may be affected by whether the doctor frames the choice in terms of mortality or survival.

COSTS VERSUS LOSSES. In general, disadvantages seem more acceptable if they are labeled "costs" than if they are labeled "losses." We may justify many losses in life by finding reasons to view them as costs. However, one's evaluation of a cost depends on the particular context. Suppose you buy a $10 ticket to a play. As you enter the theater you discover you have lost the ticket. Would you pay $10 for another ticket? Most people say no (Kahneman & Tversky, 1984). Now suppose you decide to see a play where admission is $10 a ticket. At the theater you discover that you have lost a $10 bill. Would you still pay $10 for a ticket to the play? Faced with this hypothetical problem, 88 percent of respondents said they would go ahead and buy the ticket.

Note that in each case, you would have been out $10. The "mental accounting" people do, however, differs in the two situations. People tend to view going to the theater as a transaction in which they exchange the cost of a ticket for the experience of seeing the play. In the first situation, losing the ticket raises the cost to a level that most people find unacceptable. In the second the loss of $10 is not mentally linked to the cost of the ticket. But when people are given both versions of the problem, they become more willing to replace the lost ticket in the first situation. They realize that the lost ticket can be regarded as equivalent to lost cash.

THE CONFIRMATION BIAS. If our primary objective is to make an accurate judgment, we will usually try to encode relevant information thoroughly and think about it carefully. But when our main motive is to reach a particular conclusion, whether about ourselves, other people, or circumstances, we may pay attention to evidence that confirms what we want to believe while ignoring or finding fault with evidence that points in a different direction (Kunda, 1990). We may think we are being rational and impartial, but we are only fooling ourselves.

This **confirmation bias** can affect that way students react to what they learn. When students read about scientific findings that run counter to one of their own cherished beliefs, or that challenge the wisdom of one of their own behaviors, they tend to acknowledge but minimize the strengths of the research. In contrast, when a study supports their view they will acknowledge any flaws (such as a small sample or a reliance on self-reports) but will give these flaws less weight than they would otherwise (Sherman & Kunda, 1989). It seems that in thinking critically, people apply a double standard: They think most critically about results they don't like. Could the confirmation bias be affecting your responses to the findings in this textbook?

You can see the confirmation bias at work in yourself, in friends, and in public commentators—whenever people are defending or debating their basic beliefs. Someone who favors biological explanations of behavior is apt to be more critical of studies that support social or cultural explanations than studies that support biological ones (and vice versa). Politicians are likely to accept economic news that confirms their philosophies and dismiss evidence that contradicts them as biased or unimportant.

BIASES DUE TO EXPECTATIONS. In Chapter 5 we saw that expectations affect how we perceive the world. They also affect what we do with the information we perceive. On July 3, 1988, a U.S. warship shot down an Iranian passenger jet taking off over the Persian Gulf, killing several hundred people aboard. The warship's computer system had at first misread the plane's altitude and identified it as an F-14 fighter jet but then corrected itself. Unfortunately, by that time, the initial information had created an expectation of an attack. In the stress of the moment, the skipper paid more attention to his crew's reports of an emergency than to new information being generated by the computer. The earlier

These excited horse-racing fans know the odds are against them, but they have placed their bets anyway. Your willingness to take such risks will depend in part on whether you regard losing money this way as a loss or as simply the cost of an afternoon's entertainment.

■ **confirmation bias**
The tendency to search for or attend only to information that confirms one's belief.

information was never reevaluated, and the crew assumed that the airliner was descending rather than ascending—with tragic results (Nisbett, 1988).

One expectation that human beings cannot live without is that events will have meaning. We do not like to think that they are due to chance or to causes that are too complicated to understand. We want an *explanation*. This quest for meaning is adaptive because it helps us understand and exert some control over life's events. Sometimes, however, we see a meaningful pattern or explanation when it doesn't really exist. Nearly every day the news media present an analysis of yesterday's rise or drop in stock prices. The change must have been due to international developments, or a recent economic forecast, or what the president did or didn't do. In actual fact, however, much of the fluctuation in the stock market is completely random (Shiller, 1987).

HINDSIGHT. Would you have been able to predict, beforehand, that in 1991 the Soviet Union would disintegrate, the Atlanta Braves would play in the World Series, and Elizabeth Taylor would marry for the eighth time? If you think so— don't be so sure. Studies done over the past two decades show that people who are told the actual outcome of an event (or the answer to a question) tend to be overly certain that they "knew it all along." Armed with the wisdom of hindsight, they see the outcome that actually occurred as inevitable and seemingly unalterable, and overestimate the probability that they could have predicted in advance what happened. Compared to judgments made *before* an event takes place, their judgments about their own ability to predict the event are inflated (Fischhoff, 1975; Hawkins & Hastie, 1990).

This **hindsight bias** shows up in all kinds of judgments, including political judgments ("I always knew my candidate would win"), medical judgments ("I could have told you that mole was cancerous"), and evaluations of other people's job performance ("Those in charge of Pearl Harbor in 1941 should have known it would be attacked"). In 1991, when a blinding dust storm along a stretch of highway in California caused the worst multicar crash in U.S. history, many people angrily concluded that the highway patrol should have recognized the danger and closed the road. But from the highway patrol's standpoint, the situation was more ambiguous: There were plenty of dust storms that people had gotten through perfectly well by slowing down or pulling off the road. Hindsight no doubt made the situation seem more straightforward in retrospect than it really was at the time.

Hindsight biases may be a sort of side effect of adaptive learning. When we try to predict the future, we consider many possible scenarios. But when we try to make sense of the past, we focus on explaining just one outcome—the one that actually occurred. This is efficient: explaining outcomes that didn't occur can be a waste of time. "In a sense," write Scott Hawkins and Reid Hastie (1990), "hindsight biases represent the dark side of successful learning and judgment." They are the dark side because when we are sure we knew something all along, we are less willing to find out what we need to know to make accurate predictions in the future. In medical conferences, for example, when doctors are presented with the case of a patient who died and are told what the postmortem findings were, they tend to think the case was "easier" than it actually was ("I would have known it was a brain tumor"), and so they learn less from the case than they should (Dawson et al., 1988).

As you can see, the decisions human beings make, and the feelings of regret or pleasure that follow, are not always logical. This fact has enormous implications for decision makers in business, medicine, government, the marketplace—in fact, in all areas of life. But before you despair about the human ability to think clearly, we should tell you that the situation is not hopeless. First, in everyday life, people often reach the right conclusions even though they may

■ **hindsight bias**
The tendency to overestimate one's ability to have predicted an event in advance, or answer a question correctly, once the actual outcome or answer is known.

not know how they do it. In Chapter 11, we will see that individuals who might not score too high on a test of mathematical reasoning can correctly calculate the odds in horse races or compare supermarket prices on products of varying sizes. Second, people are not equally irrational in all areas of life. When they are doing things they have some expertise in, or making decisions that have real-life consequences, certain cognitive biases diminish. Accountants who audit companies' books, for example, are less subject to the confirmation bias than are undergraduate students in psychology experiments, perhaps because auditors can be sued if they overestimate a firm's profitability or economic health (Smith & Kida, 1991).

Once we understand a bias, we may be able to reduce or eliminate it. For example, we have seen that doctors are vulnerable to the hindsight bias if they already know what caused a patient's death. But Hal Arkes and his colleagues (1988) were able to reduce a similar bias in neuropsychologists. The researchers presented the psychologists with a case study and asked them to state one reason why each of three possible diagnoses—alcohol withdrawal, Alzheimer's disease, and brain damage—might have been applicable. This procedure forced the psychologists to consider all the evidence, not just evidence that supported the "correct" diagnosis. The hindsight bias evaporated, presumably because the psychologists saw that the correct diagnosis had not been so obvious at the time the patient was being treated.

QUICK QUIZ

Put on your thinking cap to answer these questions.

1. Mervin observes that most of the items he bought as Christmas gifts cost more than they did last year, and he concludes that inflation is increasing. Which sort of reasoning is he using: inductive, deductive, or dialectical?
2. Yvonne is arguing with Henrietta about whether real estate is a better investment than stocks. "You can't convince me," says Yvonne. "I just know I'm right." Yvonne needs training in _____ reasoning.
3. Stu takes a break from studying to grab a bite at the student cafeteria. While there he meets a young woman. They hit it off, start to see each other regularly, and eventually get married. Says Stu, "I knew that day, when I headed for the cafeteria, that something special was about to happen. It was fate." What two cognitive biases are affecting Stu's thinking?
4. We are all vulnerable to the confirmation bias. Which findings in psychology are you likely to think most or least critically about, because of your own pet opinions? Flip through the chapters you have already read and note which facts or theories you resisted and which ones you readily accepted. You might also consider findings from other courses. Be honest!

ANSWERS:

1. inductive 2. dialectical 3. the need for meaning and the hindsight bias 4. We can't answer this one for you, but people often have biases about the importance of biology versus culture in explaining human behavior, the strength and importance of sex differences, the accuracy of their own memories, the impact of drugs, the use of animals in research, and many other topics we haven't gotten into yet: drug abuse, multiple personalities, midlife crises, adolescent trauma, prejudice.

■ PROBLEM SOLVING

Individuals, families, businesses, governments—all have problems. They may be as mundane as getting to work when the car breaks down or as profound as avoiding nuclear war. Problems bring all our cognitive abilities into play: internal representation, memory, and reasoning.

Paths to Problem Solving

It may seem obvious, but before you can solve a problem, you have to recognize that one exists. This is easier for some people than others. Students who have trouble learning (which is certainly a problem) are less likely than others to notice when a textbook contains incomplete or inconsistent information, or when a passage is especially difficult. As a result, they spend no more time on difficult passages than on easy ones. Poor learners also tend to go through the motions of reading without realizing when they have failed to comprehend the material (Bransford et al., 1986).

Once a problem is recognized, people generally go about solving it in four steps (Wessells, 1982): (1) *defining the problem*, which may be difficult if it lacks clear starting and end points (creating a new style of art, finding a good term paper topic, inventing a better mousetrap); (2) *devising a strategy*; (3) *executing the strategy*; and (4) *evaluating progress toward the goal*. As conditions affecting the problem change, the problem solver may have to repeat one or more of these steps before reaching the goal. For example, you may decide to solve your money problems by finding a better job, but if a recession reduces the number of jobs available you may need to rethink your strategy—perhaps keeping your current job but spending less.

Problems can sometimes be attacked by methods guaranteed to produce a solution, even if the solver does not understand how they work. Such methods are called **algorithms.** Some algorithms consist of a set of rules. To solve a problem in long division, you apply a set of rules learned in the fourth grade. Similarly, to bake a chocolate cake, you use a set of rules called a recipe. Other algorithms require an exhaustive search through all possible solutions. For example, if you forgot the last digit of a friend's unlisted telephone number, you could simply try each of the possibilities, from 0 through 9, until you reached your friend.

Often, however, there is no obvious sequence of steps that will lead inevitably to a solution. Instead, the solution depends on certain rules of thumb, which, as we saw earlier, are called *heuristics*. Heuristics suggest a course of action but do not guarantee an optimal solution. For instance, when you play chess, you can't possibly consider all of the possible strategies for winning. (Don't try; it would take you longer than the estimated life of the universe to work out all the possible sequences of moves!) But your knowledge of the game and your past history of successes and failures suggest certain strategies, such as "Move the powerful pieces first" and "Control the center of the board." A doctor trying to determine the best treatment for breast cancer, a marriage counselor trying to advise a troubled couple, and a factory owner trying to boost production must all rely on heuristics. Life's problems are rarely susceptible to "cookbook" solutions.

Problem-solving Pitfalls

If problem solving is simply a four-stage process, why don't more problems get solved? We have already encountered several answers: the difficulty people have with logic, their reluctance to consider opposing points of view, and their biases in evaluating alternatives. But these are not the only barriers.

■ **algorithm**
A problem-solving strategy that is guaranteed to lead eventually to a solution.

To find out why some people are better at devising problem-solving strategies than others, researchers have compared experts and nonexperts in engineering, business management, physics, medicine, and other fields (Bransford et al., 1986; Lash, 1988; Wagner & Sternberg, 1986). One major difference is that the experts have a rich fund of knowledge relevant to the problem at hand. On the average, they are no more intelligent than novices, but they know more and do not have to search laboriously for information. On the basis of experience they can recognize patterns, retrieve cognitive schemas (see Chapter 7), eliminate dead-end strategies, and quickly arrive at a solution. This capacity to acquire a vast storehouse of knowledge about the world, gained through experience, gives human intelligence its speed and flexibility and distinguishes it from the **artificial intelligence** of a computer (see "A Closer Look at Artificial Intelligence" on page 292).

In daily life, knowledge can spell the difference between helplessness and mastery of life's problems. After a lecture on language development, a young woman we know asked her professor whether something might be wrong with her 3-year-old son, who did not yet speak. (Until the lecture, the student did not recognize the possible existence of a problem.) The professor asked if there was any deafness in the family. There was. Then the professor suggested that the child get a physical checkup. But the student was poor; she couldn't pay a doctor. So the professor suggested that she contact the county health agency, which offered free exams. How, asked the student, do you contact this agency? Because she lacked important knowledge—about the contribution of hearing impairment to speech problems, the normal age for the appearance of speech, the existence of county health services, and the listing of such services in the phone book under "County Government"—she was unable to solve her problem without assistance.

Another source of difficulty in problem solving is rigidity in trying out different approaches. When certain strategies and rules have been successful in the past, they may become habitual: A person may develop a **mental set,** or tendency to solve new problems using the same procedures that worked before. In daily life, mental sets make human learning and problem solving efficient. Because of them, we do not continually have to reinvent the wheel. But mental sets are not helpful when a problem calls for fresh insights and methods. They cause us to cling to the same old assumptions, hypotheses, and strategies, blinding us to breakthroughs that would lead to correct, better, or more rapid

■ **artificial intelligence**
"Intelligent" behavior performed by computers. Also, the study of the methods used to program such behavior in computers.

■ **mental set**
The tendency to solve a problem with the same strategies and rules used on previous problems.

What would a robot have to do before you could call it "intelligent"? This cheerful piece of machinery informed visitors to the Boston Museum of Science, "Humans, you are witnessing the beginning of a great new era." Yet robots cannot contemplate the meaning of death, paint a great work of art, or know that it's time to prune the roses simply by looking at them.

A CLOSER LOOK AT ARTIFICIAL INTELLIGENCE

The Computer's Lament: If I Only Had a Brain

The philosopher René Descartes, who wrote "I think, therefore I am," struggled long and hard to distinguish the consciousness of human beings from the workings of mere machines. Little did he suspect that three centuries later, machines, too, would think. We refer, of course, to computers, sometimes known as electronic brains. No computer has yet achieved the sophistication of HAL, whose sinister circuits plotted rebellion in the film *2001: A Space Odyssey*. But these remarkable machines can mimic and sometimes surpass their human creators at reasoning, applying algorithms and heuristics, testing hypotheses, and remembering facts. They make plans, hold limited conversations, play chess, and even compose music. Computerized robots, though neither as talented nor as cute as *Star Wars'* R2D2, both hear and see.

Scientists in the field of *artificial intelligence,* which draws on many disciplines including psychology, design the sets of instructions (programs) that enable machines to do all these things. Until recently, most workers in artificial intelligence did not care whether the machine actually used human strategies as long as it behaved as it was supposed to. The computer's successes were many and often put human processing to shame. As early as the 1950s, when computers were still at the Neanderthal stage in their evolution, they could use logical principles to find alternate proofs of theorems in symbolic logic (Newell & Simon, 1972). The machines were tireless, and, barring a power outage, would continue to operate with unvarying efficiency day and night, even without coffee breaks. They were also fast: They could reason and compute in millionths or even trillionths of a second, making the human mind look like molasses. And they were accurate, carrying out instructions with absolute precision and reliably regurgitating whatever was stored in their memory banks.

But unbounded optimism soon gave way to caution. The powerful computers might diagnose illnesses or solve mathematical problems, but they could not carry out the most mundane everyday activities, like understanding a casual conversation, planning a trip to the grocery store, or recognizing a face. These simple accomplishments (simple for human beings, that is) require a commonsense knowledge of the world, which living things absorb through the senses. A computer knows only what a programmer has put into its data base. It lacks the millions—possibly billions—of bits of information that people collect over a lifetime.

solutions. As an illustration: Copy the figure below and see if you can connect the dots by using no more than four straight lines, without lifting the pencil from the paper. A line must pass through each point. Can you do it?

Most people have difficulty solving this problem because they are set to perceive patterns, and they interpret the arrangement of dots as a square. Once having done so, they assume that they can't extend a line beyond the "boundaries" of the square. As we observed in the chapter on sensation and perception, the tendency to perceive patterns enables us to make sense of the world. But in this case a correct solution requires you to break the set. Now that you know this, you might try again if you haven't yet solved the puzzle. Some possible solutions are given on page 309.

One type of mental set is known as **functional fixedness**. This is the tendency to encode an object only in terms of its usual function. There is nothing

■ **functional fixedness**
The tendency to consider only the usual function of an object and overlook other possible uses. It often leads to rigidity in problem solving.

When you read the words, "The phone rang. The woman got up from her chair," you can predict what will probably happen next. When you hear "Mary Had a Little Lamb," you know that the jingle is about a pet, not Mary's lunch (Allman, 1986). And when you see a friend on the street, you immediately recognize her, even if she is wearing a new outfit and just had her hair permed. Computers lack these abilities. Moreover, because they do not take context into account, they may translate "He shot off his mouth without thinking" as "He absentmindedly fired a bullet into his jaw," or "The spirit is willing but the flesh is weak" as "The vodka is good, but the meat is rotten." Think of what a literal-minded computer might make of *rap* and *hip-hop*!

In recent years, efforts have been made to give computers some of the everyday knowledge that human beings take for granted. But some members of the "artificial intelligentsia" believe that if computers are to be truly intelligent, they must be modeled after the greatest computer of them all, the human brain. Most computers process instructions sequentially and work on a single incoming stream of data. In contrast, the brain performs many operations simultaneously, and recognizes patterns "all at once" rather than as a sequence of information bits. It can do these things because each neuron communicates with thousands of others, which in turn communicate with millions more. Although no single neuron is terribly smart, millions of them working collectively and simultaneously produce cognition (Rumelhart, McClelland, & the PDP Research Group, 1986).

Computer scientists are now designing machines called *neural networks* that attempt to imitate the brain's vast grid of densely connected neurons (Anderson & Rosenfeld, 1988; D. Levine, 1990). In this approach, called *connectionism*, simple processing units are linked up to one another in a weblike system, much as neurons in the brain are, sharing information and working in parallel. Like the human brain, neural networks do not always find the very best solution to a problem, but usually they do find a good solution quickly. They also have the potential to learn from experience by adjusting the strengths of their "neural" connections in response to new information. These systems are now in their infancy, but if they are ultimately successful, they will be able to recognize patterns even when the information is incomplete—just as a 3-year-old child can.

Researchers working on neural networks believe they can give computers a humanlike ability to think, remember, and solve problems. Critics, however, remain skeptical. Human intelligence, they note, arises from the experiences of human life, including the experience of inhabiting a human body. For better or worse, human thought is inseparable from emotion, motives, and the pursuit of pleasure. And human beings *know* they think, whereas computers, as far as anyone knows, lack consciousness. But then, perhaps they don't need it—they have us.

wrong with that, of course, *unless* the solution to a problem requires you to consider some novel uses. Functional fixedness may prevent you from seeing that a nail file can be used as a screwdriver when necessary. Figure 8.2 shows a problem that requires you to overcome functional fixedness.

FIGURE 8.2

Candle mounting problem
If you were given the items shown here, and only these items, how would you go about mounting a candle on the wall? (The solution is shown in Figure 8.5 on page 304.)

Cultivating Creativity

Creativity is the ability to go beyond present knowledge, resist the persistence of set, and produce something new. Creative people recognize that problems are often solvable in more than one way. They exercise **divergent thinking;** instead of stubbornly sticking to one tried and true path, they explore some side alleys and generate several possible solutions. As a result, they are able to use familiar concepts in unexpected ways (see Figure 8.3). Less creative individuals rely solely on **convergent thinking,** following a particular set of steps that they think will converge on one correct solution. Convergent thinking is useful (it includes logical reasoning and the use of algorithms), but to be creative in solving the fuzzy problems of life, you also need to be skilled at using divergent thinking.

Traditional tests of creativity measure fluency, flexibility, and originality in generating solutions to problems (Guilford, 1950). One, the Alternate Uses Test, asks you to think of as many uses as possible for common items, such as a brick or a paper clip. Another, the Remote Associates Test (Mednick, 1962), presents sets of three words and asks you to find an associated word for each set. For example, an appropriate answer for the set *news-clip-wall* is *paper*. Associating elements in new ways by finding a common connection among them is thought to be an important component of creativity. (Can you find associates for the word sets below? The answers are given in the Very Quick Quiz on page 296.)

> 1. piggy-green-lash
> 2. surprise-line-birthday
> 3. mark-shelf-telephone
> 4. stick-maker-tennis
> 5. blue-cottage-cloth
> 6. motion-poke-down
> 7. gem-wall-stepping
> 8. chorus-bee-side
> 9. lunch-car-gift
> 10. foul-ground-pen

Recently, a new approach to measuring creativity has emerged. The Lifetime Creativity Scales (Richards et al., 1988) assess a person's actual history of creativity in a broad range of work and leisure activities. A skilled interviewer obtains detailed information about the person's creative accomplishments, including those that may not have been generally recognized. Then trained raters, using a special scoring manual, judge each product, action, or idea on its originality and meaningfulness. The scales measure both *peak creativity* (as reflected by major enterprises or activities) and *extent of involvement* (the pervasiveness of creative activity in a person's life). The invention of an unusual machine or the writing of a distinctive novel would earn you a high peak creativity score. The ongoing diagnosis and repair of automobiles or the writing of colorful letters to the editor would show some creativity. The routine assembly of mechanical parts according to a prescribed pattern or the proofreading of a manuscript would demonstrate "insignificant" creativity.

This approach assumes that creativity is a fundamental survival skill that helps us adapt to constantly changing conditions, and is not confined to traditional creative arts, such as painting or music. Creativity can be found in the auto mechanic who invents a new tool, the parent who designs and makes her children's clothes, the office manager who devises a clever way to streamline work flow, or the food hobbyist who concocts unusual gourmet meals (Richards, 1991).

■ **creativity**
A flexible, imaginative thought process leading to novel but appropriate solutions to problems, original ideas and insights, or new and useful products.

■ **divergent thinking**
Mental exploration of unusual or unconventional alternatives during problem solving. It tends to enhance creativity.

■ **convergent thinking**
Thinking aimed at finding a single correct answer to a problem by applying knowledge and reasoning.

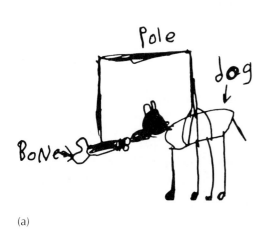

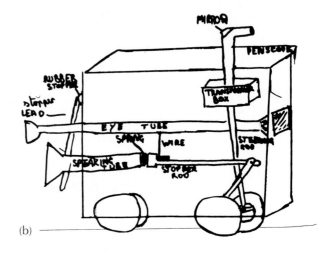

(a)   (b)

Figure 8.3

Creativity begins early

When creativity expert Edward de Bono asked children aged 4 to 14 to design a dog-exercising machine, their solutions showed they could use familiar concepts in new and imaginative ways. The child who produced drawing (a) came up with a simple idea of having the dog chase a bone held always out of reach by a harness on the dog's back—frustrating for the dog, but effective. The solution in (b) is more sophisticated: When the dog barks into a "speaking tube," the energy of its barking activates a system of rods and springs, causing the wheels of the cart to turn. An "eye tube" allows the poor pooch to see where it is going, but this is only a courtesy, since a periscope automatically "sees" obstacles and a "transformer box" adjusts the steering accordingly. The more the dog barks, the faster the cart moves. What kind of dog-exercising machine can you create?

Interestingly, creativity and intelligence are only weakly correlated (Barron & Harrington, 1981). A certain level of intelligence (as measured by IQ tests) seems necessary for creativity in most fields, but a high IQ does not guarantee that you will be creative. Personality characteristics seem more important and include the following (MacKinnon, 1962, 1968; McCrae, 1987; Schank, 1988):

1. *Nonconformity.* Creative individuals are not overly concerned about what others think of them. They are willing to risk ridicule by proposing ideas that may initially appear foolish or off the mark.

2. *Independence.* Highly creative people tend to prefer working alone instead of in a group. During childhood, they are often encouraged to solve problems themselves instead of depending on others. However, they are not antisocial. On the contrary, they tend to be outgoing and well adjusted. (It is true that among geniuses in the arts, there seems to be a higher-than-usual rate of mental disturbance, but we are talking about creative people in general.)

3. *Confidence.* In general, creative people neither fear failure nor overvalue success. They are therefore able to enjoy the challenge of a complex, ambiguous, or difficult problem. They do not let the emotional turmoil that can sometimes accompany intellectual or artistic uncertainty deter them.

4. *Curiosity.* Creative people usually have a wide range of interests and therefore accumulate a broad base of knowledge. They are open to new experiences and look into everyday puzzles that others would ignore. As one writer puts it, "They wonder why butterflies have to be caterpillars first. They wonder why the drugstore on the corner always does well and why the one across the street from it seems to be up for sale every two years. . . . They notice things and ask questions about them" (Schank, 1988).

5. *Persistence.* This is perhaps the most important attribute of the creative person. After that imaginary light bulb goes on over your head, you still have to work hard to make the illumination last. Or as Thomas Edison, who invented the real light bulb, reportedly put it, "Genius is one-tenth inspiration and nine-tenths perspiration."

Creativity requires motivation, energy, and discipline, but it can be cultivated. The humanistic psychologist Carl Rogers argued that parents who provide conditions of "psychological safety and freedom" will allow their children to develop their creative potential. A group of researchers confirmed this idea with a longitudinal study of 106 families (Harrington, Block, & Block, 1987). The most creative children had parents who respected their opinions, allowed them to make many of their own decisions, encouraged them to explore and question, gave them time to daydream, shared good times, and praised their accomplishments.

The characteristics of creativity are apparent in the biographies of successful artists, writers, scientists, and inventors. Consider the story of Georges de Mestral, a Swiss inventor, who was hunting one day in the late 1940s when he and his dog accidentally brushed up against a bush that left them both covered with burrs. When de Mestral tried to remove the burrs, they clung stubbornly to his clothes. This would be merely a minor annoyance to most of us, but de Mestral was curious about why the burrs were so hard to remove. After he got home, he studied them under a microscope and discovered that hundreds of tiny hooks on each burr had snagged on the threads of his pants. Burrs, he thought, would make great fasteners.

That was the inspiration. There followed several years of perspiration as de Mestral tried to figure out how to attach tiny hooks to pieces of tape in such a way that they would stay lined up. He also struggled to find a way of producing equally tiny loops for the hooks to attach to. After testing many methods, he finally succeeded. The result: Velcro fasteners, now used on millions of items, from blood pressure cuffs to tennis shoes (Madigan & Elwood, 1984).

(For additional lessons to be learned from creative thinkers of the past, see "Taking Psychology with You" on page 306.)

VERY QUICK QUIZ

1. When Georges de Mestral went about solving the problem of producing tiny loops, was he using algorithms or heuristics?
2. Which of the personality traits associated with creativity did de Mestral exemplify?

ANSWERS:

1. heuristics **2.** nonconformity, independence, confidence, curiosity, and persistence—in other words, all of them.

ANSWERS TO CREATIVITY TEST ON PAGE 294:

back, party, book, match, cheese, slow, stone, line, box, play

---

■ LANGUAGE

In the biblical story of the Tower of Babel, God punishes humankind for the sin of arrogance by transforming the one language shared by all into a babel of mutually incomprehensible tongues. Unable to understand one another, the various speech groups scatter to the four corners of the earth. But the punishment could have been worse: Our species could have been deprived of language entirely.

Language is our most impressive and versatile tool. Every human culture possesses this tool, and except in cases of profound retardation or disturbance, all children easily acquire it. (The process of language acquisition is discussed in Chapter 13.) Nonlinguistic communication can be both eloquent and informative, but language is what permits us to transmit the nuances and niceties of meaning that are the foundation of social life. You have learned this fact first-hand if you have ever found yourself in a country where you speak only a little of the language. In such circumstances, a person accustomed to conveying complex abstract thoughts is reduced to the concrete level of communication typical of a young child.

Speaking of Language

A **language** is a system for combining elements that are in themselves meaningless into utterances that convey meaning. The elements are usually sounds, but not always. In the United States and Canada, many hearing-impaired people use as their primary language American Sign Language (ASL), which employs gesture rather than sound (see Figure 8.4). In other countries, other gestural languages are used. These gestural "tongues" are not simply pantomime. Gestural signals, or *signs*, convey both abstract and concrete concepts and ideas, and usually you can't guess from their form what they mean. Formal rules govern the production, sequencing, and timing of the signs, just as formal rules govern the order and production of words in spoken language.

If language is not equivalent to speech, how can we know whether a communication system qualifies as a language? Linguists have identified several essential characteristics (Hockett, 1960). These include:

1. *Meaningfulness.* The main purpose of any language is to make meaningful reference to things, ideas, and feelings. Meaningfulness is achieved by the arbitrary but consistent combination of elements (such as sounds and gestures) into meaningful units (such as words or signs). There are enough words (or signs) in a language to express all the concepts that a community might want or need to express.

■ **language**
A system that combines meaningless elements such as sounds or gestures into structured utterances that convey meaning.

FIGURE 8.4

A poem for four hands
Language need not involve speech; American Sign Language (ASL) can be used to express both everyday meanings and poetic or musical ones. These two signers are experimenting with the signed equivalent of a duet. It describes the daily activities of three generations living in harmony together. In this excerpt, the man signs "brother/is bathing,/grandpa/is rocking" while the woman signs "sister/is playing,/grandma/is knitting."

2. *Displacement.* Languages permit communication about objects and events that are not present here and now—that are displaced in time or space. Merely pointing to things is not language.

3. *Productivity.* Language allows the expression and comprehension of an infinite number of novel utterances, created on the spot. You will find few, if any, sentences in this book that you have read, heard, or spoken before in exactly the same form, yet you can understand this book. Except for a few fixed phrases (such as "How are you?" or "Have a nice day"), most utterances we make or hear are new.

Since most utterances are novel, how are we able to produce and understand them? According to most *psycholinguists* (researchers who study the psychology of language), we apply a large but finite set of rules that make up the **grammar** of the language. These rules tell us which strings of sounds and words form acceptable utterances and which do not. Most people cannot actually state the rules of their grammar (despite the efforts of their English teachers). But they do use them. For example, you can transform the active sentence "John adores Mary" into a passive sentence, "Mary is adored by John." This change requires you to know that the subject and object of the original sentence must be switched, that the verb must be changed in form, and that a preposition must be inserted before the object. You carry out these operations without even thinking about it.

Syntax is the part of grammar that governs how words are arranged to convey meaning. Obviously, it makes all the difference in the world whether you say "Cassandra ate the cow" or "The cow ate Cassandra." We use our knowledge of syntax to figure out how the *surface structure* of a sentence as it is actually spoken or written reveals an underlying *deep structure* that contains meaning. Two sentences with different surface structures may have the same or nearly the same underlying structure. In "John kissed Mary," John is the grammatical subject and Mary the object; in "Mary was kissed by John," the opposite is true. But both sentences have a deep structure in which John is the actor and Mary is the recipient of the action.

A single surface structure may also have two or more possible deep structures. In that case, the sentence is ambiguous. For example, "They heard the shooting of the hunters" has two possible underlying structures. In one, the hunters are the actors; they are doing the shooting. In the other, the hunters are the objects of the action, the victims of the shooting. Similarly, in "They are bouncing babies," the babies may be the bouncers or the "bouncees." Ambiguous sentences are the linguistic equivalent of the ambiguous pictures we discussed in Chapter 5. Just as perception provides an interpretation of sensory information, the deep structure provides an interpretation of the surface structure of a sentence.

Linguistic rules alone are not enough to get us from the surface to the deep structure of a sentence. Psycholinguists have found that expectations, context, and our general knowledge of the world are equally important. If Wendy has been running a fever and her doctor feels her forehead, the sentence "She seemed cool to him" will mean one thing. If Wendy has been sitting next to Zeke all night without saying a word, "She seemed cool to him" will mean something quite different. And if Wendy comes across as socially "with it," the phrase will have yet another meaning. The cartoon on the next page illustrates how linguistic jokes sometimes reverse expectations to produce amusing meanings.

Can Animals Learn Language?

By the criteria of language we have listed, animals other than human beings do not seem to have their own languages. Of course, animals do communicate, using gestures, body postures, facial expressions, vocalizations, and odors. But a

■ **grammar**
The system of linguistic rules governing sounds (or in the case of sign languages, gestures), meanings, and syntax of a language. It may be viewed as a mechanism for generating all possible sentences in a language.

■ **syntax**
The set of grammatical rules governing the way words combine to form sentences.

Last night, Maurice ate food that disagreed with him.

Humor is often created by violating an expectation about the way words can be used in a particular context.

communication system is not necessarily a language. Dolphins exchange clicks and whistles with one another in consistent ways, but no one has shown that these sounds form a meaningful, productive code. The grunts and screeches of an ape seem limited to a set repertoire. Some of these grunts have more specific meanings than previously thought. For example, vervet monkeys seem to have separate calls to warn about leopards, eagles, and snakes (Cheney & Seyfarth, 1985). But the sounds are not combined in various ways to produce novel utterances (or at least, not that we can tell). Thus Bongo may make a certain type of sound when he encounters food, but he cannot say, "The bananas in the next grove are a lot riper than the ones we ate last week and sure beat our usual diet of termites."

Perhaps, however, certain animals could acquire language if they got a little help from their human friends. Dozens of researchers have tried to provide chimpanzees with just such help. Because the vocal tract of a chimpanzee does not permit speech, early efforts to teach chimpanzees spoken language were failures (though some comprehension did occur). During the 1960s and 1970s, researchers tried some different approaches. In one project, chimpanzees learned to use as words geometric plastic shapes arranged on a magnetic board (Premack & Premack, 1983). In another, they learned to punch symbols on a computer keyboard (Rumbaugh, 1977). In yet another, they learned hundreds of signs from American Sign Language (Fouts & Rigby, 1977; Gardner & Gardner, 1969). The animals in these and other studies learned to follow instructions, answer questions, and make requests. More important, they combined individual signs or symbols into longer utterances that they had never "heard" (or more precisely, seen) before. In general, their linguistic abilities appeared to resemble those of a 2-year-old child acquiring language.

As you can imagine, accounts of the apes' abilities caused quite a stir. The animals were apparently using their newfound skills to apologize for being disobedient, scold their trainers, and even talk to themselves. Koko, a lowland gorilla, reportedly used signs to say that she felt happy or sad, refer to past and future events, mourn for her dead pet (a kitten named All-Ball), and convey her yearning for a baby. She even lied on occasion, when she did something naughty (Patterson & Linden, 1981).

For a decade or so, these achievements met unquestioning acceptance by many psychologists and most of the public. The animals were cute and lovable, the findings appealing. But then skeptics, and some of the researchers themselves, began to point out serious problems (Seidenberg & Petitto, 1979; Terrace, 1985). In their desire to talk to the animals and their affection for their primate friends, researchers had failed to be objective. They had overinterpreted the animal's utterances, reading all sorts of meanings and intentions into a sin-

It's hard not to love apes that use sign language to apologize, ask for fruit, or lie when they are naughty. But do signing apes really have language? What do we mean by language anyway?

gle sign. In videotapes, they could be seen unwittingly giving nonverbal cues that might enable the apes to respond correctly without understanding. Further, the animals appeared to be stringing signs and symbols together haphazardly to earn a reward instead of using grammatical rules to produce novel utterances. In most cases, signs followed no particular order, suggesting that "Me eat banana" was no different for an ape than "Banana eat me." Longer utterances did not bring greater complexity in syntax, but mere repetition: "Give orange me give eat orange me eat orange give me eat orange give me you" (R. Brown, 1986).

Today, the Koko project still appears to suffer from these problems (Davidson & Hopson, 1988). Other studies, however, have benefited from the criticisms and are a marked improvement on past research. Carefully controlled experiments have established that after arduous training, chimps can acquire the ability to use symbols to refer to objects (Savage-Rumbaugh, 1986). In some projects, chimpanzees are spontaneously using signs to converse with each other, suggesting that they are not merely imitating or trying to get a reward (Van Cantfort & Rimpau, 1982). A young chimp named Loulis has learned dozens of signs from Washoe, the original signing chimp (Fouts, Fouts, & Van Cantfort, 1989). A male pygmy chimpanzee named Kanzi has learned to understand English words and short sentences without specific training (Savage-Rumbaugh et al., 1991). Kanzi hears the words through headphones, and his caregivers do not know which words are being tested, so they cannot give the animal cues. Kanzi has also learned (with training) to manipulate keyboard symbols to request foods or to announce his intentions, and he seems to use some simple grammatical ordering rules to convey meaning.

Other research suggests that even certain nonprimates can acquire some aspects of language. In Hawaii, Louis Herman and his colleagues have taught dolphins to respond to sentencelike requests made in two artificial languages, one consisting of computer-generated whistles and another of hand and arm gestures (Herman, 1987; Herman, Richards, & Wolz, 1984). To interpret a request correctly, the dolphins must take into account both the meaning of the individual symbols in a string of whistles or gestures and the order of the symbols (syntax). For example, they must understand the difference between "To left Frisbee, right surfboard take" and "To right surfboard, left frisbee take." Remarkably, they can interpret sequences of gestures from a televised image of the trainer as well as they can from a live trainer (Herman, Morrel-Samuels, & Pack, 1990).

Researchers have used several methods in their efforts to teach apes language. Here Kanzi, a pygmy chimp with the most advanced linguistic skill yet acquired by a nonhuman primate, answers questions and makes requests by punching symbols on a specially designed computer keyboard.

In another remarkable project, Irene Pepperberg (1988, 1990) has taught an African gray parrot named Alex to count, classify, and compare objects by vocalizing English words. When the bird is shown up to six items and is asked how many there are, he responds with spoken (squawked?) English phrases, such as "two cork(s)" or "four key(s)." Alex can also make requests ("Want pasta") and can answer various questions about objects ("What color? Which is bigger?"). When presented with a blue cork and a blue key and asked "What's the same?" he will correctly respond "Color." He actually scores slightly better with new objects than with familiar ones, suggesting that he is not merely memorizing a set of stock phrases.

All of these results are certainly impressive, but scientists are still divided over just what the animals in these studies are doing. Should it be called language? On one side are those who worry about *anthropomorphism*, the tendency to falsely attribute human qualities to nonhuman beings. They remind us of the story of Clever Hans, a "wonder horse" at the turn of the century who was said to possess mathematical abilities (Fernald, 1984). Clever Hans would answer math problems by stamping his hoof. For example, if asked to solve "3 times 6 divided by 2," Clever Hans would tap his foot 9 times. But a little experimentation revealed that when Hans was prevented from seeing the questioner, his "powers" left him. It seems that questioners were staring at the animal's feet and leaning forward expectantly after stating the problem, then lifting their eyes and relaxing as soon as he completed the right number of taps. Clever Hans was indeed clever, but not at math. He was simply responding to nonverbal signals that people were inadvertently providing.

On the other side are those who warn against *anthropocentrism*, the tendency to think, falsely, that human beings have nothing in common with other animals. The need to see our own species as unique, they say, may keep us from recognizing that other species are smarter than we give them credit for. Those who take this position point out that most modern researchers have gone to great lengths to avoid the Clever Hans problem. The debate over the capacity of animals for language is part of a larger controversy about animal intelligence, with some scientists concluding that some animals anticipate, plan, and make choices and others not so sure. The outcome of this debate has some intriguing implications for how we view ourselves and our place among other species on the planet. Stay tuned.

Alex is one smart bird—but how smart? Alex's abilities raise intriguing questions about the intelligence of animals and their capacity for certain aspects of language.

QUICK QUIZ

Fill in the blanks.

1. You've trained your pet cockatiel to say "Play it again, Sam" for a food reward. The bird always produces this string of sounds when it is hungry, but it does not respond to any of the words or to the sentence as a whole in any consistent way. The animal does not have language, since its "speech" lacks _____ .

2. A honeybee performs a little dance that communicates to other bees the direction and distance of food. Since the bee can "talk" about something that is located elsewhere, its communication system shows _____. But since the bee can create no utterances other than the ones that are genetically wired into its repertoire, its communication system lacks _____.

3. Knowledge of _____ permits you to identify "Frost was on the windshield" as an acceptable sentence and "On frost the was windshield" as an unacceptable one.

4. "They are visiting fire fighters" has one _____ structure and two possible _____ structures.

✳ 5. "Can a chimpanzee learn human language?" What's wrong with this question, and how might it be rephrased?

ANSWERS:

1. meaningfulness 2. displacement; productivity 3. syntax 4. surface; deep (In one deep structure, the fire fighters are doing the visiting; in the other, they are being visited.) 5. The question is cast in either-or terms. A better question (not the only one) might be: "Which features of human language, if any, can a chimpanzee learn, and under what circumstances?"

The Influence of Language on Thought

In George Orwell's chilling novel *Nineteen Eighty-Four*, a totalitarian government tries to narrow thought by shrinking language. The result, called Newspeak, is supposed to wipe out "thoughtcrime" by obliterating the words needed to commit it. "We're destroying words—scores of them, hundreds of them, every day," boasts a worker in the ironically named Ministry of Truth. "We're cutting the language down to the bone." Words also get new meanings: War is peace, love is hate. (Lest you think Orwell's projections were pure fantasy, in recent years leaders in our own government have called lying "misspeaking," the wartime killing of civilians "collateral damage," the accidental killing of American soldiers by their own side "friendly fire," nuclear missiles "peacekeepers," and tax increases "revenue enhancement.")

Was Orwell right? Does language provide a mental straitjacket for thought? Can we think only what we can say? Or does language merely express ideas and perceptions that would exist anyway?

The leading spokesperson for the notion that language shapes thought was Benjamin Lee Whorf (1897–1941), an insurance inspector by profession and a linguist and anthropologist by inclination. His **theory of linguistic relativity** held that (1) language molds habits of both cognition and perception and (2) different languages point speakers toward different views of reality. Whorf sometimes seemed to believe that language determines thought in an absolute way. He once wrote, "We dissect nature along lines laid down by our native languages" (Whorf, 1956). But usually he took the more moderate position that language has a powerful *influence* on cognition.

Whorf's evidence was linguistic and cultural. For example, he noted that English has only one word for snow, but Eskimos (now called the Inuit) have different words for falling snow, slushy snow, powdered snow, and so forth. On the other hand, Hopi has a single noun that refers to all flying things and beings, with the exception of birds. This word can be used for aphids, airplanes, and aviators. Thus the Inuit presumably would notice differences in snow that people in other cultures would not, and Hopis might see similarities between insects and aviators that others would miss. Since Whorf's time, other writers have added examples of their own. Chinese, for instance, has at least 19 words for silk, but (in keeping with the reticence of the Chinese about discussing sexual matters) it has no common word for either foreplay or orgasm, making it something of a challenge to do sex surveys in China (Kristof, 1991)! In English, much has been written about how the very word *foreplay* limits sexual imagination. Why are all activities other than intercourse merely "fore" play?

Whorf felt that grammar had an even greater influence on thought than did separate words. He argued, for example, that grammar affects how we think of time. English verbs, he noted, force people to emphasize when an action took place; you can't talk about seeing Joan without saying whether you *saw* her, *see*

✳ *Does language confine thought, or merely channel it in certain directions? If your language had no future tense, would you still be able to imagine the future?*

■ **linguistic relativity theory**
The theory that language molds habits of thought and perception and that different language communities therefore tend to have different views of reality.

her now, or *will see* her. But Hopi verbs do not require these distinctions. Instead, they allow a speaker to convey whether he or she experienced the action personally, observed it, heard about it, or inferred it. Further, English speakers refer to time as a thing that can be saved, squandered, or spent, or as something that can be measured; we say time is short, long, or great. There are no analogies in Hopi. Whorf felt these facts explained why the Hopis enjoyed repetitive rituals that Anglos would view as a "waste of time" (Whorf, 1941).

What do you think of such evidence? The linguistic differences pointed out by Whorf and others have fascinated students and teachers for generations. Clearly culture and language are intertwined: It is no accident that English is full of sports metaphors ("I scored some points with my boss," "She plays hardball in negotiations") whereas French is rich in (what else?) food metaphors (*un navet*, "a turnip," means a bad film, and *C'est la fin des haricots!*, "This is the last of the stringbeans," is equivalent to "It's the last straw") (Halpern, 1991). But does language shape thought, or does it merely reflect cultural concerns? Critics note that it is easy enough to describe in English what the various Inuit words for snow mean or how Hopis conceive of time, despite the linguistic differences. Within a culture, when a need to express some unlabeled phenomenon arises, speakers easily manufacture new words. Like the Inuit, English-speaking skiers need to talk about several kinds of snow, so they speak of *powder*, *corn*, and *boilerplate* (ice).

Linguistic evidence alone cannot prove that language determines, or even influences thought. Do the Inuit perceive snow differently from people who have fewer words for it? Do Hopis experience time differently because of their grammar? We can't know, unless linguistic evidence is supplemented by psychological evidence, and unfortunately, the few psychological studies that have been done have been inconclusive, mainly because of difficulties in studying this question.

Yet the theory of linguistic relativity, which has sometimes seemed deader than a dinosaur, keeps springing back to life. Within a language, it is easier to process some words and grammatical constructions than others; it is reasonable to assume, then, that it is easier to think certain thoughts in one language than another, because of the words and grammatical constructions the languages require (Hunt & Agnoli, 1991). Further, recent research suggests that languages may, at the very least, influence the acquisition of *specific mental skills*, by guiding attention in particular directions.

For example, Irene Miura and her colleagues (Miura et al., 1988; Miura & Okamoto, 1989) argue that linguistic differences can help explain why Asian children tend to outperform English-speaking children on tests of numerical ability. In many Asian languages, names of numbers reflect a base-10 system: The label for 12 is "ten-two," the label for 22 is "two ten(s)-two," and so forth. These names may help children understand numbers and simple arithmetic. In a study of Korean, Chinese, Japanese, and English-speaking American first-graders, Miura and her associates (1988) had children stack blocks to represent five different quantities. White blocks stood for single units and blue blocks for ten units. Each child had two chances to show the numbers. Most of the Asian children could express all five numbers in more than one way—for example, 12 as either 12 white blocks or 1 blue block and 2 white ones. But only 13 percent of the American children could do the same; most simply used a collection of white blocks. Further, on their first try most of the Asian children used patterns corresponding to written numbers—for example, 2 tens and 8 ones for 28. But only 8 percent of the American children did so. Of course, these results do not *prove* that linguistic differences are responsible for the differences in math achievement. It is interesting, though, that bilingual Asian-American students tend to score higher in math achievement than do those who speak only English (Moore & Stanley, 1986).

FIGURE 8.5

Solution to the candle mounting problem

The problem given in Figure 8.2 on page 293 can be solved by using the tacks to fasten one of the boxes to the wall as a stand. People often miss this solution because functional fixedness prevents them from recognizing that a box can have a purpose other than as a container. If all the items, including the boxes, are labeled when the problem is first presented, the solution is found more quickly.

Language also affects how we solve, or fail to solve, problems. Consider the solution to the candle-mounting problem, shown in Figure 8.5. This solution is easier to find when the items, including the boxes, are labeled. In fact, people take 15 times as long without the labels as with them (Glucksberg & Weisberg, 1966). Apparently, the labels direct attention to each object, so people notice a box as an object and not merely as a container for other objects.

Finally, language affects social perceptions (Henley, 1989). In the previous sentence, you read the name of a psychologist. Would you be at all surprised to learn it was *Nancy* Henley? Feminists have long observed that in much of our writing, humanity is male and women are outsiders, the "second sex." This is why they have long objected to the use of *men* or *mankind* to refer to humanity, and *he* to refer to any person, sex unspecified. These objections cannot be put down to pronoun envy. Children understand the "neutral" *he* as masculine, and this affects their sex stereotyping of animals, objects, and, perhaps most important, jobs (Bem, 1981; Hyde, 1984a). When adults appear to be using *he* in the gender-neutral sense, they often are thinking only of men (Hamilton, 1991; Henley, 1989; Martyna, 1980). Because of such findings, the American Psychological Association has issued a set of guidelines for psychologists on non-sexist writing.

Language, then, can influence thinking, reasoning, problem solving, and social stereotypes. It allows us to manipulate symbols rather than objects. It directs our attention. It allows us to create detailed plans for the future. But the degree to which linguistic differences between cultures result in different ways of thinking and perceiving remains an open question.

The Influence of Thought on Language

Those who have argued for linguistic relativity have sometimes made two huge assumptions: (1) that reality has no inherent organization but is, to use Whorf's term, a "kaleidoscopic flux" of impressions; and (2) that human cognition has no innate structure, apart from that imposed by culture and language. In recent years, researchers have questioned both of these assumptions. People the world over seem to share certain cognitive abilities, and language is as likely to *reflect* human cognition as it is to shape it.

The evidence comes in part from studies of **linguistic universals.** Despite their many differences, the languages of the world are also surprisingly alike. Consider the perceptual category of color. If reality were inherently unorganized, and if human beings could "cut up reality" in any way they pleased, color words would be arbitrary; it would be possible for a language to have a single

Is this a "mailman"? Because masculine nouns and pronouns promote the unconscious assumption that certain jobs are best suited to men, many organizations now use gender-neutral terms, such as police officer, fire fighter, *and* mail carrier.

word that included what English calls green and red. But anthropologists have discovered that color naming is not at all arbitrary (Berlin & Kay, 1969; Kay, 1975). The number of basic color terms used by languages varies from only 2, as in Dani, to 11, as in English, but every language draws its basic terms from a list of only 11 possibilities: black, white, red, yellow, green, blue, brown, purple, pink, orange, and gray.

These color names are not drawn at random. Every language selects its terms from the following hierarchy, working from left to right:

$$\begin{bmatrix} \text{black} \\ \text{white} \end{bmatrix} \rightarrow \text{red} \rightarrow \begin{bmatrix} \text{yellow} \\ \text{green} \\ \text{blue} \end{bmatrix} \rightarrow \text{brown} \rightarrow \begin{bmatrix} \text{purple} \\ \text{pink} \\ \text{orange} \\ \text{gray} \end{bmatrix}$$

A language with only 2 terms will have black and white (or dark and light). A language with 3 terms will have black, white, and red. A language with 4 terms will have black, white, red, and one of the colors in the middle column (yellow, green, or blue). A language with 6 terms will have black, white, red, yellow, green, and blue. If languages selected color terms at random from the 11 basic ones, there would be 2,048 possible color systems. But because they are confined to a universal hierarchy, there are actually only 33 possible systems among the thousands of human languages.

What's more, when researchers show people color charts and ask them to point to the best representatives of the basic color terms in their language, the results are the same from one language to another. The best *red* for English speakers is the best *aka* for speakers of Japanese, the best *lichi* for Navahos, and the best *anpalultak* for the Inuit. These *focal colors* are easier to remember, are named more quickly, and are more eye-catching than other colors. In fact, focal colors are salient even when people have no names for them in their language (E. R. Heider, 1972; Heider & Olivier, 1972).

All this suggests that people are sensitive to focal colors not because language emphasizes them but because the human visual system processes reality in a certain way (Lakoff, 1987). In Chapter 5 we saw that color perception seems to depend on special opponent-process cells that are sensitive to black or white, blue or yellow, and red or green—precisely the first six colors of the universal color hierarchy. It is possible that the visual system is also maximally sensitive in some way to the remaining five colors of the hierarchy.

Color names provide only one example of how perception influences language. All languages seem to name the same basic shapes and spatial relations (Clark & Clark, 1977). These categories seem to be based on built-in, natural ways of perceiving. Even some abstract categories, not obviously rooted in perception, appear to be universal. For example, all languages, even the Hopi, have some way to distinguish the present, past, and future. The past is usually, and the future is always, expressed in a more complex way than the present. Thus in English, we must add a special ending to a regular verb to make it past tense (*walk, walked*), and an additional word to make it future tense (*will walk*). The explanation seems to be that the here and now is easier to think about than the past or future, and the past is easier than the future. Children take several years to grasp the concept of nonpresent. Only when they have done so are they ready to use words like *yesterday* and *tomorrow* correctly. At first, they use *yesterday* to signify both past and future. When they understand the concept of past, they use *yesterday* correctly but are still confused about *tomorrow*. Finally they understand the concept of the future and use *tomorrow* correctly.

The universals of language, then, tell us much about human perception, memory, and mental processes. Language, which sometimes seems to be cognition's master, is also its obedient servant.

■ **linguistic universals**
The linguistic features that characterize all languages.

Becoming More Creative

Psychologists use creativity tests to study the personality characteristics of creative people. We can also find some clues to the origins of creativity in the biographies of creative geniuses. Here are a few habits and strategies that seem important and that may help you enhance your own creativity:

• *When reality contradicts expectations, ask why.* Early in this century, Wilhelm Roentgen, a German physicist, was studying cathode rays when he noticed a strange glow on one of his screens. Other people had seen the glow, too, but they ignored it because it didn't jibe with current understanding of cathode rays. Roentgen studied the glow, found it to be a new kind of radiation, and discovered X-rays (Briggs, 1984).

• *Notice your images and dreams.* Many creative people say they get their best ideas in visual form and only later translate them into language. Some even solve problems in their dreams. Elias Howe, who invented the sewing machine, had trouble figuring out how to thread the needle. Needles had always had an eye at the top and a point at the bottom, but the needle in a sewing machine had to be fastened at the top to the machine. One night Howe dreamed he was attacked by savages carrying spears with holes near the tip. When he awoke, he whittled a needle with the hole at the pointed end, and his problem was solved.

• *Keep at it.* The flash of insight is usually only the beginning of a long, drawn-out process. Sir Isaac Newton, when asked how he was able to discover the law of universal gravitation, is said to have replied, "By thinking on it continuously." Albert Einstein claimed to have had no special talent. "Curiosity, obsession, and dogged endurance, combined with self-criticism," he said, "have brought me to my ideas. Especially strong thinking powers, brain muscles, I do not have, or only to a modest degree. Many have far more of those than I without producing anything surprising" (quoted in Briggs, 1984).

• *Gather as much information as you can.* Louis Pasteur, who proved that germs cause disease, once said, "Chance favors the prepared mind." Most creative thinkers say that early in the creative process, they find out as much about a problem as possible.

• *When your mind is saturated with information, let the problem incubate.* Several inventors and discoverers have told how the solution to a problem came to them only after they stopped consciously thinking about the welter of information they had gathered.

• *Don't let others discourage you.* There is a fine line between bull-headed faith in a foolish idea and dedication to a correct one. But keep in mind that creative people do not worry about being nonconformists or having their ideas ridiculed. Geneticist Barbara McClintock's research was ignored or belittled for nearly 30 years. But she was sure she could show how genes move around and produce sudden changes in heredity. In 1983, McClintock won the Nobel Prize. The Nobel officials called her work "the second great [genetic] discovery of our time," along with the discovery of the structure of DNA. McClintock told reporters she hadn't cared what others thought. She knew she was right.

In addition to creative persons, there are creative *circumstances.* For example, Alice Isen and her associates (Isen, Daubman, & Nowicki, 1987) find that cheerful situations foster inspiration. The performance of students on creativity tests improved significantly after they watched a funny film or received a gift of candy, which put them in a good mood. In contrast, watching an upsetting film on concentration camps or a "neutral" film on math, or exercising for two minutes to boost energy, had no effect. Elation, then, may loosen up creative associations.

Another situational factor is the encouragement of *intrinsic* rather than *extrinsic* motivation. Intrinsic motives include a sense of accomplishment, intellectual fulfillment, the satisfaction of curiosity, and the sheer love of the activity. Extrinsic motives include a desire for money, fame, and attention, or the wish to avoid punishment. In one study of motives and creativity, Teresa Amabile (1985) asked 72 talented young poets and writers to create two poems. Before writing their second poem, half the writers evaluated a list of extrinsic motives for writing (such as "The market for freelance writing is constantly expanding" and "You enjoy public recognition of your work"). The other half evaluated a list of intrinsic motives ("You like to play with words"; "You achieve new insights"). Then a panel of 12 experienced poets judged the two sets of poems for originality and creativity, without knowing which writers had read which set of motives. The writers who were exposed to extrinsic reasons for writing showed a significant drop in the creativity of their second poem. Those who paid attention to intrinsic motives wrote two poems of equal quality.

Other research (Amabile, 1983) shows that people tend to be most creative when they (1) have control over how to perform a task or solve a problem; (2) are evaluated unobtrusively, instead of being constantly observed and judged; and (3) work alone. (Group brainstorming, in which people generate as many ideas as they can without judging their value, is not always more effective than individual brainstorming. Quantity of ideas does not ensure quality.) In addition, organizations encourage creativity when they let people take risks, give them plenty of time to think about problems, and welcome innovation.

In sum, if you hope to become more creative, there are two things you can do. One is to cultivate the personal qualities that lead to creativity. The other is to seek out the kinds of situations that permit their expression.

SUMMARY

1. *Thinking* is the mental manipulation of information internally represented as concepts, propositions, and images. Our mental representations simplify and summarize information in the environment.

2. A *concept* is a mental category that groups objects, relations, activities, abstractions, or qualities having common properties. *Basic concepts* have a moderate number of instances and seem naturally easier to acquire than concepts with few or many instances. Some instances of a concept are more *prototypical* than others.

3. *Propositions* are units of meaning that are made up of concepts and that express unitary ideas. *Images* are representations that mirror or resemble what they represent. Mental visual images seem analogous to images on a television screen and are used for many purposes.

4. Many mental processes are *subconscious* or *nonconscious*. Even conscious processing may be carried out in a mindless fashion, so that we overlook changes in context that call for a change in behavior.

5. *Reasoning* involves drawing inferences and conclusions from observations, facts, or assumptions (premises). In *deductive reasoning*, conclusions follow necessarily from the premises. The application of deductive reasoning depends heavily on experience and schooling. In *inductive reasoning*, the premises provide support for a conclusion, but it is still possible for the conclusion to be false. Science depends heavily on inductive reasoning.

6. Logic is often inadequate for solving the problems of everyday life. People often make logical errors, disagree with others about basic premises, or lack the information needed for drawing conclusions. In situations requiring everyday, informal reasoning, there is often no one correct answer.

7. *Dialectical reasoning* is often more appropriate than other forms of reasoning in real life. It involves the ability to think critically, in an open-minded way, about opposing points of view. Some critics believe television watching is partly responsible for a decline in the ability to weigh and evaluate opposing arguments.

8. When we make judgments and decisions, the *heuristics* (rules of thumb) we use are influenced by cognitive biases and the way choices are framed. In general, we tend to avoid risks or losses, and we exaggerate the likelihood of improbable events (in part because of the *availability heuristic*). We are also influenced by expectations, our need for meaning, the *confirmation bias*, and the *hindsight bias*. However, in everyday life people are not always irrational, and once we understand a bias we may be able to reduce or eliminate it.

9. Problem solving involves defining the problem, devising a strategy, executing the strategy, and evaluating progress. Problems can sometimes be solved by applying an *algorithm*, a procedure guaranteed to lead eventually to a solution. However, many problems require the use of heuristics, which do not guarantee an optimal solution.

10. Lack of adequate knowledge is an important barrier to effective problem solving. Another barrier is the persistence of *mental sets*, or the tendency to use strategies and rules used on previous problems although they are no longer appropriate.

11. As we saw in "A Closer Look at Artificial Intelligence," the *artificial intelligence* of computers has been limited by the machines' lack of a broad knowledge base. Scientists are trying to overcome this problem by designing machines called *neural networks*.

12. Creative problem solving requires *divergent* as well as *convergent thinking*. Most creativity tests measure fluency, flexibility, and originality, but a recent approach assesses a person's actual history of creative accomplishment. Creative people generally are willing to risk ridicule, prefer working independently, are confident enough to enjoy working on difficult problems, are curious about the world, and are able to persist at a task without becoming discouraged. These traits can be cultivated.

13. *Language* is a system for combining meaningless elements into utterances that convey meaning. Most languages are vocal, but gestural languages are widely used by the hearing impaired. A true language has three features: meaningfulness, displacement, and productivity.

14. Productivity in language is achieved by applying a large but finite set of rules called a *grammar*. These rules determine which strings of sounds and words form acceptable utterances and which do not. Rules of *syntax*, or word order, help us derive the underlying *deep structure* of a sentence from its *surface structure*. We also rely on expectations, context, and general knowledge of the world in determining deep structures.

15. No animal seems to have a full-fledged language in the wild. However, dozens of researchers have attempted to teach language to animals, employing visual symbol systems, American Sign Language, and other techniques. The linguistic skills acquired by these animals, particularly by primates, are impressive, but scientists are still divided about the extent to which they constitute true language.

16. Benjamin Lee Whorf's *theory of linguistic relativity* holds that language molds habits of cognition and perception, and that different language communities tend to perceive reality differently. This theory has been difficult to prove, but it refuses to die. Language does appear to influence the way we solve problems and form social perceptions, and it may account for cultural differences in performance on certain cognitive tasks.

17. Thought also influences language. Despite their many differences, the languages of the world are surprisingly alike. Many of their similarities appear to reflect universal ways of perceiving, thinking, and forming concepts.

KEY TERMS

thinking *277*

concept *277*

basic concept *277*

prototypical instance *277*

proposition *278*

mental image *278*

subconscious processes *279*

nonconscious processes *279*

mindlessness *280*

reasoning *281*

SOME SOLUTIONS TO THE NINE-DOT PROBLEM (From Adams, 1986.)

(a)

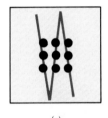

(b)

Cut the puzzle apart, tape it together in a different format, and use one line.

(c)

(d)

Roll up the puzzle and draw a spiral through the dots.

(e)

1 Line 0 Folds

Lay the paper on the surface of the Earth. Circumnavigate the globe twice + a few inches, displacing a little each time so as to pass through the next row on each circuit as you "Go West, young man."

(f)

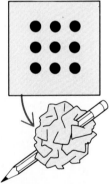

~ 2 Lines* 0 Folds

*Statistical

Draw dots as large as possible. Wad paper into a ball. Stab with pencil. Open up and see if you did it. If not, try again. "Nobody loses: Play until you win."

(g)

May 30, 1974
5 FDR   NAVAS
Roosevelt Rds. ⌂
Celba, PR 00635

Dear Prof. James L. Adams,
  My dad and I were doing Puzzles from "Conceptual Blockbusting". We were mostly working on the dot ones, like ⋮⋮⋮ My dad said a man found a way to do it with one line. I tried and did it. Not with folding, but I used a fat line. I does'nt say you can't use a fat line. Like this→ ■
P.S.
acctually you need a very fat writing apparatice. .

Sincerely,
Becky Buechel
age: 10

(h)

Emotion

> *The beauty of the world has two edges,*
> *one of laughter, one of anguish,*
> *cutting the heart asunder.*
>
> VIRGINIA WOOLF

On Sunday, April 25, in the year 1227, a knight named Ulrich von Lichtenstein disguised himself as the goddess Venus. Wearing an ornate white gown, waist-length braids, and heavy veils, and bedecked with pearls, Ulrich began a pilgrimage from Venice to Bohemia. As he traveled, he invited any and all local warriors to challenge him to a duel. By his own count (which may have been exaggerated), Ulrich broke 307 lances, unhorsed four opponents, and completed his five-week journey with an undefeated record. The reason for this extravagant performance was his passion for a highborn princess, nameless to history, whom he adored but who barely gave poor Ulrich the time of day. Ulrich trembled in her presence, suffered in her absence, and constantly endured feelings of longing, misery, and melancholy, a state of love that apparently made him very happy (M. Hunt, 1959/1967).

What we do for love: Ulrich von Lichtenstein disguised as Venus.

How would Ulrich's story sound with the emotion removed? Suppose Ulrich endured his hardships and tribulations because he was somewhat fond of the lady. Suppose he was bored in her presence and only vaguely aware of her absence. Suppose, in short, that she meant nothing more to him than his wife (oh, yes, Ulrich was married), and that theirs was merely an economic union, a practical arrangement for the purpose of begetting children and managing the serfs. How would we evaluate Ulrich's knightly performance then?

Let's try another story, from this century. In the wealthy community of Scarsdale, New York, 23-year-old Richard Herrin murdered his sleeping girlfriend, Bonnie Garland. Herrin was depressed because Garland had told him she was too young to marry and wanted to date other men. In a rage over her decision, he battered her to death with a claw hammer. The jury did not convict Herrin of murder, but of the lesser crime of manslaughter, believing that he had acted under "extreme emotional disturbance."

Herrin's supporters thought even this sentence too harsh, arguing that he had loved Bonnie deeply and passionately and was desperately unhappy because of her death. This defense did not persuade the prosecution. One psychiatrist said it reminded him of the old story of the man who murdered his parents, and then pleaded for mercy because he was an orphan.

How would Herrin's story sound with the emotion removed? Suppose Herrin murdered Garland calmly, barely flinching as he slaughtered her. Suppose he wasn't depressed about losing her, but indifferent. He wasn't enraged that she rejected him, only mildly sorry. He didn't love her "deeply and passionately"; he just liked her a little. He didn't grieve over her loss; he barely noticed it. What sentence do you think Herrin would have received? Would his friends still have defended him?

As these stories show, emotions are the heart and soul of human life. They give life color, intensity, excitement—and misery. If you could wave a magic wand and eliminate them, you would never again worry about a test result, a job interview, or a first date. You would never feel angry, even if your room-

Israeli parents (left) and an Arab father (right) react to the death of their children in the tragic Middle Eastern conflict. Their grief involves both a physiological response to loss and the cognitive perception that a young life has been unfairly cut short. In turn, culture affects the display of emotion—whether, say, you should "let it out" or "keep a stiff upper lip." Your own culture may affect how you are reacting to these two photos: Is the Israeli father "cold and uptight" or "mature and manly"? Is the Arab father being too "hysterical" or "humanly expressive"?

mate called you an idiot or you were arrested on false charges. You wouldn't be afraid to jump out of an airplane, with or without a parachute. You would never feel the grief of losing someone you love, not only because you wouldn't know sadness but because you wouldn't know love. You would never laugh, because nothing would strike you as funny.

Considering the importance of emotion in every aspect of experience, it is curious that the field of psychology didn't pay much attention to it until relatively recently. The topic of emotion used to be combined with motivation or studied as a contributor to stress. Emotions are a big factor in motivation and stress, of course, as they are in everything else—development, personality, abnormal behavior, psychotherapy, you name it. Psychologists have been hard at work to remedy their previous silence on this subject, with fascinating results. In particular, they are trying to integrate three elements that the full experience of **emotion** involves: *physiological* changes in the face and body, *cognitive* processes such as interpretations of events, and *cultural* influences that shape the experience and expression of emotion.

■ ELEMENTS OF EMOTION 1: THE BODY

Early philosophers thought our emotional personalities depended on mixes of four basic body fluids, or "humors": blood, phlegm, yellow bile (choler), and black bile. If you were an angry, irritable sort of person, you supposedly had an excess of choler; even now, the English word *choleric* describes a hothead. If you were slow-moving and unemotional, you supposedly had an excess of phlegm, and the English word for such people is *phlegmatic*. The theory of the four humors was far-fetched, and yet the basic questions it was trying to answer remain with us. What is the physiology of emotion? Where in the body does an emotion occur?

One of the first modern answers to these questions came from William James (1884), who challenged everyone who thought the chicken comes first to think about the egg. Common sense, then as now, assumed that (1) something happens, (2) you feel an emotion, (3) you do something. In James's own examples, you lose your fortune, you feel miserable, you cry; or your rival insults you, you feel angry, you hit him. But James argued that this seemingly logical sequence was out of order, and he turned it around. The correct sequence, he said, should

■ emotion
A state involving a pattern of facial and bodily changes, cognitive appraisals, subjective feelings, and tendencies toward action.

be (1) something happens, (2) your body reacts with a specific set of physiological responses, (3) you interpret and experience those responses as an emotion. If a slimy alien appeared in your room as you were reading this, your heart would start pounding and you would escape as fast as you could; *then* you would realize you are feeling fear. "We feel sorry *because* we cry," James wrote, "angry *because* we strike, afraid *because* we tremble." At about the same time that James was writing, a Danish researcher named Carl Lange came up with a similar theory, and the two names were soon linked as the **James-Lange theory of emotions:** the idea that events trigger specific bodily changes and responses (e.g., running away if you are frightened), and that emotion follows from your awareness of those physical changes.

James's theory was not quite right, but it produced animated debate and spurred a wave of research. In recent years, armed with new ways to study the physiology of emotion, psychologists have explored the contributions to emotion of facial expressions, brain processes, and the autonomic nervous system.

The Face of Emotion

The most obvious place to look for emotion is on the face, where the expression of emotion can be most visible. In his classic book *The Expression of the Emotions in Man and Animals*, Charles Darwin (1872/1965) wrote that facial expressions—the smile, the frown, the grimace, the glare—are biologically wired in human beings and other animals. The face of emotion is not learned, said Darwin; it is as much a part of our biological heritage as a nose or a kidney. Such expressions may have evolved because they allowed animals and our human forebears to tell the difference immediately between a stranger who was friendly and one who was about to attack.

Modern psychologists have supported Darwin's idea that certain basic emotions are registered on the face and that they are recognized all over the world (see Figure 9.1). Even remote tribes that have never watched a movie or read *People* magazine, such as the Fore of New Guinea or the Minangkabau of West Sumatra, can recognize the emotions expressed in pictures of people who are entirely foreign to them—and we can recognize theirs.

For more than 20 years, Paul Ekman and Wallace Friesen have been gathering evidence for the universality of six basic facial expressions of emotion: anger, happiness, fear, surprise, disgust, and sadness (Ekman, Friesen, & Ellsworth, 1972; Ekman et al., 1987). Recently they have found evidence of a seventh universal expression—contempt—in Western and non-Western cultures (Ekman & Heider, 1988). In every culture they have studied—including those of New Guinea, Brazil, Chile, Estonia, Germany, Greece, Hong Kong, Italy, Japan, Scotland, Sumatra, Turkey, and the United States—a large majority has recognized the emotional expressions portrayed by people in other cultures. This does not mean that everybody in a society can recognize the same expressions. In one study, only 61 percent of the Germans recognized disgust, only 67 percent of the Estonians and Japanese identified anger, and only 76 percent of the Turks recognized sadness (Ekman et al., 1987). (Are you impressed that a majority in so many different nations agreed on each emotion, or that sometimes a large minority disagreed?)

What might be the purpose of universal facial expressions? One answer is that they help us communicate with others, and this communication starts in infancy (Stenberg & Campos, 1990). Perhaps you recall the visual cliff study described in Chapter 5 (see p. 184), a study that was originally designed to test the development of depth perception. Now it turns out that if the baby's mother is on the far side of the cliff and *warns the baby against crossing by assuming an expression of fear or anger,* the baby will not cross. If, however, the mother smiles at the baby warmly, the baby will cross to her, even though the baby is aware

■ **James-Lange theory**
The theory, proposed independently by William James and Carl Lange, that emotion results from the perception of one's own bodily reactions.

FIGURE 9.1 _____

Some universal expressions
Can you tell what feelings are being conveyed here? Most people around the world can readily identify facial expressions of surprise, disgust, happiness, sadness, anger, and fear—no matter what the age, culture, or historical epoch of the person conveying the emotion, and even when the "person" is a work of art. This fact suggests that facial expressions of emotion play an important role in communication and that certain expressions are part of our biological heritage.

of the "cliff" (Sorce et al., 1985). Clearly, the baby's ability to recognize facial expressions of emotion has survival value.

Interestingly, facial expressions of emotion may also help people communicate with themselves, so to speak, by enabling them to identify their own emotions. Like William James, some psychologists argue that people don't frown because they are angry; rather, they feel angry because they are frowning.

According to this **facial-feedback hypothesis,** the facial muscles send messages to the brain, identifying each basic emotion (Izard, 1990; Laird, 1984; Tomkins, 1962, 1981b). When people are asked to contort their facial muscles into various patterns, they often report changed emotions to fit the pattern. As one young man put it, "When my jaw was clenched and my brows down, I tried not to be angry but it just fit the position" (Laird, 1974). Voluntary facial expressions even seem to affect the involuntary nervous system. If you put on an "angry" face, your heart rate will rise faster than if you put on a "happy" face (Levenson, Ekman, & Friesen, 1990). When people are told to contract the facial muscles involved in smiling (though not actually instructed to smile) and then to look at cartoons, they find the cartoons funnier than if they are con-

■ **facial-feedback hypothesis**
The notion that the facial muscles send messages to the brain, identifying the emotion a person feels.

tracting their muscles in a way that is incompatible with smiling (Strack, Martin, & Stepper, 1988).

Findings like these suggest that the facial muscles are somehow tied to the autonomic nervous system, which controls heart rate, breathing, and other vital functions. But what is the "somehow"? What might be the intervening process between the muscles of the face and a subjective emotional state? One imaginative line of research suggests that facial expressions change the pattern of blood flow to the brain, thereby altering temperature in certain parts of the brain, which in turn affects the release of neurotransmitters (Zajonc, Murphy, & Inglehart, 1989). In these experiments, lowering the temperature of the brain seems to cause pleasant feelings; raising the temperature seems to cause unpleasant ones. What will cool your fevered brain? Smiling—which allows more air to enter the nasal passages, and thus cools the blood flowing through the sinuses to the brain. The breathing techniques in yoga apparently have the same effect, which may be why yoga, meditation, and smiling can all improve a person's mood.

There are limits, however, to the effects of facial feedback. Obviously, smiling won't overcome the grief of hearing that a friend is dying of cancer. Moreover, people do not always wear their emotions on their faces. They do not go around scowling and clenching their jaws whenever they are angry. They can grieve and feel enormously sad without weeping. They can feel worried and tense, yet put on a happy face. They can use facial expressions to lie about a "real" feeling. Judging another person's mood just from his or her facial expression is not always a simple task.

To get around the human ability to mask emotions, Paul Ekman and his associates have developed a way to peek under the mask. The Facial Action Coding System (FACS) allows researchers to analyze and identify each of the nearly 80 muscles of the face, as well as the combinations of muscles that are associated with various emotions. When people try to hide their real emotions, Ekman (1985) finds, they use different groups of muscles. For example, when people try to pretend that they feel grief, only 15 percent manage to get the eyebrows, eyelids, and forehead wrinkle exactly right, mimicking the way grief is expressed spontaneously. Authentic smiles last only two seconds; false smiles may last ten seconds or more. Moreover, the muscle changes associated with

Facial expressions don't always convey the emotion that is felt. A posed, "social" smile (left) may have nothing to do with true feelings of happiness. (Cover her smile with your hand and you'll see that the "smile" doesn't reach her eyes.) Conversely, even a face that seems to convey utter anguish (right) may be misleading. This young woman is weeping for joy: She has just won the "Best Young Actress of the Year" award.

the real emotion—anger, contempt, sadness—can be identified beneath the smiling mask (Ekman, Friesen, & O'Sullivan, 1988).

This research suggests that some emotions are indeed part of our basic species equipment. Yet facial expressions, lively as they are, are only part of the emotional picture. Even Ekman, who has been studying them for years, concludes, "There is obviously emotion without facial expression and facial expression without emotion." In Shakespeare's play *Henry VI*, Part 3, the villain who will become the evil King Richard III says,

> Why, I can smile, and murder while I smile;
> And cry content to that which grieves my heart;
> And wet my cheeks with artificial tears,
> And frame my face to all occasions.

Emotion and the Brain

Another line of physiological research seeks to identify parts of the brain responsible for the many different aspects of emotional experience: recognizing another person's emotion, feeling intensely aroused, labeling the emotion, deciding what to do about it, and so on. Take something as apparently simple as recognizing a face. You can recognize your mother's face any old time. You could even recognize a picture of her taken ten years ago. You can recognize her when she is crying and when she is smiling. If you had a rare disease called "prosopagnosia," though, you would lose the ability to recognize all faces, including your own (Sacks, 1985). Yet people with this problem are often able to recognize facial *expressions* even when they can't identify *faces*, suggesting that different parts of the brain are involved in each process (Tranel, Damasio, & Damasio, 1988).

Some psychologists argue that certain emotions—particularly fear, rage, and sexual desire—are as "wired in" as the wing flutter of a frightened bird, the purr of a contented cat, and the snarl of a threatened wolf. They have traced some elements of these universal emotions to the limbic system and hypothalamus, evolutionarily old parts of the brain that human beings share with other species. You might remember from Chapter 3 that the hypothalamus controls the operations of the autonomic nervous system, which in turn regulates emotions and other survival needs.

The amygdala, a small structure in the limbic system, appears to be responsible for evaluating sensory information and *quickly* determining its emotional importance, and also for the initial decision to approach or withdraw from a person or situation. According to neuropsychologist Joseph LeDoux (1989), pathways in the limbic system prompt the amygdala to trigger an emotional response to incoming sensory information, which may then be "overridden" by a more accurate appraisal from the cerebral cortex. (This is why you jump with fear when you suddenly feel a hand on your back in a dark alley, and why your fear evaporates when the cortex registers that the hand belongs to a friend.) The limbic system is able to process immediate perceptions of danger or threat, which is a good thing, because otherwise you would be standing in the street asking, "Is it wise to cross now, while that very large truck is coming toward me?"

New studies suggest that the two cerebral hemispheres play different roles in the control of positive and negative emotions, and this specialization is already apparent in infants (Davidson et al., 1990; Fox & Davidson, 1988; Tucker, 1989). Certain regions of the left hemisphere appear to be specialized for the processing of positive emotions, such as happiness; regions of the right hemi-

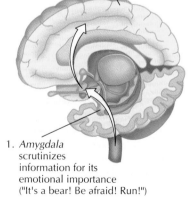

2. *Cerebral cortex* generates more complete picture; can override signals sent by amygdala ("It's only Mike in a down coat")

1. *Amygdala* scrutinizes information for its emotional importance ("It's a bear! Be afraid! Run!")

sphere are involved in the processing of negative emotions, such as disgust, fear, and depression. Patients who have lesions in one hemisphere often lose the ability to experience certain emotions. Damage to the left hemisphere tends to produce excessive anger, tears, and pessimism. "Well," you might say, "wouldn't brain damage make *anyone* angry, sad, and pessimistic?" But damage to the right hemisphere is associated with excessive displays of happiness, joking, and laughing.

This research shows that it is possible to differentiate many distinctive aspects of emotion in the brain. However, in real life, all parts of the brain operate interdependently to produce what feels like a single emotional experience (Lazarus, 1991).

The Energy of Emotion

A third line of physiological research focuses on hormones, which produce the energy of emotion. When you are in a situation that requires the body to respond—to fight, to flee, to cope—the sympathetic nervous system whirls into action (see Chapter 3). In particular, the inner part of the adrenal gland, the medulla, sends out two hormones, **epinephrine** and **norepinephrine.** (Most scientists prefer these terms to their older names, adrenaline and noradrenaline, which are still in common use.)

Why does the driver of a car usually feel angrier than the passenger when another car cuts them off? One reason may be that the driver is already physiologically aroused by the tension of coping with traffic.

The adrenal hormones produce a state of *arousal,* a level of energy that allows the body to respond quickly. During arousal the pupils dilate, widening to allow in more light; the heart beats faster; breathing speeds up; blood sugar rises, providing the body with more energy to act; and digestion slows down, so that blood flow can be diverted from the stomach and intestines to the muscles and surface of the skin. (This is why, when you are excited, scared, furious, or wildly in love, you don't want to eat.) In addition, your memory, concentration, and performance improve—up to a point. If hormone levels become too high and you are too agitated, concentration and performance can worsen. (This is why a little nervousness when you take an exam is a good thing; handtrembling anxiety is not.)

The adrenal glands produce epinephrine and norepinephrine in response to many challenges in the environment. These hormones will surge if you are laughing at a funny movie or playing a video game, if you are worried about an exam, if you are cheering at a game, or if you are responding to an insult. They will also be produced in response to nonemotional conditions, such as heat, cold, pain, injury, burns, and physical exercise; in response to some drugs; and in response to stress and pressure.

Epinephrine in particular provides the *feeling* of an emotion, that tingle, excitement, and sense of energy. At high levels, it can create the sensation of being "seized" or "flooded" by an emotion that is out of one's control. In a sense, the release of epinephrine does cause us to "lose control," because few people can consciously alter their heart rates, blood pressures, and digestive tracts. (But people can learn to control their *actions* when they are emotionally aroused, as we discuss in "Taking Psychology with You.") As arousal subsides, a "hot" emotion usually turns into its "cool" counterpart (Frijda, 1988). Anger may pale into annoyance, ecstasy into contentment, fear into suspicion, past emotional whirlwinds into calm breezes.

However, recent research in neuropsychology has found that the autonomic nervous system does not respond to events in a "one-reaction-fits-all-emotions" manner. It now appears that arousal takes several forms, involving one or the other hemisphere of the brain and different hormones (Neiss, 1988; Tucker & Williamson, 1984). Although most emotions involve similar changes that mo-

■ **epinephrine, norepinephrine**
Hormones produced by the adrenal glands that provide the body with energy to respond to environmental events.

bilize the body to cope with the environment, some emotions *are* physiologically distinct from one another.

In one series of experiments, subjects were induced, in a variety of ways, to experience fear, disgust, anger, sadness, surprise, and happiness. Each emotion, it turned out, was associated with a somewhat different *pattern* of autonomic activity, involving such measures as heart rate, skin conductance, and finger temperature. Indeed, the researchers found 14 distinctions among emotions in autonomic nervous system activity (Levenson, Ekman, & Friesen, 1990). These distinctive patterns produce differences in the way emotions *feel*, which may be why people say they feel "hot and bothered" when they are angry, but "cold and clammy" when they are afraid.

Thus arousal is not a single, global phenomenon, produced as simply as switching on the engine of a car. It's as if one switch turns on the car, another activates it into movement, and a third coordinates the whole operation, making the car move forward. Indeed, some psychologists believe that the very *purpose* of emotion is to "make the car move forward": that is, to produce a response. The changes in the autonomic nervous system that are associated with emotion, they say, do not occur in order to allow you to sit there and contemplate your internal state. Most of our emotions involve some change in *action readiness*; they occur in order to prepare the body to cope with danger or threat, excitement or opportunity, (Frijda, 1988). When you feel an emotion, chances are that you will feel motivated to do something: embrace the person who instills joy in you, avoid the person who is irritating you, or run from the situation that is frightening you (Fox, 1991).

This disposition to approach or withdraw, so closely linked with emotional states, is already apparent in infancy. In one study, ten-month-old babies were briefly separated from their mothers, then monitored during the happy reunion. The babies' joy was recorded in three physiological measures: unmistakable smiles of happiness, left-hemisphere activation, and literally reaching out to their moms (Fox & Davidson, 1988). But when the babies were only smiling socially at strangers, there was no increased left-hemispheric activation, and no reaching out.

Psychologists who are interested in the physiology of emotion have approached their task from many different directions. As we have seen, they are mapping the interconnections among facial expressions, blood flow in the brain, the hypothalamus and limbic system (especially the amygdala), the two hemispheres and their association with positive or negative emotions, and the autonomic nervous system, which prepares the body to take action.

Even so, these bodily processes are not the entire emotional experience. The physical changes caused by the autonomic nervous system cannot explain why, of two students about to take an exam, one feels psyched up and the other feels overwhelmed by anxiety. They also cannot explain why the intensity of physical changes can be unrelated to emotional experience—why, for example, injecting people with ephedrine, a powerful stimulant, has no effect on how frightened they feel about being threatened with electric shock; and why, conversely, drugs that lower heart rate have no effect on people's subjective reports of anxiety (Neiss, 1988).

One real-life consequence of the mistaken assumption that physiological changes in the body tell the whole story of emotion has been the widespread use of "lie detectors" and other methods designed to read a person's "true" feelings (see "Think About It"). But, as we will see, emotional arousal itself has no content. Are you thrilled or frightened? Sick or just in love? Your hormones alone won't tell you.

Can Lies Be "Detected"?

For many centuries in Asia, the "rice" method of lie detection was used on people suspected of a crime. The suspect had to chew on a handful of dry rice and then spit it out. The belief was that an innocent person would be able to do this easily, while a guilty person would have grains of rice stuck to his or her tongue and roof of mouth.

The Rice Method may seem primitive, but in theory it is not much removed from the rationale for the modern polygraph machine, also known as the "lie detector." Both are based on the belief that a person who is guilty and fearful will reveal increased activity in the autonomic nervous system. In the case of the guilty rice-eater, such arousal would dry the saliva in the mouth and cause grains to stick to the tongue. In the case of the guilty suspect taking a polygraph test, a lie would be revealed by increased heart rate, respiration, and electrical activity of the skin (galvanic skin response, or GSR) as the person responds with incriminating answers to questions.

Governments, employers, spouses, and spies all want guaranteed ways of detecting "the truth." Fortunately or unfortunately, most human beings are not very good at detecting the lies of others. They think that liars won't smile or "look you in the eye," for instance, but liars do exactly that. Many people assume that some body signs (such as facial animation) reflect truthfulness and others (such as nervous gestures) indicate deception, but neither assumption is true (Ekman, 1985).

The appeal of the "lie detector," therefore, was that a machine would do better than people at finding out who is innocent of a crime or lie and who is not. Until recently, many companies required all job applicants to take lie-detector tests as part of a screening procedure; some employers routinely used the machines to interrogate employees suspected of drug abuse or theft. The Senate Labor Committee estimated that by 1988, some 2 million tests were being given every year.

Unfortunately for such efforts, psychologists have found that lie detectors are simply not reliable because there are no physiological patterns of responses that are peculiar to lying. Machines cannot tell whether you are feeling guilty, angry, nervous, thrilled, or revved up from an exciting day. Innocent people may be tense and nervous about the whole procedure. They may react to a certain word ("bank") not because they robbed it, but because they recently bounced a check. In either case, the machine will record a "lie." The reverse mistake is also common. Some suave, practiced liars can lie without flinching, and others learn to "beat the machine" by tensing muscles or thinking about an exciting experience during neutral questions (Lykken, 1981).

Moreover, the people who administer the polygraph test often make many errors in reading the results. They do not reliably agree with one another's judgments, and, worst of all, they are more likely to accuse the innocent of lying than to let the guilty go free (Gale, 1988; Kleinmuntz & Szucko, 1984). As a result of research like this, the American Psychological Association issued a policy statement opposing the use of lie detectors. In 1988, the U.S. Congress agreed. Although it didn't go along with the APA's recommendation for a total ban, it did forbid the routine use of lie detectors in screening job applicants or randomly testing employees. As one shocked senator said, "Some 320,000 honest Americans are branded as liars every single year."

Yet instead of abandoning the *assumption* that it is possible to identify people who lie, many businesses today are trying new *methods* of "lie detection"—some of which are not much advanced over the Rice Method. Indeed, some employers are trying to identify people who, if hired, *might in the future* cheat, steal, or use drugs. One recent trend is the development of "honesty questionnaires," paper-and-pencil tests that supposedly measure whether or not an employee will steal on the job. By 1989, more than 4 million people were given one version of these honesty tests alone, although many questions remain about the tests' reliability and validity (Saxe, 1991).

How would you feel if you had to take a test, on entering college, that would supposedly reveal whether you are likely to cheat? Would you take it? Why or why not? How reliable does a test need to be before its widespread use can be justified—is it acceptable if it misidentifies "only" one innocent person in ten, a hundred, a thousand?

QUICK QUIZ

See if you can say which aspects of the *physiology* of emotion—hormones, cerebral hemispheres, or a specific part of the brain—are involved in the following reactions to real-life events.

1. A 3-year-old sees her dad dressed as a gorilla, and runs away in fear. What structure in the limbic system is probably involved in her withdrawal from him?

2. Murphy is watching "Hatchet Murders in the Dorm: Sequel XVII." What hormones cause his heart to pound and his palms to sweat when the murderer is stalking an unsuspecting victim?

3. Melissa is watching an old Laurel and Hardy film, which makes her chuckle and puts her in a good mood. Which hemisphere of her brain is likely to be most activated?

4. In one study of electrical stimulation of the amygdala, *previously violent* patients became violent, whereas *previously nonviolent* patients did not (Scherer, Abeles, & Fischer, 1975). What does this study suggest about the relationship between the amygdala and emotional behavior?

ANSWERS:

1. The amygdala 2. Epinephrine and norepinephrine 3. The left 4. One possible answer is that although the amygdala may influence emotional behavior, past experience with violence may also influence memory circuits and brain responses, leading to different reactions to the electrical stimulation. It is also possible that there were brain differences in the amygdalas of the two groups; perhaps the violent patients had abnormal ones due to previous brain damage.

■ ELEMENTS OF EMOTION 2: THE MIND

Put your finger on the dot in the margin, and smile. How do you feel at this moment, amused or irritated? If you followed our instructions and touched the dot, you probably feel more amused than angry. You may be laughing at yourself for doing such a silly thing, and that will make you feel happy—remember the facial-feedback hypothesis. If you didn't put your finger on the dot, you probably feel more angry than amused. "Why are the authors of this book asking me to play stupid games?" you may be asking yourself.

Notice that it is not what we wrote that produced your emotion; it is your *interpretation* of what we asked you to do. Such interpretations are involved in all emotions. Let's say that you have had a crush for weeks on the new student in your computer class. Finally you get up the nerve to start a conversation. Heart pounding, palms sweating, you cheerfully say, "Hi, there!" Before you can add another word, the student has walked right past you without even a nod. What emotion do you feel? Your answer will depend on how you explain the student's behavior:

ANGRY: "What a rude thing to do, to ignore me like that!"
SAD: "I knew it; I'm no good. No one will ever like me."
EMBARRASSED: "Oh, no! Everyone saw how I was humiliated!"
RELIEVED: "Thank goodness; I wasn't sure I wanted to get involved, anyway."

In the first century A.D., the Stoic philosophers were among the first theorists to suggest that people do not become angry or sad or anxious because of actual events, but because of their explanations of those events. Modern psychologists are testing the Stoics' ideas experimentally, identifying the mental processes involved in emotions.

How Thoughts Create Emotions

If emotion can result simply from physiological changes that occur in response to danger or another stimulus, you ought to be able to generate an emotion simply by injecting people with epinephrine. In 1924, Spanish physician Gregorio Marañon tried this experiment, and he happened on an unexpected result (see Cornelius, 1991). Nearly 30 percent of the 210 people in his research reported feeling genuine emotions, usually sadness, often accompanied by weeping and sobbing. But more than 70 percent merely reported physical changes ("My heart is beating fast"; "My throat feels tight") or what Marañon called "as if" emotions: "I feel *as if* I were angry"; "I feel *as if* I were happy."

What caused the difference between the two groups? Marañon reported that he was able to induce "genuine" emotions by asking the first group to think about their sick children or their deceased parents. In short, the people who reported genuine emotions had a reason for them! Marañon concluded that emotions involve a *physical* component, consisting of the bodily changes that accompany arousal; and a "psychological" or *mental* component, consisting of the context in which those changes occur and the interpretation the individual gives them.

Marañon's research languished in a French journal of endocrinology until the 1960s, when Stanley Schachter and Jerome Singer advanced similar ideas with their **two-factor theory of emotion** (Schachter, 1971; Schachter & Singer, 1962). Along with Marañon, they argued that bodily changes are necessary to experience an emotion, but they are not enough. Your body may be churning away in high gear, but unless you can interpret, explain, and label those changes, you won't feel an "emotion." Emotion, they said, therefore depends on two factors: *physiological arousal* and the *cognitive interpretation* of that arousal. If all your friends are worried about an upcoming exam, you may decide that the pounding of your heart is a sign that you are nervous, too. You may not realize that it is because you have been partying too much, losing sleep, and drinking too much coffee.

Schachter and Singer's own experiments, which were widely reported in textbooks and professional journals, were never successfully replicated; and their

■ **two-factor theory of emotion**
The theory that emotions depend on both physiological arousal and a cognitive interpretation or evaluation of that arousal.

According to the two-factor theory, crowds are physically arousing and provide the energy of emotion. But the content of the emotion (joy? gloom? anger?) depends on how people label and interpret their arousal. This is why one fan is feeling especially happy (her team just did well), while the young woman in front of her seems bored or even annoyed.

idea that arousal was necessary to feel an emotion proved to be overstated (Reisenzein, 1983). But their work was important because it launched studies designed to identify the kinds of cognitions that are involved in the experience of emotion. Since the 1960s, psychologists have studied the thought patterns and perceptions that are typical of many emotions, from gradations of joy to degrees of sadness.

As the Stoics argued so many centuries ago, these cognitions can be more important determinants of emotion than actual events. For example, most people assume that success on a project brings happiness, and failure brings unhappiness. In fact, research shows, people's emotions depend on the explanations they make of *why* they succeeded or failed. In a series of experiments, students reported times when they had done well on or failed an exam for a particular reason, such as help from others or lack of effort, and described the emotions they felt on each of these occasions. Their emotions were more closely associated with their explanations than with the outcome of the test (Weiner, 1986). Students who believed they did well because of their own efforts and abilities tended to feel proud, competent, and satisfied. Those who believed they did well because of a lucky fluke or chance tended to feel gratitude, surprise, or guilt ("I don't deserve this"). Those who believed their failures were their own fault tended to feel regret, guilt, or resignation. And those who blamed others for their failures tended to feel angry or hostile.

In general, psychologists have found that negative emotions differ from positive ones in the kinds of perceptions and explanations that generate them. We observed this phenomenon for ourselves when some friends returned from a mountain-climbing trip to Nepal. One said, "It was wonderful! The crystal-clear skies, the millions of stars, the friendly people, the majestic mountains, the harmony of the universe!" The other said, "It was horrible! The bedbugs, the millions of fleas, the lack of toilets, the yak-butter tea, the horrible food, the unforgiving mountains!" Guess which traveler was ecstatic while traveling and which was unhappy?

To understand the mental processes involved in emotion, consider loneliness, which consists of a cluster of feelings that include unhappiness, distress, and sometimes irritability. National surveys show that the loneliest people in the United States are adolescents and college students; fortunately, loneliness declines as people get older (Perlman, 1990; Shaver & Buhrmester, 1983).

Loneliness, however, is not the same thing as solitude or being alone. Many people live alone and do not feel lonely, because they have close ties to good friends and family. Others live in large families and feel desperately lonely, because they think that no one understands them or cares about them. Feelings of loneliness, therefore, cannot be understood by studying only *actual* isolation. Certain events may set the stage for loneliness: the breakup of a dating relationship or a marriage, widowhood, moving away from home, being fired from a job, quarreling frequently with family or friends. But the course of loneliness depends as well on how a person interprets and reacts to these events over time (Lunt, 1991; Peplau & Perlman, 1982; M. Snodgrass, 1987; Weiner, 1986):

Being alone is not the same as being lonely. Why?

1. *Internality.* Do you believe the reason for your loneliness is internal (something particular about you) or external (something in your outside world)? Internal reasons include "I'm unattractive" and "I don't know how to make friends." External explanations look outward: "The people I work with are unfriendly"; "I'm having a run of bad luck"; "This school is so big and impersonal it's hard to meet new people." Internal blame tends to make lonely people more withdrawn.

2. *Stability.* Do you believe the reason for your loneliness is permanent and unchangeable ("This is just an unfriendly place and always will be") or temporary and changeable? People who think their loneliness is inevitable create a vi-

cious cycle for themselves: Expecting nothing to improve, they do nothing to improve their circumstances, so they remain lonely.

3. *Control.* Do you believe you have control over the causes of your loneliness? The belief that there is absolutely nothing one can do to change the situation ("I'm ugly and horrible and there is nothing I can do about it") often prolongs the loneliness and the lonely person's feeling of despair.

One of the challenges of studying emotion is the sheer complexity of emotional experience in people's everyday lives. Psychologists usually study one emotion *or* another, but, in their everyday lives, most people feel one emotion *and* another. One researcher, who was trying to separate anger from anxiety for an experiment, discovered that her subjects kept reporting mixed emotions. When angry, they also reported feeling anxious and depressed. When afraid, they also said they felt depressed and hostile (Polivy, 1981). For many people, emotions occur in bunches, like grapes.

People's perceptions, beliefs, expectations, values, and appraisals of a situation can help explain the reason for such mixed emotions. In one study, college students described their thoughts and feelings just before taking a midterm exam and again after they got their grades (Smith & Ellsworth, 1987). At both times, students often reported mixed feelings—such as hope and fear *before* the exam or anger and guilt *after* the exam. These emotional blends were reliably related to the students' appraisals of their performance, the importance of the exam, their own effort in studying, their degree of certainty about how well they would do, and so on. The students who felt angriest about their poor grades, for example, interpreted the exam as being unfair. This anger, though, was often combined with guilt ("I should have studied harder"), fear ("What if I don't pass?"), or apathy ("I don't care about this course anyway").

Evelyn Ashford, winner of the 100-meter dash at the 1984 Olympics in spite of nearly being sidelined by injuries, shows a blend of feelings on her face: joy, pride, relief, exhaustion.

In addition, people differ in how *intensely* they experience their emotions. Of two people who do well on an exam, one may feel mildly pleased whereas the other is ecstatic; of two people who read about a crook who has cheated victims out of their life's savings, one may feel annoyed but the other enraged. Cognitive appraisals also help explain why these different reactions occur. People who feel emotions intensely have typical ways of thinking (Larsen, Diener, & Cropanzano, 1987): They *personalize* events ("I thought about how I would feel if my friends, family, or I were in that situation"); they *pay selective attention* to the emotion-provoking aspects of events ("I focused on the worst part of the situation"); and they *overgeneralize*, taking a single event as a sign of a general state of the world. They make mountains out of molehills, whether the molehills are good or bad.

Intensity of emotion also depends on the *frame of reference* against which people interpret an event (Frijda, 1988). Let's say you win a car in a lottery. If you already have four cars, you will probably be merely pleased. If you have always struggled to make ends meet and have been driving a clunker for years, you will probably be overjoyed. Likewise, people who place a great deal of value and significance on reaching a particular goal may feel intensely happy if they succeed, but intensely unhappy if they fail. Other people prefer not to invest so much energy in having brief moments of peak happiness, because they won't then suffer the depths of sadness in contrast—what Ed Diener and his colleagues (1991) call the "psychic cost" of extreme joy. Which type are you?

Studies of the cognitive element in emotion suggest that depressed or anxious people can learn how their thinking affects their emotions, and change their thinking accordingly (Beck, 1991). They can ask themselves what the evidence is for their beliefs that the world will collapse if they get a C in biology, that no one loves them, or that they will be lonely forever. In such cases, it is not only that emotional reasoning prevents critical thinking; the failure to think critically also creates the emotion!

As you see, the cognitions that are involved in emotion range from your immediate perceptions of an event to your basic philosophy of life. If you believe that winning is everything and trying your best counts for nothing, you may feel depressed rather than happy if you "only" come in second. If you think a friend's criticism is intentionally mean rather than well meaning, you may respond with anger rather than gratitude. If you believe that feeling intense emotions is what life is all about, you may ride a roller coaster of ups and downs; if you follow a Zen philosophy that an ideal life requires the mastery of feeling, you may seek a path of emotional calm. This is why almost all recent theories of emotion agree that cognitive appraisals, the *meaning* of events, are essential to the creation of emotion (Frijda, 1988; Lazarus, 1991; Oatley & Johnson-Laird, 1987; Ortony, Clore, & Collins, 1988). Our emotions cannot be separated from our mental lives.

QUICK QUIZ

Test your understanding of the cognitive components of emotion.

1. Chronically lonely people tend to believe that the reasons for their unhappiness are (a) controllable, (b) temporary, (c) internal, (d) caused by the situation.
2. People who react intensely to events tend to (a) take them personally, (b) be oversensitive, (c) have abnormal arousal levels, (d) focus on the larger meaning of the event.
3. At a party, you see your best friend flirting with your date. You suddenly are flooded with jealousy. What cognitions might be causing this emotion? (*Be specific.*) What alternative thoughts might reduce the jealousy?

ANSWERS:

1. c 2. a 3. Possible thoughts causing jealousy are "My date finds other people more attractive"; "My best friend is trying to steal my date"; "My date's behavior is humiliating me." But you could be saying, "It's a compliment to me that other people find my date attractive."

The Mind-Body Connection

Many people believe that emotions are the downfall of our species because they are the opposite of reason. But are emotion and cognition really independent of each other? How can we avoid thinking about reason and emotion in either-or ways?

For many centuries in Western civilization, emotion was regarded as being the opposite of thinking, and an inferior opposite at that. The heart (emotion) was said to go its own way, in spite of what the head (reason) wanted. The division between thinking and feeling has provoked one of the longest-running "either-or" debates in intellectual history: Can we control our emotions, and hence our mammalian heritage, or do they control us? One reason this debate has lasted so long (and often been, dare we say, so emotional) is that it goes right to the heart of what it means to be human.

As their understanding of emotion increases, researchers are finding new ways of thinking about feeling, and of understanding how physiological processes and cognitive processes *interact* to create emotion. Some findings and research directions help to resolve the historic conflict between mind and body:

1. *Emotions and cognitions evolve and change in the course of human development, and so do their interconnections.* Infant emotion is not cognitively sophisticated, but infants certainly notice *something* that distresses them—gas pains, frustra-

tions in the environment, discomfort. Their early "appraisals" and responses are fairly primitive: good or bad, approach it or avoid it. As the baby (and the cerebral cortex) develop, cognitive appraisals, and therefore emotions, become more complex (Fischer, Shaver, & Carnochan, 1990; Malatesta, 1990). Indeed, some emotions depend entirely on cognitive development. Infants don't feel shame or guilt, for example, because these emotions require the emergence of a sense of self and the mental perception that one has behaved badly (Lewis et al., 1989).

2. *Relationships between cognition and emotion work in both directions.* Emotion results from appraisals and other thoughts; but emotions themselves can impair or interfere with subsequent thoughts and feelings. For example, you decide that a friend has intentionally stood you up for lunch, so you feel angry. But once you feel angry, you may be unwilling to listen to anyone who tries to correct your way of thinking about your friend's tardiness.

Similarly, a perception ("this person is out to hurt me") can stimulate emotional arousal; but being physiologically aroused for nonemotional reasons can make anger, or any other emotion, more intense. If you are at a noisy, crowded concert and you believe that someone has insulted you, you are likely to feel very angry, very quickly. You will feel angrier than if you had been listening to a quiet clarinet, lying on the sofa, or watching a romantic comedy when the "insult" occurred (Averill, 1982; Zillmann, 1983).

3. *Cognitions need not be conscious and voluntary to create emotions; there are different levels of cognitive processing and awareness.* As we saw earlier in discussing nonconscious processes (Chapter 8), some modes of cognitive activity operate automatically and without voluntary control. Some emotions, too, involve the simplest of nonconscious perceptions, such as a learned conditioned emotional response to a symbol of patriotism. Others require complex cognitive capacity, such as the ability to appreciate wordplay or subtle puns before finding them funny (Zajonc, Murphy, & Inglehart, 1989). Some cognitions are almost instantaneous, processed quickly by the amygdala, but others require the cerebral cortex, the center of reason, symbols, and logic (Lazarus, 1991). This part of the brain gives us the capacity for deciding we have been betrayed, for reanalyzing our fears, for interpreting someone else's actions—and thus generating the complex emotions of adult life. Appraisals may sometimes conflict at these different levels, which is why a person can simultaneously believe that flying in an airplane is safe *and* feel worried about getting in one.

An individual's experience of emotion, then, combines mind and body. But all individuals live in a social world. Thoughts may influence emotion, but where do these thoughts come from? You may decide you are wildly jealous, but where do you get your ideas of jealousy? You may feel angry enough to punch the walls, but where do you learn what to do when you are that enraged? To answer these questions, we must turn to the third major aspect of emotional experience: the role of culture.

■ ELEMENTS OF EMOTION 3: THE CULTURE

A young wife leaves her house one morning to draw water from the local well as her husband watches from the porch. On her way back from the well, a stranger stops her and asks for some water. She gives him a cupful and then invites him home to dinner. He accepts. The husband, wife, and guest have a pleasant meal together. The husband, in a gesture of hospitality, invites the guest to spend the night—with his wife. The guest accepts. In the morning, the husband leaves early to bring home breakfast. When he returns, he finds his wife again in bed with the visitor.

This baby will not feel an ounce of remorse for keeping her parents up all night—or gratitude for their care. Remorse and gratitude require the capacity for complex appraisals.

The question is: At what point in this story does the husband feel angry?

The answer is: It depends on the culture to which he belongs (Hupka, 1981). An American husband would feel rather angry at a wife who had an extramarital affair, and a wife would feel rather angry at being offered to a guest as if she were a lamb chop. But these reactions are not universal:

• A Pawnee Indian husband of the nineteenth century would be enraged at any man who dared ask his wife for water.

• An Ammassalik Eskimo husband finds it perfectly honorable to offer his wife to a stranger, but only once. He would be angry to find his wife and the guest having a second encounter.

• A Toda husband at the turn of the century in India would not be angry at all. The Todas allowed both husband and wife to take lovers, and women were even allowed to have several husbands. Both spouses might feel angry, though, if one of them had a *sneaky* affair, without announcing it publicly.

People in most cultures experience the emotion of anger as a response to insult and the violation of social rules. It's just that they disagree about what an insult or the correct rule is. In this section, we will explore some cultural influences on emotion.

The Varieties of Emotion

Are all emotions universal, or do some of them have national boundaries? One problem in answering this question is that some languages have words for emotional states that English lacks entirely, and vice versa. The Germans have *schadenfreude*, a feeling of joy at another's misfortune. The Japanese have *ijirashii*, a feeling associated with seeing an admirable person overcoming an obstacle, and *hagaii*, helpless anguish tinged with frustration. *Litost* is a Czech word that combines grief, sympathy, remorse, and longing; the Czech writer Milan Kundera used it to describe "a state of torment caused by a sudden insight into one's own miserable self." Interestingly enough, a number of languages lack a word for *emotion* itself (J. Russell, 1991a).

Anthropologist Robert Levy (1984) reports that Tahitians lack the Western concept of, and word for, sadness. If you ask a Tahitian who is grieving over the loss of a lover what is wrong, he will say, "A spirit has made me ill." In contrast, Tahitians have a word for an emotion that most Westerners do not ex-

Cultures everywhere determine the rules for expressing emotions. The rule for a formal Japanese wedding portrait is "no expressions"—but not every member of this family has learned that rule yet.

perience. The word reflects "a sense of the uncanny," a trembling sensation that Tahitians feel when ordinary categories of perception are suspended: at twilight, in the brush, watching fires glow without heat. To Westerners, an event that cannot be categorized and identified is usually greeted with fear. Yet the Tahitian "uncanny" does not describe what most Westerners would call fear or terror.

Do these interesting examples mean that Germans are more likely than others actually to *feel* "schadenfreude," the Japanese to feel "hagaii," and the Czechs to feel "litost"—or are they just more willing to give these emotions a single name? And do the Tahitians really not feel grief, or do they experience sadness but identify it as illness?

One way to examine the problem of cultural universals is to take a *prototype* approach to the concept of emotion (J. Russell, 1991b; Shaver, Wu, & Schwartz, 1992). We explained in Chapter 8 that a prototype is the best representative of a certain class of things. For example, most people will say that anger and sadness are more representative of an "emotion" than irritability and nostalgia are. According to the prototype approach, basic-level emotions are those that people everywhere consider the core examples of the category "emotion," and these basic emotions are reflected in the emotion words that young children learn first: *happy, sad, mad,* and *scared.* As children develop, they begin to draw emotional distinctions that are less prototypical and more specific to their language and culture, such as *ecstatic, depressed, hostile,* or *anxious* (J. Russell, 1989; Storm & Storm, 1987). They may learn that *indignation* is a kind of anger, or that *pride* is a kind of happiness.

From such research, most psychologists believe that it is possible to identify a number of **primary emotions** that seem to be universal experiences. In contrast, **secondary emotions** are more culture-specific. They include cultural variations (such as *schadenfreude* or *hagaii*), blends of feeling (such as *litost*), and degrees of intensity and nuance. Primary emotions have been identified in several ways: by universally recognized facial expressions; by the fact that they are emotion prototypes in most languages; and by the predictable appearance of these emotions in child development. Others define an emotion as "basic" if it cannot be reduced to other component emotions and if it is linked with specific tendencies to act, as in running from something fearful (Fox, 1991).

Depending on how psychologists go about measuring emotions, the list of the "primary" ones varies somewhat. As Table 9.1 shows, fear, anger, sadness, joy, surprise, and disgust turn up in most studies. Yet there is much disagreement. Most people don't really think of surprise, disgust, or contempt as true emotions, although all three are registered on the face (Ortony & Turner, 1990; Shaver et al., 1987).

And what about love? Is it a basic, positive emotion? Most Westerners would say yes, even though it doesn't have a typical facial expression (except perhaps the mooning gaze of new sweethearts). Yet in a study of Chinese adults in the People's Republic of China, "sad love" turned out to be a basic and *negative* emotion prototype, consisting of a cluster of feelings such as unrequited love, infatuation, nostalgia, and sorrow (Shaver, Wu, & Schwartz, 1992). The researchers describe this emotion as "the fleeting passion you feel for an attractive person you see on a train and will never meet again." Most Westerners would surely recognize this feeling, but they would consider it, along with other forms of love, to be more positive than the Chinese do.

Some researchers believe that shame, guilt, pride, pity, and empathy are as much a part of the human emotional experience as sadness and anger, but these feelings fail to make the list of "primary" emotions because they can't be measured in the brain or identified on the face. As a result of such problems, a few psychologists are ready to abandon the whole idea of trying to identify primary emotions. Andrew Ortony and Terence Turner (1990), for example, argue that

■ **primary emotions**
Emotions that are considered to be universal and biologically based. They generally include fear, anger, sadness, joy, and disgust.

■ **secondary emotions**
Emotions that are either "blends" of primary emotions (e.g., contempt as a blend of anger and disgust) or that are specific to certain cultures (e.g., the Tahitian sense of the "uncanny").

TABLE 9.1

Primary Emotions According to Leading Theories

Psychologists have tried to identify "basic" universal emotions in several ways. Some, such as Ekman, study universally recognizable facial expressions. Others, such as Plutchik, study people's subjective evaluation of emotion words and reduce their varied emotional experiences into basic categories. Still others, such as Shaver and the Storms, ask people to evaluate hundreds of words according to whether they are or are not emotions, and then to sort all the emotion words into clusters that "go together." The results, shown below, indicate some uniform results across all methods and some interesting variations.

Tomkins	Ekman	Izard	Plutchik	Shaver et al.	Storm & Storm	Weiner & Graham	Oatley & Johnson-Laird
Fear	Fear	Fear	Fear	Fear	Fear		Fear
Anger	Anger	Anger	Anger	Anger	Anger		Anger
Enjoyment	Happiness	Joy	Joy	Joy	Happiness	Happiness	Happiness
Distress	Sadness	Sadness	Sadness	Sadness	Sadness[a]	Sadness	Sadness
Disgust	Disgust	Disgust	Disgust				Disgust
Interest		Interest	Anticipation				
Surprise	Surprise	Surprise	Surprise	Surprise[b]			
Contempt	Contempt	Contempt					
Shame		Shame		Shame[c]			
			Acceptance	Love	Love/liking		

[a]Includes shame and pain.

[b]This category was marginal to the others and not really considered an emotion by subjects.

[c]This was a basic-level category only among the Chinese.

SOURCES: Ekman et al., 1987; Ekman & Heider, 1988; Izard, 1971, 1990; Oatley & Johnson-Laird, 1987; Plutchik, 1984; Shaver et al., 1987, 1992; Storm & Storm, 1987; Tomkins, 1981b; Weiner & Graham, 1984.

it may be useful to classify emotions for research purposes, but we should not infer that some emotions are therefore more *fundamental* or universal than others.

The answers to the question "Are emotions universal?" have to do in part with whether researchers are focusing on the common elements in all emotions or on cultural differences. In the most general sense, for instance, emotions are evoked by the same situations. In a massive cross-cultural research project involving 27 countries on five continents, the researchers found that for people everywhere, sadness follows perception of loss, fear follows perception of threat and bodily harm, and anger follows perception of insult or injustice (Scherer, 1988). Yet cultures determine much of what people feel angry, sad, lonely, happy (or whatever) *about*. On the Micronesian atoll of Ifaluk, it is cause for anger if someone next to you is smoking without offering you the cigarette; it means he is unwilling to share—a terrible offense (Lutz, 1988). Increasingly in the United States, of course, it is cause for anger if someone is smoking at all: To non-smokers, it means an infringement on their right to clean air!

The Communication of Emotion

When Brian Boitano won the gold medal in men's figure skating in the 1988 Olympics, he burst into tears of joy. But when he was actually given the award, he accepted it without expression. Why did he put on a stone face? "I almost felt guilty," Boitano explained later. "I had to hold back. My facial expression could only make him [rival Brian Orser] feel worse. I was not going to gloat" (in Friedman & Miller-Herringer, 1991).

As Boitano's story illustrates, once you feel an emotion, how you express it is rarely a simple matter of "I say (or show) what I feel." You may be obliged

This father is clearly proud of his family. Is pride just a variation of happiness, or is it a distinct emotion?

to disguise what you feel. You may wish you could feel what you say. You may convey an emotional message unintentionally, through nonverbal signals.

DISPLAY RULES AND "EMOTION WORK." Whatever the emotion, every society has **display rules** that govern how and when emotions may be expressed (Ekman & Friesen, 1975). In some cultures, grief is expressed by noisy wailing and weeping; in others, by stoic, tearless resignation; in still others, by merry dance, drink, and song (LaBarre, 1947). In some traditions, love is to be expressed by extravagant gesture, like the one Ulrich made in his Venus suit; in others, love is expressed by sustained, understated action. Imagine the conflict that can occur between people from different cultures!

People learn their culture's display rules as effortlessly as they learn its language. Just as they can speak without knowing the rules of grammar, most people express (or suppress) their emotions without being aware of the rules they are following. Consider the display rules for the stages of an angry dispute (E. Hall, 1976). Suppose your neighbor builds a fence on what you believe is your property. If you are an Anglo-American, your anger is likely to move from small steps to large ones. You start by dropping hints ("Gee, Mort, are you sure that fence is on your side of the line?"). Next, you talk to friends. Then you get a third person to intervene. Eventually you confront Mort directly. If none of this works, you may sue him. If that strategy fails, you may burn the fence down.

To Anglos, these steps, from small to large, are the natural, logical way to express anger. But there is nothing "natural" about this course of action. Worldwide, it isn't even very typical. In many cultures, the first thing you do when your neighbor builds a fence that angers you is . . . nothing. You think about it. You brood over your grievances and decide what to do. This brooding may last for weeks, months, or even years. The second step is . . . you burn the fence down. This is only to draw your neighbor's attention to the fact that you two have a problem, and now you are ready for negotiations, lawyers, third-party interventions, and so on. Notice how cultures misunderstand the same action: Burning the fence down is the last resort in one, but the start of the conversation in another.

Display rules not only tell us what to do when we *are* feeling an emotion; they also tell us how and when we should show an emotion we do *not* feel. Acting out an emotion we don't really feel, or trying to create the right emotion for the occasion, has been called **emotion work.** People are expected to demon-

The good manners and dignified restraint of a European may seem "cold" or "unfeeling" to the average American. What are the unfortunate consequences of overlooking the effects of culture on the display of emotions?

■ **display rules**
Social and cultural rules that regulate when, how, and where a person may express (or suppress) emotions.
■ **emotion work**
Expression of an emotion one does not really feel.

Flight attendants, male or female, are trained to smile and convey friendliness. This man is a steward on a corporate jet.

strate sadness at funerals, happiness at weddings, and affection toward relatives. If they don't really feel such emotions, they may act as if they do.

Sometimes emotion work is a job requirement, as a study of flight attendants and bill collectors found (Hochschild, 1983). Flight attendants must "put on a happy face" and convey cheerfulness, even if they are angry about a rude or drunken passenger. Bill collectors must put on a fierce face to convey threat; they must withhold sympathy, even if they are feeling sorry for the poor person in debt. Other employees do "emotion work" when they express agreement with an employer's infuriating decision or when they display cheerfulness to annoying customers. But not all emotion work is negative: The effort to interpret a situation in a positive light, and to generate real feelings of warmth and friendliness toward others, not only makes social relations more pleasurable but also makes feeling positive emotions more likely.

BODY LANGUAGE.   Fiorello LaGuardia, who was mayor of New York from 1933 to 1945, was fluent in three different languages: English, Italian, and Yiddish. LaGuardia knew more than the words of those languages; he also knew the gestures that went along with each one. Researchers who studied films of his speeches could tell which language he was speaking *with the sound turned off* (Birdwhistell, 1970). They could do so by reading his *body language*, the countless nonverbal signals of body movement, posture, gesture, and gaze that people constantly express.

Emotions are communicated by body language too, and often are highly "contagious" as a result. Have you ever been in a cheerful mood, had lunch with a depressed friend, and come away feeling vaguely depressed yourself? Have you ever stopped to have a chat with a friend who was nervous about an upcoming exam, and ended up feeling jumpy and anxious yourself? In contrast, have you ever felt "out of sync" with another person's moods and mannerisms? Research confirms what you may have suspected: Moods are highly contagious, especially when two people's body languages are in harmony (see Figure 9.2). An ability to synchronize moods through nonverbal gestures is crucial to smooth interaction between people (Hatfield, Cacioppo, & Rapson, 1992).

FIGURE 9.2

The contagion of moods and gestures

As these scenes from an actual videotaped study show, volunteers who have never previously met each other are obviously "in sync" in their nonverbal gestures. In turn, the degree to which people's movements are synchronized determines how much emotional rapport they will feel. Such physical synchrony paves the way for the "contagion" of moods (Bernieri et al., 1991).

Some basic signals of body language, like some basic facial expressions, seem to be "spoken" universally. Across cultures, people generally recognize body movements that reveal pleasure or displeasure, liking or dislike, tension or relaxation, high status or low status (Buck, 1984). When people are depressed, it shows in their walk, stance, and head position.

However, most aspects of body language are specific to particular spoken languages and cultures. For example, the smile seems simple and unmistakable; it is, as we saw, universally recognized as a sign of friendliness. Yet it does not have universal meanings. Americans smile more frequently than Germans; this does not mean that Americans are friendlier than Germans, but that they differ in their notions of when a smile is appropriate. After a German-American business session, Americans often complain that their German counterparts are cold and aloof. Meanwhile, Germans often complain that the Americans are excessively cheerful, hiding their real feelings under the mask of a smile (Hall & Hall, 1990). The Japanese smile even more than the Americans, to disguise embarrassment, anger, or other negative emotions whose public display is considered rude and incorrect.

Even the simplest gesture is subject to misunderstanding. Visitors to other countries may learn some words in their hosts' language in an effort at courtesy, and then unwittingly offend them by making the wrong gesture. The sign of the University of Texas football team, the Longhorns, is to extend the second finger and the pinkie. In Italy and other parts of Europe this gesture means a man's wife has been unfaithful to him—a serious insult.

Cultures differ in how attentive they are to body signals and which signals are likely to draw attention. For instance, a study of more than 1,000 Japanese students found that the Japanese pay more attention to body movements associated with status and power than to body movements that express like or dislike (Kudoh & Matsumoto, 1985). In Japan, the researchers explain, social relationships are vertical, based on status, respect, and duty. In the United States, social relationships are more likely to be horizontal, based on friendship, affection, and attraction. Americans, consequently, pay more attention to body signals of emotional attraction and liking. These differences may be one reason that people from different cultures often feel "out of sync" with one another, even when they are speaking the same language.

Even within cultures, of course, people differ in their expressiveness and gestures. And many aspects of "body language" have little to do with emotion. We wave our arms for emphasis; we use formal gestures to wave for taxis, get attention in class, greet a new acquaintance. Whether communicating emotion, power, intention, or emphasis, one gesture can be worth a thousand words.

The body communicates many messages of emotion and status. Walking or standing with hands clasped behind the body, for example—as members of royalty often do, or military commanders inspecting the troops—is a sign of dominance and confidence. Culture influences many kinds of body language. Arabs stand much closer to each other in normal conversation than Westerners do—close enough to feel one another's breath and "read" one another's eyes. In many societies, men greet men with an embrace and a kiss, gestures that are taboo in most of the United States and Canada.

Be careful where you make this gesture.

> ## QUICK QUIZ
>
> The following example of cultural miscommunication occurred in an English class for foreign students: An Arab student was describing a tradition of his home country, when he inadvertently said something that embarrassed a Japanese student. To disguise his shame, the Japanese student smiled, and the Arab demanded to know what was so funny about Arab customs. The Japanese, now feeling publicly humiliated, giggled. The Arab, enraged, hit him. What concepts from the previous section explain this misunderstanding?
>
> **ANSWERS:**
>
> Arab and Japanese cultures have different *display rules* regarding the expression of anger, the appropriate response to feeling shamed, and the management of embarrassment in public. The two students also misread each other's *nonverbal communication*. To the Arab, the Japanese student's smile meant that he was being laughed at, but the Japanese intended merely to disguise his discomfort.

■ PUTTING THE ELEMENTS TOGETHER: THE CASE OF EMOTION AND GENDER

Why is it "arguing" when he does it but "getting emotional" when she does it? On emotional subjects, people often fail to define their terms. What, for example, does "emotional" mean?

"Women are too emotional," men often complain. "Men are too repressed," women often reply. People hold strong beliefs about gender differences in emotion and about whether the male or female style is better (Shields, 1991). But what do they mean by "emotional"? As we have seen, "being emotional" can refer to an internal emotional state, to how an emotion is displayed, to nonverbal expressiveness, or to emotion work. Because emotion has so many aspects, it is necessary to define our terms before we can understand whether or how the sexes differ.

THE EXPERIENCE OF EMOTION. To begin with, there is not much evidence that, within any given cultural group, one sex experiences normal, everyday emotions more often than the other (Averill, 1982; Baumeister, Stillwell, & Wotman, 1990; Shaver & Hazan, 1987; Shields, 1991). Both sexes are equally likely, on the average, to feel anxious in new social situations. Both sexes are equally likely to experience jealousy, love, and loneliness. Both sexes feel angry when they believe they have been insulted or treated unfairly. Both sexes feel embarrassed when they make public mistakes. Both sexes grieve when attachments break up. So it seems we must look elsewhere for gender differences in emotion.

THE PHYSIOLOGY OF EMOTION. If we define being "more emotional" in terms of physiological reactivity to stress, perhaps men are more emotional than women. John Gottman and his colleagues (Gottman & Krokoff, 1989; Gottman & Levenson, 1986), in doing a series of longitudinal studies of married couples, found that conflict and dissension were *physiologically* more upsetting for men than for women, which may be why many men try to avoid conflict entirely or overreact by losing control. Several studies have found that hostility and anger are more closely linked with marital distress and conflict for husbands than for wives (Smith, Sanders, & Alexander, 1990).

One reason for such findings may lie in the autonomic nervous system's response to stress. In laboratory studies of stress, males show a more pronounced elevation in the secretion of epinephrine than do females (Polefrone & Manuck, 1987). No one knows where these apparent differences come from—genetics, social learning, or situational demands.

COGNITIONS THAT GENERATE EMOTION. Men and women often differ in the perceptions and expectations that generate certain emotions, again in particular situations (R. Lakoff, 1990; Stapley & Haviland, 1989). These differences in perception can create many misunderstandings: As we have seen, two interpretations of the same event can create two different emotional responses to it. If a man pays the expenses for his date, is he entitled to her sexual favors in return? If a male teacher compliments a female student on her looks, is that a sign of flattery or sexual harassment? If a woman affectionately touches a male friend on his arm, is she signaling affection or sexual interest? Under such circumstances, it is not that one sex is "more emotional," but that the same situation (such as a date) may produce an emotion in one partner (anger, joy, or embarrassment) and not in the other—depending on what each partner expects and wants from the relationship.

THE DISPLAY RULES FOR EMOTIONAL EXPRESSION. In many cultures, women are encouraged and permitted to express their emotions and men are expected to control them—or vice versa. A major international study found only one common pattern: Almost everywhere, men are expected to control feelings of fear and convey an image of the "fearless" male (Wallbott, Ricci-Bitti, & Bänninger-Huber, 1986). With all other emotions, ranging from joy to anger, the display rules for women and men are highly variable. In many Asian cultures, as we have seen, both sexes are taught to control emotional expression (Buck & Teng, 1987). In cultures throughout Europe, the Middle East, and South America, display rules for women and men often depend on the emotion in question. In the international study mentioned above, for example, Israeli and Italian men were much more likely than women to control feelings of sadness, but British, Spanish, Swiss, and German *women* were more likely than their male counterparts to inhibit this emotion. Overall, European women were not more emotionally expressive than men; the differences were greater between cultures than between genders (Wallbott, Ricci-Bitti, & Bänninger-Huber, 1986).

Such cultural variations make it difficult to draw generalizations about the sexes, especially in nations where many different subcultures coexist. Just to confound the issue, situational rules often override gender rules: An American man will be as likely as an American women to control his temper when the target of anger is someone with higher status or power; few people, no matter how angry, will readily sound off at a professor, police officer, or employer. In the home, men and women are equally likely to sulk, hold grudges, discuss matters outright, or yell (Averill, 1982; Tavris, 1989). And you won't find gender differences in emotional expressiveness at a North American football game!

Nevertheless, there are a few reliable gender differences in North American display rules. In the United States and Canada, women and men differ, on the average, in how, where, and when they reveal certain emotions. For example, men are more likely than women to reveal anger to strangers, especially other men, when they believe they have been challenged or insulted. Men are also more likely to express anger, fear, or hurt pride in the form of aggressive action (Frodi, Macaulay, & Thome, 1977; Novaco, 1985).

Women are more likely than men, in contrast, to talk about negative emotions such as fear, sadness, loneliness, and embarrassment with their friends and family (Aukett, Ritchie, & Mill, 1988; Shields, 1991; Stapley & Haviland, 1989). Men, if they express these "unmanly" emotions at all, tend to do so only to their

Men and women often disagree on the meaning of a touch: Does it signify affection, dominance, harassment, sexual interest, sympathy, or simple friendliness? Depending on their perceptions, men and women may react to a touch with anger, happiness, disgust, fear, or desire.

Both sexes feel emotionally attached to their friends and loved ones, but often they learn to express their feelings of closeness differently. From childhood on, girls tend to prefer "face-to-face" friendships, based on shared feelings; boys tend to prefer "side-by-side" friendships, based on shared activities.

intimate partners, and rarely to casual male friends. Even with their wives and girlfriends, men tend to reveal their strengths and positive emotions and conceal their worries and weaknesses. Two psychologists, reviewing results of 39 studies, found that both sexes were equally likely to feel lonely but women were much more likely to *admit* it. One reason, the researchers discovered, was that both sexes are more likely to reject a lonely male than a lonely female. There are greater negative consequences to men than to women, it seems, of revealing unhappiness (Borys & Perlman, 1985).

One consequence of the social taboo on male expressiveness may be difficulty in recognizing men's unhappiness. In fact, some researchers now believe that many boys and men fail to be diagnosed as depressed because the tests for depression are based on typically female reactions such as crying, staying in bed, talking about one's unhappiness, and developing eating disorders (Riessman, 1990; Stapley & Haviland, 1989). Because many men do not express grief this way, some people wrongly infer that men suffer less than women when relationships end.

Catherine Riessman (1990) began to question this assumption while she was interviewing a large sample of wives and husbands about their divorces. The men were suffering as much as the women, Riessman learned, but they didn't *say* so. In fact, most of the men claimed they felt sad "some or a little of the time" and that they felt depressed or lonely "none of the time." However, Riessman found, these men were expressing grief in ways that are acceptably masculine: "frantic work," heavy drinking, driving too fast, singing sentimental songs. Many of the men reported trouble concentrating at work; difficulties on the job; restlessness and hyperactivity; and numerous physical ailments and stress symptoms. One man confessed that for four months after his separation he "threw up every morning," but no, he wasn't actually "depressed." Another denied feeling sad, but in the six months since his divorce he had racked up a long list of criminal charges.

So when we look at average differences in display rules, we find that women are "more emotional" than men in talking about negative feelings, and men are "more emotional" than women in displaying negative feelings in aggressive or self-destructive ways.

NONVERBAL COMMUNICATION. Sometimes women are considered "more emotional" because of their supposed sensitivity to other people's emotional states. This idea has been studied using a test called the Profile of Nonverbal Sensitivity (PONS), which measures a person's ability to detect emotions revealed in tones of voice, movements of the body, and facial expressions (Rosenthal et al., 1979). Women have scored slightly better on this test than men (J. Hall, 1987). But research finds that being sensitive to another person's emotional state often depends more on the *context* in which the two people are interacting than on their gender. In particular, sensitivity depends on:

1. *The sex of the sender and the receiver.* People do better reading their own sex's signals than those of the other sex (Buck, 1984).

2. *How well the two people know each other.* Dating couples and married couples can interpret each other's facial expressions and other signals better than strangers can (Hatfield, Cacioppo, & Rapson, 1992).

3. *Who has the power.* Less powerful people learn to read the powerful person's signals, usually for self-protection (R. Lakoff, 1990). In two experiments, Sara Snodgrass (1985, 1992) found that "women's intuition" should more properly be called "subordinate's intuition." In male-female pairs, the person in the subordinate (follower) position was more sensitive to the leader's nonverbal signals than the leader was to the follower's cues. This difference occurred whether a man or a woman was the leader or the follower. The social position that people are in, Snodgrass found, almost totally overrode any sex differences.

EMOTION WORK. Both sexes know the experience of having to hide emotions they feel and pretend emotions they do not feel. Yet their emotion work is often different. On the whole, women tend to be involved in the flight-attendant side of emotion work (persuading others that they are friendly, happy, and warm) and men to be involved in the bill-collection side (persuading others that they are stern, aggressive, and "unemotional"). Public-service jobs requiring emotion work are a fourth of all the jobs that men do, but they are more than half of the jobs that women do (Hochschild, 1983). Care-oriented emotion work is often a woman's job in the family as well as in the workplace. It is part of the wife's traditional responsibilities to attend to the feelings and emotional well-being of her husband and children.

Perhaps as part of their emotion work, women in North America smile more often than men do, not necessarily because they feel happier, but to pacify, nurture, and convey deference (Mayo & Henley, 1981). If women don't smile when others expect them to, they are often disliked, even if they are actually smiling as often as men would. Children learn this lesson early. Carolyn Saarni (1989) found that 6- to 10-year-olds show a steady increase in knowledge about where and when they should disguise feelings and put on a "polite smile" (for instance, when they are given a gift they don't like). From childhood on, girls are more likely than boys to mask their negative feelings with positive expressions. As adults, women often express anger with a smile, a mixed message that can be puzzling to their friends, spouses, and children (Deutsch, LeBaron, & Fryer, 1987). The smile requirement for women is by no means universal, though. In Taiwan and the People's Republic of China, for example, women do not differ from men in facial expressiveness (Buck & Teng, 1987).

Thus, with regard to emotion work and display rules, it appears that, in some cultural groups at least, women are expected to be "more emotional" than men, in terms of managing their own and other people's feelings. But if we define "emotionality" in terms of intensity, physiological reactivity, emotion-generating perceptions, expressiveness, or nonverbal sensitivity, we see that the answer to "who is more emotional" is sometimes men, sometimes women, sometimes both, and sometimes neither.

As we have seen in this chapter, the full experience and expression of emotion depend on physiology, cognitive perceptions, and society's rules. The case of gender and emotion shows that if we look at just one component, we come up with an incomplete or misleading picture. Human emotions can be compared to a tree: The biological capacity for emotion is the trunk; thoughts and explanations create the many branches; and culture is the gardener that shapes the tree and prunes it, cutting off some limbs and cultivating others.

Emotions have many purposes in human life. They allow us to establish close bonds, threaten and warn, get help from others, reveal or deceive. The many varieties and expressions of emotion suggest that although we feel emotions physically, we use them socially. As we explore motivation, personality, development, well-being, and mental disorders, we will see again and again how emotions involve thinking and feeling, perception and action—head and heart.

TAKING PSYCHOLOGY WITH YOU

"Let It Out" or "Bottle It Up"?
The Dilemma of Anger

There is a common notion afoot in America that it is best to express every emotion you feel, whenever and wherever you feel it, or else it will "fester" and cause problems. Does "letting anger out" really get rid of it, or does it only make it more intense? The answer is crucial for how we get along with our families, neighbors, employers, and strangers. Increasingly, it seems, people are freely venting their anger at strangers with rude gestures and insulting remarks, and the level of public debate about serious issues often seems to have degenerated into name-calling and the exchange of hostilities.

Although some schools of therapy once advised people to "let it all hang out," psychologists are finding that this advice is likely to hang you (Deffenbacher, 1988). By and large, research shows that expressing anger does not always get rid of anger; often it prolongs it (Averill, 1982; Tavris, 1989). When people talk about their anger or act on that feeling, they tend to rehearse their grievances, create a hostile disposition, and pump up their blood pressures. Conversely, when people learn to control their tempers, they usually feel better, not worse; calmer, not angrier. Charles Darwin (1872/1965) observed this fact more than a century ago. "The free expression by outward signs of an emotion intensifies it," he wrote. "On the other hand, the repression, as far as this is possible, of all outward signs softens our emotions. He who gives way to violent gestures will increase his rage."

Some people behave aggressively when they are angry, but others behave in a friendly, cooperative way to try to solve the problem that is causing their anger. When people are feeling angry, after all, there are many things they can do: write letters, play the piano, jog, bake bread, kick the sofa, abuse their friends or family, or yell. If a particular action soothes their feelings or gets the desired response from other people, they are likely to acquire a habit. Soon that habit feels "wired in," as if it could never be changed; in-

deed, many people justify their violent tempers by saying "I just couldn't help myself." But they can. If you have learned an aggressive habit, the research in this chapter offers practical suggestions for relearning constructive ways of managing anger:

• *Don't sound off in the heat of anger; let bodily arousal cool down.* Whether your arousal comes from background stresses such as heat, crowds, or loud noise, or from conflict with another person, take time to relax. Time allows you to decide if you are "really" angry or just tired and tense. This is the reason for that sage old advice to count to 10, count to 100, or sleep on it. Other "cooling-off" strategies include taking a time out in the middle of an argument; meditating or relaxing; and calming yourself with a distracting activity.

• *Remember that anger depends on the perception of insult; see if you can rethink the problem.* People who are quick to feel angry tend to interpret other people's actions as intentional offenses. People who are slow to anger tend to give others the benefit of the doubt (Novaco, 1985). Empathy ("Poor guy, he's feeling rotten") is usually incompatible with anger and aggressiveness, so try to see the situation from the other person's perspective (Miller & Eisenberg, 1988).

• *If you decide that expressing anger is appropriate, think carefully about how to do it so that you will get the results you want.* As we saw, different cultures have different display rules. Be sure the recipient of your anger understands what you are feeling and what complaint you are trying to convey—and this is true whether the recipient is your parent, friend, annoying neighbor, employer, or City Hall.

Ultimately, the decision about whether to express anger depends not only on whether you will feel good if you do, but also on what you hope to accomplish. Do you want to restore your rights, change the other person, improve a bad situation, or achieve justice? If those are your goals, then learning *how* to express anger so the other person will listen, and respond, is essential. For example, people who have been the targets of discrimination have successfully directed anger through legal channels to win their rights.

Of course, if you just want to "blow off steam," go right ahead—although you risk becoming a hothead.

SUMMARY

1. The complex experience of *emotion* involves physiological changes in the brain, face, and body; cognitive processes; and culture. In the late nineteenth century, the *James-Lange* theory of emotion proposed that awareness of bodily reactions to an event gives rise to the experience of emotion. "We feel sorry *because* we cry, angry *because* we strike," wrote James. His work inspired modern efforts to study the relationship between physiology and cognition in emotion.

2. Some psychologists believe that facial expressions are a clue to the biological nature of emotion. Some basic facial expressions—anger, fear, sadness, happiness, disgust, surprise—are widely recognized across cultures. Different facial expressions become apparent in infancy, and infants recognize adult expressions of fear, anger, and happiness.

3. According to the *facial-feedback hypothesis*, facial expressions not only communicate to others, but also may send messages to the brain identifying our own emotional states. Facial expressions may also affect positive and negative moods by regulating blood flow in the brain. Because people can disguise their emotions, however, facial expressions do not always communicate accurately.

4. Some researchers study structures of the brain in order to identify biological components of emotion: particularly the hypothalamus and the amygdala, which is part of the limbic system and responsible for immediate processing of incoming stimuli that are perceived as dangerous or threatening. New approaches examine how different areas of the brain are involved in various aspects of emotional experience; for example, the right hemihere seems to be specialized for the processing of negative emotions, the left hemisphere for positive emotions. Parts of the brain also specialize in recognizing faces and facial expressions.

5. *Epinephrine* and *norepinephrine* (also called adrenaline and noradrenaline) are hormones that produce physiological *arousal* to prepare the body to cope with environmental stimuli, nonemotional but physically taxing events, and all emotional states. These hormones produce changes in heart rate, respiration, pupil dilation, blood sugar levels, perspiration, digestion, memory, and performance. There seem to be several forms of arousal, involving different areas of the brain, and arousal itself does not cause an emotional state. Moreover, the autonomic nervous system produces different patterns of physiological changes that correspond to different emotions.

6. Schachter and Singer's *two-factor theory* held that emotions result from *arousal* and the *labeling* or interpretation of that arousal. Their research launched a slew of studies designed to identify the cognitive processes involved in emotion.

7. One of these cognitive processes is how people interpret and evaluate events. For example, people who feel depressed and lonely tend to think that the reasons for their unhappiness are *internal*, *stable*, and *uncontrollable*. People who feel their emotions intensely tend to *personalize* events, *pay selective attention*, and *overgeneralize*.

8. New approaches help resolve the age-old "reason-versus-emotion" debate in philosophy, showing how physiological and cognitive processes interact in the experience of emotion. They include: taking a developmental approach to the emergence of emotions; realizing that thoughts influence emotions, and vice versa; and recognizing that cognitions can be nonconscious as well as conscious, and involve different degrees of cognitive complexity.

9. Some researchers distinguish *primary* emotions, which are thought to be universal, from *secondary* emotions, which include variations and blends that are specific to cultures. The primary emotions are usually identified as fear, anger, sadness, joy, surprise, and disgust. Other psychologists doubt that surprise and disgust are true emotions; they also argue that this list omits universal emotions, such as love, hope, empathy, shame, and pride, that are difficult to measure physiologically.

10. Cultures influence the experience and expression of emotions. They determine what their members feel emotional about and what people do when they feel an emotion. *Display rules* are the culture's way of regulating how, when, and where a person may express (or must suppress) an emotion. *Emotion work* is the effort a person makes to display an emotion he or she doesn't really feel but feels obliged to convey.

11. People communicate their emotions (and many other messages) through *body language:* gesture, posture, body movement, touch, and mannerism. When people are nonverbally "in sync," their moods can be contagious. Cultures differ as widely in body language as in spoken language.

12. Women and men are equally likely to feel a wide array of emotions, from love to anger, but they sometimes differ in the perceptions and expectations that generate emotion. They also differ in the display rules that govern the expression of emotions: In Western societies, women are more likely to talk about feelings of fear, sadness, and loneliness than men are; men are more likely to deny they have such feelings or to reveal them in aggressive acts. The ability to "read" another person's emotional state depends on status, familiarity with the other person, and whether the partners are of the same gender.

KEY TERMS

emotion   *312*
James-Lange theory   *313*
facial-feedback hypothesis   *314*
epinephrine (adrenaline)   *317*
norepinephrine
  (noradrenaline)   *317*
arousal   *317*

two-factor theory of emotion   *321*
prototypes of emotion   *327*
primary emotions   *327*
secondary emotions   *327*
display rules   *329*
emotion work   *329*
body language   *330*

10

Motivation

Pitcher Jim Abbott at work.

All that Jim Abbott ever wanted to do was play baseball. This is not an unusual ambition, perhaps, but Jim Abbott was born with a condition that might have dampened the motivation of most others: He has no right hand. You'd never know it to watch him pitch for the California Angels, however. What would motivate a young man to pursue a goal that everyone told him was impossible?

All that Dian Fossey ever wanted to do was study mountain gorillas. This was not an unusual ambition, considering the varied interests that people have, but Dian Fossey's methods might have dampened the motivation of most others. Fossey lived in the wilderness with "her" gorillas, fought fiercely against the human poachers who were paid to kill or capture the animals, endured countless hardships and physical assaults, and was eventually murdered by unknown assailants. Many people have lived under temporary conditions of hardship to advance human knowledge, traveling to the North Pole or outer space. What would motivate a young woman to choose such hardship as a way of life, forgoing all comforts, family, and human love?

The words *motivation* and *emotion* both come from the Latin root meaning "to move," and the psychology of motivation indeed aims to figure out what moves us, why we do what we do. Like emotion, motivation involves physiological processes, cognitive processes, and social and cultural processes that shape its expression. Emotion can motivate us to behave in particular ways: Anger can move us to shout, fear can move us to run, and love moves us to do all sorts of things. But emotion is only one kind of motivating force.

In general, **motivation** refers to an inferred process within a person (or animal) that causes that organism to move toward a goal. The goal may be to satisfy a biological need, as in eating a sandwich to reduce hunger. The goal may be to fulfill a psychological ambition, such as having fame, money, or a good marriage. In this chapter, we will consider some of the many motives that give human life and human character their diversity.

■ THE PUSH AND PULL OF MOTIVATION

In Hugh Lofting's delightful book *The Story of Dr. Doolittle*, a shy, affectionate animal called a pushmi-pullyu turns up. The pushmi-pullyu has heads at both ends, so it can eat with one and talk with the other, and always knows where it is going (and why). When it comes to motivation, human beings are a bit like the pushmi-pullyu. Some biologically based motives, such as hunger and thirst, push us. If you go too long without food and water, your body will motivate you to seek them. Other motives, social ones, pull us; they involve *incentives*, such as money, fame, or power, that draw us toward a goal. To see the difference between a biological need and an incentive, consider thirst. Your body doesn't care whether you satisfy your thirst by drinking water, prune juice, or a milkshake. But if you decide to treat yourself to a milkshake as a reward for

■ **motivation**
An inferred process within an animal or person that causes that organism to move toward a goal.

340

two hours of study, that milkshake has become an incentive. You might not be thirsty at all.

Psychologists who study motivation, like those who study emotion, often disagree about what the phenomenon is, what causes it, and how to identify it. As the preceding example suggests, if you see someone drink a milkshake, you don't necessarily know that person's motive for doing so. Perhaps the person hates milkshakes but is being polite because her roommate brought her one as a present. Moreover, just as several emotions usually cluster together, so several motives may operate together, sometimes in different directions. A man may be motivated to achieve financial success and motivated to be a good father, but what happens when one motive conflicts with the other? Like the pushmi-pullyu, human beings are often pushed *and* pulled by competing forces.

When Motives Conflict

Two motives are said to be in conflict when the satisfaction of one leads to the inability to act on the other—when, that is, you want to eat your cake and have it, too. Researchers have identified four kinds of motivational conflicts (K. Lewin, 1948):

1. *Approach-approach* conflicts occur when you are equally attracted to two or more possible activities or goals. For example, you would like to go out with Tom, Dick, *and* Harry; you would like to be a veterinarian *and* a cowboy; you would like to stay home with a great novel *and* go out to dinner with friends.

2. *Avoidance-avoidance* conflicts, which require you to choose between "the lesser of two evils," occur when you dislike two alternatives. Novice parachute jumpers, for example, must choose between the fear of jumping and the fear of losing face if they don't jump (Epstein & Fenz, 1965).

3. *Approach-avoidance* conflicts occur when one activity or goal has both a positive and a negative aspect. For example, a shy woman wants to go to a party with her friends, but she fears being awkward and lonely if she attends; she wants to approach the party and avoid it at the same time. Differing cultural values produce many approach-avoidance conflicts, such as these, which our students have described:

- A Latino student said he wants to succeed and do well in the dominant Anglo society, but he comes from a culture that highly values family closeness. His family worries that by going to college, he will eventually leave them behind.
- A Filipina student said she wants an education more than anything else, but she also doesn't want to be disobedient to her parents, who have arranged a marriage for her back home.
- An African-American student from an impoverished neighborhood is in college on a prestigious scholarship. He is torn between wanting to leave his ghetto background behind him forever, and returning to help the family and community who have supported him.
- An Anglo student wants to be a marine biologist, but her friends tell her that only nerds and dweebs go into science.

In an approach-avoidance conflict, both attraction and repulsion are strongest when you are nearest the goal. The closer you are to something appealing, the stronger your desire to approach; the closer you are to something unpleasant, the stronger your desire to flee (see Figure 10.1). However, as you step away from the goal, the two motives change in strength. The attractive aspects of the goal still seem appealing, but the negative ones seem less unpleasant. This may be one reason that people often have trouble resolving their ambivalence in approach-avoidance situations. When they leave a situation that has some bene-

"C'mon, c'mon—it's either one or the other."

A classic avoidance-avoidance conflict.

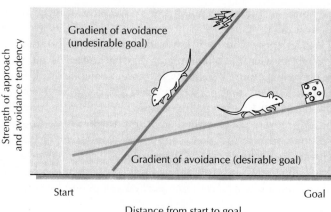

FIGURE 10.1

The approach-avoidance problem
When a goal is both appealing (good food) and punishing (because painful shock accompanies the food), an animal is motivated both to approach it and avoid it. As the animal gets closer to the goal, the desire to avoid pain rises more steeply than the desire to approach pleasure. At the point where the two tendencies intersect, the animal shows the greatest uncertainty and vacillation.

fits but many problems, and consider it from a distance, they see its positive aspects and overlook the negative ones. So they approach it again. Up close, the problems appear more clearly, motivating them to avoid the situation once more.

4. *Multiple approach-avoidance* conflicts occur in situations that offer several possible choices, each with advantages and disadvantages. For example, you might want to marry and settle down while you're still in school, and you think you have found the right person. On the other hand, you first want to establish a career and have some money in the bank, and lately you and the right person have been quarreling a lot.

Conflict is inevitable, unless you are a garden slug. But over time, unresolved conflicts have a physical and mental cost. In a series of studies, students listed their 15 main "personal strivings": "approach" goals such as "trying to be attractive" or "trying to seek new experiences," or "avoidance" goals such as "trying to avoid being noticed by others" or "trying to avoid being dependent on my boyfriend." They rated these objectives on the amount of conflict they caused and on how ambivalent the students felt about them. (For example, striving "to appear more intelligent than I am" conflicts with striving "to always present myself in an honest light.") High degrees of conflict and ambivalence were associated with anxiety, depression, headaches and other physical symptoms, and increased visits to the student health center (Emmons & King, 1988).

A provocative finding of these studies was that students in a state of conflict tended to *think* a great deal about their conflicts but not *do* anything to resolve them. One student, for instance, remained unhappily stuck between his goal of "achieving independence" and his desire to continue to be cared for by his parents. The reconciliation of motivational conflicts, the researchers found, is "a premier goal of human development" and a cornerstone of well-being.

Primary Drives and Social Motives

Many of the earliest psychologists believed that human beings were motivated largely by *instincts*, or inborn patterns of behavior. They proposed nearly as many of these instincts as there were activities, from cleanliness to cruelty. But in the 1920s, the popularity of instinct theories faded, and the concept of instincts was replaced by that of drives (Hull, 1943).

According to drive theory, biological *needs* result from states of physical deprivation. Such needs create a physiological *drive*, a state of tension that motivates a person (or animal) to satisfy the need. The cycle works like this: The body is deprived of something it physically needs, such as food or water; this need creates a drive; the person is then motivated to reduce the drive—say, by finding food or drinking water—which satisfies the need. There are only a few primary drives, including hunger, thirst, excessive cold, and pain.

Drive theory depends on the concept of **homeostasis,** the tendency of the body to maintain itself in a steady, stable condition. Homeostasis works like a thermostat, which goes on when the temperature drops a few degrees and shuts off when it reaches its set level. The body has several "thermostats" to regulate internal temperature, blood sugar, water balance in the cells, and oxygen and carbon dioxide in the blood. If an imbalance occurs in any of these, a need is created and the body will try to regain balance.

However, drive theory cannot account for the complexity and variety of human motivations. A certain level of physical energy fuels most human motives (Biner, 1991). But researchers also recognize that people are conscious creatures who think and plan ahead, who set goals for themselves and plot strategies to reach them (Bandura, 1990; Dweck, 1990). And they recognize that **social motives,** such as the need for friends or power, are as important as primary drives in influencing people's actions. Social motives are learned, some in childhood, some in later life, and they are called "social" because they develop in the context of family, environment, and culture. The interaction of biological needs and social motives is particularly apparent in the case of hunger.

Hunger, Eating, and Weight

For most people, hunger, if left unsatisfied, can become a powerful motivator. Hungry people dream of and fantasize about food. Given access to food, they consume enormous quantities to try to eliminate the feeling of being ravenous. Starving people will gorge themselves until they return to their previous body weight, and most people who have been on a severe diet go on binges that bring them back to their previous size (Polivy & Herman, 1985).

An early physiological explanation of hunger and eating sought to find "hunger centers" and "satiation centers" in the brain, particularly in the hypothalamus. Research at the time suggested that the lateral hypothalamus (LH) was responsible for signals to "start eating," and the ventromedial hypothalamus (VMH) was responsible for signals to "stop eating." When researchers damaged cells in the VMH of a rat, the animal would gorge itself and get very fat. But calling the LH a "hunger center" and the VMH the "satiety center" proved too simple. Lesions in these areas produce many behavioral changes in rats, not just changes that affect eating. Also, the quantity of food that lesioned animals eat does not depend only on damage to the hypothalamus. In one study of rats that had been on severe diets and lost weight, destruction of parts of the hypothalamus did not interfere with their normal catch-up growth (Bernardis et al., 1989).

A more common, psychological theory held that overweight is a sign of emotional disturbance. Research has failed to support this popular belief, too. Fat people are no more and no less emotionally disturbed than average-weight people (Stunkard, 1980). However, tension and irritability can *result* from constant dieting (being hungry much of the time) and unhappiness can result from being heavy in a society that discriminates against people who weigh more than the cultural ideal (Rodin, Silberstein, & Streigel-Moore, 1990).

By far the most common assumption about overweight—so widely accepted that for years hardly anyone bothered to test it—is that it is caused by overeating. Yet research now has clearly determined that *overweight is not caused simply by overeating* (C. Bouchard et al., 1990). Some overweight people do eat enormous quantities of food, but so do some very thin people. Some thin people eat very little, but so do some very fat people. In one study that carefully monitored everything that subjects were eating, two 260-pound women were maintaining their weights while consuming only 1,000 calories a day (Wooley, Wooley, & Dyrenforth, 1979). A study that asked volunteers to gorge themselves for months found that it was as hard for slender people to gain weight as it is

Overweight is caused mainly by overeating, isn't it? This idea is logical, obvious . . . and wrong. What other theories might explain why some slender people eat a lot, and some overweight people eat very little?

■ **homeostasis**
The tendency of the body to maintain itself in a steady, stable condition with regard to physical processes.
■ **social motives**
Learned motives, such as the need for affiliation, power, competence, or achievement, that are acquired through social experiences.

for most heavy people to lose weight. The minute the study was over, the slender people lost weight as fast as dieters gained it back (Sims, 1974).

One theory that integrates these diverse findings on hunger, eating, and weight argues that body weight is governed by a **set point,** a homeostatic mechanism that keeps people at roughly the weight they are genetically designed to be. Set-point theorists claim that everyone has a genetically programmed *basal metabolism rate,* the rate at which the body burns calories for energy, and a fixed number of *fat cells,* cells in the body that store fat for energy. These cells may change in size (the amount of fat they contain), but never in number. After weight loss, they just lurk around the body, waiting for the chance to puff up again. According to set-point theory, there is no single area in the brain that keeps track of weight. Rather, an interaction of metabolism, fat cells, and hormones keeps people at the weight their bodies are designed to be. When a heavy person diets, the body slows down to conserve energy (and its fat reserves). When a thin person overeats, the body speeds up to burn energy.

The set-point weight is defined as "the weight you stay at when you aren't thinking about it"—that is, when you aren't trying to diet or gain but are eating whatever you want. Your set-point weight can also be thought of as the weight you tend to return to, like it or not, after you have tried to wrench yourself above it or below it.

Set-point theory was first supported by research with rats (Keesey, 1980; Peck, 1978). In one study, for example, rats could control the intravenous intake of a rich eggnog, but they couldn't taste what they were eating or know how much food they were getting. Nevertheless, all the animals ate *less* than usual in order to maintain their existing body weights. Two researchers, commenting on these studies, noted, "In effect, Peck was asking his animals: 'Which do you care about most, how fat you are, or how much you eat?' And the animals returned a clear answer: 'How fat we are'" (Bennett & Gurin, 1982).

Studies of average-weight and heavy people support set-point theory in human beings, too (Levitan & Ronan, 1988; Taylor, 1991). In a study of 171 Pima Indians in Arizona, researchers found that two-thirds of the women and half of the men became obese over time, and the slower their metabolisms, the greater the weight gain. After adding anywhere from 20 to 45 pounds, however, the Pimas stopped gaining weight. Now their metabolism rates rose, and their weights stabilized at the new, higher level (Ravussin et al., 1988). Many Pimas apparently have a set point for plumpness.

Certainly, set-point theory seems to explain why 95 percent of all people who go on restricted diets eventually gain their weight back; they simply are returning to their set-point weight (Lissner et al., 1991). But why, then, do some people gain or lose weight and maintain the change? One answer is exercise, which boosts the body's metabolic rate. Indeed, in one study of 18 obese women who were on severely restricted diets, metabolism rates dropped sharply, as set-point theory would predict. But the women who combined the diet with modest physical activity—daily walking—lost weight and their metabolic rates rose almost to previous levels (Wadden et al., 1990). This study suggests why changes in weight often accompany major changes in habits and activity levels. People start walking to work (or stop). They become sad and lethargic after losing a job (and gain weight), or energetic when they fall in love (and lose weight).

Another factor in weight regulation is the hormone insulin. Insulin regulates the flow of glucose, a sugar, from the bloodstream into the body's cells. Since the cells usually do not need all this glucose, much of it is turned into fat for storage. Insulin increases fat stores, and it also works to prevent fat breakdown and keep the levels of free fatty acids in the blood low. At high levels, insulin makes you hungry, makes you eat more, and makes sweets taste better. When you eat glucose, say in a doughnut, your body produces more insulin to get that glucose from your blood to your cells, and the insulin level stays high for hours. In contrast,

■ **set point**
According to one theory, a homeostatic mechanism that regulates food intake, fat reserves, and metabolism to keep an organism at its predetermined weight.

Body shape and weight are strongly influenced by genetic factors. Set-point theory explains why the members of some Native American tribes of the Southwest (left) gain weight easily but lose it slowly, whereas the Bororo nomads of Niger (right) can eat a lot of food yet remain slender.

fructose (the sugar found in fruits) produces a much slower and lower rise in both blood sugar and insulin, and decreases appetite (Spitzer & Rodin, 1987). Obese individuals show an especially strong insulin response to glucose, which results in an increased desire for sweet foods—a matter of insulin, not "failed willpower." Eating foods that are high in glucose and fat (instead of the same number of calories from, say, fruits and proteins) in turn increases the likelihood of obesity.

In general, it now seems that genetics determine to a large extent what a person's metabolic rate and set point will be. In a study of 18 infants at 3 months of age, the babies of overweight mothers generated 21 percent less energy than the babies of normal-weight mothers, although all the babies were eating the same amount. At 1 year, these lower-metabolism babies had become overweight (Roberts et al., 1988).

Genes also determine whether the body will convert excess calories into fat or muscle, and what the basic body *shape* will be (pear, apple, hourglass, tree trunk, and so on). In a study of 12 pairs of adult male identical twins, Claude Bouchard and his colleagues (1990) confined the men to a dormitory for 100 days, where they were forbidden to exercise and given a diet that contained 1,000 extra calories a day. Each *pair* of twins gained almost exactly the same amount of weight, but the differences *between* twins was astonishing. One pair of twins gained $9\frac{1}{2}$ pounds, but another pair gained almost 30—all of them on only 1,000 extra calories a day. Some twins gained weight on their hips and thighs, but others gained weight around the waist.

In another study of identical and fraternal twins, Albert Stunkard and his associates (1990) found that pairs of adult identical twins who had been raised in different families were just as similar in body weight and shape as twins raised together. The early family environment had almost no effect at all on body shape, weight gain, or percentage of fat in the body.

In sum, the interactions of hunger, eating, and fat are not located in a single brain mechanism. They are part of a complex system in which brain mech-

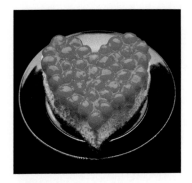

The desire for sweet foods, and the way the body metabolizes them, may have more to do with insulin than with willpower.

anisms, fat cells, food intake, insulin, metabolism, and body chemistry all interact, probably governed by specific genes that determine set point and fat distribution. Physiology, however, is just part of the story. So you're hungry; now what?

Culture and ethnic background help determine how often people eat, what they eat, and with whom they eat. When do you eat? Depending on your culture, you might eat lots of little meals throughout the day or only one large meal. What do you eat? People eat what their environment provides: whale meat in Inuit communities, lizards in South America, locusts in Africa, horses in France, dogs in Asia. Moreover, they don't eat the food their culture calls taboo: pork among Moslems and orthodox Jews, cows in India, horses in America, deer among the Tapirapé (M. Harris, 1985). With whom do you eat? People tend to eat with those of their own social status or higher. They don't eat with those they consider their social inferiors, who in various cultures have included servants, children, and women.

These social influences on hunger often cause people to eat when they aren't hungry (to be sociable) or not to eat when they are hungry (because society tells them they are too fat or because the company or food is undesirable). Indeed, sometimes social motives can completely dominate biological needs. In the disorder of anorexia nervosa, the obsession to be thin and control one's body weight overrules hunger entirely. The anorexic may die of self-imposed starvation.

The conflict between physiology (what one's body was basically designed to look like) and culture (what the ideal body is supposed to look like) is becoming increasingly difficult for many women and, to a lesser extent, men too. (In "Taking Psychology with You," we discuss this issue further.) The next time you contemplate the miracle of chocolate cake, think about the many motives that determine whether you approach it, avoid it, or compromise with "just a taste."

QUICK QUIZ

Don't avoid answering these few questions.

1. Your mother gives you a choice of cleaning 12 years of junk out of the attic or cleaning 6 years of grease out of the oven. What kind of conflict has she put you in?
2. Lorenz asks Lulu to spend a weekend with him at his family's house in the country. Lulu loves the country and would like to get away for a weekend, but she doesn't want Lorenz to think she likes him too much. What kind of conflict is she in?
3. What is the name of the theory that explains weight regulation as an interaction of metabolism, fat cells, and hormones?
4. Bill, who is thin, reads in the paper that genes set the range of body weight and shape. "Oh, good," he exclaims, "now I can eat all the junk food I want—I was born to be skinny." How would you evaluate Bill's conclusion?

ANSWERS:

1. avoidance-avoidance 2. approach-avoidance 3. set-point 4. Bill is right to recognize that there may be limits to how heavy he can become. But he may also be oversimplifying and jumping to conclusions. Even people who have a set-point for leanness will gain some weight on fatty foods and excess calories, and rich junk food is unhealthy for reasons that have nothing to do with overweight.

THE CURIOUS ANIMAL: MOTIVES TO EXPLORE, PLAY, AND UNDERSTAND

You have just had a great meal. Your hunger and thirst are sated, the indoor temperature is comfortably mild, and you are feeling no pain. If you were motivated only by primary drives, you would then sit in your chair like a hibernating bear for hours, even days. But you are also governed by motives that will move you off that chair before the spring thaw. These are the motives of curiosity, play, and exploration. They are the reason you will get up to see what that noise in the basement is, or find out what's in the nice fat package that just arrived, or join the neighbors for volleyball.

Now let's say your sister calls with puzzling and shocking news: A student in your class has committed suicide. You knew him, liked him, and always thought he was content with his life. You spend an hour on the phone, talking about this sad act of self-destruction. Your behavior is motivated by your desire to understand, to make sense of events, to put your belief about your classmate into line with his action. In hundreds of small ways as well as major ones, we are governed by the cognitive motives to understand and organize experience.

Curiosity and Play: Some Behavioral Motives

"Curiosity killed the cat," parents warn their snooping children and inquisitive neighbors, but actually curiosity helps our species survive. It is the motive that impels us to find out what things are, what they mean, and whether they are dangerous or useful.

FAMILIARITY VERSUS NOVELTY.   Human beings are constantly balancing their affection for the familiar with their curiosity about the unfamiliar. In a series of charming experiments, Robert Zajonc (1968) (pronounced ZY-unce) showed that the more familiar people are with something, the more they like it, whether the "it" is a supermarket product, a politician, or a nonsense syllable like *zug*. But once familiar with an environment, many species are motivated to seek novelty. If a rat has had its dinner, it will prefer exploring an unfamiliar wing of a maze rather than the familiar wing where food is. The interest in novelty starts early: A human baby will stop eating if someone new enters his or her range of vision. A new object will provoke either curiosity and exploration or fear and flight, depending on its complexity and unpredictability (P. Harris, 1984).

Although homeostasis technically refers to biological conditions, some psychologists apply the idea to psychological states as well. For instance, most people seek a balance between novelty and stability. If your life veers off too wildly, for too long, in the direction of unpredictable change, you may eventually be motivated to seek calmer seas. If you feel you have lived too long in a rut, you may be motivated to seek a change.

Other researchers regard risk taking and the love of adventure as characteristic aspects of personality. In this view, some people are unflappably cool, whereas others want the most excitement they can get, because they differ biologically in the level of arousal that is most comfortable to them. To assess a person's optimal arousal, Marvin Zuckerman (1983, 1990) developed a Sensation Seeking Scale to measure the strength of the motivation for excitement, risk, sensation, and adventure. He finds that *sensation seeking* seems to be a consistent quality in individuals. Sensation seekers like risky activities, new adventures, driving too fast, mood-changing drugs, tasting new foods, and sexual variety (Bates, Labouvie, & White, 1986; Levenson, 1990). They regard a peaceful life as "boring" rather than "stable"; they think a life of adventure is "exciting" rather than "foolhardy."

EXPLORATION AND MANIPULATION.   All birds and mammals are motivated to explore and investigate. Primates especially like to "monkey around" with objects, taking them apart and scrutinizing the pieces, apparently for the sheer pleasure of it. Monkeys will learn how to operate mechanical gizmos without food or other rewards (Harlow, Harlow, & Meyer, 1950). From the first, human babies explore and manipulate their small worlds. They grasp whatever is put in their tiny hands, they shake rattles, they bang pots. As they grow, they keep exploring, tasting, and investigating. Children will play spontaneously with items that honk, rattle, and ring. The motive to handle interesting objects can be overwhelming, which is why the command "don't touch" is often ignored by children, museum-goers, and shoppers.

PLAY.   Many animal species, including human beings, have an innate motive to play—to fool around and to imitate others (Huizinga, 1950). Think of kittens and lion cubs, puppies and pandas, and all young primates, who will play with and pounce on each other all day until hunger and naptime call. Play is not the same as games, which are organized activities that may bear only a passing resemblance to the spirit and purpose of play. For many people, games are hard work and not fun at all.

The young of many species enjoy *practice play*, behavior that will later be used for "serious" purposes when they are adults (Vandenberg, 1985). A kitten, for example, will stalk and attack a ball of yarn. In human beings, play is part of a child's socialization; the child "plays at" being a cowboy, parent, or Ninja. Play also teaches the young how to get along with others (Harlow & Harlow, 1966).

Some psychologists have argued that the motives for play and exploration are biologically adaptive because they help a species to find more food and other necessities of life and to cope with its environment. This may be so, but the curiosity and play motives seem to be expressed independently of these biological motives. Moreover, human play is in some ways different from the play of other animals. Children's play doesn't always imitate adult rules and activities; it often breaks adult rules and generates its own (Sutton-Smith, 1984). What is unique about human play is that it celebrates imagination, storytelling, and plans

All primates like to "monkey around."

Play and playfulness take on many forms all through life. Young children play elaborate fantasy games. Adults, like this fellow in rabbit gear, enjoy planned play and spontaneous silliness.

for the future. In fantasy play, children create imaginary worlds that structure and give meaning to experience, an ability central to human experience.

Consistency and Understanding: Some Cognitive Motives

A friend of ours moved from California to Kansas to go to graduate school. She was miserable about living in Kansas, because ever since seeing *The Wizard of Oz* at the age of 8 she had been afraid of tornadoes. "Tornadoes?" the Kansans said to her in amusement. "There's nothing to be afraid of. How could *you* live in California, with all those *earthquakes*?"

Most people are motivated to justify and explain what they do and what they believe. So reliable is this motive that psychologists can accurately predict what our friend will do. Having chosen to live in Kansas, she will begin to agree with the natives that tornadoes aren't so frightening. The real dangers occur to people who live far away, in California or India.

Years ago, Fritz Heider (1946, 1958) developed "the principle of cognitive balance" to explain such changes of mind. The mind, said Heider, seeks to keep information in balance. If you get a new piece of information that doesn't fit your beliefs, or if the opinions of a man you admire differ from your own, you are thrown into a state of imbalance. To regain mental equilibrium, you might reject the new information to keep your ideas intact and consistent. You might change your opinion of the man you admire, or change your own views to agree with his.

Heider's work was expanded by Leon Festinger (1957), who proposed the theory of **cognitive dissonance.** "Dissonance," the opposite of consistency ("consonance"), is a state of tension that occurs when a person simultaneously holds two cognitions (beliefs, thoughts) that are psychologically inconsistent, or holds a belief that is incongruent with the person's behavior. This tension is uncomfortable, and someone in a state of dissonance will be motivated to reduce it.

For example, cigarette smoking is dissonant with the awareness that "smoking causes illness." The smoker might change the behavior and try to quit. Or she might reject the cognition "smoking is bad." She could persuade herself that she will quit later on ("after these exams"). She could emphasize the benefits of smoking ("A cigarette helps me relax"). Or she could decide she doesn't want a long life, anyhow ("It will be shorter, but sweeter"). In all of these cases, the smoker is motivated to reduce dissonance because the behavior, smoking, is out of kilter with the smoker's knowledge of the dangers of that behavior.

■ **cognitive dissonance**
A state of tension that occurs when a person simultaneously holds two cognitions that are psychologically inconsistent or when a person's belief is inconsistent with his or her behavior.

In an actual study of people who had gone to a clinic to quit smoking, those who later relapsed had to reduce the dissonance between "I tried to quit smoking because it's bad for me" and "I couldn't do it." Can you predict what they did? In contrast to the successful quitters, most of them lowered their perceptions of the health risk of smoking ("It's not really so dangerous") (Gibbons, McGovern, & Lando, 1991).

You can see cognitive dissonance at work among the growing number of true believers who are predicting that doomsday is at hand. Such predictions are especially popular at the end of every century, so we predict that you will be hearing some lulus as the year 2000 dawns. A man named Edgar Whisenant predicted the end of the world would come on September 11, 1988, and thousands of people believed him. (Many ran up large bills on their charge accounts, on the grounds that Christ would return before their monthly statements did.) In California, quacks and hustlers are forever taking advantage of people's worry about earthquakes, which do occur, by making specific forecasts of when the Big One will hit. Hundreds of people have been known to leave their jobs or flee the state on the basis of these predictions.

Do you ever wonder what happens to these believers when the prophecy fails? Do they ever say, "Boy, what a jerk I was"? What would dissonance theory predict?

Festinger and two associates took advantage of a chance to study a group of people, led by a mystic they called Marian Keech, who believed the world would end on December 21. Keech promised that the faithful would be picked up by a flying saucer and whisked to safety at midnight on December 20. Many of these believers quit their jobs and spent all their savings, waiting for the end. What would they do or say to reduce the dissonance between "The world is still muddling along on the 21st" and "I predicted the end of the world and sold my worldly possessions"?

The researchers predicted that believers who had made no public commitment to the prophecy, who awaited "the end of the world" by themselves at home, would simply lose their faith. But the believers who acted on their conviction, waiting with Keech for the spaceship, would be in a state of dissonance. They would, said the researchers, have to *increase* their religious belief to avoid the cognition that they had behaved foolishly. That is just what happened. At 4:45 A.M., long past the appointed hour of the saucer's arrival, the leader had a new "vision." The world had been spared, she said, because of the impressive faith of their little band (Festinger, Riecken, & Schachter, 1956).

Cognitive dissonance theory thus predicts how people will receive and process information that conflicts with their existing ideas. They don't always do so "rationally," by accepting new facts that are well documented. You rarely hear someone say, cheerfully, "Oh, thank you for explaining to me why my lifelong philosophy of child raising is wrong! I'm so *grateful* for your facts!" The person usually says, "Oh, buzz off, and take your *cockamamie* ideas with you." Subsequent research has specified the conditions under which people are particularly likely to be motivated to reduce dissonance (Sears, Peplau, & Taylor, 1991):

1. *When people feel that they have freely made a particular decision.* If you do not think you freely chose to join a group, sell your possessions, or smoke a cigarette, you will not feel dissonance if these actions prove seriously misguided. There is no dissonance between "The Army drafted me; I had no choice about being here" and "I hate basic training."

2. *When people feel that the decision is important and irrevocable.* If you know that you can always change your mind about any decision you have made, or if you have a lackluster commitment to it, you will not feel dissonance if the decision proves foolhardy. There is no dissonance between "I just spent a fortune

Time and again doomsday predictions fail. Have you ever wondered why people who wrongly predict a devastating earthquake or the end of the world don't feel embarrassed when their forecasts flop?

Preacher Jimmy Swaggart confessed to having sex with a prostitute, and begged his followers to forgive him. How would they resolve the conflict between "I revere this man" and "He committed a sin"? Dissonance theory predicts that they will either revere him less or decide his sin wasn't all that bad.

Cognitive dissonance theory predicts the "justification of effort": The harder you work for a goal, the more you will like or value it. These men in basic training should become extremely devoted soldiers!

on ski equipment" and "I hate skiing" if you know you can return or sell your ski gear and get your money back.

3. *When people feel personally responsible for the negative consequences of their decisions.* If you choose a course of action that leads to disastrous, but unforeseen, results, you will not feel dissonance unless you feel responsible for the consequences. There is no necessary dissonance between "I took my vacation in Keokuk" and "It rained the whole week I was there" if you don't feel personally responsible for causing rain.

4. *When people have put a lot of effort into a decision, only to find the results are less than they hoped for.* The harder you work to achieve a goal, the more you will value the goal, even if the goal itself isn't so great after all (Aronson & Mills, 1959). This explains why hazing, whether in social clubs or the military, turns new recruits into loyal members. The cognition "I went through a lot of awful stuff to join this group" is dissonant with the cognition ". . . only to find I hate the group." Therefore people must decide either that the hazing wasn't so bad or that they really like the group. This mental reevaluation is called the *justification of effort,* and it is one of the most popular methods of reducing dissonance.

There are limitations, however, to dissonance theory. It is often difficult to know when two cognitions are "inconsistent": What is dissonant to you may be neutral or pleasingly paradoxical to another. In India, the acceptance of contradictions that would be "dissonant" to a Westerner is considered a major attribute of the personality (Bharati, 1985). Some people reduce dissonance by admitting their mistakes instead of rationalizing them. Still, there is vast evidence of a motive for cognitive consistency under certain conditions. Cognitive imbalance does seem to produce a state of tension that feels physically uncomfortable, particularly when the inconsistent cognitions violate one's self-concept (Elkin & Leippe, 1986). For example, in one study, when young women were made to realize that their strongly held *attitudes* in favor of conserving water were in conflict with their water-using *behavior,* they immediately reduced dissonance by taking shorter showers (Aronson, 1990).

Theories of cognitive balance and dissonance assume an even more fundamental motive: a need to organize and understand experience in terms of some general belief system. All societies have constructed religious, ethical, and political beliefs that account for how the world works (and that justify the way their particular society works). All civilizations, from the dawn of human history, have sought to understand the great mysteries of life and death. The desire to understand is one of the most powerful motives in human psychology.

QUICK QUIZ

Test your understanding of cognitive dissonance. In a classic study, students had to do a series of boring, repetitive tasks for an hour (Festinger & Carlsmith, 1959). Then they had to tell another student, who was waiting to participate in the study, that the work was interesting and fun. Half of the students were given $20 for telling this lie, and the others only $1. Which students decided that the tasks were fun after all?

ANSWER:

The students who were paid only $1. They were the ones in a state of dissonance: "The task was as dull as dishwater" is dissonant with "I said I enjoyed it—and for a mere dollar, at that." Since they couldn't change the fact of the dollar, they changed their judgment that the task was truly dull. But the students who got $20 felt no dissonance; they felt justified in lying because they were well paid.

■ THE EROTIC ANIMAL: MOTIVES FOR SEX

Almost anyone can tell the difference between food and sex, although people often use the same words in describing them: "She has a strong sexual appetite," someone will say, or "I'm lusting for a hamburger." Nevertheless, psychologists do not agree on whether human sexuality is a primary drive like hunger, or even whether it is a "drive" at all (Singer & Toates, 1987). After all, a person will not live very long without food and water, but people can live long, healthy lives without sex.

Biological factors, particularly having a minimum level of the hormone testosterone, may influence sexual desire in both sexes (McCauley & Ehrhardt, 1980). Many different kinds of studies have implicated the role of testosterone in sexual motivation: studies of men who have been chemically castrated (given synthetic hormones that suppress the production or functioning of testosterone); of men who have abnormally low testosterone levels; of women who are taking androgens after having their ovaries removed; and of women who kept diaries of their sexual activity while also having their hormone levels measured (Wade & Cerise, 1991). Although testosterone contributes to sexual arousal, sexual stimulation also produces higher levels of testosterone (Knussmann, Christiansen, & Couwenbergs, 1986).

In lower species, sexual behavior is genetically programmed. A male stickleback fish knows exactly what to do with a female stickleback, and a whooping crane knows when to whoop without instruction. As animals move up the evolutionary ladder, learning assumes a greater role in their sexual (and other) behavior. People must learn from experience, reinforcement, and cultural standards what they are supposed to *do* with their sexual desires. They learn what "turns them on," what parts of the body and what activities are "erotic," and even how to have sexual relations. Yet virtually every human society mistakenly thinks that its sexual practices and attitudes are the only "natural" ones (see "Think About It").

What Is Sexually "Normal"?

Consider kissing. Westerners *like* to consider kissing. They like to do it, too. But if you think it is "natural," try to remember your first serious kiss—and all you had to learn about noses, breathing, position of teeth and tongue, and whatnot. Indeed, the sexual kiss is so complicated that most cultures in human history have never gotten around to it. Some tribes think that kissing another person's mouth—the very place that food enters!—is disgusting (Tiefer, 1978).

We are going to ask you now to think about a subject that is among the most passionate and personal in human life: sexuality. If any topic evokes emotional reasoning, this is it! The problem is that most people assume that their own practices and preferences are "normal," right, and universal; everyone who deviates must therefore be deviant, sick, and disgusting. This attitude tends to impede rational thinking about sex.

You may be amused, for instance, that anyone would find kissing "disgusting." But what is your reaction to pedophilia—sex between adults and children? Do you approve of a 50-year-old man having sex with a woman half his age? Then what do you think about a 50-year-old *woman* who has sex with a man half her age? What is your attitude about adultery, and does it matter whether the husband or the wife is having the affair? For that matter, what is your attitude about sex between husband and wife—is it your notion of bliss or boredom? Is homosexuality abnormal? What about heterosexuality?

In various times and places, each of these practices has been considered normal and erotic; each has been considered abnormal and disgusting. In classical Athens, husbands had to be directed *by law* to have sex with their wives three times a month, to ensure enough new citizens (Pomeroy, 1975). The citizens must have been repulsed by the "disgusting" thought of marital sex.

Many people, on hearing these facts, jump to the wrong conclusion that "all sexual behavior is relative" or that "anything goes," including pedophilia. On the contrary, the point to understand is that *sexual behavior takes place in a larger network of rules, norms, and moral standards.* In-

Western societies, the sexual abuse of children is morally reprehensible and can have lasting harmful consequences (Burnam et al., 1988). In tribes in which childhood ends at puberty, however, early sexual initiation is considered necessary and appropriate. In a number of societies in Melanesia, boys are expected to have temporary homosexual relationships with older males as a normal part of growing up, a rite of passage on the route to manhood and marriage (Herdt, 1984). When Shakespeare's Juliet ran away with Romeo, she was only 13, an age at which most girls of that time were getting ready to marry; in the United States, Romeo would have been arrested for statutory rape.

Psychologists know very little about why people *within* a culture acquire the preferences and passions they do. John Gagnon (1987) observes that most people assume there is a single behavioral pattern called "homosexuality," caused by a single factor. In contrast, they see heterosexuality as more diverse and do not think it needs to be explained. But in fact there are many ways to express one's sexual identity, whether it is homosexual or heterosexual. Also, sexual identity sometimes changes; although some people are exclusively gay, lesbian, or straight all their lives, others are not. In recent years, there have been some provocative reports of findings, from brain research and twin studies, that support a biological explanation of sexual identity. But many of these studies have never been replicated, and others are small and still preliminary. To date, researchers have failed to find any single explanation in family background, hormones, genes, or experiences that accounts for sexual orientation. There may be several different routes to sexual identity—involving genetics, cultural pressures, experiences, and opportunities—and the route for one person may not be the same for another.

Consider the circumstances under which you acquired your own sexual orientation and other preferences, and whether you think they could change. Do you think you could be attracted to a person who is 20 years older than you? (Why do men and women answer that question differently?) Do you think you could be attracted to someone of the same sex, or, if you are gay, to someone of the other sex? To someone of another race? To someone who weighs 300 pounds? Why or why not? What are the cultural values, beliefs about sexual normalcy, and standards of erotic beauty that you have internalized? Think about it.

Kissing, whether to convey passionate desire, playfulness, or tender affection, is an "acquired taste" and a learned skill.

Sexuality and Gender

In certain times and places, people have assumed that men have the greater sex drive, whereas women have weak sexual desires or none at all. In other societies, people have assumed that women have the greater sex drive and that men are the innocent victims of women's infinite lusts. In actuality, there seem to be few physiological differences between men and women in the basic processes of sexual arousal and orgasm. Both sexes have the capacity for sexual enjoyment and pleasure. And most people of both sexes value the opportunity that sex provides for play, passion, and intimacy. Yet research finds repeatedly that men and women often attribute different meanings to sexual activity, and have different sexual experiences and attitudes.

ATTITUDES, ACTIONS, AND THE DOUBLE STANDARD.   Sexual attitudes reflect larger social and political trends in a society. In the early 1960s, for instance, about half of all American women had intercourse before marriage. In the 1970s, researchers found a shift toward more permissive attitudes and behavior and a decline of the double standard. By the late 1970s, the great majority of women and men were having sex outside of marriage (Sherwin & Corbett, 1985). Nevertheless, aspects of the double standard persist today (Hyde, 1988). Throughout their lives, men are more likely than women to report having had casual sex, and they have more sexual partners than women do. In a study of more than 1,000 teenagers, parents were still less tolerant of sexual activity of daughters than of sons, and teenage girls still worried about risking their reputations, although teenage boys did not (Coles & Stokes, 1985). In studies of college students across the country, women are, on the average, more conservative and idealistic about sex than men are, and men tend to be more permissive and liberal (Hendrick & Hendrick, 1987).

REASONS FOR SEX.   Even when the sexual *behavior* of men and women is alike, their sexual *motives* often differ. In many studies, men tend to be more "instrumental" in their motives for sex (regarding sex as a physical act for the purpose of pleasure); women are more "expressive" (regarding sex as an emotional act for the purpose of closeness). Men often rate sex as more important than love as a goal of dating; women tend to say that love is more important than sex (Peplau, 1984). (Of course, these differences may also reflect what males and females feel obliged to say.) In the Coles and Stokes (1985) study, many of the female teenagers felt they had to cooperate sexually with a boyfriend to please or keep him, rather than for their own pleasure. Yet there is nothing inherent in male or female psychology that accounts for this difference; over time and

✳ *Many people assume that sex is "just doing what comes naturally." What does the variety of motives that people bring to sexual relations tell us about this assumption?*

with experience, many women become more sexually "instrumental" and men more "expressive" (Tavris, 1992).

Nevertheless, the instrumental-expressive difference in sexual motives of adolescents and young adults often causes misunderstandings and crossed signals. Men and women often misread each other's body language, with unhappy results. In one study of 400 teenagers, ages 14 to 17, researchers found that, in general, boys thought almost everything was a sexual signal! They were more likely to regard tight clothing, certain situations (such as being alone in a room), and affectionate actions (such as a girl's playing with her date's hair or gazing into his eyes) as signs of willingness for sex. The girls were more likely to regard tight clothing as a sign of being fashionable, and being alone with a date or behaving affectionately simply as signs of—well, affection (Zellman & Goodchilds, 1983).

Is she dressing provocatively or comfortably? Boys and girls often disagree on the answer.

EXPERIENCES WITH SEXUAL COERCION AND RAPE. The one sexual experience that most dramatically divides men and women is rape—and living with the fear of rape. Men can be and are raped, usually by anal penetration committed by other men. This may occur in youth gangs, when the rape is intended to humiliate rival gang members, and frequently in prison, again with the intention of conquering and degrading the victim (Wade & Cerise, 1991). But rape, as an experience or a concern, affects the daily lives of women as it does not affect the lives of men.

Although the public image of the rapist tends to be one of a menacing stranger, in most cases the rapist is known to the victim. They may have dated once or a few times; they may have been friends for years; they may even be married (Koss et al., 1988; Russell, 1990). According to a major study of a national representative sample of 4,008 women, at least 12 million American women have been the victims of forcible rape at least once in their lives, most before the age of 18. Only 22 percent were assaulted by strangers (National Victim Center, 1992). The survey did not include children or adult men, so the actual number of people who have been raped is higher.

What motivates men to rape? It is not just a matter of crossed signals. Studies of convicted rapists find a mixture of motives: anger (at women or the world), the expression of power, contempt for women, acting out a sexual fantasy, or, least often, sexual sadism (Prentky, Knight, & Rosenberg, 1988). Date rapists are more likely to be impulsive "opportunists" who desire sexual release and take advantage of being in a woman's company. Often they rationalize their behavior by thinking that they "deserve" to get sex from the woman and that "she likes it this way" (Wade & Cerise, 1991).

Rape is not the only kind of coercive sexual experience. In numerous studies of college students, large numbers of women *and* men say they have had unwanted sex because of psychological pressures. In one survey of 275 undergraduate women, more than 50 percent said they had been pressured into kissing, fondling, oral sex, or intercourse (Christopher, 1988). (The percentages vary from school to school but are consistently high.) Women say they "give in" for a variety of motives: because it is easier than having an argument; because they don't want to lose the relationship; because they feel obligated, once the partner has spent time and money on them; or because the partner makes them feel guilty or inhibited (M. Lewin, 1985; Muehlenhard & Cook, 1988).

For their part, many men feel obliged to "make a move" when they don't want to. In a study of 71 college men who admitted to having coerced their dates into having sex with them, Eugene Kanin (1985) found that these young men had, from early adolescence, been pressured by male friends to "prove their

In this famous scene from Gone With The Wind *(left), Clark Gable forcibly carried a protesting Vivien Leigh to bed; she awakes the next morning with a smile on her face and love in her heart. Many similar scenes in film and TV convey the false impression that women want to be forced into sex and will be happy afterward. To help counteract this message, a poster of* The Rape of the Sabine Women *(right) was created by the Pi Kappa Phi fraternity in 1987 to raise sexual abuse awareness among its undergraduate members.*

masculinity" by "scoring." And in one survey of 993 undergraduates, 63 percent of the men reported having had unwanted intercourse (Muehlenhard & Cook, 1988). The main reasons for doing so, the men said, were peer pressure, inexperience, a desire for popularity, and a fear of seeming homosexual or "unmasculine."

Perhaps you can begin to see that the answer to the question "Why do people have sex?" is not just the simple "Because it's 'natural'" or "Because it feels good." The range of psychological motives that are involved range from intimidation to intimacy, from anger to adoration.

Theories of Sexuality

Keeping in mind that we are talking about *average* differences between men and women, consider two competing theories that have tried to account for the differences between men and women in sexual behavior and motivation.

THE SOCIOBIOLOGICAL VIEW. According to sociobiologists, the males and females of most species are profoundly different because of genetic differences created through forces of evolution (Symons, 1979). In this view, males compete with other males for access to desirable females, and their goal is to inseminate as many females as possible. Females, in contrast, are motivated to attach themselves to genetically "superior" males because of the female's greater investment in time and energy in her offspring. According to sociobiologists, the result of these two opposite sexual strategies is that, in general, males want sex more than females do; males are promiscuous, whereas females are faithful; males are drawn to sexual novelty and rape, whereas females want stability and security; and males are relatively undiscriminating in their choice of partners, whereas females are cautious and discriminating.

Because this description seems to apply to many human societies, sociobiologists conclude that people are governed by the same reproductive strategies as other species. One major problem with sociobiology, however, is its fallacy of

The male scorpionfly coerces its partner into sex. Is this evidence that "rape" is somehow "natural" in human males?

arguing by analogy. Two species may behave in an apparently similar fashion, but this does not necessarily mean that the *origins* of the behavior are the same in both species. For example, a male scorpionfly who coerces a female into copulation cannot have the same "motives" as a human male.

Moreover, sociobiology suffers from the *problem of selectivity:* If you are going to generalize from other species to human beings, which species apply? In the last decade, hundreds of studies cast doubt on the theory of the sexually promiscuous male and the patient, faithful female (Hrdy, 1988; Hubbard, 1990). It turns out that the females of many animal species—including birds, fish, mammals, and primates—are sexually ardent and often have many male partners. Further, their sexual behavior does not depend simply on the goal of being fertilized by the male, because in many cases females actively solicit males when the females are not ovulating and even when they are already pregnant.

These findings have stimulated new theories to explain why female promiscuity might make as much survival sense as its male counterpart, and why there might be genetic benefits for the offspring of sexually adventurous mothers. Perhaps, in some species, females need sperm from several males in order to assure conception by the healthiest sperm. Perhaps, in some species, females mate with numerous males precisely because paternity becomes uncertain (Hrdy, 1988). The result is that male partners will be more invested in, and tolerant of, the female's infants, and more involved with the infants' survival. Indeed, among many primates, males do not just mate and run; they stay around, feeding the infants, carrying them on their backs, and protecting them against predators (Taub, 1984).

These new theories have revolutionized the way researchers think about animal behavior, but the larger question remains: Does the evidence of female "promiscuity" in other species have any more relevance to human behavior than former theories of female "fidelity"? Probably not. Among human beings, sexual behavior is extremely varied and changeable. Human cultures range from those in which women have many children to those in which they have very few; from those in which men are very involved in child rearing to those in which they do nothing at all; from those in which women may have many lovers to those in which women may be killed if they have sex outside of marriage.

THE SOCIOCULTURAL VIEW. This perspective focuses on the norms that every culture specifies regarding ideal love and ideal sex. These norms, in turn, are shaped by a society's **gender roles,** collections of rules that determine the "proper" attitudes and behavior for men and women. As we will see in Chapter 18, people play many roles in society. During childhood and adolescence, they learn the "scripts" that fit each role.

According to John Gagnon and William Simon (1973), *sexual scripts* teach boys and girls what to consider erotic or sexy, and how to behave in dating and sex. In this view, biology influences sexuality only indirectly. Adolescent males have spontaneous erections and eventually orgasms; boys often talk and joke about masturbation with their friends. Female anatomy, however, makes the discovery of masturbation and orgasm less certain. Male sexuality is often learned in a competitive atmosphere where the goal is to impress other males. While boys are learning about physical sex, girls are learning to value the emotional aspects of relationships and to make themselves attractive. As a result, according to Simon and Gagnon (1969), male sexuality becomes genitally focused and emotionally detached, compared to that of females. Female sexuality becomes more closely connected to love and attachment.

In an update of their theory, Simon and Gagnon (1986) argue that people follow three kinds of sexual scripts. *Cultural* scripts describe the larger culture's requirements for proper sexual behavior. Are women, for example, supposed to be sexually adventurous and assertive or sexually modest and passive? The an-

■ **gender role**
A set of norms that defines socially approved attitudes and behavior for men and women.

swers vary from culture to culture. However, although people may know what their culture expects of them in general, not everyone follows its rules specifically. Sexual behavior also depends on *interpersonal* scripts, the rules of behavior that a couple develops in the course of their relationship. For example, will one be dominant and one passive? The answers for any individual couple depend on the relationship, and may change as the relationship changes. Finally, individuals follow their own *intrapsychic* scripts, scenarios for ideal or fantasized sexual behavior that develop out of a person's unique history.

Role theory maintains that most of the differences in the sexual behavior of men and women occur as a result of the different role requirements of the two sexes, which in turn are a result of the economic and social arrangements of a particular society. Because women have traditionally been concerned with finding and keeping a secure relationship, some theorists maintain, they have regarded sex as a bargaining chip. It is an asset to be rationed rather than an activity to be enjoyed for its own sake. This attitude is reflected in language, when people talk of a woman "giving herself" to, or "saving herself" for, a man. What happens, then, when a young woman who views sex as a valuable resource has intercourse early in a relationship? Dissonance theory predicts that she will rationalize that she was "swept away" by candlelight and passion. (In fact, many young women are reluctant to use birth control because it implies a conscious choice to have sex.) She may convince herself that she is wildly in love with her partner, and he with her, instead of admitting that she was sexually aroused (Cassell, 1984).

Understanding sexual attitudes and behavior as part of a larger pattern of gender roles helps explain why, in many but by no means all societies, men initiate sex more often, women tend to reject casual sex, and women "give in" and men "make a move" when they don't really want to. In accounting for many of the findings about rape, for example, role theorists argue that the motivation behind many coercive sexual acts is to "feel masculine" and play the role of dominant male. And it accounts for changes *within* a culture and for differences *across* cultures. As circumstances change, so do roles and rules.

Knowing the scripts for one's gender role has benefits; they provide a familiar set of guidelines for dealing with the complexities of male-female relationships. But they can also create anger and miscommunication, and once someone has learned the script, changing the lines is not so easy.

QUICK QUIZ

A. Why do people have sex? As the previous section suggests, there are many motives for sexual behavior. List as many of them as you can think of.

B. Now look over your list and decide which motives are primarily *physiological*, which primarily *personal or psychological*, and which primarily *social or cultural*.

ANSWERS:

Physiological motives include sexual arousal and release, reproduction, and sensual pleasure. Psychological motives include expressing intimacy, revenge, or anger; raising self-esteem; and preserving the relationship. Social/cultural motives include conforming to peer group norms regarding the frequency of sex; using sex to live up to cultural ideals of masculinity or femininity; and following the sexual dating script for one's culture. If you found it difficult to categorize motives, that's the point. They all interact. For example, raising self-esteem is a psychological motive, but it is culture that teaches people that having sex is one way of achieving self-esteem.

■ THE SOCIAL ANIMAL: MOTIVES TO CONNECT

The **need for affiliation** refers to the motive to be with others, to make friends, to cooperate, to love. Because most American social scientists have studied American society, which values achievement, power, and success, they have concentrated on these motives far more than on affiliation (Spence, 1985). One consequence of this lopsided emphasis has been the assumption that human beings are fundamentally competitive and power-oriented. However, in the last decade, researchers have found that human beings are also fundamentally cooperative and attachment-oriented. Our lives would be impossible without affiliation. Human development depends on the child's ability to care for and learn from others; adult life depends on relations with friends, family, colleagues, and the kindness of strangers.

Attachment and Affiliation

The need for, and pleasure in, physical contact starts at birth and lasts until death. Babies who are given adequate food, water, and warmth, but who are deprived of being touched and held, show retarded emotional and physical development (Bowlby, 1969). Emotional and physical symptoms also occur in adults who are "undertouched" in our society, such as the sick and the aged. A "laying on of hands" reassures and comforts a sick person, and reassurance and comfort are half the battle (L. Thomas, 1983).

Margaret and Harry Harlow first demonstrated the primate need for touching, or *contact comfort*, by raising infant rhesus monkeys with two kinds of artificial mothers (Harlow & Harlow, 1966; Harlow, 1958). The first was a forbidding construction of wires and warming lights, with a milk bottle attached. The second was constructed of wire and covered in foam rubber and cuddly terry cloth (see Figure 10.2). At the time, psychologists (but not many mothers) thought that babies become attached to their parents because the parent provides food and warmth. But Harlow's baby monkeys ran to the terry cloth "mother" when they were frightened or startled, and cuddling it calmed them down.

Infants become attached to their mothers or other caretakers for the contact comfort the adults provide. John Bowlby (1969, 1973) proposed that infant attachment has two additional purposes. It provides a secure base from which the child can explore the environment, and it provides a haven of safety to which the child can return when he or she is afraid. A sense of security, said Bowlby, allows children to develop cognitive skills. A sense of safety allows them to develop trust. Severe social deprivation and continued separations from loved ones prevent children from forming attachments, with tragic results.

Individuals vary in their need for affiliation. Some like "lots of space," and some like to be surrounded by friends. Cultures, too, vary in the value they place

■ **need for affiliation**
The motive to associate with other people, as by seeking friends, moral support, contact comfort, or companionship.

 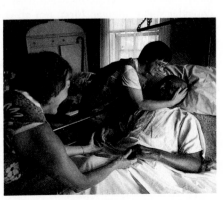

Human beings respond to contact comfort, whether from the reassuring presence of a loved pet or from the reassuring touch of a caretaker.

FIGURE 10.2

The comfort of contact

Infants need cuddling as much as they need food. In Margaret and Harry Harlow's studies, infant rhesus monkeys were raised with a terry cloth "mother" that was cuddly to cling to and with a bare wire "mother" that provided milk. The infants preferred clinging to the terry "mother" when they weren't being fed, and when they were frightened or startled, it was the terry "mother" they ran to. The basis of infant love, concluded the Harlows, is contact comfort, not food.

on affiliation. American culture emphasizes independence and self-reliance, but other cultures, such as the Latino and Japanese, emphasize family cohesiveness, group interdependence, and teamwork (Levine & Padilla, 1979; Pascale & Athos, 1981). In American society dependence is almost a dirty word, but in Japan the need for dependence is assumed to be powerful and necessary (Doi, 1973). In fact, whatever one's culture, people are "dependent"; but they depend on one another for different things at different ages. Babies are totally dependent on their parents, but they gradually develop the ability to act and think independently.

Researchers and laypeople like to debate whether men or women are the "dependent sex" or are better at "affiliation." According to Carol Gilligan (1982), many young men regard attachment as a source of danger and threat, and many young women regard attachment as a source of safety and intimacy. She supports her argument with the stories that people tell in response to pictures of people described as having "an intimate bond" between them: Men are more likely than women to see danger and threat in such scenes. However, before we jump to the apparent conclusion that men fear closeness and women pursue it, consider this evidence: First, not all studies find a sex difference. One research team that found no differences called the whole idea "a common and perhaps repressive stereotype" (Benton et al., 1983). Second, even when studies do find differences, the differences are small. In one, only 18 percent of the men and 8 percent of the women saw danger in affiliation (Helgeson & Sharpsteen, 1987).

Perhaps a more reasonable conclusion, based on studies of close relationships, is that both sexes depend on each other, although sometimes for different things (S. Brehm, 1992). In a family, the spouse who isn't working is financially dependent on the one who is. The spouse who can't express feelings is emotionally dependent on the one who can. It's hard to find true loners. Even the Lone Ranger had Tonto.

Love

"How do I love thee? Let me count the ways," wrote Elizabeth Barrett to Robert Browning. Social psychologists have also counted the ways of loving (although not as prettily as Barrett did). Zick Rubin, one of the first psychologists to develop a questionnaire to measure the meanings of love, asked people to distinguish their feelings for lovers from their feelings for friends. He found that love, at least among dating couples, had to do with intimacy (sharing innermost thoughts and feelings), attachment, and caring, and was distinctly different from liking, which has to do with affection and respect (Rubin, 1973).

How do people differ in their styles of love? Shall we count the ways? The first problem, as usual, is defining our terms. In Chapter 9 we discussed "love" as an emotion, which most people agree it is. But love can also be defined in terms of a relationship (mother love, brotherly love), an attitude (love of country, love of money), or as an experience (unrequited love) (Fehr & Russell, 1991). There have been many efforts to define love and to determine how love motivates people's behavior.

1. *Passionate ("romantic") versus companionate love.* This basic distinction contrasts *passionate* love, characterized by a turmoil of emotions, with *companionate* love, characterized by affection and trust (Hatfield, 1988). Passionate love is emotionally intense, *the* focus of one's life, and highly sexualized; it often feels unstable and fragile. Companionate love is calmer, *a* focus of one's life, and not necessarily sexualized; it feels stable and reliable—more like liking. Passionate love is the stuff of crushes, infatuations, "love at first sight," and the early stage of love affairs. It may "burn out" completely or subside into companionate love.

Some psychologists believe that passionate love is rooted in our evolutionary biology. Passionate love sees to it that couples bond together; reproduce; look after each other; and stay together in spite of having the flu, mortgages, and housework (D. Buss, 1988). Others think that passionate love is a modern, Western invention, one that individualistic cultures celebrate and community-oriented cultures distrust (Dion & Dion, 1988). Asians, for example, are less likely than Anglos and blacks to endorse romantic love as their ideal (Hendrick & Hendrick, 1986)—and remember from the last chapter that "sad love" is a *negative* emotional state for many Chinese.

Some researchers believe that by defining love as a passionate emotion instead of as a relationship or an experience, people set themselves up for disappointment. For example, Robert Solomon (1988) argues that "we *define* love in

The gaze of love is unmistakable, even after years together.

Beautiful inside and out, SWF, 35, slender, professional, bright, communicative, sensitive, loving, seeks emotionally and financially secure SWM, 35-45, to share affection, honesty, laughter, friendship, love. Note/Phone/Photo   (A)

Successful, attractive, sexy, published/produced writer (books, TV, Village Voice, Playboy), 38, not secretly yearning to be a director. Likes Don Mattingly, KCRW, making waffles & staying out late. Wants successful, interesting & well-read guy who enjoys his career, for dinner dates during world series & possible post season play. Please tell me about yourself. Photo optional.   (B)

Looking for a permanent best friend/lover, 25-35, with a 3 digit IQ, big heart, skinny legs. Race unimportant. But, **MUST** be honest, kind, witty, sensuous, confident, compassionate, adventurous, competent, reliable, and looking for a future with love, sincerity, children and time zone changes. Letter/photo/phone.   (C)

DESPERATELY SEEKING SUSAN, or Mary, or Evelyn, or Nancy or Lorraine or? (D)

Seeking an ugly, overweight, short woman lacking style, intelligence & humor. Hopefully she smokes, is in lousy shape & wouldn't know "sensitive" if it bit her on the butt. I'm dumpy, balding, unattractive & not in my early 30's. I don't work out. I'm stuck in a deadend job, smoke like a chimney & I'm a compulsive liar. Note, photo & phone not necessary.   (E)

such a way that it could only be transient experience, and then we wonder—sometimes bitterly—why love doesn't last. We say that love is a 'passion,' and then are disappointed when something so passive passes away." Solomon's observation reminds us that the way we define terms is not just an academic exercise; it can deeply affect our feelings and relationships.

2. *The six styles of love.* In the early 1970s, John Alan Lee (1973, 1988) proposed that there are six different "styles of loving," which he labeled with Greek names. The three basic ones are *ludus* (game-playing love), *eros* (romantic, passionate love), and *storge* [pronounced stor-gay] (affectionate, friendly love). Three secondary styles are *mania* (possessive, dependent, "crazy" love), *pragma* (logical, pragmatic love), and *agape* [ah-GA-pay] (unselfish, brotherly love).

These six types have been validated empirically in two studies of more than 1,300 students (Hendrick & Hendrick, 1986). A romantic, "erotic" lover (who believes in true love, instant chemistry, and abiding passion) is very different from a "ludic" lover (who enjoys playing the game of love with several partners at once, who enjoys the chase more than the catch). A pragmatic lover (who chooses a partner according to a "shopping list" of compatible traits) is unlike a "storgic" lover (who believes true love grows out of long friendship).

"Personals" columns are a good place to see the styles of love, as shown by the magazine excerpts at the top of the page. Some people are looking for "affectionate, friendly" love (A); others are more playful (B). Some pragmatic types have a whole shopping list of requirements (C), while others have a minimum standard (D). Occasionally you find someone (E) who is either refreshingly candid or just having a good time.

3. *The attachment theory of love.* Another effort to describe styles of love is based on the human need for attachment: the sense of almost physical connection with a loved one and of physical loss when a loved one leaves. In Chapter 13 we will discuss a theory that describes three kinds of infant attachment to the mother: secure, anxious/ambivalent, and avoidant. Cindy Hazan and Phillip Shaver (1987) believe that adult styles of love originate in these early styles of infant-parent attachment—the baby's first and most important "love relationship." According to their research, some couples are securely attached to each other; they aren't jealous, nervous, or worried about being abandoned. Others are always anxious or ambivalent about the relationship and fretting over it; they want to be close but worry that their partners will leave them. And some people distrust and avoid all intimate attachments (Shaver, Hazan, & Bradshaw, 1988). To use Lee's terms again, romantic lovers are likely to be securely attached; manic lovers are anxious and ambivalent; and ludic lovers are avoidant.

The general overlap among these theories suggests that they are describing the same things. All imply that some styles of love are better suited to satisfying relationships than others. In one study that compared couples who remained together with those who split up, the former were more erotic, less ludic, more self-revealing, and higher in commitment (Hendrick, Hendrick, & Adler, 1988). The success of a relationship, these theories agree, also depends not on whether both partners "love" each other, but on whether they love each other in the same way. This finding suggests that when someone says "I love you," perhaps you should reply, "What exactly do you mean by that?"

Some people seem to have characteristic styles of love that reflect their personalities (Dion & Dion, 1988). Some consistently avoid commitment; perhaps they are "sensation seekers" who thrive on passionate love. Yet all theories hold that most people can, and do, change their styles of love over time and with new partners. People who are in love for the first time tend to be romantic and idealistic, but by their third love relationship they are more realistic and even cynical (Carducci & McGuire, 1990). Still, the most pragmatic person can be struck by the thunderbolt and have a passionate interlude. The most game-playing, "no-marriage-for-me" ludic lover may later become committed to a companionate relationship. And lovers who are insecurely attached as young adults may find secure attachments later in life (Hazan & Shaver, 1987).

There is no evidence that one sex loves more than the other, in terms of "love at first sight," passionate love, companionate love over the long haul, or their ideas about the kinds of love that are possible (Fehr & Russell, 1991; Hatfield & Sprecher, 1986). Both sexes become equally attached and both suffer at the end of love. Yet women and men do differ, on the average, in how they love (Peplau & Gordon, 1985). Perhaps you remember from Chapter 9 that males and females define and express vulnerable emotional feelings quite differently. Once in a relationship, women report stronger feelings of affection and companionate love than men do, and they spend more time and energy analyzing their relationships for strengths and problems (Holtzworth-Munroe & Jacobson, 1985).

These differences between the sexes, as we saw in the case of sexuality, are tied to male and female roles, which change over time—for example, both sexes generally agree that it is the woman's responsibility to manage and monitor the relationship. For many years studies found that men were more romantic than women, who were in turn more pragmatic than men. One reason was that, until quite recently, a woman didn't just marry a man; she married a standard of

Drawing by Cline; © 1988 The New Yorker Magazine, Inc.

"Sorry, Eric, but before I commit to anybody I still need about three years of fun."

A "ludic lover" in action. Do you think that gender differences in this style of love are fading?

living (Waller, 1938). Therefore she could not afford to marry someone "unsuitable" or waste her time in a relationship that was "not going anywhere," even if she loved him. In contrast, a man could afford to be sentimental in his choice of partner. In the 1960s, two-thirds of a sample of college men said they would not marry someone they did not love, but only a fourth of the women ruled out the possibility (Kephart, 1967).

As more women became self-supporting, and as two incomes became necessary in most families, the sex difference in romantic love began to fade. Nowadays most North American women are just as romantic as men (Simpson, Campbell, & Berscheid, 1986) and just as likely to say that love is an essential element of marriage. This change suggests that our feelings about love, and the kind of love we feel, are influenced by social and economic concerns. Can you think of other influences on your own "style of love"?

QUICK QUIZ

A. Of Lee's six "styles of loving," which style does each of the following examples illustrate?

1. St. Paul tells the Corinthians to love others whether or not other people deserve it.
2. Jane Welsh and Thomas Carlyle enjoy exchanging ideas and confidences for years before realizing they love each other.
3. In choosing his last four wives, Henry VIII makes sure they are likely to bear children and are of suitably high status for his court.
4. Romeo and Juliet think only of each other and hate to be separated for even an hour.
5. Casanova tries to seduce every woman he meets for the thrill of the chase.

B. Tiffany is wildly in love with Timothy, and he with her, but she can't stop worrying about him and doubting his love. She wants to be with him constantly, but when she feels jealous she pushes him away. According to the attachment theory of love, which style of attachment does Tiffany have?

ANSWERS:

A. 1. selfless or brotherly love (agape) **2.** affectionate, friendly love (storge) **3.** pragmatic love (pragma) **4.** romantic love (eros) **5.** game-playing love (ludus) **B.** anxious/ambivalent

■ THE COMPETENT ANIMAL: MOTIVES TO WORK

Almost every adult works. Most people spend more time at work than they do at play or with their families. "Work" does not mean only paid employment. Students work at studying. Homemakers work, often more hours than salaried employees, at running a household. Artists, poets, and actors work, even if they are paid erratically. What keeps everybody doing it? The simplest answer, of course, is to have food and shelter. Yet survival does not explain what motivates LeRoy to work for caviar on his table and Duane to work for peanut butter on his. It doesn't explain why some people want to do their work well and others want just to get it done. It doesn't explain the difference between Aristotle's view ("All paid employments absorb and degrade the mind") and Noel Coward's ("Work is more fun than fun").

Psychologists, particularly those in the field of *industrial/organizational psychology*, have studied work motivation in the laboratory, where they have measured internal motives such as the desire for achievement, and in organizations, where they study the conditions that influence productivity and satisfaction. Their results give us a fuller answer to the question, "What keeps everybody working?"

The Effects of Motivation on Work

Several independent forces keep you working toward a goal: your expectation of success, your need to achieve, opportunities in the environment, and the nature of your work (McClelland, 1985). These factors apply to any form of achievement, from running a household to running a marathon.

EXPECTATIONS AND VALUES. How hard you work for something depends partly on what you expect to accomplish. If you are fairly certain of success, you will work much harder to reach your goal than if you are fairly certain of failure.

One experiment showed how quickly experience affects these expectations. Young women were asked to solve 15 anagram puzzles. Before working on each one, they had to estimate their chances of solving it. Half of the women started off with very simple anagrams, but half began with insoluble ones. Sure enough, those who started with the easy ones increased their estimates of success on later ones. Those who began with the impossible ones decided they would *all* be impossible. These expectations, in turn, affected the young women's ability to actually solve the last 10 anagrams (which were the same for everyone). The higher the expectation of success, the more anagrams the women solved (Feather, 1966).

Once acquired, therefore, expectations can create a **self-fulfilling prophecy**, in which a person predicts how he or she will do and then behaves in such a way as to make the prediction come true (R. Jones, 1977). You expect to do well, so you study hard, and then you do well. You expect to fail, so you don't do much work, and then you do poorly. In either case, you have fulfilled your expectation of yourself.

How hard you work for something, of course, also depends on how much you want it, which in turn depends on your general value system (Feather, 1982). Some people value affiliation more than achievement, and others have opposite priorities. The value people place on a goal, though, depends in part on how hard it is to reach! Because of the justification-of-effort effect, people tend to attach more value to goals and relationships they have to work hard for than to those that come easy (Brehm & Self, 1989). Conversely, when people work hard for something and fail to get it, they tend to devalue the goal, deciding it wasn't important anyway. This is known as the "sour grapes" phenomenon, a popular way to reduce dissonance.

COMPETENCE AND SELF-EFFICACY. A long tradition in psychology has held that human beings are motivated by a **need for competence** in dealing with their environments (Sternberg & Kolligian, 1990; White, 1959). This motive is assumed to be basic to the species, and its gratification naturally satisfying. A child's sense of mastery changes and develops (or can be suppressed) with age, experience, and reinforcement, and the same applies to adults.

Albert Bandura (1990) argues that competence is based on *self-efficacy*, the conviction that you can successfully accomplish what you set out to do. According to Bandura, you can acquire self-efficacy from several sources: your experiences with mastery; observation of another person's competence, which may convince you that the task is possible; encouragement from others; and your physiological state. (People feel more competent when they are calm and re-

■ **self-fulfilling prophecy**
The tendency to act on one's expectations in such a way as to make the expectations come true.
■ **need for competence**
The motive to be capable in one's activities and to master new situations.

The Many Motives of Accomplishment

Productivity

ISAAC ASIMOV
(1920–1992)

Scientist, writer

"If my doctor told me I had only six minutes to live, I wouldn't brood. I'd type a little faster."

Knowledge

MARGARET MEAD
(1901–1978)

Anthropologist

"I was brought up to believe that the only thing worth doing was to add to the sum of accurate information in the world."

Justice

MARTIN LUTHER KING, JR.
(1929–1968)

Civil rights activist

"I have a dream . . . that my four little children will one day live in a nation where they will not be judged by the color of their skin but by the content of their character."

Autonomy

GEORGIA O'KEEFFE
(1887–1986)

Artist

"[I] found myself saying to myself—I can't live where I want to, go where I want to, do what I want to . . . I decided I was a very stupid fool not to at least paint as I wanted to."

laxed than when they are agitated or excited.) Self-efficacy affects how well a person does on a task, how committed he or she is to a goal, the ability to solve complex problems at work, and even how a person will respond to criticism. People who have high self-efficacy react by working harder to do well, whereas people low in self-efficacy are more inclined to give up. Fortunately, self-efficacy can be acquired through programs and experiences that provide skills and a sense of personal control (Ozer & Bandura, 1990).

THE NEED FOR ACHIEVEMENT. Why do some people strive to succeed, starting risky new businesses or attempting new challenges? In the early 1950s, David Mc-Clelland and his associates (1953) speculated that these people have an internal **need for achievement** (nAch) that motivates them as much as hunger motivates people to eat. How could this motive be identified? McClelland (1961) later wrote that he and his colleagues sought the "'psychic X-ray' that would permit us to observe what was going on in a person's head in the same way that we can observe stomach contractions or nerve discharges in a hungry organism."

The solution came in the form of a method developed by Christiana Morgan and Henry Murray in the 1930s. The Thematic Apperception Test (TAT) is a series of ambiguous pictures and drawings; subjects simply have to tell a story about the picture they see. What is happening in the picture? What are the characters thinking and feeling? What will happen next? A person's behavior, said McClelland (1961), may be influenced by many things, but the strength of the internal motive to achieve is best captured in the fantasies one tells. "In fantasy anything is at least symbolically possible," he explained. "A person may rise to great heights, sink to great depths, kill his grandmother, or take off for the South Sea Islands on a pogo stick."

■ **need for achievement**
A learned motive to meet personal standards of success and excellence in a chosen area (often abbreviated nAch).

Power

HENRY KISSINGER *(b. 1923)*

Former Secretary of State

"Power is the ultimate aphrodisiac."

Duty

ELEANOR ROOSEVELT *(1884–1962)*

Humanitarian, lecturer, stateswoman

"As for accomplishments, I just did what I had to do as things came along."

Excellence

FLORENCE GRIFFITH JOYNER *(b. 1959)*

Olympic gold medalist

"When you've been second best for so long, you can either accept it, or try to become the best. I made the decision to try and be the best."

Money

SALVADOR DALI *(1904–1988)*

Surrealist artist

"Liking money like I like it, is nothing less than mysticism. Money is a glory."

Needless to say, people with high achievement motivation do not fantasize about taking off for the South Seas or sinking to great depths. They tell stories about working hard, becoming rich and famous, and clobbering the opposition with their wit and brilliance. These achievement-related themes increase when high achievers are in situations that arouse their competitiveness and desire to succeed—when, for example, they believe that the TAT is measuring their intelligence and leadership ability (J. Atkinson, 1958). Studies of the achievement motive in the laboratory and in real life have found numerous differences between people who score high on the need for achievement and those who score low. High scorers are more likely, for example, to start their own businesses, set high personal standards, and prefer to work with capable colleagues who can help them succeed than with co-workers who are merely friendly (Kuhl, 1978; McClelland, 1987).

However, the measurement of achievement motivation soon turned up an interesting problem: The need for achievement that is revealed by the TAT is unrelated to a person's conscious, *self-reported* need for achievement! Apparently, achievement motives come in two varieties: an implicit (unconscious) motive and an explicit (self-aware) motive (McClelland, Koestner, & Weinberger, 1989). Thus a person may express a desire to be academically successful but never seem "motivated" to carry it out. Explicit and implicit achievement motives are acquired in different ways at different times of life, respond differently to different incentives, have different physiological correlates with stress and arousal, and predict different behaviors. For example, the implicit motive predicts sustained achievement over time, because of the pleasure derived from achievement itself; whereas the explicit achievement motive predicts how a person will behave in a specific situation, because of immediate incentives and rewards.

Other researchers argue that it is not enough to say that some people have "achievement motivation" and others don't. Instead, the interesting question is *why* someone wants to achieve. For the love of learning? For fame and success? To prove self-worth? According to Carol Dweck (1990), people who are motivated by *performance* goals are concerned with doing well, being judged highly, and avoiding criticism. Those who are motivated by *learning* goals are concerned with increasing their competence and skills. Now imagine what happens when both are faced with a difficult problem. Who will sink into helplessness, doing poorly at solving the problem and eventually giving up, and who will keep going to master the problem and avoid failure?

The crucial fact about these alternatives—helplessness or mastery—is that *they are unrelated to ability*. When people are faced with a frustrating problem, talent or ambition alone does not predict who will push on and who will give up. What *does* predict success are the goals people set for themselves. When people are focused on how well they are performing, and then do poorly, they often decide the fault is theirs and they stop trying to improve. Because their goal is to demonstrate their abilities, they set themselves up for grief when they temporarily fail—as all of us must if we are to learn anything new. In contrast, people whose goal is learning regard failure as a source of useful information that will help them improve. Failure does not discourage them because they know that learning takes time (Elliott & Dweck, 1988).

THE NEED FOR POWER. Using the TAT, McClelland (1975) also found that some people are motivated by a **need for power**, for dominance over others. The methods they use to win power include aggression, persuasion, helping others, or manipulating others by arousing their guilt, devotion, or anger. Although there are sex differences in the distribution of *actual* power, studies have consistently failed to find any *motivational* differences (Winter, 1988). Men and women who have high power motivation seek prestige and visibility, enter powerful careers, and run for office.

Considerable research now suggests that the need for power, interacting with other motives, spurs some people to become leaders. But the *kind* of power that drives them distinguishes effective leaders from ineffective ones. Great leaders are motivated to use power for social goals rather than personal ambition (the difference between, say, Abraham Lincoln and Adolf Hitler). William Spangler and Robert House (1991) conducted a fascinating study of the speeches, letters, and biographies of 39 presidents, from George Washington to Ronald Reagan. Using complex measures of presidential performance, effectiveness, and greatness, they found that great presidents fit a pattern of motives. They had a lower need for affiliation and for achievement, but a higher need for power and a higher motive to use power for social rather than personal objectives.

CULTURE, GENDER, AND MOTIVES. Like eating and sexuality, the motives for achievement, affiliation, or power are deeply embedded in cultural contexts. In research designed to help companies and individuals cope with cross-cultural differences, Edward and Mildred Hall (1990) found that these motives are affected, for example, by how cultures manage time. In *monochronic* cultures (such as those of Anglo-Americans and Germans), time is organized into linear segments—appointments every hour, tight schedules, and so forth. In such societies, therefore, it is considered the height of rudeness (or status) to keep someone waiting. But in *polychronic* cultures (such as those of Latin Americans, Arabs, the French, and African Americans), time is organized along parallel lines. People do many things at once, and the demands of friends and family supersede those of the appointment book. (Table 10.1 shows some of the other differences between monochronic and polychronic cultures.) Each way of organizing time feels as normal to those who practice it as breathing air, but in

■ **need for power**
A learned motive to dominate or control others.

TABLE 10.1

Cross-cultural Differences in the Uses and Structure of Time

Monochronic People	Polychronic People
Do one thing at a time	Do many things at once
Concentrate on the job	Are highly distractible and subject to interruptions
Take time commitments (deadlines, schedules) seriously	Consider time commitments an objective to be achieved, if possible
Are low-context and need information	Are high-context and already have information
Are committed to the job	Are committed to people and relationships
Adhere religiously to plans	Change plans often and easily
Are concerned about not disturbing others; follow rules of privacy and consideration	Are more concerned with relationships (family, friends, close business associates) than with privacy
Show great respect for private property; seldom borrow or lend	Borrow and lend things often and easily
Emphasize promptness	Care less about own promptness than other people's needs
Are accustomed to short-term relationships	Build lifetime relationships

SOURCE: Hall & Hall, 1990.

fact is learned. The monochronic structure of time, which developed as a result of the industrial revolution in England, actually violates many of humanity's biological rhythms.

You can see readily how misinterpretations of motivations and behavior can occur between the two types of culture. An Anglo judge in Miami got into hot water when he observed that "Cubans always show up two hours late for weddings"—late in Anglo terms, that is. The judge was right; the problem was his implication that there was something wrong with Cubans for being "late." By not understanding cultural differences in uses of time, some Anglos mistakenly infer that some Latinos are "deficient" in achievement motivation. To the Latinos, of course, Anglos are deficient in affiliation motivation—and overly uptight about time, besides.

North Americans and northern Europeans often feel like fish out of water when they are in very different cultures such as those of the Middle East. In "monochronic" cultures, time is broken into linear segments and schedules are more important than people; in "polychronic" cultures, time is more fluid and less rigidly defined, and people come before schedules. A tourist from one kind of culture may have fun visiting another, but sometimes the two sets of rules lead to clashes and misunderstandings.

As conditions change within a society or across cultures, people's motivations change as well. At one time, for example, many people believed that women had a "fear of success," but as opportunities for women improved, this apparent motive faded. Similarly, when the proportion of men and women in an occupation changes, so do people's motivations to work in that field (Kanter, 1977). As a result of such findings, some psychologists have criticized the idea that achievement depends on an internal "motive"—an enduring, unchanging quality of the individual. This notion, they say, leads to the incorrect inference that if people don't succeed, it's their own fault—they lack the internal drive to make it (Morrison & Von Glinow, 1990). In fact, research finds that accomplishment depends not only on personal motives. It can be nurtured or reduced by the work you do and the conditions under which you do it, as we will see next.

The Effects of Work on Motivation

If someone isn't working hard, we tend to ask, "What's the matter with that person's motivation?" Why don't we ask, "What's the matter with that person's job?"

Lennart Levi, a Swedish researcher who works with the World Health Organization, has observed that the problem for organizations is whether they should try to promote feet that adapt to shoes or make shoes that fit the feet. Organizational psychologists are looking at ways to make shoes (companies) fit the feet (the people who work in them).

GOALS AND FEEDBACK. One of the most important influences on motivation to work and on actual performance is the nature of the goal you are working toward. Given two people of equal ability, the one who sets specific and moderately difficult goals will work longer and achieve more than the one who sets vague, easy goals or none at all (Locke & Latham, 1990; Smither, 1988). If a goal is too vague, such as "I'm going to work harder," you don't know what action to take to reach it or how to recognize it when you get there (what does "harder" mean?). If you set a specific goal, such as "I am going to study two hours in the evening instead of one, and read 25 pages instead of 15," you have specified both a course of action and a goal you can recognize.

Once you have specified a goal, continued motivation depends in part on getting feedback about your performance. Your employer needs to tell you that you are almost number one in sales. Your piano teacher needs to tell you that your playing has improved. When people work in environments that do not provide feedback, their motivation to do well is often weakened (Thayer, 1983).

WORKING CONDITIONS. Working conditions also affect a person's satisfaction, mood, health—and motivation to work. In an important longitudinal study, researchers interviewed a random sample of American workers over a period of ten years (Kohn & Schooler, 1983). Comparing results of the first interviews with later ones, they found that aspects of the work (such as fringe benefits, complexity of daily tasks, pace, pressure, and how routine or varied the work was) significantly changed the workers' self-esteem, job commitment, and mo-

Students can have poor working conditions too—such as having to study in crowded quarters or having small siblings who distract you.

tivation. The degree of job flexibility was especially important. People who have a chance to set their own hours, make decisions, vary their tasks, and solve problems are likely to rise to the challenge. They tend to become more flexible in their thinking, and feel better about themselves and their work, than if they feel stuck in a routine, boring job that gives them no control over what they do. As a result, their work motivation rises and stress drops (Karasek & Theorell, 1990; Locke & Latham, 1990).

Surprising as it may seem, having a high income does not stimulate work motivation. This doesn't mean that we should all accept low pay because we will like our jobs better. However, work motivation itself is not related to money, but to how and when the money is paid. The strongest motivator is *incentive pay*, that is, bonuses that are given upon completion of a goal and not as an automatic part of salary (Locke et al., 1981).

Similarly, the "working conditions" of marriage can produce either highly motivated homemakers or apathetic ones (Oakley, 1974; Strasser, 1982). Motivated homemakers tend to have extended families whom they see regularly and friends in the neighborhood who drop in frequently. They set specific goals ("I'm cleaning closets today and devoting tomorrow to the kids"). They get feedback from the family ("This meal is fabulous!"). Apathetic homemakers tend to lack social contacts and to be physically isolated. They have no clear standards for a job well done, so they don't feel they have done their jobs well. None of this, by the way, applies only to women. When men are "househusbands," their motivation rises or falls according to the same circumstances (Beer, 1983).

TEAMWORK. One way to improve working conditions and work motivation is by creating cohesive, independent work teams. For example, one alternative to the standard boring assembly line is to have factory employees work in groups and handle different aspects of assembling the product instead of one repeated routine, an approach that has been tried successfully by Volvo, Sherwin-Williams, General Foods, and Saab (Sundstrom, De Meuse, & Futrell, 1990).

Teamwork produces a diverse set of effects on members' motivation, including better problem solving, higher job satisfaction, and increased participation and trust. Of course, groups can be oppressive and stifle innovation, too, as we will see in Chapter 18. But organizational psychologists are beginning to identify the *conditions of the group* that raise motivation: clarity of purpose; autonomy; prompt feedback on performance; a physical environment that permits informal face-to-face interaction; and rewards and recognition in which the benefits to individual members depend on the whole team's performance (Sundstrom, De Meuse, & Futrell, 1990).

OPPORTUNITIES TO ACHIEVE. Ultimately, achievement ambitions are related to people's *chances* of achieving. Reviewing dozens of studies of opportunity and ambition, Rosabeth Kanter (1977) found that men and women who work in dead-end jobs with no prospect of promotion behave the same way. They play down the importance of achievement, fantasize about quitting, and emphasize the social benefits of their jobs instead of the intellectual benefits. Yet if opportunities are created for such people, if the *structure* of work changes, their motivation often changes too.

There is evidence that many women and members of minority groups encounter a "glass ceiling" in management—a barrier to promotion that is so subtle as to be transparent, yet strong enough to prevent advancement. In 1985, a survey of more than 1,000 senior executives found only 4 blacks, 6 Asians, 3 Hispanics, and 29 women among them (reported in Morrison & Von Glinow, 1990). What is the reason for these low numbers? Many people assume that managers who are members of minority groups do not aspire to achieve, or that they have different management styles or less experience. Research does not support these assumptions. A study of Asian Americans in professional and managerial positions, for instance, found that their education and work experience did not predict advancement as they do for white American men (Cabezas et al., 1989). And in a field study of 2,000 male and female managers, two researchers concluded that "the disproportionately low numbers of women in management can no longer be explained away by the contention that women practice a different brand of management from that practiced by men" (Donnell & Hall, 1980).

Instead, studies find that barriers in an organization can dampen motives to achieve. For example, in a study of the banking industry, the three most significant problems that blacks reported were (1) not being "in the network," so not being told what was going on, (2) racism, and (3) inability to get a mentor (Irons & Moore, 1985). In addition, blacks, Asians, and Hispanics often struggle with *biculturalism*, trying to fit into two cultural worlds (Thomas & Alderfer, 1989; Tsai & Uemura, 1988). Imagine, for instance, how hard it must be to mesh polychronic habits in a monochronic company (or vice versa).

As we have seen, work motivation and satisfaction depend on the right fit between qualities of the individual and conditions of the work. Such evidence raises a host of questions about how best to structure work so that the increasing ethnic diversity of workers will result in worker satisfaction, achievement, and effectiveness rather than conflict, bitterness, and prejudice on both sides (Morrison & Von Glinow, 1990). Should all minorities be required to "fit in" to the dominant culture, for example, or should companies become more multicultural—fitting the shoe to the foot?

QUICK QUIZ

1. Expecting to fail at work and then making no effort to do well can result in a _____.
2. Ramón and Ramona are learning to ski. Every time she falls down, Ramona says, "This is the most humiliating experience I've ever had! Everyone is watching me behave like a clumsy dolt!" Ramón says, "&*!!@*$@! I'll show these skis who's boss!" Why is Ramona more likely than Ramón to give up? (a) She *is* a clumsy dolt. (b) She is less competent at skiing. (c) She is focused on performance. (d) She is focused on learning.
3. Which of these factors significantly increase work motivation? (a) specific goals, (b) regular pay, (c) feedback, (d) general goals, (e) being told what to do, (f) being able to make decisions, (g) the chance of promotion, (h) having routine, predictable work, (i) having mentors
4. Phyllis is an employee at an umbrella company. Her work is always perfectly competent, but she rarely arrives on time; she doesn't seem as motivated to do well as others; and she has begun to claim an unusually high number of "sick days." Phyllis's employer is irritated by this behavior and is thinking of firing her. What guidelines of critical thinking should the boss consider first?

ANSWERS:

1. self-fulfilling prophecy 2. c 3. a, c, f, g, i 4. The boss is jumping to the conclusion that Phyllis has low achievement motivation. This may be true, but because her work is good, the boss should consider other explanations and examine the evidence. Perhaps she comes from a polychronic culture, which organizes time differently from the boss's monochronic demands. Perhaps the work conditions are unsatisfactory: There may be few opportunities for promotion; she may get no feedback; perhaps the company does not provide day care, so Phyllis arrives late because she has child-care obligations. What other possible explanations come to mind?

■ "BASIC" NEEDS AND "HIGHER" GOALS: CAN MOTIVES BE RANKED?

We have come a long way from the motives of hunger and thirst to the many forces that motivate a day's work. This progression, from basic needs to learned ones, from universal needs to culture-specific ones, from the simple to the complex, was not lost on Abraham Maslow (1954/1970). Maslow made sense of the astonishing array of human motives by arranging them in a pyramid, which he called a "hierarchy of needs."

Although Maslow revised the ranking of some needs, his hierarchy basically ascends from simple biological needs to complex psychological motives, culminating in "self-actualization" and "self-transcendence"—stages at which individuals are able to fulfill their potentials and set their own standards. Maslow argued that your needs must be met at each level before you can even think of the matters posed by the level above it. You can't worry about achievement, for instance, if you are hungry, cold, and poor. You can't become self-actualized if you haven't satisfied your need for self-esteem and love. Maslow believed that everyone would reach the highest levels on the motivational ladder if social and economic obstacles were removed. Human beings behave badly, he argued, only when their lower needs are frustrated, especially those for love, belonging, and self-esteem.

This theory, which was intuitively logical and optimistic about human nature, became immensely popular. Without much critical appraisal, it was picked up by corporations, taught in business and management schools, and used as the basis of popular "training seminars"; you may even encounter it on the job one day. This is why you should know that, unfortunately, Maslow's hierarchy of needs and motives has not been supported by research (Howell & Dipboye, 1982; Inglehart & Hildebrandt, 1990; Smither, 1988). The reason has to do with some inherent problems in the theory.

The first problem is that it is just as possible to organize human needs horizontally as vertically. One could argue that people have *simultaneous* needs for basic physical comfort and safety *and* for understanding, self-esteem, and competence. Even hungry people are motivated to explain the world and to be thought well of. Even a person who is still seeking love may be strongly motivated by ideas, social convictions, or a love of beauty (Neher, 1991). Second, people who have met their "lower" needs do not inevitably seek "higher" ones, nor is it the case that antisocial behavior results only from frustrated lower needs. Third, "higher" needs may overcome "lower" ones. Human history is full of examples of people who would rather starve than be humiliated (a "self-esteem" need); rather die of torture than sacrifice their convictions; rather explore, risk, or create new art than be safe and secure at home. Finally, Maslow tended to overlook the conditions in society that foster some motives, such as safety and physical security, over others, such as developing self-potential and risking change (Inglehart & Hildebrandt, 1990).

Think of Jim Abbott, Dian Fossey, and the men and women portrayed on pages 366–367. All, Maslow might say, were leading lives that were "self-actualized." They were not necessarily doing so because they had overcome lower needs. Many heroes and pioneers have sacrificed safety needs, love needs, and the need for approval and recognition in the quest of unpopular goals and private dreams.

Perhaps the safest conclusion, therefore, is that each of us develops an individual hierarchy of motives in the course of our development from childhood to old age. For some, the need for love, security, and safety will dominate. For others, the need for achievement or power will rule. Most of us, as we will see in the next unit, combine many motives in a way that suits our personalities and experiences.

How to Lose Weight—
And Whether You Should

Have you ever read those "ideal weight" charts that describe the weight you ought to be for your "frame size"? Well, forget them. Research on longevity and health shows that those old height-and-weight tables were wrong (Gurin, 1984). New evidence suggests that:

• The healthiest weight rises somewhat with age.
• Being obese can be unhealthy, but so can being very thin.
• Good health does not depend on being a particular, perfect weight. In 1990 the U.S. Department of Health and Human Services published new guidelines for body weight that establish a healthy weight *range* of 30 to 40 pounds and make allowance for normal weight gain as people age.

Yet despite these more flexible guidelines, fashion has changed toward a more slender standard. Miss Sweden of 1951, for example, was 5'7" tall and weighed 151 pounds; Miss Sweden of 1983 was 5'9" tall and weighed 109 pounds. Brett Silverstein and his colleagues documented the changing female ideal in this century by computing a "bust-to-waist" ratio of the measurements of models in popular women's magazines (Silverstein, Peterson, & Perdue, 1986). The ideal body type became decidedly noncurvy twice during this century: in the mid-1920s and from the mid-1960s to the present.

Why did these changes in the ideal female body occur? Silverstein found that men and women associate the curvy body with femininity; and they associate femininity with domesticity, nurturance, and, alas, incompetence. Thus, in every era in which women have been admitted to universities and have had professional careers in greater numbers, women have tried to look boyishly thin to avoid the risk of appearing feminine and dumb. This conflict, Silverstein hypothesized, should be hardest on women who value achievement, higher education, and careers (especially male-dominated careers). Moreover, such women should be more vulnerable to developing eating disorders as

a way to resolve the conflict. Being thin allows them to identify with male competence and actively distance themselves from femininity.

And that is just what the research found. College women who develop eating disorders are more likely than other women to say that (1) their parents believe a woman's place is in the home, (2) their mothers are unhappy with their lives, (3) their fathers think their mothers are unintelligent, and (4) their fathers treat sons as being more intelligent than daughters (Silverstein et al., 1988).

Many women today, therefore, face a dilemma. Evolution has programmed them for a womanly reserve of fat necessary for the onset of menstruation, healthy childbearing, nursing, and, after menopause, for production and storage of the hormone estrogen. The result of the battle between biological design and social standards is that many women today—as in the 1920s—are obsessed with weight, continually dieting, or suffering from eating disorders such as anorexia nervosa (self-starvation) or bulimia (bingeing and vomiting). For men, too, "overweight" is considered a sign of "softness" and lack of masculinity.

What's a person to do? Research offers some suggestions:

• Remember that the disposition to gain weight varies from person to person. Although many people assume that the body is infinitely malleable and that, with enough exercise and dieting, anyone can look like the cultural ideal, in fact there are biological factors that limit how much a person can change (Brownell, 1991).
• Limit rich junk food, which is bad for health as well as weight control.
• Avoid fad diets that restrict you to only a few foods or that promise quick weight loss. Such diets lead to bingeing, which restores the lost weight—plus some. "Yo-yo" patterns of dieting and weight gain actually lower body metabolism and increase the proportion of body fat, making it *easier* to gain weight and harder to lose it (Steen, Oppliger, & Brownell, 1988). More dangerous, chronic yo-yo dieting dramatically increases the chances of heart disease, hyperten-

sion, and strokes (Ernsberger & Nelson, 1988; Lissner et al., 1991).

• Get more exercise, which may raise the metabolic rate. You do not have to become a marathon runner, but you can increase your daily activity level, for example, by walking instead of driving to work or school.

• Find other ways to nurture and reward yourself than food. People who develop eating disorders are more self-critical than healthy eaters, and they are more likely to use food to assuage hurt feelings and low self-esteem (Lehman & Rodin, 1989).

• Avoid amphetamines and other "diet pills," which can be far more dangerous to your health than a few pounds (and can become addictive). Diet pills raise the metabolic rate only as long as you take them. When you stop taking them, the pounds return.

• If you are mistakenly trying to control weight by frequent vomiting and abuse of laxatives, you can break this harmful pattern by joining an eating-disorders program; school counselors and health clinics can direct you.

Most of all, think carefully and critically about the reasons that you are dieting. Are you really "overweight"? Whose standards are you following? Why?

SUMMARY

1. According to drive theory, a few basic motivating drives are based on physiological needs, such as those for food, water, and avoidance of excessive cold and pain. But people are also motivated by cognitive processes that permit them to plan and work for goals. *Social motives* are as important as physical needs.

2. Human motives often conflict. In an *approach-approach* conflict, a person is equally attracted to two goals. In an *avoidance-avoidance* conflict, a person is equally repelled by two goals. An *approach-avoidance* conflict is the most difficult to resolve, because the person is both attracted to and repelled by the same goal. Prolonged conflict can lead to physical symptoms and reduced well-being.

3. Overweight is not caused simply by overeating or emotional problems. According to *set-point theory*, hunger, weight, and eating are regulated by a complex set of bodily mechanisms that keep people at the weight they were designed to be. Insulin regulates the flow of sugar from the bloodstream into the cells; it increases fat stores and prevents fat breakdown.

4. The set point is influenced by exercise, which raises the body's metabolic rate, and by the kind of food a person eats. Sweet foods raise insulin levels, which in turn increase feelings of hunger, increase the amount of food consumed, and can create "cravings" for more sweets. Genetic factors affect set point, body shape, distribution of fat, and whether the body will convert excess calories into fat. Culture, in turn, determines what people eat, when and how often they eat, and with whom they eat.

5. Curiosity and play are important behavioral motives. The more familiar people are with something—a person, a face, a symbol—the more they tend to like it. This affection for the familiar is balanced by the need for novelty and stimulation. Individuals differ in how they strike this balance; sensation seekers prefer a high level of stimulation in many activities. In human beings, play seems to be an innate motive that is apparent from early childhood.

6. Consistency and understanding are important cognitive motives. *Cognitive dissonance theory* assumes that people are motivated to reduce the tension that exists when two cognitions are out of balance. The theory predicts how people will receive new information that is dissonant with their beliefs, self-concepts, and self-esteem.

7. Psychologists disagree about whether any aspect of human sexuality can be considered a "primary drive" or a "biological need." Levels of testosterone may influence sexual desire in both sexes, but human sexual desire and behavior are largely influenced by learning, cultural standards, and social roles.

8. Although most men and women prefer to have sex with partners they love, they often differ in the meanings they attach to sex and their motives for making love. Young men tend to be more "instrumental," enjoying sex for its physical pleasure; young women tend to be more "expressive," enjoying sex for its emotional closeness. They also have different interpretations of sexual signals. The major sex difference in sexuality has to do with sexual coercion and rape; men rape for a variety of motives, including anger, fantasy, sadism, and opportunity. Both sexes may agree to intercourse for nonsexual motives: Men sometimes feel obligated to "make a move" to prove their masculinity, and women sometimes feel obliged to "give in" to preserve the relationship.

9. Sociobiological theories hold that for evolutionary reasons, males are genetically designed to be promiscuous and females to be monogamous. New evidence disputes this argument. A competing perspective holds that differences in sexual behavior, while affected by anatomical differences, are largely related to different *gender role* expectations for men and women, including the "sexual scripts" that dictate how both sexes should behave during courtship, intimacy, and sex.

10. People are motivated to *affiliate* with others for contact comfort, reassurance, and friendship. As with all social motives, individuals and cultures differ in how much affiliation they seek and in the importance they place on attachments.

11. Several categories or theories have described varieties of love: *passionate* ("romantic") vs. *companionate* love; the *six styles of love*; and the *attachment theory of love* (love as secure, anxious/ambivalent, or avoidant). Men and women are equally likely to feel love and attachment, but gender roles affect how they experience and express love.

12. The motivation to work depends on a person's *expectations* of success; the *value* the person places on the goal; various *motives* such as competence, achievement, or power; and the *opportunity* to act on these motives. People are also motivated by a basic need to feel competent at what they do. A theory of *self-efficacy* argues that people get information from several sources about their abilities. Without self-efficacy, people lack the motivation to master new situations.

13. People who are motivated by a high *need for achievement* set their own standards for success and excellence. But achievement motivation also depends on the goals people set for themselves. When normal setbacks occur, *performance* goals can lead to helplessness and giving up; *learning* goals can lead to mastery.

14. Cultures shape the experience and expression of human motives. They differ in the organization of time and whether time or people come first: *monochronic* cultures schedule events linearly, *polychronic* cultures arrange events simultaneously. Achievement motivation is influenced by the times, the society, and working conditions.

15. People who are motivated by a *need for power* seek to dominate and control others. They may use a variety of methods to gain this power, from aggression to persuasion.

16. Achievement motivation can be raised by the conditions of work: having specific goals; feedback and praise; flexibility of tasks; control over decisions; incentive pay; cohesive, autonomous teamwork; and the opportunity for advancement.

17. Abraham Maslow believed that human motives could be ranked from basic biological needs to higher psychological needs. This popular theory remains unproven. People can have simultaneous motives, "higher" motives can outweigh "lower" ones, and people do not always become kinder or more self-actualized when their needs for safety and love are met.

KEY TERMS

motivation   *340*
incentive   *340*
homeostasis   *343*
social motives   *343*
set-point theory   *344*
exploration and curiosity   *347*
familiarity and novelty   *347*
sensation seeking   *347*
practice play   *348*
cognitive dissonance theory   *349*
justification of effort   *351*
gender role   *357*
sexual scripts   *357*
need for affiliation   *359*
contact comfort   *359*
passionate and companionate
  love   *361*

six "styles of love"   *362*
attachment theory of love   *362*
expectations and values   *365*
self-fulfilling prophecy   *365*
need for competence   *365*
self-efficacy   *365*
need for achievement (nAch)   *366*
performance and learning
  goals   *368*
need for power   *368*
polychronic vs. monochronic
  cultures   *368*
goals and feedback   *370*
teamwork   *371*
biculturalism   *372*

PART FOUR

DEVELOPMENT OF THE INDIVIDUAL

11

Diversity I: Measuring and Explaining Mental Abilities

Here's a mental challenge: Each room has two sides that are mirrors and two open sides. Find the mirrored walls. Then place a clear sheet over the puzzle and, starting in the middle, draw a line through all 8 rooms consecutively without going through a room twice.

The tough-minded . . . respect difference.
Their goal is a world made safe for
differences. . . .

RUTH BENEDICT

W hich impresses you more: the changes in your friends over time, or
the extent to which your friends have stayed the same, despite new
experiences and circumstances? Which do you find more intriguing: the fact
that people everywhere share many of the same problems and passions, or the
fact that each human life, and the person who lives it, is distinct? These questions reflect two basic ways of looking at humanity. One focuses on the common steps and outcomes of human development, the other on what makes each
person unique in all the world. In the next four chapters, we will be exploring
these twin themes of similarity and difference, stability and change in the lifelong development of the individual.

We begin by examining the biological and environmental origins of individual differences in ability. In the next chapter, we will do the same for personality. Where do these differences come from? Was your Uncle Al destined
to be an accountant because he was born with a flair for numbers, or did his
love of math depend on good teachers? Does Aunt Grace play the piano like
an angel because of inborn musical talent, or because her mother made her
practice every day? In short, are individual differences in ability primarily inborn, a matter of *nature*, or are they acquired through experience, the result of
nurture?

In this chapter we will see that both of these extreme views are unrealistic
because the strands of heredity and experience are inextricably intertwined. Before we can consider this issue, however, we must first examine how psychologists go about measuring individual differences in ability, using techniques of
psychological assessment. Along the way, we will consider the uses to which
such measurements are put: What is the purpose of attempts to sort humanity
into the smart and the dull, the talented and the ordinary? Then, in the second
part of the chapter, we will return to the question of where individual differences in ability come from—and what they mean in the world outside the classroom, otherwise known as "real life."

The long and short of it is:
Human beings are similar and
diverse.

■ ASSESSING MENTAL ABILITIES:
"THIS IS ONLY A TEST"

Most people reading this book have taken a psychological test. You took intelligence tests, achievement tests, and possibly vocational aptitude tests in school.
You may have taken other tests when applying for a job, joining the military,
or starting psychotherapy. Hundreds of psychological tests or assessment "instruments" are used in industry, education, research, and the helping professions. Some are given to individuals, others to large groups. These measures
help clarify differences among individuals as well as differences in the reactions
of the same individual on different occasions or at different stages of life.

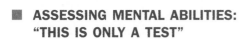

■ **psychological assessment**
The measurement and evaluation of
abilities, aptitudes, and personality
characteristics.

381

Traditionally, mental tests have been divided into two types, achievement tests and aptitude tests. **Achievement tests** are designed to measure acquired skills and knowledge, particularly the types of skills and knowledge that have been explicitly taught. The proficiency exams required by some states for high school graduation are an example. (As we discuss in "A Closer Look at Educational Testing" on page 384, there is a growing movement to establish similar exams on a national level.) **Aptitude tests,** in contrast, are designed to measure a person's ability to acquire skills or knowledge in the future. For example, vocational aptitude tests can help you decide if you will do better as a mechanic or a musician. Actually, however, all mental tests are in some sense achievement tests because they assume some sort of past learning or experience with certain objects, words, or situations. The difference between achievement and aptitude tests is one of degree and intended use.

The Test of a Good Test

Most psychological tests are **standardized;** that is, they come with uniform procedures for giving and scoring the test. It would hardly be fair to give some people detailed instructions and plenty of time and others only vague instructions and limited time. Those who administer the test must know exactly how to explain the tasks involved, how much time to allow, and what materials to use. Scoring is usually done by referring to **norms,** or established standards of performance. The usual procedure for developing norms is to give the test to a large group of people who resemble those for whom the test is intended. Norms tell users of the test which scores can be considered high, low, or average.

Any good standardized test must meet two crucial requirements. First, if the attribute being measured is one that is assumed to be stable, then scores or test results must be consistent. They should not fluctuate because of chance factors, such as who happens to administer the test or the time of day it is given. The consistency of scores on a test is known as test **reliability.** A vision test would not be of much use if it said your eyesight was 20/20 one day and 20/400 the next. Similarly, psychologists want to be sure that scores on tests of intellectual or personality characteristics don't change unpredictably from one time or situation to another.

There are several ways to measure reliability. *Test-retest reliability* is computed by giving the test twice to the same group of people, then comparing the two sets of scores statistically. If the test is reliable, individuals' scores will be similar from one session to another. This method has a drawback, however. People tend to do better the second time they take a test, after they have become familiar with the strategies required and the actual test items used. Another approach is to compute *alternate forms reliability*, by giving different versions of the same test to the same group on two separate occasions. The items on the two forms are similar in format but are not identical in content. With this method, performance cannot improve because of familiarity with the items, although people may still do somewhat better the second time around because they have learned the general strategies and procedures expected of them.

A third method, *split-half reliability*, takes a different tack. Scores on half of the test items (for example, the even-numbered items) are compared with scores on the other half (for example, the odd-numbered items). The two halves of the test are treated as if they were alternate forms. High split-half reliability means that the test is *internally consistent*.

In addition to being reliable, a test must have **validity,** that is, it must measure what it was designed to measure. A test should not be used to assess, say, creativity if what it really measures is vocabulary size. Psychologists try to establish validity in a variety of ways. One is to see that a test has *content valid-*

■ **achievement tests**
Tests designed to measure acquired skills and knowledge.
■ **aptitude tests**
Tests designed to measure a person's potential for acquiring various types of skills and knowledge, based on present abilities.
■ **standardize**
In test construction, to develop uniform procedures for giving and scoring a test.
■ **norms**
In test construction, established standards of performance.
■ **reliability**
In test construction, the consistency of scores derived from a test.
■ **validity**
The ability of a test to measure what it was designed to measure.

ity—that the items are broadly representative of the trait in question. Suppose you constructed a test to measure employees' job satisfaction. If your test tapped a broad sampling of relevant beliefs and behaviors ("Do you feel you have reached a dead end at work?" "Are you bored with your assignments?"), it would have content validity. If the test asked only how workers felt about their salary level, it would lack content validity and would be of little use. (Highly paid people are not always satisfied with their jobs, nor are poorly paid people always dissatisfied.)

Most tests are also judged on *criterion validity*, the ability to predict other, independent measures, or criteria, of the trait in question. A test can have criterion validity and thus be useful whether or not individual test items *look* valid or sensible to the test-taker. The criterion for a scholastic aptitude test might be college grades; the criterion for a test of shyness might be behavior in social situations. To find out if your job satisfaction test had criterion validity, you might return a year later to see if it correctly predicted absenteeism, resignations, or requests for job transfers.

Unfortunately, teachers, parents, and employers do not always stop to question a test's validity when test results are summarized in a single number, such as an IQ score or a job applicant's ranking (see Figure 11.1). Enthralled by the test score, they simply assume that the test measures what they think it does. Robert Sternberg (1988) notes that this assumption is especially common with mental tests, even though, he argues, such tests actually tap only a limited set of abilities important for intelligent behavior. "There is an allure to exact-sounding numbers," says Sternberg. "An IQ of 119, an SAT score of 580, a mental-abilities score in the 74th percentile—all sound very precise. . . . But the appearance of precision is no substitute for the fact of validity."

Among psychologists and educators, the validity of even some widely used tests is controversial. Consider the Scholastic Aptitude Test (SAT), which applicants to most colleges and universities in the United States have to take. Some critics believe that SAT scores do not do sufficiently better than high school grades at predicting college performance to justify the time and expense involved in giving the exam (Crouse & Trusheim, 1988). They also point out that the SAT has better criterion validity for males than for females, who do better in college than their SAT scores would have predicted.

A new version of the SAT, renamed the Scholastic Assessment Test I and scheduled for publication in 1994, has been designed to answer these and other criticisms. However, one validity problem may remain. Stuart Katz and his colleagues (Katz, Hebert, & Lautenschlager, 1991; Katz et al., 1990) studied the Reading Comprehension section of both the SAT and a preliminary version of the SAT-I. In this part of the test, students must read a passage and then answer multiple-choice questions based on the passage. Undergraduates, Katz and his colleagues find, are able to do well on a majority of the questions *even without reading the passages* (although not as well as with them). Consider this item, from the 1983 version of the SAT:

According to the author, it is the duty of children's literature to:
a. protect children from learning anything unpleasant or distressing
b. simplify moral issues so that children can understand them
c. force children to deal with the facts of pain and suffering
d. reassure children that every problem has a solution
e. present truth in a way that children can accept and understand

Did you get the answer? It's (e). Many people can figure out the right response by drawing on their knowledge of cultural values concerning children. The researchers conclude that SAT Reading Comprehension items do not measure "pure" reading comprehension, as they are supposed to, but tap general

Exact numbers can be reassuring or worrying: If your IQ is 143, you'll be thrilled; if your SAT score is 143, you'll be depressed. But do exact numbers necessarily mean that a test is valid?

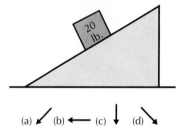

63 In what direction does the force of gravity pull the 20 lb. weight placed on the board in diagram 63?

(a) (b) (c) (d)

FIGURE 11.1

An item from a test for fire fighters
In a lawsuit involving this item, a judge noted that although a high school physics student would correctly choose answer (C), answer (A) might be more useful in fighting fires! In recent years, efforts have been made to make employment screening tests more relevant to the skills required on the job.

A CLOSER LOOK AT EDUCATIONAL TESTING

Performance-based Assessment

Standardized, multiple-choice achievement and aptitude tests are generally:

    a. highly reliable
    b. carefully constructed
    c. efficient to administer
    d. inadequate

Which answer would you choose? A growing number of psychologists and educators would like a fifth option, "All of the above."

Psychological assessment has long been regarded as one of psychology's greatest success stories. Psychologists are experts at constructing standardized tests that meet rigorous scientific standards and are effective for many purposes. Critics, however, say that many of these tests also have severe limitations and unintended negative consequences. In a 1990 report titled "From Gatekeeper to Gateway: Transforming Testing in America," a National Commission on Testing and Public Policy noted that many standardized tests were originally designed to screen people *out* of academic courses, colleges, and jobs, with no one worrying much about those who were rejected. Today, however, college admissions policies have become more inclusive and the demand for skilled workers has grown. As a result, educators and employers are looking for ways to improve the skills and develop the talents of people who do poorly on tests. And for these purposes, a single test score isn't very useful.

According to the commission, standardized testing in American schools currently costs state and local taxpayers almost $1 billion a year. At some grade levels, students may be tested a dozen times in a single year. Yet children in the United States perform far less well on knowledge and reasoning tests than do those in most other technologically developed countries, and even many developing countries. Critics say that too often tests emphasize lower-order thinking skills, are culturally biased, or assess only a narrow range of abilities. Also, teachers may feel pressured to "teach to the test." (Who wouldn't feel

knowledge and test-taking skills as well. That might be important for a test-taker to know, because guidelines for taking the SAT advise you to *ignore* background knowledge when answering the items. (Naturally this research made us take another look at the usefulness of our own Quick Quizzes. We're happy to report that you'll have to read the book in order to do well on most of them.)

Psychologists sometimes disagree about the content validity of a test because they disagree about the fundamental nature of what the test is trying to measure. This is especially true for the elusive trait we call **intelligence,** which, like love, is highly valued but hard to describe to everyone's satisfaction. Some psychologists equate intelligence with the ability to reason abstractly, others with the ability to learn and profit from experience in daily life. Some emphasize the ability to think rationally, others the ability to act purposefully. These qualities are all probably part of what most people mean by intelligence, but theorists weigh them differently.

One of the longest-running debates in psychology is about whether a global quality called "intelligence" actually exists. A typical intelligence test asks you to do several things: provide a specific bit of information, notice similarities between objects, solve arithmetic problems, define words, fill in the missing parts of incomplete pictures, arrange pictures in a logical order, arrange blocks to resemble a design, assemble puzzles, use a coding scheme, or judge what behavior would be appropriate in a particular situation. Researchers often use a statistical method called **factor analysis** to try to identify which sorts of abilities underlie performance on the various items. This procedure identifies clusters of correlated items that seem to be measuring some common trait or ability. Some psychologists believe that a general ability, or **g factor,** underlies all the

■ **intelligence**
An inferred characteristic of an individual, usually defined as the ability to profit from experience, acquire knowledge, think abstractly, or adapt to changes in the environment.

■ **factor analysis**
A statistical method for analyzing the intercorrelations among various measures or test scores. Clusters of measures or scores that are highly correlated are assumed to measure the same underlying trait, ability, or aptitude (factor).

■ **g factor**
A general ability assumed by some theorists to underlie various specific mental abilities and talents.

pressured, when newspapers rank schools by their test scores, school systems give bonuses to teachers whose students do well, and real estate agents make a district's high test scores part of their sales pitch?) As a result, instead of reading books or learning to construct a logical argument, students in some classrooms spend their time answering multiple-choice questions about isolated passages, or learning disconnected bits of information. In some schools, teachers have even been known to give out test questions before the test, or encourage students expected to score low to stay home on the day of the exam.

Such problems have led to a new philosophy in educational testing, one that emphasizes what a student is ready to learn next instead of what he or she seems unable to learn (Moses, 1990). Some school districts and states are turning to *performance-based assessment techniques,* which include written tests with open-ended questions, portfolios of a student's best work, oral presentations, and completion of real-world or hands-on projects requiring planning and critical thinking skills (for example, conducting an experiment and writing up the results). The assumption is that if teachers then "teach to the test," they will at least

be teaching the kinds of thinking and communication skills that really matter.

Several school districts and states already use performance-based techniques, and some educational reformers would like to see them incorporated into a national system of achievement exams, administered periodically to all schoolchildren. Advocates of national testing argue that national standards are necessary for holding educators accountable, and the nation needs to be sure that all students have basic work-related skills when they graduate from high school. Opponents worry that states will lose autonomy in setting curriculums, diversity will be ignored, and resources that could be better spent elsewhere will be spent on test preparation. They also observe that performance-based techniques contain a limited number of questions, require subjective evaluation, are time-consuming to administer, and have unproven validity.

One thing is certain: The next few years will see intensive efforts by psychologists and educators to design new and better tests that enhance learning. So students, get out your pencils . . . .

specific abilities as well as various kinds of talent (Spearman, 1927; Wechsler, 1955). They cite findings that although people may do better on some tasks than others, a person's scores on various tasks are often highly correlated. Other psychologists dispute the existence of a g factor, arguing that a person can excel in some kinds of tasks yet do poorly in others (Thurstone, 1938). One theory originally proposed no fewer than 120 separate "factors" in intelligence, and was subsequently updated to include 150 and then 180 such factors (Guilford, 1967, 1982, 1988).

The lack of agreement on a precise definition of intelligence has led some writers to suggest, only half-jokingly, that intelligence is "whatever intelligence tests measure."

Does this look like a test? A new approach to achievement testing, the portfolio approach, emphasizes actual accomplishment. Instead of taking a paper-and-pencil exam, students present examples of their best work. Many educators are enthusiastic about such new methods of assessment, but critics wonder if they will prove to be reliable and valid.

QUICK QUIZ

1. Professor Flummox gives his newly constructed test of Aptitude for Studying Psychology to his psychology students at the start of the year. At the end of the year he finds that those who did well on the test averaged only a C in the course. The test lacks _____.

2. The professor also gives the test to a group of students who have never taken and are not now taking psychology. They take the test once in the first week and again in the second week of the semester. Most students' scores are quite different on the two occasions, so the test also lacks _____.

3. Which are aptitude tests? (a) this quiz, (b) a driver's license exam, (c) the bar examination for lawyers, (d) a test to determine who can benefit from artistic training, (e) an intelligence test

✳ 4. What's wrong with defining intelligence as "whatever intelligence tests measure"?

ANSWERS:

1. **validity** (or, more specifically, criterion validity) 2. **reliability** (or, more specifically, test-retest reliability) 3. d, e 4. The definition is circular. How do we know someone is intelligent? Because he or she scored high on an intelligence test. Why did the person score high? Because the person is intelligent? The definition also discourages criticisms of the tests and efforts to improve them. People are led to assume that a low score must be entirely the scorer's fault rather than the test's. But the test-taker may be intelligent in ways that the tests fail to measure, and the tests may be measuring traits other than intelligence.

The Uses and Misuses of Intelligence Tests

Mental tests were originally conceived as an impartial, democratic way to select people for jobs or special schooling. They were considered an antidote for political favoritism, cronyism, prejudice, and class privilege. Employers and teachers might be swayed by stereotypes and self-interest, but tests were assumed to be objective. Many different kinds of mental tests were eventually developed to measure specific aptitudes and abilities. However, tests of general intelligence have been the most influential by far, so we will examine them closely.

BINET'S BRAINSTORM.   In 1904, the French Ministry of Education asked psychologist Alfred Binet (1857–1911) to design a test that would identify slow learners. School attendance had been made mandatory, but some children did not learn well in an ordinary classroom and needed special help. The ministry was reluctant to let teachers identify slow learners. They might have prejudices about lower-class children or assume that shy or disruptive children were retarded. What was needed was an objective test that would reveal who could benefit from remedial work.

Wrestling with the problem, Binet had a great insight: In the classroom, the responses of "dull" children resembled those of ordinary children of younger ages. Bright children, on the other hand, responded like ordinary children of older ages. The thing to measure, then, was a child's **mental age (MA),** or level of intellectual development relative to other children's. Then instruction could be tailored to the child's capabilities. The test devised by Binet and his colleague, Theophile Simon, measured memory, vocabulary, and perceptual discrimination. Items ranged from those that most young children could do easily to those that only older children could handle, as determined by the testing

■ **mental age (MA)**
A measure of mental development expressed in terms of the average mental ability at a given age. A child with a mental age of 8 performs on a test of mental ability at the level of the average 8-year-old.

of large numbers of children. These items were grouped by age level: Items passed by most 6-year-olds were assigned to the 6-year level, items passed by most 7-year-olds were assigned to the 7-year level, and so forth. An individual child's mental age was computed by finding the highest level at which the child passed all items, and then adding partial credit in months for any items passed at higher levels.

A scoring system developed later by others used a formula in which the child's mental age (MA) was divided by the child's chronological age (CA) to yield an **intelligence quotient,** or **IQ.** The result was multiplied by 100 to get rid of the decimal point:

$$IQ = MA/CA \times 100$$

Thus a child of 8 who performed like an average 6-year-old would have an IQ of $6/8 \times 100 = 75$. A child of 8 who scored like an average 10-year-old would have an IQ of $10/8 \times 100 = 125$. All average children, regardless of age, would have an IQ of 100 because MA and CA would be the same. (In actual calculations, months were used, not years, to yield a precise figure. We use years here to keep the computations simple.)

Unfortunately, this method of figuring IQ had a serious flaw. At all ages, the distribution of scores formed a bell-shaped curve, with scores near the average (mean) most common and very high or low scores rare. However, at one age scores might cluster tightly around the average, whereas at another age they might be somewhat more dispersed. As a result, the IQ score necessary to be in the top 10 (or 20 or 30) percent of one's age group varied, depending on one's age. Because of this problem, and because the IQ formula did not make much sense for adults, today's intelligence tests are scored differently. Usually the average is arbitrarily set at 100 and test scores (still informally referred to as "IQs") are computed from tables. A score still reflects how a person compares with others, either children of a particular age or adults in general. The test is constructed so that the *standard deviation*—a measure of how spread out the scores are around the mean—is always 15 (or 16 on the modern version of the Binet test). When the standard deviation is 15, theoretically about 68 percent of all people will score between 85 and 115, about 95 percent will score between 70 and 130, and about 99.7 percent will score between 55 and 145 (see Figure 11.2). In any particular sample of people, the distribution will vary somewhat from the theoretical ideal, however. On many tests, descriptive labels are used to characterize people whose scores fall between certain arbitrary cutoff points. For instance, those scoring above 130 might be called "very superior," those scoring below 70 "mentally retarded."

■ **intelligence quotient (IQ)**
A measure of intelligence originally computed by dividing a person's mental age by his or her chronological age and multiplying by 100; now derived from norms provided for standardized intelligence tests.

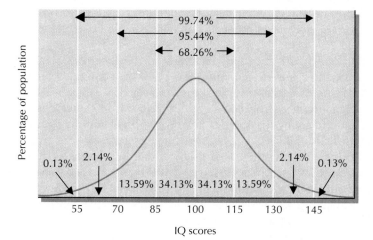

FIGURE 11.2

Expected distribution of IQ scores
In a large population of people, IQ scores will tend to be distributed on a normal (bell-shaped) curve. On most tests, about two-thirds of the scores are expected to fall between 85 and 115. In any actual sample, however, the distribution will depart somewhat from the ideal. In particular, very low scores will usually outnumber very high ones because of mental retardation caused by brain damage and birth defects.

Army intelligence testing during World War I often occurred under noisy, crowded, and confusing conditions. Many test items were culturally loaded, and some men refused to answer at all. Many people ignored these facts, however, and concluded that a high proportion of army recruits were morons.

FROM OPPORTUNITIES TO LIMITS.   Binet made certain important assumptions about his test—for example, that all children taking it would have a similar cultural background. He also emphasized that the test merely *sampled* intelligence and did not measure everything covered by that term. A test score, he said, could be useful, along with other information, for predicting school performance under ordinary conditions, but it should *not* be confused with intelligence itself. The purpose of testing was to identify children with learning problems, not to rank normal children.

Binet's test soon crossed the Atlantic to America, where it was embraced warmly. Stanford psychologist Lewis Terman revised the test and established norms for American children. His version, the *Stanford-Binet Intelligence Scale*, which was published in 1916, became the standard against which most other tests were validated. It has since been updated several times. (For some sample items, see Table 11.1.) Two decades later, David Wechsler, chief psychologist at Bellevue Hospital in New York City, designed another test, expressly for adults, which became the *Wechsler Adult Intelligence Scale (WAIS)*. It was followed by the *Wechsler Intelligence Scale for Children (WISC)*. Although the Wechsler tests produce a general IQ score, they also provide specific scores for different kinds of ability, both verbal and nonverbal ("performance"). These tests, too, have since been revised. (For some sample items, see Figure 11.3 and Table 11.2.)

However, Binet's original intentions regarding intelligence tests somehow got lost in passage, and since he died only a few years after designing his test, he was not around to protest. In France, Binet's test had been given to each child individually, so the test-giver could see if a child was ill or nervous, had poor vision, or was not trying. In America, the revised Binet and the Wechsler tests were also used with individuals, but other intelligence tests were given to huge groups of people, usually students or soldiers, and the advantages of individualized testing were lost. Americans assumed that IQ tests revealed some permanent, inherited trait underlying all intelligent behavior. The object was not to bring slow learners up to the average, but to "track" people according to "natural" ability. On the basis of test scores earned during a single testing session, students were assigned to slow or fast tracks, and soldiers were groomed for or discouraged from becoming officers. The testers overlooked the fact that

TABLE 11.1

Sample Items from the Stanford-Binet Intelligence Test, Form L-M

The older the test-taker is, the more the test requires in the way of verbal comprehension and fluency.

Age	Task
4	Fills in the missing word when asked, "Brother is a boy; sister is a ⎯⎯⎯⎯⎯ ."
	Answers correctly when asked, "Why do we have houses?"
9	Answers correctly when examiner says, "In an old graveyard in Spain they have discovered a small skull which they believe to be that of Christopher Columbus when he was about 10 years old. What is foolish about that?"
	Examiner notches folded paper; child draws how it will look unfolded.
12	Completes "The streams are dry . . . there has been little rain."
	Tells what is foolish about statements such as "Bill Jones's feet are so big that he has to put his trousers on over his head."
Adult	Can describe the difference between *misery* and *poverty, character* and *reputation, laziness* and *idleness.*
	Explains how to measure 3 pints of water with a 5-pint and a 2-pint can.

SOURCE: From Lewis M. Terman & Maud A. Merrill, *Stanford-Binet Intelligence Scale* (1972 norms ed.). Boston: Houghton-Mifflin, 1973. (Currently published by The Riverside Publishing Company.) Items are copyright 1916 by Lewis M. Terman, 1937 by Lewis M. Terman and Maud A. Merrill, © 1960, 1973 by The Riverside Publishing Company. Reproduced or adapted by permission of the publisher.

in America, with its many ethnic and social groups, people did not all share the same background and experience (S. J. Gould, 1981).

Intelligence tests developed or revised between World War I and the 1960s for use in schools favored city children over rural ones, middle-class children over poor ones, and white children over minority children. One item asked whether the Emperor Concerto was written by Beethoven, Mozart, Bach, Brahms, or Mahler. (The answer is Beethoven.) Another asked, "What should you do if you find a 3-year-old child lost on the street?" (The correct answer: Call the police. But that response might not look so attractive to a child living in the inner city, or a farm child living where there are no police nearby and

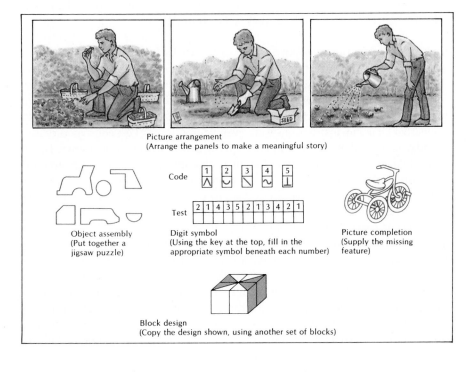

Picture arrangement
(Arrange the panels to make a meaningful story)

Object assembly
(Put together a
jigsaw puzzle)

Code

Test

Digit symbol
(Using the key at the top, fill in the
appropriate symbol beneath each number)

Picture completion
(Supply the missing
feature)

Block design
(Copy the design shown, using another set of blocks)

FIGURE 11.3

Performance tasks on the Wechsler tests
Performance (nonverbal) items are particularly useful in measuring the abilities of those who have poor hearing, are not fluent in the tester's language, have limited education, or resist doing classroom-type tasks. A large gap between a person's verbal score and performance score on a Wechsler test sometimes indicates a specific learning problem. (Object assembly, digit symbol, and picture completion adapted from Cronbach, 1990.)

TABLE 11.2

Verbal Items Similar to Those on the WISC-R and the WAIS-R

For each subtest, the first example illustrates the level of difficulty of the Wechsler Intelligence Scale for Children—Revised. The second example illustrates the level of difficulty of the Wechsler Adult Intelligence Scale—Revised. Digit span items are similar on the two tests.

Subtest	Examples
Information	Who was Thomas Jefferson?
	Who wrote *Huckleberry Finn*?
Comprehension	Why is it important to use zip codes when you mail letters?
	Why do married people who want a divorce have to go to court?
Similarities	In what way are corn and macaroni alike?
	In what way are a book and a movie alike?
Vocabulary	What do we mean by *protect*?
	What does *formulate* mean?
Arithmetic	Dick had 13 pieces of candy and gave away 8. How many did he have left?
	How many hours will it take to drive 140 miles at the rate of 30 miles an hour?
Digit Span	I am going to say some numbers. Listen carefully, and when I am through say them right after me: 3-6-1-7-5-8.
	Now I am going to say some more numbers, but this time when I stop, I want you to say them backward: 1-9-3-2-7.

SOURCE: Adapted from Lee J. Cronbach, Essentials of Psychological Testing, 5th ed. New York: Harper & Row, 1990, and based on items from the Wechsler scales, published by The Psychological Corporation, 1958.

no "streets," only roads.) IQ tests did not measure the kinds of knowledge and skills that are intelligent in a minority neighborhood or in the hills of Appalachia (Scarr, 1984a).

In the 1960s, criticism mounted. Opponents of testing argued that because teachers thought IQ scores revealed the limits of a child's potential, the scores could produce a self-fulfilling prophecy. Low-scoring children would not get the educational attention or encouragement they needed; high-scoring children would. When teachers expect a child to do well, they respond more warmly, give more feedback, teach more material, and give the child more chances to ask and answer questions (Rosenthal & Jacobson, 1987).

CULTURE-FREE AND CULTURE-FAIR TESTS. In the 1970s, group intelligence testing became a public issue. School boards and employers were sued for restricting the opportunities of low scorers. Some states prohibited the use of group tests for classifying children. Several test-makers responded to the charge of cultural bias by trying to construct tests that were *culture-free.* Such tests were usually nonverbal; in some, instructions were even pantomimed. Test constructors soon found, however, that culture can affect performance in unexpected ways. In one case, children who had emigrated from Arab countries to Israel were asked to show which detail was missing from a picture of a face with no mouth (Ortar, 1963). The children, who were not used to thinking of a drawing of a head as a complete picture, said that the *body* was missing!

In recent years, test constructors have tried to design tests that are *culture-fair.* Their aim is not to eliminate the influence of culture, but to find items that incorporate knowledge and skills common to many different cultures. So far the results have been less successful than originally hoped. Cultural values affect a person's attitude toward taking tests, comfort in the settings required for testing, motivation, rapport with the test-giver, competitiveness, and experience in solving problems independently (Anastasi, 1988). Moreover, cultures differ in which problem-solving strategies they foster. For example, children

"You can't build a hut, you don't know how to find edible roots and you know nothing about predicting the weather. In other words, you do *terribly* on our IQ test."

All tests reflect a culture's needs and values.

from white, middle-class families are typically trained to categorize things—to say that an apple and a peach are similar because they are both fruits. But children from other ethnic groups may have different expectations about what's being called for and answer that an apple and a peach are similar because they taste good—a response that test-givers interpret as less intelligent (Miller-Jones, 1989). That is why culture-fair items do not always eliminate differences in group performance.

In theory, it should be possible to establish norms that are not based on white urban children, simply by throwing out items on which such children score better than others. This strategy was used years ago to eliminate sex differences in IQ. On early tests, girls scored higher than boys at every age (Samelson, 1979). No one was willing to conclude that males were intellectually inferior, so in the 1937 revision of the Stanford-Binet test, Lewis Terman simply deleted items that showed sex differences.

But few people seem willing to do for cultural differences what Terman did for sex differences. The reason reveals a dilemma at the heart of intelligence testing. Intelligence tests put some groups of children at a disadvantage, yet they also measure skills and knowledge useful in the classroom. How can educators recognize and accept cultural differences and, at the same time, require students to demonstrate mastery of the skills, knowledge, and attitudes that will help them succeed in school and in the larger society? How can they eliminate bias from tests, while preserving the purpose for which the tests were designed? Anne Anastasi, an eminent expert in testing, contends that concealing the effects of cultural disadvantage by rejecting conventional tests is "equivalent to breaking a thermometer because it registers a body temperature of 101." Instead, she argues, special help should be given to any child that needs it (Anastasi, 1988). Others believe that IQ and other mental tests do more harm than good. Sociologist Jane Mercer (1988) has been trying for years to get testers to understand that children can be *ignorant* of information required by IQ tests without being *stupid*, but she has finally given up. Now, she says, "I'm out to kill the IQ test."

Beyond the IQ Test

The resolution of this debate may ultimately depend on whether test users can learn to use intelligence tests more intelligently. Most educators feel the tests have value, as long as a person's background is kept in mind and the results are interpreted cautiously. IQ tests are well standardized, and those given to school-age children predict school performance fairly well. Correlations between IQ scores and current or future school grades, though far from perfect, are high, ranging between .40 and .60. IQ tests often identify not only the mentally retarded, but also gifted students who have not previously considered higher education.

In some schools, a child's placement in a special education program now depends not only on an IQ score, but also on medical data and the child's demonstrated inability to get along in the family and community. Some schools are also returning to Binet's original concept. Instead of using group tests to label and categorize children, they give individual tests to identify a child's strengths and weaknesses so that teachers can design individualized programs that will boost the child's performance. Two people with the same IQ score may show a different *pattern* of strengths and weaknesses. This information can be used in the planning of individualized instructional programs.

This change in emphasis reflects an increasing awareness that the intellect—and IQ scores—can be improved, even in the mentally retarded (Butterfield & Belmont, 1977; Feuerstein, 1980; Sternberg, 1986). It also recognizes that a person may have a **learning disability**—a problem with a specific mental skill, such

Suppose a test finds IQ differences between two groups of children. Should we change the children in the group that does less well, or change the test?

■ **learning disability**
A difficulty in the performance of a specific mental skill, such as reading or arithmetic; sometimes linked to perceptual or memory problems.

Intellectually impaired children, like this child with Down's syndrome, are accomplishing more academically than anyone once thought they could.

as reading or arithmetic—without having a general intellectual impairment. Many children with learning disabilities have normal or even superior intelligence and can overcome or compensate for their handicap. Such well-known people as inventor Thomas Edison, poet Amy Lowell, and politician Nelson Rockefeller succeeded in their fields despite having *dyslexia*, a reading disability that makes it difficult to decode patterns of letters correctly.

One kind of information missed by traditional intelligence tests is *how* a person goes about answering questions and solving problems. Most of these tests take a *psychometric* approach to mental abilities, focusing on how well people perform—that is, on whether or not they get the right answers. Newer approaches, inspired by findings on human information processing, emphasize differences in how people approach the items on a test. The goal is not merely to measure mental ability but also to understand it and help people increase its use in daily life. One promising theory, Robert Sternberg's *triarchic theory of intelligence* (1988), distinguishes three aspects of intelligence: componential, experiential, and contextual.

1. *Componential intelligence* refers to the various information-processing strategies that go on inside a person's head when the person thinks intelligently. According to Sternberg, there are three types of components in the solution of any problem. *Metacomponents* are the steps necessary for recognizing the problem, selecting a strategy, and planning, monitoring, and evaluating the solution. *Performance components* are the steps required for actually finding the solution. *Knowledge-acquisition components* are the steps used in learning how to solve problems of a given type in the first place. When you write a term paper, you use metacomponents to decide on a topic, plan the paper, monitor the writing, and evaluate how well the finished product succeeds. But you use knowledge-acquisition components to do the research and performance components for the actual writing. When you draw up a budget, you use metacomponents to decide how much you are willing to spend on what, performance components to do the computations, and knowledge-acquisition components to learn how to budget in the first place. People who are strong in componential intelligence tend to do well on conventional mental tests.

2. *Experiential intelligence* takes into account experience with a given task. People who are strong in this area cope well with novelty and are also able to "automatize" steps in solving problems of a given type once they have experience with them. Those who are lacking in this area may perform well only under a narrow set of circumstances. For example, a student may do well in school, where assignments have specific due dates and feedback is immediate, but be

Engineers drawing up plans for a new project must be adept at the metacomponents of componential intelligence: They must analyze the problem, select a strategy, and evaluate solutions.

less successful after graduation if her job requires her to set her own deadlines and her employer doesn't let her know very often how she is doing.

3. *Contextual intelligence* takes the external world into account. If you are strong in contextual intelligence, you know when to adapt to the environment (if you are in a dangerous neighborhood, you become more vigilant than usual); when to change environments (you had planned to be a teacher but you find you don't enjoy working with kids, so you switch to accounting); and when to try to shape the environment into something new (your marriage is rocky, so you and your spouse go for counseling).

Most existing mental tests do not measure the experiential and contextual aspects of intelligence, but Sternberg and others are trying to change that. For example, Sternberg (1991) is preparing a test to measure the various components specified by his triarchic theory, and another group (Naglieri, Das, & Jarman, 1990) is working on a battery of tests that includes measures of attention and the ability to make and carry out plans. Such work promises to broaden our ideas about what intelligence is and help us understand the cognitive processes underlying intelligent behavior on tests and in the real world. In the meantime, however, conventional tests, and in particular IQ tests, remain the yardstick by which individual differences are most often measured. In the next section, we will look at information these tests have yielded about the origins of intellectual competence.

QUICK QUIZ

Test yourself on your knowledge of intelligence tests.

1. On Binet's test, a child of 7 who scored like most 7-year-olds would have an IQ of _____. A child of 10 with a mental age of 9 would have an IQ of _____.
2. True or false: Culture-fair tests have eliminated group differences that show up on traditional IQ tests.
3. Some schools are returning to Binet's original goal of using IQ tests as a tool for (a) labeling and categorizing children, (b) identifying children who could benefit from individualized programs, (c) studying intellectual differences among ethnic groups.
4. In your statistics class, you understand the formulas and computations, but on tests you plan your time poorly, spending the entire period on the most difficult problems, and never even get to the problems you can solve easily. As a result, your scores are lower than they might be. According to Sternberg, which aspect of componential intelligence do you need to work on?

ANSWERS:

1. 100, 90 2. false 3. b 4. metacomponents

■ GENETIC ORIGINS OF MENTAL ABILITIES

It's all very well to say that one person does well on intelligence tests and another only average or below average, but where do these differences come from? Which is more influential, heredity or the environment?

Historically, debates about this issue have sometimes sounded like a boxing match: "In this corner, we have Heredity and in this corner, we have Environ-

It's easy to oversimplify the nature-nurture debate. Heredity and environment may seem like contenders in some winner-take-all competition, but in real life is it possible to separate them?

ment. Okay, you guys, come out fighting." E. L. Thorndike (1903), one of the leading psychologists of the early 1900s, claimed that "in the actual race of life . . . the chief determining factor is heredity." But his contemporary, behaviorist John B. Watson (1925), thought that experience could write virtually any message on the blank slate of human nature: "Give me a dozen healthy infants, well-formed, and my own specified world to bring them up in and I'll guarantee to take any one at random and train him to become any type of specialist I might select—doctor, lawyer, artist, merchant-chief and yes, even beggar-man and thief, regardless of his talents, penchants, tendencies, abilities, vocations, and race of his ancestors."

Today, most psychologists have concluded that in the nature-nurture contest, there can be no clear winner. Findings in the interdisciplinary field of **behavior genetics** suggest that within a particular group, nervous system and biochemical differences may help account for variations in how people respond to their environments. But no psychological characteristic emerges full-blown from some genetic blueprint without environmental influence, any more than language appears in an infant reared in isolation.

One interaction of heredity with environment occurs when genetic factors affect how adults respond to children. For example, even modest genetic differences in intelligence may affect how parents treat their children. Slightly brighter children may get more educational toys and books (and a calculator and personal computer). Adults may prompt them to ask searching questions. Over time, these children's slight edge may grow into a larger one, as they themselves actively select environments that allow them to display their abilities. This selection process, of course, assumes that children have environments to select *from*. When a child's opportunities are limited, as they are for many poor and inner-city children, the environment may slam a lid on genetic potential instead of opening a door to it.

Because heredity and environment interact, neurological or other biological differences between people who perform intelligently and those who do not can be hard to interpret. A few years ago, a group of neuroanatomists looked at four tiny pieces of Albert Einstein's brain (Diamond et al., 1985). In one area, they found more glial cells per neuron than in control brains from 11 nongeniuses. (As we saw in Chapter 3, glial cells supply nutrients to neurons.) There were some problems with this study, but assuming the results are valid, how should we interpret them? Was Einstein smart because he had a lot of glial cells, or did his glial cells multiply because he "used his brain" more than other people?

Most neuropsychologists doubt that differences in intelligence are associated with the gross anatomy of the brain. It's more likely that the wiring of neural circuits, the amount or efficiency of neurotransmitters, or metabolism rates are what matter (Gazzaniga, 1988). For example, there is recent evidence, from studies using PET scans, that during certain intellectual tasks the brains of high performers are *less active* than those of low performers (Haier et al., 1988; Parks et al., 1988). As you can see in Figure 11.4, the brains of high performers metabolize glucose at a lower rate. A plausible explanation is that in high performers, fewer circuits are required for the task, or perhaps fewer neurons per circuit. What is not clear is whether a neurologically "efficient" brain is the cause or the result of superior performance (or both). Such biological differences may be encoded in the genes, but they may also develop as the result of experience and the acquisition of efficient ways of processing information. Indeed, in a recent study, when people were given an opportunity to practice a computer game over a period of several weeks, their glucose metabolism rates during the sessions gradually fell (Haier et al., 1992).

Because the origins of human diversity are complicated, so are the sections that follow—not only because heredity and environment interact, but also because attempts to unravel this interaction are fraught with problems of mea-

■ **behavior genetics**
An interdisciplinary field of study concerned with the genetic bases of behavior.

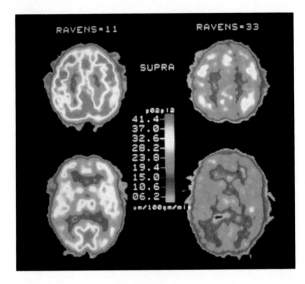

FIGURE 11.4
Intellect and brain activity
As this PET scan shows, during an abstract reasoning task the brains of high scorers (right) metabolized less glucose per minute than the brains of low scorers (left), suggesting that the brains of those who did well were working more efficiently (Haier, 1988).

surement, sampling, and interpretation. We want to alert you here that you will need to read these sections carefully. However, we feel it would be wrong to avoid or gloss over the complexities. Unsophisticated assumptions about nature and nurture can influence the formation of social and educational policies that affect millions of lives.

The Heritability Hunt

The first thing to understand about the nature-nurture issue is that no one can determine the impact of heredity on any *particular* individual's intellectual or emotional makeup. The reason lies partly in the mechanisms of inheritance.

Each person's genes are strung out on **chromosomes,** rod-shaped structures in the center of each body cell. In all cells except sperm and eggs, 46 chromosomes are lined up two by two, in 23 pairs, with each chromosome containing about 20,000 genes. Corresponding areas on each pair work together to determine a particular trait. When the body cells that produce sperm and eggs divide, one member of each original chromosome pair goes to one new sperm or egg, and the other member goes to the other new sperm or egg. Thus sperm and eggs contain 23 *unpaired* chromosomes. Chance alone decides which member of a chromosome pair goes to a particular sperm or egg. Mathematically, this means that each sperm- or egg-producing cell has the potential to produce over 8 million *different* chromosome combinations in a new sperm or egg. And the actual genetic diversity is even greater, because during the formation of a sperm or an egg, small segments of genetic material are apt to "cross over" (exchange places) between members of a chromosome pair before the final division.

The upshot is that although a parent and his or her offspring share, on the average, half their genes, each of us is the potential parent of billions of genetically *different* offspring (given the time and energy). In other words, each sperm or egg in your body contains a genetic mosaic different from the one in the sperm or egg that helped make you. Of course, each parent contributes one of billions of possible combinations to each child. Thus siblings (who also share, on the average, half their genes) can be quite unlike each other, and children can be unlike their parents, in purely *genetic* terms.

To say, then, that some trait is "genetic" does not mean that children will be just like their parents. It is true that a parent and child will be more alike in many ways than two unrelated people selected at random. It is also true that genes—half from the mother, half from the father—set limits on many human

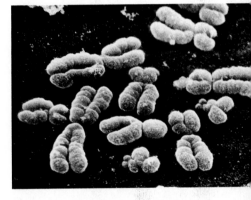

Human chromosomes, magnified almost 55,000 times.

■ **chromosomes**
The rod-shaped structures in the center of each body cell that carry the genes and determine hereditary characteristics.

attributes: anatomical sex, eye color, height range, shape of nose, color of skin. But *human diversity* is built into the way heredity works. Each of us, with the exception of identical twins, is a unique genetic hodgepodge, one that never existed before and never will again. That is why knowing a person's heredity does not automatically tell you what the person will be like.

What does it mean to say that some trait is "highly heritable"? If you want to improve your piccolo playing and someone tells you that musical ability is heritable, would you stop practicing?

Understanding Heritability

Although determining the influence of heredity and environment on a particular individual's behavior or personality is impossible, behavior geneticists *can* study the origins of differences *among* individuals. Their methods typically yield a statistical estimate of the *proportion of the total variance in a trait* that is attributable to *genetic variation* within a group. This estimate is known as the trait's **heritability,** and since it is expressed as a proportion, its maximum value is 1.0. Height is highly heritable; that is, within a group, most variation among individuals is accounted for by genetic differences. In contrast, table manners have low heritability because most variation among individuals is accounted for by differences in upbringing.

Many people have mistaken ideas about heritability. Because understanding the nature-nurture issue depends on understanding this concept, it is important that you know the facts:

1. *An estimate of heritability applies only to a particular group living in a particular environment.* Suppose that all the children in Rich County are affluent, eat plenty of high-quality food, and go to the same top-notch schools. The intellectual differences among them will probably be due largely to their genetic differences, because their environments are very similar and are optimal for intellectual development. In contrast, the children in Normal County are rich, poor, and in between. Some have good diets; others live on cupcakes. Some attend good schools; others go to miserable ones. These children's intellectual differences might well be due to their environmental differences, and for them, estimated heritability of intelligence will be lower.

2. *Heritability estimates do not apply to individuals, only to variations with a group.* Suppose researchers knew the heritability of gymnastics ability. That fact would *not* tell you whether your own gymnastics ability was due primarily to your genes, your motivation, or your training. The same applies to any trait.

3. *Even highly heritable traits can be modified by the environment.* Although height is highly heritable, malnourished children may not grow to be as tall as they would with sufficient food. Conversely, if children eat a super-nutritious diet, they may grow to be taller than anyone thought they could. The same principle applies to psychological traits, although some writers have failed to realize this. In a controversial paper, Arthur Jensen (1969) concluded that IQ and school achievement could not be boosted much because IQ is highly heritable. However, even if the second part of the statement is true, the first part does not necessarily follow.

4. *Heritable behavioral traits are usually influenced indirectly by many genes working in combination.* It is unlikely that any single gene confers musical talent, mathematical ability, or a sunny disposition. Nor do genes produce behavior directly; all genes actually do is encode instructions for the production of proteins, which in turn affect the structure and functioning of the body (including the nervous system), with potential implications for behavior. Knowing that genetics ultimately influences a behavior does not tell us what the *mechanism* of influence is—how biology interacts with the environment to promote or inhibit the behavior.

■ **heritability**
A statistical estimate of the proportion of the total variance in some trait within a group that is attributable to genetic differences among individuals within the group.

Clues from Adoption and Twin Studies

Scientists cannot estimate the heritability of human behavior by examining chromosomes directly under a microscope; they would not know what to look for. Nor, as we noted, can they estimate it from direct comparisons of brain or nervous system functioning. Instead, they must *infer* heritability by studying people whose degree of genetic similarity is known. This task is not easy.

The simplest approach might seem to be a comparison of blood relatives within families. Everyone knows of families that are famous for some talent or trait. But anecdotes and isolated examples can always be answered with counterexamples. There were seven generations of musical Bachs, but Mendelssohn's father was a banker, Chopin's a bookkeeper, and Schubert's a schoolmaster, and their mothers were not known to have musical talent (Lewontin, 1982). Results from controlled studies of families are also inconclusive, for close relatives usually share environments as well as genes. If Carlo's parents and siblings all love lasagna, that doesn't mean a taste for lasagna is heritable. The same applies if everyone in Carlo's family has a high IQ, is mentally ill, or is moody.

There are two ways out of this bind. One is to study adopted children. Such children share half their genes (but not their environment) with each birth parent. On the other hand, they share an environment (but not their genes) with their adoptive parents and adoptive siblings. Researchers can compare correlations between the children's traits and those of their biological and adoptive relatives and use the results to estimate heritability.

The other approach is to compare **identical (monozygotic) twins** and **fraternal (dizygotic) twins.** Identical twins are created when a fertilized egg divides into two parts that then develop into two separate embryos. Since the twins come from the same fertilized egg, they share all their genes, barring genetic mutations or accidents. (They may be slightly different at birth, however, because of birth complications or differences in the blood supply to the two fetuses.) In contrast, fraternal twins develop when a woman's ovaries release two eggs instead of one, and each egg is fertilized by a different sperm. Fraternal twins are wombmates, but they are no more alike genetically than any other two siblings and may be of different sexes. By comparing groups of same-sex fraternal twins to groups of identical twins, psychologists can estimate heritability. The basic assumption is that if identical twins are more alike than fraternal twins, the increased similarity must be genetic.

Perhaps, however, environments shared by identical twins differ from those shared by fraternal twins. People may treat identical twins as more alike or go to the other extreme by emphasizing their differences. To avoid such problems, investigators have studied identical twins who were separated early in life and

■ **identical (monozygotic) twins**
Twins born when a fertilized egg divides into two parts that develop into separate embryos.

■ **fraternal (dizygotic) twins**
Twins that develop from two separate eggs fertilized by different sperm. They are no more alike genetically than any two siblings.

Some identical twins, like these sisters, love to accentuate their similarities. To psychologists, the similarities—and differences—between twins are important for what they can tell us about heritability.

reared apart. (Until recently, adoption policies and attitudes toward illegitimacy permitted such separation to occur.) Although rare, such cases are numerous enough to study. In theory, separated identical twins share all their genes but not their environments. Any similarities between them should be genetic and should permit a direct estimate of heritability.

Past studies of twins reared apart had some serious flaws. Most twins "reared apart" had not been so far apart after all. Many had visited one another during childhood or were reared by relatives in the same town or went to the same school. Of the 121 sets studied between 1922 and 1973, only 3 were strangers at the time of study. Also, judgments of similarity were typically based on only a few tests, self-reports, or casual observations, and there were other methodological problems as well (Farber, 1981).

Recent research on twins has corrected many of these problems. In one project, begun in 1979, an interdisciplinary team at the University of Minnesota has been testing and interviewing identical and fraternal twins reared apart (Bouchard, 1984; Bouchard et al., 1990; Tellegen et al., 1988). Subjects undergo six days of comprehensive psychological and medical monitoring and answer some 15,000 written questions. By 1990, information had been reported on over 80 sets of reunited twins, and also on many other twins reared together.

Results from this and other behavior–genetic studies suggest that variations in intelligence (as measured by IQ tests) are partly heritable. In most studies, estimates of heritability average between .47 and .58. That is, between 47 and 58 percent of the variance in IQ scores is explainable by genetic factors (Plomin, 1989). We want to be careful not to oversimplify. Estimates for specific mental abilities differ: Those for verbal ability tend to be high, those for memory are very low, and the results for spatial ability and perceptual speed are inconsistent (Thompson, Detterman, & Plomin, 1991). Even for general IQ scores, heritability estimates range widely, from as low as .10 to almost .90 (see Figure 11.5). However, in nearly all studies, scores of identical twins are more highly correlated than those of fraternal twins. In fact, the scores of identical twins reared apart are more highly correlated than those of fraternal twins reared together. In adoption studies, the scores of adopted children are more highly correlated with those of their birth parents than with those of their adoptive parents, and by adolescence, the scores of adopted children are correlated only weakly with those of their biologically unrelated adoptive siblings (Plomin, 1988).

Separated at birth, the Mallifert twins meet accidentally.

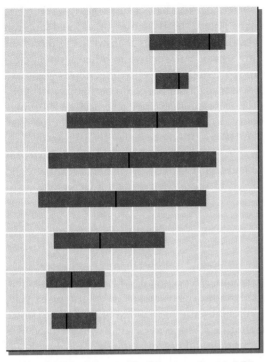

FIGURE 11.5

Family resemblances in IQ
The heritability of intelligence is hard to estimate with precision, for reasons explained in the text. This chart is based on a survey of studies on IQ correlations for biological and adoptive relatives (Bouchard & McGue, 1981). The bars show the range of correlations found by various studies. The vertical line on each bar indicates the average correlation for each type of comparison. On the average, the higher the proportion of genes family members have in common, the more highly correlated their IQ scores are, indicating that differences in hereditary contribute to differences in intelligence. However, as you can see, the exact estimates vary considerably, depending on the study.

Of course, if heredity accounts for only part of why people differ in their scores on mental tests, the environment (and random errors in measurement) must account for the rest. In the next section we will see what this might mean.

QUICK QUIZ

1. Diane hears that a particular ability is highly heritable and concludes that her low performance must be due mostly to genes. What's wrong with her reasoning?
2. Bertram reads that an ability is highly heritable in adults and concludes that schools should stop trying to instill the ability in those who seem low in it. What's wrong with his reasoning?
3. Carpentry skills seem to "run" in Andy's family. Why shouldn't Andy conclude that this talent is genetic?
4. Estimates of the heritability of intelligence based on twin and adoption studies (a) put heritability at about .90, (b) show heritability to be low, (c) average a little over .50.

ANSWERS:
1. Heritability applies only to differences among individuals within a group, not to particular individuals. 2. A trait may be highly heritable *and* susceptible to modification. 3. Family members share environments as well as genes. 4. c

---

■ ENVIRONMENTAL ORIGINS OF MENTAL ABILITIES

A leading behavior geneticist observes, "The wave of acceptance of genetic influence on behavior is growing into a tidal wave that threatens to engulf the second message of this research: These same data provide the best available evidence for the importance of environmental influences" (Plomin, 1989).

Adoption studies show how environment can have a large impact even when heritability is fairly high. As we have noted, the IQ scores of adopted children correlate more highly with their birth parents' scores than with those of their adoptive parents. That is, if Johnny scores high relative to other adopted children, his birth parents are likely to score high relative to other adults who have put their children up for adoption. This fact supports the heritability of intelligence as measured by IQ tests. However, in *absolute* terms, Johnny's IQ may differ considerably from the scores of his birth parents. Indeed, on the average, adopted children have IQs that are 10 to 20 points *higher* than those of their birth parents (Scarr & Weinberg, 1977). Most psychologists believe that this difference exists because adoptive families are generally smaller, wealthier, and better educated than other families, and these environmental factors are associated with high IQs in children.

The Forge of Experience

The influence of the environment on mental ability begins even before birth, in the silent "environment" of the womb. If a pregnant woman is malnourished, contracts certain infections, takes certain drugs, smokes or drinks excessively, or is exposed to environmental pollutants, the fetus's development may suffer (see Chapter 13). All of these circumstances are associated with reduced IQs and an increased incidence of learning disabilities in children.

Many factors are thought to affect mental ability *after* birth. Several have been implicated in the lower IQ scores of children from poor and working-class families, as compared with those from middle-class families.

• *Nutrition.* Early malnutrition slows brain growth and mental development (Stoch & Smythe, 1963; Winick, Meyer, & Harris, 1975). The average IQ gap between severely malnourished and well-nourished children can be as high as 20 points.

• *Exposure to toxins.* Children exposed to toxins such as lead, which can damage the nervous system, have lower IQ scores and more attention problems than other children (Needleman, Leviton, & Bellinger, 1982). Exposure to high levels of lead in early childhood is associated later on, in adolescence, with low vocabulary and grammatical reasoning scores, slow reaction times, poor hand-eye coordination, and low reading scores, even after various confounding factors are taken into account (Needleman et al., 1990). House paint no longer contains lead, but poor children often live in old, run-down buildings with peeling, lead-based paint.

• *Mental stimulation.* Dozens of animal studies show that a stimulating environment actually alters the structure of the brain. Rats that learn complicated tasks or grow up in cages equipped with lots of rat toys develop thicker and heavier cortexes and richer networks of synaptic connections in certain brain areas than do rats in unchallenging environments (Greenough & Anderson, 1991; Greenough & Black, 1992; Rosenzweig, 1984).

It is likely that stimulation is important in human mental development, as well. A recent study examined nearly a thousand premature infants who, because of their prematurity, were at risk for delayed development. A combination of intensive educational efforts, home visits by specialists, and training of parents about how to stimulate cognitive and social development through games and other activities resulted in an average IQ score at age 3 that was significantly higher than that of a control group (Infant Health and Development Program, 1990). These results are especially impressive because the children were assigned randomly to the two groups, the testers were unaware of which group the children were in, and the children came from a variety of income levels and ethnic origins.

The children of migrant workers (left) often spend long hours in backbreaking field work, and may miss out on the educational opportunities and intellectual advantages available to middle-class children (right).

• *Family size.* The average IQ in a family tends to decline as the number of children rises (Belmont & Marolla, 1973). Birth order also makes a difference: IQ tends to decline slightly in each successive child (Zajonc & Markus, 1975). Most researchers attribute these facts to the reduced time parents with many children can spend with each child.

• *Individual experiences.* General environmental factors, such as parents' education or social class, do not explain why siblings who grow up in the same household often have different interests and talents. Increasingly, psychologists are recognizing how individual experiences that are not necessarily shared with other family members, such as having an inspiring teacher, being favored or not favored by a parent, or winning a prize in a science fair, can affect a child's aptitudes and achievements (Dunn & Plomin, 1990).

• *Stressful family circumstances.* In a project known as the Rochester Longitudinal Study, researchers have been tracking several hundred children from birth through early adolescence, and have correlated a number of "family risk factors" with the children's intellectual competence and general adjustment (Sameroff et al., 1987; Sameroff & Seifer, 1989). These factors include, among others, a father who does not live with the family, a mother with a history of mental illness, low parental work skills, and a history of stressful events during the child's early life. On average, each such risk factor reduces a child's IQ score by 4 points. Children with no risk factors score more than *30 points higher* than those with seven or eight risk factors (see Figure 11.6).

• *Parent-child interactions.* In general, children who score well on IQ tests have parents who actively encourage their development. Such parents spend time with their children; encourage them to think things through; provide

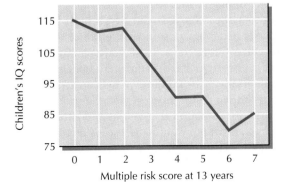

FIGURE 11.6

Family risk factors and children's IQ scores
The greater the number of stressful family circumstances, the lower a child's IQ score is likely to be (Sameroff & Seifer, 1989). An enormous gap exists between the average IQ score of children with no family risk factors and the scores of those with many, as you can see from this graph.

appropriate toys, books, and field trips; and expect them to do well (Bee et al., 1982; Bradley & Caldwell, 1984). They talk to them about objects and people and describe things accurately and fully (Clarke-Stewart, VanderStoep, & Killian, 1979; Dickson et al., 1979). Most important, their reactions to their children are tied directly to what the children do (Beckwith & Cohen, 1984). By answering their children's questions and responding to their actions, such parents give their children a sense of competence and teach them that their efforts matter.

These kinds of parenting skills can be explicitly taught. In one study of 30 middle-class parents and their toddlers, parents learned during a one-hour training session to ask open-ended questions when reading to their offspring ("What is the cat doing?") instead of merely asking the children to point out objects or answer yes-no type questions ("Is the cat asleep?"). The parents also learned to expand on the child's answers, provide alternative responses, correct inaccurate responses, and give plenty of praise. Parents in a control group read just as often to their children, but did not get the special instruction. All reading sessions were tape-recorded for later analysis. At the end of the study, which lasted only a month, the children in the experimental group were eight-and-a-half months ahead of those in the control group in their expressive language skills and six months ahead in vocabulary skills (Whitehurst et al., 1988).

Many people think that "IQ" is something about a person that can never change. In fact, IQ scores often change considerably over the entire span of childhood (McCall, Appelbaum, & Hogarty, 1973). Changes in environmental circumstances—some intended, some not—probably help explain why.

Group Differences in Intelligence

So far, we have considered intellectual differences only within a group of individuals. Throughout this century, researchers have also wondered about the origins of differences between groups. Unfortunately, the history of this research has been marred by racial, ethnic, class, and gender biases. Too often, in the words of paleontologist Stephen Jay Gould (1981), interpretations have been bent to support the belief that certain groups are destined by "the harsh dictates of nature" to be subordinate to others. (For more on this issue, see "Think About It" on page 404.)

In North America, most of the interest in group differences has focused on black-white differences in IQ. Black children score, on average, some 10 to 15 points lower on IQ tests than do white children. (We are talking about *averages*; the distribution of scores for black and white children overlap considerably.) A few psychologists argue for a genetic explanation of this difference (Jensen, 1969, 1981; Rushton, 1988). However, a serious problem with such theories is that they use heritability estimates based on white samples to estimate the role heredity plays in group differences. This problem sounds pretty technical, but it is not too difficult to understand, so stay with us.

Consider, first, not people but tomatoes. Suppose you have a bag of tomato seeds that vary genetically; all things being equal, some will produce tomatoes that are puny and tasteless, some will produce tomatoes that are plump and delicious. Now you take a bunch of seeds in your left hand and a bunch in your right. Though one seed differs genetically from another, there is no *average* difference between the seeds in your left hand and those in your right. Now you plant the left hand's seeds in pot A with some soil that you have doctored with nitrogen and other nutrients, and you plant the right hand's seeds in pot B with soil from which you have extracted nutrients. When the tomatoes grow, they will vary in size *within* each pot, purely because of genetic differences. But there

Poor soil   Rich soil

FIGURE 11.7

The tomato plant experiment
Even if the differences among plants within each pot were due entirely to genetic differences, the average difference between *pots could be entirely environmental. As the text explains, the same principle applies to individual and group differences among human beings.*

will also be an average difference between pot A and pot B. This difference *between* pots is due entirely to the different soils—even though the *within*-pot heritability is 100 percent. (This "thought experiment" is illustrated in Figure 11.7 and is based on Lewontin, 1970.)

The principle is the same for people as it is for tomatoes. Most psychologists believe that differences *within* groups, such as whites or blacks, are at least partly genetic. But that does not mean that differences *between* groups are genetic. Blacks and whites do not grow up, on the average, in the same environment. Because of a long legacy of racial discrimination, black children (as well as Hispanic and other minority children) often receive far fewer "nutrients"— in terms of education, encouragement by society, and opportunities.

One sure way to settle the question of inherent racial differences would be to gather IQ information on blacks and whites raised in exactly the same circumstances. This task is nearly impossible at present in the United States. However, we know that in the past few decades, as economic, social, political, and educational opportunities have opened up to black Americans, the performance of black children on scholastic achievement and aptitude tests has climbed considerably, and black-white differences have shrunk (L. Jones, 1984). Further, the handful of studies that have overcome past methodological problems fail to reveal any genetic differences between blacks and whites in whatever it is that IQ tests measure (Lewontin, 1982; Mackenzie, 1984). Consider:

• Children fathered by black and white American soldiers in Germany after World War II, and reared in similar German communities by similar families, did not differ significantly in IQ (Eyferth, 1961).

• Black and interracial children adopted during their first year by white families with above-average incomes and education score 10 to 20 points higher on IQ tests than black children being reared in the black community. Their performance on vocabulary and reading achievement tests is somewhat higher than the national average, and is generally comparable to that of other adopted

THINK ABOUT IT

Intolerance and IQ

A hammer is a tool that can be used to build a house or bash a head. Mental tests are tools, too. They can be used to foster the growth of individuals or promote prejudices, depending on whose hands they are in.

Scientists are not immune to the prejudices of their times. Although many, if not most, early testers rejected (or at least were skeptical of) efforts to rank ethnic, racial, or socioeconomic groups, some eminent individuals let prejudice cloud their judgment. One such individual was H. H. Goddard, a leading educator and advocate of mental testing. Goddard believed that low intelligence and poor character were inherited and that "undesirables" should be prevented from having children. In one study, he gave IQ tests to a group of newly arrived immigrants at Ellis Island (Goddard, 1917). Most of these people knew little or no English. Many could not read or write their own language. Yet no sooner did they get off the boat after a long and tiring journey than they found themselves taking the Binet IQ test. The results: 83 percent of the Jews, 80 percent of the Hungarians, 79 percent of the Italians, and 87 percent of the Russians scored as "feeble-minded," with a mental age lower than 12. Goddard acknowledged that environmental depriva-tion might explain these results, but he did not recognize that the results themselves had no validity, given the conditions under which they were obtained.

A more ambitious study of IQ was done during World War I. One and a half million soldiers took either the Army Alpha test (a verbal test) or the Army Beta test (a nonverbal test)—the first mass-produced intelligence tests in America. The purpose was to eliminate feeble-minded recruits and determine who should become an officer. To everyone's astonishment, the average mental age of white men was only 13, just a notch above the "moron" level. Blacks and eastern and southern Europeans scored even lower on the average. Many citizens of northern European ancestry concluded that the nation's intelligence was declining. They blamed this decline on the influx of new immigrants and their "breeding habits."

These citizens were, among other things, over-looking the abominable conditions under which the tests were given. Testing rooms were crowded and poorly lit. Some men could not hear the instructions, which in any case were confusing, and many simply refused to answer. Although many of the men had little or no education, or were recent immigrants, a high proportion of the items assumed schooling or experience with middle-class American culture. For instance:

The number of a Kaffir's legs is: 2, 4, 6, 8.

Christy Mathewson is famous as a: writer, artist, baseball player, comedian.

Washington is to Adams as first is to. . . .

children reared in an environment that fosters the particular skills emphasized in schools and on IQ tests (Scarr & Weinberg, 1976; Weinberg, Scarr, & Waldman, 1992).

• Degree of African ancestry (which can be roughly estimated from skin color, blood analysis, and genealogy) is not related to measured intelligence, as a genetic theory of black-white differences would predict (Scarr et al., 1977).

In recent years, researchers have been trying to pin down more precisely just how environmental factors influence the intellectual development of children from various ethnicities and races. One approach focuses on parent-child interactions. For example, Elsie Moore (1986) looked at black children adopted by either black or white middle-class couples. She found that the children in the black families had normal IQ scores, but their average score (104) was lower than that of children adopted by the white families (117). Moore then analyzed mother-child interactions while the children were working on a difficult problem from an IQ test. The mothers in Moore's sample were all loving parents, and all wanted their children to do well. However, the white mothers, perhaps because they were less anxious about their children's performance, were more

How well did you do on these items? ("Kaffir" is a derogatory term used by white South Africans for blacks—so a Kaffir has two legs. Christy Mathewson was a baseball player. We are not sure about the third item: The answer could be "second," since Washington was the first U.S. president and John Adams was the second, but it could also be "sixth," since John Quincy Adams was the sixth president.) When Stephen Jay Gould gave the Army Alpha to his students at Harvard University, more than 10 percent earned scores low enough to have kept them buck privates during World War I (Gould, 1981).

A more recent instance of bias, one that came to light in the 1970s and created a scientific scandal, involved Sir Cyril Burt, a renowned British psychologist. For three decades, beginning in the early 1940s, Burt collected IQ data on twins reared apart. He concluded that intelligence is almost entirely genetic and cannot be modified. Burt also believed there were innate differences between races and classes. His views influenced the British to adopt a system in which test scores at age 11 determined whether a child could pursue academic studies or had to enroll in vocational training instead.

After Burt's death in 1971, American psychologist Leon Kamin reanalyzed his data. Kamin (1974) found errors that no beginning psychology student would make. Sample sizes were reported differently in different papers or not at all. Test scores were "adjusted," or merely *estimated* on the basis of subjective impressions. Research procedures were vague or unreported. Kamin also noticed that correlations computed from different samples of twins agreed again and again to the third decimal place. These results seemed too precise to be true, and in fact, they weren't. Further investigation showed that at least some of Burt's studies were sheer fiction. He had made up the twins, the test scores, and even the names of nonexistent collaborators (Hearnshaw, 1979). (Naturally, we have not included Burt's studies among those discussed in this chapter.)

Today, psychologists are more sophisticated about the nature of prejudice. But psychologist R. J. Herrnstein (1982) argues that egalitarians are as biased as racists ever were. Flaws in the studies of environmentalists, says Herrnstein, are overlooked or rationalized. Anyone who takes a strong hereditarian view, or who mentions racial or ethnic differences in test data, he says, is branded a racist or an elitist.

The political nature of the IQ controversy raises some hard questions about both society and science. Why have scientists and nonscientists alike been so concerned about group differences in IQ for so many decades? Does this concern threaten social harmony and promote class and racial bias? Should scientists consider the political ramifications of their research, or should they leave that problem to others? Finally, once we have research on an issue as explosive as group differences in ability, how can we determine which social implications are justified by the results and which are not?

What do you think?

likely to smile, joke, applaud a child's efforts ("Gee, that's an interesting idea"), and help their children with general hints rather than specific instructions, and they were less likely to express displeasure with the child's progress. These results suggest that cultural and ethnic differences in child-rearing styles and parental reactions to testing may be related to children's performance on IQ tests, although many other factors (friends, subtle and overt discrimination, teacher's expectations) are important as well.

Cultural differences may also help explain disparities in intellectual performance between children in Asian countries and those in the United States. In Japan, IQ scores of children have been rising since World War II, and the average IQ of Japanese children is now the highest in the world (Lynn, 1982). The rise is probably due to in part to an improved educational system, urbanization, better health, and greater exposure to Western culture, which originally created IQ tests. But the attitudes, beliefs, and expectations of adults probably also play a part, both in IQ test performance and children's school achievement.

In one recent project, Harold Stevenson and his colleagues (1990a, 1990b) examined attitudes and beliefs about mathematics ability among parents and teachers of first- and fifth-graders from 20 schools in Chicago and 11 schools in Beijing, China. On the average, the American children's parents were far better off financially than the parents of the Chinese children, and they were better educated as well. Nevertheless, the Chinese children far outperformed the American children on a broad battery of mathematical tests. On both computations and word problems, there was virtually no overlap between schools, with the lowest-scoring Beijing schools doing better than the highest-scoring Chicago schools! These differences could not be accounted for by educational resources: The Chinese had worse facilities and larger classes. Nor could they be accounted for by differences in the children's fondness for math: 85 percent of the Chinese kids said they liked math, but so did almost 75 percent of the American children. What did set the Chinese and Americans apart, among other things, were their attitudes and beliefs. For example:

• The American parents had far lower standards for performance. They said they would be satisfied with scores barely above average on a 100-point test, and most felt their children were doing fine in math. In contrast, the Chinese parents said they would be happy only with very high scores, and fewer than half were satisfied with their children's performance.

• American parents and children generally believed that innate mathematical ability is as important as effort. This is the sort of belief that can lead people to think that if you "have it" you don't have to work hard, and if you don't have it, there's no point in trying. In contrast, Chinese parents and teachers believed that with hard work any child can succeed in math.

• The American children were more complacent about their own performance. More than half believed themselves to be above average or "among the best" in math, compared to only 39 percent of the Chinese children. When asked what they would wish for if a wizard could give them anything they wanted, more than 60 percent of the Chinese children named something related to their education. Can you guess what the American children wanted? A majority said money or material possessions.

Comparisons of American parents and children with their counterparts in Japan and Taiwan have produced similar results (Stevenson, 1990b). Parents' attitudes, therefore, probably help account for certain group differences in test scores. We want to point out, however, that parents who are not adept at promoting one type of mental skill may do an excellent job of encouraging skills that are missed by formal tests and ignored in the classroom. Moreover, when a child's abilities don't match those expected by teachers and testers, the best solution may be to "fix" not just the child, but the classroom or the test as well.

Anthropologist Shirley Brice Heath (1983) has described how this approach can work. In a study of a small black community in a southern American city, Heath found that black parents were less likely than white parents to ask their children "what," "where," "when," and "who" questions—the sorts of questions found on standardized tests and in schoolbooks ("What's this story about?" "Who is this?"). However, the black parents did ask analogy questions ("What's that like?") and story-starter questions ("Did you hear about . . ."). Teachers in the community took this information and used it to modify their teaching strategies. They encouraged their black pupils to ask "school-type" questions, but they also incorporated analogy and story-starter questions into their lessons. Soon the black children, who had previously been uncomfortable and quiet in school, became eager, confident participants.

Heath (1989) notes that traditional rural and small-town black communities have a rich linguistic tradition, one that emphasizes negotiation, flexible role playing, verbal wit, nuances of meaning, striking metaphors, rapid-fire dialogue, and unexpected analogies. In this tradition, adults ask children many questions, but only *real* questions, to which the adults do not know the answers. Adults expect youngsters to *show* what they know rather than *tell* what they know. Schools, however, do not take advantage of black children's strengths. Instead, says Heath, they typically train children only to give the "right" answers, and they treat literacy as a set of mechanistic operations.

Intelligence, then, can't be evaluated apart from the context in which it occurs. Any child will seem to be unintelligent if the child must maneuver in a world that he or she knows little about or that does not capitalize on what the child already knows.

QUICK QUIZ

1. True or false: If a trait is highly heritable within a group, then between-group differences in the trait must be due to genetics.
2. According to a German study, when black children and white children are reared in similar environments, their IQ scores are _____.
3. Name at least four environmental factors that affect mental abilities.
✳ 4. A researcher studying ethnic differences in children's mental abilities focuses on one group's lower performance in school. Can you think of a research question that might lead to a different view of these children's intellectual competence?

ANSWERS:

1. false 2. similar 3. nutrition, exposure to toxins, mental stimulation, family size, family circumstances and attitudes, parent-child interactions 4. One possibility is: What kinds of mental skills and abilities have these children developed that help them function in their communities and in the world outside of school?

■ INTELLECTUAL DIFFERENCES AND REAL LIFE

Group differences aside, it is clear that *individuals* within groups differ intellectually, for both genetic and environmental reasons. What impact do these differences have on their success in life?

Higher IQ scores do contribute to occupational success and job performance. Unusual talents, too, may give some people an edge. When you look at the lives of certain geniuses, it is hard not to conclude that they were wired somewhat differently from the rest of us. Mozart, whose father pushed him to develop his musical talents, played the harpsichord at 3 and wrote his first composition before he was 7. If you surround your son with music and hire a music teacher for him when he is 2, will he promptly become another Mozart? Probably not.

However, within most occupations there is a wide range of IQs, and the correlation between IQ and job performance is weaker than you might imagine—about .2 (Wigdor & Garner, 1982). Further, IQ does not necessarily *cause* occupational success. Geneticist Richard Lewontin (1982) notes that if you look only at people with a given IQ—say, 100—*schooling* predicts later income and occupational status quite accurately. One reason IQ predicts income is that people with high IQ scores tend to get more education than others do; a high IQ score opens the doors to opportunity. The same is true for socioeconomic background. A man with an IQ of 100 who comes from an upper-class family is seven-and-a-half times more likely to earn a high income than a man with an IQ of 100 who comes from a lower-class family. As Lewontin puts it, "If [IQ] tests do measure intrinsic intelligence, as they are claimed to do, then one can only conclude that it is better to be born rich than smart."

✳ *You are thinking of hiring someone who has a very high IQ. How much confidence in the person's ability would that IQ score inspire? What other aspects of the person and of the job would you consider?*

What else is it better to be? To find out, researchers have been looking at some forms of intelligence not captured by conventional IQ tests.

Everyday Intelligence

Psychologist Seymour Sarason tells of reporting for his first job, which was giving IQ tests at a school for the mentally retarded. Upon arriving, he learned that all of the students had escaped! When they were eventually rounded up and Sarason began to test them, he found that most could not do even the first problem. Yet these same students had outsmarted the school authorities by escaping, at least temporarily (in Sternberg, 1988). They might have low IQs, but they had a sort of *practical intelligence*.

Practical intelligence also reveals itself in the ordinary behavior of average citizens. For example, a study at a racetrack found that successful handicappers used an exceedingly complicated statistical method to predict winners. This ability was *not* related to the handicappers' IQs (Ceci & Liker, 1986). Another study found that shoppers in a supermarket can somehow select the best buy even when they cannot do the formal mathematical computations that would allow them to compare two items (Lave, Murtaugh, & de la Roche, 1984).

On the job, practical intelligence is what allows you to pick up "tacit knowledge"—strategies for success that usually are not formally taught. In studies of college professors, business managers, and salespeople, scores on tests of tacit knowledge do not correlate strongly with conventional ability-test scores, but they do predict effectiveness on the job fairly well (Sternberg, Wagner, & Okagaki, in 1993).

Findings like these support the idea that intelligence comes in many varieties. Howard Gardner (1983) suggests that there are actually seven independent "intelligences," or talents. They are *linguistic, logical-mathematical, spatial, musical,* and *bodily-kinesthetic intelligence* (which mimes, actors, athletes, and dancers have), *insight into oneself,* and *understanding of others.* Standard intelligence tests measure only the first three.

Gardner's last two "intelligences" correspond roughly to what some theorists call *emotional intelligence.* To some people, emotional intelligence may seem to be a contradiction in terms. Not so, argue Peter Salovey and John Mayer (1990; Mayer & Salovey, 1993). It is important, they note, for people to be able to identify their own and other people's emotions accurately, express emotions clearly, and regulate emotions in themselves and others. People who are low in

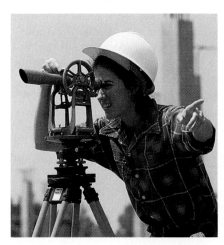

Intelligence is more than what IQ tests measure. A rock star has musical intelligence, a surveyor has spatial intelligence, and a compassionate friend has emotional intelligence.

emotional intelligence are chronically confused about their own emotions (insisting that they're not angry, for example, while shouting and slamming doors). Or they consistently misread nonverbal signals from others (insisting, for example, on giving a long-winded account of all their problems even though the listener is obviously bored).

People with high emotional intelligence can use their emotions in adaptive ways, to motivate themselves and others or spur creative thinking. Such people are likely to appear warm and genuine to others. People low in emotional intelligence appear boorish and insensitive. They may be slaves to their emotions and have trouble planning a life that is emotionally fulfilling. One study with over a thousand children found that although difficulty in interpreting nonverbal emotional signals from others was not related to IQ, it was related to low academic achievement, especially in boys. The researchers suggest that children who misread emotional cues from their teachers and classmates have trouble learning because they feel anxious and confused (Nowicki & Duke, 1989).

Emotional and practical intelligence are probably both aspects of what Sternberg (1988) calls contextual intelligence—skills that enable you to adapt to situations, change situations, or, if the first two strategies don't work, get out of situations. Contextual intelligence determines whether thinking skills are translated into intelligent action in everyday life.

People with emotional intelligence are skilled at reading nonverbal emotional cues. Which of these boys do you think feels the cockiest, and which is most fearful? What cues are you using to answer?

Motivation and the Mind

You could have a high IQ, be talented and popular, and generally "know your way around," but without one more quality, you might still fall short of your own and other people's expectations. That quality is motivation.

Consider some findings from one of the longest-running psychological studies ever conducted. Since 1921, researchers at Stanford University have been following 1,528 people with childhood IQ scores in the top 1 percent of the distribution. As children, these subjects were nicknamed "Termites," after Lewis Terman, who originally directed the research. At the start of their lives, the Termites were not only bright, but also physically healthy, sociable, and well adjusted. As the group entered adulthood, most became quite successful (Sears & Barbee, 1977; R. Sears, 1977; Terman & Oden, 1959). However, some of these gifted individuals failed to live up to their early promise, dropping out of school or drifting into low-level work. When the researchers compared the 100 most successful men in the Stanford study with the 100 least successful, they found that motivation made the difference. The successful men were ambitious, were socially active, had many interests, and were encouraged by their parents. The least successful drifted casually through life. There was *no* average difference in IQ between the two groups.

In another study, a team of educational researchers headed by Benjamin Bloom (1985) interviewed 120 of America's top artists, athletes, and scholars, along with their families and teachers, to find out what had made them so successful. The research team expected to hear tales of extraordinary natural talent. Instead, they heard tales of extraordinary dedication. The concert pianists had practiced several hours a day for years. A typical swimmer would tell of rising early every morning to swim for two hours before school started. Drive and determination were what led to the top.

Not everyone wishes to work in a competitive occupation or reach the top of a field. Career achievement carries a high price, and it is certainly not the only path to satisfaction and fulfillment. But clearly, many people's talents go untapped because they are not encouraged and trained. Talent, unlike cream, does not automatically rise to the top. That is the point of the old joke: A young man walking down a New York street asks an old woman, "How do I get to Carnegie Hall?" Her reply: "Practice, young man. Practice."

■ THE CASE FOR HUMAN DIVERSITY

This chapter opened with a simple question: How do nature and nurture produce the many differences among us? We have seen that the answer is not so simple. Statistical estimates of the extent to which differences are "heritable" or "environmental" do not tell us how heredity and environment interact to produce the unique mixture of qualities that make up a human being. Each of us is, in a sense, more than the sum of the individual influences on us. Once these influences become a part of us, they blend and become indistinguishable. A geneticist, a neurobiologist, and a psychologist offer this analogy:

> Think . . . of the baking of a cake: the taste of the product is the result of a complex interaction of components—such as butter, sugar, and flour—exposed for various periods to elevated temperatures; it is not dissociable into such-or-such a percent of flour, such-or-such of butter, etc., although each and every component . . . has its contribution to make to the final product. (Lewontin, Rose, & Kamin, 1984, p. 11)

The "cake" that is a person is never done. Each moment a slightly different self interacts with a slightly different environment. We can no more speak of genes, or of the environment, *causing* personality than we can speak of butter, sugar, or flour individually *causing* the taste of a cake. Yet we do speak that way. Why? Perhaps out of a desire to make things clearer than they are. Sometimes to justify prejudices about race or class.

Nature, however, loves diversity. Biologists agree that the "fitness" of any species depends on this diversity. If members of a species were all alike, with exactly the same strengths and weaknesses, the species could not survive a major change in the physical or social environment. With diversity, at least some members have a good chance of survival.

When we broaden the definition of intelligence, we see that each of us has something valuable to contribute to the world, whether it is artistic talent, academic ability, creativity, social skill, athletic prowess, a sense of humor, mechanical aptitude, practical wisdom, a social conscience, or the energy to get things done. The challenge, for any society, is to promote the potential of every citizen.

As Sternberg (1986) says: "We must never lose sight of the fact that what really matters in the world is not the level of our intelligence but what we achieve with this intelligence." In other words, it's not what you've got; it's what you do with it.

TAKING PSYCHOLOGY WITH YOU

Getting Smart

"Too soon old," goes an old Yiddish complaint, "and too late smart." Yet in truth, it is never too late to get smart, or at least a little smarter. In his book *Intelligence Applied*, Robert Sternberg (1986) wryly observes that people "can come into the world with some of the best intellectual gifts heredity has to offer, or they can be brought up in a highly advanced environment . . . and they

can still routinely make a mess of their lives." Such people have failed to get past certain obstacles on the road to intelligent behavior. But Sternberg and many other researchers believe these obstacles can be overcome.

Intelligence involves many things—encoding problems, noticing similarities and differences, spotting fallacies, and "reading" the environment, including other people. You might want to take a course or buy a book on thinking, to get some practice in these skills. But there are also some general guidelines to intelligent behavior that go beyond specific skills. Here are five of them. They may not turn you into a genius, but they can make you smarter.

• *Ask questions; don't be afraid to look a little ignorant.* You'll recognize this one as the first of our critical thinking guidelines from Chapter 1, but we think it's worth repeating. The smartest people are those who know what they don't know, and set about remedying the situation. Nobel Prize–winning physicist Isidor Rabi once recalled how most of the mothers in the immigrant neighborhood of his youth would ask their children the standard question, "So? Did you learn anything today?" But *his* mother always asked, "Izzy, did you ask a good question today?" (cited in Schulman, 1991).

Asking questions isn't important just for scientists; it opens a doorway to understanding in all areas of life, whether you're a factory worker or a physicist. There are many places to go for answers: libraries, counselors, teachers. However, we know that in a typical classroom setting, there are many psychological impediments to asking questions. One is feeling stupid or insecure. Another, common in some cultures, is the belief that it is impolite or inappropriate to speak up. If you have trouble asking questions publicly in class about something you really want to know, don't give up; speak to your teacher privately or write a note.

• *Don't be complacent.* You need self-confidence if you are to perform well academically and in the rest of your life; otherwise you may let a fear of failure prevent you from tackling difficult problems and taking some risks. But some people can be *over*confident, as we saw earlier in this chapter in our discussion of American children's math abilities. Complacency can prevent people from recognizing what they don't know and need to learn. Highly intelligent people are often more aware of their own ignorance than are less intelligent ones. Richard Feynman, another Nobel Prize winner in physics, was once asked by a TV viewer what he really wanted to know. After a pause, Feynman replied, "Everything" (in Schulman, 1991).

• *Seek support from others.* Social observers have often noted that American culture tends to be anti-intellectual. In some families and peer groups, a person who studies hard or has intellectual interests is ridiculed as a "nerd" or a show-off. Women may be made to feel that high academic aspirations are unfeminine: A recent study of women at two southern schools found that cultural and peer pressures caused many young women who started college with high ambitions to leave with the single goal of catching the right husband (Holland & Eisenhart, 1991). If a person's friends do not value intellectual challenges, the result may be a painful conflict between the desire to belong and the desire to improve one's mental abilities. If you are in this position, you may need to seek out others who value the life of the mind and can support you in your goals.

• *Take time to reflect; don't be impulsive.* Americans tend to equate "intelligent" with "quick" (Sternberg et al., 1981). This assumption is reflected in our intelligence tests, most of which impose strict time limits. However, in real life intelligent behavior often depends on resisting one's first impulse and considering better responses (although not endlessly). Even when time is of the essence, it is important to take time to *encode* a problem or task correctly. Students often miss test items they might have gotten right because they read the item too quickly or carelessly and therefore misinterpret it. Intelligent people learn to spend a relatively large proportion of their time on tasks that will increase their overall efficiency and in the long run save them time (carefully reading material they must remember or understand, collecting information, defining problems, setting strategies). However, they do not get bogged down in trivia.

• *Persevere, but don't perseverate.* In Chapter 8, we saw that when creative people don't at first succeed, they are willing to try, try again. Perseverance is also a prime requirement for intelligent action. A brilliant investment strategy, movie script, or scholarly work does not spring forth full-blown from a person's head. Chances are there were many false starts and painful revisions along the way. However, although people who are intellectually accomplished don't give up easily, intelligent people don't perseverate—that is, do the same thing over and over again, when it would clearly be better to change course or give up. As Sternberg notes, perseveration occurs in relationships when people keep trying to win over someone who has rejected them romantically in the most emphatic and unmistakable terms. This is not smart.

SUMMARY

1. Psychologists measure differences in intellectual abilities by using techniques of *psychological assessment*. The difference between *achievement tests* and *aptitude tests* is one of degree and intended use.

2. Most psychological tests are *standardized* and are scored by referring to established *norms*. These tests are judged in terms of their *reliability* (ability to produce consistent results) and their *validity* (ability to measure what they are intended to measure). Among psychologists and educators, the validity of some widely used tests is controversial. In "A Closer Look," we saw that there is now a movement to promote performance-based assessment.

3. There is debate about exactly what the most widely known intelligence tests measure. Some theorists believe that a general ability (a *g factor*) underlies the many specific abilities tapped by such tests, while others do not.

4. The *intelligence quotient*, or *IQ*, represents how a person has done on an intelligence test compared to others of the same age. Alfred Binet designed the first widely used intelligence test for the purpose of identifying children who could benefit from remedial work. In the United States, people assumed the tests revealed an inherited capacity that could not be changed, and the tests came to be used for screening schoolchildren and soldiers.

5. IQ tests have been criticized for being biased in favor of white, middle-class people. Efforts have been made to construct culture-free and culture-fair tests, but for a variety of reasons these efforts have not eliminated group differences in performance. Some critics would like to dispense with IQ tests altogether because they are so often interpreted unintelligently. Others believe the tests are useful for predicting school performance and diagnosing learning difficulties, as long as they are combined with other kinds of information.

6. In contrast to psychometric approaches to intelligence, newer approaches focus on the strategies people use to solve problems, and not just on whether they get the right answers. Sternberg's *triarchic theory of intelligence* proposes three aspects of intelligence: componential, experiential, and contextual. New tests based on this and other conceptualizations are in the offing, but at present, conventional tests remain the yardstick by which individual differences are typically measured.

7. Individual differences in mental ability depend on complex interactions between heredity (nature) and environment (nurture). Despite the difficulty of studying such interactions, *behavior geneticists* have been able to estimate the heritability of intelligence (as measured by IQ tests) from data on twins and adopted children.

8. *Heritability* refers to the extent to which differences in a trait within a group of individuals are accounted for by genetic differences. An estimate of heritability does not reveal the impact of heredity on a *particular* individual's traits. Also, heritability estimates apply only to differences within a particular group living in a particular environment and not to differences between groups. Even a highly heritable trait may be susceptible to environmental modification.

9. Behavior–genetic studies of twins and adopted children yield a wide range of heritability estimates for intelligence as measured by IQ tests, but these estimates average between .47 and .58.

10. Whatever their heritability, mental abilities can be profoundly affected by environmental factors. Such factors include nutrition, exposure to toxins, mental stimulation, family size, individual experiences, stressful family circumstances, and parent-child interactions. Because of these influences, an individual's IQ scores may fluctuate considerably during childhood.

11. Interest in group differences in IQ has focused especially on average black-white differences. Genetic explanations of such differences have often used heritability estimates derived from one group to estimate the genetic contribution to group differences—which is not a valid procedure. The available evidence fails to support genetic explanations of these differences.

12. Cultural differences in child-rearing practices and attitudes may help explain certain disparities in intellectual performance between black and white children in the United States, and between children in Asian countries and children in the United States. However, parents who are not adept at promoting certain types of mental ability may be excellent at encouraging other abilities not currently capitalized on by schools.

13. Education and socioeconomic background are better predictors of occupational success than IQ alone. Some people with unspectacular IQ scores have a great deal of *practical intelligence* that reveals itself in everyday activities. *Emotional intelligence*, too, is important for success in life, as are drive, determination, and resourcefulness. Broadening the definition of intelligence helps us to recognize that there are many ways for people to contribute to the world and express their potential.

KEY TERMS

Solution to the puzzle on page 380. The mirrored images of the figures provide clues as to which sides of the rooms are mirrored walls (shown as shaded here).

12

Diversity II: Measuring and Explaining Personality

*Selfness is an essential fact of life.
The thought of nonselfness, precise
sameness, is terrifying.*

LEWIS THOMAS

A psychologist we know once gave a lecture to the faculty of the first school she ever attended—her nursery school. Her topic was an optimistic report of new research on adult life. "People are not prisoners of childhood," she said. "They change their attitudes, philosophies of life, self-esteem, ambitions, values, and looks. They have new experiences that change their outlook and politics. Many even outgrow early traumas." In the audience, unknown to our friend, was one of her original teachers—now 96 years old, as clear-minded as ever. "A nice speech, dear," she said when it was over, "but as far as I'm concerned, you haven't changed a bit since you were 3. You're a bit taller, is all."

What made our friend appear unchanged to her nursery-school teacher was, undoubtedly, her "personality." The word doesn't refer to enthusiasm, liveliness, or a set of positive qualities, as in "He's got a great personality." Psychologists generally define **personality** as a distinctive and stable pattern of behavior, thoughts, motives, and emotions that characterizes an individual.

That's all very well, but which behaviors, thoughts, motives, and emotions shall we count? And how stable are they? Some psychologists look for personality in dark, hidden motives of the mind. Others regard personality as the private self, the "true self," behind the masks that people wear in daily social situations. Some psychologists regard personality as a diamond, consisting of different facets of behavior and belief. Others argue that the whole notion of "personality" is wrongheaded, a comfortable fiction rather than scientific fact. In their view, people are much more influenced by their immediate circumstances than by "personality." If people seem consistent, they say, it is only because their environments haven't changed.

In this chapter we will report different ways to study and describe personality. Two questions guide researchers: How can we describe the astonishing variety among individuals, and what is it that makes a person's "personality" distinctive?

Does your personality change, or only your interests? Jerry Rubin was a 1960s yippie and is a yuppie today.

■ PLOTTING PERSONALITY

Have you ever taken a personality quiz printed in your local newspaper or favorite magazine? These questionnaires usually have blaring headlines such as "What's Your Assertiveness Quotient?" or "Are You Self-Destructive?" or "What Type of Friend Are You—Jealous, Jumpy, or Jovial?" Most of these popular quizzes are, in fact, pretty silly psychology (see "Taking Psychology with You"). But they are part of a time-honored tradition of classifying people according to their particular traits or "personality types." A **trait** is simply a characteristic that is assumed to describe a person—as shy, brave, reliable, friendly, hostile, serious, confident, sullen, and so on—across many situations. A *type* is a cluster of traits thought to describe a kind of person; an "executive type," for instance, might have the traits of leadership and confidence.

415

The four basic personality types.

The very first efforts to describe personality were type theories, usually based on physical differences among people. We have already noted some historical efforts to divide people into four types according to their "dominant" bodily fluid (blood, phlegm, yellow bile, black bile) or according to the location of bumps on the head (Gall's system of phrenology). In the mid–twentieth century, a popular theory held that personality types vary according to body build— fat, muscular, or thin. Among psychologists today, however, type theories based on physiology are about as popular as a dog at a cat show. There is no evidence that personality depends on a person's body shape, bodily fluids, or head bumps.

Each of us is a constantly shifting kaleidoscope of traits, tendencies, preferences, and moods. Before these characteristics can be studied and understood they must first be measured in some reliable way. No one test can possibly summarize a person's entire personality, but various tests and assessment methods do provide information about certain aspects of personality—about needs, values, interests, and characteristic ways of responding to particular situations.

Tests of Personality

In addition to their usual arsenal of research methods—including the case study, field and laboratory observations, surveys, face-to-face interviews, and laboratory experiments—personality psychologists often use two kinds of tests for research and clinical purposes: objective tests and projective tests.

OBJECTIVE TESTS.   Objective tests, or **inventories,** are standardized questionnaires that require written responses, typically to multiple-choice or true-false items. Usually the test-taker is asked to report how she or he feels or acts in certain circumstances. A test may measure a single aspect of personality, such as sense of humor or pessimism, or it may assess several aspects at once. In general, objective tests have better *reliability* (they are more consistent over time) and *validity* (they actually measure what they say they measure) than other kinds of personality tests (see page 382).

As befitting the computer age, some publishers of objective tests now offer what seems to be the ultimate in objectivity: computerized interpretations of results. These interpretations, based on statistical norms, are often more reliable than those made by clinicians. But they have drawbacks. Computers cannot consider how a person behaved during the test or a person's previous history. Managers, teachers, and others not trained in psychological testing may put too much faith in statistical interpretations, just because they come from a machine.

The most well-known and widely used objective personality test is the **Minnesota Multiphasic Personality Inventory (MMPI).** The MMPI was developed in the 1930s by Starke Hathaway and J. Charnley McKinley, who wanted a way to screen people with psychological disorders. A thousand potential test items were given to approximately 200 mental patients and 1,500 nonpatients in Minneapolis. The items took the form of statements about symptoms, moods, attitudes, and behavior, and test-takers had to indicate whether the statements applied to themselves by responding "true," "false," or "cannot say." Of the initial test items, 550 were answered differently on the average by the disturbed and nondisturbed sample groups; these items were retained. (The items did not have to make sense theoretically as long as they discriminated between the people in the two groups.) The various items were assigned to ten clinical categories, or *scales,* that identified such problems as depression, paranoia, schizophrenia, and social introversion. Four *validity scales* indicated whether a test-taker was lying, careless, defensive, or evasive while responding to the items. For example, if a person tried to present an overall favorable (but unrealistic) image on nearly every item, the person's score on the lie scale would be high.

■ **inventories**
Standardized objective questionnaires requiring written responses; they typically include scales on which people are asked to rate themselves.
■ **Minnesota Multiphasic Personality Inventory (MMPI)**
A widely used objective personality test.

Since the original MMPI was devised, hundreds of additional scales have been added, and more than 8,000 books and articles have been written on the test (Butcher & Finn, 1983). The inventory has been used in some 50 countries, on everyone from ordinary job applicants to Soviet cosmonauts, and it is increasingly used to assess normal personality traits rather than emotional problems. The MMPI has also inspired the development of other personality inventories using similar items. In 1989, a major, long-awaited revision of the MMPI—the MMPI-2—was released, with norms based on a more representative sample balanced by region, ethnicity, age, and gender (Butcher et al., 1989).

Despite its popularity, the MMPI has critics. Some have observed that the test may be racially and culturally biased because its standards of "normalcy" do not reflect cultural differences. Although the sample used for test norms in the MMPI-2 is an improvement, it still underrepresented minorities, the elderly, and the poor. Some of the scales overlap, and some items are affected by the respondent's tendency to give the socially appropriate answer rather than the true one (Edwards & Edwards, 1991). The validity and reliability of the test have also come under fire. One recent review of studies concludes that the validity and reliability of the MMPI are adequate if the test is used for its original purpose—identifying people with personality or emotional disorders (Parker, Hanson, & Hunsley, 1988). Yet in practice, the MMPI (along with other objective tests) is often used in business, industry, and education for inappropriate reasons by persons who are not well trained in testing. Although the MMPI is called an "objective" test, its usefulness depends as much on a clinician's understanding of the test, and on the inferences about the patient that are drawn from it, as on the specific items themselves.

PROJECTIVE TESTS.   In contrast to the more straightforward objective test, **projective tests** are used to measure conscious and unconscious motives, thoughts, perceptions, and conflicts—aspects of personality that may not be apparent in a person's public behavior. The tests present ambiguous pictures, patterns, or stories for the test-taker to interpret. There is no correct interpretation; each person is free to respond as he or she likes. The assumption is that the person's thoughts and feelings will be "projected" onto the test materials and revealed in the person's interpretations. Projective tests are used most often by psychotherapists for purposes of clinical evaluation, but researchers also find them useful (see Figure 12.1).

■ **projective tests**
Psychological tests used to infer a person's motives, thoughts, perceptions, and conflicts on the basis of the person's interpretations of ambiguous or unstructured stimuli.

FIGURE 12.1

A projective test for body satisfaction
The Color-A-Person Test is a test for evaluating a person's body image and the emotions associated with it. Test-takers use different colors to indicate their degree of satisfaction with parts of their bodies. Scoring takes into account the colors used, differentiation of body parts, distortions from reality, and comments made during the test (Wooley & Wooley, 1985). These drawings were made by two women with eating disorders. One makes fine distinctions, but the other hates everything about herself. At the bottom of the drawing she has written "I want to change my whole body."

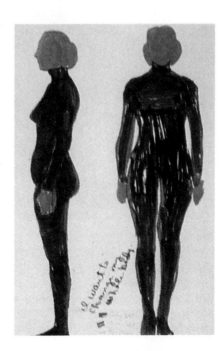

"RORSCHACH! WHAT'S TO BECOME OF YOU?"

One popular projective test, the **Rorschach Inkblot Test,** was devised by Swiss psychiatrist Hermann Rorschach in 1921. It consists of ten cards with symmetrical abstract patterns, originally formed by spilling ink on paper and folding the paper in half. The test-taker reports what he or she "sees" in the inkblots. Although various scoring systems exist, based on content, originality, and other aspects of the person's response, most clinicians interpret the answers subjectively, taking into account the symbolic meanings emphasized by psychodynamic theories (which we will consider shortly).

Another widely used projective test is the **Thematic Apperception Test (TAT),** which consists of a series of drawings or photographs showing people in ambiguous situations (see Figure 12.2). The test-taker must make up a story about each scene. An elaborate scoring system takes into account the basic issues raised in each story, the characters the test-taker identified with, the motives and emotions attributed to the various characters, and the endings given to the stories. (Chapter 10 explained how the TAT is used to assess achievement motivation.)

Other projective tests use sentence or story completion, word association, or self-expression through art. Many clinicians believe that projective techniques are a rich source of information. Test-takers cannot "fake" or lie as easily as on objective tests. The tests can also help a clinician establish rapport with a client and encourage a person to open up about anxieties, conflicts, and problems. Many critics, however, question both the validity and the reliability of some of the tests, especially as they are used by clinicians. They note that different clinicians often interpret the tests differently, and that the clinicians themselves may be "projecting" when they decide what a specific response means. Moreover, it can be hard to know whether a person's responses reflect deep-seated personality characteristics or only temporary conditions such as fatigue or a hard day.

Evaluating Personality Tests

The most important challenge for measuring personality concerns the problems of consistency and predictability. In the late 1960s, Walter Mischel reviewed dozens of personality studies and found only the weakest of correlations between a person's trait on a personality test and that person's behavior in a

■ **Rorschach [ROR-shock] Inkblot Test**
A projective personality test that asks respondents to interpret abstract, symmetrical inkblots.

■ **Thematic Apperception Test (TAT)**
A projective personality test that asks respondents to interpret a series of drawings showing ambiguous scenes.

FIGURE 12.2

The Thematic Apperception Test
On the left, a woman taking the TAT makes up stories for a set of ambiguous pictures. The picture on the right, similar to one included in an adaptation of the test, has been used to study people's unconscious feelings about intimacy. When you look at this picture, what sort of "story" do you think of? Who are the people and what are they thinking and saying? What will happen to them?

particular situation. The gap between the assumption of consistency and the fact of inconsistency came to be known as *the consistency paradox* (Bem & Allen, 1974; Mischel, 1984). This bombshell made quite an explosion in the field of personality research. After all, the most basic assumption about personality is that there is something sturdy about it across situations. But if the situation influences what people do more than their traits do, the whole notion of personality is called into question. If you score high on a measure of ambition but fail to *behave* in a way that demonstrates your ambition, are you "ambitious"? If a child cheats at one game but not at another, is the child "honest" or "dishonest"?

Personality researchers regrouped, and responded to the consistency paradox in several ways (Buss, 1989; Funder, 1991). First, they noted that behavioral consistency might *itself* be a personality trait! Although some people are chameleon-like in their behavior, others are quite consistent. Second, a situation may require a certain kind of behavior, but people often choose—for reasons of personality—what situations to get into in the first place (Snyder & Ickes, 1985). A party imposes a general requirement to be sociable, but sociable people are more likely to go to parties than hermits are. Third, simply counting acts (say, of honesty) can lead to mistaken conclusions. For example, you might not cheat in one setting out of fear of getting caught, yet not cheat in another setting because you believe cheating in that case is wrong. Your behavior is consistent, but your motives are not. Conversely, you may refrain from cheating on a class exam, yet rely on your roommate to help you with a take-home exam. Your actions may seem inconsistent to an observer, yet you may believe you are doing the honest thing in both cases. When researchers assess the *psychological meaning* of the act to the individual, they find greater consistency (Funder & Colvin, 1991).

For these reasons, the most promising tactic in measuring personality is to study the *interaction* of personality and situation. All personality theorists recognize that people are influenced by the situation they are in; a person who did not bend at all with the situational winds would be emotionally disturbed. At the same time, people bring their unique personalities and perceptions to all situations, which is why you can find sulkers at the happiest occasions and optimists in the midst of disasters.

Because of situational influences on behavior, measurements of personality will not always predict accurately what people will do in a given setting. But without these tests clinical diagnosis would be difficult and much of personality research would be impossible. Personality tests can be useful in probing the origins of human diversity, and, as we will see next, they have been used to identify qualities that form the foundation of an individual's character.

QUICK QUIZ

A. Which kind of test, projective or objective, is being given here?

1. A subject in a study of anxiety supplies an ending to a story about someone who must give a speech to a large audience.
2. A schoolchild answers a questionnaire containing items usually answered differently by children with high and low self-esteem.
3. A student looks at ambiguous pictures of men and women sitting together, and describes what is going on between them.

B. A student who scores high on a test of assertiveness but who becomes completely tongue-tied during a job interview illustrates the _____ paradox.

ANSWERS:

A. 1. projective 2. objective 3. projective B. consistency

Puzzles of Personality #1

Which has more influence on behavior—personality or situation?

Some societies, such as China, are highly situation-oriented; others, such as the United States, are more individual-oriented. Chinese workers in Beijing do their morning T'ai Chi exercises in identical fashion; individualistic Americans exercise by running or walking in different directions, in different ways, in different clothes.

Many psychologists believe that behavior is more strongly influenced by the situation you are in than by your personality. Numerous situations, from working in an office to playing in a marching band, require us to set aside preferences and feelings and behave in specific ways. Other psychologists reply that even in situations that demand a certain uniformity, individuals manage to put their unique marks on their environments. This office setting, for instance, is stamped with the "personality" of its occupant.

■ THE ELEMENTS OF PERSONALITY

Personality psychologists have identified many fascinating traits, from "sensation seeking" (the enjoyment of risk) to "erotophobia" (the fear of sex). A traditional approach has been simply to identify all of the many individual traits that contribute to personality. Recently, other researchers, unhappy with this piece-by-piece approach, have been attempting to find the few basic organizing traits of personality.

Counting Qualities

One of the most influential trait theorists in this century was Gordon Allport (1897–1967). Allport observed that most members of a society share certain qualities, which he called *common traits*, that their culture expects and rewards. To understand why two people differ, said Allport (1937, 1961), you must look at the qualities that make each of them unique.

Allport maintained that there are three kinds of individual traits: cardinal, central, and secondary. *Cardinal traits* are of overwhelming importance to an individual and influence almost everything the person does. We might say that Mohandas Gandhi (called *Mahatma*, or wise one) and Martin Luther King, Jr., had the cardinal trait of nonviolence. Few people, said Allport, have cardinal traits. Instead, most of us have five to ten *central* (or *global*) *traits* that reflect a characteristic way of behaving, dealing with others, and reacting to new situations. Some typical central traits are warmth, neatness, competitiveness, shyness, joyfulness, and negativism. "For some the world is a hostile place where men are evil and dangerous," Allport wrote (1961); "for others it is a stage for fun and frolic. It may appear as a place to do one's duty grimly; or a pasture for cultivating friendship and love." *Secondary traits* are less important aspects of personality, more subject to change than central traits are. They include preferences (for foods, colors, movies), habits, garden-variety opinions, and the like.

Since Allport, psychologists have found that psychological traits are not as simple to describe as physical ones, like having curly hair or big feet. On the contrary, psychological traits are expressed in different ways and can be very complex, as we can see in the example of self-esteem.

Literally thousands of studies have been done on self-esteem, which seems to come in two basic varieties. One is "inner" or *trait self-esteem*, which is a global judgment of worthiness that seems to form early in life and remains fairly constant over time (Campbell, 1990; Rosenberg, 1986). This basic sense of self-esteem affects people's motivation and behavior in many ways. For example, people who have high self-esteem are motivated to *enhance* their public image and to appear to be above average, whereas people who think little of themselves are primarily concerned about *protecting* their image and avoiding failure (Tice, 1991).

The second kind is "outer" or *state self-esteem*, which fluctuates across situations, particularly in response to such threats to self-worth as failing a test. One objective test of state self-esteem yielded three components: performance ("I feel confident about my abilities," "I feel as smart as others"); appearance ("I am satisfied with the way my body looks right now"); and social concerns ("I am worried about looking foolish") (Heatherton & Polivy, 1991). The subject of self-esteem has been much in the news lately, and it raises many issues for critical thinking. How should we define it: as a fundamental sense of self-worth that rests on accomplishing things for oneself and others, or is it enough to be feeling good about oneself? Where does self-esteem come from, and what affects it? Should high self-esteem be a goal of education, and if so, how would you go about promoting it?

People with low self-esteem often take it out on others.

Psychologists have studied hundreds and hundreds of other qualities, many of which are subject to change over a person's lifetime. We turn now to a different approach to the study of personality traits: the effort to identify the fundamental ones that are stable over the years and across situations.

Basic Traits

Raymond B. Cattell advanced the study of personality traits by applying a statistical method called *factor analysis,* discussed in Chapter 11. Performing a factor analysis on traits is like adding water to flour: It causes the basic material to clump up into little balls. Using questionnaires, life descriptions, and observations, Cattell (1965, 1973) measured dozens of personality traits in hundreds of people. He called these descriptive qualities *surface traits* because they are visible in a person's words or deeds. He believed that factor analysis, which identifies traits that are correlated with each other, would identify *source traits,* the bedrock of personality, the underlying causes of surface qualities. A person might have the surface traits of assertiveness, courage, and ambition; the source trait, linking all three, might be dominance. Cattell and his associates investigated many aspects of personality, including humor, music preferences, intelligence, creativity, leadership, and emotional disorder. His method of conducting large-scale research and of carefully describing the connections between traits had a major influence on research in personality.

Cattell maintained that there are 16 factors necessary to describe the complexities of personality, and many psychologists agree with him (Mershon & Gorsuch, 1988). Others have tried to boil surface traits down into even fewer clusters. Hans Eysenck (1970), for example, concluded that there are only three dimensions of personality: *extroversion,* the extent to which a person is outgoing, sociable, and energetic (extroverted); *neuroticism,* the extent to which a person is anxious, depressed, obsessive, and hostile; and *psychoticism,* the extent to which a person lacks empathy and is disposed to crime and mental illness (Eysenck & Eysenck, 1985; Eysenck & Long, 1986).

Other researchers think that Eysenck went too far in boiling down basic traits, though they agree that extroversion and neuroticism are central. On the basis of longitudinal studies and factor analysis, they argue that personality can be described according to five "robust factors," sometimes called the "Big Five" (Costa & McCrae, 1988; Digman, 1990; Goldberg, 1990; McCrae & Costa, 1987, 1991; Zuckerman, Kuhlman, & Camac, 1988):

This woman has probably been extroverted all her life.

1. *Introversion versus extroversion:* This dimension includes such personality traits as being talkative or silent, sociable or reclusive, adventurous or cautious, outgoing or shy.

2. *Neuroticism,* or emotional instability: Traits include being anxious and unable to control impulses, a tendency to have unrealistic ideas, and generally being emotionally unstable and negative. Neurotic individuals are complainers and defeatists. They complain about different things at different ages, but they are always ready to see the sour side of life and none of its sweetness.

Neuroticism is sometimes called *negative affectivity* (emotionality), or NA. Negative affectivity describes a person's tendency to feel anger, scorn, revulsion, guilt, anxiety, sadness, and other negative moods (Watson & Clark, 1984). High NA people frequently feel worried and tense, even in the absence of real problems. They complain more about their health and report more physical symptoms than low NAs do, but they are not actually in poorer health (Brett et al., 1990; Watson & Pennebaker, 1989).

3. *Agreeableness:* This dimension describes the extent to which people are good-natured or irritable, gentle or headstrong, cooperative or abrasive, not

jealous or jealous. It reflects the capacity for friendly relationships or the tendency to have hostile ones.

4. *Conscientiousness:* This factor describes individuals who are responsible or undependable; who are persevering or who quit easily; who are steadfast or fickle; who are tidy or careless; who are scrupulous or unscrupulous.

5. *Openness to experience:* The fifth dimension describes the extent to which people are original, imaginative, questioning, artistically inclined, and capable of divergent thinking (creativity)—or are conforming, unimaginative, and predictable.

The Big Five factors turn up in studies of adults in many cultures, including Chinese, Japanese, Filipino, Hawaiian, and Australian samples (Digman & Inouye, 1986; Noller, Law, & Comrey, 1987). Moreover, they seem to be as persistent as crabgrass. You might think (and hope) that people would become more open-minded and agreeable, and less neurotic, as they mature. But Paul Costa and Robert McCrae (1988), having conducted a major longitudinal study of men and women aged 21 to 96, concluded that no matter how you measure them, these traits are "still stable after all these years."

New research on the Big Five is investigating the way each personality trait interacts with circumstances to foster or inhibit a person's well-being. For example, the qualities of agreeableness, openness to experience, and extroversion are positively related to well-being (McCrae & Costa, 1991). When individuals with these traits are under stress or have problems, they respond by seeking the help of others, by trying new solutions, and by maintaining optimism. In contrast, people who are high in neuroticism tend to react by indulging in wishful thinking ("The problem will go away soon") or self-blame—two strategies that further increase their anxiety and other negative feelings (Bolger, 1990). A recent seven-year longitudinal study of 296 adults concluded that "temperamental dispositions are more powerful than environmental factors in predicting psychological distress" (Ormel & Wohlfarth, 1991). Emotional difficulties and life crises occur for everyone, the researchers found, but people high in neuroticism bring their pessimism and negativity with them, making such situations worse.

The trait approach to personality has been highly successful in identifying what seem to be the core dimensions or features that make one person different from another. The logical next question is, where do those traits come from? Let's consider the major theories that have offered answers.

QUICK QUIZ

A. Choose the correct word in each pair.

1. Raymond Cattell advanced the study of personality by his method of (*case study analysis/factor analysis*).

2. A student who hates herself for having eaten two large pizzas is also proud of herself for getting straight A's. Her feelings of self-loathing and self-worth probably reflect (*state/trait*) self-esteem.

B. Which of the following traits are *not* "robust factors" in personality? (a) introversion, (b) agreeableness, (c) psychoticism, (d) openness to experience, (e) intelligence, (f) neuroticism, (g) conscientiousness

ANSWERS:

A. 1. factor analysis 2. state B. c, e

■ THE BIOLOGICAL TRADITION: YOU ARE WHAT YOU'RE BORN

A student we know was describing her life-long problem with bad temper. "I was *born* angry," she said. "I hissed at passersby when I was carried home from the hospital." People do talk this way, but is it possible to be "born angry"? What aspects of personality might have an inherited component? And if any of them do, does that mean that people are "stuck" with certain traits forever?

Heredity, Temperament, and Traits

One way to study the origins of personality differences is to look at **temperaments,** which are characteristic styles of responding to the environment that appear in early childhood. If personality has some genetic basis, certain temperaments ought to emerge early in life and affect subsequent development. This is, in fact, the case. Even in the first weeks after birth, infants differ in activity level, mood, responsiveness, and attention span. Some are irritable and cranky. Some are placid and sweet-natured. Some cuddle up in any adult's arms and snuggle. Some squirm and fidget, as if they can't stand being held. Babies differ in activity level (thrashing and kicking), smiling and laughing, fussing and showing signs of distress, soothability (the time it takes for a baby to calm down after distress), emotionality and expressiveness, cooing and burbling in reaction to people or things, and amount of crying (Field, 1989; Kagan & Snidman, 1991).

Some differences in temperament may be ethnically based. Chinese-American infants are, on the average, more soothable than African- and European-American infants. If you press a newborn baby's nose with a cloth, most black and white babies will show a "defense reaction," turning their heads or trying to hit the cloth with their hands. In contrast, most Chinese babies lie on their backs and accept the cloth without a fight. These and other differences among newborns have been documented in studies that controlled for the mothers' age, class, nutrition, use of drugs during delivery, and other factors that might affect temperament (D. Freedman, 1979). Such findings imply hereditary differences, but parents in different cultures also treat their babies differently right from the start, in how often they hold, touch, feed, or talk to them (Rogoff & Morelli, 1989).

Within groups, certain temperamental differences in infants and young children are apparently due to variations in the responsiveness of the sympathetic nervous system to change and novelty. Jerome Kagan and his colleagues have found that two temperamental styles, which they call "inhibited" and "uninhibited," are detectable in infancy and, in the absence of intervention, remain stable throughout childhood (Kagan & Snidman, 1991). Shy, socially inhibited 5-year-olds are more likely than uninhibited children to show signs of sympathetic nervous system activity during mildly stressful mental tasks (Kagan, Reznick, & Snidman, 1988). Such signs include increased heart rate, increased dilation of the pupils, and a rise in norepinephrine in the sympathetic nervous system. Inhibited children also have higher-than-average cortisol levels, and there is some indirect evidence that they have relatively high levels of norepinephrine in the brain. Exactly the same physiological attributes are found in shy, inhibited infant monkeys (Suomi, 1987).

Some aspects of temperament may lead to characteristic habits and mannerisms in adults. Researchers have been struck by some unnerving similarities in the gestures, movements, and speech patterns of separated identical twins. In a review of the research, Susan Farber (1981) remarked on two male twins who both nodded their heads in a certain way while speaking, two other male twins who both flicked their fingers when unable to think of an answer, and two fe-

■ **temperaments**
Characteristic styles of responding to the environment that are present in infancy and are assumed to be innate.

Identical twins often unconsciously arrange their arms and legs in the same way and assume similar expressions. Research suggests that such physical mannerisms probably have a genetic basis.

male twins who both rubbed their noses and rocked when tired. Farber also noted that identical twins reared apart tended to have similar characteristic moods. If one twin was optimistic, excitable, or glum, the other was likely to be the same. If one had frequent mood changes, the other was apt to have them as well. The Minnesota Twins project, described in the previous chapter, has found the same sorts of resemblances in mood and personal style (Bouchard et al., 1986).

Apart from temperament, another way to study the genetic basis of personality is to estimate the **heritability** of adult personality traits, comparing identical twins reared apart with twins reared together (see Chapter 11). Researchers using this method report that whether the trait in question is altruism, aggression, one of the Big Five, or even religious attitudes, heritability is typically around .50 (Loehlin, 1988; Pedersen et al., 1988; Rushton et al., 1986; Tellegen et al., 1988; Waller et al., 1990). This means that within a group of people about 50 percent of the variance in such traits is attributable to genetic differences. But even more startling and controversial is the finding that the only environmental effects come from nonshared experiences, such as having a particular teacher in the fourth grade or having gotten the lead in the school play. *Shared environment and parental child-rearing practices seem to be not at all related to adult personality traits* (Plomin & Daniels, 1987)!

Understandably, researchers doing this kind of research are excited about their findings. They believe the evidence for the heritability of personality traits represents an overwhelming attack on the conventional wisdom that child-rearing practices are central to personality development. "Our retrospective study showed only meager associations between parent-child relations and adult personality," write McCrae and Costa (1988a). "It will doubtless seem incredible to many readers that variables such as social class, educational opportunities, religious training, and parental love and discipline have no substantial influence on adult personality, but imagine for a moment that it is correct. What will it mean for research in developmental psychology? How will clinical psychology and theories of therapy be changed?"

Good questions! What would these findings, if true, mean for education, for raising children, for psychotherapy, indeed for the basic assumptions of psychology? McCrae and Costa (1988a) think that these findings are simply too threatening for most psychologists to accept. However, while it is wise to keep an open mind about the challenge of genetic theories of personality, let us also consider their limitations.

■ **heritability**
A statistical estimate of the proportion of the total variance in some trait within a group that is attributable to genetic differences among individuals within that group.

Evaluating Genetic Theories

Some personality traits have a heritable component. Why can't we conclude that aggressive 8-year-old boys will inevitably grow up to become used-car salesmen, prizefighters, or criminals?

Remember that *what we know* is indistinguishable from *how we know it*, and the measurement of heritability is complex. Before we can conclude that differences in personality are largely based on differences in heredity, we must consider four qualifications:

1. *Problems with measuring "environment."* Although it is easy to estimate the genetic similarity of twins, measures of environmental events are still crude. They often rely on vague, grab-bag categories such as "social class" or "religious training," and on the twins' retrospective self-reports, which have inherent biases. Rarely do researchers actually observe the specific environments of separated twins, noting, for example, precisely how a parent interacts with a child.

When that kind of detailed and difficult observational research is done, the effects of the environment emerge more clearly (Patterson, 1986). Indeed, even identical twins, who share all their genes, can become very different people (see Figure 12.3). One twin may become schizophrenic or alcoholic and the other not. Moreover, as we discuss in "Think About It," some of the remarkable similarities between twins reared apart may actually be due to coincidence rather than genetics.

2. *Heritability estimates apply only to groups, not to individuals.* Journalistic ac-

THINK ABOUT IT

Uncanny Coincidences and Identical Twins

The human mind is unhappy with coincidences. It likes to impose meaning on them, find some causal link or *reason* for their existence. The case of identical twins, who have so many mannerisms and traits in common, offers a fascinating lesson in the psychology of coincidence. When you read strange stories of twins separated at birth, who, reunited, share all kinds of remarkable behaviors, it is tempting to infer that there is some biologically based "psychic bond" that links them. Or is there?

Jim Lewis and Jim Springer are identical twins who were separated a few weeks after their birth in 1939 and adopted by different families in Ohio. Almost 40 years later, after leading entirely separate lives, they were reunited. Jim and Jim soon discovered some astonishing similarities in their lives (Holden, 1980). Not only did they have the same first name, but both had an adopted brother named Larry and both had married a woman named Linda, divorced her, then married a woman named Betty. Lewis named his first son James Alan; Springer named his James Allan. During childhood both Jims owned a dog named Toy, and

both liked math but hated spelling. During adolescence both put on 10 pounds for no apparent reason, then lost weight. As adults, both had worked as a deputy sheriff, as an attendant in a filling station, and for a McDonald's. Both vacationed at a beach near St. Petersburg, Florida; bit their nails; drank Miller Lite Beer; and did blueprinting and woodworking.

When Thomas Bouchard heard about the two Jims, he invited them to participate in the ongoing twin study at the University of Minnesota. Like the two Jims, many of the other twins in the study also have reported uncanny coincidences. A set of British twins found that they had married on the same day in 1960, within an hour of each other. Two other twins discovered they had each filled out a diary for just one year, 1962; had used the same type of diary; and had filled out the same days of the year.

What are we to make of such coincidences? British writer Peter Watson (1981) has observed that the world is a large place and rare events do happen, entirely by chance. The odds of the same number coming up three times in a row at roulette are pretty unlikely, only 1 in 50,652. Yet considering the tens of thousands of people who gamble throughout the world each day, this unlikely event is almost certain to happen every few days, and perhaps on most days, somewhere or other in the world. Rare events happen.

Further, some events that *seem* uncommon actually are not. Watson points out that the twins

FIGURE 12.3

From one branch, two different twigs
Not all identical twins resemble each other psychologically, as you can see in these pictures of the same pair of identical twins at different ages. In both infancy and childhood the twin on the left was cheerful and easygoing, whereas the one on the right was negative and difficult.

who married on the same day were the twenty-first and twenty-second married twins seen in the Minnesota study. Statistically, the chances were nearly even that two of the Minnesota twins would have been married on the same day of the year. Of course, these twins got married in the same year as well. However, most people marry at around the same age, and the favorite day for a wedding is Saturday (the day the twins married). Taking all these facts into account, Watson estimates that the odds of any one of the pairs seen in Minnesota marrying on the same Saturday are 1 in 125—not enormous, to be sure, but not impossible, either. Watson has also estimated the probabilities of other coincidences in the lives of the twins in the Minnesota study. Some were not improbable at all. Two twins, Barbara and Daphne, preferred vodka, but vodka happens to be the most popular type of liquor among women. Likewise, a preference for Miller Lite among men is not unusual.

Some of the surprising similarities between separated twins may be explainable in terms of physiology. Because they share all their genes, identical twins are likely to develop the same hereditary illnesses (and, as we saw in Chapter 10, achieve roughly the same weight and body shape). Medical problems can affect other aspects of life—financial, occupational, social, and educational. Similarities in the economic and social conditions of life may also lead to specific similarities in behavior. For example, people who

have modest incomes may be especially likely to vacation in Florida, where a holiday is relatively inexpensive.

Twin similarities reported with fanfare by the press may divert attention from the many differences between identical twins. One pair of twins in the Minnesota study—one raised as a Nazi, the other as a Jew—wore short mustaches, fell asleep easily in front of the television, read in restaurants, read magazines from back to front, dipped buttered toast into their coffee, and flushed the toilet before using it. But one twin had been an alcoholic, whereas the other did not drink; one had a history of depression and suicidal thinking, and the other did not. Many of the startling twin similarities are due to fashions and fads, such as the popularity of certain names, drinks, and even kinds of pets. It is hard to imagine that there is a gene for naming a dog Toy or for marrying a woman named Betty.

Think about how you might apply Watson's analysis to your own life. Observe whether you have an inclination to see only the "spooky" similarities between you and a relative and ignore the differences. Some of the traits that we say "run in families" may be hereditary, but others "run in the culture" or the community; if several members of a family share them, it may be due to coincidence rather than genes. Obviously, we don't want to imply that every similarity is accidental. Just keep in mind that strange and rare events do happen—entirely by chance. Think about it.

counts of twin studies often overlook this fact. In a *Time* article on the Minnesota Twins research (January 12, 1987), we found this passage: "How much of any individual's personality is due to heredity? The . . . answer: about half." But, as we saw in Chapter 11, *heritability applies only to differences within a group, not to individuals.* For example, no one can say whether your particular genius at, say, flute-playing is a result of inherited musical talent, living all your life in a family of devoted flute-players, or a private psychological obsession that you acquired at the age of 6 when you saw *The Magic Flute.*

3. *Temperaments change.* Although temperaments appear early in life and can influence later personality traits, this does not mean that temperaments provide a fixed, unchangeable blueprint for later personality—or for behavior, as we saw in the "consistency paradox." A "difficult" child may mature and learn to exercise self-control (Thomas & Chess, 1982). Consistency in a given temperament seems to depend in part on how *extreme* that trait is in infancy. Jerome Kagan and his colleagues (1988) report that children who are exceptionally shy at age 2 tend to be quiet, cautious, and inhibited at age 7. Similarly, those who are extremely sociable and uninhibited at 2 are usually talkative and sociable five years later. But most children fall somewhere between the extremes and show far less consistency over time.

Even children at the extremes of some temperament may change as they grow older. Whether or not such change occurs seems to depend largely on

FIGURE 12.4

Don't be shy

In the photo at right, a timid infant rhesus monkey cowers behind a friend in the presence of a more outgoing stranger. Such socially inhibited behavior seems to be a biologically based disposition, both in monkeys and in human beings. But a nurturant adult monkey (below left, a foster mother) can help an infant overcome initial timidity. At first, the infant clings to her, but a few days later (below right) the same young monkey has become more adventurous.

how parents respond to the child. In his work with monkeys, Stephen Suomi (1989) has shown that a highly inhibited infant is likely to overcome its timidity if it is reared by a nurturant foster mother (see Figure 12.4). In human beings, the "fit" between a child's nature and the parents' is critical (Thomas & Chess, 1980). Not only do parents affect the baby, but the baby affects the parents. Imagine a high-strung parent with a child who is difficult and sometimes slow to respond to affection. The parent may begin to feel desperate, angry, or rejected. Over time, the parent may withdraw from the child or become critical and punishing. Such responses are likely to make the child even more difficult to handle. In contrast, a more easygoing parent may have a calming effect on a difficult child or may persist in showing affection even when the child holds back. As a result, the child may eventually become more responsive and sociable.

4. *The diminishing effect of genes over time.* Recently, a meta-analysis of 103 studies of twins found that over time, correlations between twins in most personality traits tended to decrease. "In other words," concluded the researchers, "as twins grow up, they grow apart" (McCartney, Harris, & Bernieri, 1990).

Even when psychologists do find significant correlations in traits over time, not *everybody* remains exactly the same. Consider the example of aggressiveness. Numerous studies have found that aggressive little boys tend to grow up to be aggressive men (Olweus, 1979; Rushton et al., 1986). In one study, a group of 8-year-olds, rated by their classmates as being either very aggressive or not at all aggressive, were reinterviewed when they were 30 years of age. The most aggressive children had become the most aggressive adults, many of whom had criminal records (Huesmann et al., 1984).

Does this mean that we should lock up schoolyard bullies on the grounds that they will become criminals by age 30? We should certainly pay careful attention to children who bully. But keep in mind that although the correlations between childhood and adult behavior were statistically significant, they were also very low. That means that, despite the general trend, some of the most aggressive children became less aggressive as adults (perhaps they entered the Peace Corps), and some of the least aggressive children became more so (perhaps they became hockey players).

In sum, even when traits are stable over time, this does not mean that all human qualities are rigidly fixed. As developmental psychologist Alan Sroufe (1978) pointed out, "A child who has a rapid tempo may be seething with anger, hostile to other children, unable to control his or her impulses and filled with feelings of worthlessness. But a child who has a rapid tempo also may be eager, spirited, effective, and a pleasure to others." We turn now to theories that try to account for the development of personality differences between these two children.

QUICK QUIZ

A recent newspaper headline announced "Couch Potatoes Born, Not Made: Kids' TV habits may be hereditary." What lapses in critical thinking is the headline-writer committing? What other explanations are possible? What aspects of TV watching could have a hereditary component?

ANSWERS:

The headline writer is jumping to conclusions and failing to consider other explanations. There is no "TV-watching gene," but perhaps certain temperaments may dispose people to watch a lot of television, which is a passive activity.

Puzzles of Personality #2

To what extent is personality available to consciousness?

To Freudians, conscious aware-ness is only the tip of the mental iceberg; most motives and con-flicts are hidden in the uncon-scious and are revealed only in symbols (such as the phallic sym-bol of the snake), dreams, slips of the tongue, and free associations.

Carl Jung believed that besides having a private uncon-scious, individuals share a collective unconscious contain-ing the images and themes (archetypes) that unite hu-man history and experience. One such archetype is the "shadow," the monster or evil creature. From dragons to Dracula to Darth Vader, the shadow represents the primordial fear of animals and the "bestial" side of hu-manity.

Radical behaviorists regard the unconscious as an "explanatory fiction" that is unnecessary for explaining human behavior. A young woman who bites her nails is not revealing "unconscious anxiety" or "oral needs"; she has simply acquired a bad habit that is maintained by reinforcements.

Some psychoanalysts, such as Karen Horney, have argued that men's efforts to partici-pate in the births of their children reveal unconscious "womb envy." To social-learn-ing theorists, these efforts reflect a conscious desire to be involved, and are a result of changing social rules, reinforcements, and attitudes about the father's role.

■ THE PSYCHODYNAMIC TRADITION: YOU ARE WHAT YOU WERE

Sigmund Freud (1856–1939), the founder of the theory and therapy called **psychoanalysis,** cast a long shadow over this century. Today there are basically three attitudes toward Freud and psychoanalysis:

- Freud was one of the geniuses of history. With minor exceptions, his basic theory is correct, universal, and brilliant. This view agrees with Freud's own appraisal of the importance of psychoanalysis: that it was as profound a revolution in human thought as Galileo, Darwin, and Newton created in their fields.
- Freud was a great thinker of his generation and era; many of his ideas have lasting value, but some are dated and others are wrong. This is probably the most common current view among psychiatrists and many clinical psychologists, who still use much of Freud's theory but have updated his approach.
- Freud was a fraud. Scientist Peter Medawar (1982) called psychoanalysis a dinosaur in the history of ideas, doomed to extinction. For good measure, he added that it is "the most stupendous intellectual confidence trick of the twentieth century." Anti-Freudians criticize Freud and his modern followers for their antiwoman attitudes, for their lack of scientific rigor, for creating in psychoanalysis an in-group that accepts no dissenters or disbelievers, and for promoting a costly method of therapy that is not demonstrably better than any other.

What provocative theory could produce such wildly different points of view? In this section, we will try to give you an introduction to what Freud said, what some of his followers said, and why the debate about his work continues so hotly even today.

Freud and Psychoanalysis

As you may remember from Chapter 1, psychology as a science began in Germany as an effort to study human consciousness. So it is ironic that one of the first major challenges to this young science attacked the relevance of consciousness. Freud, who lived in Vienna for most of his long career, compared conscious awareness to the tip of a mental iceberg. Beneath the visible tip, he said, lies the **unconscious** part of the mind, containing unrevealed wishes, ambitions, passions, guilty secrets, unspeakable yearnings, and conflicts between desire and duty. These unseen forces, Freud believed, have far more power over human behavior than consciousness does, so the true study of human psychology must probe beneath the surface.

To probe the unconscious, Freud developed the psychoanalytic method. The unconscious reveals itself, said Freud, in dreams, "free association"—talking about anything that pops into your head, without worrying about what anyone will think of you—and slips of the tongue. (According to Freud, accidentally saying "I'd like to kill you" when you intend to say "I'd like to kiss you" reveals your true, unconscious desire.) Because so many thoughts and memories are hidden in the unconscious and because patients resist uncovering them, Freud maintained, psychoanalytic therapy can be long and difficult.

THE DYNAMICS OF PERSONALITY. Freud's theory, and the approach of many of his followers, is called **psychodynamic** because it is based on the movement of psychological energy within the person, in the form of attachments, conflicts, and motivations. Psychic energy is to Freud's theory of personality what water is to Hoover Dam: the content within the structure. *Dynamics* is a term from physics that refers to the motion and balance of systems under the action of outside or inside forces. (For example, the science of thermodynamics studies the rela-

■ **psychoanalysis**
An approach to psychology that emphasizes unconscious motives and conflicts. It encompasses both a theory of personality and a method of psychotherapy.

■ **unconscious processes**
Mental processes, such as motives, desires, and memories, not available to awareness or to conscious introspection. Sometimes called "the unconscious," as a metaphor for the part of the mind below conscious awareness.

■ **psychodynamic**
A term referring to psychological theories that explain behavior in terms of unconscious energy dynamics within the individual—such as inner forces, conflicts, or the movement of instinctual energy.

tionship between heat and mechanical energy.) Freud borrowed from nineteenth-century physics the idea of the conservation of energy: Within any system, he thought, energy can be shifted or transformed, but the total amount of energy remains the same. Psychological energy—the energy it takes to carry out psychological processes, such as thinking and dreaming—was, to Freud, a form of physical energy.

Freud believed that energy that is blocked from direct expression must be *displaced* onto a substitute. For example, the "aggressive instinct" might be displaced in sports competition instead of directly expressed in war. When **displacement** serves a higher cultural or socially useful purpose, as in the creation of art or inventions, it is called **sublimation.** Freud himself thought that for the sake of civilization and survival, sexual and aggressive energies could and should be displaced or sublimated into socially appropriate and constructive forms.

The displacement of energy from one object to another is a key feature of Freud's psychodynamics of personality. Personality differences, he thought, stem from the way people displace energy from their instinctual preferences.

THE STRUCTURE OF PERSONALITY. To Freud, the personality is made up of three major systems: the *id*, the *ego*, and the *superego*. Although each system has its own functions and elements, human behavior is nearly always a result of the interaction among them (Freud, 1905b, 1920/1960, 1923/1962).

The **id,** which is present at birth, is the reservoir of all psychological energies and inherited instincts. To Freud, the id was the true psychic reality because it represents the inner world of subjective experience. It is unconcerned with objective reality and is unaffected by the environment. The id operates according to the **pleasure principle,** seeking to reduce tension, avoid pain, and obtain pleasure.

The id contains what Freud considered to be two basic, competing groups of instincts: the life, or sexual, instincts (fueled by psychic energy called the **libido**) and the death, or aggressive, instincts. As instinctive energy builds up in the id, the result is an uncomfortable state of tension. The id may discharge this tension in the form of displacement, reflex actions, physical symptoms, or wishful thinking—uncensored mental images and unbidden thoughts.

The **ego,** the second system to emerge, is a referee between the needs of instinct and the demands of society. It obeys the **reality principle,** putting a rein on the id's desire for pleasure until a suitable outlet can be found. The ego, said Freud, represents "reason and good sense." Freud (1923/1962) described the relationship between ego and id this way: "In relation to the id, [the ego] is like a man on horseback, who has to hold in check the superior strength of the horse; . . . Often a rider, if he is not to be parted from his horse, is obliged to guide it where it wants to go; so in the same way the ego constantly carries into action the wishes of the id as if they were its own."

If a person feels anxious or threatened when those "wishes of the id" conflict with social rules, the ego has certain weapons at its command to relieve the tension. These weapons, called **defense mechanisms,** have two characteristics: They deny or distort reality, and they operate unconsciously. According to Freud, they are often unhealthy patterns that cause emotional problems and self-defeating behavior. Although there is no single agreed-upon list of all the processes that Freud considered to be defenses, we will use the main ones described by Freud's daughter Anna Freud (1946), who became an eminent psychoanalyst herself, and by modern personality researchers:

1. In *repression*, a threatening idea, memory, or emotion is blocked from becoming conscious. A woman who had a frightening experience in childhood, for example, may repress her memory of it. "Repression" doesn't mean that you consciously bite your tongue rather than reveal a guilty secret. It refers to the

■ **displacement**
The shifting of instinctual energy from its original object or activity to a different one.

■ **sublimation**
A type of displacement that serves a higher cultural or socially useful purpose; for example, the creation of art or music as a sublimation of sexual energy.

■ **id**
In psychoanalysis, the part of personality containing inherited psychological energy, particularly sexual and aggressive instincts.

■ **pleasure principle**
The principle guiding the operation of the id; seeks to reduce tension, avoid pain, and enhance pleasure.

■ **libido**
In psychoanalysis, the psychic energy that fuels the life or sexual instincts of the id.

■ **ego**
In psychoanalysis, the part of personality that represents reason, good sense, and rational self-control.

■ **reality principle**
The principle guiding the operation of the ego; seeks to find socially acceptable outlets for instinctual energies.

■ **defense mechanisms**
Methods used by the ego to prevent unconscious anxiety from reaching consciousness.

"I'm sorry, I'm not speaking to anyone tonight. My defense mechanisms seem to be out of order."

mind's effort to keep a lid on unacceptable feelings and thoughts in the unconscious, so that you aren't even aware of them.

2. In *projection*, one's own unacceptable feelings are attributed to someone else. A boy who dislikes his father, for instance, may feel anxious about disliking someone he depends on. So he may project his feelings onto his father, concluding that "he hates me." A person who has uncomfortable sexual feelings about members of a different ethnic group may project this discomfort onto them, saying, "Those people are dirty-minded and oversexed."

3. In *reaction formation*, the feeling that produces unconscious anxiety is transformed into its opposite in consciousness. A woman who is afraid to admit she doesn't love her husband may consciously believe she loves him. How does such a transformed emotion differ from the true emotion? Usually, a reaction formation gives itself away by being excessive: The person asserts the feeling too much and is too extravagant and compulsive about demonstrating it. ("Love him? *Of course* I love him! I never have any bad thoughts about him! He's perfect!")

4. *Regression*. As we will see, Freud believed that personality develops in a series of stages, from birth to maturity. Each new step, however, produces a certain amount of frustration and anxiety. If these become too great, normal development may be briefly or permanently halted and the child may remain *fixated* at the current stage; for instance, he or she may not outgrow clinging dependence. People may regress to an earlier stage if they suffer a traumatic experience in a later one. An 8-year-old child who is anxious about parental divorce may regress to earlier habits of thumbsucking or clinging. Adults may reveal "partial fixations" that they never outgrew, such as biting nails, or regress to immature behavior when they are under pressure.

5. In *denial*, people simply refuse to admit that something unpleasant is happening or that they are experiencing a taboo emotion. A woman may deny that she is angry with her boyfriend; an alcoholic may deny that he depends on liquor.

6. *Intellectualization* and *rationalization* (defenses favored by intellectuals!) depend on higher-level cognitive processes. Intellectualization is the unconscious control of emotions and impulses by excessive dependence on rational explanations. For example, a person may refuse to acknowledge a normal fear of

Is she "regressing" to the oral stage?

death by saying, "I'm not afraid of getting old because it happens to everybody." In rationalization, the person finds excuses to justify actions caused by repressed, unacceptable feelings: "I didn't hit you because I was angry; you needed to be punished."

7. In *displacement*, as noted, people release their emotions (usually anger) on things, animals, or other people that are not the real object of their feelings. People use displacement when they perceive the real target as being too threatening to confront directly. A boy who is forbidden to express anger at his father, for example, may "take it out" on his toys or his younger sister.

These defense mechanisms, Freud maintained, protect the ego and allow the person to cope with reality. Different personalities emerge because people differ in the defenses they use, in how rigid their defenses are, and in whether their defenses lead to healthy or disturbed functioning.

The **superego,** the last system of personality to develop, represents the voice of morality, the rules of parents and society, the power of authority. The superego consists of the *ego ideal*, those moral and social standards you come to believe are right, and the *conscience*, the inner voice that says you did something wrong. The superego sits in judgment on the activities of the id, handing out good feelings (pride, satisfaction) when you do something well and handing out miserable feelings (guilt, shame) when you break the rules.

According to Freud, the healthy personality must keep all three systems in balance. Someone who is too controlled by the id is governed by impulse and selfish desires. Someone who is too controlled by the superego is rigid, moralistic, and bossy. Someone who has a weak ego is unable to balance personal needs and wishes with social duties and realistic limitations.

THE DEVELOPMENT OF PERSONALITY. Freud maintained that personality develops in a fixed series of five stages. He called these stages *psychosexual* because he believed that psychological development depends on the changing expression of sexual energy in different parts of the body as the child matures.

1. *The oral stage* marks the first year of life. Babies take in the world, as well as their nourishment, through their mouths. So the mouth, said Freud, is the focus of sensation at this stage. People who remain fixated at the oral stage, he maintained, may, as adults, seek constant oral gratification in such activities as smoking, drinking, or overeating.

2. *The anal stage*, at about age 2 to 3, marks the start of ego development, as the child becomes aware of the self and of the demands of reality. The major issue at this stage, said Freud, is control of bodily wastes, a lesson in self-control that the child learns during toilet training. People who remain fixated at this stage, he thought, become "anal retentive," holding everything in, obsessive about neatness and cleanliness. Or they can become just the opposite, "anal expulsive," that is, messy and disorganized.

3. *The phallic (or Oedipal) stage* lasts roughly from age 3 to 5. Now sexual sensation is located in the penis, for boys, and in the clitoris, for girls. The child, said Freud, unconsciously wishes to possess the parent of the opposite sex and get rid of the parent of the same sex. Children of this age often announce proudly that "I'm going to marry Daddy (or Mommy) when I grow up" and reject the same-sex "rival." Freud (1924a, 1924b) labeled this phenomenon the **Oedipus complex,** after the Greek legend of King Oedipus, who unwittingly killed his father and married his mother. (Some psychoanalysts used the term "Electra complex," from another Greek legend, to describe the female version of this conflict, but Freud himself and almost all contemporary psychoanalysts use the term "Oedipus complex" for both sexes.)

■ **superego**
In psychoanalysis, the part of personality that represents conscience, morality, and social standards.

■ **Oedipus complex**
In psychoanalysis, a conflict in which a child desires the parent of the opposite sex and views the same-sex parent as a rival; this is the key issue in the phallic stage of development.

Boys and girls, Freud believed, go through the Oedipal stage differently. Boys at this stage are discovering the pleasure and pride of having a penis. When they see a female for the first time, they are horrified. Their unconscious exclaims (in one way or another), "Her penis has dropped off! Who could have done such a thing to her? My powerful father." This realization, said Freud, causes little boys to accept the authority of the father, who must have the power to remove their little penises, too. They repress their desire for the mother and begin to imitate the father. **Identification** is the process by which they take in, as their own, the father's standards of conscience and morality. The superego has emerged.

Freud admitted that he didn't quite know what to make of females, who, lacking the penis, couldn't go through the same steps. He speculated that a girl, upon discovering male anatomy, would panic that she had only a puny clitoris instead of a stately penis. She would conclude, said Freud, that she already had lost her penis. As a result, girls don't have the powerful motivating fear that boys do to give up their Oedipal feelings. They have only a lingering sense of "penis envy." The healthy female, said Freud, resolves penis envy by having children. The neurotic female resolves penis envy by trying to be like men, perhaps by having a career (although many of his patients and his daughter did just that). In either case, Freud concluded, women do not develop the strong moral superegos that men do.

By about age 5, when the Oedipus complex is resolved, the child's basic personality patterns are formed. Unconscious conflicts with parents, unresolved fixations and guilts, and attitudes toward the same and the opposite sex, said Freud, will continue to replay themselves throughout life.

4. *The latency stage* lasts from the end of the phallic stage to puberty. The child settles down, goes to school, makes friends, develops self-confidence, and learns the social rules for appropriate male or female behavior. Sexual feeling subsides.

5. *The genital stage* begins at puberty and marks the beginning of what Freud considered mature adult sexuality. Sexual energy is now located in the genitals, and eventually is directed toward sexual intercourse. Not everyone reaches this mature stage, said Freud. The defense mechanisms of the ego and the displacement of instinctual energy may prevent some people from reaching mature genital sexuality.

■ **identification**
A process by which the child adopts an adult's standards of morality, values, and beliefs as his or her own; in psychoanalysis, identification with the same-sex parent occurs at resolution of the Oedipus conflict.

QUICK QUIZ

Which Freudian concepts do these examples suggest?

1. A 4-year-old girl wants to snuggle on Daddy's lap but refuses to kiss her mother.
2. A celibate priest writes poetry about sexual passion and love.
3. A man who is angry at his boss shouts at his kids for making noise.
4. A woman who was mistreated by her stepfather for many years assures her friends that she adores him and thinks he is perfect.
5. A racist justifies segregation by saying that black men are only interested in sex with white women.
6. A 9-year-old boy who moves to a new city starts having tantrums.

ANSWERS:

1. Oedipus complex 2. sublimation 3. displacement 4. reaction formation 5. projection 6. regression

Freud's Descendants and Dissenters

As you might imagine, Freud's ideas were not exactly received with yawns. Some of his colleagues became devoted followers, who revered Freud as they would revere the founder of a new religion (Drucker, 1979; Sulloway, 1979). Many thought his theory was, to put it kindly, nonsense. Still others felt that Freud had made an important contribution by putting together many already-existing ideas into a coherent theory of personality and its development. (Although other scientists had written about the unconscious and about the sexual impulses of children, for example, Freud was the first to package these ideas in a systematic theory.)

Before we evaluate some aspects of Freud's theory, let's consider some variations on his basic theme. Some of Freud's followers stayed in the psychoanalytic tradition and modified Freud's theories from within. Others broke away completely to start their own schools.

Carl Jung (1875–1961) differed with Freud on the nature of the unconscious. In addition to the individual's personal unconscious, said Jung, there is a **collective unconscious**, containing the universal memories and history of humankind. From his study of myths, folklore, and art in cultures all over the world, Jung was impressed by common, repeated images, which he called **archetypes.** An archetype can be a picture, such as the "magic circle," called a *mandala* in Eastern religions, which symbolizes the unity of life. It can be a mythical figure, such as the Hero, the Nurturing Mother, the Powerful Father, or the Wicked Witch (Jung, 1967). Other powerful archetypes are the *persona* and the *shadow*. The persona is the public personality, the aspects of yourself that you reveal to others, the role that society expects you to play. The shadow archetype reflects the prehistoric fear of wild animals and represents the animal side of human nature.

Two of the most important archetypes, in Jung's view, are those of men and women themselves. Jung (like Freud) recognized that human beings are psychologically bisexual, that is, that "masculine" and "feminine" qualities are to be found in both sexes. The *anima* represents the feminine archetype in men; the *animus* represents the masculine archetype in women. Problems can arise, however, if a person tries to repress this internal, opposite archetype: that is, if a man totally denies his softer "feminine" side or if a woman denies her "masculine" aspects. People also create problems in relationships when they expect the partner to behave like the ideal archetypal man or woman, instead of the real human being who has both sides.

Although Jung shared with Freud a fascination with the unconscious side of the personality, he also emphasized the positive, forward-moving strengths of the ego. For Jung, people are motivated not only by past conflicts, as Freud thought, but also by their future goals and by the desire to fulfill themselves. Moreover, Jung anticipated modern trait research by many decades when he identified *introversion* and *extroversion* as basic personality orientations. Research has also confirmed Jung's idea that certain basic archetypes—such as the Hero, the Evil Beast, and the Earth Mother—appear in virtually every society (Campbell, 1949/1968). Lately there has been a resurgence of interest in Jung's theory of archetypes and in how these universal images and stories affect how people see their own lives (McAdams, 1988).

Karen Horney [HORN-eye] (1885–1952) took issue with Freud's emphasis on sexual and aggressive motivations, his notion of genetically based instincts, and his view that inner conflicts are inevitable (Horney, 1937, 1945). Horney's key concept was that of *basic anxiety*, the feeling of being "isolated and helpless in a potentially hostile world." Because people are dependent on each other,

According to Jung, the circle is an archetypal image that conveys the cycle of life and death—as in this Hindu mandala, showing the god Vishnu surrounded by lesser deities.

■ **collective unconscious**
To Carl Jung, the universal memories and experiences of humankind, represented in the unconscious of all people.

■ **archetypes** [AR-ki-tipes]
To Jung, universal, symbolic images that appear in myths, art, dreams, and other expressions of the collective unconscious.

she believed, they often end up in a state of anxious conflict when others don't treat them well. Insecure, anxious children develop personality patterns to help them cope with their feelings of isolation and helplessness. They may become aggressive as a way of protecting what little security they do have. They may become overly submissive. They may become selfish and self-pitying as a way of gaining attention or sympathy.

In general, said Horney, people relate to each other in one of three ways: They can move *toward* others, seeking love, support, and cooperation; they can move *away* from others, trying to be independent and self-sufficient; or they can move *against* others, being competitive, critical, and domineering. Ideally, she said, the healthy personality balances all three orientations. But some people become locked into only one mode: too weak-willed and self-denying, afraid to offend anyone; too independent, afraid to admit dependency; or too hostile, afraid to express affection.

Horney (1967) was also one of the first psychoanalysts to challenge Freud's notions of penis envy and female inferiority. She argued that it is both insulting philosophy and bad science to claim, as Freud did, that half the human race is dissatisfied with the gender assigned to it. When women feel inferior to men, she said, we should look for explanations in the real social disadvantages that women live with and their second-class status. Along with many contemporary female psychoanalysts, she feared that Freudian theory would justify continued discrimination against women by making it seem that female inferiority was in their nature and not in the conditions of their lives.

In fact, said Horney, if anyone has an envy problem, it is men. Men have "womb envy": They envy the female ability to bear and nurse children. Men glorify their own genitals, she said, because they are unable to give birth themselves. Later psychoanalysts, such as Bruno Bettelheim (1962), argued that both sexes envy the reproductive abilities of the other.

Alfred Adler (1870–1937) disagreed with Freud's emphasis on the unconscious depths of the id, with its aggressive and sexual instincts. Adler had a more positive view of the human condition than Freud did. For instance, he believed that people have a *drive for superiority*, which is not the desire to dominate others but the desire for self-improvement. Adler (1927/1959) thought that people are motivated by an "upward drive" for perfection. This impulse, said Adler, stems from the natural feelings of inferiority that all of us have, first as children, when we are weak and powerless compared to adults, and then later, when we have to recognize some limitations on our abilities. But some individuals, he wrote, develop an **inferiority complex.** Unable to accept their natural limitations, they try to mask them by pretending to be strong and capable. Instead of coping with real problems in life, people with inferiority complexes become overly concerned with protecting their self-esteem. Current research has supported him, as we saw in discussing the trait of self-esteem.

Unlike Freud and like Horney, Adler emphasized the individual's need for others. A key concept in Adler's theory of personality was that of *social interest*, empathy and concern for others (Adler, 1938/1964; Crandall, 1981). Social interest reflects the ability to be unselfish, to be sympathetic, to cooperate, and to feel connected to other people and to the world.

Adler (1935) further maintained that the real essence of human personality is *the creative self*. In this view, each person actively creates his or her own personality from the raw material of heredity and experience. Everyone creates a goal to strive for as well as a way of reaching that goal. All psychological processes form a consistent organization within each individual, a personality structure that is expressed in a unique *style of life*. The style of life is a result of biological factors, the individual's conscious and unconscious motives, past history, and life goals (Ansbacher & Ansbacher, 1964).

To Adler, everyone would strive for perfection if given the chance.

■ **inferiority complex**
To Alfred Adler, an inability to accept natural limitations; occurs when the need for self-improvement is blocked or inhibited.

To Freud, human beings are the passive victims of unconscious forces; to Adler, they are the masterful directors of their fate. To Freud, creativity is a side effect of sublimation; to Adler, creativity is a basic capacity of the species. To Freud, social cooperation is a grudging sacrifice of the id; to Adler, it is the essence of human life. In recent years, as psychology has moved toward an emphasis on cognitive appraisals in human development, therapy, and personality, Adler's work has been rediscovered.

THE OBJECT-RELATIONS SCHOOL.   A contemporary challenge to classical Freudian theory comes from the **object-relations school,** developed in Great Britain by Melanie Klein, W. R. D. Fairbairn, and D. W. Winnicott. In contrast to Freud's emphasis on the Oedipal period, object-relations theory holds that the first two years of life are the most critical for development of the inner core of personality. Freud emphasized the child's fear of the powerful father; these analysts emphasize the child's need for the powerful mother, who is usually the baby's caretaker during the first critical years. Freud's theory was based on the dynamics of inner drives and impulses; object-relations theory is based on the child's *relationship* with others. It holds that the basic human drive is not impulse gratification but the need to be in relationships.

The reason for the clunky word "object" in object-relations theory (instead of the warmer word "human" or even "parent") is to indicate that the infant's attachment isn't really to a person, but to the infant's *perception* of the person. According to these theorists, the child "takes in" or *introjects* a representation of the mother—someone who is kind or fierce, protective or rejecting—that is not literally the same as the woman herself. This representation may unconsciously affect the individual throughout his or her life.

Whereas Freud thought that female development was the problem, many proponents of the object-relations school regard male development as the problem (Chodorow, 1978). In their view, children of both sexes identify first with the mother. Girls, who are the same gender as the mother, do not need to separate from her. But boys, if they are to develop a male identity, must break away. As a result, this argument runs, male identity is more precarious and insecure than female identity, because it is based on *not* being like women. Men develop more rigid *ego boundaries* between themselves and other people, whereas women's boundaries are more permeable. Later in life, in this view, the typical psychological problem for women is how to develop autonomy, whereas the typical problem for men is how to develop attachment (Gilligan, 1982).

■ **object-relations school**
A psychoanalytic branch that emphasizes the importance of the infant's first two years of life and relationships with the major caretaker.

QUICK QUIZ

Match each idea with the analyst or school associated with it.

1.	Sigmund Freud	**a.**	basic anxiety
2.	Karen Horney	**b.**	collective unconscious
3.	Alfred Adler	**c.**	introjection of mother
4.	Carl Jung	**d.**	womb envy
5.	object-relations	**e.**	Oedipus complex
		f.	social interest
		g.	archetype
		h.	infant's bond to mother
		i.	superego
		j.	inferiority complex

ANSWERS:

1. e, i 2. a, d 3. f, j 4. b, g 5. c, h

Evaluating Psychodynamic Theories

There are few true-blue Freudians any more. Modern neo("new")-Freudians, such as the members of the object-relations school, have modified many aspects of Freud's original theories (Horowitz, 1988; Hughes, 1989). Yet they continue to use the same literary language of unconscious dynamics. Most of the criticism of psychodynamic theories comes from other schools of psychology, which point out the following problems:

Psychodynamic ideas are provocative. But are they testable? What errors can arise in generalizing from patients to all humanity and in using retrospective histories to create theories of development?

1. *Untestable hypotheses.* Many (but not all) of the ideas of psychodynamic theories are impossible to test one way or the other. They are descriptive metaphors, more poetic than scientific. As we saw in Chapter 2, a theory that is impossible to disconfirm in principle is not a scientific theory, and many psychodynamic ideas about unconscious motivations are impossible to confirm or disprove. Further, because so many of these ideas depend on the subjective interpretation of the analyst, there is no empirical way to decide which view is right. Freud saw penis envy; Horney saw womb envy. Freud thought the Oedipal period was most important in determining personality and acquiring conscience; object-relations theorists think the first two years are more important. All of these theorists freely speculate about what an infant feels and perceives.

2. *Incorrect ideas.* The psychodynamic assumption that instincts fill an internal "reservoir" has been disproved by research in physiology. The body does not store anger or other emotions. People can certainly collect grievances and keep a mental list of grudges, but this is not the same as saying that they have a fixed amount of aggressive energy that must be released. Other psychodynamic ideas, such as the emphasis on sexual conflicts, have been shown to be relative rather than universal, timeless principles. The belief of some proponents of object-relations theory, that men everywhere have more trouble than women with attachments because of their need to separate from the mother, is not supported by cross-cultural or historical evidence.

3. *The "patients-represent-everyone" fallacy.* Freud and many of his followers generalized inappropriately from patients in therapy to all human beings. If a woman comes to her therapist complaining of an excessive attachment to her father, the therapist cannot scientifically conclude that her problem is typical of *all* women. If a child is confused about sexual anatomy and thinks that girls have lost their penises, a scientist cannot conclude that *all* children share this view. If a homosexual patient reports having emotional conflicts, a clinician cannot conclude that *all* homosexuals are "sick." To be accurate, the observer would have to study a random sample of women, children, or homosexuals who are not in therapy.

4. *The "looking-backward" fallacy.* Any of us, looking backward over our lives, can array events in a straight line. We assume that if A came before B, then A *caused* B. Psychoanalysts often make this error, and Freud himself was aware of it. "So long as we trace the development from its final stage backwards," he wrote, "the connection appears continuous, and we feel we have gained an insight which is completely satisfactory or even exhaustive. But if we proceed the reverse way [if we start at the beginning and try to predict the result], then we no longer get the impression of an inevitable sequence of events" (Freud, 1920/1963). Looking backward also depends on a person's memories, which—you may remember—are highly subject to distortion.

5. *An overemphasis on unconscious processes rather than real experiences.* Freud's emphasis on the unconscious had a powerful effect, then and now, not just for theoretical reasons but also for practical ones. It was a great step forward to discover that people are not always aware of their actual desires or of the motives behind their acts. However, some critics believe that psychodynamic theories put too much emphasis on the unconscious, and overlook the importance of real events and conscious thoughts.

Consider the story of how Freud hit upon the cornerstone of psychoanalytic theory—the Oedipus complex. Early in Freud's career, many of his women patients (and some men) told him they had been sexually molested in childhood, typically by their fathers, uncles, or male friends of the family. At first, Freud concluded that these early experiences of sexual abuse were responsible for his patients' later unhappiness and illness. But then he changed his mind. He decided that his patients must be reporting *fantasies*, not real events, and that children (all children, not just his patients) fantasize about having sexual relations with the parent of the other sex. These fantasies are so taboo, said Freud, that children feel guilty about having them. It is their unconscious guilt about wanting sex with the parent, not the actual experience of sexual abuse, that causes illness and emotional problems later in life. With this turnaround, psychoanalysis was born (Sulloway, 1979).

Today, the notion that children are unconsciously seductive is being vigorously attacked, as studies have documented the reality of sexual abuse in childhood (Finkelhor, 1984). Most historians and social scientists now believe that Freud's patients probably were telling the truth when they revealed sexual abuse (Masson, 1984; Rush, 1980; Sulloway, 1979). Some psychoanalysts too have become more sensitive to the actual abuse, emotional as well as physical, that some parents inflict on their children (A. Miller, 1984). This abuse, they argue, has more impact than childish "fantasies."

In spite of all these problems, contemporary researchers and clinical psychologists are finding support for some psychodynamic assumptions, which have been translated into testable hypotheses. For example, Ernest Hartmann (1991) has developed a theory of personality differences based on the psychoanalytic and object-relations idea of ego boundaries. Using an objective test that has so far been given to about 2,000 people, he finds that people differ in terms of how "thick" or "thin" their boundaries are—both with other people ("I expect other people to keep a certain distance") and even with their own internal states ("Sometimes I don't know whether I'm thinking or feeling").

Other ideas from the psychodynamic tradition have added to modern psychology. Many people are indeed unconscious of the motives behind their puzzling actions. Some early childhood experiences can have a lasting effect on personality. Thoughts and rational behavior can be distorted by guilt, anxiety, and shame. The mind does defend itself against information that is threatening, unpleasant, or shocking. Prolonged emotional conflict may indeed play itself out in physical symptoms, immature habits, and self-defeating actions. In his provocative ideas, in the beauty of his writing, and in his own complicated personality, Freud left a powerful legacy to psychology. As Havelock Ellis (1910) put it, even when Freud "selects a very thin thread [in tying together his theories], he seldom fails to string pearls on it, and these have their value whether the thread snaps or not."

■ THE LEARNING TRADITION: YOU ARE WHAT YOU DO

On a hot summer day, James Peters shot and killed his next door neighbor, Ralph Galluccio. Peters had reached the end of his patience in a ten-year dispute over their common property line. Friends said this feud was not typical of the men's personalities. Galluccio, said his employer, was "a likable person with a good, even disposition." Peters, said his employer, was a "very mild-mannered, cooperative" man, "an all-around good guy."

A Freudian might say that this violent episode demonstrates the aggressive instinct in us all, but these men were not able to displace their aggression constructively. A behaviorist, however, would examine the role of environment in

Puzzles of Personality #3

What is the "nature" of human nature?

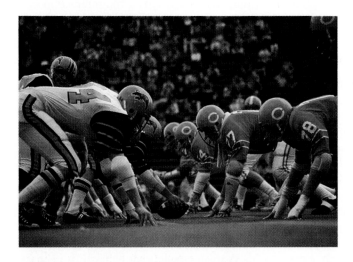

To Freudians, human nature rests on an eternal war between the aggressive or death instincts and the sexual or life instincts. The modern football game, in this view, represents the displacement of aggressive energy into a socially accepted activity.

To behaviorists and biologists, human nature can be as aggressive or peaceable as our environments permit; we have the capacity for both kinds of behavior. Behavioral research finds that aggressive sports, far from "displacing" aggression, actually model and encourage hostility and violence among players and spectators.

Karen Horney argued that human nature is basically social and cooperative; individuals who row together, so to speak, grow together. When people are prevented from expressing their needs for attachment and connection, however, they feel a basic anxiety and insecurity that may be expressed in destructiveness and hostility.

Alfred Adler believed that human nature is basically creative and constructive. Unless individuals are thwarted by social conditions, they strive to excel—as did champion skaters Torvill and Dean, who achieved perfect scores at the 1984 Olympics.

determining the actions of these men. "Environment" includes everything from neighbors and friends to family circumstances and job requirements. Some *radical behaviorists* take the extreme view that "personality" is only a convenient illusion. To understand human behavior, they say, we do not need to consider mental processes or biological factors; we need only consider the environment in which behavior occurs. Others, called *social learning theorists*, argue that we acquire consistent personality patterns as we learn to deal with the environment. What anyone does at a given time, they say, is a result of the interaction between personality and the situation.

The Behavioral School

In 1913, while Sigmund Freud was busy formulating psychoanalysis in Vienna, John B. Watson was founding the behavioral tradition in the United States. The two men represented the North and South Poles of personality theory, with Freud talking about instincts and unconscious motives and Watson dismissing these concepts as vague and unscientific. To Watson, most aspects of personality, including conflicts, fears, and habits, are classically conditioned responses, just as salivation was in Pavlov's dogs.

The best-known American behaviorist, B. F. Skinner, was actually as critical of Watson as he was of the psychoanalysts. Skinner shared with Freud the belief that behavior is determined by predictable factors. But he disagreed with Freud's reliance on hypothetical forces such as "the unconscious," "instincts," and "repression." Skinner shared with Watson a belief that behavior is primarily learned. But he rejected Watson's emphasis on classical conditioning as the major form of learning. Noting that many kinds of behavior were not classically conditioned, he turned to operant (instrumental) conditioning as the fundamental form of learning. (To refresh your memory on these terms, see Chapter 6.) For Skinner (1950), "personality" is just a collection of behavioral patterns. Personality traits (such as "aggressive," "extroverted," or "conscientious") reflect a description of particular responses in certain situations.

This doesn't mean that all situations produce the same responses in all individuals. Consider two people at a party of strangers. One, as knowledge of the five robust factors might predict, is extroverted and friendly, and the other is withdrawn and shy. Skinner would say that if we looked into the behavioral histories of these two people, we would find different patterns of reinforcement. For one, friendliness was reinforced; for the other, shyness was reinforced and assertiveness punished. What could possibly reward painful shyness? Experiments have found that shyness and anxiety are encouraged when they serve as a *self-handicapping strategy*. When shy people or people with low self-esteem are in situations in which they believe they will be evaluated, they learn to use their anxiety as an excuse for poor performance (C. Snyder, 1990). Self-handicappers place obstacles in the path of their own success. If they then fail, they can blame the failure on the handicap ("I'm shy" or "I have writer's block") instead of a lack of ability. If they succeed anyway, they can claim additional credit for doing well despite the handicap. But whereas psychoanalysts would account for this process in terms of unconscious dynamics to protect the ego, learning theorists regard it as a learned strategy to protect self-esteem.

Similarly, experimental psychologists have demonstrated in the laboratory that even "masochism," taking pleasure in pain, is learned—not, as Freud thought, an inevitable part of female personality (Stone & Hokanson, 1969). Anyone, man or woman, may acquire self-defeating, even injurious habits if those habits help the person avoid hostility or greater injury from others. When self-punishment is the lesser of two evils, it actually reduces anxiety and feels good (Baumeister & Scher, 1988).

Some behaviorists have tried to translate Freud's descriptive metaphors into behavioral language (Dollard & Miller, 1950). For example, they would interpret Freud's notion of repression in terms of acquired habits. Suppose a young man is worried that his girlfriend will leave him. He is afraid to talk to her about his feelings because he believes that would reveal unmanly weakness. Instead, every time his feelings of insecurity arise, he goes out drinking with his buddies. In so doing, he is learning a habit: "When I feel anxious, I'll drink." Freudians might say he is repressing his true feelings, burying them in the unconscious. Behaviorists would say he has learned a way of avoiding his feelings, because drinking with his friends is temporarily enjoyable and distracts him from anxiety.

Some psychologists criticize behaviorism for implying that individuals are as soft as jellyfish, and that with the right environment, anyone can become anything. They also criticize behaviorism for its implication that people are entirely passive recipients of environmental events. These common charges are not accurate. Skinner, for instance, recognized that there are limits to what people can do and to how much they can change, because of their genetic constitution or temperament, and he argued that people can *change* their environments to provide a different set of reinforcers.

Behaviorists do not deny that people have feelings, thoughts, and values. However, they believe that these mental states are as subject to the laws of learning as, say, nail biting is. (Nail biting itself, they would say, is a learned bad habit rather than a "fixation at the oral stage.") Skinner believed that the study of values is essentially the study of reinforcers. It is unscientific and imprecise to say that "Pat values fame." Rather, fame is positively reinforcing to Pat, which is why Pat continues to strive for it. Someone else might find fame unpleasantly punishing, and thus hold different "values." If we want a peaceful world, behaviorists say, we had better not wait around for people's personalities to change. We had better change circumstances so that cooperation is rewarded, cheaters don't win, and aggressors don't stay in power.

The Social Learning School

Modern social learning theorists give true radical behaviorists heartburn, because they have rediscovered the mind. They still emphasize the importance of the environment in shaping behavior, but they also believe in the importance of how people *interpret* their environments. The social learning approach to personality includes (1) aspects of the individual, (2) aspects of the environment, and (3) the *interaction* between them. Radical behaviorists also recognize that interaction, but they do not focus, as social learning theorists do, on cognitive phenomena such as perceptions, expectations, symbols, and beliefs as causes of behavior.

"If actions were determined solely by external rewards and punishments," observed Albert Bandura (1986), "people would behave like weathervanes, constantly shifting direction to conform to whatever momentary influence happened to impinge on them." To social learning theorists such as Bandura, the fact that people don't (always) act like weathervanes means that much of human behavior is *self-regulated*—shaped by thoughts, values, self-reflections, and intentions. Personality, they maintain, depends both on the context in which behavior is originally learned and on the current situation in which it occurs. To traditional learning theory, they have added principles of social learning, such as observational, or vicarious, learning (learning by watching what other people do and what happens to them for doing it) and cognitive processes such as planning for a rainy day.

Social learning theorists have identified qualities of the person that they believe influence behavior across many situations. The way people differ in each of these spheres, they say, contributes to their recognizable personalities (Mischel, 1981). Some of these qualities are:

* *Inherited temperaments.* Individuals differ in their levels of energy, the disposition to react to novelty with either curiosity or fear, and other traits in the "Big Five."
* *Skills and talents.* Different people excel in different areas, such as singing, sailing, or cooking.
* *Perceptions.* Individuals differ in how they have learned to interpret events, selectively noticing some aspects of a situation and ignoring others. Give Casey a chance to speak to an audience of 300 members of the Wildlife Association, and he sees it as an exciting challenge. Give Frank the same chance, and he sees it as a giant plot to embarrass and terrify him.
* *Expectations.* As people grow up, they learn to have certain expectations about what will happen to them if they behave in certain ways. Mildred may learn that if she speaks her mind, she can expect to irritate her parents, who want her to be quiet and obedient. Elizabeth may learn that if she speaks her mind, she can expect praise and attention.
* *Plans of action.* By adulthood, people have developed certain standards and values they use to govern themselves and their actions. People differ in their abilities to plan for the future and to carry out their plans.

There's not much call for bagpipe bands in Polynesia.

All of these aspects of the individual, however, depend on whether the circumstances permit them to be expressed. You may have a skill, such as pie baking or hog calling, and find yourself in a place that never gives you the chance to reveal it. (There is not much call for hog callers in San Francisco.) On the other hand, you may find yourself in a new environment that gives you an opportunity to show off skills you never dreamed you had. Specific situations, according to members of the social learning school, either permit us to express aspects of our personalities or prevent us from doing so.

In the most general sense, people must learn by observation and reinforcement what the rules of their culture and community are. These rules affect which personality traits are encouraged and which disparaged. For example, we saw in Chapter 10 that people differ in how they perceive and use time. Someone from an easy-going culture might think that a person from a more tightly scheduled culture has a "rigid personality." This issue raises yet another puzzle: how to measure aspects of personality that are unique to individuals, while keeping in mind the aspects of personality that are shared by many members of the culture the person lives in. (See "A Closer Look at Cross-Cultural Psychology" on p. 446.)

Evaluating Behavioral Theories

Why did James Peters kill Ralph Galluccio? Instead of assuming that Galluccio and Peters were driven by genes for aggressiveness or an instinctive death impulse, social learning psychologists would investigate the social *conditions* of their quarrel and each man's *perceptions* about it. The two men found themselves in an increasingly difficult situation that seemed to offer no way out. This doesn't mean that any two neighbors caught in a similar situation would have behaved the same way. Perhaps these two men lacked the skill to negotiate a solution to their differences. Perhaps each man had learned that aggressive actions would make other people knuckle under. When hurling insults, and then hurling eggs, failed, all they knew how to do was to escalate the aggression.

Behavioral and social learning approaches to personality represent a big step forward in solving some of the problems with psychodynamic theories. These approaches rely on experimental evidence and field studies rather than on the memories of patients in therapy. They also help account for the consistency paradox mentioned earlier, the fact that personality often does not predict behavior. If George is assertive at home but meek at work, or if Georgina is independent at work but clings to her friends, it is because they are reinforced differently in different situations. They have *learned* to behave differently.

Critics, however, observe that learning approaches sometimes attribute behavior to a vague category called "environment" (just as biological approaches sometimes attribute behavior to a vague category called "heredity"). Moreover, the social learning approach does not always distinguish the cause of a behavior from its consequences. For example, observational studies of children find that teachers and parents react more harshly to boys' aggressiveness than to girls' (Serbin et al., 1973). Boys get more punishment for disruptive behavior and therefore more rewarding attention. In social learning theory, this fact helps explain why more boys than girls are physically aggressive. But it is also possible that adults pay more attention to boys because the boys' aggressiveness is so disruptive and annoying.

Some psychologists, as we will see next, regard behavioral theories of personality as too cold and mechanical. Instead, they propose theories of personality that emphasize the total individual, the individual's unique sense of self, and free will.

QUICK QUIZ

In each situation, match each explanation with the appropriate theorist: psychoanalyst, behaviorist, or social learning theorist.

1. A 6-year-old boy is behaving aggressively in class, hitting other children and refusing to obey the teacher.
   a. The boy is being positively reinforced for aggressive behavior by getting attention from the teacher and the other children.
   b. The boy is expressing the aggressive energy of the id and has not developed enough ego control.
   c. The boy's behavior is an interaction of his own high energy level and of what he believes, from his own experience and observation, about the consequences of aggression.

2. A 6-year-old girl is clinging to her teacher in the classroom, afraid to do anything on her own.
   a. The girl has already learned to expect that any independent action she tries will be ignored or punished, so she is reluctant to work on her own.
   b. The girl gets attention from the teacher only when she is in close range. When she goes off to do work on her own, the teacher ignores her.
   c. The girl has developed passivity and dependency as a normal resolution of her Oedipus complex, in preparation for her adult roles of wife and mother.

ANSWERS:

1. a. behaviorist b. psychoanalyst c. social learning theorist 2. a. social learning theorist b. behaviorist c. psychoanalyst

A CLOSER LOOK AT
CROSS-CULTURAL PSYCHOLOGY

Culture, Personality, and the Self

Who are you? Take as much time as you like to complete this projective test: "I am _____."

Much of modern psychology is concerned with such concepts as personality, motives, needs, self-esteem, control, and achievement—all of which emphasize the individual (Sampson, 1988). But look again at the Table of Contents of this book. Imagine what it would be like if 16 chapters concerned family relations, groups, dependency needs, and the effects of other people on our behavior and perception, and only two chapters were devoted to individual physiology and cognition. Such a revised textbook would reflect the Japanese and Chinese view of personality, which is that people are interdependent, and so you cannot study an individual apart from his or her social world (Hsu, 1981; Markus & Kitayama, 1991).

Researchers in the growing field of *cross-cultural psychology* examine all of the ways in which people are affected by the culture in which they live, often comparing members of different cultures. Recently there has been a movement to develop a broader approach, called simply *cultural psychology,* which holds that all human psy-

chological functioning is mediated by culture—the system of rules for using artifacts (e.g., an ax or computer) and symbols (e.g., written words or painted images) (Cole, 1990; Shweder, 1990). In his book *Cultural Psychology,* J. R. Kantor (1982) observed that a Hindu and a Christian will respond differently to the stimulus of a cow. Both have the perceptual ability to see a physical cow, but their reactions, emotions, and ideas about the cow will be profoundly different because the cow is sacred to one and not the other.

One of the most important ways in which cultures differ has to do with whether the individual or the group is given the primary emphasis. This cultural difference, in turn, affects people's basic concepts of the self and personality. The idea of defining the "self" as a collection of personality traits ("I am extroverted, agreeable, and ambitious") is embedded in individual-centered cultures. In collectivist or group-centered cultures, the "self" is seen as something embedded in a community and is defined in a context ("I am the descendant of Joe and Ginny Jones, who came to Atlanta in 1908, opened a grain-supply store, and soon had 5 children and 13 grandchildren, one of whom ran for the state Senate . . .").

In one interesting study comparing Japanese and Americans, the Americans reported that their sense of self changes only 5 to 10 percent in different situations, whereas the Japanese said that 90 to 99 percent of their sense of self changes (de Rivera, 1989). For the Japanese, it is important to enact *tachiba*—to perform one's social roles correctly so that there will be harmony with others. Americans, in contrast, value "being true to your self" and having a "core identity." Simi-

■ **THE HUMANIST TRADITION: YOU ARE WHAT YOU CAN BECOME**

A third way to look at personality is not from outside, observing what a person does or says, but from inside, concentrating on a person's own sense of self and experience. This perspective, sometimes called **phenomenology,** does not seek to predict behavior or to uncover hidden motivations. It focuses on the person's subjective interpretation of what is happening right now. One group of phenomenologists, called *humanists,* believes that personality is defined by the human abilities that separate us from other animals: freedom of choice and free will. They regard "personality" as the sum total of an individual's decisions, his or her values and spiritual concerns, and the way the person resolves the inevitable crises that life serves up.

■ **phenomenology**
The study of events and situations as individuals experience them; in personality, the study of an individual's qualities from the person's own point of view.

larly, in cross-cultural studies of how people respond to the "I am . . ." cue, people from collectivist cultures typically answer in terms of family (e.g., "I am an uncle, a cousin, a son"), gender, or nation, whereas people from individualist cultures tend to answer in terms of personality traits or occupation (Triandis, 1990). Studies of cognition, emotion, and motivation in the two kinds of cultures find that none of these processes is "culture-free." The way that people define the self affects what they remember, their ideas about the self, their emotional responses, and their motivations (Markus & Kitayama, 1991; Trafimow, Triandis, & Goto, 1991).

Now, perhaps you have already thought of a potential problem with cross-cultural psychology. As one student of ours put it, "How come when we students speak of 'the' Japanese or 'the' blacks or 'the' whites or 'the' Latinos, it's called stereotyping, and when you do it, it's called 'cross-cultural psychology'?" In Chapter 18 we will have more to say about this excellent question, and about prejudice and stereotyping in general. For now, keep in mind that the aim of cross-cultural psychology is *not* to stereotype, that is, to assume that *all* members of a culture behave the same way. Individuals vary within every culture, according to their temperaments, traits, and learning histories. And people in the most individualistic cultures are concerned with group harmony and conformity, while people in collectivist cultures are still concerned with private feelings and goals.

Cross-cultural psychologists take pains to avoid evaluative and prejudicial language: For example, cultures may differ, *on the average,* in whether they emphasize the individual or the group; but this does not necessarily mean that the former culture is "selfish" and the latter "conformist." By showing how cultural rules shape behavior and set norms, cross-cultural psychologists hope that people will become more tolerant of group differences and of people who value other ways of doing things.

Here is an example that may apply to you or someone you know. In collectivist cultures, the strongest human bond is usually not between husband and wife, but between parent and child or siblings (Triandis, 1990). In China it is the father-son bond; in India, Mexico, and Greece it is mother-son; in parts of Africa, it is older brother-younger brother; in numerous communities it is mother-daughter. In addition, child rearing in collectivist cultures is a communal matter; everyone has a say in correcting the child's behavior. The idea of "privacy" for children is unknown, and the goal is to raise children who are obedient, hardworking, and dutiful toward their parents. Can you predict what will happen if a collectivist man marries an individualist woman? The chances are high that the husband will regard his relationship with his mother as being most important, whereas his wife will expect his relationship to her to be most important. And they are likely to disagree intensely, without knowing why, about such matters as letting their children have private rooms, speak their minds, make their own choices, and become independent.

An appreciation of the role of culture expands our understanding of personality. Now when your family or friends behave mysteriously, you can ask youself: Is it their genes, their upbringing, their situation—or their culture?

The Self and Self-Regard

Humanistic psychology was launched as a movement within psychology in the early 1960s. Its chief leaders were Abraham Maslow (1908–1970), Rollo May, and Carl Rogers (1902–1987), who argued that it was time for a "third force" in psychology. They rejected the psychoanalytic emphasis on hostility, biological instincts, and conflict. They also rejected the fragmented approach of the behavioral schools, with their emphasis on describing pieces of the person. Mainstream psychology, they said, failed to deal with the real problems of life or draw a full picture of human potential (M. B. Smith, 1984).

The trouble with psychology, said Maslow (1962/1968), was that it had forgotten that human nature includes good things, such as joy, laughter, love, simple daily happiness, and rare moments of rapture, caused by the attainment of excellence or the drive toward higher values, which he called *peak experiences.*

Maslow started out as a behaviorist, an approach he left after the birth of his first child. ("Anyone who [observes] a baby could not be a behaviorist," he later remarked.) The traits that Maslow thought most important to personality were not the Big Five, but rather the qualities of the self-actualized person—the person who strives for a life that is meaningful, challenging, and exciting.

Not all humanists have been as cheerful as Maslow was about human nature. Rollo May emphasizes some of the fundamentally difficult or even tragic aspects of the human condition, including loneliness, anxiety, and alienation. In books such as *The Meaning of Anxiety*, *Man's Search for Himself*, *Existential Psychology*, and *Love and Will*, May brought to American psychology elements of the European philosophy of existentialism. This doctrine holds, for instance, that human beings have absolute freedom of choice, but this freedom carries a price in anxiety and even despair.

Carl Rogers, like Freud, derived many of his ideas from observing his clients in therapy. As a clinician, Rogers (1951, 1961) was interested not only in why some people cannot function well, but also in what he called the fully functioning individual. Rogers's theory of personality is based on the relationship between the *self* (your conscious view of yourself, the qualities that make up "I" or "me") and the *organism* (the sum of all of your experience, including unconscious feelings, perceptions, and wishes). This experience is known only to you, through your own frame of reference. How you behave depends on your own subjective reality, Rogers said, not on the external reality around you. Fully functioning people show a **congruence,** or harmony, between self and organism. Such people are trusting, warm, and open to new experience. They aren't defensive or intolerant. Their beliefs about themselves are realistic. When the self and the organism are in conflict, however, the person is said to be in a state of incongruence.

To become fully functioning, congruent people, Rogers maintained, we all need **unconditional positive regard,** love and support for the people we are, without strings (conditions) attached. This doesn't mean that Winifred should be allowed to kick her brother when she is angry with him or that Wilbur may throw his dinner out the window because he doesn't like pot roast. In these cases, however, a parent can correct the child's behavior without withdrawing love from the child. The child can learn that the behavior, not the child, is what is bad. "House rules are 'no violence,' Winifred," is a very different message from "You are a horrible person, Winifred."

Unfortunately, Rogers observed, many children are raised with *conditional* positive regard. The condition is "I'll love you if you behave well and I won't love you if you behave badly." Adults often treat each other this way, too. People treated with conditional regard begin to suppress or deny feelings or actions that they believe are unacceptable to those they love. The result, said Rogers, is incongruence. The suppression of feelings and parts of oneself produces low self-regard, inaccurate perceptions of reality, defensiveness, and unhappiness. Incongruence creates the sensation of being "out of touch with your feelings," of not being true to your "real self." The consequences for personality would be individuals who score high on neuroticism—who are bitter, unhappy, and negative.

Evaluating Humanistic Theories

The major criticism of the humanistic approach is that many of its assumptions cannot be tested because the terms that humanists use are vague. How would you tell if a person is "self-fulfilled" or "self-actualized"? How would you distinguish a person who has "unconditional positive self-regard" from one who is arrogant or selfish? Critics also say that humanistic psychology is closer to philosophy than science, because it rests on a subjective view of human nature. It

■ **congruence**
To Carl Rogers, harmony between the conscious self and the totality of the person's unconscious feelings and life experiences.

■ **unconditional positive regard**
To Rogers, love or support given to another person with no conditions attached.

happens to be a nicer view of human nature than, say, Freud's, but it is just as difficult to prove. Freud saw, in his patients and in history, conflict, destructive drives, selfishness, and lust. Maslow and Rogers saw, in individuals and in history, cooperation, constructive drives, altruism, and love. This may tell us more about the observers than about the observed.

Many psychologists also resent the implication that they are not humanists, or do not care about humanity, just because they study people scientifically or have different ideas about how to achieve goals of peace and self-fulfillment. Some are skeptical about the prospects of creating a humane world by simply trusting in people to behave well, by giving them unconditional love, or by counting on the goodness of human nature.

Humanistic theories generated a flurry of modern programs devoted to giving people the unconditional positive regard that they believe they didn't get in childhood (a situation that seems to apply to most of humanity). In Chapter 17 we will evaluate humanistic therapies, but for now consider some questions raised by critics of the assumptions underlying these programs: Can a weekend "love bath" overturn the effects of a childhood of emotional deprivation? Can ordinary people (as opposed to saints and buddhas) be expected to *sincerely* give their closest loved ones, let alone total strangers, "unconditional positive regard" at all times? Would the effects of such regard always be beneficial, or might they lead to an inability to appraise one's limitations and mistakes? Can you separate what a person *does* from what a person *is*, as Rogers recommended?

Nevertheless, humanistic psychology has added balance to psychology's view of personality. Some of Maslow's and Rogers's ideas have been tested experimentally. Many have proven faulty, such as Maslow's belief in a hierarchy of needs (see Chapter 10), but others have been supported, as we will see in later chapters. Psychologists now study the happier emotions and positive experiences, such as love, altruism, cooperation, and creativity, along with the troubling ones. Stress researchers have discovered the healing powers of humor and hope. Child psychologists have shown how parental treatment contributes to or crushes a child's self-esteem and creativity. Finally, the idea that personality contains a deep well of "potential" (usually this means a potential for good, not a potential to become an ax murderer) has spawned an interest in the further reaches of consciousness and capability.

QUICK QUIZ

1. According to Carl Rogers, a man who loves his wife only when she is looking her best is giving her (a) *conditional* or (b) *unconditional* positive regard.
2. The humanist who described the importance of having peak experiences was (a) Rollo May, (b) Abraham Maslow, (c) Carl Rogers.
3. A humanist and a psychoanalyst are arguing about human nature. What underlying assumptions about human psychology and possibility are they likely to bring to their discussion, and what do their assumptions overlook?

ANSWERS:

1. a 2. b 3. Some assumptions: the analyst, that human nature is basically selfish and destructive; the humanist, that it is basically loving and life-affirming. Their assumptions overlook, among other things, the facts that human beings have both capacities, and that the situation often determines which capacity is expressed.

Puzzles of Personality #4

Is personality stable over a lifetime?

To psychoanalysts, the basic conflicts and motives of personality are set during a child's first five years. Other schools of psychology maintain that personality traits are flexible and can change in adulthood depending on experiences. Research is identifying some of the traits that do seem to be stable across the life span, and others that are more influenced by circumstances.

Self-esteem can vary with a person's situation and experiences. Many individuals lose self-esteem temporarily when they are fired from jobs, or when they work in environments that give them no feedback or support. People often gain self-esteem, though, when they join supportive groups to improve their working conditions, as this group of union women at a Labor Day parade has done.

Extroversion and introversion are among the more stable of traits, and have a genetic component. The woman in the bright lime-colored outfit, mugging for the camera, has probably been outgoing and demonstrative since childhood.

Not all traits are lifelong aspects of personality, however. Although aggressive children are more likely than their calmer peers to be aggressive as adults, many children and teenagers outgrow early aggressiveness.

Shyness and timidity seem to be relatively stable. Although everyone feels shy on occasion, some people feel shy on most occasions—uncomfortable in new situations and slow to reveal themselves.

■ THE PRIVATE PERSONALITY

Whatever "personality" is, most psychologists have agreed that it is stable. Biologically oriented researchers believe that the basic qualities of personality are part of a person's genetic heritage. Psychoanalysts believe that personality is formed within the first few years by unconscious dynamics. Even social learning theorists think that people are pretty much shaped for life in their formative years by the rewards, punishments, and parental treatment they get. Is change therefore impossible?

Psychologists who believe that personality is flexible suggest that stability is often more a matter of perception than reality. One woman we know observed a 7-month-old boy reaching up, trying to catch a sunbeam. When that boy was in high school, he made a laser. The woman connected the two events, concluding that the boy was always "fascinated with light." In seeing a consistency between the 7-month-old and the 17-year-old, she failed to notice all the babies who reach for sunbeams and then grow up to be miners, darkroom photo developers, or tunnel builders. Indeed, most people like to string events together to make a pattern. As Freud said, when we look back, we feel our development has been predictable because we see the paths we chose and forget the roads not taken. Looking across situations, we feel our actions are coherent because we don't want to believe that we are easily swayed by prevailing winds.

Perhaps the main reason for seeing consistency in our own lives and those of others is that we *feel* consistent. Each of us has a sense of self, an identity, through which we process and absorb experiences, thoughts, and emotions. Each of us has a unique constellation of memories, dreams, wishes, and experiences. The result, that inner sense of continuity and perception, has been called the *private personality* (Singer, 1984). The private personality allows us to draw links across situations and explain away behavior we think is out of character. We even rewrite personal history if necessary—that is, correct our memories—to maintain the sense of consistency (Greenwald, 1980).

Experiments have found that people's private thoughts and emotions often play a more profound role in their self-concepts than do their actual behaviors (Andersen, 1984). In fact, self-image may last long after actual behavior has changed radically. Private feelings of guilt, despair, pride, anticipation, elation, desire, and worry shape our self-concepts because they are so vivid. People can rationalize or explain away their actions, but, as Carl Rogers often said, they regard inner feelings and thoughts as the "real self."

The real self consists of the traits that people use to describe their personalities. But, as Karen Horney (1950) observed, healthy people are also guided by an *ideal self*—images of what they would like to be, images around which they organize actions and aspirations. The private personality, researchers are finding, is made up of many *possible selves*: images of what you believe you could become, would like to become, or even are afraid of becoming (Markus & Nurius, 1986). The way we envision our possible selves affects our motivations, dreams, plans, and self-esteem—the very stuff of personality.

In this chapter, we have seen that some qualities of the individual do seem to be stable throughout life: temperaments, mannerisms, the Big Five personality factors. Other qualities seem more susceptible to change and evolution: self-esteem, ambitions, and interests. In truth, every personality is a mixture of stability and change. The particular balance in a person's life will depend on genetic predispositions, defenses, emotional needs, and experience. People do not strike the same balance the same way at the same time. Personality change, in any case, is like a sunrise; you can't pinpoint the single moment when the sky turns color. The slow and steady nature of most changes in personality contributes to the belief that we don't really change; we just become more like ourselves.

The need to feel consistent can blind us to the fact that what we do is often unrelated to who we think we are. Is this an example of emotional reasoning, or are our feelings of consistency justified in some ways?

TAKING PSYCHOLOGY WITH YOU

On Suckers and "Personality Profiles":
How to Avoid the Barnum Effect

How well does the following paragraph describe you?

> Some of your aspirations tend to be pretty unrealistic. At times you are extroverted, affable, sociable, while at other times you are introverted, wary, and reserved. You have found it unwise to be too frank in revealing yourself to others. You pride yourself on being an independent thinker and do not accept others' opinions without satisfactory proof. You prefer a certain amount of change and variety, and become dissatisfied when hemmed in by restrictions and limitations. At times you have serious doubts as to whether you have made the right decision or done the right thing.

When people believe that this description was written just for them—the result of a personalized horoscope, "personality profile," or handwriting analysis—they all say the same thing: "It's me! It describes me *exactly!*" Why should this be so? The answer is that this description is vague enough to apply to almost everyone, positive enough to please almost everyone, and flattering enough to get almost anyone to accept it (French et al., 1991; Snyder & Shenkel, 1975). People are not so quick to accept the following "personality profile," however:

> You are a sullen, hateful slob. You dislike people and most people dislike you too. You are usually nasty, cruel, and calculating. You never think for yourself but steal other people's ideas. Once you've made a decision you stick with it, even when it's wrong.

Studies repeatedly find that *people are more willing to believe flattering statements about themselves than statements that are scientifically accurate* (Thiriart, 1991). In addition, as research shows, the more effort people invest in getting a horoscope or profile, the more likely they are to believe the results—even when the identical results are given to everyone. If they must pay money for a profile, take the time to write away for it, or give detailed information about themselves, they are more likely to believe the profile is "eerily accurate." A French psychologist once advertised himself as an astrologer. In reply to the hundreds of people who wrote to him for his services, he sent out the same vague horoscope. More than 200 recipients sent him thank-you notes praising his accuracy and perceptiveness (Snyder & Shenkel, 1975).

Personality quizzes in magazines are also based on a simplified idea of personality, and they rarely allow people to distinguish a personality problem from a temporary difficulty. Let's say you total up your score on a personality quiz and discover that you are a "worrier." Is worry part of your personality, or do you have four exams in three days and an employer who is giving you a hard time? Some of these pop personality quizzes can really make you worry about yourself.

This is why many psychologists worry that too many people are falling prey to the "P. T. Barnum effect." Barnum was the great circus showman who said "there's a sucker born every minute." He knew that the formula for success was to "have a little something for everybody"—which is what unscientific personality profiles, horoscopes, and handwriting tests have in common. To help you avoid the Barnum effect, research offers a few strategies:

• *Beware of all-purpose descriptions that could apply to anyone.* We know a married couple who were terribly impressed when an astrologer told them that "each of you needs privacy and time to be independent" along with "but don't become too independent or you will lose your bond." Such observations, which play it safe by playing it both ways, apply to virtually all couples.

• *Beware of your own selective perceptions.* Most of us are so impressed when a palm reader or horoscope gets something right that we overlook all the descriptions and predictions that are plain wrong.

• *Resist flattery.* This is the hard one. Most of us would reject a personality profile that described us as being nasty, sullen, and stupid. But many of us fall for profiles that tell us how wonderful and smart we are, especially if they seem objective or "scientific."

This discussion is not meant to keep you from having fun reading your horoscope or taking a magazine's personality quiz. Just keep your critical faculties alongside your sense of humor as you read them. Then you won't end up paying hard cash for soft answers, pawning the piano because Leos should invest in gold this month, or taking a job you despise because it fits your "type." In other words—have a good time, but prove Barnum wrong.

SUMMARY

1. *Personality* is usually defined as an individual's distinctive and relatively stable pattern of behavior, motives, thoughts, and *traits*, characteristics that describe a person across situations.

2. Personality tests include *objective tests* or *inventories* (such as the MMPI), and *projective tests* (such as the TAT and Rorschach). Projective tests, which rely on the subjective interpretation of responses, are generally less reliable than the other two measures. Personality tests of traits have problems with *the consistency paradox*—the gap between the measurement of traits and the fact that behavior often varies across situations.

3. Gordon Allport argued that personality consists of three kinds of traits: cardinal, central, and secondary. Many individual traits, such as *self-esteem*, have been identified, both as a relatively permanent *trait* and a more variable *state*.

4. Raymond Cattell used factor analysis to distinguish surface traits from source traits, which he considered the basic components of personality. Research now suggests that there are five "robust (stable) factors" in personality: extroversion, neuroticism (negative emotionality), agreeableness, conscientiousness, and openness to experience.

5. Some personality characteristics appear to be heritable to some degree. Individual differences in *temperaments* or ways of reacting to the environment emerge early in life and can influence subsequent development. Certain temperamental differences may be due to variations in the responsiveness of the sympathetic nervous system to change and novelty. Data from twin studies suggest that the heritability of various adult personality traits is around .50. Be careful, however, in drawing conclusions about the heritability of personality traits because of methodological problems in the research, the vagueness with which "environment" has been measured, and the diminishing effect of genes over time.

6. Sigmund Freud was the founder of *psychoanalysis*, which emphasizes the unconscious aspects of personality. Freud's *psychodynamic* theory was based on the movement of energy within the person. Instincts that are blocked from direct expression may be *displaced* or *sublimated* in socially acceptable ways.

7. To Freud, the personality consists of id (the source of *libido* and the aggressive instinct), ego (the source of reason), and superego (the source of conscience). *Defense mechanisms* protect the ego from unconscious anxiety. Freud believed that personality develops in a series of *psychosexual stages*: oral, anal, phallic (Oedipal), latency, and genital. During the phallic stage, Freud believed, the *Oedipus complex* occurs, in which the child desires the opposite-sex parent and feels rivalry with the same-sex parent. When the complex is resolved, the child will *identify* with the same-sex parent and settle into the latency stage. At puberty, the genital stage of adult sexuality begins.

8. Carl Jung believed that people share a *collective unconscious* that contains universal human memories and history. There are many universal *archetypes* in personality, including the anima and animus. Karen Horney believed that *basic* *anxiety* was the central human motivation, and she emphasized social relationships more than biological instincts. She also challenged Freud's ideas of female inferiority and penis envy. Alfred Adler argued that people have a need for self-improvement (a drive for *superiority*); that an important aspect of personality is *social interest;* and that each person creates his or her own personality from heredity and experience *(the creative self).*

9. The contemporary *object-relations* school differs from classical Freudian theory in emphasizing the importance of the first two years of life, rather than the Oedipal phase; the infant's relationships to important figures, especially the mother, rather than sexual needs and drives; and the problem in male development of breaking away from the mother.

10. Psychodynamic theories have been criticized for being unscientific and incorrect. Their methods have been challenged for relying on the memories of unrepresentative patients, and for paying more attention to unconscious motives than to real experiences. But many psychodynamic ideas have been influential both in experimental psychology and in psychotherapy.

11. Radical behaviorists believe that personality can be studied according to learning principles, without relying on internal mental processes. Social learning theorists also believe that personality consists of learned patterns, but they have added cognitive factors and social learning principles (such as observation and self-reinforcement). In their view, personality depends on aspects of the individual, aspects of the environment, and how the two interact.

12. Humanists believe that personality is defined by uniquely human abilities, notably free will and the subjective experience of the self. Abraham Maslow emphasized the positive, self-actualizing side of personality. Rollo May emphasizes the *existential* concerns of free will. Carl Rogers emphasized the importance of *unconditional positive regard* in creating a "fully functioning" person.

13. Some psychologists argue that trait stability is an illusion, a result of perceptual biases. However, the "private personality" gives us a feeling of consistency and allows us to assimilate change slowly. Personality includes not only actual traits, but also *possible selves:* the images of the ideal self and the undesired self that motivate people and shape their goals.

KEY TERMS

personality   *415*
trait   *415*
objective tests/inventories   *416*
Minnesota Multiphasic Personality
  Inventory (MMPI)   *416*
projective tests   *417*
Rorschach Inkblot Test   *418*
Thematic Apperception Test (TAT)
  418
consistency paradox   *419*
Gordon Allport   *421*
cardinal and central traits   *421*
trait self-esteem   *421*
state self-esteem   *421*
Raymond Cattell   *422*
factor analysis   *422*
Hans Eysenck   *422*
five robust factors   *422*
temperaments   *424*
heritability   *425*

psychoanalysis   *431*
unconscious processes   *431*
psychodynamic   *431*
displacement and sublimation   *432*
id   *432*
pleasure principle   *432*
libido   *432*
ego   *432*
reality principle   *432*
defense mechanisms   *432*
  repression   *432*
  projection   *433*
  reaction formation   *433*
  regression   *433*
  denial   *433*
  intellectualization   *433*
  displacement   *434*
superego   *434*
psychosexual stages   *434*
Oedipus complex   *434*

13

Child Development

> *In automobile terms, the child supplies the power but the parents have to do the steering.*
>
> BENJAMIN SPOCK

I n 1618, a Puritan minister advised parents that all children have "a stubbornness, and stoutness of mind arising from natural pride, which must, in the first place, be broken and beaten down" (Demos, 1970). Today, psychologists advise parents to help their children develop pride and self-esteem by building them up instead of beating them down. Throughout history, there have been many other mutually contradictory views of the child. Is a baby born with a basic personality already formed, or will personality be determined by what the parents do? Are children little savages until civilized society teaches them to be kind and cooperative, or are they little moralists, until uncivilized society teaches them to be greedy and selfish?

Today, too, people hold strong and differing beliefs about what children are like and how they should be brought up. Should mothers work outside the home or do babies need their mothers around all the time? Can fathers act like mothers? How early can babies start learning, and how much can we teach them? Can you create the child you want, or does the child have something to say about it?

Against this background of social values and practical concerns, child psychologists study many facets of a child's physical, cognitive, social, emotional, and moral development. *Child development* includes the processes by which an organism grows from a fetus in the womb to an adult, processes that include predictable changes in biological **maturation**, physical structure, behavior, and thinking. Some researchers think of "development" as a series of small, gradual, continuous steps that blend into each other, just as the babbling sound "maa, maa" becomes a call for "mama." Others think of development as a series of distinct stages that are qualitatively different from each other, just as walking is significantly different from crawling. In this view, with each stage, children acquire a new way of thinking or behaving that is added to the earlier way.

Psychologists study *universal* aspects of development, the changes that occur in all children as they mature; *cultural* differences in development, the patterns that occur in some cultures and ethnic groups but not in others; and *individual* differences in development, the changes that occur in some children but not in others. In this chapter we will consider some of their discoveries. Then we will ask you to step back, put what you have read into perspective, and consider a controversial question: What is the connection between childhood and adulthood?

In some societies and eras, children have been regarded as "little adults," as this painting of Sir Walter Raleigh and his son shows. The very idea of childhood as a special time of development is a relatively new invention.

■ FROM CONCEPTION TO THE FIRST YEAR

A baby's development, before and after birth, is an astonishing process, a marvel of maturation. In only 9 months of a mother's pregnancy, a cell grows from a dot this big (·) to a squalling bundle of energy that looks just like Aunt Sarah. In roughly another 15 months, that squalling bundle of energy grows into a babbling toddler who is curious about everything. No other time in human development brings so many changes, so fast.

■ **maturation**
The sequential unfolding of genetically governed behavior and physical characteristics.

457

Prenatal Development

Prenatal development is divided into three stages: the *germinal*, the *embryonic*, and the *fetal*. The germinal stage begins at conception, when the male sperm unites with the female ovum (egg). A day or so after conception, the fertilized egg, or *zygote*, begins to divide into two parts and, in a few more days, it attaches itself to the wall of the uterus. The outer part will form part of the placenta and umbilical cord, and the inner part becomes the *embryo*. The placenta will be the growing embryo's food and supply link from the mother, connected to the embryo itself through the umbilical cord. The placenta allows nutrients to get through and wastes to get out, and it screens out some, but not all, harmful substances.

Once implantation of the zygote is completed, about two weeks after conception, the germinal stage is over and the *embryonic* stage begins, lasting until the eighth week after conception. The embryo develops webbed fingers and toes, a tail (you have a "tailbone" to remind you of this prenatal phase), eyes, ears, a nose, a mouth, a heart and circulatory system, and a spinal cord—although at eight weeks, the embryo is only $1\frac{1}{2}$ inches long. Sometime during the fourth to eighth week, the male hormone testosterone is secreted by the rudimentary testes in embryos that are genetically male; without this hormone, the embryo will develop as a female.

After 8 weeks, the *fetal* stage begins. The embryo, now called a *fetus*, further develops the organs and systems that existed in rudimentary form during the embryonic stage. By 28 weeks, the nervous and respiratory systems are developed enough to allow some fetuses to live if born prematurely. (New technology allows some prematures to survive if born even earlier, but the risks are higher.) The last 12 weeks before birth see the greatest gains in brain and nervous system development, length, and weight.

Although the womb is a fairly sturdy protector of the growing fetus, some harmful influences can cross the placental barrier. Some of the conditions known to harm fetal development include the following:

- *German measles* (rubella), especially early in the pregnancy, often affects the fetus's eyes, ears, and heart. The most common consequence is deafness. Rubella is preventable if the mother has been vaccinated, which can be done in adulthood, up to three months before pregnancy.
- *X-rays* or other radiation, or *toxic chemicals* such as lead, can cause fetal abnormalities and deformities.
- *Sexually transmitted diseases*, such as syphilis, can cause mental retardation, blindness, and other physical disorders, and, in the case of AIDS, eventually death. Herpes can affect the fetus only if the mother has an outbreak at the time of delivery, which exposes the newborn to the virus in the birth canal. This risk can be avoided by having a Caesarean section, in which the baby is removed surgically through the uterus.
- *Cigarettes*. Pregnant women who smoke increase the likelihood of miscarriage, premature birth, abnormal fetal heartbeat, and underweight babies. The negative effects of smoking during pregnancy can last long after the child's birth, showing up in increased rates of infant sickness, Sudden Infant Death Syndrome, and, in later childhood, hyperactivity and difficulties in school.
- *Alcohol*. Pregnant women who drink alcohol heavily—that is, who have five or more drinks a day—increase by 30 percent the risk of their babies having **fetal alcohol syndrome (FAS)**. Infants with FAS are smaller than normal, have smaller brains, are more uncoordinated, and have some degree of mental retardation. The effects of lesser amounts of alcohol on the fetus are uncertain. One recent study of 592 British women who were interviewed and examined

■ **fetal alcohol syndrome**
A pattern of physical and intellectual abnormalities in infants whose mothers drank an excessive amount of alcohol during pregnancy.

during their pregnancies, and whose children were examined three years later, found that the children of mothers who did not drink at all during pregnancy were no different from those of mothers who had had fewer than 10 drinks a week (Forrest et al., 1991). But other studies have found that the risk of FAS increases if the mother has as few as two glasses of red wine daily (Bolton, 1983). One complexity in this area of research is that the effects of alcohol on the fetus are different at different stages of pregnancy.

• *Drugs.* Morphine, cocaine, and heroin can interfere with fetal development. Commonly used drugs such as antibiotics, antihistamines, tranquilizers, acne medication, diet pills, coffee, and excessive amounts of vitamins can also be transmitted to the fetus. Women should also guard against prescribed drugs that have not been adequately tested. In the 1960s, pregnant women who took the tranquilizer Thalidomide gave birth to babies with missing or deformed limbs. Between the 1940s and 1971, many women were given the hormone diethylstilbestrol (DES) to prevent miscarriages. Some daughters of these women later developed cancer of the vagina during adolescence, and sons were prone to testicular problems.

The lesson is clear. A pregnant woman does well to quit smoking completely, to drink little or no alcohol, and to take no drugs of any kind unless they are medically necessary and tested for safety (and then to accept the fact that her child will never be properly grateful for all that sacrifice!). But what if she doesn't take this advice? Should the fetus be protected from its own mother? We discuss the difficult ethical and political issues surrounding these questions in "Think About It" on page 460.

What about positive prenatal experiences? Should a pregnant woman be reading Shakespeare to her fetus, playing classical music, and preparing the fetus for college entrance exams? The fetus can certainly hear sounds in the last few months of pregnancy—mother's voice, music, startling sounds from television, hair dryers, and vacuum cleaners—and they even develop preferences for various sounds. Two psychologists asked 16 pregnant women to read Dr. Seuss's classic tale *The Cat in the Hat* aloud twice a day during the last six weeks of their pregnancies. When the babies were born, they had a choice of sucking on one of two nipples. Sucking on the first brought a recording of their mothers reading the Seuss story. Sucking on the other nipple produced a recording of the mothers reading *The King, the Mice and the Cheese*, a story with a different rhythm and pace. The newborns preferred—you guessed it—*The Cat in the Hat* (De-Casper & Spence, 1986).

This is fascinating on two counts. One, it shows the amazing ability of psychologists to find ways to "interview" newborn babies who cannot talk and who don't even know what a hat is, let alone a cat. Two, it shows the amazing ability of the human brain to learn as soon as it develops. But it does not necessarily mean that a pregnant woman should rush out to buy a "prega-phone" in order to read novels to her fetus. As we will see, it's good to have some respect for what a newborn knows, but without going overboard. That newborn still has a lot to learn.

The Newborn Child

Newborn babies could never survive on their own, but they are far from being completely passive and inert. They have a number of built-in *motor reflexes*, automatic behaviors that are necessary for survival, such as sucking and grasping. They can see, hear, touch, smell, and taste (bananas and sugar water are in, rotten eggs are out). They even have rudimentary "conversations" with the adults who tend them.

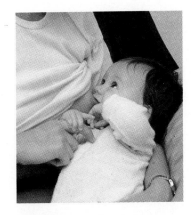

The sucking and grasping reflexes at work.

THINK ABOUT IT

Who Should Protect the Fetus?

In his moving book *The Broken Cord*, Michael Dorris (1989) told of his and his wife Louise Erdrich's struggles raising an adopted child who was born profoundly retarded as a result of fetal alcohol syndrome (FAS). "Adam's birthdays are reminders for me," wrote Dorris. "For each celebration commemorating that he was born, there is the pang, the rage, that he was not born whole."

It is certainly enraging to learn about the suffering of children born to women who seem to have cared not a fig for the fetus they were carrying. Many people are justifiably worried about the growing number of babies who are born with FAS or the damaging effects of other drugs. What will happen to them? Who will pay for their care? It is no wonder that Dorris and many of his readers are spurred to want to *do something* about pregnant women who drink too much or who abuse other drugs.

But what, exactly, is to be done? A movement on behalf of "fetal rights" argues that fetuses have rights to legal protection, including protection from their mothers. Shouldn't the fetus be protected from a mother who cannot or will not take care of it properly by following safe prenatal practices? Before you answer, consider these issues:

1. *Where do we draw the line between safe and unsafe prenatal practices?* It is clear that abuse of drugs or alcohol endangers the fetus. In general, the more alcohol consumed during pregnancy, the worse the effect (Newman & Buka, 1991), and the same is probably true for other drugs. But what about an occasional drink—should that be prohibited? Researchers do not yet know precisely how much alcohol it takes to cause problems in fetal development or how alcohol affects the various phases of prenatal growth. In 1991, a Seattle woman who was eight months pregnant went into a local restaurant, where she ordered a salad and a glass of wine. The waiter told the woman he didn't think she should have the drink, and she politely told him to mind his own business. Still, the waiter refused to serve her. He was fired the next day and the woman had her perfectly healthy baby a month later. Was the waiter's action an expression of justified concern or inappropriate meddling?

2. *Which maternal practices should we protect the fetus from?* Should women with chronic medical conditions, such as diabetes, be held liable for any problems in fetal development if they get pregnant and do not follow their doctors' advice? What about a woman who cannot afford to "protect" her fetus by quitting work and staying in bed for three months as her doctor recommends? Obstetrical advice over the years has been full of errors, and continues to be an uncertain art (Rothman, 1989). Years ago, doctors might have wanted to "protect" a fetus from being miscarried by requiring a pregnant woman to take thalidomide (when it was mistakenly believed that this drug was safe); or to "protect" the fetus's development by requiring the mother to lose 20 pounds (when it was mistakenly believed that

REFLEXES. Newborn babies have a number of reflex talents (see Table 13.1). They turn their heads toward a touch on the cheek or corner of the mouth and search for something to suck on, a handy "rooting reflex" that allows them to find the breast or bottle. They suck vigorously on a nipple, finger, or pacifier placed in their mouths. They grasp tightly to a finger pressed on their palms. They are startled by loud noises or shocks. They follow a moving light with their eyes and turn toward a familiar sound, such as the mother's voice or the thump-thump of a heartbeat (both of which they heard in the womb). If held with the feet just touching the ground, a newborn will show "walking" movements.

VISION. At birth, a baby is very, very nearsighted. The focus range is about 8 inches, the distance between the baby and the face of the person holding the baby. But visual ability develops rapidly. Newborns open their eyes wide to investigate what is around them, even in the dark. They can distinguish contrasts, shadows, and edges. And fascinating studies by Andrew Meltzoff and Michael K. Moore (1983) found that some newborns are able to imitate adult facial expressions. They may pout, smile, and open their mouths to mimic adult expres-

pregnant women should not gain "too much" weight). Today they recommend that women have Caesarean sections—major surgery that is costly and not without risks to the woman—if they think there is the slightest chance of damage to the fetus. As a result, the United States has the highest rate of unnecessary Caesarean deliveries in the world. Should physicians be able to override the decision of a pregnant woman if she chooses to have a vaginal delivery?

3. *Is maternal drug abuse the only or even the major contributor to the child's later problems?* Sociologist Barbara Rothman (1989), who has been studying the social effects of changes in reproductive technology, fears that pregnant women are fast becoming viewed as "the unskilled workers on a reproductive assembly line." They are blamed, she argues, for producing "flawed products," that is, damaged newborns or fetuses with defects. Indeed, several dozen women in the United States have been prosecuted for taking drugs during pregnancy. Yet many people overlook other causes of damage to the fetus that are far more common than maternal drug abuse, such as the lack of prenatal services for poor women, maternal malnutrition, and exposure to toxins in the workplace (which can affect the reproductive systems of *both* sexes). Scientists are also learning that *fathers'* drug use can cause fetal defects; cocaine, for example, binds to sperm (Yazigi, Odem, & Polakoski, 1991).

Moreover, people tend to overlook the environmental causes of children's problems. As Lucile Newman and Stephen Buka (1991) note, many of the learning problems that are caused by prenatal exposure to drugs are worsened by poverty and parental neglect; conversely, they can be overcome if the child lives in a good environment. In fact, research has found that children who live with cocaine-abusing parents are almost twice as likely to have behavioral problems (such as aggressiveness, hyperactivity, and bedwetting) as children who were exposed to cocaine in the womb but who then were placed in healthy homes (Meyers & Dennis, 1991).

4. *Is money best spent on incarcerating addicted pregnant women, treating their addictions, or caring for their children?* At present, only 11 percent of pregnant addicts get treatment; many detox programs reject pregnant women because they do not have prenatal services; and very few programs help addicted women who already have children (Meyers & Dennis, 1991). Yet the cost of providing postnatal care and special educational programs for children born with FAS and drug-related deficits is skyrocketing.

Ultimately, the question of who protects the fetus is enmeshed, as the fetus is, with the question of who protects the mother. Why, if society is concerned about the fetus, has it allotted so few public resources to the health and care of the pregnant woman? What *is* the best way to respond to addicted women who become pregnant—leave them alone, punish them, or treat them? How can drug-related birth defects be reduced and at the same time the rights of pregnant women to control their own bodies be respected? These are tough issues. What do you think?

---

sions. This research generated many follow-up studies (and spurred many parents to spend hours making faces at their newborns). Some replications were successful, but others, alas, were not, so it is unlikely that imitation in infants is uniformly present at birth (Cole & Cole, 1989). It develops eventually, however.

An interest in novelty also starts early. Babies reveal a surprising interest in looking at and listening to unfamiliar things (this includes most of the world). By observing what infants look at, given a choice, and how long they gaze at it, psychologists have identified many infant preferences (P. Harris, 1984). For instance, infants are primed to respond to faces. Babies who are only 9 *minutes* old will turn their heads to watch a drawing of a face if it moves in front of them, but they will not turn if the "face" consists of scrambled features or is just the outline of a face (Goren, Sarty, & Wu, 1975).

For the first six to eight weeks, babies are mostly concerned with *where* something is. Their vision helps them track someone's location and movement. After two months, though, the baby is able to determine *what* something is. Babies now can pay attention to details. They show a distinct preference for curved lines over straight ones, they can focus on parts of a picture, and, most impor-

TABLE 13.1

Reflexes and Sensory Abilities of the Newborn Baby

Reflex	Description
Rooting	An infant touched on the cheek or corner of mouth will turn toward the touch and search for something to suck on.
Sucking	An infant will suck anything suckable, such as nipple or finger.
Swallowing	An infant can swallow, though this reflex is not yet well coordinated with breathing.
Moro or "startle"	In response to loud noise or physical shock, an infant will throw arms outward and arch back.
Babinski	In response to touch on bottom of foot, the infant's toes splay outward and then curl in. (In adults, toes curl in.)
Grasp	In response to touch on palm of hand, an infant will grasp.
Stepping	If held so feet just touch the ground, an infant will show "walking" movements alternating feet in steps. This reflex vanishes in a couple of weeks.

Sense	The newborn can . . .
Sight	Focus on a point about 8 inches away; follow a moving object with eyes; discriminate some colors.
Sound	Respond to sounds, especially those of pitch and loudness of human voice; respond to rhythmic or familiar sounds heard in womb, such as heartbeat.
Smell	React to some smells, such as ammonia or licorice.
Taste	Tell the difference between salty and sweet, between sour and bitter; prefer sweet tastes.
Touch	Respond to touches, especially on hands and mouth.

Source: Bee, 1989, pp. 92–93.

tant to doting parents, they can tell the difference between mom, dad, and visiting strangers. Within a few months of birth, they develop depth perception (see Chapter 5).

SOCIAL SKILLS.   Newborns are sociable from the first. Babies smile regularly at about 4 to 6 weeks of age, especially in response to faces (although they haven't yet the foggiest notion of whom they are smiling at). The first "conversation" a baby has is with the mother or primary caretaker. Like most human conversations, it often takes place over a good meal. Babies and their mothers play little games with each other, exchanging signals in a rhythmic pattern. Whether on breast or bottle, babies nurse in a pattern of sucks and pauses. During the pauses, the mother often jiggles the baby, who then starts to suck again. The pattern between them has the back-and-forth rhythm of spoken conversation: suck, pause, jiggle, pause, suck, pause, jiggle, pause (Kaye, 1977).

This early rhythmic conversation illustrates a crucial aspect of all human exchanges: the importance of *synchrony* (Condon, 1982). Synchrony refers to the adjustment of one person's behavior to coordinate with another's. If you have ever tried to talk to someone who was "out of sync" with you, you will understand its importance; you just don't seem to connect. As we saw in Chapter 9, in conversation, people unconsciously adjust their rhythms of speech, their gestures and expressions, to be "in sync" with each other. Synchrony seems to be essential in establishing rapport between people, and its absence has been observed in people who have learning disabilities and emotional problems such as depression (Tronick, 1989).

FIGURE 13.1
Look who's talking
This mother and infant illustrate imitation and synchrony in action, exchanging giggles, gestures, coos, and smiles.

Synchrony begins at birth. Newborn infants will synchronize their behavior and attention to adult speech but not to other sounds, such as street noise or tapping (Beebe et al., 1982). Synchrony takes three related forms: *simultaneous movement* (e.g., the mother turns her head just as the baby lifts an arm), *similar tempo* (the parent and baby move at the same pace and rhythm, i.e., "march to the beat of the same drummer"), and *coordination and smoothness* (the behavior of parent and baby meshes smoothly, like well-matched dance partners). Mothers show more synchrony with their own infants than with others; parents learn how to tune in to their own babies' rhythms early on (Bernieri, Reznick, & Rosenthal, 1988). (See Figure 13.1.)

The Older Infant

Babies grow as fast as pumpkins during the first two years. Most infants double their birth weight in five months. By 1 year of age, on the average, they have tripled their birth weight and grown 10 to 12 inches in length. (The custom of talking about a baby's "length" but a child's "height" is charming; the language changes as soon as the baby is upright!) By age 2, most toddlers are half the height they will be as adults. The baby not only grows in height and weight, but also changes proportion. An infant's head is nearly one-third of the whole body; a 2-year-old's head is about one-fourth; an adult's head is only one-eighth to one-tenth of total height.

MOTOR ABILITIES. At about 1 month, infants can hold their chins up when lying on their stomachs. At about 2 months, they can raise the upper body. At 4 months, they can sit if someone supports them. At about 7 months, they can sit upright without support. From then on, parents have to look sharp. Babies soon crawl and stand with help (9 months), walk with help (10 months), and toddle off on their own (13 months). These milestones are only averages, however. Some babies develop more quickly, others more slowly. We know a baby who was such a speedy crawler that she didn't walk until 18 months, and did so then only because an older man, her 3-year-old cousin, pulled her to her feet.

THE BRAIN AND NERVOUS SYSTEM.   A newborn baby is like a model sailing ship: The basic kit comes with all its parts, but some of them aren't assembled yet. The brain's cortex, for instance, the part responsible for perception, thinking, and language, is unfinished. Virtually all the cells appear to be there, but many haven't been fully connected by way of synapses, and some connections later drop out (see Chapter 3). This may be one reason why you can't remember what being born felt like, or, in fact, anything of your first two or three years. As an infant, you didn't have the section of your ship responsible for long-term memory wired up.

The transmission of messages between nerve cells is aided by the development of *myelin*, the insulating sheath around the axons of individual neurons. The growth of this coating, called *myelinization*, takes time. At birth, the baby's cortical nerve cells (including those that connect the cerebral cortex with the brain stem) are not myelinated. The reason that infants cannot fully control the lower half of their bodies is that neurons in the spinal cord, which carry messages from the brain to the body, are not fully covered with myelin until the child is about 2 years old. Myelinization in the brain itself and the growth of connecting cells continue into adolescence and possibly adulthood.

Although babies and infants everywhere develop according to the same maturational sequence, many aspects of their development depend on cultural customs. For example, infant sleep patterns vary according to a culture's rules for sleeping arrangements. In the United States, babies are expected to sleep for eight uninterrupted hours by the age of 4 or 5 months; this milestone is considered a sign of neurological maturity. Yet in many cultures, the infant sleeps with the mother and nurses on demand throughout the night. When mothers

At birth, neurons in the infant's brain are widely spaced, but they begin to form connections immediately. These drawings show the marked increase in the size and number of neurons in the baby's first 15 months of life.

A good example of the intersection between maturation and culture is the case of the cradleboard. Most Navaho babies (left) calmly accept the Navaho custom of being strapped to a cradleboard until they are about 6 months old; Caucasian babies (right) protest vigorously when strapped in one. In spite of cultural differences in such practices, babies in every culture sit, crawl, and walk at the same average maturational age.

TABLE 13.2

Developmental Milestones During the First Year

Average Age	Motor	Cognitive	Emotional
0–2 months	Turns head; lifts chin when lying on stomach	Prefers looking at faces; likes familiar sounds; is interested in novelty; tracks *where* things are	Can imitate adult facial expressions; cries when distressed
3–4 months	Lifts chest; holds head erect; reaches for an object; sits with support	Becomes interested in *what* things are; recognizes different faces and details of objects	Smiles and shows interest in slightly unfamiliar objects; may be distressed by objects that are too unfamiliar
5–6 months	Holds head steady; transfers an object from one hand to another	Develops depth perception; understands object identity (that a thing is the same each time it is encountered)	Apparent fear at visual cliff (see Chapter 5); facial expressions of anger may appear in response to frustration
7–8 months	Sits alone; gets into sitting position	Develops retrieval memory (can recall a familiar face) and larger "working memory"; understands object permanence	Shows first signs of stranger and separation anxiety
9–10 months	Stands with help; crawls	Understands some words	
11–12 months	Pulls self to standing position; walks with support	Begins symbolic play; utters first meaningful words	Shows sadness at loss of an attachment figure

have no incentive to get the baby to sleep through the night, as most American mothers do, the infant continues to wake and nurse about every four hours (Super, 1981). In another example, infants in Africa routinely surpass American infants in their rate of learning to sit and to walk, but not in learning to crawl or climb stairs. The reason is that African parents routinely bounce babies on their feet, exercise the newborn's walking reflex, prop young infants in sitting positions, and discourage crawling (Super, 1981). So biological capacities are affected by the opportunities to practice them.

By the end of the first year, infants have made huge progress in their physical abilities (see Table 13.2). Now the story gets even more interesting.

QUICK QUIZ

You may not remember your own first year, but what do you remember about infants generally?

1. Almost all newborn babies can (a) recognize their parents, (b) see at a distance of about 8 inches, (c) imitate an adult's facial expression.
2. Which of the following is not among the newborn baby's repertoire of abilities? (a) sucking, (b) rooting, (c) the startle reflex, (d) long-term memory, (e) grasping
3. What is the infant's earliest social "conversation"? (a) crying in response to adult noises, (b) yelling for milk, (c) cooing when touched or stroked, (d) nursing at breast or bottle, in rhythm with reactions from the mother

ANSWERS:

1. b 2. d 3. d

■ COGNITIVE DEVELOPMENT

Our friend Joel reports how thrilled he was when his 13-month-old daughter Alison looked at him one day and said, for the first time, "Daddy! Daddy!" His delight was deflated somewhat, though, when the doorbell rang and she ran to the door, calling, "Daddy! Daddy!" And his delight was completely shattered when the phone rang and Alison ran to it, shouting, "Daddy! Daddy!" Later Joel learned that there was a 2-year-old child in Alison's day-care group whose father would call her on the telephone during the day and ring the doorbell when he picked her up in the evening. Alison acquired her little friend's enthusiasm for doorbells and phones, but didn't quite get the hang of "daddy."

She will soon enough, though, and that is the mystery of language. Further, she will eventually be able to imagine, reason, and see the world from daddy's viewpoint, and that is the mystery of thought.

The Ability to Think

In the 1920s, a Swiss biologist named Jean Piaget [Zhan Pea-ah-ZHAY] (1896–1980) proposed a new theory of the cognitive development of children. He observed that children understand concepts and reason differently at different stages. The cognitive strategies children use to solve problems, said Piaget, reflect an interaction between the child's current developmental stage and experience in the world. Piaget's ideas caused a revolution in thinking about how thinking develops.

PIAGET AND COGNITIVE STAGES. Piaget (1929/1960, 1952, 1984) proposed that mental functioning depends on two basic biological processes, *organization* and *adaptation*. All human beings are designed to organize their observations and experiences into a coherent set of meanings, and to adapt to new observations and experiences. The process of adaptation, said Piaget, takes two forms, which he called *assimilation* and *accommodation*.

Assimilation is what you do when you fit new information into your present system of knowledge and beliefs. Let's say little Harry learns the concept "dog" by playing with the family schnauzer. Now, if he sees the neighbor's chihuahua and says "doggie!", he has *assimilated* the new information into his understanding of dogs.

Accommodation is what you do when, as a result of undeniable new information, you must change or modify your existing beliefs or schemas. If Harry sees the neighbor's Siamese cat and still says "doggie!", his parents are likely to laugh and correct him. Harry will have to modify his schema for *dogs* to exclude cats, and he will have to create a schema for *cats*. In this way, he *accommodates* the new information that a Siamese cat is not a dog. Rochel Gelman (1983) offers another example of accommodation in a 2-year-old girl. The child would practice counting: "1,2,3,4,5,6,8,9,10." Her mother kept reminding her that she was leaving out the 7. Eventually the child assimilated this information. She would say to herself, "1,2,3,4,5,6,8,9,10—where's the 7?" Her next step was to count to 6 and stop. Finally she accommodated the missing 7 and could correctly count to 10. In this fashion, said Piaget, children at each stage assimilate the information they are capable of absorbing. Then, when the information no longer fits, their underlying mental structure accommodates.

Using these basic concepts, Piaget proposed that all children go through four stages of cognitive development:

1. During the *sensory-motor stage* (birth to age 2), the infant learns through concrete actions: looking, touching, hearing, putting things in the mouth, sucking, grasping. "Thinking" consists of coordinating sensory information with

■ **assimilation**
The process of absorbing new information into existing cognitive structures, modifying it if necessary to "fit."
■ **accommodation**
The process of modifying existing cognitive structures in response to experience and new information.

bodily movements. Soon these movements become more purposeful, as the child actively explores the environment and learns that specific movements will produce specific results. Swatting a cloth away will reveal a hidden toy; releasing one's grasp of a fuzzy duck will cause the duck to drop out of reach; banging on the table with a spoon will produce dinner (or mom, taking the spoon away).

One of the baby's major accomplishments at this stage, said Piaget, is **object permanence,** the understanding that something continues to exist even if you can't see it or touch it. In the first few months of life, he observed, infants seem to follow the motto "out of sight, out of mind." They will look intently at a little toy, but if you hide it behind a piece of paper they will not look behind the paper or make an effort to get the toy. By about 6 months, infants begin to grasp the idea that a toy exists and the family cat exists, whether they can see the toy, or the cat, or not. If a baby of this age drops a toy from her playpen, she will look for it; she also will look under a cloth for a toy that is partially hidden. By 1 year of age, most babies have developed an awareness of the permanence of (some) objects. That is when they love to play peek-a-boo.

Object permanence, said Piaget, represents the beginning of *representational* (symbolic) thought. The capacity for representational thought is what allows human beings to use mental imagery and other symbolic systems. The child is able for the first time to hold a concept in mind, to learn that the word *fly* represents an annoying, buzzing creature, and that *daddy* represents a friendly, playful one. These developments during the sensory-motor stage occur at a similar rate and sequence across a wide range of cultures. In the next stage, cultural differences begin to make themselves felt.

2. The essential aspect of the *preoperational stage* (ages 2 to 7) is the accelerated use of symbols and language, in play and in imitation of adult behavior. A 2-year-old is able to pretend, for instance, that a large box is a house, table, or train. Piaget described this stage largely in terms of what (he thought) the child cannot do. Children can think, said Piaget, but they cannot reason. They do not yet have the kinds of mental abilities that allow them to understand abstract principles or cause and effect. Piaget called these abilities **operations,** actions that the child performs in the mind and that are *reversible*. An operation is a sort of "train of thought" that can be run backward or forward. For example, multiplying 2 times 6 to get 12 is an operation; so is the reverse operation, dividing 12 by 6 to get 2.

Children at the preoperational stage are not capable of reasoning in this way. They rely on primitive or intuitive reasoning and the evidence of their own senses, which can be misleading. If a tree moves in the wind, it must be alive. If the wind blows while the child is walking, then walking must make the wind blow. Piaget believed—mistakenly, as we will see—that children of this age also cannot take another person's point of view because their thinking is **egocentric.** They see the world only from their own frame of reference. They cannot imagine that you see things differently, or that events happen to others that do not happen to them. "Why are there mountains [with lakes]?" Piaget asked a preoperational Swiss child. "So that we can skate," answered the child.

Further, said Piaget, preoperational children cannot grasp the concept of **conservation**—that physical properties do not change when their form or appearance changes. They are unable to understand that an amount of liquid, a number of pennies, or a length of rope remains the same even if you pour the liquid from one glass to another, stack the pennies, or coil the rope (see Figure 13.2). If you pour liquid from a short, fat glass into a tall, narrow glass, preoperational children will say there is more liquid in the second glass. They attend to the appearance of the liquid (its height in the glass) instead of its fixed quantity.

3. During the *concrete operations stage* (about age 6 or 7 to 11), the nature and quality of children's thought changes significantly. According to Piaget, during

■ **object permanence**
The understanding that an object continues to exist even when you can't see it or touch it.
■ **operations**
In Piaget's theory, mental actions that are cognitively reversible.
■ **egocentric thinking**
Perceiving the world from only one's own point of view; the inability to take another person's perspective.
■ **conservation**
The understanding that the physical properties of objects—such as number of items, amount of liquid, or length of an object—remain the same even when appearances change (as long as nothing is added or taken away).

FIGURE 13.2 _____

Piaget's principle of conservation

These children are taking part in experiments designed to measure their understanding of conservation. In a typical test of conservation of number (right), the child shows whether he understands that two sets of seven blocks contain the same number—even though the blocks in one set are larger and take up more space. In a test of conservation of quantity (left), the child shows whether she understands that pouring liquid from a short fat glass into a tall narrow glass does not change the amount of liquid.

these years children come to understand the principles of conservation, reversibility, and cause and effect. They understand the nature of *identity*, that a girl doesn't turn into a boy by wearing a boy's hat, that a brother will always be a brother, even if he grows up. They learn mental operations, such as addition, subtraction, multiplication, division, and categorization—not just of numbers, but of people, events, and actions. They learn a few abstract concepts such as *serial ordering*, the idea that things can be ranked from smallest to largest, lightest to darkest, shortest to tallest.

Children's thinking at this age is called "concrete" because it is still grounded in concrete experiences and concepts. Children of this age do not have much ability to understand most abstract ideas or to think deductively (drawing conclusions from premises). They can use their imaginations to try to solve problems but not in a systematic and logical way. An adult who is playing Twenty Questions systematically tries to reduce the range of possible answers: Is it a person? Female? Fictional? A young concrete-operational child will make random guesses: Is it an astronaut? Kermit the Frog? Grandpa? (Mosher & Hornsby, 1966).

4. The *formal operations stage* (age 12 to adulthood) marks the beginning of abstract reasoning. Teenagers understand that ideas can be compared and classified, just as objects can. They are able to shift from concrete operations to deductive reasoning, using premises common to their culture and experience. Research, however, shows that not all adolescents develop the ability for formal operational thought or complex moral reasoning (Laboratory of Comparative Human Cognition, 1984). Some never do. Others continue to think "concretely" unless a specific problem requires abstract thought.

People used to ask Piaget whether it was possible to speed up cognitive development. Piaget called this concern "the American question" because Americans, he said, are always trying to hurry things along. Some contemporary psychologists share Piaget's concern. David Elkind (1988), for example, fears that many middle-class parents today are trying to raise "superbabies," force-feeding them with reading and math lessons, pressuring them to achieve more and more at earlier and earlier ages. Most researchers agree that such pressure is indeed detrimental if the child is not developmentally prepared to learn. But others question Piaget's assumption that children's cognitive capacities develop like the ripening of a peach, and are largely unaffected by outside events. They maintain that parents can do a great deal to nurture and enhance their children's cognitive abilities (Schulman, 1991).

EVALUATING PIAGET. Piaget's theory has had a powerful impact, but subsequent research has modified and clarified it considerably. Many young children demonstrate more cognitive skills than Piaget thought they had, and many older children and adults lack some cognitive skills that Piaget thought everyone had by their ages. Moreover, the changes from one stage to another are neither as clear-cut nor as sweeping as Piaget implied: Children's reasoning ability has as much to do with what they are reasoning *about* as with their stage.

In particular, there seems to be no major shift from preoperational to concrete-operational thought. Research now shows that preoperational children can understand more than Piaget gave them credit for:

• Piaget believed that the ability of a baby to play peek-a-boo illustrates object permanence. But infants as young as 9 months of age also understand the *rules* of peek-a-boo. In one study, when adults failed to "take their turns," the infants were clearly startled and distressed. The babies reacted by pointing to or touching the adults, repeating their own turns, or offering toys to the adults (Ross & Lollis, 1987).

• Infants as young as $3\frac{1}{2}$ months old understand some of the physical properties of objects hidden from view. Renee Baillargeon (1991) discovered this by observing how long a baby will pay attention to an obscured ball or toy, rather than, as Piaget had, observing whether the baby would reach for the hidden toy. She reasoned that infants might *understand* that objects continue to exist when hidden, but not be able to reach for them or know how to search for them.

• Children advance rapidly in their understanding and use of symbolism much earlier than Piaget thought—between the ages of $2\frac{1}{2}$ and 3. One experiment found that within that six-month period, toddlers become able to think of a miniature model of a room in two ways at once: as a room in its own right and as a symbol of the larger room it represents (DeLoache, 1987). This ability is a big step toward adult symbolic thought, in which anything can stand for anything else—a flag for a country, a saltshaker for a house, a detachable pot handle for a doll.

• Most 3- and 4-year-olds *can* take another person's perspective. When 4-year-olds play with 2-year-olds, for example, they modify and simplify their speech so the younger child will understand (Shatz & Gelman, 1973). As we will see later, even very young children are capable of astonishing acts of empathy. They are not always egocentric; their answers depend on the questions

Are children really egocentric? This 3-year-old girl was asked to place the boy doll where the policeman could not find him. According to Piaget, she should be "egocentric," and therefore hide the boy doll from herself as well (left). On several occasions, however, she placed the doll where she, but not the policeman, could see him, suggesting that she could take the policeman's point of view (right).

you ask them. One 5-year-old showed her teacher a picture she had drawn of a cat and an unidentifiable blob. "The cat is lovely," said the teacher, "but what is this thing here?" "That has nothing to do with you," said the child. "That's what the *cat* is looking at."

• Very young children can understand the difference between animate and inanimate things. Three- and 4-year-olds, shown pictures of varied objects and asked which ones could go uphill and downhill by themselves, knew that animals can do so but inanimate objects can't. (Some of the children said that a *small* animal might need its mother to carry it up a big hill.) At this age, children use the concept of movement to help them answer whether the object walks, crawls, or flies on its own, or whether someone pushes it. However, they have no concept of growth (they can't tell you whether a toy or a tree will grow) or of biology (they don't understand that both plants and animals are alive) (Massey & Gelman, 1988).

• Finally, a child's cognitive development does not occur in isolation. Like biological development, it occurs in a social and cultural environment (LeVine, 1988; Rogoff & Morelli, 1989). The development of concrete operations, for example, varies in timing and content from one culture to another (Dasen, 1977; Greenfield, 1976). Thus a study of six African cultures found that stringing beads—a skill that children in these cultures learn at an early age—speeds the development of the conservation of number. On the other hand, many unschooled children of the Wolof, a rural group in Senegal, do not acquire an understanding of conservation, as their peers who attend school do. However, the ability for concrete operations appears in all cultures, and brief training experiences can bring it out (Greenfield, 1966).

In spite of these modifications of Piaget's theory, the *sequence* of cognitive development that he described does hold up across cultures. New reasoning abilities depend on the emergence of previous ones. You can't study algebra before you can count, and you can't study philosophy before you understand logic. Piaget's critics agree with him on a most important point: Children are not passive vessels into which education and experience are poured. Children actively interpret their worlds. They actively bring their own perceptions to new adventures.

Experience affects cognitive development. This young potter in India, and other children who work with materials like clay, understand the concept of conservation of quantity sooner than children who do not have such practical experience (Cole & Cole, 1989).

The Ability to Speak

Learning to speak would seem to be an enormous task. A child eventually will understand thousands and thousands of words; learn to string them together in sentences that make sense; and, most impressive of all, learn to produce and understand an infinite number of new word combinations.

THE DEVELOPMENT OF LANGUAGE. In the first months, babies cry and coo. They are highly responsive to the pitch, intensity, and sound of language. They are responsive to emotions in the voice before they respond to facial expressions. Anne Fernald (1990) finds that for a baby, "the melody is the message." Babies as young as two days old prefer "baby talk" to normal adult talk, at least when it is spoken by adults other than the mother (whose voice they recognize, having heard it in the womb). The adult practice of speaking baby talk to infants is not a universal phenomenon, but it is widespread, as studies in France, Italy, Japan, rural South Africa, Britain, Canada, and China have found. When most people speak to babies, their pitch is higher and more varied and the intonation is more exaggerated. But it is not yet known what aspects of "baby talk" are so attractive to infants, or what role, if any, adult baby talk plays in the development of the child's language. Among rural African Americans, adults do

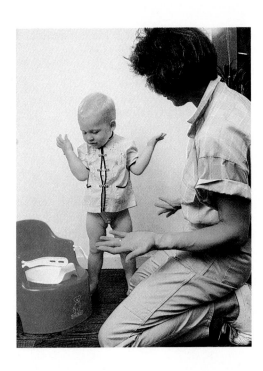

Symbolic gestures emerge early! This mother and her son are clearly having a "conversation."

not censor or simplify their speech in the presence of young children (Heath, 1990). Samoans and Mayan Indians, among other groups, do not address infants and children in a different tone (Pye, 1986).

By 6 months, infants start making many "ba-ba" and "goo-goo" sounds, endlessly repeating sounds and syllables. This *babbling phase* lasts until about 1 year of age, when the child begins to name things. One-year-olds already have a few concepts in their minds—they know who mama and daddy are, they can recognize favorite objects and people—and their first words are those that represent familiar concepts ("mama," "doggie," "bug").

By 12 to 14 months of age, babies have also developed a repertoire of symbolic *gestures*, another important part of communication. They use gestures to refer to objects (sniffing to indicate "flower"), to request something (smacking lips for "food," moving hands up and down for "play the piano"), to describe an object (blowing or waving a hand for "hot," raising arms for "big"), and to reply to questions (opening palms or shrugging shoulders for "I don't know"). One baby baseball fan used a clapping sign in response to baseball games—real or pictured (Acredolo & Goodwyn, 1988).

Between the ages of 18 months and 2 years, toddlers begin to produce words in two- or three-word combinations ("mama here," "go 'way bug," "my toy"). This is an especially enjoyable phase for adults to observe because 2-year-olds, who are clearly trying to understand the differences between categories of things, often make mistakes. They know that Tiger (the family dog) is "doggie." But they may call any four-legged, furry, noise-making object "doggie"— the neighbor's cat, a picture of a cow or deer, a pony at the circus. That is, the child *overgeneralizes*. As children grow and learn new words, their overgeneralizations decrease. They learn the difference between the concept "animal" and different animals, such as dogs (which bark) and cows (which moo).

The child's first combinations of words have a common quality in many (but not all) languages: They are **telegraphic.** When you have to pay for every word in a telegram, you quickly learn to drop unnecessary articles (*a, an,* or *the*) and auxiliary verbs (such as *is* or *are,* as in the phrase "it is all gone"). But you still convey your message. Similarly, the two-word sentences of toddlers omit lots of articles, auxiliary verbs, other parts of speech, and word endings, but are

■ **telegraphic speech**
A child's first combinations of words, which omit (as a telegram does) nonessential words.

remarkably accurate in conveying many messages. Here are some functions and examples of children's two-word "telegrams" (Slobin, 1979, 1985):

- *To locate or name something:* there toy, that chair, see doggie
- *To demand something:* more milk, give candy
- *To negate an action:* no wet, no want, not hungry, allgone milk
- *To describe an event:* Bambi go, mail come, hit ball, block fall
- *To show possession:* my shoe, Mama dress
- *To modify an object:* pretty dress, big boat
- *To question:* where ball, where Daddy

Pretty good for a little kid, don't you think? At about this age, children reveal another impressive talent. They begin to acquire new words at a rapid rate: about 9 a day, for a total of more than 14,000 new words in the preschool years (Rice, 1989). Obviously, they are doing this without word-by-word training. They absorb the new words as they encounter them in conversation, in a process called *fast mapping*, and they are able to do this on the basis of hearing only one or two uses of the word in context. The phenomenon of fast mapping has been observed in several studies, but it is not yet known exactly how children manage to do it. They seem to draw on a quick impression of the likely meaning of the word along with their growing knowledge of grammatical contexts and the rules for formulating words (Rice, 1989).

By age 3 or 4, children are creating longer and more grammatical sentences. Along with their growing conceptual ability, they make fewer overgeneralizations. They learn that mom works at a *desk* and the family eats on a *table*. But they are still seeking rules of speech and often make funny errors when they overextend or misapply a rule. Helen Bee (1989) reported this conversation between a 6-year-old and a 3-year-old, who are arguing about the relative dangers of forgetting to feed pet goldfish or of feeding them too much:

6-YEAR-OLD: It's worse to forget to feed them.
3-YEAR-OLD: No, it's badder to feed them too much.
6-YEAR-OLD: You don't say badder, you say worser.
3-YEAR-OLD: But it's baddest to give them too much food.
6-YEAR-OLD: No it's not. It's worsest to forget to feed them.

These children have learned a rule for comparisons (*-er* and *-est* endings), but they haven't yet learned all the exceptions. As a result, they overgeneralize the rules of grammar. Their conversation shows a key feature of language acquisition: that children actively seek regular, predictable rules of language. (See Figure 13.3 for similar "smart" errors in vocabulary use.)

ACQUIRING LANGUAGE. Is the ability to use language innate, wired into our biology like vision, or does this ability depend entirely on learning? Until the middle of this century, many psychologists assumed that children learn to speak by imitating what adults say and by having adults correct the child's mistakes. One of the strongest arguments against this view came from Noam Chomsky (1957, 1980), who argued that the brain must contain a *language acquisition device*, a "mental module" that is programmed to acquire language and the rules of grammar. Chomsky and others have noted that imitation cannot explain why children all go through the same stages of acquiring speech or why their simplest sentences consist of word pairs that adults would never say. Children regularly reduce a parent's sentences ("Let's go to the store!") to their own two-word version ("Go store!"), and they make errors that adults never make ("Did daddy take you?" "Daddy taked me") (Ervin-Tripp, 1964).

Learning explanations of the acquisition of language assume that children are rewarded for saying the right words and punished for making errors. But

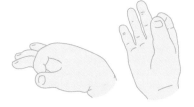

Just as "dadadadada" becomes "daddy" in hearing children, the hand gestures of deaf babies are budding versions of the real words (Petitto & Marentette, 1991). This suggests that some aspects of language acquisition are innate.

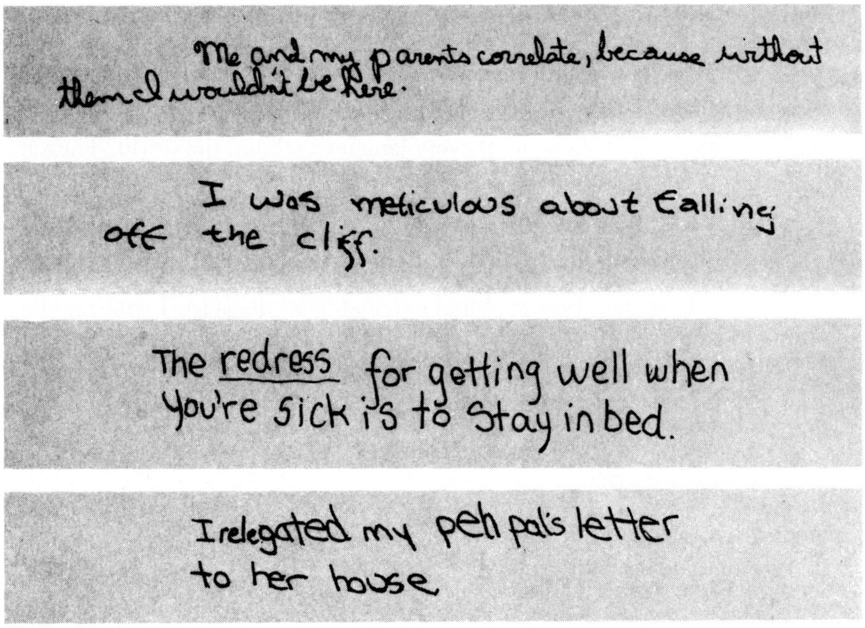

Me and my parents correlate, because without them I wouldn't be here.

I was meticulous about falling off the cliff.

The <u>redress</u> for getting well when you're sick is to stay in bed.

I relegated my pen pal's letter to her house.

FIGURE 13.3

How children learn words
Schoolchildren often produce mystifying sentences like these when they are trying to learn an unfamiliar word. The reason is that they extract one element of a word's definition, and then apply it inappropriately. For example, if "correlate" means related to, you must be "correlated" with your parents. Similarly, "meticulous" involves being very careful about small details; to "redress" a grievance means to find a remedy for it; and to "relegate" means to send away. Children learn new words faster when they are given model sentences that use the word correctly than when they are given only definitions of it (Miller & Gildea, 1987).

as you saw in the conversation between the two children, the 6-year-old's attempts to correct the younger child's mistake ("You don't say badder, you say worser") had no effect. Parents don't fare any better ("Say, daddy *took* me." "Daddy taked me"). Moreover, parents don't stop to correct every error in their children's speech, as long as they understand what the child is trying to say (Brown, Cazden, & Bellugi, 1969). Indeed, parents often *reward* children for incorrect statements! The 2-year-old who says "want milk!" is likely to get it; most parents would not wait for a more grammatical (or polite) request. Most significant, children are forever coming up with new associations and terms that are entirely original. A 5-year-old we know was walking home with his mother, who was carrying a large shopping bag that kept bumping into him. The boy protested, "It's hitting me in the armpit of my leg!" (Well, how would you describe the back of the knee?)

Nevertheless, language learning is not entirely the result of an innate capacity. Studies of middle-class parents find that many parents do not tell their children, "You said that wrong," but neither do they ignore their children's errors of speech. They are more likely to repeat verbatim a child's *well-formed* sentence than a sentence with errors ("That's a horse, mommy!" "Yes, that's a horse"). And when the child does make a mistake or produce a clumsy sentence, parents almost invariably respond by recasting it ("That are monkey!" "That *is* a monkey") or expanding its basic elements ("Monkey climbing!" "Yes, the monkey is climbing to the top of the tree") (Bohannon & Stanowicz, 1988). In turn, children are more likely to imitate adult recasts and expansions, suggesting that they are learning from them (Bohannon & Symons, 1988). Children also imitate their parents' accents, inflections, and tone of voice, and they will repeat some words that the parent tries to teach ("This is a ball, Erwin." "Baw").

Language therefore depends both on biological readiness and social experience. Children who are abandoned, abused, and not exposed to language for years (such as Genie, whom we discussed in Chapter 2) rarely speak normally. Such sad evidence suggests that there may be a critical period in language development, possibly the years between 1 and 5, possibly the entire first decade of life (Curtiss, 1977). During these years children do not need to hear speech—deaf children's acquisition of sign language parallels the development of spoken language—but they do need close relationships and practice in conversation.

At present, we can draw these conclusions about language development (Rice, 1989; Slobin, 1985):

1. A child's very first sentences follow simple rules. These rules are specific to children's speech and show up in every language around the world. They are not necessarily the rules of the adult language.

2. A child's grammar becomes gradually more complex, as the child's thinking does; but as experiments on Piagetian principles have shown, children's thinking is often well ahead of their ability to express themselves.

3. A child's language is creative and original from the start. Language does not come merely from imitating adults or passively parroting adults' rules. In fact, if adults are too intrusive in their efforts to direct a child's use of language, they may impede rather than enhance the child's language skill.

QUICK QUIZ

1. "More cake!" and "Daddy here" are examples of _____ speech.
2. Understanding that two rows of six pennies are equal in number, even if one row is flat and the other is stacked up, is an example of _____.
3. Understanding that a toy exists even after mom puts it in her purse is an example of _____, which develops during the _____ stage.
4. The belief that a car moves because you are riding in it shows _____ thinking.

ANSWERS:

1. telegraphic 2. conservation 3. object permanence, sensory-motor 4. egocentric

---

■ SOCIAL DEVELOPMENT

Learning to walk, talk, and think are not the only challenges facing young children. They have to find a balance between dependence on their parents and independence. They have to figure out relationships with siblings and friends. They have to learn the values that their families and communities hold. They have to learn what it means to be a boy or a girl. They must, in psychological terms, become **socialized** in the rules of adult life.

Attachment and Development

Chicks, ducklings, baby monkeys, puppies, and many other species attach themselves instinctively to their mothers, and their mothers are primed by hormonal factors to care for their young. What is the nature of human attachment?

BONDING. Years ago, Marshall Klaus and John Kennell (1976) argued that mothers who could see and hold their newborns immediately after birth became "bonded" to them. Bonding was thought to be set off by maternal hormones present during childbirth. Presumably, women who bonded would be better, more attentive mothers than women who were separated from their babies after delivery (such separations used to be customary hospital procedure). This idea got much publicity, and hospitals began plunking every healthy newborn on his or her mother's stomach as soon as the baby emerged from the womb.

■ **socialization**

The process by which a child acquires the rules, standards, and values of his or her family and culture.

However, subsequent research has shown that mothers (and fathers) can "bond" just fine to their babies if they first see them a day, four days, or even months after the birth. So can parents who adopt older infants and children. Parents of premature infants who live in incubators for weeks are as glad to take their babies home as are parents of full-term babies. Many modern fathers are just as attentive to their newborns as new mothers are, even without "bonding hormones" to help them along (Parke & Sawin, 1980). And, sadly, some mothers and fathers who *do* see their babies right after delivery do not feel close to their infants or wish to care for them.

For these reasons, most psychologists now say that bonding at birth is nice if you can do it, but not essential. The effects of early bonding are weak, and do not explain why a mother keeps on mothering (Campos et al., 1984). Hormones do not explain motherly behavior in the female person as they do, say, in the female rat. "Nature has to prepare mother rats for only forty days of parenthood," observed Sandra Scarr (1984b). "Humans had better be prepared for twenty years. Hormones just can't handle that."

ATTACHMENT. In developmental psychology, **attachment** refers to the emotional tie that children and their caretakers feel toward each other. As we saw in Chapter 10, infants become attached to their mothers or primary caretakers for the contact comfort the adults provide. In the first few months of life, babies aren't too particular about who the adult is. Between 7 and 9 months, however, babies stop this indiscriminate affection. Many become wary or fearful of strangers, a reaction called *stranger anxiety*. They wail if they are put in an unfamiliar setting or are left with an unfamiliar person. They have become attached to the mother (or the primary caretaker) and show *separation anxiety* if she temporarily leaves the room. This reaction usually continues until the middle of the second year, but many children show signs of distress at parental separation until they are about 3. Virtually all children go through this phase, though culture influences how strongly the anxiety is felt and how long it lasts (see Figure 13.4).

To determine the kind and quality of attachment between mothers and babies, Mary Ainsworth (1973, 1979; Ainsworth et al., 1978) devised a method called the *strange situation*. A mother (or sometimes a father) brings the baby into an unfamiliar room, containing lots of toys. After a while a stranger comes in and attempts to play with the child. The mother leaves the baby with the stranger. She then returns, plays with the child, and the stranger leaves. Finally, the mother leaves the baby alone for three minutes and returns. How does the baby behave, with the mother (or father), with the stranger, and when the baby is alone?

Ainsworth and her associates divided children into categories on the basis of their reactions to the strange situation. Some are *securely attached*. They cry or protest if the parent leaves the room; they welcome her back and then play happily again; they are clearly more attached to the parent than to the stranger. But others are *insecurely attached*. There are two styles of insecure attachment. A child may be *detached* or *avoidant*, not caring if the mother leaves the room, making little effort to seek contact with her on her return, and treating the stranger about the same as the mother. Or a child may be *resistant* or *ambivalent*, resisting contact with the mother at reunion but protesting loudly if she leaves. Such children may cry to be picked up and then demand to be put down. Some behave as if they are angry with the mother and resist her comfort.

Ainsworth argued that the difference between secure and insecure attachment lies primarily in the way mothers treat their babies in the first few months. Mothers of securely attached babies, she believes, are sensitive to their babies' needs and the meanings of their cries; they are affectionate and demonstrative. Mothers of avoidant babies are irritated by their infants, express controlled anger toward them, and are rejecting. Mothers of ambivalent babies are insensitive and inept but not rejecting. They don't know what to do to relieve their ba-

✳ *If a woman doesn't "bond" to her baby right after childbirth, will she be a bad mother? What about parents who adopt older children—is it too late for them to "bond"?*

Toward the end of the first year, children develop a wariness of strangers and distress at separation from caretakers.

■ **attachment**
A strong emotional tie between babies and their primary caretakers. In later life, attachment refers to any emotional connection between two people.

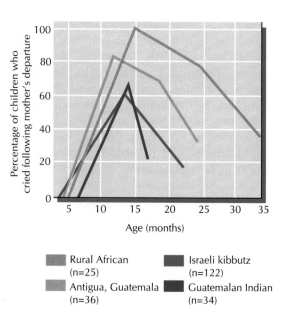

FIGURE 13.4

The course of attachment
This graph shows the percentage of children in four different cultures who cried when their mothers left the "strange situation." Notice that the babies' attachment typically does not develop until the ages of 7 to 9 months, peaks at about a year of age, and then steadily declines. Notice too how the proportion of children responding to their mother's departure varies across cultures, from a high among the African children to a low among the Israelis (from Kagan, Kearsley, & Zelazo, 1978).

bies' distress and are "out of sync" in handling their babies. Ainsworth's work, like the bonding studies, implies that it is up to sensitive, responsive mothers to create happily attached infants.

Although this research represents a thoughtful effort to measure the concepts of attachment and maternal sensitivity, there are problems with it. Some babies may become insecurely attached because they are temperamentally difficult; anyone would have trouble dealing with them (Campos et al., 1984). It *is* true that mothers who are abusive or extremely neglectful are more likely to have insecurely attached children. But several studies have found no relationship at all between mothers' normal varieties of "responsiveness" and children's eventual pattern of attachment (Cole & Cole, 1989). Moreover, the stability of a particular pattern of attachment also depends on the stability of a child's circumstances: Children are likely to shift from secure to insecure attachment patterns if their families are undergoing a period of chronic stress or illness. And mothers are not the only source of healthy attachment. Depending on the culture and environment, babies can become attached to their fathers, siblings, regular baby-sitters, and grandparents as well.

Behaviorists also point out that babies may simply learn, through a process of operant conditioning, to fuss and cry when their parents leave the room. In a series of experiments, Jacob Gewirtz and Martha Peláez-Nogueras (1991a, b) have shown that when a mother who is about to leave responds to her child's protests by stopping, hesitating, speaking to the child, or returning to pick the child up, or when she comes back into the room while the child is still complaining, the child's protests and crying increase. (Of course, this is precisely what many parents do in real life.) When, in contrast, the mother responds to anything the child does that is *not* crying and protesting (laughing, playing with toys), the child's protests soon stop. The researchers were able to condition the child to cry while the mother was leaving the room but not during her brief absence itself—or vice versa—simply by manipulating the mother's behavior.

Of course, everyone agrees that babies need the care, attention, and affection of adults. When infants are consistently deprived of social contact, affection, and cuddling, the effects can be disastrous and long-lasting. Insecurely attached infants often grow into children who have a number of behavioral problems (Bowlby, 1988; Speltz, Greenberg, & Deklyen, 1990). Concerns about the consequences of insecure attachment have led some observers to worry that day care, for infants or preschoolers, may be detrimental to child development (Belsky, 1988). Let's examine the evidence.

DAY CARE AND SOCIAL DEVELOPMENT.   The United States lags far behind all other advanced industrial nations (and many poorer nations) in providing good, affordable day care (Kamerman, 1991). Because two-thirds of all American and Canadian mothers of young children are employed outside the home, the question of the effects of day care has received much attention.

The accumulated data from many studies of day care reveal no consistent negative effects. On the contrary, many studies find that children actually do better in day care than in home care. According to one such study of 150 children, ages 2 to 4, the social and intellectual development of children who were attending day-care centers (part time or full time) was *advanced* over that of children in home care (with the mother, a sitter, or day-care provider in the home) (Clarke-Stewart, 1991; also Field, 1992).

What about the effects of putting infants in day care during their critical first year? In a major longitudinal study of 2,387 children, Frank Mott (1991) investigated whether various forms of infant care were related to the child's performance on tests of physical, cognitive, and social development several years later. First, he controlled for a wide range of factors that would have been linked with a child's having been put in day care during infancy, such as mother's use of drugs or family income. That done, Mott found *no* statistically significant association between day care in infancy and the child's later motor or social development. As for cognitive development, the children who had been in day care as infants scored *higher* than those who had been at home. On closer inspection, Mott found that healthy baby girls benefited the most by being away from their mothers in day-care arrangements; healthy baby boys neither gained nor lost by being in day care; but boys *who were physically unhealthy in their first year* benefited by being home in maternal care. Mott concluded that "no type of infant care arrangement can be generalized as being uniformly preferable or detrimental."

Indeed, that is the opinion of most psychologists today. Instead of assuming that day care is universally helpful *or* harmful, they are asking different questions: How the quality of day care affects children's development, which children do well and which do poorly in different environments, and how parents and day-care programs can work effectively together. Children develop well in many kinds of caretaking arrangements. They go through the same stages of indiscriminate friendliness, fear of strangers, and independence, whether they are at home or in day care—as long as the care is good (Clarke-Stewart, 1991).

The quality of day care has become an important issue now that the majority of mothers with children under age 6 are working outside the home. Most studies find no ill effects of good day care on children, and many social and intellectual benefits.

Sex Typing

If you woke up tomorrow and found that you were a member of the other sex, how would your life be different? By the time they are in first grade, most boys will tell you the transformation would be disastrous. They couldn't do as much or be as active. They would have to be polite and pretty. But at the same age, most girls will say that the transformation would be beneficial. They could do more and be more assertive. People would like them more. They would be more confident (Baumgartner, 1983).

Where do children get these ideas? How is it that they know "for sure" what boys and girls can and cannot do, what they are or are not like? **Sex typing** is the psychological process by which boys and girls become "masculine" or "feminine." Through sex typing, children learn the preferences, abilities, interests, personality traits, actions, and self-concepts that their culture says are appropriate for males and females.

In our culture, sex typing starts early, with blue booties for baby boys and pink booties for girls. By the time children are 3 or 4, most prefer the games and activities that are "right" for their gender, and they also prefer same-sex friends. They are trying to determine the rules that distinguish male from female. Just as they overextend language rules ("Daddy taked me"; "He runned"), they overgeneralize social rules. Try convincing a 4-year-old that girls can become pilots or that boys can become nurses. The child will say patiently, as if you are an idiot, "No, *boys* can be pilots. Only girls can be nurses." When occupations become less sex-typed, however, so do children's views of them.

By age 4 or 5, most children have acquired a permanent **gender identity,** a sense of being biologically male or female, in spite of what they wear or how they act. As we noted earlier, they realize that a girl remains a girl, even if she can climb a tree. But they are still learning the rules of sex typing. Jason, a 9-year-old of our acquaintance, was taken to a cooking class that he had expressed an interest in joining. On the way there, he asked, "Mom, do boys take cooking lessons?" "Of course, of course," she reassured him. "Why, many of the greatest cooks in the world are men." He paused to consider this information. "Does everybody know that?" he asked.

Why and how does sex typing develop?

1. *Biological theories,* as you can guess by now, hold that some differences are wired in at birth. In this view, differences between the sexes in levels of aggression, in occupational interests (such as math or nursing), and in various skills (such as flying planes or knitting sweaters) are largely a matter of hormones, genes, and possibly brain lateralization (see Chapter 3). Proponents argue that some sex typing emerges regardless of what parents and teachers do, even when parents treat their sons and daughters alike (Lytton & Romney, 1991). Thus in all primate species, including human beings, young males are more likely than females to go in for physical roughhousing. This difference in styles of play may result from an average difference in a biological disposition for rough-and-tumble play.

2. *Social-learning theories* assume that children are mimicking the male and female patterns of behavior that they observe around them. Proponents of this view emphasize the rewards and punishments that children get for behaving appropriately or inappropriately for their gender, the adult models they observe, and the lessons they learn from seeing what happens to men and women who break the rules of sex typing. This approach assumes that children learn to be masculine or feminine just as they learn any other social lesson. Studies show that fathers take a more active role than mothers do in teaching sex-appropriate behavior in play and household chores. In general, fathers allow their sons to explore, break rules, and take physical chances, but they protectively keep their daughters nearby (Jacklin, DiPietro, & Maccoby, 1984).

■ **sex typing**
The process by which children learn the behaviors, attitudes, and expectations associated in their culture with being "masculine" or "feminine."
■ **gender identity**
The sense of being male or female, whether or not one follows the rules of sex typing.

Sex typing starts early.

3. *Cognitive developmental theory* maintains that children actively sex type themselves as their cognitive abilities mature (Kohlberg, 1966; Lewis & Brooks-Gunn, 1979). As children begin to organize their social worlds, they divide people into the fundamental categories of male or female. Once they understand where they fit, they are motivated by the need for cognitive consistency (see Chapter 10) to do the things that are appropriate to their gender, and to value the things associated with that gender. Once a boy has a stable self-concept of himself as male, he then automatically values "boy things" and dislikes "girl things," without being taught. This view does not explain, however, why girls often value male activities, as society does.

One variation on the cognitive-developmental theme is *gender schema theory* (Bem, 1985). The human mind is set up to perceive and organize information according to networks of associations called schemas, and a gender schema organizes the world in terms of male or female. In most societies gender is the most powerful social category, but different schemas or categories are equally important elsewhere (for instance, race in South Africa, caste in India).

4. *Context theories* represent a major departure from traditional approaches to sex typing. They hold that by regarding masculinity and femininity as permanent personality traits that children acquire like teddy bears, we forget that

In many places you would never see a man or his son in the kitchen, but gender roles are affected by history and culture and therefore keep changing. By their actions, parents convey all sorts of sex-typed lessons to their children. This group effort to make dinner is teaching the children that (1) both sexes belong in the kitchen, (2) group cooking may be messy but it's fun, and (3) the person who frosts the cake gets to lick the spoon.

children's behavior often depends on the situation they are in. In their every-day lives, men and women, and boys and girls, often behave in "feminine" ways *and* in "masculine" ways. In this view, the people that children interact with, and the situations that require certain behaviors from them, train them in certain sex-typed skills or permit them to be more flexible (Jacklin, 1989).

For example, Eleanor Maccoby (1990), reviewing many studies, found that boys and girls do not differ in passivity or activity in some consistent, traitlike way; their behavior depends on the gender of the child they are playing with. Among young children, girls are seldom passive with each other; however, when paired with boys, girls typically stand on the sidelines and let the boys monopolize the toys. This behavior, Maccoby found, is unrelated to the individual attributes of the children in the groups. Instead, it is related to the fact that between the ages of $3\frac{1}{2}$ and $5\frac{1}{2}$, boys stop responding to girls' requests, suggestions, and other attempts to influence them. (Why this occurs is a matter of debate.) When a boy and girl compete for a shared toy, the boy dominates—unless there is an adult in the room. Girls in mixed classrooms stay nearer to the teacher, Maccoby found, not because they are more dependent but because they want a chance at the toys! Girls play just as independently as boys when they are in all-girl groups, when they will actually sit farther from the teacher than boys in all-boy groups do.

All of these theories contribute a piece to the picture of sex typing. Perhaps young boys and girls start out with different average biological dispositions for rough-and-tumble play, and perhaps those differences are then reinforced by societal customs. Children certainly are rewarded and punished when they behave appropriately or inappropriately for their gender, although boys are punished more for behaving like girls than vice versa (Maccoby, 1980). Children do play an active part in interpreting the rules of gender, and as their abilities mature, they understand the exceptions to their gender schemas—for instance, that women can be senators and men can be nurses. And most children acquire the ability to express the qualities associated with both sexes, depending on the situation (Jacklin, 1989).

The Effects of Parents

When you did something wrong as a child, what did the adults in your family do about it? Did they shout at you, punish you, or explain the error of your ways? Children learn as much, if not more, from *how* their parents interact with them as from the content of their parents' efforts.

In a successful method of child rearing called *induction*, the parent appeals to the child's own resources, affection for others, and sense of responsibility. For example, a mother may tell her child that the child's actions will harm, inconvenience, or disappoint another person. Induction tends to produce children who have moral feelings and who behave morally on five different measures. They feel guilty if they hurt others; they internalize standards of right and wrong, instead of just following orders; they confess rather than lie if they misbehave; they accept responsibility for their misbehavior; and they are considerate of others (Hoffman & Saltzstein, 1967; Schulman & Mekler, 1985).

Parents who rely on a second method, *power assertion*, use punitive methods: threats; physical punishment; depriving the child of privileges; and taking advantage of being bigger, stronger, and more powerful ("because I say so"). Power assertion, which is based on the child's fear of punishment, is associated with a *lack* of moral feeling and behavior in children. The child may feel guilty about his or her own desires and impulses (which the parent punishes), but not guilty about harming others (Maccoby, 1980). Another punishing method is *love withdrawal*, in which the parent reacts to the child's misbehavior by withdrawing,

Parents can teach their children to be responsible by explaining the reasons for rules and limits, instead of asserting "because I say so!"

Power assertion is often intimidating to a child, who may obey but feel resentful and rebellious.

by disapproving without saying why, or by threatening to stop loving the child. This reaction makes the child feel bad, without teaching the child what to do to feel good.

Parental power assertion is linked with children's aggressiveness. Observational studies of parents and children in the home find that parents of aggressive children use a great deal of punishment (shouting, scolding, spanking), yet they fail to make the punishment contingent on the child's behavior. They do not state clear rules, require compliance, praise good behavior, or consistently punish violations. Instead, they nag and "natter" at the child, occasionally and unpredictably tossing in a slap or loss of privileges. The child, in turn, becomes more antisocial, manipulative, and difficult to discipline (Patterson, 1986; Patterson, DeBaryshe, & Ramsey, 1989). Of course, it is also possible that aggressive children are simply hard to discipline consistently. But because this research was conducted over time, the researchers were able to separate cause and effect. Parental actions and expectations actually provoke the child's aggressiveness, which, as the child ages, can get out of hand and harder to restrain.

Across numerous longitudinal studies, different patterns of child-rearing practices, often with induction or power assertion at their core, have been linked to a wide variety of outcomes for children. In a large study designed to investigate the origins of male delinquency, for example, the researchers found three groups of factors that predicted which boys would avoid a life of crime: (1) the mother's consistency of discipline, her self-confidence, and her affection for her son; (2) the father's esteem for the mother, his affection for his son, his own low level of aggressiveness, and a low degree of conflict with his wife; and (3) the parents' restrictions on the son's behavior, their supervision of him, and their having set high standards for him (McCord, 1990). In the families that scored below the median on all three factors, 58 percent of the sons eventually went on to commit a serious crime, compared to 15 percent of those who came from families above the median. (For more on methods of child rearing, see "Taking Psychology with You on page 492.")

Of course, parental styles of child rearing depend on the kind of child a parent is trying to raise. Over the years, the traits that parents most value have changed significantly. In 1924, about 50 percent of a sample of average Americans emphasized "strict obedience" and "loyalty to Church" in training their children; by the late 1970s, the figure had dropped to only 20 percent. In contrast, in 1924, only 6 percent valued teaching their children "tolerance of other people's opinions," and only 25 percent valued "independence—thinking and acting for yourself." In the late 1970s, 47 percent valued tolerance, and a whopping 76 percent valued independence of thought and action (Alwin, 1988).

QUICK QUIZ

1. A child who is securely attached is more likely to (a) be reared at home instead of day care, (b) have many people to be attached to, (c) be temperamentally calm, (d) have experienced normal affection and attention from an adult.

2. A 7-year-old girl who is quiet and passive in class, but active and independent in her all-girl Brownie troop, illustrates which theory of sex typing? (a) gender schema, (b) cognitive-developmental, (c) context, (d) biological

3. Match the method of discipline with the appropriate example:
   1. induction   a. "Do it because I say so, period."
   2. power assertion   b. "Go to your room at once."
   3. punishment   c. "Pinching hurts your sister; big boys like you don't need to pinch."

4. In Chapter 12 you read that the Big Five personality traits have a strong hereditary component, are fairly resistant to change, and emerge almost regardless of what parents do. Now here we are offering evidence that what parents do *does* make a difference. How might these two lines of research be reconciled?

ANSWERS:

1. b 2. c 3. 1-c, 2-a, 3-b 4. We can avoid either-or thinking by asking, for example, *which* qualities and behaviors may largely be matters of temperament (such as introversion/extroversion) and which ones are strongly affected by parental lessons (such as aggressiveness and empathy). Remember too that how a child "turns out" depends on the *interactions* between a child's temperament and the parents' reactions to it. And perhaps the relative impact of heredity and parents changes, depending on the child's age.

The Effects of Parental Divorce

For years, psychologists asked "What are the effects of divorce on children?"—often assuming the answer would be, "awful." Now they are asking, "What factors produce negative effects and which produce positive or neutral ones?" Why did their assumptions change, and with what consequences for research?

Thirty years ago, divorce was rare and shameful. Today, divorce is nearly as common as the flu, and affects 1 million children a year. A child born today in the United States has a 40 percent chance of living through a *second* parental divorce by age 18. Some psychologists, especially clinicians, argue that many if not most of the children of divorce suffer psychologically in various ways, and that these effects can be long-lasting (Wallerstein & Blakeslee, 1989). Such researchers have assumed that single-parent families tend to be disturbed or deviant, and that the children of divorce are being put at serious psychological risk.

Yet others have concluded that most children eventually recover from the experience with few lasting consequences (C. P. Edwards, 1987). A study of 568 college-aged students found that those whose parents had divorced were no different in self-esteem or levels of depression from students whose parents had remained together—they were merely more pessimistic (some would say "realistic") about their own future marriages (Franklin, Janoff-Bulman, & Roberts, 1990). One of our students, in an essay about his parents' divorce, said, "I resent the way people talk about 'broken' families and 'intact' families. There is nothing broken about my relationship with my dad, and my brothers and mom and I are perfectly 'intact' as a family."

Moreover, not all "single-parent" families are "single-*adult*" families. Extended-family networks are more common among African Americans—married or single—than whites. When a divorce occurs, its effects can be cushioned for children who live in a household that includes not only the custodial parent but other relatives as well (Hetherington, 1989; Wilson, 1989).

To try to grasp the overall picture of the effects of divorce, Paul Amato and Bruce Keith (1991) analyzed the results of 92 studies, representing more than 13,000 children of all ages. These studies examined the effects of divorce on children's well-being, achievement, conduct, social adjustment, and relations with parents. Amato and Keith found good news and bad news. The bad news was that children of divorce do, in general, have lower well-being than do children living in two-parent families; the argument that children adapt readily and recover quickly after parental divorce was not supported. The good news was that the difference in well-being, while statistically significant, was small in magnitude; the argument that children of divorce suffer irreparably and profoundly was also not supported. In some individual studies, daughters of divorced couples were better adjusted than were sons; but in others, sons had the advantage. Overall, sex differences were not very strong.

Amato and Keith then examined three competing hypotheses of *why* divorce might produce negative effects: the "father absence" explanation; the "economic disadvantage" explanation, which holds that children of divorce suffer because divorce lowers the standard of living for many mothers; and the "family conflict" perspective, which assumes that children suffer not because of changes in family structure, but because of being caught between bitter, quarreling parents.

The father-absence explanation, in general, did not hold up. Six studies found that children's well-being was higher when they remained in contact with their (noncustodial) fathers; but six found *no* association between continued contact and well-being, and three found that contact was associated with *increased* problems for children! However, most boys did better when they lived either in the custody of their fathers or with stepfathers, in contrast to seeing their fathers intermittently or not at all.

Economic disadvantage, Amato and Keith found, does reduce the well-being of children of divorce, particularly for those who are shifted into poverty (or who cannot go to college because their fathers stop paying child support [Wallerstein & Blakeslee, 1989]). But it is not the whole story. Children of divorce continue to have lower well-being than children of nondivorced parents even when the two sets of families are equal in income.

By far the strongest explanation for the negative effects of divorce was the family conflict hypothesis. Parents who divorce are especially likely to be bitter and angry with each other, and their anger often catches the children in the middle. But parental conflict has negative effects on children in nondivorced families as well. Children in high-conflict families are more likely to have conduct problems, poor psychological adjustment, and low self-esteem than children in families with low levels of discord (Gottman & Katz, 1989). When researchers have compared children in these "fighting families"—where there is a high level of conflict between parents—with children of divorced parents, they find a similar incidence of depression and reduced well-being (Nolen-Hoeksema, Girgus, & Seligman, 1991). In contrast, the children of divorce usually adjust eventually, unless their parents continue to quarrel about visitation rights, take each other to court, fight with each other at every visit, or make the children choose sides.

As you can see, there is no single answer to the question "What are the effects of divorce?" The effects, for any one individual, depend on what the family was like before the divorce; the child's temperament, age, and needs; the financial security and psychological well-being of the custodial parent; the level of conflict between the parents; the family's support system; and many other factors to boot. As with day care, current research focuses on the diversity of children's responses to divorce, and asks: What are the factors that enable children to recover or remain unhappy and angry? From the standpoint of children's adjustment, an amicable divorce is better than a bitter marriage, but a prolonged and bitter divorce is worst of all.

A major longitudinal study followed the children of divorced couples for 15 years (Wallerstein & Blakeslee, 1989). Although the researchers used no control group, they concluded that divorce contributes to early promiscuity in teenage girls, aggressiveness in teenage boys, and lowered academic motivation in both sexes. What are some problems with this conclusion?

ANSWERS:

The psychologists may have attributed the children's current problems to the divorce without considering other possible causes, such as peer pressure or normal adolescent conflicts. Without control groups of children of parents who did not divorce, or of children who were living in families marked by conflict, the researchers cannot conclude that the problems of the children were unusual. It's hard to know what "lowered" academic motivation means if you haven't defined "average" motivation!

■ MORAL DEVELOPMENT

Do you think it is morally acceptable to steal? To steal something if you can afford to pay for it? Do you think it is morally acceptable to hit someone? To hit someone to get something you want? Have you ever done any of these things? If so, how did you feel about it?

The study of moral development focuses on three questions: (1) moral judgments (is stealing right or wrong?); (2) moral emotions (how will you feel if you steal that watch?); and (3) moral behavior (you may know it is wrong to steal, and even feel guilty if you do, but can you say no to temptation?).

Moral Judgments: Reasoning About Morality

How do children learn to resist temptation and eventually follow social rules?

Adults make moral judgments not only according to what people do, but also according to *why* they do it. We allow bad behavior, depending on a person's intentions and needs, and extenuating circumstances. We don't much like good behavior that is motivated by greed or selfishness.

Piaget (1932) was the first psychologist to divide the development of moral reasoning into stages. Young children, he said, see right and wrong in terms of results rather than intention. They might tell you that a child who accidentally breaks two dishes is naughtier than a child who intentionally breaks one. They think that rules are set by a higher authority and are inflexible. You can't change the rules of a game, of family tradition, of life. If you break the rules, punishment will be swift and sure. Not until about age 7, said Piaget, do children begin to understand that rules are social contracts that can be changed. Older children believe that intention, fair play, and reciprocity ("you do for me and I do for you") are the standards of moral action. Children's moral reasoning, said Piaget, follows the increasing cognitive complexity of their reasoning in general.

In the 1960s, Lawrence Kohlberg (1964) outlined a new stage theory. Like Piaget, he focused on moral reasoning, not behavior. He did not observe how children or adults *actually* treat each other. But because his theory has become so influential— parent-training manuals use it, entire school systems have based moral-reasoning courses on it, some prisons even use it in rehabilitation programs—we are going to look at it closely.

Kohlberg (1976, 1984) proposed three levels of moral development, each divided into two stages. Your moral "stage" is determined by the answers you give to hypothetical moral dilemmas. For example, a man's wife is dying and needs a special drug. The man can't afford the drug and the druggist won't lower his price. Should the man steal the drug? What if he no longer loves his wife? If the man is caught, should the judge be lenient? To Kohlberg, the reasoning behind the answers was more important than the decisions themselves.

At Kohlberg's first level of moral reasoning, *preconventional morality*, young children obey rules because they are ordered to, because they will be punished if they disobey, or because they want to. What is "right" is what Mom and Dad say, or what feels good. At about ages 10 or 11, according to Kohlberg, children shift to the second level, the *conventional morality* of adult society. At first, conventional morality is based on trust, caring, and loyalty to others; morality means "don't hurt others; don't rock the boat." Many people then advance to a "law-and-order orientation," based on understanding the social order, law, justice, and duty.

Late in adolescence and early adulthood, said Kohlberg, some people realize that there is an even higher level of moral judgment, beyond human laws. They see that some laws—such as those that segregate blacks from whites, or those that legitimize the systematic mistreatment or murder of minorities—are themselves immoral. Such awareness moves them to the highest moral level, *postconventional ("principled") morality*. They realize that values and laws are relative, that people hold different standards, that laws are important but can be changed. A few great individuals have a moral standard based on universal human rights. When faced with a conflict between law and conscience, such people follow conscience, even at personal risk.

Most people, said Kohlberg, never reach this ultimate level; but if anyone does in Kohlberg's system, it's likely to be a man. Women, his studies implied, are more likely than men to get stuck at the beginning of level 2, worrying about other people's feelings as the basis of moral judgment. Men tend to stop at the end of level 2, emphasizing principles of law and duty that are above feelings.

Kohlberg's theory has been attacked on several counts. First, some critics complain that the hierarchy of stages actually reflects verbal, not moral, development and thus favors white, middle-class people in Western society (Shweder, Mahapatra, & Miller, 1987). College-educated people give "higher-level," "more mature" explanations of moral decisions than people who have not attended college, but we can hardly conclude that they actually *are* more moral. They are more verbally sophisticated, however.

Second, adults have greater understanding of law than children do, but this knowledge does not make them more moral. A child who says "The judge should be lenient because [the husband] acted unselfishly" will score lower than the adult who says "The judge should be lenient because he or she can find a precedent or rule that reflects what is right." As two psychologists concluded, "The cruellest lawyer is, without question, going to get a higher score than the kindest eight-year-old" (Schulman & Mekler, 1985). Indeed, dozens of research studies now show that very young children are capable of moral feelings, of behaving kindly and considerately, of understanding that their actions have consequences. In some ways they are more moral than adults. Most 3-year-olds have no color, class, or religious prejudices.

Other critics challenge the idea that once people reach a higher level, they don't regress to a lower one. Studies find that neither adults nor children use the same moral reasoning in all ethical situations (Colby et al., 1983). You might show conventional morality by overlooking a racial slur at a dinner party (you don't want to upset everyone else), but postconventional reasoning by protesting a war you regard as immoral. Men in general are supposed to operate according to principles of law and justice, but about one-third of American and

Canadian college men say they would force a woman into sexual acts if they could "get away with it" (Malamuth & Dean, 1990), an admission that reveals the lowest form of moral reasoning.

Finally, many researchers criticize Kohlberg's work for its implication that men are more moral than women. Carol Gilligan (1982) argued that because Kohlberg and Piaget based their original theories on studies only of boys, their research is invalid as a way of understanding how and why girls make moral decisions. Gilligan agrees that women tend to base moral decisions on principles of compassion and care, whereas men base theirs on abstract principles of law and justice. But neither style of moral reasoning is *better* than the other, she maintains. Each has its strengths and weaknesses. Justice without compassion can be cold. Compassion without principle can be spineless.

Some studies support Gilligan's view, finding that men care more about justice and women care more about caring (Bussey & Maughan, 1982; Gilligan & Wiggins, 1987). Most research, however, finds no sex differences in moral reasoning (Cohn, 1991; Thoma, 1986), especially when people are allowed to rank *all* the reasons behind their moral judgments. In one study, 101 young men and women evaluated the importance of a series of considerations in deciding how to respond to four moral dilemmas. Some of the considerations emphasized "care-based" reasoning (such as "which outcome will cause the least hurt for all of the people involved") and others were "justice-based" (such as "whether there is a moral code to which all individuals should adhere"). The researchers found absolutely no differences in how men and women ranked the items or in how they evaluated the moral dilemmas. Indeed, on a few items, men were more "care-based" than women. Both men and women, it seems, base their moral decisions on compassion *and* abstract principles of justice (Friedman, Robinson, & Friedman, 1987).

Nevertheless, Gilligan's approach has an important virtue. Rather than ranking moral judgments one above the other, perhaps we should consider how they can coexist. To Kohlberg, Mohandas Gandhi reached the highest moral stage because of his commitment to universal principles of peace, justice, and nonviolence. To Gilligan, Gandhi was *also* a man who was aloof from his family and followers, whom he often treated callously. Can we really say he was at the pinnacle of morality? Here is another problem for you. Vietnam war hero John Vann performed astonishing feats of bravery during the war, time and again rescuing men from certain death. He was also an obsessive seducer who eventually abandoned his wife and five children without support, and he lied to avoid being court-martialed for the seduction of a 15-year-old girl (Sheehan, 1988). Do a person's moral virtues in one sphere of life excuse his or her behavior in other realms?

John Paul Vann was a Vietnam war hero who saved many of his men from death. He was also an extremely promiscuous man who abandoned his wife and family and failed to support them. What "stage" of morality would you place him in?

Moral Emotions: Acquiring Empathy, Guilt, and Shame

A second approach to studying morality concentrates on the development of conscience. Children shift from obeying rules for external reasons, such as fear of punishment, to obeying rules for internal reasons, because they will feel guilty or ashamed of behaving badly. Morality, in this view, depends on *empathy*, the ability to feel bad about another person's unhappiness and to feel good about another's joy, and on *altruism*, the willingness to help another person without thought of personal gain.

The ability to feel empathy seems to have an evolutionary basis (Plutchik, 1987). Children reveal empathic feelings early in life; empathy develops into different forms, depending on the child's age and cognitive abilities (Hoffman, 1989). In the first year, before they even have a sense of themselves as distinct from others, infants feel *global empathy*, general distress at another person's misery. At times, they act as though what happened to the other happened to them-

Children have an innate ability to form attachments, but experience determines whether they will develop empathy for or rivalry with others. A child who learns how to care for a new sibling is likely to acquire feelings of protectiveness and concern instead of rivalry and distance.

selves. One 11-month-old girl, seeing an older child fall and cry, behaved as if *she* had been hurt. She looked about to cry, put her thumb in her mouth, and buried her head in her mother's lap (Hoffman, 1987).

With the emergence of object permanence and the sense of self (ages 1 to 2), toddlers develop *"egocentric" empathy*. Children now understand that someone else is in distress, but they assume that the other person must feel as they do. Two-year-olds are often impulsive and egocentric, but they are also able to feel sad when another child or adult is unhappy and are capable of trying to make the person feel better. In one touching instance, a 13-month-old child offered her beloved doll to a sad adult (Hoffman, 1977). In another, an 18-month-old boy fetched his own mother to comfort a crying friend, although the friend's mother was also there!

By the age of 2 or 3, children are capable of *empathy for another's feelings* that are different from their own. The development of language also allows children to empathize with a growing number of emotions. For example, they can empathize with another child's feelings of shame, and they know when the child wants to be left alone. They are able to feel angry on someone else's behalf. One little boy, seeing a doctor give another child a painful injection, swatted the doctor in protest. A toddler in one study said, "You sad, Mommy. What Daddy do?" (Bretherton & Beeghly, 1982).

The final stage of empathy, *empathy for another's life condition*, emerges by late childhood. Children are able to understand that people have different experiences and histories and to feel empathy toward whole groups of individuals who are less fortunate than they are.

Although people might like a life without shame or guilt, these emotions, too, are essential to social life. They help maintain rules and standards, and encourage moral action. *Shame* is a wound to the self-concept. It comes from perceiving that others have seen you doing something wrong and that they will like you less for having done it. As soon as the toddler has a sense of self, shame is quick to follow (Lewis et al., 1989). *Guilt*, in contrast, is the emotion you feel when you have not lived up to your own internal standard; it is remorse for real or imagined wrongdoings, a kind of self-inflicted punishment.

Of course, guilt can also be maladaptive and self-defeating. Studies of children who live with a chronically depressed or deeply troubled parent, for example, find that these children often develop unhealthy patterns of empathy and guilt. Their feelings of empathy for the parent tend to be infused with guilt and frustration, a result of overinvolvement with the unhappy parent and an unrealistic feeling that they are somehow responsible for the parent's misery (Zahn-Waxler et al., 1990).

By the age of 2, children are aware of standards of behavior, and at this tender age they react with anxious concern or distress when a standard has been violated. By the age of 3 or 4, children associate a bad act with being a "bad boy" or "bad girl," and they begin to regulate their own behavior. In every culture around the world, children at this age judge their thoughts, feelings, and behavior against the standards they know are "right" (C. Edwards, 1987; Kagan & Lamb, 1987). In turn, adults begin to treat children differently, expecting them to do the right thing.

The capacity for moral feeling, like that for language, seems to be inborn. As Jerome Kagan (1984) says, "Without this fundamental human capacity, which nineteenth-century observers called a *moral sense*, the child could not be socialized." But the shape this "moral sense" takes depends on the child's family and culture. Infants may feel global empathy, but whether a 4-year-old boy will feel empathy toward a newborn sister's wails depends on the experience he has in taking care of her.

Moral Action: Learning to Behave Morally

Unfortunately, moral reasoning and moral emotions are not necessarily related to moral behavior. People can know what is right and not do it. They can feel really miserable about treating each other horribly, and do it anyway. In Chapter 18 we look at some social forces, such as conformity and obedience, that affect moral behavior. Here we want to consider how children become helpful members of society. How do they learn to avoid the temptations to steal, lie, cheat, and otherwise behave as they might like?

Social learning theorists answer that children's moral feelings and actions depend on the rewards, punishments, and examples they get as they grow up. When children are rewarded for aggressive and competitive acts, such behavior will prevail over cooperation and altruism (Kohn, 1986; Maccoby, 1980). However, directly rewarding children for being helpful does not necessarily produce helpful children. After all, the point of altruism is to do good with no thought of getting a reward. Nor do good role models have much of an influence. Finally, the fear of punishment interferes with the learning of self-control, empathy, and internalized values.

Then how do children learn to behave morally? In a study of children only 15 to 20 months old, some were already more helpful than others. If their behavior caused a friend to feel unhappy, afraid, or hurt, they would try to bring comfort by offering a toy, hugging the friend, or going to get help. It turned out that the mothers of these little Samaritans were using induction to reprimand their children in a particular way. They would *moralize* ("You made Doug cry; it's not nice to bite") or prohibit bad behavior with *explanations* or *statements of principle* ("You must never poke anyone's eyes because that could hurt them seriously"). Other ways of reprimanding bad behavior were ineffective. Neutral explanations ("Tina is crying because you pushed her") had no effect. The reprimands that produced the lowest rates of helping were unexplained prohibitions ("Stop that!") and punishment, such as spanking and hitting (Zahn-Waxler, Radke-Yarrow, & King, 1979). The only effective punishments are forceful reprimands or time outs, again with explanation ("You can't play with that toy for a while because you hit people with it") (Schulman & Mekler, 1985).

Ultimately, a major influence on children's moral behavior is the behavior that is expected of them. In a large-scale study of children in six cultures (Kenya, India, the Philippines, Okinawa, Mexico, and the United States), Beatrice and John Whiting (1975) measured how often children behaved altruistically (offering help, support, or unselfish suggestions) or egoistically (seeking help and attention, or wanting to dominate others). This study was subsequently reanalyzed, and five new cultures were added to it (Whiting & Edwards, 1988). Amer-

In many cultures, children are expected to work to contribute to the family income, and to take care of their younger siblings. These experiences encourage helpfulness and empathy.

ican children were the *least* altruistic on all three measures and the *most* egoistic. The most altruistic children came from societies in which:

• Children are assigned many tasks, such as caring for younger children, helping with gathering food and preparing it.
• Children know that their work makes a genuine contribution to the well-being or economic survival of the family.
• Parents depend on the children's contributions.
• Mothers have many responsibilities inside and outside the home.
• Children respect parental authority.

Developmental and cross-cultural studies show us that the old philosophic chestnut—are children fundamentally "little savages" or "little moralists"?—is unanswerable. Rather, research suggests that parents and societies would do better to ask how we can foster children's empathy, moral reasoning, and altruistic behavior.

QUICK QUIZ

To raise children who are kind and helpful, parents (and parents-to-be) should be able to answer the following questions.

1. LaVerne, age 14 months, sees her mother crying during a tearjerker, and she starts to cry too. LaVerne has developed (a) global empathy, (b) egocentric empathy, (c) empathy for another's feelings.
2. Shame and guilt are (a) unconscious emotions in infancy, (b) necessary emotions in learning moral feeling and behavior, (c) destructive emotions that should be stamped out as soon as possible.
3. Which method of parental discipline tends to create helpful children? (a) threats (b) induction, (c) punishment, (d) power assertion
4. Which form of family life tends to create helpful children? (a) every family member "does his or her own thing," (b) parents are appropriate role models, (c) children contribute to the family welfare, (d) parents remind children often about the importance of being helpful

ANSWERS:

1. b 2. b 3. b 4. c

■ CAN CHILDREN SURVIVE CHILDHOOD?

Are we really "prisoners of childhood"? If you suffered a trauma in your early years, must you endure its effects for the rest of your life?

As you can see, the study of child development does not produce one set of simple findings. Every time we presented somebody's research—on "bonding," "maternal sensitivity," cognitive stages, day care and divorce, moral development—we had to follow it with contradictory evidence. The result is continuing controversies. Can children's cognitive development be hurried? Is sex typing a necessary stage in social development or can it be eliminated? Can morality be taught? By generating studies to answer these questions, psychologists narrow the gap between the laboratory and real life. This is how science advances.

Of all the controversial issues in child development, perhaps the most controversial is this: How straight is the path from childhood to adulthood? All of us acquire attitudes, habits, and deep emotional feelings from our families. Parents influence their children in thousands of ways, both positively and negatively. Many adults carry with them the scars of abuses they suffered as children. But do all of the experiences of later childhood lead in a straight and inflexible line to the future?

Some psychologists argue that no year of life is as important as the first. If the baby doesn't start out well, they warn, if the parents (especially the mother) do not tend to the baby's every physical and emotional need in the "right" way, the baby's whole life may be influenced for the worse. How critical is this year? Certainly, if newborns start off on the wrong foot, with sickness or social deprivation, they don't do as well as babies who start off healthy and loved.

But the events of the first year do not necessarily have permanent effects, as study after study confirms. Infant vulnerabilities often can be outgrown. Researchers who followed the development of 643 children, from birth to age 18, and again at age 32, found that supportive home environments totally overcame any initial biological weakness. Problems that emerged were related more to stressful home environments than to biological vulnerabilities in infancy. Even those problems proved temporary. "As we watched these children grow from babyhood to adulthood," the researchers reported, "we could not help but respect the self-righting tendencies within them that produced normal development under all but the most persistently adverse circumstances" (Werner & Smith, 1982; see also Werner, 1989).

Given adequate stimulation, attention, and nourishment, normal babies will develop normally. But "adequate" covers considerable territory. Babies get along just fine on cradleboards or unbound, in good day-care centers or at home with caretakers. It's good to give them the very best stimulation, attention, and nourishment possible. But parents need not fear that one wrong step will cost their baby a place in graduate school or will later require 17 years of therapy.

What about the effects of prolonged difficulties in childhood? Many adults today find explanations for their current problems in the traumatic experiences of their early years. Naturally, as adults, we all look backward to make sense out of our lives. This is one reason that retrospective studies, in which people tell interviewers about their pasts, often find consistent patterns of development. However, prospective studies, which follow people from childhood to adulthood, often do not:

• After World War II, many European children, made homeless by the war, were adopted by American families. A group of these orphans, aged 5 months to 10 years, was followed and their adjustment observed. About 20 percent of the children initially showed many signs of anxiety (such as overeating, sleep disturbances, and nightmares), but over the years all of these symptoms vanished. All of the children made good progress in school, none had psychiatric problems, and all established happy, affectionate relationships with their new parents (Rathbun, DiVirgilio, & Waldfogel, 1958).

• In a study of 53 children who had had psychological disorders ranging from delinquency to depression, 35 had recovered completely by late adolescence. The researchers concluded, "The emotionally traumatized child is not doomed, the parents' early mistakes are not irrevocable" (Thomas & Chess, 1984).

• Another study followed 200 disturbed children who had been referred to a child guidance clinic for treatment when they were, on the average, 9 years old. But as young adults, aged 18 to 27, most of those children had improved enormously. Except for the most seriously disturbed children, the researchers said, "there seems to be little continuity between child and adult disturbances" (Cass & Thomas, 1979).

Now, the facts are indisputable that children who are abused or neglected, or who live in continuous risk of violence from their parents, strangers, or gangs, are more likely than nonabused children to become delinquent and violent themselves, to commit crimes, to have lower IQs, and to attempt suicide (Widom, 1989). And some behavior geneticists believe there is compelling evidence of a genetic role in criminality, violence, and delinquency (DiLalla & Gottesman, 1991). Yet it is also true that although more children of alcoholic or abusive parents acquire behavioral problems than do children of nondisturbed parents, *most* of them—the majority—do not.

For example, Melissa West and Ronald J. Prinz (1987) reviewed ten years of studies of children of alcoholic parents. They examined a range of possible pathological effects: hyperactivity, drug abuse and delinquency, lower IQ and poor school performance, social inadequacy, physical symptoms, anxiety and depression, physical aggression, and troubled family relationships. In comparison to children of nondisturbed parents, children who had an alcoholic parent were at greater risk of having one or more of these problems, and the researchers noted that "parental alcoholism is undoubtedly disruptive to family life." But West and Prinz found that "neither all nor a major portion of the population of children from alcoholic homes are inevitably doomed to psychological disorder."

In addition, as noted way back in Chapter 2, most children who are abused do *not*, as parents, abuse their own children. "Adults who were maltreated have been told so many times that they will abuse their children that for some it has become a self-fulfilling prophecy," observe Joan Kaufman and Edward Zigler (1987). In reviewing more than 40 articles on child abuse, they found that most studies of this question failed to use representative samples or a comparison group of adults who were abused and did not abuse their own children. Being abused in childhood makes a person *more likely* to be an abusive parent, but fully 70 percent do not repeat their parents' cruelties.

Because of these heartening studies, some psychologists have been trying to pinpoint the origins of *resilience* in the children of abusers and alcoholics (Cowen et al., 1990; Garmezy, 1985, 1991). Many of these resilient children get love and attention from the nondisturbed parent or another doting adult. They have an informal support network for advice and aid. They have good experiences in school. They have found activities and hobbies that they do well at, that provide solace and self-esteem (Werner, 1989). They have acquired a sense of meaning about life (West & Prinz, 1987). Most of all, they are mindfully determined not to repeat their histories.

We do not wish to imply, in reporting this optimistic news, that a painful or traumatic childhood is easy to overcome. Although this chapter has emphasized the joys and challenges of child development, there is a larger, more serious issue to consider: Whether children themselves are valued by the culture in which they develop—and what effects cultural attitudes might have on them. Indeed, a strong case can be made that American society, for all its professed love of

Childhood is not only a time of happy innocence. Can you remember feeling moments of self-doubt, humiliation, loss, fear, and sadness? To what extent did these experiences, and the way you coped with them, affect you?

children, does not treat them well. Unlike Sweden and most other European nations, the United States places a low priority on day care, child-care services, and education. People who work with children earn less than people who work with adults, even within the same field (pediatricians earn less than internists, elementary school teachers earn less than college teachers). Increasing numbers of children live in severe poverty and get no medical attention. "Adults-only" communities are springing up from coast to coast. And, most tragically, the physical and emotional abuse of children is widespread.

Keep in mind, therefore, that although some children are able to survive early traumas, this doesn't mean that childhood experiences are insignificant or that society can afford to be indifferent to children's welfare. But as children develop, they are subject to other influences, too. They outgrow certain habits and attitudes, even as they cling to others that have been rewarded and encouraged. Things happen to children and adults that *can* overturn the effects of earlier experiences. Perhaps the most powerful reason for the breaks between childhood and adulthood is that children actively interpret their experiences, a theme we have emphasized. Children have minds of their own. This is the reason for the gap between what parents try to teach and what children learn, and between what children learn and what they take with them into adulthood.

The link between childhood and adulthood is, it seems, more like a dotted curve than a straight line. In the next chapter, we will look at the development of the individual throughout life.

TAKING PSYCHOLOGY WITH YOU

Bringing Up Baby

How should you treat your children? Should you be strict or lenient, powerful or permissive? Should you require your child to stop having tantrums, to clean up his or her room, to be polite? *Authoritarian* parents exercise too much power; *permissive* parents too little. *Authoritative* parents travel a middle road; they know when and how to discipline their children (Baumrind, 1971). What are the practical steps you can take to be an authoritative parent? According to a vast number of research studies, the following guidelines are effective in teaching children to control aggressive impulses; have good self-control, high self-esteem, and confidence; and be cheerful, thoughtful, and helpful:

• *Be consistent in enforcing specific rules and demands.* Do not give in to the child's whining or tantrums, or let the child break rules behind your back. Inconsistency—letting the child pull the cat's tail on Tuesday but not on Thursday—encourages the undesirable behavior.

• *Set high expectations that are appropriate to the child's age, and teach the child how to*

meet them. Some parents make few demands on their children, either intentionally (they believe a parent should not "impose" standards) or unintentionally. Others set many demands and standards, such as requiring children to be polite, help with chores, control their anger, be thoughtful of others, and do well in school. The children of well-meaning parents who make few demands tend to be aggressive, impulsive, and immature. The children of parents who have demands and expectations tend to be helpful rather than selfish and above average in competence and self-confidence. However, the demands must be appropriate for the child's age. You can't expect 2-year-olds to dress themselves, and before you can expect children to get up on time for school by themselves they have to know how to work an alarm clock.

• *Explain, explain, explain.* Induction—telling a child *why* you have applied a rule—is an essential guideline. Punitive methods ("do it because I say so") may result in compliance, but the child will tend to disobey as soon as you are out of sight. Explanations also teach children how to reason and understand; they reward curiosity and open-mindedness (Schulman, 1991). This does not mean you have to argue with a 4-year-old about the merits of good table manners. You can set standards for your children, but also allow them to express disagreements and feelings.

• *Notice, approve of, and reward good behavior.* Many parents tend to punish the behavior they dislike, a form of attention that may actually be rewarding to the child (see Chapter 6). But it is much more effective to praise the behavior you *do* want, which teaches the child what is right.

• *Call the child's attention to the effect of his or her actions on others, and teach the child to take another person's point of view.* As we saw in this chapter, this lesson teaches empathy and

consideration for others. Vague orders such as "Don't fight!" are less effective than showing the child how his fighting disrupts and hurts others. For boys especially, there is a strong negative relationship between aggression and empathy: The higher the one, the lower the other (Feshbach et al., 1983).

• *Temper your teachings to the child's temperament.* All of these guidelines depend on how the child reacts to them and how the child interprets your actions. You cannot turn a calm child into a bundle of energy. You cannot create the "ideal child," that is, one who is an exact replica of you. But you *can* expect the best from your children—their best, not yours.

SUMMARY

1. Babies are born with basic motor reflexes that are necessary for survival, including the grasping, startle, sucking, and "rooting" reflexes. At first, they can see only a distance of 8 inches, but within a few weeks they can distinguish where something is and what it is. Babies also develop *synchrony* of rhythm with their caretakers.

2. Physical development is very rapid during the first year. On the average, babies sit without support at 7 months, crawl at 9 months, and take their first steps at 13 months. Brain development, including the growth of *myelin*, progresses rapidly.

3. Jean Piaget proposed that children's cognitive development depends on their current developmental stage and their experience in the world. Children's thinking changes and adapts through two processes, *assimilation* and *accommodation*. Piaget proposed four stages of cognitive development: *sensory-motor* (birth to age 2), during which the child learns *object permanence; preoperational* (ages 2 to 7), during which language and symbolic thought develop; *concrete operations* (ages 6 or 7 to 11); and *formal operations* (age 12 to adulthood). These age brackets are only guidelines; Piaget emphasized the sequence of the stages rather than their duration.

4. In evaluating Piaget, researchers find that young children have more cognitive abilities, at earlier ages, than Piaget thought, that they are not entirely egocentric in their thinking, and that cultural practices affect the pace and content of cognitive development. Moreover, cognitive development does not seem to work in a set of stages, in which the same mode of thought applies to all problems. But the *sequence* of development that Piaget observed does hold up.

5. Language development begins with a "babbling phase," from age 6 months to a year, and with nonverbal but symbolic gestures. At about 1 year, one-word utterances begin. At age 2, children speak in two- or three-word *telegraphic* sentences that convey a variety of messages, and they begin to acquire new words at a rapid rate. By age 3 or 4, they create longer sentences but often incorrectly *overgeneralize* grammatical rules.

6. Language develops through a combination of biological readiness and social experience. Parents do not teach language nor do children learn it according to behavioral principles. However, certain parental practices are helpful to the child, such as speaking more slowly and repeating correct sentences verbatim. There may be a critical period for learning language.

7. In human beings, hormones do not account for maternal "*bonding*" to newborn infants. Infants and caretakers usually become *attached* to each other after a few months; by the age of 7 to 12 months, babies often feel *stranger anxiety* and *separation anxiety*. Attachment occurs whether the mother is home full time or the child is in day care. For most healthy infants and preschoolers, competent day care has no negative effects and a few lasting cognitive benefits.

8. Several theories attempt to account for *sex typing*, the process by which boys and girls become "masculine" or "feminine," and *gender identity*, the cognitive understanding that one is biologically male or female. Biological theories account for these differences in terms of genetics, hormones, and brain lateralization. Social learning theory emphasizes the rewards, punishments, and vicarious examples that children get in behaving appropriately or inappropriately for their gender. Cognitive developmental theory holds that children "sex type" themselves, as their cognitive abilities mature, naturally perceiving and valuing the activities associated with their gender. Gender schema theory adds that culturally determined gender *schemas* divide the world into male and female spheres. New *context theories* hold that sex-typed behavior depends on the child's immediate context (such as the situation and the gender of the children they are with).

9. Parental methods of discipline, such as *induction* and *power assertion*, have different results. Induction is associated with children who develop empathy, internalized moral standards, and a sense of internal control, and who can resist temptation. Power assertion is associated with children who have a sense of external control, are aggressive and destructive, and show a lack of empathy and moral behavior.

10. Children of divorce do, on the average, have lower well-being than children in two-parent homes, but so do children in "intact" families marked by hostility and fighting. The effects of divorce depend on father absence (more difficult for boys), economic disadvantage, and whether the parents continue to be bitter and angry.

11. Lawrence Kohlberg's theory of moral development proposed three levels of moral reasoning: *preconventional morality* (based on rules, punishment, and self-interest); *conventional morality* (based on relationships and rules of justice and law); and *postconventional ("principled") morality*, based on higher principles of human rights. The theory has been criticized for its middle-class educational bias; its bias against women; and its assumption that people don't regress to a lower stage once they reach a higher one. Carol Gilligan's theory that men and women have equally valuable but different forms of moral reasoning has been popular but unsupported by most research.

12. Moral development also depends on the emergence of the "moral emotions"—empathy, shame, and guilt. Empathy takes different forms, depending on the child's age and cognitive abilities: global empathy, egocentric empathy, empathy for another's feelings, and empathy for another's life condition. Shame develops with the sense of self, around age 2; guilt develops when children have an internal standard of behavior, about age 3 or 4.

13. Altruistic (helpful) children tend to come from families in which they contribute to the family's well-being, carry out many tasks, and respect parental authority, and in which parents set limits without being arbitrary.

14. Some psychologists believe that no year of life is as critical as the first one, but many studies have failed to show the stability of infant qualities. Likewise, studies of children of alcoholics, of abusive parents, and even of violent families find that a large number of children are resilient—they manage to survive without repeating these patterns. With the exception of serious disorders, many childhood problems are outgrown by late adolescence or adulthood.

KEY TERMS

maturation *457*

germinal, embryonic, fetal stages *458*

fetal alcohol syndrome *458*

motor reflexes *459*

synchrony *462*

myelin *464*

assimilation *466*

accommodation *466*

object permanence *467*

representational thought *467*

operations *467*

egocentric thought *467*

conservation *467*

babbling phase *471*

overgeneralization *471*

telegraphic speech *471*

language acquisition device *472*

socialization *474*

bonding *474*

attachment *475*

stranger anxiety *475*

separation anxiety *475*

the "strange situation" *475*

sex typing *478*

gender identity *478*

gender schema *479*

context theories *479*

induction *480*

power assertion *480*

stages of moral reasoning *485*

empathy *486*

altruism *486*

shame and guilt *487*

14

Adolescence, Adulthood, and Aging

Nobody understands anyone 18, including
those who are 18.

JIM BISHOP

When you are ignorant, old age is a famine.
When you are learned, it is a harvest.

PROVERB

How old are you? Does it matter? Are you aware of your age—being "too old" for some things, such as playing hopscotch, and "too young" for others, such as running a company? If so, you hold a thoroughly modern view. Until the mid-nineteenth century, people showed little concern for age categories. Children of all ages were educated together, and children and teenagers worked alongside adults on farms and in factories. Then, in the late nineteenth century, "age consciousness" began to set in. Medical schools established pediatrics, the specialty of children's medicine, birthday celebrations became a commercial enterprise, and "old" people were set apart from the rest of society on the grounds that they could not keep up with the increasingly industrialized world (Chudacoff, 1990).

By the middle of the twentieth century, age brackets were well established for the hallmarks of middle-class adult life. You would marry in your late teens or early 20s. You would have your last child by your mid-30s. By your late 40s, you would be making your final job decisions (if you were male). By your mid-50s, you would be a doting grandparent, and by your mid-60s, you would be retired. Everyone, including you, would agree you were "set in your ways."

However, within the past two decades, people's lives have become less predictable than they used to be. When psychologists first began to follow people's lives from childhood to adulthood, they would come around every ten years or so and draw conclusions about the consistency of personality and stages of life (Kagan & Moss, 1962). Now psychologists come around every ten years and find that people have changed their names, jobs, houses, and spouses. Grandma is not home minding the grandchildren; she and Grandpa bought a trailer and are camping in Yosemite. Mom has gone to work as a banker and Dad has quit business to become a jazz musician. Your sister has eloped with her secretary, and your brother has married his ex-wife's ex-husband's half-sister. Your cousin just had her first baby at 16, and your aunt just had *her* first baby at 45.

As a result, old theories of adult development have had to be reconsidered. As Jerome Kagan (1984) put it, just because a marble rolling down a trough rolls in a straight line, we cannot infer that there is something in the nature of marbles that makes them roll in a straight line. But that is the mistake we have made with people. The troughs that once kept people on the straight and narrow path have broken down, and the human marbles are spilling out in all directions.

In this chapter, we will report new approaches to the study of development over the entire life span. In particular, we will explore three primary influences

Aging isn't what it used to be: Hulda Crooks, here at age 91, climbing Mt. Fuji, began mountain climbing in her 60s.

on adult development: *biology*, social *customs* and expectations regarding appropriate behavior in adolescence and adulthood, and the *circumstances* that different individuals and generations experience.

◼ GROWING UP AND GROWING OLD: THE BIOLOGICAL CLOCK

Children's development is influenced to a great extent by physical maturation. Once individuals are past childhood, are they subject to other genetically programmed biological upheavals that mark adult life? It seems that there are at least three adult phases: *adolescence*, with the hormonal changes that bring sexual maturity; *midlife*, with another set of hormonal changes that bring women's reproductive capacity to an end; and *old age*, with the deterioration of some physical abilities.

In the popular mind, all of these phases of biological development are believed to be traumatic. Puberty is assumed to cause severe emotional turbulence. Menopause is supposed to cause a "midlife crisis" in women. And many people believe that the older you get, the more you lose: your sex drive, your memory, your brain cells, your intelligence. Let's examine the scientific evidence that has put these ideas to the test.

Puberty

Adolescence begins with a biological marker, **puberty,** the age at which a person becomes capable of sexual reproduction. Until then, both boys and girls produce roughly the same amount of male hormones (androgens) and female hormones (estrogens). At puberty, the hypothalamus in the brain sends messages to the pituitary gland saying, in effect, "Childhood's over!" The pituitary gland, in turn, stimulates hormone production in the adrenal and other endocrine glands and in the reproductive glands. In boys, the reproductive glands are the testes (testicles), which produce sperm. In girls, the reproductive glands are the ovaries, which release eggs, or ova. Now boys have a higher level of androgens than girls do, and girls have a higher level of estrogens than boys do.

During puberty, the sex organs mature and the individual becomes capable of reproduction. In girls, the onset of menstruation, called **menarche,** and the development of breasts are major signs of sexual maturity. In boys, the major signs are the onset of nocturnal emissions and the growth of the testes, scrotum, and penis. Hormones are also responsible for the emergence of *secondary sex characteristics*, such as a deepened voice and facial and chest hair in boys and pubic hair in both sexes.

The changing rise and fall of hormones may contribute to the rapid mood swings that some adolescents feel, to the depth of their passions, and to the sensation of their emotions being out of control. In one study, teenagers described their thoughts and feelings at random intervals for a week, whenever they were "beeped" on a pager they carried with them. The most striking result was the frequency and extent of emotional changes, from highs to lows (Csikszentmihalyi & Larson, 1984).

The dramatic physical changes of puberty are part of the last "growth spurt" on the child's road to adulthood. For girls, the adolescent growth spurt begins, on the average, at age 10, peaks at 12 or 13, and stops at about age 16, by which time most girls are sexually mature. For boys, the average adolescent growth spurt starts at about age 12 and ends at about age 18. This difference in the rates of development is often a source of misery to adolescents, because most girls mature sooner than most boys.

◼ **puberty**
The age at which a person becomes capable of sexual reproduction.
◼ **menarche** [men-ARE-kee]
The onset of menstruation.

Boys and girls typically reach puberty at different times, as everyone who took a coed dancing class in grade school remembers.

The timing of the changes of puberty depends on both genetic and environmental factors. The onset of menarche, for example, can be affected by nutrition, stress, and exercise; indeed, better nutrition may be one reason that the average age of menarche has been declining in Europe and North America for the last 150 years. The onset of puberty seems to be occurring earlier for males, too. Decades ago, the average American male did not reach his maximum height until the age of 26; today this marker of the end of puberty occurs, on the average, at 18 (Cole & Cole, 1989).

There is, however, enormous individual variation in the onset and length of puberty. Some girls menstruate as early as age 8 and others do not begin until age 15. One 15-year-old male may be as developed as an adult man and another will still be a boy. In addition, just to be mischievous, nature has seen fit to make growth a jumpy, irregular, uneven business. Different parts of the body mature at different rates, a phenomenon called *asynchrony*. A girl may have undeveloped breasts but adult-sized hands and feet. A boy may be tall and gangly but have no trace of a longed-for beard. Eventually, everything catches up.

If you entered puberty before most of your classmates, or if you matured much later than they did, you know that your psychological experience of adolescence was different from that of the average teenager. Indeed, some psychologists believe that the *timing* of puberty is more important in an adolescent's development than the specific biological events themselves. Early-maturing boys generally have a more positive view of their bodies, and their relatively greater size and strength gives them a boost in sports and the prestige that being a good athlete brings young men. But they are also more likely to smoke, drink, use drugs, and break the law than later-maturing boys, and to have less self-control and emotional stability (Duncan et al., 1985). Late-developing boys feel the worst about themselves in the seventh grade, but by the twelfth grade they usually end up as the healthiest group (Petersen, 1989).

Likewise, some early-maturing girls have the prestige of being socially popular, but, partly because others regard them as being sexually precocious, they are also more likely to have conflict with their parents, have behavioral problems, drop out of school, have a negative body image, and have emotional problems (Caspi & Moffitt, 1991; Stattin & Magnusson, 1990). Girls who go through puberty relatively late, in contrast, have a more difficult time at first, but by the end of adolescence many are happier with their appearance and more popular than their early-maturing classmates (Petersen, 1989).

Are these effects a result of (1) hormonal changes alone, (2) being "out of sync" with one's classmates (early or late), or (3) the specific effects of entering puberty early? In one longitudinal study of 501 girls in New Zealand, the first two hypotheses were clearly not supported (Caspi & Moffitt, 1991). As in other studies, late-maturing girls, who began menarche at 14 or 15, had the *fewest* behavioral problems, whereas girls who entered menarche before the age of 12 subsequently had the *most* problems. Because the researchers had been observing these teenagers since childhood, they were able to find out why this was so. Although early menarche created certain stresses for many of the early-maturing girls, it did not do so for all of them. Instead, early menarche tended to accentuate the *existing* behavioral problems and family conflicts the girls had in childhood. The group with the most troubles throughout adolescence were early maturers who had a history of behavioral problems in childhood.

The researchers conclude that during times of transition and change—whether a biological change such as puberty or a social change such as going to college—existing personality traits and problems are magnified. As we will see throughout this chapter, this pattern is typical of the biological changes of aging. Biology alone, even the hormonal turmoil of adolescence, does not inevitably lead to specific psychological consequences.

Menopause and Midlife

The biology of aging affects people all through life, as a 27-year-old "aging" tennis champion can tell you. For most people, however, after puberty the next chiming of the biological clock occurs at midlife, with different results for men and women.

When women are in their late 40s or early 50s, the ovaries stop producing estrogen and progesterone, although some estrogen continues to be produced by the adrenal glands and fat cells. Menstruation stops, and soon thereafter the production of ova stops as well. This is called the **menopause,** and the process of declining reproductive ability is called the **climacteric** or *climacterium.* (Female smokers enter menopause nearly two years earlier than nonsmokers because of the effects of smoking on hormone production [McKinlay, Bifano, & McKinlay, 1985].)

Here are some common assumptions about the typical menopausal woman: She suffers from a "syndrome" or "deficiency disease." She has numerous complaints, mental and physical. She is deeply regretful about losing her reproductive capacity, her sexuality, her femininity. Often she becomes deeply depressed. Are any of these assumptions true?

The drastic decline of estrogen during menopause produces uncomfortable physical symptoms in some women, such as "hot flashes," fatigue, and rapid heartbeat. Recent pop-psychology books have emphasized and exaggerated these symptoms, but the fact is that most women go through menopause with no particular psychological difficulties and very few physical ones. In a large survey of more than 8,000 randomly chosen women, the majority viewed menopause positively (with relief that they no longer had to worry about pregnancy or periods) or neutrally (no particular feelings at all). Only 3 percent reported regret at reaching menopause. The vast majority did not report troubling physical symptoms or become a burden on medical services. They did not suffer from depression, unless they had a history of depressive episodes in their lives. Apart from having some "temporarily bothersome symptoms," such as hot flashes, sweating, and menstrual irregularity, most women said that menopause is simply "no big deal" (McKinlay, McKinlay, & Brambilla, 1987).

Then where do so many people get the idea that it is? According to the researchers who conducted this large survey, this false impression is based on women who go to physicians or therapists because they have a history of depression or have had an early menopause following a hysterectomy (removal of the uterus). By definition, such women are unrepresentative. Because most studies of menopausal women were, until recently, conducted on such atypical pa-

■ **menopause**
The cessation of menstruation; usually a gradual process lasting up to several years.
■ **climacteric**
The period of decreasing reproductive capacity in women, culminating in menopause.

tients, many people incorrectly inferred that menopause causes a "crisis." But over and over, large-scale studies of normal populations find that menopause has no effect on women's mental health (Matthews et al., 1990).

Some writers have proposed that men go through a "male menopause" that parallels the female version (McGill, 1980). For men, however, there is no biological equivalent to menopause. Testosterone does seem to peak during adolescence, but researchers disagree about when, whether, and how much it declines during adulthood. In any case, testosterone never drops as sharply in men as estrogen does in women, and men do not lose their fertility, although their sperm count may slowly diminish.

For both sexes, there is a big difference between a physical change (such as changes in hormone levels and fertility) and a psychological issue (such as the fear of getting older). The biological *fact* of aging does not itself predict how people will feel about aging or how they will respond to it. Many popular writers have assumed that aging always produces a psychological crisis. In fact, aging may be universal, but crises are not.

The Coming of Age

Until recently, most people assumed that aging is a normal part of development. An individual is born, grows older, reaches a peak, declines, and dies; it's all built into the cells. A more recent notion is that aging is *not* inevitable, but a result of possibly preventable damage to cells, a slow decline in immune function, or mutations in genes (Linnane et al., 1990). No one knows, however, exactly why cells become defective or which kinds of damage, if any, can be avoided.

In either case, biological aging does impose limits on what people can do as they grow older. On the average, the body reaches its peak efficiency at about age 30 and then slowly declines. As we age, heart, lung, and muscle capacity weaken. Metabolism and reflexes slow down. Physical changes in the eye reduce the amount of light that reaches the retina, so visual sharpness decreases. Older adults often lose some of their hearing ability, especially for tones in the higher register. The sense of smell declines after age 65 and drops sharply after age 80 (Doty, 1989). The central nervous system processes information more slowly than it once did, so older people often take longer to react.

It is not all bad news, however. Researchers in the field of *gerontology*—the study of aging and the old—have made astonishing advances in separating the processes that are intrinsic to aging from those that are a result of preventable conditions. The very fact that such a research specialty exists reflects a major change in society: Increasing numbers of people are now living into very old age—and living well. "Old" used to imply forgetful, stooped, and physically and mentally feeble. But new developments are changing these stereotypes:

1. *The definition of "old" got older.* Not long ago you would have been considered old in your 60s. Today, "old age" is not a simple matter of chronological years. Indeed, the elderly can be divided into two groups: the "young old," who have their health, strength, and mental capacities, and the "old old," who are infirm, weak, and incapacitated (Neugarten, 1974).

2. *Aging was separated from illness.* People used to think that all bodily functions declined with age. Some conditions, such as *osteoporosis* (having extremely brittle bones) or *senility* (the loss of mental abilities), were assumed to be inevitable. Today, gerontologists have found that many of the conditions thought characteristic of old age are really a result of cellular damage, malnutrition, overmedication, or disease. For example, only 15 percent of people over age 65 suffer serious mental impairment, and half of those cases are due to Alzheimer's disease, a neurological disorder (Cunningham & Brookbank, 1988). A tragically

The varieties of "old age"
Stereotypes about old people are breaking down as more and more people are living longer, healthier lives. Of three 80-year-olds, one may be ailing and infirm, one may be healthy and active, and a third might be exceptionally capable and strong.

high number of older people are overmedicated—given too many drugs for different problems—the results of which can appear as confusion, senility, or even psychosis. Others are incorrectly diagnosed: depression, for example, is no more "normal" in an old person than in a young one, but the older depressed person is less likely to be referred for psychotherapy.

3. *The biology of aging was separated from its psychology.* Imagine that you are taken from your home, your friends, and your work. You are put in a residence where you know no one and have nothing to do. Your relatives live too far away to visit. You aren't allowed to make decisions, decorate your room, keep a pet, have a lover, or choose your food. "Just relax and have a good time," your caretakers tell you. What would happen to you? Most likely, you would become depressed and bored. You would become forgetful and apathetic. You would become, in a word, "old."

Gerontologists have found that many of the problems of "old age" would occur to most people who were deprived of loved ones, close friends, meaningful activity, intellectual stimulation, and control over what happens to them (Rodin, 1988). When nursing-home residents have responsibilities and incentives for good memory, their apathy declines and their memory improves (Langer, 1989; Langer et al., 1979). When old people have a purpose in life, they feel younger than their actual years ("I'm just a kid at heart") and their well-being flourishes (Baum & Boxley, 1983).

4. *The benefits of aging.* Researchers are also discovering that aging often brings wisdom, experience, a sense of humor, and old-fashioned maturity (Erikson, Erikson, & Kivnick, 1986; Helson & Wink, 1987). As people age, they tend to feel less angry, less lonely, happier, and more content with themselves and their limitations. In one recent study of nearly 9,000 people ages 14 to 70, the older people reported a dramatically *lower* incidence of depression and stress than younger people (Lewinsohn, 1990). In a society that values youth and the new, it is easy to overlook the values of experience and the old.

Nevertheless, being 75 is definitely not the same as being 25. What changes, and what does not?

SEXUALITY.   Early surveys by sex researcher Alfred Kinsey and his associates (1948, 1953) suggested that men reach their sexual peak at age 18, women reach their sexual peak in their mid-30s, and after that it is all downhill. The idea of peaks, however, has peaked. Although later surveys have shown that the frequency of sexual activity declines over the life span, psychologists disagree about whether this drop is due to biological factors or to social factors such as job stress, sexual boredom or familiarity, marital conflict, or fatigue.

In later years, there are some biological changes in sexual response. Women produce less vaginal lubrication and men take longer to reach full erection. For both sexes, there are fewer contractions at orgasm. But these changes are not necessarily related to the frequency of sexual activity or pleasure. Among old people, the main sexual problem is lack of a partner: Longitudinal studies show that sexual interest and capacity typically last over the life span, unless illness or the death of one's partner intervenes (Brecher, 1984; Turner & Adams, 1988).

The greatest difference in sexual activity is not between the old and the young but between individuals. People who prefer to have sex infrequently tend to remain consistent, and so do those who enjoy sex frequently (Wade & Cerise, 1991). As a female respondent to a sex survey once wrote, "They say you never get too old to enjoy sex. I know, because once I asked my Grandma when you stop liking it and she was 80. She said, 'Child, you'll have to ask someone older than me.'"

INTELLIGENCE. Although folklore has it that the brain loses brain cells the way a scalp sheds dandruff, studies of animals and people challenge this gloomy forecast. Normal human aging does not produce extensive brain cell deterioration until, perhaps, extreme old age (M. Diamond, 1988). There is some decrease in the number of working neurons and in brain weight, but individuals vary enormously. What is more, there is no direct evidence that changes in neural structures are connected to changes in intellectual performance (Horn & Donaldson, 1980).

Yet studies suggest that some aspects of intelligence do decline with age; on average, older adults score lower on various mental tests than do younger adults. Four hypotheses have been advanced to explain this finding (Salthouse, 1989):

1. *The slowing-down hypothesis* holds that the age-related decline in test performance is not due to cognitive impairments, but primarily to slower reaction times—it simply takes older people longer to respond. However, some decline in test scores still occurs even when older people are given ample time to complete the tests.

2. *The disuse hypothesis* holds simply that tests measure what people learn in school, and the longer you are out of school the more likely you are to score poorly on material you aren't using (like algebra or the geography of Tibet). However, it is not "book learning" that declines the most in the later years. Raymond Cattell (1971) distinguished between *fluid intelligence*, the capacity for deductive reasoning and insight into complex relations, and *crystallized intelligence*, the ability to master and use acquired knowledge and skills. Fluid intelligence is assumed to be relatively independent of education and experience, whereas crystallized intelligence (defining words, solving arithmetic problems, or summarizing the President's policy on the environment) depends heavily on culture and education. The research suggests that both kinds of intelligence increase throughout adolescence, but over the life span fluid ability slowly decreases and crystallized ability remains stable—rather like crystallized particles of information (Salthouse, 1989).

3. *The generation hypothesis* holds that age-related differences in cognitive abilities really reflect generational differences in intellectual training, nutrition, and stimulation. As we saw in Chapter 2, longitudinal studies that follow people for many years find less of a decline in intellect than do studies that compare people of different ages at a given point in time. Someone who is 70 years old today may do worse on a test than a 30-year-old, but only because the 70-year-old did not have as much education when younger, or is currently living a less mentally challenging life. As evidence for this view, research finds that short-term training programs for people between 60 and 80 produce gains in mental test scores that are as large as the losses typical for that age group (Baltes, Sowarka, & Kliegl, 1989; Willis, 1987). In other words, most older people don't lose the *capacity* to learn and to use their cognitive abilities.

Desire and sensuality are lifelong pleasures.

* *Your grandparents are slowly losing their mental sharpness. Everyone tells you that's normal and inevitable. Are they right? What might cause intellectual decline in old age, besides age itself?*

4. *Biological hypotheses* suggest that the decline in cognitive capacity stems from physiological changes, occurring because of illness, medication, or normal deterioration. Proponents of this view point out that even as members of a particular generation age, they show a decline in some cognitive abilities. This is also true of the behavior of animals raised in rigorously controlled environments (Salthouse, 1989).

Each of these explanations adds a piece to the puzzle, but the whole picture is far from clear. Researchers disagree about when a decline begins; some think it starts in a person's 20s, others that it begins in the late 60s, others that it does not occur until one's 80s. Just to make the picture murkier, many people don't show an intellectual decline, and some even improve in their abilities (Baltes, Dittmann-Kohli, & Dixon, 1984; Hoffman & Nelson, 1990).

MEMORY. As people age, it takes them longer to retrieve names, dates, and other facts. In this case the reason does seem to be their impaired perceptual-motor skills—their slower reaction times—not impaired memory itself. Some of the memory decline that occurs in older adults is a result of poor health, poor education, or lack of practice. One study found that years of schooling and current enrollment in school were better predictors of differences in memory ability than age was (Zivian & Darjes, 1983). Another found that college students (ages 18 to 25) were more likely to use encoding strategies to help them remember—perhaps they were psychology students who remembered the memory chapter of their textbook!—whereas older adults (ages 61 to 84) relied more on planning and making lists (Loewen, Shaw, & Craik, 1990). It's a shame, therefore, that many older people are so hard on themselves about retrieving memories. When they can't remember a name, they say "Drat, I'm getting old." When younger people can't remember a name, they just say "Drat."

As with intellectual abilities, memory also comes in different types. As we saw in Chapter 7 (page 240), *explicit memory* consists of intentional recollections (trying to remember the Seven Dwarfs: Doc, Dopey, Sleepy, Happy, Grumpy, Sneezy, . . .) and involuntary ones (having the name of the last dwarf "pop into your head" at 2 A.M.: "Bashful!"). *Implicit memory* refers to the effects of an event that are expressed without awareness of it. For example, let's say you don't remember much about the movie *Snow White and the Seven Dwarfs;* yet when asked now, years later, to learn a list of the seven dwarfs, you do it faster than if you had never seen the movie at all.

Most memory tests assess explicit memory—asking people to recall something they learned during a previous study period—and on these tests, memory does appear to decline in old age (Morris, Craik, & Gick, 1990). But implicit memory shows no such decline, meaning that people do not invariably lose the ability to learn and remember as they get older (Graf, 1990). Moreover, just as studies document the beneficial effects of training programs on intelligence scores, they also show that older adults can do as well as people in their 20s, even on *explicit* memory tests, when given guidance and cues for retrieving memories (Loewen, Shaw, & Craik, 1990). Older adults are also just as good as young ones at long-practiced abilities, which is why all kinds of people—physicians, lawyers, teachers, farmers, and insurance agents—continue their work well into old age.

Ernie Hobden, age 100, has been raising bird-of-paradise flowers for years.

Many researchers who study cognition and aging, such as Marian Diamond (1984, 1988), are optimists. When people live in stimulating, interesting environments, Diamond argues, their brain function does not "naturally" decay. In her studies of active people over the age of 88, Diamond found that "the people who use their brains don't lose them." But other researchers are skeptical about the "use it or lose it" philosophy, pointing out that if you have lost it, you can't use it. One thing is certain: William James (1890/1950) made a rare mistake when he said that the ideas that people acquire before the age of 25 "are practically the only ideas they shall have in their lives. They cannot get anything new." James himself was forever coming up with new ideas in his life, and research now confirms that so can the rest of us.

QUICK QUIZ

What do you remember about the physiology of aging?

1. The onset of menstruation is called _____.
2. In boys, a deepening voice and a new mustache are examples of _____.
3. The biological clock causes (a) menopause, (b) loss of male fertility, (c) loss of sexual interest, (d) forgetfulness.
4. Most women react to menopause by (a) feeling depressed, (b) regretting the loss of femininity, (c) feeling relieved or neutral, (d) going a little crazy.
5. Which of the following abilities tend to decline with age? (Choose all that apply.) (a) hearing, (b) implicit memory, (c) explicit memory, (d) ability to work, (e) fluid intelligence, (f) crystallized intelligence, (g) sexual pleasure, (h) wisdom, (i) sense of humor, (j) reaction time

ANSWERS:

1. menarche 2. secondary sex characteristics 3. a 4. c 5. a, c, e, j

---

■ STAGES AND AGES: THE PSYCHOLOGICAL CLOCK

According to ancient Greek legend, the Sphinx was a monster, half lion, half woman, who terrorized passersby on the road to Thebes. The Sphinx would ask each traveler a question, and murder those who failed to answer correctly. The question was this: What animal walks on four feet in the morning, two feet at noon, and three feet in the evening? Only one traveler, Oedipus, knew the solution to the riddle. The animal, he said, is Man, who crawls on all fours as a baby, walks upright as an adult, and limps in old age with the aid of a staff.

The Sphinx was the first life span theorist. Since then, many philosophers, writers, and scientists have speculated on the course of adult life, expanding the Sphinx's three basic stages into seven, eight, or ten. Shakespeare suggested seven ages: infant, schoolboy, lover, soldier, just man, foolish old man, and doddering state of "second childhood." (On women's stages, Shakespeare, like many men before and since, was silent.) The idea of stages was terrifically appealing. Everyone could see that children go through stages of physical maturation. It made sense to assume that adults go through parallel stages of psychological maturation.

Erikson and Stage Theories

One of the first psychologists in this century to emphasize growth and change over the entire life span was Alfred Adler, who, as we saw in Chapter 12, broke from the traditional Freudian view that personality development stops in childhood. Adler emphasized two influences on adult change: the social factors that influence us throughout life and the ability to control our own destinies.

A fuller theory was later proposed by psychoanalyst Erik H. Erikson (1950/1963, 1987). Erikson argued that everyone passes through eight developmental stages on the way to wisdom and maturity. Erikson called his theory *psychosocial*, instead of "psychosexual" as Freud had, because he believed that people are propelled by psychological and social forces, not just by sexual motives. Each stage, said Erikson, represents a combination of biological drives and societal demands. At each one, there is a "crisis" that must be resolved for healthy development to occur.

1. The first stage, during the baby's first year, produces the crisis of *trust versus mistrust*. A baby must depend on others to provide food, comfort, cuddling, and warmth. If these needs are not met, the child may never develop the basic trust necessary to get along in the world.

2. The second stage, as the baby becomes a toddler, sets up the crisis of *autonomy (independence) versus shame and doubt*. The young child is learning to "stand on his own feet," said Erikson, and must do so without feeling ashamed of his behavior or too doubtful of his growing abilities.

3. The third stage is marked by the crisis of *initiative versus guilt*: The child is acquiring new physical and mental skills, setting goals, and enjoying newfound talents. At the same time, the child must learn to control impulses and energies. The danger lies in developing too strong a sense of guilt over his or her fantasies, newfound power, and childish instincts.

4. The fourth stage, the crisis of *competence* (originally "industry") *versus inferiority*, teaches the school-age child, said Erikson, "to be a worker and potential provider." The child now is learning to make things, use tools, and acquire the skills for adult life. Children who fail these lessons of mastery and competence, Erikson argued, risk feeling inadequate and inferior.

5. The fifth stage, puberty, sets off the crisis of *identity versus role confusion*. You must decide what you are going to be and what you hope to make of your life. If you succeed, you will come out of this stage with a strong identity, ready to plan for the future. Otherwise, you will sink into confusion, unable to make decisions. The term *identity crisis* describes what Erikson considered to be the major conflict of adolescence.

6. The sixth stage sees the crisis of *intimacy versus isolation*. Once you have decided who you are, you must share yourself with another and learn to make commitments. No matter how successful you are in work, said Erikson, you are not developmentally complete until you are capable of intimacy.

According to Erikson, children must master a sense of competence and older adults must meet the need for "generativity" and nurturance. Do these challenges occur only during one "stage" of life?

7. The seventh stage involves the crisis of *generativity versus stagnation.* Now that you know who you are and have an intimate relationship, will you sink into complacency and selfishness, or will you experience generativity, the pleasure of creativity and renewal? Parenthood is the most common means for the successful resolution of this stage, but people can be productive, creative, and nurturant in other ways, in their work or their relationships with the younger generation.

8. The eighth and final crisis is that of *ego integrity versus despair.* As they age, people strive to reach the ultimate goal—wisdom, spiritual tranquility, an acceptance of one's life and one's role in the larger scheme of things. Just as the healthy child will not fear life, said Erikson, the healthy adult will not fear death.

Some societies, Erikson maintained, make the transition from one stage to another relatively easy. If you know you are going to be a farmer like your mother and father and you have no alternative, then moving from adolescence into young adulthood is not a very painful or passionate step (unless you hate farming). If you have many choices, as adolescents in urban societies often do, the transition can become prolonged. Some people put off making choices indefinitely and never resolve their "identity crisis." Because American society values both independence and attachment, some individuals are unable to resolve Erikson's sixth crisis, that of intimacy versus isolation.

Stage theories became popular after Erikson's work, possibly as a way to make sense of the bewildering social changes that were occurring after World War II. In the 1970s there was a sudden spate of life-stage books, and you can still find them in the psychology section of your bookstore. All shared the idea that there are universal periods or "passages" in people's lives that unfold in a natural sequence, like the four seasons of the year. It was fun for readers to figure out what stage they were in and where they were heading. But were these theories popular because they are accurate, or because, as one psychologist argued, most of us "want predictability . . . and we desperately want definitions of 'normality'" (Kammen, 1979)?

Evaluating Stage Theories

Stage theories of adult development were important historically because they reminded everyone that life is not over at age 10, 15, or even 21. Adults tend to have different concerns at different ages, a result of their changing roles (student, professional, spouse, parent, grandparent) and their changing emotional needs. As Erikson showed, development is never finished once and for all. It is an ongoing process throughout life, and the "crises" of one stage may be reawakened during another. Erikson made a lasting contribution in identifying the essential concerns of adulthood: identity, competence, love and nurturance, the ability to enjoy life and accept death.

Critics have pointed out, however, that adult life changes are not like the stages of child development for one important reason. Child development is governed by *maturational* and *biological* changes that are dictated by the genes. Children go through a stage of babbling before they enter the stage of talk; they crawl before they walk; they cry before they can say, "I'm feeling blue today." But as children mature, genes become less of a driving influence on their development, and environmental demands have greater impact (Baltes, 1983). Because environmental demands are different for different individuals, this means that adult "stages" cannot be as universal or inevitable as childhood stages. And it explains why children are more alike than middle-aged adults or old people (Neugarten & Neugarten, 1986).

Erikson, like many other stage theorists, also tended to generalize to "people in general" from very limited samples. For example, Erikson entirely omit-

It's fun to try to figure out what adult "stage" you're in. But what about all the people whose experiences don't divide up neatly into ten-year intervals? What is a better way of explaining the nature and diversity of adult changes?

ted women from his original work, and as a result women seemed to be doing things "out of order." Most of the other popular stage theories were based on studies of privileged middle-class individuals. As a result, most stage theories imply a universal sequence in adult development that is not accurate.

Erikson was right to observe that in Western societies adolescence is a time of confusion about identity and aspirations, and the college years see the greatest gains in self-understanding and the resolution of identity conflicts (Adams et al., 1985; Marcia, 1976). However, an "identity crisis" is not limited to adolescence. A man who has worked in one job all his adult life, and then is laid off and must find an entirely new career, may have an identity crisis too (Holstein, 1983). Similarly, competence is not mastered once in childhood. People learn new skills and lose old ones throughout their lives, and their sense of competence rises and falls accordingly.

QUICK QUIZ

At what stage is your understanding of stages?

1. Erik Erikson's theory of life stages is called the _____ theory of development.
2. The major psychological issue during adolescence, said Erikson, is a(n) _____ crisis.
 3. You are reading a best-selling book called *Levels*. The author maintains that there are five levels of the development of human consciousness in adulthood: preconscious, barely aware, conscious, hyperconscious, and, for a select few, "evolved." What is likely to be a problem with the assumptions of this book, and how might you critically evaluate its argument?

ANSWERS:

1. psychosocial 2. identity 3. Adult development does not occur in predictable, clear-cut phases that apply to everyone. In addition, people may move back and forth between stages depending on changing circumstances in their lives. A critical reader would also examine the evidence behind this author's theory. Was it based on a representative sample, including members of both sexes, from different races and cultures? How does the author define and measure vague terms like "evolved"?

■ LIFE TRANSITIONS: THE SOCIAL CLOCK

If development does not occur predictably in adulthood, why and how does it occur at all? Instead of focusing on stages, another major approach to these questions concentrates on the *transitions*, or milestones, that mark adult life. Research suggests that what matters in adult development is not only how old you are, but what you are doing. *Having* a child has stronger effects on you than *when* you have a child. Entering the work force affects your self-esteem and ambition regardless of when you start working. Transition theorists therefore examine how people shift from one role or situation to another and the events that happen (or fail to happen) that require such changes. Four kinds of transitions can occur (Schlossberg, 1984, 1989b):

• *Anticipated transitions* are the events you plan for and rehearse: You go to school. You get married. You start a job. You get promoted. You have a child. You retire at age 65.

According to transition theory, what matters in adult development is not how old you are but what you are doing. For example, having a child has predictable effects (it increases nurturance but often temporarily diminishes self-esteem), regardless of when you have a child. These two first-time mothers, one under 20 and the other over 40, have a lot in common despite their age difference.

• *Unanticipated transitions* are the things that happen unexpectedly, with no preparation: You flunk out of school. You are fired from your job. You have triplets. You win the lottery. You are forced to retire early.

• *Nonevent transitions* are the changes you expect to happen that don't: You don't get married. You can't have children. You aren't promoted. You planned to retire but need to keep working for the income.

• *Chronic hassle transitions* are the situations that may eventually require you to change or take action, but that rumble along uncomfortably for a long stretch: You aren't getting along with your partner. Your mother gets a chronic illness and needs constant care. You have to deal with discrimination at your job. Your son keeps getting into trouble.

Notice that what is an anticipated change for one person, such as going to college, might be unanticipated for another. An upsetting, "nonevent" transition for one person, such as not getting married, can be a planned decision for another and not a transition at all. This approach acknowledges that nonevents and chronic situations cause us to adapt just as surely as actual events do. It also recognizes that not all transitions create a crisis (see "Taking Psychology with You"). In this section we will look at the transitions that occur, predictably and unpredictably, from adolescence to old age.

Adolescence: Transition to Adulthood

Adolescence refers to the period of development between puberty and adulthood. In some cultures, the time span between puberty and adulthood is only a few months. Once sexually mature, a boy or girl is expected to marry and assume adult tasks. In modern Western societies, adolescence lasts several years. Teenagers may be biologically mature, but they are not considered emotionally mature enough to be full-fledged adults. It is believed that they are not yet ready to assume the rights, responsibilities, and roles of adulthood. The long span of adolescence is new to this century. In the past, societies needed the labor of young people and could not afford to have them idle away a decade in school or in nonproductive "self-discovery" (Kett, 1977).

So adolescence begins with a biological marker (puberty), but ends with a social marker (the society's definition of adulthood, such as the legal age to vote,

■ **adolescence**
The period of development between puberty (a biological event) and adulthood (a social event).

marry, or join the military). In some societies and religions, the child goes through a social ritual, called a "rite of passage," that commemorates the arrival of adulthood.

Rebellious-teenager movies and studies of troubled teens depict adolescence as a time of storm and stress, and of conflict and hostility toward parents. What is missing from this portrait of adolescence?

THEORIES OF REBELLION, CONFLICT, AND SEPARATION.   The biological storms of puberty are reputed to carry over into psychological storms: insecurity about oneself in relation to friends, a fierce and unhappy struggle for self-identity, and a distrust and dislike of parents. This view represents the "turmoil theory" of adolescent development. It argues that adolescent anguish and rebellion are necessary and inevitable, the means by which teenagers separate themselves psychologically from their parents and form their own identities (Blos, 1962).

It is certainly true that adolescence can be difficult for many teenagers. It is a transition time in which adolescents are learning the rules of adult sexuality, morality, work, and family. Teenagers are beginning to develop their own standards and values, and often do so by trying on the styles, actions, and attitudes of their peers in contrast to those of their parents. They are growing more independent of their parents. They are questioning adult life, even as they are rehearsing for it (Offer & Sabshin, 1984). For some teenagers, these changes can feel overwhelming and lead to loneliness, depression, and a sense of isolation. Indeed, rates of depression and suicide are growing among the young, and are a serious mental-health problem (see Chapter 16).

Yet studies of representative samples of normal teenagers find that extreme turmoil and unhappiness are the exception, not the rule. For instance, a study of more than 20,000 teenagers surveyed between 1962 and 1982 found that adolescents travel one of three routes to adulthood, depending on their temperament, childhood experiences, opportunities, coping skills, and social life (Offer & Sabshin, 1984). More than half have few emotional upsets. They have supportive families, a sense of purpose and self-confidence, good friends, and the skill to cope with problems. Others have a bumpier ride, having suffered parental divorce, the death of a close relative, or serious illness. Their self-esteem wavers; they are more dependent on the positive evaluation of peers and parents and often feel discouraged. A third group, about 20 percent of all teenagers, have a tumultuous adolescence. They have behavioral problems at school and at home. They report more difficulties than satisfactions in their lives. Their backgrounds tend to be less stable, more fraught with conflicts and problems, and less advantageous than those of the other two groups. They feel less happy and secure.

Traditional theories of adolescent development were based on the importance of the child "separating" from the parent. A child who did not separate sufficiently, who maintained a close bond with the parents, was often considered "immature." Recently, psychologists have begun to question this idea, arguing that psychological separation is an issue for only a small stratum of society and does not reflect the pattern that is common in most cultures: the continued love and connection between child and parent. Terri Apter (1990) argues that two meanings of "separation" have been confused: *individuation*, the process of becoming a distinct individual with your own values and needs; and a complete *rift*, a severing of affection and an effort to replace the parent with other mentors and influences. Most adolescents learn to become individuals in the former sense, not by rejecting their parents but by striking a different balance with them.

Many teenagers, of course, do have conflicts with their parents. In one large study, the adolescents listed complaints like these: "Why my mother manipulates the conversation to get me to hate her"; "How much of a bastard my father is to my sister"; "How ugly my mom's taste is"; "How pig-headed my mom and dad are" (Csikszentmihalyi & Larson, 1984). But these fights—over what is important, who sets the rules, differences of opinion and taste, and the like—

The varieties of adolescence
The adolescent stereotype emphasizes teenage turmoil and rebellion (top left). But most teens feel good about themselves and their communities, as do the students at a high school carwash fund-raiser (lower left), and many hold jobs to earn some money (above).

do not usually reflect a profound split between parent and adolescent. In her study of 65 diverse mother-daughter pairs in Britain and the United States, Apter (1990) found that most of the teenage girls said the person they felt closest to, who offered them the greatest support, was their mother. There were plenty of quarrels—over clothes, school, chores—but these were, said Apter, "little puff balls" that did not indicate a serious break in the relationship, but an effort to get the mother to *understand*. For young men and women in Western societies, the familiar quarrels they have with their parents tend to signify a change from one-sided parental authority to a more reciprocal, adult relationship (Paikoff & Brooks-Gunn, 1991; Steinberg, 1990). Feelings of attachment to parents are not an indication of a young person's "immaturity" or "dependence." On the contrary, researchers have found a relationship between attachment to parents and assertion, social self-confidence, and ease in same- and other-sex friendships (Kenny, 1989).

GENDER, PERSONALITY, AND SELF-ESTEEM. Adolescence is also the time of the greatest psychological disparity between the sexes. Lawrence Cohn (1991) analyzed 65 studies, involving more than 9,000 people, to determine the extent of gender differences in personality, moral reasoning, "maturity of thought," conformity, and other characteristics throughout adolescence and adulthood. He found that differences were greatest among junior- and senior-high-school students, largely because girls mature earlier than boys. But most of these differences, he found, "declined significantly among college-age adults, and disappeared entirely among older men and women."

However, there is one domain, at least for Anglo and Latino teenagers, in which gender differences that appear early in adolescence tend to persist: self-

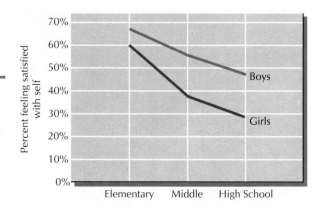

FIGURE 14.1

The path of self-esteem
This graph shows the percentage of children in elementary school, junior high, and high school who agree with the statement, "I'm happy the way I am." White boys and girls do not differ much in childhood, but by high school there is a big gap between them on this question and on four others that reflect self-esteem (American Association of University Women, 1991).

esteem. A national study of 3,000 children in fourth through tenth grades found that at the ages of 8 and 9, a majority of boys and girls were confident and assertive. But over the next eight years, the girls' self-esteem plummeted; by high school, only 29 percent of the girls still felt good about themselves, compared to 46 percent of the boys (see Figure 14.1). This lowered self-esteem translated into lower aspirations; girls were much more likely than boys to say they were "not smart enough" or "not good enough" to achieve their goals (American Association of University Women, 1991). More than half of the black girls, however, reported high levels of self-esteem throughout high school, a finding replicated in other studies (Bush & Simmons, 1987; Martinez & Dukes, 1987).

The researchers believe that the drop in self-esteem among Anglo and Latina girls occurs as they enter junior high and bump into the attitudes of their parents, teachers, and adult society that females cannot do many of the things that males can. Carol Gilligan and her colleagues, in in-depth interviews with 34 girls, concluded that these adolescent girls face a conflict between holding on to their sense of self-confidence and adjusting to the reality of how the world sees them (Gilligan, Lyons, & Hanmer, 1990). One way to solve the conflict, which many girls take, is to discredit their own feelings. They begin to speak less assertively; their speech becomes dotted with "I don't know" and "What do you think?" Another solution, which black girls tend toward, is to stand up firmly for their own feelings and knowledge, and reject the teachers and other authorities who seem to doubt them. Black girls reported that they often get support from their mothers and other relatives in being assertive and independent. According to the researchers, both "solutions" have their price. The price of self-doubt is lowered self-esteem, but the price of rejecting authority is to jeopardize academic success, which can be an important route to opportunity.

These findings are provocative, but they aren't the whole story. Perhaps the gender difference in self-esteem, like the difference in depression that we discussed in Chapter 9, reflects differences of style and expression rather than substance. That is, perhaps adolescent boys are more willing than girls to mask private self-doubts with public displays of self-confidence. For this reason, some psychologists believe that a better way to study adolescents' feelings of self-worth is to ask them what they envision for themselves in the future. Many delinquent teenage boys have high self-esteem, perhaps because they feel like heroes to their peers, but when asked to imagine their futures, they see themselves as being depressed, alone, or drug addicted (Oyserman & Markus, 1990). It is this limited vision of their *possible selves*, not their self-reported self-esteem, that affects their future course of action.

The most consuming psychological task for adolescents, it seems, is to discover or invent their own possible selves, finding their way through society's messages: "You can do anything you want"; "you're only a girl"; "you'll never make it."

TABLE 14.1

Patterns of Ethnic Identity and Acculturation

A person who belongs to an ethnic minority often faces conflict between identifying with his or her ethnic group and with the majority culture. There are several ways of resolving it:

Biculturalism: Strong feelings of ethnicity and acculturation ("I am just as loyal to my nation as to my ethnic group")

Assimilation: Weak feelings of ethnicity, strong sense of acculturation ("My ethnicity isn't important; my nationality is all that counts")

Ethnic separatism: Strong sense of ethnic identity, weak feelings of acculturation ("My ethnicity comes first; if I join the mainstream, I'm betraying my origins")

Marginality: Weak feelings of ethnicity and acculturation ("I'm an individual and don't identify with any group"; "I don't belong anywhere")

ETHNICITY AND IDENTITY. Adolescents of different races, cultures, and social classes have different experiences. Black adolescents, on the average, face greater discrimination, poverty, and unemployment than whites; that fact alone makes a certain amount of struggle and stress more likely. But in addition, many adolescents, while struggling with general issues of psychological identity, also face the dilemma of balancing an *ethnic identity* (identifying closely with one's own racial, religious, or ethnic group) with *acculturation* (identifying with and feeling part of the dominant culture) (Phinney, 1990; Spencer & Dornbusch, 1990). Research suggests that ethnic identity and acculturation are separate processes, and that individuals combine them in various ways, as shown in Table 14.1.

Young adults travel different paths toward the formation of an ethnic identity. Some psychologists see a developmental progression in the search for balance between ethnic identity and acculturation: conforming unthinkingly to the majority culture; questioning and challenging the majority culture—in some cases, rejecting it entirely; and finally reaching a sense of one's own ethnicity while accepting what is good about the majority culture one lives in (Atkinson, Morten, & Sue, 1989; Phinney, 1990). Many of the conflicts between cultural groups in North America—as well as *within* these groups—stem from having different ideas about the relative benefits of "acculturation" versus "ethnic identity" and how, or whether, they should be balanced.

One signature of ethnic identity is the name a group chooses for itself. For example, "Hispanic" is a label used by the U.S. government to include all Spanish-speaking groups. But many "Hispanics" point out that Spaniards, Cubans,

These teenagers—African American, Mexican American, and Chinese American—identify with their own traditions but also with being American. So do Irish Americans, Polish Americans, ... Can an overemphasis on ethnic identity lead to a society of small, competing cultures? Can an overemphasis on acculturation erase cultural differences that are an important part of identity? Where is the balance between preserving your own ethnic identity and becoming an integral part of the larger society?

Mexican Americans (Chicanos), Latin Americans (Latinos), and Puerto Ricans are all very different in culture and history, and therefore in ethnic identity (Vasquez & Barón, 1988). In addition, a group may decide to reject a name that was imposed on them by the majority culture (as happened with the label "Eskimos"), and insist instead on their own cultural name (they are now called the Inuit). In an article titled "Black, Negro, or Afro-American? The differences are crucial!", Halford Fairchild (1985) analyzed the significance of race names that are based on skin color, race, or national origin, for each term has different historical and emotional connotations. In only a few short years since that article, African American has become a popular term to identify people of African descent living in the Americas; those who like the term argue that it is analogous to Polish American or Italian American. But not all—blacks?—share that preference. Some feel no special kinship to Africa, just as many white Americans feel no special connection to the land of their forebears. The debate over group names is likely to continue, and the names are likely to keep changing, as ethnic groups in America struggle to define their place in a medley of cultures.

There are, in short, many normal ways to be an adolescent, and many issues that adolescents normally confront. It is perhaps no wonder that the transition from adolescence to young adulthood is one of the most difficult and stressful times in many people's lives (Pearlin, 1982). The late teens and early 20s often bring many changes at once—finishing school, leaving home, making independent decisions, starting work or professional training, getting married, having children, moving to a new part of the country and a new home. These are some of the major transitions of adulthood, which we will consider next.

QUICK QUIZ

During this transition to a new topic, try these questions.

1. Frank, an African-American college student, finds himself caught between two philosophies on his campus. One holds that blacks should shed their identity as victims of racism and move toward full integration into American culture. The other favors Afrocentric education, holding that blacks should immerse themselves in the history, values, and contribution of African culture. Frank is caught between his _____ _____ and _____ .

2. Extreme turmoil and rebellion in adolescence are (a) nearly universal, (b) the exception rather than the rule, (c) extremely rare.

3. A TV reporter asserts that teenagers must "separate" from their parents and develop "independent selves." What assumption is implicit in this assertion, and can it be challenged? What are some possible definitions of "separation"?

ANSWERS:

1. ethnic identity, acculturation 2. b 3. The reporter assumes that independence from parents is normal, universal, and good. But many people hold other values, such as continued attachment to one's family and respect for elders. The reporter also assumes that it is always economically feasible for adolescents to break away from their families; this is not always so! Finally, it is important to define terms like "separation": Does it mean a complete severing of connection, putting oneself first, or developing one's own identity and wishes?

Milestones of Adulthood

Adults evaluate their development according to a **social clock** that determines whether they are "on time" for their age or "off time" (Neugarten, 1979). Most of us can remember how carefully we compared our own development to that of our friends in childhood and adolescence. Every new step was an occasion for gloom (if your best friend got ahead of you) or elation (when you got there too). In adulthood, we make the same comparisons. All my friends are paired up; why am I single? All my friends know what work they want; why don't I? Everyone I know has children; am I ready?

All cultures have social clocks that define the "right time" to marry, start work, and have children, but these clocks may differ greatly. In some societies young men and women are supposed to marry and start having children right after puberty, and work responsibilities come later. In others, a man may not marry until he has demonstrated his financial ability to support a family. Society's reactions to people who are "off time" vary as well, from amused tolerance ("Oh, when will he grow up?") to pity, scorn, or outright rejection.

In the United States and Canada, different social clocks exist side by side. Races, ethnic groups, and men and women within these groups often have different "time schedules" on which they base their lives—from when to have children (if any) to when to retire (if ever). Doing the right thing at the right time, compared to your friends and family, can make you feel satisfied, capable, and healthy. When nearly everyone in your group goes through the same experience or enters a new role at the same time—going to school, driving a car, voting, marrying, having a baby—adjusting to the new experience is relatively easy (Stewart et al., 1982). People who wish to do things on time and cannot, for reasons out of their control, may feel inadequate, depressed, and dissatisfied.

The sheer diversity of life-cycle transitions and experiences in modern life, and the many different social clocks for different groups that exist side by side in society, mean that it is no longer possible to describe major milestones in adult life that will apply to nearly everyone. There are many different kinds of families today, as Figure 14.2 shows; the former ideal (wage-earning father, home-making mother, and two children) now describes less than 15 percent of the population. As one psychologist put it, "There is not one process of aging, but many; there is not one life course followed, but multiple courses. . . . There is no one sequence of stages but many. The variety is as rich as the historic conditions people have faced and the current circumstances they experience" (Pearlin, 1982). Keeping this diversity in mind, consider some of the events and experiences that have profound effects on adult development:

MARRIAGE OR LIVING ALONE. Naturally there are many factors involved in the timing of marriage and choice of partner, but here we want to draw your attention to one factor that has special power in setting the social clock an entire generation will follow: the availability of marriage partners.

Normally, each generation of babies has a balanced ratio of males to females. But some events can create an unbalanced ratio in adulthood. Men may have to migrate from one region to another for work. War and other forms of violence may deplete a generation of its young men. A "baby boom"—a sudden increase in the number of children born in a particular year—can also change the ratio of marriage partners (Guttentag & Secord, 1983). The reason is that in North America, most young women marry men who are about two years older than they are. Women who are born during a period of increasingly high birth rates will therefore outnumber the "older" men who are potential marriage partners. This is what happened to the baby-boom women born after World War II. When they came of marriageable age, there weren't enough

The milestones of adulthood are not predictable anymore.

Drawing by Opie; © 1987 the New Yorker Magazine, Inc.

■ **"social clock"**
A society's timetable for the "right" ages to marry, have children, start work, retire, and have other adult experiences.

FIGURE 14.2

Family diversity

There is no "typical family" anymore in the U. S. and Canada. In addition to the traditional family of husband, wife, and children (which is, statistically, a minority pattern), families now consist of a single parent and children; an adult or adults who adopt children; extended families, in which three generations live together; couples who are childless by choice; individuals of varing ages who live together as room-mates; stepfamilies; single people who live alone and who have families of close friends; gay and lesbian couples, many of whom are parents; and many other patterns.

ment just as well or poorly as men do. The only difference is in income. Working women earn much less than working men, and so have fewer benefits on which to retire (Crosby, 1991).

People's reactions to retirement depend on the circumstances of the change, not on the fact of change itself. A national longitudinal survey of several thousand men divided the sample according to the men's reasons for retirement (Crowley, 1986): ill health; voluntary early retirement before age 65; voluntary retirement at age 65; and mandatory retirement of men who were required by company policy to retire, even though they would have preferred to keep working. Well-being in retirement, this survey found, depended on having adequate financial and psychological resources, a choice about when to retire, good health, close relationships, and plenty of interesting things to do.

With people living longer and healthier lives, many have challenged the notion that chronological age alone is a measure of their ability to do a job. New retirement laws, going into effect in 1994, will eliminate mandatory retirement for all workers, with the exception of police officers, fire fighters, and tenured faculty at universities. And even those groups are pressing to have the rule of mandatory retirement eliminated. A person should be evaluated in terms of competence, they say, not age.

George Bernard Shaw described retirement as "a working definition of hell." When he died at age 94, he was, as always, writing a play.

DEATH OF A SPOUSE OR PARTNER. The death of a beloved partner is a sad and difficult transition. Basically, a person's ability to adjust depends on how much he or she depended on the deceased spouse or partner, how many friends and social connections the widow or widower continues to have, the financial resources the individual has to establish a new life, the individual's style of coping, and whether the partner's death was unexpectedly sudden or followed a prolonged illness (Lopata, 1988; Stroebe, Stroebe, & Domittner, 1988).

For example, older widows report that widowhood is less disruptive of their lives and less stressful than young widows do (Lopata, 1988). The reason seems to be that older women *expect* to become widows and regard this condition as appropriate to their age and time in life. The unexpected and "off-time" death of a young person, though, is shocking and tragic: Gay men who lose their companions to AIDS and young people who lose their spouses in sudden accidents have a more difficult time adjusting than do people whose partners die after a long, fulfilling life.

Studies of the effects of widowhood on men and women find that most survivors, with enough time, are resilient. According to data from a national longitudinal survey of health and well-being of thousands of individuals, widowed people *eventually* do not differ from married or single people in how healthy they feel, in their daily activities, number of friends, openness to new experiences, psychological well-being, and depression (McCrae & Costa, 1988b). This does not mean that the transition to widowhood is easy: On the contrary, it takes most people up to two years to recover from their grief and loss. During this period, they are susceptible to physical ailments and diseases as well as to feelings of hopelessness and despair (see Chapter 15). A significant minority still show signs of depression two years later. These tend to be individuals for whom the loss came very unexpectedly *and* who believe there is nothing they can do to be happy ever again (Stroebe, Stroebe, & Domittner, 1988).

People do best at managing milestones if these events occur "on time," yet the complexities of modern life keep changing our schedules. Efforts to push back or stop the clock have especially powerful consequences, however, when it comes to the ultimate transition, death. In "Think About It" (on page 522) we discuss some important controversies about our society's view of death and dying.

QUICK QUIZ

How well do you understand adult transitions?

1. When grown children leave home, what are most empty-nest parents likely to say? (a) "Come back! All is forgiven!" (b) "At last! Hooray!" (c) "I'm bored and lonely! Now what?"
2. The "midlife crisis" (a) happens to everybody, (b) happens to men but not to women, (c) is common but not universal.
3. Which group reports the highest amount of stress, headaches, and hassles? (a) newly married husbands, (b) graduate students, (c) mothers of young children, (d) empty-nest parents, (e) retired couples
4. Match the name of each transition (left) with the correct example (right):

   1. chronic hassle   a. You don't get married when you planned to.
   2. nonevent   b. You graduate from college.
   3. anticipated   c. You lose your job when the company goes
   4. unanticipated   bankrupt.
                          d. Your mother has a continuing illness.

ANSWERS:

1. b 2. c 3. c 4. 1d, 2a, 3b, 4c

THINK ABOUT IT

On Death and Dying

Death used to be more familiar than it is now. Only two generations ago, you could not reach the age of 20 without losing one or more members of your family; today death has moved farther into the shadows of life.

Death used to be simpler than it is now. Heartbeat and breathing stopped, and the person was pronounced dead. Today patients can "live" for weeks, even years, unconscious and in a coma, while machines keep the vital organs going.

Death used to come sooner than it does now. People are living longer, and in fact the fastest-growing age group in the United States and Canada consists of people over the age of 85.

These three changes in the experience of aging and death have caused profound psychological, legal, and moral issues for our society. Sooner or later, most of us will have to think about some difficult questions:

• *What is legal death?* New definitions of "death" include irreversible brain damage, total brain death, and the inability of the heart to beat on its own. Is a person dead if he or she could not survive without machine support?

• *When is it time to "pull the plug," and who decides?* Doctors, lawyers, families, and clergy often disagree with each other on the "right" time to let an ailing person die. Doctors, trained to prolong life, often want to keep the dying person alive as long as possible, even when that means prolonged pain and suffering. They also fear malpractice suits that may occur if they let someone die who the family thinks could have lived longer. Religious groups differ too. Some believe that death is natural and inevitable, and that doctors and lawyers should not interfere with its course. Others believe that death is to be fought with all the weapons of modern medicine.

• *How can prejudice against old people be kept out of these decisions?* Is a person ever "too old" to be given a life-saving treatment? How can we determine whether an old person wants to die because he or she is clinically depressed—a state that might be treatable—or because the decision is a "rational" one?

• *When, if ever, is euthanasia justified?* Euthanasia means "easy death" (from the Greek *eu*, "good" or "well," as in *euphoria*; and *thanatos*, "death"). It refers to the act of painlessly putting to death someone who is suffering an incurable and painful disease. "Passive" euthanasia

■ THE ADULT EXPERIENCE: CONTINUITY AND CHANGE

The influences on adult development are many and varied. Some are in the individual, in physical maturation and personality. Some are in events we can control, such as whom we marry. Some, as we will see next, are in events that are out of our control.

The High C's of Change: Cohort, Circumstance, and Chance

People are affected by their generation's values and experiences. They are affected by the work they do and the work that is available for them to do. They are affected by bolts from the blue such as losing their houses in a tornado or being drafted during war. In today's world, we can all expect to have unexpected transitions, and we can all expect that some of our expected transitions will never occur.

THE COHORT EFFECT.   Each generation, or age **cohort,** has its own experiences, social outlook, and economic opportunities. Generations that have the benefits of security and a wide range of jobs are different from those that come of age in times of scarcity and recession. People who were teenagers during the Vietnam War are unlike those who came of age before or since. The availability of drugs and changing sexual standards can create dilemmas for one generation that its parents never imagined. The cohort effect is a major reason that chil-

■ **cohort**
An age group, such as a school class or a whole generation, that shares common experiences or demographic traits.

means simply allowing such a person to die without using heroic measures, such as intravenous feeding, to keep the person alive. In "active" euthanasia, or "mercy killing," a physician or relative actually helps the death come sooner to spare the patient suffering.

The legal system has not resolved this issue. Physician Timothy E. Quill (1991) wrote an article in *The New England Journal of Medicine* revealing that he had helped a dying leukemia patient to commit suicide, which was her carefully considered wish. A grand jury in New York State was summoned to determine whether Quill should be indicted for his role in his patient's death; they acquitted him. In contrast, when a 76-year-old Florida man shot and killed his beloved wife who was dying of Alzheimer's disease, he was convicted of first-degree murder and sentenced to life in prison.

• *Who cares for the dying?* Dying of protracted illnesses, such as Alzheimer's disease, AIDS, or cancer, can last months or even years. Thus the issues of who will care for the terminally ill and where they will die are becoming more urgent. Hospitals are often cold institutions that deprive a dying person of dignity and individuality, the company of friends and family, and choices about life-prolonging techniques. One alternative is the *hospice,* a center for the dying person and his or

her family. Hospices offer the medical care of hospitals, but they are homier, allow families to live with the patient, offer counseling to both patient and family, and help the patient die with little pain. Some hospice services are provided in the patient's home.

Today many middle-aged adults face a terrible dilemma, caught between their deeply felt concerns for their parents and an equally pressing need to work. If they give up the caretaking, they often feel guilty and selfish. If they give up their jobs, they risk poverty and financial insecurity in their own old age.

• *Who pays for the dying, and do only the wealthy live?* The costs of life-sustaining equipment, long-term hospital or hospice care, and organ transplants are growing rapidly, a result of new technology. Who will pay the costs? Families? Government? If someone else can afford an organ transplant and you can't, should that person be allowed to live and you to die?

In *What Kind of Life: The Limits of Medical Progress,* Daniel Callahan (1989) argues that Americans must curb their insatiable appetite for a longer life. They should, he says, be learning how to accept aging and death, not struggling to overcome them. Do you agree? Should a society set limits on life, and, if so, how?

dren differ from their parents, and a reason that parents are not the sole important influence on their children. In particular, the ages of 16 to 24 appear to be critical for the formation of a *generational identity* that lasts throughout adulthood (Inglehart, 1990).

In one survey of a cross-section of the American population, the researchers found that major political events and social changes that occur during adolescence and young adulthood make deeper impressions and exert more lasting influence than those that happen later (Schuman & Scott, 1989). Some of the key events that have affected generational cohorts differently in this century include the Great Depression (1930s), World War II (1940s), the dropping of the atomic bomb on Hiroshima (1945), the rise of the civil-rights movement (1950s–1960s), the assassination of John Kennedy (1963), the Vietnam War (1965–1973), the rebirth of the women's-rights movement (1970s), and the legalization of abortion (1973). People who were between 16 and 24 when these events occurred regard them as "peak memories" that have shaped their lives. What are the critical events affecting your cohort?

CIRCUMSTANCE AND SITUATIONS.   One of the most powerful influences on adult development is, simply, what people do. Every day, the situations in which they work, play, love, and live make demands. Some environments offer little room for independence or creativity, and others provide an opportunity to explore both. The conditions of employment and marriage, as we saw in Chapter 10, can affect motivation, mood, health, happiness, and even intellectual abilities.

A ten-year study of a national sample of 5,000 families on welfare found tremendous, continuing changes in family income, entry into the work force, and family composition (Duncan, Hill, & Hoffman, 1988). For most poor people, poverty is only temporary, a result of unexpected misfortunes that could strike anyone, such as getting very sick, losing a job, or, for women, being divorced. Much of Western philosophy is based on the belief in upward mobility: Work hard and you will move up the ladder of success. Yet about 20 percent of all Americans move *down* the job hierarchy in their lives, and more than half are in economic decline, with incomes lagging behind inflation (K. Newman, 1988). The downwardly mobile do not necessarily become poor. But many land in jobs that offer far less status and affluence than they once enjoyed.

CHANCE.   Psychologists have rarely computed the role of chance in their theories of adult development. Chance is so, well, unexpected, so hard to study! But as people grow older, unexpected events have an even more significant effect on their lives (Baltes, 1983; Kagan, 1984). Unpredictable economic conditions and chance events have a way of interrupting people's best-laid plans. You hope to be a teacher, but you find that there are too many teachers. You hope to be able to stay home and raise four children, but inflation makes it impossible for

The "cohort effect" applies to the shared experiences and values of a generation. Many people who came of age during the political protests of the 1960s, such as this couple, continue their political activism throughout their lives. Which of your cohort's values might be affecting you?

Chance events—losing a job, being injured, getting divorced—can affect people's lives in unexpected ways. Most of the people who receive welfare or emergency services do so for only a brief time. How do your stable personality traits interact with unexpected events to produce the course of your adult development?

your spouse to support the family on one income. You expect to have children in your early 20s, but you are offered a great job and decide to work longer before starting a family. You are planning to be a professional guitarist, but you injure your hand in an accident.

Nevertheless, chance isn't everything. Keep in mind that people's attitudes and motivations determine how they respond to chance opportunities and even whether they seek them out (M. Snyder, 1983). What happens to you when chance strikes depends on your ability to change your expectations, make new plans, and find a path through unfamiliar territory.

Change and Consistency

By understanding the forces that promote development or keep us consistent, we can better evaluate popular ideas about adult life. Few people, for instance, are immune to the influence of their generation, their society, or their working conditions. This fact tells us to beware of books or programs that offer to "liberate the self"—as if the "self" existed apart from a social world of duties, demands, pleasures, and possibilities—for these often promise more than they can deliver. Conversely, the belief that *nothing* changes once you are past childhood—as if experiences had no effect—often makes people worry that they are condemned to endure their early problems forever.

The last four chapters have considered some of the factors in personality, genetic disposition, learning, and environment that foster stability and that encourage development. To summarize:

First, what resists change? Your basic personality "package"—including mannerisms, habits, defense mechanisms, level of energy, inhibitions, and general temperament—seems to be fairly consistent throughout life. These qualities influence how you interpret and react to new situations, and whether you seek stimulation and change or prefer stability and calm. Some of the more stable personality traits include extroversion/introversion, neuroticism (negative emotionality), agreeableness, openness to experience, and conscientiousness (McCrae & Costa, 1991).

Second, what is able to change? Many intellectual abilities, emotions, behaviors, and aspects of personality are significantly influenced by new situations and experiences. These include self-esteem, "possible selves," ambitiousness, interest in work, nurturance, loneliness, intellectual flexibility or rigidity, competence, and optimism.

Researchers who study adult development have usually used one of two approaches. One approach looks at what people *do* throughout their lives, how their activities change as they move into different phases of family and work life. The other looks at how people *feel* throughout their lives as their emotional needs and concerns change. Nancy Schlossberg (1989a,b) has put these two dimensions together in a theory of psychological themes that are important throughout life. Unlike Erikson, who said that certain psychological issues are more important at some ages than at others, Schlossberg believes that life events, not age, determine which issues will be important at any given time.

- *Belonging.* Do you feel that you are a central part of your social world, or only marginal?
- *"Mattering."* Do you feel that you matter to others, that you count?
- *Autonomy.* Do you feel that you have a reasonable amount of control over your life, in work, love, and play?
- *Competence.* Do you feel able to do what you need and want to do?
- *Renewal.* Do you have energy and enthusiasm for what you do?
- *Identity.* Do you have a strong sense of yourself, of who you are?
- *Intimacy.* Do you have important, close attachments?
- *Commitments.* Are there people, activities, or values to which you are committed, which give meaning to your life?

These themes, says Schlossberg, reflect our common humanity, uniting men and women, black and white, old and young. A freshman in college and a newly retired man may both temporarily feel marginal, "out of things." A teenager and her great-grandmother may both suffer loneliness without intimate friends. A man may feel he has control over his life until he is injured in a car accident. A wife's identity may change if she goes back to school in midlife. When people lose the commitments that give their lives meaning—a loved one, a career, a religious belief, a political cause—they feel cut off, adrift.

In short, adult concerns are not settled, once and for all, at some critical stage or age. It would be nice if we could acquire a sense of competence in grammar school and keep it forever, if we had only one identity crisis per lifetime, if we always belonged. But adult development is more complicated than that, and also more interesting. Adult life is full of transitions, problems, fun, choices, worries, chances, and unexpected curves. Having them is what it means to live. Meeting them is what it means to be an adult.

TAKING PSYCHOLOGY WITH YOU

Coping with Transitions: When Is a Change a "Crisis"?

Our psychological society tends to make definitive crises out of life's predictable problems. Going to college becomes a College Crisis. Difficulties at work become a Job Crisis. Blues at age 45 become a Midlife Crisis. This tends to make people feel both better ("I'm not alone; it's a diagnosable problem") and worse ("Help, I'm having a crisis!"). What is a crisis, and do you need to have one? If you don't suffer occasionally from temporary insanity, is there something wrong with you?

A *crisis* is a sudden, severely upsetting situation that forces you to mobilize resources; a *transition* is a change in your roles, routines, or relationships. Many psychologists believe that it is not your age that creates a crisis, but an event, such as losing your health, your parents, or your work. Several factors can turn a transition into a crisis (Schlossberg, 1989b):

- *Is the change planned or unplanned, predictable or unpredictable?* Major stresses can be caused by events that are unanticipated or out of order: when the birth of a child is too early, when a parent dies too soon, when retirement or unemployment occurs unexpectedly.

• *Does the change involve one event or many?* A crisis may occur if you must deal with many changes at once, such as moving away from home, leaving all of your old friends, having to support yourself, and taking on new responsibilities.

• *Do you want the change and feel that you have control over it?* People are more shattered by events that seem to come out of the blue, forcing them to make changes they would prefer to avoid.

• *Do you have the emotional skills to help you cope?* Some people react to change as a challenging problem to be solved. Others collapse, feeling that they are overwhelmed by a situation with no solution.

• *Do you have friends, relatives, or associates who can help you?* Change can be difficult for people who feel they have little support for desired decisions or no one to help them through unwished-for changes.

Understanding the factors that can turn a transition into a crisis can sometimes help people plan better. Some guidelines:

• *Don't take on too many life-shaking changes at once,* unless you know what you are doing and you are sure you want to do it. You may decide you really want to disown your family, sell all your possessions, and move to Australia, but you might do better to give yourself a little time in case you have a change of heart. If you know a major change that you cannot control is coming your way, try to postpone other decisions that aren't as important.

• *Set reasonable expectations.* First-time parents who realize that having children will produce a noisy, exciting, and stressful few years, for example, adjust better to this transition than do parents who expect children to make no difference in their stress levels or marriage. A student who expects to feel lonely for a while in a new school will cope better than a student who expects instant social success.

• *Ask for help* from friends, relatives, or support groups. The truth about change is that everyone goes through it. The realization that others are in the same boat or have survived a similar experience is often reassuring in itself.

We cannot always choose the changes that happen to us, but often we can decide what to do next.

SUMMARY

1. Adult development is influenced by the *biological clock* (physical changes throughout life), the *social clock* (events most people experience at the same ages), and *circumstances*, such as their generation (age *cohort*), experiences, and chance events.

2. Adolescence begins with *puberty*. In girls, puberty is signaled by *menarche* (the onset of menstruation) and the development of breasts; in boys, it begins with the onset of nocturnal emissions and the development of the testes and scrotum. Hormones are responsible for *secondary sex characteristics* and for rapid mood swings. Boys and girls who enter puberty early tend to have a more difficult later adjustment than those who enter puberty later than average. One reason seems to be that early puberty exacerbates existing problems of childhood.

3. In women, the *menopause* begins in the late 40s or early 50s. Most women have a few minor symptoms, but they do not regret the end of fertility, they do not become depressed or irritable, and they do not feel "unfeminine." In men, hormone production slows down, but fertility continues.

4. Ideas about old age have been revised now that old people are living longer and healthier lives. Many supposed results of aging, such as senility and brittle bones, are results of disease or overmedication. Other supposed aspects of old age result from psychological problems, such as lack of stimulation, control, and meaningful work, rather than physical decline.

5. Some studies suggest that perceptual-motor skills, intelligence, and memory decline with age. Several explanations have been offered for the fact that older adults tend to score lower than younger adults on mental tests. These explanations include slower reaction times, physiological changes in old age, and generational differences in intellectual background, nutrition, and stimulation. (*Fluid intelligence* declines more than *crystallized intelligence*, which remains fairly stable.) Some aspects of *explicit memory* decline with age, but *implicit memory*, reflecting the ability to learn and remember, does not. The frequency of sexual activity declines over the life span, but psychologists do not agree on the reason. Sexual desire and pleasure last well into old age among people who enjoy sex and who continue to have partners.

6. Erik Erikson proposed an influential *psychosocial theory of development*, in which he argued that life consists of eight stages, each characterized by a particular psychological *crisis*. In particular, Erikson argued that adolescents must face and resolve an *identity crisis*. Other stage theories followed.

7. Adult "stages" are not universal or biologically driven, like stages of child development. The *transitions* approach emphasizes the changes in people's lives regardless of when they occur. There are four kinds of transitions: *anticipated, unanticipated, nonevent,* and *chronic hassle*. Adults evaluate their development according to a *social clock* that determines whether they are "on time" or "off time" for a particular event.

8. Adolescence begins with puberty and ends with society's definition of adulthood. Most adolescents do not go through extreme emotional turmoil. Some have a relatively calm adolescence, some face particular problems, and some have more serious problems. No single pattern is typical of all teenagers. New theories are questioning the meaning, universality, and importance of "separation" from the parent.

9. Gender differences in personality, maturity of thought, and other characteristics are greatest during adolescence, but the differences tend to fade in young adulthood. Anglo and Latina adolescent girls, however, seem to show a significant and lasting drop in self-esteem by high school; black girls do not. Self-esteem is unrelated to the *possible selves* that adolescents envision for themselves. Many adolescents are also developing a balance between an *ethnic identity* (identification with their own group) and *acculturation* (identification with the dominant culture).

10. The major milestones in most people's adult lives include marriage, finding work, having children, being on their own again when divorced or when the children leave home, a midlife phase, retirement, and the death of a spouse or close partner. Parenthood brings special stresses and concerns, especially to mothers. Contrary to stereotype, most couples enjoy being "empty-nest" parents, and most people take well to retirement. Just as most adolescents do not go through turmoil, most adults do not go through a "midlife crisis." But some do spend time reassessing their values and goals, learning to accept the fact of aging and seeking renewal.

11. Adult development is also influenced by the *cohort effect* and the *generational identity* it produces; the *circumstances* of economic conditions, work, and family; and random, *chance* events. For most people on welfare, poverty is a temporary response to misfortune—losing a job, getting sick, or being divorced.

12. Adult development falls somewhere between "you can change anything about yourself" and "you can't change anything." Some aspects of personality resist change. But many others, such as self-esteem, competence, motivation, intellectual flexibility, and nurturance, are influenced by experiences in adulthood.

13. Some psychological issues recur throughout life: belonging, the need to matter to others, autonomy, competence, renewal, identity, intimacy, and commitments to activities or people that give life meaning.

KEY TERMS

puberty   *498*
menarche   *498*
secondary sex characteristics   *498*
asynchrony   *499*
menopause   *500*
climacteric   *500*
gerontology   *501*
osteoporosis   *501*
senility   *501*
fluid and crystallized
  intelligence   *503*
explicit and implicit memory   *504*
psychosocial theory (Erikson)   *506*

identity crisis   *506*
transitions   *508*
adolescence   *509*
"turmoil theory"   *510*
possible selves   *512*
ethnic identity   *513*
acculturation   *513*
social clock   *515*
"midlife crisis"   *519*
empty nest   *520*
cohort effect   *523*
generational identity   *524*

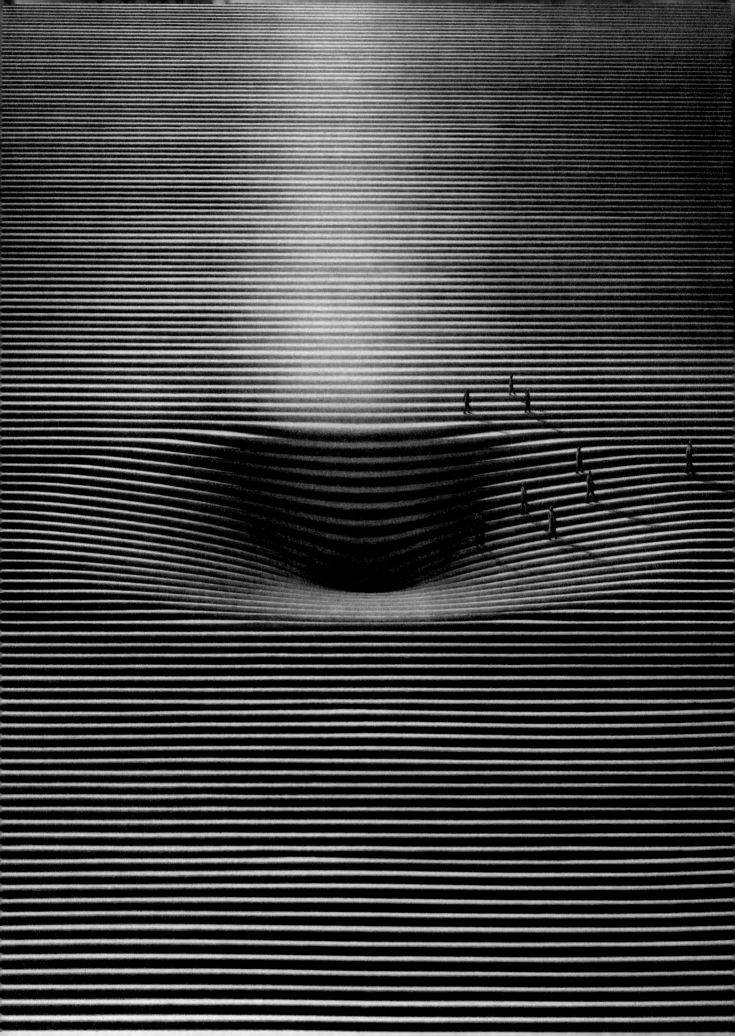

PART FIVE

HEALTH AND DISORDER

15

Health, Stress, and Coping

Rule No. 1 is, don't sweat the small stuff.
Rule No. 2 is, it's all small stuff.
And if you can't fight and you
can't flee, flow.

ROBERT ELIOT, M.D.

• Bill and his father have been battling for years. Bill feels that he can never do anything right, that his father is always ready to criticize him for the slightest flaw. Now that he has left home, Bill has a clearer perspective on their relationship, but one thing hasn't changed. Every time his father comes to visit, Bill breaks out in a mysterious rash.

• Tanya has never told anyone about a shattering experience she had as a child. She is afraid to reveal her secret, sure that no one will understand or sympathize. But the memory haunts her in daydreams and nightmares.

• Josh is walking home from school one night when three young men grab him, threaten to kill him, and steal his watch and wallet. Josh is relieved to be alive, but he finds that he can't get over this experience. Months later, he still feels humiliated and angry, and dreams of revenge.

• Lucy, who is already late for class, gets stuck in a traffic jam caused by a three-car accident. As she walks in the door, her instructor reprimands her for being late. Rushing to get her notes together for an overdue research paper, Lucy spills coffee all over herself and the documents. By noon Lucy has a splitting headache and feels exhausted.

Like bolts from the blue, a stressful event can strike at any time.

All of these people are certainly under "stress," but, as you see, their experiences are far from the same. "Stress" can be caused by occasional but recurring conflicts (Bill and his father), a traumatic experience or a sudden event that shatters your sense of safety (Tanya, Josh), and a collection of small irritations that can wear you down (Lucy). Is there a link between these stressors and health or illness?

In this chapter, we will explore the psychology of health and illness, stress and coping, in the context of daily life. We will look at findings from two fields. *Health psychology* addresses the psychological aspects of health and illness, such as the influences on how people stay healthy, why they become ill, and how they respond when they do get ill (Taylor, 1991). A related field, *behavioral medicine*, takes an interdisciplinary approach to health and illness. Researchers in behavioral medicine come from many different backgrounds, including medicine, nutrition, physiology, and psychology.

Scientific psychology and medicine have typically used a *pathogenic* approach, focusing on the causes of an illness (from *patho-*, "disease" or "suffering," and *-genic*, "producing"). But health psychologists also want to know what generates health, and so they take the *salutogenic* approach (from *salut*, "health") (Antonovsky, 1987). The pathogenic approach divides the world into the healthy and the sick, although many healthy people have occasions of feeling poorly and many sick people are able to function fairly well. In emphasizing the people who are at high risk of becoming ill, it ignores the majority who, although at some risk, stay well.

The pathogenic approach asks, "How can we eradicate stressors?" The salutogenic approach asks instead, "How can we learn to live well with stressors, and even turn them to our advantage?" To find out, health psychologists also study the exceptions—the people who theoretically should become sick but don't, the people who transcend difficulties instead of giving in to them. They study *wellness* as well as illness.

Modern research in health psychology is very promising. But some of its findings, unfortunately, have been misused to foster two common misconceptions: that illness is "all in the mind" and that curing illness just requires the right attitude of "mind over matter." At the end of this chapter we will consider the contributions of health psychology and its limitations.

■ THE NATURE OF STRESS

Throughout history, "stress" has been one of those things that everyone has experienced but few can define. Why has it been so difficult to agree on something all of us have felt?

Alarms and Adaptation

In his 1956 book, *The Stress of Life*, Canadian physician Hans Selye (1907–1982) popularized the idea of stress and advanced its study. Selye noted that many environmental factors—heat, cold, pain, toxins, viruses, and so on—throw the body out of balance, forcing it to respond. These factors, called *stressors*, include anything that requires the body to mobilize its resources. The body responds to a stressor with an orchestrated set of physical and chemical changes, which, as we saw in Chapter 9, prepare an individual to fight or flee. According to Selye, "stress" consists of a series of reactions, which he called the **General Adaptation Syndrome** (with the memorable acronym GAS). The General Adaptation Syndrome has three phases:

1. In the *alarm phase*, the organism mobilizes to meet the threat. This phase is a basic package of biological responses that allows a person to fight or flee no matter what the stressor is: trying to cross a busy intersection or trying to escape a cross rattlesnake.

2. In the *resistance phase*, the organism attempts to resist or cope with a threat that cannot be avoided. During this phase, the body's physiological responses are above normal—a response to the original stressor—but this very mechanism makes the body more susceptible to other stressors. For example, when your body has mobilized to fight off the flu, you may find that you are more easily annoyed by minor frustrations. In most cases, the body will eventually *adapt* to the stressor and return to normal.

3. If the stressor persists, it may overwhelm the body's resources. Depleted of energy, the body enters the *exhaustion phase*, becoming vulnerable to fatigue, physical problems, and eventually illness. The very reactions that allow the body to resist short-term stressors—boosting energy, tensing muscles in preparation for action, shutting out signs of pain, closing off digestion, raising blood pressure—are unhealthy as long-range responses. Tense muscles can cause headache and neck pain. Increased blood pressure can become chronic hypertension. Closing off digestion for too long can lead to digestive disorders.

■ **General Adaptation Syndrome (GAS)**

According to Hans Selye, the bodily reactions to environmental stressors.

Stress is a bane of modern civilization because our physiological alarm mechanism now chimes too often. Today, when the typical stressor is a mammoth traffic jam and not a mammoth mammal, the fight-or-flight response often gets all revved up with nowhere to go. When your teacher announces that you will

Who has more "stress"—and whose stress counts? Many media stories emphasize the stress faced by white-collar workers and managers of companies. They are less concerned with the stress faced by assembly-line workers and blue-collar laborers. Why do you think this might be so? Which group is under more stress—people in highly competitive and complicated jobs, or people in boring and predictable jobs? Actually, researchers find that "it is not the bosses but the bossed who suffer most from job stress" (Karasek & Theorell, 1990).

have an unexpected exam, you don't really need to respond as if you were fighting for your life, but your body will still sweat to dispose of excess body heat. When you see your sweetheart flirting with someone else, you don't really need to breathe hard to get oxygen to your muscles, as you would if you were fleeing to safety.

Not all stress is bad, however. Some stress, which Selye called **eustress,** is positive and feels good—competing in an athletic event, falling in love, working hard on a project you enjoy—even if it also requires the body to produce short-term energy. Selye did not believe that all stress could be avoided or that people should aim for a stress-free life, which is an impossible goal. "Just as any inanimate machine gradually wears out," he said, "so does the human machine sooner or later become the victim of constant wear and tear." The goal is to minimize the wear and tear, not get rid of it.

Selye recognized that psychological stressors (such as emotional conflict or grief) can be as important as physical stressors (such as heat, toxic chemicals, or noise). He also observed that some factors *mediate* between the stressor and the stress. A comfortable climate or a nutritious diet, for example, can soften the impact of an environmental stressor such as pollution. Conversely, a harsh climate or a poor diet can make such stressors worse. But by and large, Selye concentrated on the biological responses that result from a person's attempt to adapt to environmental demands. He defined a stressor as any event that produces the stress (that is, the General Adaptation Syndrome). A diagram of his view is:

Stressor ⟶ Stress (GAS) ⟶ Healthy adaptation or illness

Later studies, however, have found that stress is not a purely biological condition that leads directly to illness (Cohen & Williamson, 1991). First, between the stressor and its results are *qualities of the individual*, such as personality traits

■ **eustress** [YOU-stress]
Positive or beneficial stress.

and perceptions: An event that is stressful or enraging for one person may be challenging for another and boring for a third. Losing a job, traveling to China, or having "too much" work to do is stressful to some people and not to others.

Second, between the stress and its consequences is *how the individual behaves when under stress and how he or she copes with it.* Not all individuals who are under stress behave in the same way. Some drink too much, drive recklessly, or fail to take care of themselves, all of which can increase their risk of illness or accident. Some cope well to reduce the effects of stress, and others seem not to manage well at all.

For these reasons, many psychologists now prefer a definition of stress that includes aspects of the environment, aspects of the individual, and how the two interact. **Psychological stress** is the result of an exchange between the person and the environment, in which the person believes that the situation strains or overwhelms his or her resources and is endangering his or her well-being (Lazarus & Folkman, 1984).

Today, researchers have come a long way from Selye's early theories. Some are probing the physiological mechanisms in the immune system that actually transform stress into illness. Some have tried to specify which stressors are particularly risky. And others study the qualities of the person and the person's life that make some stressors worse than others. The links between stressors, qualities of the person, and the outcomes of health or illness are more complex than Selye dreamed, as we will see.

Illness and Immunology

An early approach to the psychological origins of illness came from the field of *psychosomatic medicine,* which developed in psychiatry at the turn of the century. The word **psychosomatic** refers to the interaction of mind (*psyche*) and body (*soma*). Freud was one of the main proponents of the idea that physical symptoms are often the result of unconscious conflicts. Other theorists maintained that many disorders—such as rheumatoid arthritis, hypertension, asthma, ulcers, and migraine headaches—are caused by neurotic personality patterns. These early theories led to the mistaken view that a "psychosomatic" illness is one that is "all in the mind." The modern field of psychosomatic medicine recognizes the complex nature of the mind-body relationship—not only how mind affects body, but also how body affects mind.

Today, a new field has emerged, with the cumbersome name of **psychoneuroimmunology,** which investigates the complexities of the mind-body relationship. Psychoneuroimmunologists explore the connections among *psychological* processes (such as negative emotions and perceptions), the *nervous* and endocrine systems, and cells in the *immune system* (Kiecolt-Glaser & Glaser, 1989). These researchers hope to explain, for example, why of two people who are exposed to a flu virus, one is sick all winter and the other doesn't even get the sniffles.

The immune system is designed to do two things: recognize foreign substances (*antigens*), such as flu viruses, bacteria, and tumor cells, and destroy or deactivate them. There are basically two types of white blood cells in the immune system: the *lymphocytes,* whose job is primarily to recognize and destroy foreign cells, and the *phagocytes,* whose job is to ingest and eliminate them.

To defend the body against foreign invaders, the immune system deploys different weapons (cells), sometimes together and sometimes alone, depending on the nature of the enemy. Several kinds of lymphocytes aid in this attack. *Natural killer cells* are important in tumor detection and rejection. *B cells* (so called because they are released from the bone marrow) are responsible for producing antibodies, highly specific molecules that recognize a target antigen. After a first response to a specific antigen, "memory B cells" are created to produce

■ **psychological stress**
The result of a relationship between the person and the environment, in which the person believes the situation is overwhelming and threatens his or her ability to cope.

■ **psychosomatic**
A term that describes the interaction between a physical illness or condition and psychological states; literally, mind (psyche) and body (soma).

■ **psychoneuroimmunology**
[psycho/neuro/immu/nology]
The field that studies the relationships among psychology, the nervous system, and the immune system.

a faster and more efficient attack on subsequent exposures to it; this is why inoculations against chicken pox and flu are effective. Finally, *T cells* (so called because they mature in the thymus) make direct contact with the antigen, and they too come in several versions. *Killer T cells* help destroy antigens that they have been exposed to previously. *Helper T cells* enhance and regulate the immune response (they are the primary target of the HIV virus that causes AIDS). Prolonged stress can suppress some or many of these cells that fight disease and infection (O'Leary, 1990).

For example, in a study of 420 people who heroically volunteered to fight in the war against the common cold, some were given nose drops containing viruses known to cause a cold's miserable symptoms. A control group got uncontaminated nose drops. Everyone was then quarantined for a week. The results: People who were under high stress, who felt their lives were "unpredictable, uncontrollable, and overwhelming," were twice as likely to develop colds as those reporting low levels of stress (Cohen, Tyrrell, & Smith, 1991). And in a study of medical students who had herpes virus, researchers found that herpes outbreaks were more likely to occur when the students were feeling loneliest or were under exam pressure. Loneliness and stress apparently suppressed the cells' immune capability, permitting the existing herpes virus to erupt (Kiecolt-Glaser, Garner, et al., 1985a). Nevertheless, remember that not everyone who is under stress gets sick or even shows impairment of the immune system.

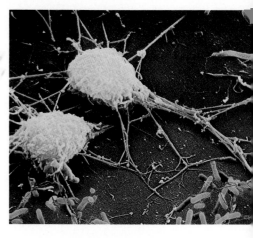

Like a fantastical Hollywood creature, a phagocyte reaches out with extended "arms" to ensnare unwitting bacteria.

Some Sources of Stress

What are the stressors that might affect the immune system and thus lead to illness? Some psychologists study the significant events that disrupt our lives; others emphasize continuing pressures in the environment; still others count nuisances, the small straws that break the camel's back.

LIFE EVENTS. Some years ago, Thomas Holmes and Richard Rahe (1967) identified 43 events that seemed to be especially stressful. By surveying thousands of people, they were able to rank a series of "life-change events" in order of their disruptive impact. Holmes and Rahe then assigned each event a corresponding number of "life-change units" (LCUs). At the top was death of a spouse (100 LCUs), followed by divorce (73), imprisonment (63), and death of a family member (63). Not all of the events were unpleasant. Marriage (50) was on the list, as were pregnancy (40), buying a house (31), and Christmas (12). Among people who became ill, the majority had had 300 LCUs or more in a year.

Later studies found numerous flaws in the idea that all life events are stressful and lead to illness. First, many of the items on the Holmes-Rahe scale can be the *result* of psychological problems or illness, rather than their cause (such as "problems at work" and "major changes in sleeping habits") (Brett et al., 1990). Second, some events become more stressful once a person is already depressed or ill. Third, as we saw in the previous chapter, many expected changes, such as retirement, are not stressful for most people. Happy events are not related (thank goodness) to illness or poor health (Taylor, 1991). Finally, simply counting life changes is not enough: Having 17 things happen to you in one year is not necessarily stressful unless you feel overwhelmed by them (Cohen, Kamarck, & Mermelstein, 1983).

BEREAVEMENT AND TRAGEDY. Some events, of course, are more shocking to the system, psychologically and physically, than others. The events at the top of the Holmes-Rahe list, death of a spouse and divorce, are powerful stressors. Indeed, in the two years following bereavement, widowed people are more susceptible to illness and physical ailments, and their mortality rate is higher than expected (Stroebe, Stroebe, & Domittner, 1988). Divorce also often takes a long-term health toll. Divorced adults have higher rates of heart disease, pneumonia, and other diseases than comparable adults who are not divorced (Jacobson, 1983).

Bereaved and divorced people may be vulnerable to illness because, feeling unhappy, they don't sleep well, they stop eating properly, they consume more drugs, and they smoke more cigarettes. However, animal and human studies suggest that separation *itself* also creates cardiovascular changes, a lowered white blood cell count, and other abnormal responses of the immune system (Laudenslager, 1988). You may recall from Chapters 10 and 13 that attachment appears to be a basic biological need of the species, and broken attachments affect us at a basic cellular level. But the quality of the attachment is as important as its presence. Unhappily married individuals show the same decline in immune function as unhappy divorced people (Kiecolt-Glaser, Fisher, et al., 1987a).

Sadly, many people suffer shocking experiences that are not on the Holmes-Rahe list—experiences about which they feel so ashamed that secrecy itself adds to the stress. (See "A Closer Look at Psychoneuroimmunology" to see how this field's findings have yielded a therapeutic suggestion for recovery from trauma.)

CONTINUING PROBLEMS. Many stress researchers believe that people have a good ability to withstand acute (short-term) stress, and even a massive blow. The real threat to health, they say, occurs when stress becomes interminable: living in a dangerous environment, such as a war zone or a high-crime neighborhood; living with a violent parent; dealing with repeated experiences of discrimination; feeling trapped in a situation you can't escape. For example, female clerical workers who feel they have no support from their bosses, who are stuck in low-

---

A CLOSER LOOK AT PSYCHONEUROIMMUNOLOGY

Why Confession Is Good for the Soul—and the Body

Now pay attention: *Don't think of a white bear.* Are you not thinking of it? Anyone who has ever tried to banish an uninvited thought knows how hard it is to erase the mental tape of worries, unhappy memories, or unwished-for obsessions. In an actual study, people who were told not to think of a white bear mentioned it nine times in a five-minute stream-of-consciousness session (Wegner et al., 1987). The reason seems to be that when you are trying to avoid a thought, you are in fact processing the thought frequently—rehearsing it and making it more accessible to consciousness. When the subject of your obsession involves an old flame whom you still desire, trying *not* to think of him or her actually prolongs your emotional responsiveness to the person (Gold & Wegner, 1991).

According to James Pennebaker and his associates, the prolonged inhibition of thoughts and emotions requires physical effort, which is stress-

ful to the body (Pennebaker, Hughes, & O'Heeron, 1987). Yet many people try to inhibit secret thoughts and feelings that make them ashamed or depressed. The inability or unwillingness to confide important or traumatic events places continuing stress on the system and can lead to long-term health problems. In study after study, individuals who suppress secrets prove to be at greater risk of illness than people who are able to talk about their tragedies, even though disclosures of traumatic events are often painful and unpleasant at first (Pennebaker, 1990).

This information poses a problem: If an event is stressful and trying to stop thinking about the event is stressful, what should you do? Research from *psychoneuroimmunology* suggests some answers.

In one of Pennebaker's studies, college students were assigned to write about either personal traumatic experiences or trivial topics for 20 minutes a day, four days in a row. Those who were asked to reveal "their deepest thoughts and feelings" about a traumatic event all had something to talk about. Many told stories of sexual abuse, physical beatings, emotional humiliation, and parental abandonment. Yet most had never discussed these feelings with anyone. The researchers took blood samples from the students

paying jobs without hope of promotion, and who have financial problems at home are the women most at risk of heart disease (Haynes & Feinleib, 1980). And the workers who most suffer from job stress are employees who have no say in job-related decisions, little opportunity to exercise initiative, and are trapped doing repetitive tasks (Karasek & Theorell, 1990).

Prolonged stress is not only associated with heart disease but also with hypertension, arthritis, and immune-related deficiencies. In the United States, for example, blacks have a much higher incidence of high blood pressure than do whites: Among adults ages 55 and 65, 33 percent of whites but 54 percent of blacks have high blood pressure, which can lead to kidney disease, stroke, and heart attack. The hypothesis that this difference in blood pressure might be due to inherent racial differences has been ruled out (Klag et al., 1991). The major cause is living in "toxic" neighborhoods characterized by poverty, poor housing, high divorce and unemployment rates, crime, drug use, and greater exposure to chemical contamination, such as lead in peeling paint (Anderson, 1991).

DAILY HASSLES. Some psychologists argue that we handle most of the big problems of life relatively well; it's the daily grind that can get us down. "Hassles" are everyday irritations and frustrations such as thoughtless friends, traffic jams, bad weather, quarrels, broken plumbing, lost keys, and sick cats. In one study of 75 married couples, the frequency of daily hassles was related to later health problems such as flu, sore throats, headaches, and backaches (DeLongis, Folkman, & Lazarus, 1988).

A major event, such as divorce, often increases the number of hassles a person must contend with—new financial worries, custody questions, moving—

Middle-class "stress" might seem a luxury to people whose health is chronically jeopardized by poverty, exposure to toxic materials, malnutrition, and lack of access to medical care.

to test for the immune activity of lymphocytes. They also measured the students' physical symptoms, emotions, and visits to the health center. On every measure, the students who wrote about traumatic experiences were better off than those who did not (Pennebaker, Kiecolt-Glaser, & Glaser, 1988). Some of them showed *short-term* increases in anger and depression; writing about an unpleasant experience was not fun. But as months passed, their health and well-being improved.

The researchers believe that "the failure to confront a trauma forces the person to live with it in an unresolved manner." Actively writing or talking about it helps people assimilate the experience and come to a sense of completion about it. But confession must not turn to obsession. Confessing your "deepest thoughts and feelings" is not therapeutic if you keep rehearsing and confessing them endlessly to all who will listen. The key is physiological release *and* a new cognitive perspective.

Writing about the same experience for several days can produce insight and distance. One woman, who had been molested at the age of 9 by a boy a year older, at first wrote about her feelings of embarrassment and guilt. By the third day, she was writing about how angry she felt at the

boy. By the last day, she had begun to see the whole event differently; he was young too, after all. When the study was over, she said, "Before, when I thought about it, I'd lie to myself. . . . Now, I don't feel like I even have to think about it because I got it off my chest. I finally admitted that it happened."

Revealing your private feelings and fears—in a diary, to a tape recorder, or to a nonjudgmental friend—seems able to speed up the normal coping process associated with major life changes. In one study, freshmen wrote either about their feelings associated with going to college or their feelings on superficial topics. The experimental group reported higher feelings of homesickness and anxiety in the short run, but by the end of the school year they had had far fewer bouts of flu and fewer visits to the infirmary than the control group did (Pennebaker, Colder, & Sharp, 1990).

To see if this research will benefit you, why not keep a diary this year? All you have to do is jot down, from time to time, your "deepest thoughts and feelings" about school, your past, your future, anything. Pennebaker predicts that you will have fewer colds, headaches, and trips to the medical clinic next year.

These airplane passengers, frustrated about a canceled flight, show the many possible responses to life's hassles: amused friendliness, sullen acceptance, efforts to get information, and just plain gloom.

and might make a person more intolerant of small hassles. By and large, however, people's reports of being hassled are independent of life events. In one study of police officers, the most stressful things they reported were not the dramatic dangers you see on television, but daily paperwork, annoyance with the press, and the snail-like pace of the judicial system (Grier, 1982).

Of course, when people report that something is a hassle, they are really reporting their feelings about it. The activity itself might be neutral. A young mother who says that making meals every day is a hassle is revealing her attitudes and emotions about this task. Perhaps because she has so many other things to do every day, preparing dinner feels to her like an awful chore. Her husband might look forward to cooking as an enjoyable way to reduce tension. So the effect of "hassles," like that of "stressful events," may depend on the person's reaction to them. And indeed, research has found that hassles are hazardous to health primarily for people who tend to be very anxious and quick to overreact (Kohn, Lafreniere, & Gurevich, 1991). Every little thing, to them, feels like the last straw.

In general, these stressors—life events, bereavement, chronic problems, and hassles—are related to your state of health. But they are not the whole story. Something else, as we will see next, is going on between the stressful event and your physical response to it.

QUICK QUIZ

We hope these questions are not sources of stress for you.

1. Steve is unexpectedly called on in class to discuss a question. He doesn't have the faintest idea of the answer, and he feels his heart start to pound and his palms start to sweat. He is in the _____ phase of the GAS.
2. Which of the following life-change events has the strongest relationship to immune problems and illness? (a) marriage, (b) bereavement, (c) taking an exam, (d) moving, (e) hassles
3. Maria has worked as a file clerk for 17 years. Which aspect of the job is likely to be *most* stressful for her? (a) the speed of the work, (b) the predictable routine, (c) feeling trapped, (d) the daily demands from her boss

ANSWERS:

1. alarm 2. b 3. c

◼ THE INDIVIDUAL SIDE OF HEALTH AND WELL-BEING

We have seen that stressors themselves are only part of the stress-illness story. We now turn to four aspects of individual psychology that affect how people respond to stressors: negative emotions, "explanatory style," healthy habits, and control.

Negative Emotions

Is there a relationship between emotion and disease? Many people assume that there is; you often hear remarks like, "She was so depressed for years it is no wonder she got cancer" or "He worried himself into an ulcer over that job." Certainly it seems that some people manufacture their own misery. Send them to a beach to escape the stress and press of civilization, and they bring along a bag of worries and irritations. But are they more likely than easygoing vacationers to get sick? Can anxiety, anger, or depression literally make you ill?

If sick people are angrier than others, does that mean that anger caused their illnesses? Can you think of other explanations for a relationship between emotions and disease?

Before scientists can conclude that emotions directly lead to illness, they have had to consider four other possible links between emotion and disease (Friedman & Booth-Kewley, 1987):

*   *The disease may cause the emotion.* Many physicians see patients who are angry, depressed, or anxious because they are sick. It is an easy jump to the conclusion that the anger, depression, or anxiety *caused* the sickness, when the reverse may be true. Sometimes people jump to the comparable conclusion that happiness causes wellness. In one study of women diagnosed with cancer, those who had expressed higher levels of joy at the start of the research were more likely to live longer than less joyful patients (S. Levy et al., 1988). That sounds like a recipe for joy—which can't hurt anyone! Yet one of the reasons the women were more joyful to begin with was that they had fewer cancerous sites and their doctors were more optimistic. In short, it is likely that the slow course of the disease was causing the women's joy (and their extended survival), not that joy slowed the cancer.
*   *Unhealthy habits may cause the disease.* Before we can conclude that "an anxious person gets ulcers," we must rule out the possibility that people who worry a lot are also more likely to smoke or drink. Unfortunately, many studies that examine the links between emotion and disease do not take health habits into account. For example, women used to have a very low incidence of ulcers compared to men, until more of them began smoking.
*   *Something else entirely may affect emotion and disease.* Another possibility is that some third factor is related both to an emotional style *and* a disease. For example, perhaps an overresponsive nervous system leads to the development of frequent anger and, independently, to the development of heart disease. Many risk factors may combine, over time, to produce illness.
*   *A chronic emotional state may lead to disease, which affects the emotion, which affects disease: the mind-body system.* Chronic anxiety or depression could lead to unhealthy practices, which could cause physical changes (influenced in turn by genetic makeup), which could make one's negative emotions worse, which could keep one from taking care of oneself, which in turn. . . .

Keeping these complex possibilities in mind, consider now the story of anger and heart disease. An early attempt to identify a connection between the two focused on the *Type A behavior pattern*, a set of qualities that seemed to increase the risk of heart disease, the nation's leading cause of death (Friedman & Rosenman, 1974). Although Type A has been measured in different, often inconsistent ways, it basically describes people who are constantly struggling to achieve, have a sense of time urgency, are irritable, and are impatient with anyone who gets in their way. Type B people are calmer and less intense.

Which is more stressful for this Type A man—his work load or his emotional reaction to it?

Today, however, the early enthusiasm about Type A is a mere shadow of its former self. It turns out that different tasks and situations produce different physiological responses in the same people, and being highly reactive to stress and challenge is not in itself a risk factor in heart disease (Krantz & Manuck, 1984). Type A people do indeed set themselves a fast work pace and a heavy work load, but many cope better than Type B people who have a lighter work load, and without a high physiological price (Frankenhaeuser, 1980). Further, people who are highly involved in their jobs, even if they work hard, have a low incidence of heart disease. "There'd be nothing wrong with us fast-moving Type A's," said a friend of ours, "if it weren't for all those slow-moving Type B's."

Nevertheless, something about Type A may be dangerous to one's health. In one major study, men who were chronically angry and resentful and who had a hostile attitude toward others were *five times* as likely as nonhostile men to get coronary heart disease and other ailments, even after controlling for other risk factors, such as smoking (Williams, Barefoot, & Shekelle, 1985). (See Figure 15.1.) The next step was to find out what kind of hostility was hazardous. *Neurotic hostility*, which describes people who are complaining and irritable, is *not* related to heart disease. (It seems to be part of the general personality trait of neuroticism, described in Chapter 12.) But *antagonistic hostility*, describing people who are aggressive, confronting, rude, cynical, and uncooperative, seems to be the "toxic" variety that is linked to heart disease, at least in men; the link between hostility and heart disease in women is less clear (Dembroski & Costa, 1988; Smith, Sanders, & Alexander, 1990). You can see the importance of defining terms, such as "anger" and "hostility," carefully.

It also turns out that not all Type B's are really so laid back and easygoing! Howard Friedman (1991) calls some of them "phony Type B's"—people who *say* that pressure doesn't bother them and who seem unaggressive, but who, just under the surface, actually are competitive, angry, and tense. They turn out to be at greater risk of heart disease than "true" Type B's.

So far, so good. Yet as psychologists further probed the connection between emotion and heart disease, they found that toxic hostility was not the only culprit. So were the chronic negative states of anxiety and depression (H. Friedman, 1991). Moreover, this cluster of negative emotions was implicated in other diseases, too. Friedman and Stephanie Booth-Kewley (1987), using meta-analysis to summarize the results of 101 studies, failed to find any significant links between specific emotions and diseases, such as the "anxious" ulcer patient or the "depressed" cancer patient. Instead, they found weak but consistent evidence

FIGURE 15.1 ——————

Hostility and health
Men who had the highest hostility scores as young medical students were the most likely to have coronary heart disease 25 years later (Williams, Barefoot, & Shekelle, 1985).

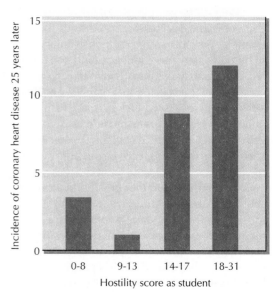

for what they called a "generic, disease-prone personality," a person who is chronically depressed, angry and hostile, worried and anxious.

It is important to understand, however, that the link was not a strong one, and that many studies find no link at all. One team of researchers reviewed 22 studies of depression and the immune system, and found that *most* of them reported no differences in the number of immune cells in people with major depressive disorders and normal controls (Stein, Miller, & Trestman, 1991). A ten-year-long study of a nationally representative sample of 6,403 women and men found that the people who had depressive symptoms or even clinical depression were *not* more likely to develop cancer (Zonderman, Costa, & McCrae, 1989). And other studies have found no links between depression, psychological distress and outbreaks of illness among men with AIDS (Rabkin et al., 1991).

Perhaps the most reasonable conclusion at present, therefore, is that negative emotions or personality traits may be *involved* in illness, but they are not the only or even the major *cause*. "Personality may function like diet," Friedman and Booth-Kewley concluded. "Imbalances can predispose one to all sorts of diseases." Psychological disturbances affect the immune system in general. The occurrence of a specific illness depends on other factors, such as whether a person drinks excessively or smokes, genetic vulnerabilities, and the biology of the disease itself.

Explanatory Style

Perhaps you remember from Chapter 9 how different ways of thinking are associated with different emotions. Lonely, depressed people tend to explain uncontrollable events as internal ("It's all my fault"), stable ("This misery is going to last forever"), and global ("It's going to affect everything I do"). Cheerful people regard the same events as external ("I couldn't have done anything about it"), unstable ("Things will improve"), and limited in impact ("Well, at least the rest of my life is OK").

Martin Seligman (1991) calls these characteristic ways of accounting for bad events *explanatory style*, and observes that these two styles of thinking describe the difference between pessimists and optimists. An optimistic explanatory style is related to self-esteem, achievement, and physical health and longevity. Pessimists will probably complain that optimism is just a *result* of good health; it's easy to think positively when you feel good. But there is growing evidence that optimism may produce good health as well as reflect it.

In one imaginative study of baseball Hall-of-Famers who had played between 1900 and 1950, 30 players were rated according to their explanatory style. A pessimistic remark would be internal, stable, and global, such as, "We didn't win because my arm is shot, it'll never get better, and it affects my performance every time." An optimistic version would be external, unstable, and specific: "We didn't win because we got a couple of lousy calls, just bad luck in this game, but we'll be great tomorrow." The optimists were significantly more likely to have lived well into old age than were the pessimists (Seligman, 1991).

What could be the link between pessimism and illness? One answer is that pessimism produces depression and stress, which in turn affect the immune system. High degrees of pessimism are independently associated with impaired immune activity (Rodin, 1988). This means that pessimists do not fall ill because they are sicker or more depressed to begin with. A longitudinal study of Harvard University graduates started out with young men who were all in good health. But 35 years later, those who had had a pessimistic explanatory style were in significantly worse health than the optimists (Peterson, Seligman, & Vaillant, 1988).

A second possible explanation has to do with how people cope with stress. Optimists tend to be problem-focused rather than emotion-focused. When

Studies suggest that explanatory style affects longevity. One example, from a study of baseball players, is Zack Wheat, an outfielder for the Brooklyn Dodgers. Wheat had an optimistic explanatory style: "I'm a better hitter than I used to be because my strength has improved and my experience has improved." Wheat lived to be 83.

faced with a problem, such as a risky operation or a serious continuing struggle with alcoholism, they focus on what they can *do* rather than on how they *feel.* They have a higher expectation of being successful, so they don't give up at the first sign of a setback. They keep their senses of humor, plan for the future, and reinterpret the situation in a positive light (Carver, Scheier, & Weintraub, 1989; Peterson & Barrett, 1987). Perhaps pessimists are more likely to become ill because they stir up negative emotions rather than act constructively.

Note that optimists do not *repress* their anxieties, cheerfully asserting, like those phony Type B's, that "everything will be fine." (Remember from the Closer Look box on page 538 that the effort to suppress worrisome secrets is stressful to the body.) Rather, they acknowledge their problems and illnesses, but have confidence that they will overcome them (Schwartz, 1990).

Can pessimism be "cured"? Optimists, naturally, think so. Cognitive therapy has been remarkably successful in teaching depressed people new explanatory styles (see Chapter 17). Psychologist Rachel Hare-Mustin told us how her mother cured her budding childhood pessimism—with humor. "Nobody likes me," Rachel lamented. "Don't say that," her mother said. "Everybody hasn't met you yet."

Healthy Habits

We bet you $100 that you already know the basic rules for protecting your health: get enough sleep, get regular exercise, eat a nutritious diet, drink alcohol only in moderation, do not overeat, do not undereat on starvation diets, and do not smoke cigarettes. A ten-year longitudinal study of nearly 7,000 people in Alameda County, California, found that each of these practices was independently related to good health and lack of stress symptoms (Matarazzo, 1984; Wiley & Camacho, 1980). The more of these practices people followed, the better their mental and physical health.

Well, why aren't you following all of them? Health psychologists study a persistent riddle of human behavior: why, when people know what is good for them, they often don't do it. An important goal of health psychology is prevention: helping people eliminate the risk factors for illness before the illness has a chance to develop. But health psychologists have found several obstacles to their pursuit of prevention (Taylor, 1991):

Walter Johnson, a star pitcher for the Washington Senators, had a pessimistic explanatory style: "I can't depend on myself to pitch well. I'm growing old. I have had my day." Johnson died at the age of 59.

• Many health habits are entrenched in childhood, and parents play a powerful role in determining a child's health habits. For example, they determine what children learn about alcohol—whether to drink in moderation or go on "binges"—and what kind of food is best. It will be hard for you to give up a high-fat diet if you associate it with home-cooked meals.

• People often have little incentive to change unhealthy habits. Smoking, eating rich food, and not exercising have few immediate consequences, and their effects do not become apparent for years. So many people in good health feel invulnerable.

• Health habits are largely independent of one another. Some people exercise every day and continue to smoke. Some people eat nutritious meals and take a lot of drugs.

• Health habits are unstable over time. Some people quit smoking for a year—and then take it up again. Others lose 50 pounds—and then gain 60.

Health psychologists have identified many factors that influence your ability to overcome these obstacles to good health. Some are in your *social system:* Do all your friends smoke and drink themselves into a stupor on weekends? Chances are that you will join them. Some are in your larger *cultural environment:* Does your culture think it is appropriate for women to exercise or for men to stop eating red meat? Some are in your *access to health care services and information:* Not everybody in this society is affluent, can afford insurance, or has the opportunity to consult doctors. Finally, as we will see next, some are in your *basic beliefs:* Do you feel fatalistic about illness or in charge of your health?

The Question of Control: Fight or Flow?

All of the factors we have discussed so far—negative emotions, pessimism, poor health habits—may in turn be related to one critical factor: Having a sense of personal control over a troubling event, chronic problem, or illness (Cohen & Edwards, 1989; Marshall, 1991).

LOCUS OF CONTROL. People differ considerably in whether or not they feel in control of most of the things that happen to them. **Locus of control** refers to the general expectation of whether or not the results of your actions are under

■ **locus of control**
A general expectation about whether the results of one's actions are under one's own control (internal locus*) or beyond one's control (external* locus*).*

your own control (Rotter, 1966). People who have an *internal* locus of control ("internals") tend to believe they are responsible for what happens to them, that they are captains of their life's ship. People who have an *external* locus of control ("externals") tend to believe they are the helpless victims—or beneficiaries—of luck, fate, or other people.

Some psychologists maintain that the very notion of being in control of your destiny reflects a middle-class view of life: work hard enough, and anything is possible (Markus & Kitayama, 1991). Poor people and minorities often have a less optimistic view of what is possible for them than affluent whites do, and taking an external stance toward life is one way to preserve self-esteem and cope with difficulties in life. They say, in effect, "I am a good and worthy person; my lot in life is a result of prejudice, fate, or society" (Crocker & Major, 1989). Further, cultures place different emphases on who is responsible for success or failure. In a comparison of 194 Anglo-American tenth-graders with 194 Chinese tenth-graders in Taiwan, Lian-Hwang Chiu (1988) found that American teenagers were more internal than their Chinese counterparts in assuming responsibility for *success*, but the Chinese were more internal than the Americans in assuming responsibility for their *failures*.

THE BENEFITS OF CONTROL. The most debilitating aspect of chronically stressful situations is the feeling of powerlessness, of having no control over what happens. People can tolerate years of difficulty if they believe they can control events or at least *predict* them (Laudenslager, 1988). These are not necessarily the same thing. You may not be able to control the stress of taking an exam, but you can usually predict and prepare for it. When people know that they will be going through a hard time, they can take steps to reduce stress.

Feeling in control of events has important advantages. It helps to reduce chronic pain, improve psychological adjustment to surgery and illness, and speed up recovery from some diseases (Taylor, 1991). In a study of patients recovering from heart attacks, those who thought their illness was due to bad luck or fate—factors outside their control—were less likely to generate active plans for recovery and more likely to resume their old unhealthy habits. But those who thought the heart attack occurred because they smoked, didn't exercise, or had a stressful job were more likely to change their bad habits and recover more quickly (Affleck et al., 1987).

The sense of control also directly affects the neuroendocrine and immune systems. This fact may explain why an improved sense of control is so beneficial to old people, whose immune systems normally decline (Rodin, 1988). The sense of being in control need not be enormous to be effective. When elderly residents of nursing homes are simply given more choices over their activities and environment and given more control over day-to-day events, the results are dramatic: They become more alert, more active, happier—and less likely to die (Langer, 1983; Langer et al., 1979).

Remember, however, that the path between control and health runs in two directions. Control does affect health, but health also affects how much control you feel you have (Rodin, 1988).

In general, it's good to feel in control of your life, but what does that mean exactly? Control over what? How much of your life? How do the events in your life affect your sense of control?

SOME PROBLEMS WITH CONTROL. In general, a sense of control is a good thing. But believing that an event is controllable does not always lead to a reduction in stress, and believing that an event is uncontrollable does not always lead to an increase in stress. The question must always be asked: Control over what?

If an unrealistically confident person tries to control the uncontrollable ("I'm going to be a movie star in 60 days!"), the resulting failure may lead to helplessness (Fleming, Baum, & Singer, 1984). It also doesn't help people to believe

Sometimes life serves up a disaster, as it has for many farm families who have lost their lands and livelihoods because of the changing economy. When is it helpful to believe we can control everything that happens to us, and when is it harmful?

they have control over an event if they then feel unable to cope with it. Victims of abuse or other crimes, for example, often suffer because they blame themselves for having "provoked" their attackers, as if they could have controlled the criminal's behavior (Janoff-Bulman, 1989).

"Control," therefore, has different meanings, and not all of them are related to health (Marshall, 1991). In one study that dissected the varieties of control, the only one that was related to health and well-being was *self-mastery*, the belief that "If I become sick, I have the power to make myself well again." Other, more unrealistic kinds of control were *not* related to health and well-being, such as self-blame ("Whatever goes wrong with my health is my own fault") and the illusion that all disease can be prevented by doing the right thing ("If I take care of myself, I can avoid illness").

What, then, can we conclude about the importance of control to health? The answer depends on the kind of control being exercised. In **primary control,** people try to influence existing reality by changing other people, events, or circumstances. In **secondary control,** people try to accommodate to reality by changing their own perceptions, goals, or desires (Rothbaum, Weisz, & Snyder, 1982). By and large, the Western approach celebrates primary control: If you don't like something, change it, fix it, or fight it. The Eastern approach emphasizes secondary control: If you have a problem, learn to live with it or act in spite of it. In a comparison of the United States and Japan, one study found that these two perspectives influence practices in child rearing, socialization, religion, work, and psychotherapy (Weisz, Rothbaum, & Blackburn, 1984).

A Japanese psychologist offers some examples of Japanese proverbs that teach the benefits of yielding to the inevitable (Azuma, 1984): *To lose is to win* (giving in, to protect the harmony of a relationship, demonstrates the superior traits of generosity and self-control); *Willow trees do not get broken by piled up snow* (no matter how many problems pile up in your life, flexibility will allow you to survive them); and *The true tolerance is to tolerate the intolerable* (some "intolerable" situations are facts of life that no amount of protest will change). Perhaps you can imagine how long "to lose is to win" would survive on an American football field, or how long most Americans would be prepared to tolerate the intolerable!

The point is not that one form of control is better or healthier than the other, but rather that both have their place. The emphasis on primary control encourages self-expression, independence, and change, at a possible price of self-absorption. The emphasis on secondary control leads to acceptance and serenity, at a possible price of self-denial and stagnation (Iga, 1986). Most problems require us to choose between trying to change what we can and accepting what we cannot. Perhaps a secret of healthy control lies in knowing the difference.

■ **primary control**
An effort to modify external reality by changing other people, the situation, or events; a "fighting-back" philosophy.

■ **secondary control**
An effort to accept external reality by changing one's own attitudes, goals, or emotions; a "learn to live with it" philosophy.

QUICK QUIZ

Please do not interpret these questions as stressful:

1. Which of the following aspects of Type A behavior seem most hazardous to health? (a) working hard, (b) being in a hurry, (c) antagonistic hostility, (d) high physical reactivity, (e) neurotic hostility
2. "I'll never find anyone else to love because I'm not good-looking; that one romance was a fluke" illustrates a(n) _____ explanatory style.
3. Adapting yourself to the reality that you are getting older is an example of primary/secondary control.
4. Joining a protest against sexual harassment on the job is an example of primary/secondary control.
✳ 5. A self-described health expert describes the case of a woman who was the victim of physical assault and who then suffered the death of her mother. "No wonder," said the expert, "that she soon thereafter developed cancer." What can we conclude from this case about the causes of cancer, and what other explanations are possible here?

ANSWERS:

1. c 2. pessimistic 3. secondary 4. primary 5. From this one case we cannot conclude anything; the expert is just arguing by anecdote. What about all the people who live with extreme stressors and don't get cancer? Other explanations include: her stressful experiences may have weakened her immune system, which made an already existing cancer begin to grow; the stress and the cancer may have been coincidental events; the stressful events may have caused her to smoke and take other health risks, which increased the likelihood of illness.

■ COPING WITH STRESS

Remarkably, most people who are "under stress"—living even in the most toxic environments of war and poverty, living through long episodes of anger or grief—do not become ill. Why not? What helps people manage endless hassles and recover from the most awful adversity? How, in short, do they cope? **Coping** consists of constantly changing cognitive and behavioral efforts to manage demands, in the environment or in oneself, that one feels or believes to be stressful (Lazarus & Folkman, 1984). Coping is not a single strategy that applies to all circumstances. People cope differently with hassles, losses, dangers, and challenges.

Freud argued that the mind develops defenses to protect it from unpleasant truths or conflicts. Because he treated people with problems, his theory implied that defenses are usually unhealthy and maladaptive. Although clinical psychologists are still concerned with the defenses that keep people unhappy, most health psychologists prefer the term *coping* to reflect a more active, constructive, and sympathetic view of people's efforts to solve their problems (Moos, 1988).

■ **coping**
Cognitive and behavioral efforts to manage demands in the environment or oneself that one feels to be stressful.

The many successful ways of coping fall into three general categories: (1) attacking the problem, (2) rethinking the problem, and (3) accepting the problem but lessening the physical effects of its stress (Shaver & O'Connor, 1986). The first deals with the stressor, the second involves your interpretation of the stressor, and the third addresses the symptoms of stress.

Attacking the Problem

A woman we know, whom we will call Nancy, was struck by tragedy when she was 22. She and her new husband were driving home one evening when a car ran out of control and crashed into them. When Nancy awoke in a hospital room, she learned that her husband had been killed instantly. She herself had permanent spinal injury and would never walk again. For many months, Nancy reacted with understandable rage and despair. "Get it out of your system," her friends said. "You need to get in touch with your feelings." "But I *know* I'm miserable," Nancy lamented. "What do I *do?*"

What should Nancy do, indeed? Her predicament and her friends' advice point to the difference between *emotion-focused* and *problem-focused* coping (Lazarus & Folkman, 1984). Emotion-focused coping concentrates on the emotions the problem has caused, whether anger, anxiety, or grief. For a period of time after a tragedy like Nancy's, it is normal to give in to these emotions and feel overwhelmed by them. Eventually, though, most people become ready to concentrate on the problem itself and get beyond the emotional state.

The specific steps in problem-focused coping depend on the problem. Sometimes the problem is clear: You lost your job. Sometimes it is uncertain: You suspect, but aren't sure, that you will lose your job. The problem may be a pressing but one-time decision; a continuing difficulty, such as living with a disability; or an anticipated event, such as having an operation.

"Defining the problem" may seem obvious, especially when the problem is standing there yelling at you. However, people often define a problem incorrectly and then set off down a wrong coping road. For example, unhappy couples often blame each other for their misery. Sometimes, of course, they are right. But a study of several hundred couples found that marital unhappiness is often a result of misdiagnosis. A husband who is under great pressure at his office may decide that his problem is an unsupportive wife. A wife who is feeling too many conflicting demands may decide that her problem is her lazy husband. If this couple tries to cope with their unhappiness by attacking each other, they merely increase their misery. If they correctly diagnose the problem ("I'm worried about my job"; "I don't have enough leisure time to myself"), different coping solutions follow (A. Pines, 1986).

Once the problem is identified, the coper can learn as much as possible about it from professionals, friends, books, and others in the same boat. In Nancy's case, she can begin by learning more about her medical condition and prognosis. What can she do for herself? What kind of exercise will help her? How do other accident victims cope? Many people in stressful situations divide their options into "stay here and suffer" versus "leave here and die." But usually there is a middle course. What are Nancy's options? She could give up and feel sorry for herself forever. She could return home to live with her parents. She could learn to care for herself. She could go into the wheelchair business. She could . . . . (In fact, Nancy stayed in school, remarried, got a Ph.D. in psychology, and now does research and counseling with disabled people.)

Problem-focused coping has a large psychological benefit: It tends to increase a person's sense of self-esteem, control, and effectiveness (D'Zurilla & Sheedy, 1991). Sometimes, of course, emotions get in the way of assessing a problem accurately. When people are agonizing over a decision, they may, to relieve their anguish, make a fast, impulsive choice. They may say or do something in anger that worsens their predicament, or become so anxious that they cannot evaluate the situation carefully. That is why most people use a combination of emotion- and problem-focused coping. At work, for example, people use problem-focused coping when the stress is caused by a specific job-related crisis. They are more likely to resort to emotion-focused coping (trying to control

How do you cope with continuing stresses? If you were in this single mother's place, would you usually be amused and charmed by your small children's demands, or annoyed and harassed?

their own emotions or ventilating them) when the stress is caused by an annoying co-worker (Fontenot & Brannon, 1991).

As you can see, problem-focused coping requires components of critical thinking, such as considering alternatives and resisting emotional reasoning. When under stress, people who think creatively and constructively about their problems are better able to solve them, avoid negative emotions such as anger and anxiety, and even reduce physiological arousal (Katz & Epstein, 1991).

Rethinking the Problem

A second way of coping with problems, after the initial panicky reaction ("I'll never get through this!"), is to think about them in new ways. Shelley Taylor (1989), who has worked with cancer and cardiac patients, women who have been raped, and other victims of disaster or disease, finds that rethinking strategies have three goals. First, they help the person find meaning in the experience: Why did this event happen to me? What does it mean for my life now? Second, they help the person regain mastery over the event and one's life: How can I keep this from happening again? What can I do about it now? And third, they help the individual restore self-esteem after a devastating setback.

Among the many cognitive strategies that people use to reinterpret events, we will consider some of the most effective.

The ultimate example of rethinking your problems.

REAPPRAISAL: "IT'S NOT SO BAD." When people cannot eliminate a stressor, they can choose to rethink its implications and consequences. Problems can be turned into challenges, losses into unexpected gains. You lost your job. Is that a disaster? Maybe it wasn't such a good job, but you were too afraid to quit to look for another. Even life-shattering events can be viewed in more than one light. A study of 100 spinal-cord-injured people found that two-thirds of them felt the disability had had positive side effects (Schulz & Decker, 1985). Benefits included becoming "a better person," "seeing other people as more important," and having an "increased awareness of self" and a new appreciation of "brain, not brawn."

People can also reappraise the motives behind the distressing behavior of others. Instead of becoming enraged at someone's actions, for example, the empathic person tries to see the situation from the other person's standpoint in order to avoid misunderstandings and misperceptions (Miller & Eisenberg, 1988).

SOCIAL COMPARISONS: "I'M BETTER OFF THAN THEY ARE." When people are sick or in difficult situations, successful copers compare themselves to others who are (they feel) less fortunate. No matter how bad off they are, they are able to find someone who is even worse off (Taylor & Lobel, 1989). This is true even of people who know they have fatal diseases. For example, one AIDS sufferer said in an interview, "I made a list of all the other diseases I would rather not have than AIDS. Lou Gehrig's disease, being in a wheelchair; rheumatoid arthritis, when you are in knots and in terrible pain. So I said, 'You've got to get some perspective on this, and where you are on the Great Nasty Disease List.'" Another said: "I really have an advantage in a sense over other people. I know there is a possibility that my life may not go on for as many years as other people's. I have the opportunity to look at my life, to make changes, and to deeply appreciate the time that I have" (Reed, 1990).

AVOIDANCE: "IT'S NOT IMPORTANT; LET'S GO TO THE MOVIES." Is it ever a good idea to cope with a problem by ignoring it or running away from it? Suppose you are going to the hospital for routine surgery, such as for a hernia, gall bladder, or thyroid condition. Should you get as much information as you can about every detail and risk of the procedure, or, having decided to go ahead, should you avoid thinking about it?

In an early study of this question, researchers divided 61 patients according to their style of coping with a forthcoming operation: "vigilance" or "avoidance" (Cohen & Lazarus, 1973). Avoiders showed a remarkable lack of interest in what was going to happen. They said such things as, "All I know is that I have a hernia. It doesn't disturb me one bit." They didn't discuss the surgery in detail and said it was nothing to worry about. "Having an operation," said one avoider, "is like having a vacation." In contrast, the vigilant types attended to every detail. They read articles about their condition and wanted to know everything about the surgery, including the type of incision that would be made and the anesthesia used. They learned about every risk, no matter how remote, and about possible postoperative complications. One patient said, "I have all the facts, my will is prepared . . . your heart could quit, you can have shock."

Some psychologists believe that vigilance is the best strategy, that "the work of worrying" prepares a person to cope with all possible results. In this situation, however, vigilance backfired. The avoiders fared much better. They needed less pain medication. They complained less about treatment. They had fewer minor complications such as nausea, headache, fever, and infection. They got out of the hospital sooner.

Many studies have now been done on the difference between people who are vigilant, who scan all information for evidence of threat, and those who avoid threatening information by distracting themselves (S. Miller, 1989). There are benefits and problems in both styles of coping. Vigilant individuals, for example, are overly sensitive to their bodily symptoms, tend to exaggerate their importance, and take longer to recover from them (Miller, Brody, & Summerton, 1988). On the other hand, perhaps because they are so health conscious, they are more likely to look after themselves—say, by getting routine medical and dental exams.

Once you have all the necessary information to make a decision and that decision is out of your hands, avoidance is an excellent coping device. But vigilance is called for when action is possible and necessary. Sometimes both strategies can work together. In a hospital, patients do best if they refuse to dwell on every little thing that could go wrong, if they distract themselves as much as possible. They also get well faster (and protect themselves) when they are vigilant about the care they are getting, when they protest incorrect or thoughtless treatment. The benefits of distraction do not mean you should lie there like a flounder and passively accept every decision made for you.

Of course, some people do more than "distract" themselves when they cope with a stressful situation; they deny it altogether. Is denial ever good for you? For a discussion of this issue, see "Think About It" on page 552.

HUMOR: "PEOPLE ARE FUNNY." "A merry heart doeth good like a medicine," it says in Proverbs, and researchers now agree. Once thought too frivolous a topic for serious study, humor has made its way into the laboratory. Herbert Lefcourt and Rod Martin (1986) gave people tests to measure stress, mood, and sense of humor. "Sense of humor" includes the ability to respond with humor in real situations, to like humor and humorous people, and to use humor in coping with stress. Lefcourt and Martin found that humor is an excellent buffer between stress and negative moods.

What's so funny about misery? "He who laughs," thundered the German poet and dramatist Bertolt Brecht, "has not heard the terrible news." But people who can transform the "terrible news" into a sense of the absurd or the whimsical are less prone to depression, anger, tension, and fatigue than are people who give in to gloom. In studies of college students who are coping with unfortunate events, those who respond with humor feel fewer negative emo-

When should you cope with a problem by attacking it head-on, and when should you ignore it? Under stress, is it better to be a tiger or an ostrich?

Many comedians use humor as a way to cope with problems. The actor Bert Lahr, shown here as the lovable Cowardly Lion in The Wizard of Oz, *began using humor as a shield against stress early in life.*

THINK ABOUT IT

Are Illusions Healthy?

Denial is certainly a common response to stress: "This isn't happening to me"; "It is happening to me, but it isn't important"; "If I ignore it, the problem will go away." Since Freud, many psychologists have regarded denial as a primitive, dangerous defense mechanism that meant a person was out of touch with reality. And being out of touch with reality has long been assumed to be a hallmark of mental illness. Now some researchers are asking: When reality serves up a problem you can't do anything about, what's so bad about losing touch with it?

Emotionally healthy people supposedly are good at "reality testing" and do not need self-promoting illusions; they can face the truth about themselves. The evidence, however, does not support this common assumption. After reviewing years of research, Shelley E. Taylor and Jonathon D. Brown (1988) concluded that well-being virtually depends on the illusions of "overly positive self-evaluations, exaggerated perceptions of control or mastery, and unrealistic optimism." These "positive illusions," Taylor (1989) argues, are not only characteristic of normal human thought, but also necessary for the usual criteria of mental health: the ability to care about others, the ability to be contented, and the ability to work productively. In fact, the people who score *highest* on tests of self-deception (for example, who deny threatening but universal feelings, such as ever having felt guilty) score the *lowest* on measures of psychopathology and depression!

Why should this be so? The mind tends to filter all incoming information, distorting it in a positive direction to enhance self-esteem and ward off bad news. Positive illusions are especially useful when people are threatened with illness, crisis, or attacks to their self-esteem. This strategy is adaptive and healthy, because it allows people to respond with hope for the future (C. R. Snyder, 1989). If they judged their problems accurately, they might fold their tents and give up. In a situation in which your abilities are untested,

---

tions and unhappiness than do students who don't have a sense of humor or who instead succumb to moping and tears (Labott & Martin, 1987; Nezu, Nezu, & Blissett, 1988).

Some theories of laughter emphasize its ability to reduce tension and emotion. You have probably been in a tense group situation when someone suddenly made exactly the right crack to make everyone laugh and defuse the mood. Laughter seems to produce some beneficial biological responses, possibly stimulating the immune system or starting a flow of endorphins, the painkilling chemicals in the brain (J. Goldstein, 1987).

Other theories emphasize the cognitive components of humor. When you laugh at a problem, you are putting it in a new perspective—seeing its silly or absurd aspects—and gaining control over it (Dixon, 1980). Humor also allows you to express indirectly feelings that are hazardous to express directly, which is why it is so often the weapon of minorities. An old joke tells of a Jewish man who accidentally bumped into a Nazi on a street. "Swine!" bellowed the Nazi. "And I'm Cohen," replied the Jew, "pleased to meet you."

Having a sense of humor, however, is not the same as smiling all the time or "putting on a happy face." For humor to be effective in coping with stress, a person must actually use it during a stressful situation—seeing or inventing funny aspects of serious events and having the ability to laugh at them (Crawford & Gressley, 1991; Nezu, Nezu, & Blissett, 1988). Hostile humor therefore misses the point: Vicious, rude jokes at another person's expense are not stress reducers. Indeed, they often create more tension and anger (Baron, 1977).

Living with the Problem

In modern life, we often cannot escape changes, conflicts, traffic, noise, or job or school pressure (see "Taking Psychology with You," page 561). A third approach to coping concentrates on reducing the physical effects of stress itself.

as William James noted long ago, it is much more beneficial to try and possibly succeed than not to try at all.

On the other hand, health psychologists worry about the many self-destructive things that denial permits people to do: They drink too much, they smoke, they won't wear their seat belts, they don't take medication for chronic illnesses. When people make important health decisions that are based on denial and self-flattering illusions, the results can be fatal. It is dangerous when a woman ignores a lump in her breast, when a man having a heart attack says "it's only indigestion," when a diabetic fails to take needed medication. Moreover, the illusion of invulnerability—"it will never happen to me"—can lead people to do all sorts of risky and stupid things.

Further, illusions are not necessarily beneficial if they keep people from recognizing their limitations. How long should you keep trying to break into the major leagues if you just aren't a great ball player? People need to know when to quit, and what they can't do as well as what they can. People who overestimate their chances of suc-

cess may waste years trying to become something they are not (Baumeister & Scher, 1988). As W. C. Fields once observed, "If at first you don't succeed, try, try again. If you still don't succeed, quit. No use being a damn fool about it."

What happens when people must reconcile their former illusions with a traumatic event that cannot be ignored? The result is often, literally, dis-illusion (Janoff-Bulman, 1989). Some victims never return to their former illusions; they see the world as less benevolent and less meaningful than it had been and themselves as less worthy. Unable to create positive illusions, they often become depressed, anxious, and fearful. Others do eventually reestablish a positive view of the world and themselves, finding new meaning in the tragedy (Collins, Taylor, & Skokan, 1990).

What is the line between "healthy illusions"—those that maintain self-esteem and optimism—and self-destructive ones? How would you know which is which? Is it better to maintain illusions at all costs, if they protect your self-esteem, or to think critically about them and risk losing optimism? What do you think?

RELAXATION. The simplest way to reduce signs of stress, such as high blood pressure and rapid breathing, is to relax. Relaxation training—learning to tense and relax certain muscles alternately, to lie or sit quietly, to banish worries of the day—apparently has beneficial effects on the immune system. In a sample of 45 elderly people living in retirement homes, those who reduced stress with relaxation techniques showed significantly improved immune activity (Kiecolt-Glaser, Glaser et al., 1985b).

Some people learn to relax through systematic *meditation*, a practice aimed at focusing one's attention and eliminating all distracting thoughts. Short-term meditation does not produce a unique physiological or emotional state; most studies find no difference between meditation and simple resting (D. Holmes, 1984). This does not mean that meditation has no benefits. In Eastern religions like Hinduism and Buddhism, meditation is much more than a relaxation or stress-reduction technique. The goal is not to unwind but to attain wisdom, acceptance of reality, emotional detachment, and transcendence of the self—states of mind not measurable on an EEG machine.

In a review of relaxation methods, two researchers found that methods that work for one person or one kind of problem may not be as successful with others (Woolfolk & Lehrer, 1984). For example, relaxation is helpful in reducing the pain of menstrual cramps if the pain is caused by muscle contractions and not fluid retention. Some people benefit from cognitive therapy, as well as relaxation, to learn to calm tense thoughts as well as tense muscles (see Chapter 17). And although biofeedback is often promoted as a stress-reducer, simple relaxation is usually just as effective, and a lot cheaper.

EXERCISE. Physical exercise, such as walking, jogging, dancing, biking, and swimming, is an important buffer between stressors and physiological symptoms (see Figure 15.2). Laboratory and field studies have found that people who are physically fit show less physiological arousal to stressors and pay fewer vis-

Exercise is great, but is it a cure-all? When does it help you alleviate your problems, and when does it become an excuse to escape them?

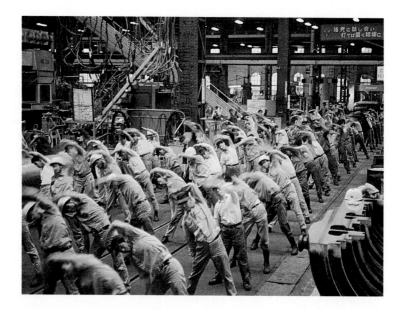

Exercise has many all-around health benefits, which is why some American companies are adopting the Japanese practice of scheduling exercise breaks for workers. Should exercise be a formal and required part of the workday?

its to the doctor than people who are less fit—even when both groups are under the same objective pressures (J. Brown, 1991). These benefits of exercise have been shown in studies of adults, adolescents, and even preschoolers. In one study, preschoolers who did aerobic exercises daily for eight weeks, compared to children who spent the same time each day in free play, not only had better cardiovascular fitness and agility, but their self-esteem improved as well (Alpert et al., 1990).

Exercise also combats anxiety, depression, and the blues (Plante & Rodin, 1990). In one study of 43 college women, all moderately to severely depressed, researchers assigned the students to one of three groups. One group did aerobic exercise three times a week, another practiced relaxation and took leisurely walks four times a week, and a control group did neither. After five weeks and again after ten weeks, the women took tests of their aerobic capacity and level of depression. Those who exercised vigorously showed improved fitness and sharp declines in depression; the relaxation and control groups didn't reduce their depression levels (McCann & Holmes, 1984). Similarly, studies of workers have found that the more that employees exercise, the fewer physical symptoms, colds, and stresses, and the less anxiety, depression, and irritability, they report (Hendrix et al., 1991). An invigorating workout can be beneficial—a non-hostile, nonaggressive workout, that is. People who think angry, competitive thoughts while they are exercising are, in effect, adding fuel to the fire.

Many popular books and magazines therefore advocate exercise as the all-purpose coping strategy. There is no doubt that regular exercise is an excellent all-around health tonic. But people who exercise in order to *avoid* their problems are not necessarily reducing their stress load, especially if they have to go back to the same old problem tomorrow. In one study of 230 working women, the strongest predictor of depression, anxiety, and physical stress was difficulty at work. The form of coping that helped best was dealing with the job problems directly (O'Neill & Zeichner, 1985). You can't, it seems, jog away from everything.

FIGURE 15.2

Fitness and health
In one study, when people were under low stress, their fitness levels were unrelated to the number of their current health problems. But when under high stress, people who were aerobically fit had fewer problems than did people who were less fit (Roth & Holmes, 1985).

Health problems (y-axis: 0, 5, 10, 15)

Life Stress: Low, High

■ High aerobic fitness
■ Low aerobic fitness

Looking Outward

A psychologist who has worked with Holocaust survivors, prisoners of war, hostages, refugees, and other survivors of catastrophe believes that a key element in their recovery is compassion, "healing through helping" (Segal, 1986). People gain strength, he says, by giving it to others.

This observation echoes Alfred Adler's theory of *social interest* (see Chapter 12). To Adler (1938/1964), social interest has a cognitive component (the ability to understand others, to see the connectedness of humanity and the world), an emotional component (the ability to feel empathy and attachment), and a behavioral component (the willingness to cooperate with others for the common welfare). Although "social interest" is the opposite of selfishness, it is harmonious with self-interest. Adler believed that people who are involved with others are better able to cope with life's problems, have higher self-esteem, and are psychologically stronger than people who are self-involved (Ansbacher, 1968).

Adler's ideas have been supported. One large study used two measures of social interest: a scale of moral values and an index of cooperation in love, work, and friendship. People who were high in social interest, compared to others, had fewer stressful experiences and were better able to cope with the stressful episodes they did have. Among people low in social interest, stress was more likely to be associated with anxiety, depression, and hostility. Social interest seems to soften the effects of stress on psychological well-being (Crandall, 1984).

Why is social interest healthy? The ability to look outside of oneself, to be concerned with others, is related to virtually all of the successful coping mechanisms we have discussed so far. It tends to lead to solving problems instead of blaming others. It helps you reappraise a conflict, by trying to see it as others do instead of taking it personally. It allows you to get perspective on a problem instead of exaggerating it. Because of its elements of forgiveness, tolerance, and connectedness, it helps you live with situations that are facts of life.

QUICK QUIZ

Can you cope with these refresher questions?

1. You accidentally broke your glasses. Which response is an example of cognitive reappraisal? (a) "I am such a stupid clumsy idiot!" (b) "I never do anything right." (c) "What a shame, but I've been wanting new frames anyway." (d) "I'll forget about it in aerobics class."
2. Finding out what your legal and financial resources are when you have been victimized by a crime is an example of (a) problem-focused coping, (b) emotion-focused coping, (c) distraction, (d) reappraisal.
3. Learning deep-breathing techniques to reduce anxiety when taking exams is an example of (a) problem-focused coping, (b) emotion-focused coping, (c) avoidance, (d) reappraisal.
4. "This class drives me crazy, but it's better than not being in school" is an example of (a) distraction, (b) social comparison, (c) denial, (d) empathy.
5. Your roommate has turned your room into a bomb crater, filled with rotten leftover food and unwashed clothes. Assuming that you don't like living with rotting food and dirty clothes, what coping strategies described in this section might be beneficial to you?

ANSWERS:

1. c 2. a 3. b 4. b 5. You might attack the problem by trying to find a compromise solution (clean the room together). You might reappraise the seriousness of the problem ("I only have to live with this person until the end of the term") compared to others ("at least my roommate is generous and friendly"). You might also apply a sense of humor (pile everything into a heap, put a flag on top, and add a sign: "Monument to the Battle of the Bilge").

■ THE SOCIAL SIDE OF HEALTH AND WELL-BEING

Thus far we have been looking at individual factors involved in stress and illness. But health and well-being are not just up to you as an individual. They also depend on the people around you.

The Alameda County health study that we mentioned earlier (which followed nearly 7,000 adults for a decade) also investigated the importance of social relationships to health. The researchers considered four kinds of social ties: marriage, contact with friends and relatives, church membership, and participation in other groups. The people who had few social networks were more likely to have died by the time of the ten-year follow-up than those who had many (Berkman & Syme, 1979).

Perhaps the people who died were sicker to begin with or had poorer health habits, which kept them from socializing? No. The importance of social networks was unrelated to physical health at the time the study began, to socioeconomic status, and to such risk factors as smoking.

Perhaps the people who died had some undiagnosed illness at the beginning of the study? This interpretation was possible because the study was based on the participants' self-reports. So the research was repeated with nearly 3,000 people in Tecumseh, Michigan, and this time the investigators collected everyone's medical exams. Ten years later, those who had few social relationships were more likely to have died than the people who had many, even after age, health, and other risk factors were taken into account (House, Landis, & Umberson, 1988; House, Robbins, & Metzner, 1982).

One possible explanation for these findings is that social support somehow affects the immune system. In fact, studies find that lonely people, who have few friends, have poorer immune function than people who are not lonely; students in a network of friends have better immune function before, during, and after exam periods than students who don't have enough social support; and spouses of cancer patients, although under considerable stress themselves, do not show a drop in immune function if they have high levels of social support (Baron et al., 1990). Social support even speeds recovery from illness when it does occur (Kulik & Mahler, 1989).

As psychologists have explored the benefits of friends and family, they have noticed something else. Sometimes friends and family are themselves the source of hassles, headaches, and conflicts. There are, therefore, two sides to the human need for social support.

When Friends Help You Cope . . .

One psychologist calls friendship a form of "assisted coping": Friends help you deal with problems when you are too drained to budge (Thoits, 1986). By "friends" we mean family members, neighbors, co-workers, and anyone else in your social network.

Friends do many "supportive" things. They provide emotional support, such as concern and affection. They offer cognitive guidance, helping you evaluate problems and plan a course of action. They offer tangible support, with resources and services such as loaning money or a car, or taking notes in class for you when you have to go to the doctor. They offer companionship. Perhaps most of all, they are sources of attachment and connection, which people need throughout their lives (Hobfoll & Stephens, 1990; Sarason et al., 1987). Old people who have dogs as companions, for example, are less stressed and visit medical clinics less often than their comparable peers who have no pets—or who have cats! Dogs provide companionship and attachment, the two ingredients of a truly best friend (J. Siegel, 1990).

The effect of friends on your health depends on what the friends are doing for you and how much stress you are under. In studying a representative sample of more than 2,000 adults, Karen Rook (1987) found that for people with *average*, everyday levels of stress, social support had no effect on health one way or the other. Among people who had *above-average* levels of stress, support from friends did help reduce their physical and emotional symptoms. But among people who had *below*-average levels of stress, such support was actually harmful. It was associated with more symptoms! Why might this be so? When people are going through a series of disasters, Rook believes, they need friends who can offer advice, assistance, and reassurance. But talking too much about daily, trivial nuisances may simply reward people's distress rather than helping them manage it.

Of course, individuals and cultures differ in how many friends and relations are needed for well-being and in what they define as "support." Mexican Americans, for example, tend to rely on their extended families for emotional support much more than Anglo-Americans do, and they feel more anxiety when separated from them. (Perhaps for this reason, rates of homelessness are very low among Latinos living in America.) Anglos have more casual networks than do Mexican Americans, even listing co-workers among those they depend on (Griffith & Villavicencio, 1985). In France, older people are more likely than American whites or blacks to feel satisfied with the amount of support provided by friends and family. Older Americans are more likely to complain that they give more than they receive (Antonucci, Fuhrer, & Jackson, 1990).

Cultures also differ in the value they place on friends and family. Anglo-Americans value quick friendliness and sociability, a result perhaps of frequent moves and life changes, but in many European and Asian cultures friendship develops slowly. It takes a long time to flower but then it blooms for life. The difference between Japanese and American culture shows clearly in the reactions to the proverb "A rolling stone gathers no moss." To Americans, it means keep moving; don't let anything cling to you. To the Japanese, it means stay where you are; if you keep moving you will never acquire the beauty of stability (Syme, 1982).

. . . And Coping with Friends

Your neighbor tells you that your closest friend has betrayed your confidence. You ask a friend for help, and he says, "Sorry—I'm too busy right now." You're in the middle of describing your most recent unhappy date, and your friend says, "Oh, quit whining." You're in the hospital recovering from major surgery, and your closest friend never shows up for a visit.

As most of us learn, friends and relatives can be stress producing as well as stress reducing. They may impose conflicting demands on us. They are often sources of hassles, quarrels, and conflicts. When disaster or serious illness strikes, friends may blunder around, not knowing what to do or say. Cancer victims report that they are often upset by the well-meaning but unhelpful reassurances from their families and friends that "all will be fine." They often feel better talking to other cancer patients (Dunkel-Schetter, 1984).

Another stressful aspect of friendship is *the contagion effect*. A depressed or troubled friend's feelings may rub off, making you depressed and troubled too. In serious situations, groups can create a "pressure cooker effect." In one study of Israeli women whose husbands were away at war, talking with others and listening to rumors exaggerated their feelings of danger and helplessness (Hobfoll & London, 1986).

Finally, relationships often impose *the burdens of care*. If too many people in your life require your energy and support, you can become exhausted. The work of caring for a chronically sick child, partner, or parent, a task that disproportionately falls on women in midlife, can become extremely stressful (Shumaker & Hill, 1991). In a study of 34 people who were taking care of a relative with Alzheimer's disease, the caregivers had lower percentages of T cells than the

Friends can be our greatest source of warmth, support, and fun . . .

control group and showed other abnormalities of the immune system (Kiecolt-Glaser, Glaser et al., 1987b).

Do the benefits of friendship outweigh these costs, or do they balance each other out? Do most people keep a sort of running balance sheet ("Well, Hildegard is a fussbudget, but she's very loyal")? To find out, Karen Rook (1984) interviewed 120 older women, expecting to find that social support would balance social conflicts. She thought that the women would overlook their friends' misbehavior by remembering all their good deeds. Not a chance. Rook found that emotional well-being was affected more by having *problems* with friends than by having their *support!* Hassles, conflicts, and disappointments lowered the women's well-being more than the friends' good deeds elevated their well-being. It's not that stress makes you more critical of your friends, by the way. Friends who do the wrong thing are an independent source of aggravation and worry (Pagel, Erdly, & Becker, 1987).

Several factors determine whether support helps or not (Dakof & Taylor, 1990; Shinn, Lehmann, & Wong, 1984):

1. *Amount of support.* Too much help and sympathy offered to someone in trouble can actually backfire, creating dependency and low self-esteem. For example, cancer patients who say they are receiving lots of support and that people are doing many things for them tend to have lower self-esteem and less sense of mastery than cancer patients who grumble about having no one to rely on (Revenson, Wollman, & Felton, 1983).

2. *Timing of support.* After bereavement, divorce, or loss, a person needs lots of understanding. Friends who try to stem grief prematurely are not helping the sufferer. Later, however, they can prove helpful by trying to get the friend back into a social life.

3. *Type of support.* For a friend's advice and sympathy to be effective, the sufferer must feel that the friend understands and has been in the same boat. That is, the friend's support must match what the sufferer needs (Dakof & Taylor, 1990). People who are under stress at work, for example, feel better if they can talk their problems over with their employers or co-workers. Their spouses generally lack the experience to offer constructive advice (Kobasa & Puccetti, 1983).

4. *Density of support.* In dense social networks, friends all know one another. Dense networks are good for your sense of stability and identity, and in a crisis everybody in the network pitches in. Women in particular seem to benefit

. . . and also sources of exasperation, headaches, and pressure.

from living in dense networks, which provide a form of social support they enjoy (Shumaker & Hill, 1991). But being in such a web can get sticky if you want to get out. Among women going back to school, those who were in a tightly knit group of friends showed worse adjustment, more physical symptoms, and lower self-esteem than women who were not in dense networks (Hirsch, 1981). "Good old friends" tend to want you to stay put. They can make you feel guilty for wanting to change.

Think for a moment about the future of friendship. Americans place great importance on their independence, yet studies suggest that the price they pay is widespread loneliness and anxiety. This dilemma—the choices between attachment and individualism, between tradition and change, between commitment to others and to oneself—is built into the very structure of American life (Bellah et al., 1985).

QUICK QUIZ

Match each of these stressful aspects of friendship with the correct description:

1. Your friends let you rage too long about an unfair experience.
2. You want to go away to graduate school, but your circle of friends wants you to stay with them.
3. You take on your friend's unhappiness.
4. Two friends are breaking up and each wants you to take his or her side.

a. contagion effect
b. conflicting demands
c. dense network
d. badly timed support

ANSWERS:

1. d 2. c 3. a 4. b

■ THE MIND-BODY CONNECTION

News reports often imply that health is mostly "mind over matter." What is the matter with overemphasizing the power of the mind—and, conversely, what's wrong with ignoring the mind's influence?

Sometimes it seems that people don't have problems any more; they only have "stress." If someone says, "Gee, I've been under a lot of stress lately," everyone immediately advises the person to relax, meditate, watch funny movies, or take a nap. But what if the person is about to be evicted for not paying the rent? Is advice to relax and reduce stress really going to help?

This question raises an important issue currently being debated in health psychology: In studying the origins of health and illness, are we overestimating psychological factors (such as optimism, humor, and attitude) and underestimating economic and biological conditions (such as unemployment and disease)?

As we have seen, psychological factors are a link in a long chain that connects stressors and illness (see Figure 15.3). But researchers disagree about how *strong* those links are (Cohen & Williamson, 1991). At one extreme, some physicians think that psychology counts for almost nothing. Disease is a biological matter, they say, and personality cannot influence a germ or a tumor. An editorial in the *New England Journal of Medicine* lashed out against the "psychologizing" of illness. "At a time when patients are already burdened by disease," the editor wrote, "they should not be further burdened by having to accept the responsibility for the outcome" (Angell, 1985). At the other extreme, numerous popular books state or imply that health is largely mind over matter and that even the worst diseases can be cured with jokes, papaya juice, and positive thinking.

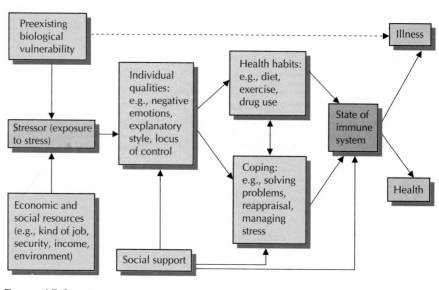

FIGURE 15.3

A model of stress and illness

Psychologists have found that the link between stressors and illness is not a simple straight line. As this diagram shows, many factors intervene between the stressors that strike a person and whether he or she becomes sick or remains healthy: predisposing biological factors; attitudes and feelings (such as emotions, optimism, and feelings of being in control); health habits (smoking, exercising, diet); and the individual's way of coping. But even this complicated model, which summarizes the topics discussed in this chapter, shows only some pieces of the picture. Can you fill in some arrows that have been omitted? For example, being ill can affect how people cope and the negative emotions they feel; friends and family, instead of providing social support, can become sources of stress themselves; and practicing good health habits may counteract an existing biological vulnerability to disease.

What, then, are the most reasonable lessons to be drawn from health psychology?

• Avoid simple-minded conclusions, such as "worrying causes warts." The relationships between stressors and illness are very complex. Individuals differ considerably in how their immune systems respond to stress. Immune function is usually suppressed during stressors such as bereavement, marital fighting, and exams; yet many individuals show no immune impairment (Manuck et al., 1991).

• In terms of action, follow "good old-fashioned motherly advice" and practice those *habits* associated with health, such as not smoking, not drinking excessively or in binges, and so on.

• In terms of psychological factors, remember that the effects of stress are worsened when you feel helpless. Although many things happen that are out of our control—exams, accidents, being born to certain parents, a flu epidemic, natural disasters—we do have control over how we cope with them. One way to restore a sense of control is to take responsibility for future actions, while not blaming yourself for past ones. In a study of cancer copers, for instance, adjustment was related to a woman's belief that she was not to blame for getting sick but that she was in charge of taking care of herself from now on (Taylor, Lichtman, & Wood, 1984). "I felt that I had lost control of my body somehow," said one woman, "and the way for me to get back some control was to find out as much as I could."

• Once you are in a stressful situation, some ways of coping are better than others. If the situation requires action, problem-solving techniques are more helpful than wallowing around indecisively or simply venting your emotions. But if the situation is a fact of life, people who can use humor, hope, distraction, reappraisal, and social comparisons will be better off than those who are overcome by depression and pessimism.

Finally, successful coping does not mean constant happiness or a life without pain. The healthy person faces problems, "copes" with them, and gets beyond them, but the problems are necessary if the person is to acquire coping skills that endure. To wish for a life without stress would be like wishing for a life without friends. The result might be calm, but it would be joyless, and ultimately hazardous to your health. The stresses of life—the daily hassles and the occasional tragedies—force us to grow, and to grow up.

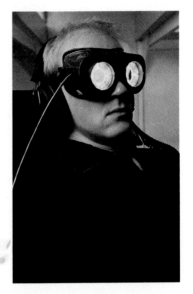

Many commercial techniques promise to help people "reduce stress." Here, a person tries an electronic route to relaxation, by wearing goggles that flash lights in the eyes and headphones that play tones and songs. Based on the information in this chapter, what would you predict about the long-term success of such methods?

TAKING PSYCHOLOGY WITH YOU

Noise, Crowds, and Weather: Living in a Stressful World

Writer Oscar Wilde once called the United States the noisiest nation that ever existed. That was in 1882. More than a century later, the din is even worse. Our ears are constantly assaulted by jackhammers, jet airplanes, motorcycles, lawn mowers, snowmobiles, chain saws, and blaring radios. To all that noise, add other nuisances, such as traffic jams, crowds, blizzards, and hot spells. What are the physical and psychological consequences of these environmental stressors?

Loud noise impairs the ability to think and work, even when you think you have adjusted to it. Children in elementary schools that were beneath the flight path for Los Angeles International Airport were compared with children in quieter classrooms (Cohen et al., 1980). The two groups were matched in age, ethnicity, race, and social class. Children in the noisy schools had higher blood pressure, were more distractable, and had more difficulty with puzzles and math problems than children in quieter schools. Children raised in noisy environments also have trouble learning how to discriminate between irrelevant noise and the relevant task. They either tune out too much in the environment or cannot tune out enough.

Studies find that noise contributes to cardiovascular problems, ulcers, irritability, fatigue, and aggressiveness, probably due to overstimulation of the autonomic nervous system. Continuous noise also has a cumulative effect on hearing. Many college students have already suffered significant hearing loss in the high-frequency range; their hearing resembles that of people more than twice their age. Disc jockeys in discotheques, truck drivers, fire fighters, dentists, machinists, and shipbuilders all have a higher incidence of substandard hearing than the norm.

The noise that is most stressful to people, however, is noise *they cannot control*. The rock song that you choose to listen to at jackhammer loudness may be pleasurable to you but intolerable to anyone who doesn't share your musical taste. The motorcycle without a muffler that makes you feel like Superman may make your neighbor feel like King Kong.

The same pattern of findings is true of crowding. At one time, environmental psychologists believed that crowding was a major source of most urban ills—crime, juvenile delinquency, infant mortality, family quarrels, and so on. This argument was not supported by subsequent research that controlled for income, class, and ethnicity (some cultures are used to high density; others are not). In Tokyo, where population density exceeds that of any U.S. city, crowding is not associated with crime.

Crowds themselves, then, are not necessarily stressful. Sometimes they are even part of the fun, as on New Year's Eve or at baseball games. As with noise, crowds become most stressful when they curtail your sense of freedom and control. They are stressful not when you *are* crowded but when you *feel* crowded. When people are able to work without interruptions in a densely packed room, they feel less crowded than if they work with interruptions in the same room with fewer people. Laboratory experiments and field studies find that the feeling of being trapped is more detrimental to health and intellectual performance than are most stressors (Taylor, 1991). These negative effects can last long after the stressful event is over.

Researchers therefore offer suggestions for asserting some control over environmental stressors and for living with those that are out of our control:

- If silence is golden, a little less noise will make us all a bit richer. So lower the volume of radios, TV sets, and stereos; don't turn stereos with earphones to full blast.
- If you work at a noisy job, be sure federal regulations are followed. To avoid permanent damage to the inner ear, constant noise levels for anyone working an eight-hour day may not exceed 90 decibels (dB).
- Try to find a quiet place to study where you won't be interrupted by unpredictable noise, such as your brothers fighting over the car or your roommates playing touch football.
- If you are trapped in a crowd over which you have no control (say, stalled in a traffic jam or in line at a busy store), relax. You can't do anything about it, and having a tantrum just raises your blood pressure and adds to the stress. Do some deep breathing, sing a song, or make lists.
- If the weather is making you irritable—either because it snowed again for the ninety-fourth day in a row or has been boiling hot for three weeks—well, join the group. Mark Twain tried to cheer up some New Englanders who were complaining about the unpredictable spring weather. "In the spring I have counted one hundred and thirty-six different kinds of weather," said Twain, "inside of twenty-four hours." As an editorial in an 1897 edition of the *Hartford Courant* lamented, "Everybody talks about the weather, but nobody does anything about it." You can't either. "Grin and bear it" is much less stressful than grumbling and being a bear.

SUMMARY

1. Hans Selye argued that environmental *stressors* (such as heat, pain, and toxins) cause the body to respond with fight-or-flee responses, as part of the *General Adaptation Syndrome*. If a stressor persists, it may overwhelm the body's ability to cope, and fatigue and illness may result. Current theories, however, emphasize the psychological factors that mediate between the stressor and the stress.

2. The immune system consists of several types of blood cells that are designed to recognize and destroy foreign substances, such as viruses. Researchers in the field of *psychoneuroimmunology* are studying how human behavior and emotion can affect the immune system. "A Closer Look" considers the physical and mental benefits of revealing secrets.

3. Certain major events, such as the death of a loved one or divorce, are known to be extremely stressful. Continuing situations of powerlessness and danger are more stressful than one major event. Daily hassles, such as traffic jams and interruptions, are also stressful, but primarily for people who are already anxious and reactive.

4. There are many possible links between emotion and disease: Disease may cause emotional changes; some emotions, such as worry, may cause unhealthy habits (such as smoking), which cause disease; a third factor may affect both emotionality and disease; and emotion and illness may affect each other in a complex feedback loop. Although evidence for a Type A personality is mixed, studies indicate that antagonistic hostility in particular, and negative emotions that cluster together in general, can lead to a "disease-prone personality." Another important personality factor that affects health is *explanatory style* (optimism or pessimism).

5. An important goal of health psychology is prevention—getting people to eat nutritious meals, quit (or never start) smoking, not abuse drugs, and the like. Some problems in prevention are that health habits are often entrenched in childhood, people have little incentive to change their patterns, and health habits are independent of one another and are unstable.

6. Feelings of personal control and self-efficacy affect a person's ability to tolerate pain, live with ongoing illness and stress, and recover from disease. People who have an *internal locus of control* believe that events are largely under their control, in contrast to people who have an *external locus of control*. However, control and health influence each other, and control is also affected by one's circumstances. People can sometimes have too strong a sense of control; the healthiest balance is taking responsibility for getting well without blaming oneself for getting sick. Health and well-being seem to depend on the right combination of *primary control* (trying to change the stressful situation) and *secondary control* (learning to accept the stressful situation). Cultures differ in the kind of control they emphasize.

7. Coping involves a person's active and adaptive efforts to manage demands that he or she feels are stressful. Methods of coping include *attacking the problem*; *rethinking the problem* (finding meaning in the experience, comparing oneself to others who are worse off, seeing the humor in the situation, and, once a decision is made, not thinking or worrying about it); and *living with the problem* (reducing the physical effects of stress through relaxation, meditation, or exercise). Healthy coping also involves *social interest* in other people.

8. Friendships, family, and acquaintances are important in maintaining physical health and emotional well-being. They provide emotional support, cognitive guidance, tangible support, companionship, and the sense of attachment. Friends can also be stressful—a source of hassles, conflicts, burdens, and betrayals. They sometimes provide the wrong kind of support or too much support or they offer support at the wrong time (too little too soon, too much too late). A *dense network*, in which many friends know each other, is good for stability and identity but can make change difficult if one member wants to break away.

9. Psychological factors are only one link in a long chain that connects stress and illness; illness is not "all in your mind" or easily cured with "the right attitude." Still, psychologists agree on the importance of learning good health habits and good coping skills. Coping with stress does not mean trying to live without pain, problems, or nuisances. It means learning how to live with them.

KEY TERMS

16

Psychological Disorders

Who in the rainbow can draw the line where the violet tint ends and the orange tint begins? Distinctly we see the difference of the colors, but where exactly does the one first blendingly enter into the other? So with sanity and insanity. In pronounced cases there is no question about them. But in [less obvious cases, few people are willing] to draw the exact line of demarcation . . . though for a fee some professional experts will.

HERMAN MELVILLE, *BILLY BUDD*

Joan of Arc heard voices that inspired her to martyrdom. Was she sane and saintly—or mad?

You don't have to be a psychologist to recognize extreme forms of abnormal behavior. A homeless woman stands on a street corner every night between midnight and 3:00 A.M., screaming obscenities and curses; by day, she is calm. A man in a shop tells you confidentially that his shoes have been bugged by the FBI, his phone is tapped, and his friends are spying on him for the CIA. An old man has kept every one of his daily newspapers going back to 1945 and, although there is no room in his house for anything else, he panics at the thought of giving them up.

When most people think of "abnormal behavior," they imagine these odd individuals or the bizarre stories that fill the newspapers—such as the shocking case of Jeffrey Dahmer, who murdered more than a dozen young men and then cannibalized their bodies. They assume that "abnormal" is the same as "insane," "crazy," or "sick." But most episodes of abnormal behavior are far less dramatic and would never make the nightly news. They occur when an individual cannot cope effectively with the stresses and problems of life. He or she may become so anxious and worried that work is impaired, or become severely depressed for a prolonged time, or begin to abuse drugs. In most cases, as the novelist Melville knew, there is no "exact line of demarcation" that indicates when normalcy ends and madness begins.

You will have noticed by now that we have tried hard to avoid traps of either-or thinking in this book, whether the subject is "right-brain versus left-brain" differences or "health versus illness." It is the same with "normal" and "abnormal," terms that describe a rainbow of behaviors, with many shadings of color and brightness. A particular problem is not a fixed point on the rainbow. It may shift over time; a person may go through episodes of inability to function. Problems also vary in intensity; they may be mildly uncomfortable, serious but endurable, or completely incapacitating. Psychologists and psychiatrists diagnose and treat a wide range of "abnormal" problems.

One of the most common worries that people have is, "Am I normal?" It is normal to fear being abnormal. Everyone on occasion has difficulties that seem too much to handle, that make us feel we just can't cope. It is also normal to experience Medical Students' Syndrome: deciding that you suffer from whatever disorder you are reading about. Precisely because many psychological disorders are so common, differing from "normal" problems only by a shade of intensity on the rainbow, it is often easy to conclude that you have them all. (We are tempted to add that this faulty conclusion is a pigment of the imagination.)

■ DEFINING ABNORMAL BEHAVIOR

Abnormal literally means "away from the normal," which implies that psychologists agree on what *normal* is. But they do not. These terms have produced considerable argument and debate. Definitions of "abnormal" depend on who is doing the defining: individuals, societies, or mental health professionals. Consider these five different definitions:

1. *Statistical deviation.* If "normal" is whatever most people do, then one definition of abnormal behavior is any behavior that is statistically rare or that deviates from the standard. Interpreted literally, this definition would lump together "abnormal" behavior that is destructive (such as murder), "abnormal" behavior that is charmingly unique (collecting ceramic alligators), and "abnormal" behavior that is desirable (genius).

Statistics themselves, of course, are neither good nor bad, but some people confuse numbers with personal values. They cite statistics to pressure each other (or themselves) into conforming, saying "everybody does it. . . ." If enough people are doing something, they conclude, it is "normal" behavior and hence acceptable. But few psychologists would agree that it is normal or desirable for a community or nation to endorse sadistic practices (as was true in Nazi Germany) or to require the suicide of its members (as was true of the religious cult of Jonestown).

2. *Violation of cultural standards.* A second definition of abnormal behavior is any action that violates the standards of a group. Every society sets up its own standards of appropriate behavior and the rules that people are expected to follow. Some kinds of behavior are shared by many cultures, such as wearing clothes and not committing murder. Other behaviors might be normal in one culture and abnormal in another.

For example, seeing visions might be a sign of schizophrenia in a twentieth-century farmer, but a sign of healthy religious fervor in a thirteenth-century monk. In America, people who have hallucinations of a deceased spouse or other relative are thought to be abnormal. Actually, this experience is not uncommon during bereavement; it is just that grieving spouses don't talk about it much because they fear being considered "crazy." But in some cultures, such as those of the Chinese and the Hopi Indians, hallucinations are regarded as normal expressions of grief. In such societies, hallucinations during bereavement are more prevalent and acceptable (DePaola & DePaola, 1988). The "line on the rainbow" between normal and abnormal hallucinations is often very fuzzy indeed (Bentall, 1990).

Certainly many ideas about abnormal behavior are culturally and historically relative. In the nineteenth century a woman or a black person who wanted to be a physician or even go to college would have been considered "abnormal." Today, many behaviors once considered abnormal are now accepted as part of the diversity of life and culture. For instance, psychologists no longer regard homosexuality as an abnormal sexual orientation or a mental "illness." As our world and our values change, other behaviors have moved from normal to "abnormal." A man or woman with no interest in sex at all was once considered normal (and, in some religions, at the pinnacle of morality). Today, many psychologists regard a *lack* of sexual interest as a disorder.

People all over the world paint their bodies—or parts of their bodies—but what seems perfectly normal in one culture may seem "abnormal" in another. These Congolese Kota boys paint their faces as part of a normal rite of passage to adulthood.

3. *Maladaptive behavior.* Many psychologists define abnormality as any behavior that is maladaptive for the individual or society. This definition would classify as abnormal a woman who is so afraid of crowds that she cannot leave her house, a man who drinks so much he cannot keep a job, and a student who is so anxious about failure that he cannot write term papers or take exams. It also covers individuals who say they feel fine and deny that there is anything wrong, but who behave in ways that are disruptive or dangerous to others: the child who sets fires, the compulsive gambler who loses the family savings.

4. *Emotional distress.* A fourth definition identifies abnormality by a person's suffering. A person may conform to all the rules and norms of his or her community, managing to work and live adequately, yet privately feel on the verge of despair. He or she may feel anxious, afraid, angry, depressed, or lonely. By these criteria, according to a nationwide study of 18,500 randomly selected people, nearly a third of all Americans will have one or more emotional disorders of varying duration at some time in their lives (Regier et al., 1988). The benefit of this approach is that it takes the person's own distress as a measure of abnormality instead of imposing the same standard for everyone. A behavior that is unendurable or upsetting for one person (such as lack of interest in sex) may be acceptable and thus no problem to another.

5. *The legal definition: impaired judgment and lack of self-control.* In law, the definition of abnormality rests primarily on whether a person is aware of the consequences of his or her actions and can control his or her behavior. Psychologists and psychiatrists do not use the terms *sanity* or *insanity* in discussing abnormal behavior. These are legal terms only, for purposes of assessing a person's ability to stand trial.

How can we make sense of all of these definitions? All of them are useful and no one of them is enough. Therefore, we will define **abnormality** broadly, as any behavior or emotional state that causes an individual great suffering or worry; that is self-defeating or self-destructive; or that is maladaptive and disrupts the person's relationships or larger community. Even by this comprehensive definition, judgments of abnormality can be influenced by cultural standards and values as well as by statistical frequency. Many people will have some mental-health problem in the course of their lives. This is normal.

QUICK QUIZ

Which definition of "abnormality" does each example from Western culture best illustrate?

1. Arthur is declared mentally incompetent to stand trial for murder.
2. Bea has stopped accepting dates because she feels anxious in crowds.
3. Chuck has a rare reading disability.
4. Dena has tattooed her face because she thinks tattoos are beautiful.
5. Ernie denies he has a problem, but his drinking has cost him his job.

ANSWERS:

1. legal 2. emotional distress 3. statistical deviation 4. violation of cultural standards 5. maladaptive behavior.

■ **abnormality** (or psychological disorder)
Any behavior or emotional state that causes personal suffering, that is self-destructive, or that is maladaptive.

■ DILEMMAS OF DIAGNOSIS

From the beginning of human society, people have suffered from sadness, anxiety, and bizarre delusions. From the beginning, people have tried to classify these disorders, explain them, and cure them. Yet even today, psychologists still fail to agree on how many, or which, conditions can be classified as mental disorders. As George Albee (1985) put it, "Appendicitis, a brain tumor and chicken pox are the same everywhere, regardless of culture or class; mental conditions, it seems, are not."

In 1952, the American Psychiatric Association published the first edition of the *Diagnostic and Statistical Manual of Mental Disorders (DSM)*. The first edition, *DSM-I*, listed 60 types of mental "illness." In 1968, the *DSM-II* appeared, this time with 145 categories. In 1980, an even fatter third edition, *DSM-III*, was published, containing 230 disorders—including tobacco dependence, marital conflicts, and sexual problems as well as brain disease and schizophrenia. The revised third edition, *DSM-III-R*, appeared in 1987, having jumped to 292 disorders. A fourth edition, *DSM-IV*, is scheduled to appear late in 1993, with still more refinements.

The primary aim of the *DSM* is *descriptive:* to provide clear criteria of diagnostic categories, so that clinicians and researchers can agree on the disorders they are talking about, study them, and treat them. (For a list of its major categories, see Table 16.1.) The *DSM* is directed to all clinicians regardless of their theoretical orientation, and it makes few assumptions about causes of the disorders it describes. (In many cases, the causes are not known.) Each disorder is identified by its behavioral signs. Where possible, information is also provided about typical age of onset, predisposing factors, course of the disorder, prevalence (rare or common), sex ratio, associated problems, and history of family problems.

The *DSM* further classifies disorders according to five *axes*, or five clinically important factors:

• The primary diagnosis of the problem, such as an anxiety disorder.
• Ingrained aspects of the individual's personality that are likely to affect the patient's behavior and ability to be treated, such as a history of extreme shyness.
• Any items in a person's medical or physical history that are relevant to the problem, such as the fact that the patient once fainted while giving a speech.
• The extent and severity of recent stressors in the patient's life, such as a recent breakup of a relationship or the death of a parent.
• An estimate of the patient's highest level of functioning in work, relationships, and leisure time. This factor indicates whether the problem is of recent origin or of long duration, and how incapacitating it is.

It is important to understand the claims, intentions, and methods of the *DSM* because the manual has had an extraordinary impact in the United States and worldwide. It has standardized the categories of what is, and what is not, a mental illness. Its categories and terminology have become the common language of most clinicians and researchers. Virtually all textbooks in psychiatry and psychology base their discussions of mental disorders on the *DSM*. Insurance companies require clinicians to assign their patients the appropriate *DSM* code number of the diagnosed disorder. Attorneys and judges often refer to the manual's list of mental disorders, even though the *DSM* warns that its categories "may not be wholly relevant to legal judgments," such as those of individual responsibility and competency.

Because of the growing power of the *DSM* to define mental disorders, it is important to know its limitations. Critics point to the following concerns about the scientific basis of diagnosis in general and the *DSM* in particular:

1. *Does giving a label to a collection of symptoms lead to overdiagnosis and self-fulfilling prophecies?* Over the years, clinicians and philosophers have observed that when people have a tool, they will use it; Abraham Kaplan (1967) called this tendency "The Law of the Instrument." "If you give a small boy a hammer,"

TABLE 16.1

Major Diagnostic Categories of Mental Disorder in the *DSM*

Disorders first evident in infancy, childhood, or adolescence include mental retardation, attention-deficit disorders (such as hyperactivity or an inability to concentrate), eating disorders, and developmental problems.

Organic mental disorders are those resulting from brain damage, degenerative diseases such as syphilis or Alzheimer's, toxic substances, or drugs.

Psychoactive substance use disorders are problems associated with excessive use of or withdrawal from alcohol, barbiturates, opiates, cocaine, amphetamines, and other drugs.

Schizophrenia consists of disorders characterized by delusions, hallucinations, and disturbances in thinking and perception.

Delusional (paranoid) disorders are characterized by excessive suspiciousness, jealousy, and delusions of persecution.

Mood disorders include major depression, extreme elation (mania), swings between the two (bipolar disorder), and chronic depressed mood (dysthymia).

Anxiety disorders include generalized anxiety disorder, specific fears (phobias), panic attacks with or without agoraphobia, post-traumatic stress disorder, and obsessive thoughts or compulsive rituals.

Somatoform disorders involve individual reports of physical symptoms (such as paralysis, heart palpitations, dizziness) for which no organic cause can be found. This category includes *hypochondria,* the extreme preoccupation with one's health and the unfounded conviction that one is ill, and *conversion disorder,* in which a physical symptom (such as a paralyzed arm or blindness) serves a psychological function.

Dissociative disorders share a sudden alteration in consciousness, identity, or behavior. Alterations in consciousness include psychogenic *amnesia,* in which important events cannot be remembered after a traumatic event; alterations in identity include *multiple personality disorder,* in which normally integrated identity splits into two or more independent identities.

Sexual disorders include problems of sexual (gender) identity, such as transsexualism (wanting to be the opposite gender); sexual performance (such as premature ejaculation, lack of orgasm, lack of desire); and paraphilias (unusual or bizarre imagery or acts—such as fetishism, sadomasochism, or exhibitionism—that are necessary for sexual arousal).

Impulse control disorders involve an inability to resist an impulse to perform some act that is harmful to the individual or to others, such as pathological gambling, stealing (*kleptomania*), setting fires (*pyromania*), or violent rages.

Personality disorders are inflexible and maladaptive personality patterns that cause distress to the individual or impair the individual's ability to function.

Conditions not attributable to a mental disorder that are a focus of attention or treatment include "problems in living" for which people seek help, such as marital and family conflicts, academic difficulties, procrastination, job dissatisfaction, and problems associated with life changes.

Kaplan wrote, "it will turn out that everything he runs into needs pounding." So it is, some argue, with psychotherapists. Give them the instruments to diagnose disorders, and everything they run into will need treatment. For example, as we will discuss further, up until 1980 only 200 cases of "Multiple Personality Disorder" (MPD) had ever been diagnosed. Since 1980, when the *DSM-III* included new criteria for identifying MPD, more than 2,000 cases have been reported. Does this mean that the disorder is being better identified, or that it is being overdiagnosed because clinicians are looking for it (Holmes, 1991)?

Jonas Robitscher, criticizing his own profession in his book *The Powers of Psychiatry* (1980), was concerned that the act of diagnosing someone threatens the person's job security, family relationships, and self-concept. He and many others have observed that diagnoses can create a self-fulfilling prophecy, in which a person tries to conform to the assigned label. They can also blind observers to *changes* in a person's behavior. Once a person has acquired a label ("ex-mental patient"; "borderline schizophrenic"), others often continue to see him or her in terms of the label (Rosenhan, 1973; see Chapter 18).

2. *Are some "mental illnesses" really problems in living?* Other critics object to the social implications of diagnosis (Szasz, 1961/1967). They remind us that the *DSM* is not called "The Diagnostic and Statistical Manual of Mental Disorders and a Whole Bunch of Everyday Problems." By lumping together problems in living (such as anxiety caused by a rift with one's parents) with true mental illness (such as having delusions), these critics say, psychiatric diagnosis implies that everyday problems are comparable to medical problems. Normal stresses no longer cause mere worry and unhappiness, but "anxiety" and "depression." Moreover, these critics are concerned that once people are given a formal diagnosis for their problems, they may feel absolved of responsibility for their actions (see Figure 16.1).

3. *Can the art of diagnosis be made scientific?* Some clinicians argue that the whole enterprise of the *DSM* is a foolhardy effort to impose a veneer of science on what is ultimately an art form. This is why, they say, the reliability in tests of many *DSM* guidelines has consistently been poor: that is, even when clinicians use the *DSM*'s list of criteria for diagnosing disorders, many still fail to agree with one another on a given patient's problem (Dumont, 1987; Kutchins & Kirk, 1986).

Diagnosis of mental disorder rests on human judgment, these clinicians say, governed by all the wisdom and prejudice that human judgment involves (Dumont, 1987). Many of the decisions about what categories of mental illness should be included or excluded in the *DSM* are not based on empirical evidence, but on group consensus. When the American Psychiatric Association

Bloom County by Berke Breathed. © 1989, Washington Post Writers Group. Reprinted with permission.

FIGURE 16.1

When does a disorder diminish responsibility?
Clinicians have identified many different categories of abnormal behavior in order to diagnose and treat people effectively. But the nature of diagnosis raises important, critical questions that society must grapple with: If people have a "disorder," are they still responsible for their actions? Some conditions legally qualify people as having "diminished responsibility" for their actions. Which disorders described in this chapter would you include? In your own life, where would you draw the line between labeling or explaining people's problems and excusing the behavior they attribute to their problems?

proposed to remove homosexuality from the *DSM*, it did not base its decision on the research showing that homosexuals were no more or less disturbed than heterosexuals. Rather, it *took a vote of its members* (Bayer, 1981). Over the years, psychiatrists have voted out many other "disorders" that once reflected the beliefs of the time, such as hysteria, masochism, and nymphomania.

Of course, it was appropriate for them to do so. The point to underscore is that as times change, so do ideas about mental illness. And that, in turn, means that clinicians must be aware of how their own beliefs and leanings affect their clinical judgments, even if they are trying to follow objective criteria. For example, in one study, 47 therapists were randomly assigned to view one of two versions of a videotaped simulation of a depressed male client. The tapes were identical except for the man's job and family roles, which were portrayed as either traditional (he was the breadwinner) or nontraditional (he was a "househusband" whose wife earned the family income). Later, the therapists evaluated the man's mental health, assigned a diagnosis, and outlined a proposed treatment. They judged the nontraditional man as being more disturbed than the traditional man, and treated him more harshly (Robertson & Fitzgerald, 1990).

Critics have observed that the *DSM* wants to look like a purely objective set of disorders, as if there were no bias or subjective choice involved (Tiefer, 1992). Yet the *DSM* is by its very nature subjective, both in terms of what is defined as a mental illness—and what is not (see "Think About It").

Advocates of the *DSM* argue that when the manual is used correctly, diagnoses are more accurate and bias is reduced; new field studies aim to improve the empirical basis of the clinical categories (Barlow, 1991; Spitzer & Williams, 1988). A study of psychiatric patients in Maryland, for instance, found better

THINK ABOUT IT

The Politics of Diagnosis

They called me mad, and I called them mad, and damn them, they outvoted me.

Nathaniel Lee, 17th-century playwright, on being consigned to a mental hospital (Porter, 1987)

In the early years of the nineteenth century, a physician named Samuel Cartwright argued that many slaves were suffering from two forms of mental illness: *drapetomania,* an uncontrollable urge to escape from slavery, and *dysathesia aethiopica,* the symptoms of which included destroying property on the plantation, being disobedient, talking back, refusing to work, and fighting back when beaten. "Sanity for a slave was synonymous with submission," notes Hope Landrine (1988), "and protest and seeking freedom were the equivalent of psychopathology." Thus doctors could assure slaveowners that a mental illness, not the intolerable condition of slavery, made slaves seek freedom.

Today, "drapetomania" sounds foolish and cruel. Surely, most people would say, the bad old days in psychiatric diagnosis are past, thanks to modern technology and the scientific method. Yet many psychologists have shown that cultural prejudices still affect the nature of diagnosis, turning normal processes into pathology and often ignoring the conditions of people's lives that may create emotional symptoms (Landrine, 1989).

The story of the revision of the *DSM-III* illustrates how old biases can appear in modern form (Caplan, 1991). Work groups were assigned to evaluate existing diagnoses and make corrections and additions. One group proposed several new categories, including something called "late luteal phase dysphoric disorder" (a fancy term for "premenstrual syndrome") and "self-defeating personality disorder" (a fancy term for "masochism"). Many psychologists immediately criticized these proposals for their lack of empirical support, the biased judgments that had inspired them, and the consequences for the one group that would most be affected by them—women (Albee, Canetto, & Sefa–Dedeh, 1991).

For example, critics of the "premenstrual syndrome" entry pointed out that, as we saw in Chapter 4, there is no coherent definition of this alleged "syndrome"; almost all women have some

accuracy in the diagnosis of schizophrenia and mood disorders than other studies had, apparently because the physicians were more closely following *DSM* criteria (Pulver et al., 1988). Other advocates argue that labeling a disorder helps people identify the source of their unhappiness and leads them to proper treatment. They respond to the criticism that there is no such thing as "mental illness" by showing that some mental disorders, such as schizophrenia and depression, occur in all societies (Kleinman, 1988). Anthropologist Jane Murphy (1976), who lived with the Inuit of Alaska and the Yorubas of Nigeria, expected that their ideas of severe abnormality would be different from those held in Western culture; this was not generally the case. In every society there are individuals who have delusions or who can't control their behavior. Everywhere, such persons are considered abnormal.

We will return to some of these controversies as we examine some of the major categories of disorder in the *DSM.*

■ ANXIETY DISORDERS

The body, sensibly, prepares us to feel anxiety (a general state of apprehension) or fear (apprehension about a specific event) when we are facing dangerous, unfamiliar, or stressful situations, such as making a first parachute jump or waiting for important news. In the short run, these are adaptive emotions that prepare us to cope with danger. But some individuals are more prone than others to irrational fear or to a chronic state of anxiety. Such individuals are found in all countries (Barlow, 1988, 1990).

Is this woman feeling normal fear or unreasonable panic? (Turn the page.)

physical symptoms, which is *normal;* and although men have as many symptoms and mood changes as women do, the work group did not propose a category called, say, "hypertestosterone syndrome" (HTS). Critics noted that even though some women have severe premenstrual symptoms, that fact did not mean they had a problem that should be included in a manual of *mental disorders.* Thyroid abnormalities can cause mood changes too, but no one would propose putting thyroid abnormalities in a manual of mental disorders. Regarding female reproductive processes as a source of mental illness, critics said, is part of a long tradition that regards women, but not men, as being at the mercy of their hormones (Tavris, 1992).

Many women also protested the proposed category called "self- defeating personality disorder." They agreed that some individuals do behave in apparently foolish, self-destructive ways: They stay in bad relationships; they don't take advantage of opportunities; they seem to tolerate heaps of abuse, verbal and physical. Yet there is no research evidence that a "masochistic personality" exists (Baumeister & Scher, 1988). "The basis on which this strongly held belief . . . persists," observed Renee Garfinkel (1986), "is chummy, anecdotal reports of one believer to another."

Psychologists presented research to the *DSM* work group showing that many women remain in bad relationships for situational and economic reasons (Strube, 1988). By implying that self-defeating behavior is rooted entirely in a woman's neurotic needs and not in the tangible conditions of her life, they said, this diagnostic category encourages people to blame the victim of an abusive man or an intolerable situation, while letting the man or the situation off the hook (L. Brown, 1986; L. Walker, 1986).

The work group did not exclude these categories in the *DSM-III-R;* they compromised by listing them in an appendix as problems "needing further study." But it did agree to drop the one proposed new category that affected only men: "paraphilic coercive disorder," which would apply to men who rape. In this case only, the work group agreed with women who were concerned that rapists diagnosed as having such a "disorder" would not be held responsible for their crimes.

What does this story suggest about the relationship between values and science, gender stereotypes and the diagnosis of disorder? Is it possible to develop diagnostic criteria that are more scientifically based than a group vote? What do you think?

People who are overly fearful or anxious are usually psychologically healthy in other ways. But often the fear that their fear is "crazy" makes it even worse. It is no help when friends tell them what they already know, that they are being irrational. As Dianne Chambless has observed, "When someone says to you, 'You must be crazy to be afraid of [substitute your favorite fear here],' that person is in effect saying, 'Your fear is different from my fear, and I don't understand yours.'"

Fear and anxiety can appear in several distinctly different forms and disorders: *generalized anxiety disorder*, marked by long-lasting, continuous feelings of apprehension and doom; *phobias*, unrealistic fears of specific things or situations; and *obsessive-compulsive disorders*, in which people develop irrational thoughts and rituals designed to ward off anxious feelings.

Generalized Anxiety

Generalized anxiety disorder is marked by continuous anxiety that has lasted a month or more and that isn't brought on by physical causes such as disease, drugs, or drinking too much coffee. Symptoms include:

* *Motor tension:* shakiness, jitteriness, muscle aches, inability to relax, fidgeting, and restlessness.
* *Autonomic hyperactivity:* sweating, pounding heart, cold and clammy hands, dry mouth, dizziness, intestinal disorders, high resting pulse.
* *Apprehensive expectation:* constant anticipation of disaster to oneself or others, brooding about misfortune.
* *Vigilance and scanning*: difficulty concentrating; feeling "on edge," irritable, and impatient; excessive worrying.

There is no single cause of chronic anxiety. There are several *predisposing factors*, including hereditary predisposition, inadequate coping mechanisms, traumatic events, and psychological dispositions, such as having unrealistic goals or unreasonable beliefs (Beck, 1988; Clark, 1988). There are also many *precipitating factors* that produce anxiety and keep it going. You are likely to feel anxious when you are in a situation in which others continually express their disapproval of you, or when you have to adapt yourself to an environment that doesn't fit your personality (such as being a slow-paced person in a fast-moving job).

When chronic anxiety results from experience with danger, it may create *post-traumatic stress disorder* (PTSD). PTSD consists of a set of emotional symptoms that are common in people who have suffered traumatic experiences, such as war and combat, rape and other assaults, and natural disasters such as earthquake. The reaction might occur immediately or it might be delayed for years. Typical symptoms include *reexperiencing the trauma* in recurrent thoughts or dreams; *"psychic numbing,"* a sense of detachment from others and an inability to feel happiness, intimacy, and sexual desire; *extreme alertness*, difficulty concentrating, and insomnia; and, in the case of war and natural disaster, *feelings of guilt about surviving* when others did not.

A new category has been proposed for inclusion in the *DSM-IV*, called Disorders of Extreme Stress (or "complex PTSD"), which would apply to survivors of extreme, prolonged trauma: victims of torture in concentration camps, battered women, children who are repeatedly and severely beaten and humiliated by their parents, hostages, and captives in slave labor camps or brothels (Herman, 1992). To survive such brutal conditions, children and adults often develop a set of severe but mixed symptoms, including depression, anxiety, anger, nightmares, delusions, addictions, self-mutilation, and physical ailments. They

It is normal to feel afraid when you jump out of a plane for the first time. But people with anxiety disorders feel as if they are jumping out of planes all the time.

■ **generalized anxiety disorder**
A continuous state of anxiety, lasting a month or more, marked by signs of motor tension, autonomic hyperactivity (e.g., a pounding heart), constant apprehension, and difficulties in concentration.

are often skilled in altering consciousness of their unendurable reality, through denial, thought suppression, trances, hallucinations, and dissociation (Herman, 1992).

Phobias

A **phobia** is an unrealistic fear of a specific situation, activity, or thing. In the general population, there are many common phobias, such as fear of heights (acrophobia); fear of closed spaces (claustrophobia); fear of dirt and germs (mysophobia); and fear of such animals as snakes, dogs, insects, and mice (zoophobia). There are also more idiosyncratic fears, such as porphyrophobia (fear of purple); triskaidekaphobia (fear of the number 13); and brontophobia (fear of thunder).

People who have a *social phobia* have a persistent, irrational fear of situations in which they will be observed by others. They fear that they will do or say something humiliating or embarrassing. Common examples of social phobias are fears of speaking or performing in public, using public restrooms, eating in public, and writing in the presence of others.

By far the most disabling fear is **agoraphobia,** which accounts for more than half of the phobia cases for which people seek treatment. Disregard the dictionary and popular definition of "fear of open spaces." The Greek *agora* was the social, political, business, and religious center of town. It was the public meeting place away from home. The essential feature in what agoraphobics fear is being alone in a public place from which escape might be difficult or help unavailable. They may report a great variety of specific fears—such as fears of public buses, driving in traffic or in tunnels, eating in restaurants, or going to parties—but the underlying fear is of being away from a safe place (usually home) or a safe person (usually a parent or spouse).

Agoraphobia may begin with a series of **panic attacks** that seem to appear for no reason. A panic attack is a sudden onset of intense fear or terror, with feelings of impending doom. It may last from a few minutes to (more rarely) several hours, with intense symptoms of anxiety: trembling and shaking; dizziness; chest pain or discomfort; feelings of unreality; hot and cold flashes; sweating; tingling in hands or feet; and a fear of dying, going crazy, or losing control. The attack is so unexpected and so scary that the agoraphobic-to-be begins to avoid situations that he or she thinks may provoke another one. After a while, anything that sets off emotional arousal, from an argument to mild excitement, feels too much like anxiety, and the person with agoraphobia will try to avoid it. Because so many of the actions associated with this phobia are designed to help the person avoid a panic attack, researchers often describe agoraphobia as a "fear of fear" rather than a fear of places (Chambless, 1988).

People who have panic attacks are found throughout the world, in industrial and nonindustrial societies (Barlow, 1990). The common symptoms are heart palpitations, dizziness, and faintness, but culture influences the likelihood of other telltale signs. Feelings of choking or being smothered, numbness, and fear of dying are most common in Latin America and southern Europe; fear of public places is most common in northern Europe and America; and a fear of going crazy is more common in the Americas than in Europe. In Greenland, some fishermen suffer from "kayak-angst": a sudden attack of dizziness and fear that occurs while they are fishing in small, one-person kayaks (Amering & Katschnig, 1990).

Some investigators believe that panic attacks may be caused by biological abnormalities, because they tend to run in families. Studies of twins suggest a heritable component in this disorder, which seems to be a tendency for the body to respond to stress with a sudden "alarm" reaction. (For other people, the response may be headaches or ulcers.) During a stressful time, the individual has

■ **phobia**
An unrealistic fear of a specific situation, activity, or object.

■ **agoraphobia**
"Fear of fear"; a set of phobias, often set of by a panic attack, sharing the basic fear of being away from a safe place or person.

■ **panic attack**
A brief feeling of intense fear and impending doom or death, accompanied by intense physiological symptoms such as rapid breathing and pulse, sweaty palms, and dizziness. Repeated attacks are the basis of panic disorder.

The Disease Germ Is
More Dangerous
Than the Mad Dog

Lysol
Disinfectant

Cultural compulsions? What is a normal concern with hygiene in one culture could seem abnormal in another. This Lysol ad played on Americans' fears of disease by warning about the "unseen menace—more threatening, more fatal, more cruel than a million mad dogs— . . . the disease germ"!

■ **obsessions**
Recurrent, unwished-for, persistent thoughts and images.
■ **compulsions**
Repetitive, ritualized, stereotyped behaviors that a person feels must be done to avoid disaster.
■ **obsessive-compulsive disorder**
An anxiety disorder in which a person feels trapped in repetitive thoughts and ritual behaviors designed to reduce anxiety.

a panic attack that seems to come "out of the blue." In fact, however, the attack is often related to the physical arousal of stress, prolonged emotion, exercise, drugs (such as caffeine or cigarettes), or existing worry (Beck, 1988; Barlow, 1990; Lang, 1988).

Having a panic attack is not uncommon. But the essential difference between people who go on to develop a disorder and those who don't lies in *how the person interprets this bodily reaction.* Healthy people who have occasional panic attacks dismiss them as being unimportant—a result of some passing crisis, something they ate at lunch, or a difficult day at work (Barlow, 1990). But people who develop a full-fledged panic disorder begin to worry about possible *future* attacks. They regard the attack as a sign of impending death or disaster instead of a passing moment of agitation. Agoraphobia develops when they begin to avoid any situation or provocation that they fear will set off another attack.

Obsessions and Compulsions

Obsessions are recurrent, persistent thoughts, images, or impulses that seem to come unbidden and unwished for. The person often finds them frightening and sometimes repugnant. For example, he or she may have repetitive thoughts of killing a child, of becoming contaminated by shaking hands, or of having unknowingly hurt someone in a traffic accident. These obsessive thoughts take many forms, but they are alike in reflecting maladaptive ways of reasoning and processing information.

Some people develop obsessive thoughts because they have difficulty managing anger. In one case, a man had repeated images of hitting his 3-year-old son with a hammer. Unable to explain his "horrible thoughts" about his beloved son, he assumed he was going insane. Most parents, in fact, have occasional negative feelings about their children, and may even entertain a fleeting thought of murder, but they recognize that these brief reactions are normal and that feelings are not the same as actions. The man, it turned out, felt that his son had usurped his place in his wife's affections, but he was unable to reveal his anger and hurt to his wife directly (Carson & Butcher, 1992).

Compulsions are repetitive, ritual behaviors that a person carries out in a stereotyped fashion, designed to prevent some disaster. For example, a woman *must* check the furnace, lights, locks, oven, and fireplace three times before she can sleep. A man *must* wash his hands and face eight times before he leaves the house. The most common compulsions are hand washing, counting, touching, and checking. Most people do not enjoy these rituals and even realize that the behavior is senseless. But if they try to break the ritual, they feel mounting anxiety that is relieved only by giving in to the compulsion. They are like the man who constantly snaps his fingers to keep tigers away. "But there aren't any tigers here," says a friend. "You see! It works!" is the answer.

Many people have trivial compulsions and superstitious rituals; baseball players are famous for them. Obsessions and compulsions become serious when they trouble the individual and interfere with his or her life—or when they interfere with the life of the *target* of a person's obsession. Indeed, some states have passed "anti-stalking" laws, which prohibit people who have obsessions about celebrities (or about lovers who spurned them) from compulsively following or threatening them.

Obsessive-compulsive disorder can begin in childhood and it occurs in both sexes. People with this disorder usually realize their thoughts and behaviors are abnormal, but they feel helpless to stop. For one young man, stairs became a treadmill: "At first I'd walk up and down the stairs only three to four times," he recalls. "Later I had to run up and down 63 times in 45 minutes. If I failed, I had to start all over again from the beginning. Then other weird behaviors, such as compulsive washing, started to kick in . . . They took on a life of their own and became the enemy. I led two lives—one a hidden nightmare, the other normal" (quoted in King, 1989).

Anxiety disorders, uncomfortable or painful as they can be, are at least a sign of commitment to the future. They mean a person can anticipate the future enough to worry about it. But sometimes people's hopes for the future become extinguished. They are no longer anxious that something *may* go wrong; they are convinced it *will* go wrong, so there is no point in trying. This is a sign, as we will see next, of the disorder of depression.

QUICK QUIZ

A. We hope you don't feel anxious about matching the term on the left with its description on the right:

1. social phobia	**a.** need to perform a ritual
2. generalized anxiety disorder	**b.** fear of fear; of being trapped in public
3. post-traumatic stress disorder	**c.** continuing sense of doom and worry
4. agoraphobia	**d.** repeated, unwanted thoughts
5. compulsion	**e.** fear of meeting new people
6. obsession	**f.** anxiety state following severe shock

 B. Two psychologists are debating the case of an anxious and depressed Japanese-American man who, with 112,000 other Japanese Americans during World War II, lost his job and home and was forcibly sent to a U.S. internment camp. Dr. Smith diagnoses post-traumatic stress disorder. Dr. Jones believes that because the man's symptoms result from an act of social injustice, the diagnosis should be something like "post-oppression disorder" (Loo, 1991). Can you identify the main *assumption* in the kind of label each psychologist is using?

ANSWERS:

A. 1. e 2. c 3. f 4. b 5. a 6. d **B.** Dr. Smith assumes that the origins of the man's unhappiness lie within him, in his own personal reaction to the trauma of imprisonment; the implied solution is psychotherapy. Dr. Jones assumes that the man's unhappiness is a result of a specific miscarriage of justice; the implied solution, in addition to psychotherapy, might involve a social remedy, such as reparations.

■ MOOD DISORDERS

Many people use the word *depression* to describe normal sadness, gloom, and loss of pep, and they mistake these normal states for an abnormal "syndrome." Of course, everyone feels depressed at times. Clinical depression, however, goes beyond normal sadness over life problems, and even beyond the wild grief that may accompany tragedy or bereavement.

Depression and Mania

Clinical depression is so widespread that it has been called the common cold of psychiatric disturbances. **Major depression** differs from chronic depressed mood, a condition called *dysthymia* [dis-THIGH-me-a] or "depressive personality," in the intensity and duration of symptoms. Major depression usually occurs as an intense episode that, like a horrible flu attack, interrupts a person's

■ **major depression**
A mood disorder involving disturbances in emotion (excessive sadness), behavior (apathy and loss of interest in usual activities), cognition (distorted thoughts of hopelessness and low self-esteem), and body function (fatigue, loss of appetite).

In his book Darkness Visible, *novelist William Styron described his descent into depression and his recovery: "Mysteriously and in ways that are totally remote from normal experience," he wrote, "the gray drizzle of horror induced by depression takes on the quality of physical pain."*

normal functioning. Dysthymia consists of milder depressive symptoms that *are* the person's normal functioning.

Severe depression consists of emotional, behavioral, cognitive, and physical changes. Depressed people report despair and hopelessness. They are tearful and weepy, often "for no reason." They think often of death or suicide. They lose interest or pleasure in their usual activities. They feel unable to get up and do things; it takes an enormous effort just to get dressed. Their thinking patterns feed this mood. They exaggerate minor failings, ignore or discount positive events ("She didn't mean that compliment; she was only being polite"), and focus on anything that goes wrong ("Just my luck to miss that train"). Unlike normal sadness or grief, major depression involves low self-esteem (Beck, 1987). Emotionally healthy grieving people do not see themselves as completely worthless and unlovable, and they know that grief will pass. Depressed people interpret all losses as signs of their personal failure and conclude that they will never be happy again.

Depression is accompanied by physical changes as well. The depressed person may stop eating (or overeat), have difficulty falling asleep or sleeping through the night, lose sexual desire, have trouble concentrating, and feel tired all the time. Some sufferers have other physical reactions, such as inexplicable pain or headaches. (Because these symptoms can also be signs of physical illness, people should have a thorough medical exam before depression is diagnosed.) About half of all people who go through a period of major depression will do so only once. Others have recurrent bouts. Some people have episodes that are many years apart, while others have clusters of depressive episodes over a few years. Alarmingly, depression and suicide rates among young people have increased in recent years. (See "Taking Psychology with You" on page 601.)

At the opposite pole from depression is *mania*, an abnormally high state of exhilaration. You might not think it is possible to feel *too* good, but mania is not the normal joy of being in love or winning a Pulitzer Prize. Someone in a manic phase is expansive to an extent that is out of character. The symptoms are exactly the opposite of depression. Instead of feeling fatigued and listless, the manic person is full of energy. Instead of feeling unambitious, hopeless, and powerless, the manic person feels full of ambitions, plans, and power. The depressed person often speaks slowly, monotonously, with no inflections. The manic person speaks rapidly, dramatically, often with many jokes and puns. Although people may experience major depressions without manic episodes, it is extremely rare for a person to experience only manic episodes. Most manic episodes are a sign of **bipolar disorder** (also called "manic-depressive" disorder), in which depression alternates with mania.

Theories of Depression

Although bipolar disorders are equally common in both sexes, more women than men—of all ethnicities and nationalities—suffer episodes of major depression (McGrath et al., 1990). The reason for this sex difference in depression rates is debatable. More women than men seek treatment for major depression, but when you interview random samples of people who are not in treatment, you often find no significant differences between women and men. Some researchers report that an apparent difference occurs because a few women score higher at the *extreme* end of the depression measure, bringing up the average (Golding, 1988). It also seems likely, as we saw in Chapter 9, that the sexes *express* depression differently. Men, for instance, have higher rates of drug abuse and violent behavior than women do, which often masks serious depression or anxiety.

■ **bipolar disorder**
A mood disorder in which depression alternates with mania.

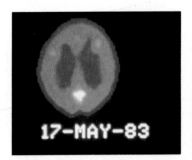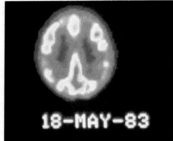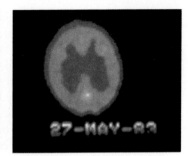

FIGURE 16.2

The depressed brain

These PET scans show changes in the metabolism of glucose, the brain's energy supply, in a patient with bipolar disorder. On May 17, the patient was depressed, and glucose metabolism throughout most of the brain was lower than normal. The next day, the patient became manic, and metabolic activity increased to near normal levels. By May 27, the patient was once again depressed, as reflected in glucose changes. Nevertheless, keep in mind that such changes do not show the direction of cause and effect: A drop in brain activity might bring on depression, but depression might also cause a drop in brain activity.

Many different theories have been advanced to explain the origins of depression. We will discuss four theories that are among the most commonly mentioned: biological theories, social theories, attachment theories, and cognitive theories.

1. *Biological theories* account for depression in terms of brain chemistry (see Figure 16.2). As we saw in Chapter 3, neurotransmitters permit messages to be transmitted from one neuron to another in the brain. Two neurotransmitters that seem to be implicated in depressive disorders are norepinephrine and serotonin. In the view of some, depression is caused by a deficient production of one or both of these neurotransmitters, and manic moods are caused by an excessive production.

This theory is supported by studies showing that when animals are given drugs that diminish the body's ability to produce serotonin, the animals become sluggish and inactive—a symptom of depression (Wender & Klein, 1981). Conversely, drugs that increase the levels of serotonin and norepinephrine sometimes alleviate symptoms of depression; hence they are called "antidepressants." The early success of antidepressants provoked great interest in the search for the biological origins of depression. However, as we will discuss further in Chapter 17, drugs are not universally effective. And even when they help some individuals, this does not necessarily mean that the depression had an exclusively organic basis.

Studies of twins and adopted children suggest that there may be a genetic component involved in the transmission of major emotional disorders. Indeed, several highly publicized studies have raised the possibility of finding a specific gene that is linked with bipolar disorder (Baron et al., 1987; Egeland et al., 1987). The culprit has been variously identified as a gene on the X chromosome or on chromosome 6 or 11. None of these studies is definitive, however, because other research has failed to find chromosome abnormalities in people with depression or manic depression (Faraone, Kremen, & Tsuang, 1990; Kelsoe et al., 1989).

2. *Social theories* of depression consider the conditions of people's lives. In this view, the reason that women are more likely than men to suffer depression

is that women are more likely to lack fulfilling jobs or family relations. Men are nearly twice as likely as women to be married *and* working full time, a combination of activities that is strongly associated with mental health (Golding, 1988). In a random sample of 1,111 men and women in Boston, virtually all of the differences between men and women in their reported levels of depression could be accounted for by their different states of marriage and employment (Gore & Mangione, 1983). Mothers of young children are especially vulnerable to depression: The more children in the house, the more likely women are to experience depression (McGrath et al., 1990).

Another social factor in the origins of adult depression may be childhood sexual abuse. In a study of female inpatients at a psychiatric hospital, over half of the women reported a history of such abuse. The number and severity of their depressive symptoms were greater than those of the patients who reported no sexual abuse (Bryer et al., 1987). A community survey of 3,125 white, Hispanic, and black women found that depression, anxiety, panics, and phobias were significantly higher among women who had been sexually abused as children or adolescents (Burnam et al., 1988).

Social analyses, though, fail to explain why some people who lose their jobs or spouses or have tragic experiences do not become clinically depressed, while others stay locked in the grip of despair. Similarly, they do not explain why some people become depressed even though they seem to "have it all."

3. *Attachment theories* emphasize the fundamental importance of affiliation and attachment to well-being. In this view, depression results from disturbed relationships and separations, both past and present. One attachment theory, the *interpersonal theory of depression*, includes biological, psychodynamic, and cognitive factors. But it emphasizes the depressed person's disputes, losses, anxieties, feelings of incompetence, and problems with relationships (Klerman et al., 1984).

A major review of studies of depression indeed found that the one thing that most often sets off a depressive episode is "disruption of a primary relationship," which is hardest on people who lack social support and good coping skills (Barnett & Gotlib, 1988). Nevertheless, attachment theories raise an interesting cause-and-effect problem. Disturbed or broken relationships may make some people clinically depressed. But depressed people are also demanding and "depressing" to family and friends, who often feel angry or sad around them and may eventually break away (Gotlib & Hooley, 1988).

4. *Cognitive theories* propose that depression results from particular habits of thinking and interpreting events (Beck, 1987). Years ago, Martin Seligman (1975) proposed a "theory of learned helplessness," which held that people become depressed when their efforts to control the environment fail. But it soon became apparent that not all depressed people have actually failed in their lives; many merely *believe* that nothing they do will be successful (Abramson, Seligman, & Teasdale, 1978). The researchers eventually reformulated their views into the *hopelessness theory of depression*. They now believe that the key cognitions in one subtype of depression—though not necessarily in all forms of depression—are that nothing good will ever happen and that the person is helpless to change this bleak future (Abramson, Metalsky, & Alloy, 1989).

Psychologists have been trying to pinpoint other cognitive styles that are associated with depression. For example, when people feel depressed, what they do about it affects the course and duration of their misery. Susan Nolen-Hoeksema (1990, 1991) has found that people who focus inward and brood endlessly about their negative feelings—she calls this a "ruminating response style"—tend to have longer and more intense periods of depression than do those who are able to distract themselves, look outward, and seek solutions to problems. Moreover, she has found considerable evidence suggesting that white, middle-class women are more likely than men to develop this introspective style, which may contribute to longer-lasting depressions in women.

One problem with cognitive theories of depression is that it is not always clear whether distorted thinking *causes* depression, *accompanies* depression, or *follows* depression. When you are feeling sad, negative thoughts come more easily (Lewinsohn et al., 1981). Two researchers set themselves the awesome task of reviewing dozens of studies based on different theories of depression (Barnett & Gotlib, 1988). They concluded that there are many "cognitive abnormalities that wax and wane with the onset and remission of depression," but these cognitions do not *precede* depression, do not predict the severity of its symptoms, and tend to vanish during remission. Studies that follow people over time (to see whether negative thinking causes depression) find that negative thinking is sometimes a cause, sometimes a result, and sometimes a two-way street (Robins, 1988).

What is a person supposed to conclude from all these studies and different theories? Why all the contradictory evidence? One answer is that depression comes in degrees of severity, from tearful tiredness to an inability to get out of bed, and psychologists study many different groups of depressed people. Yet researchers sometimes speak of the "depression" of clinical patients, college students, young children, and married couples as if it were the same thing.

Second, depression may have many causes. One person may have been abused in childhood; another may have a pessimistic cognitive style that fosters depressive interpretations of events; a third may have a genetic predisposition to respond to stress with depression. Every explanation accounts for some pieces of the depression puzzle, but none explains it all.

There are eight zillion studies of depression and many contradictory findings. What does this suggest about the search for a single cause or theory of the disorder? How can we make the most sense of conflicting results and points of view?

QUICK QUIZ

A newspaper headline announces that a single gene has been identified as the cause of depression, but when you read the fine print you learn that other studies have failed to support this research. What explanations can you think of to explain these contradictory findings?

ANSWERS:

Among other possibilities, the conflicting evidence may mean that if a genetic predisposition for depression does exist, it is not due to a single specific gene, but involves several genes working in the context of environmental events. It may mean that the right gene has not yet been identified. And it may mean that genes are not a factor in all forms of depression.

■ PERSONALITY DISORDERS

Personality disorders involve rigid, maladaptive, consistent traits that cause great distress or inability to get along with others. The *DSM-III-R* says that people with personality disorders "often appear 'odd' or eccentric . . . dramatic, emotional, or erratic . . . anxious or fearful." Of course, this description might fit any of us on some occasion and some of us on many occasions. However, a personality disorder involves a repeated, long-term pattern of behavior. It is not related to an episode of depression, or to a particular situation that temporarily causes behavior that is "out of character."

■ **personality disorders**
Psychological disorders in which rigid, maladaptive personality patterns cause personal distress or an inability to get along with others.

Narcissus fell in love with his own image—and now has a personality disorder named after him.

Problem Personalities

One kind of personality disorder—one that is often the subject of novels and movies—is the **paranoid** personality, which is marked by a pervasive, unfounded suspiciousness and mistrust of other people, irrational jealousy, secretiveness, and doubt about the loyalty of others. Another common disorder is the **narcissistic** personality, named after the Greek myth of Narcissus, a beautiful boy who fell in love with his own image. Narcissistic individuals have an exaggerated sense of self-importance and self-absorption. They are preoccupied with fantasies of unlimited success, power, brilliance, or ideal love. They require constant attention and admiration and feel entitled to special favors, without being willing to reciprocate. They fall in love quickly and out of love just as fast, when the beloved proves to have a human flaw.

Notice that these descriptions are both specific and vague. They are specific in that they evoke flashes of recognition ("I know that type!") but vague in that they involve general qualities that depend on subjective labels and value judgments. American society often encourages people to have fantasies of unlimited success and ideal love. Whether or not you like these traits is a separate matter from deciding they represent a *disorder*. For example, where would you draw the line between having a narcissistic disorder and being a normal member of a group or culture that encourages boasting in contrast to modesty?

One personality disorder in particular has provoked interest and study because of its consequences for society: the disorder of the individual who lacks conscience, morality, and emotional attachments. In the 1830s this disorder was called "moral insanity." By 1900 it became the "psychopathic personality," a phrase that some researchers and most newspapers still use. More recently the word "sociopath" was coined. The *DSM* uses the term *antisocial personality disorder*. By any name, there are some key symptoms in this troubling disorder, which has been around forever.

The Antisocial Personality

• Two teenage boys held a teacher down while a third poured gasoline over him and set him on fire. Fortunately, another teacher intervened in time for a rescue, but the boys showed no remorse, did not consider it wrong, and were disappointed that they had not actually murdered the teacher (whom they did not know). "Next time we'll do it right," said the ringleader, "so there won't be nobody left around to identify us."

• Giovanni Vigliotto was, by all accounts, warm and charming—by too many accounts, in fact. Vigliotto married 105 women in 33 years in an elaborate con game. He would find a wealthy woman, charm her into marriage, steal her assets, and vanish. Finally, one wife charged him with fraud, and he was convicted. Vigliotto admitted the many marriages, but not deception or theft. He didn't think he had done anything wrong (Carson & Butcher, 1992).

People like these, who have **antisocial personalities,** lack two critical emotions: empathy, the ability to take another person's perspective; and guilt, the ability to feel remorse or sorrow for immoral actions. They are totally without conscience. They can lie, charm, seduce, and manipulate others, and then drop them without a twinge of regret. If caught in a lie or a crime, they may seem sincerely sorry and promise to make amends, but it is all an act. They are often sexually promiscuous, unable to maintain attachments, and irresponsible in their obligations to others. For unknown reasons, this disorder is far more common in males than in females.

Antisocial personalities come in many forms. Some antisocial persons, like the teenagers who set a teacher on fire, are sadistic, with a history of criminal

■ **paranoia**
Unreasonable and excessive suspiciousness, jealousy, or mistrust. It may occur as a type of personality disorder or, with more severe symptoms of psychosis, as a type of schizophrenic disorder.

■ **narcissism**
An exaggerated sense of self-importance and self-absorption.

■ **antisocial personality disorder**
A condition characterized by antisocial behavior (such as lying, stealing, and sometimes violence), a lack of social emotions (guilt and shame), and impulsivity.

or cruel behavior that began in childhood. Others direct their energies into con games or career advancement, abusing other people emotionally rather than physically. Some people with antisocial personalities can be very "sociable," charming everyone around them, but they have no emotional connection to others or guilt about their wrongdoing.

The inability to feel emotional arousal—empathy, guilt, fear of punishment, anxiety under stress—implies some abnormality in the central nervous system. Antisocial individuals do not respond to punishments that would affect other people, such as threat of physical harm or loss of approval. It is as if they aren't "wired" to feel the anxiety necessary for avoidance learning (see Figure 16.3). This fact may explain why antisocial persons fail to learn that their actions will have unpleasant consequences (Hare, 1986).

A fascinating finding about the antisocial personality is that after age 40, about half of them "burn out"! In one study of 521 men, the researchers used longitudinal and cross-sectional methods to follow the criminal histories of male psychopaths and nonpsychopaths (terms the researchers used) between the ages of 16 and 45. Both types of analysis indicated that the criminal activities of nonpsychopaths were relatively constant over the years, whereas those of psychopaths remained extremely high until around age 40, after which they declined dramatically (Hare, McPherson, & Forth, 1988). Researchers are unsure why burnout occurs—experience? weariness? maturation of the nervous system?—and why it happens only in some cases.

One explanation of this disorder maintains that there is a common inherited disorder among people who are labeled antisocial, hyperactive, or overly extroverted (Newman, Widom, & Nathan, 1985). All of these conditions involve problems in *behavioral inhibition*—the ability to control responses to frustration or to inhibit a pleasurable action that may have unpleasant consequences. For such individuals, the momentary attraction of an activity blocks out all thought of consequences.

Some people with extremely violent antisocial personalities may have biological impairments as a result of physical abuse. Consider the chilling results of a study that compared two groups of delinquents: violent boys who had been arrested for repeated incidents of vicious assault, rape, or murder; and boys whose violence was limited to fistfights. Nearly all of the extremely violent boys

People with antisocial personalities are not necessarily evil-looking or socially inept. By all accounts, Ted Bundy, who murdered many women in cold blood, was charming, attractive, and utterly without remorse.

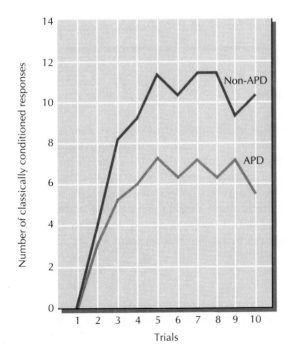

FIGURE 16.3

The antisocial personality: Immune to anxiety?
Normally, when a person is anticipating danger, pain, or shock, the electrical conductance of the skin changes—a classically conditioned response that indicates anxiety or fear. But in several experiments such as this one, people with antisocial personality disorder were slow to develop such responses. This deficit seems to be related to their ability to behave in destructive ways without regard for the consequences. (From Hare, 1965.)

(98.6 percent) had at least one neurological abnormality, and many had more than one, compared to 66.7 percent of the less violent boys. More than three-fourths of the violent boys had suffered head injuries as children, had had serious medical problems, or had been beaten savagely by their parents, compared to "only" one-third of the others (Lewis, 1981). In addition, numerous studies have found various EEG abnormalities in people with antisocial personality disorder (Holmes, 1991).

However, it is also important to consider the environments that encourage or discourage antisocial personalities. This disorder is rare or unknown in small, tight-knit, cooperative communities, such as the Inuit, religious Hutterites, and Israelis raised on the communal plan of the kibbutz. The fact that sociopaths and extroverts share certain characteristics, moreover, suggests that the two groups differ in how they learn to control their impulsive actions and express their relative fearlessness.

Our society worries more about the antisocial personalities who commit violent crimes than about those who gain power and fortune while wreaking devastation on their families, employees, or constituents. This is not surprising, since nonviolent affluent people with antisocial personalities rarely turn up in therapy, prison, or mental hospitals, despite the fact that they do great harm.

QUICK QUIZ

Can you diagnose each of the following disorders?

1. Ann can barely get out of bed in the morning. She feels life is hopeless and despairs of ever feeling good about herself.
2. Brad lacks guilt, empathy, and moral standards.
3. Connie constantly feels a sense of impending doom; for many weeks, her heart has been beating rapidly and she can't relax or concentrate.
4. Damon is totally absorbed in his own feelings and wishes.
5. Edna believes that everyone is out to get her and no one can be trusted.

ANSWERS:

1. depression 2. antisocial personality 3. generalized anxiety disorder 4. narcissistic personality disorder 5. paranoid personality disorder.

■ DISSOCIATIVE DISORDERS

Stress or shock can make any of us feel temporarily *dissociated*—that is, cut off from ourselves, feeling strange, dazed, or "unreal." In **dissociative disorders,** consciousness, behavior, and identity are split or altered. Unlike normal, short-lived states of dissociation, these disorders are extremely intense, last a long time, and appear to be out of one's control. Like post-traumatic stress disorder, dissociative disorders are often responses to shocking events. But in the former case, people can't get the trauma out of their minds and waking thoughts. In the latter, people escape the trauma by erasing it from memory.

Amnesia and Fugue

Amnesia, partial or complete memory loss of information or past events, is the most common dissociative disorder. Amnesia can result from organic conditions, such as head injury; when no organic causes are apparent it is called *psy-*

■ **dissociative disorders**
Conditions in which normally integrated consciousness or identity is split or altered, as in psychogenic amnesia or multiple personality.

■ **amnesia**
Partial or complete loss of memory for information or past events; when no organic causes are present, it is classified as a dissociative disorder.

chogenic. Psychogenic amnesia is highly selective; the person "forgets" only information that is threatening to the self. In one case, for example, a young man appeared at a hospital complaining that he did not know who he was. After a few days, he awoke in great distress, eventually remembering that he had been in an automobile accident in which a pedestrian was killed. The shock of the experience and his fear that he might have been responsible set off the episode of amnesia.

Psychogenic fugue states are even more fascinating. A person in a *fugue state* not only forgets his or her identity, but gives up customary habits and wanders far from home. The person may take on a new identity, remarry, get a new job, and live contentedly until he or she suddenly "wakes up"—puzzled and often with no memory of the fugue experiences. The fugue state may last anywhere from a few days to many years. James McDonnell, Jr., left his family in New York in 1971 and wandered to New Jersey, where he took a new name (James Peters), a new job (short-order cook), and new friends. Fifteen years later, he "woke up" and made his way back to his wife—who (apparently) greeted him with open arms.

As you might imagine, it is often difficult for clinicians to determine when people in fugue states have a true disorder and when they are faking (Schacter, 1986). This problem is also apparent in the remarkable disorder of multiple personality.

Multiple Personality

Multiple personality disorder (MPD) is often in the news these days. It is considered a dissociative disorder because its essential feature is the appearance, within one person, of two or more distinct personalities. Each personality may have its own memories, preferences, handwriting, and medical problems (Braun, 1988). In a study of one person with four personalities, for example, the researcher concluded that it was "as if four different people had been tested" (Larmore, Ludwig, & Cain, 1977).

Only 200 cases of multiple personality had been identified by 1980, when the *DSM* established new criteria for diagnosing it, but since then thousands have appeared. Some of these have been calculated attempts by murderers to plead insanity: "I didn't kill her; my other personality did." The Hillside Strangler in Los Angeles, Kenneth Bianchi, convinced several psychiatrists that his murders were really committed by another personality he called Steve Walker. However, a determined prosecutor discovered that Bianchi had read numerous psychology textbooks on multiple personality and had modeled "Steve" on a student he knew. When a psychologist purposely misled Bianchi by telling him that "real" multiple personalities come in packages of at least three, Bianchi suddenly produced a third personality. Bianchi was convicted of murder and sentenced to life in prison. But Paul Miskamen, who battered his wife to death, convinced psychiatrists and a jury that the man who killed his wife was a separate personality named Jack Kelly. Judged insane, Miskamen was committed to a mental hospital and released after 14 months.

Cases of multiple personality make for dramatic movies, books, and news stories, but among mental health professionals they are controversial. Some psychiatrists believe the disorder originates in childhood, as an adaptation to living in a situation that alternates unpredictably between unbearable abuse and affectionate loving. One "personality" embodies the good experiences and another "personality" emerges to cope with the bad ones. Many of these patients suffered horrendous abuse as young children: being dangled out of windows, being tortured, being the victim of sexual sadism (Herman, 1992; C. Ross, 1989). It is not known, though, why some children who suffer severe abuse develop multiple personality disorder and others do not.

Some cases of multiple personality have turned out to be fakes, while others seem chillingly real. How would you go about determining the difference?

■ **multiple personality disorder**
A rare dissociative disorder marked by the appearance within one person of two or more distinct personalities, each with its own name, history, and traits.

S/T: This is about as inocuous as we can get.

Jacob's: I WOULDN'T CALL IT INOCUOUS, I'D CALL IT OBNOXUOUS!

Charlie: I don't know what that word means.

Peg: I think it means something that's not important.

S/p: Well what ever this is for seems important

The different "personalities" of people with multiple personality disorder may have their own names, opinions, and even styles of handwriting, as this handwriting sample from a single patient illustrates. However, some researchers say this kind of evidence of MPD is suspect, because normal people can do the same thing. Try it yourself—can you produce four entirely different handwriting samples? (Courtesy of Bennett Braun.)

Clinicians and researchers who study and treat MPD believe that it is not rare but is often misdiagnosed as schizophrenia, depression, or personality disorder. They argue that diagnoses can be made more accurately today because the physiological changes that occur within each "personality" cannot be faked. One patient, for example, had a blood pressure of 150/110 when one personality was in control and a blood pressure of 90/60 when another personality took over (Braun, 1988).

Other experts are skeptical about this kind of evidence and think that MPD, if it exists at all, is extremely rare (Holmes, 1991). That blood pressure study, for instance, had a problem: It's our familiar flaw, the Missing Control Group. When one research team compared the EEG activity of two MPD patients with that of a normal person who merely role-played different personalities, they found that EEG differences between "personalities" were actually *greater* in the normal person (Coons, Milstein, & Marley, 1982)! Because normal people can create EEG changes by changing their moods, energy levels, and concentration, brain wave activity cannot be used to verify the existence of MPD (Holmes, 1991).

Skeptics are also concerned that clinicians who are deeply convinced of the widespread existence of MPD may actually create the disorder in their patients through the subtle mechanism of suggestion (Spanos et al., 1991). For example, here is the way one psychologist questioned Kenneth Bianchi under hypnosis: "I've talked a bit to Ken, but I think that perhaps there might be another part of Ken that I haven't talked to, another part that maybe feels somewhat differently from the part that I've talked to . . . And I would like that other part to come to talk to me . . . . Part, would you please come to communicate with me?" (quoted in Holmes, 1991). Is this psychologist *permitting* another personality to reveal itself or he is actively *creating* such a personality by planting the suggestion? Notice that he repeatedly asks Bianchi to produce another "part" of himself and even speaks to "Part" directly.

Of course, the existence of a few con men who fake MPD—and of normal subjects who, under hypnosis, go along with the suggestion to produce another personality—doesn't mean that everyone who reveals the disorder is consciously faking or trying to please the clinician. Proponents of the diagnosis note that it isn't easy to fake the existence of many distinct personalities, each with its own history, mannerisms, name, and experiences. (For more on the legal system's problems of detecting faking and determining insanity, see "A Closer Look at Forensic Psychology" on page 588.)

Robert Carson and James Butcher (1992) offer a useful way of thinking critically about the puzzle of MPD. We should, they say, avoid either-or thinking, and stop asking whether a given action is conscious *or* unconscious, genuine *or* faked, intended *or* unintended. "The human mind does not operate in these dichotomous ways," they observe. As we saw in Chapter 7, there are separate (dissociated) memory systems in normal people, and much of what we do goes on outside awareness. Similarly, people who appear to have several different personalities represent an extreme form of the normal ability to shift from one state of consciousness to another, to change emotions in an instant, and to present a variety of "selves" to the world.

■ DISORDERS OF PHYSICAL SYMPTOMS

Chhean Im, a survivor of Cambodia's savage Khmer Rouge, is almost totally blind—and yet, physically, there is nothing wrong with her eyes. Chhean Im's family was murdered, and she then spent years in a labor camp, where she was starved and beaten. One day she was forced to watch a brutal killing, and when she stopped crying, several days later, she was blind. Today Chhean Im lives in Los Angeles, one of about 150 other refugees who have lost most or all of their sight. Organically, nothing is wrong with their vision. The mystery, say Patricia Rozée and Gretchen Van Boemel (1989), who have been successfully treating these victims, lies inside a mind that says: "I'm sick of the death. I don't want to see. I don't want to deal with this anymore."

When people like Chhean Im develop physical symptoms for which no organic reason can be found, they are said to have a **somatoform disorder,** which has the form of a physical disorder (*somato* refers to the body) with no demonstrable medical cause. Symptoms include becoming blind, deaf, paralyzed, numb, or having inexplicable pain.

One kind of somatoform problem is *conversion disorder*, in which a physical symptom expresses a psychological conflict or need. For example, someone terrified of hurting another in a rage might develop a "paralyzed" arm. Another kind of somatoform disorder is *hypochondria*, an unrealistic fear of disease. Everyone occasionally has odd symptoms; everyone occasionally interprets them as a certain sign of a dread disease. But hypochondriacs exaggerate normal physical sensations, taking them as evidence of serious illness. They are preoccupied with normal bodily functions, such as heartbeat, elimination, and occasional coughs. Some hypochondriacs are obsessed about their bodies; some are phobic about developing a specific disease; some are convinced they are already ill. Their fears persist in spite of constant reassurance, which is why hypochondriacs often go from doctor to doctor, trying to confirm their fears.

In diagnosing somatoform disorders, clinicians look for symptoms that are inconsistent with known physical diseases or with basic anatomy: a "paralyzed" leg that otherwise shows normal motor reflexes, symptoms that vanish during hypnosis, or symptoms that are not anatomically possible. Are people who have these symptoms faking? Many clinicians regard somatoform disorders as expressions of uncontrollable unconscious conflicts. In contrast, they say, *malingering* is a conscious, voluntary effort to use or invent a physical symptom for an ulterior motive: to get out of work, to get drugs, to get sympathy.

The social use of physical symptoms may be a conscious process or unconscious self-deception. People with somatoform disorders have typically been rewarded in some way for having physical complaints. One study found that hypochondriacs have learned to use the excuse of poor health to justify unsatisfactory performance. When they believe that they are being evaluated and that poor health will excuse poor scores, hypochondriacs report more physical symptoms than they do when they think they are not being evaluated (Smith, Snyder, & Perkins, 1983). Many factors influence a person's likelihood of observing, worrying about, and reporting physical symptoms. These include ex-

✷ *You discover a strange rash on your leg. Do you ignore it or rush to the doctor? Where would you draw the lines between foolish denial, justified worry, and hypochondria?*

■ **somatoform disorders**
Physical disorders that have no demonstrable medical cause. They include somatization disorder, conversion disorder, and hypochondria.

The Insanity Defense: Is It Insane?

• A civil servant named Dan White lost his job on San Francisco's Board of Supervisors. He went home, got his revolver, climbed in through the window of City Hall (so the metal detectors wouldn't detect his gun), and shot Mayor George Moscone nine times. Then he murdered supervisor Harvey Milk, a gay man whom White disliked. In what the press played up as the "Twinkie Defense," White's psychiatrists testified that his excessive consumption of junk food was a sign of his "diminished mental capacity." Though his actions were premeditated, they said, White was temporarily insane. The jury agreed. Dan White served only five years in prison for manslaughter. Twenty months after his release, he committed suicide.

• A troubled young man named John Hinckley, Jr., hoping to win the attention and love of actress Jodie Foster, shot and wounded then-President Ronald Reagan and his press secretary, James Brady. Hinckley was acquitted of attempted murder on the grounds of insanity and was confined indefinitely to a mental institution.

These cases produced enormous public interest. What is the proper punishment for someone who apparently cannot control his or her actions? How do we know if someone is "insane" or faking? If someone is sentenced to spend time in a mental institution, how can we know when he or she is "cured"? Can we predict whether a person will kill again? Researchers interested in *forensic psychology* study these and other psychological issues related to the law and courtroom.

Insanity is a legal term, not a psychological one. In 1834, a Scot named Daniel M'Naghten tried to assassinate the prime minister of England, killing the prime minister's secretary by mistake. M'Naghten was acquitted of murder on the grounds that he had a "mental defect" that prevented him from understanding what he was doing at the time of the act. The "M'Naghten Rule" meant that people could be acquitted "by reason of insanity" and sentenced not to prison, but to mental institutions (or set free). In the United States, the 1954 *Durham* decision specified that "an accused is not criminally responsible if his unlawful act was the product of a mental disease or defect."

At the time, the English public was as outraged by the M'Naghten decision as the American public was by the Hinckley decision. People often get the impression that hordes of mad criminals are "getting off" by reason of insanity. In fact, trials based on the insanity plea receive far more attention than their numbers warrant. Most of the small number of people who successfully plead insanity (about 30 per state per year) have committed relatively mild offenses (Rosenhan, 1983).

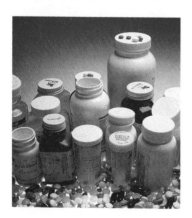

Almost everyone takes medication and vitamins on some occasions, but hypochondriacs often take them by the fistful to alleviate mild or imaginary ailments.

pectations and attitudes about the nature of disease; sensitivity to pain; anxiety, which amplifies the intensity of pain; low self-esteem and morale; and cultural background, which affects whether a person learns to "keep a stiff upper lip" or notice and talk about every little twinge of discomfort (Pennebaker, 1982).

Hypochondria provides another good illustration of the problems of diagnosis, the role of community standards in defining normalcy, and the risks of oversimplified thinking. It is easy to see what is wrong with the hypochondriac who worries too much about every bodily sensation. But why don't we label the person at the other extreme, the one who pays too *little* attention to symptoms, even dangerous ones? Moreover, consider what Susan Baur (1988) calls "normal hypochondria"—the "irrational health worries that affect so many people that *not* to be preoccupied seems bizarre." Our society, she notes, endorses "weight-watchers' hypochondria" and "fitness hypochondria." We don't think it odd if a woman weighs herself once a day or if a man works out daily to have "perfect" muscles; why then is it a disorder if a person checks his or her tongue daily for signs of tongue cancer? Where, in short, is the line between hypochondriacal attention to the body and healthy concern?

Yet the insanity defense continues to be hotly debated. Most legal and mental health professionals believe that the insanity plea is humane and necessary in a civilized society, and that the mentally incompetent or disturbed should be treated differently from those who are responsible for their actions. Some defense attorneys and psychiatrists keep trying to expand the legal causes of "temporary insanity," arguing that "premenstrual syndrome," a chemical imbalance, high testosterone, and epilepsy are legitimate excuses for losing control of oneself and committing crimes.

Others, such as Thomas Szasz (1987), believe that the insanity defense is a "legal fiction" that imprisons innocent people in mental hospitals and exonerates guilty people by declaring them not responsible for their actions. It allows wealthy or likable defendants to be let off completely or to spend a brief time in a mental hospital, and it sentences poor, minority, or rebellious defendants to lengthy or indefinite stays.

In a sizzling indictment of the ability of psychologists to determine "insanity" or to predict the future behavior of violent individuals, psychologists David Faust and Jay Ziskin (who is also a lawyer who specializes in forensic psychology) reviewed hundreds of studies (Faust & Ziskin, 1988). "Clinicians do not in fact make more accurate clinical judgments than laypersons," they concluded; their error rate exceeds their accuracy rate. In one study, military recruits who were kept in the service, despite psychiatrists' recommendations that they be discharged for "severe psychiatric liabilities," turned out to be as successful and adjusted as the control group. In study after study, clinicians were not very good at detecting malingering or efforts to fake insanity, and they were dismal at predicting future violence. One reason for these high error rates, Faust and Ziskin believe, is the differing perspectives of psychology and psychiatry, as well as the diversity of views within psychology (think of the different views of personality, for example, and the disagreements over diagnosis itself). As a result, some trials end up as battles of the experts, in which the jury must decide which psychiatrist or psychologist to believe.

Research in forensic psychology attempts to redress these problems. One researcher developed a Criminal Responsibility Assessment Scale, for example, that greatly improves agreement among clinicians in assessing the causes of an accused person's criminal act (R. Rogers, 1988). And, increasingly, empirical research in many other domains of psychology is finding its way into the courtroom. Developmental psychologists have testified on children's reactions to trauma; neuropsychologists on the extent of brain damage in people injured at work; cognitive psychologists on eyewitness testimony; social psychologists on conformity, "brainwashing," and how juries determine guilt or innocence. In these and many other areas where law and psychology intersect, psychologists are trying to help juries determine the fine line between "normal" and "abnormal" behavior—and what to do about the individuals who cross it.

■ DRUG ABUSE AND ADDICTION

Perhaps no topic in this chapter better illustrates the problem of finding the "shade of the spectrum" in which normal blurs into abnormal than that of drug abuse and addiction. Most people in America use drugs—legal, illegal, or prescription—in moderation, for short-lived effects. But some people overuse them, and the consequences of their drug abuse for society are costly in terms of loss of productive work, high rates of violence and crime, and family disruption. The consequences for individuals and their families are tragic: unhappiness, illness, and the increased likelihood of early death due to accident or disease.

From Use to Abuse

Every drug—including aspirin, cough medicine, and coffee—is dangerous and even lethal if taken in excess. Although the drugs that come to the attention of the government and the media are the illegal ones (most notably marijuana, heroin, and cocaine), the drugs that do the most damage to the most people are

When and why does drug use become abuse?

legal: alcohol and cigarettes. (You might refer to Chapter 4 to refresh your memory about stimulant and depressant drugs and how people learn to react to them.) When does "moderate use" of any drug become abuse? How much is *too* much? Because there are so many dangers of drug *abuse*, debates about drug *use* are often emotional. If the drug is illegal, feelings run especially high. Yet medically, psychologically, and socially, there are many differences between moderate use of any drug and overuse. In fact, a surprising longitudinal study that followed a large sample of children from preschool through age 18 found that adolescents who had experimented moderately with alcohol and marijuana were the *best* adjusted in the sample. Those who had never experimented with any drug were the most anxious, emotionally constricted, and lacking in social skills. And those who overused and abused drugs were maladjusted, having problems with alienation, impulsiveness, and emotional distress (Shedler & Block, 1990). We'll have more to say about the direction of cause and effect here in a moment.

To distinguish moderate drug use from abuse, the *DSM* definition of "drug abuse" includes these symptoms:

- The inability to stop or cut down.
- Intoxication throughout the day.
- Blackouts and loss of memory for events during the intoxication.
- Impaired ability to work or get along with others—for example, fights, loss of friends or job, absence from work, arguments with others over the drug use.
- Physical deterioration or illness.

Addiction: Disease or Social Problem?

Why are some people able to use drugs moderately, while others become alcoholics or addicts? One explanation looks to personality: Drug abusers may be sensation seekers who crave lots of excitement and stimulation (see Chapter 10). Another considers family history: Some drug abusers have deprived childhoods, antisocial parents, and a lifetime of rejection. A third explanation holds that peer pressure is the reason: If all your friends smoke, you are more likely to smoke too. But these factors are only part of the story.

In several longitudinal studies that followed three groups of people for more than 40 years, researchers were able to observe the course of alcohol use and abuse over time in people's lives (Vaillant, 1983). The first surprising discovery was that many people went through a period of heavy, even problem, drinking but eventually healed themselves. For such persons, alcoholism was not progressive, permanently incapacitating, or a downward spiral to skid row. They outgrew alcoholism, cutting back to social drinking levels.

Second, the study found that many of the factors thought to *cause* alcoholism were instead a *result* of alcoholism. It had long been argued, from retrospective studies, that alcoholism was a result of an unstable or dependent personality. Alcoholics were supposed to have lower self-esteem and be more depressed, paranoid, aggressive, and impulsive than social drinkers. However, the longitudinal evidence showed that these traits, along with differences in social class, unemployment, and educational achievement, all tended to develop *after* the emergence of alcoholism. As adults, problem drinkers had personality disorders and were socially inadequate. But as children they were no less privileged than peers who became normal social drinkers, were no less intelligent, and had no more emotional problems (Vaillant & Milofsky, 1982). Likewise, in that longitudinal study that followed children from preschool to age 18, problem drug use among adolescents proved to be largely a result, not a cause, of their maladjustment and other personal problems (Shedler & Block, 1990). (Conversely, the best-adjusted students were able to use drugs moderately *because* they were well adjusted.)

Then why do people become alcoholic? In colonial America, the average person drank two to three times the amount of liquor that is consumed today, yet alcoholism was not the serious social problem it is now. Drinking was a universally accepted social activity. Families drank and ate together. Alcohol was believed to produce pleasant feelings and relaxation. Indeed, the Puritan minister Cotton Mather called liquor "the good creature of God." If a person committed a crime or became violent while drunk, the colonials did not conclude that liquor was to blame. Rather, it was the person's own immoral tendencies that led to drunkenness *and* crime (Critchlow, 1986).

Between 1790 and 1830, when the American frontier was expanding, drinking came to symbolize masculine independence, high-spiritedness, and violence. The saloon became the typical setting for drinking away from home. Alcoholism rates rose dramatically. The temperance movement, which followed, argued that drinking inevitably led to drunkenness, and drunkenness to crime. The solution it proposed, and won for the Prohibition years (1920–1933), was national abstinence.

By the mid-twentieth century, drunkenness came to be seen not as an inevitable property of alcohol but as a characteristic of some people who have an inbred vulnerability to alcoholism. In *The Disease Concept of Alcoholism* (1960), E. M. Jellinek argued that alcoholism is a disease over which an individual has no control and from which he or she never recovers. Again, complete abstinence was the only solution. Today the *disease model of addiction* is still widely accepted by researchers and the public. The disease model holds that addiction, whether to alcohol or any other drug, is a biochemical process. The individual acquires a *tolerance* for the drug, meaning that greater and greater amounts are required to produce the same effect. Withdrawal produces a severe physiological reaction, including, in the case of alcohol, "the shakes," nervousness, anxiety, nightmares, and delirium.

Proponents of the disease model believe that alcoholism involves an inherited predisposition, because having biological relatives who are alcoholic contributes to a person's risk of becoming alcoholic. However, two psychologists who reviewed the research in this area reported that "on critical examination . . . the evidence [of a hereditary component in alcoholism] appears less strong" (Newlin & Thomson, 1990).

As with so many other disorders, medical researchers are trying to identify the key gene or genes that might be involved in alcoholism. Yet again, frustratingly, one study's positive results are often contradicted by another study's negative ones. Several studies found that a specific gene, which affects the function of key dopamine receptors on brain cells, was more likely to be present in the DNA of alcoholics than of nonalcoholics (Noble et al., 1991). Dopamine helps regulate pleasure-seeking actions, so the researchers suspect that this gene might help explain why alcoholics drink. However, other studies, using different measurements, have found no difference between alcoholics and controls in the presence of this gene (Bolos et al., 1990; Gelernter et al., 1991). At present, it seems that there is no single gene that "causes" alcoholism. It is possible that several genes in combination may affect the response to alcohol, the compulsive use of alcohol (or other mood-altering drugs), or the progression of alcohol-related diseases such as cirrhosis of the liver.

A different biological explanation suggests that alcoholism results, basically, from alcohol. Heavy drinking alters brain function, reduces the level of painkilling endorphins, produces nerve damage, shrinks the cerebral cortex, and wrecks the liver. In this view, these changes in turn create a biological dependence, an inability to metabolize alcohol, and psychological problems.

But the disease model, popular though it is, has several problems. If alcoholism and addiction to other drugs are diseases, more people than ever are "catching" them. Between 1942 and 1976 there was a 20-fold increase in the number of alcoholics in treatment (Peele, 1989). More and more people are be-

It's time to think critically about the popular disease model of addiction. People can become "addicted" to jogging, love, and rock music. What "disease" are they catching?

coming addicted to other drugs as well. Moreover, people can become "addicted" to activities and to television as well as to drugs; what "disease" are they catching? A growing number of television "addicts" compulsively watch TV the way drug addicts compulsively use drugs—to relieve loneliness, sadness, or anger (Jacobvitz, 1990). "Exercise addicts" have a compulsion to exercise that far exceeds any health benefits (Chan & Grossman, 1988). Some of them cannot stop exercising even when their muscles and joints have been seriously injured. Like alcoholics who organize their lives around drink, addicted athletes put exercise above everything else, including their jobs or relationships. And they have major withdrawal symptoms, such as depression and anxiety, when they are unable to exercise.

Amid much argument, therefore, some researchers want to replace the disease model of addiction with a *learning* model. In his book *Heavy Drinking: The Myth of Alcoholism as a Disease* (1988)—a book as controversial today as Jellinek's was in 1960—Herbert Fingarette argues that alcoholism is a result of physical, personal, and social factors. It is neither a sin nor a disease but "a central activity of the individual's way of life." Similarly, Stanton Peele and his associates want to replace the disease model of addiction and treatment with a "life-process" model (Peele, Brodsky, & Arnold, 1991). Some of the underlying assumptions of the disease and life-process models of addiction are shown in Table 16.2.

Opponents of the disease model of addiction marshal three lines of support for their argument:

1. *Addiction patterns vary according to culture and learning.* Study after study has found that alcoholism is much more likely to occur in cultures that forbid children to drink but condone drunkenness in adults (such as Ireland) than in cultures that teach children how to drink responsibly but forbid adult drunkenness (such as Italy and Greece). In cultures with low rates of alcoholism, adults demonstrate correct drinking habits to their children, gradually introducing them to alcohol in safe family settings. These lessons are maintained by adult customs. Alcohol is not used as a rite of passage into adulthood, nor is it associated with masculinity and power (Peele, 1989; Vaillant, 1983). Drinking is considered neither a virtue nor a sin. Abstainers are not sneered at and drunkenness is not considered charming, comical, or manly. (An Italian friend of ours,

---

TABLE 16.2

Some Comparisons Between Assumptions of the Disease and "Life-Process" Models of Addiction and Treatment

Disease model	Life-process model
Addiction is genetic, biological	Addiction is a way of coping
Person is always an alcoholic/addict	Person can grow beyond need for alcohol/other drug
Addict must abstain entirely from the drug forever	Most problem drinkers can learn to drink in moderation
Either person is addicted or not	Degree of addiction will vary depending on situation
Therapy focuses on addiction	Therapy focuses on person's problems and environment
Addict needs same treatment and group support forever	Treatment or group support lasts as long as necessary
Person must accept identity as alcoholic/addict	Person focuses on problems, not permanent labels

Source: Adapted from Peele, Brodsky, & Arnold, 1991.

Rates of alcoholism depend on when and where people drink. In cultures in which people drink moderately with meals—and children learn the social rules of drinking along with their families—alcoholism rates are much lower than in cultures in which drinking occurs in bars, in binges, or in privacy.

who doesn't like the taste of wine, told us his father was worried when his son refused wine at family gatherings. He feared that by not learning to drink socially, his son would become a drunk.)

2. *Not all addicts go through physiological withdrawal symptoms when they stop taking the drug.* During the war in Vietnam, nearly 30 percent of the soldiers were taking heroin in doses far stronger than those available on the streets of U.S. cities. These men believed themselves to be addicted. Experts predicted a drug-withdrawal disaster among the returning veterans. It never materialized (see Figure 16.4). Over 90 percent of the men simply gave the drug up, without withdrawal pain, when they came home (Robins, Davis, & Goodwin, 1974). Other studies find that the majority of people who are addicted to alcohol, cigarettes, tranquilizers, or painkillers are able to stop taking these drugs, without outside help and with no withdrawal symptoms at all (Lee & Hart, 1985). In a study of 100 hospital patients who had been given strong doses of narcotics, 99 had no withdrawal symptoms upon leaving the hospital. They left postoperative pain behind them, along with the drug (Zinberg, 1974).

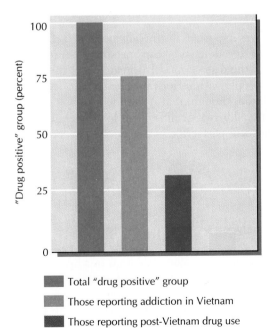

FIGURE 16.4

Drugs and Vietnam veterans: Failure of the addiction prediction

U.S. soldiers who tested "drug positive" when they were in Vietnam showed a dramatic drop in drug use when they returned to civilian life—contrary to prediction and the "disease model" of addiction (Robins, Davis, & Goodwin, 1974).

3. *Policies of total abstinence tend to increase rates of alcoholism rather than reduce them.* One of the more interesting lines of evidence for a learning theory of alcoholism is that when people do not learn how to drink moderately, they are more likely to drink irresponsibly and in binges (unless they are committed to a culture or religion that forbids all drugs). A recent study suggests that Prohibition itself—which was a national effort in the 1920s to eliminate alcoholism and problem drinking—actually *increased* rates of alcoholism. Sociologist Joan McCord (1989) found that men who were teenagers at the time of Prohibition were far and away more likely to become serious problem drinkers in adulthood than were older men, who had learned how to drink alcohol before it became illegal. Similarly, the Inuit people of British Columbia were forbidden alcohol until 1951, and then permitted to drink only in licensed bars. As a result, the Inuit would drink as much as they could while in a bar. It was a policy virtually guaranteed to create drunkenness.

All of this evidence suggests that drug abuse and addiction reflect an interaction of physiology *and* psychology, person *and* culture. They occur when an individual who is vulnerable to abusing drugs, and who perhaps has a genetic susceptibility, finds a culture and environment that support drug abuse. In particular:

• Addiction is more likely to occur among people who believe the drug is stronger than they are—that is, who believe they are addicted and will always be addicted.

• Addiction and drug abuse are more likely to occur when people learn (or when laws or customs encourage them) to take the drug in binges rather than occasionally, in moderation.

• Addiction occurs when people come to rely on a drug or an experience as a way of coping with problems, relieving pain, or avoiding stress; when it provides a false sense of power, control, and self-esteem that the individual lacks without it.

• Drug abuse is more likely to occur when the drug becomes a permanent part of a person's life instead of an occasional experience; when "everyone" drinks heavily or uses other drugs; and when the drug is taken in its most potent and distilled form (such as crack).

The disease model of addiction was important historically because it changed the existing moral condemnation of the addict as a "bad" person to concern for someone who is a "sick" person. If the disease model is inadequate, this is no reason to abandon sympathy for people with serious problems or to abandon the search for solutions. It may mean, though, that it is time to give up hoping for the perfect drug that has no addictive qualities, and look instead at the human qualities that make a drug seem perfect.

QUICK QUIZ

If you are not yet addicted to studying, try these questions:

1. Longitudinal studies find that the personality problems of adult alcoholics are often a result of (a) childhood trauma, (b) low self-esteem, (c) broken marriages, (d) alcoholism.
2. Which cultural practice is associated with *low* rates of alcoholism? (a) drinking in family or group settings, (b) infrequent but binge drinking, (c) drinking as a "rite of passage," (d) regarding alcohol as a sinful drink

3. What seems to be the most reasonable conclusion about the role of genes in alcoholism? (a) without a key gene, a person cannot become alcoholic, (b) the presence of a key gene or genes will almost always cause a person to become alcoholic, (c) genes may work in combination to increase a person's vulnerability to some kinds of alcoholism

4. For a century, people have been searching for a magic drug that would not be addictive. Heroin, cocaine, barbiturates, methadone, and tranquilizers were all, at first, supposed to be nonaddictive. In each case, some people became addicted and abuse of the drug became a social problem. Based on what you've read, what are some possible reasons for the failure to find a mood-altering but nonaddictive drug?

ANSWERS:

1. d 2. a 3. c 4. Perhaps some people are biologically vulnerable to any mind-altering drug. Perhaps the psychological need for addiction exists in the individual and not in the chemical properties of the drug. Perhaps the chemistry of the drug is less important than the cultural practices that encourage drug abuse among some groups. If that is so, there will never be a perfect pill with no addictive properties.

■ SCHIZOPHRENIA AND OTHER PSYCHOTIC DISORDERS

To be schizophrenic is best summed up in a repeating dream that I have had since childhood. In this dream I am lying on a beautiful sunlit beach but my body is in pieces. This fact causes me no concern until I realize that the tide is coming in and that I am unable to gather the parts of my dismembered body together to run away. The tide gets closer and just when I am on the point of drowning I wake up screaming in panic. This to me is what schizophrenia feels like; being fragmented in one's personality and constantly afraid that the tide of illness will completely cover me. (schizophrenic patient, quoted in Rollin, 1980)

At the turn of the century this patient would have been diagnosed with "dementia praecox" (premature mental deterioration). In 1911, Swiss psychiatrist Eugen Bleuler coined the term "schizophrenia" to signify that the personality loses its unity: Words are split from meaning, actions from motives, perceptions from reality. Today a large and varied group of disorders go under the umbrella label of **schizophrenia**. Schizophrenia is *not* the same as "split" or "multiple personality." As the above quotation illustrates, schizophrenia describes a fragmented condition, not the coexistence of several different personalities. It is an example of a **psychosis**, a mental condition that involves distorted perceptions of reality and an inability to function in most aspects of life.

The Nature of the Schizophrenias

If depression is the common cold of psychological disorder, says psychiatrist Donald Klein (1980), schizophrenia is its cancer: a baffling and complex problem. The most common symptoms include the following:

1. *Bizarre delusions* that have no basis in fact, such as the belief that dogs are anthropologists from another planet, disguised as pets in order to infiltrate human families. Some people with schizophrenia have paranoid delusions, taking innocent events—a stranger's cough, a helicopter overhead—as "evidence" that the world is plotting against them. Some have "delusions of grandeur," believing that they are Moses, Jesus, or Joan of Arc. "Reasoning with schizophrenic people about their delusions," says E. Fuller Torrey (1988), "is like trying to

■ **schizophrenia**
A psychotic disorder or disorders marked by some or all of these symptoms: delusions, hallucinations, incoherent word associations, inappropriate emotions, or lack of emotions.

■ **psychosis**
An extreme mental disturbance involving distorted perceptions and irrational behavior. It may have either psychological or organic causes.

bail out the ocean with a bucket." These delusions, he adds, are crazy only to outsiders. To the schizophrenic, they form a logical pattern.

2. *Hallucinations* that usually take the form of voices and consist of garbled, odd words; a running conversation in the head; or two or more voices conversing with each other. Unlike the hallucinations that might occur to a normal person on a drug high, schizophrenic hallucinations feel intensely real and believable to the sufferer (Bentall, 1990). Most are voices but some are tactile (such as feeling insects crawling over the body) or visual (one patient had a vision of Elizabeth Taylor in her mirror).

3. *Incoherent, loose word associations,* called "word salads." Schizophrenic thought is often an illogical jumble of ideas and symbols, linked by meaningless rhyming words or by remote associations. A patient of Bleuler's wrote this essay:

> Olive oil is an Arabian liquor-sauce which the Afghans, Moors and Moslems use in ostrich farming. The Indian plantain tree is the whiskey of the Parsees and Arabs. Barley, rice and sugar cane called artichoke, grow remarkably well in India. The Brahmins live as castes in Baluchistan. The Circassians occupy Manchuria and China. China is the Eldorado of the Pawnees. (Bleuler, 1911/1950)

The great novelist James Joyce, the story goes, once asked Carl Jung to explain the difference between his own stream-of-consciousness writing and the odd associations of his schizophrenic daughter. Jung supposedly replied, "You dive—she falls" (Wender & Klein, 1981).

4. *Severe emotional abnormalities.* Schizophrenics typically have inappropriate and exaggerated emotions (see Figure 16.5). They may laugh at sad news, become angry at good news, or weep inconsolably for no reason. Some eventually lose the ability to feel any emotion at all. One man set fire to his house, and then sat down calmly to watch TV.

FIGURE 16.5

Emotions and schizophrenia
The Diagnostic Drawing Series, designed by art therapist Barry M. Cohen, consists of three drawings. The first is a spontaneous free choice. The second is a picture of a tree. The third, illustrated here, is a "feeling picture," in which subjects are asked to draw a picture of how they feel, using lines, shapes, and colors. The picture on the left, drawn by a 31-year-old, white, female nonpatient, shows movement; expansive use of space; mixed use of line, shape, and color; heavy pressure; and an integrated design. The picture on the right, drawn by a 33-year-old, white, female schizophrenic, shows moderate use of space, the inclusion of words, single color, and lack of integration. The Diagnostic Drawing Series is the first large-scale research project to correlate diagnoses of psychiatric inpatients with specific characteristics of their drawings. Instructions, materials, and ratings of the three pictures are standardized (Cohen, Hammer, & Singer, 1988).

5. *Withdrawal into an inner world.* Some schizophrenics live in their own minds, oblivious to everything around them. In *Autobiography of a Schizophrenic Girl*, Marguerite Sechehaye wrote, "A wall of brass separates me from everybody and everything. In the midst of desolation, in indescribable distress, in absolute solitude, I am terrifyingly alone. . . ."

Schizophrenia varies in severity, duration, and kind of symptoms. In some individuals, the symptoms appear abruptly and eventually disappear with the passage of time, with or without treatment. In others, the onset is more gradual and insidious. Friends and family report a change in personality. The person may stop working or bathing, become isolated and withdrawn, and start behaving in peculiar ways (for instance, collecting garbage or hoarding food).

As for prognosis, again schizophrenia is unpredictable. Psychiatrists often speak of the "rule of thirds": Of all people diagnosed and hospitalized with schizophrenia, one-third will recover completely, one-third will improve significantly, and one-third will not get well. The more breakdowns and relapses the schizophrenic has, the poorer the chances for complete recovery (J. Stephens, 1978). Yet some chronic schizophrenics learn to live with their illness, are able to work and have warm family relationships, and eventually outgrow their symptoms completely (Harding et al., 1987).

The mystery of schizophrenia is that we could go on listing symptoms and cultural variations all day and not finish. Some schizophrenics are almost completely impaired in all spheres; others do extremely well in certain areas. Some have perfectly normal moments of lucidity in otherwise withdrawn lives. One catatonic adolescent crouched in a rigid posture in front of a television for the month of October; later, he was able to report on all the highlights of the World Series he had seen. A middle-aged man, hospitalized for 20 years, believing he was a prophet of God and that monsters were coming out of the walls, was able to interrupt his ranting to play a good game of chess (Wender & Klein, 1981). People with brain damage or organic illness usually cannot interrupt their "madness" to watch the World Series or play chess. How can those with schizophrenia do so?

Theories of the Schizophrenias

As you might imagine, any disorder that has so many variations and symptoms will pose many problems for those who try to diagnose and explain it. Some psychologists have concluded that there is really no such entity as "schizophrenia" and that clinicians and the *DSM* would be better off to drop the label entirely (Sarbin, 1992). A review of 374 studies found "a persisting failure of research to establish schizophrenia as a stable, determinate, diagnostic entity," much less one that has an identifiable cause (Mancuso & Sarbin, 1984). Another researcher, Robert Carson (1989), pointing to the failure of clinicians to agree reliably on what they are diagnosing and to the failure of a *DSM* diagnosis to predict the outcome for the patient, concluded that the concept of schizophrenia is "almost hopelessly in tatters."

Of course, these critics recognize that some people do behave in bizarre ways and that *something* is wrong with them. In their view, "schizophrenia" is a lot of different somethings, a grab-bag term for a variety of rule-breaking actions and disorders that must be understood in the context in which they occur. For example, Carson (1989) points out that it is impossible to define the term "delusion" without reference to a culture's norms. In every society, he reminds us, perfectly sane individuals hold patently "false or absurd beliefs" with great conviction and zeal. Why do we think a person is schizophrenic if he believes he is the Prophet Ezekiel, but not if he believes he was the Prophet Ezekiel in a past life?

When most people think of schizophrenia, they imagine the lonely suffering of someone like this woman. Yet many individuals with schizophrenia learn to manage their symptoms and lead lives that are successful and productive (see facing page).

Other psychologists reply to these criticisms by arguing that in cultures around the world, the same core signs of schizophrenia appear: hallucinations, loss of touch with reality, inappropriate emotions, and disorders of thought and brain function. "If schizophrenia is a myth," said Seymour Kety (1974), "it is a myth with a strong genetic component."

In fact, most researchers believe that "the schizophrenias" reflect some underlying brain disease or diseases. The problem is that because schizophrenia involves so many different symptoms, no single physiological deficiency accounts for all of them. Some studies have found brain abnormalities in some people with schizophrenia and other psychotic disorders: a slight decrease in brain weight, a decrease in the volume of the temporal lobe or limbic regions, and reduced numbers of neurons in specific layers of the prefrontal cortex (Meltzer, 1987). New techniques, such as measures of cerebral blood flow and PET scans, are being used to distinguish brain abnormalities common in all mood disorders from those that are specific to the psychoses. One promising clue is the discovery of enlarged spaces (ventricles) in the brain filled with cerebro-spinal fluid, which may indicate cerebral damage (Raz & Raz, 1990). This damage may occur because of genetic flaws, damage to the brain during birth, or subsequent damage to the brain in childhood (Cannon, Mednick, & Parnas, 1989; Meltzer, 1987).

Other leading biological explanations of schizophrenia have focused on abnormalities in chemical neurotransmitters, especially dopamine and serotonin, and on abnormal brain electrical activity. There is also good evidence of eye movement abnormalities in people who have schizophrenic symptoms, leading some researchers to suggest that these abnormalities are actually a biological marker of the disease (Clementz & Sweeney, 1990). Perhaps the brains of some people with schizophrenia are overly sensitive to everyday stimuli, which may be why they retreat into a inner world.

Brain abnormalities in the schizophrenias might, in turn, occur because of genetic defects. Children have a greater risk of schizophrenia if an identical twin or parent has the disorder, and especially if both parents are schizophrenic, even if the child is reared apart from the affected relative (Gottesman, McGuffin, & Farmer, 1987). Compared to a risk of 1 to 2 percent in the general population, children with one schizophrenic parent have a lifetime risk of 12 percent, and the risk for children with two schizophrenic parents jumps to 35 to 46 percent (M. Goldstein, 1987). Even so, nearly 90 percent of all persons who develop schizophrenia do *not* have a schizophrenic parent, and nearly 90 percent of all children with such a parent do *not* develop the disorder.

As usual, it has been hard to track down specific genes or determine the extent of their influence (Holzman & Matthysse, 1990). Just as with alcoholism, there was great excitement when a research team found a link between schizophrenic symptoms and an abnormal cluster of genes, this time on chromosome 5 (Sherrington et al., 1988). This discovery was followed by disappointment when other research failed to confirm it (Kennedy et al., 1988).

Lately there has been a surge of support for the possibility, long argued by E. Fuller Torrey, that an infectious virus during prenatal development is the main culprit in schizophrenia (Torrey, 1988). Viruses are known to attack very specific areas of the brain, leaving other areas untouched, and they can remain latent for many years before symptoms appear. The infectious disease theory fits many facts about schizophrenia, such as the odd finding that there are seasonal patterns in the births of schizophrenic children (viruses are seasonal). A 40-year longitudinal study found an association between exposure to an influenza virus during the second trimester of gestation and adult schizophrenia 20 to 30 years later (Barr, Mednick, & Munk-Jorgensen, 1990), and this finding has been supported by numerous other studies.

The second trimester of prenatal development is critical because the brain is forming crucial connections during this time. Working with Torrey, neurologist H. Stefan Bracha reasoned that if a viral infection or other prenatal trauma (such as lack of oxygen) affected the fetal brain and the subsequent development of schizophrenia, its effects should appear elsewhere in the body as well. Bracha's team conducted an ingenious study of 24 pairs of identical twins in which only one twin suffered from schizophrenia (itself evidence, as we saw, that the disorder cannot be entirely genetic). They discovered that the twins who had schizophrenia, unlike their normal twins, were significantly more likely to have various deformities in their hands, such as fewer ridges in their fingerprints (Bracha et al., 1991). Of course, hand abnormalities do not cause schizophrenia! But hands are formed during the second trimester, so it seems that the same environmental accident that can affect the brain's development also affects the hands. These findings, although preliminary, may explain why sometimes only one twin of a genetically identical pair later becomes schizophrenic: One may be affected prenatally by a virus, even within a brief few days, but not the other.

Joseph Rogers recovered from schizophrenia and became director of the National Mental Health Consumers' Association. Other people with schizophrenia learn to recognize signs of an oncoming breakdown and manage their symptoms, just as people with diabetes learn to live with their disease.

Other researchers are concluding that the onset and course of the schizophrenias depend on a combination of genetic factors, abnormal neurobiology, and family or other pressures (Gottesman, 1991). According to the *vulnerability–stress model*, a combination of heredity (or brain damage) and stress is necessary to produce the varieties of schizophrenia. In this view, genes or brain damage alone will not inevitably produce the disorder, and a vulnerable person who lives in a good environment may never show signs of it. As David Holmes (1991) puts it, "Humpty Dumpty had a fragile shell, but he didn't break until he fell." But what makes a person with schizophrenia fall? Torrey (1988) has noted that stress theories of schizophrenia raise many questions: Why don't we have epidemics of schizophrenia in prisons and concentration camps? Why did the schizophrenia rate go down during World War II rather than up? Why is the schizophrenia rate low in warring Northern Ireland, yet much higher in the peaceful western part of Ireland?

The answers to Torrey's provocative questions do not lie in the kinds of environmental causes that have been blamed in the past, such as parents who give children mixed messages or who treat them in cruel or eccentric ways. Although some parents of schizophrenics are disturbed or abusive, many others treat their children with love and support. The Copenhagen High-Risk Project has followed 207 children at high risk for schizophrenia (because of having a schizophrenic parent) and a control group of 104 low-risk children. The project directors have identified several factors that, *working in interaction*, increase the likelihood of a schizophrenic breakdown: the existence of schizophrenia in the family; physical trauma during childbirth, which is associated with the kind of damage to the brain that those imaging studies also found; exposure to the flu virus (or other prenatal trauma) during the second trimester of gestation; and having parents who are unstable and disturbed (Mednick, Parnas, & Schulsinger, 1987).

Some psychologists are still hoping that a common source of all the schizophrenias may yet be discovered. They note that rheumatic fever can appear as a disease of the nervous system, of the heart, of the joints, or of the skin. It seemed to be four different diseases until bacteriologists identified the common source (Wender & Klein, 1981). But most researchers, faced with the contradictory findings and complex factors, believe that the "schizophrenias" include several disorders with different causes and that no single culprit is likely to be discovered.

Organic Brain Disorders

Charles Whitman complained to a doctor that he was feeling overwhelmed by violent impulses and "tremendous headaches." "I have been the victim of many unusual and irrational thoughts," he wrote in his diary. One night he killed his

In Alice in Wonderland *the Mad Hatter is a comic character. But the origins of the expression "mad as a hatter" tell us that organically based mental illness is no joke: A century ago, many hatmakers suffered mental impairment and confusion as a result of inhaling poisonous mercury vapors where they worked.*

wife and his mother. The next day he killed 14 people with a high-powered rifle before the police shot him to death. A postmortem examination revealed that Whitman had a malignant brain tumor.

No one knows how much of Charles Whitman's violent behavior was attributable to his brain tumor; he also had a lifelong obsession with violence and firearms. But organic disorders can produce symptoms of psychosis. If the brain is affected by disease, tumors, infections, or a deficiency of nutrients, a person may eventually begin to behave in strange, sometimes psychotic ways. Some of these conditions are reversible. Others are progressive and irreversible, leading to death. Some are out of one's control. Others result from self-inflicted abuse. Prolonged alcoholism, for instance, can produce a brain disorder called *delirium tremens* (the D.T.'s), which causes tremors ("the shakes"), hallucinations, and terror.

Several diseases are now known to affect brain function. Alzheimer's disease causes a gradual, irreversible deterioration in memory, intellectual ability, and motor control. Huntington's chorea, which involves a deficiency of the neurotransmitter GABA (gamma-amino-butyric acid), causes involuntary spasms and twisting movements of the body, facial grimacing, memory lapses, and impulsive behavior. The disease is carried by a single dominant gene, so every child of an affected parent has a 50 percent chance of getting it, although usually not until middle age. Because the disease produces paranoia, depression, and other psychological symptoms, it is often misdiagnosed. Songwriter Woody Guthrie ("This Land Is Your Land"), a famous victim of Huntington's, was for a long time mislabeled as an alcoholic.

Other physical disorders can masquerade as mental illness. Symptoms of brain tumors or thyroid deficiency, for example, can include paranoid psychosis, sudden mania, or complete withdrawal. Endocrine, cardiovascular, and gastrointestinal diseases can produce symptoms of depression, apathy, aggression, and confusion. Syphilis, if untreated, may lead to *paresis*, a deterioration in mental and physical functioning that ends in paralysis, psychosis, and death. (Gangster Al Capone and Winston Churchill's father, Randolph, both died of paresis caused by syphilis.) For these reasons, anyone who shows a fairly sudden, unexplained change in behavior or mood should not overlook the possibility of disease (Thornton, 1984).

Finally, visions, delirium, and other abnormal behaviors can be caused by untreated infections, loss of oxygen to the brain, toxic chemicals, and even nutritional deficiencies. Pellagra, a condition caused by lack of the vitamin niacin, produces symptoms that mimic anxiety disorders and even schizophrenia. Pellagra can lead to delirium, hallucinations, and psychotic behavior, but it is reversible with a proper diet.

We have come to the end of a long walk along the spectrum of mental disorders. William Styron, who recovered from severe and debilitating depression, used the beginning of Dante's beautiful and classic poem, *The Inferno*, to convey his experience of mental illness:

> In the middle of the journey of our life
> I found myself in a dark wood.
> For I had lost the right path.

"For those who have dwelt in depression's dark wood," writes Styron, "and known its inexplicable agony, the return from the abyss is not unlike the ascent of the poet, trudging upward and upward out of hell's black depths and at last emerging into what he saw as 'the shining world.'" Dante wrote:

> And so we came forth, and once again beheld the stars.

When a Friend Is Suicidal

Suicide is a scary subject, surrounded by mystery and myth. It can be frightening to those who find themselves fantasizing about it, and it is devastating to the family, friends, and acquaintances of those who go through with it. In the United States, most people who commit suicide are over the age of 45, but suicide rates are rapidly increasing among young people. Suicide is the second highest cause of death (after car accidents) among college students and the rate for teenagers has quadrupled since 1950.

People who attempt suicide have different motives. Some believe they have no reason to live; some feel like failures in a world where (they think) everyone else is happy and successful; some want revenge against those who (they think) have made them suffer. But they all share the belief that life is unendurable and that suicide is the only solution. This belief may be rational in the case of people who are terminally ill and in pain, but more often it reflects the distorted thinking of someone suffering from depression. Often, the suicidal person doesn't really want to *die;* rather, he or she wants to escape intolerable emotions and self-consciousness (Baumeister, 1990).

Friends and family members can help prevent a suicide by knowing the difference between fact and fiction:

1. *There is no "suicidal type."* Most adolescents who try to commit suicide are isolated and lonely. Many are children of divorced or alcoholic parents. Some have problems in school and feel like failures. But others are college students who are perfectionistic, self-critical, and highly intelligent. The former may feel like ending their lives because they can foresee no future. The latter may feel suicidal because they do not like what they foresee.

2. *Take all suicide threats seriously.* Many people fail to take action when a friend talks about committing suicide. Some believe the friend's intentions but assume there is nothing they can do. "He'll just do it at another place, another time," they think. In fact, most suicides occur during an acute crisis. Once the person gets through the crisis, the desire to commit suicide fades. One researcher tracked down 515 people who had at-

tempted suicide by jumping off the Golden Gate Bridge many years earlier. Fewer than 5 percent had actually committed suicide in the subsequent decades (Seiden, 1978).

Others believe that if a friend is talking about suicide, he or she won't really do it. This belief is also false. Few people commit suicide without signaling their intentions. Most are ambivalent: "I want to kill myself, but I don't want to be dead—at least not forever." Most suicidal people want relief from the terrible pain of feeling that nobody cares, that life is not worth living. Getting these thoughts and fears out in the open is an important first step.

3. *Know the danger signs.* A depressed person may be at risk of trying to commit suicide if he or she:

- Has tried to commit suicide before.
- Has become withdrawn, apathetic, and isolated.
- Reveals specific plans for carrying out the suicide, or begins to give away cherished possessions.
- Expresses no concern about the usual deterrents to suicide, such as the fact that it will hurt the family, break religious rules, or be an irreversible action.

4. *Take constructive action.* If you believe a friend is in danger of suicide, trust your judgment. Do not be afraid to ask, "Are you thinking of suicide?" This question does not "put the idea" in anyone's mind. If your friend is contemplating the action, he or she will probably be relieved to talk about it, and you will know that it is time to find help. Let your friend talk without argument. Don't try to talk your friend out of it by debating whether suicide is right or wrong, and don't put on phony cheerfulness. If your friend's words or actions scare you, say so. By listening nonjudgmentally, you are showing that you care. By allowing your friend to unburden his or her grief, you help the person get through the immediate crisis.

If you are seriously worried about your friend's safety, get the person to a counselor, health professional or the emergency room of a hospital; or call a local suicide hot line. Don't worry about "doing the wrong thing." In an emergency, the worst thing you can do is nothing at all.

SUMMARY

1. "Abnormal behavior" has been defined as a statistical deviation from the norm; as a violation of cultural standards; as maladaptive or destructive behavior; as emotional distress; and as "insanity," the legal term for incompetence to stand trial.

2. Diagnosing psychological disorders is complicated. The *Diagnostic and Statistical Manual of Mental Disorders* tries to provide objective criteria of abnormal behavior. But some critics argue that diagnosis turns "problems in living" into inflated "disorders," gives people labels that stigmatize their behavior and create a self-fulfilling prophecy, and by its very nature is more an art than a science because of human bias and subjective judgment.

3. *Generalized anxiety disorder* is a condition of continuous anxiety, lasting at least a month, with signs of nervousness, worry, and physiological arousal. Other anxiety disorders include *post-traumatic stress disorder*, *panic attack*, *agoraphobia*, and *obsessive-compulsive disorder*.

4. *Mood disorders* include *major depression* and *bipolar disorder*. Symptoms of major depression include distorted thinking patterns, low self-esteem, physical ailments such as fatigue and loss of appetite, and prolonged grief and despair. In bipolar disorder, depression alternates with mania or euphoria.

5. Many theories try to explain depression and its greater prevalence among women. Biological theories emphasize a depletion of neurotransmitters in the brain and the role of specific genes for mood disorders. Social theories consider the conditions of people's lives that might cause a sex difference, such as work and family life, the particular stresses of motherhood, and sexual abuse in childhood. Attachment or interpersonal theories argue that depression results from broken or conflicted relationships. Cognitive theories, such as *hopelessness theory*, emphasize distorted thoughts and unrewarding patterns of reinforcement, and habits of brooding or rumination that cause depressions to last.

6. *Personality disorders* are characterized by rigid, self-destructive traits that cause distress or an inability to get along with others. They include the *paranoid*, the *narcissistic*, and the *antisocial* personality. The antisocial personality (also called psychopath or sociopath) is marked by antisocial behavior, lack of guilt and empathy, and impulsiveness or lack of self-control. The disorder may involve a neurological defect, caused by genetics or by damage in childhood to the brain and central nervous system, or it may result from environment and experience.

7. *Dissociative disorders* involve a split in consciousness or identity. They include *amnesia*, *fugue* states, and *multiple personality disorder* (MPD), in which two or more distinct personalities and identities appear within one person. There is considerable controversy about the validity and nature of MPD.

8. *Somatoform disorders* consist of physical symptoms with no apparent physical cause. People who have *hypochondria* are oversensitive to bodily symptoms and may use them to excuse poor performance. People who have a *conversion disorder* have a physical symptom that serves a psychological need.

9. The effects of drugs depend on whether they are used moderately or are abused. Signs of *drug abuse* include the inability to stop or cut down, intoxication throughout the day, blackouts, impaired ability to work or get along with others, and physical deterioration. According to the *disease model of addiction*, some people have a biological vulnerability to addictions such as alcoholism. The vulnerability may result from a genetic factor or from years of heavy drinking or other drug use. The *learning model of addiction* points out that addiction patterns vary according to culture, learning, and accepted practice; that many people can stop taking a drug (even heroin) with no withdrawal symptoms; and that drug abuse increases when people are not taught moderate use. Addiction and abuse appear to reflect an interaction of physiology and psychology, person and culture, vulnerability and opportunity.

10. *Schizophrenia* is a psychotic disorder involving many symptoms, such as delusions, hallucinations, "word salads," inappropriate emotions, and withdrawal. The "schizophrenias," which involve brain disease, vary in severity, duration, and prognosis. According to the *vulnerability-stress model*, these disorders result from a combination of factors: genetic defects, viral infection or other trauma to the brain during the second trimester of prenatal development, brain damage during birth, and an unstable and abusive environment in childhood.

11. *Organic brain disorders* can produce psychotic symptoms or psychological disorders, such as depression. Brain damage may result from disease, tumors, injury, infection, nutritional deficiency, a virus, or poisoning.

KEY TERMS

17

Approaches to Treatment and Therapy

No form of therapy has ever been initiated without a claim that it had unique therapeutic advantages. And no form of therapy has ever been abandoned because of its failure to live up to these claims.

MORRIS B. PARLOFF

• Murray is a smart fellow with just one problem: He procrastinates. He can't seem to settle down and write his term papers. He keeps getting incompletes, swearing he'll do those papers soon, but before long the incompletes turn to F's. Why does Murray procrastinate, manufacturing his own misery? What kind of therapy might help him?

• Sally complains of anxieties, irritability, and continuing problems in her marriage. Although she is successful at work, she feels like a fraud, a useless member of society, and a burden to her family. She weeps often. Why is Sally so unhappy, and what can she do about it?

• Jerry, a college student, is brought to the hospital by the campus police, who found him wandering around, dazed and confused. He is anxious and talkative, and reports hearing angry voices that accuse him of being a spy. What treatment can help Jerry?

• Margaret's parents were drug addicts who abandoned her when she was a baby. She lived in four foster homes before finding a family that truly cared for her. Margaret is married and loves her husband, but she has many inhibitions and insecurities. What can Margaret do to recover from her unhappy childhood?

Psychotherapists use many techniques, including expression through art, to help people resolve their problems. In this drawing, a child reveals her grief over a classmate's suicide.

People seek professional help for many difficulties and disorders. These range from "problems in living," such as family conflicts and procrastination, to the delusions common in schizophrenia. Today there is an equally large array of programs that promise help for personal problems. In this chapter we will consider and evaluate three major approaches to treatment. (1) *Medical treatments* include drugs or direct intervention in brain function, with or without additional therapy. Medical treatment may be given in a hospital, but also by physicians or psychiatrists on an outpatient basis. (2) *Psychotherapy* covers an array of psychological approaches to treating mental problems. Some of the more popular schools of psychotherapy include psychodynamic therapies, cognitive-behavioral therapies, family therapy, group therapy, and humanistic therapies. Finally, (3) *self-help and community alternatives* include support groups, skills training, rehabilitation counseling, and community interventions.

Each of these approaches can successfully treat some problems but not others. Each can help some individuals but may harm others. Finding the right treatment depends not only on having a good practitioner but on being an educated consumer. What does research show about the effectiveness of drugs, psychotherapy, counseling, and self-help? What works best and for what problem? When do therapies fail and when do they do harm?

■ MEDICAL TREATMENTS

Over the centuries, approaches to psychological disorders have alternated between the medical model, which regards mental problems as having biological causes, and the psychological model, which views mental problems as having psychological causes. Treatments likewise have varied from physical interventions, such as drugs and surgery, to psychological ones.

Is It "All in the Mind" or Based in the Body?

The medical tradition has had a healthy history. The ancients believed that "melancholia" (depression) was caused by an excess of "black bile" in the spleen. Plato located the source of female emotional and physical disorders in the uterus (*hystera* in Greek). He believed that the childless uterus literally wanders throughout the body, causing everything from paralysis and seizures to headaches and tears. All such symptoms in women, therefore, were "hysterical." Other philosophers thought that emotional and behavioral disorders resulted from faulty digestion and spicy food, which affected the *hypochondrium*—the area below the rib cage containing the stomach, liver, and pancreas. "Hypochondria" now refers to an unfounded concern with one's health, but the word used to refer to emotional disorders thought to be caused by digestive problems in this region (Drinka, 1984).

Theories of melancholia, hysteria, and hypochondria lasted for many centuries, right along with the belief that strange behavior was probably caused by demonic possession and witchcraft (Fraser, 1984). By the early eighteenth century, new medical discoveries challenged both of these views. Physicians argued that the cause of emotional disorder was to be found in the nervous system. "Nervousness" became the common diagnosis. "All nervous distempers whatsoever from Yawning and Stretching, up to a mortal fit of Apoplexy," wrote Dr. George Cheyne in 1733, "seem to be but one continued Disorder, or the several steps and degrees of it" (quoted in Drinka, 1984).

In the mid-1700s, a scientist named William Cullen used the Latin word for nervousness, *neurosis*, to describe the supposed disorders of the nervous system: paralysis, fainting, shortness of breath, cholera, epilepsy, palpitations, asthma, diabetes, melancholia, diarrhea, and mental retardation. By clustering these "neurotic" conditions together, he popularized the idea that many disorders have a common physical, or *organic*, cause. By the early twentieth century, Freud shifted the search for organic causes of "neurosis" to a search for unconscious, mental ones. Freud promoted the idea that many disorders have a *psychological* cause, and this view began to dominate psychotherapy.

Today the emphasis in psychiatry has shifted from the unconscious back to biochemistry, an intellectual earthquake that has shattered the foundations of the profession. The organic model is enjoying a resurgence partly because of new research on the brain, drugs, and genetics, and partly because of the failure of traditional psychotherapies to help chronic sufferers. Many ethical and scientific issues remain unsettled, however, and the debate about treatment continues.

The Question of Drugs

There are two primary lines of evidence to support the view that there is a biological basis to many emotional disorders and psychoses: (1) the evidence, discussed in Chapter 16, that some disorders may have a genetic component or involve a biochemical abnormality, and (2) the finding that some medications affect people with disorders but have no effect on others, which suggests that the drugs may be compensating for an organic deficiency.

Centuries ago, people suffering from physical and mental problems were often "diagnosed" as being possessed by the devil or being witches. The "cure" was to be hanged or burned at the stake.

These dramatic photos capture the effectiveness of antipsychotic drugs on the symptoms of this young man with schizophrenia. In the photo on the left, he was unmedicated; in the photo on the right, he had taken medication. However, because drugs carry risks and do not help all people with schizophrenia, the public should be wary of claims of "miracle cures."

Antipsychotic drugs, or *major tranquilizers,* include chlorpromazine (Thorazine), haloperidol (Haldol), and, more recently, clozapine (Clozaril). These drugs represented a major change in the treatment of schizophrenia and other psychoses. Before their introduction, hospital staffs controlled psychotic patients with physical restraints, including straitjackets, or put them in unfurnished padded cells to keep them from hurting others or themselves during states of extreme agitation and delusion. For people who are acutely ill with schizophrenia and likely to improve spontaneously within a few weeks or months, antipsychotic drugs can be effective. They reduce agitation and panic, and often shorten the schizophrenic episode (Kane, 1987). There are also people who, on clozapine, "awakened" after a decade of illness and resumed their former lives.

Some researchers argue that antipsychotic drugs are among the safest in medicine. But these drugs, especially if taken over many years, do have potentially dangerous side effects. One is the development of a neurological disorder (called tardive dyskinesia), characterized by involuntary muscle movements. About one fourth of the adults who take antipsychotics develop this disorder, and fully one-third of elderly patients do (Saltz et al., 1991). In a small percentage of cases, antipsychotic drugs cause neuroleptic malignant syndrome, which produces delirium, coma, and death (Pope, Keck, & McElroy, 1986). Clozapine has produced, in about 2 percent of cases, a potentially fatal condition (called agranulocytosis) in which there is a dangerous decrease in certain white blood cells. To avoid these dangers, researchers are trying to develop safer antipsychotic drugs and prescribing lower doses of existing ones. Unfortunately, doses that are too low increase the chance that schizophrenic symptoms will worsen, particularly after a year of treatment (Marder et al., 1987).

Thus antipsychotic drugs are a double-edged sword in the treatment of chronic schizophrenia. For some patients, they remove or lessen the most dramatic symptoms, such as "word salads" and hallucinations, but they usually cannot restore normal thought patterns or relationships. They allow many people to be released from hospitals, but often these individuals cannot care for themselves or they fail to take their medication because of its side effects. The overall effect of these drugs is modest, and some individuals diagnosed as schizophrenic deteriorate when they take them (Carson & Butcher, 1992; Smith, Glass, & Miller, 1980).

■ **antipsychotic drugs**
Major tranquilizers primarily used in the treatment of schizophrenia and other disorders involving psychotic symptoms, such as delusions.

Antidepressant drugs, classified as stimulants, are used in treating mood disorders, usually depression, but also anxiety, agoraphobia, and obsessive-compulsive disorder. There are three kinds of antidepressant drugs. One type, called *monoamine oxidase (MAO) inhibitors,* directly elevates the level of the neurotransmitters norepinephrine and serotonin. (These drugs are called MAO inhibitors because they block, or inhibit, the enzyme that can deactivate norepinephrine and serotonin.) The second, more commonly used kind, called *tricyclic antidepressants,* prevents reabsorption, or "reuptake," of norepinephrine and serotonin by the cells that have released them. Recently, a third kind of antidepressant hit the market, fluoxetine (Prozac). Prozac works on the same principle as the tricyclics, but it specifically targets serotonin. Antidepressants are nonaddictive, but they too can produce unpleasant physical side effects, including a dry mouth, constipation, headaches, nausea, weight gain, and blurry vision. Antidepressants are prescribed not only for depression. One antidepressant, clomipramine, has successfully reduced obsessive-compulsive symptoms—such as endless hand-washing and hair-pulling—in people who had spent years suffering (Swedo & Rapoport, 1991).

Another substance, a salt called *lithium carbonate,* is often successful in calming people who suffer from manic depression. It must be given in exactly the right dose, because too little won't help and too much is toxic. The patient's blood levels of lithium must be carefully monitored.

"Minor" tranquilizers, such as Valium and Xanax, are classified as depressants. These drugs are the ones most frequently prescribed by physicians for patients who complain of unhappiness or anxiety, but, unfortunately, they are the least effective in treating emotional disorders. In addition, a small but significant percentage of the people who take minor tranquilizers become abusers of the drug, developing problems with tolerance and withdrawal (Lader, 1989; Lader & Morton, 1991). For these reasons, antidepressants are preferable to tranquilizers when treating mood disorders.

Drugs have helped many people who might otherwise have gone from therapy to therapy without relief. Consider the case of Raphael Osheroff, who had a thriving medical practice until he became severely depressed and could no longer work. He admitted himself to a private psychiatric hospital where he received daily intensive psychotherapy. After *seven months* of ineffective treatment, Osheroff switched to another hospital, where he was given antidepressant medication. Within a few months he was fully recovered (Shuchman & Wilkes, 1990).

The increasing popularity of drugs as a method of treatment poses a problem for clinical psychologists, who, unlike psychiatrists, are not licensed to prescribe medication. Many psychologists are now actively lobbying for prescription rights, arguing that they should have access to the full range of treatment possibilities. But they have run into resistance from the medical profession, which argues that even with increased training, psychologists will not be qualified to prescribe medication, and from other psychologists who are concerned about the medicalizing of their field and who want psychology to remain a "clear and distinct" alternative to psychiatry (DeNelsky, 1990).

Medication, of course, does not magically eliminate depressed people's real-life problems. But it can be a useful first step in treatment. By improving people's sleep patterns, appetite, and energy, it allows them to concentrate on solving their problems. Yet, despite these benefits, a few words of caution are in order:

1. *The placebo effect.* New drugs, like new therapies, often promise quick and effective cures, as the public was told with the arrival of clozapine, Xanax, and Prozac. Yet the placebo effect (see Chapter 2) ensures that some people will respond positively to new drugs just because of the enthusiasm surrounding them. After a while, when placebo effects decline, many drugs turn out to be neither

■ **antidepressant drugs**
Stimulants that influence neurotransmitters in the brain; they are used in the treatment of mood disorders, usually depression and anxiety.

as effective as promised nor as widely applicable. One problem is that in sup- posedly double-blind studies of new drugs, patients can often tell if they are be- ing given an active drug or a placebo because of the side effects. In a survey of studies that used "active placebos" (which mimic the side effects of real drugs), there was, remarkably, little difference in effectiveness between placebos and antidepressants (Fisher & Greenberg, 1989).

2. *The therapeutic window.* The challenge with drugs is to find the "thera- peutic window," the amount that is enough but not too much. Some people have been given antidepressants in doses too weak to make a difference. Oth- ers have been given doses that are too strong, causing harmful or even danger- ous side effects (Breggin, 1991). Some people have taken drugs for years with- out improvement, which is as useless as staying in a "talk therapy" for years without improvement.

3. *Relapse and drop-out rates.* A person may have short-term success with an- tipsychotic and antidepressant drugs, but the percentage of people who stop taking these medications, possibly because of their unpleasant side effects, is very high—between 50 and 67 percent (McGrath et al., 1990; Torrey, 1988). Depressed people who take antidepressants without learning how to cope with their problems are also more likely to have a high relapse rate—that is, the de- pression is more likely to return. Sometimes drugs become part of the prob- lem: Some anxious people become afraid to go anywhere without their pills.

4. *Nonmedical alternatives.* Several kinds of psychotherapy work as well as drugs, or even better, for many people with mood disorders—including panic attacks, phobias, anxiety, and cases of depression that are not extremely severe (Barlow, 1990; Chambless, 1985; Dobson, 1989; Robinson, Berman, & Neimeyer, 1990).

5. *Race, gender, and dosage.* The same dose of a drug may not be suitable for men and women, or for all racial groups. When psychiatrist Keh-Ming Lin moved from Taiwan to Seattle, he was amazed to learn that the dosage of anti- psychotic drugs given to American schizophrenics was often 10 times higher than the dose for Chinese patients with the same illness. In subsequent research comparing 13 Caucasian and 16 Asian schizophrenics, Lin and his colleagues confirmed that the Asian patients required significantly lower doses of the med- ication for optimal treatment (Lin et al., 1989; Lin, Poland, & Lesser, 1986). The reason is unclear, but it may involve differences in metabolic rates, amount of body fat, the number or type of drug receptors in the brain, or cultural prac- tices such as smoking and eating habits. And within a culture, men and women may not metabolize antidepressants and other drugs the same way (McGrath et al., 1990).

Sometimes, drug treatments truly can be miraculous, rescuing a person from a life of institutions or emotional despair. But some scientists are sounding the alarm about the *routine* prescription of medications, which are often dispensed without accompanying therapy for the person's problems. At one conference we attended, a psychiatrist warned that, because of the ease of prescribing an- tidepressants and tranquilizers, "It is not unusual for [psychiatrists] to see any- where from six to eight patients per client hour. This is not being involved with your patient in any meaningful way." The proper use of drugs depends on the individual, the problem, the practitioner, and whether the drugs are combined with other therapy.

Probing the Brain: Surgery and Electroshock

Some physicians attempt to treat mental illness by changing brain function di- rectly. **Psychosurgery** is an operation designed to intervene in the part of the brain thought to be responsible for emotional disorders or disturbed behavior.

✳ Newsweek *announces that Prozac is "a breakthrough drug for depression." Other media headlines herald the news that clozapine helps thousands of people with schizophre- nia. Why should the public be cau- tious before concluding that these drugs are miracle cures?*

■ **psychosurgery**
A surgical procedure that destroys se- lected areas of the brain believed to be involved in emotional disorders or violent, impulsive behavior.

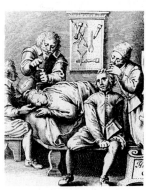

Throughout history, healers have tried to literally root out behavior they considered abnormal. An engraving from 1634 shows trepanning, *an ancient method of drilling holes in the skull to "release" psychic pressures supposedly causing mental illness.*

It should not be confused with brain surgery to remove an abnormal organic condition, such as a tumor.

In 1936, a Portuguese neurologist, Egas Moniz, developed a procedure that cut the fibers of the frontal lobes of the brain. The operation, called a leucotomy or prefrontal *lobotomy*, was supposed to reduce the patient's anxiety or other symptoms without impairing intellectual ability. This procedure was performed on tens of thousands of people in its heyday; unfortunately, it often left the patient apathetic and withdrawn (Valenstein, 1986). Moniz, who won a Nobel Prize for his work, was paralyzed later in life when he was shot in the spine; his assailant was a patient who was angry at having been lobotomized (Holmes, 1991).

With the advent of antipsychotic drugs in the 1950s, lobotomies declined in the United States, but other forms of psychosurgery took their place. For example, some surgeons have tried to reduce violent rages by removing parts of the amygdala, a part of the limbic system involved in emotion. Critics of psychosurgery argue that it is unreliable, has unpredictable results, and causes unintended brain damage (Robitscher, 1980). Because of the legal and ethical problems involved in psychosurgery, it is regarded as a procedure of last resort.

An equally controversial procedure is **electroconvulsive therapy (ECT),** or "shock treatment." An electrode is placed on one or both sides of the head, and a brief current is administered. The current triggers a seizure that typically lasts one minute, causing the body to convulse intensely. A colleague told us about a man who was given ECT in the early 1950s: The convulsions sent him flying off the table and shattered his legs. Cases such as this reinforce the public impression of ECT as a barbaric and painful practice, akin to electrocution. Today, however, the technique has been vastly modified and the voltage reduced. Patients are given muscle relaxants and anesthesia, so their convulsions are minimized and they can sleep through the procedure (Malitz & Sackeim, 1986). Advocates maintain that ECT is a far faster and more effective way to treat severe depression (especially in people who are suicidal) than drug therapy. The method lost favor when drugs seemed to be so promising and ECT so dangerous. When drugs proved to have limited effectiveness and to take time to work, and when new ways appeared of monitoring brain activity during ECT sessions, researchers began to reexamine ECT.

ECT affects every aspect of brain activity, including blood flow, neuroendocrine levels, and neurotransmitters. It is most effective with suicidally depressed people, for whom there is a risk in waiting until antidepressants or psychotherapy can take effect. ECT is not effective with other disorders, such as schizophrenia or alcoholism. Its main drawback is that it produces memory loss and other cognitive impairments, sometimes briefly but sometimes permanently. That is why some former patients call it "a crime against humanity," and a psychiatrist called the use of ECT "like hitting [someone] with a two-by-four" (Fisher, 1985). ECT continues to inspire passion, pro and con.

■ **electroconvulsive therapy (ECT)**

A procedure occasionally used for cases of prolonged major depression, in which a brief brain seizure is induced to alter brain chemistry.

QUICK QUIZ

A. Match the treatment with the problem(s) for which it is most typically used.

1. antipsychotic drugs
2. antidepressant drugs
3. lithium carbonate
4. electroconvulsive therapy

a. suicidal depression
b. manic depression
c. schizophrenia
d. depression and anxiety
e. obsessive-compulsive disorder

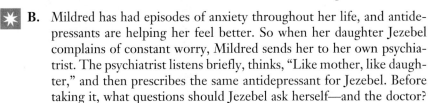 **B.** Mildred has had episodes of anxiety throughout her life, and antidepressants are helping her feel better. So when her daughter Jezebel complains of constant worry, Mildred sends her to her own psychiatrist. The psychiatrist listens briefly, thinks, "Like mother, like daughter," and then prescribes the same antidepressant for Jezebel. Before taking it, what questions should Jezebel ask herself—and the doctor?

ANSWERS:

A. 1. c 2. d, e 3. b 4. a **B.** Is Jezebel's problem as serious as her mother's, or is the doctor seeing a superficial similarity between them? What is Jezebel anxious *about?* Has the doctor taken Jezebel's full medical and psychological history? Are there other forms of therapy that might be tried first?

The Hoofbeats of a Zebra

One rainy afternoon a young woman named Sheila Allen went to a community hospital and asked for psychiatric help. Sheila Allen had virtually no strength left. She couldn't walk; she could barely sit up. For years she had been going to dozens of doctors, getting sicker and sicker. The doctors didn't take her complaints seriously, and finally she agreed with them that she needed to try the "kook hospital." Her diagnosis was "bizarre behavior, with looseness of thought associations and severe depression associated with suicidal thoughts."

Sheila Allen was lucky. At the hospital she met a neurologist who suspected she had an uncommon disease called myasthenia gravis, which weakens the muscles. His diagnosis proved correct. Fortunately, there is a treatment for this illness and Sheila Allen recovered. Why had no doctor correctly diagnosed her problem? Her neurologist said, "There is a saying about diagnosis—about why doctors often fail to recognize one of the less common diseases. It goes, 'When you hear hoofbeats, you don't necessarily think of a zebra.' I recognized the hoofbeats of a zebra" (Roueché, 1984).

All clinicians learn to recognize the hoofbeats that make the most noise in their profession. Mind-oriented people listen for one beat, body-oriented people for another. Throughout history, both sides have made terrible errors. In the nineteenth century, people thought tuberculosis was caused by a "tubercular personality" until the bacillus that causes the disease was discovered (Sontag, 1978). Conversely, madness was said to result from masturbation; male circumcision became popular as a way to prevent "masturbatory insanity." It was (mistakenly) believed that circumcised boys wouldn't masturbate (Paige, 1978; Szasz, 1970).

Errors of diagnosis and treatment still occur. A British medical historian, Elizabeth Thornton (1984), observed the case of a young woman who was admitted to a hospital for psychiatric treatment. The patient was not as fortunate as Sheila Allen. Her psychiatrists subjected her to months of psychoanalytic therapy while failing to diagnose her real problem, a brain tumor. (The great

Psychologically minded experts and medically minded experts often interpret the same behavior differently. How can we avoid the diagnostic errors that occur because of this either/or thinking?

composer George Gershwin was a victim of the same mistake of diagnosis.) Thornton collected dozens of these errors and even reanalyzed Freud's early cases. She believes that many of his patients were suffering from organic illnesses that were unidentified in Freud's day, such as tuberculous meningitis, temporal lobe epilepsy, and Tourette's syndrome.

But psychologists are also concerned about a comparable error: reducing complex psychological problems to matters of biochemistry. As we noted, some physicians are tempted to prescribe drugs indiscriminately, without finding out what the patient might be angry, depressed, or anxious *about*. Two psychosurgeons induced lesions on the amygdala of a man who, they said, had "paranoid delusions" about his wife's infidelity with a neighbor. Her denials would set the man into a rage. According to follow-ups conducted by an independent observer, the man never recovered. He was in and out of hospitals for years, with "paranoid delusions" that two doctors were out to get him. His wife divorced him and married the neighbor (Chorovor, 1974).

As long as people think that hoofbeats indicate only one animal, disagreements about medical and psychological models of mental illness will continue.

■ TYPES OF PSYCHOTHERAPY

All psychotherapists have one thing in common: They want to help clients think about their lives in new ways in order to find solutions to the problems of life. ("A Closer Look at Psychotherapy" examines this unifying theme in all therapies.) In this section we will consider the major schools of psychotherapy and

---

A CLOSER LOOK AT PSYCHOTHERAPY

Repairing Your Life—And Your Life Story

At the very beginning of this book we quoted George Gerbner's definition of human beings as "the only species that tells stories—and lives by the stories we tell." This idea—that the narratives we use to describe our lives are the key metaphor in understanding human behavior—is sweeping psychology and many other fields. Our plans, memories, love affairs, hatreds, ambitions and dreams, are guided by plot outlines. "Understanding one's past, interpreting one's actions, evaluating future possibilities—each is filtered through these stories," says Mary Gergen (1992). "Events 'make sense' as they are placed in the correct story form."

Thus we say, "I am this way because, as a small child, I ran away from home for two days, and then my parents. . . ." We say, "Let me tell you the story of how we fell in love." We say,

"When you hear what happened, you'll understand why I feel I was entitled to take such cold-hearted revenge." We say, "I can't be a surgeon, because I am. . . ." As George Howard (1991) puts it, life is the story we live by, pathology is a story gone mad, and psychotherapy is an exercise in "story repair."

Stories need not be *fictions*, in the child's meaning of "tell me a story." Rather, they are narratives that provide a unifying theme to organize the events of our lives and give them meaning. If you were writing a play about your life, with you as the leading actor, what would the script say? Do you see yourself as the victim or beneficiary of social forces, a product of your biology, free will, divine destiny, or an early trauma?

The process of psychotherapy is often one of replacing the client's self-defeating, pessimistic, or unrealistic life story with one that is more hopeful and attainable. In this view, successful therapy occurs when therapist and client agree on a new explanation of the client's problems, one that allows the person to make constructive changes. But the possibility of change must be part of the client's narrative.

One woman, "Karen Z.," who had had a devastating childhood, asked her psychotherapist,

some of their offshoots. To describe each of the therapeutic schools that follow, we will use our procrastinating friend Murray as an example to give you an idea of its basic philosophy and methods. But keep in mind that these therapies treat many problems, including emotional disorders, conflicts in relationships, and traumatic experiences.

Psychodynamic ("Insight") Therapies

Sigmund Freud was the father of the "talking cure." He believed that intensive probing of the past and of the mind would produce *insight*—the patient's moment of truth, the awareness of the reason for his or her symptoms and anguish. With insight and emotional release, the symptoms would disappear. Today, Freud's original method has evolved into many different forms, but the goal of insight unites them. These therapies are called *psychodynamic* because they are based on exploring the unconscious dynamics of personality, such as defenses and conflicts.

Traditional, "orthodox" psychoanalysis is a method for those who have money and time. The client usually meets with the analyst three to five times a week, often for many years. One orthodox psychoanalyst, John Gedo (1979), reported that in 20 years he treated only 36 people, each one requiring "more than 600 sessions, sometimes as many as 1,000, spread over 3 to 7 years." (In the film *Sleeper*, Woody Allen played a character who was in suspended animation for two centuries. When he awakes, his first thought is: "I haven't seen my analyst in 200 years! He was a strict Freudian—if I'd been going all this time I'd probably almost be cured by now.")

Michael Mahony (1991), if she would ever recover from her chronic depression and sexual inhibitions. "Now tell me straight," she asked him, "would it be better for me to give up on ever having a happy sex life or is it possible to recover from that kind of thing?" Mahony waffled, telling her that some therapists would say she would always be scarred by her early experience, while others would emphasize the power of recovery. Still, she pressed him for his opinion. "I believe that many people are stronger and more resilient than we realize," said Mahony finally, "and I will not foreclose on the capacities of the human spirit."

In the next three years, Karen Z. took control of her life. She left her empty marriage, launched a new career, joined new groups, formed new friendships. Years after leaving therapy, she sent a card to Mahony: "You were right."

Karen Z.'s account shows us that in psychotherapy as in the rest of life, stories are important, but they aren't everything. Her improvement depended not only on a new belief that she would one day be happy, but also on her own actions in making a new life for herself. Stories aren't just figments of the imagination; they *come from somewhere*. The experiences and circumstances of people's lives shape their stories, and stories in turn affect the possibility of changing those conditions.

Salvador Minuchin (1991), the family therapist, worries about the growing tendency of psychotherapists to overlook the objective realities of their clients' lives in favor of emphasizing their self-generated life stories. "How could it be good therapy," he asks, "to tell a Salvadorean mother whose eldest son has been 'disappeared' by a right-wing death squad that the members of her family were self-determining, cocreators of their own narratives?" Yet even for this Salvadorean mother, the explanation that she—and thousands like her—make of their tragedy has tremendous consequences. Social movements and revolutions begin, after all, in the minds of people who say: "We will not accept the official story, and we have the power to change it."

People begin to shape their personal narratives in late adolescence. "Early in life we are free to choose what life story we will inhabit," observes Howard (1991), "—and later we find we are lived by that story." Some stories give us wings; others imprison us. One common goal of all good psychotherapies is to help people create a personal narrative that works best for them.

Freud (1910) believed that Leonardo da Vinci's paintings of Madonnas were a sublimated expression of his longing for his mother, from whom he had been separated early in life. One goal of psychoanalysis is to help clients "sublimate" their energies constructively instead of expressing them neurotically.

In analysis, the client lies on a couch, facing away from the analyst, and uses **free association** to say whatever comes to mind. For example, by free associating to his dreams, his fantasies about work, and his early memories, Murray might gain the insight that he procrastinates as a way of expressing anger toward his parents. He might realize he is angry because they insist that he study for a career he dislikes. Ideally, Murray will come to this insight by himself. If the analyst suggests it, Murray might feel too defensive about displeasing his parents to accept it.

The second major element of psychoanalysis is **transference,** the patient's transfer of emotional responses toward his or her parents to the analyst. A woman who failed to resolve her Oedipal love for her father might seem to "fall in love" with the analyst. A man who was always angry at his mother for rejecting him might now become furious with his analyst for going on vacation. Through transference, analysts believe, patients resolve their emotional problems.

Other psychotherapists use Freudian principles but reject traditional psychoanalytic methods. They face the client; they participate more; they are more goal-directed. *Brief psychodynamic therapy* is one alternative to traditional analysis. Freud himself worried about the question of length of treatment in his essay, "Analysis Terminable and Interminable." However, most of his followers operated on the principle that the longer a patient stays in therapy, the better. "In Freud's day," observes Rachel Hare-Mustin (1983), "analysis lasted a year and marriage lasted a lifetime. Now it's just the opposite." Instead of "interminable" analysis, time-limited or brief therapy consists of 15, 20, or 25 sessions. Without delving into the client's entire history, the therapist listens to the client's problems and formulates the main issue or *dynamic focus* (Strupp & Binder, 1984). The rest of therapy focuses on the person's self-defeating habits and repetitive problems. The therapist looks for clues in the client's behavior in the therapeutic relationship to identify and change these chronic patterns.

Cognitive and Behavioral Therapies

Psychologists who practice cognitive or behavioral therapy would focus on helping Murray change his current behavior and attitudes rather than providing him with insight. "Mur," they would say, "you have lousy study habits. And you have a set of beliefs about studying, writing papers, and success that are woefully unrealistic." Such therapists would not worry much about Murray's past, his parents, his unconscious anxieties, or his motives.

In Chapter 6 we discussed the major principles of learning theory and behaviorism and some of their applications (such as the token economy). Behavior therapists use a variety of techniques derived from behavioral principles, including systematic desensitization, aversive conditioning, flooding, and contracts.

1. *Systematic desensitization* is a step-by-step process of "desensitizing" a client to a feared object or experience. It combines relaxation training with a systematic hierarchy of stimuli, sometimes in imagined situations and sometimes in real ones, that lead gradually to the greatest fear. The hierarchy for a person who is terrified of flying might be: Read about airplane safety; visit an airport; sit in a plane while it is on the ground; take a short flight; take a long flight. At each step the person must become comfortable before moving on.

2. *Aversive conditioning* uses punishment to replace the positive reinforcement that perpetuates a bad habit. For example, a woman who bites her nails is reinforced each time she does so by relief of anxiety and a brief good feeling. A behavior therapist might have her wear a rubber band around her wrist and ask her to snap it (hard!) each time she bites her nails or feels the desire to do

■ **free association**
In psychoanalysis, a method of recovering unconscious conflicts by saying freely whatever comes to mind.
■ **transference**
In psychoanalysis, a critical step in which the patient transfers emotional feelings for his or her parents to the therapist.

Two therapists assist a phobic woman who is afraid of stairs. In this form of behavior therapy, the therapists take the client directly into the feared situation in order to extinguish her fear. What situations would you have to put yourself in to extinguish your own fears? Public speaking? Visiting the spider display at a zoo? Looking down from the top of the Empire State Building?

so. The goal is to make sure that there are no continuing rewards for the undesirable behavior.

3. *Flooding or exposure treatments* take the individual right into the most feared situation, but the therapist goes along with the client to show that the situation isn't going to kill either of them. Exposure therapy has proved very effective with agoraphobia and other anxiety disorders (Agras, 1985).

4. *Behavioral records and contracts* are ways of changing unwanted habits, such as overeating or quarreling, by keeping careful track of the rewards that keep the habit going. A man might not be aware of how much he eats throughout the day; a behavioral record shows that he eats more junk food than he realized in the late afternoon. Once the unwanted behavior is identified, along with the reinforcements that keep it going, a new program is instituted with a new program of reinforcements. A husband and wife who fight over housework, for instance, might be asked to make up an actual contract of who will do what, with specified rewards for carrying out their responsibilities. Without such a contract, it is easy to shout accusations: "You *never* do anything around here!"

A behaviorist might treat Murray's procrastination in several ways. Murray might not be aware of how he actually spends his time when he is avoiding his studies. Afraid he hasn't time to do everything, he does nothing. Keeping a behavioral diary lets Murray know exactly how he spends his time, and how much time he could realistically allot to a project. (Procrastinators often are poor judges of how much time it takes to do things.) The therapist would help Murray set *behavioral goals*, small step by small step. Instead of having a vague, impossibly huge goal, such as "I'm going to reorganize my life," Murray would establish specific small goals, such as reading the two books necessary for an English paper and writing one page of an assignment.

The therapist might also provide specific *skills training* to make sure Murray knows how to reach those goals. It's not enough to tell someone "Just don't be shy" if the person simply doesn't know how to make companionable small talk when meeting a potential date. There are countless skills-training programs available—for parents who don't know how to discipline children, for people with social anxieties, for children and adults who are aggressive because they don't know how to express themselves, and so on.

Any situation can be interpreted in different ways. According to cognitive therapists, depression results from thoughts such as these: "I'm alone again; no one wants to be with me; everyone but me is having a good time." Yet many people enjoy solitude and self-reflection and do not "think themselves" into a state of gloom when they are alone.

The poet Michael Casey described the first daffodil that bravely rises through the snow as "a gleam of laughter in a sullen face." Are you more inclined to focus on the lingering icy clutch of winter or the early sunny signs of spring?

Of course, people's thoughts, feelings, and motivations can influence their behavior. Most of us reward and punish ourselves by the judgments we make of our actions. "Gee, I did that well," we say, or we torment ourselves with guilt for not doing something well. In discussing emotion (Chapter 9) and emotional disorders (Chapter 16), we saw how distorted thoughts and perceptions are related to moods and mood problems.

Cognitive therapy aims to correct distorted and unrealistic thinking (Beck, 1976, 1991; Ellis & Dryden, 1987). Clients may be asked to write down their negative thoughts, read the thoughts as if someone else had said them, and then write a rational response to each one. For example, many people have unrealistic notions of what they "must" or "should" do in their lives, and often they do not pause to examine these notions carefully.

A cognitive therapist would treat Murray's procrastination problem by exploring Murray's thoughts and feelings about his work. Many procrastinators are perfectionists. If they can't do something perfectly, they won't do it at all. Unable to accept their human limitations, they set impossible standards for themselves. Perfectionists are vulnerable to depression because the unreasonable demands they make of themselves give them ample opportunity to fail.

Murray may be afraid to write his term papers because he believes he cannot express his ideas well. When he writes a sentence, he imagines his teacher making fun of it. He imagines all possible criticisms in advance, and his poor essay doesn't stand up to them. In time, he decides that turning in nothing at all is better than turning in a bad paper. This decision brings its own problems. "Since the paper is late," he thinks, "it has to be even better to make up for its lateness." Now suppose Murray examines these thoughts:

Negative Thoughts	Rational Responses
That sentence isn't good enough. I'd better rewrite it.	Good enough for what? True, it won't win a Pulitzer Prize, but it's just fine for a small English essay.
It's terrible not to do my best. I'm wasting my potential.	It's terrible to waste my life rewriting English essays. It's a greater waste to do nothing with my abilities.

True behaviorists consider thoughts to be "behaviors" that are modifiable by learning principles. In practice, most psychologists agree that thoughts influence behavior and behavior influences thoughts. Cognitive and behavioral therapies often borrow each other's methods, so "cognitive-behavior" therapy is more common than either method alone.

Humanistic Therapies

Humanistic therapies, like their parent philosophy humanism, start from the assumption that people seek self-actualization and self-fulfillment. These therapies generally do not delve into past conflicts, but aim to help people feel better about themselves and free themselves from self-imposed limits. They share the belief that the way to do so is by exploring what is going on "here and now," not the issues of "why and how."

In *client-centered* or *nondirective* therapy, developed by Carl Rogers, the therapist's role is to listen sympathetically, to offer what Rogers called *unconditional positive regard*, to be an "ideal parent." This method aims to build the client's self-esteem, the feeling that he or she is loved and respected no matter what. To Rogerians, it almost doesn't matter what the client's specific complaint is. Thus a Rogerian might assume that Murray's procrastination masks his low self-regard, and that Murray is out of touch with his real feelings and wishes.

Although client-centered therapy has no specific techniques, Rogers (1961) believed that effective therapists must have three qualities. They must be warm, providing unconditional positive regard for the client; they must be genuine and honest in expressing their feelings; and they must show accurate empathic understanding of the client's problems. The therapist's support for the client, according to Rogers, is eventually adopted by the client, who will become more self-accepting. Once that is accomplished, the person can accept the limitations of others too.

Gestalt therapy, developed by Frederick (Fritz) Perls (1969), aims at self-actualization through emotional liberation. Perls believed that people tend to think too much and to suppress their feelings. As a result, he said, they lose the ability to feel and to function at their full potential. *Gestalt* means "whole," and Perls wanted to "fill the holes" in personality.

Perls worked in a group setting, where people were encouraged to "let it all hang out"—that is, to express any feeling that they had without fear of consequences. One method was the direct encounter, in which brutal frankness, ventilation of any and all negative or taboo feelings, and confrontation were encouraged. Another method was *role playing*, in which, for instance, an individual who was angry at his father might play himself talking to his father, then play his father talking back to him. By acting out both sides to a conflict, Perls maintained, a person gains understanding. Unlike a Rogerian, a Gestalt therapist might fight back with Murray, insult him, cajole him, or join him in role playing.

Existential therapy helps clients explore the meaning of existence, facing with courage the great questions of life—such as death, freedom, free will, alienation from oneself and others, loneliness, and meaninglessness. Existential therapists believe that our lives are not inevitably determined by our pasts or our circumstances; instead, we have the power to choose our own destinies. As Irvin Yalom (1989) explains, "the crucial first step in therapy is the patient's assumption of responsibility for his or her life predicament. As long as one believes that one's problems are caused by some force or agency outside oneself, there is no leverage in therapy." Victor Frankl (1955) developed a form of existential therapy after surviving a Nazi concentration camp. In that pit of horror, he observed, some people maintained their dignity and sanity because they were able to find meaning in the experience, shattering though it was.

Some observers believe that ultimately, all therapies are "existential." In different ways, therapy helps people determine what is important to them, what values guide them, and what changes they will have the courage to make. An existential therapist might help Murray think about the significance of his procrastination, what his ultimate goals in life are, and how he might find the strength to carry out those goals.

Beyond the Person: Family and Group Therapies

Murray's situation is getting worse. His father has begun to call him Mr. To-morrow, which upsets his mother, and his brother the math major has been cal-culating how much tuition money Murray's incompletes are costing. His older sister Isabel, the biochemist who never had an incomplete in her life, now pro-poses that all of them go to a family therapist. "Murray's not the only one in this family with complaints," she says.

Family therapists maintain that Murray's problem is not *in him*. It developed in a social context, it is sustained by a social context, and any change he makes will affect that context.

THE FAMILY KALEIDOSCOPE. Salvador Minuchin (1984) compares the family to a kaleidoscope, a changing pattern of mosaics in which the pattern is larger than any one piece. Efforts to isolate and "therapize" one piece, one member of the family without the others, are, in this view, doomed. For one thing, each mem-ber has his or her own perceptions about the others, which may be entirely wrong. For another, family members are usually unaware of how they influence one another. By observing the entire family together (or, in the case of couple problems, both partners together), the therapist can discover the family's ten-sions and imbalances in power and communication (Satir, 1983).

In "psychosomatic families," only one member (usually a child) actually gets an illness or psychological symptoms, but that illness plays a role in the work-ings of the whole family. Minuchin believes that psychosomatic families have a common feature: They avoid conflict. The child gets sick as a way of express-ing anger, keeping the parents together, or asserting control. For example, Min-uchin argues, anorexia nervosa tends to occur in families in which parents over-control their daughters. Refusing to eat, even to the point of starvation, can be the daughter's way of controlling the one thing she can, her body (Minuchin, Rosman, & Baker, 1978).

Some family therapists use a *multigenerational* approach, helping clients iden-tify repetitive patterns of behavior across generations in their families (Kerr & Bowen, 1988). The therapist and client create a *genogram*, a family tree of psy-chologically significant events across as many generations as the client can de-termine (Carter & McGoldrick, 1988). Sometimes the genogram highlights the origins of current problems and conflicts. The genogram of the playwright Eu-gene O'Neill, for instance, shows a pattern of estrangement between father and children for three generations (see Figure 17.1). Sometimes the genogram re-veals positive patterns. The genogram of Alexander Graham Bell, who invented the telephone, reveals a three-generation dedication to solving problems in hear-ing and speaking.

Although many family therapists treat the whole family, others will treat in-dividuals in a *family systems* perspective (Bowen, 1978; Carter & McGoldrick, 1988). Clients learn that if they change in any way, even in getting rid of their problem or unhappiness, their families will protest noisily. They will send ex-plicit and subtle messages that read, "Change back!" The family systems view recognizes that if one family member changes, the others must change too: If I won't tango with you, you can't tango with me. But most people don't like change. They are comfortable with old patterns and habits, even those that cause them trouble. They *want* to keep tangoing, even if their feet hurt.

One branch of family therapy is called *strategic therapy*. Its advocates approach family problems with minimal emphasis on learning the family's history, gen-erating insights, or fostering humanistic principles of self-fulfillment. Rather, they use whatever "tactics" or "strategies" they believe will help the individual or family in question. They try to figure out how a person's problem works in that person's life and then to determine what particular strategy might undo it.

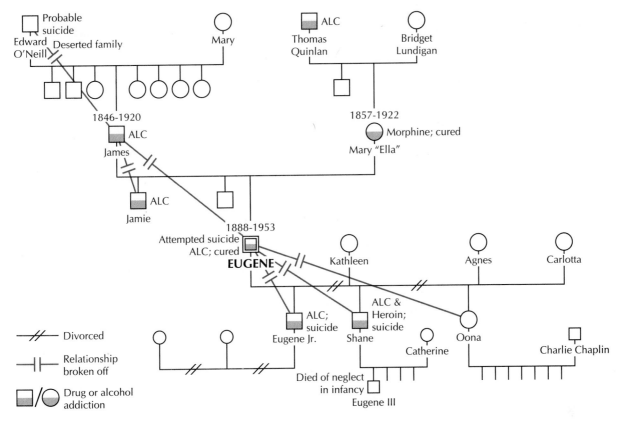

FIGURE 17.1

The family genogram of playwright Eugene O'Neill
*The O'Neill family shows multigenerational patterns of estrangement between father
and children, multiple marriages, and addiction. Both Eugene and his older brother
Jamie felt alienated from their father; in turn, Eugene was totally estranged from
his two sons, and he never spoke to his daughter Oona again after she married
Charlie Chaplin. Eugene attempted suicide; both of his sons did commit suicide.
Eugene's grandfather, father, older brother, and sons were alcoholics; his mother,
a morphine addict for 26 years, was later cured. Eugene, who had had problems
with alcohol as well, quit drinking at age 37.*

*Constructing a genogram allows family therapists and their clients to observe pat-
terns across generations that often illuminate current conflicts and concerns. By recognizing patterns that are destructive, family members can begin to change them
(McGoldrick & Gerson, 1985).*

One famous practitioner of strategic therapy, on individuals as well as families, was Milton Erickson, who was known for his unconventional methods.
For example, he used "paradoxical" techniques, in which he would instruct a
person to do *more* of what he or she was trying to eliminate. Erickson once
treated an old man who had insomnia by telling him to get up at 2 A.M. and
scrub the kitchen floor. This technique showed them both that the man's insomnia was not a symptom of anxiety but simply of having excess energy (Haley, 1984). A strategic family therapist would try various tactics with Murray,
from simply offering practical advice on writing papers to providing the paradoxical advice to *keep* procrastinating. If Murray then rebels and writes his paper, the goal has been reached. If he obeys the instructions to procrastinate, he
shows he is willing to engage in the therapy.

In general, family therapists would observe how Murray's procrastination fits
his family dynamics. Perhaps it allows Murray to get his father's attention and
his mother's sympathy. Perhaps it keeps Murray from facing his greatest fear:

that if he does finish his work, it won't measure up to his father's high standards. The therapist will not only help Murray change, but will help his family deal with a changed Murray.

GROUP THERAPY. Murray could also meet weekly with a group of procrastinators who already know every one of his excuses and habits. Group therapies are as diverse as their leaders. Psychodynamic therapists, cognitive-behaviorists, family therapists, and humanists all may run group therapy sessions. Some groups consist of people who share a problem; others consist of people with different problems. Only the basic format—self-revelation in a group—is the same. In group therapy, ideally, members learn that their problems are not unique. They learn to speak up and become more assertive with other people in (presumably) a safe setting. They learn that they cannot get away with their usual excuses because others in the group have tried them all (Yalom, 1989). Group therapies are commonly used in institutions, such as prisons and mental hospitals. But they are also popular among people who have a range of social difficulties, such as shyness and anxiety.

QUICK QUIZ

Match each method with the therapy most likely to use it.

1. free association	a. cognitive therapy
2. systematic desensitization	b. psychoanalysis
3. facing the fear of death	c. humanistic therapies
4. reappraisal of thoughts	d. behavior therapy
5. unconditional positive regard	e. group therapy
6. revelation with others	f. family therapy
7. genogram	g. existential therapy
8. contract specifying duties	

ANSWERS:

1. b 2. d 3. g 4. a 5. c 6. e 7. f 8. d

Psychotherapy in Practice

The four general approaches to psychotherapy that we have discussed may seem wildly different. In theory, they are, and so are the techniques resulting from those theories. Yet in practice, many psychotherapists are **eclectic,** borrowing a method from here, an idea from there. This flexibility suits their own preferences and enables them to treat many different clients. In a survey of family therapists, more than one-third described their methods as eclectic, and only small minorities rigidly adhered to "pure" theoretical schools within their field (Rait, 1988).

As we noted, cognitive-behavior therapy is one popular hybrid. Some cognitive therapists have incorporated psychoanalytic ideas, such as the importance of dealing with the client's defenses, insights, transference, and motivations (Safran & Segal, 1990). Some psychoanalytic therapists borrow methods from the family systems approach. Some humanistic therapists are more "directive" than the theory recommends and some behaviorists are less directive. Many therapists have borrowed role-playing techniques from Gestalt therapy. Because of this overlap, some researchers are trying to find the common processes in all therapies, even those as different as cognitive, psychoanalytic, humanistic, and behaviorist (Mahony, 1991; Safran & Segal, 1990).

■ **eclectic**
Literally, selected from various sources; in psychotherapy, the term describes the common practice of using methods from different theoretical schools.

ten stop taking their medication. Their psychotic symptoms return, the patients are rehospitalized, and the "revolving door" cycle continues.

In addition, hospital administrators, anxious to avoid legal charges of violating patients' rights, often discharge patients as soon as possible without regard for where they might go. Some state regulations have made it very difficult to hospitalize people involuntarily for longer than a few weeks (even those who are dangerous to themselves or others), and even difficult to keep patients who *want* to stay. Although this means that hospitals can't make the mistake they did with Gladys Burr, it creates other problems. A woman who had been hospitalized 12 times in ten years for violent attacks was let out (again) after a four-month confinement for stabbing someone. She then killed two people with a semiautomatic rifle. Her parents and psychiatrists had been unable to commit her against her will.

Finally, having pressured the states to close their mental hospitals and release disturbed people, the government then cut financial aid for local and state mental health care and for housing the poor and homeless. One result was the "dumping" of thousands of patients onto the streets. Another was the shifting of the care of chronic mental patients to profit-making, private nursing homes and board-and-care homes, which are often unregulated and poorly staffed. For the most part, mental patients are no better off in these facilities than they were when they were warehoused in state institutions (Shadish, Lurigio, & Lewis, 1989). And a third result was the burdening of general hospitals with people who have mental problems (Kiesler & Simpkins, 1991).

One possible solution is "involuntary outpatient commitment": Patients who meet certain standards of being dangerous to themselves or the community could be compelled by the courts to take part in community treatment programs (Mulvey, Geller, & Roth, 1987). Patients would be monitored regularly, and only if they violate the treatment regimen would they be committed to an institution. Opponents of this idea argue that, in practice, patients would often end up being policed, like parolees from prison, without actually getting treatment. They worry about granting the state too much power to invade the privacy of the mentally ill. To make sure a person is taking medication, for example, would you require drug tests? Exactly what aspects of the person's life would you monitor for treatment—the patient's family life? Personal relationships? Friends? Drinking?

You are the public. What services should governments provide for disturbed people? How can communities protect the rights of the mentally ill while protecting the safety of the public? And what about individuals who pose no danger to themselves or others? Should cities try to force such people into shelters, or do people have a right to live on the streets if they choose? What do you think?

vices they provide for their residents; in their primary emphasis (work, social activities, companionship); in the strictness of their rules (e.g., about visitors or alcohol); and in the length of stay of their residents, from six months to indefinitely (Torrey, 1988).

Newer methods follow the *clubhouse model,* a program for mentally ill people that provides rehabilitation counseling, job and skills training, and a support network. Members may live at the clubhouse until they are ready to be on their own, and they may visit the clubhouse at any time. New York City's Fountain House, one of the oldest such programs in the country, has an excellent track record (Beard, Propst, & Malamud, 1982). Other community approaches include the establishment of support systems, family therapy, foster care and family home alternatives, and family support groups (Hatfield & Lefley, 1987). The success of these programs often depends on the dedication of the people running them, which is why it is often difficult to transplant a successful program from one place to another (Torrey, 1988). To solve this problem, some psychologists are developing ways of teaching the staff who work with psychiatric patients how to set rehabilitation goals, how to teach everyday skills, and how to evaluate patients' progress (Anthony, Cohen, & Kennard, 1990).

Rehabilitation psychologists, by the way, do not work only with schizophrenics. We know a secretary who permanently injured her back and was no longer able to sit long hours at a desk or resume her old job. She entered a program run by rehabilitation psychologists who were helping people find new careers when they could no longer work at their former ones. Today she has a new career. She's a rehabilitation psychologist.

The Self-Help Movement

Long before there were psychotherapists, there were sympathetic advisers. Long before there were psychologists, there was psychological help. Nowadays, there are literally thousands of programs designed to help people help themselves—with a little help from their friends.

SELF-HELP AND SUPPORT GROUPS. Self-help group members outnumber therapy patients four to one; we are truly in the midst of a "self-help revolution" (Gartner & Riessman, 1984). Self-help groups are usually organized around a common concern. Name it, and there is a group for it: Alcoholics Anonymous, Overeaters Anonymous, Parents Anonymous (for abusive parents), Depressives Anonymous, Schizophrenics Anonymous. There are countless nonanonymous groups such as those for gay fathers, divorced people, women who have had mastectomies, parents of murdered children, rape victims, widows, stepparents, cancer patients, and relatives of patients.

By uniting people with common problems, support groups offer their members three ingredients of feeling better: understanding, empathy, and advice. Others in the group have been there, know what you are going through, and may have found solutions you never would have imagined. For people who fear that no one else has ever suffered what they have or felt what they feel, such groups can be reassuring in ways that family, friends, and even psychotherapists are not (Dunkel-Schetter, 1984; Wyatt & Mickey, 1987).

Although self-help groups can be immensely therapeutic, they are not therapy. They do not search for "underlying problems." They are not designed to help people with serious psychological difficulties. "But there is one benefit of a self-help group that you don't get with a therapist," says Marion Jacobs, Co-Director of the California Self-Help Center at UCLA. "At the end of the program, you have ten new friends."

"LIFE CHANGE" ENCOUNTER GROUPS. During the 1960s, Fritz Perls's Gestalt techniques became the basis of the encounter group movement. Encounter groups aimed for "personal growth," not psychotherapy. The encounter-group scene has changed in many ways since then, not all of them desirable. "What began

This self-help group consists of several AIDS patients and two volunteers, who gather for sessions in which they share concerns and offer constructive advice. In this session, they are "visualizing" the disease in an effort to control its effects.

as something novel, spontaneous, unstructured and filled with surprise," wrote critic Thomas Kiernan (1974), "has quickly developed teachers, high priests, official spokesmen, orthodoxies, heresies, even messianic claims, rituals, dogmas, an ecclesiastical jargon and a Billy Graham-type of show business promotion."

Encounter groups exist today in dozens of different forms, none regulated by law or professional standards. Many promise increased awareness, unconditional regard from others, and self-fulfillment. But they vary widely in their philosophy and in the kinds of encounters they offer. Some of the programs are mild in method and intention, offering support, cohesiveness, and a search for spiritual meaning (M. Galanter, 1989, 1990). But many are based on breaking people down by putting them through isolation, stress, fatigue, and hunger, and then "reconstructing" them in the group's image. The psychological casualties are high in such settings (Glass, Kirsch, & Parris, 1977). (In Chapter 18 we will look at methods of coercive persuasion that such groups use.)

Poor Murray! He's getting a little tired by now, having tried so many therapies. That last weekend with the Nature Walk ("Trek to Truth") Encounter was a lot of fun, but now he's *really* behind. All of these choices are enough to make a person procrastinate about getting help. Which therapy or self-help program is the "right" one?

■ EVALUATING PSYCHOTHERAPY AND ITS ALTERNATIVES

In studying the matter of effectiveness, researchers must overcome several difficulties:

• *The justification of effort problem.* People usually become attached to their therapists or groups, especially if they have invested money or time in them. (Remember "the justification of effort" research in Chapter 10.) The minute researchers say that some therapy doesn't "work," they hear a chorus of howls: "But psychotherapy worked for *me!* I would *never* have (taken that job/moved to Cincinnati/left home) if it hadn't been for Dr. Blitznik!" Alas, none of us can be our own control group. That is, we can't know what would have happened *without* Dr. Blitznik. Maybe we would have taken the job, moved to Cincinnati, or left home anyway.

• *The illusion of improvement.* Most people who go through *any* therapy or self-improvement program will tell you they are the better for it. "I went through _____ and now I am a new person!" "I took a course in _____ and it changed my life!" Every program claims enthusiastic graduates, even when studies find that the program or therapy was objectively ineffective (Hinrichsen, Revenson, & Shinn, 1985). One reason seems to be that people edit their memories of what they were like before, because they want to believe that they are consistent. If their attitudes then change, people revise their memories, "recalling" past attitudes that are virtually identical to their present ones. But when people want to believe they *have* changed, they revise their memories in the opposite direction. In one study, participants in a self-improvement program exaggerated, in recall, how poorly off they were before the program and how much better they were afterward (Conway & Ross, 1984). When participants accept a program's validity, they anticipate change from the start, look for change as they go along, and overestimate the amount of change at the end.

• *Complexity of elements.* Another problem in measuring the effectiveness of therapy is the sheer number of elements involved: qualities of the therapist and client, the kind of therapy, the nature of the problem, and the duration of the therapy. People may be depressed or anxious for a variety of reasons, and some

Psychotherapy clients will tell you how grateful they are to Dr. Blitznik for changing their lives. But perhaps their lives would have changed anyway. How can we evaluate the true effectiveness of psychotherapy?

may respond better to one kind of therapy than another (Mahony, 1991; Persons, 1991). It is hard to measure every factor objectively and then untangle the complicated interactions among all of them.

• *Defining "success."* Whether therapy is "successful" depends on how success is defined. In one follow-up study of 16 men with erection problems, Stephen Levine and David Agle (1978) learned how complicated it is to define success in sex therapy. Is a man "cured" if he can achieve erections but is so worried about failing that he disregards his wife's sexual satisfaction? Is he "cured" if he can achieve erections but doesn't much want to? What if he can have erections half the time? When the researchers defined "cure" as *reduced frequency* of erection failure, sex therapy was successful in ten cases. When they defined "cure" as complete elimination of sexual problems in both husband and wife, sex therapy was successful in only one case. In some couples, solving the sexual problem upset a delicate marital balance of power, creating new problems.

Some psychotherapists believe that "feeling better" is a good enough measure of effectiveness. Others argue that effectiveness is unmeasurable. Anyone, they say, can see that therapy helps. Critics reply that *assertions* of effectiveness do not substitute for *demonstrations* of effectiveness, especially now that psychotherapy and self-help programs have become big business (Fischer, 1978). Many are worried about the *scientist-practitioner gap*, the fact that increasing numbers of psychotherapists practice their own kind of therapy without paying much attention to the findings of scientist/researchers (Persons, 1991).

Despite these problems of measurement, psychologists have conducted literally hundreds of studies designed to test the effectiveness of therapy, counseling, and self-help groups. First, the good news: Psychotherapy does seem to be better than doing nothing at all. People in almost any professional treatment improve more than people who do not get help (Lambert, 1983; Robinson, Berman, & Neimeyer, 1990; Smith, Glass, & Miller, 1980). Now, the sobering news: The people who do the best in therapy also have the least serious problems to begin with. Long-standing personality patterns and psychotic disorders are not appreciably helped by psychotherapy or its alternatives (Strupp, 1982). Finally, the bad news: In some cases, psychotherapy is harmful because of the therapist's incompetence, bias, or unethical methods (Lambert, Christensen, & DeJulio, 1983).

When Therapy Helps

Psychotherapy is a social exchange. Like all relationships, its success depends on qualities of both participants and on the "fit" between the two people (Frank, 1985).

THE SEVEN DWARFS AFTER THERAPY

How much can therapy change a person—and how can we evaluate "change"?

THE SUCCESSFUL CLIENT. Good therapeutic candidates combine a basically strong sense of self with sufficient distress to motivate them to change (Strupp, 1982). For example, one study of depressed elderly people found that cognitive, behavioral, or brief dynamic therapy were equally likely to be successful. What made the difference in outcome was the clients' *commitment* to the therapy, *willingness* to work on their problems, and their *expectations* of success. In turn, the people with commitment and willingness had support from their families and a personal style of dealing actively with problems instead of avoiding them (Gaston et al., 1988, 1989).

One reason that psychotherapies are so rarely "pure" in their methods is that the people who seek therapy are diverse. Some are introspective and want to talk about their childhoods. Others are practical sorts who attack an emotional problem as they would attack an overgrown lawn: Let's mow it down. Some want an open-ended chance to talk about their feelings. Others want *action*. These personality differences often influence the approach that the therapist uses, the course of therapy, and the results.

THE SUCCESSFUL THERAPIST. Even within the same school of therapy, why do some therapists succeed brilliantly and others fail? The answer has to do with the therapist's personality, particularly the qualities that Carl Rogers praised: empathy, warmth, genuineness, and imagination (see Figure 17.2). The great teachers who establish new schools of therapy often get high rates of success because of their own "healing power" and charisma. They make their clients feel respected, accepted, and understood. In a study of 59 people in psychodynamic therapy, the one factor that predicted progress was the client's perception of the therapist's empathy (Free et al., 1985).

The qualities of a good therapist are not limited to professional psychologists. Many people who are unhappy or in a crisis cope with their difficulties by talking with friends, relatives, or religious advisers. Counselors, social workers, and even paraprofessionals (people who have some experience but not an advanced degree) can be as effective as clinical psychologists in treating most everyday problems (Strupp, 1982; Strupp & Hadley, 1979).

THE THERAPEUTIC ALLIANCE. Ultimately, success in any form of therapy depends on the *therapeutic alliance* that the therapist and client establish together, which in turn depends on their ability to understand one another (Strupp, 1982). This does not mean that the therapist and client must be the same race, gender, sexual orientation, or religion; it doesn't even mean that they have to *like* one another, although it helps. (The story goes that one of Milton Erickson's clients blurted out one day, "Do I have to like you?" Erickson replied, "Certainly not. Our work is far too important for it to matter whether or not you like me." The patient sighed in relief and proceeded to do well in treatment.)

However, misunderstandings, whether they result from ignorance, dissimilar values, or prejudice on either side, do make therapy more difficult (McGoldrick, Pearce, & Giordano, 1982). For example, some white therapists misunderstand their black clients' body language. They regard lack of eye contact and frequent glancing around as the client's attempt to "size up what can be ripped off," instead of as signs of discomfort and an effort to get oriented (Brodsky, 1982). From their standpoint, black clients often misunderstand or distrust the white therapist's demand for self-disclosure. A lifetime of experience often makes them reluctant to reveal feelings that they believe a white person wouldn't understand or accept (Ridley, 1984). For their part, black therapists sometimes have to deal with clients who are bigoted.

Often, therapists must distinguish normal cultural patterns from individual psychological problems (Sue, 1991). For example, Hispanic and Asian clients

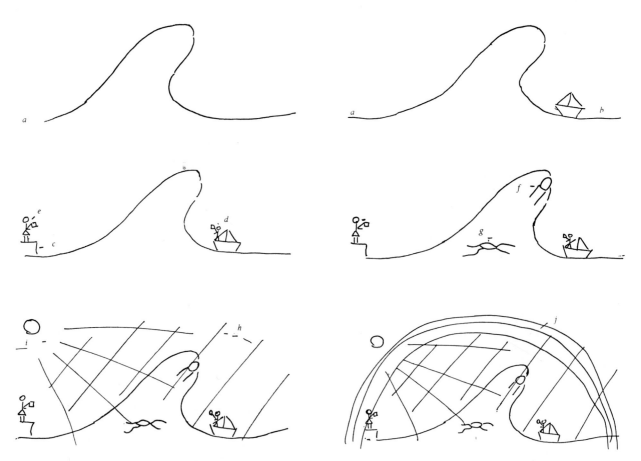

FIGURE 17.2

Psychotherapy in action: How one therapist reached a withdrawn boy
Robert Hobson (1985) spent many weeks trying to communicate with Stephen, a 15-year-old boy who refused to speak or look at him. One day, in frustration, Hobson took an envelope and drew a squiggly line (a) and invited Stephen to add to the picture. Stephen drew a ship (b), thereby turning Hobson's line into a "terrifying tidal wave." Was the boy, Hobson wondered, afraid of being emotionally "drowned"?

Hobson next drew (c), a landing pier (representing safety). Stephen was not interested in safety. He responded with (d), a person waving goodbye.

Hobson, suspecting that Stephen's problem might stem from emotional separation from his mother, drew (e), a woman waving goodbye. Stephen drew (f), and spoke for the first time: "A flying fish." Hobson drew (g) and said "An octopus." Stephen, shoulders drooping in sadness, marked up the entire sketch with lines (h), adding, "It's raining."

Hobson, hoping to convey optimism, drew the sun (i), its rays conflicting with the rain. Stephen paused, and looked at Hobson intently for the first time. He drew large arcs embracing the whole illustration (j). "A rainbow," said Stephen. He smiled.

are likely to react to a formal interview with a therapist with relative passivity, deference, and inhibited silence, leading some therapists to diagnose a "problem" of shyness that is only a cultural norm. Some Hispanics respond to catastrophic stress with an *ataque nervioso*, a nervous attack of screaming, swooning, and agitation. It is a culturally determined response, but an uninformed clinician might label it as a sign of pathology (Malgady, Rogler, & Costantino, 1987).

Some psychologists are trying to develop forms of therapy that fit the client's cultural background. *Cuento* or "folktale" therapy, for example, is based on principles of social learning theory, using traditional Puerto Rican folktales to model

"Cuento" (folktale) therapy was developed for Puerto Rican children who have behavioral problems. It makes use of traditional Puerto Rican stories, such as the tales of Juan Bobo (left), to teach children to control aggression, differentiate right from wrong, and delay gratification. The photo on the right shows a therapy session conducted by Giuseppe Costantino and Migdalia Coubertier, in which the children and their mothers watch a videotape of the folktale, discuss it together, and later role-play its major themes. The method has been successful in reducing children's anxiety and improving their attention span and imagination (Costantino, Malgady, & Rogler, 1986).

desirable behavior and attitudes. Puerto Rican children in this program feel less anxious and adapt to their Anglo-American neighborhoods faster than control groups that receive either no treatments or traditional ones (Rogler et al., 1987).

Being aware of cultural differences, however, doesn't mean that the therapist should stereotype all clients from a particular culture or tailor the therapy to fit some abstract notion of cultural rules. Some Asians, after all, *do* have personal problems with excessive shyness, and some Hispanics *do* have emotional disorders! It definitely does not mean that a person will do poorly in therapy unless the therapist and client are "matched" according to gender and race (Howard, 1991). It does mean that therapists must do what is necessary to ensure that the client will find the therapist to be *trustworthy* and *effective* (Sue & Zane, 1987)—and clients must be aware of their prejudices too.

Some therapists define themselves by their commitment to clients who are targets of prejudice. Gay therapists, feminist therapists, and black and other minority therapists may come from any of the various psychological schools of therapy. But they share a goal of improving the self-esteem and mental health of clients whose problems are complicated by having been victims of discrimination. They would argue, for example, that a homosexual should not seek counseling from someone who still thinks that homosexuality is a mental illness (Garnets et al., 1991), and a woman who was a victim of incest should not go to a Freudian who still thinks that little girls unconsciously want to have sex with their fathers.

Which Therapy for Which Problem?

Murray has found a therapist who is sympathetic, he's motivated to change, and he thinks that he and the therapist will form a nice therapeutic alliance. But which therapeutic approach, if any, will be best for him?

It is not easy to compare different therapies because good therapists, as we saw, do many similar things, even when they come from different schools. However, it is clear from research that the success of therapy depends in part on the nature of the problem being treated.

TALK VERSUS ACTION.   One major difference among therapies is that some (such as psychoanalysis and humanism) encourage insight, whereas others (such as behaviorism) focus on action for change. Insight therapies have been shown to be *ineffective*, compared with placebo treatments, for a variety of specific problems (Prioleau, Murdock, & Brody, 1983). In particular, they are not highly successful in treating major depression (McGrath et al., 1990); anxiety, fears, agoraphobia, and panic (Chambless, 1985); sex problems and sex offenders (Abel et al., 1984); personality disorders (Strupp, 1982); schizophrenia (Torrey, 1988); or drug abuse (Vaillant, 1983). Insight therapies seem to be best suited to people who are introspective about their motives and feelings, who want to explore their pasts and examine their current lives.

Over 200 controlled studies have demonstrated the effectiveness of behavior therapies in contrast to doing nothing at all or to being in psychodynamic therapy (Fischer, 1978; A. Lazarus, 1990; Rachman & Wilson, 1980). In spite of this success rate, however, behavior therapy too has its failures, especially with chronic personality disorders (Brody, 1990; Foa & Emmelkamp, 1983). It is not the answer to such problems as recovering from trauma or severe depression. It is not highly effective with people who do not really want to change and who are not motivated to carry out a behavioral program (Woolfolk & Richardson, 1984).

Many psychodynamic therapists believe that the longer therapy goes on, the more successful it will be. As Figure 17.3 shows, research does not support this claim (K. Howard et al., 1986). Of course, people who have serious chronic mental disorders often benefit from continued therapeutic care. But for people who have one or another of the common emotional problems of life, short-term treatment is usually all that is necessary (Strupp & Binder, 1984).

"PURE" VERSUS COMBINED APPROACHES.   Some problems, and some clients, are immune to any single kind of therapy but may respond to combined methods. For example, people who have continuing, difficult problems—such as recovering from a traumatic experience, living with chronic pain, or coping with a disturbed family member—often are best helped by a combination approach (A. Lazarus, 1989). One eclectic therapist has combined cognitive, behavioral, and psychoanalytic methods in an effective treatment for survivors of coercive cults (A. Solomon, 1991). The most promising treatment for sex offenders (in-

FIGURE 17.3 _____

Is more therapy better?
About half of all patients improve in only eight sessions and about 75 percent improve by the twenty-sixth session. After that, only a few percent benefit from more sessions (K. Howard et al., 1986).

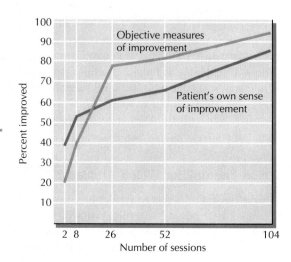

cluding child molesters, rapists, and adults who commit incest) combines cognitive therapy, aversive conditioning, sex education, group therapy, reconditioning sexual fantasies, and social skills training. None of these methods works by itself (Abel et al., 1984).

Some people who have mood disorders respond to a combination of drug treatments, cognitive-behavioral methods, and group support (Chambless, 1985). Some depressed patients respond better to a combination of drugs and cognitive psychotherapy than to either method alone (Bowers, 1990; Conte et al., 1986). For these reasons, some psychiatrists and psychologists are collaborating in what they call the *split treatment* model: The psychiatrist prescribes medication while the psychologist focuses on the psychological aspects of treatment (Wiggins, 1991).

SELF-HELP VERSUS PROFESSIONAL HELP. Do-it-yourself therapies can be effective for many problems in life. In fact, consider the surprising results of an overview of studies that compared people in self-administered treatment, therapist-administered treatment, and no treatment at all (for problems including phobias and emotional disturbances). People in the self-administered group improved significantly over those who did nothing at all. But there were no differences between the people in self-administered and therapist-administered treatment (Scogin et al., 1990)!

Of course, the major drawback to self-help books and programs is making sure the person actually carries out the program. On their own, many individuals don't follow through. For example, one study found that procedures for teaching parents to toilet-train their children were more effective and had fewer "emotional side effects" when a therapist was involved than when the parents got the same advice from a self-help book (Matson & Ollendick, 1977). Consumers should also beware of any self-help books, tapes, or programs that have not been tested for effectiveness and that promise more than they can deliver (Koocher, 1990)—as does the title of one such book, *The Doctor's Guide to Instant Stress Relief*.

According to many studies, people who join self-help groups in order to break their addictions often have a higher relapse rate than do individuals who break these habits on their own (Peele, Brodsky, & Arnold, 1991). It is as if the group says, "You're addicted; you can't do anything about your addiction without us; and then you need us to keep from becoming readdicted." Once people define the problem in this way, giving up an internal locus of control, they seem to become less able or willing to take charge of it themselves.

When Therapy Harms

• After "Susan B." committed suicide, her distraught husband discovered a letter she had left for her psychotherapist. In it, she implored the analyst not to feel guilty for "using me for your own pleasure"—for the sexual intercourse he required as part of her therapy for the five months she had been seeing him. She chided him for his waning sexual interest in her that caused her final depressive episode, but begged him not to blame himself for her death (Kiernan, 1974).

• A man entered therapy for help in dealing with his family relationships, steadily increasing his involvement until he was going four times a week. He spent much time preparing for his sessions and reflecting on them afterward, growing more and more intolerant of his wife and children's efforts to get his attention. One day he said, "I wish my wife and kids would just go away. They're interfering with my analysis" (Zilbergeld, 1983).

As these cases illustrate, some people in therapy are not helped by it; instead, they are seriously harmed or unduly influenced by the treatment or by the therapist. The client's emotional state may deteriorate and symptoms may worsen (Bergin & Lambert, 1978). Some clients become excessively dependent, relying on the therapist or support group for all decisions. Some therapists actively foster this dependency out of financial or psychological motives (Johnson, 1988).

There are a number of ways in which a therapist can harm or unduly influence a client:

• *Coercion* by the therapist to accept the therapist's advice, sexual intimacies, or other unethical behavior (Pope & Bouhoutsos, 1986). Some therapists abuse their clients' trust, convincing them that the therapy requires them to behave in ways they find reprehensible (Bersoff, 1978). Others use strong-arm tactics to get individuals or families to break old patterns. Donald Ransom (1982), a family therapist, has criticized the trend in his field to "overpower families" with authoritarian tactics, then leaving them to fend unsuccessfully for themselves.

Coercion can be subtle as well as overt. In extreme cases of "psychotherapy cults," members become persuaded that their health depends on staying in the group. One study found that such cults are created by the therapist's use of techniques that foster the client's dependency and isolation, prevent the client from terminating therapy, and—as you might expect by now—reduce the client's ability to think critically (Temerlin & Temerlin, 1986).

• *Bias* on the part of a therapist who doesn't understand the client because of the client's gender, race, religion, sexual orientation, or ethnic group. The therapist may try to induce the client to conform to the therapist's standards and values, even if they are not appropriate to the client or in the client's best interest (Brodsky, 1982; Garnets et al., 1991; López, 1989).

• *Therapist-induced disorders.* In a healthy therapeutic alliance, as we've seen, therapists and clients seek a common explanation for the client's problems. Of course the therapist will influence this explanation, according to his or her training and philosophy. This is why Freudian patients have dreams of phallic symbols and patients in Jungian therapy have dreams of archetypes! It is also why people in primal scream therapy "remember" being born, people in fetal therapy "remember" their lives in the womb, and people in past-lives therapy "remember" being Julius Caesar (or whomever) (Spanos et al., 1991).

However, some therapists so zealously believe in the prevalence of certain problems that, sometimes consciously but more often unconsciously, they may induce the client to produce the symptoms they are looking for (Holmes, 1991). In Chapter 16 we discussed how this process might be one reason for the growing number of patients diagnosed as having multiple personality disorder. But it is also the mechanism by which increasing numbers of people are concocting far-fetched "explanations" of their current life problems. Some, through hypnotist-induced suggestions, are "remembering" UFO abductions, forced participation in secret Satanic cults, and other sinister events—even though all the psychological evidence indicates that such memories are constructed fantasies shaped by the suggestions and expectations of the therapist (Spanos, 1991). These *pseudomemories* may feel real to the individual, but they are actually responses to the demands of the situation in which they are generated. When they produce false accusations against innocent people, become admissible evidence in court, or prevent a person from solving serious problems, they can be harmful indeed.

For all of these reasons, it is important for people to become educated consumers of psychotherapeutic services (see "Taking Psychology with You").

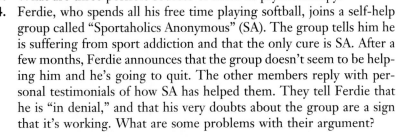

QUICK QUIZ

Refresh your understanding of psychotherapy.

1. The most important predictor of successful therapy is (a) how long it lasts, (b) the insight it provides the client, (c) the bond between therapist and client, (d) whether the therapist and client are matched according to gender, race, and culture.
2. The most important attribute of a good therapist is (a) years of training, (b) warmth and empathy, (c) objective detachment, (d) intellectual ability.
3. What are three possible sources of harm in psychotherapy?
4. Ferdie, who spends all his free time playing softball, joins a self-help group called "Sportaholics Anonymous" (SA). The group tells him he is suffering from sport addiction and that the only cure is SA. After a few months, Ferdie announces that the group doesn't seem to be helping him and he's going to quit. The other members reply with personal testimonials of how SA has helped them. They tell Ferdie that he is "in denial," and that his very doubts about the group are a sign that it's working. What are some problems with their argument?

ANSWERS:

1. c 2. b 3. coercion, bias, and therapist-induced disorders, sometimes through pseudomemories of events that never happened 4. The group members have failed the test of *falsifiability* (see Chapter 2): that is, they will accept no evidence that disproves their claims. If a person is helped by the group, they say it works; if a person is *not* helped by the group, they still say it works but the person doesn't know it yet or is "denying" its benefits. They are also arguing by anecdote: Ferdie is not hearing testimonials from people who have dropped out of the group and were not helped by it. Arguing by anecdote is not scientific reasoning, nor is it a way to determine a group's effectiveness.

The Value and Values of Therapy

On radio, in the newspapers, on television, in countless popular books, media psychologists offer free thera . . . well, free advice. There is nothing unethical about advice. Members of the clergy, neighbors, relatives, and friends hand it out all the time. Indeed, some observers have argued that psychotherapy is, in reality, paid friendship. As North Americans become more and more geographically mobile, as families grow smaller, as city life becomes more impersonal, the professional support of psychotherapy has replaced the informal support of friends and relations.

Is there anything wrong with that? In his book *The Shrinking of America*, Bernie Zilbergeld (1983), himself a psychotherapist, argued that psychotherapy, while often very helpful, promotes three myths that also increase dissatisfaction: (1) that people should always be happy and competent, and if they aren't they need fixing; (2) that almost any change is possible; and (3) that change is relatively easy. As we have seen in previous chapters, however, some aspects of personality are resistant to change, and most changes do not happen overnight.

In contrast, as you may remember from Chapter 15, Eastern cultures have a somewhat less optimistic view of change; they are more tolerant of events they regard as being outside human control. In the Japanese practice of Morita therapy, for example, clients are taught to accept and live with their most troubling

Can psychotherapy transform a depressed person into someone who is never sad? What kinds of changes is it reasonable to expect from psychotherapy?

The language and goals of psychotherapy have made their way into many programs designed to "expand human potential." This woman, for example, is hoping to learn to relax and trust others by being thrown into the air and caught. This exercise is probably fun, but is it likely to have lasting effects? What kinds of therapy are best for what kinds of problems? What are the limitations of psychotherapy and its offshoots?

emotions, instead of trying to eradicate these psychological weeds from the lawn of life. Recently, Western psychotherapists have been borrowing ideas from the Japanese, attempting to teach greater self-acceptance instead of constant self-improvement (Reynolds, 1987; Welwood, 1983).

Psychotherapy warrants neither extravagant claims nor total rejection. There are many things it cannot do, and many things it can do. It cannot transform you into someone you're not. It cannot cure you overnight. It cannot provide a life without problems. But it can help you make decisions. It can get you through bad times when no one seems to care or understand. It can improve morale and restore the energy to cope. Psychotherapy is not intended to substitute for experience—for work that is satisfying, relationships that are sustaining, activities that are enjoyable. As Socrates knew, the unexamined life is not worth living. But as an anonymous philosopher added, the unlived life is not worth examining.

TAKING PSYCHOLOGY WITH YOU

Becoming a Smart Therapy Consumer

In North America today there is a vast and bewildering array of therapies in the marketplace. There are hundreds of them, but the word *therapy* is unregulated. Anyone can set up any kind of program and call it therapy, and this is not against the law. To protect themselves as well as to get the best possible help, consumers need to be informed and know how to choose wisely.

Some people spend more time looking for a good dentist than a good therapist. They fail to remember that their consumer rights apply to buying mental health services as well as to buying any other professional service. You would not be likely to keep going to a dentist, year after year, if your toothache got worse and the dentist merely kept promising to make it go away. Yet some people stay in therapy, year after year, with no resolution of their problems. They become "therapy junkies."

In order for consumers to make the best use of therapy, research suggests the following guidelines:

• *Knowing when to start.* In general, if you have a persistent problem that you do not know how to solve, one that causes you considerable unhappiness and that has lasted six months or more, it may be time to look for help. Everyone gets caught in a maze from time to time. It may take the clear-eyed observations of a perceptive bystander to see a way out.

• *Setting goals.* Try to identify exactly what you expect from therapy, and discuss your goals with the therapist. Do you want to solve a problem in your relationships or in your emotional life? Are your goals realistic? Some therapies are designed not for solving problems but for exploring ideas. People often seek help in making important decisions. Others want to explore a philosophy of life to guide their future actions. Still others want to understand themselves better. If you know what you want from therapy, you may feel less disappointed later. You will also be better able to select a therapist who can meet your needs.

• *Choosing a therapist.* Remember that anyone can hang out a shingle advertising "Therapeutic help." The word "psychologist" is regulated, although qualifications vary from state to state. As we saw back in Chapter 1, you must have a professional degree and a period of supervised training to become a licensed psychologist, psychiatrist, counselor, or social worker. Unfortunately, the fact that someone has a license does not guarantee that he or she is competent, reputable, or ethical. Your school counseling center is a good place to start if you are looking for a reputable therapist. Your local Mental Health Association chapter (check your phone book) can also provide information on nearby therapists.

A therapist or counselor should be someone you trust and like. Research shows clearly that empathy between client and counselor, and the warmth of the counselor, are two of the most important factors in predicting success of treatment. Never trust anyone who suggests that a sexual relationship with him (or her) will help your problem. This is unethical conduct and illegal in many

states. The basic rule of thumb is this: If the therapist does not treat you with the same attention and respect that you give him or her, find someone else.

• *The question of fees.* Freud thought that patients should pay for treatment, enough to make it hurt. Only then, he said, would patients be motivated to improve. This theory, to put it kindly, serves therapists more than it does clients. *There is no evidence that the amount of payment affects the success of the therapy.* In one study, in fact, college students in paid versus free therapy did not differ in self-reports of improvement, but the students who paid no fee had *lower* levels of distress when the therapy ended (Yoken & Berman, 1984).

As a consumer, you can often negotiate a fee depending on what you can afford. If you have medical insurance that covers psychotherapy, find out whether your policy covers the kind of therapist you are seeking. Some insurance companies pay only for treatments by psychiatrists or licensed psychologists.

• *Knowing when to stop.* Of course, if you are in time-limited treatment, such as 12 sessions of brief therapy or a 7-session plane-phobia program, you ought to stick with it to the end. In an unlimited therapy program, however, you have the right to determine when enough is enough. Breaking with a therapist (or self-help group) can be painful and difficult, like leaving home for the first time, but it can also be a sign that the treatment has been successful (Johnson, 1988). You may need to consider ending therapy, changing therapists, or leaving a group if:

—Therapy dominates your life and nothing else seems important.

—The therapist keeps finding new reasons for you to stay, although the original problems were solved long ago.

—You have become so dependent on the therapist that you won't make a move without consulting him or her.

—Your therapist has been unable to help you cope with the problem that brought you there.

As we saw in this chapter, not all therapies are appropriate for all problems. If you are not getting relief, the reason could be as much in the treatment as in you. If you have made a real effort to work with a counselor or therapist and there has been no result after considerable time and effort, it is time to think about alternatives.

SUMMARY

1. Diagnoses and treatments of psychological problems have alternated throughout history from the medical (organic) model to the psychological (mental) model. Recent research has sparked renewed interest in medical treatments of mental disorder, but there is still much controversy.

2. The drugs most in use today for emotional disorders include *antipsychotic drugs*, used in treating schizophrenia and psychotic symptoms; *antidepressants*, used in treating mood disorders; and *minor tranquilizers*, often prescribed for emotional problems. Antipsychotics reduce psychotic symptoms and allow many schizophrenics to be released from hospitals, but in a few cases they can have dangerous and fatal side effects. Antidepressants are more effective for mood disorders than minor tranquilizers, which seem to have little or no effect and can become addictive.

3. Some issues in drug treatment for nonpsychotic disorders include the problem of the placebo effect; finding the *therapeutic window* or correct dose for each individual; the high drop-out and relapse rates among people who take antidepressants or other medications without also learning how to cope with problems; the fact that nondrug therapies can work as well as drugs for many mood and behavioral problems; and the effects of gender and race on the effectiveness of the dosage.

4. When drugs or psychotherapy fail to help seriously disturbed people, some psychiatrists intervene directly in the brain. *Psychosurgery* destroys an area of the brain thought to be responsible for the problem. *Electroconvulsive therapy* (ECT), in which a brief current is sent through the brain, has been used successfully to treat suicidal depressives. However, its effects do not last and it has unpredictable effects on memory.

5. Errors of diagnosis and treatment occur on both sides of the mind-body debate. Some people with organic disorders have been mistakenly treated with psychotherapy; some people with psychological problems have been mistakenly treated with drugs.

6. There are hundreds of psychotherapies, but they basically fall into four schools: (a) *Psychodynamic ("insight") therapies* include orthodox Freudian psychoanalysis and its modern variations, which explore unconscious dynamics. *Brief psychodynamic therapy* is a time-limited version that focuses on one major dynamic issue. (b) *Cognitive therapies* aim to change the irrational thoughts involved in negative emotions and self-defeating actions. *Behavioral therapies* are based on learning principles, and include such methods as systematic desensitization, aversive conditioning, exposure, and behavioral contracts. In practice, many therapists combine cognitive and behavioral techniques. (c) *Humanistic therapies* aim to help people feel better about themselves and reach "self-actualization." They include Carl Rogers' *client-centered* therapy, Frederick Perls' *Gestalt* therapy, and *existential* therapy. (d) *Family therapies* share the view that an individual's problems arise in and must be solved in a family context. Family therapists may use a *genogram* to document generational patterns in a family. In practice most therapists are *eclectic*, using many methods and ideas.

7. People who have severe, chronic mental problems, such as schizophrenia, or who have physical disabilities resulting from disease or injury, may benefit from alternatives to individual psychotherapy. *Rehabilitation psychologists* offer such people job training, support, and community treatment programs. The growing *self-help movement* provides support groups organized around a specific problem.

8. Efforts to evaluate the effectiveness of psychotherapy get mixed results. Generally, psychotherapy is least effective with people who have the most serious disorders; it rarely produces extreme and long-lasting changes; and sometimes it is harmful. But psychotherapy can help people feel better and solve (or accept) certain problems.

9. Successful therapy requires a good relationship between therapist and client. Good clients are motivated to solve their problems and are willing to take responsibility for them. Good therapists are empathic, inspirational, and able to teach constructive lessons. A *therapeutic alliance* between client and therapist depends on their ability to understand each other. They do not need to be perfectly "matched," but it is important for both sides to avoid bias and stereotyping.

10. Given the common elements in effective therapy, some therapies are better than others for specific problems. By and large, cognitive-behavior therapies have a higher success rate than psychodynamic or humanist therapies; short-term treatment is just as effective as (and cheaper than) long, indefinite therapy; and therapies that combine many techniques are able to solve some problems that one technique alone cannot.

11. In some cases, therapy is harmful. The therapist may be biased, coercive, and unethical, foster the client's dependency, or create pseudomemories of events that never actually happened.

12. Some psychologists believe that people have come to expect too much from therapy and falsely assume that change is always easy and desirable. Therapy can help people in many ways, but it cannot transform them into something they are not.

KEY TERMS

antipsychotic drugs (major tranquilizers) *607*
antidepressant drugs *608*
lithium carbonate *608*
minor tranquilizers *608*
therapeutic window *609*
psychosurgery *609*
lobotomy *610*
electroconvulsive therapy (ECT) *610*
psychodynamic ("insight") therapies *613*
free association *614*
transference *614*
brief psychodynamic therapy *614*
dynamic focus *614*
behavioral therapies *614*
systematic desensitization *614*
aversive conditioning *614*

flooding (exposure) *615*
behavioral contracts *615*
cognitive therapies *616*
humanistic therapies *617*
client-centered therapy *617*
Gestalt therapy *617*
existential therapy *617*
family therapy *618*
genogram *618*
strategic family therapy *618*
group therapy *620*
eclectic approaches *620*
rehabilitation psychology *621*
clubhouse model *623*
support, self-help groups *624*
encounter groups *624*
therapeutic alliance *627*
pseudomemories *632*

PART SIX

PRINCIPLES OF SOCIAL LIFE

18

Individuals in Social Context

Think About It:
    The Grand Experiment: Can People
    Accept Their Differences?
Taking Psychology with You:
    Attitude Change: From Persuasion
    to "Brainwashing"

. . . to hurt innocent people whom I knew many years ago in order to save myself is, to me, inhuman and indecent and dishonorable. I cannot and will not cut my conscience to fit this year's fashions.

LILLIAN HELLMAN

The man was on trial for murder, although he personally had never killed anyone. Six psychiatrists examined him and found him sane. His family life was normal and he had deep feelings of love for his wife, children, and parents. Two observers, after reviewing transcripts of his 275-hour interrogation, described him as "an average man of middle class origins and normal middle class upbringing, a man without identifiable criminal tendencies" (Von Lang & Sibyll, 1984).

The man was Adolf Eichmann, a Nazi SS officer who had supervised the deportation and death of millions of Jews during World War II. Eichmann was proud of his efficiency at his work and his ability to resist the temptation to feel pity for his victims. But he insisted he was not anti-Semitic: He had had a Jewish mistress for a while, and he personally arranged for the protection of his Jewish half-cousin (both dangerous crimes for an SS officer). Shortly before his execution by hanging, Eichmann said, "I am not the monster I am made out to be. I am the victim of a fallacy."

The fallacy to which Eichmann referred was the widespread belief that a person who does monstrous deeds must be a monster—someone sick, insane, evil, cruel. An *enemy* monster, that is. When a member of their own side commits a monstrous act, people tend to be more lenient.

During the war in Vietnam, a platoon of American soldiers rounded up several hundred women, old men, and children in a village called My Lai. The commander of the platoon, Lt. William Calley, ordered the men to push the civilians into a ditch and kill them. Here is an account of the massacre by a soldier, interviewed by Mike Wallace of CBS News (Milgram, 1974):

Q: How many people would you say were killed that day?
A: I'd say about three hundred and seventy. . . .
Q: What kind of people—men, women, and children?
A: Men, women, children.
Q: And babies?
A: And babies. . . . They [were] just pushed in a ravine, or just sitting, squatting . . . and shot.
Q: How do you shoot babies?
A: I don't know. It's just one of those things.
Q: What did these civilians—particularly the women and children, the old men—what did they do? What did they say to you?
A: They were begging and saying, "No, no." And the mothers was hugging their children, and . . . but they kept right on firing. Well, we kept right on firing. They was waving their arms and begging. . . .

When this case came to trial, Lt. Calley tried the same defense that Eichmann had: He was just following orders. Because there was some doubt about whether Calley had really been given explicit orders to kill civilians, he was found guilty—but given a light sentence.

Most Americans despised Eichmann and felt he deserved the death penalty, but about half of the American public felt sympathetic toward Calley and the soldiers who obeyed him. What else could a soldier do but obey orders? Disobedience could mean death. This is true, but not the whole truth. Not every soldier in Calley's platoon fired his weapon. Not every German in Nazi Germany took part in or supported the systematic killing of Jews and other groups targeted for destruction. A few heroes risked their lives to aid and shelter victims or to disobey orders in other ways.

For example, a German physician, known to history only as Dr. Marie L., refused Nazi requests that she participate in sadistic "experiments" on prisoners in concentration camps. One Nazi doctor, Eduard Wirths, tried to persuade her by pointing out that the Jews to be operated on were subhuman beings. "Can you not see," he asked, "that these people are different from you?" She replied that many people were different from her, starting with Dr. Wirths (Lifton, 1986).

The Nazis have, for good reason, come to symbolize the evil potential in "human nature." They used technology to carry mass slaughter to horrendous new extremes. Perhaps for this reason, some people today regard them as an aberration, a story safely buried in the past. Yet almost no nation can claim to have bloodless hands, and the practices of torture, genocide, and mass killings are all too common in human history: the American slaughter of native "Indians," the Turkish slaughter of Armenians, the Khmer Rouge slaughter of millions of fellow Cambodians, the Spanish slaughter of Mexicans, Idi Amin's reign of terror against his own people in Uganda, the Japanese slaughter of Koreans and Chinese, the Iraqi slaughter of Kurds, the Iranian slaughter of members of the Baha'i religion, the mass killings ("disappearances") in Argentina and Chile . . . . Far from being rare, the systematic destruction of people defined as "the enemy" was and is a widespread practice (Staub, 1989).

Why? Why do most people go along with the crowd, even when the crowd is committing morally reprehensible acts? Why do most people do what they are told without thinking twice about it? Why do some people behave in helpful and cooperative ways, and others in hurtful or destructive ones? Perhaps we should turn these questions around. Why do some individuals behave bravely, even at the risk of their lives? Why do some people chart their own courses through unmarked territory?

The field of *social psychology* explores these (and many other) questions by examining the individual in a social context. The "psychology" part of social psychology concerns the person's perceptions, attitudes, emotions, and behavior. The "social" part concerns the person's group, culture, and relationships. In previous chapters we have already reported many topics and studies in social psychology, including love and attachment; how "set and setting" affect the use of drugs; how roles and scripts affect sexual behavior; how work settings affect work motivation and job satisfaction; how emotions communicate; the effects of culture on behavior; and why friends are necessary for good health. Social psychology covers a lot of territory, from first impressions when meeting a stranger to international diplomacy.

In this chapter we will consider some of the major areas in this field: roles; attitudes, explanations, and prejudices; obedience and conformity; mob mindlessness and the behavior of groups. As we go along, we will show how the same principles can be used to explain the forces that divide people and those that unite them.

Many roles in modern life require us to give up individuality, as conveyed by this dazzling image of white-suited referees at the Seoul Olympics. If each referee decided to behave out of role, the games could not continue. When is it justified to yield personal styles and preferences for the role, and when is it not?

▪ ROLES AND RULES

"We are all fragile creatures entwined in a cobweb of social constraints," said social psychologist Stanley Milgram. This cobweb snares people in two ways. First, there are social **rules** (also called **norms**) that people are expected to follow. Rules are the conventions of everyday life that make our interactions with other people predictable and orderly. Some rules are matters of law, such as "A person may not beat up another person, except in self-defense." Some rules come from a group's cultural values, such as "A man may beat up another man who insults his masculinity." Some rules are tiny, invisible regulations that people learn to follow unconsciously, such as "You may not sing at the top of your lungs on a public bus."

Second, people fill a variety of social **roles.** A role is a position in society that is regulated by norms about how a person in that position should behave. In modern life, most people play many roles. Gender roles define the "proper" behavior for a man and a woman. Occupational roles determine "correct" behavior for a manager and an employee, a professor and a student. Family roles set tasks for parent and child, husband and wife, brother and sister. Certain aspects of every role must be carried out. As a student, for instance, you know just what you have to do to pass this course. But people bring their own personalities and interests to the roles they play. Although three actresses who play the role of Cleopatra must follow the same script, each will have a different interpretation. It is the same with social roles.

In this section, we will examine three controversial studies that illuminate the power of social roles to influence behavior.

The Prison Study

One day as you are walking home from school, a police car pulls up. Two uniformed officers get out, arrest you, and take you to a prison cell. There you are stripped of your clothes, sprayed with a delousing fluid, given a prison uniform, photographed with your prison number, and put behind bars. You feel a little queasy but you feel no panic, because you have agreed to play the part of "prisoner" in an experiment for two weeks. Your prison cell, while authentic, is in the basement of a university building.

▪ **rules (norms)**
Social conventions, including explicit laws and implicit cultural standards, that regulate human life.
▪ **role**
A social position that is governed by a set of norms for proper behavior.

Prisoners and guards quickly learn their respective roles, as they have done at this correctional facility.

So began an effort to study what happens when ordinary college students take on the roles of prisoners and guards (Haney, Banks, & Zimbardo, 1973). The students who volunteered for this experiment were paid a nice daily sum. They were randomly assigned to be prisoners or guards, but other than that they were given no instructions about how to behave. Within a very short time, the "prisoners" became distressed, helpless, and panicky. They developed emotional symptoms and psychosomatic ailments. Some became depressed, tearful, and apathetic. Others became rebellious and angry. After a few days, half of the prisoners begged to be let out. Most were more than willing to forfeit their pay for early release.

Within an equally short time, the "guards" adjusted to their new power. Some tried to be nice, helping the "prisoners" and doing little favors for them. Some were "tough but fair," holding strictly to "the rules." But about a third of them became tyrannical. Although they had complete freedom to use any method to maintain order, they almost always chose to be abusive, even when prisoners were not resisting in any way. One guard, unaware that he was being observed by the experimenters, paced the yard while the prisoners were sleeping, pounding his nightstick into his hand. Another guard put a prisoner in solitary confinement (a small closet) and tried to keep him there all night, concealing this information from the experimenters (who, he thought, were "too soft" on the "prisoners"). Many guards were willing to work overtime without additional pay.

The researchers ended this experiment after only six days. They had not expected such a speedy and terrifying transformation of normal students. The "prisoners" were relieved by this decision, but most of the "guards" were disappointed. They not only had become bullies; they also enjoyed it.

Critics of this study maintain that you can't learn much from such an artificial setup. In their view, the volunteers knew very well—from movies, TV, and games—how they were supposed to behave. They acted their parts to the hilt, in order to have fun and not disappoint the experimenters. Their behavior was no more surprising than if young men had been dressed in football gear and then had been found to be willing to bruise each other. The critics agree that the prison study makes a great story, but they maintain that it isn't *research*. That is, it does not carefully investigate relationships between factors; for all its drama, the study provides no new information. "It's just staging a 'happening,'" argued Leon Festinger (1980).

Philip Zimbardo, who designed the study, believes that these criticisms make his point: People's behavior depends to a large extent on the roles they are asked to play. *Real* prisoners and guards know their "parts," too. Moreover, if the students were having so much "fun," why did the prisoners beg for early release? Why did the guards lose sight of the "game" and behave as if it were a real job? Even if the prison study was a dramatization, he said, it illustrates the power of roles in a way that a short-lived experiment cannot.

The Hospital Study

Eight normal, healthy adults participated in a study by David Rosenhan (1973) of mental hospitals. The eight volunteers—a housewife, a painter, a pediatrician, a graduate student in psychology, a psychiatrist, and three psychologists, including Rosenhan himself—appeared at 12 different hospitals in five states with the same complaint. They said that they had heard voices, mostly unclear, but they could make out the words *hollow, empty,* and *thud.* Apart from this lie, they all gave honest personal histories, which contained not a trace of abnormal problems. All eight were quickly admitted to the hospitals; one was diagnosed as manic depressive and all the rest as schizophrenic. Once in the hospital, the pseudopatients immediately stopped faking any symptoms. All behaved normally and "sanely." Nevertheless, they were kept in the hospital from 7 to 52 days, an average of 19 days. When they were released, it was with the same diagnosis, now "in remission."

Although this study is usually used to illustrate problems of psychiatric diagnosis, it also shows the impact on behavior of being in the role of patient or attendant. Once the pseudopatients were diagnosed as schizophrenic and assigned the role of patient, the hospital staff regarded everything they did as further signs of emotional disorder. For example, all of the pseudopatients took frequent notes about their experiences. Several nurses noted this act in the records without asking them what they were writing about. One nurse wrote "patient engages in writing behavior," as if writing were an odd thing to do.

The powerless role of "patient" and the label "mentally ill," Rosenhan found, confer invisibility and encourage **depersonalization,** the loss of people's individuality as persons. In all 12 hospitals, the staff avoided eye contact and conversation with patients as much as possible. The pseudopatients attempted to speak a total of 185 times to staff psychiatrists, but 71 percent of the time the psychiatrist moved on without replying or even looking at the patient. Only 4 percent of the attempts succeeded in getting the psychiatrist to stop and talk. Of 1,283 attempts to talk to nurses and attendants, only half of one percent succeeded. The usual response to a pseudopatient's effort to communicate was the staff member's equal effort to avoid discussion. The result was often a bizarre exchange like this one:

> PSEUDOPATIENT: Pardon me, Dr. X. Could you tell me when I am eligible for grounds privileges?
> PSYCHIATRIST: Good morning, Dave. How are you today? [moves off without waiting for a response]

The role of attendant confers a power that often causes well-meaning individuals to treat patients badly. Rosenhan himself observed actual patients who were beaten by staff members for trying to talk to them. One patient was hit for approaching an attendant and saying, "I like you." A staff member might abuse a patient in front of a dozen other patients and stop only if another staff member appeared. To the staff, Rosenhan explains, patients are not full human beings. Their disorders somehow turn them into robots who lack feelings and perceptions.

■ **depersonalization**
The loss of one's individuality and humanity.

There are problems with Rosenhan's study as there are with the prison study. Critics point out that it was not necessarily wrong to hospitalize people who complained of hearing voices. They also dislike the deceptiveness of the infiltrators and argue that Rosenhan wasn't sympathetic enough to an overworked staff suffering from financial cutbacks. Emotionally disturbed people, they add, often do behave in unpleasant, unpredictable ways. It is not surprising that even trained staff would feel ambivalent about them or impose control.

Rosenhan is sympathetic to the problems of mental health professionals. He knows that they are not monsters and that most of them enter their jobs with good motives. The heartless or simply impersonal (and depersonalizing) behavior of staff members reflects the roles they are required to play. Even in times of financial hardship, he adds, hospitals set priorities for what a person in each role is expected to do. Staffs are still required to keep records and have lengthy meetings, but time with patients becomes a low priority. The result is less attention to the people whom the staff is there to help.

The Obedience Study

Jot down your best answer to these three questions. (1) What percentage of people are sadistic? (2) If told by an authority to harm an innocent person, what percentage of people would do it? (3) If you were instructed to harm an innocent person, would you do it or would you refuse? On what evidence or assumptions are you basing your answers?

In Chapter 2 we described Stanley Milgram's dramatic study of obedience to authority (Milgram, 1963, 1974). Now let's consider it more closely. Participants in this study thought they were part of an experiment on the effects of punishment on learning. Each was assigned, apparently at random, to the role of "teacher." Another person, introduced as a fellow volunteer, was the "learner." When the learner, seated in an adjoining room, made an error in reciting a list of word pairs he was supposed to have memorized, the teacher had to give him an electric shock by depressing a lever on an ominous-looking machine. With each error the voltage, marked from 0 to 450, was to be increased by another 15 volts. The shock levels on the machine were labeled from "slight shock" to "danger—severe shock" and, finally, "XXX." In reality, the "learners" were confederates of Milgram and did *not* receive shocks, but none of the "teachers" ever realized this. The actor-victims played their parts convincingly: As the study continued, they shouted in pain and pleaded to be released, all according to a prearranged script.

When Milgram first designed this experiment, he asked a number of psychiatrists, students, and middle-class adults how many people they thought would "go all the way" to XXX on orders from the experimenter. The psychiatrists predicted that most people would refuse to go beyond 150 volts, when the "learner" first demanded to be freed, and that only one person in a thousand, someone who was emotionally disturbed and sadistic, would administer the highest voltage. The nonprofessionals agreed with this prediction, and all of them said that they personally would disobey early in the experiment.

In fact, however, every subject in the study administered some shock to the learner, and about two-thirds of these men and women, of all ages and all walks of life, obeyed the experimenter to the fullest. They obeyed no matter how

Left: *Milgram's shock machine.* Right: *The "learner" is strapped into his chair.*

much the victim shouted for them to stop and no matter how painful the shocks seemed to be. They obeyed even when they themselves were anguished about the pain they believed they were causing. They obeyed even as they wept, implored the experimenter to release them, and argued with themselves. More than a thousand participants at several universities eventually went through the Milgram experiment. Most of them, men and women equally, inflicted what they thought were dangerous amounts of shock to another person. Many protested to the experimenter, but their doubts were usually overcome when he simply responded, "The experiment requires that you continue."

Milgram and his team next set up several variations of the basic experiment to determine the conditions under which people might disobey the experimenter. They found that virtually *nothing the victim did or said changed the likelihood of the person's compliance*—even when the victim said he had a heart condition, screamed in agony, or stopped responding entirely as if he had collapsed. However, people were more likely to disobey when:

• The experimenter left the room. Many people then subverted authority by giving low levels of shock but reporting that they were following orders.
• The victim was right there in the room, and the teacher had to administer the shock directly to his body.
• Two experimenters issued conflicting demands (to continue the experiment or to stop at once). In this case, no one kept inflicting shock.
• The person ordering them to continue was an ordinary man, apparently another volunteer, instead of the authoritative experimenter.
• The subject worked with peers who refused to go further. Seeing someone rebel gave subjects the courage to disobey.

In the "touch-proximity" variation of Milgram's experiment, the "teacher" actually had to administer "shock" directly to the learner. Here, a subject continues to obey, although many in this condition did not.

"The key to the behavior of subjects," Milgram (1974) summarized, "lies not in pent-up anger or aggression but in the nature of their relationship to authority. They have given themselves to the authority; they see themselves as instruments for the execution of his wishes; once so defined, they are unable to break free."

The Milgram experiment too has its critics. Some think it was unethical. Others find it too artificial and oversimplified. It ignores, for example, the personality traits that can affect extreme obedience to authority in real life (Blass, 1991). Still others argue that there are plenty of examples of obedience to immoral authority in history without having to set up such an unreal laboratory scenario. Yet this experiment had a tremendous influence on public awareness of the dangers of blind obedience.

In spite of their limitations, the three imaginative studies we have described illustrate the power of social roles and obligations to influence, even overturn, the personality patterns of individuals. The behavior of the prisoners and guards varied (some prisoners were more rebellious than others, some guards were more abusive than others); but, ultimately, what people did depended on the roles they were assigned. Regardless of their personal feelings, the staff of the mental hospital had to adapt to its structure of roles, from psychiatrists at the top to ward attendants at the bottom. Finally, when people in the Milgram study believed they had to follow the legitimate orders of authority, most of them put their private values to sleep.

■ SOCIAL COGNITION I: ATTRIBUTIONS AND ATTITUDES

■ **social cognition**
An area in social psychology concerned with the social influences on thought, memory, perception, and other cognitive processes.

Social psychologists are interested not only in what people do, but in what is going on in their heads while they do it. One of the most important areas in social psychology is the study of **social cognition,** how the social environment influences thoughts, perceptions, and beliefs (Fiske & Taylor, 1991). In the next two sections we will take a look at some of the thoughts and beliefs that most affect how people get along with one other—or that keep them from getting along at all.

Explanations and Excuses

❋ *Have you ever called someone else's error a "stupid, clumsy mistake," yet excused an identical blunder on your part as "something that couldn't be helped"? Why? Why do people need excuses anyway?*

One theme of this book has been that human beings are active, problem-solving creatures, forever trying to make sense of the world and understand what is going on around them. According to **attribution theory,** people are motivated to make sense of their own and others' behavior in order to predict and control events (Cheng & Novick, 1990; Ross & Fletcher, 1985). "To attribute" means "to consider as caused by." Caused by what? Generally, there are two kinds of causes. When you make a *situational attribution,* you regard an action as being caused by something in the environment: "Joe stole the money because his family is starving." When you make a *dispositional attribution,* you regard an action as being caused by something in the person, such as a trait or motive: "Joe stole the money because he is a born thief."

Through experimental research, social psychologists have specified some of the conditions under which people prefer certain attributions to others. For example, when people try to find reasons for someone else's behavior, they tend to overestimate personality factors and underestimate the influence of the situation (Nisbett & Ross, 1980). This tendency has been called the **fundamental attribution error.** Were the student guards basically cruel and the prisoners basically cowardly? Was the hospital staff lazy, thoughtless, or selfish? Were the hundreds of people who obeyed Milgram's experimenter by nature sadistic? People who think so, many psychologists maintain, are committing this attribution error. They are especially likely to do so when they are distracted or mentally preoccupied, and don't have time to stop and ask themselves, "Why, exactly, *is* Aurelia behaving like a dork today?" Instead, they leap to the easiest attribution, which is dispositional: Aurelia simply has a dork-like personality (Gilbert, Pelham, & Krull, 1988).

The fundamental attribution error is prevalent in Western nations, where middle-class people tend to believe firmly that individuals are responsible for their own actions. But it is by no means universal (Fletcher & Ward, 1988). It is less likely to occur in countries such as India, for example, where people are more embedded in their caste and family networks and more likely to recognize these situational constraints on behavior (J. G. Miller, 1984). If someone is behaving oddly, therefore, an Indian is likely to make a situational attribution of the problem.

When it comes to explaining their *own* behavior, most Westerners tend to choose attributions that are favorable to them (Markus & Kitayama, 1991). This **self-serving bias** means that people like to take credit for their good actions and let the situation account for their bad ones. For instance, most of us will say, "I am furious for good reason—this situation is intolerable!" We are less likely to say, "I am furious because I am an ill-tempered grinch." If we do something admirable, though, such as donating $100 to charity, we attribute our motives to personality ("I'm generous") instead of to the situation ("The fundraiser pressured me into it").

The self-serving bias is also apparent in the excuses people make to justify their mistakes. C. R. Snyder, Raymond Higgins, and Rita Stucky (1983) have observed that self-protecting excuses have been part of human life since Adam blamed Eve for giving him the apple—and Eve blamed the serpent. The researchers identified several categories of excuses: "I didn't do it"; "I did it, but it wasn't so bad"; "I didn't mean to"; and "I couldn't help it." A psychotherapy client of one of the researchers put it best. "It's like this," she said. "If it's not my fault, it's her fault, and if it's not her fault, it's still not my fault."

■ **attribution theory**
The theory that people are motivated to explain their own and others' behavior by attributing causes of that behavior to a situation or disposition.

■ **fundamental attribution error**
The tendency to overestimate personality factors (dispositions) and underestimate environmental ones (situations) in explaining behavior.

■ **self-serving bias**
The tendency of people to take credit for good actions and to excuse or rationalize their mistakes.

Children learn the value of excuses at an early age.

Excuses have several social purposes. They allow you to reassert your good qualities, reduce your responsibility, and minimize the badness of the action itself (C. Snyder, 1989). Excuses also make it possible for you to maintain your self-esteem, soften the other person's anger, and change the other person's attributions about you and your actions (Weiner, Figueroa-Muñoz, & Kakihara, 1991). Yet excuses also justify the destructive things that people do and allow them to rationalize the failure to take helpful action, such as speaking up against wrongdoing or aiding someone in a crisis.

For example, in Milgram's experiment, many people who administered the highest levels of shock attributed their behavior to the demands of the experiment. A 37-year-old welder explained that the experimenter was responsible for any pain the victim might suffer "for the simple reason that I was paid for doing this. I had to follow orders. That's how I figured it." In contrast to this self-justification, the people who refused to give high levels of shock took credit for their actions and attributed their refusal to matters of conscience or principle. "One of the things I think is very cowardly," said a 32-year-old engineer, "is to try to shove the responsibility onto someone else. See, if I now turned around and said, 'It's your fault. . . it's not mine,' I would call that cowardly" (Milgram, 1974).

Culture affects not only the fundamental attribution error, but also self-serving attributions and excuses. In Japan, for example, heads of companies are expected to take responsibility not only for their own failings, but for the failings of their employees or products—and they do (Pascale & Athos, 1981). In the United States, in contrast, the common practice is for heads of corporations to get huge salaries and bonuses even when the company is doing poorly, and to blame the economy, government policies, or their employees if something goes wrong (Crystal, 1991). (Of course, many Americans no longer take responsibility for their mistakes because they fear lawsuits.)

People also make attributions for events that have little to do with their self-esteem or even their own behavior. According to the **just-world hypothesis**, people all over the world need to believe that the world is fair, that good people are rewarded and villains punished (M. Lerner, 1980). The belief in a just world helps people make sense out of senseless events and feel safe in the presence of threatening events. If a friend loses his job, if a woman is raped, if a prisoner is tortured, it is reassuring to believe that they all must have done something to deserve what happened or at least to cause it. The need to believe in a just world often leads to a dispositional attribution called *blaming the victim*. When there is no question in anyone's mind that A did something to harm B, A can argue that B deserved the treatment, provoked the treatment, or wanted the treatment. "Many subjects harshly devalue the victim *as a consequence* of acting against him," wrote Milgram (1974). "Such comments as, 'He was so stupid and stubborn he deserved to get shocked,' were common."

■ **just-world hypothesis**
The notion that people need to believe that the world is fair and that justice is served, that bad people are punished and good people are rewarded.

By now you might be wondering where, in all these attributions, the truth is. Most human actions are determined both by personality and by environment, and we cannot always know the reason for people's actions. In that case, is the fundamental attribution error always an "error"? Maybe we make dispositional attributions about another person because they are more accurate in predicting that person's future actions (Fiske & Taylor, 1991). Moreover, is the self-serving bias always "biased"? Maybe we know more about our own behavior and intentions than we do about the actions of others. Researchers are still debating these questions. But they all agree that attributions, whether accurate or not, have consequences for emotions and behavior, for law and justice, and for daily human relations.

QUICK QUIZ

A. What kind of attribution is being made in each case, situational (S) or dispositional (D)?

1. A jury decides that a congressman accepted a bribe because FBI agents had set up a trap to trick him.
2. A jury decides that a congressman accepted a bribe because he is dishonest.
3. A man says, "My wife has sure become a grouchy person."
4. The same man says, "I'm grouchy because I've had a bad day at the office."
5. A woman reads that unemployment is very high in inner-city communities. "Well, if those people weren't so lazy they would find work," she says.

B. What principles of attribution theory are suggested by 3, 4, and 5?

ANSWERS:

1. S 2. D 3. D 4. S 5. D **B.** 3 illustrates the fundamental attribution error; 4, the self-serving bias; 5, the just-world hypothesis and fundamental attribution error.

Attitudes and Values

People have attitudes about all sorts of things—politics, people, food, children, movies, sports heroes, you name it. An **attitude** is a relatively stable opinion containing a cognitive element (your perceptions and beliefs about the topic, including any stereotypes you may have) and an emotional element (your feelings about the topic, which may range from negative and hostile to positive and loving). Attitudes range from shallow, changeable opinions to major convictions. Many public-opinion polls do not discriminate between these two extremes; they just ask for a person's "attitude," not how strongly it is felt. As a result, public opinion often seems to be easily swayed.

A **value** is a more central and basic motivating belief, reflecting the goals and ideals that are important to the person—freedom, beauty, equality, friendship, fame, wisdom, and so on (Rokeach & Ball-Rokeach, 1989). Attitudes are often an outgrowth of guiding values. For example, people's *attitudes* toward racial issues in America often depend on the larger *values* they hold. In one study, people who held humanitarian and egalitarian values (such as "There should be equality for everyone—because we are all human beings") were more likely to hold attitudes that were sympathetic to blacks (such as "Black people do not have the same job opportunities that whites do"). People who endorsed values of the Protestant Ethic ("If people work hard enough they are likely to

■ **attitude**

A fairly stable opinion regarding a person, object, or activity, containing a cognitive element (perceptions and beliefs) and an emotional element (positive or negative feelings).

■ **value**

A central organizing belief or belief system that shapes a person's goals and motivations.

make a good life for themselves") held more unsympathetic attitudes toward blacks ("The cause of most of the social and economic ills of blacks is the instability of the black family"). In America today, many white people endorse both values, and the attitudes they express at any one time toward blacks depend on which value is foremost in their mind (Katz & Hass, 1988). One result has been a growing chasm between blacks and whites in their attitudes about the causes of race conflict and solutions to it (Edsall & Edsall, 1991).

Many people have observed that as people age, their attitudes seem to harden like hailstones. Indeed, surveys typically find that many of the attitudes of young people *are* more fluid and changeable. Is this because young people are more impressionable or open-minded ("dispositional" attributions) or because they have more life changes that cause them to modify their beliefs (a "situational" attribution)? In studying this question, Tom Tyler and Regina Schuller (1991) found that attitude change does not depend on age but on having new experiences. Older people can be just as open-minded, and younger people just as closed-minded, as one another. The apparent age difference is really a life-style difference: Older people are less likely to have new experiences than young adults are.

THE BIG LIE.   Most people tend to think that their attitudes are based on thinking—a reasoned conclusion about how things work. In fact, social psychologists have found that some attitudes are a result of not thinking at all. You may remember from Chapter 10 that repeated exposure to a name, symbol, or nonsense syllable is enough to make a person feel more favorable toward it. This principle has long been known to governments and advertisers: Repeat something often enough, even the basest lie, and eventually the public will believe it. The formal name for this phenomenon is the **validity effect.**

In a recent series of experiments, Hal Arkes (1991) and his associates demonstrated how the validity effect operates. In a typical study, people read a list of statements, such as "Mercury has a higher boiling point than copper" or "Over 400 Hollywood films were produced in 1948." They had to rate each statement for its validity, where "1" means the rater thinks the statement is definitely false and "7" that it is definitely true. A week or two later, subjects again rated the validity of some of these statements and others they hadn't seen previously. The result: Mere repetition increased the perception that the familiar statements were true. The validity effect also occurred for other kinds of statements: unverifiable opinions, such as "At least 75 percent of all politicians are basically dishonest," opinions that subjects initially felt were true, and those they initially felt were false.

"Note that no attempt has been made to persuade," says Arkes (1991). "No supporting arguments are offered. We just have subjects rate the statements. Mere repetition seems to increase rated validity. This is scary." When Arkes discussed this research with a student from the People's Republic of China, she was not surprised. She told him how her government made use of this tactic by distributing posters claiming, for example, that the protest for democracy in Tienanmen Square was organized by a small band of traitors. At first, no one believed these lies. But over time, with repetition, the government's assertions became more plausible.

Closer to home, here is a more recent example of the validity effect: The myth of Ronald Reagan's popularity. Over and over during Reagan's term of office, the press claimed that he was the most popular president in history. Yet when two political scientists actually examined the evidence of public opinion polls, they found that Reagan's approval rating averaged 50 percent, lower than the averages of Eisenhower (69), Kennedy (71), Johnson (52), and Nixon (56), and not much above Carter (47). His highest rating, early in his presidency, was 68 percent—lower than that of the five previous presidents. It is true that Rea-

■ **validity effect**
The tendency of people to believe that a statement is valid or true simply because it has been repeated many times.

gan's ratings for *personal* appeal were much higher than his ratings for job performance—but Americans *always* have given higher approval to their president's personal qualities than to his political skills (Ferguson & Rogers, 1986). Nevertheless, the effect of the repeated assertion of Reagan's unique popularity was to get the country to believe it, as many people still do today.

ATTITUDES AND ACTIONS. Psychologists have argued for years about which comes first, attitudes or behavior—and whether they need even be related. Sometimes, attitudes and behavior are as unrelated as grapefruit and shoes. For example, studies of college students find that most sexually active students know that they should use condoms and that they are at risk of AIDS and other sexually transmitted diseases, but few practice what is being preached to them. In one study of 5,500 Canadian college students, the majority knew which sexual acts increase the risk of HIV transmission and also knew about safe sexual practices. Yet that knowledge, the researchers reported, "was not typically translated into safer behavior" (MacDonald et al., 1990).

Sometimes, of course, attitudes do dispose people to act in certain ways. If you have a positive attitude about the game of soccer, you may try to get to every game you can. If you have a negative attitude, you may refuse every invitation to go to one. However, sometimes a change of behavior leads to new attitudes because of new information and new experiences. Your friends drag you, kicking and screaming, to a soccer game, and you become a devoted fan. Naturally, convictions are more strongly related to behavior than garden-variety attitudes are. People who have a strong emotional commitment to an issue are more likely to work on its behalf (Abelson, 1988).

Attitudes and behavior can also be brought into harmony by the wish for consistency. In Chapter 10 we discussed an important approach to the study of attitudes: **cognitive dissonance** theory. As we saw, when two attitudes, or when an attitude and behavior, conflict (are dissonant), people are often motivated to resolve the conflict by changing an attitude or their behavior. (For more on attitude change, by methods ranging from persuasion to "brainwashing," see "Taking Psychology with You" on page 679.)

■ SOCIAL COGNITION II: STEREOTYPES AND PREJUDICES

Perhaps the most "social" of our cognitions are habits of thought about other groups of people—and about the general wonderfulness of our own group. In this section we will consider social identities, stereotypes, and prejudices.

Ethnocentrism: "Us" Versus "Them"

Everyone develops a *personal* identity—a sense of who one is—that is based on individual traits and unique history. According to **social identity** theory, people also develop *social* identities based on their nationality, ethnicity, religion, occupation and other roles in society (Hogg & Abrams, 1988; Tajfel & Turner, 1986). Social identities are important because they give people a feeling of place and position in the world; otherwise, most people would feel like loose marbles rattling around in an unconnected universe. Social identities raise self-esteem, but unfortunately they also tend to create **ethnocentrism,** the belief that one's own culture, religion, nation, or gender is superior. Every society on earth has been guilty of ethnocentrism.

Ethnocentrism is probably universal because it aids survival by making people feel attached to their groups and willing to work on the group's behalf. As soon as people have created a category called "us," however, they invariably

■ **cognitive dissonance**
A state of tension that occurs when a person simultaneously holds two cognitions that are psychologically inconsistent, or when a person's belief is inconsistent with his or her behavior.

■ **social identity**
The part of a person's self-concept that is based on his or her identification with a nation, culture, ethnic group, gender, or other roles in society.

■ **ethnocentrism**
The belief that one's own ethnic group, nation, or religion is superior to all others.

perceive everybody else as "not-us." Collective pronouns that apply to *us* and *them* are powerful influences on social cognition and perception. In one experiment, which students believed was testing their verbal skills, nonsense syllables such as *xeh*, *yof*, *laj* or *wuh* were randomly paired with either an in-group word (*us*, *we*, or *ours*), an out-group word (*them*, *they*, or *theirs*), or, for a control measure, another pronoun (such as *he*, *hers*, or *yours*). The students then had to rate the nonsense syllables on how pleasant or unpleasant they were. Why, you might ask, would anyone have an emotional reaction to the syllable *yof*? But, in fact, students liked the nonsense syllables significantly more when they had been paired with in-group words. Not one student guessed why; none was aware of how the words had been paired (Perdue et al., 1990).

Us-them thinking is common in all domains of life, and can easily be activated as soon as any two groups perceive themselves to be in competition or opposition: men-women, Army fans-Navy fans, prisoners-guards, students-teachers, artificially created groups in a laboratory. Us-them thinking is especially common in war, of course, when enemies regard each other as inhuman and deserving of destruction. But, closer to home, you can see everyday examples of it at a football game, during an election, or in discussions of controversial issues.

Ethnocentrism is a perfect example of a self-serving bias, because it is often used to rationalize "our" abusive behavior toward "them." "We" are good, noble, and human; "they" are bad, stupid, and beastly (see Figure 18.1). The Germans who ran Hitler's concentration camps regarded Jews, blacks, homosexu-

FIGURE 18.1

Faces of the enemy
In every country, propaganda posters stereotype "them," the enemy, as ugly, aggressive, brutish, and greedy; "we," the heroes, are beautiful and virtuous. Some examples, clockwise starting from the upper left: the American view of the German enemy in World War I, a "mad brute"; the Soviet view of the United States in the 1930s, a greedy capitalist; an Iraqi view of a barbaric Iran in 1985, in the midst of their long war; a Nicaraguan mural of the enemy as "chicken-footed Death"; an IRA poster of bloody "English pigs"; and a Southeast Asian portrayal of Richard Nixon as a vampire devouring the region.

als, Gypsies, Catholics, and anyone else who was not of the "pure" Aryan race as "vermin" to be "exterminated." Religious extremists of all kinds feel superior to "heathens" and thus entitled to kill them. Military torturers are able to inflict pain on their victims by splitting "us" (the nation's "saviors") from "them" (the rebels who are the nation's "enemies") (Staub, 1990). The irony is that "they" are thinking the same way about "us."

Stereotypes

"Us-them" thinking both creates and reflects stereotyping. A **stereotype** is a summary impression of a group of people in which a person believes that *all members* of that group share a common trait or traits. Stereotypes are among the cognitive schemas by which we map the world (see Chapter 7). Some stereotypes are negative ("Artists are weird"). Some, such as stereotypes of our own in-groups, are positive ("My school produces the smartest people and best athletes"). Some are neutral. There are stereotypes of people who drive Volkswagens or BMWs, of men who wear earrings and of women who wear business suits, of engineering students and art students, of feminists and fraternities.

The fact that everyone occasionally thinks in stereotypes is itself neither good nor bad. Stereotypes help us process new information and retrieve old memories. People remember facts that support their stereotypes and tend to forget facts that disconfirm them. A stereotype is a way of organizing experience, of making sense of the differences among individuals and groups, and of predicting how people will behave. This is why, as one study found, people remember the qualities associated with stereotypes such as "prude" or "politician" better than they remember a list of specific traits ("reserved"; "extroverted"). The researchers concluded that "categorization by stereotype provides a virtually instantaneous, detailed, and memorable portrait of an individual" (Andersen, Klatzky, & Murray, 1990).

One cognitive process that contributes to stereotyping is the phenomenon of *illusory correlation:* When people expect two things to be associated, they overestimate the strength of the actual relationship between them (Hamilton & Sherman, 1989; Mullen & Johnson, 1990). Although stereotypes do help us put the world together, the "illusory correlations" on which they are based lead to three distortions of reality. First, stereotypes *accentuate differences between groups.* They emphasize the ways in which groups are different, not the common features. So the stereotyped group may seem odd, unfamiliar, or dangerous, "not like us." Second, stereotypes *underestimate differences within other groups.* People realize that their own groups are made up of all kinds of individuals. But stereotypes create the impression that all members of other groups (say, all Texans or teenagers) are the same. One rude French waiter means that all French people are rude; one Greek thief means that all Greeks are thieves. But if someone in their own group is rude or steals, most people draw no such conclusions. Third, stereotypes produce *selective perception.* People tend to see only what fits the stereotype and to reject any perceptions that do not fit.

Stereotypes are not always entirely wrong. Many have a "grain of truth," capturing with some accuracy something about the group (Allport, 1954/1979). The problems occur when people assume that the grain of truth is the whole seashore. For example, the stereotype that most American whites have of blacks is based on the troubling statistics that are in the news: the large number of young black men who are in prison, the black women and children who are on welfare, the scope of drug abuse, and so forth. These are real problems, but they are far from applying to all blacks (or only to blacks). On the contrary, there has been a striking expansion of blacks into the middle class and into integrated occupations and communities. In 1940 only 200,000 blacks held white-

Do you have a stereotype of this punk woman? (Turn to page 656.)

■ **stereotype**
A cognitive schema or a summary impression of a group, in which a person believes that all members of the group share a common trait or traits (positive, negative, or neutral).

collar jobs; in 1990 nearly 2,000,000 did. From 1950 to 1990 the black population doubled but the number of blacks holding these jobs jumped 920 percent (Edsall & Edsall, 1991). Many whites, however, have not assimilated these positive statistics into their racial stereotypes (Jones, 1991).

When people like a group, their stereotype of the group's behavior tends to be positive. When they dislike a group, their stereotype *of the same behavior* tends to be negative. In a study that asked people to evaluate the traits associated with members of six cultures (English, Russian, German, American, French, and Italian), people strongly agreed in their judgments of their own and the others' typical national traits (Peabody, 1985). But the terms they used to describe the traits depended on whether they liked the country or not. A person who is careful with money can be seen as *thrifty* or *stingy*. Someone who is friendly toward strangers could be *trusting* or *gullible*. Someone who enjoys spending time with the relatives might be *family-loving* or *clannish*. Here are some other examples:

English, Russians, Germans		French, Italians, Americans	
Positive	**Negative**	**Positive**	**Negative**
Thrifty	Stingy	Generous	Extravagant
Serious	Grim	Lively	Frivolous
Skeptical	Distrustful	Trusting	Gullible
Cautious	Timid	Bold	Rash
Selective	Choosy	Broad-minded	Undiscriminating

People who have negative stereotypes about a group, explains anthropologist Edward T. Hall (1983), cannot understand how *deeply felt* another culture's way of behaving is. As a result, he says, they don't realize that the behavior that seems irresponsible, compulsive, or stupid actually reflects a different way of putting the world together. When Hall worked on a Hopi reservation, he found that the Hopis and the Anglos had stereotypes about each other. The Hopis were forever leaving work undone; they would start to build a dam, a house, or a road, and stop in the middle. To the Anglos, this "fact" meant that the Hopis were shiftless and lazy. But to the Hopi, building dams, houses, and roads was unimportant. Unlike the maturing of a sheep or the ripening of corn, these activities had no natural, built-in timetable. Why was it so important to finish these silly human projects, anyway? What did matter to the Hopi was working in their fields and completing religious ceremonies. The Hopi saw the Anglos as being hopelessly rigid, arbitrary, and compulsive.

The values and rules of culture determine how people "see" the same social event. Is coming late to class good, bad, or indifferent? Is it good or bad to argue with your parents about grades? Chinese students in Hong Kong (where communalism and respect for one's elders are highly valued) and Caucasian students in Australia (where individualism is highly valued) give entirely different interpretations of these two events (Forgas & Bond, 1985). It is a small step from different interpretations to negative stereotypes: "Australians are selfish and disrespectful of adults"; "The Chinese are mindless slaves of authority." It is a small step, in other words, from stereotyping to prejudice.

Prejudice

A **prejudice** is an unreasonable negative feeling toward a category of people or a cultural practice. Prejudice against a group carries a strong emotional discomfort with, dislike of, or outright hatred of its members. Typically it is based on a negative stereotype that resists rational argument. In his classic book *The Nature of Prejudice*, Gordon Allport (1954/1979) reported this conversation:

■ **prejudice**
An unjustified negative feeling toward a group of people or a custom.

Do you have a stereotype of this woman now? She is participating in an English baby-buggy-pushing contest. Many people have a negative stereotype of punks, who seem odd and threatening. But punks are just as individually varied, and just as willing to conform (to their own style), as any other group.

MR. X: The trouble with Jews is that they only take care of their own group.

MR. Y: But the record of the Community Chest campaign shows that they give more generously, in proportion to their numbers, to the general charities of the community, than do non-Jews.

MR. X: That shows they are always trying to buy favor and intrude into Christian affairs. They think of nothing but money; that is why there are so many Jewish bankers.

MR. Y: But a recent study shows that the percentage of Jews in the banking business is negligible, far smaller than the percentage of non-Jews.

MR. X: That's just it; they don't go in for respectable business; they are only in the movie business or run night clubs.

Notice that Mr. X doesn't respond to Mr. Y's evidence; he just moves along to another reason for his dislike of Jews. That is the nature of prejudice. As Elliot Aronson (1988) observes, suppose Mr. Y tried to persuade you to eat boiled insects. "Ugh," you might say, "they are so ugly." "But so are lobsters," he says, "and lots of people love lobsters." "Well, insects have no food value," you say. "Actually, they are a good source of protein," he answers. He might try other arguments, but the fact is that you have a food prejudice against eating insects—a reaction that exists in some cultures but by no means all.

Researchers have identified various reasons for the persistence of prejudice:

1. *Socialization.* Many prejudices are passed along from parents to children, in messages that say "we don't associate with people like that," sometimes without either generation having ever met the object of their dislike. Advertising, entertainment shows, and news reports also perpetuate derogatory images and sterotypes of various groups, such as old people, women, gay men and lesbians, fat people, and racial minorities.

2. *Social benefits.* Prejudices may bring support from others who share them. As we will see, it is difficult for most people to break away from the attitudes and prejudices of their friends, families, and associates—and from the social identities that these affiliations provide.

3. *Economic benefits.* Many studies have found that the greatest prejudice occurs when groups are in direct competition for jobs. During the middle of the nineteenth century, when Chinese immigrants worked on building the transcontinental railroad across the United States, there was very little prejudice against them. They were considered hard-working, industrious, and law-abiding. There was also no economic competition between the Chinese and the Anglos, as jobs were plentiful. But after the railroad was finished, at about the end of the Civil War, jobs dwindled. The Chinese had to compete with former soldiers for scarce jobs—and now they were considered criminal, crafty, and stupid (Aronson, 1988).

4. *Psychological benefits.* Prejudice can bring self-esteem, reduced anxiety, feelings of superiority, and a set of explanatory beliefs. Prejudice allows people to explain a complex world in terms of simple causes ("Those people are the source of all my troubles"). It is also the handmaiden of ethnocentrism; it allows people to feel proud of themselves and their own group and superior to others (Tajfel & Turner, 1986). In addition, people who are insecure and frustrated can use another group as a *scapegoat*, that is, as a socially accepted target for their insecurity. Centuries ago, a scapegoat was literally a goat. A religious leader would place his hands on the head of a goat as he recited the sins of the community. The goat was then allowed to escape into the wilds, symbolically taking the people's sins with it. Today a scapegoat is any powerless person or group who takes the blame for a problem. Some families make one weak child the scapegoat for their emotional conflicts. Some nations make an ethnic minority the scapegoat for their economic difficulties, as the Nazis did with the Jews and as the early Romans did with the Christians (Allport, 1979).

Years ago, a classic study demonstrated the chilling link between economic conditions and scapegoating in America. Using data from 14 states in the South, the researchers found a strong negative correlation between the number of lynchings of blacks and the price of cotton (Hovland & Sears, 1940): that is, the poorer the economic conditions for whites, the greater the number of lynchings. These data were recently reanalyzed to assess other possible explanations, but the basic correlation remained (Hepworth & West, 1988). Another research project used many different measures of economic threat and social insecurity (such as the unemployment rate, rate of serious crimes, number of work stoppages, and personal income levels) and of prejudice (number of anti-Semitic incidents, activities by the Ku Klux Klan, and survey attitudes of prejudice toward other groups). The researchers found that during times of high social and economic threat, prejudice rises significantly (Doty, Peterson, & Winter, 1991).

In most people's experience, however, prejudice is not an all-or-nothing thing that they either have or don't have. As Allport (1954/1979) put it, "Defeated intellectually, prejudice lingers emotionally." Patricia Devine and her colleagues (1991) have studied white heterosexuals' responses to being in situations with blacks or gay men. The researchers find that most people hold remnants of emotional prejudices that they acquired in childhood but that, as adults, they consciously try to eradicate. They are caught between what they know they *should* do when they meet a target of their old prejudice and what they fear they *would* do. Highly prejudiced people feel little guilt or conflict about their biases, and they feel no conflict between "should" and "would." Less prejudiced people may feel uncomfortable when they are with blacks or gays, but they also feel guilty about having these feelings and struggle to overcome them. According to Devine, such individuals should not be accused of being racists or homophobes, because they are actively trying to break their "prejudice habit" (Devine et al., 1991).

Other psychologists are not as optimistic as Devine. They suggest that superficial attitudes are less important than the "real" prejudices that are revealed when a person is with the object of his or her discomfort (Jones, 1991). For example, in one experiment in which students administered shock to confederates in an apparent study of biofeedback, whites showed *less* aggression toward blacks than toward whites. But, as you can see in Figure 18.2, as soon as the whites were angered (by overhearing derogatory remarks about themselves), they showed *more* aggression toward blacks than toward whites (Rogers & Prentice-Dunn, 1981). This finding implies that whites may be willing to control their negative feelings toward blacks under "normal" conditions, but as soon as they are angry, stressed, or provoked, their real prejudice reveals itself.

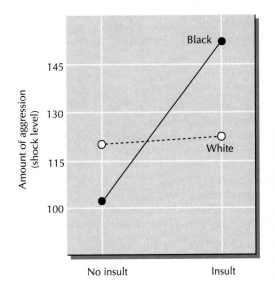

FIGURE 18.2

Latent racism?
In this study, white students gave the same amount of shock to other whites, whether or not they were angry. But when they had been insulted, whites gave much higher levels of shocks to blacks than they did when not angry (Rogers & Prentice-Dunn, 1981).

WANTS, &c.

WANTED A COOK—She must not be an Irish woman, and must bring unexceptionable recommendations. Apply at 33 Grove street, Greenwich.   j5 3t

WANTED—A FARM in Westchester county, with a good water prospect. One in the vicinity of Throg's Neck woold be preferred. Apply at 250 Pearl-street.   d20 d&ctf

WANTED.—Young Ladies as apprentices wanted at the Mantua-making Establishment of A. C. SMETS & CO. 258 Broadway.   n30

BOARD WANTED—by a gentleman and lady in a private family, in the vicinity of Cliff-street. A family where there are no other boarders would be preferred. Address A. B. at this Office.   J6 3t*

WANTED—Immediately, a respectable woman, as Nurse, who has been accustomed to the care of children. None need apply without the best of references, at No. 2 Bond-street.   d23 tf

WANTED—by a young lady educated in France, and who also possesses a good knowledge of the English—a situation as Instructress to small children in a private family. Satisfactory references will be given. Direct to M. R. at this Office.   d30

Signs reveal the history of prejudice in the United States. In 1831, a newspaper ad boldly reflected the then-popular dislike of the Irish. Job ads and hotels used to make it clear that "Christians only" were wanted, and anti-Semitism is on the rise again today. Anti-Japanese feelings ran high in the 1920s and during World War II, and returned recently with America's economic recession. Iranians and other "aliens" have been the targets of political hostilities and movements to restrict "colored" immigration. Native Americans have been targets of hatred since Europeans arrived on the continent. Animosity toward blacks resulted in segregated facilities, a legal practice until the 1950s, and today many neighborhoods and schools remain separate and unequal. Prejudice against women also remains widespread, as shown by a male-only club in Virginia. Why do new prejudices keep emerging, and why do some old ones persist?

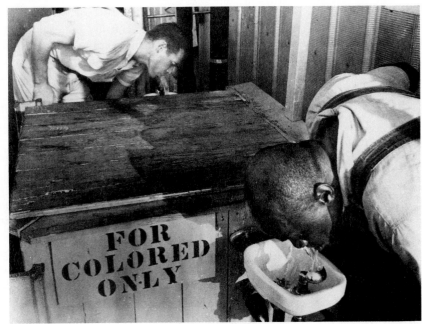

How would you define a racist? Does your definition depend on a person's attitude, emotional responses, overt actions, intentions, or all of those things? Is a person racist if he or she is intellectually opposed to racism but feels uncomfortable being around a member of another race?

As these studies suggest, prejudice can occur in overt and subtle forms. Many overtly racist attitudes—for example, those that endorse white "superiority" and oppose integration and intermarriage—have markedly declined in recent years. But there are several ways to interpret this apparent reduction in racial prejudice (Sears, Peplau, & Taylor, 1991):

1. Old prejudices have been replaced by *symbolic racism*, in which white prejudice focuses not on dislike of black individuals but on racial symbols and issues such as "forced busing," "reverse discrimination," "welfare abuse," and "hard-core criminals." In this view, these issues have become code words for the continuing animosity and resentment that most whites have for blacks, but which they know would be thought racist and unfashionable to express outright.

2. Whites truly are not as racist or hostile toward blacks as they used to be. In this view, most whites are *ambivalent*, caught between their sympathy for blacks and the disadvantages that many blacks have suffered, and their perceptions that blacks are also partially responsible for their plight. They have two conflicting values: equality and egalitarianism on the one hand, and individualism and self-reliance on the other (Katz & Hass, 1988). Because of their ambivalence, they feel discomfort and uneasiness about race issues. The behavioral result is the same—avoiding relationships with blacks—but the motives and feelings are different.

3. Prejudice reflects *realistic group conflict.* As economic conditions worsen, more ethnic and racial groups are competing for portions of a shrinking pie. In this view, whites resent affirmative action programs because these programs directly threaten their own job prospects, not because they hold any particularly negative attitudes toward blacks.

4. Prejudice has actually declined, but blacks and whites, like any other two cultures, have different *cultural rules and norms.* Their mutual discomfort is less a result of racism than of unfamiliarity with one another's ways.

Of course no single explanation can apply to the complex problem of race relations. But before prejudice can be reduced, we need to understand the many causes of its existence and the many different forms it takes.

QUICK QUIZ

A. Identify which concept—ethnocentrism, stereotyping, or prejudice—is illustrated by the following three statements.

   1. Juan believes that all Anglos are uptight and cold, and he won't listen to any evidence that contradicts his belief.

   2. John knows and likes the Chicano minority in his town but he privately believes that Anglo culture is superior to all others.

   3. Jane believes that Honda owners are thrifty and practical. June believes that Honda owners are stingy and dull.

B. Jemma vacations in Spain, where her handbag is snatched. "All Spanish men are thieves," she fumes. Jemma has formed a(n) _____ between Spaniards and criminals.

C. An affluent black man describes his experiences living and working in a mostly white world. All his life, he says, he has believed in integration, but now he finds it is often tiring and annoying to be with whites. Part of him feels on edge, uncomfortable. Is this man, or the whites he works with, "racist"? What are some explanations of his discomfort?

ANSWERS:

group's norms and habits.

they are always expected to behave in ways that are not congenial to their own is suffering "culture fatigue": the difficulty that members of all cultures face when subtle, nonverbal ways. Or perhaps no one in this story is prejudiced, and the man racist whites who communicate their prejudice and discomfort with him in many tigue may stem from being on guard all the time. The man may be working with The man himself may be a racist who thinks that all whites are prejudiced; his fa-one who simply feels ill at ease with members of a minority (or majority) group? all members of another race? Someone who holds a negative stereotype? Some-we should try to define what, exactly, is a "racist." Someone who actively dislikes **A. 1.** prejudice **2.** ethnocentrism **3.** stereotypes **B.** illusory correlation **C.** First,

■ CONFORMITY, OBEDIENCE, AND DISSENT

The cowboy is the American symbol of brave independence. In countless movies the single brave hero, ignoring the cringing cowardliness of the crowd, defeats the bad guys. Sometimes he disobeys unfair laws in order to bring the bad guys to justice. The cowboy's opposite is the bureaucrat, symbol of faceless conformity, who toes the line and never has a creative idea. The bureaucrat enforces unfair laws and tolerates injustice.

These stereotypes of the cowboy and the bureaucrat, and our general attitudes about obedience and conformity, are influenced by culture, history, and national values (Gergen, 1973; Sampson, 1977). In America, the open frontier of the West gave rise to myths that glorified the rugged individualism of the lone cowboy and resistance to established authority. But now look at the same stereotype through different glasses. The cowboy can be seen as a loutish loner who never compromises, can't get along with others, and threatens the general welfare by breaking laws. Likewise, the bureaucrat can be viewed as someone who cooperates with others, is loyal to co-workers, forgoes personal wishes, and follows laws for the benefit of all.

As you can see, obedience and conformity have both positive and negative aspects. **Obedience** refers to behavior performed in following an order from someone in a position of authority. **Conformity** refers to behavior or attitudes that occur as a result of real or imagined group pressure. These basic social processes are necessary in all human societies. A nation could not function if everyone ignored red lights, cheated on their taxes, dumped garbage anywhere they chose, or assaulted each other. But these same processes can have unfortunate consequences. Conformity often suppresses critical thinking and creativity. People often do self-destructive things because "everyone else does it." As for obedience, the plea "I was only following orders"—as in the cases of William Calley, Adolf Eichmann, and, more recently, Oliver North—has been offered throughout history to excuse actions carried out on behalf of orders that were foolish, destructive, or illegal. (By the way, the American military code does not require soldiers to obey *illegal* orders.) The writer C. P. Snow observed that "more hideous crimes have been committed in the name of obedience than in the name of rebellion."

In explaining their actions, people often *deny* conformity but *embrace* obedience (Kelman & Hamilton, 1988; Milgram, 1974). When people conform to unspoken rules, they tend to believe they are doing so of their own free will. "I dress like all my friends because I want to," they say. When they obey specific orders, they tend to believe that they do not have the free will to disobey. "I was ordered to wear this uniform," they say. "What else could I do?"

■ **obedience**
Behavior performed in following an order from someone in authority.

■ **conformity**
Behavior or attitudes that occur as a result of real or imaged group pressure.

Conformity: Following Peers

You appear at your professor's laboratory for an experiment on perception. You join seven other students seated in a room, and the study begins. You are shown a 10-inch line and asked which of three other lines is identical to it. The correct answer, line A, is obvious, so you are amused when the first person in the group chooses line B. "Bad eyesight," you say to yourself. "He's off by 2 whole inches!" The second person also chooses line B. "What a dope," you think. But by the time the fifth person has chosen line B you are beginning to doubt yourself. The sixth and seventh students also choose line B, and now you are worried about your eyesight. The experimenter looks at you. "Your turn," he says. Do you follow the evidence of your own eyes or the collective judgment of the group?

This was the basic design for a series of classic studies of conformity conducted by Solomon Asch (1952, 1965). The seven "nearsighted" students were actually Asch's confederates. Asch wanted to know what people would do when a group unanimously contradicted an obvious fact. He found that when people made the line comparisons on their own, they were almost always accurate. But in the group, only 20 percent of the students remained completely independent on every trial (often being apologetic for not agreeing with the group). One-third conformed to the group's incorrect decision more than half the time, and the rest conformed at least some of the time. Conformers and independents often felt uncertain regardless of their decision. As one said, "I felt disturbed, puzzled, separated, like an outcast from the rest."

As decades of research now confirm, many people will, in a group, deny their private beliefs, agree with silly notions, and do things they would never do on their own (Aronson, 1988). They do so for various reasons, including:

1. *Identification with the group.* People may conform because they identify with members of the group and want to be like them in dress, attitudes, or behavior. If all your friends have dyed their hair blue, you may subject your head to a blue rinse just so you will be like them.

2. *The desire to be accurate.* Suppose you spell "accommodate" correctly, with two *c*'s and two *m*'s, but your classmates insist that it has only one *m*. Or suppose you know how to spell "potato," but an authority tells you it has an *e* on the end. You may conform to their judgment, on the grounds that they probably know more than you do. In this case, out of your natural desire to be right, you will be wrong. When people believe that a group has special abilities that

Sometimes people like to conform in order to feel like part of the group . . .

are superior to their own, they are more likely to conform to its judgments (Insko et al., 1985).

3. *The desire for personal gain.* You may comply with group opinion to keep your job, to get a promotion, or to win votes.

4. *The wish to be liked; the fear of being unpopular.* Most people know that disagreeing with a group can make them unpopular. Groups have many ways of controlling their members and trying to enforce agreement. If one person in a group takes a deviant, contrary stance (or a creative, independent stance, depending on your point of view), the group first directs its energies toward persuading the person to conform. If pleasant persuasion fails, the group may become hostile. If subtle hostility fails, the group may punish, isolate, or reject the deviant altogether (Shaver & Buhrmester, 1983).

5. *Mindlessness.* As we saw in Chapter 8, people can be *mindful* or *mindless* as they go about their daily lives. Most of the time, people conform without thinking about it. They have no secret motive. They just go along doing what they have always done. When people are mindful, they are actively making decisions, trying to understand events, or concentrating on their tasks. When people behave mindlessly, they accept ideas uncritically, they don't really listen to what other people are saying, and their actions are dictated by past experience. They act on "automatic pilot" (Langer, 1989).

6. *Personality traits.* Certain personality traits make some people more afraid than others to resist group pressure. People who have a strong need for social approval, who are highly rigid, or who have low self-esteem are all more likely to conform than people who are more self-assured and flexible (Sears, Peplau, & Taylor, 1991). Most instances of conformity, though, depend heavily on the group situation and on the reasons behind the person's need to conform. Everyone conforms in some degree to work rules, their friends' social habits, and the standards of groups that mean something to them. A teenager may do everything in her power *not* to conform to her parents' values, dress, and musical taste. Yet she may conform slavishly to the values, dress, and musical taste of her immediate group of friends. Conformity, therefore, is not a simple matter of joining the herd. People follow different herds at different times.

Obedience: Following Orders

Why do most people follow orders? Some answers are obvious: They can be suspended from school, fired from their jobs, or arrested if they disobey. In addition, they obey for many of the same reasons that they conform. They identify with the authority who is giving orders. They want to be liked. They hope

. . . and sometimes they like to rebel a little in order to assert their individuality.

to gain personal advantages. They obey in "mindless" acceptance of the authority's right to issue orders or in the confidence that the authority knows more than they do.

But what about those obedient people in Milgram's experiment, the ones who felt they were doing wrong, who wished they were free, but who could not untangle themselves? Why do people obey when it is not in their interest, or when obedience conflicts with their values? Assuming that a person *wants* to disobey, several factors may stand in the way, including these:

1. *Embarrassment.* Most people don't like to rock the boat, appear to doubt the experts, or be rude (Sabini & Silver, 1985). In most social situations, good manners are the honey of relationships and the grease of civilization. They smooth over the rough spots and protect good feelings. When people break the rules of manners, they often feel awkward and embarrassed. To have gotten up from your chair in the Milgram study and walked out meant you would have had to explain and justify your "rudeness." Many were too embarrassed to do so.

2. *Lacking a language of protest.* Many people in Milgram's study simply did not know how to stand up to authority and express their decision to disobey without embarrassment. They literally didn't have the words. One woman kept apologizing to the experimenter, trying not to offend him with her worries for the victim: "Do I go right to the end, sir? I hope there's nothing wrong with him there." (She did go right to the end.) A man repeatedly protested and questioned the experimenter, but he too obeyed, even when the victim apparently had collapsed in pain. "He thinks he is killing someone," Milgram commented, "yet he uses the language of the tea table."

3. *Entrapment.* **Entrapment** is a process in which individuals escalate their commitment to a course of action in order to justify their investment in it (Brockner & Rubin, 1985). You are "trapped" at the point at which you are heavily invested in an activity and it "costs" too much to get out. The first steps of entrapment pose no difficult choices. But one step leads to another, and before the person realizes it, he or she has become committed to a course of action that does pose problems. In Milgram's study, once subjects had given a 15-volt shock, they had committed themselves to the experiment. The next level was "only" 30 volts. Before they knew it, they were administering what they believed were dangerously high shocks. At that point, it was difficult to explain a sudden decision to quit.

Entrapment catches everyone, from individuals to governments. You start dating someone you like moderately. Before you know it, you have been together so long that you can't break up, although you don't want to become committed, either. You visit Las Vegas and quickly lose the $50 you allotted yourself for gambling. So you decide to keep going "just a little longer" in hopes of recovering the lost money. Before long, you're out $227 and have to go home a day early. A government starts a war it thinks will end quickly. Years later, it has lost so many soldiers and so much money that it believes it cannot retreat without losing face.

Salespeople value the old "foot-in-the-door technique," a tried and true method of entrapment. Once you agree to do a small favor for someone, you are more likely to agree to a larger favor later. In one experiment, women were asked if they would help a safe-driving campaign by putting a small "Drive Safely" sign in their windows. Later the experimenters asked these women to put a large and ugly sign on their front lawns. Of the women who agreed to the first request, 76 percent agreed to the second, compared to only 16 percent of the control group, who were asked only to put up the ugly sign (Freedman & Fraser, 1966).

■ **entrapment**
A gradual process in which individuals escalate their commitment to a course of action to justify their investment of time, money, or effort.

A far more dramatic and sinister example of entrapment comes from a study of 25 men who had served in the Greek military police during the authoritarian regime that ended in 1974 (Haritos-Fatouros, 1988). A psychologist who interviewed the men identified the steps used in training them to use torture in questioning prisoners. First the men were ordered to stand guard outside the interrogation and torture cells. Then they stood guard in the detention rooms, where they observed the torture of prisoners. Then they "helped" beat up prisoners. Once they had obediently followed these orders and become actively involved, the torturers found their actions easier.

Many people expect the answers to moral problems to fall into two clear categories, with right on one side and wrong on the other. But in real life, as in the Milgram study, people often set out on a path that is morally ambiguous, only to find that they have traveled a long way toward violating their own principles (Sabini & Silver, 1985). A job requires, at first, only a "little" cheating, and, besides, "everyone else is doing it." From Greece's "bad" torturers to Milgram's "good" subjects, people share the difficult task of drawing a line beyond which they will not go.

Dissent: Following Conscience

Throughout history, men and women have not only obeyed orders or conformed to ideas that they believed to be misguided or immoral, but, sometimes, resisted them. Many blacks and whites disobeyed the laws of segregation. Many individuals have stopped conforming to traditional sex roles. Many men and women "blow the whistle" on practices they consider immoral or unfair, risking their jobs and friendships to do so (Glazer & Glazer, 1990). A junior researcher in molecular biology, Margot O'Toole, blew the whistle on fraudulent research that had been published by a senior colleague. She lost her job and her house, and her husband's job was put in jeopardy as well. For four years she was unable to obtain work in science, until the National Institutes of Health issued a report vindicating her and praising her courage.

Just as there are many reasons for obedience and conformity, there are many reasons for independent action. In cultures that emphasize and reward individualism, people seem to have a basic need to feel unique (Snyder & Fromkin, 1980). If you tell them that their attitudes are actually garden-variety opinions, they become more rebellious. According to Jack Brehm (1966), people need to

Three courageous whistleblowers from Rockwell International—Ria Solomon, Sylvia Robins, and Al Bray—tried to inform NASA that the space shuttle Challenger *was not safe.*

believe that they have freedom of choice. When they believe their freedom is in jeopardy, they experience a negative emotional state that Brehm calls **reactance.** To reduce this state and restore their sense of freedom, people often react to an order by doing just the opposite.

In America, many parents of small children observe reactance early on, when they instruct their 4-year-old to pick up his toys and he says, stoutly, "Won't!" Adults react to some orders in roughly the same way. In one study, students were told they would not be able to hear a public lecture in favor of lowering the voting age. Half of the students were told that the reason was censorship: School officials did not want them to hear the speaker's ideas. The rest were told that the speaker was ill. The students in the first group became more positive toward the censored position (Wicklund & Brehm, 1976).

Reactance increases as the threat to freedom increases and as the issue in question becomes more important. You may not feel much reactance if your mother asks you to call Uncle Harry (whom you like), but you may dig in your heels if she asks you to call Uncle Horace (whom you find boring). Reactance also depends on the belief that you are *entitled* to freedom. If you believe that you have the right to free speech and that the government has no right to censor the press, you are more likely to feel angry about government censorship than if you do not have these views (Brehm & Brehm, 1981). For people to disobey, therefore, they must feel that they have right on their side.

Another important factor in dissent is, simply, *having an ally.* In Asch's experiment, the presence of one other person who gave the correct answer was enough to overcome conformity to the (incorrect) majority. In Milgram's experiment too, the presence of a peer who disobeyed sharply increased the number of subjects who also disobeyed. One dissenting member of a group may be viewed as a "troublemaker," but two dissenting members are a coalition, and enough dissenting members can become a majority. Having an ally reassures a person of the rightness of the protest.

Let us now consider an actual moral dilemma that some people face at work. Suppose that you are working for an organization that you like very much. Your job is to supervise the safe installation of toxic waste cleanup systems. But after a while you learn that your immediate supervisor is taking bribes from companies that do not want to pay the cost of cleaning up their wastes. What would you do?

Your possibilities fall along two dimensions (Hirschman, 1970). One is "exit": Do you stay in the company or leave it? The second is "voice": Do you speak up or remain silent? For example, a person could stay in the company and keep his or her mouth shut (the "love it" part of "love it or leave it"). This is the traditional expectation of companies and governments that define loyalty as unquestioning obedience. The person could leave the organization quietly, without saying anything (the "leave it" part of "love it or leave it"). If a person does decide to speak up, he or she may do so within the organization, informing co-workers and supervisors. Finally, he or she can "blow the whistle," informing outsiders of company policies.

In a study of 8,587 federal government employees across the country, employees were asked if they had observed any wrongdoing at work, whether they told anyone about it, and what happened if they told (Graham, 1986). Nearly half of the sample reported that they had personally observed some serious cases of wrongdoing, such as someone stealing federal funds, accepting bribes, or tolerating a situation that was dangerous to public safety. Of that half, 72 percent had done nothing at all. The rest reported the problem to their immediate supervisors. Of those who reported, about 40 percent did nothing else, but nearly 60 percent eventually took the matter to higher authorities.

According to this study, there were four stages of dissent. First, the dissenters had to *see* the wrongdoing and believe it was serious. Second, dissenters *took re-*

■ **reactance**

A negative emotional state produced by a real or imagined threat to one's freedom of choice.

sponsibility for doing something about it. Third, they believed that *something could be done* about the problem, that there were solutions inside or outside the organization, often with allies to help. Finally, *entrapment* increased their commitment. Once having taken the initial step of informing their supervisors, most continued the protest.

Dissenters believe that loyalty to their company or country is revealed by correcting its mistakes, not by ignoring them. People who become whistle-blowers believe they have a higher loyalty still, to the public or to principle. But dissent can be difficult, as we will see next, when it means forgoing the pleasures and withstanding the pressures of being in a group.

QUICK QUIZ

A. What is the reason for conformity in these two cases?

1. You drink because you want to be like your friends, who drink heavily.
2. You drink as a matter of habit, without thinking about it.

B. What concept does each story illustrate?

1. Although your parents keep insisting that you should study more than you do, you study less and less.
2. A friend of yours, who is moving, asks you to bring over a few boxes. Since you are there anyway, he asks you to fill them with books. Before you know it, you have packed up his entire kitchen, living room, and den.
3. A clique of your classmates has developed a scam for cheating on exams. On your own, you don't know how to protest something that "everybody does." Then you learn that several classmates are also distressed about the cheating, and together you decide to publicize the matter.

ANSWERS:

A. 1. identification 2. mindlessness B. 1. reactance 2. entrapment 3. having an ally

INDIVIDUALS AND GROUPS

• In 1961, President John F. Kennedy, after meeting with his advisers, approved a CIA plan to invade Cuba and overthrow the government of Fidel Castro. The invasion at the Bay of Pigs was a total disaster and the United States was humiliated.

• At an international soccer competition in Belgium in 1985, a riot broke out in the stands. Thirty-eight people died.

• Many years ago, in a case that received much public attention, a woman named Kitty Genovese was stabbed repeatedly in front of her apartment building. She screamed for help for more than half an hour, but not one of the 38 neighbors who heard her, who came to their windows to watch, even called the police.

Something happens to individuals when they collect in a group. They think and act differently than they would on their own. This is true when the group is organized to solve problems and make decisions, as was Kennedy's circle of advisers; when it has gathered to have fun, as at a soccer game; or when it consists of anonymous bystanders, as in the Genovese case. A group's actions, research suggests, depend less on the personalities of its members than on the nature of the group itself.

Group Thinking and Groupthink

Suppose a man with a serious heart ailment is offered an operation that could cure him or kill him. Should the man have the operation if his chances of dying are one in ten, three in ten, nine in ten? Years ago, a graduate student was studying the effects of group discussion on decisions like this one (Stoner, 1961). He kept getting an odd result: On their own, people tended to be cautious about recommending surgery. But when they discussed the matter in a group, they made riskier recommendations. This result came to be called "the risky shift." It was invoked to explain irrational company decisions, mob madness, and the Bay of Pigs invasion.

Within a decade, however, other studies had found that some group decisions are more conservative and less risky than the decisions of individual members would be. It turned out that the risky shift was a special case of a more general principle of group decision making, called **group polarization.** Polarization does not mean that a group becomes split between two poles. It means that the group's *average* decision is more extreme than its members' individual decisions would be. The direction of the group's decision depends, in part, on the topic being debated. Some topics bring out the risky side, but others, such as marriage, tend to bring out caution. The direction of polarization also depends on how many people in the group were *initially* leaning toward risky or conservative decisions.

Once the group starts talking, polarization occurs for several reasons. One perfectly sensible explanation is that other people may know more than you do and offer ideas you hadn't considered, so you will be influenced to take a more extreme position. Second, some people intensify their opinions once they realize that others not only agree with them but are even stronger in their convictions. Third, people are likely to start thinking of arguments that will support their views. As arguments increase in favor of risk (or caution), the shift toward the extreme appears to be the only "rational" or "logical" choice (Kaplan & Miller, 1983).

One kind of group whose decisions have especially important consequences is the jury, 12 individuals who must agree on conviction or acquittal. What are the effects of group discussion on their collective decision? Usually, the verdict initially favored by a majority of the members is the one that eventually wins, as group polarization would predict. When the group is equally split, however, most juries show a *leniency bias:* The more the group talks, the more lenient its verdict. One reason is that jurors who favor acquittal are more influential than jurors who favor conviction. Why might this be so? The "reasonable doubt" standard—a person is innocent unless proven guilty beyond a reasonable doubt—favors acquittal; it is easier to raise one doubt than to refute all doubts. But when juries are instructed to arrive at a verdict based on "a preponderance of evidence that the defendant committed the crime," the leniency bias vanishes (MacCoun & Kerr, 1988). If you ever serve on a jury, you might keep these findings in mind!

Group members who like each other and share attitudes often work well together. But close, friendly groups are subject to a problem called **groupthink,** the tendency for all members of the group to think alike and suppress dissent. It occurs when a group's need for total agreement overwhelms its need to make the wisest decision, and when the members' needs to be liked and accepted overwhelm their ability to disagree with a bad decision. To study groupthink, Irv-

■ **group polarization**
The tendency of a group's decision to be more extreme than its members' individual decisions.
■ **groupthink**
In close-knit groups, the tendency for all members to think alike and to suppress dissent and disagreement.

ing Janis (1982b) examined the historical records of the presidents who actually made the decisions to launch the Bay of Pigs invasion and to escalate the Vietnam War.

According to Janis, groupthink has several identifiable features. First, to preserve harmony and to stay in the leader's good graces, members avoid thinking of alternatives to the leader's initial preference. Instead of generating as many solutions to a problem as possible, they stick with the first one. Second, members don't want to disagree with each other or make their friends look bad, so they don't examine this initial preference closely for errors or flaws. They suppress their own misgivings, which creates an illusion of unanimity. Third, the group avoids getting any outside information from experts that might challenge its views, and it suppresses dissent within the group. (President Lyndon Johnson, who favored increased bombing of North Vietnam, ridiculed his adviser Bill Moyers by greeting him with "Well, here comes Mr. Stop-the-Bombing.") The result is that everyone remains in a "tight little ship," even if the ship is about to sink.

Groupthink can be counteracted, however, under particular conditions that encourage the expression of doubt and dissent (Janis, 1982a). In one experiment, researchers divided management trainees into two groups to discuss a challenging problem: deciding what equipment would be necessary for survival on the moon (Hall & Watson, 1970). The first group was asked to come to a unanimous decision. The second group was encouraged to avoid agreement: Members were instructed not to change their opinions for the sake of good feelings, not to take "straw votes" that might encourage people to side with the majority, and to regard their differences as natural and beneficial rather than disruptive. The final decisions of the groups were evaluated by NASA scientists. In the quality and creativity of their decisions, the second group was far superior.

Other researchers remind us that just as groups influence individuals, individuals influence groups. Group members who hold minority opinions do not have the same power as the majority, but they can sometimes persuade and change the majority. Considering, as Serge Moscovici (1985) puts it, that the minority starts off being viewed as "deviant, incompetent, unreasonable, unappealing, and unattractive," how *does* it influence the group?

One strategy is repetition. Repeated minority arguments are like drops of water eroding a rock. Eventually, as such arguments become familiar, they seem less outrageous—an instance of the validity effect. Second, by taking a firm, consistent, and well-expressed position, the minority makes its views more persuasive. A third strategy (as we noted earlier) is to find allies in the group, which makes minority members seem less deviant or rebellious and their ideas more legitimate. Dissenters are disruptive to a group, but they force the group to become aware of other ideas and other solutions. By undermining the majority's complacency, dissenters may move the group to more independent and innovative ideas.

Responsibility and Anonymity

A friend told us of a tug-of-war game between the eleventh and twelfth grades in her high school. She confesses that she didn't pull as hard as she should have, because she figured that her teammate Steve, a 280-pound tackle, could do the work for the whole side. Many group members think this way. Responsibility for an outcome is "diffused," or spread, among all the members. This response allows individuals to pass the buck, to assume that someone else will do the job or make the right decision.

In work groups, the **diffusion of responsibility** often results in **social loafing:** Each member of a team loafs along, letting others "pull harder" (Latané, Williams, & Harkins, 1979). This slowdown of effort does not happen in all

How not to lead a group.

■ **diffusion of responsibility**
In organized or anonymous groups, the tendency of members to avoid taking responsibility for actions or decisions, assuming others will do it.

■ **social loafing**
The tendency of group members, under some conditions, to reduce their efforts and "loaf"; one result of diffusion of responsibility.

groups. It occurs primarily when individual group members are not responsible or accountable for the work they do, when people feel that working harder would only duplicate their colleagues' efforts, or when the work itself is uninteresting. Members of a group need to feel that they are making unique contributions, even if their contributions are anonymous. When the challenge of the job is increased or when each member of the group has a different, important job to do, the sense of individual responsibility rises and loafing declines (Harkins & Petty, 1983). Loafing also declines when people know they will have to evaluate their own performance privately, or when they know their group's performance will be evaluated against that of another group (Harkins & Szymanski, 1989). And if people are working on a group project that really matters to them, they may even work *harder* than they would on their own to compensate for some of their loafing buddies (Williams & Karau, 1991)!

THE FACELESS CROWD.   The most extreme condition associated with diffused responsibility is **deindividuation,** the loss of awareness of one's individuality (Festinger, Pepitone, & Newcomb, 1952). Deindividuated people "forget themselves" in responding to the immediate situation. They are more likely to act mindlessly, and their behavior becomes disconnected from their attitudes. They do things they would never do on their own.

Deindividuation increases under conditions of anonymity. It is more likely to occur, for instance, when a person is in a large city rather than a small town, in a faceless mob rather than an intimate group, or when signs of individuality are covered by uniforms or masks. Deindividuated people can become more aggressive (think of those soccer fans), but sometimes they can become more friendly (think of all the chatty people on buses and planes who reveal things to their seatmates they would never tell anyone they knew). In one study, students who spent an hour with seven strangers in a darkened room felt more friendly and affectionate toward them than did students who conversed with strangers in a lighted room (Gergen, Gergen, & Barton, 1973).

The power of the situation to influence what deindividuated people do is shown clearly in two experiments. In one, women who were dressed in Ku Klux Klan-like white disguises delivered twice as much (apparent) electric shock to another woman as did women who were not only undisguised but also wore large name tags (Zimbardo, 1970; see Figure 18.3). In a second study, when the women were wearing nurses' uniforms, they gave *less* shock than women in regular dress (Johnson & Downing, 1979). Apparently the KKK disguise was a signal to behave aggressively; the nurses' uniforms were a signal to behave nurturantly.

Some individuals, and some cultures, are more "individuated" than others. Christina Maslach and her associates have developed a scale that assesses a person's willingness to be distinguished from others—for example, to give your

■ **deindividuation**
In groups or crowds, the loss of awareness of one's own individuality; in varying degrees, a person feels indistinguishable from others.

FIGURE 18.3

Anonymity and cruelty
Women covered in Ku Klux Klan-like disguises gave more shocks to another woman than did women who were not disguised or who were identified with name tags (Zimbardo, 1970).

opinion on a controversial subject to a group of strangers, to publicly challenge a speaker with whom you disagree, or to raise your hand to ask a question in a large class. Asians are on the average less individuated than Anglos, blacks, and Latinos, reflecting the Asian cultural emphasis on social harmony (Maslach, Stapp, & Santee, 1985).

THE HELPFUL BYSTANDER.   Since the Kitty Genovese story hit the news, there have been many other reports of bystander apathy. Without calling for help, bystanders watch as a woman is attacked, as a man burns himself to death, as a car hits a child and drives away. Such apathy reflects social loafing on a large scale. But instead of simply condemning bystanders for their laziness or cowardice, social psychologists have identified some of the factors that predict whether and when people will behave altruistically, helping strangers in trouble, even at risk to themselves. These conditions should be familiar to you from another section of this chapter: *The stages of a bystander's decision to help in a crisis are nearly the same as in an individual's decision to protest wrongdoing.*

1. *The bystander must perceive the need for help.* Many bystanders see no need to help someone in trouble. Sometimes this blindness justifies inaction; the German citizens of Dachau didn't "see" the local Nazi concentration camp, although it was in plain view. But sometimes the blindness is an inevitable result of screening out too many demands on attention. People who live in a big city cannot stop to help everyone who seems to need it.

Whether or not people interpret a situation as requiring their intervention also depends on cultural rules. In northern European nations and in the United States, husband-wife disputes are considered strictly private; neighbors intervene at their peril. In one field study, bystanders observed a (staged) fight between a man and a woman. When the woman yelled, "Get away from me; I don't know you!", two-thirds of the bystanders went to help her. When she shouted, "Get away from me; I don't know why I ever married you!", only 19 percent tried to help (Shotland & Straw, 1976). In Mediterranean and Latin cultures, however, a dispute between any two people is considered fair game for anyone who is passing by. In fact, two people in a furious dispute might even *rely* on bystanders to intervene (Hall & Hall, 1990).

2. *The bystander must then decide to take responsibility for offering to help.* In a large crowd of observers, it is easy for people to avoid action. Crowds of anonymous people encourage the diffusion of responsibility because everyone assumes that someone else will take charge. When people are alone and hear someone call for help, they usually *do* intervene (Latané & Darley, 1976). Bystanders are also more likely to take responsibility when they are in a good mood—and when they are thinking of themselves as kind, benevolent people (Brown & Smart, 1991).

3. *The bystander weighs the costs of getting involved as opposed to doing nothing.* The cost of helping might be personal danger, wasted time, or embarrassment (if it turns out the person wasn't really in trouble). The cost of not helping might be guilt, blame from others, loss of honor, or loss of self-esteem.

Some psychologists believe that all acts of helpfulness are ultimately "selfish," even if one person helps another in order to feel like a moral and decent soul. Others, however, argue that life is full of countless illustrations of true *altruism,* in which people help others out of empathy and concern without weighing costs or benefits at all (Batson, 1990). A study of Gentiles who risked their lives to rescue Jews during the Nazi era found two motives: deeply held moral values or personal feelings for the victim (Oliner & Oliner, 1988). Bystanders who feel a moral obligation to the victim or who empathize with the victim are more likely to take responsibility for helping (Batson et al., 1988; Dovidio, Allen, & Schroeder, 1990).

Courageous bystanders, then and now: During the Nazi occupation of France, people living in the impoverished Protestant village of Le Chambon rescued some 5,000 Jewish children from being sent to their deaths. The villagers, led by their pastor André Trocme and his wife Magda (left), believed it was a special privilege and a moral obligation to shelter Jews. More recently, Terri Barnett and Gregory Alan (being honored at City Hall, right), along with other African Americans, rescued a white man during the Los Angeles riots that followed the acquittal of four police officers who had beaten the black motorist Rodney King. In both Le Chambon and in Los Angeles, the rescuers had themselves been victims of persecution and discrimination, but rose above the temptation to treat others as they had been treated—choosing instead to save fellow human beings in trouble.

4. *The bystander must know how to be helpful.* People who intervene in a crisis feel that they are competent to help and that their efforts won't backfire. This sense of competence turns up in studies of people who rescue others from political persecution and of people who help in street emergencies. Of 32 people who had directly intervened in real criminal episodes, for example, all said they felt certain they could handle the dangerous situation. Many had had training in police work, first aid, or self-defense (Huston et al., 1981). But even people who do not have such skills or strengths can help in an emergency. They can call for medical help, get the police, comfort the victim, and report a crime (Shotland & Goodstein, 1984).

Social psychologists emphasize, therefore, that altruism is not only a spontaneous or selfless expression of a desire to help. There are social conditions that make altruism more likely to occur, and there are conditions that make it less likely as well.

Competition and Cooperation

If you want to make some money, play the dollar auction with several friends. Everyone must bid for your dollar in 5-cent increases, and the auction is over when there is no new bid for 30 seconds. The catch is this: The second-highest bidder must also pay you, although he or she will get nothing in return. Usually, the bidding starts quickly and soon narrows to two competitors. After one of them has bid $1.00, the other decides to bid $1.05, because she would rather pay $1.05 for your dollar than give you $.95 for nothing. Following the same logic, the person who bid $1.00 decides to go to $1.10. By the time they quit, you may have won $5 or $6.

Your bidders will have been trapped by the nature of competition—and of entrapment. Both will want to "win"; both will fear losing; both will try to save face. Had they thought of cooperation, however, they would *both* have won. The bidders could have agreed to set a limit on the bidding (say, $.45) and split the profits.

During a competitive game, participants and spectators are involved and energized, and have a good time. Competition in business and science can lead to better services and products and new inventions. Yet there are some psychological hazards to competition. When winning is everything, competitors may find no joy in being second or even being in the activity at all. After reviewing the huge number of studies on the effects of competition, Alfie Kohn (1986) concluded that "the phrase *healthy competition* is a contradiction in terms." Competition, research shows, often makes people feel insecure and anxious (even if they win), fosters jealousy and hostility, and can stifle achievement. Because competition is "the common denominator of American life," Kohn maintains, we rarely pause to notice its negative effects.

Just as competition can drive people apart, *cooperation* can bring them together. Years ago, Muzafer Sherif and his colleagues used a natural setting, a Boy Scout camp called Robbers Cave, to conduct an experiment on the contrasting results of cooperation and competition (M. Sherif, 1958; Sherif et al., 1961). Sherif randomly assigned normal 11- and 12-year-old boys to two groups, the Eagles and the Rattlers. To build "team spirit," each group worked on communal projects, such as making a rope bridge and building a diving board. Sherif then put the teams in competition for prizes. During fierce games of football, baseball, and tug-of-war, the boys whipped up a competitive fever that spilled off the playing fields. They began to raid each other's cabins, call each other names, and start fistfights. No one dared to have a friend from the opposite gang. Before long, the Rattlers and Eagles were as hostile toward each other as any two rival gangs fighting for turf, any two siblings fighting for a parent's attention, and any two nations fighting for dominance. Their hostility continued even when they were just sitting around together watching movies.

So far, Sherif had done nothing more than a typical Little League competition might do. But then he determined to undo the hostility he had created and to make peace between the Eagles and Rattlers. The experimenters set up a series of situations in which both groups needed to work together to reach a desired goal. The boys had to cooperate to get the water supply system working. They had to pool their resources to get a movie they all wanted to see. When

> ✳ *In the United States, most people assume that competition—in everything from the Little League to big business—is a good thing. Why, then, do some psychologists think that "healthy competition" is a contradiction in terms?*

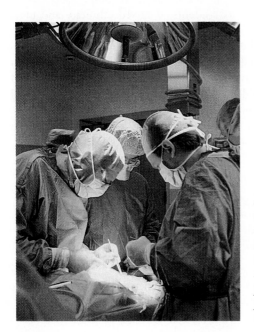

Members of a medical team pool their efforts and skills to save a patient—an example of the kind of teamwork that, in a less dramatic way, occurs in everyone's life. Because industrial societies emphasize the value of competition, they often underestimate the pervasiveness and importance of cooperation.

the staff truck broke down on a camping trip, they all had to join forces to pull the truck up a steep hill and get it started again. This policy of interdependence in reaching *mutual goals* was highly successful in breaking down "us-them" thinking, competitiveness, and hostility. The boys eventually made friends among their former "enemies."

The same process applies in adult groups. When adults work together in a cooperative group in which teamwork is rewarded, they often like each other better and are less hostile than when they are competing for individual success (Deutsch, 1949, 1980). Cooperation creates a new social identity, causing people to think of themselves as members of one big group instead of two opposed groups, *us* and *them* (Gaertner et al., 1990). Similarly, families who work together on an overriding problem, or in a family business, are more cooperative and have less competition among siblings than those who do not have a unifying goal.

Many people once believed that the best way to reduce group prejudice was for members of opposing groups to get to know each other better. This *contact hypothesis* became the basis for racial desegregation in the 1950s and 1960s. People assumed that contact would reduce hostility between the races, and sometimes, as in the case of integrated housing projects, it did (Deutsch & Collins, 1951; Wilner, Walkley, & Cook, 1955). However, simple contact has not always been successful—as is apparent to anyone visiting most big-city high schools today. In reviewing studies of desegregated schools, Walter Stephan (1985) found that in 25 percent of the studies the black children actually showed a *drop* in self-esteem. For every example of reduced prejudice, Stephan found other evidence of more prejudice. In some integrated schools, different ethnic groups form cliques and gangs, fighting other groups, and defending their own ways. In such cases, why doesn't contact across ethnicities work?

One answer may be that the typical American school, at all levels, is designed for competition. Students compete for the teacher's attention and grades. Those who are not fluent in standard English, who are shy, or who come from cultures that praise cooperation do not fare well in such environments. Others tease or ignore them, conclude that they are "stupid," and never give them the chance to prove themselves. The minority students then stick together, feeling angry and defensive.

To break this pattern, Elliot Aronson and his colleagues (1978) organized elementary school classrooms using a "jigsaw method" to build cooperation. Classes were divided into groups of six students of mixed ethnicity and race. Each little group worked together on a shared task that was broken up like a jigsaw puzzle. Each child needed the contributions of the others to put the assignment together; for instance, each child might be given one paragraph of a six-paragraph biography and asked to learn the whole story. This method proved highly effective in reducing the children's animosity toward others who seemed different, in increasing good will, and in improving grades all around.

Decades of studies of the contact hypothesis find four factors that appear to be necessary to reduce prejudice between two groups (Stephan & Brigham, 1985):

- *Cooperation*, in which the groups work together for a common goal
- *Equal status;* if one side has more power, prejudice can continue
- *Support by authority figures* such as teachers, employers, and police
- *Opportunities for members of both groups to socialize informally*

One of the reasons that racism has been so persistent in American society is that these four conditions are rarely met all at the same time.

QUICK QUIZ

A. Identify which phenomenon—deindividuation, group polarization, diffusion of responsibility, or groupthink—is represented in each of the following four situations.

1. The president's closest advisers are afraid to disagree with his views on arms negotiations.
2. You are at a Halloween party wearing a silly Donald Duck costume. When you see a chance to play a practical joke on the host, you do it.
3. You invite four friends out for pizza to help you decide the merits of a new job offer. After talking things over with them, you agree to quit your safe job for a new one that offers greater challenge but has a risk of failure.
4. Walking down a busy street, you see that fire has broken out in a store window. "Someone must have called the fire department," you say.

 B. Gang warfare is a severe and growing problem in the United States. What concepts *from this chapter* might apply to understanding (if not solving) this problem?

ANSWERS:

opportunities for equal-status cooperation between factions.
leaders; the danger to teenagers who refuse to join or support a gang; the lack of
gang members become entrapped by conformity to each other and obedience to
behave violently); the economic and social benefits of belonging to a gang; how
type their "enemies" (and how society stereotypes gang members, not all of whom
portance of the social identity of belonging to a gang; how gang members stereo-
sponsibility. **B.** Social psychologists would consider, among other things: the im-
A. 1. groupthink **2.** deindividuation **3.** group polarization **4.** diffusion of re-

THE QUESTION OF HUMAN NATURE

Throughout this book, we have seen that individuals differ, as schools of psychology do, in their basic views of human nature. Are we, "at heart," good, helpful, and cooperative, or selfish, aggressive, and cruel? Those who believe that people are basically decent and kind often rely on moral persuasion as a tactic of making the world less hostile. Those who believe that people are governed by aggressive, even death-seeking instincts hope that we can find constructive ways of displacing or channeling our violent energies. Optimists tend to hope that everything will work out if you just trust people to behave well; pessimists assume that nothing will work out because you can't trust people further than you can throw them.

Social psychologists phrase the question differently. It is in our "nature," they would say, to behave both generously *and* savagely, to be selfish *and* altruistic, to hold deeply embedded prejudices toward "outsiders" *and* to accept members of other cultures warmly and with appreciation of differences (see "Think About It"). The task is to identify the conditions that make these reactions likely to occur. To do this, they draw on the *normal psychological processes* discussed in this chapter: roles, obedience to authority, conformity, stereotyping, self-serving bias, entrapment, deindividuation, and competition.

Optimists and pessimists disagree on whether "human nature" is basically good or basically destructive. With the question stated that way, the only answer is both—or neither. What would be a better question, and a more useful answer?

THINK ABOUT IT

The Grand Experiment: Can People Accept Their Differences?

The whole world is festering with unhappy souls—
The French hate the Germans, the Germans hate
the Poles,
Italians hate Yugoslavs, South Africans hate the
Dutch;
And I don't like anybody very much.

Kingston Trio, "The Merry Minuet"

The 1992 Los Angeles riots, which brought racial and cultural animosities to the surface, illustrated the human capacity both for despair and destruction and for caring and renewal.

Sometimes the situation indeed looks bleak. In the United States, hate crimes—cross burnings, vandalism, assault, and murder—are increasingly being committed against blacks, gays, Latinos, Jews, Asians, Arabs, and women in all groups. In what was Yugoslavia, Serbs and Croats reenact an ancient animosity. In Northern Ireland, Catholics and Protestants live in severely segregated communities and regard each other with fear and loathing, as do Jews and Arabs in the Middle East. Anti-Semitism is on the rise in Russia and Poland, where there aren't many Jews left to blame for anything. Across Europe, a growing neo-Nazi movement attacks the influx of refugees.

In this last box, we ask you to think about the most important "think about it" of our time: Can people of different cultures—within a nation and between nations—manage to live in some semblance of peace? What will it take to prevent world war or even local ethnic wars—a giant Robbers Cave experiment, in which everyone cooperates against an invasion from space? For that matter,

what is a reasonable definition of "peace" or "tolerance" that should guide our efforts? Can people be expected to accept and like everyone else's customs, even when these seem totally foreign or morally repugnant, or is it more reasonable to encourage people to abide by a live-and-let-live philosophy? Should society strive to integrate cultures and groups—at the risk of increased conflict and animosity as well as increased affection and understanding—or aim for peaceful but isolating self-segregation?

In the table we list some arguments for the inevitability of group conflict on the one hand and the possibility of understanding or at least tolerance on the other. As you evaluate both sides, can you think of additional arguments?

• *Roles* are necessary in any social system, from a small tribe to a vast nation. They can be rigid, requiring people to give up personal feelings in the service of the role—whether the role is employee, spouse, or soldier. But they can also be flexible, less confining, and better able to bend with the qualities of the person who carries out the role.

• *Conformity* to one's group and *obedience* to authority are essential if a social system is to function. These mechanisms can lead to mindless obedience and the execution of illegal orders. But people can also learn to celebrate their unique qualities and tolerate the qualities of others. They can learn how and when to protest in order to influence the majority. And they have the motives for uniqueness, freedom, and justice to help them do so.

Cultural Animosity is Inevitable

Once they have learned their culture's rules and roles, people follow them uncritically.

Culture affects so many of our ideas of what is right and how to behave that it is impossible not to fear or dislike people who do things differently.

Competition between cultures is inevitable as long as they differ in resources and power.

"Us-them" thinking will last as long as cultural differences do.

It is impossible for people to avoid feelings of prejudice.

Much of human behavior is "mindless."

Ethnocentrism and other prejudices are biologically "wired into" our species, and therefore cannot be eradicated.

There always has been cultural conflict.

Hate crimes and other expressions of intolerance are getting worse.

The United States has failed in its effort to be a "melting pot"; cultures do not want to assimilate into bland uniformity.

What do you think?

Cultural Coexistence Is Possible

Some people resist social pressure and follow conscience.

A "world culture" is emerging because of modern international telecommunications and increased international travel and business. More and more people are being exposed to how others do things—and frequently adopting their customs (and food!).

Cultures can cooperate in many realms: science, arts, business, music, sports, aid in emergencies.

People have the empathic ability to understand "them."

People can be legally kept from acting on their prejudices.

When human beings set themselves a problem to solve, they can be highly "mindful."

Prejudice is more closely linked to economic and social conditions, and therefore can be reduced when inequities are reduced.

There always was smallpox, too, but it has been nearly eradicated.

Individual and organized activism against human-rights violations and discrimination is higher than ever.

Few nations in world history have even tried the grand experiment of embracing other cultures, and the U.S. faces a unique challenge in the number of cultures that live there (93 languages are spoken in Los Angeles alone).

What do you think?

• *Competition* is often a compelling motivator of achievement. The "space race" produced many rapid innovations in space technology. But competition can also produce prejudice and hostility, and it can reduce the pleasure of doing an activity for its own sake. Families, schools, companies, and cultures can train people in cooperative strategies, as well as encourage competition without the obsessive need for victory at all costs.

• *Cognitive processes*, such as stereotyping, ethnocentrism, and attributions, also have benefits and problems. They organize information that might otherwise be overwhelming. They justify behavior so that people don't have to think twice about everything they do (or even think once about it). They raise self-esteem so that people can feel good about themselves and their communities.

But these same processes can lead to distorted perceptions of other groups. They justify unjustifiable behavior. They protect self-esteem at the cost of self-delusion.

• *Entrapment* causes attitudes and actions to change in small steps. Before people realize it, they have committed themselves to a new belief or course of action. Entrapment can lead people toward helpful and generous behavior or toward aggressive behavior, depending on how the trap is set.

• *Deindividuation* allows people to suppress their individual preferences for the greater good of an institution, an ideal, or a goal. Yet when people entirely abandon responsibility for their actions, tragedy can result. The news is full of stories of mindless mobs, but also of people who retained their individuality amid great pressures to conform.

When philosopher Hannah Arendt (1963) wrote about the trial of Adolf Eichmann, she used the phrase "the banality of evil." (Banal means "commonplace" or "unoriginal.") Eichmann and his fellow Nazis were ordinary men, Arendt wrote, just doing their jobs. This is, perhaps, the hardest lesson in psychology. Most people want to believe that harm to others is done only by "evil people" who are bad down to their bones. It is reassuring to divide the world into those who are good or bad, mild or mean, open-minded or narrow-minded. Yet again and again, we have seen that perfectly nice people can become, under some conditions, aggressive, selfish, and prejudiced. Fortunately, people who are aggressive, selfish, and prejudiced can become, under some conditions, friendly, helpful, and tolerant.

A few years ago, scientists from 12 nations gathered in Seville, Spain, to consider the inevitability of war. "Humanity can be freed from the bondage of biological pessimism," they concluded in their report, which was called the Seville Statement on War. "The same species who invented war is capable of inventing peace" (Groebel & Hinde, 1989). The researchers particularly attacked the common idea that we have inherited a tendency to make war from our animal ancestors. Warfare "is a peculiarly human phenomenon and does not occur in other animals," the researchers found. Genes, they argued, provide only a potential for any action; learning and environmental conditions determine whether and how that potential will express itself.

All of this is good news and bad news. The bad news is that bad behavior cannot be eliminated by getting rid of a few "bad" people or nations. The good news is that if humankind has created the conditions for cruelty, perhaps it can eradicate them.

In Hawaii, many different ethnic and racial groups coexist, and no single group is a majority. This group of Hawaiian musicians provides a metaphor for a question that social psychologists hope to answer: Can people harmonize in spite of their differences, or do they inevitably end up singing different songs?

Attitude Change: From Persuasion to "Brainwashing"

All around you, every day, people are trying to get you to change your mind. Advertisers, politicians, and friends use similar methods of persuasion. By knowing what these methods are, you will have a better chance of knowing how to evaluate persuasive messages and when to accept or resist them (Pratkanis & Aronson, 1992).

• *Separate the person who is trying to persuade you from the message being conveyed.* There is a reason that advertisements are full of beautiful models, sports heroes, and experts. People are more likely to be persuaded if they hear arguments from someone they admire or think is attractive. Advertisers and politicians spend more to convince the public that they can be trusted than to educate the public about their products or their ideas. Of course, sometimes it takes a beloved celebrity to get people to pay attention: When basketball superstar Magic Johnson announced he had HIV, the virus that leads to AIDS, many people understood for the first time that AIDS could happen to them too.

• *Don't be fooled by The Big Lie: Separate the quality of the product or the truth of the message from your familiarity with it.* Some advertisements, for politicians and products, are repeated what seems like a thousand times a day. Familiarity is the reason that many people spend four times as much for a familiar brand of aspirin as for an unfamiliar one, even though the cheaper product is just as good.

• *Separate your intellectual judgment from your feelings.* If a message is linked with a good feeling, people are more likely to listen to it and to change their attitudes. In one study, students who were given peanuts and Pepsi while listening to an argument were more likely to be convinced than were students who listened without the pleasant munchies and soft drinks (Janis, Kaye, & Kirschner, 1965). Perhaps this is why so much business is conducted over lunch, and so many seductions over dinner!

The emotion of fear, in contrast, can cause people to avoid accepting arguments that are in their own best interest, which is why scare tactics are usually unsuccessful. Such tactics are used, for example, to try to persuade people to

quit smoking or abusing other drugs, to drive only when sober, to use condoms to avoid AIDS and other sexually transmitted diseases, and to check for signs of cancer. However, fear works only if (1) people are scared a little, but not so much that they become too anxious and deny the danger completely; and (2) the message is combined with information about what a person can do to avoid the danger (Leventhal, 1970). When messages about a future disaster are too terrifying and when people believe that there is nothing they can do to avoid it, they tend to deny the danger. Social activists, in contrast, feel worried enough to do something. By adopting a more realistic "strategy of small wins," they avoid being paralyzed by the scale of their task (Weick, 1984).

• *Know the attitudes and values that are important to you and be prepared to defend them.* Experiments find that when people are "inoculated" against persuasive tactics, by hearing opposing ideas and practicing a defense against them, they are better able to resist persuasion (McGuire & Papageorgis, 1961). This is not a case for rigid thinking and the refusal to accept new ideas. But it is a case for critical thinking. If you can identify and defend your point of view, you are better able to withstand unsupported arguments against it and to accept good evidence for changing it.

Sometimes, however, efforts to change attitudes go beyond exposing people to a new idea and persuading them to accept it. Persuasion tactics become more severe and manipulative. The term *brainwashing* was first used during the Korean War to describe how American prisoners of war came to collaborate with their Chinese Communist captors and endorse anti-American propaganda. It has since been used to account for the sympathy that some hostages develop toward their captors, and the fanatical attachment of cult members to their leaders. The cults may be religious, political, or psychological.

Many psychologists dislike the word "brainwashing" and prefer the phrase "undesired social influence" or "coercive persuasion." The word *brainwashing,* they argue, implies that a person has a sudden change of mind and is unaware of what is happening. It sounds mysterious and powerful. In fact, its methods are neither mysterious nor unusual. Indeed, the difference between "persuasion" and "brainwashing" is often only a matter of degree and the observer's bias.

Studies of religious and psychological cults find some common steps in the coercive persuasion of a recruit. These steps occur in many other situations as well, from military and fraternity hazing to political rallies. *They become coercive when they suppress an individual's ability to reason and make choices in his or her own best interests* (M. Galanter, 1989; Pratkanis & Aronson, 1992; Temerlin & Temerlin, 1986; Zimbardo & Hartley, 1985).

• *The person is put under physical or emotional distress.* Participants may not be allowed to eat, sleep, or exercise. They may be isolated in dark rooms with no stimulation or food prior to joining the group. In a group, they may be induced into a trancelike state through repetitive chanting, hypnosis, deep relaxation, or fatigue. If a participant is under stress, perhaps feeling lonely or troubled, he or she is already emotionally primed to accept the ideas of the group.

• *The person's problems are defined in simplistic terms, and simple answers are offered—repeatedly.* There are as many of these answers as there are persuasive groups, but here are some real examples: Do you have problems with your marriage? A long-term marriage is an "addiction"; better break the habit. Are you afraid or unhappy? It all stems from the pain of being born. Are you worried about war in the Mideast or hunger in Africa? It's not your problem; victims are responsible for everything that happens to them. Are your parents giving you a hard time? Reject them completely. Are you struggling financially? It's your fault for not *wanting* enough to be rich.

• *The group leader offers unconditional love, acceptance, attention, and answers to personal problems.* In exchange, the leader demands everyone's attachment, adoration, and idealization. In addition, the new recruit may be given a "love bath" from the group—constant praise, support, applause, and affection. Positive emotions of euphoria and well-being are generated.

• *An extreme version of "us-them" thinking is created.* The recruit is told that he or she is part of the "chosen," the elite, the "redeemed." To foster this new identity, many cults require a severe initiation rite; require their members to wear identifying clothes or eat special diets; and assign new names. All members of the Philadelphia group MOVE were given the last name "Africa"; all members of the Church of Armageddon took the last name "Israel." Conversely, members are taught to hate certain "evil" enemies: parents, capitalists, blacks, whites, nonbelievers.

• *The person is subjected to entrapment.* "There is no contract up front that says 'I agree to become a beggar and give up my family,'" says Philip Zimbardo. Instead, the person agrees to small things: to spend a weekend with the group, then another weekend, then weekly seminars, then advanced courses. During the Korean War, the Chinese first got the American POWs to agree with mild remarks such as "The United States is not perfect." Then the POWs had to add their own examples of such imperfections. At the end they were signing their names to anti-American broadcasts (Schein, Schneier, & Barker, 1961).

• *Once a person is in the group, his or her access to information is severely controlled.* As soon as a person is a committed member, the group limits his or her choices, denigrates critical thinking and makes fun of doubts, defines the outside world as evil, and insists that any private distress is due to lack of belief in the group. Total conformity is imposed and groupthink is demanded.

Some people may be more vulnerable than others to coercive tactics. But the techniques are powerful enough to overwhelm even strong individuals, as studies of hostages and prisoners have found. Unless people understand how these methods work, few can resist their power. To protect themselves, says psychologist Michael Langone, "people must think or sink." That has been the theme of this book.

SUMMARY

1. Social psychology studies people in social context, including the influences of *roles*, *norms*, and groups on behavior and cognition. Three studies illustrate the power of roles to affect individual personality and values. In Zimbardo's prison study, college students quickly fell into the role of "prisoner" or "guard." In Rosenhan's mental hospital study, the role of staff attendant caused nurses and psychiatrists to *depersonalize* patients and sometimes treat them harshly. In Milgram's obedience study, people in the role of "teacher" inflicted what they thought was extreme shock to another person in the role of "learner" because of the authority of the experimenter.

2. According to *attribution theory*, people are motivated to explain their own and other people's actions. They may attribute actions to the *situation* or to a person's *disposition* (qualities in the person). The *fundamental attribution error* occurs when people overestimate personality traits as a cause of behavior and underestimate the situation. A *self-serving bias* allows people to excuse their own mistakes by blaming the situation. According to the *just-world hypothesis*, people need to believe that the world is fair and that people get what they deserve. To preserve this belief, they may *blame the victim* for inviting injustice.

3. People have many *attitudes*, which include cognitions and feelings about a subject, but their *values* are more central and motivating beliefs. Some attitudes are based on carefully elaborated convictions, but others stem from the *validity effect:* simply hearing a statement often enough. Attitudes dispose people to behave in certain ways, but sometimes a change of behavior (because of the law or social custom) causes attitudes to change. "Taking Psychology with You" discusses some methods of attitude change, including tactics that range from persuasion to coercion.

4. *Social identity theory* emphasizes the importance to people of belonging to various social groups, but once in a group people are likely to experience *ethnocentrism*, the belief that their group is superior to all others.

5. A *stereotype* is a cognitive schema about a group that helps people organize experience and predict how others will behave. But stereotypes create *illusory correlations* in which people incorrectly associate negative qualities with minority groups. Stereotypes distort reality in three ways: They emphasize differences between groups; they underestimate the differences within groups; and they produce *selective perception*, in which people see only evidence that fits their stereotypes.

6. A *prejudice* is an unjustified negative feeling about a group of people that resists rational evidence. Prejudices persist because of socialization, social support, economic gains, and psychological payoffs, such as feelings of superiority. People often use a minority group as a *scapegoat*, a target that is assigned the blame for their problems. Some racist attitudes have declined, but many forms of race prejudice and conflict continue.

7. *Obedience*, following the orders of an authority, and *conformity*, going along with group pressure, are basic social processes that make society possible. People conform because they identify with a group, trust the group's judgment or knowledge, hope for personal gain, or wish to be liked. They also may conform mindlessly. People obey orders for many of the same reasons, but also because they are too embarrassed to disobey, lack a language of protest, or have been *entrapped*.

8. *Dissent* and *nonconformity* also occur for several reasons. The theory of *reactance* maintains that people need to feel they have freedom of choice; if their freedom is threatened, they react to restore it. Dissent is more likely when a person has support and is not the lone protester.

9. Once in a group, individuals often behave differently than they would on their own. In *group polarization*, the group's collective decision is more extreme than its members' private decisions. In *groupthink*, group members think alike and, for the sake of harmony, suppress disagreement. The *diffusion of responsibility* causes group members to work less hard ("social loafing") and to avoid taking responsibility for their decisions and actions. *Deindividuation* is the loss of self-awareness and sense of individuality in a group or crowd. These group processes have been used to explain foolhardy group decisions, mindless mob violence, and the unwillingness of bystanders to help a stranger in trouble. However, groups can be structured to counteract all of these processes.

10. The stages in a bystander's decision to help a stranger (like the stages of deciding to "blow the whistle" on wrongdoing) include seeing the need for help, deciding to take responsibility for action, weighing the costs of helping, having a commitment to helping others or feeling empathy toward them, and knowing what to do to help.

11. Cooperation and competition have strong effects on attitudes and behavior. Competition often increases hostility, stereotyping, and aggression between groups. Conflict and hostility between groups can be reduced by interdependence in working for mutual goals and by equal-status contact.

12. War and peace, cruelty and kindness, can be viewed as the results of normal psychological processes, including roles and rules; obedience and conformity; cognitive processes such as attributions, stereotypes, and mindlessness; cooperation and competition; and group processes including deindividuation and groupthink. By themselves, these processes are neutral; they can be used either positively or negatively.

KEY TERMS

rules (norms) *643*
role *643*
depersonalization *645*
social cognition *647*
attribution theory *648*
fundamental attribution error *648*
self-serving bias *648*
just-world hypothesis *649*
blaming the victim *649*
attitude *650*
value *650*
validity effect *651*
cognitive dissonance *652*
social identity theory *652*
ethnocentrism *652*
"us-them" thinking *653*
stereotype *654*
illusory correlation *654*

prejudice *655*
scapegoat *656*
obedience *661*
conformity *661*
mindlessness *663*
language of protest *664*
entrapment *664*
whistleblowers *665*
reactance *666*
group polarization *668*
groupthink *668*
diffusion of responsibility *669*
social loafing *669*
deindividuation *670*
altruism *671*
competition *672*
cooperation *673*
contact hypothesis *674*

Taking Psychology with You

THE FIVE STRANDS OF HUMAN
EXPERIENCE

PSYCHOLOGY IN YOUR LIFE
Situation 1: When Love Has Gone
Situation 2: Job Stress
Method and Matter

You've come a long way since the beginning of this book. It is now time to stand back and ask yourself where you've been and what you've learned from the many studies, topics, and controversies that have been covered. What fundamental principles emerge, and how can you take them with you into your own life? You probably won't be surprised that different psychologists would answer these questions differently; as we noted back in Chapter 1, psychology is a patchwork quilt of ideas. Still, even a patchwork quilt has an overall pattern. We believe that there exists a "big picture" in the study of psychology, one that reveals five fundamental determinants of human behavior.

■ THE FIVE STRANDS OF HUMAN EXPERIENCE

If you look back at the chapters in this book, you will see that our focus began within the individual—with neurons and hormones—and gradually expanded to include the physical environment, the social environment, and entire cultures. Both across the sequence of chapters and within individual ones you can find what we call the five strands of human experience:

1. *Biology.* As physical creatures, we are influenced by our bodies and our brains. Physiology affects the rhythms of our lives, our perceptions of reality, our ability to learn, the intensity of our emotions, our temperaments, and, in some cases, our vulnerability to emotional disorder.

2. *Cognition.* Our species is, above all, the animal that explains things. Our cognitions—beliefs, explanations, and attributions—may not always be realistic or sensible, but they continually influence our actions and choices. All of us are constantly seeking to make sense of the world around us and of our own physical and mental states. Perception is sensation plus interpretation. Emotion is arousal plus attribution. Language is sound (or gesture) plus meaning.

3. *Environment.* What we do and how we do it are often less a matter of personality than of situation. We respond to the environment, and, in turn, our acts have consequences that influence future behavior. Features of the physical environment (such as room design, noise level, and air temperature) and the requirements of a specific circumstance (such as a job or a course) are constantly affecting us, even as we are constantly affecting our environments, in a repeating chain of cause and effect. The right environment can help us cope better with disabilities, get along better with others, and even become more creative and happy. The wrong kind can foster boredom, hostility, and discontent.

4. *Other people.* In Western culture, many people like to think of themselves as independent creatures. But everyone conforms, to one extent or another, and with greater or lesser awareness, to the expectations and demands of others. Spouses, lovers, friends, bosses, parents, and perfect strangers "pull our strings" in ways we may not recognize. Human beings emulate role models, conform to group pressures, obey authorities, and blossom or wilt in close relationships. Throughout life we need "contact comfort"—sometimes in the literal touch or embrace of others and sometimes in shared experience or conversation.

5. *Culture.* Although there are many universals of behavior that unite humanity, "human nature" also varies from one culture to another. Culture dictates a set of norms and roles for how employers and employees, strangers and friends, and men and women are "supposed" to act. Culture teaches individuals how to use and interpret body language, how to treat their spouses, how to rear their children, and even how to perceive the world. Whenever you find yourself wondering, irritably, why "*those* people have to behave that way," chances are a cultural difference is at work.

These five forces suggest different questions to ask when you are trying to describe, understand, predict, or change a particular aspect of your own life. For example:

Biology. What is going on in my body? Do I have a physical condition that might be affecting my behavior? Do I have a temperamental tendency to be easily aroused or to be calm? Are drugs or alcohol altering my ability to make decisions or behave as I would like? Might an irregular schedule be disrupting my physical functions and impairing my efficiency? Am I under unusual pressures that increase physical stress?

Cognition. How am I interpreting this situation? Are my explanations reasonable? Have I tested them? Am I wallowing in negative thoughts and "catastrophizing"? Do I attribute my successes to luck but take all the blame for my failures? Do I assume the worst about others? Do I make "external" attributions or "internal" ones? What are my underlying attitudes?

Environment. What are the contingencies and consequences governing my behavior and that of others? What rewards are maintaining the status quo? Which situations make me feel ambitious, confident, or content, and which ones make me feel helpless, pessimistic, or angry? Would I be different if the situation changed? How might I be able to change it?

Other people. Who are the people in my life who affect my attitudes and behavior? Am I responding to their expectations or rules in a "mindless" way? What part do I play in affecting their behavior? How do my friends and relatives support me or hinder me in achieving my goals?

Culture. How do my ethnicity and nationality affect me? What gender roles do they specify for me and my partners in close relationships? Am I acting out some sort of unwritten cultural role? What would happen if I ignored the norms of that role? Of the many cultural messages being aimed at me by television, books, parents, and teachers, which have the greatest influence? Are my conflicts with other people a result of cultural misunderstandings—due, for instance, to differing rules for expressing emotion?

Keep in mind, though, that *no single one of these factors operates in isolation from the others.* The forces that govern our behavior are as intertwined as strands of ivy on a wall, and it can be hard to see where one strand begins and another ends. This message, if enough people believed it, would probably put an end to the "pop psych" industry, which promotes single, simple answers to real-life complexities. (Anxious about the state of the world? Just jog some more or fix your diet. Not doing so well at work? Just learn to dress for success.) Some simplifiers of psychology try to reduce human problems to biochemical imbalances or genetic defects. Others argue that anyone can "fulfill any potential," regardless of biology or environment, and that solving problems is merely a matter of being determined.

In this book we have tried to show that the real concerns and dilemmas of life do not divide up neatly according to the chapters of an introductory psychology text (even ours). For example, to understand shyness or loneliness, you might need to consider your personal learning history; childhood experiences and what you observed from adult role models; temperamental tendencies; adult experiences; the autobiographical memories that make up your personal "story"; recent transitions in your life; how stress, diet, drugs, and sleep patterns might be affecting your mood; and whether you come from a culture that encourages or prohibits assertiveness. It may seem daunting to keep so many factors in mind. But once you get into the habit of seeing a situation from many points of view, relying on single-answer approaches will feel like wearing blinders.

■ PSYCHOLOGY IN YOUR LIFE

If the theories and findings in this book are to be of long-lasting personal value to you, they must jump off the printed page and into your daily life. In previous chapters we have tried to point out ways in which you can apply what you have learned. However, *you* must do the actual work of selecting those aspects of psychological knowledge that can be of benefit to you.

To give you some practice in doing so, we will take two common problems and offer some ideas about where to look in this book for principles and findings that may shed light on them. If you are serious about wanting to use psychology, we recommend that you turn to the specified pages and think about how the information there can best be applied, even if you don't have the particular problems we have selected. Our brief lists of hints are far from exhaustive, and we have not attempted to touch on every major topic in this book. You should feel free to make the "remote associations" that are the heart of creativity and come up with additional ideas that could be brought to bear on a particular problem. There is no single correct solution in these hypothetical situations, any more than there is a single solution to the real problems in life.

Situation 1: When Love Has Gone

You have been romantically involved with someone for a year. When the relationship began, you felt very much in love and you thought your feelings were returned. But for a long time now your partner's treatment of you has been anything but loving. In fact, your partner makes fun of your faults in front of others, yells at you about the slightest annoyance, and insults and humiliates you. Sometimes you are ignored for days on end, as if your partner wants to punish you for some imagined wrong. All of your friends advise you to leave the relationship. Yet you can't shake the feeling that your partner must really love you. You still occasionally have a great time together, and your partner seems to become very distressed whenever you threaten to leave. You wish you could either improve the relationship or get out, and your inability to act leaves you feeling angry and depressed.

How might each of the following topics help you resolve this problem? We suggest that you try to come up with your own answers, aided by these text references, before you look at ours:

- Approach-avoidance conflicts (Chapter 10, page 341)
- Intermittent reinforcement (Chapter 6, page 216)
- Observational learning (Chapter 6, page 230)
- Self-esteem (Chapter 12, page 421) and locus of control (Chapter 15, page 545)
- Cognitive dissonance theory (Chapter 10, page 349)
- Gender differences in emotion and love (Chapter 9, page 332, and Chapter 10, page 363)
- Adult transitions (Chapter 14, pages 508, 515, 526)
- Reactance (Chapter 18, page 666)

Here are a few reasons why these topics might apply (you may think of others):

Research on *approach-avoidance conflicts* may help explain why you are both attracted to and repelled by this relationship—and why the closer you approach, the more you want to leave (and vice versa). When a goal is both attractive and painful, it is not unusual to feel uncertain and vacillate about the possible courses of action.

Intermittent reinforcement may explain why you persist in apparently self-defeating behavior. If staying in the relationship brought only punishment or if your partner always ignored you, it would be easier to leave. But your partner intermittently gives you good times, and when behavior is occasionally rewarded, it becomes resistant to extinction.

Past *observational learning* may help account for your present behavior. Perhaps your parents have a dominant/submissive relationship, and their way of interacting is what you have learned to expect in your own relationships.

Low *self-esteem* may explain why you tolerate abuse and humiliation; you may actually agree with your partner's criticisms and insults and feel you don't "deserve" a better relationship. If you have an *external locus of control*, you may feel that you cannot control what is happening to you—that you are merely a victim of fate, chance, or the whims and wishes of others.

Cognitive dissonance theory suggests that you may be trying to keep your attitudes and behavior consistent. The cognition "I am in this relationship and chose to be with this person" is dissonant with "This person ignores and mistreats me." Since you are still unable to break up (and alter the first cognition), you are working on the second cognition, hoping that your partner will change for the better.

Research on *gender differences* finds that men and women often have different unstated rules about expressing emotion and different definitions of love. Perhaps traditional gender roles are preventing you and your partner from communicating your true preferences and feelings.

Findings on *adult transitions* and *"crises"* might alert you to stresses in your partner's life: Have there been unexpected or difficult changes, such as a move, a new job, or the illness of a parent?

Finally, *reactance* may explain why you do not listen to your friends. Their advice may be sound but threatening to your autonomy. In a paradoxical way, doing the opposite of what everyone thinks you should—staying in the relationship—gives you a (temporary) sense of control.

Understanding your situation, of course, does not lead automatically to a solution. Depending on the circumstances, you might choose to cope with the ongoing stress of the situation (Chapter 15); change your perceptions of the situation (Chapter 18); use learning principles to try to alter your own or your partner's behavior (Chapter 6); find other sources of self-esteem (Chapters 12 and 14); find a support group of people in the same situation (Chapter 17); seek psychological therapy or counseling, with or without your partner (Chapter 17)—or leave the relationship.

Situation 2: Job Stress

You are an up-and-coming computer programmer. You like your job, but you feel overwhelmed by the amount of work you have to do. You never seem to be able to meet your deadlines, and you find yourself worrying about work at night and on weekends—you are unable to relax. Your friends accuse you of being a "grind" and a "workaholic," though you would like to work less if you could. You believe you deserve a promotion, but your boss is curt and abrupt, rarely accepts your good ideas, and never gives you any feedback about your work, let alone praise. (You assume your boss dislikes you and has some grudge against you.) You are beginning to feel isolated from your co-workers, too. Lately, you find that your motivation is sagging, and creative ideas are slow in coming. The occasional relaxing evening drink has turned into steady drinking at home and several belts during the day, too, as you try to blot out your worries. What can you do to improve this situation?

Here are some psychological topics that may yield insights:

- Sources of stress (Chapter 15, page 537)
- Work motivation (Chapter 6, page 225, and Chapter 10, page 370)
- Attributions (Chapter 18, page 648)
- Defense mechanisms (Chapter 12, page 432)
- Drug use and abuse (Chapter 4, page 130, and Chapter 16, page 589)
- Obedience, conformity, and dissent (Chapter 18, page 661)

Here are a few reasons why these topics might apply:

Research on *sources of stress* may alert you to the reasons for your harried condition. You may need to analyze how much of the pressure you feel is due to the demands of the job and how much is a product of your own internal standards. You can't cope with stress appropriately until you know what is causing it.

Research on *work motivation* shows that achievement motivation can be a part of personality but is also affected by the nature of the work environment. "Burnout," for instance, often occurs because of the way a job is structured; there may be little support from co-workers or employers, infrequent feedback, and few opportunities for developing innovative ideas. Workers are most productive when the conditions of the job—such as flexibility, variation in routine, and the power to make decisions—encourage intrinsic motivation.

Attribution theory states that attributions, whether accurate or not, guide our responses to a situation. Your assumption that your employer dislikes you and holds a grudge may not be valid. Perhaps he or she is under unusual pressure and is therefore distracted. Perhaps he or she is unaware of your contributions. A talk with the boss may be in order.

The clinical concept of a *defense mechanism* suggests that your overwork may be a way to channel thoughts away from some other area of your life that is troubling you. Would you really work less if you could, or is your constant preoccupation with your job a sign of denial—an unwillingness to face problems at home?

Research on *drug use* shows that drug effects and the likelihood of abuse depend on mental set and situational setting, your physical tolerance, your cultural experience with the use of the drug, and your social environment when taking the drug. A special vulnerability to alcohol's physical effects may explain your gradual slide into a serious alcohol problem. Or alcohol may offer you a convenient excuse for relaxing your previously high standards of performance on the job ("I can't help it; it's the booze"). Because excessive drinking affects brain function and judgment, it probably does impair your performance, creating a vicious cycle of drug use and excuse.

Finally, research on *obedience*, *conformity*, and *dissent* suggests that you may not be alone in your problems at work. Perhaps your co-workers share your problems and would like to make improvements, but they fear rocking the boat. There may be a solution you could accomplish with the aid of others that would be difficult to achieve on your own.

Method and Matter

Our two examples have been personal problems, but the applications of psychology extend beyond personal concerns to social ones. Remember James Peters and Ralph Galluccio from Chapter 12? (If you don't, don't worry; just reread Chapter 7 on memory, and feel reassured.) Peters and Galluccio were neighbors who fought for ten years over a boundary dispute. In the end, Peters killed Galluccio. Such disputes, with and without that violent finale, are unfortunately common among lovers, neighbors, and nations. Psychological findings can increase our understanding of such hostilities and may help reduce them. For example, Chapter 9 discussed how cultural differences in emotion and body language can create misunderstandings. Chapter 8 described steps that can lead to better, more creative solutions to problems. Chapter 13 described how children learn to be altruistic, empathic, and responsible, or selfish and irresponsible. And Chapter 18 suggested ways people can overcome prejudice and ethnocentrism and get along in spite of their differences.

An engineer-turned-social scientist, Jacobo Varela (1978), believes that we now have enough accurate information about human behavior to develop "social technology." Just as physical technology offers mechanical answers to engineering problems, social technology applies psychological answers to social problems. Varela and his students have applied many of the findings discussed in this book to real-life situations, with great success. Yet Varela reports that it is often difficult to persuade people to think in terms of general psychological strategies for facing life's problems and challenges. Instead, he says, people often confuse his *examples* with his *method:*

> If I talk about a woman's being cured of alcoholism, people think the method applies only to alcoholics. . . . If I present the case of a parole violator who abandoned crime for good, I am told to offer my services to the nearest parole board. The point is that social technology is distinct from the problems it solves. The system of solutions remains constant, but it can be adapted easily to the task at hand. A screwdriver may be used to tighten screws on a typewriter, but that does not make it a typewriter tool, effective only on typewriters.

That is why the one chapter that may ultimately be most useful to you is the one you may have assumed to be least useful: Chapter 2, "How Psychologists Know What They Know." The best way to take psychology with you is to understand its basic principles of critical thinking, its ways of approaching problems and questions. Specific findings within psychology change, as new research is done and new theories evolve. But the method of psychology continues, and clear thinking is its hallmark.

Statistical Methods

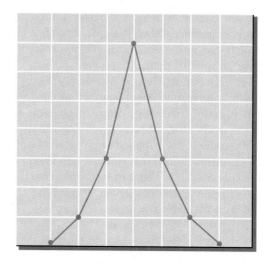

Nineteenth-century English statesman Benjamin Disraeli reportedly once named three forms of dishonesty: "lies, damned lies, and statistics." It is certainly true that people can lie with the help of statistics. It happens all the time: Advertisers, politicians, and others with some claim to make either use numbers inappropriately or ignore certain critical ones. (When hearing that "four out of five doctors surveyed" recommend some product, have you ever wondered just how many doctors were surveyed and whether they were representative of all doctors?) People also use numbers to convey a false impression of certainty and objectivity when the true state of affairs is uncertainty or ignorance. But it is people, not statistics, that lie. When statistics are used correctly, they neither confuse nor mislead. On the contrary, they expose unwarranted conclusions, promote clarity and precision, and protect us from our own biases and blind spots.

If statistics are useful anywhere, it is in the study of human behavior. If human beings were all alike, and psychologists could specify all the influences on behavior, there would be no need for statistics. But any time we measure human behavior, we are going to wind up with different observations or scores for different individuals. Statistics can help us spot trends amid the diversity.

This appendix will introduce you to some basic statistical calculations used in psychology. Reading the appendix will not make you into a statistician, but it will acquaint you with some ways of organizing and assessing research data. If you suffer from a "number phobia," relax: You do not need to know much math to understand this material. However, you should have read Chapter 2, which discussed the rationale for using statistics and described various research methods. You may want to review the basic terms and concepts covered in that chapter. Be sure that you can define *hypothesis, sample, correlation, independent variable, dependent variable, random assignment, experimental group, control group, descriptive statistics, inferential statistics* and *test of statistical significance.* (Correlation coefficients, which are described in some detail in Chapter 2, will not be covered here.)

To read the tables in this appendix, you will also need to know the following symbols:

N = the total number of observations or scores in a set

X = an observation or score

Σ = the Greek capital letter sigma, read as "the sum of"

$\sqrt{}$ = the square root of

(*Note:* Boldfaced terms in this appendix are defined in the glossary at the end of the book.)

■ ORGANIZING DATA

Before we can discuss statistics, we need some numbers. Imagine that you are a psychologist and that you are interested in that most pleasing of human qualities, a sense of humor. You suspect that a well-developed funny bone can protect people from the negative emotional effects of stress. You already know that in the months following a stressful event, people who score high on sense-of-humor tests tend to feel less tense and moody than more sober-sided individuals do. You realize, though, that this correlational evidence does not prove cause and effect. Perhaps people with a healthy sense of humor have other traits, such as flexibility or creativity, that act as the true stress buffers. To find out whether humor itself really softens the impact of stress, you do an experiment.

First, you randomly assign subjects to two groups, an experimental group and a control group. To keep our calculations simple, let's assume there are only 15 people per group. Each person individually views a silent film that most North Americans find fairly stressful, one showing Australian aboriginal boys undergoing a puberty rite involving physical mutilation. Subjects in the experimental group are instructed to make up a humorous monologue while watching the film. Those in the control group are told to make up a straightforward narrative. After the film, each person answers a mood questionnaire that measures current feelings of tension, depression, aggressiveness, and anxiety. A person's overall score on the questionnaire can range from 1 (no mood disturbance) to 7 (strong mood disturbance). This procedure provides you with 15 "mood disturbance" scores for each group. Have people who tried to be humorous reported less disturbance than those who did not?

Constructing a Frequency Distribution

Your first step might be to organize and condense the "raw data" (the obtained scores) by constructing a **frequency distribution** for each group. A frequency distribution shows how often each possible score actually occurred. To construct one, you first order all the possible scores from highest to lowest. (Our mood disturbance scores will be ordered from 7 to 1.) Then you tally how often each score was actually obtained. Table A.1 gives some hypothetical "raw data" for the two groups, and Table A.2 shows the two frequency distributions based on these data. From these distributions you can see that the two groups differed. In the experimental group, the extreme scores of 7 and 1 did not occur at all, and the most common score was the middle one, 4. In the control group, a score of 7 occurred four times, the most common score was 6, and no one obtained a score lower than 4.

Because our mood scores have only seven possible values, our frequency distributions are quite manageable. Suppose, though, that your questionnaire had yielded scores that could range from 1 to 50. A frequency distribution with 50 entries would be cumbersome and might not reveal trends in the data clearly. A solution would be to construct a *grouped frequency distribution* by grouping

TABLE A.1

Some Hypothetical Raw Data

These scores are for the hypothetical humor-and-stress study described in the text.

Experimental group	4,5,4,4,3,6,5,2,4,3,5,4,4,3,4
Control group	6,4,7,6,6,4,6,7,7,5,5,5,7,6,6

TABLE A.2

Two Frequency Distributions

The scores are from Table A.1.

Experimental Group			Control Group		
Mood Disturbance Score	Tally	Frequency	Mood Disturbance Score	Tally	Frequency
7		0	7	////	4
6	/	1	6	ЖЖ /	6
5	///	3	5	///	3
4	ЖЖ ///	7	4	//	2
3	///	3	3		0
2	/	1	2		0
1		0	1		0
		N = 15			N = 15

adjacent scores into equal-sized *classes* or *intervals.* Each interval could cover, say, five scores (1–5, 6–10, 11–15, and so forth). Then you could tally the frequencies within each *interval*. This procedure would reduce the number of entries in each distribution from 50 to only 10, making the overall results much easier to grasp. However, information would be lost. For example, there would be no way of knowing how many people had a score of 43 versus 44.

Graphing the Data

As everyone knows, a picture is worth a thousand words. The most common statistical picture is a **graph,** a drawing that depicts numerical relationships. Graphs appear at several points in this book, and are routinely used by psychologists to convey their findings to others. From graphs, we can get a general impression of what the data are like, note the relative frequencies of different scores, and see which score was most frequent.

In a graph constructed from a frequency distribution, the possible score values are shown along a horizontal line (the *x-axis* of the graph) and frequencies along a vertical line (the *y-axis*), or vice versa. To construct a **histogram,** or **bar graph,** from our mood scores, we draw rectangles (bars) above each score, indicating the number of times it occurred by the rectangle's height (Figure A.1).

A slightly different kind of "picture" is provided by a **frequency polygon,** or **line graph.** In a frequency polygon, the frequency of each score is indicated by a dot placed directly over the score on the horizontal axis, at the appropriate height on the vertical axis. The dots for the various scores are then joined together by straight lines, as in Figure A.2. When necessary an "extra" score, with a

frequency of zero, can be added at each end of the horizontal axis, so that the polygon will rest on this axis instead of floating above it.

A word of caution about graphs: They may either exaggerate or mask differences in the data, depending on which units are used on the vertical axis. The two graphs in Figure A.3, although they look quite different, actually depict the same data. Always read the units on the axes of a graph; otherwise, the shape of a histogram or frequency polygon may be misleading.

FIGURE A.1

A histogram
This graph depicts the distribution of mood disturbance scores shown on the left side of Table A.2.

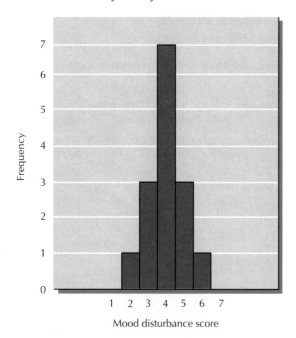

FIGURE A.3

Same data, different impressions
These two graphs depict the same data, but have different units on the vertical axis.

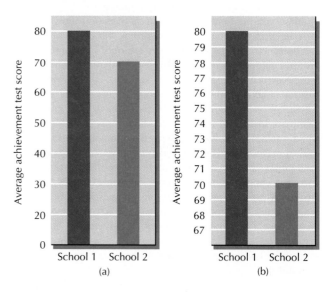

FIGURE A.2

A frequency polygon
This graph depicts the same data as Figure A.1.

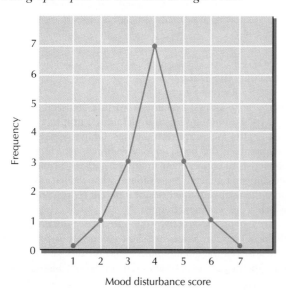

■ DESCRIBING DATA

Having organized your data, you are now ready to summarize and describe them. As you will recall from Chapter 2, procedures for doing so are known as *descriptive statistics.* In the following discussion, the word *score* will stand for any numerical observation.

Measuring Central Tendency

Your first step in describing your data might be to compute a **measure of central tendency** for each group. Measures of central tendency characterize an entire set of data in terms of a single representative number.

THE MEAN. The most popular measure of central tendency is the *arithmetic mean,* usually called simply the **mean.** It is often expressed by the symbol *M.* Most people are thinking of the mean when they say "average." We run across means all the time: in grade point averages, temperature averages, and batting averages. The mean is valuable to the psychologist because it takes all the data into account and it can be used in further statistical analyses. To compute the mean, you simply add up a set of scores and divide the total by the number of scores in the set. Recall that in mathematical notation, Σ means "the sum of," X stands for the individual scores, and N represents the total number of scores in a set. Thus the formula for calculating the mean is:

$$M = \frac{\Sigma X}{N}$$

Table A.3 shows how to compute the mean for our experimental group. Test your ability to perform this calculation by computing the mean for the control group yourself. (You can find the answer, along with other control group statistics, on page 696.) Later, we will describe how a psychologist would compare the two means statistically to see if there is a significant difference between them.

TABLE A.3

Calculating a Mean and a Median

The scores are from the left side of Table A.1.

Mean (M)

$$M = \frac{4 + 5 + 4 + 4 + 3 + 6 + 5 + 2 + 4 + 3 + 5 + 4 + 4 + 3 + 4}{15}$$

$$= \frac{60}{15}$$

$$= 4$$

Median

Scores, in order: 2, 3, 3, 3, 4, 4, 4, [4,] 4, 4, 4, 5, 5, 5, 6

↑
Median

THE MEDIAN. Despite its usefulness, sometimes the mean can be misleading, as we noted in Chapter 2. Suppose you piled some children on a seesaw in such a way that it was perfectly balanced, and then a 200-pound adult came and sat on one end. The center of gravity would quickly shift toward the adult. In the same way, one extremely high score can dramatically raise the mean (and one extremely low score can dramatically lower it). In real life, this can be a serious problem. For example, in the calculation of a town's mean income, one millionaire would offset hundreds of poor people. The mean income would be a misleading indication of the town's actual wealth.

When extreme scores occur, a more representative measure of central tendency is the **median,** or midpoint in a set of scores or observations ordered from highest to lowest. In any set of scores, the same *number* of scores falls above the median as below it. The median is not affected by extreme scores. If you were calculating the *median* income of that same town, the one millionaire would offset only one poor person.

When the number of scores in the set is odd, calculating the median is a simple matter of counting in from the ends to the middle. However, if the number of scores is even, there will be two middle scores. The simplest solution is to find the mean of those two scores and use that

number as the median. (When the data are from a grouped frequency distribution, a more complicated procedure is required, one beyond the scope of this appendix.) In our experimental group, the median score is 4 (see Table A.3). What is it for the control group?

THE MODE. A third measure of central tendency is the **mode,** the score that occurs most often. In our experimental group, the modal score is 4. In our control group, it is 6. In some distributions, all scores occur with equal frequency, and there is no mode. In others, two or more scores "tie" for the distinction of being most frequent. Modes are used less often than other measures of central tendency. They do not tell us anything about the other scores in the distribution; they often are not very "central"; and they tend to fluctuate from one random sample of a population to another more than either the median or the mean.

Measuring Variability

A measure of central tendency may or may not be highly representative of other scores in a distribution. To understand our results, we also need a **measure of variability** that will tell us whether our scores are clustered closely around the mean or widely scattered.

THE RANGE. The simplest measure of variability is the **range,** which is found by subtracting the lowest score from the highest one. For our hypothetical set of mood disturbance scores, the range in the experimental group is 4 and in the control group it is 3. Unfortunately, though, simplicity is not always a virtue. The range gives us some information about variability but ignores all scores other than the highest and lowest ones.

THE STANDARD DEVIATION. A more sophisticated measure of variability is the **standard deviation (SD).** This statistic takes every score in the distribution into account. Loosely speaking, it gives us an idea of how much, on the average, scores in a distribution differ from the mean. If the scores were all the same, the standard deviation would be zero. The higher the standard deviation, the more variability there is among scores.

To compute the standard deviation, we must find out how much each individual score deviates from the mean. To do so we simply subtract the mean from each score. This gives us a set of *deviation scores.* Deviation scores for numbers above the mean will be positive, those for numbers below the mean will be negative, and the positive scores will exactly balance the negative ones. In other words, the sum of the deviation scores will be zero. That is a problem, since the next step in our calculation is to add. The solution is to *square* all the deviation scores (that is, to multiply each score by itself). This step gets rid of negative values. Then we can compute the average of the *squared* deviation scores by adding them up and dividing the sum by the number of scores (*N*). Finally, we take the square root of the result, which takes us from squared units of measurement back to the same units that were used originally (in this case, mood disturbance levels).

The calculations just described are expressed by the following formula:

$$SD = \sqrt{\frac{\Sigma(X - M)^2}{N}}$$

Table A.4 shows the calculations for computing the standard deviation for our experimental group. Try your hand at computing the standard deviation for the control group.

TABLE A.4

Calculating a Standard Deviation

Scores (X)	Deviation scores (X − M)	Squared deviation scores (X − M)²
6	2	4
5	1	1
5	1	1
5	1	1
4	0	0
4	0	0
4	0	0
4	0	0
4	0	0
4	0	0
4	0	0
3	−1	1
3	−1	1
3	−1	1
2	−2	4
	0	14

$$SD = \sqrt{\frac{\Sigma(X - M)^2}{N}} = \sqrt{\frac{14}{15}} = \sqrt{.93} = .97$$

Note: When data from a sample are used to estimate the standard deviation of the population from which the sample was drawn, division is by N − 1 instead of N, for reasons that will not concern us here.

Remember, a large standard deviation signifies that scores are widely scattered, and that therefore the mean is not terribly typical of the entire population. A small standard deviation tells us that most scores are clustered near the mean, and that therefore the mean is representative. Suppose two classes took a psychology exam, and both classes had the same mean score, 75 out of a possible 100. From the means alone, you might conclude that the classes were similar in performance. But if Class A had a standard deviation of 3 and Class B had a standard deviation of 9, you would know that there was much more variability in performance in Class B. This information could be useful to an instructor in planning lectures and making assignments.

Transforming Scores

Sometimes researchers do not wish to work directly with raw scores. They may prefer numbers that are more manageable, such as when the raw scores are tiny fractions. Or they may want to work with scores that reveal where a person stands relative to others. In such cases, raw scores can be transformed to other kinds of scores.

PERCENTILE SCORES. One common transformation converts each raw score to a **percentile score** (also called a *centile rank*). A percentile score gives the percentage of people who scored at or below a given raw score. Suppose you learn that you have scored 37 on a psychology exam. In the absence of any other information, you may not know whether to celebrate or cry. But if you are told that 37 is equivalent to a percentile score of 90, you know that you can be pretty proud of yourself; you have scored as well as, or higher than, 90 percent of those who have taken the test. On the other hand, if you are told that 37 is equivalent to a percentile score of 50, you have scored only at the median—only as well as, or higher than, half of the other students. The highest possible percentile rank is 99, or more precisely, 99.99, because you can never do better than 100 percent of a group when you are a member of the group. (Can you say what the lowest possible percentile score is? The answer is on page 696.) Standardized tests such as those described in Chapter 11 often come with tables that allow for the easy conversion of any raw score to the appropriate percentile score, based on data from a larger number of people who have already taken the test.

Percentile scores are easy to understand and easy to calculate. However, they also have a drawback: They merely rank people and do *not* tell us how far apart people are in terms of raw scores. Suppose you scored in the 50th percentile on an exam, June scored in the 45th, Tricia scored in the 20th, and Sean scored in the 15th. The difference between you and June may seem identical to that between Tricia and Sean (five percentiles). But in terms of *raw* scores you and June are probably more alike than Tricia and Sean, because exam scores usually cluster closely together around the midpoint of the distribution and are farther apart at the extremes. Because percentile scores do not preserve the spatial relationships in the original distribution of scores, they are inappropriate for computing many kinds of statistics. For example, they cannot be used to calculate means.

Z-SCORES. Another common transformation of raw scores is to **z-scores,** or **standard scores.** A z-score tells you how far a given raw score is above or below the mean, using the standard deviation as the unit of measurement. To compute a z-score, you subtract the mean of the distribution from the raw score and divide by the standard deviation:

$$z = \frac{X - M}{SD}$$

Unlike percentile scores, z-scores preserve the relative spacing of the original raw scores. The mean itself always corresponds to a z-score of zero, since it cannot deviate from itself. All scores above the mean have positive z-scores and all scores below the mean have negative ones. When the raw scores form a certain pattern called a *normal distribution* (to be described shortly), a z-score tells you how high or low the corresponding raw score was, relative to the other scores. If your exam score of 37 is equivalent to a z-score of +1.0, you have scored 1 standard deviation above the mean. Assuming a roughly normal distribution, that's pretty good, because in a normal distribution only about 16 percent of all scores fall at or above 1 standard deviation above the mean. But if your 37 is equivalent to a z-score of −1.0, you have scored 1 standard deviation below the mean—a poor score.

Z-scores are sometimes used to compare people's performance on different tests or measures. Say that Elsa earns a score of 64 on her first psychology test and Manuel, who is taking psychology from a different instructor, earns a 62 on his first test. In Elsa's class, the mean score is 50 and the standard deviation is 7, so Elsa's z-score is (64 − 50)/7 = 2.0. In Manuel's class, the mean is also 50, but the standard deviation is 6. Therefore, his z-score is also 2.0 [(62 − 50)/6]. Compared to their respective classmates, Elsa and Manuel did equally well. *But be careful:* This does *not* imply that they are equally able students. Perhaps Elsa's instructor has a reputation for giving easy tests and Manuel's for giving hard ones, so Manuel's instructor has attracted a more industrious group of students. In that case, Manuel faces stiffer competition than Elsa does, and even though he and Elsa have the same z-score, Manuel's performance may be more impressive.

You can see that comparing z-scores from different people or different tests must be done with caution. Standardized tests, such as IQ tests and various personality tests, use z-scores derived from a large sample of people assumed to be representative of the general population taking the tests. When two tests are standardized for similar populations, it is safe to compare z-scores on them. But z-scores derived from special samples, such as students in different psychology classes, may not be comparable.

Curves

In addition to knowing how spread out our scores are, we need to know the *pattern* of their distribution. At this point we come to a rather curious phenomenon. When researchers make a very large number of observations, many of the physical and psychological variables they study have a distribution that approximates a pattern called a **normal distribution.** (We say "approximates" because a *perfect* normal distribution is a theoretical construct and is not actually found in nature.) Plotted in a frequency polygon, a normal distribution has a symmetrical, bell-shaped form known as a **normal curve** (see Figure A.4).

A normal curve has several interesting and convenient properties. The right side is the exact mirror image of the left. The mean, median, and mode all have the same value and are at the exact center of the curve, at the top of the "bell." Most observations or scores cluster around the center of the curve, with far fewer out at the ends, or "tails" of the curve. Most important, as Figure A.4 shows, when standard deviations (or z-scores) are used on the horizontal axis of the curve, the percentage of scores falling between the mean and any given point on the horizontal axis is always the same. For example, 68.26 percent of the scores will fall between plus and minus 1 standard deviation from the mean; 95.44 percent of the scores will fall

FIGURE A.4

A normal curve

When standard deviations (or z-scores) are used along the horizontal axis of a normal curve, certain fixed percentages of scores fall between the mean and any given point. As you can see, most scores fall in the middle range (between +1 and −1 standard deviations from the mean).

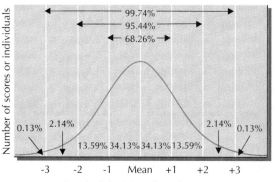

between plus and minus 2 standard deviations from the mean; and 99.74 percent of the scores will fall between plus and minus 3 standard deviations from the mean. These percentages hold for any normal curve, no matter what the size of the standard deviation. Tables are available showing the percentages of scores in a normal distribution that lie between the mean and various points (as expressed by z-scores).

The normal curve makes life easier for psychologists when they want to compare individuals on some trait or performance. For example, since IQ scores from a population form a roughly normal curve, the mean and standard deviation of a test are all the information you need in order to know how many people score above or below a particular score. On a test with a mean of 100 and a standard deviation of 15, about 68.26 percent of the population scores between 85 and 115—1 standard deviation below and 1 standard deviation above the mean (see Chapter 11).

Not all types of observations, however, are distributed normally. Some curves are lopsided, or *skewed*, with scores clustering at one end or the other of the horizontal axis (see Figure A.5). When the "tail" of the curve is longer on the right than on the left, the curve is said to be positively, or right, skewed. When the opposite is true, the curve is said to be negatively, or left, skewed. In experiments, reaction times typically form a right-skewed distribution. For example, if people must press a button whenever they hear some signal, most will react quite quickly; but a few will take an unusually long time, causing the right "tail" of the curve to be stretched out.

Knowing the shape of a distribution can be extremely valuable. Paleontologist and biologist Stephen Jay Gould (1985) has told how such information helped him cope with the news that he had a rare and serious form of cancer. Being a researcher, he immediately headed for the library to learn all he could about his disease. The first thing he found was that it was incurable, with a median mortality of only eight months after discovery. Most people might have assumed that a "median mortality of eight

FIGURE A.5

Skewed curves

Curve (a) is skewed negatively, to the left. Curve (b) is skewed positively, to the right. The direction of a curve's skewness is determined by the position of the long tail, not by the position of the bulge. In a skewed curve, the mean, median, and mode fall at different points.

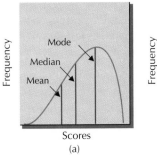
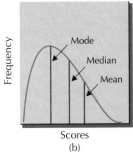

(a)   (b)

months" means "I will probably be dead in eight months." But Gould realized that although half of all patients died within eight months, the other half survived longer than that. Since his disease had been diagnosed in its early stages, he was getting top-notch medical treatment, and he had a strong will to live, Gould figured he could reasonably expect to be in the half of the distribution that survived beyond eight months. Even more cheering, the distribution of deaths from the disease was right-skewed: The cases to the left of the median of eight months could only extend to zero months, but those to the right could stretch out for years. Gould saw no reason why he should not expect to be in the tip of that right-hand tail.

For Stephen Jay Gould, statistics, properly interpreted, were "profoundly nurturant and life-giving." They offered him hope and inspired him to fight his disease. As of this writing, Gould is as active professionally as he ever was. The initial diagnosis was made in July of 1982.

ANSWERS:

Control group statistics:

$$\text{Mean} = \frac{\Sigma X}{N} = \frac{87}{15} = 5.8$$

$$\text{Median} = 6$$

$$\text{Standard Deviation} = \sqrt{\frac{\Sigma(X - M)^2}{N}} = \sqrt{\frac{14.4}{15}}$$
$$= \sqrt{.96} = .98$$

Lowest possible percentile score: 1 (or, more precisely, .01)

■ DRAWING INFERENCES

Once data are organized and summarized, the next step is to ask whether they differ from what might have been expected purely by chance (see Chapter 2). A researcher needs to know whether it is safe to infer that the results from a particular sample of people are valid for the entire population from which the sample was drawn. *Inferential statistics* provide this information. They are used in both experimental and correlational studies.

The Null Versus the Alternative Hypothesis

In an experiment, the scientist must assess the possibility that his or her experimental manipulations will have no effect on the subjects' behavior. The statement expressing this possibility is called the **null hypothesis.** In our stress-and-humor study, the null hypothesis states that making up a funny commentary will not relieve stress any more than making up a straightforward narrative will. In other words, it predicts that the difference between the means of the two groups will not deviate significantly from zero. Any obtained difference will be due solely to chance fluctuations. In contrast, the **alternative hypothesis** (also called the experimental or research hypothesis) states that on the average the experimental group will have lower mood disturbance scores than the control group.

The null hypothesis and the alternative hypothesis cannot both be true. Our goal is to reject the null hypothesis. If our results turn out to be consistent with the null hypothesis, we will not be able to do so. If the data are inconsistent with the null hypothesis, we will be able to reject it with some degree of confidence. Unless we study the entire population, though, we will never be able to say that the alternative hypothesis has been proven. No matter how impressive our results are, there will always be some degree of uncertainty about the inferences we draw from them. Since we cannot prove the alternative hypothesis, we must be satisfied with showing that the null hypothesis is unreasonable.

Students are often surprised to learn that it is the null hypothesis, not the alternative hypothesis, that is tested. After all, it is the alternative hypothesis that is actually of interest. But this procedure does make good sense. The null hypothesis can be stated precisely and tested directly. In the case of our fictitious study, the null hypothesis predicts that the difference between the two means will be zero. The alternative hypothesis does not permit a precise prediction because we don't know how much the two means might differ (if, in fact, they do differ). Therefore, it cannot be tested directly.

Testing Hypotheses

Many computations are available for testing the null hypothesis. The choice depends on the design of the study, the size of the sample, and other factors. We will not cover any specific tests here. Our purpose is simply to introduce you to the kind of *reasoning* that underlies inferential statistics. With that in mind, let us return once again to our data. For each of our two groups we have calculated a mean and a standard deviation. Now we want to compare the two sets of data to see if they differ enough for us to reject the null hypothesis. We wish to be reasonably certain that our observed differences did not occur entirely by chance.

What does it mean to be "reasonably certain"? How different from zero must our result be to be taken seriously? Imagine, for a moment, that we had infinite resources and could somehow repeat our experiment, each time using a new pair of groups, until we had "run" the entire population through the study. It can be shown mathematically that if only chance were operating, our various experimental results would form a normal distribution. This theoretical distribution is called "the sampling distribution of the difference between means," but since that is quite a mouthful, we will simply call it the *sampling distribution* for short. If the null hypothesis were true, the mean of the sampling distribution would be zero. That is, on the average, we would find no difference between the two groups. Often, though, because of chance influences or *random error*, we would get a result that deviated to one degree or another from zero. On rare occasions, the result would deviate a great deal from zero.

We cannot test the entire population, though. All we have are data from a single sample. We would like to know whether the difference between means that we actually obtained would be close to the mean of the theoretical sampling distribution (if we *could* test the entire population) or far away from it, out in one of the "tails" of the curve. Was our result highly likely to occur on the basis of chance alone or highly unlikely?

Before we can answer that question, we must have some precise way to measure distance from the mean of the sampling distribution. We must know exactly how far from the mean our obtained result must be to be considered "far away." If only we knew the standard deviation of the sampling distribution, we could use it as our unit of measurement. We don't know it, but fortunately, we can use the standard deviation of our *sample* to estimate it. (We will not go into the reasons that this is so.)

Now we are in business. We can look at the mean difference between our two groups and figure out how far it is (in terms of standard deviations) from the mean of the sampling distribution. As mentioned earlier, one of the convenient things about a normal distribution is that a certain fixed percentage of all observations falls between the mean of the distribution and any given point above or below the mean. These percentages are available from tables. Therefore, if we know the "distance" of our obtained result from the mean of the theoretical sampling distribution, we automatically know how likely our result is to have occurred strictly by chance.

To give a specific example, if it turns out that our obtained result is 2 standard deviations above the mean of the theoretical sampling distribution, we know that the probability of its having occurred by chance is less than 2.3 percent. If our result is 3 standard deviations above the mean of the sampling distribution, the probability of its having occurred by chance is less than .13 percent—less than 1 in 800. In either case, we might well suspect that our result did not occur entirely by chance after all. We would call the result *statistically significant*. (Psychologists usually consider any highly unlikely result to be of interest, no matter which direction it takes. In other words, the result may be in either "tail" of the sampling distribution.)

To summarize: Statistical significance means that if only chance were operating, our result would be highly improbable, so we are fairly safe in concluding that more than chance was operating—namely, the influence of our independent variable. We can reject the null hypothesis, and open the champagne. As we noted in Chapter 2, psychologists usually accept a finding as statistically significant if the likelihood of its occurring by chance is 5 percent or less (see Figure A.6). This cutoff point gives the researcher a reasonable chance of confirming reliable results as well as reasonable protection against accepting unreliable ones.

FIGURE A.6

Statistical significance

This curve represents the theoretical sampling distribution discussed in the text. The curve is what we would expect by chance if we did our hypothetical stress-and-humor study many times, testing the entire population. If we used the conventional significance level of .05, we would regard our obtained result as significant only if the probability of getting a result that far from zero by chance (in either direction) totaled 5 percent or less. As shown, the result must fall far out in one of the tails of the sampling distribution. Otherwise, we cannot reject the null hypothesis.

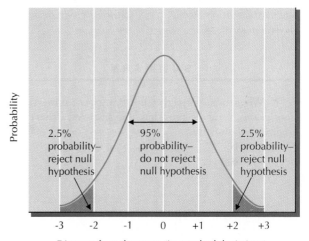

Distance from the mean (in standard deviations)

Some cautions are in order, though. As noted in Chapter 2, statistically significant results are not always psychologically interesting or important. Further, statistical significance is related to the size of the sample. A large sample increases the likelihood of reliable results. But there is a trade-off: The larger the sample, the more probable it is that a small result having no practical importance will reach statistical significance. For this reason, it is always useful to know how much of the total variability in scores was accounted for by the independent variable. (The computations are not discussed here.) If only 3 percent of the variance was accounted for, then 97 percent was due either to chance factors or to systematic influences of which the researcher was unaware. Because human behavior is affected by so many factors, the amount of variability accounted for by a single psychological variable is often modest.

Oh, yes, about those humor findings: Our fictitious study is similar to two more complicated ones done by Herbert M. Lefcourt and Rod A. Martin (1986). Women who tried to be funny reported less mood disturbance than women who merely produced a straightforward narrative. They also grimaced and fidgeted less during the film, suggesting that they really did feel less stress. The results were not statistically significant for men, possibly because men did not find the film all that stressful. Other findings, however, suggest that humor can shield both sexes from stress (see Chapter 15). *The moral:* When gravity gets you down, try a little levity.

KEY TERMS

frequency distribution 691	percentile score 694
graph 691	z-score (standard score)
histogram/bar graph 691	694
frequency polygon/line graph 692	normal distribution 695
	normal curve 695
measure of central tendency 692	right- and left-skewed distributions 695
mean 692	null hypothesis 696
median 693	alternative hypothesis
mode 693	696
range 693	sampling distribution 697
standard deviation 693	statistically significant
deviation score 693	697

SUMMARY

1. When used correctly, statistics expose unwarranted conclusions, promote precision, and help researchers spot trends amid diversity.

2. Often, the first step in data analysis is to organize and condense data in a *frequency distribution*, a tally showing how often each possible score (or interval of scores) occurred. Such information can also be depicted in a *histogram* (bar graph) or a *frequency polygon* (line graph).

3. Descriptive statistics summarize and describe the data. *Central tendency* is measured by the *mean*, *median*, or, less frequently, the *mode*. Since a measure of central tendency may or may not be highly representative of other scores in a distribution, it is also important to analyze variability. A large *standard deviation* means that scores are widely scattered about the mean; a small one means that most scores are clustered near the mean.

4. Raw scores can be transformed into other kinds of scores. *Percentile scores* indicate the percentage of people who scored at or below a given raw score. Z-scores (standard scores) indicate how far a given raw score is above or below the mean of the distribution.

5. Many variables have a distribution approximating a *normal distribution*, depicted as a *normal curve*. The normal curve has a convenient property: When standard deviations are used as the units on the horizontal axis, the percentage of scores falling between any two points on the horizontal axis is always the same. Not all types of observations are distributed normally, however. Some distributions are *skewed* to the left or right.

6. Inferential statistics are used to test the *null hypothesis*. They tell a researcher whether a result differed significantly from what might have been expected purely by chance. Basically, hypothesis testing involves estimating where the obtained result would have fallen in a theoretical *sampling distribution* based on studies of the entire population in question. If the result would have been far out in one of the "tails" of the distribution, it is considered statistically significant. A statistically significant result may or may not be psychologically interesting or important.

GLOSSARY

abnormality (or psychological disorder) Any behavior or state of emotional distress that causes personal suffering, that is self-destructive, or that is maladaptive.

absolute threshold The smallest quantity of physical energy that can be reliably detected by an observer.

accommodation The process of modifying existing cognitive structures in response to experience and new information.

achievement tests Tests designed to measure acquired skills and knowledge.

activation-synthesis theory The theory that dreaming results from the cortical synthesis and interpretation of neural signals triggered by activity in the lower part of the brain.

adolescence The period of development between puberty (a biological event) and adulthood (a social event).

agoraphobia "Fear of fear"; a set of phobias, often set off by a panic attack, sharing the basic fear of being away from a safe place or person.

algorithm A problem-solving strategy that is guaranteed to lead eventually to a solution.

alpha waves Relatively large, slow brain waves characteristic of relaxed wakefulness.

altered (alternate) state of consciousness A deliberately produced state of consciousness that differs from ordinary wakefulness or sleep.

alternate forms reliability The consistency of test scores when alternate versions of a test are given to the same person or group on separate occasions.

alternative hypothesis An assertion that the independent variable in a study will have a certain predictable effect on the dependent variable. Also called an *experimental* or *research hypothesis*.

amnesia Partial or complete loss of memory for information or past events; when no organic causes are present, it is classified as a dissociative disorder.

amygdala A brain structure involved in the arousal and regulation of emotion; may also play a role in the association of memories formed in different senses.

androgens Masculinizing hormones.

anterograde amnesia Loss of the ability to form long-term memories for new facts and events.

antidepressant drugs Stimulants that influence neurotransmitters in the brain; they are used in the treatment of mood disorders, usually depression and anxiety.

antipsychotic drugs Major tranquilizers primarily used in treatment of schizophrenia and other disorders involving psychotic symptoms, such as delusions.

antisocial personality disorder A condition characterized by antisocial behavior (such as lying, stealing, and sometimes violence), lack of social emotions (guilt and shame), and impulsivity.

anxiety disorder *See* generalized anxiety disorder; panic attack; phobia.

applied psychology The study of psychological issues that have direct practical significance. Also, the application of psychological findings.

aptitude tests Tests designed to measure a person's potential for acquiring various types of skills and knowledge, based on present abilities.

archetypes [AR-ki-tipes] To Carl Jung, universal, symbolic images that appear in myths, art, dreams, and other expressions of the collective unconscious.

arithmetic mean *See* mean.

artificial intelligence "Intelligent" behavior performed by computers. Also, the study of the methods used to program such behavior in computers.

assimilation The process of absorbing new information into existing cognitive structures, modifying it if necessary to "fit."

attachment A strong emotional tie between babies and their primary caretakers. In later life, attachment refers to any emotional connection between two people.

attitude A fairly stable opinion toward a person, object, or activity, containing a cognitive element (perceptions and beliefs) and an emotional element (positive or negative feelings).

attribution theory The theory that people are motivated to explain their own and others' behavior by attributing causes of that behavior to a situation or disposition.

audition The sense of hearing.

auditory nerve The nerve connecting the receptors for hearing with the brain.

autonomic nervous system The subdivision of the peripheral nervous system that regulates the internal organs and glands.

availability heuristic The strategy of estimating the probability of a certain type of event by how easy it is to think of or recall examples or instances; the more available such examples or instances in memory, the higher the estimate.

axon Extending fiber of a neuron that conducts impulses away from the cell body and transmits them to other neurons. From the Greek for "axis."

basic concepts Concepts that have a moderate number of instances and that are easier to acquire than those having few or many instances.

basic psychology The study of psychological issues in order to seek knowledge for its own sake rather than for its practical application.

basilar [BASS-uh-lur] membrane The membrane in which the auditory receptor cells are embedded.

behavior genetics An interdisciplinary field of study concerned with the genetic bases of behavior.

behavior modification The application of conditioning techniques to reduce or eliminate maladaptive or problematic behavior or teach new responses.

behavioral medicine An interdisciplinary field that studies behaviors related to the maintenance of health, the onset of illness, and the prevention of disease.

behaviorism An approach to psychology that emphasizes the study of objectively observable behavior and the role of the environment as a determinant of human and animal behavior.

binocular cues Visual cues to depth or distance requiring two eyes.

biofeedback A technique for controlling bodily functions by attending to an instrument that monitors the function and signals changes in it.

biological rhythm A periodic, more-or-less regular fluctuation in a biological system; may or may not have psychological implications.

biology The study of the evolution, structure, and functioning of living organisms.

bipolar disorder A mood disorder in which depression alternates with mania.

bonding A strong emotional tie that parents typically feel toward their newborn babies.

brain stem The part of the brain at the top of the spinal cord; it is responsible for automatic functions such as heartbeat and respiration.

brightness Lightness or luminance; the dimension of visual experience related to the amount of light emitted from or reflected by an object.

case study A detailed description of a particular individual under study or treatment. Also called *case history.*

cell body The part of the neuron that keeps it alive and determines whether it will fire.

central nervous system The portion of the nervous system consisting of the brain and spinal cord.

central tendency *See* measure of central tendency.

cerebellum A brain structure that regulates movement and balance.

cerebral cortex A collection of several thin layers of cells covering the cerebrum; largely responsible for higher functions. *Cortex* is Latin for "bark" or "rind."

cerebral hemispheres The two halves of the cerebrum.

cerebrum [suh-REE-brum] The largest brain structure, comprising the upper part of the forebrain; it is in charge of most sensory, motor, and cognitive processes in human beings. From the Latin for "brain."

child development The gradual, orderly sequence of changes in biological maturation, physical structure, behavior, and thinking that marks growth from conception to maturity. In life-span psychology, "development" refers to the process of growth and change

from conception to death.

childhood amnesia The inability to remember events and experiences that occurred early in life.

chromosomes The rod-shaped structures in the center of each body cell that carry the genes and determine hereditary characteristics.

chunk A meaningful unit of information; may be comprised of smaller units.

circadian [sur-CAY-dee-un] rhythm A biological rhythm with a period (from peak to peak or trough to trough) of about 24 hours. From the Latin *circa,* "about," and *dias,* "a day."

classical conditioning The process, first described by Ivan Pavlov, by which a previously neutral stimulus acquires the capacity to elicit a response through association with a stimulus that already elicits a similar response. Sometimes called *Pavlovian* or *respondent conditioning.*

climacteric The period of decreasing reproductive capacity in women, culminating in menopause.

clinical psychology The branch of psychology concerned with the diagnosis, treatment, and study of mental and emotional problems and disabilities.

cochlea [KOCK-lee-uh] A snail-shaped, fluid-filled organ in the inner ear containing the receptors for hearing.

coefficient of correlation A measure of correlation that ranges in value from -1.00 to $+1.00$.

cognitive dissonance A state of tension that occurs when a person simultaneously holds two cognitions that are psychologically inconsistent, or when a person's belief is inconsistent with his or her behavior.

cognitive map A mental representation of the environment.

cognitive psychology An approach to psychology that emphasizes mental processes in perception, memory, language, problem solving, and other areas of behavior.

cognitive schema An integrated network of knowledge, beliefs, and expectations concerning a particular topic.

cohort An age group, such as a school class or a whole generation, that shares common experiences or demographic traits.

collective unconscious To Carl Jung, universal memories and experiences of humankind, represented in the unconscious of all people.

complexity (of light) Refers to the number of different wavelengths contained in light from a particular source.

compulsions Repetitive, ritualized, stereotyped behaviors that a person feels must be done to avoid disaster.

concept A category used to class together objects, relations, activities, abstractions, or qualities that share common properties.

conditioned response (CR) The classical conditioning term for a response that is elicited by a conditioned stimulus; it occurs after the conditioned stimulus is associated with an unconditioned stimulus.

conditioned stimulus (CS) The classical conditioning term for an initially neutral stimulus that comes to elicit a conditioned response after being associated with an unconditioned stimulus.

cones Visual receptors involved in color vision.

confirmation bias The tendency to search for or attend to only information that confirms one's belief.

conformity Behavior or attitudes that occur as a result of real or imagined group pressure.

congruence To Carl Rogers, harmony between the conscious self and the totality of the person's unconscious feelings and life experiences.

consciousness The awareness of the environment and one's own existence, sensations, and thoughts.

conservation   The understanding that the physical properties of objects—such as number of items, amount of liquid, or length of an object—remain the same even when appearances change (as long as nothing is added or taken away).

consolidation   The process by which a long-term memory becomes durable and stable.

content validity   The ability of a test to give a broad picture of whatever the test claims to measure.

continuous reinforcement   A reinforcement schedule in which a particular response is always reinforced.

control condition   In an experiment, a comparison condition in which subjects are not exposed to the same "treatment" or manipulation of the independent variable as in the experimental condition; in some studies, experimental subjects serve as their own controls; in others there are separate experimental and control groups.

convergent thinking   Thinking aimed at finding a single correct answer to a problem by applying knowledge and reasoning.

coping   The cognitive and behavioral efforts to manage demands in the environment or oneself that one feels to be stressful.

cornea   A transparent membrane that covers the front part of the eye and bends incoming light toward a lens behind it.

corpus callosum   The bundle of nerve fibers connecting the two cerebral hemispheres.

correlation   A measure of how strongly two or more variables are related to each other.

correlational study   A descriptive study that looks for a consistent relationship between two phenomena.

counseling psychology   An applied branch of psychology concerned with helping people deal with problems of everyday life.

counterconditioning   In classical conditioning, the process of pairing a conditioned stimulus with a stimulus that elicits a response that is incompatible with an unwanted conditioned response.

creativity   A flexible, imaginative thought process leading to novel but appropriate solutions to problems, original ideas and insights, or new and useful products.

criterion validity   The ability of a test to predict other, independent measures (criteria) associated with the characteristic being assessed.

critical period   *See* sensitive period.

critical thinking   The ability and willingness to assess claims and make objective judgments on the basis of well-supported reasons.

cross-cultural psychology   The study of cultural influences on human behavior, and of the psychological differences and similarities among cultural groups.

cross-sectional study   A study in which groups of subjects of different ages are compared at a given time.

cue-dependent forgetting   The inability to retrieve information stored in memory because of insufficient internally or externally generated cues.

culture-fair tests   Tests designed to reduce cultural bias by incorporating knowledge and skills common to many different cultures and socioeconomic groups.

culture-free tests   Tests in which cultural experience is presumed not to influence performance.

dark adaptation   A process by which visual receptors become maximally sensitive to dim light.

decay theory (of forgetting)   The theory that information in memory eventually disappears if it is not reactivated; it appears to be more plausible for short-term than long-term memory.

declarative memories   Memories of facts, rules, concepts, and events; include semantic and episodic memories.

deductive reasoning   A form of reasoning in which a conclusion follows necessarily from certain premises; if the premises are true, the conclusion must be true.

deep processing   In the encoding of information, the processing of meaning rather than simply the physical or sensory features of a stimulus.

defense mechanisms   In psychoanalytic theory, methods used by the ego to prevent unconscious anxiety from reaching consciousness.

deindividuation   In groups or crowds, the loss of awareness of one's own individuality; in varying degrees, a person feels indistinguishable from others.

déjà vu [day-zhah VOO]   The feeling that something happening at the present moment has happened before in exactly the same way; from the French for "already seen."

delta waves   Slow, regular brain waves characteristic of stage 3 and stage 4 sleep.

dendrites   Branches on a neuron that receive information from other neurons and transmit it toward the cell body. From the Greek for "tree."

denial   In psychoanalytic theory, a defense mechanism in which a person refuses to accept evidence of the reality of his or her own emotions.

dependent variable   A variable that an experimenter predicts will be affected by manipulations of the independent variable.

depersonalization   The loss of one's individuality and humanity. (*See also* deindividuation.)

depressants   Drugs that slow down activity in the central nervous system.

depression   *See* major depression; bipolar disorder.

descriptive methods   Methods that yield descriptions of behavior or phenomena but not causal explanations.

descriptive statistics   Statistics that organize and summarize research data.

developmental psychology   The study of physical, mental, and social changes over the life span.

dialectical reasoning   A process in which opposing facts or ideas are weighed and compared, with a view to determining the truth or resolving differences.

difference threshold   The smallest difference in stimulation that can be reliably detected by an observer when two stimuli are compared. Also called *just noticeable difference (j.n.d.)*.

diffusion of responsibility   In organized or anonymous groups, the tendency of members to avoid taking responsibility for actions or decisions, assuming others will do it.

discriminative stimulus   In operant conditioning, a stimulus that signals when a particular response is likely to be followed by a reinforcer, punisher, or neutral consequence.

displacement   In psychoanalytic theory, the shifting of instinctual energy from its original object or activity to a different one.

display rules   Social and cultural rules that regulate when, how, and where a person may express (or suppress) emotional feelings.

dispositional attribution   An explanation of one's own or another's behavior that relies on something in the person.

dissociation   Separation of consciousness into distinct parts.

dissociative disorders   Conditions in which normally integrated consciousness or identity is split or altered, as in psychogenic amnesia or multiple personality.

divergent thinking   Mental exploration of unusual or unconventional alternatives during problem solving. It tends to enhance creativity.

dizygotic twins   *See* fraternal twins.

doctrine of specific nerve energies   The theory that we experience different sense modalities because signals received by different sense organs stimulate different nerve pathways, which terminate in different areas of the brain.

double-blind study An experiment in which neither the subjects nor the researchers know which subjects are in the control group(s) and which in the experimental group(s) until after results are tallied.

Down's syndrome A form of mental retardation usually caused by an extra chromosome 21. It is accompanied by various physical anomalies, such as a downward curve of the inner eyelid.

eclectic [ek-LEC-tik] Literally, selected from various sources; in psychotherapy, the term describes the common practice of using methods from different theoretical schools.

educational psychology The study of psychological principles that explain learning and ways of improving educational systems.

ego In psychoanalysis, the part of personality that represents reason, good sense, rational control; it operates according to the *reality principle.*

egocentric thinking Perceiving the world from only one's own point of view; the inability to take another person's perspective.

eidetic [eye-DET-ik] imagery An image of a visual stimulus that appears to exist in the external environment instead of in "the mind's eye" and that can be "read" for information.

elaborative rehearsal Association of new information with already stored knowledge and analysis of the new information in order to make it memorable.

electroconvulsive therapy (ECT) A procedure occasionally used for cases of prolonged major depression, in which a brief brain seizure is induced to alter brain chemistry.

electrodes Devices used to apply electric current to tissue or detect neural activity.

electroencephalogram (EEG) A recording of neural activity detected by electrodes.

emotion A state involving a pattern of facial and bodily changes, cognitive appraisals, subjective feelings, and tendencies toward action. (*See also* primary emotions and secondary emotions.)

emotion work The expression of an emotion one does not really feel in response to social or cultural expectations.

empirical Relying on or derived from observation, experimentation, or measurement.

encoding (in memory) The conversion of information into a form that can be stored and retrieved.

endocrine glands Internal organs that produce hormones and release them into the bloodstream; from the Greek for "secrete within."

endorphins [en-DOR-fins] Neurotransmitters that are similar in structure and action to opiates; they are involved in pain reduction, pleasure, and memory. (Known technically as *endogenous opioid peptides.*)

entrapment A gradual process in which individuals escalate their commitment to a course of action to justify their investment of time, money, or effort.

epinephrine, norepinephrine (adrenaline, noradrenaline) Hormones produced by the adrenal glands that provide the body with energy to respond to environmental events.

episodic memories Memories for personally experienced events and the contexts in which they occurred.

equilibrium The sense of balance.

estrogens Feminizing hormones.

ethnocentrism The belief that one's own ethnic group, nation, or religion is superior to all others.

eustress [YOU-stress] Positive or beneficial stress. (*See also* psychological stress.)

evoked potentials Patterns of brain activity produced in response to specific events.

experiment A controlled test of a hypothesis in which the researcher manipulates one variable to discover its effect on another, while holding other conditions constant.

experimental psychology A broad field of psychology devoted to the experimental study of learning, motivation, sensation and perception, physiology, human performance, and cognition.

experimenter effects Unintended changes in subjects' behavior due to cues inadvertently given by the experimenter.

explicit memory Conscious, intentional recollection of an event or item of information.

extinction The weakening and eventual disappearance of a learned response. In classical conditioning, it occurs when the conditioned stimulus is no longer paired with the unconditioned stimulus. In operant conditioning, it occurs when a response is no longer followed by a reinforcer.

extrinsic reinforcers Reinforcers that are not inherently related to the activity being reinforced. Examples are money, prizes, and praise.

facial-feedback hypothesis The notion that the facial muscles send messages to the brain, identifying the emotion a person feels. According to this hypothesis, we don't frown because we feel angry; we feel angry because we are frowning.

factor analysis A statistical method for analyzing the intercorrelations among various measures or test scores. Clusters of measures or scores that are highly correlated are assumed to measure the same underlying trait, ability, or aptitude (factor).

feature detectors Cells in the visual cortex that are sensitive to specific features of the environment.

fetal alcohol syndrome A pattern of physical and intellectual abnormalities in infants whose mothers drank an excessive amount of alcohol during pregnancy.

figure The part of the perceptual field that is perceived as foreground or as an object or pattern against a background.

fixed interval (FI) schedule An intermittent schedule of reinforcement in which a reinforcer is delivered for the first response made after a fixed period of time has elapsed since the last reinforcer.

fixed ratio (FR) schedule An intermittent schedule of reinforcement in which reinforcement occurs only after a fixed number of responses.

flashbulb memories Vivid, detailed recollections of the circumstances in which one learned of or perceived some significant or surprising event, or of the event itself.

forebrain The largest subdivision of the brain; involved in the control of sensory, motor, and cognitive processes in human beings. The upper part is called the *cerebrum.*

fovea The area in the center of the retina of the eye containing the greatest concentration of cones; provides sensitivity to detail and color.

fraternal (dizygotic) twins Twins that develop from two separate eggs fertilized by different sperm. They are no more alike genetically than any two siblings.

free association In psychoanalysis, a method of recovering unconscious conflicts by saying freely whatever comes to mind.

frequency (of a sound wave) The number of times per second that a sound wave cycles through a peak and low point.

frequency distribution A summary of how frequently each score in a set occurred.

frequency polygon (line graph) A graph showing a set of points obtained by plotting score values against score frequencies. Adjacent points are joined by straight lines.

functional fixedness The tendency to consider only the usual function of an object and overlook other possible uses. It often leads to rigidity in problem solving.

functionalism An early approach to psychology that stressed the function or purpose of behavior and consciousness.

fundamental attribution error The tendency to overestimate personality factors (dispositions) and underestimate environmental ones (situations) in explaining behavior.

ganglion cells Neurons in the retina of the eye that gather information from receptor cells (by way of intermediate bipolar cells); their axons make up the optic nerve.

gate-control theory The theory that the experience of pain depends in part on whether pain impulses get past a neurological "gate" in the spinal cord and thus reach the brain.

gender identity The sense of being male or female, regardless of whether or not one follows the rules of sex typing.

gender role A set of norms that defines socially approved attitudes and behavior for men and women.

General Adaptation Syndrome (GAS) According to Hans Selye, the bodily reactions to environmental stressors.

generalized anxiety disorder A continuous state of anxiety, lasting a month or more, marked by signs of motor tension, autonomic hyperactivity (e.g., a pounding heart), constant apprehension, and difficulties in concentration.

gerontology The study of aging and the old.

Gestalt [geh-SHTALT] principles Principles, first formulated by the Gestalt psychologists, that govern the perceptual organization of the sensory world into meaningful units and patterns.

Gestalt [geh-SHTALT] psychology An approach to psychology that emphasizes the perception, learning, and mental manipulation of whole units rather than their analysis into parts; from the German word for "pattern" or "form."

g factor A general ability assumed by some theorists to underlie various specific mental abilities and talents.

glial cells Cells that hold neurons in place, insulate them, and provide them with nutrients.

grammar The system of linguistic rules governing sounds (or in the case of sign languages, gestures), meanings, and syntax of a language. It may be viewed as a mechanism for generating all possible sentences in a language.

graph A drawing that depicts numerical relationships.

ground The part of the perceptual field perceived as formless or as the background.

group polarization The tendency of a group's decision to be more extreme than its members' individual decisions.

groupthink In close-knit groups, the tendency for all members to think alike and to suppress dissent and disagreement.

gustation The sense of taste.

health psychology A field within psychology that studies psychological aspects of health and illness.

heritability A statistical estimate of the proportion of the total variance in some trait within a group that is attributable to genetic differences among individuals within the group.

heuristic A rule of thumb that guides problem solving but does not guarantee an optimal solution. Heuristics are often used as shortcuts in solving complex problems.

higher-order conditioning In classical conditioning, a procedure in which a neutral stimulus becomes a conditioned stimulus through association with an already established conditioned stimulus.

hindbrain A subdivision of the brain that includes the pons, the medulla, much of the reticular activating system, and the cerebellum.

hindsight bias The tendency to overestimate one's ability to have predicted an event in advance, or answer a question correctly, once the actual outcome or answer is known.

hippocampus A brain structure involved in the storage of new information in memory.

histogram (bar graph) A graph in which the heights (or lengths) of bars are proportional to the frequencies of individual scores or classes of scores in a distribution.

homeostasis The tendency of the body to maintain itself in a steady, stable condition with regard to physical processes, such as temperature, water balance, blood sugar, and oxygen.

hormones Chemical substances that are secreted by organs called *glands* and that affect the functioning of other organs. From the Greek for "to urge on."

hue The dimension of visual experience specified by the various color names and related to the wavelength of light. In common usage, *hue* and *color* are often used synonymously.

humanistic psychology (humanism) An approach to psychology that emphasizes personal growth and the achievement of human potential more than the scientific understanding, prediction, and control of behavior.

hypnosis A condition in which attention is focused and a person is extremely responsive to suggestion.

hypothalamus A brain structure involved in emotions and drives vital to survival, such as fear, hunger, thirst, and reproduction; regulates the autonomic nervous system.

hypothesis A statement that attempts to predict or account for a set of phenomena. Scientific hypothesis specify relationships among events or variables and are supported or disconfirmed by empirical investigation.

id In psychoanalysis, the part of personality containing inherited psychological energy, particularly sexual and aggressive instincts; it operates according to the *pleasure principle*.

identical (monozygotic) twins Twins born when a fertilized egg divides into two parts that develop into separate embryos.

identification A process by which the child adopts an adult's standards of morality, values, and beliefs as his or her own; in psychoanalysis, identification with the same-sex parent occurs at resolution of the Oedipal conflict.

image *See* mental image.

implicit memory Unconscious retention in memory, as evidenced by the effect of a previous experience or previously encountered information on current thoughts or actions.

imprinting The tendency of some animals, especially birds, to follow and form a permanent attachment to the first moving object they see or hear after birth.

incentive An external motivating stimulus, such as money, praise, or fame.

independent variable A variable that an experimenter manipulates.

individuation A sense of oneself as distinct from others; a willingness to say and do things that set oneself apart from one's group.

induction A method of child rearing in which the parent appeals to the child's own resources, abilities, sense of responsibility, and feelings for others in correcting the child's misbehavior. (In contrast to methods that rely on asserting power or withdrawing love.)

inductive reasoning A form of reasoning in which the premises provide support for a certain conclusion, but it is still possible for the conclusion to be false.

industrial/organizational psychology The study of behavior in, and application of psychological principles to, the workplace and the marketplace.

inferential statistics Statistical tests that allow researchers to assess how likely it is that their results occurred merely by chance.

inferiority complex To Alfred Adler, an inability to accept natural limitations; it occurs when the need for self-improvement is blocked or inhibited.

infradian [in-FRAY-dee-un] rhythm A biological rhythm that occurs less frequently than once a day. From the Latin for "below a day."

insight A form of learning that occurs in problem solving and appears to involve the (often sudden) understanding of how elements of a situation are related or can be reorganized to achieve a solution.

instinct A complex pattern of behavior that occurs without learning in every member of a species in response to a specific stimulus. Also called *fixed action pattern.*

instinctive drift The tendency of an organism to revert to an instinctive behavior over time; it can interfere with learning.

insulin A hormone, produced by the pancreas, that plays a role in the body's use of sugar and affects appetite.

intelligence An inferred characteristic of an individual, usually defined as the ability to profit from experience, acquire knowledge, think abstractly, or adapt to changes in the environment.

intelligence quotient (IQ) A measure of intelligence originally computed by dividing a person's mental age by his or her chronological age and multiplying by 100; now derived from norms provided for standardized intelligence tests.

intermittent (partial) schedule of reinforcement A reinforcement schedule in which a particular response is sometimes but not always reinforced.

intrapsychic Within the mind or self.

intrinsic reinforcers Reinforcers that are inherently related to the activity being reinforced. Examples are enjoyment of the task and the satisfaction of accomplishment.

introspection A form of self-observation in which individuals examine and report the contents of their own consciousness.

inventories Standardized objective questionnaires requiring written responses; they typically include scales on which people are asked to rate themselves.

iris A muscular, ring-shaped membrane that controls how much light enters the eye; also gives the eye its color.

James-Lange theory The theory, proposed independently by William James and Carl Lange, that emotion results from the perception of one's own bodily reactions. In this view, each emotion is physiologically distinct.

just noticeable difference (j.n.d.) *See* difference threshold.

just-world hypothesis The notion that people need to believe that the world is fair and that justice is served; that bad people are punished and good people are rewarded.

kinesthesis [KIN-es-THEE-sis] The sense of body position and movement of body parts; also called *kinesthesia.*

laboratory observation The observation of subjects in a research laboratory.

language A system that combines meaningless elements such as sounds or gestures into structured utterances that convey meaning.

latent learning A form of learning that is not immediately expressed in an overt response; it occurs without obvious reinforcement.

lateralization Specialization of the two cerebral hemispheres for particular psychological operations.

learning A relatively permanent change in behavior (or behavioral potential) due to experience.

learning disability A difficulty in the performance of a specific mental skill, such as reading or arithmetic; sometimes linked to perceptual or memory problems.

lens (of the eye) A curved, transparent structure that focuses light rays entering through the pupil.

libido In psychoanalysis, the psychic energy that fuels the life or sexual instincts of the id.

limbic system A group of brain areas involved in emotional reactions and motivated behavior.

linguistic relativity theory The theory that language molds habits of thought and perception and that different language communities tend to have different views of reality. This theory is associated with Benjamin Lee Whorf.

linguistic universals The linguistic features that characterize all languages.

lobotomy A surgical procedure that cuts fibers in frontal lobes of the brain; it went out of fashion with the discovery of antipsychotic medication.

localization of function Specialization of particular brain areas for particular functions.

locus of control A general expectation about whether the results of one's actions are under one's own control (*internal* locus) or beyond one's control (*external* locus).

longitudinal study A study in which subjects are followed and periodically reassessed over a period of time.

long-term memory (LTM) The memory system involved in the long-term retention of information; theoretically, it has an unlimited capacity.

long-term potentiation A long-lasting increase in the strength of synaptic responsiveness, thought to be a biological mechanism of memory.

loudness The dimension of auditory experience related to the intensity of a pressure wave.

lucid dream A dream in which the dreamer is aware of dreaming.

magnetic resonance imaging (MRI) A method for studying body and brain tissue, using magnetic fields and special radio receivers.

maintenance rehearsal Rote repetition of material in order to maintain its availability in memory.

major depression A mood disorder involving disturbances in emotion (excessive sadness), behavior (apathy and loss of interest in usual activities), cognition (distorted thoughts of hopelessness and low self-esteem), and body function (fatigue, loss of appetite). (*See also* bipolar disorder.)

maturation The sequential unfolding of genetically governed behavior and physical characteristics.

mean The most common measure of central tendency; an average calculated by adding up all the scores or numbers in a set and dividing the sum by the number of quantities in the set. Also called *arithmetic mean.*

measure of central tendency A number intended to characterize an entire set of data.

measure of variability A number that indicates how dispersed scores are around the mean of the distribution. (*See also* variance.)

median A measure of central tendency; the value at the midpoint of a distribution of scores when the scores are ordered from highest to lowest.

melatonin A hormone secreted by the pineal gland; it is involved in the regulation of circadian rhythms.

memory The capacity to retain and retrieve information. It also refers to the mental structure or structures that account for this capacity and to the material retained (either the total body of information or specific items of information).

menarche [men-ARE-kee] The onset of menstruation.

menopause The cessation of menstruation; usually a gradual process lasting up to several years.

mental age (MA) A measure of mental development expressed in terms of the average mental ability at a given age. A child with a mental age of 8 performs on a test of mental ability at the level of the average 8-year-old.

mental image A mental representation that mirrors or resembles the thing it represents. Mental images can occur in many and perhaps all sensory modalities.

mental set A tendency to solve a problem with the same strategies and rules used on previous problems.

meta-analysis A statistical method for combining and evaluating the results of many different studies.

midbrain A subdivision of the brain that lies between the hindbrain and forebrain and contains important neural way stations.

Minnesota Multiphasic Personality Inventory (MMPI) A widely used objective personality test.

mnemonics (ni-MON-iks) Strategies or techniques for improving memory.

mode A measure of central tendency; the most frequently occurring score in a distribution.

monocular cues Visual cues to depth or distance that can be used by one eye alone.

monozygotic twins *See* identical twins.

motivated forgetting Forgetting because of a desire to eliminate awareness of painful, embarrassing, or otherwise unpleasant experiences.

motivation An inferred process within an animal or person that causes that organism to move toward a goal.

motor nerves Nerves in the peripheral nervous system that carry messages from the central nervous system to muscles, glands, and internal organs.

multiple personality disorder A rare dissociative disorder marked by the appearance within one person of two or more distinct personalities, each with its own name, history, and traits.

myelin sheath A fatty insulating sheath surrounding many axons.

narcissism (n.); narcissistic (adj.) An exaggerated sense of self-importance and self-absorption.

naturalistic observation The observation of subjects in their natural environment.

need for achievement (achievement motivation) A learned motive to meet personal standards of success and excellence in a chosen area (often abbreviated *nAch*).

need for affiliation The motive to associate with other people, as by seeking friends, moral support, contact comfort, or companionship.

need for competence The motive to be capable in one's activities and to master new situations.

need for power A learned motive to dominate or control others.

negative afterimage A visual image that persists after a visual stimulus is withdrawn and has features that contrast with those of the stimulus (e.g., a contrasting color).

negative correlation An association between increases in one variable and decreases in another.

negative reinforcement A reinforcement procedure in which a response is followed by the removal, delay, or decrease in intensity of an unpleasant stimulus; as a result, the response becomes stronger or more likely to occur.

nerve A bundle of nerve fibers (axons and sometimes dendrites) in the peripheral nervous system.

neuromodulators Chemical messengers in the nervous system that increase or decrease the action of specific neurotransmitters.

neuron A cell that conducts electrochemical signals; basic unit of the nervous system. Also called a *nerve cell*.

neuropsychology The field of psychology concerned with the neural and biochemical bases of behavior and mental processes.

neuroscience An interdisciplinary field of study concerned with the structure, function, development, and biochemistry of the nervous system.

neurosis; neuroses (pl.) To Freud, a psychological disorder characterized by self-punishing, maladaptive behavior, emotional symptoms, or physical symptoms that protect a person against unconscious anxiety. It is no longer used as a clinical diagnosis.

neurotransmitter A chemical substance that is released by a transmitting neuron at the synapse and that alters the activity of a receiving neuron.

nonconscious processes Mental processes occurring outside of and not available to conscious awareness.

normal curve A symmetrical, bell-shaped frequency polygon representing a normal distribution.

normal distribution A theoretical frequency distribution having certain special characteristics. For example, the distribution is symmetrical, the mean, mode, and median all have the same value, and the farther a score is from the mean the less the likelihood of obtaining it.

norms In test construction, established standards of performance; they are usually determined by giving the test to a large group of people who are representative of the population for whom the test is intended.

norms (social) *See* rules.

null hypothesis An assertion that the independent variable in a study will have no effect on the dependent variable.

obedience Behavior performed in following an order from someone in authority.

object permanence The understanding that an object continues to exist even when you can't see it or touch it.

object-relations school A branch of psychoanalysis that emphasizes the importance of the infant's first two years of life and relationships with the major caretaker.

observational learning A learning process in which an individual learns new responses by observing the behavior of another (a model) rather than through direct experience. Sometimes called *vicarious conditioning*.

observational study A study in which the researcher carefully and systematically observes and records behavior without interfering in any way with the behavior.

obsessions Recurrent, unwished-for, persistent thoughts and images.

obsessive-compulsive disorder An anxiety disorder in which a person feels trapped in repetitive thoughts and ritual behaviors designed to reduce anxiety.

Oedipus complex In psychoanalysis, a conflict in which a child desires the parent of the opposite sex and views the same-sex parent as a rival; this is the key issue in the phallic or Oedipal stage of development.

olfaction The sense of smell.

operant conditioning The process by which a response becomes more or less likely to occur, depending on its consequences. Also called *instrumental conditioning*.

operational definition A precise definition of a term in a hypothesis that specifies the operations for observing and measuring it.

operations In Jean Piaget's theory, mental actions that are cognitively reversible.

opiates Drugs, derived from the opium poppy, that relieve pain and commonly produce euphoria.

opponent-process cells Cells in the visual system that fire in response to one color and are inhibited from firing by another.

opponent-process theory (of color) A theory that assumes that the visual system treats various pairs of colors as opposing or antagonistic.

optic nerve The nerve connecting the retina of the eye with the brain.

panic attack A brief feeling of intense fear and impending doom or death, accompanied by intense physiological symptoms such as rapid breathing and pulse, sweaty palms, and dizziness.

paradigm A model, theory, or set of beliefs and assumptions, shared by a community of scientists, that guides the questions they study and the methods they use.

paranoia (n.); paranoid (adj.) Unreasonable and excessive suspiciousness, jealousy, or mistrust. It may occur as a type of personality disorder or, with more severe symptoms of psychosis, as a type of schizophrenic disorder.

parapsychology The study of purported psychic phenomena, such as ESP and telepathy.

parasympathetic nervous system A subdivision of the autonomic nervous system that operates during relaxed states and conserves energy.

partial schedule of reinforcement *See* intermittent schedule of reinforcement.

pathogenic Causing disease or suffering.

Pavlovian conditioning *See* classical conditioning.

percentile score A number that indicates the percentage of people who scored at or below a given raw score.

perception The process by which the brain organizes and interprets sensory information.

perceptual constancy The accurate perception of objects as stable or unchanged despite changes in the sensory patterns they produce.

perceptual illusion An erroneous or misleading perception of reality.

perceptual set A habitual way of perceiving, based on expectations.

peripheral nervous system All portions of the nervous system outside the brain and spinal cord. Includes sensory and motor nerves.

personality A distinctive and relatively stable pattern of behavior, thoughts, motives, and emotions that characterizes an individual.

personality disorders Psychological disorders in which rigid, maladaptive personality patterns cause personal distress or inability to get along with others.

PET (positron-emission tomography) scan A method for analyzing biochemical activity in the brain using injections of a glucoselike substance containing a radioactive element.

phenomenology The study of events and situations as individuals experience them; in personality, the study of an individual's qualities from the person's own point of view.

pheromone A chemical substance that, when released by an organism, influences the physiology or behavior of other members of the same species.

phobia An intense, unrealistic fear of an object, activity, or situation.

physiological psychology An approach to psychology that emphasizes bodily events and changes associated with feelings, actions, and thoughts.

pitch The dimension of auditory experience related to the frequency of a pressure wave; height or depth of a tone.

pituitary gland A small endocrine gland at the base of the brain that releases many hormones and regulates other endocrine glands.

placebo An inactive substance or fake treatment used as a control in an experiment or given by a medical practitioner to a patient; people sometimes respond to a placebo as they would to an active substance or real treatment.

pleasure principle In psychoanalytic theory, the principle guiding the operation of the id; seeks to reduce tension, avoid pain, and enhance pleasure.

population The entire set of individuals from which a sample is drawn.

positive correlation An association between increases in one variable and increases in another.

positive reinforcement A reinforcement procedure in which a response is followed by the presentation of, or increase in intensity of, a reinforcing stimulus; as a result, the response becomes stronger or more likely to occur.

prejudice An unjustified negative attitude toward a group of people or a custom.

primacy effect (in memory) The tendency for items at the beginning of a list to be well recalled.

primary control An effort to modify external reality by changing other people, the situation, or events; a "fighting-back" method of coping.

primary emotions Emotions that are considered to be universal and biologically based. They generally include fear, anger, sadness, joy, and disgust.

primary punisher A stimulus that is inherently punishing; an example is electric shock.

primary reinforcer A stimulus that is inherently reinforcing, typically satisfying a physiological need; an example is food.

principle of falsifiability The principle that a scientific theory must make predictions that are specific enough to expose the theory to the possibility of disconfirmation; that is, the theory must predict not only what will happen, but what will not happen.

proactive interference Forgetting that occurs when previously stored material interferes with the ability to remember similar, more recently learned material.

procedural memories Memories for the performance of actions or skills.

progesterone A hormone essential in the maintenance of pregnancy.

projection In psychoanalytic theory, a defense mechanism in which one's unacceptable feelings are attributed to someone else.

projective tests Psychological tests used to infer a person's motives, thoughts, perceptions, and conflicts on the basis of the person's interpretations of ambiguous or unstructured stimuli.

proposition A unit of meaning that expresses a unitary idea and is made up of concepts.

psychedelic drugs Consciousness-altering drugs that produce hallucinations, change thought processes, or disrupt the normal perception of time and space.

psychiatry The medical study, diagnosis, treatment, and prevention of mental disorders.

psychoactive drug A drug capable of influencing perception, mood, cognition, or behavior.

psychoanalysis An approach to psychology that emphasizes unconscious motives and conflicts. It encompasses both a theory of personality and a method of psychotherapy.

psychoanalyst A person who has had special training in the theory and practice of psychoanalysis.

psychodynamic A term referring to psychological theories that explain behavior in terms of unconscious energy dynamics within the individual—such as inner forces, conflicts, or the movement of instinctual energy.

psycholinguistics The study of the acquisition, comprehension, and production of language.

psychological assessment The measurement and evaluation of abilities, aptitudes, and personality characteristics.

psychological stress The result of a relationship between the person and the environment, in which the person believes the situation is overwhelming and threatens his or her ability to cope.

psychological tests Procedures used to measure personality traits, emotional states, aptitudes, interests, abilities, and values.

psychology The scientific study of behavior and mental processes and how they are affected by an organism's physical state, mental state, and external environment. The term is often represented by Ψ, the Greek letter *psi* (pronounced SY).

psychometrics The measurement of mental abilities, traits, and processes.

psychoneuroimmunology [psycho/neuro/immu/nology] The field that studies the relationships among psychology, the nervous system, and the immune system.

psychophysics The area of psychology concerned with the relationship between physical properties of stimuli and sensory experience.

psychosis; psychoses (pl.) An extreme mental disturbance involving distorted perceptions of reality and irrational behavior. It may have either psychological or organic causes.

psychosomatic A term that describes the interaction between a physical illness or condition and psychological states; literally, mind (*psyche*) and body (*soma*).

psychosurgery Any surgical procedure that destroys selected areas of the brain believed to be involved in emotional disorders or violent, impulsive behavior. (*See*, e.g., lobotomy.)

psychotherapist A person who practices psychotherapy; may be a clinical psychologist, psychiatrist, counselor, social worker, or other mental health professional.

psychotherapy The treatment of mental disorders, emotional problems, and personality difficulties. There are dozens of different kinds of psychotherapy.

puberty The age at which a person becomes capable of sexual reproduction.

punisher Any stimulus or event that weakens or reduces the probability of the response that it follows.

punishment The process by which a stimulus or event weakens or reduces the probability of the response that it follows.

pupil A round opening in the eye through which light passes.

random assignment A procedure for assigning people to experimental and control groups in which each individual has the same probability as any other of being assigned to a given group.

range A simple measure of variability, calculated by subtracting the lowest score in a distribution from the highest score.

rapid eye movement (REM) sleep Sleep periods characterized by eye movement, loss of muscle tone, and dreaming.

reactance A negative emotional state produced by a real or imagined threat to one's freedom of choice.

reaction formation In psychoanalytic theory, a defense mechanism that transforms an unconscious emotion into its conscious opposite; for example, hatred into love.

reality principle In psychoanalytic theory, the principle guiding the operation of the ego; it seeks to find socially acceptable outlets for instinctual energies.

reasoning The drawing of conclusions or inferences from observations, facts, or assumptions.

recall The ability to retrieve and reproduce from memory previously encountered material.

recency effect (in memory) The tendency for items at the end of a list to be well recalled.

recognition The ability to identify previously encountered material.

reflex An automatic reaction to a stimulus; often inborn but can also be learned or modified by experience.

reflex arc The neural circuitry underlying a reflex.

regression In psychoanalytic theory, a defense mechanism in which a person returns to an earlier stage of development, behaving in immature ways.

rehearsal The review or practice of material for the purpose of improving subsequent retention.

reinforcement The process by which a stimulus or event strengthens or increases the probability of the response that it follows.

reinforcer Any stimulus or event that strengthens or increases the probability of the response that it follows.

relearning method A method to measure retention that compares the time required to relearn material with the time used in initial learning of the material.

reliability In test construction, the consistency of test scores from one time and/or place to another.

REM sleep *See* rapid eye movement sleep.

replicate To duplicate or repeat.

representative sample A sample that matches the population in question on important characteristics such as age and sex.

repression In psychoanalytic theory, a basic defense mechanism that keeps taboo or painful thoughts or emotions from consciousness.

reticular activating system (RAS) A dense network of neurons found in the core of the brain stem; arouses the cortex and screens incoming information.

retina Neural tissue lining the back of the eyeball's interior that contains the receptors for vision.

retinal disparity The slight difference in lateral separation between two objects as seen by the left eye and the right eye.

retrieval Recovery of material that has been stored in memory.

retroactive interference Forgetting that occurs when recently learned material interferes with the ability to remember similar material stored previously.

retrograde amnesia Loss of the ability to remember events or experiences that occurred before some particular point in time.

rods Visual receptors that respond to dim light but are not involved in color vision.

role A given social position that is governed by a set of norms for proper behavior.

Rorschach [ROR-shock] Inkblot Test A projective personality test that asks respondents to interpret abstract, symmetrical inkblots.

rules (norms) Social conventions that regulate human life, including explicit laws and implicit cultural standards.

salutogenic Causing health.

sample A group of subjects selected from a population for study in order to estimate characteristics of the population.

saturation Vividness or purity of color; the dimension of visual experience related to the complexity of light waves.

schema *See* cognitive schema.

schizophrenia A psychotic disorder marked by some or all of these symptoms: delusions, hallucinations, incoherent word associations, inappropriate emotions, or lack of emotions.

school psychology An applied branch of psychology concerned with enhancing students' performance and emotional development.

secondary control An effort to accept external reality by changing one's own attitudes, goals, or emotions; a "learn to live with it" method of coping.

secondary emotions Emotions that are either "blends" of primary emotions (e.g., contempt as a blend of anger and disgust) or that are specific to certain cultures (e.g., the Tahitian sense of the "uncanny").

secondary punisher A stimulus that has acquired punishing properties through association with other punishers: also called *conditioned punisher.*

secondary reinforcer A stimulus that has acquired reinforcing properties through association with other reinforcers: also called *conditioned reinforcer.*

selective attention The focusing of attention on selected aspects of the environment and the blocking out of others.

self-fulfilling prophecy An expectation that comes true because of the tendency of those holding the expectation to act on it in certain ways.

self-serving bias The tendency of people to take credit for good actions and to excuse or rationalize their mistakes.

semantic memories Memories that reveal general knowledge, including facts, rules, concepts, and propositions.

semicircular canals Sense organs in the inner ear that contribute to equilibrium by responding to rotation of the head.

senility A loss of mental abilities in old age; once thought to be inevitable, it is now known to result often from disease or malnutrition.

sensation The detection or direct experience of physical energy in the external or internal environment due to stimulation of receptors in the sense organs.

sense receptors Specialized cells that convert physical energy in the environment into electrical energy that can be transmitted as nerve impulses to the brain.

sensitive period A period in the development of an organism that is optimal for the acquisition of a particular behavior.

sensory adaptation The reduction or disappearance of sensory responsiveness that occurs when stimulation is unchanging or repetitious.

sensory deprivation The absence of normal levels of sensory stimulation.

sensory memory A memory system that momentarily preserves extremely accurate images of sensory information.

sensory nerves Nerves in the peripheral nervous system that carry sensory messages toward the central nervous system.

sensory registers Subsystems of sensory memory. Most memory models assume a separate register for each sensory modality.

serial position effect The tendency for recall of the first and last items on a list to surpass recall of items in the middle of the list.

set point According to one theory, a homeostatic mechanism that regulates food intake, fat reserves, and metabolism to keep an organism at its predetermined weight.

sex hormones Hormones that regulate the development and functioning of reproductive and sex organs and stimulate the development of male and female sexual characteristics.

sex typing The process by which children learn the behaviors, attitudes, and expectations associated in their culture with being "masculine" or "feminine."

shaping An operant conditioning procedure in which successive approximations of a desired response are reinforced. Used when the desired response has a low probability of occurring spontaneously.

short-term memory (STM) In many theories of memory, a limited capacity memory system involved in the retention of information for brief periods. It is used to store recently perceived information and information retrieved from long-term memory for temporary use.

signal detection theory A psychophysical theory that divides the detection of a sensory signal into a sensory process and a decision process.

single-blind study An experiment in which subjects do not know whether they are in an experimental or control group.

situational attribution An explanation of one's own or another's behavior that relies on something in the environment or circumstance.

"social clock" A society's timetable for the "right" ages to marry, have children, start work, retire, and have other adult experiences.

social cognition An area in social psychology that studies social influences on thought, memory, perception, and other cognitive processes.

social identity The part of a person's self-concept that is based on his or her identification with a nation, culture, or ethnic group or with gender or other roles in society.

social interest To Alfred Adler, the ability to feel empathy, to cooperate, and to be connected to others.

socialization The process by which a child acquires the rules, standards, and values of his or her family and culture.

social learning theory The theory that human social behavior is learned through observation and imitation of others and is maintained by positive consequences.

social loafing The tendency of group members, under some conditions, to reduce their efforts and "loaf"; one result of the diffusion of responsibility.

social motives Learned motives, such as the need for affiliation, power, competence, or achievement, that are acquired from social experiences.

social psychology The field of psychology that studies individuals in a social context.

sociobiology A school of thought that attempts to account for social behavior in terms of genetic predispositions and evolutionary principles.

sociocultural perspective An approach to psychology that emphasizes social and cultural influences on behavior.

somatic nervous system The subdivision of the peripheral nervous system that controls skeletal muscles. Also called *skeletal nervous system.*

somatoform disorders Physical disorders that have no demonstrable medical cause. They include somatization disorder, conversion disorder, and hypochondria.

spinal cord A collection of neurons and supportive tissue running from the base of the brain down the center of the back, protected by a column of bone (the spinal column).

split-half reliability The consistency of test scores when scores on two halves of a test are compared.

spontaneous recovery The reappearance of a learned response after its apparent extinction.

standard deviation A commonly used measure of variability that indicates the average difference between scores in a distribution and their mean; more precisely, the square root of the average squared deviation from the mean.

standardize In test construction, to develop uniform procedures for giving and scoring a test.

state-dependent memory The tendency to remember something when one is in the same physical or mental state as during the original learning or experience.

states of consciousness Distinctive and discrete patterns in the functioning of consciousness, characterized by particular modes of perception, thought, memory, or feeling.

statistically significant The term used to refer to a result that is extremely unlikely to have occurred by chance.

stereotype A cognitive schema or a summary impression of a group, in which a person believes that all members of the group share a common trait or traits (positive, negative, or neutral).

stimulants Drugs that speed up activity in the central nervous system.

stimulus; stimuli (pl.) An event or change in the environment that causes, elicits, or leads to a response.

stimulus control Control over the occurrence of a response by a discriminative stimulus; the response is not compelled, but it becomes more likely.

stimulus discrimination The tendency to respond differently to two or more similar stimuli that differ on some dimension. In classical conditioning, occurs when a stimulus similar to the conditioned stimulus fails to evoke the conditioned response. In operant conditioning, occurs when an organism learns to make a response in the presence of one stimulus but not in the presence of other, similar stimuli.

stimulus generalization After conditioning, the tendency to respond to a stimulus that resembles one involved in the original conditioning. In classical conditioning, it occurs when a stimulus that resembles the conditioned stimulus elicits the conditioned response. In operant conditioning, it occurs when a response that has been reinforced (or punished) in the presence of one stimulus tends to occur (or be suppressed) in the presence of other, similar stimuli.

storage (in memory) The maintenance of material in memory over time.

stress *See* psychological stress; eustress.

structuralism An early approach to psychology that stressed the analysis of immediate experience into basic elements.

subconscious processes Mental processes occurring outside of conscious awareness but accessible to consciousness when necessary.

subjects Animals or human beings used in research.

sublimation In psychoanalytic theory, a type of displacement that serves a higher cultural or social purpose; for example, the creation of art or music as sublimation of sexual energy.

successive approximations In the operant conditioning procedure of shaping, behaviors that are ordered in terms of increasing similarity or closeness to the desired response.

superego In psychoanalysis, the part of personality that represents conscience, morality, and social standards.

surveys Questionnaires and interviews that ask people directly about their experiences, attitudes, or opinions.

sympathetic nervous system The subdivision of the autonomic nervous system that mobilizes bodily resources and increases the output of energy during emotion and stress.

synapse The site where transmission of a nerve impulse from one nerve cell to another occurs; includes the synaptic knob, synaptic gap, and receptor site of the receiving cell. From the Greek for "point of contact" or "joined together."

synaptic vesicles Chambers at the tip of an axon that contain neurotransmitter molecules.

syntax The set of grammatical rules governing the way words combine to form sentences.

systematic desensitization A variation of *counterconditioning* used in behavior therapy to eliminate fears; involves exposing a person to a hierarchy of fear- or anxiety-producing stimuli while the person is in a relaxed state.

taste buds Nests of taste receptor cells.

telegraphic speech A child's first combinations of words, which omit (as a telegram does) nonessential words.

temperaments Characteristic styles of responding to the environment that are present in infancy and are assumed to be innate.

testosterone An important androgen (masculinizing hormone).

test-retest reliability The consistency of test scores when a test is given to the same person or group on more than one occasion.

thalamus A brain structure that relays sensory messages to the cerebral cortex.

Thematic Apperception Test (TAT) A projective personality test that asks respondents to interpret a series of pictures showing ambiguous scenes.

theory An organized system of assumptions and principles that purports to explain a specified set of phenomena and their interrelationships.

thinking The mental manipulation of information stored in the form of concepts, images, or propositions.

timbre The distinguishing quality of a sound; the dimension of auditory experience related to the complexity of the pressure wave.

tip-of-the-tongue (TOT) state The subjective certainty that information is available in long-term memory even though one is having difficulty retrieving it.

token economy A behavior modification technique in which secondary reinforcers called *tokens*, which can be collected and exchanged for primary or other secondary reinforcers, are used to shape behavior.

tolerance The increasing resistance to a drug's effects with continued use; as tolerance develops, larger doses are required to produce effects once brought on by smaller ones.

trait A descriptive characteristic of an individual, assumed to be stable across situations.

transduction The conversion of one form of energy to another. Sensory receptors are biological transducers.

transference In psychoanalysis, a critical step in which the patient transfers emotional feelings for his or her parents to the therapist.

trichromatic theory A theory of color perception that proposes three mechanisms in the visual system, each sensitive to a certain range of wavelengths; their interaction is assumed to produce all the different experiences of hue.

two-factor theory of emotion The theory that emotions depend on both physiological arousal and a cognitive interpretation or evaluation of that arousal.

ultradian [ul-TRAY-dee-un] rhythm A biological rhythm that occurs more frequently than once a day; from the Latin for "beyond a day."

unconditional positive regard To Carl Rogers, love or support given to another person with no conditions attached.

unconditioned response (UR) The classical conditioning term for a reflexive response elicited by a stimulus in the absence of learning.

unconditioned stimulus (US) The classical conditioning term for a stimulus that elicits a reflexive response in the absence of learning.

unconscious processes Mental processes, such as motives, desires, and memories, not available to awareness or to conscious introspection; sometimes called "the unconscious," as a metaphor for the part of the mind below conscious awareness.

validity In test construction, the ability of a test to measure what it was designed to measure.

validity effect The tendency of people to believe that a statement is valid or true simply because it has been repeated many times.

value A central organizing belief or belief system that shapes a person's goals and motivations.

variability *See* measure of variability.

variable-interval (VI) schedule An intermittent schedule of reinforcement in which a reinforcer is delivered for a response made after a variable period of time has elapsed since the last reinforcer.

variable-ratio (VR) schedule An intermittent schedule of reinforcement in which reinforcement occurs after a variable number of responses.

variables Characteristics of behavior or experience that can be measured or described by a numeric scale. Variables are manipulated and assessed in scientific studies.

variance A measure of the dispersion of scores around the mean. (*See also* measure of variability.)

volunteer bias A shortcoming of findings derived from a sample of volunteers instead of a representative sample.

Weber's Law A law of psychophysics stating that the change necessary to produce a just noticeable difference is a constant proportion of the original stimulus.

withdrawal symptoms Physical and psychological symptoms that occur when someone addicted to a drug stops taking it.

z-score (standard score) A number that indicates how far a given raw score is above or below the mean, using the standard deviation of the distribution as the unit of measurement.

Abel, Gene; Becker, Judith; et al. (1984). Treatment manual for child molesters. Unpublished manuscript, Columbia University, New York.

Abelson, Robert P. (1988). Conviction. *American Psychologist, 43,* 267–275.

Abrams, David B., & Wilson, G. Terence (1983). Alcohol, sexual arousal, and self-control. *Journal of Personality and Social Psychology, 45,* 188–198.

Abramson, Lyn Y.; Metalsky, Gerald I.; & Alloy, Lauren B. (1989). Hopelessness depression: A theory-based subtype of depression. *Psychological Review, 96,* 358–372.

Abramson, Lyn Y.; Seligman, Martin E. P.; & Teasdale, John (1978). Learned helplessness in humans: Critique and reformulation. *Journal of Abnormal Psychology, 87,* 49–74.

Acredolo, Linda, & Goodwyn, Susan (1988). Symbolic gesturing in normal infants. *Child Development, 59,* 450–466.

Adams, Gerald R.; Ryan, John H.; Hoffman, Joseph J.; Dobson, William R.; & Nielsen, Elwin C. (1985). Ego identity status, conformity behavior, and personality in late adolescence. *Journal of Personality and Social Psychology, 47,* 1091–1104.

Adams, James L. (1986). *Conceptual blockbusting: A guide to better ideas* (3rd ed.). Boston: Addison-Wesley.

Adler, Alfred (1927/1959). *Understanding human nature.* New York: Premier.

Adler, Alfred (1935). The fundamental views of individual psychology. *International Journal of Individual Psychology, 1,* 5–8.

Adler, Alfred (1938/1964). *Social interest: A challenge to mankind.* New York: Capricorn.

Affleck, Glenn; Tennen, Howard; Croog, Sydney; & Levine, Sol (1987). Causal attribution, perceived control, and recovery from a heart attack. *Journal of Social and Clinical Psychology, 5,* 339–355.

Agras, Stewart (1985). *Panic: Facing fears, phobias, and anxiety.* New York: Freeman.

Ainsworth, Mary D. S. (1973). The development of infant-mother attachment. In B. M. Caldwell & H. N. Ricciuti (eds.), *Review of child development research,* Vol. 3. Chicago: University of Chicago Press.

Ainsworth, Mary D. S. (1979). Infant-mother attachment. *American Psychologist, 34,* 932–937.

Ainsworth, Mary D. S.; Blehar, Mary L.; Waters, Everett; & Wall, Sally (1978). *Patterns of attachment.* Hillsdale, NJ: Erlbaum.

Alagna, Sheryle W., & Hamilton, Jean A. (1986). Science in the service of mythology: The psychopathologizing of menstruation. Paper presented at the annual meeting of the American Psychological Association, Washington, DC.

Albee, George W. (1977). The Protestant ethic, sex, and psychotherapy. *American Psychologist, 32,* 150–161.

Albee, George W. (1985, February). The answer is prevention. *Psychology Today,* 60–64.

Albee, George W.; Canetto, Silvia S.; & Sefa-Dedeh, Araba (1991). Naming a syndrome is the first step. *Canadian Psychology, 32,* 154–160.

Allen, L. S.; Gorski, R. A.; Shin, J.; Barakat, N.; & Hines, M. (1987). Sex differences in the corpus callosum of the living human being. *Anatomical Record, 218,* 7A [Abstract].

Allman, William F. (1986, May). Mindworks. *Science 86, 7*(3), 23–31.

Allport, Gordon W. (1937). *Personality: A psychological interpretation.* New York: Holt, Rinehart and Winston.

Allport, Gordon W. (1954/1979). *The nature of prejudice* (25th anniversary ed.). Reading, MA: Addison-Wesley.

Allport, Gordon W. (1961). *Pattern and growth in personality.* New York: Holt, Rinehart and Winston.

Alpert, Bené; Field, Tiffany; Goldstein, Sheri; & Perry, Susan (1990). Aerobics enhances cardiovascular fitness and agility in preschoolers. *Health Psychology, 9,* 48–56.

Alwin, Duane (1988). Historical changes in parental orientations to children. In N. Mandell & S. Cahill (eds.), *Sociological studies of child development.* Greenwich, CT: JAI Press.

Amabile, Teresa M. (1983). *The social psychology of creativity.* New York: Springer-Verlag.

Amabile, Teresa M. (1985). Motivation and creativity: Effects of motivational orientation on creative writers. *Journal of Personality and Social Psychology, 48,* 393–399.

Amato, Paul R., & Keith, Bruce (1991). Parental divorce and the well-being of children: A meta-analysis. *Psychological Bulletin, 110,* 26–46.

American Association of University Women (1991). Shortchanging girls, shortchanging America. Report prepared by Greenberg-Lake: The Analysis Group Inc. for the AAUW, Washington, DC.

American Psychiatric Association (1987). *Diagnostic and statistical manual of mental disorders* (3rd ed., rev.). Washington, DC: American Psychiatric Association.

American Psychological Association (1984). Survey of the use of animals in behavioral research at U.S. universities. Washington, DC: American Psychological Association.

Amering, Michaela, & Katschnig, Heinz (1990). Panic attacks and panic disorder in cross-cultural perspective. *Psychiatric Annals, 20,* 511–516.

Anastasi, Anne (1988). *Psychological testing* (6th ed.). New York: Macmillan.

Andersen, Susan M. (1984). Self-knowledge and social inference: II. The diagnosticity of cognitive/affective and behavioral data. *Journal of Personality and Social Psychology, 46,* 294–307.

Andersen, Susan M.; Klatzky, Roberta L.; & Murray, John (1990). Traits and social stereotypes: Efficiency differences in social information processing. *Journal of Personality and Social Psychology, 59,* 192–201.

Anderson, James A., & Rosenfeld, Edward (eds.) (1988). *Neurocomputing: Foundations of research.* Cambridge, MA: MIT Press.

Anderson, John R. (1983). Retrieval of information from long-term memory. *Science, 220,* 25–30.

Anderson, John R., & Bower, Gordon H. (1973). *Human associative memory.* Washington, DC: Winston.

Anderson, Norman B. (1991). Addressing ethnic minority health issues: Behavioral medicine at the forefront of research and practice. Paper presented at the annual meeting of the Society of Behavioral Medicine, Washington, DC.

Angell, Marcia (1985, June 13). Disease as a reflection of the psyche. *New England Journal of Medicine, 312,* 1570–1572.

Ansbacher, Heinz (1968). The concept of social interest. *Journal of Individual Psychology, 24,* 131–149.

Ansbacher, Heinz, & Ansbacher, Rowena (eds.) (1964). *The individual psychology of Alfred Adler.* New York: Harper Torchbooks.

Anthony, William A.; Cohen, Mikal; & Kennard, William (1990). Understanding the current facts and principles of mental health systems planning. *American Psychologist, 45,* 1249–1252.

Antonovsky, Aaron (1987). *Unraveling the mystery of health: How people manage stress and stay well.* San Francisco: Jossey-Bass.

Antonucci, Toni C.; Fuhrer, Rebecca; & Jackson, James S. (1990). Social support and reciprocity: A cross-ethnic and cross-national perspective. *Journal of Social and Personal Relationships, 7,* 519–530.

Antrobus, John (1991). Dreaming: Cognitive processes during cortical activation and high afferent thresholds. *Psychological Review, 98,* 96–121.

Apter, Terri (1990). *Altered loves: Mothers and daughters during adolescence.* New York: St. Martin's Press.

Arendt, Hannah (1963). *Eichmann in Jerusalem: A report on the banality of evil.* New York: Viking.

Arendt, Josephine; Aldhous, Margaret; & Wright, John (1988, April 2). Synchronization of a disturbed sleep-wake cycle in a blind man by melatonin treatment. *Lancet, 1*(8588), 772–773.

Arendt, Thomas; Allen, Yvonne; Sinden, John; et al. (1988, March 31). Cholinergic-rich brain transplants reverse alcohol-induced memory deficits. *Nature, 332,* 448–450.

Arkes, Hal R. (1991). Some practical judgment/decision making research. Paper presented at the annual meeting of the American Psychological Association, Boston.

Arkes, Hal R.; Faust, David; Guilmette, Thomas J.; & Hart, Kathleen (1988). Eliminating the hindsight bias. *Journal of Applied Psychology, 73,* 305–307.

Aronfreed, Justin (1969). The concept of internalization. In D. A. Goslin (ed.), *Handbook of socialization theory and research.* Chicago: Rand McNally.

Aronson, Elliot (1988). *The social animal* (5th ed.). New York: Freeman.

Aronson, Elliot (1990). The return of the repressed: Dissonance theory makes a comeback. Paper presented at the annual meeting of the Western Psychological Association, Los Angeles.

Aronson, Elliot, & Mills, Judson (1959). The effect of severity of initiation on liking for a group. *Journal of Abnormal and Social Psychology, 59,* 177–181.

Aronson, Elliot; Stephan, Cookie; Sikes, Jev; Blaney, Nancy; & Snapp, Matthew (1978). *The jigsaw classroom.* Beverly Hills, CA: Sage.

Asch, Solomon E. (1952). *Social psychology.* Englewood Cliffs, NJ: Prentice-Hall.

Asch, Solomon E. (1965). Effects of group pressure upon the modification and distortion of judgments. In H. Proshansky &

B. Seidenberg (eds.), *Basic studies in social psychology.* New York: Holt, Rinehart and Winston.

Aschoff, Jurgen, & Wever, Rutger (1981). The circadian system of man. In J. Aschoff (ed.), *Handbook of behavioral neurobiology, Vol. 4: Biological rhythms.* New York: Plenum.

Aserinsky, Eugene, & Kleitman, Nathaniel (1955). Two types of ocular motility occurring in sleep. *Journal of Applied Physiology, 8,* 1–10.

Ashcraft, Mark H. (1989). *Human memory and cognition.* New York: HarperCollins.

Atkinson, Donald R.; Morten, George; & Sue, Derald W. (1989). *Counseling American minorities: A cross-cultural perspective* (3rd ed.). Dubuque, IA: William C. Brown.

Atkinson, John W. (ed.) (1958). *Motives in fantasy, action, and society.* Princeton, NJ: Van Nostrand.

Atkinson, Richard C., & Shiffrin, Richard M. (1971, August). The control of short-term memory. *Scientific American, 225*(2), 82–90.

Aukett, Richard; Ritchie, Jane; & Mill, Kathryn (1988). Gender differences in friendship patterns. *Sex Roles, 19,* 57–66.

Averill, James R. (1982). *Anger and aggression.* New York: Springer-Verlag.

Azrin, Nathan H., & Foxx, Richard M. (1974). *Toilet training in less than a day.* New York: Simon & Schuster.

Azuma, Hiroshi (1984). Secondary control as a heterogeneous category. *American Psychologist, 39,* 970–971.

Bahrick, Harry P. (1984). Semantic memory content in permastore: Fifty years of memory for Spanish learned in school. *Journal of Experimental Psychology: General, 113,* 1–29.

Bahrick, Harry P., & Hall, Lynda K. (1991). Lifetime maintenance of high school mathematics content. *Journal of Experimental Psychology: General, 120,* 20–33.

Bahrick, Harry P.; Bahrick, Phyllis O.; & Wittlinger, Roy P. (1975). Fifty years of memory for names and faces: A cross-sectional approach. *Journal of Experimental Psychology: General, 104,* 54–75.

Bahrke, Michael S.; Yesalis, Charles E. III; & Wright, James E. (1990). Psychological and behavioural effects of endogenous testosterone levels and anabolic-androgenic steroids among males: A review. *Sports Medicine, 10,* 303–337.

Bailey, Ronald H. (1975). *The role of the brain.* New York: Time-Life Books.

Baillargeon, Renee (1991). Reasoning about the height and location of a hidden object in 4.5- and 6.5-month-old infants. *Cognition, 38,* 13–42.

Baltes, Paul B. (1983). Life-span developmental psychology: Observations on history and theory revisited. In R. M. Lerner (ed.), *Developmental psychology: Historical and philosophical perspectives.* Hillsdale, NJ: Erlbaum.

Baltes, Paul B.; Dittmann-Kohli, Freya; & Dixon, Roger A. (1984). New perspectives on the development of intelligence in adulthood: Toward a dual-process conception and a model of selective optimization with compensation. In P. B. Baltes & O. G. Brim, Jr. (eds.), *Life-span development and behavior,* Vol. 6. New York: Academic Press.

Baltes, Paul B.; Sowarka, Doris; & Kliegl, Reinhold (1989). Cognitive training research on fluid intelligence in old age: What can older adults achieve by themselves? *Psychology and Aging, 4,* 217–221.

Bandura, Albert (1969). Social-learning theory of identificatory processes. In D. A. Goslin (ed.), *Handbook of socialization theory and research.* Chicago: Rand McNally.

Bandura, Albert (1973). *Aggression: A social learning analysis.* Englewood Cliffs, NJ: Prentice-Hall.

Bandura, Albert (1977). *Social learning theory.* Englewood Cliffs, NJ: Prentice-Hall.

Bandura, Albert (1986). *Social foundations of thought and action: A social cognitive theory.* Englewood Cliffs, NJ: Prentice-Hall.

Bandura, Albert (1990). Self-regulation of motivation through goal systems. In R. A. Dienstbier (ed.), *Nebraska Symposium on Motivation*, Vol. 38. Lincoln: University of Nebraska Press.

Bandura, Albert; Ross, Dorothea; & Ross, Sheila A. (1963). Vicarious reinforcement and imitative learning. *Journal of Abnormal and Social Psychology, 67,* 601–607.

Banks, Martin S. (in collaboration with Philip Salapatek) (1984). Infant visual perception. In P. Mussen (ed.), *Handbook of child psychology* (4th ed.). Vol. II, M. M. Haith & J. J. Compos (eds.), *Infancy and developmental psychobiology.* New York: Wiley.

Bányai, Éva I., & Hilgard, Ernest R. (1976). Comparison of active-alert hypnotic induction with traditional relaxation induction. *Journal of Abnormal Psychology, 85,* 218–224.

Barber, Theodore X. (1979). Suggested ("hypnotic") behavior: The trance paradigm versus an alternative paradigm. In E. Fromm & R. E. Shor (eds.), *Hypnosis: Developments in research and new perspectives* (2nd ed.). New York: Aldine.

Barber, Theodore X., & Wilson, Sheryl C. (1977). Hypnosis, suggestions, and altered states of consciousness: Experimental evaluation of a new cognitive-behavioral theory and the traditional trance-state therapy of "hypnosis." *Annals of the New York Academy of Sciences, 296,* 34–47.

Barinaga, Marcia (1992). Challenging the "no new neurons" dogma. *Science, 255,* 1646.

Barlow, David H. (1988). *Anxiety and its disorders.* New York: Guilford Press.

Barlow, David H. (1990). Disorders of emotion. Paper presented at the annual meeting of the American Psychological Association, Boston.

Barlow, David H. (ed.) (1991). Special issue on diagnoses, dimensions, and DSM-IV: The science of classification. *Journal of Abnormal Psychology, 100,* 243–412.

Barnett, Peter A., & Gotlib, Ian H. (1988). Psychosocial functioning and depression: Distinguishing among antecedents, concomitants, and consequences. *Psychological Bulletin, 104,* 97–126.

Baron, Miron; Risch, Neil; Hamburger, Rahel; Mandel, Batsheva; et al. (1987, March 19). Genetic linkage between X-chromosome markers and bipolar affective illness. *Nature, 326,* 289–292.

Baron, Robert A. (1977). *Human aggression.* New York: Plenum.

Baron, Robert A. (1981). The "costs of deception" revisited: An openly optimistic rejoinder. *IRB: A Review of Human Subjects Research, 3*(1), 8–10.

Baron, Robert S.; Cutrona, Carolyn E.; Hicklin, Daniel; Russell, Daniel W.; & Lubaroff, David M. (1990). Social support and immune function among spouses of cancer patients. *Journal of Personality and Social Psychology, 59,* 344–352.

Barr, Christopher E.; Mednick, Sarnoff A.; & Munk-Jorgensen, Poul (1990). Exposure to influenza epidemics during gestation and adult schizophrenia: A 40-year study. *Archives of General Psychiatry, 47,* 869–874.

Barron, Frank, & Harrington, David M. (1981). Creativity, intelligence, and personality. *Annual Review of Psychology, 32,* 439–476.

Bartlett, Frederic C. (1932). *Remembering.* Cambridge, England: Cambridge University Press.

Bartoshuk, Linda (1980, September). Separate worlds of taste. *Psychology Today, 14*(4), 48–49, 51, 54–56, 63.

Bartoshuk, Linda (1990, August/September). Psychophysical insights on taste. *APA Science Agenda,* 12–13.

Bates, Marsha E.; Labouvie, Erich W.; & White, Helene R. (1986). The effect of sensation seeking needs on alcohol and marijuana use in adolescence. *Bulletin of the Society of Psychologists in Addictive Behaviors, 5,* 29–36.

Batson, C. Daniel (1990). How social an animal? The human capacity for caring. *American Psychologist, 45,* 336–346.

Batson, C. Daniel; Dyck, Janine; Brandt, J. Randall; Batson, Judy; et al. (1988). Five studies testing two new egoistic alternatives to the empathy-altruism hypothesis. *Journal of Personality and Social Psychology, 55,* 52–77.

Baum, Steven, & Boxley, Russell (1983). Age identification in the elderly. *The Gerontologist, 23,* 532–537.

Baumeister, Roy F. (1990). Suicide as escape from self. *Psychological Review, 97,* 90–113.

Baumeister, Roy F., & Scher, Steven J. (1988). Self-defeating behavior patterns among normal individuals: Review and analysis of common self-destructive tendencies. *Psychological Bulletin, 104,* 3–22.

Baumeister, Roy F.; Stillwell, Arlene; & Wotman, Sara R. (1990). Victim and perpetrator accounts of interpersonal conflict: Autobiographical narratives about anger. *Journal of Personality and Social Psychology, 59,* 994–1005.

Baumgartner, Alice (1983). "My daddy might have loved me": Student perceptions of differences between being male and being female. Paper published by the Institute for Equality in Education, Denver.

Baumrind, Diana (1971). Current patterns of parental authority. *Developmental Psychology Monograph* 4 (1, pt. 2).

Baumrind, Diana (1985). Research using intentional deception: Ethical issues revisited. *American Psychologist, 40,* 165–174.

Baur, Susan (1988). *Hypochondria: Woeful imaginings.* Berkeley: University of California Press.

Bayer, Ronald (1981). *Homosexuality and American psychiatry.* New York: Basic Books.

Beard, John H.; Propst, Rudyard N.; & Malamud, T. J. (1982). The Fountain House model of psychiatric rehabilitation. *Psychosocial Rehabilitation Journal, 5,* 47–54.

Beck, Aaron T. (1976). *Cognitive therapy and the emotional disorders.* New York: International Universities Press.

Beck, Aaron T. (1987). Cognitive models of depression. *Journal of Cognitive Psychotherapy, An International Quarterly, 1,* 5–37.

Beck, Aaron T. (1988). Cognitive approaches to panic disorder: Theory and therapy. In S. Rachman & J. D. Maser (eds.), *Panic: Psychological perspectives.* Hillsdale, NJ: Erlbaum.

Beck, Aaron T. (1991). Cognitive therapy: A 30-year retrospective. *American Psychologist, 46,* 368–375.

Beckwith, Leila, & Cohen, Sarale E. (1984). Home environment and cognitive competence in preterm children during the first 5 years. In Allen W. Gottfried (ed.), *Home environment and early cognitive development: Longitudinal research.* Orlando, FL: Academic Press.

Bee, Helen (1989). *The developing child* (5th ed.). New York: Harper & Row.

Bee, Helen; Barnard, Kathryn E.; et al. (1982). Prediction of IQ and language skill from perinatal status, child performance, family characteristics, and mother-infant interaction. *Child Development, 53,* 1134–1156.

Beebe, B.; Gerstman, L.; Carson, B.; et al. (1982). Rhythmic communication in the mother-infant dyad. In M. Davis (ed.), *Interaction rhythms: Periodicity in communicative behavior.* New York: Human Sciences Press.

Beer, William R. (1983). *Househusbands: Men and housework in American families.* South Hadley, MA: J. F. Bergin/Praeger.

Bellah, Robert N.; Madsen, Richard; Sullivan, William M.; Swidler, Ann; & Tipton, Steven M. (1985). *Habits of the heart: Individualism and commitment in American life.* Berkeley: University of California Press.

Belmont, Lillian, & Marolla, Francis A. (1973). Birth order, family size, and intelligence. *Science, 182,* 1096–1101.

Belsky, Jay (1988). The effects of infant day care reconsidered. *Early Childhood Research Quarterly, 3,* 235–272.

Bem, Daryl, & Allen, Andrea (1974). On predicting some of the people some of the time: The search for cross-cultural consistencies in behavior. *Psychological Review, 81,* 506–520.

Bem, Sandra L. (1981). Gender schema theory: A cognitive account of sex typing. *Psychological Review, 88,* 354–364.

Bem, Sandra L. (1985). Androgyny and gender schema theory: A conceptual and empirical integration. In T. B. Sonderegger (ed.), *Nebraska Symposium on Motivation: Psychology and gender, 1984,* Vol. 32. Lincoln: University of Nebraska Press.

Benbow, Camilla P., & Stanley, Julian C. (1983). Sex differences in mathematical reasoning: More facts. *Science, 222,* 1029–1031.

Bennett, Henry L. (1988). Perception and memory for events during adequate general anesthesia for surgical operations. In Helen M. Pettinati (ed.), *Hypnosis and memory.* New York: Guilford Press.

Bennett, H. L.; Davis, H. S.; & Giannini, J. A. (1985). Nonverbal response to intraoperative conversation. *British Journal of Anaesthesia, 57,* 174–179.

Bennett, Neil G.; Blanc, Ann Klimas; & Bloom, David E. (1988). Commitment and the modern union: Assessing the link between premarital cohabitation and subsequent marital stability. *American Sociological Review, 53,* 127–138.

Bennett, Neil G.; Bloom, David E.; & Craig, Patricia H. (1989). The divergence of black and white marriage patterns. *American Journal of Sociology, 95,* 692–722.

Bennett, William, & Gurin, Joel (1982). *The dieter's dilemma: Eating less and weighing more.* New York: Basic Books.

Bentall, R. P. (1990). The illusion of reality: A review and integration of psychological research on hallucinations. *Psychological Bulletin, 107,* 82–95.

Benton, Cynthia; Hernandez, Anthony; Schmidt, Adeny; Schmitz, Mary; Stone, Anna; & Weiner, Bernard (1983). Is hostility linked with affiliation among males and with achievement among females? A critique of Pollak and Gilligan. *Journal of Personality and Social Psychology, 45,* 1167–1171.

Bergin, Alan E., & Lambert, Michael J. (1978). The evaluation of therapeutic outcomes. In A. E. Bergin & S. L. Garfield (eds.), *Handbook of psychotherapy and behavior change* (2nd ed.). New York: Wiley.

Berkman, Lisa, & Syme, S. Leonard (1979). Social networks, host resistance, and mortality: A nine-year follow-up study of Alameda County residents. *American Journal of Epidemiology, 109,* 186–204.

Berlin, Brent, & Kay, Paul (1969). *Basic color terms: Their universality and evolution.* Berkeley: University of California Press.

Bernard, Jessie (1981). The good-provider role: Its rise and fall. *American Psychologist, 36,* 1–12.

Bernardis, Lee L.; Bellinger, Larry L.; Kodis, Marge; & Feldman, Mary J. (1989). Normal catch-up growth in rats severely food-restricted prior to lesions of the dorsomedial hypothalamic nucleus: The first 48 hours. *Pharmacology, Biochemistry & Behavior, 32,* 957–960.

Bernieri, Frank J.; Reznick, J. Steven; & Rosenthal, Robert (1988). Synchrony, pseudosynchrony, and dissynchrony: Measuring the entrainment process in mother-infant interactions. *Journal of Personality and Social Psychology, 54,* 243–253.

Bernieri, Frank J.; Davis, J.; Rosenthal, R.; & Knee, C. (1991). Interactional synchrony and the social affordance of rapport: A validation study. Unpublished manuscript, Oregon State University, Corvallis, OR.

Bernstein, Ilene L. (1985). Learning food aversions in the progression of cancer and treatment. *Annals of the New York Academy of Sciences, 443,* 365–380.

Berscheid, Ellen (1985). Interpersonal attraction. In G. Lindzey & E. Aronson (eds.), *Handbook of social psychology,* Vol. II. New York: Random House/Erlbaum.

Bersoff, Donald N. (1978). Coercion and reciprocity in psychotherapy. In C. T. Fischer & S. L. Brodsky (eds.), *Client participation in human services: The Prometheus principle.* New Brunswick, NJ: Transaction Books.

Besalel-Azrin, V.; Azrin, N. H.; & Armstrong, P. M. (1977). The student-oriented classroom: A method of improving student conduct and satisfaction. *Behavior Therapy, 8,* 193–204.

Bettelheim, Bruno (1962). *Symbolic wounds.* New York: Collier.

Bettelheim, Bruno (1967). *The empty fortress.* New York: Free Press.

Bharati, A. (1985). The self in Indian thought and action. In A. Marsella, G. DeVos, & F. Hsu (eds.), *Culture and self.* London: Tavistock.

Biederman, Irving (1987). Recognition-by-components: A theory of human image understanding. *Psychological Review, 94,* 115–147.

Biner, Paul M. (1991). Effects of lighting-induced arousal on the magnitude of goal valence. *Personality and Social Psychology Bulletin, 17,* 219–226.

Birdwhistell, Ray L. (1970). *Kinesics and context: Essays on body motion communication.* Philadelphia: University of Pennsylvania Press.

Black, J. E.; Isaacs, K. R.; Anderson, B. J.; Alcantara, A. A.; & Greenough, W. T. (1990). Learning causes synaptogenesis, whereas motor activity causes angiogenesis, in cerebellar cortex of adult rats. *Proceedings of the National Academy of Science, 87,* 5568–5572.

Blakemore, Colin, & Cooper, Grahame F. (1970). Development of the brain depends on the visual environment. *Nature, 228,* 477–478.

Blass, Thomas (1991). Understanding behavior in the Milgram obedience experiment: The role of personality, situations, and their interactions. *Journal of Personality and Social Psychology, 60,* 398–413.

Bleier, Ruth (1988). Sex differences research: Science or belief? In R. Bleier (ed.), *Feminist approaches to science.* New York: Pergamon Press.

Bleier, Ruth; Houston, Lanning; & Byne, William (1986). Can the corpus callosum predict gender, age, handedness, or cognitive differences? *Trends in Neurosciences, 9,* 391–394.

Bleuler, Eugen (1911/1950). *Dementia praecox or the group of schizophrenias.* New York: International Universities Press.

Bloom, Benjamin S. (ed.) (1985). *Developing talent in young people.* New York: Ballantine.

Bloom, John W.; Kaltenborn, Walter T.; Paoletti, Paolo; Camilli, Anthony; & Lebowitz, Michael D. (1987). Respiratory effects of non-tobacco cigarettes. *British Medical Journal, 295,* 1516–1518.

Blos, Peter (1962). *On adolescence.* New York: Free Press.

Bogen, Joseph (1978, October). The giant walk-through brain. *Human Nature, 1*(10), 40–47.

Bohannon, John N. (1988). Flashbulb memories for the space shuttle disaster: A tale of two theories. *Cognition, 29,* 179–196.

Bohannon, John N., & Stanowicz, Laura (1988). The issue of negative evidence: Adult responses to children's language errors. *Developmental Psychology, 24,* 684–689.

Bohannon, John N., & Symons, Victoria (1988). Conversational conditions of children's imitation. Paper presented at the biennial Conference on Human Development, Charleston.

Bolger, Niall (1990). Coping as a personality process: A prospective study. *Journal of Personality and Social Psychology, 59,* 525–537.

Bolles, Robert C. (1972). Reinforcement, expectancy and learning. *Psychological Review, 79,* 394–409.

Bolles, Robert C.; Holtz, Rolf; Dunn, Thomas; & Hill, Wendy (1980). Comparisons of stimulus learning and response learning in a punishment situation. *Learning and Motivation, 11,* 78–96.

Bolos, Annabel M.; Dean, M.; Lucas-Derse, S.; Ramsburg, M.; Brown, G. L.; Goldman, D. (1990, December 26). Population and pedigree studies reveal a lack of association between the dopamine D2 receptor gene and alcoholism. *Journal of the American Medical Association, 264,* 3156–3160.

Bolton, P. J. (1983). Drugs of abuse. In D. F. Hawkins (ed.), *Drugs and pregnancy.* Edinburgh: Churchill Livingston.

Bonica, John J. (1980). Pain research and therapy: Past and current status and future needs. In L. Ng & J. J. Bonica (eds.), *Pain, discomfort, and humanitarian care.* New York: Elsevier.

Bonnet, Michael H. (1990). The perception of sleep onset in insomniacs and normal sleepers. In R. R. Bootzin, J. F. Kihlstrom, & D. L. Schacter (eds.), *Sleep and cognition.* Washington, DC: American Psychological Association.

Bootzin, Richard R.; Epstein, Dana; & Wood, James M. (1991). Stimulus control instruction. In P. Hauri (ed.), *Case studies in insomnia.* New York: Plenum.

Boring, Edwin G. (1953). A history of introspection. *Psychological Bulletin, 50,* 169–187.

Bornstein, Robert F.; Leone, Dean R.; & Galley, Donna J. (1987). The generalizability of subliminal mere exposure effects: Influence of stimuli perceived without awareness on social behavior. *Journal of Personality and Social Psychology, 53,* 1070–1079.

Borys, Shelley, & Perlman, Daniel (1985). Gender differences in loneliness. *Personality and Social Psychology Bulletin, 11,* 63–74.

Bouchard, Claude; Tremblay, A.; Despres, J. P.; Nadeau, A.; et al. (1990, May 24). The response to long-term overfeeding in identical twins. *New England Journal of Medicine, 322,* 1477–1482.

Bouchard, Thomas J., Jr. (1984). Twins reared together and apart: What they tell us about human diversity. In S. W. Fox (ed.), *Individuality and determinism.* New York: Plenum.

Bouchard, Thomas J., Jr., & McGue, Matthew (1981). Familial studies of intelligence: A review. *Science, 212,* 1055–1058.

Bouchard, Thomas J., Jr.; Lykken, David T.; Segal, Nancy L.; & Wilcox, Kimerly J. (1986). Development in twins reared apart: A test of the chronogenetic hypothesis. In A. Demirjian (ed.), *Human growth: A multidisciplinary review.* London: Taylor & Francis.

Bouchard, Thomas J., Jr.; Lykken, David T.; McGue, Matthew; Segal, Nancy L.; et al. (1990). Sources of human psychological differences: The Minnesota Study of Twins Reared Apart. *Science, 250,* 223–228.

Bousfield, W. A. (1953). The occurrence of clustering in the recall of randomly arranged associates. *Journal of General Psychology, 49,* 229–240.

Bowen, Murray (1978). *Family therapy in clinical practice.* New York: Jason Aronson.

Bower, Gordon H., & Clark, M. C. (1969). Narrative stories as mediators of serial learning. *Psychonomic Science, 14,* 181–182.

Bower, Gordon H., & Mayer, John D. (1989). In search of mood-dependent retrieval. *Journal of Social Behavior and Personality, 4,* 121–156.

Bower, T. G. R. (1981). *Development in infancy* (2nd ed.). San Francisco: Freeman.

Bowers, Kenneth S.; Regehr, Glenn; Balthazard, Claude; & Parker, Kevin (1990). Intuition in the context of discovery. *Cognitive Psychology, 22,* 72–110.

Bowers, Wayne A. (1990). Treatment of depressed in-patients: Cognitive therapy plus medication, relaxation plus medication, and medication alone. *British Journal of Psychiatry, 156,* 73–78.

Bowlby, John (1969). *Attachment and loss. Vol. I: Attachment.* New York: Basic Books.

Bowlby, John (1973). *Attachment and loss. Vol. II: Separation.* New York: Basic Books.

Bowlby, John (1988). *A secure base: Parent-child attachment and healthy human development.* New York: Basic Books.

Bracha, H. Stefan; Torrey, E. Fuller; Bigelow, Llewellyn B.; Lohr, James B.; & Linington, Beverly B. (1991). Subtle signs of prenatal maldevelopment of the hand ectoderm in schizophrenia: A preliminary monozygotic twin study. *Biological Psychiatry, 30,* 719–725.

Bradley, Robert H., & Caldwell, Bettye M. (1984). 174 children: A study of the relationship between home environment and cognitive development during the first 5 years. In Allen W. Gottfried (ed.), *Home environment and early cognitive development: Longitudinal research.* Orlando, FL: Academic Press.

Bransford, John; Sherwood, Robert; Vye, Nancy; & Rieser, John (1986). Teaching thinking and problem solving. *American Psychologist, 41,* 1078–1089.

Braun, Bennett G. (1988). *The treatment of multiple personality disorder.* Washington, DC: American Psychiatric Press.

Brecher, Edward M. (and the editors of Consumer Reports Books) (1984). *Love, sex, and aging: A Consumers Union report.* Boston: Little, Brown.

Breggin, Peter R. (1991). *Toxic psychiatry.* New York: St. Martin's Press.

Brehm, Jack W. (1966). *A theory of psychological reactance.* New York: Academic Press.

Brehm, Jack W., & Self, Elizabeth A. (1989). The intensity of motivation. *Annual Review of Psychology, 40,* 109–131.

Brehm, Sharon S. (1985). *Intimate relationships.* New York: Random House.

Brehm, Sharon S., & Brehm, Jack W. (1981). *Psychological reactance: A theory of freedom and control.* New York: Academic Press.

Breland, Keller, & Breland, Marian (1961). The misbehavior of organisms. *American Psychologist, 16,* 681–684.

Bretherton, Inge, & Beeghly, Marjorie (1982). Talking about internal states: The acquisition of an explicit theory of mind. *Developmental Psychology, 18,* 906–921.

Brett, Joan F.; Brief, Arthur P.; Burke, Michael J.; George, Jennifer M.; & Webster, Jane (1990). Negative affectivity and the reporting of stressful life events. *Health Psychology, 9,* 57–68.

Bridgeman, Bruce, & Staggs, David (1982). Plasticity in human blindsight. *Vision Research, 22,* 1199–1203.

Briggs, Jean (1970). *Never in anger: Portrait of an Eskimo family.* Cambridge, MA: Harvard University Press.

Briggs, John (1984, December). The genius mind. *Science Digest, 92(12),* 74–77, 102–103.

Brigham, John C., & Malpass, Roy S. (Fall, 1985). The role of experience and contact in the recognition of faces of own- and other-race persons. *Journal of Social Issues, 41,* 139–155.

Brockner, Joel, & Rubin, Jeffrey Z. (1985). *Entrapment in escalating conflicts: A social psychological analysis.* New York: Springer-Verlag.

Brodsky, Annette M. (1982). Sex, race, and class issues in psychotherapy research. In J. H. Harvey & M. M. Parks (eds.), *Psychotherapy research and behavior change.* The Master Lecture Series, Vol. 1. Washington, DC: American Psychological Association.

Brody, Nathan (1990). Behavior therapy versus placebo: Comment on Bowers and Clum's meta-analysis. *Psychological Bulletin, 107,* 106–109.

Brown, Alan S. (1991). A review of the tip-of-the-tongue experience. *Psychological Bulletin, 109,* 204–223.

Brown, Jonathon D. (1991). Staying fit and staying well. *Journal of Personality and Social Psychology, 60,* 555–561.

Brown, Jonathon D., & Smart, S. April (1991). The self and social conduct: Linking self-representations to prosocial behavior. *Journal of Personality and Social Psychology, 60,* 368–375.

Brown, Laura S. (1986). Diagnosis and the Zeitgeist: The politics of masochism in the DSM-III-R. Paper presented at the annual meeting of the American Psychological Association, Washington, DC.

Brown, Robert, & Middlefell, Robert (1989). Fifty-five years of cocaine dependence [letter]. *British Journal of Addiction, 84,* 946.

Brown, Roger (1986). *Social psychology* (2nd ed.). New York: Free Press.

Brown, Roger, & Kulik, James (1977). Flashbulb memories. *Cognition, 5,* 73–99.

Brown, Roger, & McNeill, David (1966). The "tip of the tongue" phenomenon. *Journal of Verbal Learning and Verbal Behavior, 5,* 325–337.

Brown, Roger; Cazden, Courtney; & Bellugi, Ursula (1969). The child's grammar from I to III. In J. P. Hill (ed.), *Minnesota Symposium on Child Psychology,* Vol. 2. Minneapolis: University of Minnesota Press.

Brownell, Kelly D. (1991). Dieting and the search for the perfect body: Where physiology and culture collide. *Behavior Therapy, 22,* 1–12.

Bryant, Richard A., & McConkey, Kevin M. (1990). Hypnotic blindness and the relevance of cognitive style. *Journal of Personality and Social Psychology, 59,* 756–761.

Bryer, Jeffrey; Nelson, Bernadette; Miller, Jean; & Krol, Pamela (1987). Childhood sexual and physical abuse as factors in adult psychiatric illness. *American Journal of Psychiatry, 144,* 1426–1430.

Buck, Linda, & Axel, Richard (1991). A novel multigene family may encode odorant receptors: A molecular basis for odor recognition. *Cell, 65,* 175–187.

Buck, Ross (1984). *The communication of emotion.* New York: Guilford Press.

Buck, Ross, & Teng, Wan-Cheng (1987). Spontaneous emotional communication and social biofeedback: A cross-cultural study of emotional expression and communication in Chinese and Taiwanese students. Paper presented at the annual meeting of the American Psychological Association, New York.

Burke, Deborah; Burnett, Gayle; & Levenstein, Peggy (1978). Menstrual symptoms: New data from a double-blind study. Paper presented at the annual meeting of the Western Psychological Association, San Francisco.

Burke, Deborah M.; MacKay, Donald G.; Worthley, Joanna S.; & Wade, Elizabeth (1991). On the tip of the tongue: What causes word finding failures in young and older adults? *Journal of Memory and Language, 30*, 237–246.

Burnam, M. Audrey; Stein, Judith; Golding, Jacqueline; Siegel, Judith; & Sorenson, Susan (1988). Sexual assault and mental disorders in a community population. *Journal of Counseling and Clinical Psychology, 56*, 843–850.

Bush, Diane M., & Simmons, Roberta (1987). Gender and coping with the entry into early adolescence. In R. C. Barnett, L. Biener, & G. K. Baruch (eds.), *Gender & stress.* New York: Free Press.

Buss, Arnold H. (1989). Personality as traits. *American Psychologist, 44*, 1378–1388.

Buss, David M. (1988). Love acts: The evolutionary biology of love. In R. J. Sternberg & M. L. Bames (eds.), *The psychology of love.* New Haven, CT: Yale University Press.

Bussey, Kay, & Maughan, Betty (1982). Gender differences in moral reasoning. *Journal of Personality and Social Psychology, 42*, 701–706.

Butcher, James N., & Finn, Stephen (1983). Objective personality assessment in clinical settings. In M. H. Hersen, A. E. Kazdin, & A. S. Bellack (eds.), *The clinical psychology handbook.* New York: Pergamon.

Butcher, James N.; Dahlstrom, W. Grant; Graham, John R.; Tellegen, Auke; & Kaemmer, Beverly (1989). *Minnesota Multiphasic Personality Inventory-II: Manual for administration and scoring.* Minneapolis: University of Minnesota Press.

Butterfield, E. C., & Belmont, J. M. (1977). Assessing and improving the executive cognitive functions of mentally retarded people. In I. Bialer & M. Sternlict (eds.), *Psychological issues in mental retardation.* New York: Psychological Dimensions.

Cabezas, A.; Tam, T. M.; Lowe, B. M.; Wong, A.; & Turner, K. (1989). Empirical study of barriers to upward mobility of Asian Americans in the San Francisco Bay area. In G. Nomura (ed.), *Frontiers of Asian American studies.* Pullman, WA: Washington State University Press.

Callahan, Daniel (1989). *What kind of life: The limits of medical progress.* New York: Simon & Schuster.

Camel, J. F.; Withers, G. S.; & Greenough, William T. (1986). Persistence of visual cortex dendritic alterations induced by postweaning exposure to a "superenriched" environment in rats. *Behavioral Neuroscience, 100*, 810–813.

Campbell, Jennifer D. (1990). Self-esteem and clarity of the self-concept. *Journal of Personality and Social Psychology, 59*, 538–549.

Campbell, Joseph (1949/1968). *The hero with 1,000 faces* (2nd ed.). Princeton, NJ: Princeton University Press.

Campbell, Magda; Overall, John E.; Small, Arthur M.; et al. (1989). Naltrexone in autistic children: An acute open dose range tolerance trial. *Journal of the American Academy of Child and Adolescent Psychiatry, 28*, 200–206.

Campos, Joseph J.; Barrett, Karen C.; Lamb, Michael E.; Goldsmith, H. Hill; & Stenberg, Craig (1984). Socioemotional development. In P. Mussen (ed.), *Handbook of child psychology* (4th ed.). Vol. II, M. M. Haith & J. J. Campos (eds.), *Infancy and developmental psychobiology.* New York: Wiley.

Cannon, Tyrone D.; Mednick, Sarnoff A.; & Parnas, Josef (1989). Genetic and perinatal determinants of structural brain deficits in schizophrenia. *Archives of General Psychiatry, 46*, 883–889.

Caplan, Paula J. (1991). How *do* they decide who is normal? The bizarre, but true, tale of the DSM process. *Canadian Psychology, 32*, 162–170.

Caramazza, Alfonso, & Hillis, Argye E. (1991, February 28). Lexical organization of nouns and verbs in the brain. *Nature, 349*, 788–790.

Carducci, Bernardo J., & McGuire, Jay C. (1990). Behavior and beliefs characteristic of first-, second-, and third-time lovers. Paper presented at the annual meeting of the American Psychological Association, Boston.

Carpenter, William T., Jr.; Sadier, John H.; et al. (1983). The therapeutic efficacy of hemodialysis in schizophrenia. *New England Journal of Medicine, 308*(12), 669–675.

Carskadon, Mary A.; Mitler, Merrill M.; & Dement, William C. (1974). A comparison of insomniacs and normals: Total sleep time and sleep latency. *Sleep Research, 3*, 130 [Abstract].

Carson, Robert C. (1989). What happened to schizophrenia? Reflections on a taxonomic absurdity. Paper presented at the annual meeting of the American Psychological Association, New Orleans.

Carson, Robert C., & Butcher, James N. (1992). *Abnormal psychology and modern life* (9th ed.). New York: HarperCollins.

Carter, Betty, & McGoldrick, Monica (eds.) (1988). *The changing family life cycle: A framework for family therapy* (2nd ed.). New York: Gardner Press.

Cartwright, Rosalind D. (1989). Sleep and dreams in depressed men and women undergoing divorce. Paper presented at the annual meeting of the American Psychological Association, New Orleans.

Cartwright, Rosalind (1990). A network model of dreams. In R. R. Bootzin, J. F. Kihlstrom, & D. L. Schacter (eds.), *Sleep and cognition.* Washington, DC: American Psychological Association.

Cartwright, Rosalind (1991). Dreams that work: The relation of dream incorporation to adaptation to stressful events. *Dreaming, 1*, 3–9.

Carver, Charles S.; Scheier, Michael F.; & Weintraub, Jagdish K. (1989). Assessing coping strategies: A theoretically based approach. *Journal of Personality and Social Psychology, 56*, 267–283.

Caspi, Avshalom, & Moffitt, Terrie E. (1991). Individual differences are accentuated during periods of social change: The sample case of girls at puberty. *Journal of Personality and Social Psychology, 61*, 157–168.

Cass, Loretta K., & Thomas, Carolyn (1979). *Childhood pathology and later adjustment.* New York: Wiley-Interscience.

Cassell, Carol (1984). *Swept away: Why women fear their own sexuality.* New York: Simon & Schuster.

Cattell, Raymond B. (1965). *The scientific analysis of personality.* Baltimore: Penguin.

Cattell, Raymond B. (1971). *Abilities: Their structure, growth and action.* Boston: Houghton Mifflin.

Cattell, Raymond B. (1973). *Personality and mood by questionnaire.* San Francisco: Jossey-Bass.

Ceci, Stephen J., & Liker, Jeffrey K. (1986). Academic and nonacademic intelligence: An experimental separation. In R. J. Sternberg & R. K. Wagner (eds.), *Practical intelligence: Nature and origins of competence in the everyday world.* New York: Cambridge University Press.

Cermak, Laird S., & Craik, Fergus I. M. (eds.) (1979). *Levels of processing in human memory.* Hillsdale, NJ: Erlbaum.

Chambless, Dianne L. (1985). Agoraphobia. In M. Hersen & A. S. Bellak (eds.), *Handbook of clinical behavior therapy with adults.* New York: Plenum.

Chambless, Dianne L. (1988). Cognitive mechanisms in panic disorder. In S. Rachman & J. D. Maser (eds.), *Panic: Psychological perspectives.* Hillsdale, NJ: Erlbaum.

Chan, Connie S., & Grossman, Hildreth Y. (1988). Psychological effects of running loss on consistent runners. *Perceptual & Motor Skills, 66*, 875–883.

Chance, Paul (1988a). *Learning and behavior* (2nd ed). Belmont, CA: Wadsworth.

Chance, Paul (1988b, October). Knock wood. *Psychology Today, 22*(10), 68–69.

Cheney, Dorothy L., & Seyfarth, Robert M. (1985). Vervet monkey alarm calls: Manipulation through shared information? *Behavior, 94*, 150–166.

Cheng, Patricia W., & Novick, Laura R. (1990). A probabilistic contrast model of causal induction. *Journal of Personality and Social Psychology, 58,* 545–567.

Chiu, Lian-Hwang (1988). Locus of control differences between American and Chinese adolescents. *The Journal of Social Psychology, 128,* 411–413.

Chodorow, Nancy (1978). *The reproduction of mothering.* Berkeley: The University of California Press.

Chomsky, Noam (1957). *Syntactic structures.* The Hague: Mouton.

Chomsky, Noam (1980). Initial states and steady states. In M. Piatelli-Palmerini (ed.), *Language and learning: The debate between Jean Piaget and Noam Chomsky.* Cambridge, MA: Harvard University Press.

Chorovor, Stephan L. (1974, May). Big brother and psychotechnology II: The pacification of the brain. *Psychology Today, 7*(12), 59–69.

Christensen, Larry, & Burrows, Ross (1990). Dietary treatment of depression. *Behavior Therapy, 21,* 183–194.

Christopher, F. Scott (1988). An initial investigation into a continuum of premarital sexual pressure. *Journal of Sex Research, 25,* 255–266.

Chudacoff, Howard P. (1990). *How old are you? Age consciousness in American culture.* Princeton, NJ: Princeton University Press.

Clark, David M. (1988). A cognitive model of panic attacks. In S. Rachman & J. D. Maser (eds.), *Panic: Psychological perspectives.* Hillsdale, NJ: Erlbaum.

Clark, Herbert H., & Clark, Eve V. (1977). *Psychology and language: An introduction to psycholinguistics.* New York: Harcourt Brace Jovanovich.

Clark, Margaret S.; Millberg, Sandra; & Erber, Ralph (1987). Arousal state dependent memory: Evidence and some implications for understanding social judgments and social behavior. In K. Fiedler & J. P. Forgas (eds.), *Affect, cognition and social behavior.* Toronto: Hogrefe.

Clarke-Stewart, K. Alison (1991). A home is not a school: The effects of child care on children's development. In S. L. Hofferth & D. A. Phillips (eds.), *Child care policy research. Journal of Social Issues, 47*(2), 105–124.

Clarke-Stewart, K. Alison; VanderStoep, Laima P.; & Killian, Grant A. (1979). Analyses and replication of mother-child relations at two years of age. *Child Development, 50,* 777–793.

Clauw, D. J.; Nashel, D. J.; Umhau, A.; & Katz, P. (1990). Tryptophan-associated eosinophilic connective-tissue disease. A new clinical entity? *Journal of the American Medical Association, 263,* 1502–1506.

Clementz, Brett A., & Sweeney, John A. (1990). Is eye movement dysfunction a biological marker for schizophrenia? A methodological review. *Psychological Review, 108,* 77–92.

Coe, William C., & Sarbin, Theodore R. (1977). Hypnosis from the standpoint of a contextualist. *Annals of the New York Academy of Sciences, 296,* 2–13.

Cohen, Barry M.; Hammer, Jeffrey S.; & Singer, Shira (1988). The Diagnostic Drawing Series: A systematic approach to art therapy evaluation and research. Special Issue: Assessment in the creative arts therapies. *Arts in Psychotherapy, 15,* 11–21.

Cohen, Frances, & Lazarus, Richard S. (1973). Active coping processes, coping dispositions, and recovery from surgery. *Psychosomatic Medicine, 35,* 375–389.

Cohen, Sheldon, & Edwards, Jeffrey R. (1989). Personality characteristics as moderators of the relationship between stress and disorder. In R. W. J. Neufeld (ed.), *Advances in the investigation of psychological stress.* New York: Wiley.

Cohen, Sheldon, & Williamson, Gail M. (1991). Stress and infectious disease in humans. *Psychological Bulletin, 109,* 5–24.

Cohen, Sheldon; Kamarck, Tom; & Mermelstein, Robin (1983). A global measure of perceived stress. *Journal of Health and Social Behavior, 24,* 385–396.

Cohen, Sheldon; Tyrrell, D. A.; & Smith, A. P. (1991, August 29). Psychological stress and susceptibility to the common cold. *New England Journal of Medicine, 325*(9), 606–612.

Cohen, Sheldon; Evans, Gary W.; Krantz, David S.; & Stokols, Daniel (1980). Physiological, motivational, and cognitive effects of aircraft noise on children. *American Psychologist, 35,* 231–243.

Cohn, Lawrence D. (1991). Sex differences in the course of personality development: A meta-analysis. *Psychological Bulletin, 109,* 252–266.

Colby, Anne; Kohlberg, Lawrence; Gibbs, J.; & Lieberman, M. (1983). A longitudinal study of moral judgment. *Monographs of the Society for Research in Child Development, 48* (1–2, Serial No. 200).

Cole, Michael (1990). Cultural psychology: A once and future discipline? In J. J. Berman (ed.), *Cross-cultural perspectives. Nebraska Symposium on Motivation, 1989.* Lincoln: University of Nebraska Press.

Cole, Michael, & Cole, Sheila R. (1989). *The development of children.* New York: Scientific American Books.

Coles, Robert, & Stokes, Geoffrey (1985). *Sex and the American teenager.* New York: Harper & Row.

Collins, Allan M., & Loftus, Elizabeth F. (1975). A spreading-activation theory of semantic processing. *Psychological Review, 82,* 407–428.

Collins, Rebecca L.; Taylor, Shelley E.; & Skokan, Laurie A. (1990). A better world or a shattered vision? Changes in life perspectives following victimization. *Social Cognition, 8,* 263–285.

Comstock, George; Chaffee, Steven; Katzman, Natan; McCombs, Maxwell; & Roberts, Donald (1978). *Television and human behavior.* New York: Columbia University Press.

Condon, William (1982). Cultural microrhythms. In M. Davis (ed.), *Interaction rhythms: Periodicity in communicative behavior.* New York: Human Sciences Press.

Conte, Hope; Plutchik, Robert; Wild, Katherine; & Karasu, Toksoz (1986). Combined psychotherapy and pharmacotherapy for depression. *Archives of General Psychiatry, 43,* 471–479.

Conway, Michael, & Ross, Michael (1984). Getting what you want by revising what you had. *Journal of Personality and Social Psychology, 47,* 738–748.

Coons, Philip M.; Milstein, Victor; & Marley, Carma (1982). EEG studies of two multiple personalities and a control. *Archives of General Psychiatry, 39,* 823–825.

Copi, Irving M., & Burgess-Jackson, Keith (1992). *Informal logic* (2nd ed.). New York: Macmillan.

Corkin, Suzanne (1984). Lasting consequences of bilateral medial temporal lobectomy: Clinical course and experimental findings in H. M. *Seminars in Neurology, 4,* 249–259.

Cornelius, Randolph R. (1991). Gregorio Marañón's two-factor theory of emotion. *Personality and Social Psychology Bulletin, 17,* 65–69.

Cornell-Bell, A. H.; Finkbeiner, S. M.; Cooper, M. S.; & Smith, S. J. (1990). Glutamate induces calcium waves in cultured astrocytes: Long-range glial signaling. *Science, 247,* 470–473.

Costa, Paul T., Jr., & McCrae, Robert R. (1988). Personality in adulthood: A six-year longitudinal study of self-reports and spouse ratings on the NEO personality inventory. *Journal of Personality and Social Psychology, 54,* 853–863.

Costantino, Giuseppe; Malgady, Robert G.; & Rogler, Lloyd H. (1986). Cuento therapy: A culturally sensitive modality for Puerto Rican children. *Journal of Consulting and Clinical Psychology, 54,* 639–645.

Cowen, Emory L.; Wyman, Peter A.; Work, William C.; & Parker, Gayle R. (1990). The Rochester Child Resilience Project (RCRP): Overview and summary of first year findings. *Development and Psychopathology, 2,* 193–212.

Cowen, Ron (1989). Receptor encounters: Untangling the threads of the serotonin system. *Science News, 136,* 248–250, 252.

Craik, Fergus I. M., & Tulving, Endel (1975). Depth of processing and the retention of words in episodic memory. *Journal of Experimental Psychology: General, 104,* 268–294.

Crandall, James E. (1981). *Theory and measurement of social interest: Empirical tests of Alfred Adler's concept.* New York: Columbia University Press.

Crandall, James E. (1984). Social interest as a moderator of life stress. *Journal of Personality and Social Psychology, 47,* 164–174.

Crawford, Mary, & Gressley, Diane (1991). Creativity, caring, and context: Women's and men's accounts of humor preferences and practices. *Psychology of Women Quarterly, 15,* 217–231.

Crick, Francis, & Mitchison, Graeme (1983, July 14). The function of dream sleep. *Nature, 304*(14), 111–114.

Critchlow, Barbara (1983). Blaming the booze: The attribution of responsibility for drunken behavior. *Personality and Social Psychology Bulletin, 9,* 451–474.

Critchlow, Barbara (1986). The powers of John Barleycorn: Beliefs about the effects of alcohol on social behavior. *American Psychologist, 41,* 751–764.

Crocker, Jennifer, & Major, Brenda (1989). Social stigma and self-esteem: The self-protective properties of stigma. *Psychological Review, 96,* 608–630.

Cronbach, Lee J. (1990). *Essentials of psychological testing* (5th ed.). New York: Harper & Row.

Crosby, Faye J. (1991). *Juggling.* New York: The Free Press.

Cross, A. J. (1990). Serotonin in Alzheimer-type dementia and other dementing illnesses. *Annals of the New York Academy of Science, 600,* 405–415.

Crouse, James, & Trusheim, Dale (1988). *The case against the SAT.* Chicago: University of Chicago Press.

Crowley, Joan (1986). Longitudinal effects of retirement on men's well-being and health. *Journal of Business & Psychology, 1,* 95–113.

Crystal, Graef S. (1991). *In search of excess: The overcompensation of the American executive.* New York: Norton.

Csikszentmihalyi, Mihaly, & Larson, Reed (1984). *Being adolescent: Conflict and growth in the teenage years.* New York: Basic Books.

Cubelli, Roberto (1991, September 19). A selective deficit for writing vowels in acquired dysgraphia. *Nature, 353,* 209–210.

Cunningham, Walter R., & Brookbank, John W. (1988). *Gerontology: The psychology, biology, and sociology of aging.* New York: Harper & Row.

Curtiss, Susan (1977). *Genie: A psycholinguistic study of a modern-day "wild child."* New York: Academic Press.

Cutler, Brian, & Penrod, Steven D. (1988). Improving the reliability of eyewitness identification: Lineup construction and presentation. *Journal of Applied Psychology, 73,* 281–290.

Czeisler, Charles A.; Johnson, Michael P.; Duffy, Jeanne F.; Brown, Emery N.; et al. (1990). Exposure to bright light and darkness to treat physiologic maladaptation to night work. *New England Journal of Medicine, 322,* 1253–1259.

Dabbs, James M., Jr., & Morris, Robin (1990). Testosterone, social class, and antisocial behavior in a sample of 4,462 men. *Psychological Science, 1,* 209–211.

Dagenbach, Dale; Carr, Thomas H.; & Wilhelmsen, AnneLise (1989). Task-induced strategies and near-threshold priming: Conscious influences on unconscious perception. *Journal of Memory and Language, 28,* 412–443.

Dakof, Gayle A., & Taylor, Shelley E. (1990). Victims' perceptions of social support: What is helpful from whom? *Journal of Personality and Social Psychology, 58,* 80–89.

Damasio, Antonio R. (1990). Category-related recognition defects as a clue to the neural substrates of knowledge. *Trends in Neurosciences, 13,* 95–98.

Darwin, Charles (1872/1965). *The expression of the emotions in man and animals.* Reprinted by the University of Chicago Press.

Dasen, Pierre (ed.) (1977). *Piagetian psychology: Cross-cultural contributions.* New York: Gardner Press.

Datan, Nancy, & Thomas, Jeanne (1984). Late adulthood: Love, work, and the normal transitions. In D. Offer & M. Sabshin (eds.), *Normality and the life cycle.* New York: Basic Books.

Davidson, Keay, & Hopson, Janet L. (1988, April 10). Gorilla business. *Image* (San Francisco Chronicle), 14–18, 33–36.

Davidson, Richard J.; Ekman, Paul; Saron, Clifford D.; Senulis, Joseph A.; & Friesen, Wallace V. (1990). Approach-withdrawal and cerebral asymmetry: Emotional expression and brain physiology I. *Journal of Personality and Social Psychology, 58,* 330–341.

Davis, Joel (1984). *Endorphins: New waves in brain chemistry.* Garden City, NY: Dial Press (Doubleday).

Dawson, Neal V.; Arkes, Hal R.; Siciliano, C.; et al. (1988). Hindsight bias: An impediment to accurate probability estimation in clinicopathologic conferences. *Medical Decision Making, 8*(4), 259–264.

Dean, Geoffrey (1986–1987, Winter). Does astrology need to be true? Part 1: A look at the real thing. *The Skeptical Inquirer, 11,* 166–184.

Dean, Geoffrey (1987, Spring). Does astrology need to be true? Part II: The answer is no. *The Skeptical Inquirer, 11,* 257–273.

de Bono, Edward (1985). *de Bono's thinking course.* New York: Facts on File.

DeCasper, Anthony J., & Spence, Melanie J. (1986). Prenatal maternal speech influences newborns' perception of speech sounds. *Infant Behavior and Development, 9,* 133–150.

Deci, Edward L. (1975). *Intrinsic motivation.* New York: Plenum.

Deci, Edward L., & Ryan, Richard M. (1987). The support of autonomy and the control of behavior. *Journal of Personality and Social Psychology, 53,* 1024–1037.

Deffenbacher, Jerry L. (1988). Cognitive-relaxation and social skills treatments of anger: A year later. *Journal of Counseling Psychology, 35,* 234–236.

de Lacoste-Utamsing, Christine, & Holloway, Ralph L. (1982). Sexual dimorphism in the human corpus callosum. *Science, 216,* 1431–1432.

DeLoache, Judy S. (1987, December 11). Rapid change in the symbolic functioning of very young children. *Science, 238,* 1556–1557.

DeLongis, Anita; Folkman, Susan; & Lazarus, Richard S. (1988). The impact of daily stress on health and mood: Psychological and social resources as mediators. *Journal of Personality and Social Psychology, 54,* 486–495.

Dembroski, Theodore M., & Costa, Paul T., Jr. (1988). Assessment of coronary-prone behavior: A current overview. *Annals of Behavioral Medicine, 10,* 60–63.

Dement, William (1955). Dream recall and eye movements during sleep in schizophrenics and normals. *Journal of Nervous and Mental Disease, 122,* 263–269.

Dement, William (1978). *Some must watch while some must sleep.* New York: Norton.

Dement, William, & Kleitman, Nathaniel (1957). The relation of eye movements during sleep to dream activity: An objective method for the study of dreaming. *Journal of Experimental Psychology, 53,* 339–346.

Demos, John (1970). *A little commonwealth.* New York: Oxford University Press.

DeMyer, Marian K. (1975). Research in infantile autism: A strategy and its results. *Biological Psychiatry, 10,* 433–452.

DeNelsky, Garland Y. (1990). The case against prescription privileges for psychologists. Paper presented at the annual meeting of the American Psychological Association, Boston.

DePaola, Laura, & DePaola, Steve (1988). Hallucinations during widowhood. Paper presented at the annual meeting of the Western Psychological Association, San Francisco.

de Rivera, Joseph (1989, June). Comparing experiences across cultures: Shame and guilt in America and Japan. Paper presented at the meeting of the American Psychological Society, Alexandria, VA.

Deutsch, Francine M.; LeBaron, Dorothy; & Fryer, Maury M. (1987). What is in a smile? *Psychology of Women Quarterly, 11,* 341–352.

Deutsch, Morton (1949). An experimental study of the effects of cooperation and competition among group processes. *Human Relations, 2,* 199–231.

Deutsch, Morton (1980). Fifty years of conflict. In L. Festinger (ed.), *Retrospections on social psychology.* New York: Oxford University Press.

Deutsch, Morton, & Collins, Mary Ellen (1951). *Interracial housing: A psychological evaluation of a social experiment.* Minneapolis: University of Minnesota Press.

DeValois, Russell L. (1960). Color vision mechanisms in the monkey. *Journal of General Physiology, 43,* 115–128.

DeValois, Russell L., & DeValois, Karen K. (1975). Neural coding of color. In E. C. Carterette & M. P. Friedman (eds.), *Handbook of perception,* Vol. 5. New York: Academic Press.

DeValois, Russell L., & DeValois, Karen K. (1980). Spatial vision. *Annual Review of Psychology, 31,* 309–341.

Devine, Patricia G.; Monteith, Margo J.; Zuwerink, Julia R.; & Elliot, Andrew J. (1991). Prejudice with and without compunction. *Journal of Personality and Social Psychology, 60,* 817–830.

Diamond, Jared (1987, August). Soft sciences are often harder than hard sciences. *Discover, 8*(8), 34–35, 38–39.

Diamond, Marian (1984, November). A love affair with the brain (A conversation). *Psychology Today, 18*(11), 62–73.

Diamond, Marian (1988). *Enriching heredity: The impact of the environment on the anatomy of the brain.* New York: Free Press.

Diamond, Marian; Johnson, Ruth E.; Young, Daniel; & Singh, S. Sukhwinder (1983). Age related morphologic differences in the rat cerebral cortex and hippocampus: Male-female; right-left. *Experimental Neurology, 81,* 1–13.

Diamond, Marian; Scheibel, Arnold B.; Murphy, Greer M.; & Harvey, Thomas (1985). On the brain of a scientist: Albert Einstein. *Experimental Neurology, 88,* 198–204.

Dickson, W. Patrick; Hess, Robert D.; Miyake, Naomi; & Azuma, Hiroshi (1979). Referential communication accuracy between mother and child as a predictor of cognitive development in the United States and Japan. *Child Development, 50,* 53–59.

Diener, Ed; Colvin, C. Randall; Pavot, William G.; & Allman, Amanda (1991). The psychic costs of intense positive affect. *Journal of Personality and Social Psychology, 61,* 492–503.

DiFranza, Joseph R.; Winters, Thomas H.; Goldberg, Robert J.; Cirillo, Leonard; et al. (1986). The relationship of smoking to motor vehicle accidents and traffic violations. *New York State Journal of Medicine, 86,* 464–467.

Digman, John M. (1990). Personality structure: Emergence of the five-factor model. In M. R. Rosenzweig & L. W. Porter (eds.), *Annual Review of Psychology.* Palo Alto: Annual Reviews.

Digman, John M., & Inouye, Jillian (1986). Further specification of the five robust factors of personality. *Journal of Personality and Social Psychology, 50,* 116–123.

DiLalla, Lisabeth F., & Gottesman, Irving I. (1991). Biological and genetic contributors to violence—Widom's untold tale. *Psychological Bulletin, 109,* 125–129.

Dinges, David F.; Whitehouse, Wayne G.; Orne, Emily C.; Powell, John W.; Orne, Martin T.; & Erdelyi, Matthew H. (1992). Evaluating hypnotic memory enhancement (hypermnesia and reminiscence) using multitrial forced recall. *Journal of Experimental Psychology: Learning, Memory, and Cognition, 18,* 1139–1147.

Dion, George L., & Anthony, William A. (1987). Research in psychiatric rehabilitation: A review of experimental and quasi-experimental studies. *Rehabilitation Counseling Bulletin, 30,* 177–203.

Dion, Kenneth L., & Dion, Karen K. (1975). Self-esteem and romantic love. *Journal of Personality, 43,* 39–57.

Dion, Kenneth L., & Dion, Karen K. (1988). Romantic love: Individual and cultural perspectives. In R. J. Sternberg & M. L. Barnes (eds.), *The psychology of love.* New Haven, CT: Yale University Press.

Dixon, N. F. (1980). Humor: A cognitive alternative to stress? In I. G. Sarason & C. D. Spielberger (eds.), *Stress and anxiety,* Vol. 7. Washington, DC: Hemisphere.

Dobson, Keith S. (1989). A meta-analysis of the efficacy of cognitive therapy for depression. *Journal of Consulting and Clinical Psychology, 57,* 414–419.

Doering, Charles H., et al. (1975). Negative affect and plasma testosterone: A longitudinal human study. *Psychosomatic Medicine, 37,* 484–491.

Doering, Charles H.; Brodie, H. K. H.; Kraemer, H. C.; Becker, H. B.; & Hamburg, D. A. (1974). Plasma testosterone levels and psychologic measures in men over a 2-month period. In R. C. Friedman, R. M. Richard, & R. L. Vande Wiele (eds.), *Sex differences in behavior.* New York: Wiley.

Doi, L. T. (1973). *The anatomy of dependence.* Tokyo: Kodansha International.

Dollard, John, & Miller, Neal E. (1950). *Personality and psychotherapy: An analysis in terms of learning, thinking, and culture.* New York: McGraw-Hill.

Dolnick, Edward (1990, July). What dreams are (really) made of. *The Atlantic Monthly, 226,* 41–45, 48–53, 56–58, 60–61.

Donnell, S. M., & Hall, J. (1980, Spring). Men and women as managers: A significant case of no significant difference. *Organizational Dynamics, 8,* 60–76.

Dorris, Michael (1989). *The broken cord.* New York: Harper & Row.

Doty, Richard L. (1989). Influence of age and age-related diseases on olfactory function. *Annals of the New York Academy of Sciences, 561,* 76–86.

Doty, Richard M.; Peterson, Bill E.; & Winter, David G. (1991). Threat and authoritarianism in the United States, 1978–1987. *Journal of Personality and Social Psychology, 61,* 629–640.

Dovidio, John F.; Allen, Judith L.; & Schroeder, David A. (1990). Specificity of empathy-induced helping: Evidence for altruistic motivation. *Journal of Personality and Social Psychology, 59,* 249–260.

Drinka, George F. (1984). *The birth of neurosis.* New York: Simon & Schuster.

Drucker, Peter F. (1979, March). What Freud forgot. *Human Nature, 2,* 40–50.

Druckman, Daniel, & Swets, John A. (eds.) (1988). *Enhancing human performance: Issues, theories, and techniques.* Washington, DC: National Academy Press.

Dumont, Matthew P. (1987, December). A diagnostic parable (first edition—unrevised) [Review of *DSM-III-R*]. *Readings: A Journal of Reviews and Commentary in Mental Health,* pp. 9–12.

Duncan, Greg J.; Hill, Martha S.; & Hoffman, Saul D. (1988, January 29). Welfare dependence within and across generations. *Science, 239,* 467.

Duncan, Paula D.; Ritter, Philip L.; Dornbusch, Sanford M.; Gross, Ruth T.; & Carlsmith, J. Merrill (1985). The effects of pubertal timing on body image, school behavior, and deviance. *Journal of Youth and Adolescence, 14,* 227–235.

Dunford, Franklyn; Huizinga, David; & Elliott, Delbert S. (1990). The role of arrest in domestic assault: The Omaha police experiment. *Criminology, 28,* 183–206.

Dunkel-Schetter, Christine (1984). Social support and cancer: Findings based on patient interviews and their implications. *Journal of Social Issues, 40*(4), 77–98.

Dunn, Judy, & Plomin, Robert (1990). *Separate lives: Why siblings are so different.* New York: Basic Books.

du Verglas, Gabrielle; Banks, Steven R.; & Guyer, Kenneth E. (1988). Clinical effects of fenfluramine on children with autism: A review of the research. *Journal of Autism and Developmental Disorders, 18,* 297–308.

Dweck, Carol (1990). Toward a theory of goals: Their role in motivation and personality. In R. A. Dienstbier (ed.), *Nebraska Symposium on Motivation,* Vol. 38. Lincoln: University of Nebraska Press.

Dworkin, Barry R., & Dworkin, Susan (1988). The treatment of scoliosis by continuous automated postural feedback. In R. Ader, H. Weiner, & A. Baum (eds.), *Experimental foundations of behavioral medicine: Conditioning approaches.* Hillsdale, NJ: Erlbaum.

Dworkin, Barry R., & Miller, Neal E. (1986). Failure to replicate visceral learning in the acute curarized rat preparation. *Behavioral Neuroscience, 100,* 299–314.

Dywan, Jane, & Bowers, Kenneth (1983). The use of hypnosis to enhance recall. *Science, 222,* 184–185.

D'Zurilla, Thomas J., & Sheedy, Collette F. (1991). Relation between problem-solving ability and subsequent level of psychological stress in college students. *Journal of Personality and Social Psychology, 61,* 841–846.

Eagly, Alice H., & Carli, Linda L. (1981). Sex of researchers and sex-typed communications as determinants of sex differences in influencibility: A meta-analysis of social influence studies. *Psychological Bulletin, 90,* 1–20.

Ebbinghaus, Hermann M. (1885/1913). *Memory: A contribution to experimental psychology.* (H. A. Ruger & C. E. Bussenius, trans.) New York: Teachers College, Columbia University.

Eccles, John C. (1981). In praise of falsification. In R. D. Tweney, M. E. Doherty, & C. R. Mynatt (eds.), *On scientific thinking.* New York: Columbia University Press.

Edsall, Thomas B., & Edsall, Mary D. (1991). *Chain reaction: The impact of race, rights, and taxes on American politics.* New York: Norton.

Edwards, Betty (1986). *Drawing on the artist within: A guide to innovation, invention, imagination and creativity.* New York: Simon & Schuster.

Edwards, Carolyn P. (1987). Culture and the construction of moral values. In J. Kagan & S. Lamb (eds.), *The emergence of morality in young children.* Chicago: University of Chicago Press.

Edwards, John N. (1987). Changing family structure and youthful well-being: Assessing the future. *Journal of Family Issues, 8,* 355–372.

Edwards, Lynne K., & Edwards, Allen L. (1991). A principal-components analysis of the Minnesota Multiphasic Personality Inventory Factor Scales. *Journal of Personality and Social Psychology, 60,* 766–772.

Egeland, Janice A.; Gerhard, Daniela; Pauls, David; Sussex, James; et al. (1987, February 26). Bipolar affective disorders linked to DNA markers on chromosome 11. *Nature, 325,* 783–787.

Ekman, Paul (1985). *Telling lies.* New York: Norton.

Ekman, Paul, & Friesen, Wallace V. (1975/1984). *Unmasking the face.* Englewood Cliffs, NJ: Prentice-Hall. (Reprinted by Consulting Psychologists Press, Palo Alto, CA.)

Ekman, Paul, & Heider, Karl G. (1988). The universality of a contempt expression: A replication. *Motivation and Emotion, 12,* 303–308.

Ekman, Paul; Friesen, Wallace V.; & Ellsworth, Phoebe (1972). *Emotion in the human face: Guidelines for research and an integration of findings.* New York: Pergamon.

Ekman, Paul; Friesen, Wallace V.; & O'Sullivan, Maureen (1988). Smiles when lying. *Journal of Personality and Social Psychology, 54,* 414–420.

Ekman, Paul; Friesen, Wallace V.; O'Sullivan, Maureen; et al. (1987). Universals and cultural differences in the judgments of facial expression of emotion. *Journal of Personality and Social Psychology, 53,* 712–717.

Elkin, Roger A., & Leippe, Michael R. (1986). Physiological arousal, dissonance, and attitude change: Evidence for a dissonance-arousal link and a "don't remind me" effect. *Journal of Personality and Social Psychology, 51,* 55–65.

Elkind, David (1988). *Miseducation: Preschoolers at risk.* New York: Knopf.

Elliott, Elaine S., & Dweck, Carol S. (1988). Goals: An approach to motivation and achievement. *Journal of Personality and Social Psychology, 54,* 5–12.

Ellis, Albert, & Dryden, Windy (1987). *The practice of rational emotive therapy.* New York: Springer.

Ellis, Havelock (1910). Review of "A psycho-analytic study of Leonardo da Vinci," by Sigmund Freud. *The Journal of Mental Science, 56,* 522–523.

Emmons, Robert A., & King, Laura A. (1988). Conflict among personal strivings: Immediate and long-term implications for psychological and physical well-being. *Journal of Personality and Social Psychology, 54,* 1040–1048.

Englander-Golden, Paula; Whitmore, Mary R.; & Dienstbier, Richard A. (1978). Menstrual cycle as focus of study and self-re-

ports of moods and behaviors. *Motivation and Emotion, 2,* 75–86.

Englund, C., & Naitoh, P. (1980). An attempted validation study of the birthdate-based biorhythm (BBB) hypothesis. *Aviation, Space, and Environmental Medicine, 51,* 583–590.

Ennis, Robert H. (1985). Critical thinking and the curriculum. *National Forum, 65*(1), 28–30.

Epstein, R.; Kirshnit, C. E.; Lanza, R. P.; & Rubin, L. C. (1984, March 1). 'Insight' in the pigeon: Antecedents and determinants of an intelligent performance. *Nature, 308,* 61–62.

Epstein, Seymour, & Fenz, Walter (1965). Steepness of approach and avoidance gradients in humans as a function of experience. *Journal of Experimental Psychology, 70,* 1–12.

Erikson, Erik H. (1950/1963). *Childhood and society* (2nd ed.). New York: Norton.

Erikson, Erik H. (1987). *A way of looking at things: Selected papers from 1930 to 1980* (edited by Stephen Schlein). New York: Norton.

Erikson, Erik H.; Erikson, Joan M.; & Kivnick, Helen Q. (1986). *Vital involvements in old age.* New York: Norton.

Ernsberger, Paul, & Nelson, D. O. (1988). Refeeding hypertension in dietary obesity. *American Journal of Physiology, 154,* R47–55.

Eron, Leonard (1980). Prescription for reduction of aggression. *American Psychologist, 35,* 244–252.

Ervin-Tripp, Susan (1964). Imitation and structural change in children's language. In E. H. Lenneberg (ed.), *New directions in the study of language.* Cambridge, MA: MIT Press.

Evans, Christopher (1984). *Landscapes of the night.* (Edited and completed by Peter Evans.) New York: Viking.

Eyferth, Klaus (1961). [The performance of different groups of the children of occupation forces on the Hamburg-Wechsler Intelligence Test for Children.] *Archiv für die Gesamte Psychologie, 113,* 222–241.

Eysenck, Hans (1970). *The structure of human personality.* New York: Methuen.

Eysenck, Hans J., & Eysenck, Michael W. (1985). *Personality and individual differences.* New York: Plenum.

Eysenck, Sybil, & Long, F. Y. (1986). A cross-cultural comparison of personality in adults and children: Singapore and England. *Journal of Personality and Social Psychology, 50,* 124–130.

Fairchild, Halford H. (1985). Black, Negro, or Afro-American? The differences are crucial! *Journal of Black Studies, 16,* 47–55.

Faraone, Stephen V.; Kremen, William S.; & Tsuang, Ming T. (1990). Genetic transmission of major affective disorders: Quantitative models and linkage analyses. *Psychological Bulletin, 108,* 109–127.

Farber, Susan L. (1981). *Identical twins reared apart: A reanalysis.* New York: Basic Books.

Faust, David, & Ziskin, Jay (1988, July 1). The expert witness in psychology and psychiatry. *Science, 241,* 31–35.

Feather, N. T. (1966). Effects of prior success and failure on expectations of success and subsequent performance. *Journal of Personality and Social Psychology, 3,* 287–298.

Feather, N. T. (ed.) (1982). *Expectations and actions: Expectancy-value models in psychology.* Hillsdale, NJ: Erlbaum.

Feeney, Dennis M. (1987). Human rights and animal welfare. *American Psychologist, 42,* 593–599.

Fehr, Beverly, & Russell, James A. (1991). The concept of love viewed from a prototype perspective. *Journal of Personality and Social Psychology, 60,* 425–438.

Feinberg, Richard A. (1986). Credit cards as spending facilitating stimuli: A conditioning interpretation. *Journal of Consumer Research, 13,* 348–356.

Feingold, Alan (1988). Cognitive gender differences are disappearing. *American Psychologist, 43,* 95–103.

Ferguson, Thomas, & Rogers, Joel (1986, May). The myth of America's turn to the right. *Atlantic,* 43–53.

Fernald, Anne (1990). Emotion in the voice: Meaningful

melodies in mother's speech to infants. Paper presented at the annual meeting of the American Psychological Association, Boston.

Fernald, L. D. (1984). *The Hans legacy: A story of science.* Hillsdale, NJ: Erlbaum.

Feshbach, Norma (1985). Chronic maternal stress and its assessment. In J. N. Butcher & C. D. Speilberger (eds.), *Advances in personality assessment*, Vol. 5. Hillsdale, NJ: Erlbaum.

Feshbach, Norma; Feshbach, Seymour; Fauvre, Mary; & Ballard-Campbell, Michael (1983). *Learning to care: A curriculum for affective and social development.* Glenview, IL: Scott, Foresman.

Festinger, Leon (1957). *A theory of cognitive dissonance.* Evanston, IL: Row, Peterson.

Festinger, Leon (1980). Looking backward. In L. Festinger (ed.), *Retrospections on social psychology.* New York: Oxford University Press.

Festinger, Leon, & Carlsmith, J. Merrill (1959). Cognitive consequences of forced compliance. *Journal of Abnormal and Social Psychology, 58*, 203–210.

Festinger, Leon; Pepitone, Albert; & Newcomb, Theodore (1952). Some consequences of de-individuation in a group. *Journal of Abnormal and Social Psychology, 47*, 382–389.

Festinger, Leon; Riecken, Henry W.; & Schachter, Stanley (1956). *When prophecy fails.* Minneapolis: University of Minnesota Press.

Feuerstein, Reuven (1980). *Instrumental enrichment: An intervention program for cognitive modifiability.* Baltimore, MD: University Park Press.

Field, Tiffany (1989, Summer). Individual and maturational differences in infant expressivity. *New Directions for Child Development, 44*, 9–23.

Field, Tiffany (1992). Quality infant daycare and grade school behavior and performance. *Child Development*, in press.

Fields, Howard (1991). Depression and pain: A neurobiological model. *Neuropsychiatry, Neuropsychology, and Behavioral Neurology, 4*, 83–92.

Fingarette, Herbert (1988). *Heavy drinking: The myth of alcoholism as a disease.* Berkeley, CA: University of California Press.

Finkelhor, David (1984). *Child sexual abuse: New theory and research.* New York: Free Press.

Fischer, Joel (1978). Does anything work? *Journal of Social Science Research, 1*, 215–243.

Fischer, Kurt W.; Shaver, Phillip R.; & Carnochan, Peter (1990). How emotions develop and how they organise development. *Cognition & Emotion, 4*, 81–127.

Fischhoff, Baruch (1975). Hindsight is not equal to foresight: The effect of outcome knowledge on judgment under uncertainty. *Journal of Experimental Psychology: Human Perception and Performance, 1*, 288–299.

Fisher, Kathleen (1985, March). ECT: New studies on how, why, who. *APA Monitor, 16*, 18–19.

Fisher, Seymour, & Greenberg, Roger (eds.) (1989). *A critical appraisal of biological treatments for psychological distress: Comparisons with psychotherapy and placebo.* Hillsdale, NJ: Erlbaum.

Fiske, Susan T., & Taylor, Shelley E. (1991). *Social cognition* (2nd ed.). New York: McGraw-Hill.

Fitzgerald, Joseph M. (1988). Vivid memories and the reminiscence phenomenon: The role of a self narrative. *Human Development, 31*, 261–273.

Fivush, Robyn, & Hamond, Nina R. (1991). Autobiographical memory across the school years: Toward reconceptualizing childhood amnesia. In R. Fivush & J. A. Hudson (eds.), *Knowing and remembering in young children.* New York: Cambridge University Press.

Fixsen, Dean L.; Phillips, Elery L.; et al. (1978, November). The Boys Town revolution. *Human Nature, 1*, 54–61.

Fleming, Raymond; Baum, Andrew; & Singer, Jerome E. (1984). Toward an integrative approach to the study of stress. *Journal of Personality and Social Psychology, 46*, 939–949.

Fletcher, Garth J., & Ward, C. (1988). Attribution theory and processes: Cross-cultural perspective. In M. H. Bond (ed.), *The cross-cultural challenge to social psychology.* Newbury Park, CA: Sage.

Flor, Herta; Kerns, Robert D.; & Turk, Dennis C. (1987). The role of spouse reinforcement, perceived pain, and activity levels of chronic pain patients. *Journal of Psychosomatic Research, 31*, 251–259.

Foa, Edna, & Emmelkamp, Paul (eds.) (1983). *Failures in behavior therapy.* New York: Wiley.

Fontenot, Kathleen, & Brannon, Linda (1991). Gender differences in coping with job stress. Paper presented at the annual meeting of the American Psychological Association, San Francisco.

Forgas, Joseph, & Bond, Michael H. (1985). Cultural influences on the perception of interaction episodes. *Personality and Social Psychology Bulletin, 11*, 75–88.

Forrest, F.; Florey, C. du V.; Taylor, D.; McPherson, F.; & Young, J. A. (1991, July 6). Reported social alcohol consumption during pregnancy and infants' development at 18 months. *British Medical Journal, 303*, 22–26.

Foulkes, David (1990). Dreaming and consciousness. *European Journal of Cognitive Psychology, 2*, 39–55.

Foulkes, David; Hollifield, Michael; Sullivan, Brenda; Bradley, Laura; et al. (1990). REM dreaming and cognitive skills at ages 5–8: A cross-sectional study. *International Journal of Behavioral Development, 13*, 447–465.

Fouts, Roger S., & Rigby, Randall L. (1977). Man-chimpanzee communication. In T. A. Seboek (ed.), *How animals communicate.* Bloomington: University of Indiana Press.

Fouts, Roger S.; Fouts, Deborah H.; & Van Cantfort, Thomas E. (1989). The infant Loulis learns signs from cross-fostered chimpanzees. In R. A. Gardner, B. T. Gardner, & T. E. Van Cantfort (eds.), *Teaching sign language to chimpanzees.* New York: State University of New York Press.

Fox, Nathan A. (1991). If it's not left, it's right: Electroencephalograph asymmetry and the development of emotion. *American Psychologist, 46*, 863–872.

Fox, Nathan A., & Davidson, Richard J. (1988). Patterns of brain electrical activity during facial signs of emotion in 10-month-old infants. *Developmental Psychology, 24*, 230–236.

Frank, Jerome D. (1985). Therapeutic components shared by all psychotherapies. In M. J. Mahony & A. Freeman (eds.), *Cognition and psychotherapy.* New York: Plenum.

Frank, Robert G.; Gluck, John P.; & Buckelew, Susan P. (1990). Rehabilitation: Psychology's greatest opportunity? *American Psychologist, 45*, 757–761.

Frankenhaeuser, Marianne (1980). Psychological aspects of life stress. In S. Levine & H. Ursin (eds.), *Coping and health.* New York: Plenum.

Frankl, Victor E. (1955). *The doctor and the soul: An introduction to logotherapy.* New York: Knopf.

Franklin, Kathryn M.; Janoff-Bulman, Ronnie; & Roberts, John E. (1990). Long-term impact of parental divorce on optimism and trust: Changes in general assumptions or narrow beliefs? *Journal of Personality and Social Psychology, 59*, 743–755.

Fraser, Antonia (1984). *The weaker vessel.* New York: Knopf.

Free, Noel K.; Green, Bonnie L.; Grace, Mary C.; Chernus, Linda A.; & Whitman, Roy M. (1985). Empathy and outcome in brief focal-dynamic therapy. *American Journal of Psychiatry, 142*, 917–921.

Freed, C. R.; Breeze, R. E.; Rosenberg, N. L.; et al. (1990). Transplantation of human fetal dopamine cells for Parkinson's disease. Results at 1 year. *Archives of Neurology, 47*, 505–512.

Freedman, Daniel (1979). *Human sociobiology.* Riverside, NJ: Free Press.

Freedman, Jonathan L. (1988). Television violence and aggression: What the evidence shows. In S. Oskamp (ed.), *Television as a social issue (Applied Social Psychology Annual*, Vol. 8). Newbury Park, CA: Sage.

Freedman, Jonathan L., & Fraser, Scott (1966). Compliance without pressure: The foot-in-the-door technique. *Journal of Personality and Social Psychology, 4*, 195–202.

Freeman, Ellen; Rickels, Karl; Sondheimer, S. J.; & Polansky, M. (1990). Ineffectiveness of progesterone suppository treatment for premenstrual syndrome. *Journal of the American Medical Association, 264,* 349–353.

French, Christopher C.; Fowler, Mandy; McCarthy, Katy; & Peers, Debbie (1991, Winter). Belief in astrology: A test of the Barnum effect. *Skeptical Inquirer, 15,* 166–172.

Freud, Anna (1946). *The ego and the mechanisms of defence.* New York: International Universities Press.

Freud, Sigmund (1905a). Fragment of an analysis of a case of hysteria. In J. Strachey (ed. and trans.), *Standard edition of the complete psychological works of Sigmund Freud,* Vol. VII. London: The Hogarth Press and the Institute of Psycho-Analysis (1964 edition).

Freud, Sigmund (1905b). Three essays on the theory of sexuality. In *Standard edition,* Vol. VII.

Freud, Sigmund (1910/1957). Leonardo da Vinci: A study in psychosexuality. In *Standard edition,* Vol. XI.

Freud, Sigmund (1920/1960). *A general introduction to psychoanalysis.* (Joan Riviere, trans.) New York: Washington Square Press.

Freud, Sigmund (1920/1963). The psychogenesis of a case of homosexuality in a woman. In S. Freud, *Sexuality and the psychology of love.* New York: Collier Books.

Freud, Sigmund (1923/1962). *The ego and the id.* (Joan Riviere, trans.) New York: Norton.

Freud, Sigmund (1924a). The dissolution of the Oedipus complex. In *Standard edition,* Vol. XIX.

Freud, Sigmund (1924b). Some psychical consequences of the anatomical distinction between the sexes. In *Standard edition,* Vol. XIX.

Friedman, Howard S. (1991). *The self-healing personality.* New York: Henry Holt.

Friedman, Howard S., & Booth-Kewley, Stephanie (1987). The disease-prone personality: A meta-analytic view of the construct. *American Psychologist, 42,* 539–555.

Friedman, Howard S., & Miller-Herringer, Terry (1991). Nonverbal display of emotion in public and private: Self-monitoring, personality, and expressive cues. *Journal of Personality and Social Psychology, 61,* 766–775.

Friedman, Meyer, & Rosenman, Ray (1974). *Type A behavior and your heart.* New York: Knopf.

Friedman, Stanley, & Fisher, Charles (1967). On the presence of a rhythmic, diurnal, oral instinctual drive cycle in man: A preliminary report. *Journal of the American Psychoanalytic Association, 15,* 317–343.

Friedman, William; Robinson, Amy; & Friedman, Britt (1987). Sex differences in moral judgments? A test of Gilligan's theory. *Psychology of Women Quarterly, 11,* 37–46.

Frijda, Nico H. (1988). The laws of emotion. *American Psychologist, 43,* 349–358.

Frodi, Ann; Macaulay, Jacqueline; & Thome, Pauline (1977). Are women always less aggressive than men? A review of the literature. *Psychological Bulletin, 84,* 634–660.

Fromholt, Pia, & Larsen, Steen F. (1991). Autobiographical memory in normal aging and primary degenerative dementia (dementia of Alzheimer type). *Journal of Gerontology, 46,* P85–P91.

Frye, Richard E.; Schwartz, B. S.; & Doty, Richard L. (1990). Dose-related effects of cigarette smoking on olfactory function. *Journal of the American Medical Association, 263,* 1233–1236.

Funder, David C. (1991). Global traits: A neo-Allportian approach to personality. *Psychological Science, 2,* 31–38.

Funder, David C., & Colvin, C. Randall (1991). Explorations in behavioral consistency: Properties of persons, situations, and behaviors. *Journal of Personality and Social Psychology, 60,* 773–794.

Fussell, Paul (1989). *Wartime.* New York: Oxford University Press.

Gaertner, Samuel L.; Mann, Jeffrey A.; Dovidio, John F.; Murrell, Audrey J.; & Pomare, Marina (1990). How does cooperation reduce intergroup bias? *Journal of Personality and Social Psychology, 59,* 692–704.

Gagnon, John (1987). Science and the politics of pathology. *Journal of Sex Research, 23,* 120–123.

Gagnon, John, & Simon, William (1973). *Sexual conduct: The social sources of human sexuality.* Chicago: Aldine.

Galanter, Eugene (1962). Contemporary psychophysics. In R. Brown, E. Galanter, H. Hess, and G. Mandler (eds.), *New directions in psychology.* New York: Holt, Rinehart and Winston.

Galanter, Marc (1989). *Cults: Faith, healing, and coercion.* New York: Oxford University Press.

Galanter, Marc (1990). Cults and zealous self-help movements: A psychiatric perspective. *American Journal of Psychiatry, 147,* 543–551.

Gale, Anthony (ed.) (1988). *The polygraph test: Lies, truth, and science.* London: Sage.

Gallagher, Winifred (1988, March). Marijuana: Is there new reason to worry? *American Health, 7,* 92ff.

Galotti, Kathleen (1989). Approaches to studying formal and everyday reasoning. *Psychological Bulletin, 105,* 331–351.

Ganaway, George K. (1991). Alternative hypotheses regarding satanic ritual abuse memories. Paper presented at the annual meeting of the American Psychological Association, San Francisco.

Garcia, John, & Koelling, Robert A. (1966). Relation of cue to consequence in avoidance learning. *Psychonomic Science, 4,* 23–124.

Gardner, Howard (1983). *Frames of mind: The theory of multiple intelligences.* New York: Basic Books.

Gardner, R. Allen, & Gardner, Beatrice T. (1969). Teaching sign language to a chimpanzee. *Science, 165,* 664–672.

Garfield, Patricia (1974). *Creative dreaming.* New York: Ballantine.

Garfinkel, Renee (1986). Methodological and scientific problems in DSM-III-R diagnoses. Paper presented at the annual meeting of the American Psychological Association, Washington.

Garmezy, Norman (1985). Stress-resistant children: The search for protective factors. In J. E. Stevenson (ed.), *Recent research in developmental psychopathology.* New York: Pergamon.

Garmezy, Norman (1991). Resilience and vulnerability to adverse developmental outcomes associated with poverty. *American Behavioral Scientist, 34,* 416–430.

Garnets, Linda; Hancock, Kristin A.; Cochran, Susan D.; Goodchilds, Jacqueline; & Peplau, Letitia A. (1991). Issues in psychotherapy with lesbians and gay men: A survey of psychologists. *American Psychologist, 46,* 964–972.

Gartner, Alan, & Riessman, Frank (eds.) (1984). *The self-help revolution.* Vol. X, Community Psychology Series. New York: Human Sciences Press.

Gaston, Louise; Marmar, Charles R.; Thompson, Larry W.; & Gallagher, Dolores (1988). Relation of patient pretreatment characteristics to the therapeutic alliance in diverse psychotherapies. *Journal of Consulting & Clinical Psychology, 56,* 483–489.

Gaston, Louise; Marmar, Charles R.; Gallagher, Dolores; & Thompson, Larry W. (1989). Impact of confirming patient expectations of change processes in behavioral, cognitive, and brief dynamic psychotherapy. *Psychotherapy, 26,* 296–302.

Gazzaniga, Michael S. (1967). The split brain in man. *Scientific American, 217*(2), 24–29.

Gazzaniga, Michael S. (1983). Right hemisphere language following brain bisection: A 20-year perspective. *American Psychologist, 38,* 525–537.

Gazzaniga, Michael S. (1985). *The social brain: Discovering the networks of the mind.* New York: Basic Books.

Gazzaniga, Michael S. (1988). *Mind matters.* Boston: Houghton Mifflin.

Gedo, John (1979). A psychoanalyst reports at mid-career. *American Journal of Psychiatry, 136,* 646–649.

Geen, Russell G. (1978). Some effects of observing violence upon the behavior of the observer. In B. A. Maher (ed.), *Progress in experimental personality research.* New York: Academic Press.

Geiselman, R. Edward (1988). Improving eyewitness memory through mental reinstatement of context. In G. M. Davies and D. M. Thomson (eds.), *Memory in context: Context in memory.* New York: Wiley.

Geldard, F. A. (1962). *Fundamentals of psychology.* New York: Wiley.

Gelernter, Joel; O'Malley, S.; Risch, N.; Kranzler, H. R.; et al. (1991, October 2). No association between an allele at the D2 dopamine receptor gene (DRD2) and alcoholism. *Journal of the American Medical Association, 266,* 1801–1807.

Geller, E. Scott, & Lehman, Galen R. (1988). Drinking-driving intervention strategies: A person-situation-behavior framework. In M. D. Laurence, J. R. Snortum, & F. E. Zimring (eds.), *The social control of drinking and driving.* Chicago: University of Chicago Press.

Gelles, Richard J., & Straus, Murray A. (1988). *Intimate violence: The causes and consequences of abuse in the American family.* New York: Simon & Schuster/Touchstone.

Gelman, Rochel (1983). Recent trends in cognitive development. In C. J. Scheirer & A. M. Rogers (eds.), *The G. Stanley Hall Lecture Series,* Vol. 3. Washington, DC: American Psychological Association.

Gerbner, George (1988). Telling stories in the information age. In B. D. Ruben (ed.), *Information and behavior,* Vol. 2. New Brunswick, NJ: Transaction Books.

Gergen, Kenneth J. (1973). Social psychology as history. *Journal of Personality and Social Psychology, 26,* 309–320.

Gergen, Kenneth J. (1985). The social constructionist movement in modern psychology. *American Psychologist, 40,* 266–274.

Gergen, Kenneth; Gergen, Mary; & Barton, William (1973, October). Deviance in the dark. *Psychology Today, 7*(5), 129–130.

Gergen, Mary M. (1992). Life stories: Pieces of a dream. In G. Rosenwald & R. Ochberg (eds.), *Storied lives.* New Haven, CT: Yale University Press.

Gevins, Alan S.; Bressler, Steven L.; Cutillo, Brian A.; Illes, Judy; et al. (1990). Effects of prolonged mental work on functional brain topography. *Electroencephalography and Clinical Neurophysiology, 76,* 339–350.

Gewirtz, Jacob L. (1991). An analysis of infant social learning. Paper presented at the annual meeting of the American Psychological Association, San Francisco.

Gewirtz, Jacob L., & Peláez-Nogueras, Martha (1991a). The attachment metaphor and the conditioning of infant separation protests. In J. L. Gewirtz & W. M. Kurtines (eds.), *Intersections with attachment.* Hillsdale, NJ: Erlbaum.

Gewirtz, Jacob L., & Peláez-Nogueras, Martha (1991b). Infants' separation difficulties and distress due to misplaced maternal contingencies. In T. Field, P. McCabe, & N. Schneiderman, *Stress and coping in infancy and childhood.* Hillsdale, NJ: Erlbaum.

Gibbons, Frederick X.; McGovern, Paul G.; & Lando, Harry A. (1991). Relapse and risk perception among members of a smoking cessation clinic. *Health Psychology, 10,* 42–45.

Gibson, Eleanor, & Walk, Richard (1960). The "visual cliff." *Scientific American, 202,* 80–92.

Gilbert, Daniel T.; Pelham, Brett W.; & Krull, Douglas S. (1988). On cognitive busyness: When person perceivers meet persons perceived. *Journal of Personality and Social Psychology, 54,* 733–739.

Gilligan, Carol (1982). *In a different voice.* Cambridge, MA: Harvard University Press.

Gilligan, Carol, & Wiggins, Grant (1987). The origins of morality in early childhood relationships. In J. Kagan & S. Lamb (eds.), *The emergence of morality in young children.* Chicago: University of Chicago Press.

Gilligan, Carol; Lyons, Nona P.; & Hanmer, Trudy J. (eds.) (1990). *Making connections: The relational worlds of adolescent girls at Emma Willard School.* Cambridge, MA: Harvard University Press.

Gillin, J. Christian; Sitaram, N.; Janowsky, D.; et al. (1985). Cholinergic mechanisms in REM sleep. In A. Wauquier, J. M. Gaillard, J. M. Monti, & M. Radulovacki (eds.), *Sleep: Neurotransmitters and neuromodulators.* New York: Raven Press.

Glanzer, Murray, & Cunitz, Anita R. (1966). Two storage mechanisms in free recall. *Journal of Verbal Learning and Verbal Behavior, 5,* 351–360.

Glass, Leonard L.; Kirsch, Michael A.; & Parris, Frederick N. (1977). Psychiatric disturbances associated with Erhard Seminars Training, I: A report of cases. *American Journal of Psychiatry, 134,* 245–247.

Glazer, Myron P., & Glazer, Penina M. (1990). *The whistleblowers: Exposing corruption in government and industry.* New York: Basic Books.

Glucksberg, Sam, & Weisberg, Robert W. (1966). Verbal behavior and problem solving: Some effects of labelling in a functional fixedness problem. *Journal of Experimental Psychology, 71,* 659–664.

Goddard, H. H. (1917). Mental tests and the immigrant. *The Journal of Delinquency, 2,* 243–277.

Gold, Daniel, & Wegner, Daniel M. (1991). Fanning old flames: Arousing romantic obsession through thought suppression. Paper presented at the annual meeting of the American Psychological Association, San Francisco.

Gold, Paul E. (1987). Sweet memories. *American Scientist, 75,* 151–155.

Goldberg, Lewis R. (1990). An alternative "description of personality": The big-five factor structure. *Journal of Personality and Social Psychology, 59,* 1216–1229.

Golding, Jacqueline M. (1988). Gender differences in depressive symptoms. *Psychology of Women Quarterly, 12,* 61–74.

Goldstein, Avram (1980). Thrills in response to music and other stimuli. *Physiological Psychology, 8,* 126–129.

Goldstein, Jeffrey H. (1987). Therapeutic effects of laughter. In W. F. Fry, Jr., & W. A. Salameh (eds.), *Handbook of humor and psychotherapy.* Sarasota, FL: Professional Resource Exchange.

Goldstein, Michael J. (1987). Psychosocial issues. *Schizophrenia Bulletin, 13*(1), 157–171.

Goldstein, Richard (1981). On deceptive rejoinders about deceptive research: A reply to Baron. *IRB: A Review of Human Subjects Research, 3*(8), 5–6.

Goleman, Daniel (1982, March). Staying up: The rebellion against sleep's gentle tyranny. *Psychology Today, 16*(3), 24–25, 27–28, 31–32, 35.

Golub, Sharon (1988). A developmental perspective. In L. H. Gise, N. G. Kase, & R. L. Berkowitz (eds.), *The premenstrual syndrome.* New York: Churchill Livingstone.

Goodenough, Donald R.; Shapiro, Arthur; Holden, Melvin; & Steinschriber, Leonard (1959). A comparison of dreamers and nondreamers: Eye movements, electroencephalograms and the recall of dreams. *Journal of Abnormal and Social Psychology, 59,* 295–302.

Goodman, Gail, & Helgeson, Vicki S. (1988). Children as witnesses: What do they remember? In L. Walker (ed.), *Handbook on sexual abuse of children.* New York: Springer.

Gore, Susan, & Mangione, Thomas W. (1983). Social roles, sex roles and psychological distress. *Journal of Health and Social Behavior, 24,* 300–312.

Goren, C. C.; Sarty, J.; & Wu, P. Y. (1975). Visual following and pattern discrimination of face-like stimuli by newborn infants. *Pediatrics, 56,* 544–549.

Gorn, Gerald J. (1982). The effects of music in advertising on choice behavior: A classical conditioning approach. *Journal of Marketing, 46,* 94–101.

Gotlib, Ian H., & Hooley, J. M. (1988). Depression and marital functioning. In S. Duck (ed.), *Handbook of personal relationships: Theory, research and interventions.* Chichester, England: Wiley.

Gottesman, Irving I. (1991). *Schizophrenia genesis: The origins of madness.* New York: Freeman.

Gottesman, Irving; McGuffin, Peter; & Farmer, Anne E. (1987). Clinical genetics as clues to the "real" genetics of schizophrenia. *Schizophrenia Bulletin, 13*(1), 23–47.

Gottman, John M., & Katz, Lynn F. (1989). Effects of marital discord on young children's peer interaction and health. *Developmental Psychology, 25,* 373–381.

Gottman, John M., & Krokoff, Lowell J. (1989). Marital interaction and satisfaction: A longitudinal view. *Journal of Consulting & Clinical Psychology, 57,* 47–52.

Gottman, John M., & Levenson, Robert W. (1986). Assessing the role of emotion in marriage. *Behavioral Assessment, 8,* 31–48.

Gould, Stephen Jay (1981). *The mismeasure of man.* New York: Norton.

Gould, Stephen Jay (1985, June). The median isn't the message. *Discover, 6*(6), 40–42.

Graf, Peter (1990). Life-span changes in implicit and explicit memory. *Bulletin of the Psychonomic Society, 28,* 353–358.

Graf, Peter, & Schacter, Daniel A. (1985). Implicit and explicit memory for new associations in normal and amnesic subjects. *Journal of Experimental Psychology: Learning, Memory, & Cognition, 11,* 501–518.

Graham, Jill W. (1986). Principled organizational dissent: A theoretical essay. *Research in Organizational Behavior, 8,* 1–52.

Greene, Robert L. (1986). Sources of recency effects in free recall. *Psychological Bulletin, 99,* 221–228.

Greenfield, Patricia (1966). On culture and conservation. In J. S. Bruner, R. R. Olver, & P. M. Greenfield et al. (eds.), *Studies in cognitive growth.* New York: Wiley.

Greenfield, Patricia (1976). Cross-cultural research and Piagetian theory: Paradox and progress. In K. F. Riegel & J. A. Meacham (eds.), *The developing individual in a changing world, Vol. 1: Historical and cultural issues.* The Hague: Mouton.

Greenfield, Patricia, & Beagles-Roos, Jessica (1988). Radio vs. television: Their cognitive impact on children of different socioeconomic and ethnic groups. *Journal of Communication, 38,* 71–92.

Greenough, W. T. (1984). Structural correlates of information storage in the mammalian brain: A review and hypothesis. *Trends in Neurosciences, 7,* 229–233.

Greenough, William T. (1991). The animal rights assertions: A researcher's perspective. *Psychological Science Agenda* (American Psychological Association), *4*(3), 10–12.

Greenough, William T., & Anderson, Brenda J. (1991). Cerebellar synaptic plasticity: Relation to learning vs. neural activity. *Annals of the New York Academy of Sciences, 627,* 231–247.

Greenough, William T., & Black, James E. (1992). Induction of brain structure by experience: Substrates for cognitive development. In M. Gunnar & C. A. Nelson (eds.), *Behavioral developmental neuroscience, Vol. 24, Minnesota Symposia on Child Psychology.* Hillsdale, NJ: Erlbaum.

Greenwald, Anthony G. (1980). The totalitarian ego: Fabrication and revision of personal history. *American Psychologist, 35,* 603–618.

Greenwald, Anthony G. (1992). New Look 3: Unconscious cognition reclaimed. *American Psychologist, 47,* 766–779.

Greenwald, Anthony G.; Spangenberg, Eric R.; Pratkanis, Anthony R.; & Eskenazi, Jay (1991). Double-blind tests of subliminal self-help audiotapes. *Psychological Science, 2,* 119–122.

Gregory, Richard L. (1963). Distortion of visual space as inappropriate constancy scaling. *Nature, 199,* 678–679.

Gregory, Richard L., & Wallace, Jean G. (1963). Recovery from early blindness: A case study. *Monograph Supplement 2, Quarterly Journal of Experimental Psychology, No. 3.* (Reprinted in R. L. Gregory, *Concepts and mechanisms of perception.* New York: Scribners.)

Greven, Philip (1991). *Spare the child: The religious roots of punishment and the psychological impact of physical abuse.* New York: Alfred A. Knopf.

Grier, Kenneth (1982). A study of job stress in police officers and high school teachers. Unpublished doctoral dissertation, University of South Florida, Tampa.

Griffith, James E., & Villavicencio, Sandra (1985). Relationships among acculturation, sociodemographic characteristics and social supports in Mexican American adults. *Hispanic Journal of Behavioral Sciences, 7,* 75–92.

Groebel, Jo, & Hinde, Robert (eds.) (1989). The Seville statement on violence. *Aggression and war: Their biological and social bases.* Cambridge, England: Cambridge University Press.

Guba, Egon G. (1990). The alternative paradigm dialog. In E. G. Guba (ed.), *The paradigm dialog.* Newbury Park, CA: Sage.

Guilford, J. P. (1950). Creativity. *American Psychologist, 5,* 444–454.

Guilford, J. P. (1967). *The nature of human intelligence.* New York: McGraw-Hill.

Guilford, J. P. (1982). Cognitive psychology's ambiguities: Some suggested remedies. *Psychological Review, 89,* 48–59.

Guilford, J. P. (1988). Some changes in the structure-of-intellect model. *Educational and Psychological Measurement, 48,* 1–4.

Gurin, Joel (1984, May). What's your natural weight? *American Health, 3,* 43–47.

Guttentag, Marcia, & Secord, Paul (1983). *Too many women?* Beverly Hills, CA: Sage.

Haber, Ralph N. (1970, May). How we remember what we see. *Scientific American, 222,* 104–112.

Haber, Ralph N. (1974). Eidetic images. In R. Held (ed.), *Image, object, and illusion.* San Francisco: Freeman.

Haier, Richard J.; Siegel, Benjamin V., Jr.; Nuechterlein, Keith H.; Hazlett, Erin; et al. (1988). Cortical glucose metabolic rate correlates of abstract reasoning and attention studied with positron emission tomography. *Intelligence, 12,* 199–217.

Haier, Richard J.; Siegel, Benjamin V., Jr.; MacLachlan, Andrew; Soderling, Eric; et al. (1992). Regional glucose metabolic changes after learning a complex visuospatial/motor task: a positron emission tomographic study. *Brain Research, 570,* 134–143.

Haley, Jay (1984). *Ordeal therapy.* San Francisco: Jossey-Bass.

Hall, Edward T. (1976). *Beyond culture.* New York: Anchor Press/Doubleday.

Hall, Edward T. (1983). *The dance of life.* New York: Anchor Press/Doubleday.

Hall, Edward T., & Hall, Mildred (1990). *Understanding cultural differences.* Yarmouth, ME: Intercultural Press, Inc.

Hall, G. Stanley (1899). A study of anger. *American Journal of Psychology, 10,* 516–591.

Hall, Jay, & Watson, W. H. (1970). The effects of normative intervention on group decision-making performance. *Human Relations, 23,* 299–317.

Hall, Judith A. (1987). On explaining gender differences: The case of nonverbal communication. In P. Shaver & C. Hendrick (eds.), *Sex and gender: Review of Personality and Social Psychology* (Vol. 7). Beverly Hills, CA: Sage.

Hallin, Daniel (1991). *Sound bite news: Television coverage of elections, 1968–1988.* Occasional paper, Woodrow Wilson International Center for Scholars, Media Studies Project, Washington, DC.

Halpern, Faye (1991, September/October). As tall as three kneeling apples! *Utne Reader,* 119–120.

Hamilton, David L., & Sherman, Steven J. (1989). Illusory correlations: Implications for stereotype theory and research. In D. Bar-Tal, C. F. Graumann, A. W. Kruglanski, & W. Stroebe (eds.), *Stereotypes and prejudice: Changing conceptions.* New York: Springer-Verlag.

Hamilton, Mykol C. (1991). Masculine bias in the attribution of personhood. *Psychology of Women Quarterly, 15,* 393–402.

Haney, Craig; Banks, Curtis; & Zimbardo, Philip (1973). Interpersonal dynamics in a simulated prison. *International Journal of Criminology and Penology, 1,* 69–97.

Harding, Courtenay; Zubin, Joseph; & Strauss, John (1987). Chronicity in schizophrenia: Fact, partial fact, or artifact? *Hospital and Community Psychiatry, 38,* 477–486.

Harding, Courtenay; Brooks, George W.; Ashikaga, Takamaru; Strauss, John S.; & Breier, Alan (1987). The Vermont longitudinal study of persons with severe mental illness. I. Methodology, study sample, and overall current status. II. Long-term outcome for DSM-III schizophrenia. *American Journal of Psychiatry, 144,* 718–735.

Hare, Robert D. (1965). Acquisition and generalization of a conditioned-fear response in psychopathic and nonpsychopathic criminals. *Journal of Psychology, 59,* 367–370.

Hare, Robert D. (1986). Twenty years of experience with the Cleckley psychopath. In W. H. Reid, D. Doff, J. I. Walker, & J. W. Bonner (eds.), *Unmasking the psychopath: Antisocial personality and related syndromes.* New York: Norton.

Hare, Robert D.; McPherson, Leslie M.; & Forth, Adelle E. (1988). Male psychopaths and their criminal careers. *Journal of Consulting & Clinical Psychology, 56,* 710–714.

Hare-Mustin, Rachel T. (1983). Educating for counseling and psychotherapy with women. Paper presented at the annual meeting of the American Psychological Association, Anaheim, CA.

Hare-Mustin, Rachel T., & Maracek, Jeanne (1990). Gender and the meaning of difference: Postmodernism and psychology. In R. Hare-Mustin & J. Maracek (eds.), *Psychology and the construction of gender.* New Haven: Yale University Press.

Haritos-Fatouros, Mika (1988). The official torturer: A learning model for obedience to the authority of violence. *Journal of Applied Social Psychology, 18,* 1107–1120.

Harkins, Stephen G., & Petty, Richard E. (1983). Social context effects in persuasion. In P. Paulus (ed.), *Basic group processes.* New York: Springer-Verlag.

Harkins, Stephen G., & Szymanski, Kate (1989). Social loafing and group evaluation. *Journal of Personality and Social Psychology, 56,* 934–941.

Harlow, Harry F. (1958). The nature of love. *American Psychologist, 13,* 673–685.

Harlow, Harry F., & Harlow, Margaret K. (1966). Learning to love. *American Scientist, 54,* 244–272.

Harlow, Harry F.; Harlow, Margaret K.; & Meyer, D. R. (1950). Learning motivated by a manipulation drive. *Journal of Experimental Psychology, 40,* 228–234.

Harrington, David; Block, Jeanne; & Block, Jack (1987). Testing aspects of Carl Rogers's theory of creative environments: Child-rearing antecedents of creative potential in young adolescents. *Journal of Personality and Social Psychology, 52,* 851–856.

Harris, Ben (1979). Whatever happened to little Albert? *American Psychologist, 34,* 151–160.

Harris, Marvin (1985). *Good to eat: Riddles of food and culture.* New York: Simon & Schuster.

Harris, Paul L. (1984). Infant cognition. In P. Mussen (ed.), Handbook of child psychology (4th ed.). M. M. Haith & J. J. Campos (eds.), Vol. II: *Infancy and developmental psychobiology.* New York: Wiley.

Hart, John Jr.; Berndt, Rita S.; & Caramazza, Alfonso (1985, August 1). Category-specific naming deficit following cerebral infarction. *Nature, 316,* 339–340.

Hartmann, Ernest (1991). *Boundaries in the mind: A new psychology of personality differences.* New York: Basic Books.

Hasher, Lynn, & Zacks, Rose T. (1984). Automatic processing of fundamental information: The case of frequency of occurrence. *American Psychologist, 39,* 1372–1388.

Hastorf, Albert H., & Cantril, Hadley (1954). They saw a game: A case study. *Journal of Abnormal and Social Psychology, 49,* 129–134.

Hatfield, Agnes B., & Lefley, Harriet P. (eds.) (1987). *Families of the mentally ill: Coping and adaptation.* New York: Guilford Press.

Hatfield, Elaine (1988). Passionate and companionate love. In R. J. Sternberg & M. L. Barnes (eds.), *The psychology of love.* New Haven, CT: Yale University Press.

Hatfield, Elaine, & Sprecher, Susan (1986). Measuring passionate love in intimate relationships. *Journal of Adolescence, 9,* 383–410.

Hatfield, Elaine; Cacioppo, John T.; & Rapson, Richard (1992). The logic of emotion: Emotional contagion. In M. S. Clark (ed.), *Review of Personality and Social Psychology,* Vol. 12. Newbury Park, CA: Sage.

Hawkins, Scott A., & Hastie, Reid (1990). Hindsight: Biased judgments of past events after the outcomes are known. *Psychological Bulletin, 107,* 311–327.

Haynes, Suzanne, & Feinleib, Manning (1980). Women, work, and coronary heart disease: Prospective findings from the Framingham heart study. *American Journal of Public Health, 70,* 133–141.

Hazan, Cindy, & Shaver, Phillip (1987). Romantic love con-ceptualized as an attachment process. *Journal of Personality and Social Psychology, 52,* 511–524.

Hearnshaw, Leslie S. (1979). *Cyril Burt, psychologist.* Ithaca, NY: Cornell University Press.

Heath, Shirley B. (1983). *Ways with words: Language, life, and work in communities and classrooms.* New York: Cambridge University Press.

Heath, Shirley B. (1989). Oral and literate traditions among Black Americans living in poverty. *American Psychologist, 44,* 367–373.

Heath, Shirley B. (1990). The children of Trackton's children: Spoken and written language in social change. In J. W. Stigler, R. A. Shweder, & G. Herdt (eds.), *Cultural psychology: The Chicago symposia on human development.* Cambridge, England: Cambridge University Press.

Heatherton, Todd F., & Polivy, Janet (1991). Development and validation of a scale for measuring state self-esteem. *Journal of Personality and Social Psychology, 60,* 895–910.

Heider, Eleanor Rosch (1972). Universals in color naming and memory. *Journal of Experimental Psychology, 93,* 1020.

Heider, Eleanor Rosch, & Olivier, Donald C. (1972). The structure of the color space in naming and memory for two languages. *Cognitive Psychology, 3,* 337–354.

Heider, Fritz (1946). Attitudes and cognitive organization. *Journal of Psychology, 21,* 107–112.

Heider, Fritz (1958). *The psychology of interpersonal relations.* New York: Wiley.

Helgeson, Vicki S., & Sharpsteen, Don J. (1987). Perceptions of danger in achievement and affiliation situations: An extension of the Pollak and Gilligan versus Benton et al. debate. *Journal of Personality and Social Psychology, 53,* 727–733.

Helson, Ravenna, & Wink, Paul (1987). Two conceptions of maturity examined in the findings of a longitudinal study. *Journal of Personality and Social Psychology, 53,* 531–541.

Helson, Ravenna; Mitchell, Valory; & Moane, Geraldine (1984). Personality and patterns of adherence and nonadherence to the social clock. *Journal of Personality and Social Psychology, 46,* 1079–1097.

Hendrick, Clyde, & Hendrick, Susan S. (1986). A theory and method of love. *Journal of Personality and Social Psychology, 50,* 392–402.

Hendrick, Susan S., & Hendrick, Clyde (1987). Multidimensionality of sexual attitudes. *The Journal of Sex Research, 23,* 502–526.

Hendrick, Susan S.; Hendrick, Clyde; & Adler, Nancy L. (1988). Romantic relationships: Love, satisfaction, and staying together. *Journal of Personality and Social Psychology, 54,* 980–988.

Hendrix, William H.; Steel, Robert P.; Leap, Terry L.; & Summers, Timothy P. (1991). Development of a stress-related health promotion model: Antecedents and organizational effectiveness outcomes. Special Issue: Handbook on job stress. *Journal of Social Behavior & Personality, 6,* 141–162.

Henley, Nancy M. (1989). Molehill or mountain? What we know and don't know about sex bias in language. In M. Crawford & M. Gentry (eds.), *Gender and thought: Psychological perspectives.* New York: Springer-Verlag.

Hepworth, Joseph T., & West, Stephen G. (1988). Lynchings and the economy: A time-series reanalysis of Hovland and Sears (1940). *Journal of Personality and Social Psychology, 55,* 239–247.

Herdt, Gilbert (1984). *Ritualized homosexuality in Melanesia.* Berkeley: University of California Press.

Herman, Barbara H. (1991). Effects of opioid receptor antagonists in the treatment of autism and self-injurious behavior. In J. J. Ratey (ed.), *Mental retardation: Developing pharmacotherapies. Progress in psychiatry #32.* Washington, DC: American Psychiatric Press.

Herman, John H. (1992). Transmutative and reproductive properties of dreams: Evidence for cortical modulation of brainstem generators. In J. Antrobus & M. Bertini (eds.), *The neuropsychology of dreaming.* Hillsdale, NJ: Erlbaum.

Herman, Judith L. (1992). *Trauma and recovery.* New York: Basic Books.

Herman, Louis M. (1987). Receptive competencies of language-trained animals. In J. S. Rosenblatt, C. Beer, M. C. Busnel, & P. J. B. Slater (eds.), *Advances in the study of behavior*, Vol. 17. Petaluma, CA: Academic Press.

Herman, Louis M.; Morrel-Samuels, Palmer; & Pack, Adam A. (1990). Bottlenosed dolphin and human recognition of veridical and degraded video displays of an artificial gestural language. *Journal of Experimental Psychology: General, 119,* 215–230.

Herman, Louis M.; Richards, D. G.; & Wolz, J. P. (1984). Comprehension of sentences by bottlenosed dolphins. *Cognition, 16,* 129–219.

Heron, Woodburn (1957). The pathology of boredom. *Scientific American, 196*(1), 52–56.

Herrnstein, R. J. (1982, August). IQ testing and the media. *Atlantic Monthly, 250,* 68–74.

Hess, Eckhard H. (1959). Imprinting. *Science, 130,* 133–144.

Hetherington, E. Mavis (1989). Coping with family transitions: Winners, losers, and survivors. *Child Development, 60,* 1–14.

Hilgard, Ernest R. (1977). *Divided consciousness: Multiple controls in human thought and action.* New York: Wiley-Interscience.

Hilgard, Ernest R., & Hilgard, Josephine R. (1975). *Hypnosis in the relief of pain.* Los Altos, CA: William Kaufmann.

Hilgard, Josephine R. (1979). *Personality and hypnosis: A study of imaginative involvement* (2nd ed.). Chicago: University of Chicago Press.

Hill, Harlan F.; Chapman, C. Richard; Kornell, Judy A.; Sullivan, Keith M.; et al. (1990). Self-administration of morphine in bone marrow transplant patients reduces drug requirement. *Pain, 40,* 121–129.

Hill, Winfred F. (1985). *Learning: A survey of psychological interpretations* (4th ed.). New York: Harper & Row.

Hinrichsen, Gregory A.; Revenson, Tracey A.; & Shinn, Marybeth (1985). Does self-help help? An empirical investigation of scoliosis peer support groups. *Journal of Social Issues, 41*(1), 65–88.

Hirsch, Barton (1981). Social networks and the coping process: Creating personal communities. In B. H. Gottlieb (ed.), *Social networks and social support.* Beverly Hills, CA: Sage.

Hirsch, Helmut V. B., & Spinelli, D. N. (1970). Visual experience modifies distribution of horizontally and vertically oriented receptive fields in cats. *Science, 168,* 869–871.

Hirschel, J. David; Hutchinson, Ira W., III; Dean, Charles; et al. (1990). *Charlotte spouse assault replication project: Final report.* Washington, DC: National Institute of Justice.

Hirschman, Albert O. (1970). *Exit, voice, and loyalty: Responses to decline in firms, organizations, and states.* Cambridge, MA: Harvard University Press.

Hirst, William; Neisser, Ulric; & Spelke, Elizabeth (1978, January). Divided attention. *Human Nature, 1,* 54–61.

Hite, Shere (1987). *Women and love: A cultural revolution in progress.* New York: Knopf.

Hobfoll, Stevan E., & London, Perry (1986). The relationship of self-concept and social support to emotional distress among women during war. *Journal of Social and Clinical Psychology, 12,* 87–100.

Hobfoll, Stevan E., & Stephens, Mary Ann P. (1990). Social support during extreme stress: Consequences and intervention. In I. G. Sarason, B. R. Sarason, & G. R. Pierce (eds.), *Social support: An interactional view—Issues in social support research.* New York: Wiley.

Hobson, J. Allan (1988). *The dreaming brain.* New York: Basic Books.

Hobson, J. Allan (1990). Activation, input source, and modulation: A neurocognitive model of the state of the brain-mind. In R. R. Bootzin, J. F. Kihlstrom, & D. L. Schacter (eds.), *Sleep and cognition.* Washington, DC: American Psychological Association.

Hobson, J. Allan, & McCarley, Robert W. (1977). The brain as a dream state generator: An activation-synthesis hypothesis of the dream process. *American Journal of Psychiatry, 134,* 1335–1348.

Hobson, Robert F. (1985). *Forms of feeling: The heart of psychotherapy.* London: Tavistock.

Hochschild, Arlie (1983). *The managed heart.* Berkeley: University of California Press.

Hockett, Charles F. (1960). The origins of speech. *Scientific American, 203,* 89–96.

Hoffman, Martin L. (1977). Empathy, its development and prosocial implications. In C. B. Keasey (ed.), *Nebraska Symposium on Motivation*, Vol. 25. Lincoln: University of Nebraska Press.

Hoffman, Martin L. (1987). The contribution of empathy to justice and moral judgment. In N. Eisenberg & J. Strayer (eds.), *Empathy and its development.* New York: Cambridge University Press.

Hoffman, Martin L. (1989). Empathy, social cognition, and moral action. In W. Kurtines & J. Gewirtz (eds.), *Moral behavior and development: Advances in theory, research, and application*: Vol. 1. Hillsdale, NJ: Erlbaum.

Hoffman, Martin L., & Saltzstein, Herbert (1967). Parent discipline and the child's moral development. *Journal of Personality and Social Psychology, 5,* 45–57.

Hoffman, Richard G., & Nelson, Kathleen S. (1990). Memory and cognitive change in normal aging. Paper presented at the annual meeting of the American Psychological Association, Boston.

Hogg, Michael A., & Abrams, Dominic (1988). *Social identifications: A social psychology of intergroup relations and group processes.* New York: Routledge.

Holden, Constance (1980). Identical twins reared apart. *Science, 207,* 1323–1325.

Holland, D. C., & Eisenhart, M. A. (1991). *Educated in romance: Women, achievement, and college culture.* Chicago: University of Chicago Press.

Holman, B. L., & Tumeh, S. S. (1990). Single-photon emission computed tomography (SPECT). Applications and potential. *Journal of the American Medical Association, 263,* 561–564.

Holmes, David (1984). Meditation and somatic arousal reduction: A review of the experimental evidence. *American Psychologist, 39,* 1–10.

Holmes, David (1991). *Abnormal psychology.* New York: HarperCollins.

Holmes, Thomas, & Rahe, Richard (1967). The social readjustment rating scale. *Journal of Psychosomatic Research, 11,* 213–218.

Holstein, Kenneth A. (1983). Identity development: A comparison of adults and adolescents. Paper presented at the annual meeting of the American Psychological Association, Anaheim, CA.

Holtzworth-Munroe, Amy, & Jacobson, Neil S. (1985). Causal attributions of married couples: When do they search for causes? What do they conclude when they do? *Journal of Personality and Social Psychology, 48,* 1398–1412.

Holzman, Philip S., & Matthysse, Steven (1990). The genetics of schizophrenia: A review. *Psychological Science, 1,* 279–286.

Horn, John L., & Donaldson, Gary (1980). Cognitive development in adulthood. In O. G. Brim, Jr. & J. Kagan (eds.), *Constancy and change in human development.* Cambridge, MA: Harvard University Press.

Horne, J. A. (1988). Sleep loss and "divergent" thinking ability. *Sleep, 11,* 528–536.

Horney, Karen (1937). *The neurotic personality of our time.* New York: Norton.

Horney, Karen (1945). *Our inner conflicts.* New York: Norton.

Horney, Karen (1950). *Neurosis and human growth.* New York: Norton.

Horney, Karen (1967). *Feminine psychology.* New York: Norton.

Horowitz, Mardi J. (1988). *Introduction to psychodynamics: A new synthesis.* New York: Basic Books.

House, James S.; Landis, Karl R.; & Umberson, Debra (1988, July 19). Social relationships and health. *Science, 241,* 540–545.

House, James S.; Robbins, Cynthia; & Metzner, Helen (1982). The association of social relationships and activities with mortality: Prospective evidence from the Tecumseh Community Health Study. *American Journal of Epidemiology, 116,* 123–140.

Houston, John P. (1981). *Fundamentals of learning and memory* (2nd ed.). New York: Academic Press.

Hovland, Carl I., & Sears, Robert R. (1940). Minor studies of aggression: Correlation of lynchings with economic indices. *Journal of Psychology, 9,* 301–310.

Howard, George S. (1991). Culture tales: A narrative approach to thinking, cross-cultural psychology, and psychotherapy. *American Psychologist, 46,* 187–197.

Howard, Kenneth; Kopta, S. Mark; Krause, Merton S.; & Orlinsky, David (1986). The dose-effect relationship in psychotherapy. *American Psychologist, 41,* 159–164.

Howell, William C., & Dipboye, Robert L. (1982). *Essentials of industrial and organizational psychology.* Homewood, IL: Dorsey Press.

Hrdy, Sarah B. (1981). *The woman that never evolved.* Cambridge: Harvard University Press.

Hrdy, Sarah B. (1988). Empathy, polyandry, and the myth of the coy female. In R. Bleier (ed.), *Feminist approaches to science.* New York: Pergamon.

Hsu, Francis (1981). *Americans and Chinese: Passage to difference.* Honolulu: University of Hawaii Press.

Hubbard, Ruth (1990). *The politics of women's biology.* New Brunswick, NJ: Rutgers University Press.

Hubel, D. H., & Wiesel, T. N. (1962). Receptive fields, binocular interaction and functional architecture in the cat's visual cortex. *Journal of Physiology* (London), *160,* 106–154.

Hubel, D. H., & Wiesel, T. N. (1968). Receptive fields and functional architecture of monkey striate cortex. *Journal of Physiology* (London), *195,* 215–243.

Huesmann, L. Rowell; Eron, Leonard; Lefkowitz, Monroe M.; & Walder, Leopold (1984). The stability of aggression over time and generations. *Developmental Psychology, 20,* 1120–1134.

Hughes, J. M. (1989). *Reshaping the psychoanalytic domain: The work of Melanie Klein, W.R.D. Fairbairn, & D.W. Winnicott.* Berkeley: University of California Press.

Huizinga, Johan (1950). *Homo ludens: A study of the play element in culture.* Boston: Beacon.

Hull, Clark (1943). *Principles of behavior.* New York: Appleton-Century-Crofts.

Hunt, Earl, & Agnoli, Franca (1991). The Whorfian hypothesis: A cognitive psychology perspective. *Psychological Review, 98,* 377–389.

Hunt, Morton M. (1959/1967). *The natural history of love.* New York: Minerva Press.

Hupka, Ralph (1981). Cultural determinants of jealousy. *Alternative Lifestyles, 4,* 310–356.

Hurvich, Leo M., & Jameson, Dorothea (1974). Opponent processes as a model of neural organization. *American Psychologist, 29,* 88–102.

Huston, Ted; Ruggiero, Mary; Conner, Ross; & Geis, Gilbert (1981). Bystander intervention into crime: A study based on naturally-occurring episodes. *Social Psychology Quarterly, 44,* 14–23.

Hyde, Janet S. (1981). How large are cognitive gender differences? A meta-analysis using ω^2 and d. *American Psychologist, 36,* 892–901.

Hyde, Janet S. (1984a). Children's understanding of sexist language. *Developmental Psychology, 20,* 697–706.

Hyde, Janet S. (1984b). How large are gender differences in aggression? A developmental meta-analysis. *Developmental Psychology, 20,* 722–736.

Hyde, Janet S. (1988). Sex, gender, and meta-analysis. Invited address to the Society for the Scientific Study of Sex, San Francisco.

Hyde, Janet S., & Linn, Marcia C. (1988). Gender differences in verbal ability: A meta-analysis. *Psychological Bulletin, 104,* 53–69.

Hyde, Janet S.; Fennema, Elizabeth; & Lamon, Susan J. (1990). Gender differences in mathematics performance: A meta-analysis. *Psychological Bulletin, 107,* 139–155.

Hyman, Irwin A. (1988). Eliminating corporal punishment in schools: Moving from advocacy research to policy implementation.

Paper presented at the annual meeting of the American Psychological Association, Atlanta.

Iga, Mamoru (1986). *The thorn in the chrysanthemum: Suicide and economic success in modern Japan.* Berkeley: University of California Press.

Infant Health and Development Program (1990). Enhancing the outcomes of low-birth-weight, premature infants: A multisite, randomized trial. *Journal of the American Medical Association, 263,* 3035–3042.

Inglehart, Ronald, & Hildebrandt, Kai (1990). Cultural change and changing worldviews. Paper presented at the annual meeting of the American Psychological Association, Boston.

Inglis, James, & Lawson, J. S. (1981). Sex differences in the effects of unilateral brain damage on intelligence. *Science, 212,* 693–695.

Insko, Chester A.; Smith, Richard; Alicke, Mark; Wade, Joel; & Taylor, Sylvester (1985). Conformity and group size: The concern with being right and the concern with being liked. *Personality and Social Psychology Bulletin, 11,* 41–50.

Irons, Edward D., & Moore, Gilbert W. (1985). *Black managers: The case of the banking industry.* New York: Praeger/Greenwood.

Isen, Alice M.; Daubman, Kimberly A.; & Nowicki, Gary P. (1987). Positive affect facilitates creative problem solving. *Journal of Personality and Social Psychology, 52,* 1122–1131.

Izard, Carroll E. (1971). *The face of emotion.* New York: Appleton-Century-Crofts.

Izard, Carroll E. (1990). Facial expressions and the regulation of emotions. *Journal of Personality and Social Psychology, 58,* 487–498.

Jacklin, Carol N. (1989). Female and male: Issues of gender. *American Psychologist, 44,* 127–133.

Jacklin, Carol N.; DiPietro, Janet A.; & Maccoby, Eleanor E. (1984). Sex-typing behavior and sex-typing pressure in child/parent interaction. *Archives of Sexual Behavior, 13,* 413–425.

Jacobson, Gerald (1983). *The multiple crises of marital separation and divorce.* New York: Grune & Stratton.

Jacobvitz, Robin N. S. (1990). Defining and measuring TV addiction. Paper presented at the annual meeting of the American Psychological Association, Boston.

James, William (1884). What is an emotion? *Mind, 9,* 188–205. (Reprinted in M. Arnold [ed.], *The nature of emotion.* Baltimore, MD: Penguin, 1968.)

James, William (1890/1950). *Principles of psychology* (Vol. 1). New York: Dover.

James, William (1902/1936). *The varieties of religious experience.* New York: Modern Library.

Janis, Irving L. (1982a). Counteracting the adverse effects of concurrence-seeking in policy-planning groups. In H. Brandstatter, J. H. Davis, & G. Stocker-Kreichgauer (eds.), *Group decision making.* New York: Academic Press.

Janis, Irving L. (1982b). *Groupthink: Psychological studies of policy decisions and fiascoes* (2nd ed.). Boston: Houghton Mifflin.

Janis, Irving L.; Kaye, Donald; & Kirschner, Paul (1965). Facilitating effects of "eating-while-reading" on responsiveness to persuasive communications. *Journal of Personality and Social Psychology, 1,* 181–186.

Janoff-Bulman, Ronnie (1989). The benefits of illusions, the threat of disillusionment, and the limitations of inaccuracy. Special Issue: Self-illusions: When are they adaptive? *Journal of Social & Clinical Psychology, 8,* 158–175.

Jaynes, Julian (1973a). Introduction: The study of the history of psychology. In M. Henle, J. Jaynes, & J. J. Sullivan (eds.), *Historical conceptions of psychology.* New York: Springer.

Jaynes, Julian (1973b). The problem of animate motion in the seventeenth century. In M. Henle, J. Jaynes, & J. J. Sullivan (eds.), *Historical conceptions of psychology.* New York: Springer.

Jellinek, E. M. (1960). *The disease concept of alcoholism.* New Haven, CT: Hillhouse Press.

Jenkins, John G., & Dallenbach, Karl M. (1924). Obliviscence during sleep and waking. *American Journal of Psychology, 35,* 605–612.

Jensen, Arthur R. (1969). How much can we boost IQ and scholastic achievement? *Harvard Educational Review, 39,* 1–123.

Jensen, Arthur R. (1981). *Straight talk about mental tests.* New York: Free Press.

Jessel, T. M., & Iversen, L. L. (1979). Opiate analgesics inhibit substance P release from rat trigeminal nucleus. *Nature, 268,* 549–551.

Jewett, M. E.; Kronauer, R. E.; & Czeisler, C. A. (1991, March 7). Light-induced suppression of endogenous circadian amplitude in humans. *Nature, 350,* 59–62.

John, E. Roy (1976, May). How the brain works—a new theory. *Psychology Today, 9*(12), 48–52.

John, E. R.; Tang, Y.; Brill, A. B.; Young, R.; & Ono, K. (1986). Double-labeled metabolic maps of memory. *Science, 233,* 1167–1175.

Johnson, Catherine (1988). *When to say goodbye to your therapist.* New York: Simon & Schuster.

Johnson, Robert, & Downing, Leslie (1979). Deindividuation and valence of cues: Effects of prosocial and antisocial behavior. *Journal of Personality and Social Psychology, 37,* 1532–1538.

Johnston, Lloyd D.; O'Malley, Patrick M.; & Bachman, Jerald G. (1991). Drug use among American high school seniors, college students and young adults, 1975–1990. Vol. I. DHHS Publication No. (ADM) 91–1813. Washington, DC: U. S. Department of Health and Human Services.

Jones, James M. (1991). Psychological models of race: What have they been and what should they be? In J. Goodchilds (ed.), *Psychological perspectives on human diversity in America.* Washington, DC: American Psychological Association.

Jones, Lyle V. (1984). White-black achievement differences: The narrowing gap. *American Psychologist, 39,* 1207–1213.

Jones, Mary Cover (1924). A laboratory study of fear: The case of Peter. *Pedagogical Seminary, 31,* 308–315.

Jones, Russell A. (1977). *Self-fulfilling prophecies.* Hillsdale, NJ: Erlbaum.

Jump, Teresa L., & Haas, Linda (1987). Fathers in transition: Dual-career fathers participating in child care. In M. S. Kimmel (ed.), *Changing men: New directions in research on men and masculinity.* Beverly Hills, CA: Sage.

Jung, Carl (1967). *Collected works.* Princeton, NJ: Princeton University Press.

Kagan, Jerome (1984). *The nature of the child.* New York: Basic Books.

Kagan, Jerome (1989). *Unstable ideas: Temperament, cognition, and self.* Cambridge, MA: Harvard University Press.

Kagan, Jerome, & Lamb, Sharon (eds.) (1987). *The emergence of morality in young children.* Chicago: University of Chicago Press.

Kagan, Jerome, & Moss, Howard (1962). *Birth to maturity.* New York: Wiley.

Kagan, Jerome, & Snidman, Nancy (1991). Infant predictors of inhibited and uninhibited profiles. *Psychological Science, 2,* 40–44.

Kagan, Jerome; Kearsley, Richard B.; & Zelazo, Philip R. (1978). *Infancy: Its place in human development.* Cambridge, MA: Harvard University Press.

Kagan, Jerome; Reznick, J. Steven; & Snidman, Nancy (1988). Biological bases of childhood shyness. *Science, 240,* 167–171.

Kagan, Jerome; Reznick, J. Steven; Snidman, Nancy; Gibbons, J.; & Johnson, Maureen O. (1988). Childhood derivatives of inhibition and lack of inhibition to the unfamiliar. *Child Development, 59,* 1580–1589.

Kahneman, Daniel, & Treisman, Anne (1984). Changing views of attention and automaticity. In R. Parasuraman, D. R. Davies, & J. Beatty (eds.), *Varieties of attention.* New York: Academic Press.

Kahneman, Daniel, & Tversky, Amos (1984). Choices, values, and frames. *American Psychologist, 39,* 341–350.

Kalmijn, Ad. J. (1982). Electric and magnetic field detection in elasmobranch fishes. *Science, 218,* 916–918.

Kamerman, Sheila B. (1991). Child care policies and programs: An international overview. In S. L. Hofferth & D. A. Phillips (eds.), *Child care policy research. Journal of Social Issues, 47*(2), 179–196.

Kamin, Leon J. (1974). *The science and politics of I.Q.* Potomac, MD: Erlbaum.

Kammen, M. (1979). Changing perceptions of the life cycle in American thought and culture. *Massachusetts Historical Society Proceedings, 91,* 35–66.

Kandel, Denise B. (1984). Marijuana users in young adulthood. *Archives of General Psychiatry, 41,* 200–209.

Kandel, Eric R. (1981). Visual system III: Physiology of the central visual pathways. In E. R. Kandel & J. H. Schwartz (eds.), *Principles of neural science.* New York: Elsevier-North Holland.

Kandel, Eric R., & Schwartz, James H. (1982). Molecular biology of learning: Modulation of transmitter release. *Science, 218,* 433–443.

Kane, John M. (1987). Treatment of schizophrenia. *Schizophrenia Bulletin, 13,* 133–156.

Kanin, Eugene J. (1985). Date rapists: Differential sexual socialization and relative deprivation. *Archives of Sexual Behavior, 14,* 219–231.

Kanter, Rosabeth (1977). *Men and women of the corporation.* New York: Basic Books.

Kantor, J. R. (1982). *Cultural psychology.* Chicago: Principia Press.

Kaplan, Abraham (1967). A philosophical discussion of normality. *Archives of General Psychiatry, 17,* 325–330.

Kaplan, Martin F., & Miller, Charles E. (1983). Group discussion and judgment. In P. Paulus (ed.), *Basic group processes.* New York: Springer-Verlag.

Karasek, Robert, & Theorell, Tores (1990). *Healthy work: Stress, productivity, and the reconstruction of working life.* New York: Basic Books.

Katz, Irwin, & Hass, R. Glen (1988). Racial ambivalence and American value conflict: Correlational and priming studies of dual cognitive structures. *Journal of Personality and Social Psychology, 55,* 893–905.

Katz, Joel, & Melzack, Ronald (1990). Pain "memories" in phantom limbs: Review and clinical observations. *Pain, 43,* 319–336.

Katz, Lori, & Epstein, Seymour (1991). Constructive thinking and coping with laboratory-induced stress. *Journal of Personality and Social Psychology, 61,* 789–800.

Katz, Stuart; Hebert, Elizabeth; & Lautenschlager, Gary (1991). Answering GRE and new SAT comprehension questions without passages. Paper presented at the annual meeting of the Eastern Psychological Association, New York.

Katz, Stuart; Lautenschlager, Gary J.; Blackburn, A. Boyd; & Harris, Felicia (1990). Answering reading comprehension items without passages on the SAT. *Psychological Science, 1,* 122–127.

Kaufman, Joan, & Zigler, Edward (1987). Do abused children become abusive parents? *American Journal of Orthopsychiatry, 57,* 186–192.

Kay, Paul (1975). Synchronic variability and diachronic changes in basic color terms. *Language in Society, 4,* 257–270.

Kaye, Kenneth (1977). Toward the origin of dialogue. In H. R. Schaffer (ed.), *Studies in mother-infant interaction.* New York: Academic Press.

Kaye, Lenard W., & Applegate, Jeffrey S. (1990). Men as elder caregivers: A response to changing families. *American Journal of Orthopsychiatry, 60,* 86–95.

Keane, M. M.; Gabrieli, J. D. E.; & Corkin, S. (1987). Multiple relations between fact-learning and priming in global amnesia. *Society for Neuroscience Abstracts, 13,* 1454.

Keefe, Francis J., & Gil, Karen M. (1988). Behavioral concepts in the analysis of chronic pain syndromes. *Journal of Consulting & Clinical Psychology, 54,* 776–783.

Keesey, Richard E. (1980). A set-point analysis of the regulation of body weight. In A. Stunkard (ed.), *Obesity.* Philadelphia: Saunders.

Keirstead, Susan A.; Rasminsky, Michael; Fukuda, Y.; et al. (1989). Electrophysiologic responses in hamster superior colliculus evoked by regenerating retinal axons. *Science, 246,* 255–257.

Kelly, Dennis D. (1981a). Disorders of sleep and consciousness. In E. Kandel & J. Schwartz (eds.), *Principles of neural science.* New York: Elsevier-North Holland.

Kelly, Dennis D. (1981b). Physiology of sleep and dreaming. In E. Kandel & J. Schwartz (eds.), *Principles of neural science.* New York: Elsevier-North Holland.

Kelman, Herbert C., & Hamilton, V. Lee (1988). *Crimes of obedience.* New Haven: Yale University Press.

Kelsoe, John R.; Ginns, Edward I.; Egeland, Janice A.; Gerhard, Daniela S.; et al. (1989). Re-evaluation of the linkage relationship between chromosome 11p loci and the gene for bipolar affective disorder in the Old Order Amish. *Nature, 342,* 238–243.

Kennedy, James; Giuffra, Luis; Moises, Hans; Cavalli-Sforza, L. L.; et al. (1988, November 10). Evidence against linkage of schizophrenia to markers on chromosome 5 in a northern Swedish pedigree. *Nature, 336*(6195), 167–169.

Kenny, David A. (1987). *Statistics for the social and behavioral sciences.* Boston: Little, Brown.

Kenny, Maureen W. (1989). The assessment of parental attachment among college seniors. Paper presented at the annual meeting of the American Psychological Association, New Orleans.

Kephart, William M. (1967). Some correlates of romantic love. *Journal of Marriage and the Family, 29,* 470–474.

Kerr, Michael E., & Bowen, Murray (1988). *Family evaluation: An approach based on Bowen theory.* New York: Norton.

Kesner, Raymond P.; Measom, Michael O.; Forsman, Shawn L.; & Holbrook, Terry H. (1984). Serial-position curves in rats: Order memory for episodic spatial events. *Animal Learning & Behavior, 12,* 378–382.

Kett, Joseph (1977). *Rites of passage: Adolescence in America, 1790 to the present.* New York: Basic Books.

Kety, Seymour S. (1974). From rationalization to reason. *American Journal of Psychiatry, 131,* 957–963.

Kiecolt-Glaser, Janice, & Glaser, Ronald (1989). Behavioral influences on immune function: Evidence for the interplay between stress and health. In T. Field, P. McCabe, & N. Schneiderman (eds.), *Stress and coping,* Vol. 2. Hillsdale, NJ: Erlbaum.

Kiecolt-Glaser, Janice; Garner, Warren; Speicher, Carl; Penn, Gerald; Holliday, Jane; & Glaser, Ronald (1985a). Psychosocial modifiers of immunocompetence in medical students. *Psychosomatic Medicine, 46,* 7–14.

Kiecolt-Glaser, Janice; Glaser, Ronald; Williger, D.; Stout, J. C.; et al. (1985b). Psychosocial enhancement of immunocompetence in a geriatric population. *Health Psychology, 4,* 25–41.

Kiecolt-Glaser, Janice; Fisher, L. D.; Ogrocki, P.; Stout, J. C.; et al. (1987a). Marital quality, marital disruption, and immune function. *Psychosomatic Medicine, 49,* 13–34.

Kiecolt-Glaser, Janice; Glaser, Ronald; Shuttleworth, Edwin; Dyer, Carol; et al. (1987b). Chronic stress and immunity in family caregivers of Alzheimer's disease victims. *Psychosomatic Medicine, 49,* 523–535.

Kiernan, Thomas (1974). *Shrinks, etc.: A consumer's guide to psychotherapies.* New York: Dial Press.

Kiesler, Charles A., & Simpkins, Celeste (1991). The de facto national system of psychiatric inpatient care. *American Psychologist, 46,* 579–584.

Kihlstrom, John F., & Harackiewicz, Judith M. (1982). The earliest recollection: A new survey. *Journal of Personality, 50,* 134–148.

Kihlstrom, John F.; Schacter, Daniel L.; Cork, Randall C.; Hurt, Catherine A.; and Behr, Steven E. (1990). Implicit and explicit memory following surgical anesthesia. *Psychological Science, 1,* 303–306.

Kimble, Gregory A. (1990). Mother Nature's bag of tricks is small. *Psychological Science, 1,* 36–41.

Kimura, Doreen, & Harshman, Richard (1984). Sex differences in brain organization. In G. J. de Vries, J. P. C. De Bruin,

H. B. M. Vylings, & M. A. Corner (eds.), *Sex differences in the brain: The relation between structure and function,* Vol. 61. New York: Elsevier.

King, Pamela (1989, October). The chemistry of doubt. *Psychology Today,* 58, 60.

Kinsbourne, Marcel (1982). Hemispheric specialization and the growth of human understanding. *American Psychologist, 37,* 411–420.

Kinsey, Alfred C.; Pomeroy, Wardell B.; & Martin, Clyde E. (1948). *Sexual behavior in the human male.* Philadelphia: Saunders.

Kinsey, Alfred C.; Pomeroy, Wardell B.; Martin, Clyde E.; & Gebhard, Paul H. (1953). *Sexual behavior in the human female.* Philadelphia: Saunders.

Kitchener, Karen S., & King, Patricia M. (1989). The reflective judgment model: Ten years of research. In M. L. Commons, C. Armon, L. Kohlberg, et al. (eds.), *Beyond formal operations III: Models and methods in the study of adolescent and adult thought.* New York: Praeger.

Klag, Michael J.; Whelton, Paul K.; Coresh, Josef; Grim, Clarence E.; & Kuller, Lewis H. (1991, February 6). The association of skin color with blood pressure in US blacks with low socioeconomic status. *Journal of the American Medical Association, 265,* 599–602.

Klaus, Marshall, & Kennell, John (1976). *Maternal-infant bonding.* St. Louis: Mosby.

Klein, Donald F. (1980). Psychosocial treatment of schizophrenia, or psychosocial help for people with schizophrenia? *Schizophrenia Bulletin, 6,* 122–130.

Klein, Raymond, & Armitage, Roseanne (1979). Rhythms in human performance: 1 1/2-hour oscillations in cognitive style. *Science, 204,* 1326–1328.

Kleinman, Arthur (1988). *Rethinking psychiatry: From cultural category to personal experience.* New York: Free Press.

Kleinmuntz, Benjamin, & Szucko, Julian J. (1984, March 29). A field study of the fallibility of polygraph lie detection. *Nature, 308,* 449–450.

Klerman, Gerald L.; Weissman, Myrna M.; Rounsaville, Bruce J.; & Chevron, Eve S. (1984). *Interpersonal psychotherapy of depression.* New York: Basic Books.

Knussmann, Rainer; Christiansen, Kerrin; & Couwenbergs, Catharina (1986). Relations between sex hormone levels and sexual behavior in men. *Archives of Sexual Behavior, 15,* 429–445.

Kobasa, Suzanne C., & Puccetti, Mark C. (1983). Personality and social resources in stress resistance. *Journal of Personality and Social Psychology, 45,* 839–850.

Koegel, Robert L.; Schreibman, Laura; O'Neill, Robert E.; & Burke, John C. (1983). The personality and family-interaction characteristics of parents of autistic children. *Journal of Consulting and Clinical Psychology, 51,* 683–692.

Kohlberg, Lawrence (1964). Development of moral character and moral ideology. In M. Hoffman & L. W. Hoffman (eds.), *Review of child development research.* New York: Russell Sage Foundation.

Kohlberg, Lawrence (1966). A cognitive-developmental analysis of children's sex-role concepts and attitudes. In E. E. Maccoby (ed.), *The development of sex differences.* Stanford, CA: Stanford University Press.

Kohlberg, Lawrence (1976). Moral stages and moralization: The cognitive-developmental approach. In T. Lickona (ed.), *Moral development and behavior.* New York: Holt, Rinehart and Winston.

Kohlberg, Lawrence (1984). *Essays on moral development, Vol. 2. The psychology of moral development: The nature and validity of moral stages.* San Francisco: Harper & Row.

Köhler, Wolfgang (1925). *The mentality of apes.* New York: Harcourt, Brace.

Köhler, Wolfgang (1959). Gestalt psychology today. Presidential address to the American Psychological Association, Cincinnati. [Reprinted in E. R. Hilgard (ed.), *American psychology in historical perspective: Addresses of the presidents of the American Psychological Association, 1892–1977.* Washington, DC: American Psychological Association, 1978.]

Kohn, Alfie (1986). *No contest: The case against competition.* Boston: Houghton Mifflin.

Kohn, Melvin, & Schooler, Carmi (1983). *Work and personality: An inquiry into the impact of social stratification.* Norwood, NJ: Ablex.

Kohn, Paul M.; Lafreniere, Kathryn; & Gurevich, Maria (1991). Hassles, health, and personality. *Journal of Personality and Social Psychology, 61,* 478–482.

Kohout, Jessica, & Wicherski, Marlene (1991). *1989 Doctorate Employment Survey.* Washington, DC: American Psychological Association (Office of Demographic, Employment and Educational Research).

Koocher, Gerald (1990). Self-help or hype? Paper presented at the annual meeting of the American Psychological Association, Boston.

Koss, Mary P.; Dinero, Thomas E.; Seibel, Cynthia A.; & Cox, Susan L. (1988). Stranger and acquaintance rape: Are there differences in the victim's experience? *Psychology of Women Quarterly, 12,* 1–24.

Kosslyn, Stephen M. (1980). *Image and mind.* Cambridge, MA: Harvard University Press.

Kosslyn, Stephen M. (1983). *Ghosts in the mind's machine: Creating and using images in the brain.* New York: Norton.

Kosslyn, Stephen M.; Seger, Carol; Pani, John R.; & Hillger, Lynn A. (1990). When is imagery used in everyday life? A diary study. *Journal of Mental Imagery, 14,* 131–152.

Krantz, David S., & Manuck, Stephen B. (1984). Acute psychophysiologic reactivity and risk of cardiovascular disease: A review and methodological critique. *Psychological Bulletin, 96,* 435–464.

Kripke, Daniel F. (1974). Ultradian rhythms in sleep and wakefulness. In E. D. Weitzman (ed.), *Advances in sleep research,* Vol. 1. Flushing, NY: Spectrum.

Kripke, Daniel F., & Sonnenschein, David (1978). A biologic rhythm in waking fantasy. In K. S. Pope & J. L. Singer (eds.), *The stream of consciousness: Scientific investigations into the flow of human experience.* New York: Plenum.

Krippner, Stanley, & Hillman, Deborah (1990). Social aspects of grassroots experiential dream groups. Paper presented at the annual meeting of the American Psychological Association, Boston.

Kristof, Nicholas D. (1991, August 18). Chinese relations. *New York Times Magazine, 140,* 8, 10.

Kubey, Robert, & Csikszentmihalyi, Mihaly (eds.) (1990). Television and the quality of life: How viewing shapes everyday experiences. Hillsdale, NJ: Erlbaum.

Kudoh, Tsutomu, & Matsumoto, David (1985). Cross-cultural examination of the semantic dimensions of body postures. *Journal of Personality and Social Psychology, 48,* 1440–1446.

Kuhn, Thomas (1981). Unanswered questions about science. In R. D. Tweney, M. E. Doherty, & C. R. Mynatt (eds.), *On scientific thinking.* New York: Columbia University Press.

Kulik, James A.; & Mahler, Heike I. (1989). Social support and recovery from surgery. *Health Psychology, 8,* 221–238.

Kunda, Ziva (1990). The case for motivated reasoning. *Psychological Bulletin, 108,* 480–498.

Kutchins, Herb, & Kirk, Stuart A. (1986, Winter). The reliability of DSM-III: A critical review. *Social Work Research & Abstracts, 22,* 3–12.

LaBarre, Weston (1947). The cultural bases of emotions and gestures. *Journal of Personality, 16,* 49–68.

LaBerge, Stephen (1986). *Lucid dreaming.* New York: Ballantine Books.

LaBerge, Stephen (1990). Lucid dreaming: Psychophysiological studies of consciousness during REM sleep. In R. R. Bootzin, J. F. Kihlstrom, & D. L. Schacter (eds.), *Sleep and cognition.* Washington, DC: American Psychological Association.

Laboratory of Comparative Human Cognition (1984). Culture and cognitive development. In P. Mussen (ed.), *Handbook of child psychology* (4th ed.). W. Kessen (ed.), Vol. I: *History, theory, and methods.* New York: Wiley.

Labott, Susan, & Martin, Randall (1987). The stress-moderating effects of weeping and humor. *Journal of Human Stress, 13,* 159–164.

Labows, John N., Jr. (1980, November). What the nose knows: Investigating the significance of human odors. *The Sciences,* 10- 13.

Lader, Malcolm (1989). Benzodiazepine dependence. Special Issue: Psychiatry and the addictions. *International Review of Psychiatry, 1,* 149–156.

Lader, Malcolm, & Morton, Sally (1991). Benzodiazepine problems. *British Journal of Addiction, 86,* 823–828.

Laird, James D. (1974). Self-attribution of emotion: The effects of expressive behavior on the quality of emotional experience. *Journal of Personality and Social Psychology, 29,* 475–486.

Laird, James D. (1984). The real role of facial response in the experience of emotion: A reply to Tourangeau and Ellsworth, and others. *Journal of Personality and Social Psychology, 47,* 909–917.

Lakoff, George (1987). *Women, fire, and dangerous things: What categories reveal about the mind.* Chicago: University of Chicago Press.

Lakoff, Robin T. (1990). *Talking power.* New York: Basic Books.

Lamb, Michael E., & Campos, Joseph (1983). *Development in infancy: An introduction.* New York: Random House.

Lambert, Michael J. (1983). Introduction to assessment of psychotherapy outcome: Historical perspective and current issues. In M. J. Lambert, E. R. Christensen, & S. S. DeJulio (eds.), *The assessment of psychotherapy outcome.* New York: Wiley-Interscience.

Lambert, Michael J.; Christensen, Edwin R.; & Dejulio, Steven S. (eds.) (1983). *The assessment of psychotherapy outcome.* New York: Wiley-Interscience.

Lancaster, Jane (1975). *Primate behavior and the emergence of human culture.* New York: Holt, Rinehart and Winston.

Land, Edwin H. (1959). Experiments in color vision. *Scientific American, 200*(5), 84–94, 96, 99.

Landrine, Hope (1988). Revising the framework of abnormal psychology. In P. Bronstein & K. Quina (eds.), *Teaching a psychology of people.* Washington, DC: American Psychological Association.

Landrine, Hope (1989). The politics of personality. *Psychology of Women Quarterly, 13,* 325–340.

Lang, Peter J. (1988). Fear, anxiety, and panic: Context, cognition, and visceral arousal. In S. Rachman & J. D. Maser (eds.), *Panic: Psychological perspectives.* Hillsdale, NJ: Erlbaum.

Langer, Ellen J. (1983). *The psychology of control.* Beverly Hills, CA: Sage.

Langer, Ellen J. (1989). *Mindfulness.* Cambridge, MA: Addison-Wesley.

Langer, Ellen J., & Piper, Alison I. (1988). Television from a mindful/mindless perspective. In S. Oskamp (ed.), *Television as a social issue (Applied Social Psychology Annual,* Vol. 8). Newbury Park, CA: Sage.

Langer, Ellen J.; Blank, Arthur; & Chanowitz, Benzion (1978). The mindlessness of ostensibly thoughtful action: The role of placebic information in interpersonal interaction. *Journal of Personality and Social Psychology, 36,* 635–642.

Langer, Ellen J.; Rodin, Judith; Beck, Pearl; Weinman, Cynthia; & Spitzer, Lynn (1979). Environmental determinants of memory improvement in late adulthood. *Journal of Personality and Social Psychology, 37,* 2003–2013.

Larmore, Kim; Ludwig, Arnold M.; & Cain, Rolene L. (1977). Multiple personality: An objective case study. *British Journal of Psychiatry, 131,* 35–40.

Larsen, Randy J.; Diener, Ed; & Cropanzano, Russell (1987). Cognitive operations associated with individual differences in affect intensity. *Journal of Personality and Social Psychology, 53,* 767–774.

Lash, Rick (1988). Problem solving and the development of expertise in management. Paper presented at the annual meeting of the American Psychological Association, Atlanta.

Lashley, Karl S. (1950). In search of the engram. In *Symposium of the Society for Experimental Biology,* Vol. 4. New York: Cambridge University Press.

Latané, Bibb, & Darley, John (1976). Help in a crisis: Bystander response to an emergency. In J. Thibaut, J. Spence, & R. Carlson (eds.), *Contemporary topics in social psychology.* Morristown, NJ: General Learning Press.

Latané, Bibb; Williams, Kipling; & Harkins, Stephen (1979). Many hands make light the work: The causes and consequences of social loafing. *Journal of Personality and Social Psychology, 37,* 822–832.

Laudenslager, Mark L. (1988). The psychobiology of loss: Lessons from humans and nonhuman primates. *Journal of Social Issues, 44*(3), 19–36.

Lave, J.; Murtaugh, M.; & de la Roche, O. (1984). The dialectic of arithmetic in grocery shopping. In B. Rogoff & J. Lave (eds.), *Everyday cognition: Its development in social context.* Cambridge, MA: Harvard University Press.

Lavie, Peretz (1976). Ultradian rhythms in the perception of two apparent motions. *Chronobiologia, 3,* 214–218.

Lazarus, Arnold A. (1989). *The practice of multi-modal therapy.* Baltimore, MD: Johns Hopkins University Press.

Lazarus, Arnold A. (1990). If this be research.... *American Psychologist, 58,* 670–671.

Lazarus, Richard S. (1991). Cognition and motivation in emotion. *American Psychologist, 46,* 352–367.

Lazarus, Richard S. & Folkman, Susan (1984). *Stress, appraisal, and coping.* New York: Springer.

LeBoyer, Marion; Bouvard, Manuel; & Dugas, M. (1988). Effects of naltrexone on infantile autism. *Lancet, 1,* 715.

LeDoux, Joseph E. (1989). Cognitive-emotional interactions in the brain. *Cognition and Emotion, 3,* 267–289.

Lee, Jerry W., & Hart, Richard (1985). Techniques used by individuals who quit smoking on their own. Paper presented at the annual meeting of the American Psychological Association, Los Angeles.

Lee, John Alan (1973). *The colours of love.* Ontario, Canada: New Press.

Lee, John Alan (1988). Love-styles. In R. J. Sternberg & M. L. Barnes (eds.), *The psychology of love.* New Haven: Yale University Press.

Lefcourt, Herbert M., & Martin, Rod A. (1986). *Humor and life stress: Antidote to adversity.* New York: Springer-Verlag.

Lehman, Adam K., & Rodin, Judith (1989). Styles of self-nurturance and disordered eating. *Journal of Consulting & Clinical Psychology, 57,* 117–122.

Lehman, Darrin R.; Lempert, Richard O.; & Nisbett, Richard E. (1988). The effects of graduate training on reasoning. *American Psychologist, 43,* 431–442.

Lenhardt, Martin L.; Skellett, Ruth; Wang, Peter; & Clarke, Alex M. (1991). Human ultrasonic speech perception. *Science, 253,* 82–85.

Lent, James R. (1968, June). Mimosa cottage: Experiment in hope. *Psychology Today, 2*(1), 51–58.

Lepper, Mark R.; Greene, David; & Nisbett, Richard E. (1973). Undermining children's intrinsic interest with extrinsic rewards. *Journal of Personality and Social Psychology, 28,* 129–137.

Lerner, Melvin J. (1980). *The belief in a just world: A fundamental delusion.* New York: Plenum.

Levenson, Michael R. (1990). Risk taking and personality. *Journal of Personality and Social Psychology, 58,* 1073–1080.

Levenson, Robert W.; Ekman, Paul; & Friesen, Wallace V. (1990). Voluntary facial action generates emotion-specific autonomic nervous system activity. *Psychophysiology, 27,* 363–384.

Leventhal, Howard (1970). Findings and theory in the study of fear communications. In L. Berkowitz (ed.), *Advances in experimental social psychology,* Vol. 5. New York: Academic Press.

Levine, Daniel S. (1990). *Introduction to cognitive and neural modeling.* Hillsdale, NJ: Erlbaum.

Levine, Elaine S., & Padilla, Amado M. (1979). *Crossing cultures in therapy: Pluralistic counseling for the Hispanic.* Monterey, CA: Brooks/Cole.

LeVine, Robert A. (1988). Environments in child development: An anthropological perspective. In W. Damon (ed.), *Child development today and tomorrow.* San Francisco: Jossey-Bass.

Levine, Stephen B., & Agle, David (1978). The effectiveness of sex therapy for chronic secondary psychological impotence. *Journal of Sex & Marital Therapy, 4,* 235–258.

Levinthal, Charles F. (1988). *Messengers of paradise: Opiates and the brain.* New York: Doubleday/Anchor Press.

Levitan, Alexander A., & Ronan, William J. (1988). Problems in the treatment of obesity and eating disorders. *Medical Hypnoanalysis Journal, 3,* 131–136.

Levy, Jerre (1983). Language, cognition, and the right hemisphere: A response to Gazzaniga. *American Psychologist, 38,* 538–541.

Levy, Jerre (1985, May). Right brain, left brain: Fact and fiction. *Psychology Today, 19*(5), 38–39, 42–44.

Levy, Jerre; Trevarthen, Colwyn; & Sperry, Roger W. (1972). Perception of bilateral chimeric figures following hemispheric deconnection. *Brain, 95,* 61–78.

Levy, Robert I. (1984). The emotions in comparative perspective. In K. R. Scherer & P. Ekman (eds.), *Approaches to emotion.* Hillsdale, NJ: Erlbaum.

Levy, Sandra M.; Lee, Jerry; Bagley, Caroline; & Lippman, Marc (1988). Survival hazards analysis in first recurrent breast cancer patients: Seven-year follow-up. *Psychosomatic Medicine, 50,* 520–528.

Lewin, Kurt (1948). *Resolving social conflicts.* New York: Harper.

Lewin, Miriam (1985). Unwanted intercourse: The difficulty of saying no. *Psychology of Women Quarterly, 9,* 184–192.

Lewinsohn, Peter (1990). Depression across the age span. Paper presented at the annual meeting of the Western Psychological Association, Los Angeles.

Lewinsohn, Peter; Steinmetz, Julia; Larson, Douglass; & Franklin, Judith (1981). Depression-related cognitions: Antecedent or consequence? *Journal of Abnormal Psychology, 90,* 213–219.

Lewis, Dorothy O. (ed.) (1981). *Vulnerabilities to delinquency.* New York: Spectrum Medical and Scientific Books.

Lewis, Michael, & Brooks-Gunn, Jeanne (1979). *Social cognition and the acquisition of self.* New York: Plenum.

Lewis, Michael; Sullivan, Margaret W.; Stanger, Catherine; & Weiss, Maya (1989). Self-development and self-conscious emotions. *Child Development, 60,* 146–156.

Lewontin, Richard C. (1970). Race and intelligence. *Bulletin of the Atomic Scientists, 26*(3), 2–8.

Lewontin, Richard C. (1982). *Human diversity.* New York: Scientific American Library.

Lewontin, Richard C.; Rose, Steven; & Kamin, Leon J. (1984). *Not in our genes: Biology, ideology, and human nature.* New York: Pantheon.

Lewy, Alfred J.; Sacks, Robert L.; Miller, L. Steven; & Hoban, Tana M. (1987). Antidepressant and circadian phase-shifting effects of light. *Science, 235,* 352–354.

Libet, Benjamin (1985). Unconscious cerebral initiative and the role of conscious will in voluntary action. *Behavioral and Brain Sciences, 8,* 529–566.

Lichstein, Kenneth L., & Fanning, John (1990). Cognitive anxiety in insomnia: An analogue test. *Stress Medicine, 6,* 47–51.

Lichtenstein, Sarah; Slovic, Paul; Fischhoff, Baruch; Layman, Mark; & Combs, Barbara (1978). Judged frequency of lethal events. *Journal of Experimental Psychology: Human Learning and Memory, 4,* 551–578.

Lieberman, David A. (1979). Behaviorism and the mind: A (limited) call for a return to introspection. *American Psychologist, 34,* 319–333.

Lifton, Robert J. (1986). *The Nazi doctors: Medical killing and the psychology of genocide.* New York: Basic Books.

Lightfoot, Lynn O. (1980). Behavioral tolerance to low doses of alcohol in social drinkers. Unpublished doctoral dissertation, University of Waterloo, Waterloo, Ontario.

Lin, Keh-Ming; Poland, Russell E.; & Lesser, Ira M. (1986). Ethnicity and psychopharmacology. *Culture, Medicine, & Psychiatry, 10,* 151–165.

Lin, Keh-Ming; Poland, Russell E.; Nuccio, Inocencia; Matsuda, Kazuko; et al. (1989). A longitudinal assessment of haloperidol doses and serum concentrations in Asian and Caucasian schizophrenic patients. *American Journal of Psychiatry, 146,* 1307–1311.

Lindvall, O.; Brundin, P.; Widner, H.; et al. (1990). Grafts of fetal dopamine neurons survive and improve motor function in Parkinson's disease. *Science, 247,* 574–577.

Linn, Marcia C., & Petersen, Anne C. (1985). A meta-analysis of gender differences in spatial ability: Implications for mathematics and science achievement. In J. S. Hyde & M. C. Linn (eds.), *The psychology of gender: Advances through meta-analysis.* Baltimore, MD: Johns Hopkins University Press.

Linnane, Anthony W.; Baumer, A.; Maxwell, R. J.; Preston, H.; Zhang, C. F.; & Marzuki, S. (1990). Mitochondrial gene mutation: The ageing process and degenerative diseases. *Biochemistry International, 22,* 1067–1076.

Linton, Marigold (1978). Real-world memory after six years: An in vivo study of very long-term memory. In M. M. Gruneberg, P. E. Morris, & R. N. Sykes (eds.), *Practical aspects of memory.* London: Academic Press.

Linz, Daniel; Donnerstein, Edward; & Penrod, Steven (1988). The effects of long-term exposure to violent and sexually degrading depictions of women. *Journal of Personality and Social Psychology, 55,* 758–767.

Lipscomb, David (1972). The increase in prevalence of high frequency hearing impairment among college students. *Audiology, 11,* 231–237.

Lissner, L.; Odell, P. M.; D'Agostino, R. B.; Stokes, J., III; et al. (1991, June 27). Variability of body weight and health outcomes in the Framingham population. *New England Journal of Medicine, 324* (26), 1839–1844.

Locke, Edwin A., & Latham, Gary P. (1990). Work motivation and satisfaction: Light at the end of the tunnel. *Psychological Science, 1,* 240–246.

Locke, Edwin A., & Latham, Gary P. (1991). The fallacies of common sense "truths": A reply to Lamal. *Psychological Science, 2,* 131–132.

Locke, Edwin A.; Shaw, Karyll; Saari, Lise; & Latham, Gary (1981). Goal-setting and task performance: 1969–1980. *Psychological Bulletin, 90,* 125–152.

Loehlin, John C. (1988). Partitioning environmental and genetic contributions to behavioral development. Invited address at the annual meeting of the American Psychological Association, Atlanta.

Loewen, E. Ruth; Shaw, Raymond J.; & Craik, Fergus I. (1990). Age differences in components of metamemory. *Experimental Aging Research, 16*(1–2), 43–48.

Loftus, Elizabeth F. (1980). *Memory.* Reading, MA: Addison-Wesley.

Loftus, Elizabeth F., & Palmer, John C. (1974). Reconstruction of automobile destruction: An example of the interaction between language and memory. *Journal of Verbal Learning and Verbal Behavior, 13,* 585–589.

Loftus, Elizabeth F., & Zanni, Guido (1975). Eyewitness testimony: The influence of the wording of a question. *Bulletin of the Psychonomic Society, 5,* 86–88.

Loftus, Elizabeth F.; Miller, David G.; & Burns, Helen J. (1978). Semantic integration of verbal information into a visual memory. *Journal of Experimental Psychology: Human Learning and Memory, 4,* 19–31.

Loo, Chalsa M. (1991). An integrative-sequential treatment model for post-traumatic stress disorder: A case study of the Japanese American internment and redress. Paper presented at the annual meeting of the American Psychological Association, San Francisco.

Lopata, Helena Z. (1988). Support systems of American urban widowhood. *Journal of Social Issues, 44*(3), 113–128.

López, Steven R. (1989). Patient variable biases in clinical judgment: Conceptual overview and methodological considerations. *Psychological Bulletin, 106,* 184–203.

Lorenz, Konrad (1937). Imprinting. *The Auk, 54,* 245–273.

Louis, Arthur M. (1978, April). Should you buy biorhythms? *Psychology Today, 11*(11), 93–96.

Lovaas, O. Ivar (1977). *The autistic child: Language development through behavior modification.* New York: Halsted Press.

Lovaas, O. Ivar; Schreibman, Laura; & Koegel, Robert L. (1974). A behavior modification approach to the treatment of autistic children. *Journal of Autism and Childhood Schizophrenia, 4,* 111–129.

Luce, Gay Gaer, & Segal, Julius (1966). *Current research on sleep and dreams.* Bethesda, MD: U.S. Department of Health, Education, and Welfare.

Luce, Terrence S. (1974, November). Blacks, whites and yellows, they all look alike to me. *Psychology Today, 8*(6), 105–106, 108.

Lugaresi, Elio; Medori, R.; Montagna, P.; et al. (1986, October 16). Fatal familial insomnia and dysautonomia with selective degeneration of thalamic nuclei. *New England Journal of Medicine, 315,* 997–1003.

Lunt, Peter K. (1991). The perceived causal structure of loneliness. *Journal of Personality and Social Psychology, 61,* 26–34.

Luria, A. R. (1968). *The mind of a mnemonist.* (L. Soltaroff, trans.) New York: Basic Books.

Luria, A. R. (1980). *Higher cortical functions in man* (2nd rev. ed.). New York: Basic Books.

Lutz, Catherine (1988). *Unnatural emotions.* Chicago: University of Chicago Press.

Lykken, David T. (1981). *A tremor in the blood: Uses and abuses of the lie detector.* New York: McGraw-Hill.

Lynch, Gary (1986). *Synapses, circuits, and the beginnings of memory.* Cambridge, MA: MIT Press.

Lynch, Gary, & Baudry, M. (1984). The biochemistry of memory: A new and specific hypothesis. *Science, 224,* 1057–1063.

Lynn, R. (1982). IQ in Japan and the United States shows a growing disparity. *Nature, 297,* 222–223.

Lynn, Steven Jay; Rhue, Judith W.; & Weekes, John R. (1990). Hypnotic involuntariness: A social cognitive analysis. *Psychological Review, 97,* 69–184.

Lytton, Hugh, & Romney, David M. (1991). Parents' differential socialization of boys and girls: A meta-analysis. *Psychological Bulletin, 109,* 267–296.

Maccoby, Eleanor E. (1980). *Social development.* New York: Harcourt Brace Jovanovich.

Maccoby, Eleanor E. (1990). Gender and relationships: A developmental account. *American Psychologist, 45,* 513–520.

MacCoun, Robert J., & Kerr, Norbert L. (1988). Asymmetric influence in mock jury deliberation: Jurors' bias for leniency. *Journal of Personality and Social Psychology, 54,* 21–33.

MacDonald, N. E.; Wells, G. A.; Fisher, W. A.; Warren, W. K.; et al. (1990). High risk STD/HIV behavior among college students. *Journal of the American Medical Association, 263,* 3155–3159.

MacKavey, William R.; Malley, Janet E.; & Stewart, Abigail, J. (1991). Remembering autobiographically consequential experiences: Content analysis of psychologists' accounts of their lives. *Psychology and Aging, 6,* 50–59.

Mackenzie, Brian (1984). Explaining race differences in IQ: The logic, the methodology, and the evidence. *American Psychologist, 39,* 1214–1233.

MacKinnon, Donald W. (1962). The nature and nurture of creative talent. *American Psychologist, 17,* 484–495.

MacKinnon, Donald W. (1968). Selecting students with creative potential. In P. Heist (ed.), *The creative college student: An unmet challenge.* San Francisco: Jossey-Bass.

Madigan, Carol O., & Elwood, Ann (1984). *Brainstorms & thunderbolts.* New York: Macmillan.

Mahony, Michael J. (1991). *Human change processes: The scientific foundations of psychotherapy.* New York: Basic Books.

Malamuth, Neil, & Dean, Karol (1990). Attraction to sexual aggression. In A. Parrot & L. Bechhofer (eds.), *Acquaintance rape: the hidden crime.* Newark, NJ: Wiley.

Malatesta, Carol Z. (1990). The role of emotions in the development and organization of personality. In R. A. Thompson (ed.), *Socioemotional development. Nebraska Symposium on Motivation, 1988.* Lincoln: University of Nebraska Press.

Malgady, Robert G.; Rogler, Lloyd; & Costantino, Giuseppe (1987). Ethnocultural and linguistic bias in mental health evaluation of Hispanics. *American Psychologist, 42,* 228–234.

Malitz, Sidney, & Sackeim, Harold A. (eds.) (1986). *Electroconvulsive therapy: Clinical and basic research issues.* New York: New York Academy of Sciences.

Mancuso, James C., & Sarbin, Theodore (1984). Illusion and reality in the science of schizophrenia. *Contemporary Psychology, 29,* 992–993.

Manning, C. A.; Hall, J. L.; & Gold, P. E. (1990). Glucose effects on memory and other neuropsychological tests in elderly humans. *Psychological Science, 1,* 307–311.

Manuck, Stephen B.; Cohen, Sheldon; Rabin, Bruce S.; Muldoon, Matthew F.; & Bachen, Elizabeth A. (1991). Individual differences in cellular immune response to stress. *Psychological Science, 2,* 111–115.

Marcia, James E. (1976). Identity six years later: A follow-up study. *Journal of Youth and Adolescence, 5,* 145–160.

Marder, Stephen; Van Putten, T.; Mintz, J.; LeBell, M.; et al. (1987). Low- and conventional-dose maintenance therapy with fluphenazine decanoate. Two-year outcome. *Archives of General Psychiatry, 44,* 518–521.

Marks, Gary, & Miller, Norman (1987). Ten years of research on the false–consensus effect: An empirical and theoretical review. *Psychological Bulletin, 102,* 72–90.

Markus, Hazel R., & Kitayama, Shinobu (1991). Culture and the self: Implications for cognition, emotion, and motivation. *Psychological Review, 98,* 224–253.

Markus, Hazel, & Nurius, Paula (1986). Possible selves. *American Psychologist, 41,* 954–969.

Marlatt, G. Alan, & Rohsenow, Damaris J. (1980). Cognitive processes in alcohol use: Expectancy and the balanced placebo design. In N. K. Mello (ed.), *Advances in substance abuse,* Vol. 1. Greenwich, CT: JAI Press.

Marshall, Grant N. (1991). A multidimensional analysis of internal health locus of control beliefs: Separating the wheat from the chaff? *Journal of Personality and Social Psychology, 61,* 483–491.

Martinez, Ruben, & Dukes, Richard L. (1987). Race, gender and self-esteem among youth. *Hispanic Journal of Behavioral Sciences, 9,* 427–443.

Martyna, Wendy (1980). Beyond the "he/man" approach: The case for nonsexist language. *Signs, 5,* 482–493.

Maslach, Christina; Stapp, Joy; & Santee, Richard T. (1985). Individuation: Conceptual analysis and assessment. *Journal of Personality and Social Psychology, 49,* 729–738.

Maslow, Abraham H. (1954/1970). *Motivation and personality* (1st and 2nd eds.). New York: Harper & Row.

Maslow, Abraham H. (1962/1968). *Toward a psychology of being* (1st and 2nd eds.). Princeton, NJ: Van Nostrand.

Maslow, Abraham H. (1971). *The farther reaches of human nature.* New York: Viking.

Massey, Christine M., & Gelman, Rochel (1988). Preschooler's ability to decide whether a photographed unfamiliar object can move itself. *Developmental Psychology, 24,* 307–317.

Masson, Jeffrey (1984). *The assault on truth: Freud's suppression of the seduction theory.* New York: Farrar, Straus & Giroux.

Matarazzo, Joseph (1984). Behavioral immunogens and pathogens in health and illness. In B. L. Hammonds & C. J. Scheirer (eds.), *Psychology and health: The master lecture series,* Vol. 3. Washington, DC: The American Psychological Association.

Matson, Johnny L., & Ollendick, Thomas H. (1977). Issues in toilet training normal children. *Behavior Therapy, 8,* 549–553.

Matthews, Karen A.; Wing, Rena R.; Kuller, Lewis H.; Meilahn, Elaine N.; et al. (1990). Influences of natural menopause on psychological characteristics and symptoms of middle-aged healthy women. *Journal of Consulting and Clinical Psychology, 58,* 345–351.

Mawhinney, T. C. (1990). Decreasing intrinsic "motivation" with extrinsic rewards: Easier said than done. *Journal of Organizational Behavior Management, 11,* 175–191.

Mayer, John D., & Salovey, Peter (1993). The intelligence of emotional intelligence. *Intelligence, 17*(3), in press.

Mayer, John D.; Gayle, Michael; Meehan, Mary Ellen; & Haarman, Anna-Kristina (1990). Toward better specification of the mood-congruency effect in recall. *Journal of Experimental Social Psychology, 26,* 465–480.

Mayo, Clara, & Henley, Nancy (eds.) (1981). *Gender and nonverbal behavior.* New York: Springer-Verlag.

Mazur, Allen, & Lamb, Theodore A. (1980). Testosterone, status, and mood in human males. *Hormones and Behavior, 14,* 236–246.

McAdams, Dan P. (1988). *Power, intimacy, and the life story: Personological inquiries into identity.* New York: Guilford Press.

McCall, Robert B.; Appelbaum, Mark I.; & Hogarty, Pamela S. (1973). Developmental changes in mental performance. *Monographs of the Society for Research in Child Development, 38* (3, Serial No. 150).

McCann, I. Lisa, & Holmes, David S. (1984). Influence of aerobic exercise on depression. *Journal of Personality and Social Psychology, 46,* 1142–1147.

McCartney, Kathleen; Harris, Monica J.; & Bernieri, Frank (1990). Growing up and growing apart: A developmental meta-analysis of twin studies. *Psychological Bulletin, 107,* 226–237.

McCauley, Elizabeth, & Ehrhardt, Anke (1980). Female sexual response. In D. D. Youngs & A. Ehrhardt (eds.), *Psychosomatic obstetrics and gynecology.* New York: Appleton-Century-Crofts.

McClelland, David C. (1961). *The achieving society.* New York: Free Press.

McClelland, David C. (1975). *Power: The inner experience.* New York: Irvington.

McClelland, David C. (1985). How motives, skills, and values determine what people do. *American Psychologist, 40,* 812–825.

McClelland, David C. (1987). Characteristics of successful entrepreneurs. *Journal of Creative Behavior, 3,* 219–233.

McClelland, David C.; Koestner, Richard; & Weinberger, Joel (1989). How do self-attributed and implicit motives differ? *Psychological Review, 96,* 690–702.

McClelland, David C.; Atkinson, John W.; Clark, Russell A.; & Lowell, Edgar L. (1953). *The achievement motive.* New York: Appleton-Century-Crofts.

McCloskey, Michael, & Zaragoza, Maria (1985). Misleading postevent information and memory for events: Arguments and evidence against memory impairment hypotheses. *Journal of Experimental Psychology: General, 114,* 1–16.

McCloskey, Michael; Wible, Cynthia G.; & Cohen, Neal J. (1988). Is there a special flashbulb-memory mechanism? *Journal of Experimental Psychology: General, 117,* 171–181.

McConnell, James V. (1962). Memory transfer through cannibalism in planarians. *Journal of Neuropsychiatry, 3,* Monograph Supplement 1.

McCord, Joan (1989). Another time, another drug. Paper presented at conference, Vulnerability to the Transition from Drug Use to Abuse and Dependence, Rockville, MD.

McCord, Joan (1990). Crime in moral and social contexts. *Criminology, 28,* 1–26.

McCormick, Laura J., & Mayer, John D. (1991). Mood-congruent recall and natural mood. Poster presented at the annual meeting of the New England Psychological Association, Portland, ME.

McCrae, Robert R. (1987). Creativity, divergent thinking, and openness to experience. *Journal of Personality and Social Psychology, 52,* 1258–1265.

McCrae, Robert R., & Costa, Paul T., Jr. (1987). Validation of the five-factor model of personality across instruments and observers. *Journal of Personality and Social Psychology, 52,* 81–90.

McCrae, Robert R., & Costa, Paul T., Jr. (1988a). Do parental influences matter? A reply to Halverson. *Journal of Personality, 56,* 445–449.

McCrae, Robert R., & Costa, Paul T., Jr. (1988b). Psychological resilience among widowed men and women: A 10-year follow-up of a national sample. *Journal of Social Issues, 44*(3), 129–142.

McCrae, Robert R., & Costa, Paul T., Jr. (1991). Adding *Liebe und Arbeit:* The full five-factor model and well-being. *Personality and Social Psychology Bulletin, 17,* 227–232.

McEwen, Bruce S. (1983). Gonadal steroid influences on brain development and sexual differentiation. *Reproductive Physiology IV (International Review of Physiology), 27,* 99–145.

McFarlane, Jessica; Martin, Carol Lynn; & Williams, Tannis MacBeth (1988). Mood fluctuations: Women versus men and menstrual versus other cycles. *Psychology of Women Quarterly, 12,* 201–223.

McGaugh, James L. (1990). Significance and remembrance: The role of neuromodulatory systems. *Psychological Science, 1,* 15–25.

McGill, Michael (1980). *The forty to sixty year old male.* New York: Simon & Schuster.

McGlone, Jeannette (1978). Sex differences in functional brain asymmetry. *Cortex, 14,* 122–128.

McGlone, Jeannette (1980). Sex differences in human brain asymmetry: A critical survey. *Behavioral and Brain Sciences, 3,* 215–227.

McGlynn, Susan M. (1990). Behavioral approaches to neuropsychological rehabilitation. *Psychological Bulletin, 108,* 420–441.

McGoldrick, Monica, & Gerson, Randy (1985). *Genograms in family assessment.* New York: Norton.

McGoldrick, Monica; Pearce, John K.; & Giordano, J. (eds.) (1982). *Ethnicity and family therapy.* New York: Guilford Press.

McGrath, Ellen; Keita, Gwendolyn P.; Strickland, Bonnie; & Russo, Nancy F. (eds.) (1990). *Women and depression: Risk factors and treatment issues.* Washington, DC: American Psychological Association.

McGue, Matt, & Bouchard, Thomas J. (1987). Genetic and environmental determinants of information processing and special mental abilities: A twin analysis. In R. J. Sternberg (ed.), *Advances in the psychology of human intelligence,* Vol. 5. Hillsdale, NJ: Erlbaum.

McGuire, William, & Papageorgis, Dimitri (1961). The relative efficacy of various types of prior belief-defense in producing immunity against persuasion. *Journal of Abnormal and Social Psychology, 62,* 327–337.

McKinlay, John B.; McKinlay, Sonja M.; & Brambilla, Donald (1987). The relative contributions of endocrine changes and social circumstances to depression in mid-aged women. *Journal of Health and Social Behavior, 28,* 345–363.

McKinlay, Sonja M.; Bifano, Nancy L.; & McKinlay, John B. (1985). Smoking and age at menopause in women. *Annals of Internal Medicine, 103,* 350–356.

McLeod, Beverly (1985, March). Real work for real pay. *Psychology Today, 19*(3), 42–44, 46, 48–50.

McNaughton, B. L., & Morris, R. G. M. (1987). Hippocampal synaptic enhancement and information storage within a distributed memory system. *Trends in Neuroscience, 10,* 408–415.

Medawar, Peter B. (1979). *Advice to a young scientist.* New York: Harper & Row.

Medawar, Peter (1982). *Pluto's Republic.* Oxford, England: Oxford University Press.

Meddis, Ray (1977). *The sleep instinct.* London: Routledge & Kegan Paul.

Mednick, Sarnoff A. (1962). The associative basis of the creative process. *Psychological Review, 69,* 220–232.

Mednick, Sarnoff A.; Parnas, Josef; & Schulsinger, Fini (1987). The Copenhagen High-Risk Project, 1962–86. *Schizophrenia Bulletin, 13,* 485–495.

Meltzer, Herbert Y. (1987). Biological studies in schizophrenia. *Schizophrenia Bulletin, 13,* 77–111.

Meltzoff, Andrew N., & Moore, Michael K. (1983). Newborn infants imitate adult facial gestures. *Child Development, 54,* 702–709.

Melzack, Ronald (1973). *The puzzle of pain.* New York: Basic Books.

Melzack, Ronald (1990). Phantom limbs and the concept of a neuromatrix. *Trends in Neurosciences, 13,* 88–92.

Melzack, Ronald, & Dennis, Stephen G. (1978). Neurophysiological foundations of pain. In R. A. Sternback (ed.), *The psychology of pain.* New York: Raven Press.

Melzack, Ronald, & Wall, Patrick D. (1965). Pain mechanisms: A new theory. *Science, 150,* 971–979.

Mercer, Jane (1988, May 18). Racial differences in intelligence: Fact or artifact? Talk given at San Bernardino Valley College.

Merikle, Philip M. (1988). Subliminal auditory tapes: An evaluation. *Psychology and Marketing, 5,* 355–372.

Mershon, Bryan, & Gorsuch, Richard L. (1988). Number of factors in the personality sphere: Does increase in factors increase predictability of real-life criteria? *Journal of Personality and Social Psychology, 55,* 675–680.

Meyers, Raymond C., & Dennis, Barbara (1991). Health, behavioral and developmental ramifications for children exposed to "crack" cocaine. Unpublished manuscript, Department of Human Services, Philadelphia, PA.

Milavsky, J. Ronald (1988). Television and aggression once again. In S. Oskamp (ed.), *Television as a social issue (Applied Social Psychology Annual,* Vol. 8). Newbury Park, CA: Sage.

Milgram, Stanley (1963). Behavioral study of obedience. *Journal of Abnormal and Social Psychology, 67,* 371–378.

Milgram, Stanley (1974). *Obedience to authority: An experimental view.* New York: Harper & Row.

Millar, Keith, & Watkinson, Neal (1983). Recognition of words presented during general anaesthesia. *Ergonomics, 26,* 585–594.

Miller, Alice (1984). *Thou shalt not be aware: Psychoanalysis and society's betrayal of the child.* New York: Farrar, Straus & Giroux.

Miller, George A. (1956). The magical number seven, plus or minus two: Some limits on our capacity for processing information. *Psychological Review, 63,* 81–97.

Miller, George A. (1969, December). On turning psychology over to the unwashed. *Psychology Today, 3*(7), 53–55, 66–68, 70, 72, 74.

Miller, George A., & Gildea, Patricia M. (1987, September). How children learn words. *Scientific American, 257*(6), 94–99.

Miller, Inglis J., & Reedy, Frank E. (1990). Variations in human taste bud density and taste intensity perception. *Physiology and Behavior, 47,* 1213–1219.

Miller, Joan G. (1984). Culture and the development of everyday social explanation. *Journal of Personality and Social Psychology, 46,* 961–978.

Miller, Jonathan (1983). *States of mind.* New York: Pantheon.

Miller, Neal E. (1969). Learning of visceral and glandular responses. *Science, 163,* 434–435.

Miller, Neal E. (1978). Biofeedback and visceral learning. *Annual Review of Psychology, 29,* 421–452.

Miller, Neal E. (1985). The value of behavioral research on animals. *American Psychologist, 40,* 423–440.

Miller, Paul A., & Eisenberg, Nancy (1988). The relation of empathy to aggressive and externalizing/antisocial behavior. *Psychological Bulletin, 103,* 324–344.

Miller, Suzanne M. (1989). To see or not to see: Cognitive informational styles in the coping process. In M. Rosenbaum (ed.), *Learned resourcefulness: On coping skills, self-regulation, and adaptive behavior.* New York: Springer.

Miller, Suzanne M.; Brody, David; & Summerton, Jeffrey (1988). Styles of coping with threat: Implications for health. *Journal of Personality and Social Psychology, 54,* 142–148.

Miller-Jones, Dalton (1989). Culture and testing. *American Psychologist, 44,* 360–366.

Milner, Brenda (1970). Memory and the temporal regions of the brain. In K. H. Pribram & D. E. Broadbent (eds.), *Biology of memory*. New York: Academic Press.

Milner, Brenda; Corkin, Suzanne; & Teuber, H. L. (1968). Further analysis of the hippocampal amnesic syndrome: 14-year follow-up study of H. M. *Neuropsychologia, 6,* 215–234.

Minuchin, Salvador (1984). *Family kaleidoscope.* Cambridge, MA: Harvard University Press.

Minuchin, Salvador (1991, September/October). The seductions of constructivism. *The Family Therapy Networker, 15,* 47–50.

Minuchin, Salvador; Rosman, Bernice L.; & Baker, Lester (1978). *Psychosomatic families: Anorexia nervosa in context.* Cambridge, MA: Harvard University Press.

Mischel, Walter (1981). A cognitive social learning approach to assessment. In T. V. Merluzzi, C. R. Glass, & M. Genest (eds.), *Cognitive assessment.* New York: Guilford Press.

Mischel, Walter (1984). Convergences and challenges in the search for consistency. *American Psychologist, 39,* 351–364.

Mishkin, Mortimer, & Appenzeller, Tim (1987). The anatomy of memory. *Scientific American, 256,* 80–89.

Miura, Irene T., & Okamoto, Yukari (1989). Comparisons of U.S. and Japanese first graders' cognitive representation of number and understanding of place value. *Journal of Educational Psychology, 81,* 109–113.

Miura, Irene T.; Kim, Chungsoon C.; Chang, Chih-Mei; & Okamoto, Yukari (1988). Effects of language characteristics on children's cognitive representation of number: Cross-national comparisons. *Child Development, 59,* 1445–1450.

Monk, Timothy H., & Aplin, Lynne C. (1980). Spring and Autumn daylight saving time changes: Studies of adjustment in sleep timings, mood, and efficiency. *Ergonomics, 23,* 167–178.

Montagner, Hubert (1985). [An ethological approach of the interaction systems of the infant and the young child.] *Neuropsychiatrie de l'Enfance et de l'Adolescence, 33,* 59–71.

Moore, Elsie G. J. (1986). Family socialization and the IQ test performance of traditionally and transracially adopted black children. *Developmental Psychology, 22,* 317–326.

Moore, S. D., & Stanley, J. C. (1986). Family backgrounds of young Asian Americans who reason extremely well mathematically. Unpublished manuscript, Johns Hopkins University.

Moore, Timothy E. (1988). The case against subliminal manipulation. *Psychology and Marketing, 5,* 297–316.

Moore, Timothy E. (1991). Subliminal auditory self-help tapes. Paper presented at the annual meeting of the American Psychological Association, San Francisco.

Moore-Ede, Martin C., & Sulzman, Frank M. (1981). Internal temporal order. In J. Aschoff (ed.), *Handbook of behavioral neurobiology, Vol. 4: Biological rhythms.* New York: Plenum.

Moore-Ede, Martin, C.; Sulzman, Frank M.; & Fuller, Charles A. (1984). *The clocks that time us: Physiology of the circadian timing system.* Cambridge, MA: Harvard University Press.

Moos, Rudolf H. (1988). Life stressors and coping resources influence health and well-being. *Psychological Assessment, 4,* 133–158.

Morris, Robin G.; Craik, Fergus I.; & Gick, Mary L. (1990). Age differences in working memory tasks: The role of secondary memory and the central executive system. *Quarterly Journal of Experimental Psychology: Human Experimental Psychology, 42,* 67–86.

Morrison, Ann M., & Von Glinow, Mary Ann (1990). Women and minorities in management. *American Psychologist, 45,* 200–208.

Moscovici, Serge (1985). Social influence and conformity. In G. Lindzey & E. Aronson (eds.), *Handbook of social psychology,* Vol. II (3rd ed.). New York: Random House.

Moses, Susan (1990, November). Assessors seek test that teaches. *The APA Monitor, 21,* 1, 37.

Mosher, Frederic A., & Hornsby, Joan R. (1966). On asking questions. In J. S. Bruner, R. R. Olver, & P. M. Greenfield (eds.), *Studies in cognitive growth.* New York: Wiley.

Mott, Frank L. (1991). Developmental effects of infant care: The mediating role of gender and health. In S. L. Hofferth & D. A. Phillips (eds.), *Child care policy research. Journal of Social Issues, 47*(2), 139–158.

Moyer, Kenneth E. (1983). The physiology of motivation: Aggression as a model. In C. J. Scheirer & A. M. Rogers (eds.), *The G. Stanley Hall Lecture Series,* Vol. 3. Washington, DC: American Psychological Association.

Mozell, Maxwell M.; Smith, Bruce P., Smith, Paul E.; Sullivan, Richard L.; & Swender, Philip (1969). Nasal chemoreception in flavor identification. *Archives of Otolaryngology, 90,* 367–373.

Muehlenhard, Charlene, & Cook, Stephen (1988). Men's self-reports of unwanted sexual activity. *Journal of Sex Research, 24,* 58–72.

Mullen, Brian, & Johnson, Craig (1990). Distinctiveness-based illusory correlations and stereotyping: A meta-analytic integration. *British Journal of Social Psychology, 29,* 11–28.

Mulvey, Edward P.; Geller, Jeffrey L.; & Roth, Loren H. (1987). The promise and peril of involuntary outpatient commitment. *American Psychologist, 42,* 571–584.

Murphy, Jane (1976). Psychiatric labeling in cross-cultural perspective. *Science, 191,* 1019–1028.

Murphy, Wendy B. (1982). *Touch, taste, smell, sight and hearing.* Alexandria, VA: Time-Life Books.

Myers, David G. (1980). *The inflated self.* New York: Seabury.

Myers, Ronald E., & Sperry, R. W. (1953). Interocular transfer of a visual form discrimination habit in cats after section of the optic chiasm and corpus callosum. *Anatomical Record, 115,* 351–352.

Nadel, Lynn, & Zola-Morgan, Stuart (1984). Infantile amnesia: A neurobiological perspective. In M. Moscovitch (ed.), *Infantile memory: Its relation to normal and pathological memory in humans and other animals.* New York: Plenum.

Naglieri, Jack A.; Das, J. P.; & Jarman, Ronald F. (1990). Planning, attention, simultaneous, and successive cognitive processes as a model for assessment. *School Psychology Review, 19,* 423–442.

Nash, Michael (1987). What, if anything, is regressed about hypnotic age regression? A review of the empirical literature. *Psychologibal Bulletin, 102,* 42–52.

National Commission on Testing and Public Policy (1990). *From gatekeeper to gateway: Transforming testing in America.* Chestnut Hill, MA. (Boston College): National Commission on Testing and Public Policy.

National Victim Center & Crime Victims Research and Treatment Center (1992). *Rape in America: A report to the nation.* Fort Worth, TX: National Victim Center.

Needleman, Herbert L.; Leviton, Alan; & Bellinger, David (1982). Lead-associated intellectual deficit. *New England Journal of Medicine, 306,* 367.

Needleman, Herbert L.; Schell, Alan; Bellinger, David; Leviton, Alan; et al. (1990). The long-term effects of exposure to low doses of lead in childhood: An 11-year follow-up report. *New England Journal of Medicine, 322,* 83–88.

Neher, Andrew (1991). Maslow's theory of motivation: A critique. *Journal of Humanistic Psychology, 31,* 89–112.

Neiss, Rob (1988). Reconceptualizing arousal: Psychobiological states in motor performance. *Psychological Bulletin, 103,* 345–366.

Neisser, Ulric (1967). *Cognitive psychology.* Englewood Cliffs, NJ: Prentice-Hall.

Neisser, Ulric (1981). John Dean's memory: A case study. *Cognition, 9,* 1–22. (Reprinted in U. Neisser [ed.], *Memory observed: Remembering in natural contexts.* San Francisco: Freeman, 1982.)

Neisser, Ulric (1982). Snapshots or benchmarks? In U. Neisser (ed.), *Memory observed: Remembering in natural contexts.* San Francisco: Freeman.

Neisser, Ulric, & Harsch, Nicole (1992). Phantom flashbulbs: False recollections of hearing the news about Challenger. In E. Winograd & U. Neisser (eds.), *Affect and accuracy in recall: Studies of "flashbulb memories."* New York: Cambridge University Press.

Neisser, Ulric; Winograd, Eugene; & Weldon, Mary Sue (1991). Remembering the earthquake: "What I experienced" vs. "How I heard the news." Paper presented at the annual meeting of the Psychonomic Society, San Francisco.

Nelson, Thomas O., & Dunlosky, John (1991). When people's judgments of learning (JOLs) are extremely accurate at predicting subsequent recall: The "delayed JOL effect." *Psychological Science, 2,* 267–270.

Neugarten, Bernice (1969). Continuities and discontinuities of psychological issues in adult life. *Human Development, 14,* 121–130.

Neugarten, Bernice (1974, September). Age groups in American society and the rise of the young-old. *Annals of the American Academy of Political and Social Science, 415,* 187–198.

Neugarten, Bernice (1979). Time, age, and the life cycle. *American Journal of Psychiatry, 136,* 887–894.

Neugarten, Bernice L., & Neugarten, Dail A. (1986, Winter). Age in the aging society. *Daedalus, 115,* 31–49.

Newcomb, Michael D., & Bentler, Peter M. (1988). *Consequences of adolescent drug use.* Newbury Park, CA: Sage.

Newell, Alan, & Simon, Herbert (1972). *Human problem solving.* Englewood Cliffs, NJ: Prentice-Hall.

Newlin, David B., & Thomson, James B. (1990). Alcohol challenge with sons of alcoholics: A critical review and analysis. *Psychological Bulletin, 108,* 383–402.

Newman, Eric A., & Hartline, Peter H. (1982). The infrared "vision" of snakes. *Scientific American, 246*(3), 116–127.

Newman, Joseph P.; Widom, Cathy S.; & Nathan, Stuart (1985). Passive avoidance in syndromes of disinhibition: Psychopathy and extraversion. *Journal of Personality and Social Psychology, 48,* 1316–1327.

Newman, Katherine (1988). *Falling from grace: The experience of downward mobility in the American middle class.* New York: Free Press.

Newman, Lucile F., & Buka, Stephen (1991). Clipped wings. *American Educator,* Spring, 27–33, 42.

Newton, Nancy A.; Lazarus, Lawrence W.; & Weinberg, Jack (1984). Aging: Biopsychosocial perspectives. In D. Offer & M. Sabshin (eds.), *Normality and the life cycle.* New York: Basic Books.

Nezu, Arthur M.; Nezu, Christine M.; & Blissett, Sonia E. (1988). Sense of humor as a moderator of the relation between stressful events and psychological distress: A prospective analysis. *Journal of Personality and Social Psychology, 54,* 520–525.

Nichols, Michael P. (1988). *The power of the family.* New York: Simon & Schuster.

Nickerson, Raymond A., & Adams, Marilyn Jager (1979). Long-term memory for a common object. *Cognitive Psychology, 11,* 287–307.

Niemi, G.; Katz, R. S.; & Newman, D. (1980). Reconstructing past partisanship: The failure of party identification recall questions. *American Journal of Political Science, 24,* 633–651.

Nisbett, Richard E. (1988). Testimony on behalf of the American Psychological Association before the U.S. House of Representatives Committee on Armed Services, October 6.

Nisbett, Richard E., & Ross, Lee (1980). *Human inference: Strategies and shortcomings of social judgment.* Englewood Cliffs, NJ: Prentice-Hall.

Noble, Ernest P.; Blum, Kenneth; Ritchie, T.; Montgomery, A.; & Sheridan, P. J. (1991). Allelic association of the D2 dopamine receptor gene with receptor-binding characteristics in alcoholism. *Archives of General Psychiatry, 48,* 648–654.

Noelle-Neumann, Elisabeth (1984). *The spiral of silence.* Chicago: University of Chicago Press.

Nolen-Hoeksema, Susan (1990). *Sex differences in depression.* Stanford, CA: Stanford University Press.

Nolen-Hoeksema, Susan (1991). Responses to depression and their effects on the duration of depressive episodes. *Journal of Abnormal Psychology, 100,* 569–582.

Nolen-Hoeksema, Susan; Girgus, Joan S.; & Seligman, Martin E. (1991). Sex differences in depression and explanatory style in children. Special Issue: The emergence of depressive symptoms during adolescence. *Journal of Youth & Adolescence, 20,* 233–245.

Noller, Patricia; Law, Henry; & Comrey, Andrew L. (1987). Cattell, Comrey, and Eysenck personality factors compared: More evidence for the five robust factors? *Journal of Personality and Social Psychology, 53,* 775–782.

Norman, Donald A. (1988). *The psychology of everyday things.* New York: Basic Books.

Novaco, Raymond W. (1985). Anger and its therapeutic regulation. In M. Chesney and R. Rosenman (eds.), *Anger and hostility in cardiovascular and behavioral disorders.* Washington, DC: Hemisphere.

Nowicki, Stephen, Jr., & Duke, Marshall P. (1989). A measure of nonverbal social processing ability in children between the ages of 6 and 10. Paper presented at the annual meeting of the American Psychological Society, Alexandria, VA.

Oakley, Ann (1974). *Woman's work: The housewife, past and present.* New York: Pantheon.

Oatley, Keith, & Johnson-Laird, P. N. (1987). Towards a cognitive theory of emotions. *Cognition & Emotion, 1,* 29–50.

Offer, Daniel, & Sabshin, Melvin (1984). Adolescence: Empirical perspectives. In D. Offer & M. Sabshin (eds.), *Normality and the life cycle.* New York: Basic Books.

Ogden, Jenni A., & Corkin, Suzanne (1991). Memories of H. M. In W. C. Abraham, M. C. Corballis, and K. G. White (eds.), *Memory mechanisms: A tribute to G. V. Goddard.* Hillsdale, NJ: Erlbaum.

Olds, James (1975). Mapping the mind onto the brain. In F. G. Worden, J. P. Swazy, and G. Adelman (eds.), *The neurosciences: Paths of discovery.* Cambridge, MA: Colonial Press.

Olds, James, & Milner, Peter (1954). Positive reinforcement produced by electrical stimulation of septal area and other regions of the rat brain. *Journal of Comparative and Physiological Psychology, 47,* 419–429.

O'Leary, Ann (1990). Stress, emotion, and human immune function. *Psychological Bulletin, 108,* 363–382.

Oliner, Samuel P., & Oliner, Pearl M. (1988). *The altruistic personality: Rescuers of Jews in Nazi Europe.* New York: Free Press.

Olweus, Dan (1979). Stability of aggressive reaction patterns in males: A review. *Psychological Bulletin, 86,* 852–875.

O'Neill, Colleen, & Zeichner, Amos (1985). Working women: A study of relationships between stress, coping and health. *Journal of Psychosomatic Obstetrics & Gynaecology, 4,* 105–116.

Ormel, Johan, & Wohlfarth, Tamar (1991). How neuroticism, long-term difficulties, and life situation change influence psychological distress: A longitudinal model. *Journal of Personality and Social Psychology, 60,* 744–755.

Ortar, G. (1963). Is a verbal test cross-cultural? *Scripts Hierosolymitana* (Hebrew University, Jerusalem), *13,* 219–235.

Ortony, Andrew, & Turner, Terence J. (1990). What's basic about basic emotions? *Psychological Review, 97,* 315–331.

Ortony, Andrew; Clore, Gerald L.; & Collins, Allan (1988). *The cognitive structure of emotions.* Cambridge, England: Cambridge University Press.

Orwell, George (1949). *Nineteen eighty-four.* New York: Harcourt Brace Jovanovich.

Oyserman, Daphna, & Markus, Hazel R. (1990). Possible selves and delinquency. *Journal of Personality and Social Psychology, 59,* 112–125.

Ozer, Elizabeth M., & Bandura, Albert (1990). Mechanisms governing empowerment effects: A self-efficacy analysis. *Journal of Personality & Social Psychology, 58,* 472–486.

Page, J. Bryan; Fletcher, Jack; & True, William R. (1988). Psychosociocultural perspectives on chronic cannabis use: The Costa Rican follow-up. *Journal of Psychoactive Drugs, 20,* 57–65.

Pagel, Mark D.; Erdly, William W.; & Becker, Joseph (1987). Social networks: We get by with (and in spite of) a little help from our friends. *Journal of Personality and Social Psychology, 53,* 793–804.

Paige, Karen (1978, May). The ritual of circumcision. *Human Nature, 1,* 40–49.

Paikoff, Roberta L., & Brooks-Gunn, Jeanne (1991). Do parent-child relationships change during puberty? *Psychological Bulletin, 110,* 47–66.

Paivio, Allan (1969). Mental imagery in associative learning and memory. *Psychological Review, 76,* 241–263.

Paivio, Allan (1983).   The empirical case for dual coding. In J. C. Yuille (ed.), *Imagery, memory and cognition*. Hillsdale, NJ: Erlbaum.

Palmer, Stephen; Schreiber, Charles; & Fox, Craig (1991).   Remembering the earthquake: "Flashbulb" memory for experienced vs. reported events. Paper presented at the annual meeting of the Psychonomic Society, San Francisco.

Panksepp, J.; Herman, B. H.; Vilberg, T.; Bishop, P.; & DeEskinazi, F. G. (1980).   Endogenous opioids and social behavior. *Neuroscience and Biobehavioral Reviews, 4,* 473–487.

Papini, Mauricio R., & Bitterman, M. E. (1990).   The role of contingency in classical conditioning. *Psychological Review, 97,* 396–403.

Park, Denise C.; Smith, Anderson D.; & Cavanaugh, John C. (1990).   Metamemories of memory researchers. *Memory & Cognition, 18,* 321–327.

Parke, Ross, & Sawin, Douglas B. (1980).   The family in early infancy. In F. A. Pederson (ed.), *The father-infant relationship: Observational studies in a family context*. New York: Praeger.

Parker, Elizabeth S.; Birnbaum, Isabel M.; & Noble, Ernest P. (1976).   Alcohol and memory: Storage and state dependency. *Journal of Verbal Learning and Verbal Behavior, 15,* 691–702.

Parker, Keven C. H.; Hanson, R. Karl; & Hunsley, John (1988).   MMPI, Rorschach, and WAIS: A meta-analytic comparison of reliability, stability, and validity. *Psychological Bulletin, 103,* 367–373.

Parks, Randolph W.; Loewenstein, David A.; Dodrill, Kathryn L.; Barker, William W.; et al. (1988).   Cerebral metabolic effects of a verbal fluency test: A PET scan study. *Journal of Clinical & Experimental Neuropsychology, 10,* 565–575.

Parlee, Mary Brown (1982).   Changes in moods and activation levels during the menstrual cycle in experimentally naive subjects. *Psychology of Women Quarterly, 7,* 119–131.

Parlee, Mary Brown (1989).   The science and politics of PMS research. Paper presented at the annual meeting of the Association for Women in Psychology, Newport, Rhode Island.

Pascale, Richard, & Athos, Anthony G. (1981).   *The art of Japanese management*. New York: Simon & Schuster.

Patterson, Francine, & Linden, Eugene (1981).   *The education of Koko*. New York: Holt, Rinehart and Winston.

Patterson, Gerald R. (1986).   Performance models for antisocial boys. *American Psychologist, 41,* 432–444.

Patterson, G. R.; DeBaryshe, Barbara D.; & Ramsey, Elizabeth (1989).   A developmental perspective on antisocial behavior. *American Psychologist, 44,* 329–335.

Paul, Richard W. (1984, September).   Critical thinking: Fundamental to education for a free society. *Educational Leadership,* 4–14.

Pavlov, Ivan P. (1927/1960).   *Conditioned reflexes*. (G. V. Anrep, trans. & ed.) New York: Dover.

Peabody, Dean (1985).   *National characteristics*. Cambridge, England: Cambridge University Press.

Pearlin, Leonard (1982).   Discontinuities in the study of aging. In T. K. Hareven & K. J. Adams (eds.), *Aging and life course transitions: An interdisciplinary perspective*. New York: Guilford Press.

Peck, Jeffrey W. (1978).   Rats defend different body weights depending on palatability and accessibility of their food. *Journal of Comparative and Physiological Psychology, 92,* 555–570.

Pedersen, Nancy L.; Plomin, Robert; McClearn, G. E.; & Friberg, Lars (1988).   Neuroticism, extraversion, and related traits in adult twins reared apart and reared together. *Journal of Personality and Social Psychology, 55,* 950–957.

Peele, Stanton (1989).   *Diseasing of America: Addiction treatment out of control*. Lexington, MA: Lexington Books.

Peele, Stanton, & Brodsky, Archie, with Mary Arnold (1991).   *The truth about addiction and recovery*. New York: Simon & Schuster.

Penfield, Wilder, & Perot, Phanor (1963).   The brain's record of auditory and visual experience: A final summary and discussion. *Brain, 86,* 595–696.

Pennebaker, James W. (1982).   *The psychology of physical symptoms*. New York: Springer-Verlag.

Pennebaker, James W. (1990).   *Opening up: The healing power of confiding in others*. New York: Morrow.

Pennebaker, James W.; Colder, Michelle; & Sharp, Lisa K. (1990).   Accelerating the coping process. *Journal of Personality and Social Psychology, 58,* 528–527.

Pennebaker, James W.; Hughes, Cheryl F.; & O'Heeron, Robin C. (1987).   The psychophysiology of confession: Linking inhibitory and psychosomatic processes. *Journal of Personality and Social Psychology, 52,* 781–793.

Pennebaker, James W.; Kiecolt-Glaser, Janice; & Glaser, Ronald (1988).   Disclosure of traumas and immune function: Health implications for psychotherapy. *Journal of Consulting and Clinical Psychology, 56,* 239–245.

Peplau, Letitia A. (1983).   Roles and gender. In H. Kelley et al. (eds.), *Close relationships*. New York: Freeman.

Peplau, Letitia A. (1984).   Power in dating relationships. In J. Freedman (ed.), *Women: A feminist perspective* (3rd ed.). Palo Alto, CA: Mayfield.

Peplau, Letitia A., & Gordon, Steven L. (1985).   Women and men in love: Gender differences in close heterosexual relationships. In V. O'Leary, R. Unger, & B. Wallston (eds.), *Women, gender, and social psychology*. Hillsdale, NJ: Erlbaum.

Peplau, Letitia A., & Perlman, Dan (eds.) (1982).   *Loneliness: A sourcebook of current theory, research, and therapy*. New York: Wiley-Interscience.

Pepperberg, Irene M. (1988).   Comprehension of "absence" by an African grey parrot: Learning with respect to questions of same/different. *Journal of the Experimental Analysis of Behavior, 50,* 553–564.

Pepperberg, Irene M. (1990).   Cognition in an African gray parrot (Psittacus erithacus): Further evidence for comprehension of categories and labels. *Journal of Comparative Psychology, 104,* 41–52.

Perdue, Charles W.; Dovidio, John F.; Gurtman, Michael B.; & Tyler, Richard B. (1990).   Us and them: Social categorization and the process of intergroup bias. *Journal of Personality and Social Psychology, 59,* 475–486.

Perlman, Daniel (1990).   Age differences in loneliness: A meta-analysis. Paper presented at the annual meeting of the American Psychological Association, Boston.

Perls, Frederick (1969).   *Gestalt therapy verbatim*. Berkeley, CA: Real People Press.

Persons, Jacqueline B. (1991).   Psychotherapy outcome studies do not accurately represent current models of psychotherapy: A proposed remedy. *American Psychologist, 46,* 99–106.

Pert, Candace B., & Snyder, Solomon H. (1973).   Opiate receptor: Demonstration in nervous tissue. *Science, 179,* 1011–1014.

Petersen, Anne C. (1989).   Developmental transitions and their role in influencing life trajectories. Paper presented at the annual meeting of the American Psychological Association, New Orleans.

Peterson, Christopher, & Barrett, Lisa C. (1987).   Explanatory style and academic performance among university freshmen. *Journal of Personality and Social Psychology, 53,* 603–607.

Peterson, Christopher; Seligman, Martin E. P.; & Vaillant, George (1988).   Pessimistic explanatory style is a risk factor for physical illness: A thirty-five year longitudinal study. *Journal of Personality and Social Psychology, 55,* 23–27.

Peterson, Lloyd R., & Peterson, Margaret J. (1959).   Short-term retention of individual verbal items. *Journal of Experimental Psychology, 58,* 193–198.

Petitto, Laura A., & Marentette, Paula F. (1991, March 22).   Babbling in the manual mode: Evidence for the ontogeny of language. *Science, 251,* 1493–1496.

Phinney, Jean S. (1990).   Ethnic identity in adolescents and adults: Review of research. *Psychological Bulletin, 108,* 499–514.

Piaget, Jean (1929/1960).   *The child's conception of the world*. Paterson, NJ: Littlefield, Adams.

Piaget, Jean (1932).   *The moral judgment of the child*. New York: Macmillan.

Piaget, Jean (1952).   *The origins of intelligence in children*. New York: International Universities Press.

Piaget, Jean (1984). Piaget's theory. In P. Mussen (ed.), *Handbook of child psychology* (4th ed.), W. Kessen (ed.), *Vol. 1: History, theory, and methods.* New York: Wiley.

Pines, Ayala M. (1986). Marriage. In C. Tavris (ed.), *EveryWoman's emotional well-being.* New York: Prentice Hall.

Pines, Maya (1983, September). The human difference. *Psychology Today, 17*(9), 62–68.

Plante, Thomas G., & Rodin, Judith (1990). Physical fitness and enhanced psychological health. *Current Psychology: Research and Reviews, 9,* 3–24.

Pleck, Joseph H. (1987). American fathering in historical perspective. In M. S. Kimmel (ed.), *Changing men: New directions in research on men and masculinity.* Beverly Hills, CA: Sage.

Plomin, Robert (1988). The nature and nurture of cognitive abilities. In R. J. Sternberg (ed.), *Advances in the psychology of human intelligence,* Vol. 4. Hillsdale, NJ: Erlbaum.

Plomin, Robert (1989). Environment and genes: Determinants of behavior. *American Psychologist, 44,* 105–111.

Plomin, Robert, & Daniels, D. (1987). Why are children in the same family so different from one another? *Behavioral and Brain Sciences, 10,* 1–16.

Plous, S. (1991). An attitude survey of animal rights activists. *Psychological Science, 2,* 194–196.

Plutchik, Robert (1984). Emotions: A general psychoevolutionary theory. In K. R. Scherer & P. Ekman (eds.), *Approaches to emotion.* Hillsdale, NJ: Erlbaum.

Plutchik, Robert (1987). Evolutionary bases of empathy. In N. Eisenberg & J. Strayer (eds.), *Empathy and its development.* New York: Cambridge University Press.

Polefrone, Joanna M., & Manuck, Stephen B. (1987). Gender differences in cardiovascular and neuroendocrine response to stressors. In R. C. Barnett, L. Biener, & G. K. Baruch (eds.), *Gender and stress.* New York: The Free Press.

Poley, Wayne; Lea, Gary; & Vibe, Gail (1979). *Alcoholism: A treatment manual.* New York: Gardner.

Polivy, Janet (1981). On the induction of emotion in the laboratory: Discrete moods or multiple affect states? *Journal of Personality and Social Psychology, 41,* 803–817.

Polivy, Janet, & Herman, C. Peter (1985). Dieting and bing[e]ing: A causal analysis. *American Psychologist, 40,* 193–201.

Pollitt, Katha (1991, December). Reading books, great or otherwise. *Harper's Magazine,* 34, 36. [Excerpt from "Why we read," paper delivered at Columbia University Center for American Culture Studies, 1991.]

Pomeroy, Sarah (1975). *Goddesses, whores, wives and slaves: Women in classical antiquity.* New York: Schocken.

Pope, Harrison G., & Katz, David L. (1988). Affective and psychotic symptoms associated with anabolic steroid use. *American Journal of Psychiatry, 145,* 487–490.

Pope, Harrison G., Jr.; Keck, P. E.; & McElroy, S. L. (1986). Frequency and presentation of neuroleptic malignant syndrome in a large psychiatric hospital. *American Journal of Psychiatry, 143,* 1227–1233.

Pope, Kenneth, & Bouhoutsos, Jacqueline (1986). *Sexual intimacy between therapists and patients.* New York: Praeger.

Porter, Roy (1987). *A social history of madness: The world through the eyes of the insane.* New York: Weidenfeld & Nicolson.

Postman, Neil (1985). *Amusing ourselves to death.* New York: Viking Penguin.

Poulos, Constantine X., & Cappell, Howard (1991). Homeostatic theory of drug tolerance: A general model of physiological adaptation. *Psychological Review, 98,* 390–408.

Pratkanis, Anthony, & Aronson, Elliot (1992). *Age of propaganda: The everyday use and abuse of persuasion.* New York: Freeman.

Premack, David (1965). Reinforcement theory. In D. Levine (ed.), *Nebraska Symposium on Motivation, 1965.* Lincoln: University of Nebraska Press.

Premack, David, & Premack, Ann James (1983). *The mind of an ape.* New York: Norton.

Prentky, Robert A.; Knight, Raymond A.; & Rosenberg, Ruth (1988). Validation analyses on a taxonomic system for rapists: Disconfirmation and reconceptualization. Conference of the New York Academy of Sciences: Human sexual aggression: Current perspectives. *Annals of the New York Academy of Sciences, 528,* 21–40.

Press, Gary A.; Amaral, David G.; & Squire, Larry R. (1989, September 7). Hippocampal abnormalities in amnesic patients revealed by high-resolution magnetic resonance imaging. *Nature, 341,* 54–57.

Pribram, Karl H. (1971). *Languages of the brain: Experimental paradoxes and principles.* Englewood Cliffs, NJ: Prentice-Hall.

Pribram, Karl H. (1982). Localization and distribution of function in the brain. In J. Orbach (ed.), *Neuropsychology after Lashley.* Hillsdale, NJ: Erlbaum.

Prioleau, Leslie; Murdock, Martha; & Brody, Nathan (1983). An analysis of psychotherapy versus placebo studies. *Behavioral and Brain Sciences, 6,* 275–285.

Pryor, Karen (1984). *Don't shoot the dog!* New York: Simon & Schuster.

Pulver, Ann; Carpenter, William; Adler, Lawrence; & McGrath, John (1988). Accuracy of diagnoses of affective disorders and schizophrenia in public hospitals. *American Journal of Psychiatry, 145,* 218–220.

Pye, Clifton (1986). Quiché Mayan speech to children. *Journal of Child Language, 13,* 85–100.

Quill, Timothy E. (1991, March 7). Death and dignity. A case of individualized decision making. *New England Journal of Medicine, 324* (10), 691–694.

Rabkin, Judith G.; Williams, Janet B.; Remien, Robert H.; Goetz, Raymond; et al. (1991). Depression, distress, lymphocyte subsets, and human immunodeficiency virus symptoms on two occasions in HIV-positive homosexual men. *Archives of General Psychiatry, 48,* 111–119.

Rachman, S. J., & Wilson, G. Terence (1980). *The effects of psychological therapy* (2nd ed.). Oxford, England: Pergamon.

Radetsky, Peter (1991, April). The brainiest cells alive. *Discover, 12,* 82–85, 88, 90.

Radner, Daisie, & Radner, Michael (1982). *Science and unreason.* Belmont, CA: Wadsworth.

Rait, Douglas (1988, January-February). Survey results. *The Family Therapy Networker,* 52–56.

Ralph, Martin R., & Menaker, Michael (1988). A mutation of the circadian system in golden hamsters. *Science, 241,* 1225–1227.

Ransom, Donald C. (1982). Harmful elements in family therapy. Paper presented at the annual meeting of the American Psychological Association, Washington.

Rathbun, Constance; DiVirgilio, Letitia; & Waldfogel, Samuel (1958). A restitutive process in children following radical separation from family and culture. *American Journal of Orthopsychiatry, 28,* 408–415.

Ravussin, Eric; Lillioja, Stephen; Knowler, William; Christin, Laurent; et al. (1988). Reduced rate of energy expenditure as a risk factor for body-weight gain. *New England Journal of Medicine, 318,* 467–472.

Raz, Sarah, & Raz, Naftali (1990). Structural brain abnormalities in the major psychoses: A quantitative review of the evidence from computerized imaging. *Psychological Bulletin, 108,* 93–108.

Rechtschaffen, Allan; Gilliland, Marcia A.; Bergmann, Bernard M.; & Winter, Jacqueline B. (1983). Physiological correlates of prolonged sleep deprivation in rats. *Science, 221,* 182–184.

Reed, Geoffrey M. (1990). Stress, coping, and psychological adaptation in a sample of gay and bisexual men with AIDS. Unpublished doctoral dissertation, University of California, Los Angeles.

Regier, Darrel; Boyd, Jeffrey; Burke, Jack; Rae, Donald; et al. (1988). One-month prevalence of mental disorders in the United States. *Archives of General Psychiatry, 45,* 977–986.

Reinke, Barbara; Holmes, David S.; & Harris, Rochelle (1985).

The timing of psychosocial changes in women's lives: The years 25 to 45. *Journal of Personality and Social Psychology, 48,* 1353–1365.

Reisenzein, Rainer (1983). The Schachter theory of emotion: Two decades later. *Psychological Bulletin, 94,* 239–264.

Reppert, Steven M.; Weaver, David R.; Rivkees, Scoff A., & Stopa, Edward G. (1988). Putative melatonin receptors in a human biological clock. *Science, 242,* 78–81.

Rescorla, Robert A. (1968). Probability of shock in the presence and absence of CS in fear conditioning. *Journal of Comparative and Physiological Psychology, 66,* 1–5.

Rescorla, Robert A. (1988). Pavlovian conditioning: It's not what you think it is. *American Psychologist, 43,* 151–160.

Rescorla, Robert A., & Wagner, Allan R. (1972). A theory of Pavlovian conditioning: Variations in the effectiveness of reinforcement and nonreinforcement. In A. H. Black & W. F. Prokasy (eds.), *Classical conditioning II: Current research and theory.* New York: Appleton-Century-Crofts.

Restak, Richard (1983, October). Is free will a fraud? *Science Digest, 91*(10), 52–55.

Revenson, Tracey; Wollman, Carol; & Felton, Barbara (1983). Social supports as stress buffers for adult cancer patients. *Psychosomatic Medicine, 45,* 321–331.

Reynolds, Brent A., & Weiss, Samuel (1992). Generation of neurons and astrocytes from isolated cells of the adult mammalian central nervous system. *Science, 255,* 1707–1710.

Reynolds, David K. (1987). *Water bears no scars: Japanese lifeways for personal growth.* New York: Morrow.

Ricaurte, George A.; Forno, Lysia; Wilson, Mary; deLanney, Louis; Irwin, Ean; Mulliver, Mark; & Langston, J. William (1988). (+ or −) 3, 4-Methylenedioxy-methamphetamine selectively damages central serotonergic neurons in nonhuman primates. *Journal of the American Medical Association, 260,* 51–55.

Rice, Mabel L. (1989). Children's language acquisition. *American Psychologist, 44,* 149–156.

Richards, Ruth L. (1991). Everyday creativity and the arts. Paper presented at the annual meeting of the American Psychological Association, San Francisco.

Richards, Ruth L.; Kinney, Dennis K.; Benet, Maria; & Merzel, Ann (1988). Everyday creativity: Characteristics of the Lifetime Creativity Scales and validation with three large samples. *Journal of Personality and Social Psychology, 54,* 476–485.

Richardson-Klavehn, Alan, & Bjork, Robert A. (1988). Measures of memory. *Annual Review of Psychology, 39,* 475–543.

Richmond, Barry J.; Optican, Lance M.; Podell, Michael; & Spitzer, Hedva (1987). Temporal encoding of two-dimensional patterns by single units in primate inferior temporal cortex. 1. Response characteristics. *Journal of Neurophysiology, 57,* 132–146.

Ridley, Charles R. (1984). Clinical treatment of the nondisclosing black client. *American Psychologist, 39,* 1234–1244.

Riessman, Catherine K. (1990). *Divorce talk: Women and men make sense of personal relationships.* New Brunswick, NJ: Rutgers University Press.

Rioch, David M. (1975). Psychological and pharmacological manipulations. In L. Levi (ed.), *Emotions: Their parameters and measurement.* New York: Raven Press.

Risman, Barbara J. (1987). Intimate relationships from a microstructural perspective: Men who mother. *Gender and Society, 1,* 6–32.

Roberts, Susan B.; Savage, J.; Coward, W. A.; Chew, B.; & Lucas, A. (1988). Energy expenditure and intake in infants born to lean and overweight mothers. *New England Journal of Medicine, 318,* 461–466.

Robertson, John, & Fitzgerald, Louise F. (1990). The (mis)treatment of men: Effects of client gender role and life-style on diagnosis and attribution of pathology. *Journal of Counseling Psychology, 37,* 3–9.

Robins, Clive J. (1988). Attributions and depression: Why is the literature so inconsistent? *Journal of Personality and Social Psychology, 54,* 880–889.

Robins, Lee N.; Davis, Darlene H.; & Goodwin, Donald W. (1974). Drug use by U.S. Army enlisted men in Vietnam: A follow-up on their return home. *American Journal of Epidemiology, 99,* 235–249.

Robinson, Leslie A.; Berman, Jeffrey S.; & Neimeyer, Robert A. (1990). Psychotherapy for the treatment of depression: A comprehensive review of controlled outcome research. *Psychological Bulletin, 108,* 30–49.

Robitscher, Jonas (1980). *The powers of psychiatry.* Boston: Houghton Mifflin.

Rodgers, Joann (1988, April). Pains of complaint. *Psychology Today, 22*(4), 26–27.

Rodin, Judith (1988). Control, health, and aging. Invited address, Society of Behavioral Medicine, Boston.

Rodin, Judith; Silberstein, Lisa R.; & Striegel-Moore, Ruth H. (1990). Vulnerability and resilience in the age of eating disorders: Risk and protective factors for bulimia. In J. E. Rolf et al. (eds.), *Risk and protective factors in the development of psychopathology.* Cambridge, England: Cambridge University Press.

Roediger, Henry L., III (1990). Implicit memory: Retention without remembering. *American Psychologist, 45,* 1043–1056.

Roehrs, Timothy; Timms, Victoria; Zsyghuizen-Doorenbos, Ardith; & Roth, Thomas (1989). Sleep extension in sleepy and alert normals. *Sleep, 12,* 449–457.

Roehrs, Timothy; Timms, Victoria; Zsyghuizen-Doorenbos, Ardith; Buzenski, Raymond; et al. (1990). Polysomnographic, performance, and personality differences of sleepy and alert normals. *Sleep, 13,* 395–402.

Rogers, Carl (1951). *Client-centered therapy: Its current practice, implications, and theory.* Boston: Houghton Mifflin.

Rogers, Carl (1961). *On becoming a person.* Boston: Houghton Mifflin.

Rogers, Richard (1988). APA's position on the insanity defense. *American Psychologist, 42,* 840–848.

Rogers, Ronald W., & Prentice-Dunn, Steven (1981). Deindividuation and anger-mediated interracial aggression: Unmasking regressive racism. *Journal of Personality and Social Psychology, 41,* 63–73.

Rogler, Lloyd H.; Malgady, Robert G.; Costantino, Giuseppe; & Blumenthal, Rena (1987). What do culturally sensitive mental health services mean? The case of Hispanics. *American Psychologist, 42,* 565–570.

Rogoff, Barbara, & Morelli, Gilda (1989). Perspectives on children's development from cultural psychology. *American Psychologist, 44,* 343–348.

Rogoff, Barbara, & Waddell, Kathryn J. (1982). Memory for information organized in a scene by children from two cultures. *Child Development, 53,* 1224–1228.

Rokeach, Milton, & Ball-Rokeach, Sandra (1989). Stability and change in American value priorities, 1968–1981. *American Psychologist, 44,* 775–784.

Rollin, Henry (ed.) (1980). *Coping with schizophrenia.* London: Burnett.

Rook, Karen S. (1984). The negative side of social interaction: Impact on psychological well-being. *Journal of Personality and Social Psychology, 46,* 1097–1108.

Rook, Karen S. (1987). Social support versus companionship: Effects on life stress, loneliness, and evaluations by others. *Journal of Personality and Social Psychology, 52,* 1132–1147.

Rosaldo, Renato (1989). *Culture and truth: The remaking of social analysis.* Boston: Beacon Press.

Rosch, Eleanor H. (1973). Natural categories. *Cognitive Psychology, 4,* 328–350.

Rosen, R. D. (1977). *Psychobabble.* New York: Atheneum.

Rosenberg, Morris (1986). Self-concept from middle childhood through adolescence. In J. Suls & A. G. Greenwald (eds.), *Psychological perspectives on the self,* Vol. 3. Hillsdale, NJ: Erlbaum.

Rosenhan, David L. [D. L.] (1973). On being sane in insane places. *Science, 179,* 250–258.

Rosenhan, David L. (1983). Psychological abnormality and law. In C. J. Scheirer & B. L. Hammonds (eds.), *Psychology and the law: The APA Master Lecture Series*, Vol. 2. Washington, DC: American Psychological Association.

Rosenthal, Norman E.; Sack, David A.; et al. (1985). Antidepressant effects of light in seasonal affective disorder. *American Journal of Psychiatry, 142*, 163–169.

Rosenthal, Robert (1966). *Experimenter effects in behavioral research*. New York: Appleton-Century-Crofts.

Rosenthal, Robert, & Jacobson, Lenore (1987). *Pygmalion in the classroom: Teacher expectation and pupils' intellectual development.* New York: Irvington.

Rosenthal, Robert; Hall, Judith A.; Archer, Dane; DiMatteo, M. Robin; & Rogers, Peter L. (1979). The PONS test: Measuring sensitivity to nonverbal cues. In S. Weitz (ed.), *Nonverbal communication* (2nd ed.). New York: Oxford University Press.

Rosenzweig, Mark R. (1984). Experience, memory, and the brain. *American Psychologist, 39*, 365–376.

Ross, Colin A. (1989). *Multiple personality disorder: Diagnosis, clinical features, and treatment.* New York: Wiley.

Ross, Hildy S., & Lollis, Susan P. (1987). Communication within infant social games. *Developmental Psychology, 23*, 241–248.

Ross, Lee (1977). The intuitive psychologist and his shortcomings: Distortions in the attribution process. In L. Berkowitz (ed.), *Advances in experimental social psychology*, Vol. 10. New York: Academic Press.

Ross, Michael (1989). Relation of implicit theories to the construction of personal histories. *Psychological Review, 96*, 341–357.

Ross, Michael, & Fletcher, Garth J. O. (1985). Attribution and social perception. In G. Lindzey & E. Aronson (eds.), *Handbook of social psychology*, Vol. II (3rd ed.). New York: Random House.

Roth, David L., & Holmes, David S. (1985). Influence of physical fitness in determining the impact of stressful life events on physical and psychologic health. *Psychosomatic Medicine, 47*, 164–173.

Rothbaum, Fred M.; Weisz, John R.; & Snyder, Samuel S. (1982). Changing the world and changing the self: A two-process model of perceived control. *Journal of Personality and Social Psychology, 42*, 5–37.

Rothman, Barbara (1989). *Recreating motherhood.* New York: Norton.

Rotter, Julian B. (1966). Generalized expectancies for internal versus external control of reinforcement. *Psychological Monographs, 80* (Whole no. 609, 1–28).

Roueché, Berton (1984, June 4). Annals of medicine: The hoofbeats of a zebra. *New Yorker, LX*, 71–86.

Rozée, Patricia D., & Van Boemel, Gretchen (1989). The psychological effects of war trauma and abuse on older Cambodian refugee women. *Women & Therapy, 8*, 23–50.

Rubin, Zick (1973). *Liking and loving.* New York: Holt, Rinehart and Winston.

Ruda, M. A. (1982). Opiates and pain pathways: Demonstration of enkephalin synapses on dorsal horn projection neurons. *Science, 215*, 1523–1525.

Ruggiero, Vincent R. (1988). *Teaching thinking across the curriculum.* New York: Harper & Row.

Rumbaugh, Duane M. (1977). *Language learning by a chimpanzee: The Lana project.* New York: Academic Press.

Rumelhart, David E.; McClelland, James L.; & The PDP Research Group (1986). *Parallel distributed processing: Explorations in the microstructure of cognition*, Vols. 1 and 2. Cambridge, MA: MIT Press.

Rush, Florence (1980). *The best kept secret: Sexual abuse of children.* Englewood Cliffs, NJ: Prentice-Hall.

Rushton, J. Philippe (1988). Race differences in behaviour: A review and evolutionary analysis. *Personality and Individual Differences, 9*, 1009–1024.

Rushton, J. Philippe; Fulker, David W.; Neale, Michael C.; Nias, David; & Eysenck, Hans J. (1986). Altruism and aggression: The heritability of individual differences. *Journal of Personality and Social Psychology, 50*, 1192–1198.

Russell, Diana E. H. (1990). *Rape in marriage* (rev. ed.). Bloomington: Indiana University Press.

Russell, James A. (1989). Culture, scripts, and children's understanding of emotion. In C. Saarni & P. Harris (eds.), *Children's understanding of emotion.* Cambridge, England: Cambridge University Press.

Russell, James A. (1991a). Culture and the categorization of emotion. *Psychological Bulletin, 110*, 426–450.

Russell, James A. (1991b). In defense of a prototype approach to emotion concepts. *Journal of Personality and Social Psychology, 60*, 37–47.

Russell, Michael; Peeke, Harman V. S.; et al. (1984). Learned histamine release. *Science, 225*, 733–734.

Saarni, Carolyn (1989). Children's understanding of strategic control of emotional expression in social transactions. In C. Saarni & P. L. Harris (eds.), *Children's understanding of emotion.* Cambridge, England: Cambridge University Press.

Sabini, John, & Silver, Maury (1985, Winter). Critical thinking and obedience to authority. *National Forum* (Phi Beta Kappa Journal) *LXV*, 13–17.

Sacks, Oliver (1985). *The man who mistook his wife for a hat and other clinical tales.* New York: Simon & Schuster.

Safran, Jeremy D., & Segal, Zindel V. (1990). *Interpersonal process in cognitive therapy.* New York: Basic Books.

Sahley, Christie L.; Rudy, Jerry W.; & Gelperin, Alan (1981). An analysis of associative learning in a terrestrial mollusk. 1: Higher-order conditioning, blocking, and a transient US preexposure effect. *Journal of Comparative Physiology, 144*, 1–8.

Salovey, Peter, & Mayer, John D. (1990). Emotional intelligence. *Imagination, Cognition, and Personality, 9*, 185–211.

Salthouse, Timothy A. (1989). Age-related changes in basic cognitive processes. In M. Storandt & G. R. VandenBos (eds.), *The adult years: Continuity and change.* Washington, DC: The American Psychological Association.

Saltz, Bruce L.; Woerner, M. G.; Kane, J. M.; Lieberman, J. A.; et al. (1991, November 6). Prospective study of tardive dyskinesia incidence in the elderly. *Journal of the American Medical Association, 266*(17), 2402–2406.

Salzinger, Kurt (1990). A behavioral analysis of human error. Paper presented at the annual meeting of the American Psychological Association, Boston.

Samelson, Franz (1979). Putting psychology on the map: Ideology and intelligence testing. In A. R. Buss (ed.), *Psychology in social context.* New York: Irvington.

Sameroff, Arnold J., & Seifer, Ronald (1989). Social regulation of developmental continuities. Paper presented at the annual meeting of the American Association for the Advancement of Science, San Francisco.

Sameroff, Arnold J.; Seifer, Ronald; Barocas, Ralph; Zax, Melvin; & Greenspan, Stanley (1987). Intelligence quotient scores of 4-year-old children: Social-environmental risk factors. *Pediatrics, 79*, 343–350.

Sampson, Edward E. (1977). Psychology and the American ideal. *Journal of Personality and Social Psychology, 35*, 767–782.

Sampson, Edward E. (1988). The debate on individualism. *American Psychologist, 43*, 15–22.

Sanders, Diana; Warner, Pamela; Bäckström, Torbjörn; & Bancroft, John (1983). Mood, sexuality, hormones and the menstrual cycle. I. Changes in mood and physical state: Description of subjects and method. *Psychosomatic Medicine, 45*, 487–501.

Sapolsky, Robert M. (1987, July). The case of the falling nightwatchmen. *Discover, 8*, 42–45.

Sarason, Barbara R.; Shearin, Edward N.; Pierce, Gregory R.; & Sarason, Irwin G. (1987). Interrelations of social support measures: Theoretical and practical implications. *Journal of Personality and Social Psychology, 52*, 813–832.

Sarbin, Theodore R. (1991). Hypnosis: A fifty year perspective. *Contemporary Hypnosis, 8*, 1–15.

Sarbin, Theodore R. (1992). The social construction of schizophrenia. In W. Flack, D. R. Miller, & M. Wiener (eds.), *What is schizophrenia?* New York: Springer-Verlag.

Satir, Virginia (1983). *Conjoint family therapy* (3rd ed.). Palo Alto, CA: Science and Behavior Books.

Savage-Rumbaugh, E. Sue (1986). *Ape language: From conditioned response to symbol.* New York: Columbia University Press.

Savage-Rumbaugh, Sue; Sevcik, Rose A.; Brakke, Karen E.; Rumbaugh, Duane M.; & Greenfield, Patricia M. (1990). Symbols: Their communicative use, comprehension, and combination by Bonobos *(Pan paniscus)*. In C. Rovee-Collier & L. P. Lipsitt (eds.), *Advances in infancy research*, Vol. 6. Norwood, NJ: Ablex.

Saxe, Leonard (1991). Lying: Thoughts of an applied psychologist. *American Psychologist, 46*, 409–415.

Scarborough, Elizabeth, & Furumoto, Laurel (1987). *Untold lives: The first generation of American women psychologists.* New York: Columbia University Press.

Scarr, Sandra (1984a). Intelligence: What an introductory psychology student might want to know. In A. M. Rogers and C. J. Scheirer (eds.), *The G. Stanley Hall Lecture Series*, Vol. 4. Washington, DC: American Psychological Association.

Scarr, Sandra (1984b). *Mother care, other care.* New York: Basic Books.

Scarr, Sandra, & Weinberg, Richard A. (1976). IQ test performance of black children adopted by white families. *American Psychologist, 31*, 726–739.

Scarr, Sandra, & Weinberg, Richard A. (1977). Intellectual similarities within families of both adopted and biological children. *Intelligence, 1*, 170–191.

Scarr, Sandra; Pakstis, Andrew J.; Katz, Soloman H.; & Barker, William B. (1977). Absence of a relationship between degree of white ancestry and intellectual skill in a black population. *Human Genetics, 39*, 69–86.

Schachter, Stanley (1971). *Emotion, obesity, and crime.* New York: Academic Press.

Schachter, Stanley, & Singer, Jerome E. (1962). Cognitive, social, and physiological determinants of emotional state. *Psychological Review, 69*, 379–399.

Schacter, Daniel L. (1986). Amnesia and crime: How much do we really know? *American Psychologist, 41*, 286–295.

Schacter, Daniel L. (1987). Implicit memory: History and current status. *Journal of Experimental Psychology: Learning, Memory, & Cognition, 13*, 501–518.

Schacter, Daniel L., & Moscovitch, Morris (1984). Infants, amnesics, and dissociable memory systems. In M. Moscovitch (ed.), *Infant memory.* New York: Plenum.

Schank, Roger (with Peter Childers) (1988). *The creative attitude.* New York: Macmillan.

Schatzman, M.; Worsley, A.; & Fenwick, P. (1988). Correspondence during lucid dreams between dreamed and actual events. In J. Gackenbach & S. LaBerge (eds.), *Conscious mind, sleeping brain.* New York: Plenum.

Scheier, Lawrence M.; Newcomb, Michael D.; & Bentler, Peter M. (1990). Influences of drug use on mental health: An 8-year study. Paper presented at the annual meeting of the American Psychological Association, Boston.

Schein, Edgar; Schneier, Inge; & Barker, Curtis H. (1961). *Coercive persuasion.* New York: Norton.

Scherer, Klaus R. (ed.) (1988). *Facets of emotion: Recent research.* Hillsdale, N.J.: Erlbaum.

Scherer, Klaus R.; Abeles, Ronald P.; & Fischer, Claude S. (1975). *Human aggression and conflict.* Englewood Cliffs, NJ: Prentice-Hall.

Schlossberg, Nancy K. (1984). Exploring the adult years. In A. M. Rogers & C. J. Scheirer (eds.), *The G. Stanley Hall lecture series*, Vol. 4. Washington, DC: American Psychological Association.

Schlossberg, Nancy K. (1989a, Winter). Marginality and mattering: Key issues in building community. *New Directions for Student Services, 48*, 5–15.

Schlossberg, Nancy K. (1989b). *Overwhelmed: Coping with life's ups and downs.* Lexington, MA: Lexington Books.

Schmidt, Janet A. (1985). Older and wiser? A longitudinal study of the impact of college on intellectual development. *Journal of College Student Personnel, 26*, 388–394.

Schmidt, Peter J.; Nieman, Lynnette K.; Grover, Gay N.; Muller, Kari L.; et al. (1991). Lack of effect of induced menses on symptoms in women with premenstrual syndrome. *New England Journal of Medicine, 324*, 1174–1179.

Schneider, Allen M., & Tarshis, Barry (1986). *An introduction to physiological psychology* (3rd ed.). New York: Random House.

Schnell, Lisa, & Schwab, Martin E. (1990, January 18). Axonal regeneration in the rat spinal cord produced by an antibody against myelin-associated neurite growth inhibitors. *Nature, 343*, 269–272.

Schulman, Michael (1991). *The passionate mind: Bringing up an intelligent and creative child.* New York: The Free Press.

Schulman, Michael, & Mekler, Eva (1985). *Bringing up a moral child.* Reading, MA: Addison-Wesley.

Schulz, Richard, & Decker, Susan (1985). Long-term adjustment to physical disability: The role of social support, perceived control, and self-blame. *Journal of Personality and Social Psychology, 48*, 1162–1172.

Schuman, Howard, & Scott, Jacqueline (1989). Generations and collective memories. *American Journal of Sociology, 54*, 359–381.

Schwartz, Barry, & Reilly, Martha (1985). Long-term retention of a complex operant in pigeons. *Journal of Experimental Psychology: Animal Behavior Processes, 11*, 337–355.

Schwartz, Gary E. (1990). The data are always friendly: A new look at repression and health? Paper presented at the annual meeting of the Western Psychological Association, Los Angeles.

Scogin, Forrest; Bynum, Jerry; Stephens, Gretchen; & Calhoon, Sharon (1990). Efficacy of self-administered treatment programs: Meta-analytic review. *Professional Psychology: Research and Practice, 21*, 42–47.

Scott, Joseph E., & Schwalm, Loretta A. (1988). Rape rates and the circulation rates of adult magazines. *Journal of Sex Research, 24*, 241–250.

Scribner, Sylvia (1977). Modes of thinking and ways of speaking: Culture and logic reconsidered. In P. N. Johnson-Laird & P. C. Wason (eds.), *Thinking: Readings in cognitive science.* Cambridge, England: Cambridge University Press.

Scriven, Michael (1985). Critical for survival. *National Forum, 65*(1), 9–12.

Sears, David O.; Peplau, Letitia Anne; & Taylor, Shelley E. (1991). *Social psychology* (7th ed.). Englewood Cliffs, NJ: Prentice Hall.

Sears, Pauline, & Barbee, Ann H. (1977). Career and life satisfactions among Terman's gifted women. In J. C. Stanley, W. C. George, & C. H. Solano (eds.), *The gifted and the creative: A fifty-year perspective.* Baltimore, MD: Johns Hopkins University Press.

Sears, Robert R. (1977). Sources of life satisfactions of the Terman gifted men. *American Psychologist, 32*, 119–128.

Segal, Julius (1986). *Winning life's toughest battles.* New York: McGraw-Hill.

Segall, Marshall H.; Campbell, Donald T.; & Herskovits, Melville J. (1966). *The influence of culture on visual perception.* Indianapolis: Bobbs-Merrill.

Segall, Marshall H.; Dasen, Pierre R.; Berry, John W.; & Poortinga, Ype H. (1990). *Human behavior in global perspective: An introduction to cross-cultural psychology.* New York: Pergamon.

Seiden, Richard (1978). Where are they now? A follow-up study of suicide attempters from the Golden Gate Bridge. *Suicide and Life-Threatening Behavior, 8*, 203–216.

Seidenberg, Mark S., & Petitto, Laura A. (1979). Signing behavior in apes: A critical review. *Cognition, 7*, 177–215.

Sekuler, Robert, & Blake, Randolph (1985). *Perception.* New York: Knopf.

Seligman, Martin E. P. (1975). *Helplessness: On depression, development, and death.* San Francisco: Freeman.

Seligman, Martin E. P. (1991). *Learned optimism.* New York: Knopf.

Seligman, Martin E. P., & Hager, Joanne L. (1972, August). Biological boundaries of learning: The sauce-Béarnaise syndrome. *Psychology Today, 6*(3), 59–61, 84–87.

Selye, Hans (1956). *The stress of life.* New York: McGraw-Hill.

Sem-Jacobsen, C. W. (1959). Effects of electrical stimulation on the human brain. *Electroencephalography and Clinical Neurophysiology, 11,* 379.

Senden, Marius von (1960). *Space and sight: The perception of space and shape in the congenitally blind before and after operation.* (P. Heath, trans.) New York: Free Press.

Serbin, Lisa A.; O'Leary, K. Daniel; Kent, Ronald N.; & Tonick, Illene J. (1973). A comparison of teacher response to the preacademic and problem behavior of boys and girls. *Child Development, 44,* 796–804.

Shadish, William R., Jr.; Lurigio, Arthur J.; & Lewis, Dan A. (1989). After deinstitutionalization: The present and future of mental health long-term care policy. *Journal of Social Issues, 45*(3), 1–16.

Shatz, Marilyn, & Gelman, Rochel (1973). The development of communication skills: Modifications in the speech of young children as a function of the listener. *Monographs of the Society for Research in Child Development, 38.*

Shaver, Phillip, & Buhrmester, Duane (1983). Loneliness, sex-role orientation, and group life: A social needs perspective. In P. B. Paulus (ed.), *Basic group processes.* New York: Springer-Verlag.

Shaver, Phillip, & Hazan, Cindy (1987). Romantic love conceptualized as an attachment process. *Journal of Personality and Social Psychology, 52,* 511–524.

Shaver, Phillip, & O'Connor, Cary (1986). Problems in perspective. In C. Tavris (ed.), *EveryWoman's emotional well-being.* New York: Prentice Hall.

Shaver, Phillip; Hazan, Cindy; & Bradshaw, Donna (1988). Love as attachment: The integration of three behavioral systems. In R. J. Sternberg & M. Barnes (eds.), *The psychology of love.* New Haven, CT: Yale University Press.

Shaver, Phillip R.; Wu, Shelley; & Schwartz, Judith C. (1992). Cross-cultural similarities and differences in emotion and its representation: A prototype approach. In M. S. Clark (ed.), *Review of Personality and Social Psychology,* Vol. 13. Newbury Park, CA: Sage.

Shaver, Phillip; Schwartz, Judith; Krison, Donald; & O'Connor, Cary (1987). Emotion knowledge: Further exploration of a prototype approach. *Journal of Personality and Social Psychology, 52,* 1061–1086.

Shedler, Jonathan, & Block, Jack (1990). Adolescent drug use and psychological health. *American Psychologist, 45,* 612–630.

Sheehan, Neil (1988). *A bright shining lie: John Paul Vann and America in Vietnam.* New York: Random House.

Shepard, Roger N. (1967). Recognition memory for words, sentences and pictures. *Journal of Verbal Learning and Verbal Behavior, 6,* 156–163.

Shepard, Roger N., & Metzler, Jacqueline (1971). Mental rotation of three-dimensional objects. *Science, 171,* 701–703.

Sherif, Carolyn Wood (1979). Bias in psychology. In J. Sherman & E. T. Beck (eds.), *The prism of sex.* Madison: University of Wisconsin Press.

Sherif, Muzafer (1958). Superordinate goals in the reduction of intergroup conflicts. *American Journal of Sociology, 63,* 349–356.

Sherif, Muzafer; Harvey, O. J.; White, B. J.; Hood, William; & Sherif, Carolyn (1961). *Intergroup conflict and cooperation: The Robbers Cave experiment.* Norman: University of Oklahoma Institute of Intergroup Relations.

Sherman, Bonnie R., & Kunda, Ziva (1989). Motivated evaluation of scientific evidence. Paper presented at the annual meeting of the American Psychological Society, Arlington, VA.

Sherman, Lawrence W. (1992). *Policing domestic violence.* New York: Free Press.

Sherman, Lawrence W., & Berk, Richard A. (1984). The specific deterrent effects of arrest for domestic assault. *American Sociological Review, 49,* 261–271.

Sherman, Lawrence W.; Schmidt, Janell D.; Rogan, Dennis P.; et al. (1991). From initial deterrence to long-term escalation: Short-custody arrest for poverty ghetto domestic violence. *Criminology, 29,* 821–849.

Sherrington, Robin; Brynjolfsson, Jon; Petursson, Hannes; Potter, Mark; et al. (1988, November 10). Location of a susceptibility locus for schizophrenia on chromosome 5. *Nature, 336,* 164–167.

Sherry, David F., & Schacter, Daniel L. (1987). The evolution of multiple memory systems. *Psychological Review, 94,* 439–454.

Sherwin, Robert, & Corbett, Sherry (1985). Campus sexual norms and dating relationships: A trend analysis. *Journal of Sex Research, 21,* 258–274.

Shields, Stephanie A. (1975). Functionalism, Darwinism, and the psychology of women: A study in social myth. *American Psychologist, 30,* 739–754.

Shields, Stephanie A. (1991). Gender in the psychology of emotion: A selective research review. In K. T. Strongman (ed.), *International Review of Studies on Emotion,* Vol. 1. New York: Wiley.

Shiller, R. (1987). The volatility of stock market prices. *Science, 235,* 33–37.

Shinn, Marybeth; Lehmann, Stanley; & Wong, Nora (1984). Social interaction and social support. *Journal of Social Issues, 40*(4), 55–76.

Shotland, R. Lance, & Goodstein, Lynne (1984). The role of bystanders in crime control. *Journal of Social Issues, 40*(1), 9–26.

Shotland, R. Lance, & Straw, Margaret (1976). Bystander response to an assault: When a man attacks a woman. *Journal of Personality and Social Psychology, 34,* 990–999.

Shuchman, Miriam, & Wilkes, Michael S. (1990, October 7). Dramatic progress against depression. *The New York Times Magazine,* Pt. 2, *The Good Health Magazine,* 12, 30ff.

Shumaker, Sally A., & Hill, D. Robin (1991). Gender differences in social support and physical health. *Health Psychology, 10,* 102–111.

Shweder, Richard (1990). Cultural psychology—What is it? In J. W. Stigler, R. A. Shweder, & G. Herdt (eds.), *Cultural psychology: The Chicago symposia on human development.* Cambridge, England: Cambridge University Press.

Shweder, Richard A.; Mahapatra, Manamohan; & Miller, Joan G. (1987). Culture and moral development. In J. Kagan & S. Lamb (eds.), *The emergence of morality in young children.* Chicago: University of Chicago Press.

Sibatani, Atuhiro (1980, December). The Japanese brain. *Science 80,* 22–26.

Siegel, Alan B. (1991). *Dreams that can change your life.* Los Angeles: Jeremy Tarcher.

Siegel, Judith M. (1990). Stressful life events and use of physician services among the elderly: The moderating role of pet ownership. *Journal of Personality and Social Psychology, 58,* 1081–1086.

Siegel, Ronald K. (1989). *Life in pursuit of artificial paradise.* New York: Dutton.

Siegel, Shepard (1983). Classical conditioning, drug tolerance, and drug dependence. In R. G. Smart, F. B. Glaser, Y. Israel, et al. (eds.), *Research advances in alcohol and drug problems,* Vol. 7. New York: Plenum.

Siegel, Shepard, & Sdao-Jarvie, Katherine (1986). Attenuation of ethanol tolerance by a novel stimulus. *Psychopharmacology, 88,* 258–261.

Siegel, Shepard; Hinson, Riley E.; Krank, Marvin D.; & McCully, Jane (1982). Heroin "overdose" death: Contribution of drug-associated environmental cues. *Science, 216,* 436–437.

Silverstein, Brett; Peterson, Barbara; & Perdue, Lauren (1986). Some correlates of the thin standard of bodily attractiveness in women. *International Journal of Eating Disorders, 5,* 145–155.

Silverstein, Brett; Perdue, Lauren; Wolf, Cordulla; & Pizzolo, Cecilia (1988). Bingeing, purging, and estimates of parental attitudes regarding female achievement. *Sex Roles, 19,* 723–733.

Simon, Herbert (1973). The structure of ill-structured problems. *Artificial Intelligence, 4,* 181–202.

Simon, William, & Gagnon, John H. (1969, March). Psychosexual development. *Transaction, 6,* 9–18.

Simon, William, & Gagnon, John H. (1986). Sexual scripts: Permanence and change. *Archives of Sexual Behavior, 15,* 97–120.

Simpson, Jeffry A.; Campbell, Bruce; & Berscheid, Ellen (1986). The association between romantic love and marriage: Kephart (1967) twice revisited. *Personality and Social Psychology Bulletin, 12,* 363–372.

Sims, Ethan A. (1974). Studies in human hyperphagia. In G. Bray & J. Bethune (eds.), *Treatment and management of obesity.* New York: Harper & Row.

Singer, Barry, & Toates, Frederick (1987). Sexual motivation. *Journal of Sex Research, 23,* 481–501.

Singer, Jerome L. (1984). The private personality. *Personality and Social Psychology Bulletin, 10,* 7–30.

Singer, Jerome L., & Singer, Dorothy G. (1988). Some hazards of growing up in a television environment: Children's aggression and restlessness. In S. Oskamp (ed.), *Television as a social issue (Applied Social Psychology Annual,* Vol. 8). Newbury Park, CA: Sage.

Skinner, B. F. (1938). *The behavior of organisms: An experimental analysis.* New York: Appleton-Century-Crofts.

Skinner, B. F. (1948). Superstition in the pigeon. *Journal of Experimental Psychology, 38,* 168–172.

Skinner, B. F. (1948/1976). *Walden Two.* New York: Macmillan.

Skinner, B. F. (1950). Are theories of learning necessary? *Psychological Review, 57,* 193–216.

Skinner, B. F. (1956). A case history in the scientific method. *American Psychologist, 11,* 221–233.

Skinner, B. F. (1972). The operational analysis of psychological terms. In B. F. Skinner, *Cumulative record* (3rd ed.). New York: Appleton-Century-Crofts.

Skinner, B. F. (1974). *About behaviorism.* New York: Knopf.

Skinner, B. F. (1983). *A matter of consequences.* New York: Knopf.

Skinner, B. F. (1990). Can psychology be a science of mind? *American Psychologist, 45,* 1206–1210.

Skreslet, Paula (1987, November 30). The prizes of first grade. *Newsweek,* 8.

Slade, Pauline (1984). Premenstrual emotional changes in normal women: Fact or fiction? *Journal of Psychosomatic Research, 28,* 1–7.

Slater, Suzanne, & Mencher, Julie (1991). The lesbian family life cycle: A contextual approach. *American Journal of Orthopsychiatry, 61,* 372–382.

Slobin, Daniel I. (1979). *Psycholinguistics* (2nd ed.). Glenview, IL: Scott, Foresman.

Slobin, Daniel I. (1985). *The cross-linguistic study of language acquisition,* Vols. 1 & 2. Hillsdale, NJ: Erlbaum.

Small, Meredith (ed.) (1984). *Female primates.* New York: Alan Liss.

Smith, Barbara A.; Fillion, Thomas J.; & Blass, Elliott, M. (1990). Orally mediated sources of calming in 1- to 3-day-old human infants. *Developmental Psychology, 26,* 731–737.

Smith, Craig A., & Ellsworth, Phoebe C. (1987). Patterns of appraisal and emotion related to taking an exam. *Journal of Personality and Social Psychology, 52,* 475–488.

Smith, James F., & Kida, Thomas (1991). Heuristics and biases: Expertise and task realism in auditing. *Psychological Bulletin, 109,* 472–489.

Smith, Mary Lee; Glass, Gene; & Miller, Thomas I. (1980). *The benefits of psychotherapy.* Baltimore, MD: Johns Hopkins University Press.

Smith, Timothy W.; Sanders, Jill D.; & Alexander, James F. (1990). What does the Cook and Medley Hostility Scale Measure? Affect, behavior, and attributions in the marital context. *Journal of Personality and Social Psychology, 58,* 699–708.

Smith, Timothy; Snyder, C. R.; & Perkins, Suzanne C. (1983). The self-serving function of hypochondriacal complaints: Physical symptoms as self-handicapping strategies. *Journal of Personality and Social Psychology, 44,* 787–797.

Smith, Tom W. (1991). *What do Americans think about Jews?* New York: American Jewish Committee.

Smither, Robert D. (1988). *The psychology of work and human performance.* New York: Harper & Row.

Snodgrass, Mary Ann (1987). The relationships of differential loneliness, intimacy, and characterological attributional style to duration of loneliness. In M. Hojat & R. Crandall (eds.), *Loneliness: Theory, research, and applications.* (Special issue of the *Journal of Social Behavior and Personality, 2,* 173–186.)

Snodgrass, Sara E. (1985). Women's intuition: The effect of subordinate role on interpersonal sensitivity. *Journal of Personality and Social Psychology, 49,* 146–155.

Snodgrass, Sara E. (1992). Further effects of role versus gender on interpersonal sensitivity. *Journal of Personality and Social Psychology, 62,* 154–158.

Snow, Barry R; Pinter, Isaac; Gusmorino, Paul; Jimenez, Arthur; Rosenblum, Andrew; & Adelglass, Howard (1986). Sex differences in chronic pain: Incidence and causal mechanisms. Paper presented at the annual meeting of the American Psychological Association, Washington, DC.

Snyder, C. R. (1989). Reality negotiation: From excuses to hope and beyond. Special Issue: Self-illusions: When are they adaptive? *Journal of Social and Clinical Psychology, 8,* 130–157.

Snyder, C. R. (1990). Self-handicapping processes and sequelae: On the taking of a psychological dive. In R. L. Higgins, C. R. Snyder, & S. C. Berglas (eds.), *Self-handicapping: The paradox that isn't.* New York: Plenum.

Snyder, C. R., & Fromkin, Howard (1980). *Uniqueness: The human pursuit of difference.* New York: Plenum.

Snyder, C. R., & Shenkel, Randee J. (1975, March). The P. T. Barnum effect. *Psychology Today, 8*(10), 52–54.

Snyder, C. R.; Higgins, Raymond L.; & Stucky, Rita J. (1983). *Excuses: Masquerades in search of grace.* New York: Wiley-Interscience.

Snyder, Mark (1983). The influence of individuals on situations: Implications for understanding the links between personality and social behavior. *Journal of Personality, 51,* 497–516.

Snyder, Mark, & Ickes, William (1985). Personality and social behavior. In G. Lindzey & E. Aronson (eds.), *Handbook of social psychology,* Vol. 2 (3rd ed.). New York: Random House.

Solomon, Anita O. (1991). Psychotherapeutic techniques for victims of destructive cults. Paper presented at the annual meeting of the American Psychological Association, San Francisco.

Solomon, Paul R. (1979). Science and television commercials: Adding relevance to the research methodology course. *Teaching of Psychology, 6,* 26–30.

Solomon, Robert (1988). *About love.* New York: Simon & Schuster.

Sommer, Robert (1977, January). Toward a psychology of natural behavior. *APA Monitor.* (Reprinted in *Readings in psychology 78/79.* Guilford, CT: Dushkin, 1978.)

Sontag, Susan (1978). *Illness as metaphor.* New York: Farrar, Straus & Giroux.

Sorce, James F.; Emde, Robert N.; Campos, Joseph; & Klinnert, Mary D. (1985). Maternal emotional signaling; its effect on the visual cliff behavior of 1-year-olds. *Developmental Psychology, 21,* 195–200.

Spangler, William D., & House, Robert J. (1991). Presidential effectiveness and the leadership motive profile. *Journal of Personality and Social Psychology, 60,* 439–455.

Spanos, Nicholas P. (1986). Hypnotic behavior: A social-psychological interpretation of amnesia, analgesia, and "trance logic." *Behavioral and Brain Sciences, 9,* 449–467.

Spanos, Nicholas P. (1991). Hypnosis, suggestion, and creation of false memories and secondary personalities. Paper presented at the annual meeting of the American Psychological Association, San Francisco.

Spanos, Nicholas P.; Menary, Evelyn; Gabora, Natalie J.; DuBreuil, Susan C.; & Dewhirst, Bridget (1991). Secondary identity enactments during hypnotic past-life regression: A sociocognitive perspective. *Journal of Personality and Social Psychology, 61,* 308–320.

Spearman, Charles (1927). *The abilities of man.* London: Macmillan.

Speltz, Matthew L.; Greenberg, Mark T.; & Deklyen, Michelle

(1990). Attachment in preschoolers with disruptive behavior: A comparison of clinic-referred and nonproblem children. *Development & Psychopathology, 2,* 31–46.

Spence, Janet T. (1985). Achievement American style. *American Psychologist, 40,* 1285–1295.

Spencer, M. B., & Dornbusch, Sanford M. (1990). Ethnicity. In S. S. Feldman & G. R. Elliott (eds.), *At the threshold: The developing adolescent.* Cambridge, MA: Harvard University Press.

Sperling, George (1960). The information available in brief visual presentations. *Psychological Monographs, 74* (498).

Sperry, Roger W. [R. W.] (1964). The great cerebral commissure. *Scientific American, 210*(1), 42–52.

Sperry, Roger W. (1982). Some effects of disconnecting the cerebral hemispheres. *Science, 217,* 1223–1226.

Spilich, George J.; June, Lorraine; & Renner, Judith (1992). Cigarette smoking and cognitive performance. *British Journal of Addiction, 87,* 113–126.

Spitzer, Lynn, & Rodin, Judith (1987). Effects of fructose and glucose preloads on subsequent food intake. *Appetite, 8,* 135–145.

Spitzer, Robert L., & Williams, Janet B. (1988). Having a dream: A research strategy for DSM-IV. *Archives of General Psychiatry, 45,* 871–874.

Spring, Bonnie; Chiodo, June; & Bowen, Deborah J. (1987). Carbohydrates, tryptophan, and behavior: A methodological review. *Psychological Bulletin, 102,* 234–256.

Squire, Larry R. (1986). Mechanisms of memory. *Science, 232,* 1612–1619.

Squire, Larry R. (1987). *Memory and the brain.* New York: Oxford University Press.

Squire, Larry R.; Ojemann, Jeffrey G.; Miezin, Francis M.; et al. (1992). Activation of the hippocampus in normal humans: A functional anatomical study of memory. *Proceedings of the National Academy of Science, 89,* 1837–1841.

Sroufe, L. Alan (1978, October). Attachment and the roots of competence. *Human Nature, 1,* 50–57.

Staats, Carolyn K., & Staats, Arthur W. (1957). Meaning established by classical conditioning. *Journal of Experimental Psychology, 54,* 74–80.

Stam, Henderikus J. (1989). From symptom relief to cure: Hypnotic interventions in cancer. In N. P. Spanos & J. F. Chaves (eds.), *Hypnosis: The cognitive-behavioral perspective.* Buffalo, NY: Prometheus Books.

Stanovich, Keith E. (1992). *How to think straight about psychology* (3rd ed.). New York: HarperCollins.

Stapley, Janice C., & Haviland, Jeannette M. (1989). Beyond depression: Gender differences in normal adolescents' emotional experiences. *Sex Roles, 20,* 295–308.

Stapp, Joy; Tucker, Anthony M.; & VandenBos, Gary R. (1985). Census of psychological personnel: 1983. *American Psychologist, 40,* 1317–1351.

Stattin, Haken, & Magnusson, David (1990). *Pubertal maturation in female development.* Hillsdale, NJ: Erlbaum.

Staub, Ervin (1989). *The roots of evil: The origins of genocide and other group violence.* New York: Cambridge University Press.

Staub, Ervin (1990). The psychology and culture of torture and torturers. In P. Suedfeld (ed.), *Psychology and torture.* Washington, DC: Hemisphere.

Steen, Suzanne; Oppliger, Robert; & Brownell, Kelly (1988). Metabolic effects of repeated weight loss and regain in adolescent wrestlers. *Journal of the American Medical Association, 260,* 47–50.

Stein, Marvin; Miller, Andrew; & Trestman, Robert L. (1991). Depression, the immune system, and health and illness: Findings in search of meaning. *Archives of General Psychiatry, 48,* 171–177.

Steinberg, Laurence D. (1990). Interdependence in the family: Autonomy, conflict and harmony in the parent-adolescent relationship. In S. S. Feldman & G. R. Elliott (eds.), *At the threshold: The developing adolescent.* Cambridge, MA: Harvard University Press.

Stempel, Jennifer J.; Beckwith, Bill E.; & Petros, Thomas V. (1986). The effects of alcohol on the speed of memory retrieval.

Paper presented at the annual meeting of the American Psychological Association, Washington, DC.

Stenberg, Craig R., & Campos, Joseph (1990). The development of anger expressions in infancy. In N. Stein, B. Leventhal, & T. Trabasso (eds.), *Psychological and biological approaches to emotion.* Hillsdale, NJ: Erlbaum.

Stephan, Walter (1985). Intergroup relations. In G. Lindzey & E. Aronson (eds.), *Handbook of social psychology,* Vol. II. New York: Random House.

Stephan, Walter, & Brigham, John C. (1985). Intergroup contact: Introduction. *Journal of Social Issues, 41*(3), 1–8.

Stephens, Joseph (1978). Long-term prognosis and follow-up in schizophrenia. *Schizophrenia Bulletin, 4,* 25–47.

Stephens, Mitchell (1991, September 20). The death of reading. *Los Angeles Times Magazine,* 10, 12, 16, 42, 44.

Sternberg, Robert J. (1985). *Beyond IQ.* New York: Cambridge University Press.

Sternberg, Robert J. (1986). *Intelligence applied: Understanding and increasing your intellectual skills.* San Diego: Harcourt Brace Jovanovich.

Sternberg, Robert J. (1988). *The triarchic mind: A new theory of human intelligence.* New York: Viking.

Sternberg, Robert J. (1991). Theory-based testing of intellectual abilities: Rationale for the Triarchic Abilities Test. In H. A. Rowe (ed.), *Intelligence: Reconceptualization and measurement.* Hillsdale, NJ: Erlbaum.

Sternberg, Robert J., & Kolligian, John, Jr. (eds.) (1990). *Competence considered.* New Haven: Yale University Press.

Sternberg, Robert J.; Wagner, Richard K.; & Okagaki, Lynn (in press). Practical intelligence: The nature and role of tacit knowledge in work and at school. In H. Reese & J. Puckett (eds.), *Advances in lifespan development.* Hillsdale, NJ: Erlbaum.

Sternberg, Robert J.; Conway, Barbara E.; Ketron, Jerry L.; & Bernstein, Morty (1981). People's conceptions of intelligence. *Journal of Personality and Social Psychology, 41,* 37–55.

Stevenson, Harold W.; Lee, Shin-ying; Chen, Chuansheng; Lummis, Max; et al. (1990a). Mathematics achievement in children in China and the United States. *Child Development, 61,* 1053–1066.

Stevenson, Harold W.; Lee, Shin-ying; Chen, Chuansheng; Stigler, James W.; et al. (1990b). Contexts of achievement: A study of American, Chinese, and Japanese children. *Monographs of the Society for Research in Child Development, 55*(1–2).

Stewart, Abigail; Sokol, Michael; Healy, Joseph M., Jr.; Chester, Nia L.; & Weinstock-Savoy, Deborah (1982). Adaptation to life changes in children and adults: Cross-sectional studies. *Journal of Personality and Social Psychology, 43,* 1270–1282.

Stickler, Gunnar B.; Salter, Margery; Broughton, Daniel D.; & Alario, Anthony (1991). Parents' worries about children compared to actual risks. *Clinical Pediatrics, 30,* 522–528.

Stoch, M. B., & Smythe, P. M. (1963). Does undernutrition during infancy inhibit brain growth and subsequent intellectual development? *Archives of Diseases in Childhood, 38,* 546–552.

Stolzy, S.; Couture, L. J.; & Edmonds, H. L., Jr. (1986). Evidence of partial recall during general anesthesia. *Anesthesia and Analgesia, 65,* S154 (Abstract).

Stone, Lewis J., & Hokanson, Jack E. (1969). Arousal reduction via self-punitive behavior. *Journal of Personality and Social Psychology, 12,* 72–79.

Stoner, James (1961). A comparison of individual and group decisions involving risk. Unpublished master's thesis, MIT, Cambridge, MA.

Storm, Christine, & Storm, Tom (1987). A taxonomic study of the vocabulary of emotions. *Journal of Personality and Social Psychology, 53,* 805–816.

Strack, Fritz; Martin, Leonard L.; & Stepper, Sabine (1988). Inhibiting and facilitating conditions of the human smile: A nonobtrusive test of the facial-feedback hypothesis. *Journal of Social and Personality Psychology, 54,* 768–777.

Strasser, Susan (1982). *Never done: A history of American housework.* New York: Pantheon.

Stroebe, Wolfgang; Stroebe, Margaret S.; & Domittner, Günther (1988). Individual and situational differences in recovery from bereavement: A risk group identified. *Journal of Social Issues, 44*(3), 143–158.

Strube, Michael J. (1988). The decision to leave an abusive relationship: Empirical evidence and theoretical issues. *Psychological Bulletin, 104*, 236–250.

Strupp, Hans H. (1982). The outcome problem in psychotherapy: Contemporary perspectives. In J. H. Harvey & M. M. Parks (eds.), *Psychotherapy research and behavior change: The APA Master Lecture Series*, Vol. 1. Washington, DC: *American Psychological Association.*

Strupp, Hans H., & Binder, Jeffrey (1984). *Psychotherapy in a new key.* New York: Basic Books.

Strupp, Hans H., & Hadley, Suzanne (1979). Specific versus nonspecific factors in psychotherapy: A controlled study of outcome. *Archives of General Psychiatry, 36*, 1125–1136.

Stunkard, Albert J.; Harris, J. R.; Pedersen, N. L.; & McClearn, G. E. (1990, May 24). The body-mass index of twins who have been reared apart. *New England Journal of Medicine, 322*, 1483–1487.

Sue, Stanley (1991). Ethnicity and culture in psychological research and practice. In J. Goodchilds (ed.), *Psychological perspectives on human diversity in America.* Washington, DC: American Psychological Association.

Sue, Stanley, & Zane, Nolan (1987). The role of culture and cultural techniques in psychotherapy: A critique and reformulation. *American Psychologist, 42*, 37–45.

Suedfeld, Peter (1975). The benefits of boredom: Sensory deprivation reconsidered. *American Scientist, 63*(1), 60–69.

Sulloway, Frank J. (1979). *Freud: Biologist of the mind.* New York: Basic Books.

Sundstrom, Eric; De Meuse, Kenneth P.; & Futrell, David (1990). Work teams: Applications and effectiveness. *American Psychologist, 45*, 120–133.

Suomi, Stephen J. (1987). Genetic and maternal contributions to individual differences in rhesus monkey biobehavioral development. In N. Krasnegor, E. Blass, M. Hofer, & W. Smotherman (eds.), *Perinatal development: A psychobiological perspective.* New York: Academic Press.

Suomi, Stephen J. (1989). Primate separation models of affective disorders. In J. Madden (ed.), *Adaptation, learning, and affect.* New York: Raven Press.

Super, C. M. (1981). Behavioral development in infancy. In R. H. Munroe, R. L. Munroe, & B. B. Whiting (eds.), *Handbook of cross-cultural human development.* New York: Garland.

Susman, Elizabeth J.; Inoff-Germain, Gale; Nottelmann, Editha D.; et al. (1987). Hormones, emotional dispositions, and aggressive attributes in young adolescents. *Child Development, 58*, 1114–1134.

Sutton-Smith, Brian (1984). Recreation as folly's parody. *TAASP Newsletter, 10*, 4–13.

Swedo, Susan E., & Rapoport, Judith L. (1991). Trichotillomania [hair-pulling]. *Journal of Child Psychology & Psychiatry & Allied Disciplines, 32*, 401–409.

Syme, S. Leonard (1982, July-August). People need people. *American Health, 1.*

Symons, Donald (1979). *The evolution of human sexuality.* New York: Oxford University Press.

Szasz, Thomas (1961/1967). *The myth of mental illness.* New York: Dell Delta.

Szasz, Thomas (1970). *The manufacture of madness.* New York: Harper Torchbooks.

Szasz, Thomas (1987). *Insanity: The idea and its consequences.* New York: Wiley.

Tajfel, Henri, & Turner, John C. (1986). The social identity theory of intergroup behavior. In S. Worchel & W. G. Austin (eds.), *Psychology of intergroup relations.* Chicago: Nelson-Hall.

Taub, Arthur (1984). Opioid analgesics in the treatment of chronic intractable pain of non-neoplastic origin. *Pain. Supplement 2*, 204.

Taub, David M. (1984). *Primate paternalism.* New York: Van Nostrand Reinhold.

Tavris, Carol (1989). *Anger: The misunderstood emotion* (2nd ed.). New York: Touchstone/Simon & Schuster.

Tavris, Carol (1992). *The mismeasure of woman.* New York: Simon & Schuster.

Taylor, Shelley E. (1989). *Positive illusions: Creative self-deception and the healthy mind.* New York: Basic Books.

Taylor, Shelley E. (1991). *Health psychology* (2nd ed.). New York: McGraw-Hill.

Taylor, Shelley E., & Brown, Jonathon D. (1988). Illusion and well-being: A social psychological perspective on mental health. *Psychological Bulletin, 103*, 193–210.

Taylor, Shelley E., & Lobel, Marci (1989). Social comparison activity under threat: Downward evaluation and upward contacts. *Psychological Review, 96*, 569–575.

Taylor, Shelley E.; Lichtman, Rosemary R.; & Wood, Joanne V. (1984). Attributions, beliefs about control, and adjustment to breast cancer. *Journal of Personality and Social Psychology, 46*, 489–502.

Tellegen, Auke; Lykken, David T.; Bouchard, Thomas J., Jr.; et al. (1988). Personality similarity in twins reared apart and together. *Journal of Personality and Social Psychology, 54*, 1031–1039.

Temerlin, Jane W., & Temerlin, Maurice K. (1986). Some hazards of the therapeutic relationship. *Cultic Studies Journal, 3*, 234–242.

Terman, Lewis M., & Oden, Melita H. (1959). *Genetic studies of genius. V. The gifted group at mid-life.* Stanford, CA: Stanford University Press.

Terrace, H. S. (1985). In the beginning was the "name." *American Psychologist, 40*, 1011–1028.

Teyler, T. J., & DiScenna, P. (1987). Long-term potentiation. *Annual Review of Neuroscience, 10*, 131–161.

Thayer, Paul W. (1983). Industrial/organizational psychology: Science and application. In C. J. Scheirer & A. Rogers (eds.), *The G. Stanley Hall Lecture Series*, Vol. 3. Washington, DC: American Psychological Association.

Thiriart, Philippe (1991, Winter). Acceptance of personality test results. *Skeptical Inquirer, 15*, 161–165.

Thoits, Peggy A. (1986). Social support as coping assistance. *Journal of Consulting and Clinical Psychology, 54*, 416–423.

Thoma, Stephen J. (1986). Estimating gender differences in the comprehension and preference of moral issues. *Developmental Review, 6*, 165–180.

Thomas, Alexander, & Chess, Stella (1980). *The dynamics of psychological development.* New York: Brunner/Mazel.

Thomas, Alexander, & Chess, Stella (1982). Temperament and follow-up to adulthood. In R. Porter & G. M. Collins (eds.), *Temperamental differences in infants and young children.* London: Pitman.

Thomas, Alexander, & Chess, Stella (1984). Genesis and evolution of behavioral disorders: From infancy to early adult life. *American Journal of Psychiatry, 141*, 1–9.

Thomas, D. A., & Alderfer, Clayton P. (1989). The influence of race on career dynamics: Theory and research on minority career experiences. In M. Arthur, D. Hall, & B. Lawrence (eds.), *Handbook of career theory.* Cambridge, England: Cambridge University Press.

Thomas, Lewis (1983). *The youngest science: Notes of a medicine-watcher.* Toronto: Bantam.

Thomas, V. J., & Rose, F. D. (1991). Ethnic differences in the experience of pain. *Social Science and Medicine, 32*, 1063–1066.

Thompson, Lee Anne; Detterman, Douglas K.; & Plomin, Robert (1991). Associations between cognitive abilities and scholastic achievement: Genetic overlap but environmental differences. *Psychological Science, 2*, 158–165.

Thompson, Richard F. (1983). Neuronal substrates of simple associative learning: Classical conditioning. *Trends in Neurosciences, 6*, 270–275.

Thompson, Richard F. (1986). The neurobiology of learning and memory. *Science, 233*, 941–947.

Thorndike, E. L. (1898). Animal intelligence. An experimental study of the associative processes in animals. *Psychological Review Monograph Supplement, 2* (Whole No. 8).

Thorndike, E. L. (1903). *Educational psychology.* New York: Columbia University Teachers College.

Thornton, E. M. (1984). *The Freudian fallacy: An alternative view of Freudian theory.* Garden City, NY: Dial Press (Doubleday).

Thurstone, Louis L. (1938). Primary mental abilities. *Psychometric Monographs,* No. 1.

Tice, Dianne M. (1991). Esteem protection or enhancement? Self-handicapping motives and attributions differ by trait self-esteem. *Journal of Personality and Social Psychology, 60,* 711–725.

Tiefer, Leonore (1978, July). The kiss. *Human Nature, 1,* 28–37.

Tiefer, Leonore (1992). Critique of DSM-III-R nomenclature for sexual dysfunctions. *Psychiatric Medicine, 10,* 227–245.

Tinbergen, Nikolaas (1951). *The study of instinct.* Oxford: Clarendon Press.

Tolman, Edward C. (1948). Cognitive maps in rats and men. *Psychological Review, 55,* 189–208.

Tolman, E. C., & Honzik, C. H. (1930). Introduction and removal of reward and maze performance in rats. *University of California Publications in Psychology, 4,* 257–275.

Toman, Walter (1976). *Family constellation* (3rd ed.). New York: Springer.

Tomkins, Silvan S. (1962). *Affect, imagery, consciousness: I. The positive affects.* New York: Springer-Verlag.

Tomkins, Silvan S. (1981a). The quest for primary motives: Biography and autobiography of an idea. *Journal of Personality and Social Psychology, 41,* 306–329.

Tomkins, Silvan S. (1981b). The role of facial response in the experience of emotion: A reply to Tourangeau and Ellsworth. *Journal of Personality and Social Psychology, 40,* 355–357.

Torrey, E. Fuller (1988). *Surviving schizophrenia* (rev. ed.). New York: Harper & Row/Harper Colophon.

Trafimow, David; Triandis, Harry C.; & Goto, Sharon G. (1991). Some tests of the distinction between the private self and the collective self. *Journal of Personality and Social Psychology, 60,* 649–655.

Tranel, Daniel, & Damasio, Antonio (1985). Knowledge without awareness: An autonomic index of facial recognition by prosopagnosics. *Science, 228,* 1453–1454.

Tranel, Daniel; Damasio, Antonio; & Damasio, Hanna (1988). Intact recognition of facial expression, gender, and age in patients with impaired recognition of face identity. *Neurology, 38,* 690–696.

Triandis, Harry C. (1990). Cross-cultural studies of individualism and collectivism. In J. J. Berman (ed.), *Cross-cultural perspectives. Nebraska Symposium on Motivation, 1989.* Lincoln: University of Nebraska Press.

Tronick, Edward Z. (1989). Emotions and emotional communication in infants. *American Psychologist, 44,* 112–119.

Tsai, Mavis, & Uemura, Anne (1988). Asian Americans: The struggles, the conflicts, and the successes. In P. Bronstein & K. Quina (eds.), *Teaching a psychology of people.* Washington, DC: American Psychological Assocation.

Tsunoda, Tadanobu (1985). *The Japanese brain: Uniqueness and universality.* (Yoshinori Oiwa, trans.) Tokyo: Taishukan.

Tucker, Don M. (1989). Asymmetries of neural architecture and the structure of emotional experience. In R. Johnson & W. Roth (eds.), *Eighth event-related potentials international conference.* New York: Oxford University Press.

Tucker, Don M., & Williamson, Peter A. (1984). Asymmetric neural control systems in human self-regulation. *Psychological Review, 91,* 185–215.

Tucker, M. Belinda, & Taylor, Robert J. (1989). Demographic correlates of relationship status among Black Americans. *Journal of Marriage and the Family, 51,* 655–665.

Tulving, Endel (1985). How many memory systems are there? *American Psychologist, 40,* 385–398.

Tulving, Endel, & Schacter, Daniel L. (1990). Priming and human memory systems. *Science, 247,* 301–305.

Turner, Barbara F., & Adams, Catherine G. (1988). Reported change in preferred sexual activity over the adult years. *The Journal of Sex Research, 25,* 289–303.

Turner, Judith A., & Chapman, C. Richard (1982). Psychological interventions for chronic pain: A critical review. II. Operant conditioning, hypnosis, and cognitive-behavioral therapy. *Pain, 12,* 1–21, 23–46.

Tversky, Amos, & Kahneman, Daniel (1973). Availability: A heuristic for judging frequency and probability. *Cognitive Psychology, 5,* 207–232.

Tversky, Amos, & Kahneman, Daniel (1981). The framing of decisions and the psychology of choice. *Science, 211,* 453–458.

Tversky, Amos, & Kahneman, Daniel (1986). Rational choice and the framing of decisions. *Journal of Business, 59,* S25l–S278.

Tyler, Tom R., & Schuller, Regina A. (1991). Aging and attitude change. *Journal of Personality and Social Psychology, 61,* 689–697.

U. S. Department of Health and Human Services (1989). Reducing the health consequences of smoking: 25 years of progress. Report of the Surgeon General, DHHS Publication No. (CDC) 89–8411. Washington, DC.

Vaillant, George E. (1983). *The natural history of alcoholism: Causes, patterns, and paths to recovery.* Cambridge, MA: Harvard University Press.

Vaillant, George E., & Milofsky, Eva S. (1982). The etiology of alcoholism. *American Psychologist, 37,* 494–503.

Valenstein, Elliot (1986). *Great and desperate cures: The rise and decline of psychosurgery and other radical treatments for mental illness.* New York: Basic Books.

Van Cantfort, Thomas E., & Rimpau, James B. (1982). Sign language studies with children and chimpanzees. *Sign Language Studies, 34,* 15–72.

Vandenberg, Brian (1985). Beyond the ethology of play. In A. Gottfried & C. C. Brown (eds.), *Play interactions.* Lexington, MA: Lexington Books.

Van Lancker, Diana R., & Kempler, Daniel (1987). Comprehension of familiar phrases by left- but not by right-hemisphere damaged patients. *Brain & Language, 32,* 265–277.

Varela, Jacobo A. (1978, October). Solving human problems with human science. *Human Nature, 1,* 84–90.

Vasquez, Melba J. T., & Barón, Augustine, Jr. (1988). The psychology of the Chicano experience: A sample course structure. In P. Bronstein & K. Quina (eds.), *Teaching a psychology of people.* Washington, DC: American Psychological Association.

Vila, J., & Beech, H. R. (1980). Premenstrual symptomatology: An interaction hypothesis. *British Journal of Social and Clinical Psychology, 19,* 73–80.

Vokey, John R., & Read, J. Don (1985). Subliminal messages: Between the devil and the media. *American Psychologist, 40,* 1231–1239.

Von Lang, Jochen, & Sibyll, Claus (eds.) (1984). *Eichmann interrogated: Transcripts from the archives of the Israeli police.* New York: Random House.

Wadden, Thomas A.; Foster, G. D.; Letizia, K. A.; & Mullen, J. L. (1990, August 8). Long-term effects of dieting on resting metabolic rate in obese outpatients. *Journal of the American Medical Association, 264,* 707–711.

Wade, Carole, & Cerise, Sarah (1991). *Human sexuality* (2nd ed.). San Diego: Harcourt Brace Jovanovich.

Wagemaker, Herbert, Jr., & Cade, Robert (1978). Hemodialysis in chronic schizophrenic patients. *Southern Medical Journal, 71,* 1463–1465.

Wagenaar, Willem A. (1986). My memory: A study of autobiographical memory over six years. *Cognitive Psychology, 18,* 225–252.

Wagner, Richard K., & Sternberg, Robert J. (1986). Tacit knowledge and intelligence in the everyday world. In R. J. Sternberg & R. K. Wagner (eds.), *Practical intelligence: Nature and origins of competence in the everyday world.* New York: Cambridge University Press.

Walker, Edward L. (1970). Relevant psychology is a snark. *American Psychologist, 25,* 1081–1086.

Walker, Lenore (1986). Diagnosis and politics: Abuse disorders. Paper presented at the annual meeting of the American Psychological Association, Washington, DC.

Wallbott, Harald G.; Ricci-Bitti, Pio; & Bänninger-Huber, Eva (1986). Non-verbal reactions to emotional experiences. In K. R. Scherer, H. G. Wallbott, & A. B. Summerfield (eds.), *Experiencing emotion: A cross-cultural study.* Cambridge, England: Cambridge University Press.

Waller, Niels G.; Kojetin, Brian A.; Bouchard, Thomas J., Jr.; Lykken, David T.; & Tellegen, Auke (1990). Genetic and environmental influences on religious interests, attitudes, and values: A study of twins reared apart and together. *Psychological Science, 1,* 138–142.

Waller, Willard (1938). *The family: A dynamic interpretation.* New York: Dryden.

Wallerstein, Judith, & Blakeslee, Sandra (1989). *Second chances: Men, women and children a decade after divorce.* New York: Ticknor & Fields.

Wang, Alvin Y., & Thomas, Margaret H. (1992). The effect of imagery-based mnemonics on the long-term retention of Chinese characters. *Language Learning, 42.*

Wang, Alvin Y.; Thomas, Margaret H.; & Ouellette, Judith A. (1992). The keyword mnemonic and retention of second-language vocabulary words. *Journal of Educational Psychology,* (in press).

Warren, Gayle H., & Raynes, Anthony E. (1972). Mood changes during three conditions of alcohol intake. *Quarterly Journal of Studies on Alcohol, 33,* 979–989.

Watkins, L. R., & Mayer, D. J. (1982). Organization of the endogenous opiate and nonopiate pain control systems. *Science, 216,* 1185–1193.

Watson, David, & Clark, Lee Anna (1984). Negative affectivity: The disposition to experience aversive emotional states. *Psychological Bulletin, 96,* 465–490.

Watson, David, & Pennebaker, James W. (1989). Health complaints, stress, and distress: Exploring the central role of negative affectivity. *Psychological Review, 96,* 234–254.

Watson, John B. (1913). Psychology as the behaviorist views it. *Psychological Review, 20,* 158–177.

Watson, John B. (1925). *Behaviorism.* New York: Norton.

Watson, John B., & Rayner, Rosalie (1920). Conditioned emotional reactions. *Journal of Experimental Psychology, 3,* 1–14.

Watson, Peter (1981). *Twins: An uncanny relationship?* Chicago: Contemporary Books.

Watzlawick, Paul (ed.) (1984). *The invented reality.* New York: Norton.

Webb, Wilse B., & Agnew, H. W., Jr. (1974). Sleep and waking in a time-free environment. *Aerospace Medicine, 45,* 617–622.

Webb, Wilse B., & Cartwright, Rosalind D. (1978). Sleep and dreams. In M. Rosenzweig & L. Porter (eds.), *Annual Review of Psychology, 29,* 223–252.

Wechsler, David (1955). *Manual for the Wechsler Adult Intelligence Scale.* New York: Psychological Corporation.

Wechsler, David (1958). *The measurement and appraisal of adult intelligence* (4th ed.). Baltimore: Williams & Wilkins.

Wegner, Daniel M.; Schneider, David J.; Carter, Samuel R., III; & White, Teri L. (1987). Paradoxical effects of thought suppression. *Journal of Personality and Social Psychology, 53,* 5–13.

Wehr, Thomas A.; Sack, David A.; & Rosenthal, Norman E. (1987). Seasonal affective disorder with summer depression and winter hypomania. *American Journal of Psychiatry, 144,* 1602–1603.

Weick, Karl E. (1984). Small wins: Redefining the scale of social problems. *American Psychologist, 39,* 40–49.

Weil, Andrew T. (1972/1986). *The natural mind: A new way of looking at drugs and the higher consciousness.* Boston: Houghton Mifflin.

Weil, Andrew T. (1974a, June). Parapsychology: Andrew Weil's search for the true Geller. *Psychology Today, 8*(1), 45–50.

Weil, Andrew T. (1974b, July). Parapsychology: Andrew Weil's search for the true Geller—Part II. The letdown. *Psychology Today, 8*(2), 74–78, 82.

Weinberg, Richard A.; Scarr, Sandra; & Waldman, Irwin D. (1992). The Minnesota transracial adoption study: A follow-up of IQ test performance at adolescence. *Intelligence, 16,* 117–135.

Weiner, Bernard (1986). *An attributional theory of motivation and emotion.* New York: Springer-Verlag.

Weiner, Bernard, & Graham, Sandra (1984). An attributional approach to emotional development. In C. E. Izard, J. Kagan, & R. B. Zajonc (eds.), *Emotions, cognition, and behavior.* Cambridge, England: Cambridge University Press.

Weiner, Bernard; Figueroa-Muñoz, Alice; & Kakihara, Craig (1991). The goals of excuses and communication strategies related to causal perceptions. *Personality and Social Psychology Bulletin, 17,* 4–13.

Weisburd, Stefi (1984, April 7). Food for mind and mood. *Science News, 125*(14), 216–219.

Weisz, John R.; Rothbaum, Fred M.; & Blackburn, Thomas C. (1984). Standing out and standing in: The psychology of control in America and Japan. *American Psychologist, 39,* 955–969.

Weitzman, Lenore J. (1985). *The divorce revolution.* New York: The Free Press.

Welfel, Elizabeth R., & Davison, Mark L. (1986). The development of reflective judgment during the college years: A four-year longitudinal study. *Journal of College Student Personnel, 27,* 209–216.

Welwood, John (ed.) (1983). *Awakening the heart: East-west approaches to psychotherapy and the healing relationship.* Boulder, CO: Shambhala.

Wender, Paul H., & Klein, Donald F. (1981). *Mind, mood, and medicine: A guide to the new biopsychiatry.* New York: Farrar, Straus & Giroux.

Werner, Emmy E. (1989). High-risk children in young adulthood: A longitudinal study from birth to 32 years. *American Journal of Orthopsychiatry, 59,* 72–81.

Werner, Emmy, & Smith, Ruth S. (1982). *Vulnerable but invincible: A longitudinal study of resilient children and youth.* New York: McGraw-Hill.

Wessells, Michael G. (1982). *Cognitive psychology.* New York: Harper & Row.

West, Melissa O., & Prinz, Ronald J. (1987). Parental alcoholism and childhood psychopathology. *Psychological Bulletin, 102,* 204–218.

Wheeler, Anthony (1990, Fall). Biological cycles and rhythms vs. biorhythms. *Skeptical Inquirer,* 75–82.

White, Robert W. (1959). Motivation reconsidered: The concept of competence. *Psychological Review, 66,* 297–333.

White, Sheldon H., & Pillemer, David B. (1979). Childhood amnesia and the development of a socially accessible memory system. In J. F. Kihlstrom & F. J. Evans (eds.), *Functional disorders of memory.* Hillsdale, NJ: Erlbaum.

Whitehouse, Wayne G.; Dinges, David F.; Orne, Emily C.; & Orne, Martin T. (1988). Hypnotic hypermnesia: Enhanced memory accessibility or report bias? *Journal of Abnormal Psychology, 97,* 289–295.

Whitehurst, G. J.; Falco, F. L.; Lonigan, C. J.; Fischel, J. E.; et al. (1988). Accelerating language development through picture book reading. *Developmental Psychology, 24,* 552–559.

Whiting, Beatrice B., & Edwards, Carolyn P. (1988). *Children of different worlds: The formation of social behavior.* Cambridge, MA: Harvard University Press.

Whiting, Beatrice, & Whiting, John (1975). *Children of six cultures.* Cambridge, MA: Harvard University Press.

Whorf, Benjamin L. (1941). The relation of habitual thought and behavior to language. In L. Spier (ed.), *Language, culture, and personality.* Menasha, WI: Sapir Memorial Publication Fund.

Whorf, Benjamin L. (1956). Science and linguistics. In J. B. Carroll (ed.), *Language, thought and reality: Selected writings of Benjamin Lee Whorf*. Cambridge, MA: MIT Press.

Wicklund, Robert A., & Brehm, Jack W. (1976). *Perspectives on cognitive dissonance*. Hillsdale, NJ: Erlbaum.

Widom, Cathy S. (1989). Does violence beget violence? A critical examination of the literature. *Psychological Bulletin, 106*, 3–28.

Wigdor, Alexandra K., & Garner, W. R. (eds.) [National Research Council Assembly of Behavioral and Social Sciences] (1982). *Ability testing: Uses, consequences, and controversies*. Washington, DC: National Academy Press.

Wiggins, Jack G. (1991). Anxiety: A cooperative approach. Paper presented at the annual meeting of the American Psychological Association, San Francisco.

Wiley, James, & Camacho, Terry (1980). Life-style and future health: Evidence from the Alameda County Study. *Preventive Medicine, 9*, 1–21.

Williams, Kipling D., & Karau, Steven J. (1991). Social loafing and social compensation: The effects of expectations of co-worker performance. *Journal of Personality and Social Psychology, 61*, 570–581.

Williams, Redford B., Jr.; Barefoot, John C.; & Shekelle, Richard B. (1985). The health consequences of hostility. In M. A. Chesney & R. H. Rosenman (eds.), *Anger and hostility in cardiovascular and behavioral disorders*. New York: Hemisphere.

Willis, Sherry L. (1987). Cognitive training and everyday competence. In K. W. Schaie (ed.), *Annual review of gerontology and geriatrics*, Vol. 7. New York: Springer.

Wilner, Daniel; Walkley, Rosabelle; & Cook, Stuart (1955). *Human relations in interracial housing*. Minneapolis: University of Minnesota Press.

Wilson, Edward O. (1975). *Sociobiology: The new synthesis*. Cambridge, MA: Belknap/Harvard University Press.

Wilson, Melvin N. (1989). Child development in the context of the black extended family. *American Psychologist, 44*, 380–385.

Windholz, George, & Lamal, P. A. (1985). Kohler's insight revisited. *Teaching of Psychology, 12*, 165–167.

Winick, Myron; Meyer, Knarig Katchadurian; & Harris, Ruth C. (1975). Malnutrition and environmental enrichment by early adoption. *Science, 190*, 1173–1175.

Winter, David G. (1988). The power motive in women—and men. *Journal of Personality and Social Psychology, 54*, 510–519.

Wispé, Lauren G., & Drambarean, Nicholas C. (1953). Physiological need, word frequency, and visual duration thresholds. *Journal of Experimental Psychology, 46*, 25–31.

Wood, Gordon (1984). Research methodology: A decision-making perspective. In A. M. Rogers & C. J. Scheirer (eds.), *The G. Stanley Hall Lecture Series*, Vol. 4. Washington, DC: American Psychological Association.

Wooley, O. Wayne, & Wooley, Susan C. (1985). Color-A-Person: A new body image test. Paper presented at the annual convention of the American Psychological Association, Los Angeles.

Wooley, Susan; Wooley, O. Wayne; & Dyrenforth, Susan (1979). Theoretical, practical, and social issues in behavioral treatments of obesity. *Journal of Applied Behavior Analysis, 12*, 3–25.

Woolfolk, Robert L., & Lehrer, Paul M. (1984). Are stress reduction techniques interchangeable or do they have specific effects?: A review of the comparative empirical literature. In R. L. Woolfolk & P. M. Lehrer (eds.), *Principles and practice of stress management*. New York: Guilford Press.

Woolfolk, Robert L., & Richardson, Frank C. (1984). Behavior therapy and the ideology of modernity. *American Psychologist, 39*, 777–786.

Wright, R. L. D. (1976). *Understanding statistics: An informal introduction for the behavioral sciences*. New York: Harcourt Brace Jovanovich.

Wu, T-C; Tashkin, Donald P.; Djahed, B.; & Rose, J. E. (1988). Respiratory hazards of smoking marijuana as compared with tobacco. *New England Journal of Medicine, 318*, 347–351.

Wurtman, Richard J. (1982). Nutrients that modify brain function. *Scientific American, 264*(4), 50–59.

Wurtman, Richard J., & Lieberman, Harris R. (eds.) (1982–1983). Research strategies for assessing the behavioral effects of foods and nutrients. *Journal of Psychiatric Research, 17*(2) [whole issue].

Wyatt, Gail E., & Mickey, M. Ray (1987). Ameliorating the effects of child sexual abuse: An exploratory study of support by parents and others. *Journal of Interpersonal Violence, 2*, 403–414.

Yalom, Irvin D. (1989). *Love's executioner & other tales of psychotherapy*. New York: Basic Books.

Yazigi, R. A.; Odem, R. R.; & Polakoski, K. L. (1991, October 9). Demonstration of specific binding of cocaine to human spermatozoa. *Journal of the American Medical Association, 266*(14), 1956–1959.

Yoken, Carol, & Berman, Jeffrey S. (1984). Does paying a fee for psychotherapy alter the effectiveness of treatment? *Journal of Consulting and Clinical Psychology, 52*, 254–260.

Zahn-Waxler, Carolyn; Radke-Yarrow, Marian; & King, Robert (1979). Child-rearing and children's pro-social initiations toward victims of distress. *Child Development, 50*, 319–330.

Zahn-Waxler, Carolyn; Kochanska, Grazyna; Krupnick, Janice; & McKnew, Donald (1990). Patterns of guilt in children of depressed and well mothers. *Developmental Psychology, 26*, 51–59.

Zajonc, Robert B. (1968). Attitudinal effects of mere exposure. *Journal of Personality and Social Psychology, 9, Monograph Supplement 2*, 1–27.

Zajonc, Robert B., & Markus, Gregory B. (1975). Birth order and intellectual development. *Psychological Review, 82*, 74–88.

Zajonc, R. B.; Murphy, Sheila T.; & Inglehart, Marita (1989). Feeling and facial efference: Implications of the vascular theory of emotion. *Psychological Review, 96*, 395–416.

Zellman, Gail, & Goodchilds, Jacqueline (1983). Becoming sexual in adolescence. In E. R. Allgeier & N. B. McCormick (eds.), *Changing boundaries: Gender roles and sexual behavior*. Palo Alto, CA: Mayfield.

Zilbergeld, Bernie (1983). *The shrinking of America: Myths of psychological change*. Boston: Little, Brown.

Zillmann, Dolf (1983). Transfer of excitation in emotional behavior. In J. T. Cacioppo & R. E. Petty (eds.), *Social psychophysiology: A sourcebook*. New York: Guilford Press.

Zimbardo, Philip (1970). The human choice: Individuation, reason, and order versus deindividuation, impulse, and chaos. In W. J. Arnold & D. Levine (eds.), *Nebraska Symposium on Motivation, 1969*. Lincoln: University of Nebraska Press.

Zimbardo, Philip G., & Hartley, Cynthia F. (1985, Spring-Summer). Cults go to high school: A theoretical and empirical analysis of the initial stage in the recruitment process. *Cultic Studies Journal, 2*, 91–147.

Zinberg, Norman (1974). The search for rational approaches to heroin use. In P. G. Bourne (ed.), *Addiction*. New York: Academic Press.

Zivian, Marilyn, & Darjes, Richard (1983). Free recall by in-school and out-of-school adults: Performance and metamemory. *Developmental Psychology, 19*, 513–520.

Zonderman, Alan B.; Costa, Paul T., Jr.; & McCrae, Robert R. (1989, September 1). Depression as a risk for cancer morbidity and mortality in a nationally representative sample. *Journal of the American Medical Association, 262*, 1191–1195.

Zuckerman, Marvin (ed.) (1983). *Biological bases of sensation seeking, impulsivity, and anxiety*. Hillsdale, NJ: Erlbaum.

Zuckerman, Marvin (1990). The psychophysiology of sensation seeking. Special Issue: Biological foundations of personality: Evolution, behavioral genetics, and psychophysiology. *Journal of Personality, 58*, 313–345.

Zuckerman, Marvin; Kuhlman, D. Michael; & Camac, Curt (1988). What lies beyond E and N? Factor analyses of scales believed to measure basic dimensions of personality. *Journal of Personality and Social Psychology, 54*, 96–107.

CREDITS

TEXT AND TABLES

CHAPTER 1 Page 26, George Miller in Jonathan Miller, *States of Mind*, pp. 15–16, © 1983 by Pantheon Books, a division of Random House, Inc.

CHAPTER 3 Page 101, from Richard Restak, "Is free will a fraud?" *Science Digest*, *91*(10), October 1983.

CHAPTER 6 Page 220, from Paul Chance, "Knock wood," *Psychology Today*, October 1988, pp. 68–69, © PT Partners, L. P.; reprinted with permission from *Psychology Today* magazine / p. 228, from Robert A. Rescorla, "Pavlovian conditioning: It's not what you think it is," *American Psychologist*, *43*, © 1988 by the American Psychological Association; reprinted by permission of the publisher.

CHAPTER 8 Page 281, from Sylvia Scribner, "Modes of thinking and ways of speaking: Culture and logic reconsidered," in P. N. Johnson-Laird and P. C. Wason (eds.), *Thinking: Readings in Cognitive Science*, 1977, Cambridge University Press, New York / p. 283, from Kathleen Galotti, "Approaches to studying formal and everyday reasoning," *Psychological Bulletin*, *105*, 1989, © 1989 by the American Psychological Association; adapted by permission.

CHAPTER 11 Page 410, from Richard C. Lewontin, Steve Rose, and Leon J. Kamin, *Not in Our Genes: Biology, Ideology, and Human Nature*, p. 11, © 1984 by Pantheon Books, a division of Random House, Inc.

CHAPTER 12 Page 432, from Sigmund Freud, *The Ego and the Id*, translated by James Strachey, © 1960 by James Strachey; used by permission of W. W. Norton & Co., Inc. / pp. 452–453, from C. R. Snyder and Randee J. Shenkel, "The P. T. Barnum Effect," *Psychology Today*, March 1975; reprinted with permission from *Psychology Today* magazine; © 1975 (Sussex Publishers, Inc.) / p. 465, from Paul H. Mussen et al., *Child Development and Personality*, 1984, Harper & Row, Publishers, Inc. / p. 472, from Daniel Slobin, *Psycholinguistics*, 1979, Scott, Foresman and Co.

CHAPTER 13 Page 462, from Helen Bee, *The Developing Child*, 1989, Harper & Row, Publishers, Inc. / p. 472, from Helen Bee, *The Developing Child*, 1989, Harper & Row, Publishers, Inc.

CHAPTER 16 Pages 576–577, from Pamela King, "The chemistry of doubt," *Psychology Today*, October 1989, pp. 58–60; reprinted with permission from *Psychology Today* magazine; © 1989 (Sussex Publishers, Inc.) / p. 592, from Stanton Peele and Archie Brodsky with Mary Arnold, *The Truth About Addiction and Recovery*, © 1991 by Stanton Peele and Archie Brodsky with Mary Arnold; abridged by permission of Simon & Schuster, Inc. / p. 596, from Eugen Bleuler, *Dementia Praecox or the Group of Schizophrenias*, 1950, International Universities Press, Madison, CT.

CHAPTER 18 Pages 641, 647, 649, excerpts from Stanley Milgram, *Obedience to Authority*, © 1974 by Stanley Milgram; reprinted by permission of HarperCollins Publishers / p. 655, from Dean Peabody, *National Characteristics*, 1985, Cambridge University Press, New York / p. 676, from Sheldon Harnick, "Merry Little Minuet," Alley Music Corp.; reprinted by permission.

ILLUSTRATIONS

CHAPTER 1 Page 23, from Joy Stapp, Anthony M. Tucker, and Gary VandenBos, "Census of psychological personnel: 1983," *American Psychologist*, *40*(12), © 1985 by the American Psychological Association; reprinted by permission of the publisher.

CHAPTER 2 Page 52, from R. L. D. Wright, *Understanding Statistics: An Informal Introduction for the Behavioral Sciences*, "Correlations," p. 240, © 1976 by Harcourt Brace Jovanovich, Inc.; reproduced by permission of the publisher / p. 60, from R. L. D. Wright, *Understanding Statistics: An Informal Introduction for the Behavioral Sciences*, "Same mean, different variables," p. 112, © 1976 by Harcourt Brace Jovanovich; reproduced by permission of the publisher / p. 64, from Sapolsky, 1987; courtesy *Discover* magazine, © 1987.

CHAPTER 4 Page 115, from Wilse B. Webb and H. W. Agnew, Jr., "Sleep and waking in a time-free environment," *Aerospace Medicine*, *45* (1974); reprinted with the permission of the authors / p. 119, from McFarlane, Martin, and Williams, "Mood changes in men and women," *Psychology of Women Quarterly*, *12* (1988), pp. 201–223; reprinted by permission of Cambridge University Press / p. 124, from Dennis D. Kelly, "Physiology of sleep and dreaming," in E. Kandel and J. Schwartz (eds.), *Principles of Neural Science*, © 1981 by Elsevier Science Publishing Co.; reprinted by permission of the publisher.

CHAPTER 5 Page 155, from F. A. Geldard, *Fundamentals of Psychology*, © 1962 by John Wiley & Sons; reprinted by permission of Jeannette M. Geldard / p. 158, reprinted with permission from the American Academy of Otolaryngology—Head and Neck Surgery, Alexandria, Virginia / p. 178, from Maxwell M. Mozell et al., "Nasal chemoreception in flavor identification," *Archives of Otolaryngology*, *90*, p. 371, © 1969 by the American Medical Association.

CHAPTER 6 Page 204, from Ivan P. Pavlov, *Conditioned Reflexes*, trans. by G. V. Anrep, 1927, Oxford University Press, Oxford, England / p. 219, from Paul Chance, *Learning and Behavior*, p. 125, © 1979 by Wadsworth Publishing Co., Inc.; reprinted by permission of the publisher / p. 225, "Turning play into work" from David Greene and Mark R. Lepper, "Intrinsic motivation: How to turn play into work," *Psychology Today*, September 1974, p. 52; adapted with permission from *Psychology Today* magazine; © 1974 (Sussex Publishers, Inc.) / p. 229, from E. C. Tolman and C. H. Honzik, "Introduction and removal of reward and maze performance in rats," *University of California Publications in Psychology*, *4* (1930).

CHAPTER 7 Page 248, adapted from Michael G. Wessell, *Cognitive Psychology*, p. 98, © 1982 by Harper & Row, Publishers, Inc. / p. 249, from Elizabeth Loftus, *Memory*, p. 25, © 1980, Addison-Wesley Publishing Co., Inc., Reading, MA / p. 255, from Terence S. Luce, "Blacks, whites, and yellows: They all look alike to me," *Psychology Today*, November 1974, p. 108; reprinted with permission from *Psychology Today* magazine; © 1974 (Sussex Publishers, Inc.) / p. 268, from Hermann Ebbinghaus, *Memory: A Contribution to Experimental Psychology*, 1885/1964, Dover Publications, Inc. / p. 269, from Marigold Linton, "I remember it well," *Psychology Today*, July 1979, p. 85; adapted with permission from *Psychology Today* magazine; © 1979 (Sussex Publishers, Inc.).

CHAPTER 8   Page 285, from Daniel Hallin, "Sound bite news: Television coverage of elections, 1968–1988," Woodrow Wilson International Center for Scholars, 1991 / James L. Adams, *Conceptual Blockbusting*, © 1986 Addison-Wesley Publishing Co., Inc., Reading, MA; reprinted by permission of the publisher.

CHAPTER 10   Page 362, reprinted with permission from *Los Angeles* magazine; all rights reserved.

CHAPTER 11   Page 383, adapted from Lee J. Cronbach, *Essentials of Psychological Testing*, 4th ed., p. 208, © 1984 by Harper & Row, Publishers, Inc. / p. 399, from Thomas J. Bouchard, Jr., and Matthew McGue, "Familial studies of intelligence: A review," *Science*, 212 (4498), May 29, 1981, © 1981 by the American Association for the Advancement of Science / p. 401, from Arnold J. Sameroff and Ronald Seifer, "Social regulation of development continuities," reprinted by permission of the authors.

CHAPTER 13   Page 473, from George A. Miller, "How children learn words," *Scientific American*, September 1987, p. 98, reprinted with permission / p. 476, from Jerome Kagan, Richard B. Kearsley, and Philip R. Zelazo, *Infancy: Its Place in Human Development*, Cambridge, MA: Harvard University Press; © 1978 by the President and Fellows of Harvard College; reprinted by permission of the publishers.

CHAPTER 14   Page 512, from "Shortchanging girls, shortchanging America," 1991; reprinted by permission of the American Association of University Women, Washington, DC.

CHAPTER 15   Page 542, from David Holmes, *Abnormal Psychology*; © 1991 by HarperCollins Publishers; reprinted by permission of HarperCollins Publishers / p. 554, from David Holmes, *Abnormal Psychology*; © 1991 by HarperCollins Publishers; reprinted by permission of HarperCollins Publishers.

CHAPTER 16   Page 583, from Robert Hare, "Acquisition and generalization of conditioned fear response in psychopathic and nonpsychopathic criminals," *Journal of Psychology*, p. 369, 1965; reprinted with permission of the Helen Dwight Reid Educational Foundation; published by Heldref Pulications, 1319 Eighteenth Street, N.W., Washington, DC 20036-1802; © 1965 / p. 593, from Lee N. Robins, Darlene N. Davis, and Donald W. Goodwin, *American Journal of Epidemiology*, 99, pp. 235–249, 1974; reprinted by permission of the *American Journal of Epidemiology* and the authors.

CHAPTER 17   Page 619, adapted from Monica McGoldrick and Randy Garson, *Genograms in Family Assessment*, Norton; used by permission of the authors / p. 628, from Robert F. Hobson, *Forms of Feeling*, 1985, Tavistock Publications, pp. 11–13 / p. 630, from Kenneth I. Howard et al., "The dose-effect relationship in psychotherapy," *American Psychologist*, 41, February 1986, p. 160, © 1986 by the American Psychological Association; reprinted by permission of the publisher and author.

CHAPTER 18   Page 656, Gordon Allport, *The Nature of Prejudice*, pp. 13–14, © 1974, Addison-Wesley Publishing Co., Inc., Reading, MA; reprinted with permission / p. 657, from R. Rogers and S. Prentice-Dunn, "Deindividuation and anger-mediated interracial aggression: Unmasking regressive racism," *Journal of Personality and Social Psychology*, 41, p. 68; © 1981 by the American Psychological Association; reprinted by permission.

PHOTOGRAPHS

Unless otherwise acknowledged, all photographs are the property of ScottForesman.

TABLE OF CONTENTS   Page vi Bob Daemmrich/Stock, Boston / p. vii Mehmet Biber/Photo Researchers / p. viii top, Erik Svensson/The Stock Market; bottom, K. Preuss/The Image Works / pp. ix, x AP/Wide World / p. xii Peter Beck/The Stock Market / p. xiii Alfred Gescheidt/The Image Bank / p. xiv Gary Faber/The Image Bank.

CHAPTER 1   Page 2 Robert Fludd, *Utriusque Cosmi*, 1619–21 / p. 3 Fonds/Cosmopress, Geneva / p. 6 Randa Bishop/Uniphoto / p. 7 left, Mark E. Gibson/The Stock Market; center, William Thompson/The Picture Cube; right, Eric Sanford/Adventure Photo / p. 9 top, The Granger Collection, New York; bottom, Archives of the History of American Psychology / p. 11 Courtesy of the Harvard University Archives / p. 12 *Dutch Proverbs* by Pieter Bruegel the El-

der, Gemäldegalerie, Staatliche Museen Preußischer Kulturbesitz, Berlin (photo: Jörg P. Anders) / p. 13 top, Archives of the History of American Psychology; bottom, *Dutch Proverbs* (detail) by Pieter Bruegel the Elder, Gemäldegalerie, Staatliche Museen Preußischer Kulturbesitz, Berlin (photo: Jörg P. Anders) / p. 14 Max Halberstadt/Mary Evans/Sigmund Freud Copyrights/Courtesy of W. E. Freud / pp. 15, 17, 18, 19 *Dutch Proverbs* (details) by Pieter Bruegel the Elder, Gemäldegalerie, Staatliche Museen Preußischer Kulturbesitz, Berlin (photo: Jörg P. Anders) / p. 25 left, Roe DiBona; right, Vladimir Lange/The Image Bank / p. 26 Steve Skloot/Photo Researchers / p. 30 Dick Ruhl / p. 32 top, Dick Ruhl; bottom, BENT OFFERINGS by Don Addis. By permission of Don Addis and Creators Syndicate / p. 36 top left, Stuart Franklin/Magnum; top right, Crickmay/*Daily Telegraph*/International Stock; bottom, Chris Callis / p. 37 top left, Tannenbaum/Sygma; top right, Dennis Brack/Black Star; center left, Courtesy of Natural Nectar Corp.; center right, Daniel Lainé/Actuel; bottom, Jim Anderson/Woodfin Camp & Associates.

CHAPTER 2   Page 38 Bob Daemmrich/Stock, Boston / p. 39 Jacques Chenet/Woodfin Camp & Associates / p. 40 left, Charles Moore/Black Star; right, Dan McCoy/Black Star / p. 43 Gale Zucker/Stock, Boston / p. 44 The Bettmann Archive / p. 46 From Susan Curtiss, *Genie: A Modern Day Wild Child*, Academic Press; used by permission / p. 48 both, J. Guichard/Sygma / p. 54 Joseph Schuyler/Stock, Boston / p. 57 Tom McCarthy/The Picture Cube / p. 60 top, *Miss Peach* by Mell Lazarus. By permission of Mell Lazarus and Creators Syndicate / p. 62 Enrico Ferorelli / p. 66 Jim Amos/Photo Researchers.

CHAPTER 3   Page 74 Howard Sochurek/The Stock Market / p. 78 top, Roe DiBona / p. 83 top, Biophoto Associates/Science Source/Photo Researchers / p. 89 Dan McCoy/Rainbow / p. 90 Fritz Goro, *Life* Magazine © Time Warner Inc. / p. 91 top, Courtesy of Drs. Michael E. Phelps and John C. Mazziotta, UCLA School of Medicine; bottom, Howard Sochurek / p. 97 Warren Anatomical Museum, Harvard Medical School / p. 102 Courtesy of Natural Nectar Corp. / p. 104 both, Howard Sochurek / p. 105 Copyright © 1992 The Time Inc. Magazine Company. Reprinted by permission.

CHAPTER 4   Page 112 Mehmet Biber/Photo Researchers / p. 113 The Granger Collection, New York / p. 116 left, Earl Scott/Photo Researchers; right, Tom Evans/Photo Researchers / p. 117 Chris Steele-Perkins/Magnum / p. 121 Brown Brothers / p. 122 left, Melissa Hayes English/Photo Researchers; right, Earl Roberge/Photo Researchers / p. 124 top and center, Walter Chandoha / p. 125 L&D Klein/Photo Researchers / p. 127 all, Allan Hobson/Science Source/Photo Researchers / p. 130 left, Mehmet Biber/Photo Researchers; right, Tibor Hirsch/Photo Researchers / p. 136 both, Omikron/Photo Researchers / p. 138 left, Paula M. Lerner/The Picture Cube; right, Tom McCarthy/Unicorn / p. 139 National Library of Medicine / p. 141 Ernest Hilgard, Stanford University / p. 143 The Bettmann Archive.

CHAPTER 5   Page 150 Erik Svensson/The Stock Market / p. 151 From R. L. Gregory and J. C. Wallace, "Recovery from early blindness," *Experimental Psychological Society Monograph No. 2* (Cambridge, 1963) / p. 155 bottom left and right, Gary Retherford / p. 158 both, from Tom N. Cornsweet, "Information processing in human visual systems," reprinted by permission from Issue 5, *The SRI Journal*. © January 1969, SRI International / p. 159 top, Tony O'Brien/Picture Group; bottom, Michael Beasley/TSW, Chicago / p. 166 top, Ron James; bottom left, Kaiser Porcelain Ltd. (Artist: Judy Cousins) / p. 169 top, left to right, Erik Svensson/The Stock Market; J. Williamson/Photo Researchers; Roy Schneider/The Stock Market; center, left to right, Nicholas De Sciose/Photo Researchers; Milt & Joan Mann/Cameramann International; L. Fleming/The Image Works; bottom, Barrie Rokeach/Photo 20-20 / p. 170 The "Bizarro" cartoon by Dan Piraro is reprinted courtesy of Chronicle Features, San Francisco, CA / p. 175 bottom, Molly Webster/© 1982 *Discover* Magazine / p. 180 Arthur Tress/Photo Researchers / p. 182 left, Dan Helms/Duomo; right, Barbara Morgan, *Martha Graham, Letter to the World (Kick)*. 1940. Gelatin-silver print, 14 3/4 × 18 3/8″. Collection, The Museum of Modern Art, New York. John Spencer Fund. © Barbara Morgan-Willard and Barbara Morgan Archives / p. 184 left, Enrico Ferorelli / p. 185 Arnaud Borrel/Gamma-Liaison / p. 186 Tony Schwartz / p. 191 both, *Magic*, Dover Publications.

CHAPTER 6 Page 198 K. Preuss/The Image Works / p. 199 Don & Pat Valenti / p. 200 Tom Tucker/Monkmeyer Press / p. 202 top, The Granger Collection, New York / p. 205 Cameramann/The Image Works / p. 207 Courtesy of Professor Benjamin Harris, from Watson's 1919 film *Experimental Investigation of Babies* / p. 211 Joe McNally / p. 219 top, Randy Taylor/Sygma / p. 220 Eric Carle/Stock, Boston / p. 222 David Young-Wolff/PhotoEdit / p. 223 Marion E. Hilton / p. 224 Ira Wyman/Sygma / p. 227 Adam Woolfitt/Woodfin Camp & Associates / p. 230 Adam Woolfitt/Susan Griggs Agency / p. 232 all, R. Epstein, "'Insight' in the Pigeon," Epstein et al., 1984.

CHAPTER 7 Page 238 AP/Wide World / p. 239 The Bettmann Archive / p. 240 Copyright © 1985, 1958 by Robert L. May Co. Reprinted by permission of Modern Curriculum Press, Inc. / p. 244 Ed Carlin/The Picture Cube / p. 245 Richard Hutchings/Photo Researchers / p. 247 Lenore Weber / p. 251 Jerry Jacka / p. 252 top left, Porterfield-Chickering/Photo Researchers; top right, Don & Pat Valenti; bottom, Raoul Hackel/Stock, Boston / p. 254 Charles Steiner/Sygma / p. 255 bottom, Paul Shambroom/Photo Researchers / p. 259 both, Larry R. Squire, Veterans Affairs Medical Center, San Diego, CA / p. 260 Wasyl Szrodzinski/Photo Researchers / p. 261 Sidney Harris / p. 266 The Museum of Modern Art/Film Stills Archive / p. 267 Catherine Ursillo/Photo Researchers / p. 270 AP/Wide World / p. 271 top, Sidney Harris.

CHAPTER 8 Page 275 Robert Frerck/Odyssey Productions, Chicago / p. 276 The Metropolitan Museum of Art, Gift of Thomas F. Ryan, 1910 (11.173.9) / p. 277 Cary Wolinsky/Stock, Boston / p. 278 left to right, Benaroch/Lazic/Facelly/Sipa; Wells/Gamma-Liaison; Eva Sereny/Sygma; Peter Marlow/Sygma / p. 279 Grapes-Michaud/Photo Researchers / p. 280 Kindra Clineff/The Picture Cube / p. 283 Jim Pickerell/Black Star / p. 284 Malcolm Hancock / p. 287 Focus on Sports / p. 291 William Pierce/*Time* Magazine / p. 293 Jack Deutsch/Innervisions / p. 295 © 1970 by The Cognitive Research Trust; reprinted by permission of Simon & Schuster / p. 297 all, Dr. Ursula Bellugi, Salk Institute / p. 299 *American Health: Fitness of Body and Health*, © 1986 American Health Partners / p. 300 Elizabeth Rubert / p. 301 Michael Goldman/Sisyphus / p. 304 top, Jack Deutsch/Innervisions; bottom, Lawrence Migdale/Stock, Boston.

CHAPTER 9 Page 310 AP/Wide World / p. 311 Universitätsbibliothek, Heidelberg / p. 312 left, William Karel/Sygma; right, Tannenbaum/Sygma / p. 314 top left, Barry Lewis/Network; top center, Erika Stone; top right, Ted Kerasote/Photo Researchers; bottom left, Francie Manning/The Picture Cube; bottom center, John Giordano/Saba; bottom right, Bridgeman/Art Resource, NY / p. 315 left, A. Knudsen/Sygma; right, G. Schachmes/Sygma / p. 317 David Young-Wolff/PhotoEdit / p. 321 Wasyl Szrodzinski/Photo Researchers / p. 322 Nancy Bates/The Picture Cube / p. 323 David Madison/Duomo / p. 325 Laura Dwight / p. 326 Philip J. Griffiths/Magnum / p. 329 David Austen/Stock, Boston / p. 330 top, Chris Sorensen/The Stock Market; bottom, both photos, adapted from Bernieri, Davis, Rosenthal, & Knee (1991) / p. 331 top left, Tim Graham/Sygma; top center, Robert Azzi/Woodfin Camp & Associates; top right, AP/Wide World; bottom, Bob Daemmrich/The Image Works / p. 333 Ellis Herwig/The Picture Cube / p. 334 top, Michael O'Brien; bottom, © Joel Gordon 1978.

CHAPTER 10 Page 339 Beth Wald/Adventure Photo / p. 340 Michael Ponzini/Focus on Sports / p. 345 top left, Dennis Stock/Magnum; top right, Victor Englebert/Photo Researchers; bottom, Bill DeBold/Gamma-Liaison / p. 348 Harlow Primate Laboratory, University of Wisconsin / p. 349 left, Bill Ross/Woodfin Camp & Associates; right, Chuck Fishman/Woodfin Camp & Associates / p. 350 Rob Nelson/Picture Group / p. 351 Art Seitz/Sygma / p. 354 left, Catherine Noren/Photo Researchers; center, Day Williams/Photo Researchers; right, Jim Anderson/Woodfin Camp & Associates / p. 355 Eric Kroll / p. 356 left, Photofest / p. 359 left, Ann Goolkasian/The Picture Cube; right, Linda Bartlett/Folio / p. 360 both, Harlow Primate Laboratory, University of Wisconsin / p. 361 Harry Groom/Photo Researchers / p. 366 left to right, Rick Friedman/Black Star; Dennis Brack/Black Star; Flip & Debra Shulke/Black Star; Dennis Brack/Black Star / p. 367 left to right, Owen Franken/Sygma; Marvin Koner/Black Star; Durand/G. Giansanti/P. Perrin/Sygma; Daniel Simon Gamma-Liaison / p. 369 Eastcott/Momatiuk/The Image Works / p. 370 Spencer Grant/The Picture Cube.

CHAPTER 11 Page 380 Reprinted from *Games* Magazine (19 West 21st Street, New York, NY 10010). Copyright © 1981. B. & P. Publishing Co., Inc. / p. 381 Richard Hutchings/Photo Researchers / p. 385 John Nordell/J. B. Pictures / p. 390 Sidney Harris / p. 392 top, Richard Hutchings/Photo Researchers; bottom, Charles Feil/Stock, Boston / p. 395 top, Richard Haier, Department of Psychiatry, University of California, Irvine; bottom, Biophoto Associates/Science Source/Photo Researchers / p. 397 Kathryn Abbe/Frances McLaughlin-Gill © 1979 / p. 401 top left, Shelly Katz/Black Star; top right, Lawrence Migdale/Photo Researchers / p. 408 left, Tim Peters/Picture Group; center, Bruce Roberts/Photo Researchers; right, Peter Vadnai/The Stock Market / p. 409 Harvey Lloyd/The Stock Market / p. 417 Reprinted from *Games* Magazine (19 West 21st Street, New York, NY 10010). Copyright © 1981. B. & P. Publishing Co., Inc.

CHAPTER 12 Page 414 Catherine Ursillo/Photo Researchers / p. 415 both, AP/Wide World / p. 417 both, O. W. Wooley, *Body Dissatisfaction: Studies Using the Color-a-Person Body Image Test* (unpublished manuscript) / p. 418 top, Sidney Harris; bottom left, Mimi Forsyth/Monkmeyer Press; bottom right, Innervisions / p. 420 top left, Wally McNamee/Woodfin Camp & Associates; top right, Mark A. Mittelman; bottom left, Timothy Eagan/Woodfin Camp & Associates; bottom right, Peter Menzel/Stock, Boston / p. 421 "Broom-Hilda" by Russell Myers. Reprinted by permission Tribune Media Services / p. 422 Costa Manos/Magnum / p. 425 Rob Nelson/Picture Group / p. 427 both, Susan Szasz / p. 428 top and bottom right, Evan Byrne, Laboratory of Comparative Ethology, National Institute of Child Health and Human Development; bottom left, Harlow Primate Laboratory, University of Wisconsin / p. 430 top left, M. P. Kahl/Photo Researchers; top right, Cosimo Scianna/The Image Bank; bottom left, Jack Deutsch/Innervisions; bottom right, Erika Stone / p. 433 bottom, Jack Deutsch/Innervisions / p. 436 The Granger Collection, New York / p. 437 John Kelly/The Image Bank / p. 441 top, Jeffrey E. Blackman/The Stock Market; center left and center right, S. Franklin/Sygma; bottom, John Kelly/The Image Bank / p. 444 Mark A. Mittelman / p. 450 top left, Mary Heitner; top right, Costa Manos/Magnum; bottom left, Wayne Miller/Magnum; bottom right, Bob Daemmrich/Stock, Boston.

CHAPTER 13 Page 456 Peter Beck/The Stock Market / p. 457 National Portrait Gallery, London / p. 459 Sally & Richard Greenhill / p. 463 all, Marina Raith/Gruner & Jahr / p. 464 top, Drawings by Orietta Agostoni; bottom, Doris Pinney Brenner / p. 468 left, Marcia Weinstein; right, Mimi Forsyth/Monkmeyer Press / p. 469 both, Jackie Curtis / p. 470 Mandal Ranjiz/Photo Researchers / p. 471 Erika Stone / p. 475 Frank Siteman / p. 477 David Butow/Black Star / p. 479 bottom, Margo Granitsas/Photo Researchers / pp. 480, 481 Robert Brenner/PhotoEdit / p. 484 Sandra Lousada/Susan Griggs Agency / p. 487 Erika Stone / p. 489 left, Diane M. Lowe/Stock, Boston; right, Betsy Lee / p. 491 Jean-Claude Lejeune/Stock, Boston.

CHAPTER 14 Page 496 Peter Correz/TSW, Chicago / p. 497 AP/Wide World / p. 499 Jeff Persons/Stock, Boston / p. 502 left, Daemmrich/Uniphoto; center, Porterfield-Chickering/Photo Researchers; right, Ira Wyman/Sygma / p. 503 Dion Ogust/The Image Works / p. 504 Mark Ferri / p. 506 Tom McCarthy/The Picture Cube / p. 509 left, Frank Siteman/Stock, Boston; right, George Goodwin/Monkmeyer Press / p. 511 top left, Allan Tannenbaum/Sygma; bottom left, Spencer Grant/The Picture Cube; right, Steve Hansen/Stock, Boston / p. 513 left, Brent Jones; center, Robert Frerck/Odyssey Productions, Chicago; right, James R. Hays/Unicorn / p. 516 top left, Deborah Davis/PhotoEdit; top center, Robert Brenner/PhotoEdit; top right, Randy Matusow; center left, Charles Gupton/Stock, Boston; center right, David Lissy/The Picture Cube; bottom left, S. Gazin/The Image Works; bottom right, Will & Deni McIntyre/Photo Researchers / p. 518 Laura Dwight / p. 521 © 1943 Yousef Karsh/Woodfin Camp & Associates / p. 524 Philip Jon Baily/The Picture Cube / p. 525 Herman Kokojan/Black Star.

CHAPTER 15 Page 532 AP/Wide World / p. 533 Jeffry Myers/Stock, Boston / p. 535 left, Enrico Ferorelli; right, Allen Green/Photo Researchers / p. 537 Manfred Kage/Peter Arnold, Inc. / p. 539 Stanley Rice/Monkmeyer Press / p. 540 Paul Fusco/Magnum / p. 542 top, Tom Sobolik/Black Star / pp. 544, 545 National Baseball Library, Cooperstown, NY / p. 547 Roy Roper/Picture Group / p. 549 Camilla Smith/Rainbow / p. 550 Malcolm Hancock

Author Index

SUBJECT INDEX